ISBN 978-1-397-31933-3
PIBN 11374718

1 MONTH OF
FREE
READING

at

www.ForgottenBooks.com

By purchasing this book you are
eligible for one month membership to
ForgottenBooks.com, giving you
unlimited access to our entire
collection of over 1,000,000 titles via
our web site and mobile apps.

To claim your free month visit:

www.forgottenbooks.com/free1374718

English
Français
Deutsche
Italiano
Español
Português

www.forgottenbooks.com

Mythology Photography **Fiction**
Fishing Christianity **Art** Cooking
Essays Buddhism Freemasonry
Medicine **Biology** Music **Ancient**
Egypt Evolution Carpentry Physics
Dance Geology **Mathematics** Fitness
Shakespeare **Folklore** Yoga Marketing
Confidence Immortality Biographies
Poetry **Psychology** Witchcraft
Electronics Chemistry History **Law**
Accounting **Philosophy** Anthropology
Alchemy Drama Quantum Mechanics
Atheism Sexual Health **Ancient History**
Entrepreneurship Languages Sport
Paleontology Needlework Islam
Metaphysics Investment Archaeology
Parenting Statistics Criminology
Motivational

CALENDAR

OF THE

ROYAL COLLEGE OF SURGEONS

OF ENGLAND.

AUGUST 1, 1923.

LONDON:

TAYLOR AND FRANCIS, RED LION COURT, FLEET STREET.

[*Price One Shilling.*]

CALENDAR

OF THE

OYAL COLLEGE OF SURGEONS

OF ENGLAND.

QUÆ PROSUNT OMNIBUS ARTES

AUGUST 1, 1923.

LONDON:

TAYLOR AND FRANCIS, RED LION COURT, FLEET STREET.

1923.

ROYAL COLLEGE OF SURGEONS

LINCOLN'S INN FIELDS,
LONDON, W.C. 2.

———— ♦♦♦ ————

Telephone Number - - - - - - Holborn 4699.

7

CONTENTS.

ALMANACK.

8th Month.		AUGUST xxxi days.	1923.
1.	W.		
2.	Th.		
3.	F.		
4.	S.	College closed.	
5.	S.	TENTH SUNDAY AFTER TRINITY.	
6.	M.	College closed.	
7.	Tu.		
8.	W.		
9.	Th.		
10.	F.		
11.	S.	Half-Quarter Day.	
12.	S.	ELEVENTH SUNDAY AFTER TRINITY.	
13.	M.		
14.	Tu.		
15.	W.		
16.	Th.		
17.	F.		
18.	S.		
19.	S.	TWELFTH SUNDAY AFTER TRINITY.	
20.	M.		
21.	Tu.		
22.	W.		
23.	Th.		
24.	F.		
25.	S.		
26.	S.	THIRTEENTH SUNDAY AFTER TRINITY.	
27.	M.		
28.	Tu.		
29.	W.		
30.	Th.		
31.	F.		

9th Month.		SEPTEMBER xxx days.	1923.
1.	S.	Museum and Library closed this month.	
2.	S.	FOURTEENTH SUNDAY AFTER TRINITY.	
3.	M.		
4.	TU.		
5.	W.		
6.	TH.		
7.	F.		
8.	S.		
9.	S.	FIFTEENTH SUNDAY AFTER TRINITY.	
10.	M.		
11.	TU.		
12.	W.		
13.	TH.		
14.	F.		
15.	S.		
16.	S.	SIXTEENTH SUNDAY AFTER TRINITY. Summer time ends.	
17.	M.		
18.	TU.		
19.	W.		
20.	TH.		
21.	F.	First Professional Examination for L.D.S. begins.	
22.	S.		
23.	S.	SEVENTEENTH SUNDAY AFTER TRINITY.	
24.	M.		
25.	TU.	First Conjoint Examination begins.	
26.	W.		
27.	TH.	Second Conjoint Examination begins.	
28.	F.		
29.	S.	MICHAELMAS DAY.	
30.	S.	EIGHTEENTH SUNDAY AFTER TRINITY.	

10th Month.		OCTOBER xxxi days.	1923.

1.	M.	Museum and Library re-opened.
2.	Tu.	Committee of Management: 8.30 P.M. [Fund: 5 P.M.
3.	W.	Jenks Scholarship Committee: 4.45 P.M. Exec. Comm., Cancer
4.	Th.	Library Comm.: 4 P.M. Committee on Annual Report: 4.45 P.M.
5.	F.	[Pass Exam. for Membership begins.
6.	S.	
7.	S.	NINETEENTH SUNDAY AFTER TRINITY.
8.	M.	
9.	Tu.	
10.	W.	Museum Committee: 4 P.M. General Purposes Comm.: 5 P.M.
11.	Th.	
12.	F.	Museum Demonstration: Sir Arthur Keith: 5 P.M.
13.	S.	
14.	S.	TWENTIETH SUNDAY AFTER TRINITY.
15.	M.	Museum Demonstration: Mr. S. G. Shattock: 5 P.M.
16.	Tu.	John Hunter died, 1793.
17.	W.	
18.	Th.	Quarterly Council: 4 P.M.
19.	F.	Museum Demonstration: Sir Arthur Keith: 5 P.M.
20.	S.	
21.	S.	TWENTY-FIRST SUNDAY AFTER TRINITY.
22.	M.	Museum Demonstration: Mr. S. G. Shattock: 5 P.M.
23.	Tu.	
24.	W.	
25.	Th.	
26.	F.	Museum Demonstration: Sir Arthur Keith: 5 P.M.
27.	S.	
28.	S.	TWENTY-SECOND SUNDAY AFTER TRINITY.
29.	M.	Museum Demonstration: Mr. S. G. Shattock: 5 P.M.
30.	Tu.	
31.	W.	

11th Month.		NOVEMBER xxx days.	1923.
1.	Th.	Finance Committee : 4 P.M.	
2.	F.	Second Professional Examination for L.D.S. begins.	
3.	S.		
4.	S.	Twenty-third Sunday after Trinity. [and Members.	
5.	M.	Last day for notices of Motion for Annual Meeting of Fellows	
6.	Tu.	Court of Examiners at Examination Hall : 5 P.M.	
7.	W.	Executive Committee, Cancer Fund : 5 P.M.	
8.	Th.	Ordinary Council: 4 P.M. Bradshaw Lecture : Mr. W. G.	
9.	F.	[Spencer : 5 P.M.	
10.	S.	Vacancy on Court of Examiners advertised.	
11.	S.	Twenty-fourth Sunday after Trinity. Half-Quarter Day.	
12.	M.	[Armistice signed, 1918.	
13.	Tu.		
14.	W.	Hunterian Trustees : 4 P.M.	
15.	Th.	Annual Meeting of Fellows and Members : 3 P.M. Final	
16.	F.	[Fellowship : Written Examination.	
17.	S.		
18.	S.	Twenty-fifth Sunday after Trinity.	
19.	M.	Final Fellowship Examination continued this week.	
20.	Tu.		
21.	W.		
22.	Th.		
23.	F.		
24.	S.		
25.	S.	Twenty-sixth Sunday after Trinity.	
26.	M.		
27.	Tu.		
28.	W.		
29.	Th.		
30.	F.		

12th Month.		DECEMBER xxxi days. 1923.
1.	S.	
2.	☾.	First Sunday in Advent.
3.	M.	D.L.O. Examination, Part I, begins.
4.	Tu.	Committee of Management : 8.30 p.m.
5.	W.	Last day for applications for election to Court of Examiners.
6.	Th.	[Exec. Comm., Cancer Fund : 5 p.m.
7.	F.	Thomas Vicary Lecture : Sir Arthur Keith : 5 p.m. D.L.O.
8.	S.	[Examination, Part II, begins.
9.	☾.	Second Sunday in Advent.
10.	M.	D.P.M. Examination, Part I, begins.
11.	Tu.	Primary Fellowship : Written Examination.
12.	W.	
13.	Th.	Ordinary Council : 4 p.m. Election to Court of Examiners.
14.	F.	F.R.C.S. with Ophthalmology Examination begins. D.P.M.
15.	S.	[Examination, Part II, begins.
16.	☾.	Third Sunday in Advent. [and D.T.M. & H. Exam. begin.
17.	M.	Primary Fellowship : Vivâ voe Exam. begins. D.P.H. Exam., Pt. I,
18.	Tu.	Committee of Management : 8.30 p.m.
19.	W.	
20.	Th.	
21.	F.	
22.	S.	
23.	☾.	Fourth Sunday in Advent.
24.	M.	
25.	Tu.	Christmas Day. College closed.
26.	W.	College closed.
27.	Th.	
28.	F.	
29.	S.	
30.	☾.	First Sunday after Christmas. [D.O.M.S. Exam. Pt. I, begin.
31.	M.	Last day for Jacksonian Prize Essays. D.P.H. Exam. Pt. II, and

1.	Tu.	First Conjoint Examination begins.
2.	W.	Exec. Comm., Cancer Fund: 5 P.M. [Conjoint Exam. begins.
3.	Th.	Museum Comm.: 4 P.M. Gen. Purposes Comm.: 5 P.M. Second
4.	F.	Library Comm.: 5 P.M. D.O.M.S. Exam., Part II, begins.
5.	S.	
6.	S.	EPIPHANY.
7.	M.	Court of Examiners at Examination Hall: 5 P.M.
8.	Tu.	
9.	W.	
10.	Th.	Quarterly Council: 4 P.M.
11.	F.	Pass Examination for Membership begins.
12.	S.	
13.	S.	FIRST SUNDAY AFTER EPIPHANY.
14.	M.	
15.	Tu.	
16.	W.	
17.	Th.	
18.	F.	
19.	S.	
20.	S.	SECOND SUNDAY AFTER EPIPHANY.
21.	M.	Hunterian Lecture: Prof. R. St. L. Brockman: 5 P.M.
22.	Tu.	
23.	W.	Hunterian Lecture: Prof. R. M. Handfield-Jones: 5 P.M.
24.	Th.	
25.	F.	Hunterian Lecture: Prof. Sidney Forsdike: 5 P.M.
26.	S.	
27.	S.	THIRD SUNDAY AFTER EPIPHANY.
28.	M.	Hunterian Lecture: Prof. Frank Cook: 5 P.M.
29.	Tu.	
30.	W.	Hunterian Lecture: Prof. Alexander Fleming: 5 P.M.
31.	Th.	

2nd Month.		FEBRUARY xxix days. 1924.
1.	F.	Hunterian Lecture: Prof. Geoffrey Jefferson: 5 P.M.
2.	S.	
3.	S.	FOURTH SUNDAY AFTER EPIPHANY.
4.	M.	Hunterian Lecture : Prof. K. M. Walker : 5 P.M.
5.	Tu.	
6.	W.	Hunterian Lecture : Prof. C. Max Page : 5 P.M. Exec. Comm.,
7.	Th.	[Cancer Fund: 5 P.M.
8.	F.	Half-Quarter Day. Finance Committee : 4.30 P.M. Hunterian [Lecture : Prof. W. H. Ogilvie : 5 P.M. First
9.	S.	[Professional Examination for L.D.S. begins.
10.	S.	FIFTH SUNDAY AFTER EPIPHANY. Lord Lister died, 1912.
11.	M.	Hunterian Lecture : Prof. W. Sampson Handley : 5 P.M.
12.	Tu.	[ford Knaggs : 5 P.M.
13.	W.	Hunterian Trustees : 4 P.M. Hunterian Lecture : Prof. R. Law-
14.	Th.	John Hunter born, 1728. Ordinary Council : 4 P.M.
15.	F.	Arris and Gale Lecture : Mr. V. E. Negus : 5 P.M.
16.	S.	
17.	S.	SEPTUAGESIMA SUNDAY.
18.	M.	Arris and Gale Lecture : Mr. C. P. G. Wakeley : 5 P.M.
19.	Tu.	
20.	W.	Arris and Gale Lecture : Mr. H. E. Griffiths : 5 P.M.
21.	Th.	
22.	F.	Second Professional Examination for L.D.S. begins.
23.	S.	
24.	S.	SEXAGESIMA SUNDAY.
25.	M.	
26.	Tu.	
27.	W.	
28.	Th.	
29.	F.	

3rd Month.		MARCH xxxi days.	1924.
1.	S.		
2.	S.	QUINQUAGESIMA SUNDAY.	
3.	M.		
4.	Tu.	Committee of Management: 8.30 P.M.	
5.	W.	Executive Committee, Cancer Fund: 5 P.M.	
6.	Th.		
7.	F.	Date of Council Election announced.	
8.	S.		
9.	S.	FIRST SUNDAY IN LENT.	
10.	M.		
11.	Tu.	Committee of Management: 8.30 P.M.	
12.	W.		
13.	Th.	Ordinary Council: 4 P.M.	
14.	F.		
15.	S.		
16.	S.	SECOND SUNDAY IN LENT.	
17.	M.	Last day for nomination of Candidates for Council.	
18.	Tu.	First Conjoint Examination begins.	
19.	W.		
20.	Th.	Second Conjoint Examination begins. Competition for Begley	
21.	F.	[Studentship.	
22.	S.		
23.	S.	THIRD SUNDAY IN LENT.	
24.	M.		
25.	Tu.	LADY DAY.	
26.	W.		
27.	Th.		
28.	F.	Museum Demonstration: Sir Arthur Keith: 5 P.M.	
29.	S.		
30.	S.	FOURTH SUNDAY IN LENT. [Examiners at Examination Hall.	
31.	M.	Museum Demonstration: Mr. S. G. Shattock: 5 P.M. Court of	

4th Month.		APRIL xxx days.	1924.
1.	Tu.	Voting-papers for Council Election issued.	
2.	W.	Executive Committee, Cancer Fund : 5 P.M.	
3.	Th.	Museum Committee : 4 P.M. Library Commiteee : 5 P.M.	
4.	F.	General Purposes Comm.: 4.30 P.M. Museum Demonstration : Sir [Arthur Keith : 5 P.M. Pass Exam. for Membership begins.	
5.	S.	Vacant annual Examinerships advertised.	
6.	S.	FIFTH SUNDAY IN LENT.	
7.	M.	Museum Demonstration : Mr. S. G. Shattock : 5 P.M. D.T.M. &	
8.	Tu.	[H. Examination begins.	
9.	W.		
10.	Th.	Quarterly Council : 4 P.M.	
11.	F.	Museum Demonstration : Sir Arthur Keith : 5 P.M.	
12.	S.	Vacancy on Court of Examiners advertised.	
13.	S.	PALM SUNDAY.	
14.	M.	Museum Demonstration : Mr. S. G. Shattock : 5 P.M.	
15.	Tu.		
16.	W.		
17.	Th.		
18.	F.	GOOD FRIDAY. College closed.	
19.	S.	College closed.	
20.	S.	EASTER SUNDAY.	
21.	M.	College closed.	
22.	Tu.	D.P.H. Exam., Part I, begins.	
23.	W.		
24.	Th.		
25.	F.		
26.	S.	Last day for applications for annual Examinerships.	
27.	S.	FIRST SUNDAY AFTER EASTER.	
28.	M.	D.P.H. Exam., Part II, begins.	
29.	Tu.	[applications for election to Court of Examiners.	
30.	W.	Huntcrian Lecture : Prof. W. E. Gullie : 5 P.M. Last day for	

5th Month.		MAY xxxi days.	1924.
1.	Th.		
2.	F.	First Professional Examination for L.D.S. begins.	
3.	S.		
4.	S.	Second Sunday after Easter.	
5.	M.	Finance Committee: 4.30 p.m.	
6.	Tu.		
7.	W.	Executive Committee, Cancer Fund: 5 p.m.	
8.	Th.	Ordinary Council: 4 p.m. Election to Court of Examiners.	
9.	F.	Half-Quarter Day.	
10.	S.	Vacant Lectureships advertised.	
11.	S.	Third Sunday after Easter.	
12.	M.		
13.	Tu.		
14.	W.	Hunterian Trustees : 4 p.m.	
15.	Th.		
16.	F.		
17.	S.		
18.	S.	Fourth Sunday after Easter.	
19.	M.		
20.	Tu.		
21.	W.		
22.	Th.	Final Fellowship: Written Examination.	
23.	F.		
24.	S.		
25.	S.	Rogation Sunday.	
26.	M.	Final Fellowship Examination continued this week.	
27.	Tu.		
28.	W.		
29.	Th.	Ascension Day.	
30.	F.		
31.	S.		

6th Month.		JUNE xxx days.	1924.
1.	**S.**	SUNDAY AFTER ASCENSION.	
2.	M.	D.L.O. Examination, Part I, begins.	
3.	Tu.	Committee of Management: 8.30 P.M.	
4.	W.	Exec. Comm., Cancer Fund: 5 P.M. Last day for applications for	
5.	TH.	[election to Lectureships.	
6.	F.	D.L.O. Examination, Part II, begins.	
7. ·	S.	College closed.	
8.	**S.**	WHIT SUNDAY.	
9.	M.	College closed.	
10.	Tu.	Primary Fellowship: Written Examination.	
11.	W.		
12.	TH.	Ordinary Council: 4 P.M. Annual Election of Examiners.	
13.	F.	Second Professional Examination for L.D.S. begins.	
14.	S.		
15.	**S.**	TRINITY SUNDAY.	
16.	M.	Primary Fellowship: *Vivâ voce* Examination begins.	
17.	Tu.		
18.	W.	Library Committee: 5 P.M.	
19.	TH.	Museum Committee: 4 P.M. General Purposes Committee: 5 P.M.	
20.	F.	F.R.C.S. with Ophthalmology Examination begins.	
21.	S.		
22.	**S.**	FIRST SUNDAY AFTER TRINITY.	
23.	M.	D.P.H. Exam., Part I, and D.P.M. Exam., Part I, begin.	
24.	Tu.	MIDSUMMER DAY.	
25.	W.		
26.	TH.	Second Conjoint Examination begins.	
27.	F.	D.P.M. Examination, Part II, begins.	
28.	S.		
29.	**S.**	SECOND SUNDAY AFTER TRINITY.	
30.	M.	D.P.H. Examination, Part II, begins. Court of Examiners at [Examination Hall, 5 P.M.	

7th Month.		JULY xxxi days.	1924.
1.	Tu.		
2.	W.	Executive Committee, Cancer Fund : 5 P.M.	
3.	Th.	Election of Members of Council.	
4.	F.	Pass Examination for Membership begins.	
5.	S.		
6.	S.	THIRD SUNDAY AFTER TRINITY.	
7.	M.	D.O.M.S. Examination, Part I, begins.	
8.	Tu.		
9.	W.	Hunterian Trustees : 4 P.M. [Presidents and Lecturers.	
10.	Th.	Quarterly Council : 4 P.M. Election of President and Vice-	
11.	F.	D.O.M.S. Examination, Part II, begins.	
12.	S.		
13.	S.	FOURTH SUNDAY AFTER TRINITY.	
14.	M.		
15.	Tu.	First Conjoint Examination begins.	
16.	W.		
17.	Th.		
18.	F.		
19.	S.		
20.	S.	FIFTH SUNDAY AFTER TRINITY.	
21.	M.	D.T.M. & H. Examination begins.	
22.	Tu.		
23.	W.		
24.	Th.		
25.	F.		
26.	S.		
27.	S.	SIXTH SUNDAY AFTER TRINITY.	
28.	M.		
29.	Tu.		
30.	W.		
31.	Th.	Ordinary Council : 4 P.M.	

HISTORICAL SUMMARY.

THE early history of the ROYAL COLLEGE OF SURGEONS OF ENGLAND is the history of two Companies, which, existing at first as separate fraternities or guilds, were for a time united into one body corporate, and finally became resolved again into two distinct Corporations. One of these, the Barbers' Company of London, is first definitely mentioned, in the records preserved at the Guildhall, in the year 1308, when Richard le Barber was presented and sworn before the Court of Aldermen as Master and Supervisor of the Barbers' Guild; and from an Ordinance of the City made in the previous year it is evident that the Barbers of London were at that time engaged in the practice of at least some branches of Surgery. The other Company, known as the Fellowship or Guild of Surgeons, is mentioned in the City records in the year 1369, when two Masters were sworn before the Court of Aldermen and given power to report the faults of unskilful Surgeons.

Between these two bodies there was for many years a keen rivalry and jealousy. Each tried by turns to attain supremacy of authority and jurisdiction in matters relating to the practice of Surgery. In the year 1376 the Barbers made a complaint to the Mayor and Aldermen against unskilled practitioners in Surgery, and obtained an Ordinance providing that two Masters should be appointed annually to direct and rule the Craft, to inspect instruments, and to see that none should be admitted to the franchise of the City except after attestation of their skill by good examination. Fourteen years later, however, four Masters of the Surgeons' Guild were sworn before the Court of Aldermen, and *they* were invested with the power of scrutiny among persons practising Surgery and with authority to present defaults. But in the year 1410 the Barbers obtained from the Court of Aldermen confirmation of the privileges granted to them in 1376 with the addition that they should be enjoyed " without the scrutiny of any person or persons of any other craft or trade under any name whatsoever other than the craft or trade of the said Barbers."

The Barbers' Company was by this time assuming a twofold character, for it consisted of two classes of members, those who were Barbers simply or practised only the minor branches of Surgery, such as blood-letting and

1923.

Origin of the College.

The Barbers' Company first mentioned in 1308.

The Surgeons' Guild mentioned in 1369.

Rivalry between the two Companies.

Barbers' Ordinance of 1376.

Surgeons' Ordinance of 1390.

Barbers' Ordinance confirmed in 1410.

Barbers' Company assumes two-fold character.

tooth-drawing, and those who exercised the faculty of Surgery. In the year 1415 the Mayor and Aldermen required the Company to furnish them with a list of all the latter class of members, from which they selected two as Masters of those practising Surgery, leaving to the Company itself the election of the Masters of the Barbers. Meanwhile the Guild of Surgeons sought an alliance with the Physicians. About the year 1423, probably through the influence of Thomas Morstede (a Surgeon who accompanied Henry V. to Agincourt and who was afterwards Surgeon to Henry VI.), they obtained an Ordinance from the Court of Aldermen having for its object an association or Commonalty of Physicians and Surgeons. Fortified by the support of the Physicians, the Surgeons once more challenged the surgical privileges of the Barbers, but these were again confirmed by the Mayor and Aldermen in 1424. The scheme for a combination of Physicians and Surgeons fell through, but the Surgeons continued a separate body with Ordinances for the government of their Society. The volume containing these Ordinances, which were made in the year 1435, is still in existence and is now in the possession of the Barbers' Company.

Temporary alliance of Surgeons' Guild with Physicians in 1423.

Freed from opposition, the Barbers' Company continued to grow in importance. and in the year 1462 the right of its members to practise Surgery was definitely established by LETTERS PATENT granted by EDWARD IV. in the first year of his reign. This Charter, from which the Royal College of Surgeons of England, as recited in the Charter of 1800, dates its constitutional history as a body corporate, was granted to the Freemen of the Mystery of Barbers of the City of London practising Surgery. They were made one Body and Perpetual Community with a Common Seal and with power to hold lands and make Bye-Laws. Provision was made for the annual election of two Masters to rule the Community, to have the scrutiny and government of all persons practising Surgery in London and its suburbs, as well as the supervision of their instruments and medicines, and to have power to inflict punishment upon offenders by fines, imprisonment and other reasonable means. No person was to be allowed to practise Surgery within the City of London and its suburbs unless first approved by the Masters of the Company. The surgical rights of the Barbers' Company were thus firmly established, and, as testimony to the eminence attained by the Surgeons of the Company, it is worthy of note that the Senior Warden of the Company, when the Charter was granted, was WILLIAM HOBBES, Serjeant-Surgeon to the King—probably the first to hold that office.

The Barbers incorporated by Edward IV. in 1462.

Provisions of the Charter of 1st Edward IV.

In the year 1493 the Guild of Surgeons, which had continued as a separate body, entered into an alliance or "Composition" with the Barbers' Company, by which the two Companies agreed each to appoint two Wardens, the four so appointed to act together in all matters relating to Surgery and to the examination and government of its practitioners.

Alliance between the Barbers' Company and Surgeons' Guild made in 1493.

The Charter granted by Edward IV. to the Barbers' Company was confirmed by Henry VII. and also by Henry VIII., but in 1511 an Act (3 Henry VIII. cap. 11) was passed, constituting a further licensing authority by enacting that no person should practise as a Physician or Surgeon in London, or within seven miles of the same, unless first examined and approved by the Bishop of London, or the Dean of St. Paul's, with the assistance of four Physicians or Surgeons. Two years later, upon the petition of the Guild of Surgeons, another Act (5 Henry VIII. cap. 6) was passed, providing that a limited number of members of the Fellowship (or Guild) of Surgeons, as also of members of the Barbers' Company duly admitted as Surgeons, should be exempt from Constableship and Watch and from bearing arms and serving upon inquests and juries within the City of London.

Of the Act 3rd Henry VIII. relating to the Bishop's Licence; 1511.

Of the Act 5th Henry VIII. relating to exemption of Surgeons from bearing arms and serving on juries; 1513.

IN THE YEAR 1540 the two Companies, which had so long been associated by voluntary agreement, were formally united by Act of Parliament, and thus entered upon a new era in their career. The Act (32nd HENRY VIII. cap. 42) after reciting that there were two distinct Companies of Surgeons in London, one called the Barbers of London and the other the Surgeons of London, enacted that the two Companies should from thenceforth be united and made one Body Corporate, to be called by the name of the Masters or Governors of the Mystery and Commonalty of the Barbers and Surgeons of London. The United Company was to enjoy all the rights and privileges at any time granted to the two separate Companies. Four Masters or Governors, two to be Surgeons and two to be Barbers, were to be appointed annually; barbers were forbidden to perform any surgical operations, except the drawing of teeth, and surgeons were not to exercise the craft of barbery and shaving. Provision was also made for the study of Anatomy by giving the Company the right to claim four bodies annually of persons executed for felony. THOMAS VICARY, Serjeant-Surgeon to Henry VIII. and afterwards to Mary and to Elizabeth, was elected the first Master. The United Company shared the possession of Barbers' Hall, which is known to have occupied its present site in Monkwell Street since 1490 and was probably there even before that. The Hall,

The two Companies united by Henry VIII. in 1540.

Provisions of the Act of incorporation

The first Master of the United Company and its Hall.

subsequently added to by Inigo Jones in 1636, is still standing, having escaped destruction in the Great Fire of London.

Of the Act 34th and 35th Henry VIII. regarding treatment of minor ailments by unlicensed persons.

The Union thus effected was destined to last for more than two hundred years. At first, however, the privileges conferred on the Surgeons of the Company appear to have excited opposition, for in the 34th and 35th years of Henry VIII. an Act was passed allowing unlicensed persons to treat outward sores and swellings with herbs and ointments.

Origin of Court of Examiners in 1555.

During the reign of QUEEN MARY, in the year 1555, Regulations were drawn up relating to the examination of persons for the Company's Licence to practise. These Regulations provided for the appointment of thirteen Examiners, including the Master and two Governors. This is the origin of the Court of Examiners of the Royal College of Surgeons of England, although it was not until the time of Charles I. that the appointment of ten Examiners—the number continued to this day—was provided for by Charter.

Letters Patent of James I. and provisions thereof, 1605.

In the year 1605 the Company obtained a Charter from JAMES I. providing that the Governing Body of the Company should consist of four Masters or Governors, two of whom were to be Surgeons, and twenty-six Assistants. The Company was given power to examine Barbers and Surgeons, and to prohibit ignorant persons, or such as wilfully refused to be examined, from practising.

Letters Patent of Charles I. and provisions thereof, 1629.

In the year 1629 CHARLES I. granted a further Charter to the Company, providing that ten Freemen of the Company should be elected and constituted Examiners of Surgeons in London. No one was to practise Surgery in London, or within seven miles of it, except Members of the College of Physicians, unless examined and approved by the Examiners of the Company, and every person so approved might practise Surgery anywhere in England. Apprentices were to serve for not less than seven years, to be sound in body and limbs, and to read and understand Latin. The duty was also assigned to the Court of Examiners of examining Surgeons and Surgeons' Assistants for the Royal Navy and Merchant Service and of inspecting their instruments and chests of medicines. This duty they and their successors, the Company of Surgeons and the Royal College of Surgeons, continued to discharge until other arrangements were made at a comparatively recent date.

Surgeons object to their union with the Barbers, 1684.

For many years the union between the two Companies appears to have worked smoothly, but as early as 1684 there were signs that the Surgeons were beginning to find their association with the Barbers irksome and inconvenient. In that year a Petition for the dissolution of the United Company was presented to the King, but the agitation died out, and it was not until many years later that further steps were taken in the matter. The dissatisfaction, however, continued. From the year 1540 the practice of Surgery had been entirely separated from that of barbery, and much progress had been made in surgical skill and knowledge. Under the United Company several of the Surgeons had attained great eminence in their profession, and among these may be mentioned Richard Ferris, Thomas Gale, the two Clowes', Wiseman, Amyand, Cheselden, Sir Caesar Hawkins, and Percivall Pott. The Surgeons resented the presence of Barbers at their examinations, and objected to the signatures of Barbers appearing upon Surgical Diplomas. In 1744 they informed the Barbers that they intended to petition Parliament for the dissolution of the union. The Barbers protested against this, and both parties presented Petitions to Parliament. The Surgeons prevailed, and in the year 1745 an Act of Parliament was passed dissolving the union and establishing two separate Companies. The Barbers were allowed to retain the whole of the Corporate property, real and personal, with the exception of the Arris Bequest and Gale's Annuity for Anatomy Lectures founded in 1646 and 1655 respectively. These Trusts the Act vested in the Company of Surgeons, and they are now administered by the Royal College of Surgeons.

Petition for dissolution of union presented, 1744.

The union dissolved in 1745.

This Act of the 18th George II. dissolving the union of the Barbers and the Surgeons incorporated the Surgeons under the name of the Master, Governors and Commonalty of the Art and Science of Surgeons of London, and constituted a governing body consisting of twenty-one Assistants appointed for life, of whom one was to be Master and two Governors or Wardens elected annually, and of whom ten were to be Examiners appointed for life. John Ranby, Serjeant-Surgeon to George II. (whom he accompanied to the battle of Dettingen in 1743), became the first Master of the Company, and upon taking his seat he presented a handsome silver cup, which is still in the possession of the College. The First Wardens were Joseph Sandford and William Cheselden. These appointments were made by the Act, which also specified by name the ten Examiners and sixteen Members of the Court of Assistants. The sixteen thus appointed were directed to meet forthwith, and select from the Freemen of the Company five others to complete the number of the Court. Thereafter, the Court were to meet on the first Thursday in July in each succeeding year for the election of the Master and Governors, and to fill up any vacancies, which from time to time might occur from death or resignation among the Examiners and Assistants. In addition to

Act of 18th George II. dissolves union and constitutes Company of Surgeons.

The first Master and Wardens.

The Examiners and the Court of Assistants.

examining Surgeons for the Navy the Examiners were also required to examine all candidates for the posts of Surgeon or Surgeons' Mate in the Army. The Freemen of the Company were to enjoy the same Surgical privileges as approved Surgeons of the United Company had enjoyed under the Act of Union and Charter of Charles I., and, while in the practice of their profession, were to be exempt from all Parish, Ward, and Leet Offices and from serving upon Juries.

Surgeons Hall built. The Surgeons had to find a new home, and, after holding their first meetings at Stationers' Hall, eventually secured premises in the Old Bailey and there built Surgeons' Hall, entering into occupation in 1751. Here the business of the Company was transacted until 1796, when the Court of Assistants, finding the building in need of substantial repair and their tenure of the premises secured for not more than fifty-five years, determined to dispose of the property and erect a new building upon a freehold site.

Difficulties caused by irregular meeting of Court of Assistants in 1796. About this time the Company became involved in difficulties in consequence of a provision in the Act of Incorporation which had unfortunately been framed without due regard to possible eventualities. This provision required that the Master and Governors, or any two of them, with nine or more members of the Court of Assistants, should constitute a Court for the despatch of business. On the 7th July, 1796, a meeting was held at which the Master, Mr. Gunning, presided, but at which no Governor was present, one having died in the previous May and the other being too ill to attend. Consequently it was impossible to obtain a properly constituted quorum. Nevertheless the Court conducted its ordinary business, and among other matters elected Henry Cline to the Court of Assistants. In spite of this technical defect in their constitution, the Court of Assistants continued to transact the business of the Company. They disposed of **Property in Old Bailey sold and site in Lincoln's Inn Fields acquired.** their property in the Old Bailey and acquired a freehold site in Lincoln's Inn Fields, upon which part of the present building of the Royal College of Surgeons of England now stands. The business of the Company was not suspended. Examinations were held and Diplomas were issued. The Examinations of Surgeons for the Navy and Army were also continued. **Endeavour to reconstitute Company by Act of Parliament abandoned, and petition for Charter presented.** It became, however, necessary to find some means of removing the legal difficulties which had arisen, and, for this purpose and also with the object of acquiring additional powers and authority, a Bill was introduced into Parliament. The Bill passed through the Commons, but was thrown out in the House of Lords; and after further deliberation it was determined to abandon the Bill and to petition for a Charter from the Crown.

Meanwhile Parliament entrusted to the care of the Company the Hunterian Collection purchased for the Nation at a cost of £15,000. The Collection was delivered to the Company under an Order of the Treasury, dated 28th November, 1799, and in March 1800 the Company was re-incorporated and constituted by the name of the Royal College of Surgeons in London, by Charter granted by George III. In the year 1806 Parliament voted a sum of £15,000, and subsequently a further sum of £12,500, in aid of the erection of a building for the display of the Hunterian Collection. A contribution of £21,000 was at the same time made from the funds of the College, and the Museum was opened to visitors in 1813.

Hunteria Collection entrusted to Company in 1799.

The Charter of the 40th GEORGE III. definitively severed the connexion of the College with the Corporation of the City of London. Members of the College were not entitled to any franchise belonging to the Freemen of the City, but all other privileges and possessions acquired under former Acts and Charters, and not altered by the Charter then granted, were continued and ratified. The Court of Assistants still consisted of twenty-one Members appointed for life with power to fill up vacancies as they might happen, and from them were chosen the ten Examiners, the Master and two Governors or Wardens being selected from these ten. The two principal Serjeant-Surgeons and the Surgeon-General to the Forces, if not already on the Courts of Assistants and Examiners, were always to be admitted into those Courts in preference to all other persons, when any vacancy should occur.

Charter of George III. constitutes Royal College of Surgeons of London in 1800.

The Court of Assistants and Court of Examiners.

CHARLES HAWKINS, Serjeant-Surgeon to George III., was appointed the First Master, and WILLIAM LONG and GEORGE CHANDLER became the first Governors. All Members of the old Company of Surgeons, on signifying their acceptance of the Charter, were entitled to become Members of the College, and any person in the future desiring to become a Member was required to pass an examination and obtain " Letters Testimonial of his Qualification to practise the Art and Science of Surgery under the Common Seal of the College." In addition to examining candidates for the Membership, the Court of Examiners were required, as under the former Acts and Charters, to examine all Army and Navy Surgeons, their Assistants and Mates, and to inspect their instruments.

The first Master and Governors.

Members of the late Company incorporated, and all future Members to pass examination.

Court of Examiners to examine all Army and Navy Surgeons and Assistants and Mates.

A further Charter, granted by GEORGE IV. in 1822, changed the titles Master and Governors to President and Vice-Presidents, and provided that the Court of Assistants should in future be styled the Council of the College.

Titles of Master and Governors changed to President and Vice-Presidents, and Court of Assistants to be called Council.

Name of College changed to Royal College of Surgeons of England and Fellowship instituted in 1843.

No change was, however, made in the constitution of the College until the year 1843, when a new Charter (7th VICTORIA) was obtained, which changed the name of the College to The Royal College of Surgeons of England, and instituted a new class of Members, who were to be called FELLOWS, from and by whom the Council were to be elected. The

Number of Council increased.

number of the Council was increased to twenty-four, and, while the existing Members of the Council were allowed to continue in office for life, provision was made that three elected Members should retire annually, so that, when no more life-Members were left, it would not be possible for a Member to retain his seat for a longer period than eight years without re-election.

Constitution of Court of Examiners altered.

A great change was also effected by this Charter in the constitution of the Court of Examiners. They were no longer to be necessarily selected from the Council, but any Fellow, whether on the Council or not, was made eligible. The Examiners then in office were to continue for life, but all future Examiners were to hold office only during the pleasure of the Council. The Serjeant-Surgeons and Surgeon-General to the Forces were no longer to have any preference of being admitted Examiners, and the President and Vice-Presidents were not to be chosen exclusively from the Examiners but from all the Members of the Council indifferently, whether Examiners of the College or not.

Provision for election of the first Fellows.

The Charter further provided that the President, Vice-Presidents and Members of the Council should be Fellows, and directed them to elect, within three months from the date of the Charter, not less than 250 and not more than 300 Members of the College to be Fellows. They were also given power to appoint other Members to be Fellows within one year from the date of the Charter. With these exceptions no persons were to be admitted to the Fellowship except by examination, nor until attaining the age of twenty-five years. The first Fellows, 300 in number, were chosen mainly from the Surgeons, Assistant-Surgeons and Lecturers of the Metropolitan and Provincial Hospitals. They were elected under one general Diploma on December 11th, 1843. A further election of 242 Fellows took place on the 26th August, 1844, and these included a considerable number of representatives of the Naval, Military and Indian Forces.

Further provision for the election of Fellows in 1852.

In the year 1852 further extension of the principle of election to the Fellowship without examination was made by a Supplemental Charter (15th VICTORIA), which enabled the Council to elect Members of fifteen years' standing to the Fellowship, provided they were Members when the Charter of 1843 was enacted. The Council were also empowered to admit annually to the Fellowship, without examination, two Members of the College of twenty years' standing, and authority was given for the *ad eundem* admission to the Fellowship, under certain conditions, of Fellows by examination of the Dublin and the Edinburgh Colleges of Surgeons, and the Faculty of Physicians and Surgeons of Glasgow. This Charter also provided that Members of the Court of Examiners thereafter elected should go out of office at the end of five years, but should be eligible for immediate re-election. Provision was also made for the appointment of a Board of Examiners in Midwifery for testing the fitness of persons to practise Midwifery, and Licences in Midwifery were granted to persons passing the Examinations of the Board until the year 1875, after which the Examinations were discontinued. Examiners to retire at end of five years. Licence in Midwifery instituted.

In the year 1859 the Licence in DENTAL SURGERY was instituted under the Charter of the 23rd VICTORIA, which empowered the Council to appoint a Board of Examiners for testing the fitness of persons to practise as Dentists. Licence in Dental Surgery instituted in 1859.

In the year 1875 an Act of Parliament was passed to enable the College to associate itself with one or more of the Colleges or Bodies named in Medical Acts for the purpose of conducting joint examinations for qualifications to be registered under the Acts. In pursuance of the provisions of this Act the College subsequently entered into an Agreement with the Royal College of Physicians of London, establishing a CONJOINT EXAMINING BOARD and requiring that all candidates for the Licence of the Royal College of Physicians of London and the Membership of the Royal College of Surgeons of England, commencing professional study after the 1st October, 1884, should pass the Examinations of the Board before becoming entitled to their Diplomas. Thus was constituted the present Examining Board of the two Colleges. The lease of a site on the Victoria Embankment was acquired from the Duchy of Lancaster, and on this an Examination Hall for the Board was erected at the joint expense of the two Colleges. The foundation-stone was laid by QUEEN VICTORIA on the 24th March 1886, and the Hall was first used for examinations in the year 1887. In addition to the examinations for the L.R.C.P. Lond. and M.R.C.S. Eng., examinations are also conducted by the Board for a Diploma in Public Health, granted jointly by the two Colleges, the first examination for this Diploma being held in 1887. Further, in 1904, the question of establishing an examination and Diploma in Tropical Medicine and Hygiene was considered, at the suggestion of the Secretary of State for the Colonies, but, while the 1923. Enabling Act of 1875. Conjoint Examining Board in England established. Examination Hall built. Diploma in Public Health instituted. Diploma in Tropical Medicine instituted.

Royal College of Surgeons was in favour of the proposal then made, it was not until 1911 that arrangements were finally adopted for an examination in these subjects to be conducted by the Board and a Diploma to be granted jointly by the two Colleges to candidates approved by the examiners.

Charter of 1888 allows Fellows to record votes at Council Elections by papers sent through Post.

In the year 1888 a Supplemental Charter was obtained, mainly with the objects of enabling the College to hold lands and hereditaments of a greater yearly value than that previously sanctioned, and of allowing Fellows to record their votes at elections to the Council by voting-papers sent through the Post, instead of by personal attendance at the College, as required up to that time.

Honorary Fellowship instituted by Charter in 1899.

The last Charter, obtained by the College in 1899, the 63rd year of Queen Victoria's reign, enables the Council to elect persons, whom they shall deem to be sufficiently distinguished for the purpose, to be Honorary Fellows of the College. These Honorary Fellows, the number of whom must not exceed fifty at any time, are not eligible for the Council or for the Court of Examiners, nor are they entitled to vote at Elections to the Council. Their status is purely honorary and does not confer the right to practise Surgery. The first to become an Honorary Fellow was KING EDWARD VII., who, when Prince of Wales, was graciously pleased to accept the Diploma. At the head of a list of distinguished names the College now has the honour to place that of KING GEORGE V., followed by those of H.R.H. the Prince of Wales and H.R.H. the Duke of Connaught. His Majesty, when Prince of Wales, became an Honorary Fellow of the College, and, after ascending the Throne, signified his pleasure to retain the title.

New Examination Hall built.

In the year 1908 the Examination Hall on the Victoria Embankment was sold, and a freehold site in Queen Square, Bloomsbury, was subsequently purchased. Upon this site a new Examination Hall has been built by the two Colleges, and since May 1912 the Examinations of the Conjoint Board have been conducted in this building.

CHARTERS.

40TH GEORGE III.

22ND MARCH, 1800.

GEORGE THE THIRD, by the Grace of God, of Great Britain, France, and Ireland, King, Defender of the Faith, &c. To ALL TO WHOM these Presents shall come, WHEREAS our Royal Predecessor, King Edward IV., by certain Letters Patent, under the Great Seal of England, bearing date the 24th Day of February, in the first Year of his Reign, did at the Supplication of the Freemen of the Mystery of Barbers of the City of London, using the Mystery or Faculty of Surgery, grant to them, among other Things, that the said Mystery, and all the Men of the same Mystery of the said City, should be one Body and Perpetual Community, and that two Principals of the same Commonalty, of the most expert Men in the Mystery of Surgery, might, with the assent of twelve or eight Persons at the least, of the same Community, every Year elect and make out of the Community, two Masters, or Governors, being the most expert in the Mystery of Surgery, to oversee, rule, and govern, the Mystery and Commonalty aforesaid.

Recital of the Letters Patent of 1st Edward 4th; incorporating the Freemen of the Mystery of Barbers of the City of London.

AND WHEREAS by an Act of Parliament, made and passed in the 32d Year of the late King Henry VIII. intitled for Barbers and Surgeons, after reciting, that, within the City of London, there were then two several and distinct Companies of Surgeons, occupying and exercising the Faculty of Surgery, one Company called the Barbers of London, and the other Company called the Surgeons of London. It was thereby enacted, That the said two several and distinct Companies of Surgeons should from thenceforth be united, and made one intire and whole Body Corporate, and one Commonalty Perpetual, which at all times thereafter should be called by the Name of the Masters or Governors of the Mystery and Commonalty of the Barbers and Surgeons of London; and by the same Name to implead and be impleaded before all manner of Justices, in all Courts, and in all manner of Suits.

Of the Act 32d Henry 8th.

By which the two Companies of Barbers of London, and Surgeons of London were united.

d

Of the Letters Patent of 5th Charles 1st.

AND WHEREAS, in and by certain Letters Patent, under the Great Seal of England, bearing Date the 15th Day of August, in the 5th Year of the Reign of His late Majesty, King Charles I., reciting that the Men of the same Companies enjoyed divers Liberties and Franchises within the City of London, the Suburbs and Liberties thereof, by virtue of divers

Which confirmed to such united Company all the possessions, franchises and liberties which the said Company then held and enjoyed,

Acts of Parliament, and divers Charters, and Letters Patent, His said Majesty did grant and confirm unto the said Masters and Governors of the Mystery and Commonalty aforesaid, and their Successors, all and singular the Manors, Messuages, Lands, Tenements, Customs, Liberties, Franchises, Immunities, Jurisdictions, and Hereditaments, whatsoever, which the Men of the said Companies then held, used, and enjoyed, by any lawful Means

with power to make annual Elections of Masters or Governors whereof two to be Professors in Surgery; and to elect ten Freemen to be Examiners.

or Title whatsoever: And his said late Majesty did thereby give power to the said Corporation, to make annual Elections of Masters or Governors of the said Commonalty, whereof two to be Professors in the Art and Science of Surgery; and also to elect and constitute ten of the Freemen of the said Society to be Examiners of Surgeons in London.

Recital of the Act of 18th of George 2nd

AND WHEREAS, by an Act of Parliament, made and passed in the 18th Year of the Reign of our late Royal Grandfather, King George II., intitled "An Act for making the Surgeons of London, and the Barbers of London,

by which the Union of the two Companies was dissolved;

two separate and distinct Corporations," It was enacted, that the said Union and Incorporation of the Barbers and Surgeons of London, made and effected by the aforesaid Act of the 32d Year of King Henry VIII. should, from and after the 24th Day of June, 1745, be dissolved and declared void and of no effect; and that such of the Members of the said united Company who were Freemen of the said Company, and admitted and approved Surgeons, within the Rules of the said Company, and their

and which constituted a distinct Company of Surgeons, by the Name of "The Master, Governors, and Commonalty of the Art and Science of Surgeons of London."

Successors, should from thenceforth be made, and they were thereby made and constituted, a separate and distinct Body Corporate and Commonalty Perpetual, which at all times thereafter were to be called by the Name of Master, Governors and Commonalty of the Art and Science of Surgeons of London, and by the same Name might implead and be impleaded before all manner of Justices, in all Courts. and in all manner of Actions and Suits, and take to them and their Successors, Lands, Tenements, Rents, or Hereditaments, not exceeding the yearly Value of £200 in the whole.

Recital that such Corporation was dissolved.

AND WHEREAS, we are informed that the said Corporation of Master, Governors, and Commonalty of the Art and Science of Surgeons of Lon-

don, hath become and now is dissolved: AND WHEREAS, it is of great consequence to the Commonweal of this Kingdom, that the Art and Science
of Surgery should be duly promoted: AND WHEREAS, it appears to us, that
the Establishment of a College of Surgeons will be expedient for the due
promotion and encouragement of the Study and Practice of the said Art
and Science, Now WE, of our special Grace and mere Motion, and at the
humble Petition of JAMES EARLE, Esquire, the late Master, and divers
other Members of the aforesaid late Corporation of Surgeons; have willed,
ordained, constituted, declared, given and granted, and by these Presents,
for Us, Our Heirs, and Successors, do will, ordain, constitute, and declare,
give and grant; unto the aforesaid JAMES EARLE, and unto all the Members
of the said late Company or Corporation of Master, Governors, and Commonalty of the Art and Science of Surgeons of London; having been admitted and approved Surgeons, within the Rules of the said Company;
and also unto all such Persons, who upon, or since, the dissolution of the
said Corporation, shall have obtained Letters Testimonial, under a Seal
purporting to be the Seal of the said late dissolved Corporation, authoriz-
ing them to practise the Art and Science of Surgery; and they, from
henceforth for ever hereafter, shall be and remain by virtue of these Presents,
one Body Corporate and Politic; by the Name of THE ROYAL COLLFGE OF
SURGEONS IN LONDON, and by the same Name shall and may have perpetual
Succession, and a Common Seal; with power to break, alter, and make
anew the said Seal, from time to time at their will and pleasure; and by
the same Name shall and may implead, and be impleaded, before all manner of Justices, in all Courts, and in all manner of Actions and Suits;
and shall be at all times for ever hereafter persons able and capable in
Law to take, purchase. possess, hold, and enjoy, and shall and may take,
purchase, possess, hold and enjoy, a Hall or Council-house, with its Appurtenances, situate within the Cities of London or Westminster, or within
one Mile of either of them, for the use and purposes of the said College;
and also any other Lands, Tenements, Rents, or Hereditaments, wheresoever situate, lying and being; not exceeding, together with the aforesaid
Hall or Council-house, and its appurtenances, the yearly value of one
thousand Pounds in the whole; without incurring any of the Penalties in
any Statute of Mortmain, or any Thing, in any Statute of Mortmain, to
the contrary notwithstanding.

And it is Our further Will and Pleasure, that nothing in these Presents

d 2

That it is of great consequence that the Science of Surgery should be duly promoted,

and that a College will be expedient for the due encouragement thereof.

Therefore His Majesty- was pleased to in-corporate the Members of the late Company, and all such Persons who since the Dissolution thereof have ob-tained Letters Testimonial &c.

By the name of "The Royal College of Surgeons in London." With perpetual succession and a common seal;

and power to hold and enjoy a Council-house within London or Westminster cr one mile of either of them; and to possess lands and tene-ments, includ-ing such Coun-cil-House of the yearly value of £1000 in mort-main.

Proviso.—That the City of Lon-

don shall not have any jurisdiction over the College.

shall be construed to give the Corporation of the City of London any Power or Jurisdiction over the said College hereby established and incorporated;

Nor the Members of the College enjoy any franchise belonging to the Freemen of the City of London.

and that no Person, by virtue of these our Letters Patent, constituted or ordained, or hereafter to be admitted a Member of the said College, shall be thereby entitled to any Franchise belonging to the Freemen of the City of London.

The College to enjoy all other privileges and possessions by any former Acts or Letters Patent, given to, or otherwise acquired by, the late Company, not hereby altered, &c.

And it is Our further Will and Pleasure, and we do hereby, so far as We lawfully can or may, grant and ordain, that the said Royal College of Surgeons hereby incorporated, shall and may exercise and enjoy all and singular other the Gifts, Grants, Liberties, Privileges and Immunities, Possessions, real and personal, whatsoever and wheresoever, hereinbefore mentioned, or by any Act or Acts of Parliament, or by any Letters Patent, of Our Royal Predecessors, Kings and Queens of England given, granted, and confirmed unto, or otherwise lawfully acquired by, and belonging to the said late Master, Governors, and Commonalty of the Art and Science of Surgeons; or any of them, and not hereby altered, taken away, changed, or abridged, made void, or annulled.

The College liable to perform such Duties as the late Company did perform by the Act of 25th George 2d. "For the better preventing the horrid Crime of Murder."

And it is Our further Will and Pleasure, that the College of Surgeons hereby established, shall be liable to, and shall perform, such Duties as the late dissolved Corporation of Surgeons was at any time heretofore liable to, and did perform, by virtue of an Act made in the 25th Year of the Reign of Our Royal Grandfather, King George II., intituled, " An Act for the better preventing the horrid Crime of Murder."

To provide a proper place within four hundred yards from the place of execution for dissecting the Bodies of Murderers.

And further We Will, that the said College shall, and by these Presents they are required to purchase or provide a proper Room, House, or Building, with suitable Conveniences, within four hundred Yards, at the farthest, from the usual Place of Execution for the County of Middlesex, or the City of London, and the Suburbs thereof; for the purpose of more conveniently Dissecting and Anatomizing the Bodies of such Murderers as shall at any time hereafter be delivered to them, by virtue of the last mentioned Act.

Power to elect twenty - one persons to be the Court of Assistants of the College;

And it is Our further Will and Pleasure, that it shall and may be lawful, to and for the said College, hereby established and incorporated, from time to time in the Manner hereinafter mentioned, to elect, choose and appoint twenty-one Persons to be the Court of Assistants of the said College: of which Court of Assistants ten Persons shall at all times be consti-tuted and appointed Examiners of Surgeons for the said College; and of such ten Persons one shall be Principal Master, and two others shall be Governors; to be respectively qualified and admitted in such manner, and to continue in the said Offices respectively, for such time or times as by these Our Letters Patent is hereinafter ordered and appointed. And it shall and may be lawful for the Master and Governors of the said College, or for one of them, together with ten or more of the Members of the said Court of Assistants for the time being, when and as often as to any one of the Master or Governors shall seem meet, to hold Courts and Assemblies, in order to treat and consult about, and concerning, the Rule, Order, State, and Government of the said College. And also that it shall and may be lawful to and for the said Master and Governors, and Court of Assistants, so assembled, or the major part of them, to make, ordain, confirm, annul, or revoke, from time to time, such Bye-Laws, Ordinances, Rules, and Constitutions, as to them shall seem requisite and convenient, for the Regulation, Government, and Advantage of the said College: so as such Bye-Laws, Ordinances, Rules, and Constitutions be not contrary to Law: and in all such cases as shall be necessary, be examined, approved of, and allowed, as by the Laws and Statutes of this Realm is provided and required: and also to transact and ordain all such other Matters and Things as the Master, Governors and Court of Assistants, of the late dissolved Company or Corporation, of the Master, Governors, and Commonalty of the Art and Science of Surgeons of London, might heretofore lawfully do, transact, or ordain.

And further We Will, that CHARLES HAWKINS, Esquire, one of Our Principal Serjeant-Surgeons, shall be and he is hereby constituted and appointed the first Master of the said College of Surgeons: and that WILLIAM LONG and GEORGE CHANDLER, Esquires, shall be, and they are hereby constituted and appointed the first Governors of the same: And that the said CHARLES HAWKINS, WILLIAM LONG, and GEORGE CHANDLER, together with JOSEPH WARNER, WILLIAM LUCAS, SAMUEL HOWARD, and WILLIAM COOPER, Esquires, the said JAMES EARLE, THOMAS KEATE, Esquire, the Surgeon-General to our Forces, and CHARLES BLICKE, Esquire, shall be, and they are hereby constituted and appointed the first Examiners of Surgeons for the said College. And also that the said CHARLES HAWKINS, WILLIAM LONG, GEORGE CHANDLER, and JOSEPH WARNER, JONATHAN

Marginal notes:

of which Number ten shall be Examiners. and of such ten, one shall be Principal Master, and two others Governors.

The Master and Governors, or one of them with ten other Members of the Court of Assistants, may hold Courts to treat and consult about the Government of the College;

and make and annul Bye-Laws,

and transact all such other business as the Court of Assistants of the late dissolved Company might or could do.

Charles Hawkins, Esq., the first Master.

William Long and George Chandler, Esqs., the first Governors.

The first Court of Examiners.

WATHEN, Esquire; the said WILLIAM LUCAS, SAMUEL HOWARD, WILLIAM COOPER, JAMES EARLE, and CHARLES BLICKE, THOMPSON FORSTER, Esquire; JOHN BIRCH, Esquire; the said THOMAS KEATE, JOHN HEAVISIDE, JOHN HOWARD, WILLIAM BLIZARD, and HENRY CLINE, Esquires; DAVID DUNDAS, Esquire; the other of our Principal Serjeant-Surgeons; and such three other Persons as shall be elected to that Office on the day whereon the Court of Assistants of the said College, hereby incorporated. shall first meet, after the Date of these our Letters Patent, or at a Court of Assist-

The first Court of Assistants. ants to be holden within one Month then next after: shall be and they. are hereby constituted the first Court of Assistants of the said College of Surgeons, hereby incorporated and established.

The Master and Governors to enjoy their Offices until the first Thursday in July next, and until a new Election of Master and Governors. And it is Our further Will, that the said Master and Governors shall respectively hold and enjoy their said Offices of Master and Governors from henceforth until the first Thursday in July next after the Day of the Date of these Presents; and from thenceforth until a new Election of a Master and Governors of the said Corporation shall take place, as is hereinafter expressed.

The Examiners and Assistants and their Successors to enjoy their Offices for their natural lives, or until removed. And We also Will, that the said Persons, so before named and constituted Examiners of Surgeons of the said College, and their Successors in that Office, duly chosen, nominated, or appointed, and that the said Persons so before named and constituted Assistants of the said College, established by these our Letters Patent, and their Successors in that Office, duly chosen, nominated or appointed, shall respectively hold and enjoy their said Offices during their natural lives, or until they shall be lawfully removed out of the said Offices for any reasonable cause.

The two principal Serjeant-Surgeons and the Surgeon-General to the Forces to be always admitted into the Courts of Assistants and Examiners when any vacancy shall happen in those Courts in preference to all other persons And it is Our further Will and Pleasure, that the two Principal Serjeant-Surgeons to Us, and to Our Heirs and Successors, and the Surgeon-General to our Forces, and to the Forces of Our Heirs and Successors, if they, or any of them, at the times of their Appointments respectively, shall not be Members of the Courts of Assistants and Examiners of the said College, shall be from time to time admitted Members of the said Court of Assistants, and also Examiners of the said College hereby incorporated, when and so soon as any Vacancy shall happen, from time to time. after the Appointment of every such Serjeant-Surgeon, or Surgeon-General respectively, in preference to all other Persons.

And further it is Our Will and Pleasure that the Master and Governors of the said College, hereby incorporated and established, or one of them, together with the Assistants of the said College, hereby nominated, or the major part of them, shall, within thirty Days next after the Date of these Our Letters Patent, meet at such place at which the Persons, Members of the said late Corporation, shall have usually held their Meetings, for the space of six Months next before the Day of the Date of these Presents, or at such other place within the Cities of London or Westminster, or within one Mile of either of those Cities, as the Master or Governors, or any two of them, hereby constituted, shall in that behalf, by notice to be by them given and published in the London Gazette, fourteen Days before the Day of holding such Meeting for that purpose, appoint; and shall then and there hold a Court of Assistants, for carrying into effect these Our Letters Patent; and at such Court the said Master and Governors, Examiners and Assistants, or such of them as shall be then present, shall administer unto each other respectively, and each of them shall take the respective Oaths following, that is to say, the said Master and Governors shall take the following Oath:—" You do swear that, according to the best of your " Skill and Knowledge, you will discharge the several Trusts and Powers " vested in you, as Master (or Governor, as the Case may be) of the Royal " College of Surgeons in London; and that you will diligently maintain " the Honor and Welfare of the said College; and in all Things, which " shall in any Sort concern your Office, you will act faithfully and honestly, " without Favor or Affection, Prejudice or Partiality, to any Person or " Persons whomsoever.—So HELP YOU GOD."

The Court of Assistants to meet within thirty days and hold a Court for the purpose of carrying into effect this Charter; and at such Court, the said Master, Governors, Examiners, and Assistants to take the following Oaths.

The Oath of the Master and Governors.

And that each of such Examiners and Assistants shall take the following Oath, that is to say—" You do swear, that so long as you shall remain in " the Office of Examiner (or Assistant, as the Case may be) of the Royal " College of Surgeons in London, you will diligently maintain the Honor " and Welfare of the said College; and in all Things relating to your " Office, and with all Manner of Persons, act equally and impartially, ac- " cording to the best of your Skill and Knowledge.—So HELP YOU GOD."

The Oath of the Examiners and Assistants.

And no Person hereby appointed or hereafter to be elected Master, Governor, Examiner, or Assistant of the said College, hereby established and incorporated, shall proceed to act in the execution of such Office, until he and they shall have taken the respective Oath and Oaths hereinbefore

No Person to act in either of those Offices without having first taken the Oath appointed

mentioned, which shall be duly administered to them respectively, at a Court of Assistants to be holden in pursuance of these Our Letters Patent.

The Court of Assistants upon the first Thursday in July in every year, or within one month then after, to meet and chuse out of the Examiners one person to be Master, and two others to be Governors for the succeeding year.

And We further Will, that the Master, Governors, and Assistants, for the time being, of the said College, hereby made and established, shall, upon the first Thursday in the Month of July next after the Date of these Our Letters Patent, or within one Month then after, and upon the first Thursday in July, in every succeeding Year, or within one Month then after, meet in the Place which shall from time to time be used, or appointed to be used as their Hall or Council-house, or as near to such Hall or Council-house as conveniently may be; and then and there elect, chuse, and appoint out of the Examiners, by the Majority of Votes of such of the Court of Assistants as shall be then present, one Person to be Principal Master, and two other Persons to be Governors of the said College, for the then succeeding Year; and then and there also, in like manner, chuse and

And to appoint the Serjeant-Surgeons or the Surgeon-General, if not already Examiners, and if they are, then some other of the Court of Assistants, to fill up such Vacancies as shall be in the Court of Examiners, unless such Vacancies have been previously filled up, which it shall be lawful to do at a special Court of Assistants.

appoint one or more of Our Principal Serjeant-Surgeons, or the Surgeon-General of Our Forces, if not already an Examiner or Examiners of Surgeons of the said College; or otherwise shall chuse and appoint out of their own Body, some other Person or Persons, to be Examiner or Examiners of Surgeons for the said College, in the place and stead of such Examiner or Examiners as shall have happened to die, or have been removed from the said Office of Examiner in the then next preceding Year, unless such Vacancies in the Office of Master or Governor, and in that Court, shall have been previously filled up within the then preceding Year, which it shall be lawful for the said Court of Assistants to do, at any

And also to chuse out of the Members of the College, some Person or Persons to be of the Court of Assistants in the place of such of the Assistants as shall have died or been removed in the then next preceding year, unless previously filled up in that year.

special Court to be held for that purpose. And also in like manner chuse and appoint, out of the Members of the said College established by these Presents, such Person or Persons to be of the Court of Assistants of the same College, in the place of such Person or Persons who shall have happened to die in or have been removed from the said Office of one of the Court of Assistants in the then next preceding Year: unless such Vacancies in that Court shall have been previously filled up within the then preceding Year; which it shall be lawful for the said Court of Assistants to do, at a special Court to be held for that purpose.

The Master or one of the Governors, with ten Assistants, suffi-

And it is our Will and Pleasure, that the Master, or one of the Governors, together with ten Assistants at the least, shall be at all times sufficient to constitute a Court of Assistants for the purpose of such Elections, or for the purpose of transacting any other Business belonging to the said Court. But that no Court of Assistants shall be holden for the special purpose of electing any Person to be Master, Governor, Examiner, or Assistant; without seven Days previous Notice to be given for that purpose, by Summons to the Members of the Court of Assistants for the time being.

cient to constitute a Court of Assistants for the purpose of such Elections, and for all other Purposes. But no Court shall be holden for the special purpose of any such Election, without seven Days' notice to the Court of Assistants.

And furthermore it is Our Will and Pleasure, that if, at any time or times hereafter, it shall happen that the Master and both the Governors of the said College hereby established, shall die, or become incapable of acting before the Election of a new Master and Governors, according to the Provisions hereinbefore contained, that then, and in every such case, it shall and may be lawful for the senior Member of the Court of Assistants who shall be capable of attending, to summon, convene, and hold a Court of Assistants which shall be held as soon as may be next after the Death or Incapacity of the last of such of them the said Master and Governors, who shall be so dead or incapable of acting; and that at such Court, a Master and Governors of the said College shall be elected for the remainder of the then current Year; and that it shall and may be lawful for the senior Assistant of the said College who shall be then present, to preside at and hold such Court, and to administer to the new Master and Governors, who shall be then and there elected, the Oath appointed to be taken by the Master and Governors of the said College as aforesaid, any thing herein contained to the contrary thereof notwithstanding: And in case it shall so happen that on the Day appointed for the ordinary Election of Master and Governors for the ensuing Year, the Master and both the Governors shall be dead, or incapable of attending, the senior Member of the Court of Assistants, who shall be present at the Court of Assistants to be held for the purpose of such Election, shall preside at, and hold such Court, and administer to the new Master and Governors, who shall then and there be elected, the Oath appointed to be taken by the Master and Governors of the said College as aforesaid, any thing herein contained to the contrary notwithstanding: And in case it shall at any time happen, that the Persons who shall assemble at the Day and Place appointed for any Court of Assistants to be holden in pursuance of these our Letters Patent, shall not be capable of holding such Court, by reason of the Absence of any of the Members of the said Court whose Presence shall be required

If the Master and Governors shall die or be incapable of acting at the same time,

the senior Member of the Court of Assistants may convene and hold a Court within fourteen days next after the death or incapacity of the last of such Master or Governors.

And at such Court the Master and Governors for the remainder of the then current year shall be elected, and the senior Member who shall be present shall preside at, and hold such Court, and administer to the new Master and Governors the Oath to be taken by them.

If, on the ordinary day of Election of Master and Governors, the Master and both the Governors shall be dead or incapable of attending, the senior Member present shall hold such Court and administer the Oaths.

If it shall at any time happen that no Court of Assistants can be held by reason of the absence of any of the Members whose presence shall be required; the senior Member present may adjourn the Court to a future day; but no such adjournment shall take place until after the expiration of one hour, from the time appointed for holding the Court.

for that purpose, it shall be lawful for the senior Member present to adjourn such Court to a future Day, provided that no such Adjournment shall be made until after the Expiration of one hour at the least, from the Hour appointed for holding such Court.

No person shall be capable of becoming a Member of the College, except the Members of the late dissolved Company, and persons who have since the dissolution thereof obtained Letters Testimonial. &c., unless he shall have obtained Letters Testimonial under the Seal of the College.

And it is our further Will and Pleasure, that after the Day of the Date of these Presents, no Person except those who before the Day of the Date of these Presents were Members of the late Corporation of Surgeons, established by the said Act, made and passed in the eighteenth Year of the Reign of Our Royal Grandfather, King George II. ; and also excepting such Persons as shall have received such Letters Testimonial as aforesaid, under a Seal purporting to be the Seal of the late dissolved Company or Corporation of Surgeons, shall be capable of becoming a Member of the said College hereby established, unless he shall have obtained Letters Testimonial of his Qualification to practise the Art and Science of Surgery, under the Common Seal of the College hereby established; but every

But every person who shall hereafter obtain such Letters Testimonial, shall become a Member of the College.

Person who shall hereafter obtain such Letters Testimonial, under the Common Seal of the College aforesaid, shall thereby, by virtue of such Letters Testimonial, become and be constituted a Member of the said College, subject to all the Regulations, Provisions, and Bye-Laws of the said College.

The Court of Examiners from time to time, upon request of the Commander in Chief and Lords of the Admiralty, to examine all army and navy Surgeons and their Assistants and Mates,

And it is our further Will and Pleasure, that from and after such Day on which the Court of Assistants of the College hereby established shall first meet, in the manner before-mentioned, the Examiners of the College of Surgeons hereby established, shall, and they are hereby required from time to time, upon Request to them made by the Commander in Chief of our Forces, and by the Lord High Admiral or Commissioners for executing the Office of Lord High Admiral, or any other Officer of Us, Our Heirs or Successors, properly authorized to examine every Person who shall be a Candidate to be appointed to serve as a Surgeon or Assistant Surgeon in any Regiment, Troop, Company, Hospital, or Garrison of Soldiers, in the Service of Ourselves, Our Heirs or Successors, or to serve as a Surgeon or Surgeon's Mate, appointed on Board any Ship or Ships in the Service of Ourselves, Our Heirs or Successors, or any other Service in

and for such Examinations to receive such Fee as shall be allowed them from time to time by the Om

which We, Our Heirs or Successors shall think fit to employ any Persons to act in any such Capacities, and shall accept and receive for each such Examination, from the Persons so examined respectively, such Fee or

Reward as shall from time to time be allowed by such Officer or Officers of Us, Our Heirs or Successors, as shall be authorized to require such Examinations, to be had respectively, and no more ; and shall also in like manner examine all Surgeons' Instruments to be used in Our Service, which they shall be required in like manner to examine, and shall return such Instruments, when examined, to such Person or Persons as shall be appointed to receive the same, with such Certificate, in such Form, and properly sealed up, or otherwise authenticated in such manner as the Officer or Officers, from time to time, to be appointed by Us for such Purposes, shall require ; and taking for the same Examination such Fee or Reward as shall be allowed from time to time by such our Officer or Officers respectively, and no more.

Provided always, that the Fees or Rewards from time to time to be appointed as aforesaid, for the Examination of any such Person or Instruments as aforesaid, shall not be less than the Fees or Rewards heretofore paid for the like Examinations respectively.

And further We Will that no Court or Courts for the Examination of any Person or Persons touching their Skill in Surgery, shall ever be held but in the Presence of the Master or one of the Governors, and five of the Members, at least, of the Court of Examiners of the said College, hereby established and incorporated as aforesaid.

And it is Our further Will and Pleasure, that the Members of the said late Corporation and such other Persons who, since the Dissolution thereof, shall have obtained such Letters Testimonial under a Seal, purporting to be the Seal of the late dissolved Company or Corporation as aforesaid ; and who shall be willing to become and be Members of the said College hereby established and incorporated, shall testify their Acceptance of these Our Letters Patent, and their Consent to become Members of the said College, by signifying such their Acceptance and Consent in Writing to the Court of Assistants, within six calendar Months after the Date of these Our Letters Patent, who shall cause such Acceptance and Consent to be entered in certain Books to be kept for that purpose, at the Hall or Council-house of the said College ; and the said Court of Assistants are hereby required to keep such Books, and have such Entries made therein accordingly.

who shall be authorized to require such Examinations,

and shall also in like manner, examine Surgeons' Instruments,

and shall return the same when examined, authenticated in such manner as shall be required,

taking for such Examinations such Fees as shall be allowed by such Officers from time to time.

Provided that such Fees so to be from time to time appointed for the Examination of any such person or instruments, shall not be less than the Fees heretofore paid for the like Examinations.

No Court of Examiners to be held unless in the presence of the Master, or one of the Governors and five Members of the Court of Examiners at least.

The Members of the late Company and such persons who have, since the dissolution thereof, obtained Letters Testimonial, &c. who shall be willing to become Members of the College, to testify their consent in writing to the Court of Assistants, within six months after the date of the Charter.

Which acceptance and consent shall be entered in proper books to be kept at the College.

And such persons who shall not signify their consent within the time limited, shall not be deemed Members of the College, unless admitted Members thereof by the Court of Assistants upon special application made to them for that purpose.

And it is Our further Will and Pleasure, that such and so many of the Members of the said late Corporation, and of such Persons as shall have obtained such Letters Testimonial as aforesaid, as shall not, within the time aforesaid, signify in manner aforesaid their Acceptance of these Our Letters Patent, shall not be deemed or be Members of the said College, unless they shall be duly admitted to be Members thereof by the said Court of Assistants, upon special application made to them for that purpose.

But all persons beyond the seas at the time of the date of the Charter may signify their consent within six months after their return

Provided always, that if any of such Persons shall happen to be beyond the Seas at the Date of these Our Letters Patent, it shall be lawful for such Persons respectively to signify their Acceptance thereof, in manner aforesaid, within six calendar Months after they shall return respectively to this Kingdom.

But the Master, Governors and Court of Assistants may proceed to hold a Court to carry the Charter into effect, without having first signified their consent and acceptance of the Charter.

Nevertheless, it is Our Will and Pleasure, that the Master, Governors, and Assistants, of the College hereby established, and hereinbefore specially named and appointed, shall and may proceed to hold a Court for the purpose of carrying these Our Letters Patent into Execution, as aforesaid, without having testified their Assent to, and Acceptance of, such Letters Patent, by any Writing, or by any Entry to be made in manner aforesaid.—Witness HIS MAJESTY, at Westminster, the 22d Day of March, in the fortieth Year of His Reign,

By Writ of Privy Seal,

WILMOT.

3RD GEORGE IV.

13TH FEBRUARY, 1822.

GEORGE THE FOURTH, by the Grace of God, of the United Kingdom of Great Britain and Ireland, King, Defender of the Faith, &c. To ALL TO WHOM these Presents shall come, greeting. WHEREAS our late Royal Father King George the Third, by certain Letters Patent under the Great Seal of Great Britain, bearing date the twenty-second day of March in the Fortieth Year of his Reign ; Reciting (among other things) that a certain then late Corporation of Master, Governors, and Commonalty of the Art and Science of Surgeons of London, had become and then was dissolved ; and .nat it was of great consequence to the Common Weal of the Kingdom that the Art and Science of Surgery should be duly promoted ; and that the establishment of a College of Surgeons would be expedient for the due promotion and encouragement of the study and practice of the said Art and Science ; of his special grace and mere motion, and at the humble Petition of James Earle, Esq., then late Master, and divers other Members of the aforesaid then late Corporation of Surgeons ; for himself, his Heirs and Successors, did (among other things) will, ordain, constitute and declare, give. and grant unto the aforesaid James Earle, and unto all the Members of the said then late Company or Corporation of Master, Governors, and Commonalty of the Art and Science of Surgeons of London, having been admitted and approved Surgeons, within the Rules of the said Company, and also unto all such persons, who upon, or since the dissolution of the said Corporation, should have obtained Letters Testimonial, under a Seal purporting to be the Seal of the said then late dissolved Corporation, authorising them to practise the Art and Science of Surgery ; that they, from thenceforth for ever thereafter, should be and remain, by virtue of the said Letters Patent, one Body Corporate and Politic, by the name of THE ROYAL COLLEGE OF SURGEONS IN LONDON, and should be at all times, for ever thereafter, persons able and capable in law to take, purchase, possess, hold, and enjoy, and should and might take, purchase, possess, hold and enjoy, a Hall, or Council-House, with its appurtenances, situate within the Cities of London or Westminster, or within one mile of either of them, for the use and purposes of the said College ; and also

Recital of Letters Patent of 40th George III.

any other Lands, Tenements, Rents, or Hereditaments, wheresoever situate, lying, and being; not exceeding, together with the aforesaid Hall or Council-house and its appurtenances, the yearly value of One thousand Pounds in the whole, without-incurring any of the Penalties in any Statute of Mortmain, or any thing, in any Statute of Mortmain, to the contrary notwithstanding.

Further recital of Letters Patent of 40th George III.

AND WHEREAS in and by the said Letters Patent our said late Royal Father did further Will that the said College should, and by the said Letters Patent they were required to purchase or provide a proper Room, House, or Building, with suitable conveniences, within four hundred yards, at the furthest, from the usual place of Execution for the County of Middlesex, or the City of London, and the suburbs thereof, for the purpose of more conveniently dissecting and anatomizing the Bodies of such Murderers as should at any time thereafter be delivered to them, by virtue of a certain Act passed in the Twenty-fifth Year of the Reign of His Majesty King George the Second, entitled, "An Act for the better preventing the horrid Crime of Murder."

Further recital of Letters Patent of 40th George III.

AND WHEREAS in and by the said Letters Patent it was further declared to be the Will and Pleasure of our said late Royal Father, that it should and might be lawful to and for the said College, thereby established and incorporated, from time to time in the manner thereinafter mentioned, to elect, choose and appoint twenty-one persons to be the Court of Assistants of the said College; of which Court of Assistants ten persons should at all times be constituted and appointed Examiners of Surgeons for the said College; and of such ten persons one should be principal Master, and two others should be Governors, to be respectively qualified and admitted in manner thereby provided.

Further recital of Letters Patent of 40th George III.

AND WHEREAS in and by the said Letters Patent it was further declared to be the Will and Pleasure of our said late Royal Father, that the two principal Sergeant-Surgeons to our said late Royal Father, his Heirs and Successors, and the Surgeon-General to the Forces of our said late Royal Father, his Heirs and Successors, if they, or any of them, at the times of their appointments respectively, should not be Members of Courts of Assistants and Examiners of the said College, should be from time to time admitted Members of the said Court of Assistants and also Examiners of the said College thereby incorporated, when and so soon as any vacancy should happen, from time to time, after the appointment of every such Serjeant-Surgeon or Surgeon-General respectively, in preference to all other persons.

AND WHEREAS it appears to Us to be expedient, in order more effectually to promote and encourage the study and practice of the said Art and Science of Surgery, that further powers and privileges be granted to the said Royal College: Now KNOW YE, that WE of our especial grace and mere motion, at the humble petition of the said Royal College, have willed, ordained, constituted, declared, and granted, and by these Presents for Us, Our Heirs and Successors, do will, ordain, constitute, declare, and grant unto the said Royal College, that the said Royal College of Surgeons in London shall and may take, purchase, possess, hold, and enjoy, any Lands, Tenements, Rents, or Hereditaments, wheresoever situate, lying, and being; not exceeding, together with the aforesaid Hall or Council-house and its appurtenances, and the Lands, Tenements, Rents, or Hereditaments now held by them, the yearly value of Two thousand Pounds, in the whole, without incurring any of the Penalties in any Statute of Mortmain, or any thing, in any Statute of Mortmain, to the contrary notwithstanding.

Preamble

The College may hold Lands or Rents to the yearly value of £2000.

AND WE do hereby also for Us, Our Heirs and Successors, give and grant our especial licence, full power, and lawful and absolute authority, to any Person or Persons, Bodies Politic or Corporate, their Heirs and Successors respectively, to grant, alien, sell, convey and dispose of in Mortmain, in perpetuity or otherwise, to or to the use and benefit of, or in trust for, the said Royal College of Surgeons any Lands, Tenements, Rents, or Hereditaments whatsoever not exceeding, together with the aforesaid Hall or Council-house and its appurtenances, and the Lands, Tenements, Rents, or Hereditaments now held by them, the yearly value aforesaid of Two thousand Pounds in the whole. And it is our further Will and Pleasure that the said College shall not be hereafter required to purchase or provide a proper Room, House or Building, as hereinbefore mentioned, within four hundred yards at the farthest from the said usual place of Execution, but that in lieu thereof it shall be sufficient for the said College, and by these Presents they are required, to purchase or provide such Room, House or Building, with suitable conveniences, within

Persons may convey Lands or Rents to the College.

The College to provide for the dissection of the Bodies of Murderers within half a mile from the usual place of Execution.

half a mile at the farthest from the said usual place of Execution for the purpose in the said Letters Patent mentioned.

AND IT IS our further Will and Pleasure that the Names, Styles, and Titles of Office of the principal Master, Governors, and Court of Assistants of the said Royal College shall be altered respectively in manner follow-

The title of Master changed to President. ing, that is to say ; the principal Master shall in future be called and denominated the President of the said Royal College ; the Governors shall

The title of Governors changed to Vice - Presidents, and Court of Assistants to Council. in future be called and denominated the Vice-Presidents of the said Royal College ; and the Court of Assistants shall in future be called and denominated the Council of the said Royal College.

The two principal Serjeant-Surgeons and the Surgeon-General if on the Council to be admitted to the Court of Examiners on the first vacancy. AND IT IS our further Will and Pleasure that if any Person who shall at any time hereafter be appointed one of the two principal Serjeant-Surgeons to Us, or to Our Heirs and Successors, or Surgeon-General to the Forces of Us, Our Heirs and Successors, shall be at the time of such Appointment or shall at any time thereafter be chosen a Member of the Council of the said College, he shall in that case, when and so soon as any vacancy shall happen in the Court of Examiners of the said College, be admitted a Member of the said Court in preference to each and every other Member of the Council ; and that such principal Serjeant-Surgeons and Surgeon-General shall not have any other preference whatever either in respect of admission to the said Council or the Court of Examiners of the said College, any thing in the said Letters Patent to the contrary notwithstanding.

The College to enjoy the right of having a Mace. AND IT IS our further Will and Pleasure that it shall and may be lawful to and for the said College at all times hereafter, and upon all such occasions as they shall think proper and expedient to exercise and enjoy the Right and Privilege of having a Mace, and of causing the same to be borne by such Officer as they shall appoint for that purpose. IN WITNESS whereof We have caused these Our Letters to be made Patent. WITNESS Ourself, at Our Palace of Westminster, this thirteenth Day of February, in the Third Year of Our Reign.

By Writ of Privy Seal,

SCOTT.

7th VICTORIA.

14th September, 1843.

VICTORIA, by the Grace of God, of the United Kingdom of Great Britain and Ireland, Queen, Defender of the Faith, To ALL TO WHOM THESE PRESENTS SHALL COME, GREETING, WHEREAS the Body Politic and Corporate of THE ROYAL COLLEGE OF SURGEONS IN LONDON was incorporated or re-established under or by virtue of a certain Charter or Letters Patent, bearing date at Westminster, the twenty-second day of March, in the Fortieth Year of the Reign of King George the Third, or otherwise, as in such Letters Patent mentioned or referred to, and the said College is now regulated and governed by and according to the Provisions of such Charter or Letters Patent, and a certain other or Supplemental Charter, granted by Letters Patent bearing date at Westminster the thirteenth day of February in the Third year of the Reign of King George the Fourth, and also by or according to certain Bye-Laws and Ordinances made by the said College for its regulation and better government.

Recites—That the College was incorporated or re-established by Charter of 40th George III.

Recites—That a supplemental Charter was granted 3rd George IV.

AND WHEREAS the Body Politic and Corporate of the said College at present consists of persons created Members of the said College by the said first-mentioned Charter, or constituted such Members by Letters Testimonial, under the Common Seal of the said College, of the respective qualifications of such persons to practise the Art and Science of Surgery. And the Governing Body of the said College consists of a Council of twenty-one of the Members of the College, ten of them being also Examiners of Surgeons for the College, and one of such ten persons being also the President and two of them the Vice-Presidents of the College and the two principal Serjeant-Surgeons to us and to our Heirs and Successors and the Surgeon-General to the Forces, of us, our Heirs and Successors, provided they shall have been chosen Members of the Council, have at present a preference of being admitted Examiners of the said College before all other persons whenever vacancies happen in the Court of Examiners of the College.

Recites—That the College at present consists of Members constituted by Letters Testimonial. Recites—That the Governing Body consists of a Council of Twenty-one, ten of them being Examiners, one of such ten persons being also the President, and two of them the Vice-Presidents. Recites—That the two principal Serjeant-Surgeons and the Surgeon-General (provided they shall have been chosen Members of the Council) have a preference of being admitted Examiners

Declares that it is expedient to create a new class of Members, to be called Fellows.

AND WHEREAS, in order more effectually to promote and encourage the study and practice of the said art and science of Surgery, It appears to us expedient, that a new class of Members of the said College, to be called Fellows, should be created, and (with the exception of the first Fellows hereinafter named and directed and authorized respectively to be appointed) be required, in order to obtain the Diploma of their Fellowship, to have attained a greater age than is at present necessary in the case of Ordinary Members of the said College, and to have complied with such Rules and

That the number of the Council should be increased, and that all future Members be chosen from the Fellows, and hold office for a limited period only, instead of for life, and the Fellows to have the right of electing the Council, and that alterations be also made as regards the election, admission, and continuance in office of future Examiners.

Regulations, and passed such Examination as hereinafter mentioned; That the number of the Members of the Council of the said College should be increased, and that all future Members of the Council be chosen from the Fellows of the College and hold their office for a limited period only, instead of for life, and that the right of electing Members of the Council be transferred from the Council (with whom such right now resides) to the Body of such Fellows; That alterations be also made as regards the election and admission and continuance in office of the future Examiners of the College, and that certain further powers and privileges should also be granted to the said College. Now KNOW YE, That WE, of our especial grace and mere motion, at the Humble Petition of the said Royal College, HAVE willed, ordained, constituted, and declared and granted, and by these presents for us, our Heirs and Successors, DO will, ordain, constitute and declare, and unto the said ROYAL COLLEGE OF SURGEONS in LONDON do grant, in manner following, to wit:

1. The name of the College to be the Royal College of Surgeons of England, and a portion of the Members to be Fellows thereof.

1. That from henceforth the Corporate Name or Style of the said College shall be—THE ROYAL COLLEGE OF SURGEONS OF ENGLAND, and that a portion of the Members of the said College shall be Fellows thereof by the name or style of THE FELLOWS OF THE ROYAL COLLEGE OF SURGEONS OF ENGLAND.

2. First Fellows.

2. That the present President and two Vice-Presidents, and all other the present Members of the Council of the said College, and also such several other persons, not being less than two hundred and fifty nor more than three hundred in number, and being Members of the said College, as the Council of the said College, at any time or times before the expiration of three calendar months from the date hereof, shall elect and declare to be Fellows in manner hereinafter directed, together with any such other persons as the Council of the said College, after the expiration of the said three calendar months, and within one year from the date hereof, shall

thınk fit and shall appoint in manner hereinafter authorized, snall be
Fellows of the said College.

3. That the Council of the said College, with all convenient speed after
the date of these our Letters Patent, and before the expiration of three
calendar months from the date hereof, and in such manner as the said
Council shall deem best, shall elect to be Fellows of the said College any
such number of persons, being Members of the said College, and not being
in the whole less than two hundred and fifty nor more than three hundred,
as the said Council shall think proper: And also shall, before the expiration of such three calendar months, by one general Diploma, under the
Seal of the said College, and in such form as the Council shall think fit
declare, or cause such persons to be declared Fellows of the Royal College
of Surgeons of England accordingly ; but the names of all such persons, so
declared Fellows, shall be contained and set forth in a Schedule to such
general Diploma. And such general Diploma shall also, within two
calendar months after the Seal of the said College shall have been affixed
thereto, be enrolled in our High Court of Chancery.

3. The Council shall within three months elect not less than 250 nor more than 300 Membersof the College to be Fellows.

4. That it shall also be lawful for the Council of the said College, at
any time or times after the expiration of the said three calendar months
and before the expiration of one year from the date hereof, by Diploma or
Diplomas under the Seal of the said College, and in such form as the said
Council shall think fit, and without any Fee, to appoint any other person
or persons (being a Member or Members of the said College) to be a Fellow
or Fellows of the said Royal College of Surgeons of England.

4. Power of the Council within one year to ap-point other Members to be Fellows.

5. That, except as hereinbefore mentioned, no person shall become or
be admitted a Fellow of the said College until after he shall have attained
the age of Twenty-five years, and shall also have complied with such Rules
and Regulations as the Council of the said College shall from time to time
consider expedient, and by a Bye-Law or Bye-Laws direct, nor unless he
shall have passed such special Examination by the Examiners of the said
College, as the Council shall from time to time think fit, and by a Bye-Law
or Bye-Laws direct, that Candidates for a Fellowship of the said College
shall undergo ; but every fit and proper person having attained such age,
and complied with such Rules and Regulations, and passed such special
Examination, shall be entitled to be admitted a Fellow of the said College.

5. Except as hereinbefore mentioned, no person tobe ad-mitted aFellow until he shall have attained the age of twen-ty-five, have complied with such Rules ano Regulations as shall be consi-dered expe-dient, and have passed a special Examination.

Admission of a Fellow to be by Diploma, and every Fellow (not being already a Member) to be a Member by virtue of his Fellowship.

6. That the admittance of every such new Fellow as last mentioned, shall be by Diploma under the Seal of the said College, in such form as the Council of the College shall from time to time think fit and direct; and that every person so admitted a Fellow of the said College, and not being already a Member thereof, shall also, by virtue of such his admittance as a Fellow, become and be considered admitted as a Member of the said College.

7. Admission-Fee of a Fellow to be any sum not exceeding Thirty Guineas.

7. That the Fee to be paid on the admittance of every such new Fellow as last aforesaid (over and besides the stamp-duty on his admittance or Diploma), shall be any such sum not exceeding the sum of Thirty-one Pounds Ten Shillings, as the Council of the said College shall from time to time think fit, and by a Bye-Law or Bye-Laws direct.

8. Diplomas of Fellows granted the same day to be numbered to show priority.

8. That where several Diplomas shall be granted on the same day (whether to such new Fellows as last aforesaid, or to any Fellows to be created after the said first three calendar months, and within the first year from the date hereof as aforesaid), such Diplomas shall be numbered under such Regulations as the Council may think fit, in order to show the order and priority of such Diplomas among themselves.

9. A Register to be kept of the Fellows according to their several seniorities, and to be open to the inspection of Members.

9. That the Council of the said College shall cause the name of every Fellow for the time being of the said College, and if thought fit by the Council, together also with the place of residence of every such Fellow, to be entered according to their several seniorities (in the manner and to be determined or ascertained respectively as hereinafter mentioned), in a Book or Register to be kept for that purpose at the Hall of the said College, or such other place for the time being as the said Council shall direct; and such Book or Register of Fellows, at such times and subject to such reasonable and proper Regulations as the Council for the time being shall think fit and direct, shall be open to the inspection of any Member of the said College (whether Fellow or not), at the Hall of the said College, or

How seniority of Fellows is to be determined.

other place appointed for the time being for the custody of the same. And the Seniority of such Fellows to be entered in such Book or Register as aforesaid, shall be and be determined or ascertained respectively as follows, that is to say, The present President shall be entered first, the two present Vice-Presidents, according to their respective seniority next after him, and then all the other present Members of the Council according to their

respective seniorities, and immediately after such the present Members of
the Council; the Fellows to be elected within three calendar months from
the date hereof as hereinbefore directed, according to the order and priority
of their names, as the same shall be contained and set forth in the Schedule to such general Diploma, whereby they shall be so declared Fellows
as hereinbefore directed; and, with respect to all other Fellows, their
names shall be entered according to the dates of their respective Diplomas;
and when the Diplomas of any Fellows shall bear date on the same day,
then as regards or between such Fellows according to the order and
priority in which the Diplomas shall be so numbered, as hereinbefore
directed.

10. That from henceforth no Member of the said College, who shall not
also be a Fellow of the same, shall be eligible as a Member of the Council
of the said College; nor (but subject and without prejudice to the validity
of any Election to be made as hereinafter directed) shall any Fellow be so
eligible whilst practising Midwifery or Pharmacy, or who shall have practised Midwifery or Pharmacy at any time during the five years next preceding the day of Election, nor unless he shall reside and *bonâ fide* practise
his profession of Surgeon within five miles by highway or road from the
General Post-Office in St. Martin's-le-Grand. And if any Member of the
Council shall at any time after his Election practise Midwifery or Pharmacy, or shall cease to reside and *bonâ fide* practise his profession of
Surgeon within five miles of the General Post-Office, as aforesaid, he shall
be liable to removal from the Council.

10. No Member not a Fellow to be eligible as a Member of the Coun-cil.

No Fellow to be eligible as a Member of Coun-cil whilst prac-tising Midwifery or Pharmacy, or who shall have so practised during five years next preceding elec-tion, nor unless he shall reside and practise within five miles of the General Post-Office.

11. That the present Members of the Council of the said College shall
be and continue Life Members thereof as heretofore, and that the number
of the Members of the Council shall in the manner hereinafter mentioned
be increased from twenty-one to twenty-four, and that all future Members
of the Council shall be elective and be elected periodically, in the manner
and subject to the regulations hereinafter mentioned and directed.

11. Present Mem-bers of Council to continue for life, the number of the Council to be in-creased to twen-ty-four; future Members to be elective and elect-ed periodically, as after mentioned.

12. That upon the first Thursday in the Month of July in the year
one thousand eight hundred and forty-four, or within one calendar month
afterwards, and in the manner hereinafter mentioned, three Fellows of
the said College shall be chosen to be additional Members of the Council
of the said College; and that upon the first Thursday in July in every

12. Upon the first Thursday in July next ensuing date hereof (or within one month) in manner after mentioned, three Fellows to I eho-sen to be addi-tional Members of the Council.

And at the same period in every succeeding year three Fellows shall be chosen Members of Council. In each year in which there shall be no vacancy, or less than three, among the Life Members, three of the Elective Members, or such less number as with the vacancies among Life Members shall make the number three, shall go out of office, and when more than three vacancies among Life Members, none of the Elective Members to go out of office, and three Fellows only to be chosen to fill up three of the Life vacancies, and the remaining vacancies to be treated as Life vacancies for following year or years, as the case may require. When the number of Elective Members shall be completed to twenty-four three of the Council to go out of office annually. In all cases Fellows going out of office to be eligible for re-election.

succeeding year, for ever thereafter, or within one calendar month afterwards, and in the manner hereinafter mentioned, three Fellows shall be chosen to be members of the Council; and in every such succeeding year in which there shall be no vacancy, or less than three vacancies among the Life Members of the Council, three of the Elective Members of the Council, or such less number of such Elective Members as, with the number of vacancies in that year among the Life Members, will make up the number three, shall go out of office upon the day whereon such three Fellows shall be chosen to be Members as aforesaid, so that the number of the Council shall at no time exceed twenty-four; and in every such succeeding year in which there shall be three or more than three vacancies among the Life Members, none of the Elective Members shall go out of office in that year, and three Fellows, and three only, shall be chosen to fill up three of such vacancies among the Life Members, and the remaining vacancy or vacancies of that year (if any) shall be considered and treated as a vacancy or vacancies among the Life Members in the following year or years, as the case may be or require. But from and after the period when the number of the Elective Members of the Council shall be completed and made up to twenty-four, three of the Members of the Council shall go out of office every year, upon the day whereon three new Members shall be elected, as aforesaid. But in all cases Fellows going out of office shall notwithstanding be eligible for nomination and immediate re-election, and, continuing eligible in other respects, their names shall be announced to the Meeting accordingly in the order and manner hereinafter directed.

13. Those Members to go out of office who have been longest on the Council.

13. That the Elective Members of the Council, who shall from time to time go out of office in the manner hereinbefore mentioned and directed, shall be those who shall have been longest on the Council without re-election; and in the case of Fellows elected upon the Council in the same year, those shall first go out of office whose names stand lowest (among those elected of the same year) on the Book or Register of the Fellows of the College.

14. Substitute Members to be from time to time elected to fill up vacancies taking place among Elective Members in any other way

14. That whenever any vacancy or vacancies shall take place among the Elective Members in any other way than by their going out of office by rotation as aforesaid, such vacancy or vacancies shall be filled up by the election (upon some early and convenient day to be fixed by the Council

for that purpose\ of a substitute Member or Members in the room of the person or persons whose place or places shall have so become vacant; and every person, so elected to fill up any such vacancy, shall hold such office until the time when the person in whose room he shall be chosen would have been liable to go out of office, and he shall then go out of office accordingly, but shall notwithstanding be eligible for nomination **and** immediate re-election, and continuing eligible in other respects, his name shall be announced to the Meeting accordingly in the order and manner hereinafter directed.

than by going out of office by rotation; every person so elected to hold office until the time when the person in whose room he shall have been chosen would have gone out of office, but to be re-eligible.

15. That the Members of the Council of the College shall hereafter be elected by the Fellows of the said College, including the Members of the Council as such; and such Fellows, whether Members of the Council or not, shall be allowed to vote in person only and not by proxy; and that any number of Fellows (not being less than fifteen present) at a Meeting convened for the purpose of electing a Member or Members of Council, shall be competent to proceed to such Election.

15. Mode of Election of Council. No proxies allowed.

Any number of Fellows not less than fifteen present at a Meeting, competent to proceed to an Election.

16. That the Chair at every such Meeting shall be taken by the President of the said College, or in his absence by one of the Vice-Presidents, or in case also of their absence, then by the senior Member of the Council of the said College then present. And if it shall so happen that from any cause the business of the day cannot be concluded upon such the day fixed for election as aforesaid, then and in every such case an adjournment of the Meeting shall take place to the next day, at an hour to be named by the Chairman (Sundays, Christmas-days and Good Fridays excepted, and being passed over when occasion shall require), and so from day to day (except as aforesaid) until the business of the Meeting shall be completed; but no other business shall be discussed or attended to at any such Meeting besides the election of a Member or Members of the Council, for which the same shall have been convened. PROVIDED ALSO, that if upon the day fixed for any such Election there shall not be fifteen or more Fellows assembled and continuing together for the purpose of such Election, then at any time after the space of one hour after the time of day fixed for such Election the Chair may be taken as aforesaid, and it shall be lawful for the Chairman to adjourn the Meeting to the next day, and so from day to day (except as aforesaid) if necessary, in the man-

16. At every Meeting convened for election of a Member of Council the Chair to be taken by the President or one of the Vice-Presidents, or by senior Member of Council present. Adjournments may take place from day to day.

No other business than that of Election to be discussed or attended to.

Chairman may adjourn the Meeting from day to day if not fifteen Fellows present within one hour after the time fixed.

ner hereinbefore mentioned with respect to adjournments of such Meetings in case of the business thereof not being concluded as aforesaid.

17. *Such notices of Election to be given as the Council shall think fit and shall determine by Bye-Laws. Subject to these presents, Elections to be conducted as the Council shall by Bye-Laws determine. But such Election to be always by Ballot, and to be decided by a majority of votes.*

17. That such previous notice or notices of every election of a Member or Members of the Council shall be given as the Council shall from time to time think fit, and shall by a Bye-Law or Bye-Laws determine and appoint, and that, subject only to the regulations and restrictions in these our Letters Patent mentioned or contained, the election of Members of the Council shall be conducted in such way and manner as the Council shall from time to time think fit, and shall by a Bye-Law or Bye-Laws also determine or regulate and appoint, but such Election shall always be by Ballot, and be decided by a majority of balls or votes, and every Fellow who shall be eligible to be elected according to the regulations and restrictions contained or mentioned and authorized in or by these our Letters Patent, shall be announced to the Meeting as a Fellow eligible in the order and according to the priority in which his name shall stand in the book or registry of Fellows; and if he shall be thereupon nominated in such mode as the Council shall by Bye-Law or Bye-Laws provide for the general nomination of Members at Elections, he shall be balloted for accordingly, but not otherwise.

Every eligible Fellow shall be announced to the Meeting according to the priority of his name on the Register of Fellows. Fellow, if nominated as provided for by Bye-Laws, shall be balloted for accordingly.

18. *When any eligible Fellow shall have been passed over for want of nomination or for non-election, he shall be re-eligible on such special terms as shall be provided for by Bye-Laws; but if passed by a second time, he shall cease to be eligible.*

18. That when any eligible Fellow shall have been passed by for want of any such nomination as aforesaid, or having been balloted for shall not be elected a Member of the Council, he shall cease to be eligible to be elected, except upon such special terms of nomination as shall by the Council by Bye-Law be for the time being provided for such cases, and upon such special terms any Fellow so passed by or not elected may be re-nominated for and be elected a Member of the Council, but if he shall be on such second occasion either passed by or not elected, he shall for ever thereafter cease to be eligible for election upon the Council.

19. *No Fellow eligible to the Council unless at time of his nomination there shall be delivered in a Certificate that he is a fit and proper person to be a Member of the Council, and particularly that he does not and has not within five*

19. That no Fellow whatever shall be eligible to be a Member of the Council unless at the time of his nomination for election as such there shall also be produced and delivered in, in such way and manner and in such form as the Council shall from time to time think fit and by Bye-Law regulate and appoint accordingly, a Certificate in writing signed by such number of Fellows as by such Bye-Law shall be required, that, or to the effect that such Fellow so nominated is a fit and proper person to be a Member of the Council, and particularly that he does not practise and has not within five years practised Midwifery or Pharmacy, and that he resides and *bond fide* practises his profession of a Surgeon within five miles by highway or road from the General Post-Office in St. Martin's-le-Grand, and such nomination and certificate being delivered in, in the manner required, the same (as regards the matters or particulars so to be certified as aforesaid, but no further) shall be final and conclusive as to the right of such Fellow to be balloted for as a Member of the Council, and also to be elected such Member if upon the Ballot he shall be so elected.

years practised Midwifery or Pharmacy, and that he resides and practises his profession of Surgeon within five miles from the General Post-Office.

20. That there shall be Ten Examiners of Surgeons for the said College, and the present Examiners shall be and continue such Examiners for life as heretofore. But that the two principal Serjeant-Surgeons to Us and to our Heirs and Successors, and the Surgeon-General to the Forces of Us our Heirs and Successors, or any of them, and although they may be chosen Members of the Council of the said College, shall no longer have any preference of being admitted Examiners of the said College before other persons; and that all future Examiners of the said College shall be elected by the Council of the College, either from the Members of the Council or from the other Fellows of the said College, or from both or either of them; and that all future Examiners of the said College shall hold their office of Examiners during the pleasure of the Council, and so long only as the Council of the College shall think fit.

20. The present Examiners to continue for life; but the Serjeant-Surgeons and the Surgeon-General no longer to have any preference of being admitted Examiners.

All future Examiners to be elected either from the Council or from the Fellows, or both or either, and shall hold office during the pleasure of the Council.

21. That the President and Vice-Presidents of the said College shall no longer be chosen exclusively from or out of the Examiners of the said College, but from or out of all the Members of the Council indifferently, and whether Examiners of the College or not. And that any number of Examiners of the College, not being less than Six, shall be sufficient to form a Court of Examiners, and with or without the President or Vice-Presidents of the College, or any of them (and whether or not the President or Vice-Presidents, or any of them, may be Examiners).

21. President and Vice-Presidents no longer to be chosen exclusively from the Examiners, but from all the Council indifferently, and whether Examiners or not. Any number of Examiners, not less than Six, sufficient to form a Court, and with out President or Vice-Presidents (although Examiners) being present.

22. That if it shall at any time hereafter appear that any present or future Member, or any Fellow of the said College, to be appointed or admitted at any time after the expiration of the said first three calendar months from the date hereof, shall have obtained his Letters Testimonial or his Diploma respectively by any fraud, false statement, or imposition

22. Diploma or Letters Testimonial obtained by fraud may be declared void after such previous notice and hearing as the Council shall think proper; and there-

upon such Member or Fellow shall cease to be so.

or that, either before or after obtaining such his Letters Testimonial or Diploma, he shall have violated any Bye-Law, Rule, or Regulation of the said College, then and in every such case, and after such previous notice to and such hearing of, such Member or Fellow as, under the circumstances, the Council of the said College shall think proper, it shall be lawful for such Council to recall and to declare the Letters Testimonial or Diploma respectively of such Member or Fellow to be void, and thereupon every such Member or Fellow shall cease to be a Member, or a Member and Fellow of the said College, as the case may be accordingly.

Confirmation of existing Powers except as hereby altered.

AND WE DO FURTHER DECLARE OUR WILL AND PLEASURE TO BE, That, except in the respects hereby altered, the said College and the Council of the same shall continue to have all such and the same jurisdiction, powers, authorities and discretions for and with respect to the government of the said College and the election and choice of the Officers of the same, as well as the admission and expulsion of Members and Fellows, and for the making, ordaining, confirming, annulling, or revoking Bye-Laws, Ordinances, Rules, and Constitutions, and transacting and ordaining all other matters and things whatsoever for the regulation, government and advantage of the said College, as such College and the Council thereof respectively now have under or by virtue of the said two several hereinbefore recited or mentioned Charters or Letters Patent, or either of them respectively, or in any other lawful manner.

No future Bye-Law or Ordinance to be of any force until approved of by the Crown or otherwise, as shall be directed.

AND WE DO HEREBY FOR Us, our Heirs and Successors, grant and confirm unto them all such jurisdictions, powers, authorities and discretions accordingly ; PROVIDED ALWAYS, and it is our further Will and Pleasure, that no Bye-Law or Ordinance hereafter to be made by the said Council shall be of any force until our approval thereof shall have been signified to the said College under the hand of one of our Principal Secretaries of State, or the same shall have been otherwise approved in such manner as shall be directed by Us, with the advice and consent of the Lords Spiritual and Temporal and Commons of our Realm, in Parliament assembled.

AND WE DO HEREBY FOR Us, our Heirs and Successors, further grant unto the said College, that these our Letters Patent, or the enrolment or exemplification thereof, shall be in and by all things, good, firm, valid, sufficient, and effectual in the Law, according to the true intent and meaning thereof, notwithstanding the not fully or not duly reciting the said several Letters Patent, or the dates thereof, or any other omission, imperfection, defect, matter, cause or thing whatsoever, the same or any Rule or Law to the contrary thereof, in anywise notwithstanding. In witness whereof, We have caused these Our Letters to be made Patent.

Witness Ourself at Our Palace at Westminster, this Fourteenth day of September in the Seventh year of Our Reign.

By Writ of Privy Seal,

EDMUNDS.

15TH VICTORIA.

18TH MARCH, 1852.

VICTORIA, by the Grace of God, of the United Kingdom of Great Britain and Ireland, Queen, Defender of the Faith, To ALL TO WHOM THESE PRESENTS SHALL COME, GREETING, WHEREAS the Body Politic and Corporate of THE ROYAL COLLEGE OF SURGEONS IN LONDON was incorporated or re-established under or by virtue of a certain Charter or Letters Patent, bearing date at Westminster the Twenty-second day of March in the Fortieth year of the Reign of King George the Third, or otherwise, as in such Letters Patent mentioned or referred to, and further powers and privileges were granted to the said College by a certain other or Supplemental Charter granted by Letters Patent, bearing date at Westminster the Thirteenth day of February in the Third Year of the Reign of King George the Fourth. And by our Letters Patent, bearing date at Westminster the Fourteenth day of September in the Seventh year of our Reign, the name or style of the said College was altered to "The Royal College of Surgeons of England," by which name or style the said College is now called or known, and divers further powers and privileges were granted to the said College by our said Letters Patent: And the said College is now regulated and governed by and according to the provisions of the said several Charters or Letters Patent, and also by or according to certain Bye-Laws and Ordinances made by the said College for its regulation and better government.

Recital That the College was incorporated or re-established by Charter of 40th George III.

Recital That further powers were granted by Charter of 3rd George IV.

Recital That the name of the College was altered and divers further powers granted by Charter of 7th Victoria.

Recital
Of government
and constitu-
tion of the
College.

AND WHEREAS the Body Politic and Corporate of the said College at present consists of persons created Members of the said College by the said first-mentioned Charter, or constituted such Members by Letters Testimonial, under the Common Seal of the said College, of the respective qualifications of such Persons to practise the Art and Science of Surgery, and also of persons created Fellows of the said College under the provisions of our said Letters Patent, and elected and declared to be Fellows of the said College by one General Diploma, under the Seal of the said College, enrolled in our High Court of Chancery, and also of other persons appointed under the powers of our said Letters Patent, by the Council of the said College, to be Fellows of the said College by Diplomas under the Seal of the said College, and also of other persons, who after having attained the age of Twenty-five years, and complied with the Rules and Regulations directed by the Bye-Laws of the said College, and having passed a special Examination by the Examiners of the said College, have been admitted Fellows by Diplomas under the Seal of the said College. And the governing body of the said College consists of a Council of twenty-four persons, some of whom, being Members of the said Council at the date of our said Letters Patent, were thereby continued, and are Life Members thereof, and others of them are elective Members of the said Council, chosen from the Fellows of the said College in manner mentioned and directed by our said Letters Patent, and hold their office for a limited period only, and one of such twenty-four persons is the President, and two of them are the Vice-Presidents of the said College; and the Court of Examiners of the said College consists of ten persons, some of whom, being Examiners at the date of our said Letters Patent, were thereby continued and are such Examiners for life, and others of them have been elected by the Council of the said College since the date of our said Letters Patent and under the directions therein contained, and hold their office of Examiners during the pleasure of the Council of the said College.

Declares
it to be expe-
dient that the
right of admis-
sion to the Fel-
lowship be ex-
tended to
Members at
date of late
Charter.

AND WHEREAS, it appears to us expedient that the right of admission to the Fellowship of the said College be extended to such persons as were Members of the said College at the date of our said Letters Patent, subject to certain conditions and regulations hereinafter mentioned, and that the Council of the said College have power annually to elect certain Members of the College to be Fellows, without Examination, in manner

hereinafter mentioned.   That certain restrictions now existing upon the
eligibility of Fellows to be Members of the Council of the said College be
removed, and that certain other qualifications be required of Fellows
offering themselves as Candidates for the Council.   That certain alterations be made in the electing of Members of the Council.   That power be
given for admission to the College as hereinafter mentioned of Fellows,
Members and Licentiates of certain other Corporate Bodies, as hereinafter
mentioned.   That certain alterations be made as to the continuance in
office of all future Examiners of the said College, and as to the continuance of the President in certain cases as a Member of the Council,
and that a Board of Examiners in Midwifery be established, as hereinafter mentioned.   Now KNOW YE, That WE of Our special grace and mere
motion, at the humble Petition of the said Royal College, have willed,
ordained, constituted, and declared and granted, and by these Presents,
for Us, Our Heirs and Successors, do, will, ordain, constitute and declare,
and unto the said Royal College of Surgeons of England do grant in
manner following, to wit,—

That certain restrictions be removed and other qualifications required as to admission to the Council.

1. THAT it shall be lawful for the Council of the said College at any
time or times hereafter, by Diploma or Diplomas under the Seal of the
said College, in such form as the said Council may think fit and direct, and
without any previous examination, to appoint any person or persons who
at the date of our said Letters Patent was or were a Member or Members
of the said College of Fifteen Years' standing ; and also any person or
persons who, being at the date of our said Letters Patent a Member or
Members of the said College of less than Fifteen Years' standing, shall
have attained at the time of such appointment the standing of Fifteen
Years, to be a Fellow or Fellows of the said College, subject to the regulations hereinafter mentioned and directed.

1. Power of Council to appoint Members of 15 years' standing to the Fellowship without examination.

2. THAT the appointment of every person to the Fellowship of the said
College under the powers herein contained, shall be determined by the
Vote or Ballot of the Council, and be decided by a majority of votes or
balls, and that every such person seeking to be admitted to the Fellowship shall transmit or deliver to the Secretary of the said College, at such
time before the day appointed for the Ballot or Election as the Council
may think proper and direct, a Certificate, signed by such persons as
hereinafter mentioned, of the moral character and professional attainments
of the person applying for admission to the Fellowship, and that he does

2. Appointment of Members to the Fellowship to be by vote of Council, and Persons seeking such admission to deliver a Certificate and Declaration as to Character, Attainments and Practice.

not sell or supply Drugs or Medicines otherwise than in the due exercise or practice of his Profession of an Apothecary: and shall also at such time, so to be appointed as aforesaid, transmit or deliver to the said Secretary a Declaration signed by himself, to the effect that he does not sell or supply Drugs or Medicines otherwise than in the due exercise or practice of his Profession of an Apothecary; and such Certificate and Declaration shall be in such form as the Council of the said College shall from time to time direct.

3. Persons by whom such Certificates are to be signed. 3. THAT the Certificate to be produced by the persons seeking admission to the Fellowship of the said College, as last aforesaid, shall be signed by Six Fellows of the said College; or in the case of persons absent from the United Kingdom in the service of our Royal Army or Navy, by Two Fellows of the said College, and by the Director-General or other Officer superintending the Medical Department of the service to which such persons shall respectively belong; or in the service of the Honourable East India Company by Two Fellows of the said College, and by the Secretary to the Military Department of the said Company; or in the case of Persons resident in any of our Colonies, Plantations or Dependencies, by Two Fellows of the said College, and by the Governor, Lieutenant-Governor, or Superintendent thereof, whose signature shall be certified by our Secretary, or one of our Under Secretaries of State for the Colonies.

4. Fee on admission of such Fellows to be Ten Guineas. 4. THAT the Fee to be paid upon the admittance of every Fellow of the said College, to be appointed under the powers hereinbefore contained (over and besides any Stamp Duty on his admittance or Diploma), shall be the sum of Ten Guineas.

5. Lawful for Council to admit annually to the Fellowship without examination two Members of twenty years' standing. 5. THAT it shall be lawful for the Council of the said College, by Diploma or Diplomas under the Seal of the said College, in such form as the Council may think proper, to admit to the Fellowship of the said College in each and every year from the date of these our Letters Patent, without examination, but subject to such conditions and regulations as the said Council may think fit, and by any Bye-Law or Bye-Laws direct, any Two persons, being at the time of such admittance Members of the said College of not less than Twenty Years' standing; and that the Fee to be paid upon the admittance of each such Fellow as last aforesaid shall be the same as the Fee payable upon the admittance of Members of the said College to the Fellowship under the authority of our said Letters Patent.

6. THAT it shall be lawful for the Council of the College, by Diploma under the Seal of the College, to admit without examination to the Membership or Fellowship of the said College, on such conditions, and on the payment of such respective Fees as the Council of the College shall by Bye-Law determine, the Fellows, Members and Licentiates respectively of the Royal College of Surgeons in Ireland, the Royal College of Surgeons of Edinburgh, and the Faculty of Physicians and Surgeons of Glasgow provided such Fellows, Members and Licentiates shall be, at the time of their application for admission, in the *bonâ fide* practice of the Profession of a Surgeon in England or Wales, and shall have obtained their respective Diplomas or Licences after examination, and such persons so admitted, to such Membership or Fellowship shall take rank amongst the Members or Fellows of the said College, according to the date of such last-mentioned Diplomas or Licences.

6. Lawful for the Council to admit without examination to the Membership or Fellowship of the College, the Fellows, Members, and Licentiates of Colleges of Surgeons of Dublin and Edinburgh, and Faculty of Glasgow, practising Surgery in England or Wales.

7. THAT from henceforth no Fellow of the said College who shall not have been a Fellow of the same for Fourteen Years, or a Member of the same for Twenty Years, and no Fellow of the said College who at the time of election shall not be in the *bonâ fide* practice of his Profession of a Surgeon, or who shall be practising as an Apothecary, shall be eligible as a Member of the Council of the said College; but every Fellow of the said College of such standing as a Fellow or Member of the same as last aforesaid, and who at the time of such election shall be in the *bonâ fide* practice of his Profession of a Surgeon, and shall not be practising as an Apothecary, shall be eligible as a Member of the said Council, any restriction or disqualification in respect of the practice or residence of such Fellow or otherwise in the said Letters Patent contained to the contrary notwithstanding. But if any Member of the Council shall at any time after his Election cease to be in the *bonâ fide* practice of his Profession of a Surgeon, or shall practise as an Apothecary, he shall thereupon cease to be such Member of the Council, and shall forfeit all his rights and privileges as such Member thereof; and it shall be lawful for the Council of the said College to declare the place of such Member in the Council to be vacant, and the same shall be filled up in manner hereinafter directed respecting vacancies in the Council.

7. Eligibility of Fellows to the Council.

Member of Council ceasing to practise Surgery, or practising as an Apothecary, shall thereupon cease to be a Member of Council.

8. Vacancies in Council to be filled up on the first Thursday in July (or within one month), unless Members of Council shall be reduced below eighteen, in which case vacancies to be filled up at such time as Council shall appoint.

8. THAT all vacancies which shall from henceforth occur in the Council of the said College, either by reason of any of the Members thereof going out of Office by rotation or from any other cause, shall be filled up in manner hereinafter mentioned on the first Thursday in the month of July in every year, or within one Calendar Month afterwards, unless at any time the number of Members of the said Council shall be reduced below eighteen, in which case it shall be lawful for the Council of the said College to appoint such day for filling up the vacancies as they may think proper: and that the Council of the said College shall cause a notice of the day appointed for the election of Members into the Council to supply the vacancies occasioned either by Members going out of office by rotation, or by any other cause, and of the number of vacancies to be filled up, to be advertized in the 'London Gazette' at such time as the Council shall from time to time direct, before the day appointed for such Election, and shall also cause such notice to be published or announced in such other manner as the said Council may from time to time direct.

9. Candidates for Seats in Council to transmit certain Notices, Nominations, Certificates and Declarations.

9. THAT every eligible Fellow who shall intend to offer himself as a Candidate for a Seat in the Council of the said College shall within such time as the Council shall from time to time direct from the publication of the 'London Gazette,' in which the day of Election shall be announced, transmit or deliver to the Secretary of the said College a notice signed by himself of such his intention, together with a nomination signed by six Fellows of such person as a fit person to be elected into the Council, and a Certificate that he is in the *bonâ fide* practice of his Profession as a Surgeon, and that he does not practise as an Apothecary, which Certificate shall be signed by three Fellows of the said College; and the person so intending to offer himself as a Candidate for the Council shall at the same time transmit or deliver to the said Secretary a Declaration signed by himself, that he is in the *bonâ fide* practice of his Profession as a Surgeon, and that he does not practise as an Apothecary ; and such Nomination and Certificate, and also such Declaration as last aforesaid, shall be in such form as the Council of the said College shall from time to time direct.

10 Fellows nominating a greater number of Candidates for Council than vacancies to be filled up, incapacitated from voting at Election.

10. THAT no Fellow shall have power to nominate at any one election any greater number of persons as Candidates for the Council than the number of vacancies which shall be to be filled up at such Election ; and if any Fellow shall at any such Election nominate any greater number of Candidates than as last aforesaid, then such Fellow shall be incapacitated from voting at that Election.

11. THAT no Member of Council shall go out of Office by rotation whilst holding the Office of President; and that as often as it shall happen that the President shall be one of the Members who would at any Annual Meeting go out of Office by rotation, two Members of Council only, instead of three as prescribed by the Charter, shall be elected at such Meeting— and that at the next Annual Meeting such Member shall go out of Office in addition to any other Members of Council going out of Office by rotation according to our said Letters Patent—but any Member whose going out of Office shall have been postponed as above provided, shall in case of his re-election into the Council on his going out of Office at such succeeding Annual Meeting as aforesaid, on all future occasions go out of Office in the same order as if he had been re-elected at the time when he would, but for this provision, have gone out of Office.

11. Member of Council not to go out of Office by rotation whilst President, but to go out of Office at next Annual Election—and on future occasions to go out of Office as if he had gone out of office while President.

12. That the Council of the said College shall cause lists of the names of all eligible Fellows of the said College who shall in manner hereinbefore directed be nominated as Candidates for the Council, and shall have complied with the provisions hereinbefore contained respecting the Notice, Certificate and Declaration to be transmitted to the Secretary of the said College, together with the names of the Fellows by whom they shall respectively be so nominated, to be published in the 'London Gazette' and in two London Daily Newspapers, at such time before the day appointed for the Election as the Council shall from time to time direct.

12. Lists of Candidates eligible to Council, together with names of Fellows by whom nominated, to be published in Gazette and in two London Daily Newspapers.

13. THAT henceforth, instead of the name of every Fellow eligible to be elected being announced to the Meeting in the order and according to the priority in which his name shall stand in the Register of Fellows, as directed by our said Letters Patent, the names of all Fellows included in the Lists so published as aforesaid, shall be announced to the Meeting as the Candidates for Election.

13. Mode of announcement at Election of names of Candidates.

14. THAT the names of the Members of the Council who shall in each year retire from Office by rotation, shall, if they shall be desirous of re-election, and shall intimate such their desire in writing to the Secretary of the said College within such period as the Council shall determine before the day appointed for the Election, be placed at the head of the Lists of Candidates to be published as hereinbefore directed; and that such persons, if re-elected into the Council, shall take precedence of all other persons

14. Names of Members retiring from Council by rotation and desirous of re-election to be placed at the head of List of Candidates.

f

who shall be elected into the Council on the same day, and shall with respect to each other take precedence according to their former seniority in the Council.

15. Required Certificate and Declaration to be conclusive as to eligibility to Council, but if afterwards they shall appear untrue or fraudulent, lawful for the Council to declare the Member of Council to be no longer a Member, and thereupon such Member shall cease to be a Member of Council.

15. That any Nomination and Certificate or Declaration hereinbefore required to be made or produced upon or previously to the election of any Fellow into the Council of the said College, being transmitted or delivered in the manner hereinbefore required, the same (as regards the matters or particulars so to be certified and declared as aforesaid, but no further) shall be final and conclusive as to the eligibility of such Fellow. But if it shall afterwards appear to the satisfaction of the Council of the said College that any such Nomination or Certificate or Declaration is in any respect untrue or fraudulent, then it shall be lawful for the Council of the said College to declare the Member of the Council, to whom such Nomination and Certificate may relate, or by whom such Declaration may have been made, to be no longer a Member of the said Council ; and thereupon every such Member of the Council of the said College shall cease to be such Member thereof, and shall forfeit all his rights and privileges as such Member thereof ; and it shall be lawful for the Council of the said College to declare the place of such Member in the Council to be vacant, and the same shall be filled up in manner hereinbefore directed respecting Vacancies in the said Council.

16. Examiners hereafter elected to go out of office at end of Five Years, but immediately re-eligible, and to take precedence according to former standing.

16. That every Fellow of the said College who shall from henceforth be elected to the Office of Examiner of the said College, shall go out of office at the end of Five Years from the day of his election ; but that it shall be lawful for the Council of the said College immediately to re-elect such person to the said office, and every such person being so re-elected, shall take precedence in the Court of Examiners, according to his former standing as a Member thereof.

17. Board of Examiners in Midwifery for testing the fitness of persons to practise Midwifery to consist of not less than Three Persons, to be

17. And it is our further will and pleasure, That a Board of Examiners be appointed by the said College for the purpose of testing the fitness of persons to practise in Midwifery, and of granting Certificates of such fitness ; and that such Board shall consist of not less than Three persons. And we do hereby authorize and require the Council of the said College, within Twelve Months from the date of these our Letters Patent, to appoint not less than Three persons to be such Examiners in

Midwifery, who shall continue in office for such period, and shall conduct *appointed within Twelve Months.* tne examinations in such manner, and shall grant Certificates in such form as the Council of the said College shall determine and from time to time direct. And it shall be lawful for the Council of the said College, from time to time, as vacancies shall occur in such last-mentioned Board of Examiners, to appoint any persons to fill up the same.

18. AND WE DO HEREBY FURTHER DECLARE OUR WILL AND PLEASURE TO BE, That all and every direction, provision, regulation, clause, matter or thing whatsoever, in the said several recited Letters Patent of our Royal Predecessors and Ourselves, or in any Bye-Laws, or Bye-Law of the said College, contained, which may be repugnant to or inconsistent, or at variance with the several directions, provisions, and regulations herein contained, or any of them, in so far as the same are repugnant thereto, inconsistent or at variance therewith, shall be, and the same are hereby abrogated, repealed, and rendered of none effect. But that, except in the respects hereby altered, the said College and the Council of the same shall continue to have all such, and the same jurisdiction, powers, authorities, and discretions for and with respect to the Government of the said College, and the election and choice of the Officers of the same, as well as the admission and expulsion of Members and Fellows, and for the making, ordaining, confirming, annulling, or revoking Bye-Laws, Ordinances, Rules, and Constitutions, and transacting and ordaining all other matters and things whatsoever, for the regulation, government, and advantage of the said College, as such College and the Council thereof respectively now have, under or by virtue of the said three several hereinbefore recited Charters or Letters Patent, or either of them respectively, or in any other lawful manner.

18. Confirmation of existing powers except as hereby altered.

AND WE DO HEREBY for Us, Our Heirs and Successors, grant and confirm unto them all such jurisdictions, powers, authorities and discretions accordingly.

AND WE DO HEREBY for Us, Our Heirs and Successors, further grant unto the said College, that these, our Letters Patent, or tne enrolment or exemplification thereof, shall be in and by all things, good, firm, valid, sufficient and effectual in the Law, according to the true intent and meaning thereof, notwithstanding the not fully or not duly reciting the said several Letters Patent, or the dates thereof, or any other omission, imperfection. defect, matter, cause or thing whatsoever, the same or any Rule or Law to the contrary thereof, in anywise notwithstanding. In witness whereof We have caused these Our Letters to be made Patent.

Witness Ourself at Our Palace at Westminster, this Eighteenth day of March in the Fifteenth year of Our Reign.

By Her Majesty's Command,

EDMUNDS.

23RD VICTORIA.

8TH SEPTEMBER, 1859.

VICTORIA, by the Grace of God, of the United Kingdom of Great Britain and Ireland Queen, Defender of the Faith, To ALL TO WHOM THESE PRESENTS SHALL COME GREETING, WHEREAS the Body Politic and Corporate of THE ROYAL COLLEGE OF SURGEONS IN LONDON was incorporated or re-established under or

Recital—That the College was incorporated or re-established by Charter of 40th George III. by virtue of a certain Charter or Letters Patent, bearing date at Westminster the Twenty-second day of March in the Fortieth year of the Reign of King George the Third, or otherwise as in such Letters Patent mentioned or referred to, and further powers and privileges were granted to the said

Recital — That further power were granted by Charter of 3rd George IV. College by a certain other or Supplemental Charter granted by Letters Patent, bearing date at Westminster the Thirteenth day of February in the Third Year of the Reign of King George the Fourth. And by our Letters Patent, bearing date at Westminster the Fourteenth day of September in the Seventh year of our Reign, the name or style of the said College was altered to " The Royal College of Surgeons of England," by which name or style the

Recital—That the name of the College was altered and divers further powers were granted by Charter of 7th Victoria. said College is now called or known, and divers further powers and privileges were granted to the said College by our said Letters Patent. And by our further Letters Patent, bearing date at Westminster the Eighteenth day of March in the Fifteenth year of our Reign, divers further powers and privileges were granted to the said College, and alterations were in certain

Recital—That divers other powers were granted by Charter of 15th Victoria. of the provisions and regulations contained in the said former Letters Patent of Ourself and our Royal Predecessors: and the said College is now regulated and governed by and according to the provisions of the said

Recital—Of government and constitution of the College. several Charters or Letters Patent, and also by or according to certain Bye-Laws and Ordinances made by the said College for its regulation and better government.

AND WHEREAS by the Medical Act, made and passed in the Twenty-first and Twenty-second years of our Reign, it is amongst other things enacted " that it shall, notwithstanding anything therein contained, be lawful for Ourself by Charter to grant to the Royal College of Surgeons of England power to institute and hold Examinations for the purpose of testing the fitness of persons to practise as Dentists who may be desirous of being so examined, and to grant Certificates of such Fitness." Recital—Of Medical Act of 21st and 22nd Victoria.

AND WHEREAS, in order to provide for the due qualification of persons practising as Dentists, it appea.s to us expedient that the said Royal College of Surgeons of England should have power to institute and hold Examinations for the purpose of testing the fitness of such persons, subject to the regulations and directions hereinafter mentioned. Now KNOW YE, That WE of our especial grace and mere motion, at the humble Petition of the said Royal College, have willed, ordained, constituted, and declared and granted, and by these Presents for Us, Our Heirs and Successors, do will, ordain, constitute and declare, and unto the said Royal College of Surgeons of England do grant in manner following, to wit,— Declares it to be expedient that this College should have power to institute examinations of persons to practise as Dentists.

1. That it shall be lawful for the Council of the said College to appoint a Board of Examiners for the purpose of testing the fitness of persons to practise as Dentists who may be desirous of being so examined, and to grant Certificates of such fitness. And it is our will and pleasure that such Board of Examiners be called the Board of Examiners in Dental Surgery, and consist of not less than six Members, to be appointed as hereinafter mentioned, three of whom shall be Members of the Court of Examiners for the time being of the said College, and the others of them shall be such persons skilled in Dental Surgery as the Council of the said College shall from time to time think proper to appoint. 1. Power of Council to appoint a Board of Examiners for testing the fitness of persons to practise as Dentists, and to grant Certificates of such fitness. That such Board consist of not less than 6 Members, 3 to be Members of the Court of Examiners of the College, and the others to be persons skilled in Dental Surgery.

2. AND we do hereby authorize and require the Council of the said College, within six calendar months from the date of these our Letters Patent, to appoint three persons, being Members of the Court of Examiners of the said College, and also three such other persons skilled in Dental Surgery as they may think fit, to be such Examiners in Dental Surgery, who shall continue in Office for such period, and shall conduct the Examinations in such manner, and shall grant Certificates in such form, as the Council of the said College shall determine and from time to time direct. And it shall be lawful for the said Council of the said College 2. That the Council shall appoint such Board within six months from this date, to continue in office for such period, to conduct the examinations in such manner and to grant Certificates in such form as the Council shall determine.

from time to time, as vacancies shall occur in such last-mentioned Board of Examiners, to appoint any persons to fill up the same, nevertheless so that the said Board of Examiners shall always be constituted as hereinbefore directed.

3. AND IT IS OUR FURTHER WILL AND PLEASURE, That the said College do admit all persons who shall be desirous of being examined as aforesaid, whether Members of the said College or not Members thereof, to examination by the said Board of Examiners in Dental Surgery. PROVIDED nevertheless that such persons shall have attained the age of Twenty-one years, and shall also have complied with such Rules and Regulations as to education as the Council of the said College shall from time to time consider expedient.

4. THAT such reasonable Fees shall be paid for the Certificates of the said Board of Examiners in Dental Surgery as the Council of the said College shall from time to time think fit, and by any Bye-Law or Bye-Laws direct.

PROVIDED ALWAYS, AND IT IS OUR FURTHER WILL AND PLEASURE, That these Presents shall not operate to create, or be taken or deemed to confer upon any person who shall obtain such Certificate of fitness as aforesaid, any right or title to be registered under the said Medical Act in respect of such Certificate. IN WITNESS whereof, We have caused these Our Letters to be made Patent.

Witness Ourselves at our Palace at Westminster, this Eighth day of September in the Twenty-third year of Our Reign.

By Her Majesty's Command,

EDMUNDS.

52ND VICTORIA.

20TH JULY, 1888.

VICTORIA, by the Grace of God, of the United Kingdom of Great Britain and Ireland, Queen, Defender of the Faith, To ALL TO WHOM THESE PRESENTS SHALL COME, GREETING, WHEREAS the Body Politic and Corporate of THE ROYAL COLLEGE OF SURGEONS IN LONDON was incorporated or re-established under or by virtue of a certain Charter or Letters Patent, bearing date at Westminster the Twenty-second day of March in the Fortieth year of the Reign of King George the Third, or otherwise, as in such Letters Patent mentioned or referred to, and further powers and privileges were granted to the said College by a certain other or Supplemental Charter granted by Letters Patent, bearing date at Westminster the Thirteenth day of February in the Third Year of the Reign of King George the Fourth. And by our Letters Patent, bearing date at Westminster the Fourteenth day of September in the Seventh year of our Reign, the name or style of the said College was altered to " The Royal College of Surgeons of England," by which name or style the said College is now called or known, and divers further powers and privileges were granted to the said College by our said Letters Patent: And by our further Letters Patent, bearing date at Westminster the Eighteenth day of March in the Fifteenth year of our Reign, divers further powers and privileges were granted to the said College, and alterations were made in certain of the provisions and regulations contained in the said former Letters Patent of ourselves and our Royal Predecessors. And by our further Letters Patent, bearing date at Westminster the Eighth day of September in the Twenty-third year of our Reign, divers further powers and privileges were granted to the said College.

AND WHEREAS the Governing Body of the said College consists of a 1923.

Recital—That the College was incorporated or re-established by Charter of 40th George III.

Recital—That further powers were granted by Charter of 3rd George IV.

Recital—That the name of the College was altered and further powers granted by Charter of 7th Victoria.

Recital—That further powers were granted by Charter of 15th Victoria.

Recital—That further powers were granted by Charter of 23rd Victoria.

Recital—That

g

the Governing Body of the College consists of a Council of twenty-four persons elected by the Fellows. Council of twenty-four persons, and vacancies therein are filled up by election by the Fellows of the said College, and one of such twenty-four persons is the President, and two of them are the Vice-Presidents of the said College ; and the Court of Examiners of the said College consists of ten persons, and the said College is now regulated and governed by and according to the provisions of the said several Charters or Letters Patent, and also by or according to certain Bye-Laws and Ordinances made by the said College for its regulation and better government.

Recital—That the College may hold Lands of the yearly value of £2000.

Recital—That in elections for the Council the Fellows may vote in person only, and not unless fifteen be present.

Recital — Of qualifications required of Candidates for the Council.

AND WHEREAS, under and by virtue of the provisions and regulations contained in the said former Letters Patent of Ourselves and our Royal Predecessors, the amount of lands, tenements, rents or hereditaments which may be taken and held by the said College, including the Hall or Council-house thereof, is limited to lands, tenements, rents or hereditaments not exceeding the yearly value of £2000 in the whole; and at the election of the Members of the Council of the said College by the Fellows thereof, the said Fellows are allowed to vote in person only, and not by proxy or voting-papers, and no such election can be proceeded with unless there be Fifteen or more Fellows assembled and continuing together; and Candidates for the Council of the said College are required to be Fellows of the said College of not less than Fourteen years' standing as Fellows, or Twenty years' standing as Members thereof, and to fulfil certain conditions as to practice, and to be nominated for election to the said Council by six Fellows of the said College, and to transmit or deliver to the Secretary thereof certain Certificates and Declarations, and a Fee of Ten Guineas (over and besides any Stamp Duty on his admittance or Diploma), is payable on the admittance to the Fellowship of the College of any such

Recital—That the College is required to maintain a Board of Examiners in Midwifery and a Board of Six Examiners in Dental Surgery.

Member of not less than Twenty years' standing ; and the said College is required to appoint and maintain a Board of Three Examiners in Midwifery for the purpose of testing by examination the fitness of persons to practise in Midwifery, and of granting Certificates of such fitness; and the said College is required to appoint and maintain a Board of Examiners in Dental Surgery for the purpose of testing the fitness of persons to practise as Dentists who may be desirous of being so examined, and to grant Certificates of such fitness, and three of such Examiners in Dental Surgery are to be Members of the Court of Examiners of the said College for the time being, and three such other persons skilled in Dental Surgery as the Council of the said College shall think fit.

AND WHEREAS it appears to us expedient that the amount of land which may be taken, purchased, possessed, holden, and enjoyed by the said College should be increased; that the election of Members of the Council of the said College by the Fellows thereof should henceforth be by means of voting-papers as well as in person, and that the number of Fellows required to be present at any meeting for the election of a Member or Members of the Council of the said College should henceforth be determined and fixed by Bye-Law and not as hereinbefore-mentioned; that modifications and alterations should be made in the length of standing and method of Nomination required of Candidates for the Council of the said College, and that the said conditions as to practise and the said Certificates and Declarations should cease to be required or exist; that the said College should not henceforth be required to appoint a Board of Examiners, or to hold examinations for the purpose of testing the fitness of persons to practise in Midwifery, or of granting Certificates of such fitness. That the number of the Members of the said Board of Examiners in Dental Surgery should, if at any time the Council of the said College should think fit, be increased beyond the number of six, and that such Members thereof as shall not be Members of the Court of Examiners for the time being of the said College should be persons duly registered under the provisions of the "Dentists' Act, 1878." Now KNOW YE, That WE of Our especial grace and mere motion, at the humble Petition of the said Royal College, have willed, ordained, constituted, and declared and granted, and by these Presents for Us, Our Heirs and Successors, do will, ordain, constitute and declare, and unto the said Royal College of Surgeons of England do grant in manner following, to wit,—

1. That the said Royal College of Surgeons of England shall and may take, purchase, possess, hold, and enjoy any lands, tenements, and rents or hereditaments, wheresoever situate, lying, and being, not exceeding at any one time, together with the aforesaid Hall or Council-house and its appurtenances, and the lands, tenements, rents, or hereditaments now held by them, the yearly value of £20,000 in the whole.

AND WE do hereby also for Us, Our Heirs and Successors, give and grant our especial license, full power, and lawful and absolute authority, to any Person or Persons, and any Bodies Politic or Corporate, to grant

g 2

Marginal notes:

Recital—That it is expedient that the College should be enabled to hold more Land.

That in elections for the Council the Fellows should be allowed to vote by voting-papers, and that the number of Fellows required to be present should be determined by Bye-Law.

That the qualifications required of Candidates for the Council should be modified

That the College should not be required to appoint a Board of Examiners in Midwifery, and that the number of Examiners in Dental Surgery should be increased at the discretion of the Council.

Grant.

1. Power to the College to hold Land of the yearly value of £20,000.

alien, sell, convey, or dispose of, in perpetuity or otherwise, to or to the use and benefit of, or in trust for, the said Royal College of Surgeons of England, any lands, tenements, rents, or hereditaments whatsoever, not exceeding at any one time, together with the aforesaid Hall or Council-house and its appurtenances, and the lands, tenements, rents, or hereditaments now held by them, the yearly value aforesaid of £20,000 in the whole.

2. In Elections for the Council the Fellows may vote by means of voting papers, and as to quorum.

2. THAT the Members of the Council of the said College shall be elected by the Fellows of the said College including the Members of the Council who are Fellows, and such Fellows, whether Members of the Council or not, shall be allowed to vote either in person or by voting papers, to be signed, authenticated, delivered, and recorded in such form and manner as the Council of the said College shall from time to time think fit and direct, but no such election shall be proceeded with unless there shall be such number of Fellows, exclusive of the Members of the Council, then actually present at a meeting convened for the purpose of electing a Member or Members of the said Council, as the Council of the said College shall from time to time by Bye-Law fix and direct.

3. Proceedings at meetings for Election to the Council and adjournments thereof.

3. THAT the chair at every such meeting shall be taken by the President of the said College, or in his absence by one of the Vice-Presidents, or in case also of their absence then by the senior Member of the Council of the said College then present. And if it shall so happen that from any cause the business of the day cannot be concluded upon such the day fixed for election as aforesaid, then and in every such case an adjournment of the meeting shall take place to the next day, at an hour to be named by the Chairman (Sundays, Christmas days and Good Fridays being excepted and passed over when occasion shall require) and so from day to day (except as aforesaid) until the business of the meeting shall be completed; but no business shall be discussed or attended to at any such meeting except the election of a Member or Members of the Council for which the same shall have been convened: PROVIDED ALSO that if upon the day fixed for any such election there shall not be such number of Fellows as is hereinbefore provided, assembled and continuing together for the purpose of such election, then at any time after the space of one hour after the time of day fixed for such election the chair may be taken as aforesaid

and it shall be lawful for the Chairman to adjourn the meeting to the next day, and so from day to day (except as aforesaid) if necessary, in the manner hereinbefore mentioned with respect to adjournments of such meetings in case of the business thereof not being concluded as aforesaid.

4. THAT from henceforth no Fellow of the said College who shall not have been a Fellow of the same for Ten years, or a Member of the same for Twenty years, shall be eligible as a Member of the Council of the said College, but every Fellow of the said College, of such standing as aforesaid, shall be eligible as a Member of the said Council, any restriction or disqualification in respect of the standing or practice of such Fellow or otherwise in the said hereinbefore recited Letters Patent or any of them contained to the contrary notwithstanding.

4. Fellows of Ten years and Members of Twenty years' standing to be eligible for the Council.

5. THAT every eligible Fellow who shall intend to offer himself as a candidate for a seat in the Council of the said College, shall, within such time from the publication of the 'London Gazette,' in which the day of election shall be announced, as the Council shall from time to time by Bye-Law direct, transmit or deliver to the Secretary of the said College a notice, signed by himself, of such his intention, together with a nomination signed by three Fellows of such person as a fit person to be elected into the Council, and such notice and nomination shall be in such form as the Council of the said College shall from time to time direct.

5. Nomination of Candidates for Election to the Council.

6. THAT the Council of the said College shall cause lists of the names of all eligible Fellows of the said College who shall, in manner hereinbefore directed, be nominated as Candidates for the Council, and shall have complied with the provisions hereinbefore contained respecting the notice to be transmitted to the Secretary of the said College, together with the names of the Fellows by whom they shall respectively be so nominated, to be published in the 'London Gazette' and in two London daily newspapers, at such time before the day appointed for the election, as the Council shall from time to time by Bye-Law direct. That Section 15 of our hereinbefore recited Letters Patent, bearing date at Westminster the 18th day of March in the Fifteenth year of our Reign, shall be and the same is hereby repealed, abrogated, and rendered of none effect.

6. Lists of Candidates for Election to the Council to be published in the 'London Gazette.'

Repeal of Section 15 of Charter of 15th Victoria.

7. The existing Board of Examiners in Midwifery to be dissolved, and no such Examiners to be hereafter appointed.

7. THAT the existing Board of Examiners appointed by the said College or the Council thereof, under or by virtue of our said Letters Patent bearing date at Westminster the 18th day of March in the Fifteenth year of our reign, for the purpose of testing the fitness of persons to practise in Midwifery and of granting Certificates of such fitness, be and the same is hereby dissolved, and that from and after the date of these our Letters Patent, no such Examiners in Midwifery shall be appointed by the Council of the said College, or examinations held, or certificates granted or vacancies filled up as are authorised and required to be appointed, held, granted, and filled up respectively by our said first-named Letters Patent.

8. Power to the Council to increase or diminish the number of Members of the Board of Examiners in Dental Surgery.

8. THAT it shall be lawful for the Council of the said College from time to time to increase or diminish the number of Members of the said Board of Examiners in Dental Surgery to such number, not being less than six, as the said Council shall think fit and determine: PROVIDED ALWAYS that, subject as hereinafter mentioned, the said Board shall henceforth always be constituted of such number (not being less than three) of Members of the Court of Examiners of the College for the time being, as the Council of the said College shall from time to time by Bye-Law determine, together with such number (not being less than three) of persons duly registered under the "Dentists' Act, 1878," as the said Council shall from time to time by Bye-Law determine: PROVIDED ALSO, that nothing herein contained shall affect or alter the rights or position of the present Members of the said Board of Examiners in Dental Surgery (if any) who are not registered under the "Dentists Act,' 1878," but such Members shall remain in office for the same period and exercise the same rights and powers pertaining to such office as if these our Letters Patent had not been granted.

9. Power to the Council to appoint Members of the Board of Examiners in Dental Surgery.

9. THAT it shall be lawful for the Council of the said College from time to time to appoint persons to be Members of the said Board of Examiners in Dental Surgery, either in order to increase the number thereof or to fill up vacancies therein, and such persons shall continue in office for such period, and shall conduct the examinations in such manner, and shall grant certificates in such form, as the Council of the said College shall determine and from time to time direct, nevertheless so that the

said Board of Examiners shall always be constituted as hereinbefore
directed.

10. AND WE DO HEREBY FURTHER DECLARE OUR WILL AND PLEASURE TO BE,
That all and every direction, provision, regulation, clause, matter, or thing
whatsoever, in the said several recited Letters Patent of our Royal Predecessors and Ourselves, or in any Bye-Laws or Bye-Law of the said College
contained, which may be repugnant to or inconsistent or at variance with
the several directions, provisions, and regulations herein contained, or any
of them, so far as the same are repugnant thereto, inconsistent or at
variance therewith, shall be and the same are hereby abrogated, repealed,
and rendered of none effect. But that except in the respects hereby
altered, the said College and the Council of the same shall continue to
have all such and the same jurisdictions, powers, authorities, and discretions, for and with respect to the Government of the said College, and the
election and choice of the officers of the same, as well as the admission
and expulsion of Members and Fellows, and for the making, ordaining,
confirming, annulling, or revoking bye-laws, ordinances, rules, and
constitutions, and transacting and ordaining all other matters and things
whatsoever for the regulation, government and advantage of the said
College as such College and the Council thereof respectively now have,
under or by virtue of the said several hereinbefore recited Charters or
Letters Patent or either of them respectively, or in any other lawful
manner :

Repeal of provisions in existing Charters inconsistent herewith.

AND WE DO HEREBY, for Us, our Heirs and Successors, grant and confirm
unto them all such jurisdictions, powers, authorities, and discretions
accordingly, and direct that except as hereby varied the said Charters or
Letters Patent shall be and continue of full force and effect :

Confirmation of existing Charters.

AND WE DO HEREBY, for Us, our Heirs and Successors, further grant under
the said College that these our Letters Patent, or the enrolment or exemplification thereof, shall be in and by all things good, firm, valid, sufficient
and effectual in the law according to the true intent and meaning hereof,
notwithstanding the not fully or not duly reciting the said several Letters
Patent, or the dates thereof, or any other omission, imperfection, defect,

matter, cause, or thing whatsoever, the same, or any rule or law to the contrary thereof, in anywise notwithstanding:

IN WITNESS whereof we have caused these our Letters to be made Patent:

WITNESS Ourself, at Westminster, the Twentieth day of July, in the Fifty-Second year of Our Reign.

By Warrant under the Queen's Sign Manual,

MUIR MACKENZIE.

63RD VICTORIA.

22nd December, 1899.

VICTORIA, by the Grace of God, of the United Kingdom of Great Britain and Ireland, Queen, Defender of the Faith, To ALL TO WHOM THESE PRESENTS SHALL COME GREETING: WHEREAS the Body Politic and Corporate of the ROYAL COLLEGE OF SURGEONS IN LONDON was incorporated or re-established under or by virtue of a certain Charter or Letters Patent bearing date at Westminster the Twenty-second day of March in the Fortieth year of the Reign of King George the Third or otherwise as in such Letters Patent mentioned or referred to, and further powers and privileges were granted to the said College by a certain other or Supplemental Charter granted by Letters Patent bearing date at Westminster the Thirteenth day of February in the Third year of the Reign of King George the Fourth, and by our Letters Patent bearing date at Westminster the Fourteenth day of September in the Seventh year of our Reign the name or style of the said College was altered to " The Royal College of Surgeons of England " by which name or style the said College is now called or known and divers further powers and privileges were granted to the said College by our said Letters Patent. And by our further Letters Patent bearing date at Westminster the Eighteenth day of March in the Fifteenth year of our Reign divers further powers and privileges were granted to the said College and alterations were made in certain of the provisions and regulations contained in the said former Letters Patent of Ourselves and Our Royal Predecessors. And by our further Letters Patent bearing date at Westminster the Eighth day of September in the Twenty-third year of our Reign divers further powers and privileges were granted to the said College. And by our further Letters Patent bearing date at Westminster the Twentieth day of July in the Fifty-second year of our Reign divers further powers and privileges were granted to the

said College and divers provisions of the hereinbefore recited Letters
Patent were repealed abrogated or altered.

AND WHEREAS the said College consists of Fellows and Members thereof
and the Governing Body of the said College consists of a Council of
twenty-four persons being Fellows and elected Members of the said
Council, by the Fellows of the said College and one of such twenty-four
persons is the President and two of them are the Vice-Presidents of the
said College such President and Vice-Presidents being elected by the said
Council, and the Court of Examiners consists of ten Fellows of the said
College elected by the said Council, and the said College is now regulated
and governed by and according to the provisions of the said several
Charters or Letters Patent and also by or according to certain Bye-Laws
Ordinances and Regulations made by the said College for its regulation
and better government.

AND WHEREAS by virtue of our hereinbefore recited Letters Patent bearing
date at Westminster the Eighteenth day of March in the Fifteenth year
of our Reign the Council of the said College have power to appoint or
admit to the Fellowship of the said College without examination but
subject to certain conditions and regulations and the payment of certain
fees persons who were Members of the said College on the Fourteenth day
of September 1843, also two persons in each and every year being at the
time of such admission Members of the said College of not less than
Twenty years' standing, and also Fellows of the Royal College of Surgeons
in Ireland the Royal College of Surgeons of Edinburgh or of the Faculty
of Physicians and Surgeons of Glasgow practising in England or Wales,
but no other persons can be admitted to the Fellowship of the said College
unless they shall have attained the age of Twenty-five years and complied
with the rules and regulations directed by the Bye-Laws of the said College
and passed a special examination by the examiners of the said College.

AND WHEREAS it appears to us expedient that a new class of Fellows
of the said College with limited rights and privileges should be created or
instituted to be and be called Honorary Fellows of the Royal College of
Surgeons of England and to be elected by the Council of the said College
in manner hereinafter appearing. Now KNOW YE that We of Our Special
Grace and mere motion at the humble Petition of the said College have

willed ordained constituted and declared and granted and by these Presents do will ordain constitute and declare and unto the said Royal College of Surgeons of England do grant in manner following, to wit:—

1. THAT it shall be lawful for the Council of the said College from time to time without examination or compliance with the rules and regulations by the hereinbefore mentioned Bye-Laws of the College in that behalf directed but subject to such rules and regulations, if any, as the said Council shall from time to time think fit and direct to elect such persons whether British subjects or not and whether of the age of Twenty-five years or not as the said Council shall deem sufficiently distinguished for the purpose to be and such persons shall be and be called Honorary Fellows of the Royal College of Surgeons of England anything to the contrary in any of the hereinbefore recited Letters Patent of Ourselves or Our Royal Predecessors or in the Bye-Laws or Regulations of the said College notwithstanding. Provided always that the number of such Honorary Fellows existing at one and the same time shall never exceed fifty.

2. THAT the fitness and election of each such person shall be determined by the vote or ballot of the said Council and be decided by a majority of votes or balls.

3. THAT every person so elected shall receive such Diploma or other evidence of his election as the Council shall from time to time think fit and direct but no fee shall be payable by any such person in respect of his election or of such Diploma or other evidence of election.

4. THAT no such Honorary Fellow shall be eligible as a Member of the Council or Court of Examiners of the said College or entitled to vote at any election of a Member or Members of the said Council but every such Honorary Fellow shall have and enjoy such of the other Corporate rights and privileges attaching to the Fellowship of the said College and be subject to such Rules and Regulations as the said Council may from time to time think fit and direct.

5. THAT no person so elected an Honorary Fellow of the said College shall thereby acquire any right to practise Surgery or to be registered

as a registered Medical Practitioner under or by virtue of the Medical Acts or any of them.

6. THAT save in so far as concerns the election admission rights and privileges of such Honorary Fellows the qualifications conditions and methods of admission rights and privileges of Fellows of the said College shall be and remain the same as are prescribed by or by virtue of the hereinbefore recited Letters Patent and the Bye-Laws Rules and Regulations of the said College for the time being in force.

IN WITNESS whereof we have caused these our Letters to be made Patent:

WITNESS Ourself at Westminster the Twenty-second day of December in the Sixty-third year of Our Reign.

By Warrant under the Queen's Sign Manual,

MUIR MACKENZIE.

CHAPTER 43.

An Act to amend the Medical Acts so far as relates to the Royal   A.D. 1875.
College of Surgeons of England.   [19th July 1875.]
                                                                    ——

WHEREAS by the Medical Act (hereinafter called the principal Act)   21 & 22 Vict.
and Acts amending the same every person becoming possessed of any   c. 90.
one or more of the qualifications mentioned in the said Acts is to be
entitled to be registered under the principal Act, and one of such qualifications is that of fellow or member or licentiate in midwifery of the
Royal College of Surgeons of England :

And whereas by the principal Act it is further provided that any two
or more of the colleges and bodies in the Medical Acts in that behalf
mentioned may, with the sanction and under the direction of the general
council, unite and co-operate in conducting the examinations required for
qualifications to be registered under the principal Act :

And whereas the Royal College of Surgeons of England is one of
such bodies, but doubts are entertained whether it is able to take
advantage of the hereinbefore recited provisions of the principal Act
unless it receives further powers from Parliament, and accordingly it
is expedient to amend the Medical Acts so far as relates to the said
college :

Be it enacted by the Queen's most Excellent Majesty, by and with the
advice and consent of the Lords Spiritual and Temporal, and Commons,
in this present Parliament assembled, and by the authority of the same,
as follows :

1. If in pursuance of the principal Act the Royal College of Surgeons   Power to
of England unites or co-operates with any of the colleges or bodies in   the Royal
that behalf mentioned in the Medical Acts in conducting the examinations   College of
required for qualifications to be registered under the principal Act, then,   Surgeons of
                                                                              England to
                                                                              make bye-

A.D. 1875.

laws with a view to the Medical Act.

notwithstanding anything in any statute or charter contained, it shall be lawful for the council for the time being of the said college to prescribe, by a bye-law under the common seal of the said college, that no person shall become a fellow or member or licentiate in midwifery of the said college unless (in addition to passing such examination (if any) and complying with such other conditions (if any) as may be prescribed by any bye-laws in force for the time being made in pursuance of any charter of the said college) he shall have passed such examinations, hereinafter called the joint examinations, for qualification to be registered under the Medical Act, and complied with such conditions relating thereto as may be agreed upon between the said college and the college or body, colleges or bodies, with whom the said college may be united or co-operating as aforesaid ; and every person who shall have passed such joint examinations and complied with such conditions as aforesaid shall be entitled to receive letters testimonial of his qualification to practise the art and science of surgery under the common seal of the said college, on obtaining which he shall become and be constituted a member of the said college, subject to all the regulations, provisions, and bye-laws in force for the time being of the said college :

Saving power of council to admit to the fellowship in certain cases.

Provided that nothing in this Act contained shall diminish or affect any power which the council of the said college at the time of passing this Act may have, under any charter, of appointing or electing to be fellows of the said college, without examination, any of the present members of the said college who if this Act had not passed would be or might become eligible, by reason of their standing as members, to be appointed or elected fellows of the said college without examination, or any fellows or members or licentiates respectively of the Royal College of Surgeons in Ireland, the Royal College of Surgeons of Edinburgh, or the Faculty of Physicians and Surgeons of Glasgow, who shall at the time of passing this Act be in the bonâ fide practice of the profession of a surgeon of England or Wales, and shall have obtained their respective diplomas or licenses after examination :

Bye-laws to be approved by the Privy Council.

Provided also, that no bye-law made in pursuance of this Act shall be of any force unless it has the approval of the Lords of Her Majesty's Most Honourable Privy Council, and that it shall be lawful for said Lords of the Council at any subsequent time, if they shall think fit, to revoke such assent.

2. Nothing in this Act contained shall deprive the said college of the right (if any) existing at the passing of this Act, or relieve them from the obligation (if any) existing at the passing of this Act, to admit women to the examinations required for letters testimonial of the college, or for a qualification to be registered under "The Medical Act, 1858," or to grant letters testimonial to any woman who has satisfactorily passed the examinations and fulfilled the other general conditions imposed upon persons seeking to obtain from the said college such letters testimonial or qualification.

A.D. 1875.

Saving rights of the college to admit women to certain examinations.

3. This Act may be cited for all purposes as " The Medical Act, Royal College of Surgeons of England, 1875," and shall be construed as one with the Medical Acts.

Title and construction of Act.

CHAPTER 41.

An Act to remove Restrictions on the granting of Qualifications for Registration under the Medical Act on the ground of Sex.

[11th August 1876.]

BE it enacted by the Queen's most Excellent Majesty, by and with the advice and consent of the Lords Spiritual and Temporal, and Commons, in the present Parliament assembled, and by the authority of the same :

1. The powers of every body entitled under the Medical Act to grant qualifications for registration shall extend to the granting of any qualification for registration granted by such body to all persons without distinction of sex : Provided always, that nothing herein contained shall render compulsory the exercise of such powers, and that no person who but for this Act would not have been entitled to be registered shall, by reason of such registration, be entitled to take any part in the government, management, or proceedings of the universities or corporations mentioned in the said Medical Act.

2. This Act shall be taken to be incorporated with the Medical Act, as amended by the Act of the twenty-second year of Her Majesty, chapter twenty-one, and the Medical Act as so amended and any other Act amending the Medical Act shall be construed and have effect accordingly.

BYE-LAWS.

SECT. I.—COMMON SEAL*.

1. THE COMMON SEAL of the ROYAL COLLEGE of SURGEONS of ENGLAND shall consist of the Armorial Bearings, Crest, Supporters and Motto of the College, as registered in Her Majesty's College of Arms; and of which a fac-simile is here given.

2. The Seal shall be in the custody of the President and Vice-Presidents.

3. The Seal shall not be affixed to any instrument, except in the presence of the President or one of the Vice-Presidents, or in their absence in the presence of the Senior Member of the Council.

SECT. II.—HONORARY MEDAL.

1. There shall be an Honorary Medal of the College, to be awarded by the Council under such Rules and Conditions as the Council shall from time to time determine.

2. The Honorary Medal shall not be awarded to any Member of the Council.

SECT. III.—BYE-LAWS.

The making, altering or abrogating any Bye-Law shall be in the following manner :—

A written Formula for any proposed Bye-Law, or for altering or for abrogating any existing Bye-Law, being delivered by a Member of the Council to the President

---

* The Common Seal of the Royal College of Surgeons of England shall consist of the Armorial Bearings, Crest, Supporters, and Motto of the College as registered in Her Majesty's College of Arms *as follows, viz.* :—" *Quarterly a Cross of St. George thereon, an Imperial Crown between two Anchors erect in pale and two Portcullises in fess ; in the first and fourth Quarters a Serpent nowed; in the second and third a Lion couchant guardant,*" with " *a Chief thereon, a lion of England.*" and " *on a wreath an Eagle reguardant, an imperial Crown on the head, and a Mace in the Dexter claw,*" with the Motto " *Quæ prosunt omnibus Artes;*" " *on the dexter side the figure of Machaon, holding in the exterior hand a broken arrow, and on the Sinister the figure of Podalirius, in his exterior hand a staff entwined by a Serpent ;*" of which Armorial Bearings &c. a representation is here given.

1923.   *h*

or presiding Member at any Meeting of the Council, shall thereupon be read ; and if seconded, be taken into consideration; the Council shall then decide by Ballot, whether the said Formula shall be referred to a Committee ; and if a Majority be in favour of such reference, a Committee of three Members of the Council shall immediately be elected, by marking lists, to whom the said Formula shall be referred : and such Committee shall thereupon take the said Formula into consideration and report their opinion thereon to the next Meeting of the Council.

At which next or any succeeding Meeting, the Council, having considered the report of the said Committee, shall ballot for the acceptance or rejection of the said Formula ; and if the same be then approved and accepted, it shall be again referred to the said Committee, in order that the Opinion of Counsel may be taken upon any point therein, if in the judgment of the said Council or Committee such Opinion be necessary.

And the said Committee shall report to the next Meeting of the Council their determination in the matter, with the Opinion of Counsel, if any have been taken ; and if the said Formula be again approved by a Majority of the said Council or of any succeeding Council, the same shall be ordained by such Council, signed by the Members present, and submitted to the proper authority, for sanction and ratification.

SECT. IV.—ELECTION AND ADMISSION OF MEMBERS OF COUNCIL.

1. The place and time appointed for every Meeting of the Fellows for the Election of Members or a Member of the Council shall be announced in the ' London Gazette,' and in two London daily Newspapers, not less than one hundred and ten days and not more than one hundred and twenty before the day of Meeting.

2. Every eligible Fellow desirous of a seat in the Council shall, within ten days from the publication of the ' London Gazette ' in which the day of Meeting for the Election shall be announced, transmit or deliver to the Secretary of the College, a notice signed by himself in the following Terms :—

I, A. B., of C., Fellow of the Royal College of Surgeons of England, do hereby declare, that I am a Candidate for a Seat in the Council of the said College ;

Together with a Nomination signed by three Fellows of the College in the following Terms :—

We, the undersigned Fellows of the Royal College of Surgeons of England, do hereby certify that A. B., of C., is in our estimation a fit person to be elected into the Council of the said College ; and we do hereby nominate him a Candidate for a seat in the said Council.

3. The names of the eligible Fellows who shall have been nominated as Candidates for the Council in the manner hereinbefore required, and shall have complied with the provisions respecting the said notice, together with the names of the three Fellows by whom they shall respectively have been nominated, shall be published in the ' London Gazette,' and in two London daily Newspapers, not less than ten days before the day appointed for the Election.

4. Members of the Council retiring from Office by rotation, and desirous of re-election, shall intimate such their desire in writing, addressed to the Secretary, within ten days from the publication of the ' London Gazette ' in which the day of Meeting for the Election shall be announced ; and the names of such Members shall

be published in the ' London Gazette' and in the said two London daily Newspapers at the head of the list of the names of the several other Candidates to be therein published as aforesaid.

5. Not less than ninety days prior to the day fixed for such Meeting, the Secretary shall deliver or send by the post to every Fellow of the College, whose address is registered at the College, a voting-paper, in such form as the Council of the College may from time to time direct.

6. Every such Fellow, if he desires to vote at such Election, by voting-paper, and not in person, shall return such voting-paper marked, enclosed, sealed, authenticated and attested in such manner as the Council shall from time to time direct and require, and so as the same shall be received by the Secretary, or person acting for him, not later than the time appointed for the commencement of such Election.

7. At every Meeting for Election into the Council, not less than six Fellows of the College exclusive of the Members of Council being actually present, the Chairman having declared the business of the day, and appointed two of the Fellows present to act as Scrutineers in taking the result of the Ballot, the Secretary or person acting for him shall announce to the Meeting the names of the several Candidates so published as aforesaid in the order in which such names were so published, except the name or names of such of the said Candidates as shall previously have signified to the Secretary in writing his or their desire not to proceed to the Election, whereupon a Ballot shall be forthwith taken for the Election of such a number of Members as shall be required to fill up the vacancies in the Council, and the Secretary or person acting for him shall thereupon deposit in the Ballot-box the voting-papers which he shall have duly received, and such Ballot shall be kept open for two hours; and at the expiration of such two hours, the Balloting-box shall, in the presence of the two Scrutineers, be opened by the Chairman, who shall, in the presence and with the concurrence and assistance of the two Scrutineers, ascertain the result of such Ballot, and shall forthwith declare the names of the Fellows elected into such vacancies, and thereupon the Election of such Fellows to be Members of the Council shall be deemed to be and be complete.

8. If at any Election two or more Candidates for one or more vacancies shall obtain an equal number of votes, the right of such Candidates to be elected shall be determined by their seniority in standing as Fellows of the College, the senior of such Fellows being preferred.

9. When there shall be any vacancy in the Council by the death or resignation of a Member, the Fellow, of those elected, who shall have been so elected by the smallest number of votes, shall be the substitute Member of Council in the room of such Member; and when more than one such vacancy shall be required to be so filled up, the Fellow elected by the smallest number of votes shall be the substitute in the room of that Member whose period of Office would have first terminated, and so in regard to each of such vacancies respectively. And if it shall at any time happen that more than one Member shall be elected by the same number of votes, being with reference to the other Fellows elected the smallest number of votes, the youngest in standing as a Fellow of the persons so elected by such equal number of votes shall be the substitute Member, and so in regard to each of such vacancies respectively.

———

SECT. V.—ABSENCE OR MISCONDUCT OF MEMBERS OF COUNCIL.

1. Should any Member of the Council be absent from more than four consecutive Meetings, without leave of the Council, he shall *ipso facto* cease to be a Member of the Council, unless a reason for such absence satisfactory to the Council be assigned.

2. Any Member of the Council who shall wilfully disobey any Bye-Law, Ordinance, Rule, or Constitution of the College, shall be liable to censure or removal from the Council, by resolution thereof.

3. If any Member of the Council, ceasing to be or removed from being a Member of the Council, by virtue of either of the two preceding Clauses, shall be the President, or one of the Vice-Presidents of the College, he shall on so ceasing to be, or being removed from being a Member of the Council, also cease to hold the office of President or Vice-President, as the case may be.

SECT. VI.—RESIGNATION OF MEMBERS OF COUNCIL.

1. The Resignation of a Member of the Council shall not be effectual until the acceptance thereof by the Council.

2. Every Member of the Council, whose Resignation shall have been accepted, or who shall have been removed, or who shall have gone out of office by rotation, shall, *ipso facto*, cease to be a Member of every Committee of which he shall have been elected a Member.

SECT. VII.—MEETINGS OF COUNCIL.

1. A Meeting of the Council shall be holden upon the first Thursday in January, April, July, and October in every year; or within one Calendar Month after each of those days.

2. The President may call a Meeting of the Council whenever he shall judge the same to be necessary.

3. The President may call a Meeting of the Council upon a Requisition, signed by eight or more Members of the Council.

4. Upon the demand of three Members, any question under consideration by the Council shall be decided by Ballot.

5. Every Resolution of the Council relating to Censure or Removal shall be submitted to the Council at a Meeting specially to be holden for that purpose; of which Meeting seven days' Notice, by summons, stating such purpose, shall be given to the Members of the Council.

6. Every question in the Council relating to Censure or Removal shall be determined by Ballot.

7. Every Member present from the commencement until the termination of any Meeting of the Council shall be entitled to One Guinea.

SECT. VIII.—ELECTION OF EXAMINERS.

1. Every Election into the Court of Examiners shall take place at a Meeting of the Council, of which Meeting not less than seven days' notice shall be given to the Members of the Council by Summons, and notice of such Meeting and the purpose thereof and the number of vacancies to be filled up thereat shall further be given

by advertisement in such Public Journals or Newspapers as the Council of the College shall from time to time determine and direct, a reasonable time before the date fixed for such Meeting.

2. No Fellow of the College shall be eligible for election as a Member of the Court of Examiners, unless not less than three clear days before the Meeting of the Council for the election he shall have been nominated in writing by a Member of the Council, or unless not less than seven clear days before the Election he shall have made application in writing to the Secretary, to be admitted as a Candidate for election into the Court of Examiners.

3. No Fellow of the College shall be elected a Member of the Court of Examiners unless, in addition to having been nominated or having made such application as aforesaid, he shall obtain a number of votes representing an absolute majority of the Members of the Council then present at the Meeting for such Election whether voting or not. Such votes to be taken by Ballot in manner following:—

4. On the day and at the time appointed for the Election, the Secretary, or person acting for him, shall announce to the Meeting the names of all the Fellows of the College who shall have been duly nominated, or made application as hereinbefore provided, whereupon a Ballot shall be taken in manner following: that is to say, every Member of the Council present and desiring to vote, shall put into the Balloting-box a slip of paper containing one of the names so announced to the Meeting, the papers shall then be severally examined by the President or Presiding Member, and the names written thereon read aloud by the Secretary or person acting for him, and the Candidate. if any, who shall obtain a majority of votes representing an absolute majority of the Members of the Council then present at the Meeting, whether voting or not, shall be declared to be and be duly elected a Member of the Court of Examiners for the period of five years.

5. If at the first Ballot for the election of a Member of the Court of Examiners, no Candidate shall obtain a number of votes representing such absolute majority, a second Ballot shall be taken, the name of the Candidate obtaining the smallest number of votes in the first Ballot being omitted and excluded from such second Ballot, and if on such second Ballot no Candidate shall receive a number of votes representing an absolute majority of the Members of the Council then present at the Meeting, whether voting or not, a third Ballot shall be taken, the name of the Candidate obtaining the smallest number of votes in the second Ballot being omitted and excluded from such third Ballot, and so on until some Candidate shall have obtained a number of votes representing an absolute majority of the Members of the Council then present at the Meeting, whether voting or not, when he shall be declared to be and be duly elected a Member of the Court of Examiners for the period of five years.

6. If at any Ballot two or more Candidates shall obtain an equal number of votes, being with respect to the other Candidates the smallest number of votes obtained by any Candidate, the Junior or Juniors on the Roll of Fellows shall be omitted and excluded from the succeeding Ballot.

7. If at the first Ballot there be more than two Candidates, and all of them shall obtain an equal number of votes, the Junior on the Roll of Fellows shall be omitted and excluded from the second Ballot, and so on at each succeeding Ballot.

8. The above procedure shall be adopted with regard to the Election of as many Candidates as there are vacancies to be filled up at such Meeting, the name of any Candidate already elected being omitted and excluded from all subsequent Ballots.

SECT. IX.—ABSENCE OF EXAMINERS.

Should a Member of the Court of Examiners be absent from that Court more than six successive Meetings without assigning a Reason satisfactory to the Court, such Absence shall be reported to the Council holden next after the said six Meetings; and the Member so absenting himself shall be liable to removal from the Court by resolution of the Council.

SECT. X.—RESIGNATION OF EXAMINERS.

The Resignation of a Member of the Court of Examiners shall not take effect until the acceptance thereof by the Council.

SECT. XI.—MEETINGS OF COURT OF EXAMINERS.

1. The Court of Examiners shall be authorized to hold such Courts for the Examination of Candidates for the Fellowship of the College and to make such adjournments thereof as may by them be judged necessary.

2. The Court of Examiners shall constitute and be the Examiners in Surgery appointed by the College for the Joint Examinations to be conducted by the College and the Royal College of Physicians of London, and shall receive in respect thereof such remuneration as the Council shall from time to time determine and direct. Six at least of the said Court of Examiners shall attend each Examination in Surgery forming part of such Joint Examinations.

3. Every Member of the Court of Examiners present from the commencement to the termination of any meeting of the Court of Examiners relative to Examinations, but not for the purpose of conducting any of the above Examinations, shall be entitled to One Guinea.

4. In every case of Examination for the Diploma of Fellow the Examiners present from the commencement to the termination of such Examination shall be entitled to an equal division of such a sum as the Council shall from time to time determine whether the person examined be approved or not.

SECT. XII.—ELECTION OF PRESIDENT AND VICE-PRESIDENTS.

The mode of Election of President and Vice-Presidents shall be as follows:—

1. Every Member of the Council present at the Meeting for such Election, having been furnished with a list of the Members of the Council, shall, if desirous of voting, put a mark against the name of one person in such list, and put the same into the Balloting-box; the papers shall then be severally examined by the President (or Presiding Member), and every name against which such mark shall have been put shall be read aloud by the Secretary, or person acting for him; and the person (if any) against whose name there shall have been affixed a number of marks representing an absolute majority of the Members of the Council then present at the Meeting whether voting or not, shall be, and be declared to be duly elected President.

2. In case it shall appear that no name in the said lists has a number of marks representing such absolute majority affixed against it, a second Ballot shall be taken, the name against which the smallest number of marks was affixed in the first Ballot being omitted and excluded from the second Ballot, and so on with subsequent Ballots, until some name shall have a number of marks affixed against it representing an absolute majority of the Members of the Council then present at the Meeting, whether voting or not, when the person against whose name such number of marks shall have been affixed shall be, and be declared to be, duly elected President.

3. If any difficulty shall arise with respect to any such Ballot by reason of the names of two or more persons having an equal number of marks affixed against them, the question shall be decided according to the seniority of such persons as Members of the Council, the name of the Junior being omitted and excluded from the succeeding Ballot.

4. The same procedure shall be adopted with regard to the Election of each of the Vice-Presidents.

SECT. XIII.—EXAMINERS AND EXAMINATIONS IN ANATOMY AND PHYSIOLOGY.

1. The Council shall, under such Regulations, and for such time or period as to them shall seem proper (but always subject to removal at the pleasure of the Council), appoint such persons as they shall think proper for the purpose of conducting Examinations in Anatomy and Physiology of Candidates for the Diploma of Fellow.

2. The Council shall further appoint such persons for such periods and on such terms as they shall think fit to be the Examiners in Anatomy and Physiology to be appointed by the College for the Joint Examinations conducted by the College and the Royal College of Physicians of London. No person shall be ineligible under this clause by reason of having been appointed under the preceding clause.

3. The Examinations in Anatomy and Physiology to be required of all Candidates for the Diploma of Fellow shall be held at such time and conducted in such manner as the Council of the College shall from time to time direct.

4. The Council shall have power to accept from any Candidate for the Diploma of Fellow, in lieu of such Examination in Anatomy and Physiology, any Degree, Diploma. Licence, or Certificate of any University, College, or other public body whose Degree, Diploma, Licence, or Certificate the Council shall deem to be equivalent to the passing of such Examination.

SECT. XIV.—EXAMINATION AND ADMISSION OF MEMBERS.

1. No person under the age of Twenty-one years shall become a Member of the College nor unless and until he shall have passed the Examinations for Qualifications to be registered under the Medical Act, held by the Examining Board for the time being constituted under the Scheme and Regulations approved and adopted by the Royal College of Physicians of London on March 12th, 1883, and by the College on April 29th, 1883 (herein called the Joint Examinations), and complied with the conditions relating thereto contained in the said Scheme and Regulations, or

such conditions as may be agreed upon between the College of Physicians and the College for the time being.   Nothing contained in this Section shall diminish or affect the right of any person who shall have commenced professional study before the 1st of October, 1884, to be examined for and to receive the Diploma of Member of the College; but such right, where it exists, shall remain and continue, to all intents and purposes, as if this Bye-Law had not been enacted.

2. The Diploma of Member shall be in such Form as the Council may from time to time judge proper.

3. The Seal of the College shall be affixed to the Diploma of every Member of the College.

4. Every person, prior to his admission as a Member of the College, shall, in the presence of an Officer of the College, make and subscribe his name to the following Declaration: —

" I, A. B., do solemnly and sincerely declare, that, while a Member of the Royal College of Surgeons of England, I will observe the Bye-Laws thereof: that I will obey every lawful Summons issued by order of the Council of the said College, having no reasonable excuse to the contrary: and that I will demean myself honourably in the practice of my Profession ; and to the utmost of my power maintain the dignity and welfare of the College."

5. Every person, prior to his admission as a Member, shall subscribe his name to a Copy of the Bye-Laws of the College, in testimony of his having engaged himself to the observance thereof.

6. The fee for the Diploma of Member, exclusive of the fees payable for the Licence of the Royal College of Physicians of London under the Scheme and Regulations for the Joint Examinations, shall be such sum not exceeding Twenty Guineas and shall be payable in such manner and at such times as the Council from time to time direct, and in addition thereto there shall be paid the Stamp Duty, if any, on such Diploma and such reasonable fees for and in case of re-examination as shall be in like manner directed.

7. If the Court of Examiners shall find any circumstance in the Character, Conduct, or mode of Practice of any Candidate for Examination which in their opinion renders such Candidate unfit to be admitted a Member of the College, the said Court shall have the power of declining to examine him until the opinion of the Council shall have been taken thereon.

SECT. XV.—RIGHTS OF FELLOWS AND MEMBERS.

The Council will, at all times, protect and defend every Fellow and Member of the College who may be disturbed in the exercise and enjoyment of the Rights, Privileges, Exemptions, and Immunities, acquired by him as a Fellow and Member or Member thereof.

SECT. XVI.—MISCONDUCT OF FELLOWS AND MEMBERS.

1. If any Fellow or Member of the College shall after due enquiry be judged by the Council to have been guilty of disgraceful conduct in any professional respect, he shall be liable to removal by resolution of the Council from being a Fellow and Member or Member of the College.

2. Should any Fellow or Member of the College be convicted of any Criminal Offence, or have his name removed from the Medical Register by the General Medical Council under Section XXIX. of the Medical Act of 1858, the Council of the College may, if they should consider the offence of which he shall have been so convicted, or for which his name shall have been so removed, to be of such a nature as to render him unfit to remain a Fellow and Member or a Member of the College, remove such Fellow or Member by resolution to that effect, from being a Fellow and Member or a Member of the College.

3. Any Fellow or Member who shall have been removed by Resolution of the Council as aforesaid shall thereby forfeit all his rights and privileges as a Fellow and Member or a Member of the College; and his Diplomas or Diploma shall thereupon be void and shall become the property of the College, and be delivered up by such Fellow or Member to the College on demand, provided that if at any subsequent time the Council of the College by Resolution, and subject to such conditions as they may think proper, rescind any Resolution which may have been passed under any of the preceding Bye-Laws for removing any person from being a Fellow and Member or Member of the College, such rescinding of the former Resolution shall have the effect of restoring such person to the Fellowship or Membership of the College, and such person shall, notwithstanding such removal or forfeiture as aforesaid, but subject to such conditions as the Council may in the particular case see fit to impose, be restored to his rights and privileges as a Fellow and Member or a Member of the College.

SECT. XVII.—MEETINGS OF FELLOWS AND MEMBERS.

1. No business whatever shall be transacted, nor any matter be discussed or debated, at any meeting or assemblage convened by or under the authority of the President or Council, or before or after the business thereof shall have commenced, other than the particular business or matter in respect of which such meeting or assemblage shall have been convened; nor shall any debate or discussion whatsoever be had or allowed at any meeting convened by the President or Council for the delivery of Lectures or Orations, either before or after the same shall have commenced or terminated. And no meeting or assemblage of Fellows or Members of the College shall be held in the Hall or Council House of the College, or in any of its appurtenances, unless convened by or under the authority of the President or Council; and no Fellow or Member of the College shall advertise, or convene or attend, or combine with others to advertise, or convene or attend, any meeting or assemblage in the Hall or Council House of the College, or in any of its appurtenances, not authorized by the President or Council. And any Fellow or Member of the College who may in any manner offend herein shall be liable to be restrained and excluded by the Council from attending any Oration and Lectures at the Theatre, and from any use of or admission to the Library and Museum, and to be suspended from any or all other Privileges which he may have as a Fellow and Member or a Member of the College, for any such period as the Council may adjudge, or to removal by resolution of the Council from being a Fellow and Member or a Member of the College. And every Fellow or Member of the College who shall thereupon be removed as aforesaid shall forfeit all his rights and privileges as a Fellow and Member or a Member thereof.

2. All meetings convened by or under the authority of the President or Council

of the College. as well for general business as for the delivery of Orations or Lec_ tures, or for the distribution of Prizes, shall be under the control and direction of the President or other Member of the Council presiding at such Meeting. And any Fellow or Member of the College who shall interrupt, impede, or interfere with the proceedings at any such Meeting, or shall propose any matter for discussion or de_ bate without the leave of the President or other person so presiding, shall, upon being required by the President or other person so presiding, immediately withdraw from such Meeting; and shall be moreover liable to be restrained and excluded by the Council from attending any Orations and Lectures at the Theatre, and from any use of or admission to the Library and Museum, and to be suspended from any or all other privileges which he may have as a Fellow and Member or a Mem_ ber of the College, for any such period as the Council may adjudge. And any Fellow or Member of the College who shall so offend a second time, or during any suspension by the Council shall attempt to exercise any of the privileges from which he shall be suspended, shall be liable to removal by resolution of the Council from being a Fellow and Member or a Member of the College. And every Fellow or Member of the College who shall thereupon be removed as aforesaid shall forfeit all his rights and privileges as a Fellow and Member or a Member thereof.

SECT. XVIII.—RESIGNATION AND RELEASE OF FELLOWS AND MEMBERS.

1. Any Fellow or Member of the College, desirous of ceasing to be a Fellow or Member thereof. shall tender his resignation to the Council; and upon the accept_ ance of his Resignation, he shall pay Ten Guineas, over and above all charges of Stamps.

2. No resignation shall be complete and valid until an Instrument under the Seal of the College, declaratory thereof. in such form as the Council shall from time to time direct, be delivered to the Fellow or Member resigning.

SECT. XIX.—CERTIFICATE OF DIPLOMA.

A Certificate that a Diploma has been obtained by any Member shall not be granted to or for any Person whomsoever without the Authority of the Council; and for which Certificate Five Guineas shall be paid, over and above all charges of Stamps, unless it shall appear to the Council that such Diploma has been destroyed or irrevocably lost by fire, shipwreck, or other accident; in which case the fee of Five Guineas may be remitted.

SECT. XX.—ADMISSION TO THE FELLOWSHIP BY EXAMINATION.

1. No person shall be entitled to the Diploma of Fellow unless he (a) shall have produced evidence satisfactory to the Council that he has attained the age of twenty-five years: (b) shall have complied with clause 1 of the Section relating to the Examination and Admission of Members or possess a qualification or qualifications in Medicine and Surgery recognized by the Council in lieu thereof; (c) shall have passed the examinations and complied with the conditions herein- after prescribed. Provided always that nothing herein contained shall diminish

or affect the right of any person who shall have commenced professional study before the first day of October One thousand Eight hundred and Eighty-four to be examined for and to receive the Diploma of Fellow ; but such right where it exists shall remain and continue to all intents and purposes as if this Bye-Law had not been enacted.

2. The Council shall have power from time to time to make or alter such Rules and Regulations respecting the professional education of Candidates for the Fellowship as they may think proper.

3. The Examination for the Fellowship shall be divided into two parts, viz. :—

The first Examination to be on Anatomy and Physiology.

The second Examination to be on Pathology, Therapeutics, and Surgery, and on such other subjects as the Council may from time to time consider necessary.

In order to be admitted to the First Examination, the Candidate shall produce evidence—

That he has been engaged during not less than three Winter Sessions in the acquirement of professional knowledge, in such manner as the Council shall from time to time direct.

In order to be admitted to the Second Examination, the Candidate shall produce evidence—

(If a Member) that he has been engaged for six years in the acquirement of professional knowledge, in such manner as the Council shall from time to time direct.

(If not a Member) that he has been engaged in the acquirement of professional knowledge, in such manner as the Council shall from time to time direct, for at least four years subsequent to the date of having obtained a qualification or qualifications in Medicine and Surgery recognized by the Council for the purpose.

4. The fee to be paid for admission to the Fellowship shall be Thirty Guineas over and above all charges, if any, for stamps, and shall be payable in such manner as the Council shall from time to time direct.

Provided always that the Council may, if they think fit, remit Ten Guineas of such fee in the case of a Candidate who is a Member of the College.

5. Examinations for the Fellowship shall be held at such periods as the Council shall from time to time determine.

6. The Examinations shall be conducted in such manner as the Council shall from time to time direct.

7. Every Member of the College shall, prior to his admission as a Fellow by Examination, make and subscribe his name to the following Declaration, in the presence of an Officer of the College, viz. :—

" I, A. B., of C., Member of the Royal College of Surgeons of England, do solemnly and sincerely declare that, while a Fellow of the said College, I will observe the Bye-Laws thereof relating to the Fellowship. and will obey every lawful Summons issued by order of the Council of the said College, having no reasonable excuse to the contrary."

8. Every Member of the College shall, prior to his admission as a Fellow. subscribe his name to a Copy of the Bye-Laws relating to the Fellowship, in testimony of having engaged himself to the observance thereof.

9. Every person not previously a Member of the College shall, prior to his

admission as a Fellow, make and subscribe his name to the following Declaration, in the presence of an Officer of the College, viz. :—

"I, A. B., of C., do solemnly and sincerely declare that, while a Fellow or Member of the Royal College of Surgeons of England, I will observe the Bye-Laws thereof, and will obey every lawful Summons issued by the Council of the said College, having no reasonable excuse to the contrary, and will to the utmost of my power maintain the welfare and dignity of the College."

10. Every person not previously a Member of the College shall, prior to his admission as a Fellow, subscribe his name to a copy of the Bye-Laws of the College.

11. The Diploma of a Fellow shall be in such form as the Council may from time to time direct.

12. The Seal of the College shall be affixed to the Diploma of every Fellow.

13. When more than one Member of the College shall be admitted to the Fellowship at the same time, their names shall be entered upon the Register of Fellows according to the priority of the dates of their respective Diplomas as Members; and should a person not previously a Member be admitted a Fellow at the same time as a Member or Members, such previous Member or Members shall take the precedence.

SECT. XXI.—ADMISSION OF MEMBERS TO THE FELLOWSHIP BY ELECTION.

1. The proposition for the admission of a Member of twenty years' standing to the Fellowship under the authority of the Fifth Section of the Charter of the fifteenth of Victoria shall be made at the Quarterly Meeting of the Council in January.

2. At the time of any such proposition being made, a recommendation for the admission to the Fellowship of the Member proposed shall be laid before the Council; which recommendation shall be signed by six Members of the Council, and shall declare that he is in their opinion a fit and proper person to be admitted into the Fellowship.

3. The Council shall ballot upon the admission of any person so proposed at the Quarterly Meeting of the Council in April next succeeding.

4. A fee of Ten Guineas shall be payable upon the admission of Members to the Fellowship by Election, and shall be paid at or before the issue of the Diploma of Fellowship.

5. The Names of such Fellows as shall be elected as aforesaid shall be entered upon the List or Register of Fellows according to the dates of their election; and when more than one shall be elected upon the same day, their names shall take precedence according to the priority of their Diplomas as Members.

6. No Member of the College, admitted to the Fellowship by election, shall exercise any right or privilege he shall have acquired as a Fellow until he shall have signed a copy of the Bye-Laws of the College, in testimony of having engaged himself to the observance thereof, and made and subscribed the following Declaration in the presence of the Council, viz. :—

"I, A. B., of C., Member of the Royal College of Surgeons of England, do solemnly and sincerely declare that, while a Fellow of the said College, I will observe the Bye-Laws thereof, and will obey every lawful summons issued by order of the Council of the said College, having no reasonable excuse to the contrary. And I make this solemn Declaration by virtue of the provisions of the Statutary Declarations Act 1835."

SECT. XXII.—AD EUNDEM ADMISSIONS.

1. Any Fellow of the Royal College of Surgeons in Ireland, of the Royal College of Surgeons of Edinburgh, or of the Faculty of Physicians and Surgeons of Glasgow, who shall be desirous of Admission to the Fellowship of this College, shall transmit or deliver to the Secretary of this College, or person acting for him, his Diploma, an Application to be so admitted, and a Declaration signed by himself in the following terms:—

" I. A. B., of C., Fellow of D., do hereby declare that I was duly admitted to such Fellowship, having previously passed the necessary Examination or Examinations required by the Bye-Laws or Regulations of the said Royal College (or Faculty), and that I am in the bonâ fide Practice of the Profession of a Surgeon in England (or Wales), and that I do not sell or supply Drugs or Medicines, (or, that I do not sell or supply Drugs or Medicines otherwise than in the due exercise or practice of my profession as an Apothecary)."

Together with the foregoing Declaration shall be transmitted or delivered the following Certificate:—

" We, the undersigned Fellows of the Royal College of Surgeons in Ireland (or of Edinburgh), (or of the Faculty of Physicians and Surgeons of Glasgow), do hereby certify that A. B., of C., Fellow of the said Royal College (or Faculty), is, from his moral character and professional attainments, a fit and proper person to be admitted to the Fellowship of the Royal College of Surgeons of England, and that he does not sell or supply Drugs or Medicines, (or, that he does not sell or supply Drugs or Medicines otherwise than in the due exercise or practice of his profession of an Apothecary); and we accordingly recommend him to the Council of the said College to be admitted a Fellow thereof."

2. The foregoing Certificate shall be signed by six Fellows of the College (or Faculty) of which the said Applicant shall be a Fellow.

3. A similar Certificate signed by six Fellows of this College shall also be transmitted or delivered with the foregoing Declaration and Certificate.

4. The Fellows of the Royal College of Surgeons in Ireland, of the Royal College of Surgeons of Edinburgh, or of the Faculty of Physicians and Surgeons of Glasgow, shall not be admissible to the Fellowship of this College unless the Council of this College shall be satisfied that the course of professional Study for such Fellowship required by the said Colleges or Faculty to which such Fellow shall belong shall be equal to the Course of professional Study required for the Fellowship of this College.

5. The Fellows of the Royal Colleges of Surgeons in Ireland and of Edinburgh, and of the Faculty of Physicians and Surgeons of Glasgow, shall pay on their Admission to the Fellowship of this College the sum of Thirty Guineas over and above all charges for Stamps which shall be necessary.

6. No person admitted ad eundem a Fellow of this College shall exercise any right or privilege he shall have acquired by such admission until he shall have

signed a copy of the Bye-Laws of the College, in testimony of having engaged himself to the observance thereof, and made and subscribed the following Declaration in the presence of the Council, viz.:—

"I, A. B., of C., Fellow of D., do solemnly and sincerely declare that, while a Fellow of the Royal College of Surgeons of England, I will observe the Bye-Laws thereof, and will obey every lawful summons issued by order of the Council of the said College, having no reasonable excuse to the contrary."

SECT. XXIII.—TREASURERS.

1. The President and Vice-Presidents for the time being shall be joint Treasurers of the College.

2. All Payments, Contributions, and Fines shall be paid to the Treasurers of the College.

3. All Drafts upon the Banker of the College shall be signed by two of the Treasurers at least.

4. The Accounts of the College shall be audited at least once in each year, at such date or dates as the Council shall direct, by a Professional Auditor to be nominated by the Council.

SECT. XXIV.—PROPERTY OF THE COLLEGE.

1. The Moneys belonging to the College shall not be invested otherwise than upon Government or Real Security, or upon such Securities as may from time to time be permitted to Trustees under the authority of Parliament.

2. All investments shall be made in the Name of the "Royal College of Surgeons of England."

3. All Moneys, the property of or belonging to the College, shall be paid to the President, or, by his order or in his absence, to one of the Vice-Presidents, by the Secretary or any other Person holding or having received the same, as soon as such payment can be made.

4. All Payments, Contributions, and Fines shall be to the use of the College.

SECT. XXV.—DENTAL SURGERY.

1. The Board of Examiners in Dental Surgery shall consist of four Members of the Court of Examiners of the College for the time being, and four other persons duly registered under "The Dentists Act 1878," together with such additional Members of the Board, if any, as the Council may from time to time determine, not being more than four additional Members of the Court of Examiners, and not more than four additional persons duly registered under "The Dentists Act 1878."

2. The Members of the Board shall be elected by the Council of this College for the period of five years, or for such shorter period as the Council may determine, and shall be re-eligible.

3. Should a vacancy occur in the Board from the death or resignation of a Member thereof, or from any other cause, such vacancy shall be reported to the Council of this College, and filled up at a meeting of the Council, of which meeting seven days' notice shall be given by summons.

4. Should a Member of the Board be absent from more than three consecutive Meetings, such absence shall be reported to the Council holden next after the said three Meetings ; and the Member so absenting himself, without assigning a reason satisfactory to the Council, shall be liable to removal from the Board by resolution of the Council.

5. The Board shall hold such meetings. and shall conduct its proceedings in such manner, as the Council of this College shall from time to time direct.

6. The Senior Member of the Court of Examiners of this College. on the Board, shall act as Chairman thereof; and in his absence the next Senior Member of the said Court shall preside.

7. Candidates for the Certificate of fitness to practise as a Dentist shall comply with such regulations, as regards Professional Study and Examination, as shall from time to time be required by the Council of this College.

8. The Fee for the Certificate of fitness to practise as a Dentist shall be Twenty Guineas over and above any Stamp Duty.

9. The Certificate shall be in such form as the Council of this College shall from time to time direct.

10. No person shall be admitted to the Final Examination for the Certificate of fitness to practise as a Dentist until he shall have completed the twenty-first year of his age.

SECT. XXVI.—ADMISSION OF WOMEN.

1. Pursuant to the powers conferred by the Medical Act 1876 and subject to the provisions therein and hereinafter contained, women may be admitted as Members and Fellows of the College and may obtain Diplomas in Dental Surgery on the same terms and conditions as men ; and so far as it is necessary to give effect to this Bye-Law words in the Bye-Laws and Regulations of the College which import the masculine gender shall also import the feminine gender and all proper alterations shall be made in the form of the Letters Testimonial, Diplomas, Certificates and Licences granted by the College.

2. Women shall not be eligible as Members of the Council and shall not vote at or take any part in any election of a Member or Members of the Council, or attend any Meeting of Fellows or of Fellows and Members (except Meetings convened for the delivery of Lectures or Orations), or otherwise take any part in the government, management or proceedings of the College.

3. Women shall not be eligible as Members of the Court of Examiners or for any Examinership to which the Council appoint.

INDEX TO THE BYE-LAWS.

OFFICERS, ETC.

TRUSTEES OF THE HUNTERIAN COLLECTION.

BY OFFICE. 17.

COUNCIL.

PRESIDENT.

SIR JOHN BLAND-SUTTON, 47 *Brook-street*, W. 1.

VICE-PRESIDENTS.

SIR BERKELEY GEORGE ANDREW MOYNIHAN, Bt., K.C.M.G., C.B., 33 *Park-sq.*, *Leeds*.

HOLBURT JACOB WARING, 37 *Wimpole-street*, W. 1.

SIR ANTHONY ALFRED BOWLBY, Bt., K.C.B., K.C.M.G., K.C.V.O., 25 *Manchester-sq.*, W. 1.

WILLIAM FREDERIC HASLAM, 8 *Vicarage-road, Edgbaston, Birmingham*.

SIR CHARLES ALFRED BALLANCE, K.C.M.G., C.B., M.V.O., 106 *Harley-street*, W. 1.

SIR D'ARCY POWER, K.B.E., 10 A *Chandos-street*, W. 1.

WALTER GEORGE SPENCER, O.B.E., 2 *Portland-place*, W. 1.

THOMAS HORROCKS OPENSHAW, C.B., C.M.G., 16 *Wimpole-street*, W. 1.

RAYMOND JOHNSON, O.B.E., *Chobham Farm, Chobham, Surrey*.

VINCENT WARREN LOW, C.B., 76 *Harley-street*, W. 1.

JAMES SHERREN, C.B.E., 6 *Devonshire-place*, W. 1.

SIR JOHN LYNN-THOMAS, K.B.E., C.B., C.M.G., *Llwyndyrys, Llechryd, Cardiganshire*.

ERNEST WILLIAM HEY GROVES, 25 *Victoria-square, Clifton, Bristol*.

SIR CUTHBERT SIDNEY WALLACE, K.C.M.G., C.B., 26 *Upper Wimpole-street*, W. 1.

FRANCIS JAMES STEWARD, 98 *Portland-place*, W. 1.

WILLIAM THELWALL THOMAS, M.B.E., 84 *Rodney-street, Liverpool*.

CHARLES HERBERT FAGGE, 3 *Devonshire-place*, W. 1.

ROBERT PUGH ROWLANDS, O.B.E., 12 *Queen Anne-street*, W. 1.

JAMES BERRY, 21 *Wimpole-street*, W. 1.

JOHN HERBERT FISHER, 83 *Wimpole-street*, W. 1.

WILLIAM SAMPSON HANDLEY, 36 *Harley-street*, W. 1.

PERCY SARGENT, C.M.G., D.S.O., 20 *Harley-street*, W. 1.

GEORGE ERNEST GASK, C.M.G., D.S.O., 4 *York-gate*, N.W. 1.

MUSEUM COMMITTEE.

Thomas Horrocks Openshaw, C.B., C.M.G., *Chairman.*
Raymond Johnson, O.B.E.
Sir Anthony Alfred Bowlby, Bt.

The President,
The Vice-Presidents, } *ex officio.*

LIBRARY COMMITTEE.

Charles Herbert Fagge, *Chairman.*
Robert Pugh Rowlands, O.B.E.
Sir D'Arcy Power, K.B.E.

The President,
The Vice-Presidents, } *ex officio.*

COMMITTEE FOR GENERAL PURPOSES.

James Sherren, C.B.E., *Chairman.*
John Herbert Fisher.
George Ernest Gask, C.M.G., D.S.O.

The President,
The Vice-Presidents, } *ex officio.*

FINANCE COMMITTEE.

Walter George Spencer, O.B.E., *Chairman.*
Sir Cuthbert S. Wallace, K.C.M.G.
James Berry.

The President,
The Vice-Presidents,
The Chairmen of the Museum, Library, and General Purposes Committees, } *ex officio.*

COMMITTEE ON ANNUAL REPORT OF THE COUNCIL.

Charles Herbert Fagge, *Chairman.*
Sir Anthony Alfred Bowlby, Bt.
Sir D'Arcy Power, K.B.E.
Vincent Warren Low, C.B.
William Sampson Handley.

The President,
The Vice-Presidents, } *ex officio.*

HUNTERIAN PROFESSORS.

Robert Lawford Knaggs.
William Sampson Handley.
Charles Max Page, D.S.O.
Kenneth Macfarlane Walker, O.B.E.
Alexander Fleming.
Geoffrey Jefferson.

Frank Cook.
William Edward Gallie.
Sidney Forsdike.
William Heneage Ogilvie.
Ranald Montagu Handfield-Jones.
Ralph St. Leger Brockman.

ARRIS AND GALE LECTURERS.

Hugh Ernest Griffiths.
Cecil Pembrey Grey Wakeley.

Victor Ewings Negus.

ARNOTT DEMONSTRATOR.

Sir Arthur Keith.

ERASMUS WILSON LECTURER.

Samuel George Shattock.

BRADSHAW LECTURER.
WALTER GEORGE SPENCER, O.B.E.

THOMAS VICARY LECTURER.
SIR ARTHUR KEITH.

CONSERVATOR OF THE MUSEUM.
SIR ARTHUR KEITH, M.D., C.M., LL.D., F.R.S., F.R.C.S.

PHYSIOLOGICAL CURATOR.
RICHARD HIGGINS BURNE, M.A.Oxon.

PATHOLOGICAL CURATOR.
SAMUEL GEORGE SHATTOCK, F.R.S., F.R.C.S.

ASSISTANT PATHOLOGICAL CURATOR.
CECIL FOWLER BEADLES, M.R.C.S.

PATHOLOGICAL ASSISTANT.
CLEMENT EDWARD SHATTOCK, M.S., M.D., F.R.C.S.

PROSECTOR.
HENRY CECIL WILSON.

HONORARY CURATOR OF THE ODONTOLOGICAL COLLECTION.
SIR FRANK COLYER, K.B.E., F.R.C.S., L.D.S.

LIBRARIAN.
VICTOR GUSTAVE PLARR, M.A.Oxon.

CLERK IN THE LIBRARY.
ARTHUR FUSEDALE.

SECRETARY.
SIBERT FORREST COWELL, M.A.Oxon.

CLERK IN THE SECRETARY'S OFFICE.
DOROTHY GERTRUDE SARGANT.

DIRECTOR OF EXAMINATIONS.
FREDERIC GREVILLE HALLETT, O.B.E.

SOLICITOR.
E. HUGH N. WILDE, M.A.Cantab.

COURT OF EXAMINERS.

RAYMOND JOHNSON, O.B.E., *Chairman, Chobham Farm, Chobham, Surrey.*
JOHN MURRAY, 110 *Harley-street*, W. 1.
VINCENT WARREN LOW, C.B., 76 *Harley-street*, W. 1.
SIR CUTHBERT SIDNEY WALLACE, K.C.M.G., C.B., 26 *Upper Wimpole-street*, W. 1.
HERBERT STRINGFELLOW PENDLEBURY, 44 *Brook-street*, W. 1.
CHARLES HERBERT FAGGE, 3 *Devonshire-place*, W. 1.
LOUIS BATHE RAWLING, 16 *Montagu-street*, W. 1.
HERBERT SHERWELL CLOGG, 41 *Devonshire-street*, W. 1.
HUGH LETT, C.B.E., 6 *Lower Berkeley-street*, W. 1.
THOMAS PERCY LEGG, C.M.G., 139 *Harley-street*, W. 1.

BOARD OF EXAMINERS IN ANATOMY AND PHYSIOLOGY FOR THE FELLOWSHIP.

Anatomy.

JOHN ERNEST SULLIVAN FRAZER, 2 *Pembridge-crescent*, W. 11.
GORDON GORDON-TAYLOR, O.B.E., 80 *Harley-street*, W. 1.
WILLIAM FREDERIC HASLAM, 8 *Vicarage-road, Edgbaston, Birmingham.*
WILLIAM WRIGHT, D.Sc., *Villa Candens, Gerrard's Cross, Bucks.*

Physiology.

ARTHUR RENDLE SHORT, 69 *Pembroke-road, Clifton, Bristol.*
JOHN MELLANBY, M.D., *The Laurels, Englefield-green, Surrey.*
DAVID HENRIQUES DE SOUZA, M.D., 1 *Belsize-grove, Hampstead*, N.W. 3.
FFRANGCON ROBERTS, M.D., *The Gables, Histon, Cambs.*

BOARD OF EXAMINERS IN DENTAL SURGERY.

Surgical Section.

JOHN MURRAY.
RAYMOND JOHNSON, O.B.E.
VINCENT WARREN LOW, C.B.
SIR CUTHBERT SIDNEY WALLACE, K.C.M.G., C.B.
HERBERT STRINGFELLOW PENDLEBURY.
CHARLES HERBERT FAGGE.
LOUIS BATHE RAWLING.
HERBERT SHERWELL CLOGG.

Dental Section.

EVELYN SPRAWSON, M.C., 68 *Southwood-lane, Highgate*, N. 6.
JOSEPH LEWIN PAYNE, O.B.E., 18 *Portland-place*, W. 1.
DOUGLAS GABELL, 9 *Portland-place*, W. 1.
ARTHUR BAYFORD GUY UNDERWOOD, 19 *Upper Wimpole-street*, W. 1.

EXAMINERS FOR THE F.R.C.S. (WITH OPHTHALMOLOGY).

JOHN HERBERT FISHER, 83 *Wimpole-street*, W. 1.
SIR WILLIAM TINDALL LISTER, K.C.M.G., 24 *Devonshire-place*, W. 1.

EXAMINING BOARD IN ENGLAND BY THE ROYAL COLLEGE OF PHYSICIANS OF LONDON AND THE ROYAL COLLEGE OF SURGEONS OF ENGLAND.

EXAMINATION HALL, QUEEN SQUARE, BLOOMSBURY, W.C. 1.

Telegraphic Address : "Conjoint" Holb. London.   Telephone Number : Museum 1492.

EXAMINERS IN CHEMISTRY.   EXAMINERS IN PHYSICS.

(Appointed by the Royal College of Physicians.)

WILLIAM BRADSHAW TUCK, D.Sc., 45 *Bartholomew-road*, N.W. 5.
CHARLES STANLEY GIBSON, O.B.E., B.Sc., *Medical School, Guy'sHospital*, S.E. 1.

FREDERICK WOMACK. M.B., B.Sc., *The Croft, Finchampstead, Wokingham, Berks.*
WILLIAM EDWARD CURTIS, D.Sc., *King's College, Strand*, W.C.

EXAMINERS IN ELEMENTARY BIOLOGY.

(Appointed by the Royal College of Surgeons.)

THOMAS WILLIAM SHORE, O.B.E., M.D., *"Woodlawn," Kingswood-road, Upper Norwood*, S.E. 19.
JAMES P. HILL, D.Sc., F.R.S., *"Kanimbla," Dollis-avenue, Finchley*, N. 3.

EXAMINERS IN ANATOMY.

(Royal College of Physicians.)   (Royal College of Surgeons.)

THOMAS BAILLIE JOHNSTON, M.B., *Anatomical Department, Guy's Hospital Medical School*, S.E. 1.

DAVID HEPBURN, C.M.G., M.D., 61 *Ninian-road, Cardiff.*
JOHN BASIL HUME, *Connaught-club, Seymour-street*, W. 1.
HENRY ALBERT HARRIS, 52 *Claremont-road, Highgate*, N. 6.

EXAMINERS IN PHYSIOLOGY.

(Royal College of Physicians.)   (Royal College of Surgeons.)

JOHN BERESFORD LEATHES, M.B., F.R.S., 2 *Manchester-road, Sheffield.*
JOHN MELLANBY, M.D., *The Laurels, Englefield-green, Surrey.*

HERBERT ELDON ROAF, M.D., 5 *Heathgate*, N.W. 11.
CHARLES ARTHUR LOVATT EVANS, 57 *Ashbourne-avenue,Golder's-green*,N.W. 11.

EXAMINERS IN MATERIA MEDICA AND PHARMACOLOGY.

(Appointed by the Royal College of Physicians.)

ALFRED ERNEST RUSSELL, M.D., 7 *Upper Wimpole-street*, W. 1.
EDWARD ALFRED COCKAYNE, M.D., 33 *Weymouth-street*, W. 1.
PHILIP HAMILL, M.D., 74 *Harley-street*, W. 1.
ALFRED JOSEPH CLARK, M.C., M.D., *University-college, Gower-street*, W.C. 1.
WALTER ERNEST DIXON, O.B.E., M.D., *Whittlesford, Cambridge*.

EXAMINERS IN MEDICAL ANATOMY AND THE PRINCIPLES AND PRACTICE OF MEDICINE.

(Appointed by the Royal College of Physicians.)

SIR ARCHIBALD EDWARD GARROD, K.C.M.G., M.D., 133 *Banbury-road, Oxford.*
JOHN HANNAH DRYSDALE, M.D., 11 *Devonshire-place*, W. 1.
ARTHUR PHILIP BEDDARD, M.D., 117 *Gloucester-place*, W. 1.
WILLIAM CECIL BOSANQUET, M.D., 16 *Nottingham-place*, W. 1.
JAMES WILLIAM RUSSELL, M.D., 72 *Newhall-street, Birmingham*.
CHARLES RICHARD BOX, M.D., 2 *Devonshire-place*, W. 1.
SIR JAMES PURVES STEWART, K.C.M.G, C.B., M.D., 94 *Harley-street*, W. 1.
CHARLES BOLTON, C.B.E., M.D., F.R.S., 9 *Wimpole-street*, W. 1.
LEWIS ALBERT SMITH, M.D., 25 *Queen Anne-street*, W. 1.
SIR WILLIAM HENRY WILLCOX, K.C.I.E., C.B., C.M.G., M.D., 40 *Welbeck-street*, W. 1.

EXAMINERS IN SURGICAL ANATOMY AND THE PRINCIPLES AND PRACTICE OF SURGERY.

(Appointed by the Royal College of Surgeons.)

THE COURT OF EXAMINERS. (See page 5.)

EXAMINERS IN MIDWIFERY AND DISEASES PECULIAR TO WOMEN.

(Royal College of Physicians.)

JOHN PRESCOTT HEDLEY, M.B., 65 *Harley-street*, W. 1.
SIR EWEN JOHN MACLEAN, M.D., 12 *Park-place, Cardiff*.
THOMAS GEORGE STEVENS, M.D., 20 *Queen Anne-street*, W. 1.
JOHN DAVIS BARRIS, M.B., 50 *Welbeck-street*, W. 1.
HENRY JOHN FORBES SIMSON, M.B., 86 *Brook-street*, W. 1.

(Royal College of Surgeons.)

GEORGE DRUMMOND ROBINSON, M.D., 17 *Seymour-street*, W. 1.
CHARLES HUBERT ROBERTS, M.D., 48 *Harley-street*, W. 1.
EARDLEY LANCELOT HOLLAND, M.D., 55 *Queen Anne-street*, W. 1.
DONALD WHATLEY ROY, M.B., 10 *Chandos-street*, W. 1.

EXAMINERS FOR DIPLOMA IN PUBLIC HEALTH.

(Royal College of Physicians.)   (Royal College of Surgeons.)

PART I.   PART I.

HENRY WILSON HAKE, Ph.D., *Westminster*   SIR FREDERICK WILLIAM ANDREWES,
Hospital Medical School, S.W. 1.   O.B.E., F.R.S., 1 *North-grove, High-*
                                                                gate, N.

PART II.   PART II.

DAVID SAMUEL DAVIES, M.D., 6 *Lans-*   FRANCIS JOSEPH STEVENS, M.D., *Town*
down-place, Clifton, Bristol.   *Hall, Camberwell,* S.E. 5.

EXAMINERS FOR DIPLOMA IN TROPICAL MEDICINE AND HYGIENE.

.(Royal College of Physicians.)   (Royal College of Surgeons.)

EXAMINERS IN BACTERIOLOGY.

SIR PERCY WILLIAM BASSETT-SMITH,   HUGH BASIL GREAVES NEWHAM, C.M.G.,
K.C.B., C.M.G., 18 *Queen Anne-*   M.D., *London School of Tropical*
street, W. 1.   *Medicine, Endsleigh-gardens,* N.W. 1.

EXAMINERS IN DISEASES AND HYGIENE OF THE TROPICS.

SIR LEONARD ROGERS, C.I.E., M.D.,   GEORGE CARMICHAEL LOW, M.D., 86
21 *Cavendish-square*, W. 1.   *Brook-street*, W. 1.

EXAMINERS FOR DIPLOMA IN OPHTHALMIC MEDICINE AND SURGERY.

PART I.

(Appointed by the Royal College of Surgeons.)

SIR JOHN HERBERT PARSONS, C.B.E., 54 *Queen Anne-street*, W. 1.
HERBERT WILLOUGHBY LYLE, M.D., " *Speldhurst*," *Elmfield-road, Bromley.*

PART II.

(Royal College of Physicians.)   (Royal College of Surgeons.)

GORDON MORGAN HOLMES, C.M.G.,   MALCOLM LANGTON HEPBURN, M.D.. 111
C.B.E., M.D., 101 *Harley-street*, W. 1.   *Harley-street*, W. 1.

EXAMINERS FOR DIPLOMA IN PSYCHOLOGICAL MEDICINE.

PART I.

(Royal College of Physicians.)

HENRY DEVINE, O.B.E., M.D., *Corporation Mental Hospital, Portsmouth.*

(Royal College of Surgeons.)

SIR FREDERICK WALKER MOTT, K.B.E., M.D., *25 Nottingham-place,* W. 1.

PART II.

(Appointed by the Royal College of Physicians.)

JAMES TAYLOR, C.B.E., M.D., 49 *Welbeck-street,* W. 1.

CHARLES HUBERT BOND, C.B.E., M.D., *Board of Control,* 66 *Victoria-street,* S.W. 1.

COMMITTEE OF MANAGEMENT.

(Royal College of Physicians.)

JOSEPH ARDERNE ORMEROD, M.D., 25 *Upper Wimpole-street,* W. 1.
SIR WILLIAM HALE WHITE, K.B.E., M.D., 38 *Wimpole-street,* W. 1.
ROBERT ARTHUR YOUNG, C.B.E., M.D., 57 *Harley-street,* W. 1.

(Royal College of Surgeons.)

SIR CHARLES ALFRED BALLANCE, K.C.M.G., C.B., M.V.O., 106 *Harley-street,* W. 1.
HOLBURT JACOB WARING, 37 *Wimpole-street,* W. 1.
WALTER GEORGE SPENCER, O.B.E., 2 *Portland-place,* W. 1.

SECRETARY TO THE EXAMINING BOARD.

FREDERIC GREVILLE HALLETT, O.B.E.

ASSISTANT SECRETARY TO THE EXAMINING BOARD.

HORACE HAYTER REW.

REPRESENTATIVE IN THE GENERAL COUNCIL OF MEDICAL EDUCATION AND REGISTRATION.

HOLBURT JACOB WARING.

REPRESENTATIVE ON CENTRAL MIDWIVES BOARD.

WALTER SPENCER ANDERSON GRIFFITH, C.B.E., M.D.

REPRESENTATIVE ON CENTRAL COUNCIL FOR THE LONDON BLIND.

JOHN HERBERT FISHER.

REPRESENTATIVES IN UNIVERSITIES.

University of London.	{ RAYMOND JOHNSON, O.B.E. { VINCENT WARREN Low, C.B.
University of Birmingham.	SIR BERKELEY GEO. ANDREW MOYNIHAN, Bt., K.C.M.G., C.B.
University of Liverpool.	*Vacant.*
University of Sheffield.	SIR BERKELEY GEO. ANDREW MOYNIHAN, Bt., K.C.M.G., C.B.
University of Wales.	SIR JOHN LYNN-THOMAS, K.B.E., C.B , C.M.G.
University of Bristol.	SIR D'ARCY POWER, K.B.E.

REPRESENTATIVES ON EXECUTIVE COMMITTEE OF IMPERIAL CANCER RESEARCH FUND.

SIR JOHN BLAND-SUTTON.
SIR ANTHONY ALFRED BOWLBY, Bt., K.C.B., K.C.M.G., K.C.V.O.
SIR D'ARCY POWER, K.B.E.
SIR CHARLES ALFRED BALLANCE, K.C.M.G., C.B., M.V.O.

REPRESENTATIVE ON MANAGING COMMITTEE OF SCHIFF HOME OF RECOVERY.

SIR HERBERT FURNIVALL WATERHOUSE.

REPRESENTATIVE ON COUNCIL OF QUEEN VICTORIA'S JUBILEE INSTITUTE FOR NURSES.

Vacant.

REPRESENTATIVE ON MANAGING COMMITTEE OF BRITISH HOSPITAL FOR MOTHERS AND BABIES.

GUY BELLINGHAM SMITH, M.B.

REPRESENTATIVE ON CENTRAL COUNCIL FOR DISTRICT NURSING IN LONDON.

WALTER GEORGE SPENCER, O.B.E.

TRUSTEES OF THE ODONTOLOGICAL COLLECTION.

JOHN HOWARD MUMMERY, C.B.E.	CHARLES FREDERICK RILOT.
FREDERICK JOSEPH BENNETT.	JOSEPH LEWIN PAYNE.
WILLIAM ADOLPHUS MAGGS.	

ORIGINAL APPOINTMENT AND SUCCESSION

OF

TRUSTEES OF THE HUNTERIAN COLLECTION.

BY ORIGINAL APPOINTMENT.

William, Lord Auckland.
George Henry, Earl of Euston (Duke of Grafton).
Charles Small Pybus, Esq.
Right Hon. George Rose.
Dr. Matthew Baillie.
Alleyne, Lord St. Helens.
Charles George, Lord Arden.
Sir Charles Blagden.
Isaac Hawkins Brown, Esq.
Sir Archibald Macdonald, Bt.
Dr. Watson, Bishop of Llandaff.
Dr. Edward Whitaker Gray.
Right Hon. Charles Long (Lord Farnborough).
Sir George Augustus Shuckburgh Evelyn, Bt.

BY ELECTION.

Succession.
1805. George John, Earl Spencer.
1809. George G. L. Gower, Marquess of Stafford (Duke of Sutherland).
1811. William Wyndham, Lord Grenville.
1815. Edward Adolphus, Duke of Somerset.
1817. Sir Everard Home, Bt.
    „ Charles, Lord Colchester.
1818. Charles William, Earl of Charleville.
1820. Davies Gilbert, Esq.
1824. Right Hon. Robert Peel (Sir Robert Peel, Bt.).
1827. Dr. Blomfield, Bishop of Chester (Bishop of London).
1830. Charles Hatchett, Esq.
1832. Sir Astley Paston Cooper, Bt.
1834. Sir Robert Harry Inglis, Bart. (Right Hon.).
    „ Arthur, Duke of Wellington.
1835. Sir George Thomas Staunton, Bt.
1836. Edward Geoffrey Smith, Lord Stanley (Earl of Derby).
1838. Sir John Frederick William Herschel, Bt.

Succession.
1840. William Willoughby (Earl of Enniskillen).
   „   Sir Philip de Malpas Grey-Egerton, Bt.
   „   William, Earl of Burlington (Duke of Devonshire).
1841. Joseph Henry Green, Esq.
   „   Sir Benjamin Collins Brodie, Bt.
1845. Walter Francis, Duke of Buccleuch and Queensberry.
1847. Dr. Buckland, Dean of Westminster.
1851. Samuel Wilberforce, Bishop of Oxford (Bishop of Winchester).
1853. Lord John Russell (The Earl Russell).
1856. Sir Roderick Impey Murchison, Bt.
   „   Right Hon. Sir James R. G. Graham, Bt.
1857. Sir Charles Lyell, Bt.
   „   Henry John, Earl of Ducie.
1860. William Hunter Baillie, Esq.
1862. William Sharpey, Esq., M.D.
1863. George Douglas, Duke of Argyll.
1864. George Grote, Esq.
1870. Robert Arthur Talbot, Marquess of Salisbury.
1871. Cæsar Henry Hawkins, Esq.
   „   Sir John Lubbock, Bt. (Right Hon.).
1873. George Busk, Esq.
1875. Right Hon. William Ewart Gladstone.
1879. Lord Arthur John Edward Russell.
1881. Allen Thomson, Esq., M.D.
   „   Henry Austin, Lord Aberdare.
1885. William Henry Flower, Esq. (Sir W. H. Flower, K.C.B.).
   „   Thomas, Lord Walsingham.
   „   Sir James Paget, Bt.
   „   William Hunter Baillie, Esq., Jun.
1886. Thomas Henry Huxley, Esq. (Right Hon.).
1887. James Ludovic, Earl of Crawford.
1892. Lieut.-General Augustus Henry Lane-Fox Pitt-Rivers.
1893. Sir William Scovell Savory, Bt.
1894. Right Hon. Sir Edward Fry.
1895. William Hillier, Earl of Onslow.
   „   Sir John Eric Erichsen, Bt.
   „   Right Hon. George Denman.
   „   Sir Joseph Lister, Bt. (Lord Lister).
1897. Hon. Lionel Walter Rothschild (Lord Rothschild).
   „   Jonathan Hutchinson, Esq. (Sir Jonathan Hutchinson).
1899. Frederick Temple, Marquess of Dufferin and Ava.
1900. Sir Michael Foster, K.C.B.
   „   Sir Thomas Smith, Bt.
   „   Archibald Philip, Earl of Rosebery.
   „   Sir Joseph Fayrer, Bt., K.C.S.I.
   „   Right Hon. Sir Herbert Eustace Maxwell, Bt.
1902. Herbrand Arthur, Duke of Bedford.
1904. Sir Harry Hamilton Johnston, G.C.M.G.

Succession.
1907. German Sims Woodhead, Esq., M.D. (Sir G. S. Woodhead, K.B.E.).
  „   Sir John Tweedy.
1910. Arthur Everett Shipley, Esq., D.Sc. (Sir A. E. Shipley, G.B.E.).
1912. Right Hon. Sir Herbert Hardy Cozens-Hardy (Lord Cozens-Hardy).
  „   Right Hon. Sir Joseph Cockfield Dimsdale, Bt., K.C.V.O.
1913. John, Viscount Morley of Blackburn, O.M.
  „   Sir John Wolfe Barry, K.C.B.
  „   Sir William Selby Church, Bt., K.C.B., M.D.
1915. Charles Wallace Alexander Napier, Lord Lamington.
1918. Sir Henry Morris, Bt.
1920. William Frederick Danvers, Viscount Hambleden.
  „   Sir Thomas Wrightson, Bt.
1921. James William, Viscount Ullswater.
1922. Sir James Dewar, LL.D., D.Sc., F.R.S.
  „   Sir George Henry Makins, G.C.M.G., C.B.

[The names of existing Trustees are printed in heavy type.]

[The names of existing Officers are printed in heavy type.]

MASTERS AND PRESIDENTS.

MASTERS *.

1745. John Ranby.
1746. William Cheselden.
1747. John Freke.
1748. Cæsar Hawkins.
1749. Peter Sainthill.
1750. Peter Sainthill.
1751. John Ranby.
1752. John Ranby.
1753. Legard Sparham.
1754. James Hickes.
1755. Noah Roul.
1756. John Westbrook.
1757. William Singleton.
1758. Mark Hawkins.
1759. Christopher Fullagar.
1760. Edward Nourse.
1761. David Middleton.
1762. John Townsend.
1763. John Blagden.
1764. Robert Young.
1765. Percivall Pott.
1766. Stafford Crane.
1767. Robert Adair.
1768. Benjamin Cowell.
1769. William Bromfield.
1770. Wentworth Gregory.
1771. Wentworth Gregory.
1772. John Pyle.
1773. Joseph Warner.
1774. Matthew Spray.
1775. Richard Grindall.
1776. Robert Young.
1777. Robert Young.
1778. Pennell Hawkins.
1779. Fleming Pinkstan.

1780. Joseph Warner.
1781. Peter Triquet.
1782. Richard Grindall.
1783. Richard Grindall.
1784. Joseph Warner.
1785. Henry Watson.
1786. Isaac Minors.
1787. Edmund Pitts.
1788. Henry Watson.
1789. John Gunning.
1790. Charles Hawkins.
1791. William Lucas.
1792. Samuel Howard.
1793. John Wyatt.
1794. William Walker.
1795. William Cooper.
1796. Isaac Minors.
1797. John Gunning.
1798. James Earle.
1799. Charles Hawkins.
1800. Charles Hawkins.
  ,,   William Long.
1801. George Chandler.
1802. Thomas Keate.
1803. Sir Charles Blicke, Kt.
1804. David Dundas.
1805. Thompson Forster.
1806. Charles Hawkins.
1807. Sir James Earle, Kt.
1808. George Chandler.
1809. Thomas Keate.
1810. Sir Charles Blicke, Kt.
1811. David Dundas.
1812. Thompson Forster.
1813. Sir Everard Home, Bt.

* Masters of the Company of Surgeons from 1745 to 1799.

MASTERS (continued).

1814. Sir William Blizard, Kt.
1815. Henry Cline.
1816. William Norris.
1817. Sir James Earle, Kt.
  „ George Chandler.

1818. Thomas Keate.
1819. Sir David Dundas, Bt.
1820. Thompson Forster.
1821. Sir Everard Home, Bt.

PRESIDENTS.

1822. Sir Everard Home, Bt.
  „ Sir William Blizzard, Kt.
1823. Henry Cline.
1824. William Norris.
1825. William Lynn.
1826. John Abernethy.
1827. Sir Astley Paston Cooper, Bt.
1828. Sir Anthony Carlisle, Kt.
1829. Honoratus Leigh Thomas.
1830. Richard Clement Headington.
1831. Robert Keate.
  „ Robert Keate.
1832. John Painter Vincent.
1833. George James Guthrie.
1834. Anthony White.
1835. John Goldwyer Andrews.
1836. Sir Astley Paston Cooper, Bt.
1837. Sir Anthony Carlisle, Kt.
1838. Honoratus Leigh Thomas.
1839. Robert Keate.
1840. John Painter Vincent.
1841. George James Guthrie.
1842. Anthony White.
1843. John Goldwyer Andrews.
1844. Sir Benjamin Collins Brodie, Bt.
1845. Samuel Cooper.
1846. William Lawrence.
1847. Benjamin Travers.
1848. Edward Stanley.
1849. Joseph Henry Green.
1850. James Moncrieff Arnott.
1851. John Flint South.

1852. Cæsar Henry Hawkins.
1853. James Luke.
1854. George James Guthrie.
1855. William Lawrence.
1856. Benjamin Travers.
1857. Edward Stanley.
1858. Joseph Henry Green.
1859. James Moncrieff Arnott.
1860. John Flint South.
1861. Cæsar Henry Hawkins.
1862. James Luke.
1863. Frederic Carpenter Skey.
1864. Joseph Hodgson.
1865. Thomas Wormald.
1866. Richard Partridge.
1867. John Hilton.
1868. Richard Quain.
1869. Edward Cock.
1870. Sir William Fergusson, Bt.
1871. George Busk.
1872. Henry Hancock.
1873. Thomas Blizard Curling.
1874. Frederick Le Gros Clark.
1875. Sir James Paget, Bt.
1876. Prescott Gardner Hewett.
1877. John Birkett.
1878. John Simon.
1879. Luther Holden.
1880. John Eric Erichsen.
1881. Sir Wm. James Erasmus Wilson.
1882. Thomas Spencer Wells.
1883. John Marshall.

PRESIDENTS (continued).

1884. John Cooper Forster.
1885. William Scovell Savory.
1886. William Scovell Savory.
1887. William Scovell Savory.
1888. William Scovell Savory.
1889. Jonathan Hutchinson.
1890. Thomas Bryant.
1891. Thomas Bryant.
1892. Thomas Bryant.
1893. John Whitaker Hulke.
1894. John Whitaker Hulke.
1895. Christopher Heath.
  „ Christopher Heath.
1896. Sir William Mac Cormac, Kt.
1897. Sir William Mac Cormac, Bt.
1898. Sir William Mac Cormac, Bt.
1899. Sir William Mac Cormac, Bt.
1900. Sir William Mac Cormac, Bt.
1901. Henry Greenway Howse.
1902. Sir Henry Greenway Howse, Kt.
1903. John Tweedy.

1904. John Tweedy.
1905. John Tweedy.
1906. Henry Morris.
1907. Henry Morris.
1908. Sir Henry Morris, Bt.
1909. Henry Trentham Butlin.
1910. Henry Trentham Butlin.
1911. Sir Henry Trentham Butlin, Bt.
  „ Rickman John Godlee.
1912. Sir Rickman John Godlee, Bt.
1913. Sir Rickman John Godlee, Bt.
1914. Sir William Watson Cheyne, Bt.
1915. Sir William Watson Cheyne, Bt.
1916. Sir William Watson Cheyne, Bt.
1917. Sir Geo. Henry Makins, G.C.M.G.
1918. Sir Geo. Henry Makins, G.C.M.G.
1919. Sir Geo. Henry Makins, G.C.M.G.
1920. Sir Anthony Alfd. Bowlby, K.C.B.
1921. Sir Anthony Alfd. Bowlby, K.C.B.
1922. Sir Anthony Alfred Bowlby, Bt.
1923. **Sir John Bland-Sutton.**

MEMBERS OF THE COURT OF ASSISTANTS AND OF THE COUNCIL.

COURT OF ASSISTANTS *.

1745–73. John Ranby.
,, −48. Joseph Sandford.
,, −52. William Cheselden.
,, −47. Ambrose Dickins.
,, −53. William Petty.
,, −46. John Shipton.
,, −63. John Hayward.
,, −56. John Freke.
,, −48. William Pyle.
,, −56. Legard Sparham.
,, −58. James Hickes.
,, −73. Peter Sainthill.
,, −60. Noah Roul.
,, −58. John Westbrook.
,, −61. William Singleton.
,, −51. James Phillips.
,, −47. Harry Holdip.
,, ,, Thomas Bigg.
,, −57. Joseph Webb.
,, −60. Mark Hawkins.
,, −71. Christopher Fullagar.
1746–61. Edward Nourse.
1747–51. John Girle.
,, −66. John Townsend.
,, −78. Cæsar Hawkins. (Bt.)
1748–68. Walter Jones.
,, −68. John Blagden.
1751–85. John Belchier.
,, −78. David Middleton.
1752–65. Samuel Sharp.
1753–83. Robert Young.
1756–61. John Girle.
,, −88. Percivall Pott.
1757–84. Stafford Crane.
1758–71. Benjamin Cowell.
,, −62. Edmund Sanxay.
1760–89. Robert Adair.
,, −80. William Bromfield.
1761–67. Henry Grundy.
,, −72. Wentworth Gregory.
,, −93. John Pyle.

1762–65. John Torr.
1763–1764. Mileson Hingeston.
1764–1800. Joseph Warner.
1765–1768. Thomas Gataker.
,, −1787. Matthew Spray.
1766–1797. Richard Grindall.
1767–1776. Thomas Tomkyns.
1768–1792. Fleming Pinkstan.
,, −1776. James Burnett.
1769–1788. Peter Triquet.
1771–1793. Henry Watson.
,, −1784. Thomas Smith.
1772–1791. Archdall Harris.
1773–1784. William Sharpe.
,, −1797. Isaac Minors.
1776–1784. Pennell Hawkins.
,, −1780. Joseph Else.
1778–1791. Edmund Pitts.
,, −1800. Jonathan Wathen.
1780–1796. William Graves.
,, −1782. James Frank.
1783–1789. Richard Crowther.
1784–1798. John Gunning.
1784–1800. William Lucas.
,, ,, Samuel Howard.
,, −1797. John Wyatt.
1785–1792. James Patch.
,, −1796. William Walker.
1787–1800. Charles Hawkins.
1788 ,, William Cooper.
1789–1793. John Hunter.
,, −1800. James Earle.
,, ,, William Long.
1791 ,, George Chandler.
,, ,, Charles Blicke.
1792 ,, Thompson Forster.
,, ,, John Birch.
1793 ,, Thomas Keate.
,, ,, John Heaviside.
,, ,, John Howard.
1796 ,, William Blizard.

* Members of the Court of Assistants under the Company of Surgeons from 1745 to 1800.

1923.

COURT OF ASSISTANTS (continued).

1796–1800. Henry Cline.
1800–13. Charles Hawkins.
  „ –18. William Long.
  „ –22. George Chandler.
  „ –01. Joseph Warner.
  „ –10. Samuel Howard.
  „   William Cooper.
  „ –05. Jonathan Wathen.
  „ –10. William Lucas.
  „ –17. Sir James Earle, Kt.
  „ –15. Sir Charles Blicke, Kt.
  „ –27. Thompson Forster.
  „ –15. John Birch.
  „ –21. Thomas Keate.
  „ –28. John Heaviside.
  „ –08. John Howard.
  „ –35. Sir William Blizard, Kt.
  „ –27. Henry Cline.
  „ –26. Sir David Dundas, Bt.
  „ –16. John Samuel Charlton.

1800–10. Edward Ford.
  „ –27. William Norris.
1801–15. James Ware.
  „ –27. Sir Everard Home, Bt.
1805–32. John Adair Hawkins.
1808–27. Francis Knight.
1810–27. Sir Ludford Harvey, Kt.
  „ –35. William Lynn.
  „ –30. John Abernethy.
1813–30. William Lucas.
1815–41. Sir Astley Paston Cooper, Bt.
  „ –40. Sir Anthony Carlisle, Kt.
1816–17. Thomas Blizard.
  „ –24. Thomas Chevalier.
1817–21. James Wilson.
  „ –24. John Gunning.
1818–45. Honoratus Leigh Thomas.
1821–31. Richard Clement Headington.
1822–57. Robert Keate.

COUNCIL.

1822–51. John Painter Vincent.
1824–56. George James Guthrie.
  „ –29. William Wadd.
1826–28. Sir Patrick Macgregor, Bt.
1827–30. Henry Jeffreys.
  „ –46. Anthony White.
  „ –49. John Goldwyer Andrews.
  „ –48. Samuel Cooper.
  „ –54. Thomas Copeland.
1828–41. John Howship.
  „ –48. James Briggs.
  „ –67. Sir William Lawrence, Bt.
1829–62. Sir Benjamin Collins Brodie, Bt.
1830–58. Benjamin Travers.
  „ –38. Henry Earle.
  „ –36. Sir Charles Bell, Kt.
1831–70. Joseph Swan.
1832–62. Edward Stanley.
1835–63. Joseph Henry Green.
  „ –48. Thomas Callaway.
1836–45. George Gisborne Babington.
1838–43. Frederick Tyrrell.
1840–47. Robert Liston.
1841–65. James Moncrieff Arnott.
  „ –73. John Flint South.

1843–47. John Morgan.
1844–49. Richard Welbank.
  „ –46. John Scott.
  „ –51. Edward Cutler.
1845–49. Charles Aston Key.
1846–63. Cæsar Henry Hawkins.
  „ –50. Richard Dugard Grainger.
  „ –66. James Luke.
1848–67. Frederic Carpenter Skey, C.B.
  „ –52. Richard Anthony Stafford.
  „ –53. Bransby Blake Cooper.
1849–68. Joseph Hodgson.
  „ –67. Thomas Wormald.
  „ –55. George Pilcher.
  „ –61. John Bishop.
1850–69. Gilbert Wakefield Mackmurdo.
  „ –67. Francis Kiernan.
1851–69. William Coulson.
  „ –52. John Dalrymple.
1852–64. George Gulliver.
  „ –68. Richard Partridge.
1854–78. John Hilton.
  „ –73. Richard Quain.
1856–71. Edward Cock.
  „ –72. Samuel Solly.

COUNCIL (*continued*).

1857–63. Thomas Tatum.
1858–65. Alexander Shaw.
1861–77. Sir William Fergusson, Bt.
1862–70. Thomas Paget.
,, –69. John Adams.
1863–71. Samuel Armstrong Lane.
,, –80. George Busk.
,, - 80. Henry Hancock.
1864–80. Thomas Blizard Curling.
,, –79. Frederick Le Gros Clark.
1865–73. Thomas Turner.
,, –89. Sir James Paget, Bt.
1866–73. Charles Hawkins.
1867–83. Prescott Gardner Hewett. (Bt.)
,, –75. Henry Spencer Smith.
,, –83. John Birkett.
1868–80. John Simon. (K.C.B.)
,, –84. George Murray Humphry. (Kt.)
,, –84. Luther Holden.
1869–77. John Gay.
,, –85. John Eric Erichsen. (Bt.)
1870–84. Sir Wm. Jas. Erasmus Wilson, Kt.
,, –78. Henry Lee.
1871–95. Sir Thomas Spencer Wells, Bt.
,, –79. George Critchett.
1872–78. Barnard Wight Holt.
1873–81. Haynes Walton.
,, –90. John Marshall.
,, –76. George Southam.
1874–82. Alfred Baker.
1875–86. John Cooper Forster.
1876–81. Claudius Galen Wheelhouse.
1877 -93. Sir Wm. Scovell Savory, Bt.
,, –85. Timothy Holmes.
1878–84. John Gay.
,, –94. Edward Lund.
1879–87. John Wood.
,, –90. Henry Power.
,, –95. Jonathan Hutchinson. (Kt.)
1880–96. William Cadge.
,, –1888. Sir Joseph Lister, Bt.
,, –1904. Thomas Bryant.
,, –1900. Sir Thomas Smith, Bt.
1881–1895. John Whitaker Hulke.
,, –1897. Christopher Heath.
1882–1890. John Croft.
1883–1891. Sydney Jones.
,, –1901. Sir William Mac Cormac, Bt.

1884–1886. William Allingham.
,, –1892. George Lawson.
,, –1892. Matthew Berkeley Hill.
,, –1895. Arthur Edward Durham.
1885–1901. Nottidge Charles Macnamara.
,, –1897. Oliver Pemberton.
1886–1891. Septimus William Sibley.
,, –1902. Reginald Harrison.
1887–1903. Alfred Willett.
1888–1903. Thomas Pickering Pick.
1889–1905. Sir Henry Greenway Howse.
1890–1906. John Langton.
,, –1893. Marcus Beck.
,, –1898. Wm. Mitchell Banks. (Kt.)
1891–1897. Walter Rivington.
,, –1903. Thomas Richard Jessop.
1892–1908. Frederick Howard Marsh.
,, –1907. Sir John Tweedy.
1893–1914. Sir Henry Morris, Bt.
,, –1909. Arthur W. Mayo Robson. (Kt.)
1894–1902. James Hardie.
1895–1895. John Ward Cousins.
,, –1905. Sir Alfred Cooper, Kt.
,, –1912. Sir Henry Trentham Butlin, Bt,
,, –1903. Sir Frederick Treves, Bt.
1896–1900. John Neville C. Davies-Colley.
1897–1913. Edmund Owen.
,, –1915. Sir Rickman John Godlee, Bt.
,, –1918. Sir Wm. Watson Cheyne, Bt.
1898–1914. Francis Richardson Cross.
1899–1907. Herbert William Page.
1900–08. John Ward Cousins.
,, –16. Sir Alfred Pearce Gould, K.C.V.O.
1901–14. Richard Clement Lucas.
1902–10. John Hammond Morgan, C.V.O.
,, –10. Henry Hugh Clutton.
,, –15. Charles Wm. Mansell Moullin.
1903–12. Clinton Thomas Dent.
,, –21. Sir George Henry Makins.
1904–16. Sir Frederic Samuel Eve, Kt.
,, –28. **Sir Anthony Alfd. Bowlby, Bt.**
,, –12. Harry Gilbert Barling. (Bt.)
1905–13. Cuthbert Hilton Golding-Bird.
,, –08. William Harrison Cripps.
1906–10. George Arthur Wright.
1907–13. William Bruce Clarke.
,. -23. Sir Charters James Symonds.
1908–24. **William Frederic Haslam.**

COUNCIL (continued).

1908-14. Charles Barrett Lockwood.
„ -16. Sir Wm. Arbuthnot Lane, Bt.
1909-20. William Harrison Cripps.
1910-18. Bilton Pollard.
„ -30. Sir Charles Alfred Ballance.
·„ -26. Sir John Bland-Sutton.
1912-28. Sir D'Arcy Power.
„ -27. Sir Berkeley Geo. A. Moynihan.
1913-21. James Ernest Lane.
„ -18. Louis Albert Dunn.
„ -14. Jonathan Hutchinson.
·„ -29. Holburt Jacob Waring.
1914-16. James Stanley Newton Boyd.
„ -23. Sir William Thorburn.
„ -22. William McAdam Eccles.
„ -22. Sir Charles Ryall.
1915-26. Walter George Spencer.
„ -23. Frédéric François Burghard.

1915-23. Sir Herbert F. Waterhouse.
1916-24. Thomas Horrocks Openshaw.
„ -24. Raymond Johnson.
„ -25. Vincent Warren Low.
1917-25. James Sherren.
1918-25. Sir John Lynn-Thomas.
„ -26. Ernest William Hey Groves.
1919-27. Sir Cuthbert Sidney Wallace.
1920-28. Francis James Steward.
1921-27. William Thelwall Thomas.
„ -29. Charles Herbert Fagge.
1922-30. Robert Pugh Rowlands.
1923-31. James Berry.
„ -31. John Herbert Fisher.
„ -29. William Sampson Handley,
„ -30. Percy Sargent.
„ -31. George Ernest Gask.

COURT OF EXAMINERS.

1745-73. John Ranby.
„ -52. William Cheselden.
„ -47. Ambrose Dickins.
|„ -53. William Petty.
„ -46. John Shipton.
„ -56. John Freke.
„ -48. William Pyle.
„ -56. Legard Sparham.
„ -58. James Hickes.
„ -64. Peter Sainthill.
1746-60. Noah Roul.
1747-78. Cæsar Hawkins.
1748-58. John Westbrook.
1752-61. William Singleton.
1753-57. Joseph Webb.
1756-60. Mark Hawkins.
„ -71. Christopher Fullagar.
1757-61. Edward Nourse.
1758-61. John Girle.
„ -66. John Townsend.
1760-68. John Blagden.
„ -78. David Middleton.
1761-68. Robert Adair.
„ -84. Robert Young.
, -89. Percivall Pott.
1764-84. Stafford Crane.

1766-1771. Benjamin Cowell.
1768-1780. William Bromfield.
„ -1772. Wentworth Gregory.
1771-1793. John Pyle.
„ -1800. Joseph Warner.
1772-1787. Matthew Spray.
1773-1797. Richard Grindall.
1778-1784. Pennell Hawkins.
„ -1792. Fleming Pinkstan.
1780-1788. Peter Triquet.
1784-1793. Henry Watson.
„ -1797. Isaac Minors.
„ -1791. Edmund Pitts.
1787-1800. Charles Hawkins.
1788-1789. Richard Crowther.
1789-1798. John Gunning.
„ -1800. William Lucas.
1791-1800. Samuel Howard.
1792-1797. John Wyatt.
1793-1796. William Walker.
„ -1800. William Cooper.
1796-1800. James Earle.
1797-1800. William Long.
„ -1800. George Chandler.
1799-1800. Thomas Keate.
„ -1800. Charles Blicke.

Note.—The above-named were Members of the Court of Examiners under the Company of Surgeons.

COURT OF EXAMINERS (continued).

1800–13. Charles Hawkins.
  „ –10. William Long.
  „ –22. George Chandler.
  „ –01. Joseph Warner.
  „ –09. William Lucas.
  „ –10. Samuel Howard.
  „ . William Cooper.
  „ –17. Sir James Earle, Kt.
  „ –21. Thomas Keate.
  „ –15. Sir Charles Blicke, Kt.
1801–26. Sir David Dundas, Bt.
  „ –27. Thompson Forster.
1809–27. Sir Everard Home, Bt.
1810–35. Sir William Blizard, Kt.
  „ –27. Henry Cline.
1813–27. William Norris.
1816–25. Sir Ludford Harvey, Kt.
1817–35. William Lynn.
1821–29. John Abernethy.
1822–41. Sir Astley Paston Cooper, Bt.
1825–40. Sir Anthony Carlisle, Kt.
1826–44. Honoratus Leigh Thomas.
1827–28. Sir Patrick Macgregor, Bt.
  „ –31. Richard Clement Headington.
  „ –55. Robert Keate.
1828–51. John Painter Vincent.
  „ –56. George James Guthrie.
1829. William Wadd.
  „ –46. Anthony White.
1831–49. John Goldwyer Andrews.
1835–46. Sir Benjamin Collins Brodie, Bt.
  „ –48. Samuel Cooper.
1840–67. Sir William Lawrence, Bt.
1841–58. Benjamin Travers.
1844–62. Edward Stanley.
1846–63. Joseph Henry Green.
  „ –47. Robert Liston.
1847–65. James Moncrieff Arnott.
1849–68. John Flint South.
  „ –66. Cæsar Henry Hawkins.
1851–68. James Luke.
1855–70. Frederic Carpenter Skey, C.B.
1856–65. Joseph Hodgson.
1858–68. Thomas Wormald.
1862–67. Francis Kiernan.
1864–73. Richard Partridge.
1865–75. John Hilton.
  „ –70. Richard Quain.
1867–71. Edward Cock.

1867–72. Samuel Solly.
  „ –70. Sir William Fergusson, Bt.
1868–72. John Adams.
  „ –73. Samuel Armstrong Lane.
  „ –72. George Busk.
1870–75. Henry Hancock.
  „ –80. Frederick Le Gros Clark.
  „ –84. William Scovell Savory.
1871–79. Thomas Blizard Curling.
1872–77. Henry Spencer Smith.
  „ –82. John Birkett.
1873–83. Luther Holden.
  „ –81. John Marshall.
  „ –83. Timothy Holmes.
  „ –84. John Cooper Forster.
1875–79. John Eric Erichsen.
1877–87. George Murray Humphry.
1879–89. John Wood.
1880–89. John Whitaker Hulke.
  „ –87. Jonathan Hutchinson.
1881–86. John Croft.
1882–92. Thomas Bryant.
1883–92. Christopher Heath.
  „ –87. Edward Lund.
1884–94. John Langton.
  „ –94. Thomas Pickering Pick.
1886–92. Matthew Berkeley Hill.
1887–97. Henry Greenway Howse.
  „ –92. William Morrant Baker.
  „ –97. Sir William Mac Cormac, Kt.
1889–99. Jeremiah McCarthy.
  „ 99. Edmund Owen.
1892–93. Marcus Beck.
  „ –97. Frederick Howard Marsh.
  „ –1900. John Neville C Davies-Colley.
  „ –1894. Frederick Treves.
1893–1903. Rickman John Godlee.
1894–1904. Henry Morris.
  „ –1900. William Anderson.
  „ –1902. Herbert William Page.
1897–1902. William Johnson Walsham.
  „ –1902. Sir William Henry Bennett.
  „ –1907. Cuthbert Hilton Golding-Bird.
1899–1909. Alfred Pearce Gould.
  „ –1909. Bernard Pitts.
1900–1905. Walter H. Acland Jacobson.
1901–1908. George Henry Makins, C.B.
1902–1911. Sir Frederic Samuel Eve, Kt.
  „ –1907. William Watson Cheyne, C.B.

COURT OF EXAMINERS (continued).

1902–1911. Clinton Thomas Dent.
1903–1913. William Frederic Haslam.
1904.   Arthur Quarry Silcock.
1905–1915. Bilton Pollard.
„ –1910. William Bruce Clarke.
1907–1917. James Ernest Lane.
„   „   Louis Albert Dunn.
1908–1918. Walter George Spencer.
1909–1919. Sir Charles Alfred Ballance.
„   „   Sir Hbt. Furnivall Waterhouse.
1911–1920. Holburt Jacob Waring.
„ –1921. Robert Lawford Knaggs.
„   „   Jonathan Hutchinson.

1913–1923. Sir William Thorburn.
1915–1925. John Murray.
1917–1927. Raymond Johnson.
„ –1923. Frédéric François Burghard.
1918–1923. Vincent Warren Low.
1919–1924. Sir Cuthbert Sidney Wallace.
„   „   Herbert S. Pendlebury.
1920–1925. Charles Herbert Fagge.
1921–1923. James Sherren.
„ –1926. Louis Bathe Rawling.
1923–1928. Herbert Sherwell Clogg.
„   „   Hugh Lett.
„   „   Thomas Percy Legg.

BOARD OF EXAMINERS IN ANATOMY AND PHYSIOLOGY.

1875. William Scovell Savory.
„ John Birkett.
„ Luther Holden.
„ Timothy Holmes.
„ John Cooper Forster.
„ John Wood.
„ Henry Power.
„ George Green Gascoyen.
„ Christopher Heath.
1876. John Whitaker Hulke.
„ Arthur Edward Durham.
„ Thomas Pickering Pick.

1877. William Warwick Wagstaffe.
1878. Walter Rivington.
„ William Morrant Baker.
1879. Benjamin Thompson Lowne.
1880. Edward Bellamy.
„ Jeremiah M‘Carthy.
„ John Langton.
„ Gerald Francis Yeo.
1881. Henry Power.
1883. Henry Greenway Howse.
„ Edmund Owen.

BOARD OF EXAMINERS IN ANATOMY AND PHYSIOLOGY FOR THE FELLOWSHIP.

ANATOMY.

1884. Henry Greenway Howse.
„ William Anderson.
„ Edmund Owen.
„ Henry Morris.
„ Rickman John Godlee.
1887. John Neville Colley Davies-Colley.
1888. William Henry Bennett.
„ Frederick Treves.
1889. Alfred Pearce Gould.
„ George Henry Makins.
„ William Bruce Clarke.
1893. Walter Hamilton Acland Jacobson.
1894. William Anderson.
„ William Frederic Haslam.
„ Charles Barrett Lockwood.
1895. John Bland Sutton.

1898. James Ernest Lane.
„ Frederick Gymer Parsons.
1899. Alfred Harry Young.
„ Berkeley G. Andrew Moynihan.
1903. Louis Albert Dunn.
„ Arthur Keith.
„ Christopher Addison.
1904. William McAdam Eccles.
1907. Alfred Harry Young.
1908. Frederick Gymer Parsons.
„ Arthur Thomson.
1909. Charles Herbert Fagge.
„ James Sherren.
1913. Robert William Reid.
„ Gordon Taylor.
1914. William Wright.

BOARD OF EXAMINERS IN ANATOMY AND PHYSIOLOGY FOR THE FELLOWSHIP (continued).

ANATOMY (continued).

1914. William Henry Clayton Greene.
1918. Arthur Ralph Thompson.
„ Andrew Melville Paterson.
1919. John Ernest Sullivan Frazer.

1919. Gordon Gordon-Taylor.
1920. William Frederic Haslam.
1923. William Wright.

PHYSIOLOGY.

1884. Henry Power.
„ William Morrant Baker.
„ Cuthbert Hilton Golding-Bird.
„ Gerald Francis Yeo.
1885. Jeremiah McCarthy.
1886. Benjamin Thompson Lowne.
1887. Gerald Francis Yeo.
1889. D'Arcy Power.
1890. John Barlow.
1891. Chas. William Mansell Moullin.
1892. Benjamin Thompson Lowne.
„ Cuthbert Hilton Golding-Bird.
„ William Stirling.
1895. Edward Albert Schäfer.
„ Ernest Henry Starling.
1897. D'Arcy Power.
„ William Henry Thompson.
„ Thomas Gregor Brodie.
1900. William Dobinson Halliburton.
1902. Edward Waymouth Reid.

1902. Ernest Henry Starling.
„ Leonard Erskine Hill.
„ de Burgh Birch.
1907. William Henry Thompson.
„ George Alfred Buckmaster.
„ Thomas Gregor Brodie.
„ Charles Frederick Myers-Ward.
1909. Edmund William Wace Carlier.
1911. Herbert Willoughby Lyle.
1912. Francis Gotch.
„ John Sidney Edkins.
1913. Arthur Rendle Short.
1914. George Alfred Buckmaster.
1916. John Beresford Leathes.
1917. Herbert Willoughby Lyle.
„ Francis Arthur Bainbridge.
1919. Arthur Rendle Short.
1921. John Mellanby.
1922. David Henriques de Souza.
„ Ffrangcon Roberts.

BOARD OF EXAMINERS IN MIDWIFERY.

1852. James Luke.
„ Arthur Farre, M.D.
„ Henry Oldham, M.D.
„ James Reid, M.D.
1853. George James Guthrie.
1854. William Lawrence.
„ Charles West, M.D.
1855. Benjamin Travers.
1856. Edward Stanley.
1857. Joseph Henry Green.
1858. James Moncrieff Arnott.
1859. John Flint South.
1860. Cæsar Henry Hawkins.
„ Robert Lee, M.D.
1861. James Luke.
1862. Frederic Carpenter Skey.
1863. Joseph Hodgson.

1864. Thomas Wormald.
1865. Richard Partridge.
1866. John Hilton.
1866. Robert Barnes, M.D.
„ Wm. Overend Priestley, M.D.
1867. Richard Quain.
1868. Edward Cock.
1869. Samuel Solly.
1870. George Busk.
1871. Henry Hancock.
1872. Thos. Blizard Curling.
1873. Fredk. Le Gros Clark.
1874. Sir James Paget, Bart.
1875. Prescott Gardner Hewett.
1876. Election deferred.
1888. Board abolished.

BOARD OF EXAMINERS IN DENTAL SURGERY.

COURT OF EXAMINERS' SECTION.

1860. William Lawrence.
„ Joseph Henry Green.
„ James Moncrieff Arnott.
1864. John Flint South.
1865. Frederic Carpenter Skey.
„ James Luke.
1868. Richard Partridge.
„ John Hilton.
1870. Edward Cock.
1872. Frederick Le Gros Clark.
1873. Henry Hancock.
„ William Scovell Savory.
1875. John Birkett.
1879. Luther Holden.
1880. Timothy Holmes.
1882. John Cooper Forster.
1883. John Wood.
„ John Whitaker Hulke.
1885. Jonathan Hutchinson.
1887. Thomas Bryant.
1888. Christopher Heath.
1889. John Langton.
„ Thomas Pickering Pick.
1892. Henry Greenway Howse.
„ Sir William Mac Cormac, Kt.
1895. Jeremiah McCarthy.
1896. Edmund Owen.
1897. John Neville C. Davies-Colley.
„ Rickman John Godlee.
1899. Henry Morris.

1900. William Anderson.
„ Herbert William Page.
„ William Johnson Walsham.
1902. Sir William Henry Bennett.
„ Cuthbert Hilton Golding-Bird.
„ Alfred Pearce Gould.
1903. Bernard Pitts.
1904. Walter H. Acland Jacobson.
1906. George Henry Makins, C.B.
1907. Sir Frederic Samuel Eve, Kt.
1909. Clinton Thomas Dent.
„ William Frederic Haslam.
1910. Bilton Pollard.
1911. James Ernest Lane.
„ Louis Albert Dunn.
1913. Walter George Spencer.
1915. Sir Charles Alfred Ballance.
1917. Sir Hbt. Furnivall Waterhouse.
„ Holburt Jacob Waring.
1918. Robert Lawford Knaggs.
1919. Jonathan Hutchinson.
„ John Murray.
1920. Raymond Johnson.
1921. Frédéric François Burghard.
„ Vincent Warren Low.
1923. Sir Cuthbert Sidney Wallace.
„ Herbert S. Pendlebury.
„ Charles Herbert Fagge.
„ Louis Bathe Rawling.
„ Herbert Sherwell Clogg.

DENTAL SECTION.

1860. Thomas Bell.
„ John Tomes.
„ Arnold Rogers.
1865. Samuel Cartwright.
„ William Anthony Harrison.
1870. George Augustus Ibbetson.
1871. Samuel James Augustus Salter.
1875. Thomas Arnold Rogers.
„ Henry John Barrett.
1880. Alfred Coleman.
„ Augustus Winterbottom.
1881. Charles Sissmore Tomes.
1884. Henry Moon.
1886. James Smith Turner.
1888. Samuel John Hutchinson.
1889. Morton Alfred Smale.

1890. Ashley William Barrett.
1893. John Howard Mummery.
1895. Frederick Canton.
1900. Storer Bennett.
„ Arthur Swayne Underwood.
1902. William Bromfield Paterson.
1903. William Adolphus Maggs.
„ Peter Sidney Spokes.
1910. Sir James Frank Colyer.
1912. William Henry Dolamore.
1913. Montagu Frank Hopson.
„ Norman Godfrey Bennett.
1920. Evelyn Sprawson.
1922. Joseph Lewin Payne.
1923. Douglas Gabell.
„ Arthur Bayford Guy Underwood.

EXAMINERS IN MEDICINE.

1868. Thomas Bevill Peacock.
  „ Samuel Wilks.
1876. Edward Henry Sieveking.
  „ George Johnson.
  „ John Syer Bristowe.
1879. William Howship Dickinson.

1881. Samuel Jones Gee.
  „ Frederick Thomas Roberts.
1886. Walter Moxon.
  „ Joseph Frank Payne.
  „ James Frederick Goodhart.

EXAMINERS IN MIDWIFERY.

1881. John Williams.

1881. George Ernest Herman.

CONJOINT EXAMINING BOARD IN ENGLAND.

EXAMINERS APPOINTED BY
THE ROYAL COLLEGE OF SURGEONS.

EXAMINERS IN ELEMENTARY ANATOMY.

1884. John Neville Colley Davies-Colley.
  „ Alfred Pearce Gould.
  „ Charles William Mansell Moullin.
  „ James Black.
  „ Robert William Reid.
1886. William Bruce Clarke.
1887. Arthur Hensman.
  „ William Arbuthnot Lane.
  „ Charles Alfred Ballance.
  „ Charles Stonham.

1889. Charles Barrett Lockwood.
1891. James Stanley Newton Boyd.
  „ William Frederic Haslam.
  „ Bilton Pollard.
  „ James Ernest Lane.
1892. Louis Albert Dunn.
1894. Walter Hamilton Hylton Jessop.
  „ Herbert Furnivall Waterhouse.
1895. Jonathan Hutchinson, Jun.
  „ Edmund Wilkinson Roughton.

EXAMINERS IN ELEMENTARY PHYSIOLOGY.

1884. Cuthbert Hilton Golding-Bird.
1885. Edwin Hurry Fenwick.
1886. William Dobinson Halliburton.

1888. Frederick Walker Mott.
1889. Walter George Spencer.
  „ John Rose Bradford.

EXAMINERS IN ELEMENTARY BIOLOGY.

1892. Frank Evers Beddard.
  „ Thomas William Shore.
1893. Henry Percy Dean.
1895. George Alfred Buckmaster.
1896. Peyton Todd Bowman Beale.
  „ Thomas George Stevens.
  „ Thomas William Shore.
1898. Frederick Gymer Parsons.
1901. Herbert Willoughby Lyle.
  „ Peter Chalmers Mitchell.

1901. Walter G. Ridewood.
1903. Thomas George Stevens.
  „ Henry Wm. Marett Tims.
1908. Thomas William Shore.
  „ James P. Hill.
1913. Walter G. Ridewood.
  „ George P. Mudge.
1918. Thomas William Shore.
  „ James P. Hill.

EXAMINERS IN ANATOMY.

1884.	Henry Greenway Howse.	1902.	Holburt Jacob Waring.
„	Edmund Owen.	„	Arthur Keith.
„	Rickman John Godlee.	„	Christopher Addison.
„	William Henry Bennett.	1904.	James Ernest Lane.
1887.	Frederick Howard Marsh.	1907.	William Wright.
1888.	John Neville Colley Davies-Colley.	„	William Henry Clayton Greene.
1889.	William Anderson.	„	Arthur Robinson.
„	George Dancer Thane.	1912.	John Ernest Sullivan Frazer.
1892.	Alfred Harry Young.	„	Andrew Melville Paterson.
„	Richard Clement Lucas.	„	John Cameron.
1894.	William Johnson Walsham.	1916.	Arthur Thomson.
„	George Henry Makins.	1917.	Frederic Wood Jones.
1897.	William Bruce Clarke.	1918.	Frederick Gymer Parsons.
„	Stanley Boyd.	1920.	**David Hepburn.**
„	Arthur Robinson.	1922.	**John Basil Hume.**
1899.	Arthur Thomson.	1923.	**Henry Albert Harris.**

EXAMINERS IN PHYSIOLOGY.

1884.	Henry Power.	1901.	Ernest Henry Starling.
„	William Morrant Baker.	1902.	William Henry Thompson.
„	Gerald Francis Yeo.	„	Thomas Gregor Brodie.
1885.	Jeremiah McCarthy.	1904.	John Beresford Leathes.
1886.	Cuthbert Hilton Golding-Bird.	1907.	Bertram Louis Abrahams.
1887.	Benjamin Thompson Lowne.	1908.	Benjamin Moore.
1889.	Vincent Dormer Harris.	1909.	Ernest Henry Starling.
1891.	William Dobinson Halliburton.	1913.	Charles Frederick Myers-Ward.
1892.	D'Arcy Power.	1914.	Herbert Eldon Roaf.
1894.	Walter George Spencer.	„	Conrad Meredyth Hinds Howell.
1896.	John Rose Bradford.	1917.	George Alfred Buckmaster.
1897.	Leonard Erskine Hill.	1919.	**Herbert Eldon Roaf.**
1899.	George Alfred Buckmaster.	1922.	**Charles Arthur Lovatt Evans.**

EXAMINERS IN SURGERY.

1884. The Court of Examiners. (See page 20.)

EXAMINERS IN MIDWIFERY.

1884.	George Ernest Herman.	1893.	C. Montagu Handfield-Jones.
„	Alfred Lewis Galabin.	1894.	Amand Routh.
„	Francis Henry Champneys.	1896.	Arthur H. Nicholson Lewers.
„	William Duncan.	1897.	Herbert Ritchie Spencer.
1886.	John Baptiste Potter.	1898.	William Radford Dakin.
„	John Williams.	1899.	Walter Spencer Anderson Griffith.
1887.	Walter Spencer Anderson Griffith.	1901.	William Duncan.
1889.	Peter Horrocks.	1901.	James Henry Targett.
1891.	George Ernest Herman.	1902.	George Francis Blacker.
1892.	William Duncan.	1903.	Arthur H. Nicholson Lewers.

EXAMINERS IN MIDWIFERY (*continued*).

1906. William Rivers Pollock.
„   Walter William Hunt Tate.
1907. Hugh James Moore Playfair.
1908. James Henry Targett.
1909. George Francis Blacker.
1911. William Blair Bell.
1912. George Drummond Robinson.
1913. Henry Russell Andrews.

1914. Charles Hubert Roberts.
1916. John Shields Fairbairn.
1917. George Frederick Darwall Smith.
1918. Cuthbert Lockyer.
1919. **George Drummond Robinson.**
1921. **Charles Hubert Roberts.**
1922. **Eardley Lancelot Holland.**
1923. **Donald Whatley Roy.**

EXAMINERS FOR DIPLOMA IN PUBLIC HEALTH.

PART I.

1887. William Henry Corfield.
1890. Thomas Stevenson.
1891. George Turner.
1895. Arthur Pearson Luff.
1900. Christopher Childs.
1901. Alex. Grant Russell Foulerton.
1906. Harold Robert Dacre Spitta.
1911. Richard Tanner Hewlett.
1916. John William Henry Eyre.
1920. **Sir Frederick Wm. Andrewes.**

PART II.

1887. Richard Thorne Thorne.
1890. Edward Ballard.
1891. Sir George Buchanan.
1894. Edward Seaton.
1899. Syd. Arthur Monckton Copeman.
1904. Herbert Timbrell Bulstrode.
1909. Richard Deane Sweeting.
1914. Sir Shirley Forster Murphy.
1917. Frederick Norton Kay Menzies.
1922. **Francis Joseph Stevens.**

EXAMINERS FOR DIPLOMA IN TROPICAL MEDICINE.

BACTERIOLOGY.

1911. John William Henry Eyre.
1920. **Hugh Basil Greaves Newham.**

DISEASES AND HYGIENE OF TROPICS.

1911. Charles Wilberforce Daniels.
1920. **George Carmichael Low.**

REPRESENTATIVES ON COMMITTEE OF MANAGEMENT.

1884. John Cooper Forster.
„   John Marshall.
„   William Scovell Savory.
1886. Sir Joseph Lister, Bt.
1888. Jonathan Hutchinson.
1890. John Whitaker Hulke.
1892. Thomas Bryant.
„   Christopher Heath.
1895. Thomas Pickering Pick.
1897. Sir William MacCormac, Bt.
1900. John Langton.
1901. Henry Greenway Howse.
1902. Edmund Owen.

1905. Sir Rickman John Godlee, Bt.
1906. Sir Henry Morris, Bt.
1908. Sir Wm. Watson Cheyne, Bt.
1912. Sir Alfred Pearce Gould.
1913. Sir George Henry Makins.
1914. Sir Frederic Samuel Eve.
1916. William Frederic Haslam.
1916. Bilton Pollard.
1918. James Ernest Lane.
1919. **Sir Charles Alfred Ballance.**
1921. **Holburt Jacob Waring.**
„   **Walter George Spencer.**

OFFICERS.

MUSEUM.

CONSERVATORS.

1800. William Clift.	1861. William Henry Flower.
1842. Richard Owen.	1884. Charles Stewart.
1852. John Thomas Quekett.	1908. Sir Arthur Keith.

ASSISTANT CONSERVATORS.

1824. William Home Clift.	1843. John Thomas Quekett.
1827. Richard Owen.	1908. Richard Higgins Burne.

PATHOLOGICAL CURATORS.

1831. Frederic Samuel Eve.	1897. Samuel George Shattock.
1890. James Henry Targett.	

ASSISTANT PATHOLOGICAL CURATOR.

1917. Cecil Fowler Beadles.

PHYSIOLOGICAL CURATOR.

1912. Richard Higgins Burne.

ASSISTANTS IN THE MUSEUM.

1858. Thomas Howard Stewart.	1877. George Arthur Wright.
„ James Murie.	1878. Walter Pye.
1860. Charles Bader.	„ John George Garson.
1863. James Bell Pettigrew.	1888. James Henry Targett.
1868. Litchfield Jones Moseley.	1892. Richard Higgins Burne.
1871. James Frederick Goodhart.	1909. Cecil Fowler Beadles.
„ James Lidderdale.	1922. Clement Edward Shattock.
1873. Alban Henry Griffiths Doran.	

STUDENTS IN HUMAN AND COMPARATIVE ANATOMY.

1839. William Crozier.	1848. Charles Henry Hallett.
1840. John Thomas Quekett.	1849. George Robert Skinner.
1841. William Augustus Hillman.	1850. David Henry Monckton.
1842. James Dunn.	1851. John Falconer.
1843. John Williams.	1852. John Henry Sylvester.
1844. Simon Rood Pittard.	1853. Henry Vandyke Carter.
1845. George Hansbrow.	1854. John Lizars Lizars.
1846. Edward Charles Hulme.	1855. Henry Robert Silvester.
1847. John Thomas Arlidge.	„ Thomas Howard Stewart.

PROSECTORS.

1890. William Edward Pearson.
1914. Henry Cecil Wilson.

LIBRARY.

LIBRARIANS.
1828. Robert Willis.
1853. John Chatto.

1887. James Blake Bailey.
1897. Victor Gustave Plarr.

ASSISTANTS IN THE LIBRARY.
1832. Thomas Madden Stone.
1892. Charles Richard Hewitt.

COLLEGE DEPARTMENT.

SECRETARIES.
1800. Okey Belfour.
1811. Edmund Belfour.

1865. Edward Trimmer.
1901. Sibert Forrest Cowell.

ASSISTANT-SECRETARIES.
1859. Edward Trimmer.
1882. Frederic Greville Hallett.

1888. Sibert Forrest Cowell.

BEADLES.
1800. William Pass.
1802. Jeremiah Gibbeson.

1807. William Taylor.
1811. William Stone.

CLERKS.
1842. Henry Poole Gregg.
1853. Thomas Madden Stone.
1871. Richard Smith.
1874. Charles Stewart Loch.

1876. Bowen Pottinger Woosnam.
  ,, Henry Francis Searle.
1877. Frederic Greville Hallett.
1887. Sibert Forrest Cowell.

DIRECTOR OF EXAMINATIONS.
1914. Frederic Greville Hallett.

REPRESENTATIVES IN THE GENERAL COUNCIL OF MEDICAL EDUCATION AND REGISTRATION.

1858. Joseph Henry Green.
1860. James Moncrieff Arnott.
1865. Cæsar Henry Hawkins.
1870. Richard Quain.
1876. Sir James Paget, Bt.

1881. John Marshall.
1891. Thomas Bryant.
1904. Sir Henry Morris, Bt.
1917. Holburt Jacob Waring.

HUNTERIAN ORATION.

In the year 1813 Dr. Matthew Baillie and Sir Everard Home, Bart., Executors of John Hunter, "being desirous of showing a lasting mark of respect to the memory of the late Mr. John Hunter," gave to the College the sum of £1684 4s. 4d. Three per cent Consolidated Bank Annuities for the endowment of an annual Oration, to be called the Hunterian Oration, and to be delivered in the Theatre of the College on the 14th of February, the Birthday of John Hunter, by the Master, or one of the Governors for the time being, or such other Member of the Court of Assistants as should be appointed by the Master and Governors or any two of them—such Oration to be expressive of the merits in Comparative Anatomy, Physiology, and Surgery, not only of John Hunter, but also of all such persons, as should be from time to time deceased, whose labours have contributed to the improvement or extension of Surgical Science.

The Endowment was accepted by the College under a Deed of Trust dated the 9th October 1813, containing, amongst others, the following conditions:—That the Fund should be vested in the names of three Members of the Court of Assistants ; that £10, part of the interest accruing from the Fund, should be given to the Orator ; and that the remainder of the interest should be expended in providing a Dinner, on the day of the delivery of the Oration, for the Members of the Court of Assistants and such other persons as the Master and Governors for the time being should think proper to invite.

In 1853, after consultation with the representatives of the founders of the Trust, it was decided that the Oration should in future be delivered biennially instead of annually.

The fund was re-invested in 1900, and at the present time consists of £1850 India Three per Cent. Stock.

HUNTERIAN ORATORS.

1814. Sir Everard Home, Bt.	1831. Anthony White.
1815. Sir William Blizard, Kt.	1832. Samuel Cooper.
1816. Henry Cline.	1833. John Howship.
1817. William Norris.	1834. William Lawrence.
1818. Sir David Dundas, Bt.	1837. Sir Benjamin Collins Brodie, Bt.
1819. John Abernethy.	1838. Benjamin Travers.
1820. Sir Anthony Carlisle, Kt.	1839. Edward Stanley.
1821. Thomas Chevalier.	1840. Joseph Henry Green.
1822. Sir Everard Home, Bt.	1841. Thomas Callaway.
1823. Sir William Blizard, Kt.	1842. George Gisborne Babington.
1824. Henry Cline.	1843. James Moncrieff Arnott.
1825. William Norris.	1844. John Flint South.
1826. Sir Anthony Carlisle, Kt.	1846. William Lawrence.
1827. Honoratus Leigh Thomas.	1847. Joseph Henry Green.
1828. Sir William Blizard, Kt.	1848. Richard Dugard Grainger.
1829. John Painter Vincent.	1849. Cæsar Henry Hawkins.
1830. George James Guthrie.	1850. Frederic Carpenter Skey.

HUNTERIAN ORATORS (continued).

1851.*Richard Anthony Stafford.
1852. James Luke.
1853. Bransby Blake Cooper.
1855. Joseph Hodgson.
1857. Thomas Wormald.
1859. John Bishop.
1861. William Coulson.
1863. George Gulliver.
1865. Richard Partridge.
1867. John Hilton.
1869. Richard Quain.
1871. Sir William Fergusson, Bt.
1873. Henry Hancock.
1875. Frederick Le Gros Clark.
1877. Sir James Paget, Bt.
1879. George Murray Humphry.
1881. Luther Holden.
1883. Sir Thomas Spencer Wells, Bt.
1885. John Marshall.

1887. William Scovell Savory.
1889. Henry Power.
1891. Jonathan Hutchinson.
1893. Thomas Bryant.
1895. John Whitaker Hulke.
1897. Christopher Heath.
1899. Sir William Mac Cormac, Bt.
1901. Nottidge Charles Macnamara.
1903. Sir Henry Greenway Howse, Kt.
1905. John Tweedy.
1907. Henry Trentham Butlin.
1909. Henry Morris.
1911. Edmund Owen.
1913. Sir Rickman John Godlee, Bt.
1915. Sir William Watson Cheyne, Bt.
1917. Sir George Henry Makins.
1919. Sir Anthony Alfred Bowlby.
1921. Sir Charters James Symonds.
1923. Sir John Bland-Sutton.

* Oration not delivered, but published subsequently.

HUNTERIAN LECTURES.

Clause 2 of the Terms and Conditions, on which the Hunterian Collection was delivered to the Company of Surgeons, provided " that one Course of Lectures, not less than twenty-four in number, on Comparative Anatomy and other subjects, illustrated by the preparations, shall be given every year by some Member of the Company."

In 1894, by permission of the Lords of the Treasury, this Clause was altered to the following, viz.:—

" That one Course of Lectures, not less than twelve in number, on Comparative Anatomy and other subjects, illustrated by preparations from the Hunterian Collection and the other contents of the Museum, shall be given every year by Fellows or Members of the College."

An honorarium of Ten Guineas per lecture is provided from the general funds of the College.

HUNTERIAN PROFESSORS.

COMPARATIVE ANATOMY.

1800–09. Lectures suspended.
1810. Everard Home.
1811–12. Lectures suspended.
1813. Sir Everard Home, Bt.
1814–15. Astley Paston Cooper.
1816–19. William Lawrence.
1820–21. Benjamin Collins Brodie.
1822. Sir Everard Home, Bt.

1823. Benjamin Collins Brodie.
1824–28. Joseph Henry Green.
1829–30. Herbert Mayo.
1831. Lectures suspended.
1832–33. Sir Charles Bell, Kt.
1834–36. Lectures suspended.
1837–55. Richard Owen.
1856. Lectures suspended.

HUNTERIAN PROFESSORS (continued).

SURGERY.

1800–09.	*Lectures suspended.*	1823–24.	Thomas Chevalier.
1810.	Sir William Blizard, Kt.	1825–28.	Charles Bell.
1811–12.	*Lectures suspended.*	1829–30.	George James Guthrie.
1813.	„ „	1831.	*Lectures suspended.*
1814–17.	John Abernethy.	1832.	George James Guthrie.
1818.	Anthony Carlisle.	1833.	Henry Earle.
1819–21.	James Wilson.	1834–36.	*Lectures suspended.*
1822.	Benjamin Collins Brodie.	1839.	Frederick Tyrrell.

HISTOLOGY.

1857–61. *John Thomas Quekett.
1862. *Lectures suspended.*

COMPARATIVE ANATOMY AND PHYSIOLOGY.

1857–59.	George Busk.	1887.	Francis Warner.
1860–61.	William Scovell Savory.	„ ·	Anthony Alfred Bowlby.
1862–63.	George Gulliver.	„ –89.	Charles Barrett Lockwood.
1863–69.	Thomas Henry Huxley.	„ –88.	Walter H. Hylton Jessop.
1870–73.	William. Henry Flower.	1888.	William Watson Cheyne.
1874–85.	William Kitchen Parker.	„ –89.	John Bland Sutton.
1876–84.	William Henry Flower.	1889.	Mark Purcell Mayo Collier.
1885–94.	Charles Stewart.	1890–91.	William Watson Cheyne.
„ –86.	Frederick Treves.	„ –93.	Benjamin Thompson Lowne.
„ „	William Arthur Brailey.	1891–94.	Charles Bagge Plowright.
„ „	Alex Hill.	1893.	Henry Johnstone Campbell.

SURGERY AND PATHOLOGY.

1869.	Frederick Le Gros Clark.	1890.	John Langton.
1870–71.	John Birkett.	„	Walter Pye.
1872–74.	Timothy Holmes.	„	William Henry Battle.
1875.	Henry Lee.	1891.	Reginald Harrison.
1876–77.	Robert Brudenell Carter.	„	William Anderson.
1878.	Thomas Spencer Wells.	„	James Berry.
1879–83.	Jonathan Hutchinson.	1892.	Henry Trentham Butlin.
1884.	Sir Henry Thompson, Knt.	„	Chas. Wm. Mansell Moullin.
1885.	Edward Lund.	„	William Watson Cheyne.
„	John Wood.	„	Henry Betham Robinson.
1886–87.	Henry Power.	1893.	Bernard Pitts.
„	William Cadge.	„	Jonathan Hutchinson, Jun.
1887.	Christopher Heath.	1894.	Thomas Pickering Pick.
1888. –89.	Thomas Bryant.	„	William Thorburn.
„ –89	Arthur Edward James Barker.	„	Raymond Johnson.
1889.	Matthew Berkeley Hill.	„	Edward Treacher Collins.
„	Frederick Howard Marsh.		

* During the years 1850–55 twelve lectures on Histology, in addition to the twenty-four Hunterian Lectures delivered by Professor Owen, were delivered by Professor Quekett.

HUNTERIAN PROFESSORS (continued).

1895. Number of Lectures reduced from 24 to 12 and old division of Lecture abolished.

1895–1902. Charles Stewart.
„ Charles Barrett Lockwood.
„ Joseph Griffiths.
1896. John Alfred Coutts.
„ Leonard Erskine Hill.
1897. Arthur Wm. Mayo Robson.
„ D'Arcy Power.
1898. Henry Morris.
„ –99. Frederick Gymer Parsons.
1899. Leonard Erskine Hill.
1900. Arthur Wm. Mayo Robson.
„ Arthur Keith.
1901. Percy Furnivall.
„ Christopher Addison.
1902. Frederick Gymer Parsons.
„ –03. William McAdam Eccles.
1903–04. Arthur Keith.
„ Andrew Melville Paterson.
„ Arthur Robinson.
1904. Arthur Wm. Mayo Robson.
„ Louis Bathe Rawling.
„ Thomas Crisp English.
1905. Clinton Thomas Dent.
„ William Sampson Handley.
„ John P. Lockhart Mummery.
„ Marmaduke Stephen Mayou.
1906. John Warrington Haward.
„ Arthur Henry Cheatle.
„ Herbert John Paterson.
„ Charles Gabriel Seligmann.
1907–08. William Sampson Handley.
„ John Wm. Thomson Walker.
„ John Howell Evans.
„ William Wright.
„ Cecil Fowler Beadles.
1908. William Francis Victor Bonney.
„ Donald John Armour.
„ Arthur Ralph Thompson.
„ Frank Charles Shrubsall.
1909–23. Sir Arthur Keith.
„ –11. Samuel George Shattock.
„ William Wright.
„ Cecil William Rowntree.
1923.

1910. William Sampson Handley.
„ George Coats.
„ Richard Horace Paramore.
„ Charles Bolton.
1911. Fredc. Wm. Edridge-Green.
„ Walter d'Este Emery.
„ Kenneth Weldon Goadby.
„ Benjamin Moore.
„ Sir Henry Trentham Butlin, Bart.
1912. Herbert Cumming French.
„ Richard Horace Paramore.
„ William Girling Ball.
„ John William Henry Eyre.
1913. Wilfred Batten Lewis Trotter
„ William Wright.
„ Joseph Ebenezer Adams.
„ Kenneth Macfarlane Walker.
1914. Charles Wm. Mansell Moullin.
„ Hastings Gilford.
„ Ernest Wm. Hey Groves.
„ Arthur Rendle Short.
„ Harold Beckwith Whitehouse.
1915. William Sampson Handley.
„ John Howell Evans.
„ Rupert Farrant.
„ Frederick Charles Pybus.
„ Harry Blakeway.
1916. Sir John Bland-Sutton.
„ John Ernest Sullivan Frazer.
„ Jas. Eustace Radclyffe McDonagh.
„ Vincent Zachary Cope.
„ William Blair Bell.
1917–18. Jonathan Hutchinson.
„ Robert Henry Elliot.
„ William Sampson Handley.
„ Alfred Edward Webb-Johnson.
„ Frank Cook.
1918. William Tindall Lister.
„ Percival Pasley Cole.
„ Edward Kenneth Martin.
„ Hildred Carlill.
1919. Gordon Taylor.
„ Albert James Walton.

D

HUNTERIAN PROFESSORS (continued).

1919. David Ligat.
,, Thomas Bramley Layton.
,, Alexander Fleming.
,, Edward Gustave Schlesinger.
1920. Sir Berkeley Moynihan.
,, Walter George Spencer.
,, James Sherren.
,, Harry Tyrrell Gray.
,, Rupert Farrant.
,, Vincent Zachary Cope.
1921. William Sampson Handley.
,, Walter Goldie Howarth.
,, Charles Walter Gordon Bryan.
,, Harry Platt.
,, -22. Alfred Geo. Timbrell Fisher.
1922. Harold Burrows.
,, Kenneth Macfarlane Walker.
,, Charles Aubrey Pannett.

1922. Alan Herapath Todd.
1923-24. Robert Lawford Knaggs.
,, Louis Bathe Rawling.
,, Edward Musgrave Woodman.
,, Cecil Augustus Joll.
,, Hugh Ernest Griffiths.
,, Geoffrey Langdon Keynes.
1924. William Sampson Handley.
,, Charles Max Page.
,, Kenneth Macfarlane Walker.
,, Alexander Fleming.
,, Geoffrey Jefferson.
,, Frank Cook.
,, William Edward Gallie.
,, Sidney Forsdike.
,, William Heneage Ogilvie.
,, Ranald Montagu Hanfield-Jones.
,, Ralph St. Leger Brockman.

ARRIS AND GALE LECTURES.

The Arris Lectures were founded in 1646 by Mr. Edward Arris, a Member of the Company of Barbers and Surgeons, of which he became Master in 1651. He was also an Alderman of the City of London in that year. He died on the 28th May 1676. His portrait in one picture with a portrait of Sir Charles Scarborough, who was appointed to deliver the Arris Lectures in 1649, is in the possession of the Barbers' Company.

From the Minute Books of the Company of Barbers and Surgeons it appears that on the 24th March 1646 Mr. Edward Arris paid to the Company a sum of £300 "for the use of the new publique Anatomy." This sum was subsequently repaid to Mr. Arris, and in lieu thereof he settled upon the Company an annuity of £30, which shortly before his death he redeemed by the payment of £510. By the Act of Parliament of the 18th George II (1745) for dissolving the Union between the Barbers and Surgeons this sum of £510 was given and vested in the Company of Surgeons then incorporated, and upon the dissolution of that Company became vested in the College. The fund now consists of £433 6s. 8d, Metropolitan Consolidated Three per Cent. Stock.

In the final settlement of the Trust no conditions appear to have been imposed save an understanding that the Anatomy Lectures of the Company were to be continued. By an Act of Parliament passed in 1540 the Company were entitled to claim four bodies annually of persons executed for felony, and to make use of them for the study of Anatomy. The bodies were dissected, and lectures on the muscles and other subjects were given. The Surgeons of the Company were required to attend these lectures and demonstrations, which were called "Public Anatomies." The intention of Mr. Arris was to assist the Company in this work, and the lecturers appointed under this foundation were at first called "Readers of the Muscular Lecture."

Under the Company of Surgeons the Arris Lectures were from 1753 to 1766 delivered by the Masters of Anatomy, of whom the first to be appointed were

Percivall Pott and John Hunter. In 1767 the office of Professor of Anatomy was created, and the Arris Lectures were assigned to him.

The Gale Lectures were founded by Mr. John Gale of Bushey, a Member of the Company of Barbers and Surgeons, who, by his Will, dated 13th August 1655, left to the Company an Annuity of £16, payable out of the rents of certain premises on Snow Hill in the City of London, for one Lecture in Anatomy every year to be called Gale's Anatomy.

This Annuity, together with the Arris Bequest, was by the Act of Parliament of 1745 vested in the Company of Surgeons, and upon the dissolution of that Company became vested in the College. In pursuance of Acts of Parliament passed in the 35th and 44th years of George III for the improvement of Snow Hill, the Rent Charge of £16 per annum was purchased by the City of London for the sum of £432, which sum, in accordance with the directions of those Acts, was invested in the name of the Accountant General of the Court of Chancery, until the same shall again be invested in some Real Estate, and the same was laid out in the purchase of £689 16s. 5d. Consolidated Bank Annuities (re-invested in £703 0s. 1d. 2½ per Cent. Consols in 1891), the interest thereof being paid to the College.

The earliest record of a lecture under this Trust is dated 30th June 1698, when it was " ordered that there be an Anatomy Lecture called Gale's Anatomy," and Dr. Havers, well known for his description of the canals in bone, since called Haversian, was appointed the first Reader. The Lecture was afterwards called the Osteology Lecture.

Under the Company of Surgeons the Lecture was at first allotted to the senior Master of Anatomy, and afterwards to the Professor of Anatomy.

At the beginning of the Nineteenth Century, lectures were for a time suspended at the College owing to building operations, but were resumed in 1810. It was then determined that six lectures should be delivered annually under the Arris and Gale Trusts. The lectures were no longer distinguished as " muscular " and " osteological," but were united into one course delivered by a Professor of Anatomy and Surgery. In 1857 the title of the lecturer was altered to Professor of Human Anatomy and Surgery, and in 1868 to Arris and Gale Lecturer. In 1864 the number of lectures was reduced to three. Honorarium for the three lectures, the amount of the dividends received from the Arris Bequest and Gale Annuity— about £30.

LECTURERS SINCE 1800.

1800–09. *Lectures suspended.*	1837–38. Edward Stanley.
1810. Sir William Blizard.	1839–40. Frederick Tyrell.
1811–13. *Lectures suspended.*	1841. George James Guthrie.
1814–17. John Abernethy.	1842–45. Bransby Blake Cooper.
1818. Anthony Carlisle.	1846. John Flint South.
1819–21. James Wilson.	1847–52. James Paget.
1822. Benjamin Collins Brodie.	1853–54. Frederic Carpenter Skey.
1823–24. Thomas Chevalier.	1855–59. Prescott Gardner Hewett.
1825–28. Charles Bell.	1860–62. John Hilton.
1829–32. George James Guthrie.	1863. Samuel Solly.
1833. Henry Earle.	1864–65. William Fergusson.
1834–36. *Lectures suspended.*	1866–67. Henry Hancock.

LECTURERS SINCE 1860 (*continued*).

1868.	Frederick Le Gros Clark.	1910.	Sydney Richard Scott.
1869–71.	John Whitaker Hulke.	,,	Peter Thompson.
1872–73.	George Murray Humphry.	1911.	Grafton Elliot Smith.
1874.	George William Callender.	1912.	Harry Tyrrell Gray.
1875–76.	William Turner.	,,	Leonard Gregory Parsons.
1877–80.	Benjamin Thompson Lowne.	,,	Edward Fawcett.
1881–82.	Gerald Francis Yeo.	1913.	William Blair Bell.
1883.	Henry Power.	,,	Charles Gabriel Seligmann.
1884–85.	Edward Albert Schäfer.	1914–16.	Frederic Wood Jones.
1886–87.	Leonard Charles Wooldridge.	,, –15.	David Waterston.
1888.	Robert Marcus Gunn.	1917.	Ernest William Hey Groves.
1889–90.	William Hunter.	,,	Wilfred Harris.
1891–93.	John Rose Bradford.	1918.	Frederick Gymer Parsons.
1894.	Ernest Henry Starling.	,,	William Wright.
1895.	Walter George Spencer.	1919.	Edred Moss Corner.
1896–97.	Ernest Henry Starling.	,,	Ernest Marshall Cowell.
1898.	Thomas Gregor Brodie.	,,	John Charlton Briscoe.
1899–1900.	Berkeley George Andrew Moynihan.	1920.	Frederic Wood Jones.
		,,	Grafton Elliot Smith.
1901–02.	Thomas Gregor Brodie.	1921–22.	Fred. Wm. Edridge-Green.
1903–04.	John Herbert Parsons.	,,	Joseph Faulkner Dobson.
1904.	Percy John Cammidge.	,,	John Howell Evans.
1905.	Donald John Armour.	1922.	Vincent Zachary Cope.
1906.	John Harry Watson.	,,	Thomas Swale Vincent.
,,	Sydney Walter Curl.	1923.	Leonard Ralph Braithwaite.
1907.	Joseph Faulkner Dobson.	,,	Ethelbert Rest Flint.
,,	Bertram Louis Abrahams.	1924.	Hugh Ernest Griffiths.
1908.	Francis Arthur Bainbridge.	,,	Cecil Pembrey Grey Wakeley.
,,	Major Greenwood, Jun.		
1909.	Grafton Elliot Smith.	,,	Victor Ewings Negus.

ERASMUS WILSON LECTURES.

With the object of promoting the study of the Pathology together with the Anatomy and Physiology, human and comparative, of the Skin and its Appendages, the late Sir Erasmus Wilson gave to the College the sum of £5000 New Three per cent. Consols, under a Deed of Trust, dated the 8th July 1869, to found and endow a Professorship of Dermatology. The Council appointed Sir Erasmus Wilson to the Professorship, and during the period 1870–78 he delivered six lectures annually, and presented to the Museum a large collection of casts and models used in illustration of his lectures.

In 1879 certain alterations in the terms of the Trust were effected with the approval of the Founder, providing that the income derived from the Fund should be devoted to the promotion of original researches by lectures delivered at the College, the number of such lectures not to exceed three in any one year, and to be given by one or more persons to be called Erasmus Wilson Professors of Pathology.

In 1881 further alterations were thought desirable, and under a new Deed of Trust, dated the 13th April 1882, it is now provided that the income of the Fund

shall be appropriated in part towards the payment of the salary of a Pathological
Curator of the Museum, and in part for the payment of Lectures on the Pathological
contents of the Museum to be delivered by the Pathological Curator or some other
person appointed for the purpose with the title of Erasmus Wilson Lecturer.
Three lectures were delivered annually from 1882 to 1908. In July 1908 it was
decided to institute a series of lectures or demonstrations on advanced Surgical
Pathology, illustrated by specimens in the Museum, and from 1909 to 1918 and
since 1921 the Erasmus Wilson Lectures have formed part of this Series, six
demonstrations being given annually by Mr. S. G. Shattock, the Pathological
Curator. Honorarium £30.

In 1900 the fund was re-invested in £4731 13s. Metropolitan Consolidated
Three per Cent. Stock, and this amount has since been increased to £5250 by the
investment of an unexpended income balance accumulated mainly in the early
years of the Trust.

LECTURERS.

1870–78.	Erasmus Wilson.	1900.	Edward Treacher Collins.
1880.	Henry Trentham Butlin.	1901.	Walter Edmunds.
1881.	Henry Trentham Butlin.	1902.	Charles Powell White.
„	Frederick Treves.	1903.	Sir Charles Bent Ball.
1882–84.	Frederick Samuel Eve.	1904.	Edred Moss Corner.
1885.	Charles Stewart.	1905.	Leonard Stanley Dudgeon.
1886–87.	John Bland Sutton.	„	Percy Wm. George Sargent.
1888.	Lectures postponed.	1906.	James Sherren.
1889.	Charles Alfred Ballance.	1907.	Willmott Henderson Evans.
„	Joseph Priestley Smith.	„	Reginald Cheyne Elmslie.
1890–91.	John Bland Sutton.	„	Kenneth Weldon Goadby.
1892.	Jonathan Hutchinson, Jun.	1908.	John William Henry Eyre.
1893–95.	James Henry Targett.	„	Leonard Stanley Dudgeon.
1896–97.	Walter George Spencer.	„ –18.	Samuel George Shattock.
1898.	Holburt Jacob Waring.	1919–20.	Lectures suspended.
1899.	Thomas Gregor Brodie.	1921–24.	Samuel George Shattock.

BRADSHAW LECTURE.

The Bradshaw Lecture was founded in memory of her husband by the late
Mrs. Sally Hall Bradshaw, widow of Dr. William Wood Bradshaw, M.A.Oxon.,
D.C.L., LL.D., a Fellow of the College for many years in practice at Reading.
She bequeathed to the College by Will, dated 6th September 1875 and proved
26th August 1880, a sum of £1000 Three per Cent. Consols, the income thereof to be
expended upon a lecture on Surgery to be called "The Bradshaw Lecture," and to
be delivered annually on the 18th August, the anniversary of Dr. Bradshaw's death.

In 1882 an Order of Administration of the Bequest was obtained from the
Charity Commissioners, which provided that the Lecture should be delivered on
the 18th day of August, or on such other day as might be expressly substituted in
each year for that day by the President, and a sum of £900 Three per Cent.
Consols was transferred to the College in satisfaction of the Bequest. The fund
was re-invested in 1900, and at the present time consists of £900 Metropolitan
Consolidated Three per Cent. Stock. Honorarium of Lecturer, £27.

LECTURERS.

1882. Sir James Paget, Bt.	1903. Henry Morris.
1883. John Marshall.	1904. Arthur William Mayo Robson.
1884. William Scovell Savory.	1905. Henry Trentham Butlin.
1885. John Wood.	1906. Edmund Owen.
1886. Henry Power.	1907. Rickman John Godlee.
1887. Sir Joseph Lister, Bt.	1908. Sir William Watson Cheyne, Bt.
1888. Jonathan Hutchinson.	1909. Francis Richardson Cross.
1889. Thomas Bryant.	1910. Sir Alfred Pearce Gould, K.C.V.O.
1890. Sir Thomas Spencer Wells, Bt.	1911. Richard Clement Lucas.
1891. John Whitaker Hulke.	1912. Charles Wm. Mansell Moullin.
1892. Christopher Heath.	1913. George Henry Makins.
1893. Sir William MacCormac.	1914. Sir Frederic Samuel Eve.
1894. Oliver Pemberton.	1915. Sir Anthony Alfred Bowlby.
1895. Nottidge Charles Macnamara.	1916. Charters James Symonds, C.B.
1896. Reginald Harrison.	1917. Sir John Bland-Sutton.
1897. Alfred Willett.	1918. D'Arcy Power.
1898. Thomas Pickering Pick.	1919. Sir Charles Alfred Ballance.
1899. Henry Greenway Howse.	1920. Sir Berkeley Moynihan.
1900. John Langton.	1921. Holburt Jacob Waring.
1901 Thomas Richard Jessop.	1922. Sir William Thorburn.
1902. Frederick Howard Marsh.	1923. **Walter George Spencer.**

MORTON LECTURE ON CANCER.

In 1887 Mr. J. T. Morton of Cedar Grange, Caterham Valley, provided a sum of Ninety Guineas for the endowment for three years of a lecture on Cancer and Cancerous Diseases. In 1890 he provided a further sum of Ninety Guineas for three more annual lectures.

LECTURERS.

1887. Sir James Paget, Bt.	1892. German Sims Woodhead.
1888. Sir Thomas Spencer Wells, Bt.	„ James Galloway.
1889. John Marshall.	1893. Samuel George Shattock.

THOMAS VICARY LECTURE.

In 1919 the Barbers' Company undertook to provide an annual sum of £10 10s. for five years for the purpose of instituting at the Royal College of Surgeons an historical lecture in Anatomy or Surgery to be called the Thomas Vicary Lecture, the appointment of the lecturer being in the gift of the College.

LECTURERS.

1919. Sir John Tweedy.	1922. Walter George Spencer.
1920. Sir D'Arcy Power.	1923. **Sir Arthur Keith.**
1921. Sir Charles Alfred Ballance.	

ARNOTT DEMONSTRATIONS.

Mr. James Moncrieff Arnott, F.R.S., President of the College in 1850 and 1859, died in 1885, and by his Will left to the College the sum of £1000, to the end that the annual interest or income thereof should be applied annually to the purposes of the Museum and the Lectures connected therewith, the bequest to be payable after the death of his daughter, Miss Jane Moncrieff Arnott.

Miss Arnott died in June 1907, and the bequest was paid to the College and invested in £1081 0s. 6d. Transvaal Government Three per cent. Stock in November 1907.

In July 1908 it was decided to institute a series of Lectures or Demonstrations on advanced Surgical Pathology, illustrated by specimens in the Museum, and to apply the income derived from the Arnott Bequest to the payment of part of the cost of these Lectures or Demonstrations. In 1908–09 nine Demonstrations were given under this Trust, and Section XXI. of the Standing Rules now provides that under the Arnott Bequest not less than six Demonstrations of the contents of the Museum shall be given annually by the Conservator of the Museum or some other duly qualified person or persons. Honorarium £32 8s. 6d.

DEMONSTRATORS.

1908–09. Arthur Keith.	1909–24. **Sir Arthur Keith.**
„ „ Samuel George Shattock.	

BLICKE BEQUEST.

Sir Charles Blicke, Master of the College in 1803 and 1810, died in 1815, and by his Will left to the College £300 Three per cent. Consols "for the distinct purpose of applying the annual interest thereof for the purchase of books for ever."

The fund was transferred to the College in 1817, and vested in the names of three Members of the Court of Assistants as Trustees.

In 1900 the fund was re-invested, and at the present time consists of £300 India Three per cent. Stock.

CLINE TRUST.

Mr. Henry Cline, Master of the College in 1815 and President in 1823, died in 1827, and by his Will bequeathed to the College, on trust, such an amount of his Three per cent. French Rentes as should at the time of his death produce £600 per annum, the dividends thereof to be received by his children, grandchildren, and great grandchildren, and after the death of the survivor of them, to be applied to the improvement of the Science of Surgery in such manner as the Council of the College should from time to time direct. In satisfaction of this Bequest a Rente of 15,000 francs per annum was entered in the Books of the Bank of France.

Of this annuity 535 francs were sold in 1908 to pay Estate Duty and interest thereon claimed by the Commissioners of Inland Revenue upon one-fifth of the 15,000 francs passing on the death of each of four of the five great grandchildren.

The surviving great grandchild died on the 5th August, 1917, and the balance of 14,465 francs per annum has been transferred into the name of the College. These Rentes, which now form the Trust, were valued by the Inland Revenue Authorities at £10,366 11s. 6d., and Estate and Legacy Duties thereon, amounting to £1,525 19s. 11d. were paid out of general funds of the College, as the regulations of the French Government forbade any portion of the Rentes forming the Bequest being sold and the proceeds transmitted abroad during the War.

This sum having now been repaid to the general funds of the College out of the income from the Trust, it has been decided by the Council of the College to apply the income from the Trust to the development of the Army Medical War Collection of pathological and other specimens, entrusted to the care of the College under an Agreement with the Secretary of State for War, dated the 11th November, 1921.

LISTER MEMORIAL FUND.

This Fund was raised by public subscription with the object of showing a lasting mark of respect to the memory of the Right Hon. Lord Lister, O.M., F.R.S., F.R.C.S., and in grateful appreciation of his eminent services to the science of surgery and the signal benefit thereby conferred on mankind.

In the year 1920 the Royal College of Surgeons of England undertook to become the Trustees and Administrators of the Fund, and with the approval of the General Committee of the Fund the trust was transferred to the College subject to the following provisions :—

(1) That out of the General Fund a sum of £500, together with a bronze medal, be awarded every three years, irrespective of nationality, in recognition of distinguished contributions to surgical science, the recipient being required to give an Address in London under the auspices of the Royal College of Surgeons.

(2) That the award be made by a Committee constituted as follows :—
Two members nominated by the Royal Society.
Two members nominated by the Royal College of Surgeons of England.
One member nominated by the Royal College of Surgeons in Ireland.
One member nominated by the University of Edinburgh.
One member nominated by the University of Glasgow.

(3) That any surplus income of the General Fund, after providing for the erection of a monument, and after defraying administrative expenses, be either devoted to the furtherance of surgical science by means of grants or be invested to increase the capital of the Fund.

The following stocks have been transferred into the name of the College as the capital sum to produce the income required to make the award referred to in paragraph (1) of the scheme, viz. :—

£1,000 Canada 4 p.c. Registered Stock 1940–1960.
£1,000 Ceylon Government 4 p.c. Inscribed Stock 1939–1959.
£1,000 New South Wales 4 p.c. Stock 1942–1962.
£1,000 Victorian Government 4 p.c. Consolidated Inscribed Stock 1940–1960.
£1,000 South Indian Railway 4 p.c. Registered Debenture Stock 1945.

JACKSONIAN PRIZE.

In the year 1800 Mr. Samuel Jackson, F.R.S., a Member of the College, announced his intention of giving a sum of £10 annually as a Prize to the Author of the best Dissertation on a practical subject in Surgery. In order to make the donation perpetual, he subsequently gave to the College a sum of £333 6s. 8d. Consolidated Bank Annuities, which he vested in the name of three Members of the Court of Assistants under a Deed of Trust, dated the 13th April 1806.

On the 13th May, 1869, it was resolved " that in any year in which the Jacksonian Prize is not adjudged the interest arising from the Jacksonian Fund be added to the principal of the Fund," and through additions thus made and reinvestment in 1891 the Fund now consists of £616 13s. 4d. India Three per cent. Stock, and the annual dividend of £18 10s. received on this sum now constitutes the Prize.

JACKSONIAN PRIZEMEN
WITH THE SUBJECTS OF THEIR DISSERTATIONS.

1801. On the diseases of Joints, particularly of the Knee, and the best mode of treating them. *No Dissertation received.*

1802. On Gunshot wounds and the best mode of treating them. *No Award.*

1803. THOMAS CHEVALIER.—Gunshot wounds and the best mode of treating them.

   „   THOMAS NOBLE ELWYN.—Diseases of the Urethra and the best method of treatment.

1804. WILLIAM CHANDLER.—Aneurism and the best method of treatment.

   „   On Herniæ, particularly Femoral Hernia, and the best method of treatment. *No Award.*

1805. JOHN HYSLOP.—Injuries of the Head from external violence.

1806. SAMUEL COOPER. —The Diseases of Joints, particularly of the Hip and Knee and the best mode of treatment.

   „   WILLIAM LAWRENCE.—Hernia and the best mode of treatment.

1807. JOHN HYSLOP.—Diseases of the Eye and its appendages, with the treatment of them.

1808. CHRISTOPHER T. JOHNSON.—On Cancer and its treatment.

1809. GABRIEL J. M. DE LYS.—Fractures of the Bones of the Trunk, and the treatment of them.

1810. JOHN SMITH SODEN.—The Bite of a Rabid Animal.

   „   JAMES GILLMAN.—*Honorarium* for Dissertation on the same subject.

1811. JOSEPH HODGSON.—Wounds and Diseases of Arteries and Veins.

1812. WILLIAM GOODLAD.—Diseases of the Vessels and Glands of the Absorbent System.

1813. DANIEL PRING.—Injuries and Diseases of Nerves.

   „   HENRY EARLE.—*Honorarium* for Dissertation on the same subject.

1814. On Injuries and Diseases of Muscle. *No Award.*

1815. EDWARD STANLEY.—On Diseases of Bone.

1816. On Scrofula. *No Dissertation received.*

   „   On Syphilis. *No Award.*

1817. Joseph Swan.—On Deafness and Diseases and Injuries of the Organ of Hearing.
1818. Eusebius Arthur Lloyd.—On Scrofula.
„   John Haddy James.—On Inflammation.
„   On Diseases of the Skin.   *No Dissertation received.*
1819. Joseph Swan.—On the Treatment of morbid local affections of Nerves.
1820. On Diseases of the Skin.   *No Dissertation received.*
  .   On Diseases of the Rectum.   *No Dissertation received.*
1821. Robert Bingham.—On Injuries and Diseases of the Bladder.
1822. Thomas William Chevalier.—On Injuries and Diseases of Muscle.
„   Samuel Plumbe.—On Disease of the Skin.
„   George Calvert.—On Diseases of the Rectum.
1823. George Calvert.—On Fungus Hæmatodes.
1824. George Calvert.—On Tic Douloureux.
1825. On Reparation of Fractured Bone, and the special treatment of fracture of
      the neck of the Scapula, of the Olecranon, of the neck of the Thigh-bone,
      of the Patella, and of the Malleoli.   *No Award.*
1826. Richard Anthony Stafford.—On Spina Bifida and Injuries and Diseases of
      the Spine and the Medulla Spinalis.
1827. Edward Browne.—On Reparation of Fractured Bone, and the special treat-
      ment of fracture of the neck of the Scapula, of the Olecranon, of the neck
      of the Thigh-bone, of the Patella, and of the Malleoli.
„   On Injuries and Morbid Affections of the Maxillary bones and Antrum.   *No
      Dissertation received.*
1828. George Rogerson.—The causes, consequences, and treatment of Inflamma-
      tion of the several distinctions of Membrane.
1829. James Reid.—On Bronchocele.
  ,   On Encysted Tumours.   *No Award.*
1830. On Injuries and Diseases of the Nose and of the Nasal Sinuses.   *No Disser-
      tation received.*
1831. Richard Radford Robinson.—On Fractures of the Ribs, of the Sternum,
      and of the Pelvis, their influence on the several viscera, and the treatment
      of such cases.
„   Richard Middlemore.—On Diseases of the Eye and its appendages, and the
      treatment of them.
1832. Benjamin Phillips.—The mode of union of simple and compound Fractures.
„   On the symptoms occasioned by the different Mineral Poisons when taken
      into the Stomach ; the proper Antidotes and treatment which experience
      or science affords for each ; and, when the event is fatal, the appearances
      or effects which are generally found in the dead body   *No Dissertation
      received.*
1833. John Green Crosse.—On the formation, constituents and extraction of
      . Urinary Calculi.
„   Richard Radford Robinson. ⎱ *Honoraria* for their Dissertations on the same
  - „   George Thompson Morgan. ⎰ subject.
1834. Dickinson Webster Crompton.—Injuries and Diseases the Nose and of
      the Nasal Sinuses.
„   Thomas Blizard Curling.—On Tetanus.
1835. Frederick Ryland.— On Injuries and Diseases of the Larynx, also of the
      Trachea, and treatment.

1836. On Hæmorrhage, spontaneous and accidental, with treatment. *No Award.*

1837. SAMUEL GASKELL.—An Enquiry into the nature of the Processes of Suppuration and Ulceration.

1838. EDWIN LEE.—On the comparative advantages of Lithotomy and Lithotrity, and on the circumstances under which one method should be preferred to the other.

„ On the structure and treatment of Nævi and other Erectile Tumours. *No Award.*

1839. RUTHERFORD ALCOCK.—The nature, symptoms, and treatment of Concussion of the Brain, and of the other forms of Cerebral injury from external violence.

1840. On the structure and treatment of Nævi and other Erectile Tumours. *No Dissertation received.*

„ On Hæmorrhage, spontaneous and accidental, with treatment. *No Dissertation received.*

1841. RUTHERFORD ALCOCK.—Injuries of the Thorax, and Operations on its Parietes.

1842. WILLIAM PIERS ORMEROD.—The comparative value of the Preparations of Mercury and Iodine in the treatment of Syphilis.

„ On injuries and morbid affections of the Maxillary Bones, including those of the Antrum. *No Dissertation received.*

1843. JOHN WILLIAM GRIFFITH.—Derangements in the Secretion of Urine, their causes, consequences, and treatment.

1844. EDWARDS CRISP.—The Anatomical structure and diseases of the larger Blood-vessels.

„ On the injuries and diseases of the Scalp. *No Award.*

1845. THOMAS SAFFORD LEE.—Tumours of the Uterus and its appendages, their structure, pathology, and treatment.

1846. THOMAS CALLAWAY.—On Luxations and Fractures of the Clavicle, Scapula, and Scapular End of the Humerus, and treatment.

„ EDWARD HULME.—On Asphyxia, its various causes and forms, and Treatment.

1847. On the nature and treatment of permanent contraction of Muscles, especially in relation to distortion and disability. *No Dissertation received.*

1848. JOHN BIRKETT.—On Diseases of the Mammary Gland, Male and Female, and the treatment thereof.

1849. HENRY LEE.—On the causes, consequences, and treatment of Purulent Deposits.

„ PETER HINCKES BIRD.—Erysipelas, its nature and treatment.

1850. CHARLES TOOGOOD DOWNING.—Neuralgia, its various forms, pathology, and treatment.

1851. EDWARDS CRISP.—The causes, diagnosis, and treatment of Obstructions of the Intestines within the Abdomen.

1852. HENRY THOMPSON.—The pathology and treatment of Stricture of the Urethra.

1853. HARVEY LUDLOW.—Diseases of the Testis and its coverings, and their treatment.

1854. On the structure and treatment of Erectile Tumours. *No Dissertation received.*

1855. On Gunshot wounds and their treatment. *No Dissertation received.*

1856. VICTOR DE MERIC.—The pathology and treatment of Syphilis.

„ An enquiry into the nature and treatment of the different forms of Gangrene. *No Award.*

1857. ALFRED POLAND.—Gunshot wounds and their treatment.

„   On the effects produced in Man by the introduction into the system of
     Poisons from the Lower Animals; excluding Hydrophobia and Cowpox.
     No Award.

1858. On the pathology and treatment of diseases of the Ovary. *No Dissertation
     received.*

„   On Vegetable Poisons   their effects means of detection and treatment. *No
     Award.*

1859. JOHN WHITAKER HULKE.—The morbid changes of the Retina as seen in the
     Eye of the living person and after removal from the Body, together with
     the symptoms associated with the several morbid conditions.

„   CHARLES BADER.—*Honorarium* for Dissertation on the same subject.

„   On the structure and treatment of vascular Nævi. *No Dissertation received.*

„   HENRY THOMPSON.—The healthy and morbid anatomy of the Prostate Gland.

1860. A description of the diseased conditions of the Knee-joint which require am-
     putation of the limb, and of those conditions which are favourable for the
     excision of the joint; with an explanation of the relative advantages of
     both operations as far as can be ascertained by cases properly authenticated.
     No Award.

1861. JOHN WOOD.—The best method of effecting the radical cure of Inguinal
     Hernia, explaining the principle of the operation adopted.

„   On the structure and diseases of the Lachrymal Passages at the inner side of
     the Orbit, being those between the Conjunctiva and the Nasal Cavity.
     No Dissertation received.

1862. On the relative value of the treatment of Popliteal Aneurism by Ligature
     and by Compression. *No Award.*

„   On the healthy and morbid anatomy of the Tonsils and the appropriate treat-
     ment of their diseases. *No Dissertation received.*

1863. MORELL MACKENZIE.—The pathology and treatment of Diseases of the Larynx ;
     the Diagnostic Indications to include the appearances as seen in the
     living person.

„   On the normal and pathological anatomy of the various Synovial Bursæ con-
     nected with the Muscles and Tendons of the upper Extremity, and the
     treatment of their diseases. *No Dissertation received.*

1864. WILLIAM ADAMS.—Club Foot, its causes, pathology, and treatment.

„   JOHN CROWN AGNIS.—*Honorarium* for Dissertation on the same subject.

„   THOMAS ANNANDALE.—The malformation, diseases, and injuries of the fingers
     and toes, with their surgical treatment.

„   On the diseases of the Ankle-joint and of the joints and bones of the Tarsus
     requiring surgical treatment; stating the treatment (including operative)
     most suitable in each case, with the results thereof. *No Dissertation
     received.*

1865. WILLIAM PAUL SWAIN.— The diseased conditions of the Knee-joint which
     require amputation of the limb, and those conditions which are favourable
     for excision of the joint.

„   On the relative value of the various modes of treatment of Popliteal Aneur-
     ism. *No Dissertation received.*

1866. JOHN CLAY.—Ovariotomy; pathology and diagnosis of cases suitable for this
     operation, with the best method of performing it and the results of
     recorded cases.

1866. On Fractures into Joints ; their modes of union, with the treatment and result. *No Dissertation received.*

1867. CHRISTOPHER HEATH.—The injuries and diseases of the Jaws, including those of the Antrum, with the treatment by operation or otherwise.

„ WM. JOHNSON SMITH.—The various deformities resulting from severe Burns on the surface of the body, the structural changes occasioned by these injuries, the best modes of preventing demforities, and the treatment, operative or otherwise, adapted to correct them.

1868. On Pyæmia after injuries and operations ; its pathology, causes, symptoms, prevention, and treatment. *No Award.*

„ On Amputations of the Limbs ; the various modes of operation practised, their relative advantages, and the methods of arresting Primary Hæmorrhage, and of dressing the Stump. *No Dissertation received.*

1869. Aneurism by Anastomosis ; the various forms of this disease, and the different methods of treatment, with the Author's experience and views thereon. *No Dissertation received.*

1870. Hæmorrhagic Diathesis and Spontaneous and accidental Hæmorrhage. *No Dissertation received.*

1871. The treatment of Wounds after Operations, including the arrest of Hæmorrhage, Primary and Secondary. *No Award.*

1872. The Diseases of the Nose, including those of the Sinuses connected with it and their treatment. *No Award.*

1873. HENRY TRENTHAM BUTLIN.—Ununited Fractures.

1874. Tracheotomy, with particular reference to the causes of death after the operation, and the rules for rendering the operation more generally successful. *No Award.*

1875. The use of the Galvano-Caustic in the removal of Morbid Growths. *No Dissertation received.*

1876. WILLIAM HARRISON CRIPPS.—The treatment of Cancer of the Rectum, particularly as regards the possibility of curing or relieving the Patient by excision of the affected part.

1877. The Disease of the Lymphatic System known as Hodgkin's Disease, or Lymphadenoma. *No Award.*

1878. JOSEPH PRIESTLEY SMITH.—Glaucoma, its causes, symptoms, pathology, and treatment.

1879. The Disease of the Lymphatic System known as Hodgkin's Disease, or Lymphadenoma. *No Dissertation received.*

1880. WILLIAM WATSON CHEYNE.—The history, principles, practice, and results of Antiseptic Surgery.

1881. WILLIAM ALEXANDER.—The pathology and surgical treatment of Diseases of the Hip-Joint.

1882. ANTHONY ALFRED BOWLBY.—Wounds and other Injuries of Nerves, their symptoms, pathology, and treatment.

1883. FREDERICK TREVES.—The Pathology, Diagnosis, and Treatment of Obstruction of the Intestines in its various forms in the Abdominal Cavity.

1884. The Surgical Treatment of Uterine Tumours, both Innocent and Malignant. *No Dissertation received.*

1885. WILLIAM BRUCE CLARKE.—The Diagnosis and Treatment of such Affections of the Kidney as are amenable to direct Surgical Interference.

1886. JAMES BERRY.—The Pathology, Diagnosis, and Surgical treatment of Diseases of the Thyroid Gland.
1887. EDWIN HURRY FENWICK.—The Pathology, Diagnosis, and Treatment of Tumours of the Bladder.
      FREDERICK ARMITAGE SOUTHAM.—*Certificate of Honourable Mention* for Dissertation on the same subject.
1888. JONATHAN HUTCHINSON, Jun.—The Diagnosis, Effects, and Treatment of Injuries to the Epiphyses of the Long Bones.
1889. WALTER GEORGE SPENCER.—The Pathology, Diagnosis, and Surgical Treatment of Intracranial Abscess and Tumour.
1890. WILLIAM THORBURN.—The Nature and Treatment of Injuries to the Spinal Column and the Consequences arising therefrom.
1891. The Pathology and Treatment of Diseases of the Knee-Joint. *No Dissertation received.*
1892. JOHN BLAND-SUTTON.—Diseases of the Ovaries and the Uterine Appendages, their Pathology, Diagnosis, and Treatment.
1893. Hydrophobia. *No Dissertation received.*
1894. HOLBURT JACOB WARING.—The Diagnosis and the Surgical Treatment of Diseases of the Liver, Gall-Bladder, and Biliary Ducts.
1895. ALFREDO ANTUNES KANTHACK. —Tetanus.
1896. ROBERT COZENS BAILEY.—The Pathology, Diagnosis, and Treatment of Diseases of the Prostate Gland.
1897. PERCY FURNIVALL.—The Pathology, Diagnosis, and Treatment of the various Neoplasms met with in the Stomach, Small Intestine, Cæcum, and Colon.
1898. Hydrophobia. *No award*
1899. HARRY LAMBERT LACK.—The Pathology, Diagnosis, and Treatment of Inflammatory Affections of the Nasal Fossæ and the Associated Sinuses and Air-Cells.
1900. WILLIAM McADAM ECCLES.—The Pathology, Diagnosis, and Treatment of the Diseases caused by and connected with Imperfect Descent of the Testicle.
1901. The Diagnosis and Treatment of Bullet Wounds of the Chest and Abdomen. *No Dissertation received.*
1902. THOMAS CRISP ENGLISH.— Fracture of the Skull, its Consequences immediate and remote, including Pathology and Treatment.
  ,,   LOUIS BATHE RAWLING.—*Honorarium* for Dissertation on the same subject.
1903. MARMADUKE STEPHEN MAYOU.—The various forms of Conjunctivitis, their Pathology and Treatment.
1904. HERBERT JOHN PATERSON.—The Diagnosis and Treatment of such Affections of the Stomach as are amenable to direct Surgical Interference.
1905. REGINALD CHEYNE ELMSLIE.—The Pathology and Treatment of Deformities of the Long Bones due to Disease occurring during and after Adolescence.
1906. DONALD JOHN ARMOUR.—The Diagnosis and Treatment of those Diseases and Morbid Growths of the Vertebral Column, Spinal Cord and Canal, which are amenable to Surgical Operations.
1907. The Operative Surgery of the Heart and Lungs, including the Pericardium and Pleura. *No Award.*
1908. JOHN PERCY LOCKHART MUMMERY.—The Pathology and Treatment of those Conditions and Diseases of the Colon which are relievable by Operative Measures.

1909. WILLIAM GIRLING BALL.—The Treatment of Surgical Affections by Vaccines and Antitoxins.
1910. KENNETH MACFARLANE WALKER.—Tuberculous Disease of the Urinary Bladder and Male Genital Organs.
1911. The Diseases of the Pancreas, with special reference to their surgical treatment. *No Award.*
1912. FRANCIS WILLOUGHBY GOYDER.—The Embryology and Treatment of Cleft Palate.
1913. JOHN HOWELL EVANS.—Malformations of the Small Intestine : their mode of origin, the morbid conditions which arise from them, and their treatment.
1914. JONATHAN HUTCHINSON.—The Pathology, Diagnosis, and Treatment of Trigeminal Neuralgia.
1915. Congenital Dislocations of the Joints, their pathology and treatment. *No Award.*
1916. ERNEST WILLIAM HEY GROVES.—Methods and results of Transplantation of Bone in the repair of defects caused by injury or disease.
1917. The Causation, Diagnosis, and Treatment of Traumatic Aneurysm, including Arterio-Venous Aneurysm. *No Dissertation received.*
1918. JOHN ANDREW CAIRNS FORSYTH.—Injuries and Diseases of the Pancreas, and their surgical treatment.
1919. The Investigation and Treatment of Injuries of the Thorax received in War. *No Dissertation received.*
1920. HAROLD BURROWS, C.B.E.—The Results and Treatment of Gunshot Injuries of the Blood-Vessels.
1921. The Pathology, Diagnosis, and Treatment of Tuberculous Disease of the Spinal Column with its complications. *No Award.*
1922. SIDNEY FORSDIKE.—The Effects produced by Radium upon Living Tissues with special reference to its use in the Treatment of Malignant Disease.

JOHN HUNTER MEDAL

AND

TRIENNIAL PRIZE.

The Triennial Prize was founded by the Court of Assistants in the year 1820, and was first offered for competition in 1822. The honorarium, provided from the funds of the College, at first amounted to Thirty Pounds, but in 1840 was increased to Fifty Guineas.

In 1864 a life-size statue of John Hunter by H. Weekes, R.A., was erected in the Museum of the College by public subscription, and with the residue of the subscriptions the Statue Committee founded the John Hunter Medal, which in the year 1867 they entrusted to the College for award to the person to whom the Triennial Prize shall from time to time be adjudged.

The Prize, which now consists of the John Hunter Medal executed in bronze with an honorarium of Fifty Pounds, was offered triennially from 1822 to 1922 as an award for the best essay on a subject in human or comparative anatomy and physiology, but in 1925 and thereafter triennially may be awarded to some Fellow or Member of the College, who has, during the preceding ten years, done such work in Anatomy, Physiology, Histology, Embryology, or Pathological Anatomy as, in the opinion of the Committee of adjudication, deserves special recognition.

LIST OF RECIPIENTS
WITH THE SUBJECTS OF THEIR DISSERTATIONS.

1822–24. JOSEPH SWAN.—A minute dissection of the Nerves of the Medulla Spinalis from their origin to their terminations, and to their conjunctions with the Cerebral and Visceral Nerves ; authenticated by preparations of the dissected parts.

1825–27. JOSEPH SWAN.—A minute dissection of the Cerebral Nerves frrm their origin to their termination, and to their conjunction with the Nerves of the Medulla Spinalis and Viscera; authenticated by preparations of the dissected parts.

1828–30. An inquiry into the ultimate terminations of the Sanguiferous System and the commencement and terminations of the Lymphatic System, explanatory of the means by which parts of the Body are formed, maintained, altered, and removed ; authenticated by preparations. *No Dissertation received.*

1831–33. On the effects produced by complete or partial Division of the various Nerves, or by other Injuries to those Structures. *No Dissertation received.*

1834–36. To determine the diameters, disposition, and modes of communication of the continuous capillary arteries and veins, both in the pulmonic and systemic circulations ; and also the disposition of the vascular system in the Spleen, Corpus Cavernosum and Corpus Spongiosum; the subject to be illustrated by injected and other preparations of the human capillaries and those of inferior animals. *No Dissertation received.*

1837–39. To determine the diameters, disposition, and modes of communication of the continuous capillary arteries and veins, both in the pulmonic and general circulations; the subject to be illustrated by injected and other preparations both of the human body and of inferior animals. *No Dissertation received.*

1840–42. THOMAS WILLIAMS.—The structure and functions of the Lungs.

1843–45. HOLMES COOTE.—The Anatomy of the fibres of the Cerebrum, Cerebellum, and Spinal Cord in the Human Subject, together with the origins of the cerebral, spinal, and sympathetic nerves, specially illustrated by the anatomy of the same parts in the lower vertebrate animals.

1846–48. HENRY GRAY.—The origin, connection, and distribution of the Nerves of the Human Eye and its appendages, illustrated by comparative dissections of the Eye in the other vertebrate animals.

„ ALFRED POLAND.—*Honorarium* for Dissertation on same subject.

1849–51. The functions of the several parts of the large Intestines in animals of the class Mammalia. *No Dissertation received.*

1853–55. The structure and functions of the Ganglionic Systems of Nerves in Man illustrated by reference to Comparative Anatomy. *No Award.*

1856–58. The structure and functions of the Lymphatic and Lacteal Systems illustrated by reference to Comparative Anatomy. *No Award.*

1859–61. GEORGE HARLEY.—The anatomy and physiology of the Suprarenal Bodies illustrated by drawings and preparations.

1862–64. The Structural Anatomy and Physiology of the Lymphatic Vessels and Glands (the anatomical distribution not being required); the communications (if any) between the Lymphatics and the Blood-vessels to be demonstrated; and the influence (if any) which the Lymphatic Vessels or Glands exercise on the fluids they transmit to be elucidated. The dissertation to be illustrated by preparations and drawings. *No Dissertation received.*

1865–67. The anatomical structure of those parts of the Eyeball which are contained within the Sclerotic and Cornea; with illustrations drawn from each of the five great divisions of the Vertebrata. *No Award.*

1868–70. The Anatomy and Physiology of the organs of Taste and Smell in the Mammalia. *No Dissertation received.*

1871–73. The Structure and Functions of the Medulla Oblongata, including the connections of the Central Nerve-Roots. *No Award.*

1874–76. The Radicles of the Lymphatic System in relation to the external and internal surfaces of the Body. *No Dissertation received.*

1877–79. GEORGE ARTHUR WOODS.—The Anatomy and Physiology of the third, fourth, and sixth Nerves, as illustrated by observation and experiment in health, and by reference to the effects of injury and disease.

1880–82. The Relations between the Radicles and the Lymphatic System and Capillary Vessels. *No Award.*

1883–85. The Nature of Inhibitory Action in the Animal Body, to be elucidated by original research. *No Dissertation received.*

1886–88. The Structure and Functions of the Sympathetic System of Nerves in Man, to be illustrated by reference to Comparative Anatomy. *No Award.*

1889–91. The Anatomy of the 3rd, 4th, 5th, and 6th Cranial Nerves in the Vertebrata; including an Account of their development and relations to the Sympathetic System. *No Dissertation received.*

1892–94. The Spleen, its Anatomy and Physiology, illustrated by Comparative Anatomy. *No Dissertation received.*

1895–97. The Arrangement and Topography of the different parts of the Gastrointestinal Canal in Man, with special reference to the Variations in their relation to the Peritoneum and the occurrence of Abnormalities; the the subject to be illustrated from Development and a comparison with the customary arrangement in other Mammalian Animals. *No Award.*

1898–1900. The Thyroid Gland—its Structure, Comparative Anatomy, and Physiology. *No Award.*

1901–1903. THOMAS RUPERT HAMPDEN BUCKNALL.—The Pathological Conditions arising from Imperfect Closure of the Visceral Clefts.

1904–1906. The Effects of Nerve-Lesions on Growth and Development. *No Dissertation received.*

1907–1909. The Histological Anatomy of the Lymphatic and Hæmo-Lymphatic Glands, more especially with reference to the changes which these Glands undergo in acute infective processes. *No Award.*

1910–1912. WILLIAM BLAIR BELL.—The Anatomy and Physiology of the Pituitary Body, and the relationship with disease of its abnormal and morbid conditions.

1913–1915. The Human and Comparative Anatomy and Physiology of the Cerebellum. *No Award.*

1916–1918. The Development of the Hip-Joint and the Knee-Joint of Man. *No Dissertation received.*

1919–1921. The Anatomy, Morphology, and Age-changes of Cervical Ribs in Man, including a description of the associated Ligaments, Blood-Vessels, and Nerves. *No Dissertation received.*

HONORARY MEDAL.

The Honorary Medal of the College was instituted under a Bye-Law made in the year 1802.

It is a Gold Medal with the following design, viz. :—On the obverse, the Armorial Bearings, Crest, Supporters, and Motto of the College; and on the reverse, Galen contemplating a Human Skeleton.

The leading considerations in awarding the Honorary Medal are liberal acts or distinguished labours, researches, and discoveries, eminently conducive to the improvement of natural knowledge and of the healing art.

LIST OF RECIPIENTS.

1822. JAMES PARKINSON.	1884. SIR WM. JAMES ERASMUS WILSON.
1825. JOSEPH SWAN.	1897. SIR JAMES PAGET, Bt.
1834. GEORGE BENNETT.	,, LORD LISTER.
1869. WILLIAM LODEWYK CROWTHER.	1906. SIR RICHARD HAVELOCK CHARLES.
1876. THOMAS BEVILL PEACOCK.	1910. ROBERT FLETCHER.
1883. RICHARD OWEN.	

HONORARY MEMBERSHIP.

The Honorary Membership of the College was instituted under a Bye-Law made in the year 1802.

The leading considerations in the choice of Honorary Members were similar to those influencing the selection of recipients of the Honorary Medal.

The Bye-Law was abrogated after the institution of the Fellowship in 1843.

HONORARY MEMBERS.

1812. Rt. Hon. Sir Joseph Banks, Bt., K.B.
1818. Georges Cuvier.
1821. Sir Humphry Davy, Bt.
1830. Sir Gilbert Blane, Bt.

BLANE MEDALS.

This Medal was founded by Sir Gilbert Blane, Bt., F.R.S., a distinguished physician, best known for the sanitary reforms which he effected in the Navy, and the success of the measures which he introduced for the prevention of scurvy.

Under a Deed of Trust, dated the 13th March 1830, he transferred to the College the sum of £300 three per Cent. Consolidated Bank Annuities to provide for two Gold Medals to be conferred once in every two years on two Medical Officers of the Royal Navy " who in the time required shall have delivered to the proper office Journals evincing the most distinguished proofs of skill, diligence, humanity, and learning in the exercise of their professional duties." The Journals were to be submitted for adjudication to the President of the Royal College of Physicians of London, the President of the Royal College of Surgeons of England, and the Senior Medical Commissioner of the Royal Navy (Director-General of the Medical Department of the Navy).

In 1913, in pursuance of authority given to them under the Deed, the Presidents of the Colleges and the Director-General of the Medical Department of the Navy decided, with the approval of the Lords of the Admiralty, to make certain alterations in the Regulations for the award of the Medals, and it is now provided "that one Medal be awarded annually to the Medical Officer who obtains the highest aggregate marks at the examination for promotion to the rank of Surgeon Lieutenant Commander, now held twice a year in connection with the Courses at the Medical School of the Royal Naval College, Greenwich—the award to be subject to the approval of the Presidents of the Colleges of Physicians and Surgeons respectively, and the Director General of the Medical Department of the Navy."

The fund has been re-invested, and at the present time consists of £300 Metropolitan Consolidated 3½ per cent. Stock.

E 2

BLANE MEDALLISTS.

1832. John Liddell.
„ William Donnelly.
1833. John Wilson.
„ R. P. Hillyar.
1835. Samuel Irvine.
„ Evan Bowen.
1837. William Martin.
„ Charles McArthur.
1839. Alexander McKechnie.
„ Robert H. Brown.
1841. J. O. McWilliam.
„ John Tarn.
1843. William Lindsay.
„ Robert Austin Bankier.
1845. T. R. Dunn.
„ J. Wingate Johnston.
1847. Peter Leonard.
„ Henry W. Mahon.
1849. T. R. H. Thomson.
„ Fitzwilliam Mansell.
1851. George Mackay.
„ William McKinlay.
1853. R. T. C. Scott.
„ James Salmon.
1855. Alexander Armstrong.
„ Charles D. Steel.
1857. W. R. E. Smart.
„ A. E. Mackay.
1859. William Duvis.
„ Walter Dickson.
1861. C. K. Ord.
„ William Macleod.
1864. Andrew Graham.
„ Charles Forbes.
1866. William H. Sloggett.
„ Stephen Bowden.
1868. John Jack.
„ Henry Hadlow.
1870. Alexander Rattray.
„ D. L. Morgan.
1873. D. McEwan.
„ R. C. P. Lawrenson.
1874. J. D. Macdonald.
„ Thomas Colan.

1875. T. J. Haran.
„ Richard Eustace.
1877. Adam Brunton Messer.
„ F. W. Davis.
1880. Henry Frederick Norbury.
„ W. D. Longfield.
1881. Alex. McDonald.
„ Belgrave Ninnis.
1883. George Maclean.
„ Robert Hall More.
1886. Henry Scott Lauder.
„ Miles O'Connel McSwiney.
1888. T. J. Preston.
„ T. D. Gimlette.
1890. Richard Wm. Coppinger.
„ Thomas Henry Knott.
1892. Charles C. Godding.
„ John D. Menzies.
1894. Alex. G. P. Gipps.
„ Gilbert Kirker.
1896. Everard Home Saunders.
„ Vidal Gunson Thorpe.
1898. Francis H. A. Clayton.
„ Percy Wm. Bassett-Smith.
1900. James Macdonald Rogers.
„ Oswald Rees.
1902. Chris. Louis White Bunton.
„ John Falconer Hall.
1905. Sidney Thomas Reid.
„ Robert Wm. Glennan Stewart.
1907. Jas. Wm. Wilcocks Stanton.
„ Bernard Ley.
1909. Charles Rowley Nicholson.
„ Arthur William Bligh Livesay.
1910. George Trevor Collingwood.
„ Arthur Reginald Bankart.
1913. Richard Cleveland Munday.
„ Edward Sutton.
1914. Gilbert Francis Syms.
1922. Sidney Wilfred Grimwade.
„ Robert William Basil Hall.
„ Sheldon Francis Dudley.
„ Reginald St. George S. Bond.

WALKER PRIZE.

Under a Deed of Trust, dated the 10th May 1894, the late Mr. Charles Clement Walker of Lilleshall Old Hall, near Newport, Salop, transferred to the College the sum of £540 Victoria Three and a half per cent. Inscribed Stock for the endowment of a Prize intended to encourage the investigation of Cancer.

The Prize, which is open to foreigners as well as to British subjects, consists of a gift of £100, and is awarded quinquennially by the Council, upon the recommendation of a Committee, to the person, if any, who shall be deemed to have done the best work during the preceding five years in advancing the knowledge of the Pathology and Therapeutics of Cancer.

LIST OF RECIPIENTS.

1891–1895. HAROLD JALLAND STILES.
1896–1900. *No award.*
1901–1905. CARL OLUF JENSEN.
1906–1910. ERNEST FRANCIS BASHFORD.
1911–1915. WILLIAM SAMPSON HANDLEY.
1916–1920. *No award.*

JOHN TOMES PRIZE.

This Prize was founded in 1894 by Members of the Dental Profession in memory of the late Sir John Tomes, F.R.S., F.R.C.S., and his services in promoting the study of Dental Surgery and improving the status of its practitioners.

The sum of £310 India Three per cent. Stock (since increased to £337 6s. 7d. Stock) was entrusted to the College, and it was agreed that the income thence derived should be expended in awarding triennially a Prize to such person, holding a Diploma in Dental Surgery of one of the Licensing Bodies in Great Britain or Ireland, as should be deemed by the Committee of adjudication to have done, during the preceding three years, original or other scientific work, worthy of special recognition on the subjects of Dental Surgery and Pathology, Dental Anatomy and Physiology (including Histology), or Dental Mechanics. The value of the honorarium or prize is £30 7s.

LIST OF RECIPIENTS.

1894–96. CHARLES SISSMORE TOMES.
1897–99. JOHN HOWARD MUMMERY.
1900–02. KENNETH WELDON GOADBY.
1903–05. *No award.*
1906–08. ARTHUR SWAYNE UNDERWOOD.
1909–11. ARTHUR HOPEWELL-SMITH.
1912–14. JAMES FRANK COLYER.
1915–17. JOSEPH GEORGE TURNER.
1918–20. JAMES SIM WALLACE.

CARTWRIGHT PRIZE AND MEDAL.

This Prize was founded in 1884 by the " Association of Surgeons practising Dental Surgery " with the object of commemorating the services of Samuel Cartwright, F.R.C.S., in improving the status of the Dental Profession, not only by inducing many of those engaged in its practice to become fully qualified Surgeons, but also by assisting to gain the recognition of Dentistry as a special branch of Surgery by the institution of a Licence in Dental Surgery by the Royal College of Surgeons of England.

The " Association of Surgeons practising Dental Surgery " having been dissolved, the administration of the Fund for the endowment of the Prize has been entrusted to this College under an order of the Charity Commissioners of the 31st July 1900, establishing a scheme approved by the Council of the College and the surviving members of the Association.

The Fund (at present amounting to £822 8s. 7d. 2½ per cent. Consols) is invested in the name of " The Official Trustees of Charitable Funds," and the dividends are paid to the President and Vice-Presidents of the College as Trustees of the Fund.

The Prize, consisting of the Cartwright Medal in bronze and an honorarium of £85, is to be awarded quinquenially to the author of the best essay upon a subject relating to Dental Surgery to be selected by the Council upon the recommendation of a Committee. Candidates must be persons engaged in the study or practice of Dental Surgery and possessing qualifications capable of registration under the Medical Acts of the United Kingdom.

PRIZEMEN AND SUBJECTS OF ESSAYS.

1901–05. The Surgical Diseases having their origin in abnormal or diseased conditions of the Teeth and their Structures, the essay to be illustrated by pathological and microscopical specimens. *No Award.*

1906–10. Henry Percy Pickerill.— The prevention of Dental Caries.

1911–15. Oral Sepsis as a factor in the causation of general and local diseases. *No Essay received.*

1916–20. William Kelsey Fry, M.C.— The Treatment of Injuries of the Jaws, and the restoration by mechanical means of parts of the Jaws lost as the result of injury or removed on account of disease.

JENKS SCHOLARSHIPS.

In 1893 Miss Johnstone of Bath bequeathed £5000 in trust for founding five Scholarships for Medical Students in memory of George Samuel Jenks, M.D., F.R.C.P., a former Member of the College.

The Will assigns the nomination to these Scholarships to the President and Censors of the Royal College of Physicians and to the Council of the Royal College of Surgeons alternately, with a first claim or preference for students educated at and leaving Epsom College ; and directs that one Scholarship be awarded annually, tenable for five years. The value of each Scholarship is about £27 per annum.

SCHOLARS.

1893. James Alfred Patrick Cullen.	1909. Philip Denis Scott.
1894. Thomas Chetwood.	1910. Gerald Gibbons.
1895. Douglas Duke Turner.	1911. Arthur Lloyd Davies.
1896. Arthur Whitehead Smith.	1912. Graham Selby Wilson.
1897. George Archibald Bosson.	1913. Frank Caldecott.
1898. William Hardy Fleetwood.	1914. John Douglas Magor Cardell.
1899. Chas. Henry Burton Thompson.	1915. Ralph Stanley Swindell.
1900. Alfred George Sworn.	1916. John St. Clair Shadwell.
1901. Rupert Farrant.	1917. Tom Forbes Jeffery (died).
1902. John Webster Bride.	1918. Charles Richardson McClure.
1903. Alfred Richardson.	„ Thomas Haines Sims.
1904. Charles Gibson.	1919. Jack William Jeffery.
1905. Eric Alfred Charles Fazan.	1920. Rupert Hadley Scott.
1906. Godfrey Alan Walker.	1921. Ronald Henry Knight.
1907. William Henry Price Saunders.	1922. Douglas Stanley-Jones.
1908. Ernest Haines Walker.	

BEGLEY STUDENTSHIP.

Under the Will of the late Mrs. Jane Begley of Hammersmith, widow of Dr. William Chapman Begley, a Member of the College, who for 34 years was in charge of the male department at the Hanwell Asylum, the College in 1905 became possessed of a sum of £800 2½ per cent Consols for the benefit of students studying Medicine, Surgery, and Anatomy.

In accordance with Mrs. Begley's expressed wish a Studentship in Surgery and Anatomy of £20 per annum tenable for three years has been founded.

STUDENTS.

1906. Walter Burford Johnson.	1915. Joseph Clinton Collins.
1909. John Robert Douglas Webb.	1918. Edith Marjorie Rooke.
1912. Alan Cecil Perry.	1921. Kenneth Owen Parsons.

STREATFEILD RESEARCH SCHOLARSHIPS.

In 1916, under a Deed of Trust, Mrs. Eliza Streatfeild of Park Street, Mayfair, transferred into the joint names of the Royal College of Physicians of London and the Royal College of Surgeons of England a sum of £10,000 2½ per cent. Annuities to be held on trust and the income thereof to be applied to promote, assist, and encourage research in Medicine and Surgery, or either of those arts or sciences.

SCHOLARS AND SUBJECTS OF RESEARCH.

1919. Frederick Gordon Cawston, M.D.—" Snails as a Cause of Disease."

1922. Kenneth Norman Grierson Bailey, M.B.—" Infection of the Urinary Tract by Coliform Bacilli."

DONORS AND BENEFACTORS.

A LIST OF THOSE WHO HAVE GIVEN, OR BEQUEATHED, SUMS OF MONEY
TO THE COLLEGE.

		£	s.	d.
1646.	Edward Arris.......................	510	0	0
1655.	John Gale	689	16	5
1806.	Samuel Jackson	333	6	8
,,	Parliament	15,000	0	0
1810.	Parliament	12,500	0	0
1813.	Dr. Matthew Baillie } ,, Sir Everard Home, Bart. }	1,684	4	4
1817.	George Cruttenden	500	0	0
,,	Sir Charles Blicke	300	0	0
1827.	Henry Cline	10,366	11	6
1852.	Parliament	15,000	0	0
1869.	Sir Erasmus Wilson	5,000	0	0
1880.	Mrs. S. H. Bradshaw	1,000	0	0
1884.	Sir Erasmus Wilson	209,617	16	8
1885.	James Moncrieff Arnott	1,000	0	0
1894.	Charles Clement Walker	536	0	0
,,	Subscribers to John Tomes Memorial	308	9	0
1900.	Subscribers to Cartwright Memorial	644	15	1
1905.	Mrs. Jane Begley	718	10	0
1922.	H.M. War Department	7,500	0	0

1916. Mrs. Eliza Streatfeild .. £10,000 2½ per cent. Annuities,
entrusted to the Royal College of Physicians of London and
the Royal College of Surgeons of England jointly.

CONTINGENT BEQUESTS.

1902. Mr. James William Groves bequeathed to the College by Will ¾ths of his
residuary estate, subject to the life-interests therein of his wife, Mrs. Florence
Mary Jane Groves, and his sister, Miss Frederica Harriet Groves, for the general
purposes and objects of the Museum (including in such purposes and objects the
purchase of collections or the defraying of the expenses of the Conservator incurred
in journeys abroad for the inspection of other Collections). It was expected that the
sum ultimately placed at the disposal of the College under this Bequest would
amount to about £30,000.

1910. Sir George Sutherland Mackenzie, K.C.M.G., C.B., left by Will a sum
of £30,000, the income therefrom to be paid to his two brothers for their joint
lives and the life of the survivor, and, on the death of the survivor, to be paid to
the President and Council of the Royal College of Physicians and the President
and Council of the Royal College of Surgeons for the purpose of providing the
means of assisting qualified medical persons to pursue scientific medical investigation.

Regulations relating to the Preliminary Examination in General Education and to the Pre-Medical Examination in Chemistry and Physics, both of which must be passed previous to the commencement of Medical Study.

SECTION I.

PRELIMINARY EXAMINATION IN GENERAL EDUCATION.

(*This Examination may be passed in two, but no more than two, Parts, and must be completed before the Pre-Medical Examination in Chemistry and Physics is taken, except as provided in paragraph 2, Section II., on page 62.*)

The Preliminary Examination in General Education must include the following subjects :—

(*a*) ENGLISH (Grammar ; Composition ; Literature).

(*b*) MATHEMATICS (Arithmetic ; Algebra, including easy quadratic equations ; Geometry, including the subject-matter of *Euclid*, books i., ii., iii., and simple deductions).

(*c*) One of the following languages, namely :—Greek ; Latin ; French ; Russian ; German ; Italian ; Dutch or Spanish. (The examination must include Grammar, translation into English from unprescribed books, and translation from English.)

[*Note.*—A Candidate desiring to offer any other language than those specified in Section (*c*) must make application in writing to the Committee of Management.]

(*d*) A second language selected from the foregoing list or one of the following subjects, namely :—Higher Mathematics ; History ; Geography ; Physical Science ; Natural Science ; Botany ; Biology ; Geology.

The following is a List of Examining Bodies whose Examinations in General Education are recognized by the Examining Board in England :—

I.—UNIVERSITY EXAMINATIONS HELD IN THE UNITED KINGDOM.

A.

Final Examination for a Degree in Arts or Science of any University in the United Kingdom.

B.

These Examinations may be passed in two, but no more than two, Parts.

UNIVERSITY OF OXFORD :—
    Responsions.
    Moderations.
Oxford Delegacy for Local Examinations :
    Higher School Certificate Examination.
    *School Certificate Examination.

    * For conditions of recognition—see English Board of Education.

UNIVERSITY OF CAMBRIDGE :—
Previous Examination.
General Examination.
Cambridge Local Examinations and Lectures Syndicate :
Higher School Certificate Examination.
*School Certificate Examination.
OXFORD AND CAMBRIDGE SCHOOLS EXAMINATION BOARD :—
Higher Certificate Examination.
*School Certificate Examination.
UNIVERSITY OF DURHAM :—
Matriculation Examination of the Faculties of Medicine, Science, Letters,
and Music.
Higher Certificate Examination.
*School Certificate Examination.
UNIVERSITY OF LONDON :—
Matriculation Examination.
Higher Senior School Examination.
*General School Examination.
VICTORIA UNIVERSITY OF MANCHESTER, UNIVERSITY OF BIRMINGHAM, UNIVERSITY
OF LIVERPOOL, UNIVERSITY OF LEEDS, AND UNIVERSITY OF SHEFFIELD, JOINT
MATRICULATION BOARD OF :—
Matriculation Examination.
Higher School Certificate Examination.
*School Certificate Examination.
UNIVERSITY OF BRISTOL :—
Matriculation Examination.
Higher School Certificate Examination.
*School Certificate Examination.
UNIVERSITY OF WALES :—
Matriculation Examination.
UNIVERSITIES OF SCOTLAND :—
Preliminary Examination of the Joint Board of Examiners of the Scottish
Universities for Graduation in Medicine and Surgery.
Preliminary Examination of the Joint Board of Examiners of the Scottish
Universities for Graduation in Arts or Science.
UNIVERSITY OF ST. ANDREWS :—
Final Examination for the Diploma of L.L.A.
UNIVERSITY OF DUBLIN :—
Junior Freshman Term Examination (exclusive of Trigonometry).
Special Preliminary Examination to be held in March, the standard and
subjects of which shall be those of a Junior Freshman Examination
(exclusive of Trigonometry).
Junior Exhibition Examination on obtaining marks of sufficient merit in
the subjects of (a) or (b).
Examination for the First, Second, Third, or Fourth Year in Arts.
(Certificate to be signed in the approved form by the Medical Registrar
of the University.)

* For conditions of recognition—see English Board of Education.

QUEEN'S UNIVERSITY OF BELFAST :—
Matriculation Examination.
NATIONAL UNIVERSITY OF IRELAND :—
Matriculation Examination.

II.—GOVERNMENT EXAMINATIONS HELD IN THE UNITED KINGDOM.

ENGLISH BOARD OF EDUCATION :—
First School Examination Certificate to include a "pass with credit" in English, and in one Language in Group II. or in Mathematics in Group III.

The following examinations are recognized under this certificate :—

(1) The School Certificate Examination of the Oxford and Cambridge Schools Examination Board.
(2) The School Certificate Examination of the Oxford Delegacy for Local Examinations.
(3) The School Certificate Examination of the Cambridge Local Examination and Lectures Syndicate.
(4) The School Certificate Examination of the University of Bristol.
(5) The School Certificate Examination of the University of Durham.
(6) The General School Examination of the University of London.
(7) The School Certificate Examination of the Northern Universities Joint Matriculation Board.

SCOTTISH EDUCATION DEPARTMENT :—
Leaving Certificate Examination.
INTERMEDIATE EDUCATION BOARD OF IRELAND :—
Middle Grade Examination with Honours in three subjects.
Senior Grade Examination.
CENTRAL WELSH BOARD :—
Senior Certificate Examination.

III.—EXAMINATIONS BY CHARTERED BODIES HELD IN THE UNITED KINGDOM.

COLLEGE OF PRECEPTORS :—
Senior Certificate Examination.
EDUCATIONAL INSTITUTE OF SCOTLAND :—
Preliminary Examination for Medical Students.
ROYAL COLLEGES OF PHYSICIANS AND SURGEONS IN IRELAND :—
Preliminary Examination.

IV.—EXAMINATIONS HELD OUT OF THE UNITED KINGDOM.

UNIVERSITY OF MALTA :—
Matriculation Examinasion.
UNIVERSITY OF CALCUTTA :—
*Preliminary Scientific or Intermediate Examination.

* In addition to the Matriculation Examination.

UNIVERSITY OF MADRAS :—
  *Intermediate Examination.
UNIVERSITY OF BOMBAY :—
  *Preliminary Scientific Examination or Previous Examination.
PUNJAB UNIVERSITY :—
  *Intermediate Examination in Arts or Science.
UNIVERSITY OF ALLAHABAD :—
  *Intermediate Examination in Arts.
UNITED PROVINCES (INDIA) EDUCATION DEPARTMENT :—
  Leaving Certificate (if supplemented by one of the Previous or Intermediate
  Examinations).
CEYLON MEDICAL COLLEGE :—
  Preliminary Examination.
UNIVERSITY OF M'GILL COLLEGE, MONTREAL :—
  Matriculation Examination.
COLLEGE OF PHYSICIANS AND SURGEONS OF THE PROVINCE OF QUEBEC :—
  Matriculation Examination.
UNIVERSITIES AND COLLEGES OF THE PROVINCE OF ONTARIO :—
  Junior Matriculation Examination.
UNIVERSITY OF MANITOBA :—
  Matriculation Examination.
UNIVERSITY OF NEW BRUNSWICK, FREDERICTON :—
  Matriculation Examination.
COLLEGE OF PHYSICIANS AND SURGEONS OF NEW BRUNSWICK :—
  Matriculation Examination.
DALHOUSIE UNIVERSITY, HALIFAX, NOVA SCOTIA :—
  Matriculation Examination.
PROVINCIAL MEDICAL BOARD OF NOVA SCOTIA :—
  Preliminary Examination.
NEWFOUNDLAND MEDICAL BOARD :—
  Preliminary or Matriculation Examination.
UNIVERSITY OF MELBOURNE :—
  Matriculation Examination.
UNIVERSITY OF SYDNEY :—
  Matriculation Examination for the Faculty of Medicine.
  First Year Examination in Arts.
  Senior Public Examination.
UNIVERSITY OF ADELAIDE :—
  Senior Public Examination.
UNIVERSITY OF TASMANIA :—
  Senior Public Examination.

* In addition to the Matriculation Examination.

UNIVERSITY OF WESTERN AUSTRALIA :—
Matriculation Examination.

UNIVERSITY OF OTAGO :—
Preliminary Medical Examination.

UNIVERSITY OF NEW ZEALAND :—
Preliminary Examination for Medical Students.

UNIVERSITIES OF SOUTH AFRICA :—
The Examination of the Joint Matriculation Board of the Universities of Cape Town, South Africa, Stellenbosch, and Witwatersrand.

UNIVERSITY OF HONG KONG :—
Matriculation Examination in Medicine.

FOREIGN UNIVERSITIES IN EUROPE :—
Examinations entitling to the French Diplomas of Bachelier ès Lettres and Bachelier ès Sciences; the German Abiturienten-Examen of the Gymnasia and Real-gymnasia; and other corresponding Entrance Examinations to the Universities in Europe.

EGYPTIAN GOVERNMENT :—
Examination for the Secondary Education Certificate.

SECTION II.

PRE-MEDICAL EXAMINATION IN CHEMISTRY AND PHYSICS.

(*This Examination may not be taken until after the Preliminary Examination in General Education has been completed, except in the case mentioned in paragraph 2 below.*)

1. An examination, recognized or conducted by the Board, in Chemistry and Physics must be passed before Medical Study can be commenced.

Candidates who produce satisfactory evidence that they have passed in Chemistry and Physics or in either subject at one of the following Examinations will be exempted from further examination in the subject or subjects in which they have passed, viz. :—

Oxford University Higher School Certificate.
Cambridge University Higher School Certificate.
Oxford and Cambridge Schools Examination Board Higher Certificate.
London University Higher School Certificate.
Bristol University Higher School Certificate.
Joint Matriculation Board of the Northern Universities Higher School Certificate.
Durham University Higher School Certificate (provided the optional paper in Organic Chemistry is taken).

2. Candidates who may have passed the required subjects of the Preliminary Examination in General Education in any of the examinations mentioned in paragraph 1, and at the same time have also passed in Chemistry and Physics, will be held to have completed both the Preliminary Examination in General Education and the Pre-Medical Examination in Chemistry and Physics.

3. Candidates who produce satisfactory evidence that they have passed an examination in Chemistry and Physics or in Chemistry or Physics which exempts them from further examination in one or both subjects for the Degree in Medicine of any University in the British Empire, or of a Foreign University recognised by the Examining Board in England, will be exempted from the subject or subjects in which they have passed.

4. Before admission to the Pre-Medical Examination in Chemistry and Physics conducted by the Board, Candidates must produce evidence of having received not less than 180 hours' instruction and laboratory work in Chemistry and 120 hours' instruction and laboratory work in Physics, to the satisfaction of their Teachers. These courses may be commenced or attended before the required Preliminary Examination in General Education is passed.

5. The Examination is partly written, partly oral, and partly practical.

Synopses indicating the range of subjects in the Pre-Medical Examination will be found on pages 63–66.

6. Candidates may present themselves for the Pre-Medical Examination immediately after passing the Preliminary Examination in General Education, provided they are able to produce the Certificates required by paragraph 4.

7. Candidates must present themselves for examination in Chemistry and Physics together (unless they claim exemption from one of them under the conditions of paragraphs 1 and 3) until they have reached the required standard to pass in both or in one subject, but they will not be allowed to pass in one subject unless they obtain at the same time at least half the number of marks required to pass in the other subject.

8. Candidates referred in either subject or in both subjects will be required, before being admitted to re-examination, to produce Certificates that they have received further instruction in the subject or subjects in which they have been referred, to the satisfaction of their Teachers, for a period of three months.

9. The Fee for admission to the Pre-Medical Examination is £3 3s.; for re-examination in Chemistry, £2 2s.; and for re-examination in Physics, £1 1s.

10. The Examination will be held in the months of January, March or April, July, September or October.

11. Applications and inquiries with reference to the Preliminary Examination in General Education, the Pre-Medical Examination in Chemistry and Physics, as well as to the Professional Examinations for the Licence of the Royal College of Physicians of London and the Diploma of Member of the Royal College of Surgeons of England should be addressed to the Secretary, Examination Hall, 8–11 Queen Square, Bloomsbury, London, W.C. 1, from whom forms of the required Certificates may be obtained.

SYNOPSES.

PRE-MEDICAL EXAMINATION.

I. Chemistry and Practical Chemistry.

INORGANIC CHEMISTRY.

The General Elementary Principles of Chemistry :—

Simple substances. Mixtures. Chemical Compounds. Laws of Chemical Combination. Atomic Theory. Meaning and Use of Chemical Symbols. Equations and Simple Calculations.

Classification of the Elements. The General Characters of the Chief Types of Compounds. Acids, Bases and Salts.

The Elements of Physical Chemistry. Elementary Properties of Solutions, such as, Diffusion; Osmotic Pressure; Determination of Molecular Weights in Solution; Colloidal State; Electrical Conductivity; Hydrolysis in Aqueous Solution; Strengths of Acids and Bases; Use of Indicators; Nature of Chemical Equilibrium ; Catalysis ; Elements of Thermochemistry.

(It is understood that the Principles of Physical Chemistry should be treated in an elementary manner and with due regard to the future work of the medical student.)

The General Characters of the Chief Types of Inorganic Matter, as illustrated by the following :—

Hydrogen and Oxygen. Oxidation and Reduction. Ozone. Composition and Properties of Water. Hydrogen Peroxide.

Nitrogen. Composition of the Atmosphere. Ammonia and Ammonium Salts. Nitrous Oxide and Nitric Acid.

Carbon. Carbon Monoxide and Carbon Dioxide. Carbonates.

Halogens. Chlorine and Hydrochloric Acid. Hypochlorous Acid and Sodium Hypochlorite. Bleaching Powder. Potassium Chlorate. Bromine and Iodine. Hydrobromic and Hydriodic Acids.

Sulphur. Hydrogen Sulphide. Sulphur Dioxide and Sulphur Trioxide. Sulphurous and Sulphuric Acids. Sodium Thiosulphate.

Phosphorus. Phosphorus Pentoxide and Orthophosphoric Acid. Alkali Phosphates.

The following metals:—

Sodium, Potassium, Calcium, Magnesium, Mercury, Iron, Lead, Arsenic, Antimony, Bismuth, and their more important compounds.

(A knowledge of Metallurgical Processes, as such, is not required.)

ORGANIC CHEMISTRY.

The Ultimate Analysis of Organic Compounds as regards Carbon, Hydrogen, and Nitrogen. Determination of Empirical Formulæ and Molecular Weight. Graphical, or Structural, Formulæ. Homologous Series. Isomerism.

The General Character of the Chief Types of Organic Compounds, as illustrated by the following members of the various classes :—

Methane and Ethane. Ethylene. Acetylene. Benzene. Chloroform and Iodoform. Methyl and Ethyl Alcohols. Phenol. Ethyl Ether. Formic and Acetic Aldehydes. Acetone. Formic and Acetic Acids. Ethyl Acetate. Acetamide. Glycine. Hydrocyanic Acid and the Alkali Cyanides. Urea and its Synthesis. Lactic and Acetoacetic Acids. Glycerol. Fats and Saponification. Glucose and Fermentation.

PRACTICAL CHEMISTRY.

(a) Qualitative Analysis.

Candidates will be expected to possess such a knowledge of the properties of Inorganic Substances as will enable them to identify Simple Salts, Individual Metals and their Oxides, and Free Acids. The constituents of the salts, the free metals and their oxides, and the acids are included in the following :—

Metals : Sodium, Potassium, Ammonium, Calcium, Barium, Magnesium, Iron, Lead, Mercury, Arsenic, Antimony, Bismuth.

Acids : Hydrochloric Hydriodic, Nitric, Carbonic, Sulphuric, Phosphoric, Hydrogen Sulphide.

(b) Quantitative Analysis.

Volumetric determination involving simple applications of Alkalimetry and Acidimetry. Volumetric estimation of Chlorides by the Thiocyanate and Chromate methods. Volumetric examinations by means of the Iodine and Thiosulphate reaction.

(c) Organic Chemistry.

The study of the reactions, with a view to the identification, of the following typical Organic Compounds :—

Ethyl Alcohol, Acetone, Acetic Acid, Ethyl Acetate, Acetamide, Glycine, Urea, Glucose, Phenol.

II. Physics (including Mechanics.)

GENERAL PHYSICS.

Units of length, mass, and time in the metric and British systems. Uniform velocity and variable velocity. Relative velocity. Acceleration. Newton's laws of motion. Absolute and gravitational measures of force. Parallelogram of forces. Simple Machines. Principle of moments or torques. Friction. Work and energy. Conservation of energy.

Specific gravity and density. Principle of Archimedes. Hydrometers. Surface tension. Young's modulus of elasticity.

Atmospheric pressure and the barometer. Air pumps. Siphon. Boyle's law. Diffusion in gases and liquids. Kinetic theory of gases. Osmotic pressure. Viscosity. Laws of pressure of moving fluids in uniform tubes.

HEAT.

Thermometry. Expansion of solids, liquids, and gases. Constant volume air thermometer.
Calorimetry. Specific Heat.
Change of state. Latent Heat.
Conduction, convection, and radiation.
Vapour-pressure. Hygrometry.
Relation between heat and work.

SOUND.

Characteristics of wave motion. Longitudinal and transverse waves.
Pitch, loudness, and timbre of musical notes and their physical correspondents.
Experimental determinations of pitch.
Vibrations of stretched strings and air columns. Resonance.
Measurement of wave velocity in solids, liquids, and gases.

LIGHT.

Laws of reflection and refraction. Images formed by reflection at plane and spherical surfaces. Prisms. Convex and concave lenses. Combinations of lenses.
Magnifying glass, telescope and microscope. Spectacles.
The eye as an optical instrument. Ophthalmoscope.
Visible and invisible regions of the spectrum. Spectroscope. Varieties of spectra.
Wave theory of light. Polarisation of light. Measurement of the rotation of the plane of polarisation. Polarimeter.
Photometry.

ELECTRICITY.

Electrification by friction and induction. Electroscopes. Electrophorus.
Frictional machines and the Wimshurst machine. Condensers. Disruptive and brush discharges.
Properties of magnets. Molecular theory of magnetism.
Magnetic effects of electric currents. Tangent galvanometer. Sensitive galvanometers of the suspended needle and moving coil types. Ammeters. Electromagnet. Telephone.
Electrolysis and its interpretation by the theory of dissociation. Primary cells. Accumulator.
Electrical potential or pressure. Measurement of potential difference or voltage. Voltmeters.
Ohm's Law. Resistance and electromotive force. Units of measurement. Arrangement of cells in series and in parallel. Simple methods of comparing electromotive forces and resistances. Resistance of conductors in parallel. Potentiometer. Wheatstone's bridge.
Induced currents. Magneto machine and dynamo. Electric motor. Induction coil. Alternating currents. Transformers.
Rate of expenditure of electrical energy in watts and ergs per second. Heat developed by current. Efficiency of electric lamps. Electric arc.
Cathode and X-rays. Simple phenomena of radioactivity.
1923.

PRACTICAL EXAMINATION.

Candidates will be required to carry out such experiments as are indicated in the following list, which is not intended to be exhaustive, but rather to indicate the general type of questions that may be set.

Candidates may be called upon to undergo a *vivâ voce* examination on the use of the usual types of physical apparatus :—

Measurements of length by callipers, micrometer screw, and vernier.
Simple determinations of areas and volumes.
Use of balance weighing to a centigramme.
Determinations of density and specific gravity of solids and liquids.
Hydrometers.
Determination of " g " by the simple pendulum.
Friction.
Velocity of sound by resonance.
Simple measurements by the sonometer.
Comparison of the frequencies of tuning-forks.
The mercury thermometer. Determination of fixed points.
Simple methods for determining specific heat and latent heats.
Determination of dew point and humidity.
Curves of cooling.
Use of simple photometers.
Verification of the laws of reflection and refraction.
Measurements of the focal lengths of mirrors and lenses.
Arrangement of slit, prism, and lenses to obtain a pure spectrum.
Arrangement of two lenses to represent a simple form of telescope or microscope.
Estimation of magnification by simple methods.
Mapping a magnetic field. Null points.
Comparison of magnetic moments.
Measurements of electrical resistance by substitution and by Wheatstone's bridge.
Comparison of electromotive forces of cells.
Electrochemical equivalents.
Simple measurements with ammeters and voltmeters.

Regulations and Synopses relating to the several Examinations of the Examining Board in England by the Royal College of Physicians of London and the Royal College of Surgeons of England applicable to Candidates who have not passed the required Preliminary Examination in General Education before the 1st of January, 1923.

(M.R.C.S., L.R.C.P.)

CHAPTER I.

I. Candidates who desire to obtain the Licence of the Royal College of Physicians of London and the Diploma of Member of the Royal College of Surgeons of England are required:—(1) To complete five years of professional study after passing a recognised Preliminary Examination in General Education, and an Examination in Chemistry and Physics conducted or recognised by the Examining Board in England; (2) to comply with the following Regulations; and to pass the Examinations hereinafter set forth in Chapter II.

II. The Regulations relating to the Preliminary Examination in General Education together with a list of recognised Examinations and the Regulations relating to the Pre-Medical Examination in Chemistry and Physics with a list of Examinations which are recognised by the Board in lieu thereof will be found on pages 57–66.

III. Candidates who have passed the Matriculation Examination of any University recognised for the purpose by the Examining Board in England are exempted from passing any further Preliminary Examination in General Education.

IV. Applications and enquiries with reference to the Examinations for the Licence of the Royal College of Physicians of London and the Diploma of Member of the Royal College of Surgeons of England should be addressed to the Secretary, Examination Hall, 8–11, Queen Square, Bloomsbury, London, W.C. 1, from whom forms of the required Certificates may be obtained.

V. Any communication relating to the Regulations should contain the Candidate's names in full and the date of passing the Preliminary Examination in General Education, and of passing the Pre-Medical Examination or of registration as a Medical Student.

VI. The Examinations will be held in the months of January, March or April, June or July, and September or October, unless otherwise appointed.

VII. Candidates intending to present themselves are required to give notice in writing to the Secretary of the Examining Board in England fourteen clear days before the day on which the Examination commences, transmitting at the same time the required Certificates.

VIII. All fees must be paid three days prior to the day on which the Examination commences.

IX. Exemptions from the conditions of admission to the several Examinations can be granted only by the Committee of Management.

CHAPTER II.

I. There are two Professional Examinations, called herein the First Examination and the Final Examination.

II. The courses of study for these Examinations must not be commenced until the Pre-Medical Examination in Chemistry and Physics or some other Examination in these subjects recognised by the Board has been passed.

III. The Certificates of Professional Study will be required to show that Students have attended the courses to the satisfaction of their Teachers, and that they have attended such examinations as are held during the courses.

FIRST PROFESSIONAL EXAMINATION.

IV. The Subjects of this Examination are:—
   Section I. (a) Anatomy, including Histology and Embryology.
          (b) Physiology, including Bio-Chemistry.
   Section II. Pharmacology, Practical Pharmacy, and Materia Medica.

V. In Section I. the Examination is partly written, partly oral, and partly practical: in Section II. the Examination is oral only.

Synopses indicating the range of the subjects of this Examination will be found on pages 73 and 74.

VI. Candidates may present themselves for the two Sections together or separately, but they must take Parts (a) and (b) of Section I. together until they have passed in one or both Parts. Candidates will not be allowed to pass in one Part unless they obtain at the same time at least half the number of marks required to pass in the other Part.

Section II. of the Examination may be passed at any time before the Candidate enters for the Final Professional Examination.

VII. Before admission to the First Professional Examination Candidates must produce evidence
   Of having attended:—
For Section I.
   1. Courses of instruction in Anatomy, including Embryology, during five terms, during which they must have dissected the whole body.
   2. Courses of instruction in Physiology, including General Biology, Bio-Chemistry, and Bio-Physics, during five terms.
   3. A course of instruction in Histology.
For Section II.
   4. Courses of instruction in Pharmacology, Practical Pharmacy, and Materia Medica.

   [Instruction in Practical Pharmacy must be given by a registered Medical Practitioner, or by a Member of the Pharmaceutical Society of Great Britain, or in a Public Infirmary, or Dispensary.]

VIII. Candidates referred in either or both Parts of Section I. will be required, before being admitted to re-examination, to produce a Certificate that they have pursued, to the satisfaction of their Teachers, in a recognised Medical School, their studies in one or both Parts as the case may be, during a period of not less than three months subsequent to the date of their reference.

IX. Candidates referred in Section II. will be required, before being admitted to re-examination, to produce a Certificate that they have pursued, to the satisfaction of their Teachers, in a recognised Medical School, their studies in this Section during a period of not less than three months subsequent to the date of their reference.

X. The fees for admission to the First Examination are as follows:—

	£	s.
For the whole Examination on first admission to either Section	10	10
For re-examination after rejection in Section I.	6	6
For re-examination after rejection in either part of Section I.	3	3
For re-examination after rejection in Section II.	3	3

XI. Candidates who produce satisfactory evidence of having passed an Examination for a Degree in Medicine in the subjects of Section I. or of either Part of Section I. and of Section II. of the First Examination conducted at any University in the British Empire, or at a Foreign University recognised by the Examining Board in England, will be exempted from further examination in such subject or subjects.

FINAL PROFESSIONAL EXAMINATION.

XII. The subjects of the Final Professional Examination are:—

Section I. (a) Pathology, including Morbid Anatomy, Morbid, Histology, and Clinical Pathology.

(b) Bacteriology.

Section II. Part I. Medicine, including Medical Anatomy, Forensic Medicine, and Public Health.

Part II. Surgery, including Surgical Anatomy and the use of Surgical Appliances.

Part III. Midwifery and Gynæcology.

XIII. The Examination in Section I. is partly written, partly practical, and partly oral.

XIV. The Examination in Section II. Parts I. & II. is partly written, partly clinical, partly practical, and partly oral.

XV. The Examination in Section II. Part III. is partly written and partly oral.

XVI. Candidates may take Sections I. & II. and the three Parts of Section II. of this Examination separately, or they may present themselves for the whole Examination at one time. They will be required to produce the Certificates mentioned in Paragraph XIX. before being admitted to the respective Parts of the Examination.

XVII. Candidates who have passed· both Sections of the First Professional Examination will be admissible to either Section or any Part of Section II. of the Final Examination at the expiration of two and a half years (30 months) from the date of passing Section I. of the First Professional Examination on production of the Certificates required for the Section or Parts (see Paragraph XIX. p. 71), provided that the whole Examination is not completed before the expiration of five academic years of professional study (57 months) including three academic years of Clinical Work at a recognised Medical School and Hospital after passing Section I. of the First Professional Examination.

XVIII. Before admission to the Final Examination, Candidates will be required to produce evidence that they have completed the following courses of study after passing Section I. of the First Professional Examination :—

1. Of having attended at a recognised Medical School and Hospital—
   (*a*) A course. of Pathology, including Morbid Anatomy and Histology.
   (*b*) A course of instruction in the performance of post-mortem examinations. (Candidates will be required to produce evidence that they themselves have performed post-mortem . examinations.)
   (*c*) A course of Clinical Pathology.
   (*d*) A course of Bacteriology.
   (*e*) A course of practical instruction in Clinical Medicine.
   (*f*) A course of Practical Surgery, including Mechano-therapeutics.
   (*g*) A course of instruction in Forensic Medicine.
   (*h*) A course of instruction in Mental Diseases.
   (*i*) A course of instruction in Public Health, including Preventive Medicine and Hygiene, with practical demonstrations.
   (*j*) A course of instruction in the administration of Anæsthetics, the Certificate to include evidence that the Candidate himself has administered anæsthetics under supervision.
   (*k*) A course of instruction in Midwifery and· Gynæcology.
   (*l*) Instruction in Applied Anatomy and Applied Physiology.
   (*m*) A course of Operative Surgery.

2. Of having attended at a recognised Hospital—
   (*a*) General Out-patient and In-patient Hospital Practice, including Clinical Lectures, during 21 months.
   (*b*) Six months' Medical Clinical Clerkship, of which not less than three months shall have been in the Wards.
   (*c*) Six months' Surgical Dressership, of which not less than three months shall have been in the Wards.
   (*d*) Three months' Gynæcological Clerkship.
       Candidates will be required to produce the following Certificate, viz. :—
       " It is hereby certified that.................has attended as Clinical Clerk in the Obstetric and Gynæcological Wards and Out-patient Department for a period of three months, and has under my supervision carried out his Clinical Studies, including the examination of such a number of pregnant women and Gynæcological patients as in my opinion qualifies him to present himself for the Final Examination in Midwifery and Gynæcology."

3. Of having attended 5 Labours conducted by a Teacher or Member of the Staff of an approved Hospital and of having subsequently conducted 15 other Labours.

NOTE.—This Certificate must be signed by a Member of the Staff of of a Lying-in Hospital or of a Maternity Department of a General Hospital, or by the Dean of the Medical School attached to the General Hospital.

4. Of having received instruction in Children's Diseases and in the care of Infants for a period of three months at a recognised General Hospital or at a Children's Hospital recognised by the Examining Board in England for the purpose.

5. Of having attended for three months in each of the following Special Departments of recognised General Hospitals or at Special Hospitals recognised for the purpose :—

  (a) Eye.
  (b) Throat, Nose, and Ear.
  (c) Skin.

6. Of having received instruction in Venereal Diseases at a recognised Hospital.

7. Of having received instruction in Radiology at a recognised Hospital

8. Of having attended a course of instruction, including Clinical Demonstrations, at a recognised Fever Hospital.

9. Of having attended a course of instruction, including Clinical Demonstrations, at a recognised Mental Hospital.

10. Of having received instruction in Vaccination.

  The certificate must be such as will qualify its holder to contract as a Public Vaccinator under the Regulations, at the time in force, of the Ministry of Health.

11. Of being 21 years of age.

XIX. Candidates will be required to produce the following Certificates before being admitted to the respective parts of the Examination, viz. :—

Section I. (a) & (b). Pathology and Bacteriology.
  Of having attended the courses prescribed in Chapter II. Paragraphs XVIII.
  Clauses 1 (a) (b) (c) (d), 2 (a) (b) (c) (d).

Section II. Part I. Medicine.
  Of having attended the courses prescribed in Chapter II. Paragraph XVIII.
  Clauses I (a) (b) (c) (d) (e) (g) (h) (i) (l), 2 (a) (b), 4, 5 (a) & (c), 6, 7, 8, 9, 10, & 11.

Section II. Part II. Surgery.
  Of having attended the courses prescribed in Chapter II. Paragraph XVIII.
  Clauses 1 (a) (b) (c) (d) (f) (g) (j) (l) (m), 2 (a) (c), 5 (a) (b) (c), 6, 7, 10, & 1¹.

Section II. Part III. Midwifery and Gynæcology.
  Of having attended the courses prescribed in Chapter II. Paragraph XVIII.
  Clauses 1 (a) (b) (c) (d) (g) (h) (j) (k) (l), 2 (a) (b) (c) (d), 3, 4, 6, 9, 10, & 11.

XX. Candidates referred in the Final Examination, or in one or more of the Sections or Parts into which they may have divided it, will not be admitted to re-examination until after the lapse of a period of not less than three months from the date of rejection. They will be required, before being admitted to re-examination, to produce a Certificate in regard to Pathology and Bacteriology of having received further instruction in these subjects at a recognised Medical School during the period of their reference ; in regard to Medicine and Surgery, of having attended the Medical and Surgical Practice, or the Medical or Surgical Practice as the case may be, at a recognised Hospital during the period of their reference ; and in regard to Midwifery and Gynæcology, of having received further instruction in these subjects from a recognised Teacher during the period of their reference.

NOTE.—A Candidate who possesses a registrable qualification is admissible to re-examination without producing additional Certificates.

XXI. The fees for admission to the Final Examination are as follows :—

	First admission.	Each subsequent admission.
	£ s.	£ s.
Section I. Pathology and Bacteriology	4 4	3 3
Section II. { Part I. Medicine	10 10	6 6
Part II. Surgery	10 10	6 6
Part III. Midwifery and Gynæcology	6 6	4 4

XXII. Candidates who produce satisfactery evidence of having passed an Examination for a Degree in Medicine in the subjects of Pathology and Bacteriology at any University in the British Empire or at a Foreign University recognised by the Examining Board in England will be exempted from passing Section I. of the Examination.

XXIII. Every Candidate who shall have passed the Final Examination and who shall have paid the required fees, including the fee for any part of a Professional Examination from which he may have been exempted is, subject to the Bye-laws of the two Royal Colleges, entitled to receive :—

The Licence of the Royal College of Physicians of London, and

The Diploma of Member of the Royal College of Surgeons of England.

CHAPTER III.

SPECIAL REGULATIONS.

I. Candidates who have obtained Qualifications in the British Empire or in Foreign Countries which entitle them to practise Medicine or Surgery in the country where such Qualifications have been conferred, after a course of study and examination equivalent to that required by the Regulations of the Board, will, on the production of satisfactory evidence as to age, and proficiency in Vaccination, and on payment of the required fees, be admissible to the First and Final Examinations without any intervals between them.

II. Members of English, Scottish, or Irish Universities who have passed such an examination or examinations at their Universities as shall comprise the subjects of the First Examination and of Section I. of the Final Examination of the Examining Board in England, and who have completed the curriculum of Medical

Study according to the Regulations required by the Board or by their Universities, will be eligible for admission to a Part or Parts of Section II. of the Final Examination of the Board at the expiration of 30 months from the date of passing in Anatomy and Physiology, provided they do not complete the Examination until the full curriculum of five academic years of study from the date of passing in Chemistry and Physics has been completed including three years of clinical study after passing the Examination in Anatomy and Physiology.

Any Candidate so admitted to examination will be required to pay a fee of Five Guineas on first admission, which will cover his examination in all three parts of Section II., and, on completion of the Examination, such Candidate shall, on further payment of not less than Thirty-five Guineas and subject to the Bye-Laws of each College, be entitled to receive the Licence of the Royal College of Physicians of London and the Diploma of Member of the Royal College of Surgeons of England.

III. Members of other Universities in the British Empire or in Foreign Countries recognised from time to time for the purpose* who have passed such an Examination or Examinations at their Universities for the Degree of Doctor or Bachelor of Medicine or Surgery as shall comprise the subjects of the First Examination and of Section I. of the Final Examination of the Examining Board in England, and who have completed the curriculum of Medical Study required by the Regulations of the Board, will be admissible to a Part or Parts of Section II. of the Final Examination of the Board 30 months after passing in Anatomy and Physiology, provided that the Examination is not completed until the full curriculum of five academic years of study from the date of passing in Chemistry and Physics has been completed, including three years of Clinical Study after passing the Examination in Anatomy and Physiology.

Any Candidate so admitted to examination will be required to pay the fees prescribed in Paragraph XXI. Chapter II. of the Regulations; and any such Candidate who shall have passed the Final Examination shall, on further payment of not less than Fourteen Guineas and subject to the Bye-Laws of each College, be entitled to receive the Licence of the Royal College of Physicians of London and the Diploma of Member of the Royal College of Surgeons of England.

Forms of Certificates required under the conditions of Paragraph II. may be obtained of the Secretary of the Examining Board in England, Examination Hall, Queen Square, Bloomsbury, London, W.C. 1.

SYNOPSES.

FIRST PROFESSIONAL EXAMINATION.

I. Anatomy.

The Examination in Anatomy will include

1. Descriptive and Topographical Anatomy.
2. Histology. The structure of the tissues of the body : the structure of the organs of the body : recognition of microscopical preparations of the tissues and organs.

* A list of these Universities will be found on pp. 106–108.

3. Embryology. (*a*) The maturation and fertilization of the ovum: (*b*) The development of the ovum until the formation of the membranes: (*c*) The broad outlines of the development of the organs and systems of the human body.

Candidates are expected to have practised, and to be familiar with, general histological methods, including the examination of fresh tissues, the fixing and hardening of tissues and organs, the cutting, staining, and mounting of sections. They may be called upon either to perform or to describe any of these methods.

II. Physiology.

The Examination in Physiology will include

1. The Physiology of Digestion, Absorption, Circulation, Respiration, Secretion, Nutrition, Animal Heat, and Animal Motion. The Function of the Nervous System and Sense-Organs. Reproduction.
2. Bio-Chemistry. The composition of Food, and of the Tissues, Secretions, Excretions, and other Fluids of the body.

Candidates are expected to be able to practise at the Examination the usual methods of chemical and physical examination of the various fluids and solids of the food and of the animal body, as well as the special tests by which the more important substances (both inorganic and organic) occurring in the body are detected and estimated.

Candidates may further be required to show an acquaintance with the mode of action and methods of employment of the commoner kinds of apparatus which are used in physiological work, especially in regard to the investigation of muscle, the heart, the pulse, and respiration.

III. Pharmacology, Practical Pharmacy, and Materia Medica.

1. Candidates will be required to recognise the drugs and preparations in Schedule A.
2. Candidates will be required to know the constitution and the chemical and physical properties of the drugs in Schedule B, in so far as these properties are of practical importance in Medicine.

Candidates will be required to show a competent knowledge of the pharmacological action and doses of the drugs in Schedule B, and of the prepaiations of these drugs. Experimental evidence as to the mode of action of drugs, therapeutics, pharmacy, and pharmaceutical details as to the modes of preparation of drugs will form no part of the examination.

SCHEDULE A.

Mercury subchloiide.
Mercury with chalk.
Arsenious anhydride.
Arsenical solution.
Potassium permanganate.
Ferrous sulphate.
Iron and ammonium citrate.
Iodine.
Ether.
Chloroform.

Paraldehyde.
Amyl nitrite.
Aromatic spirit of ammonia.
Chloral hydrate.
Carbolic acid.
Camphor.
Liniment of camphor.
Quinine sulphate.
Opium.
Ergot.
Oil of turpentine.
Creosote.
Compound senna mixture.

SCHEDULE B.

Ammonium carbonate, ammonium chloride, ammonium acetate.
Potassium carbonate, potassium bicarbonate, potassium citrate.
Sodium sulphate, acid sodium phosphate.
Magnesia, magnesium sulphate.
Calcium carbonate.
Silver nitrate.
Copper sulphate.
Zinc sulphate.
Lead acetate.
Alum.
Bismuth carbonate, bismuth oxychloride.
Barium sulphate.
Sodium hypochlorite, chloramine-T.
Iron, iron sulphate, iron perchloride, iron and ammonium citrate.
Potassium permanganate, hydrogen peroxide.
Mercury, mercury subchloride, mercuric chloride.
Arsenious anhydride.
Arsenobenzol, neoarsenobenzol.
Antimony tartrate.
Potassium bromide, potassium iodide, iodine, iodoform.
Hydrochloric acid, citric acid, caustic potash.
Gentian, calumba, senega.
Croton oil, castor oil, phenolphthalein. cascara sagrada, aloes, senna, rhubarb,
    jalap, colocynth, sulphur, liquid paraffin.
Tannic acid, kino.
Male fern, santonin, pelletierine tannate, oil of chenopodium.
Cod-liver oil, dried thyroid, pituitary extract, adrenalin hydrochloride.
Colchicum.
Digitalis, strophanthus, squill.
Caffeine, theobromine, theocine.
Amyl nitrite, sodium nitrite, nitroglycerin.
Ipecacuanha, emetine.
Nux vomica, strychnine.
Opium, morphine, codeine, apomorphine.
Belladonna, atropine, hyoscine, homatropine.
Physostigmine.
Cocaine, ethocaine (novocaine).

Cinchona bark, quinine.
Rectified spirit, ether, chloroform, ethyl chloride, nitrous oxide.
Chloral hydrate, paraldehyde, barbitone.
Hexamine, oil of copaiba.
Ergot.
Carbolic acid, cresol, creosote.
Phenacetin, sodium salicylate, salol, acetylsalicylic acid.
Formaldehyde solution, paraform, menthol, camphor, thymol, oil of turpentine, cantharidin, mustard.

IV. Syllabus of the course of GENERAL BIOLOGY required under Chapter II. Paragraph VII. 2 on page 68.

1. The Cell—its structure and properties.
2. The general structure, comparative physiology, and life-history of lower types of plants and animals (e. g., Hæmatococcus, Spirogyra, Saccharomyces, Bacteria, Amœba, Paramœcium, and Monocystis).
3. The general structure of Hydra and Lumbricus as illustrative of the diploblastic and triploblastic Invertebrata.
4. The general structure and elementary physiology of Vertebrata, as illustrated by Scyllium and Rana. The elements of the structure and functions of the chief animal tissues.
5. The elementary facts of evolution, heredity, and variation. The relations of plants and animals to their environment, parasitism, and saprophytism.

FINAL PROFESSIONAL EXAMINATION.

Synopsis of Forensic Medicine.

Privileges and obligations of Medical Practitioners. Medical Registration. Medical Certificates and Notifications. Medical Evidence. Dying Declarations. Procedure relating to Coroners' Inquests.

Signs of death and the phenomena which follow death. Putrefaction in air. Putrefaction in water. Mummification. Formation of Adipocere. Inspection of the dead body and post-mortem examination.

Medico-legal aspects of identification.

Modes of dying. Causes of sudden death.

Death from the following causes :—Wounds and mechanical injuries. Hanging. Strangulation. Suffocation. Drowning. Electrical current and Lighting. Starvation.

Indications of death from Accident, Suicide or Homicide. Methods of recognition of blood-stains.

Poisoning.—Medico legal duties of Medical Practitioners in cases of poisoning. Symptoms and post-mortem appearances produced by the common inorganic, organic, and gaseous poisons, and the treatment of the patient.

Method of post-mortem examination in cases of poisoning, and reservation of parts of the body for analysis.

Simple tests for common poisons. The Sale of Poisons.

Medico-legal questions relating to Pregnancy, Delivery, Rape, Criminal Abortion, Infanticide.

The Lunacy Laws in so far as they affect the Medical Practioner in relation to the signing of Certificates of Lunacy.

Regulations relating to the Education and Examination of Candidates for the Diploma of Fellow.

(F.R.C.S.)

SECTION I.

EXAMINATIONS.

1. The Examination for the Fellowship is divided into two parts, viz.: The First Examination and the Second Examination.

2. The subjects of the First Examination are Anatomy and Physiology, and the questions on these subjects may require an elementary acquaintance with Comparative Anatomy and Physiology. The Examination is partly written and partly *vivâ voce*, and is held twice in the year, in the months of June and December.

3. The subjects of the Second Examination are Surgery, including Surgical Anatomy and Pathology. The Examination is partly written and partly *vivâ voce*, and includes the examination of Patients and the performance of operations on the dead body. It is held twice in the year, in the months of May and November.

SECTION II.

FEES.

·1. The fees for examination are as follows :—

	First admission.	Re-examination.
	£ s. d.	£ s. d.
First Examination	8 8 0	5 5 0
Second do.	12 12 0	12 12 0

2. Of such examination-fees Twenty Guineas will be reckoned as the fee or part of the fee payable upon admission to the Fellowship.

3. The fee to be paid upon admission to the Fellowship is Thirty Guineas, except when the Candidate is a Member of the College, in which case the fee is Twenty Guineas.

SECTION III.

Conditions of admission to the First Examination.

I. A Member of the College is admissible to the First Examination at any time after receiving his Diploma of Membership.

II. A Candidate, who is not a Member of the College but who has passed Parts I, II, and III (Chemistry, Physics, and Elementary Biology) of the First Examination and Part I (Anatomy and Physiology) of the Second Examination of the Examining Board in England by the Royal College of Physicians of London· and the Royal College of Surgeons of England is admissible to the First Examination on the production of the following Certificates, viz.:—

1. Of having been engaged in the acquirement of professional knowledge during not less than three Winter Sessions after registration as a Medical Student by the

General Medical Council or after passing a Preliminary Examination in General Education recognized by the Conjoint Examining Board in England.

2. Of having dissected at a recognized Medical School or Schools for a period of not less than eighteen months.

Note.—Dissections during the regular vacations will be accepted, provided the Certificate shows that they have been performed under the superintendence of an authorized Teacher in a Medical School.

III. A Candidate, who is neither a Member of the College nor has passed the First and Second Examinations of the Conjoint Examining Board in England, but who is a Member of a University recognized under the Regulations of the Conjoint Examining Board, is admissible to the First Examination on the production of the following Certificates, viz. :—

1. Of registration as a Medical Student by the General Medical Council or of having passed a Preliminary Examination in General Education recognized by the Conjoint Examining Board in England.

2. Of having passed Examinations for a Degree in Medicine at a recognized University comprising the subjects of Parts I, II, and III (Chemistry, Physics, and Elementary Biology) of the First Examination, and Part I (Anatomy and Physiology) of the Second Examination of the Conjoint Examining Board in England.

3. Of having been engaged in the acquirement of professional knowledge during not less than three Winter Sessions after registration as a Medical Student or after passing a recognized Preliminary Examination in General Education.

4. Of having attended lectures on Anatomy during one Winter Session at a recognized Medical School.

5. Of having dissected at a recognized Medical School or Schools for a period of not less than eighteen months during the ordinary Sessions or Terms.

Note.—Dissections during the regular vacations will be accepted, provided the Certificate shows that they have been performed under the superintendence of an authorised Teacher in a Medical School.

6. Of having attended lectures on Physiology during one Winter Session at a recognized Medical School.

7. Of having attended at a recognized Medical School :—(a) a course of Experimental Physiology, (b) a course of Chemical Physiology, (c) a course of Histology.

NOTE.—By (a) it is meant that the learners themselves shall, individually, be engaged on the necessary experiments, manipulations, &c.; but it is not hereby intended that the learners shall perform vivisections.

SECTION IV.

Conditions of admission to the Second Examination.

I. A Member of the College is admissible to the Second Examination at any time after having passed the First Examination, on producing satisfactory evidence of having been engaged not less than six years in the study (or study and practice) of the profession.

II. A Candidate, who is not a Member of the College but who possesses a qualification recognized by the Council for the purpose *, is admissible to the Second Examination, after having passed the First Examination, on the production of evidence of having been engaged in the study (or study and practice) of the profession for not less than four years subsequent to the date of obtaining the recognized qualification, one year of which shall have been spent in attendance upon the Surgical Practice of a recognized Hospital or Infirmary.

Note I.—*In compliance with the conditions of the Charter, the Diploma of Fellow is not conferred upon successful Candidates until they have attained the age of twenty-five years.*

Note II.—*The Diploma of Fellow is granted to successful Women Candidates, subject to the provisions of the Medical Act,* 1876, *and of the Bye-Laws of the College.*

N.B.—All communications with reference to the Examinations for the Diploma of Fellow should be addressed to Mr. F. G. Hallett, Secretary of the Examining Board in England, Examination Hall, Queen Square, Bloomsbury, London, W.C. 1, to whom intending Candidates should send applications and certificates at least 14 days before the commencement of an Examination.

Fees should be paid at least three days before an Examination.

N.B.—Books of Questions set at the Examinations for the Diploma of Fellow from 1912 to 1920 may be had on application to the Publishers, Messrs. Taylor and Francis, Red Lion Court, Fleet Street, E.C., price 2s. 6d. each; Post-free, 2s. 7d. Books of Questions for 1921 and 1922 may also be obtained from Messrs. Taylor and Francis, price 9d. each; Post-free, 10d.

---

* These qualifications are the registrable Surgical and Medical Degrees of the following Universities, viz.:—Oxford, Cambridge, Durham, London, Victoria University of Manchester, Birmingham, Liverpool, Leeds, Sheffield, Bristol, Wales, Edinburgh, Aberdeen, Glasgow, St. Andrews, Dublin, Royal University of Ireland, National University of Ireland, Queen's University of Belfast, Sydney, Melbourne, Adelaide, New Zealand, Allahabad, Calcutta, Bombay, Madras, Punjab, McGill University of Montreal, Laval University of Quebec, Dalhousie University of Nova Scotia, University of Manitoba, University of Malta, University of Hong Kong, the Italian Royal Universities, and the Imperial University of Japan; and the Surgical and Medical Degrees of the University of Toronto and the Queen's University of Kingston, Ontario, if held together with the Diploma of the College of Physicians and Surgeons of the Province of Ontario.

Regulations relating to the Special Course of Study and Examination in Ophthalmology for Fellows of the College.

F.R.C.S. (with Ophthalmology).

1. The Examination comprises Anatomy, Physiology, and Optics in their relation to Ophthalmology; Clinical and Pathological Ophthalmology and Ophthalmic Operations.

2. The Examination consists of (a) two written papers; (b) a written and *vivâ voce* examination on patients; (c) operations; (d) *vivâ voce* examination upon pathological and anatomical specimens, and upon Ophthalmology in general.

3. The Examination will be held in June and December.

4. Candidates must be Fellows of the Royal College of Surgeons of England, or have passed the Second Professional Examination for the Diploma of Fellow.

5. Candidates must produce evidence of having held the Office of Clinical Assistant, House Surgeon, or Registrar for a period of two years, at an Ophthalmic Hospital recognised by the College for the purpose or in the Ophthalmic Department of a recognised General Hospital, after obtaining a registrable Medical and Surgical Qualification.

(NOTE.—*No Hospital or Department containing less than ten beds for eye cases will be recognised.*)

6. The conditions of clause 5 may be modified at the discretion of the Court of Examiners in the case of a candidate (a) who holds, or has held, the appointment of Ophthalmic Surgeon or Assistant Ophthalmic Surgeon to a Hospital, Infirmary, or Dispensary; (b) who has carried out original investigations in any branch of the Examination; (c) who has written a thesis or published work on any subject of the Examination; (d) whose studies or practice have extended over a prolonged period of time without fulfilling the exact conditions.

7. Candidates must give four weeks' notice of their intention to present themselves for examination to the Director of Examinations, Examination Hall, 8–11 Queen Square, Bloomsbury, London, W.C. 1, and forward at the same time the evidence required by clause 5.

8. The fee for admission or re-admission to the Examination is £10 10s., and must be paid to the Director of Examinations three days before the Examination commences.

9. A Candidate who passes the Examination will receive a Certificate entitling him to describe himself as F.R.C.S. (with Ophthalmology).

Regulations of the Council.

ELECTION TO THE FELLOWSHIP OF MEMBERS OF TWENTY YEARS' STANDING.

1. The chief ground of recommendation for this mode of admission to the Fellowship shall be distinction in Surgery or in the Sciences relating to Surgery ; but under certain special circumstances, to be stated by the Members of the Council proposing the Candidate, other grounds of recommendation may be entertained.

2. The recommendation of Members for this mode of admission to the Fellowship shall be made on a printed form prepared for the purpose.

3. The forms shall be bound in a book, to be called the BOOK OF RECOMMENDATIONS, each form being duly numbered, and on no account to be removed from the book, which is to be accessible only to Members of the Council and to the Secretary.

4. No other form of recommendation shall be permitted ; no personal application to the Council or to the Secretary shall be entertained ; and no direct Candidature shall be sanctioned.

5. On the election of a Member to the Fellowship in this manner, the fact of his admission, with the date, shall be entered in the Recommendation Book and be signed by the President and the Secretary, and the election shall be recorded by a distinctive mode of entry in the List of Fellows.

6. A book shall be kept by the Secretary, in which Members of the Council may enter names of Members of the College who may be possible nominees for election to the Fellowship in this manner.

7. The description of a Fellow elected in this manner shall be F.R.C.S. or F.R.C.S.Eng., and not F.R.C.S.Eng. (*hon. causâ*).

See also Bye-Laws, Sect. XXI. p. xcii.

Regulations relating to the Licence in Dental Surgery.

(L.D.S., R.C.S.Eng.)

(*These Regulations apply to all Candidates who pass the Preliminary Examination in General Education on or after the 1st January, 1923.*)

CHAPTER I.

PRELIMINARY EXAMINATION IN GENERAL EDUCATION AND PRE-MEDICAL EXAMINATION IN CHEMISTRY AND PHYSICS.

1. Candidates for the Licence in Dental Surgery of the Royal College of Surgeons of England are required to pass one of the Examinations in General Education recognized by the Conjoint Examining Board in England, and the Pre-Medical Examination in Chemistry and Physics conducted by that Board or one of the examinations recognized in lieu thereof, before they commence the curriculum of professional study for the Licence extending over four years.

2. Candidates who produce evidence of having been registered by the General Medical Council as Medical or Dental Students on or after the 1st January, 1923, will be considered to have passed the required Preliminary Examination in General Education and the Pre-Medical Examination.

3. Candidates who hold the Degree of D.M.D. Harvard, D.D.S. Pennsylvania, D.D.S. Michigan, D.D.S. Illinois, D.D.S. St. Louis, Missouri, D.D.S. North Western University, Chicago, D.D.S. Minnesota, or the Licence of the Dental Board of Victoria, Australia, are not required to pass these Examinations. 1923.

G

CHAPTER II.

FIRST PROFESSIONAL EXAMINATION.

1. The First Professional Examination consists of Part I. Dental Mechanics, Part II. Dental Metallurgy, and Part III. Section (a) General Anatomy and Physiology, Section (b) Dental Anatomy and Physiology, and is held in January or February, April, and September or October in each year.

2. Candidates may present themselves for the several Parts of the First Professional Examination together or separately, but before admission to any part of the Examination they must produce evidence of having passed the required Preliminary Examination in General Education and the required Pre-Medical Examination or a certificate of having been registered as a Medical or Dental Student by the General Medical Council.

Part I.—Dental Mechanics.

3. This Examination is a practical one, conducted in the Mechanical Laboratory of one of the Dental Hospitals in London.

4. Candidates must give twenty-one days' notice in writing of their intention to present themselves for the Examination, and at the same time forward certificates :—

(1) Of having been engaged, during a period of not less than two years, in acquiring a practical familiarity with the details of Dental Mechanics. One year at least of this study must be taken in the Mechanical Department of a recognized Dental Hospital where the arrangements for teaching Dental Mechanics are satisfactory to the Board of Examiners in Dental Surgery. Part or the whole of the rest of the course may be taken as a pupil with a competent dentist provided that time spent as a private pupil shall be at least twice the time required for the corresponding instruction taken at a Dental School.

This instruction may be taken prior to the date of passing the Examination in General Education and the Pre-Medical Examination, but will not be counted as part of the required four years of professional study unless taken after passing the Pre-Medical Examination.

(2) Of having attended at a recognized Dental Hospital and School :—

(a) A course of lectures on Dental Mechanics.

(b) A course of Practical Dental Mechanics, including the manufacture and adjustment of 6 dentures and 6 crowns.

5. At the Examination in Dental Mechanics candidates will be required to provide themselves with the following instruments :—Wax spatula, double-ended : sculptors : gouge : vulcanite files : gold files : pliers, pin-roughing, bending, and collar : metal cutting shears : plate cutters : plate perforator : broaches : chasing punches : riveting hammer : fret saw frame and saws : Melotte's moldine outfit : mouth blowpipe : solder tweezers : crown holder : borax slab : dividers.

The following instruments will be supplied by the Hospital at which the candidates are examined :—Hammers for striking up plates : horn mallets : ordinary casting materials and apparatus : Bunsen burner.

6. Any candidate referred at this Examination, who does not hold a registrable Dental Qualification, will be required, before admission to re-examination, to produce a certificate of having received three months' further instruction under the conditions specified in Certificate (1) paragraph 4.

Part II.—*Dental Metallurgy.*

7. This Examination is conducted by written paper. A synopsis will be found on pages 88–89.

8. Candidates must give twenty-one days' notice in writing of their intention to present themselves for the Examination, and at the same time forward a certificate :—

Of having attended at a recognized Dental Hospital and School:—

(a) A course of lectures on Dental Metallurgy.

(b) A course of Practical Dental Metallurgy.

9. Any candidate referred at this Examination, who does not hold a registrable Dental Qualification, will be required, before admission to re-examination, to produce a certificate of having received, subsequently to the date of reference, not less than three months' instruction in Dental Metallurgy in a recognized Dental School.

Part III.—(a) *General Anatomy and Physiology.*

(b) *Dental Anatomy and Physiology.*

10. This Examination is partly written and partly oral. Synopses for Section (a) will be found on pages 90–91.

11. Candidates may enter for Section (a) only or for Sections (a) and (b) together on producing the required certificates, but they will not be allowed to proceed with Section (b) until they have passed in Section (a). In the case of a Candidate who enters for both Sections and fails in Section (a) the fee paid for admission to Section (b) will not be forfeited, but will be credited to the candidate on re-admission to examination in that Section. Candidates who enter for both Sections together may pass in Section (a) although failing to pass in Section (b).

12. Candidates must give twenty-one days' notice in writing of their intention to present themselves for the whole or for one Section of this Examination and at the same time forward certificates :—

(1) For Part III (a).

Of having attended at a recognized Medical School :—

(a) Courses of instruction in Anatomy, including special demonstrations on prepared dissections during three terms.

(b) A course of dissections, to include, if possible, the head, and neck, during one term.

(c) Courses of instruction in Physiology, including General Biology, Bio-Chemistry, and Bio-Physics, during three terms.

(d) A course of instruction in Histology.

(2) For Part III (b).

Of having attended at a recognized Dental School :—

(a) A course of instruction in Dental Anatomy and Physiology.

(b) A separate course of instruction in Dental Histology, including the preparation of Microscopical Sections.

13. A candidate referred at this examination, who does not hold a registrable Dental Qualification, will be required before re-admission to Section (a) to produce a certificate of three months' additional study of Anatomy and Physiology at a recognized Medical School, and will be required before re-admission to Section (b) to produce a certificate of three months' additional study of Dental Anatomy and Physiology at a recognized Dental School.

Exemptions.

14. Candidates who have passed Section I. of the Professional Examination of the Conjoint Examining Board in England, or who produce evidence of having passed the examination in Anatomy and Physiology for a degree, or other qualification, in Medicine or Surgery, registrable under the Medical Act of 1886, or for the degree of M.B. or M.D. of a Foreign or Colonial University recognized by the Conjoint Examining Board in England, are not required to pass Section (a).

CHAPTER III.

Second Professional Examination.

1. The Second Professional Examination is held in February, May or June, and November in each year, and consists of:—

Part I. General Surgery and Pathology.

Part II. Dental Surgery and Pathology, and Practical Dental Surgery.

2. Candidates who have passed the First Professional Examination at least six months previously may present themselves for Part I. only on producing the certificates mentioned in paragraph 6 of this Chapter, or they may enter for the whole Examination at one time on producing the certificates mentioned in paragraphs 6 and 10 of this Chapter.

(*The interval of six months is not required in the case of a Colonial or Foreign Dentist.*)

3. Candidates must pass in Part I. before proceeding to Part II.

4. Candidates who enter for the whole Examination at one time may pass in Part I. although failing to pass in Part II.; but, if they fail to pass in Part I., they will not be allowed to proceed with the Practical and Oral Examinations in Part II. In such cases the fee paid for admission to Part II. will not be forfeited, but will be held over until such time as the candidate is re-admitted to examination in that Part.

Part I.—*General Surgery and Pathology.*

5. This Examination is partly written and partly oral. Synopses will be found on pages 91–93.

6. Candidates must give twenty-one days' notice in writing of their intention to present themselves for this Examination, and at the same time forward certificates :—

(1) Of having attended at a recognized Medical School —:

(a) A course of instruction in Surgery during two terms.

(b) A course of instruction in Medicine during two terms.

(c) A course of instruction in General Pathology (including Bacteriology) during two terms.

These courses of instruction must be attended after the completion of the courses in Anatomy and Physiology.

(2) Of having acted as Surgical Dresser in the Out-Patient Department of a recognized Hospital for three months.

(3) Of having attended, at a recognized Hospital or Hospitals, the practice of Medicine and Surgery, including clinical lectures, for 12 months.

(4) Of being 21 years of age.

7. Any candidate referred at this Examination, who does not hold a registrable Dental Qualification, will be required, before admission to re-examination, to produce a certificate of such additional study during three months at a recognized Medical School and Hospital as the Teachers of the School may determine.

EXEMPTIONS.

8. Candidates, who are Members of the College, or who have passed the Examination in Surgery of the Conjoint Examining Board in England, or who produce evidence of having passed the Examination in Surgery for a Degree, or other Qualification, in Medicine or Surgery registrable under the Medical Act of 1886, are not required to pass Part I. of the Second Professional Examination.

Part II.—*Dental Surgery and Pathology.*

9. This Examination is partly written, partly oral, and partly practical. The oral examination is conducted by the use of preparations, casts, drawings, &c. At the practical examination candidates may be examined :—

(a) On the treatment of Dental Caries, on the preparation and treatment of teeth by filling with gold or other material, by inlaying or by crowning, and on other operations in Dental Surgery.

(*Candidates must provide their own instruments.*)

(b) On the treatment of abnormalities of position of the teeth of children.

(c) On Clinical cases.

10. Candidates must give twenty-one days' notice in writing of their intention to present themselves for this Examination, and at the same time forward certificates :—

(1) Of having been engaged during four years in the acquirement of professional knowledge subsequently to the date of registration as a Medical or Dental Student, or of having passed the Pre-Medical Examination conducted or recognized by the Conjoint Examining Board in England.

(2) Of having attended at a recognized Dental Hospital and School :—

    (a) A course of Dental Surgery and Pathology.
    (b) A separate course of Practical Dental Surgery.
    (c) A course of Dental Bacteriology.
    (d) A course of Dental Materia Medica.
    (e) A course of practical instruction in the administration of such Anæsthetics as are in common use in Dental Surgery.

(3) Of having attended at a recognized Dental Hospital and School, or in the Dental Department of a recognized General Hospital, the practice of Dental Surgery during two years.

. 11. Any candidate referred at this Examination, who does not hold a registrable Dental Qualification, will be required before admission to re-examination to produce a certificate of three months' additional study at a recognized Dental Hospital.

CHAPTER IV.

FEES.

. 1. The fee for the Diploma in Dental Surgery is Twenty Guineas.

. 2. The fees payable before admission to the several Examinations are as follows :—

	Each admission.		
	£	s.	d.
First Professional Examination :			
Part I.—Dental Mechanics	5	5	0
Part II.—Dental Metallurgy	1	1	0
Part III.—(a) Anatomy and Physiology..	3	3	0
(b) Dental Anatomy and Physiology	3	3	0
Second Professional Examination :			
Part I.—General Surgery	3	3	0
Part II.—Dental Surgery	5	5	0
	£21	0	0

3. Fees paid on first admission to the several Examinations, or Parts thereof, will be counted as the fee, or part of the fee, of Twenty Guineas for the Diploma according to the amount so paid.

4. The balance of the fee of Twenty Guineas must be paid before the grant of the Diploma in cases in which candidates have been exempted from some part of the Examinations.

Note.—*A ticket of admission to the Museum, to the Library, and to the College Lectures will be presented to each Candidate who obtains the Diploma.*

Candidates are requested to note that they do not become Licentiates in Dental Surgery of the College on passing the Second Professional Examination; that it rests with the Council of the College to confer the Diploma upon candidates who have become qualified for the Licence by fulfilling the requirements of the Regulations and by paying the required fees; and that, until the grant of the Diploma by the Council, they are not entitled to make use of the description L.D.S., R.C.S.Eng. (or L.D.S.Eng.), the right to which is only acquired with the grant of the Diploma.

N.B.— All applications with reference to the Examination for the Licence in Dental Surgery should be addressed to Mr. F. G. Hallett, O.B.E., Secretary of the Examining Board in England, Examination Hall, Queen Square, Bloomsbury, London. W.C. 1.

Books of Questions set at the Examinations for the Licence in Dental Surgery from 1912 to 1920 may be obtained on application to Messrs. Taylor and Francis, Red Lion Court, Fleet Street, London, E.C. 4, price 2s. 6d. each; Post-free 2s. 8d. Books of Questions for 1921 and 1922 may also be obtained from Messrs. Taylor and Francis, price 9d. each; Post-free, 10d.

LIST OF RECOGNIZED DENTAL HOSPITALS AND SCHOOLS.

LONDON.

Royal Dental Hospital of London.—University College Hospital Dental School. —Guy's Hospital Dental School.—London Hospital Dental School.

PROVINCIAL.

Birmingham Dental Hospital and Birmingham University Dental Department.—Liverpool Dental Hospital, and Liverpool University Dental School.— Dental Hospital of Manchester, and Victoria University of Manchester Dental Department.—Newcastle-on-Tyne Dental Hospital.—Bristol Royal Infirmary and General Hospital and Bristol University Dental Department—Sheffield Royal Hospital, and Sheffield University Dental Department.—Leeds General Infirmary, and Leeds University Dental Department.

SCOTLAND.

Edinburgh Dental Hospital and School; Glasgow Dental Hospital and School.

IRELAND.

Dental Hospital and School of Ireland, Dublin; University College, Cork.

UNITED STATES OF AMERICA.

Harvard University Dental Department and Hospital.—Pennsylvania University Dental Department and Hospital.—Michigan University Dental Department and Hospital.—University of Illinois Dental Department and Hospital.—St. Louis University School of Dentistry.—North-Western University Dental Department, Chicago.—University of Minnesota Dental Department.

LIST OF HOSPITALS RECOGNIZED FOR DENTAL HOSPITAL
PRACTICE BUT UNATTACHED TO A DENTAL SCHOOL.

LONDON.

St. Thomas' Hospital Dental Department. — Westminster Hospital Dental
Department.

PROVINCIAL.

Newcastle-on-Tyne Royal Infirmary Dental Department.— Plymouth Denta l
Hospital.—Exeter Dental Hospital.

SYNOPSES.

(These Synopses will shortly be revised.)

FIRST PROFESSIONAL EXAMINATION.

DENTAL METALLURGY.

The physical properties of the Metals--Gold, Platinum, Palladium, Silver, Tin,
Antimony, Mercury, Lead, Bismuth, Zinc, Cadmium, Copper, Aluminium, Iron,
Nickel : viz. :—Lustre ; Tenacity ; Elasticity ; Malleability ; Ductility ; Conductivity for Heat and Electricity ; Fusibility: Specific gravity ; Specific heat ; Expansion by heat ; Brittleness ; Hardness ; Crystalline character ; Change of Volume
on Solidification.

Action of Air (either hot or cold), of Water, of Acids, of Alkalis and of
Sulphuretted Hydrogen on the above metals and their principal alloys and
amalgams.

Effect of the exposure of the above metals, their alloys and amalgams, in the
mouth.

Gold.—Preparation and properties of pure Gold. Cohesive and non-cohesive Gold.
Precipitated and spongy Gold. Assay of Gold. Calculation of amount of
base metal to be added to reduce the fineness of Gold to a given carat, or of
the amount of fine Gold or of Gold of high carat needed to be added to raise
the fineness of an Alloy to a given carat. The detection and estimation of
Gold in Alloys. The Purple of Cassius. The effect of impurities on the
properties of Gold. The properties of the alloys of Gold. Composition of
Solders for Gold.

Platinum —Preparation and properties of Platinum. Platinum-Black and spongy
Platinum. Detection and estimation of Platinum in Alloys. Alloys of
Platinum with Iridium, Gold, Silver, and other metals. Dental Alloy.

Palladium.—Preparation and properties of Palladium and its combination with
Silver, Gold, and Mercury.

Silver.—Preparation and properties of pure Silver. Assay of Silver by cupellation and in the wet way. Preparation and properties of the combinations of Silver and Copper, Gold, Platinum, and Mercury. Composition and preparation of Solders for Silver. Electroplating.

Tin.—Preparation and properties of Tin. Detection of Tin in Alloys. Preparation and properties of the Alloys of Tin. Its combinations with Zinc, Copper, and Mercury. Composition and melting-points of readily fusible Alloys.

Antimony.—Preparation and properties. Properties of Alloys.

Mercury.—Preparation and properties of pure Mercury. Testing the purity of Mercury. Vermilion and detection of impurities therein. Preparation and properties of Amalgams of the various Metals mentioned in this Synopsis. Composition and preparation of the principal Alloys which have been used for preparing Dental Amalgams. Methods of testing such Amalgams, as to the causes of their change of volume, permanence in the mouth, and change of colour. Effects of different Metals in these Amalgams. Possible action of Amalgam fillings on other metals used in the mouth.

Lead.—Preparation and properties. Effect of alloying on its properties. Solders and soft Soldering.

Bismuth.—Preparation and properties. Alloys.

Zinc.—Preparation, purification, and properties. Preparation of Zinc Oxide, Zinc Chloride, and the various materials for the Oxychloride, Oxyphosphate, and Oxysulphate Cements. Action of Acids and Alkaline Solutions on Cements in the Mouth. Alloys of Zinc.

Cadmium.—Properties, its advantages and disadvantages in Alloys and Amalgams.

Copper.—Preparation and properties. Effect of impurities on its properties. Alloys. Modes of preparation and properties of Copper Amalgams. Preparation of Sullivan's Amalgam and its modifications.

Aluminium.—Preparation and properties of Aluminium and Aluminium-Bronze. Solders for Aluminium and Aluminium-Bronze.

Nickel.—Preparation and properties. Alloys. German Silver. Nickel-plating.

Iron.—Differences between Cast Iron, Wrought Iron, and Steel. Effect of presence of impurities in Iron. Hardening, tempering, annealing, and burning Steel.

Methods of testing Metals and Alloys for their various properties as described in the first paragraph.

Methods of testing Dental Amalgams for changes of volume. Effect of Sulphuretted Hydrogen, Water, Air, Acids, and Alkalis on Dental Amalgams.

Methods of parting Gold from Silver ; rough tests for fineness of Gold Alloys (touchstone) ; of preparation of Gold Alloy of required fineness ; of recovery of Gold from scraps ; of preparation of Solders for Gold ; of recovery of Platinum and Silver from scraps ; of preparation of pure Silver ; of preparation of Amalgam Alloys containing two or more of the following metals—Silver, Tin, Gold, Platinum, Copper, Zinc ; of preparation of readily fusible Alloys, containing two or more of the metals Tin, Lead, Bismuth, Mercury, Cadmium, Antimony, and Zinc.

Methods of determining melting-points of readily fusible Alloys ; of preparation of Alloys recommended for Dies and Counter Dies.

Description of Furnaces and Muffles used in Metallurgy.

Theory and varieties of Blow-pipes and Fluxes.

Colouring and Gilding Gold.

Purification of Sweep or Lemel.

ANATOMY.

The Bones.—Classification, structure, development, and uses of Bones. Identification of the bones (excluding hand and foot). Precise knowledge of the Bones of the Head and Neck.

Joints.—Varieties of Joints ; structures entering into a joint. Temporo-Mandibular Joint ; Joints of the Spine, Clavicle, and Shoulder.

Muscles and Fasciæ.—The naked-eye anatomy of a Muscle. Modes of attachment. Relations and actions of Muscles of mastication, deglutition, expression, and respiration. The Fasciæ of the Upper Limb and of the Head and Neck.

Circulatory System.—The Heart, its structure ; the arrangement of its cavities ; valves ; relations of the Heart. Pericardium. The arrangement of the principal arteries and veins of the body. Position, course, relations, and distribution of the vessels of the Head and Neck.

Nervous System.—Main divisions of the Brain. Naked-eye anatomy of the Spinal Cord, and of a Spinal Segment with its nerve-roots. Cranial and Spinal nerves. General arrangement of the Sympathetic Nervous System. Course, relations, and distribution of the Cranial Nerves. The Cervical and Dorsal Spinal Nerves. Cervical and Brachial Plexuses.

Organs of Special Sense. The **Eye**—Structure of the eyeball ; its vascular and nerve supply ; intrinsic and extrinsic muscles. **The Eyelids**—Lacrymal Apparatus. The **Nose**—Nasal Fossæ, and accessory cavities. Nasal Mucous Membrane ; vascular and nervous supply. The **Ear**—An elementary knowledge of the External, Middle, and Internal Ear.

The Face and Neck.—Lips, Mouth, Tongue, Salivary Glands, Palate, Tonsils, Pharynx, Œsophagus. Larynx, Trachea, Thyroid Body, Thyro-lingual Duct. Cervical Lymphatic Glands with the areas drained by them. The Triangles of the Neck with their boundaries and contents.

Thoracic and Abdominal Viscera.—Their structure, general arrangement, and relations. The Thoracic Duct.

PHYSIOLOGY.

Histology.—The Epithelial, Connective, Muscular, and Nervous tissues. The Buccal and Lingual Mucous Membranes and the Salivary Glands.

Contractile Tissues.—Their mode of action and relation to nerves ; Voluntary and Involuntary Muscular contraction ; Tetanus ; Rigor mortis.

The Blood.—Its structure, composition, and uses. Coagulation ; arterial and venous blood. The chemistry and combinations of Hæmoglobin. The gases of the blood.

Circulatory System.—Mechanics of the circulation of the blood. Blood pressure. The pulse.

Structure and mode of action of the Heart, Arteries, Veins, Capillaries. General plan of the Systemic, Pulmonary, and Portal circulations. Influence of the Vagus and Sympathetic Nerves on the actions of the heart and vessels.

Lymphatic System. — General arrangement of the Lymphatic and Lacteal Systems. Structure and function of Lymphatic Glands and Tonsil.

Respiration.— Mechanism of Respiration. Principal muscles concerned in tranquil and in forced respiration. Control of respiration by the Nervous system. Chemical changes in blood and air. Interchange of gases. Dyspnœa : Death by suffocation.

Alimentation. Digestion.—Composition and uses of the various secretions discharged into the mouth, stomach, and intestines. Chemistry of simple foods, *e. g.* bread, meat, milk ; their digestion, absorption, and destination. Classification of food-stuffs.

The muscular and nervous mechanism of Mastication, Deglutition, Peristalsis, Defæcation, Vomiting.

Nutrition.—General plan and action of a secreting gland, with its nerves and vessels. Secretion and Excretion. The Liver as a secretory and excretory organ. Glycogen. Metabolism in general.

The Urine.—Its composition ; variations in amount and specific gravity. Sources and meaning of its components.

The Skin and its Appendages.—Structure and Functions.

Animal Heat.—Maintenance and regulation of animal heat. The normal temperature. Cold-blooded and warm-blooded animals.

Nervous System.—General plan of Cerebro-spinal and Sympathetic systems. White and grey nerve-matter, and their general disposition in brain and cord. Nerve-centres and their uses. Actions of various kinds of nerves, *e. g.* motor, sensory, vasomotor. Reflex action.

Special Senses.—Component parts of the eyeball. The eye as an optical instrument. Variations in the pupil; how affected. Reception of an image by the eye. Vision.

Ear.—Its general structure. Mode of conduction of sound-vibrations.

Taste. Touch. Smell.—The special Structures for the reception of the impressions for these senses.

The Vocal Apparatus.—The production of voice. Speech.

Development.—An elementary knowledge of the development of the face and neck.

SECOND PROFESSIONAL EXAMINATION.

SURGERY AND SURGICAL PATHOLOGY.

Micro-organisms.—Elementary knowledge of, in their relation to Pathological processes.

Inflammation.—Causes. Vascular and structural changes. Clinical signs and constitutional symptoms. Terminations.

Boil. Abscess. Carbuncle.

Ulceration.—Nature of process. Chief varieties of Ulcers of Skin.

Sinus and Fistula.

Gangrene.—Causes. Varieties.

Erysipelas.—Sapræmia. Septicæmia. Pyæmia.

Tetanus.—Causes and symptoms.

Tuberculosis.—Modes of infection. Changes in the tissues. Terminations. General principles of treatment.

Tuberculosis of Lymphatic glands and of Bone.

Actinomycosis.—Modes of infection. Signs and treatment when occurring in head and neck.

Syphilis.—Modes of infection.   Stages, symptoms, and treatment of acquired and congenital forms.
Hæmorrhage.—Varieties.   Arrest of Hæmorrhage.
Hæmophilia.
Syncope. Collapse. Shock.
Wounds.—Classification.   Processes of healing.   Treatment.
Fractures.—Causes, varieties, signs, and symptoms.   Process of union.
General principles of treatment.
Signs and treatment of fractures of the bones of the face.
Joints.—General signs and treatment of Dislocations.   Special knowledge of dislocation of Shoulder-joint and of Temporo-maxillary joint.
Blood-vessels.—Injuries of vessels and their consequences.   Atheroma.
Calcification of Arteries.   Causes and chief forms of Aneurism.
Varicose veins.   Thrombosis and Embolism.
Nerves.—Results of injury to nerves.   Common causes of Paralysis.
Neuritis. Neuralgia.
Special knowledge of affections of Vth and VIIth cranial nerves.
New Growths.—Meaning of terms " innocent " and " malignant."
General structure and classification of Tumours.   Diagnosis and treatment of the more common Tumours.
Cysts.—Varieties and classification.   Diagnosis and treatment of Cysts of the Head and Neck.
Diseases of Bones.—Periostitis, osteitis, osteomyelitis, caries, necrosis.   Symptoms and treatment of diseases of the bones of the face.
Tumours of Bone.
Rickets.—Causes and signs.   Changes in bone.
Scurvy.
Surgical affections of the Head and Neck.—Wounds of Head and Neck.   Cut-throat.   Foreign bodies in the air-passage and in the food-passage.   Dysphagia, Dyspnœa.   Laryngotomy and Tracheotomy.
Diseases of the Lymphatic Glands in the Neck.
Diseases of Temporo-Mandibular Joint.   Closure of Jaws.
Mouth and Lips. — Stomatitis — causes, varieties, symptoms, treatment.
Salivary calculus.   Ranula and other cysts of mouth.   Hare-lip.
Epithelioma.   Herpes.   Syphilis.   Tubercle.   Nævus.   Papilloma.
Cancrum oris.
Oral sepsis; its influence in the causation of disease.
Tongue.—Glossitis, acute and chronic.   Papilloma.   Epithelioma.   Ulcers.
Gumma.   Wounds of Tongue.
Palate.—Cleft Palate.   Tumours of Palate.   Ulceration.   Necrosis.
Tonsils.—Varieties of Tonsillitis, diagnosis, consequences, and treatment.
Chronic enlargement of tonsils.   Ulceration of Fauces.
Gums.—Surgical affections, causes, diagnosis, and treatment.
Maxillary and Frontal Sinuses.—Surgical affections, causes, diagnosis, and treatment.
Nose and Pharynx.—Inflammatory affections.   Ozœna.   Polypi.   Foreign body in Nose.   Lupus and syphilis of Nose.   Rodent ulcer of Nose and Face.
Epistaxis.
Adenoid vegetations.
Parotid and Submaxillary Salivary Glands.—Surgical affections.

Submaxillary Cellulitis.
Larynx.—Scald. Spasm of glottis. Œdematous Laryngitis. Diphtheritic membrane in nose, throat, or larynx.
Neck.—Torticollis. Causes of Stiff-neck. Caries of cervical vertebræ. Cervical abscess. Bronchocele.
Eye.—Conjunctivitis. Iritis. Corneal ulcers and opacities. Ptosis. Strabismus.
Anæsthetics: with special reference to their use in Dental Surgery.
Preparation of a patient for the administration of an anæsthetic.
Artificial Respiration.

Regulations for obtaining the Diploma in Public Health of the Royal College of Physicians of London and the Royal College of Surgeons of England.

(D.P.H., R.C.P.S.Eng.)

(Revised Regulations to apply to all candidates who have not obtained a registrable qualification and commenced the special study of Public Health before the 1st of January, 1924, will shortly be issued.)

Section I.—EXAMINATION.

1. Candidates must have obtained a registrable Qualification in Medicine, Surgery, and Midwifery.
2. The Examination consists of two Parts. Part I. will be held in the months of April, June, and December, and Part II. in the months of January, April, and July, in each year.
3. Candidates must pass Part I. before being admitted to Part II.
4. Candidates may enter for Parts I. and II. separately, or at the same time, but no Candidate's name will be published until both parts of the Examination have been passed.
5. The Examination in each part will be written, oral, and practical *.
* Note.—*The Practical Examination in Part II. may include a visit to, and report on, some selected premises.*
6. The Fee for each admission to either Part of the Examination, which must be paid three days before the Examination commences, is £10 10s., except in the case of Candidates who possess Diplomas granted by the Royal College of Physicians of London or the Royal College of Surgeons of England, who will be required to pay £6 6s. only.
7. Candidates who fail to satisfy the Examiners in either part may present themselves again at the next Examination on payment of the same Fees.
8. The Diploma awarded is entitled "Diploma in Public Health of the Royal College of Physicians of London and the Royal College of Surgeons of England."
9. Candidates intending to present themselves for either part of the Examination must give 14 days' notice in writing to the Secretary, at the Examination Hall Queen Square, Bloomsbury, London, W.C. 1.

Section II.—CONDITIONS OF ADMISSION TO EXAMINATION.

I. *For Candidates who obtained a registrable Qualification on or before the*
1st of January, 1890.

Candidates entitled to be registered under the Medical Act on or before the
1st of January, 1890, will be admissible to the Examination on producing evidence
of the above Qualification.

II. *For Candidates who obtained a registrable Qualification after the*
1st of January, 1890.

Candidates will be admissible to examination in Part I.on producing evidence:—

1. Of having been in possession of a registrable Qualification in Medicine,
Surgery, and Midwifery for at least 12 months.

2. Of having attended, after obtaining such registrable Qualification, practical
instruction in Chemistry, Bacteriology, and the Pathology of the diseases of
Animals transmissible to Man, in a Laboratory or Laboratories recognized by the
Examining Board in England, during a period of six months.

[*Note.*—The certificate of attendance on this course must show that the candidate has worked in the Laboratory for at least 240 hours, of which not more than
half have been devoted to Chemistry.]

Candidates will be admitted to Part II. of the Examination on producing
evidence :—

3. Of having spent not less than nine months in the special study of Public
Health since obtaining a registrable Qualification.

4. Of having, after obtaining a registrable Qualification, been diligently engaged
in acquiring a practical knowledge in the duties, routine and special, of Public
Health Administration on not less than 60 working days during six months under
the supervision of

(*a*) In England and Wales, the Medical Officer of Health of a County or
of a single Sanitary District having a population of not less than 50,000, or
a Medical Officer of Health devoting his whole time to Public Health work ; or

(*b*) In Scotland, a Medical Officer of Health of a County or Counties, or of one
or more Sanitary Districts having a population of not less than 30,000 ; or

(*c*) In Ireland, a Medical Superintendent Officer of Health of a District or
Districts having a population of not less than 30,000 ; or

(*d*) In the British Dominions outside the United Kingdom, a Medical Officer of
Health of a Sanitary District having a population of not less than 30,000, who
himself holds a registrable Diploma in Public Health ; or

(*e*) A Medical Officer of Health who is also a Teacher in the Department ·of
Public Health of a recognized Medical School ; or

(*f*) A Sanitary Staff Officer of the Royal Army Medical Corps having charge of
an Army Corps, District, Command, or Division recognized for this purpose by the
General Medical Council. †

† The following Districts have been recognized by the General Medical Council, viz.:—
 Aldershot; Salisbury Plain; Southern and Western Districts; Dublin and Cork Districts;
  Chatham, Home, and Eastern Districts; North-Eastern and North-Western
  Districts; Scottish District; Gibraltar; Peshawar, Rawalpindi, Lahore, Mhow,
  Poona, Meerut, Lucknow, Secunderabad, and Burma.

(g) An Assistant Medical Officer of Health of a County or of a single Sanitary District having a population of not less than 50,000, provided the Medical Officer of Health of the County or District in question permits the Assistant Officer to give the necessary instruction and to issue Certificates.

₊ Provided that the period of six months may be reduced to a period of three months, including attendance on at least 30 working days in the case of a Candidate who produces evidence that, after obtaining a registrable Qualification, he has attended a course or courses of instruction in sanitary law, vital statistics, epidemiology, school hygiene, and other subjects bearing on Public Health Administration, given by a Teacher or Teachers in the Department of Public Health of a recognized Medical School, or in the case of a Candidate who produces evidence of having been resident Medical Officer in a Hospital for Infectious Diseases containing not less than 100 beds during a period of three months.

Note.—Candidates who shall have produced evidence that they have themselves held for a period of not less than three years appointments as Medical Officer of Health of a Sanitary District within the British Dominions, and having a population of not less than 15,000, may be exempted from the requirement of paragraph 4.

5. Of having attended, twice weekly during three months, after obtaining a registrable Qualification, the practice of a Hospital for Infectious Diseases at which he has received instruction in the methods of Administration.

Note (1).—Methods of Administration shall include the methods of dealing with patients at their admission and discharge, as well as in the wards and the Medical Superintendence of the Hospital generally.

Note (2).—In the case of a Medical Officer of the Royal Army Medical Corps a certificate from a Principal Medical Officer under whom he has served, stating that he has during a period of at least three months been diligently engaged in acquiring a practical knowledge of Hospital Administration in relation to Infectious Diseases, may be accepted as evidence under Regulation 5.

SYLLABUS FOR THE EXAMINATION.

PART I.

Syllabus of Written and Oral Examinations.

Air. Examination of air, recognition and determination of impurities. Moisture in air.

Meteorology. Meteorological instruments and their construction. Causes and conditions which influence climate.

Water. Sources and characters of water. The purification and softening of water supplies. Methods of chemical analysis. Distribution and supply.

Soils. Varieties of, and their relation to geological formations. Interpretation of geological and ordnance survey maps. The relation of soil to Public Health.

Buildings. Principles of building construction in their application to dwellings, hospitals, schools, &c., and the interpretation of plans.

The principles of Ventilation, Warming, and Lighting.
The general principles of Sanitary Engineering, including treatment and disposal of sewage and refuse.
The chemical analysis of sewage and sewage effluents.
Personal Hygiene in relation to diet, exercise, and clothing.
Food. The chemical analysis and microscopical examination of food. The detection of the commoner adulterants, preservatives, and poisons in foodstuffs. The pathology of diseases caused by unwholesome food.
The employment of poisonous substances in various trade processes.
Disinfection.
Bacteriology. General characteristics of micro-organisms. Biology, classification, and morphology of bacteria. Ordinary methods of cultivation and staining. Separation of micro-organisms. Saprophytism and Parasitism. Fermentation and Putrefaction. Specific Toxins. Antitoxins—their preparation and standardization. The preparation of bacterial vaccines. Immunity. General pathology of infection.
Causation and pathology of the specific infective diseases affecting man and common to man and the lower animals.
The pathology and causation of diseases due to moulds and yeasts, and of protozoal infections.
Methods of bacteriological examination of :—
   (a) Air, dust, soil, and sewage ;
   (b) Water (quantitative and qualitative), including methods in use for isolating and identifying the common organisms associated with organic pollution ;
   (c) Milk, butter, and other foods ;
   (d) Animals dead of bacterial disease.
The Animal Parasites infesting man and foodstuffs.

Practical Examination.

Candidates must show a practical knowledge of the ordinary method of bacteriological and chemical analysis as illustrated by the above syllabus.

PART II.

Syllabus of Written and Oral Examinations.   ·

Laws and statutes relative to Public Health and the Model Bye-laws and Regulations of the Ministry of Health : the Statutes relating to the control of Foods and Drugs and the supervision of Midwives. In these subjects the Candidate will be expected to show that he possesses an adequate knowledge of those portions of the Public Health statutes which relate more particularly to sanitary provisions.

The origin, history, pathology, symptoms, methods of propagation, geographical distribution, and control of epidemic, endemic and other preventable diseases at home and abroad.

Unwholesome and dangerous trades, the diseases and conditions to which they give rise, and the prevention of nuisances arising therefrom.

General effects of climate, acclimatisation.

Effects on health of overcrowding, vitiated air, impure air, polluted soil, contaminated water, and bad or insufficient food. Control of meat, milk, and other food supplies. Infantile mortality, its causes and the remedies. The sanitary supervision of Public Elementary Schools, and the general principles of School Hygiene.

Duties and powers of Sanitary Authorities and their officers, in connection with which the Candidate will be expected to show a good knowledge of the routine duty of the Medical Officer of Health and Sanitary Inspector.

Vital Statistics :—Fallacies attending their employment. Calculation of population, birth rate, marriage rate, and death rate ; mortality rates of various diseases ; sickness rates ; relation between occupation and mortality ; life tables,·their construction and interpretation ; the value of statistical facts, averages, and methods.

Practical Examination.

Candidates must show that in knowledge and judgment as to the framing of Reports they are qualified for the work of Medical Officer of Health.

Books of Questions set at the Examinations for the Diploma in Public Health during the years 1887 to 1918 may be obtained on application to Messrs. Taylor and Francis, Publishers, Red Lion Court, Fleet Street, London, E.C.4. Price 6*d.* each, post-free 7*d.* Books of Questions for the years 1919, 1920, 1921, and 1922 may also be obtained from Messrs. Taylor and Francis. Price 9*d.* each, post-free 10*d.*

Regulations for obtaining the Diploma in Tropical Medicine and Hygiene of the Royal College of Physicians of London and the Royal College of Surgeons of England.

(D.T.M. & H. Eng.)

I. The Examination will be held in the months of April, July, and December.

II. The Examination will comprise :—

Written questions, oral questions, and practical work in the following subjects in relation to Tropical Medicine :—pathology, protozoology, helminthology, entomology, clinical medicine, clinical surgery, and hygiene.

III. The fee for admission to the Examination is £9 9*s.*

IV. Candidates must give 14 days' notice in writing to the Secretary, at the Examination Hall, Queen Square, Bloomsbury, London, W.C.1, and produce at the same time the necessary certificates of study.

1923. H

V. Candidates must produce evidence of being in possession of a registrable qualification in Medicine, Surgery, and Midwifery, and of having attended subsequently to obtaining such registrable qualification :—

> (1) practical instruction in pathology, protozoology, helminthology, entomology, bacteriology, and hygiene in relation to Tropical Medicine in an institution recognized for this purpose during not less than three months;
>
> (2) the clinical practice of a hospital recognized for the study of Tropical Diseases during not less than three months.

VI. Graduates in Medicine or Surgery of Indian, Colonial, and Foreign Universities recognized by the Examining Board in England, whose degrees are not registrable in this country, may enter for the Examination for the Diploma in Tropical Medicine and Hygiene on fulfilling the same conditions in regard to study.

VII. The above conditions of study may be modified at the discretion of the Committee of Management in the cases of a candidate (*a*) who has been employed in Foreign or Colonial Medical Service; (*b*) who has been engaged in professional work in tropical countries; (*c*) who produces evidence of having been engaged in original investigations in Tropical Medicine or Hygiene.

Syllabus of the Examination.

(1) The methods of examination of tissues, blood, secretions, excretions, parasites, and other organisms in relation to Tropical Medicine.

The characters and life-history of protozoa, helminths, arthropoda, fungi, bacteria, and other organisms in relation to tropical diseases.

(2) Medicine in relation to tropical diseases.

(3) Hygiene of the Tropics in relation to climate, race, food, water, soil, and waste matter.

(4) Hygiene of the Tropics in relation to towns, buildings, plantations, irrigation, and shipping.

(5) Reclaiming of swamps and low-lying lands.

(6) Sanitary measures dealing with communicable tropical diseases.

Books of Questions set at the Examinations for the Diploma in Tropical Medicine during the years 1912-1915 may be obtained on application to Messrs. Taylor and Francis, Red Lion Court, Fleet Street, London, E.C. 4.   Price 6*d.*, post-free 7*d.* each.   Books of Questions for 1920, 1921 and 1922 may also be obtained from Messrs. Taylor and Francis.   Price 9*d.* each, post-free 10*d.*

Regulations for obtaining the Diploma in Ophthalmic Medicine and Surgery of the Royal College of Physicians of London and the Royal College of Surgeons of England.

(D.O.M.S., R.C.P.& S.Eng.)

I. Both Parts of the Examination will be held in the months of January and July.

II. The Examination shall comprise :—

Part I. (*a*) Anatomy and Embryology of the Visual apparatus (including the contents of the orbit, the bones in the neighbourhood thereof, and the central nervous system so far as it relates to vision).

(*b*) Physiology of Vision.

(*c*) Elementary Optics.

Part II. (*a*) Optical defects of the eye.

(*b*) Ophthalmic Medicine and Surgery.

(*c*) Pathology with special reference to Medical and Surgical Ophthalmology.

III. The Examination will be written, oral, and practical in Part I. and Part II. (*a* & *c*), and written, oral, and clinical in Part II. (*b*).

IV. Candidates may enter for Part I. of the Examination at any time after a registrable qualification in Medicine, Surgery, and Midwifery has been obtained.

(Candidates must present themselves for the whole of Part I. In the event of failure in one division only, candidates will be allowed to present themselves for re-examination in that division.)

V. Candidates may enter for Part II. of the Examination on the completion of one year of special study of Opthalmology after a registrable qualification in Medicine, Surgery, and Midwifery has been obtained, provided that Part I. has been previously passed, and on production of the following certificates :—

(*a*) Of having specially studied Ophthalmic Medicine and Surgery and General Medicine in its relation to Ophthalmology for a period of twelve months.

(*b*) Of having been engaged in the investigation and correction of error of refraction.

(*c*) Of having attended the Clinical practice of a recognized Ophthalmic Hospital or of the Ophthalmic Department of a recognized General Hospital for twelve months.

(The conditions of this certificate (*c*) will be fulfilled by holding the appointment as House Surgeon or House Physician or as Clinical

Assistant at one of the above Hospitals or Departments, provided that in the case of a Clinical Assistant the certificate shows that he has attended for at least three hours a day on two days of the week.)

(d) Of having attended a practical course of Operative Ophthalmic Surgery.

(e) Of having attended a course of Pathology and Bacteriology with special reference to Ophthalmic Medicine and Surgery.

VI. The fee for admission or re-admission to each part of the examination is £6 6s.

VII. Candidates must give 14 days' notice in writing of their intention to present themselves for Examination, to the Secretary at the Examination Hall, 8–11 Queen Square, Bloomsbury, London, W.C. 1, forwarding at the same time, in the case of Part I., evidence and date of obtaining a registrable qualification, and, in the case of Part II., the necessary certificates of study.

VIII. Graduates in Medicine or Surgery of Indian, Colonial, and Foreign Universities recognized by the Examining Board in England, but whose degrees are not registrable in this country, may enter for the examination for the Diploma in Ophthalmic Medicine and Surgery on fulfilling the same conditions in regard to study.

IX. The above conditions of study may be modified at the discretion of the Committee of Management in the case of a candidate (a) who has carried out original investigations in any branch of the examination, (b) who has written a thesis on the Pathology of the Eye, (c) whose studies have extended over a prolonged period of time without fulfilling the exact conditions ; but exemption will not be granted from any part of the Examination.

Books of Questions set at the Examinations for the Diploma in Ophthalmic Medicine and Surgery during the years 1920, 1921, and 1922 may be obtained on application to Messrs. Taylor and Francis, Red Lion Court, Fleet Street, London, E.C. 4. Price 9d. each, post-free 10d.

Regulations for obtaining the Diploma in Psychological Medicine of the Royal College of Physicians of London and the Royal College of Surgeons of England.

(D.P.M., R.C.P. & S.Eng.)

I. Both Parts of the Examination will be held in the months of June and December.

II. The Examination shall comprise the following subjects, with special regard to their relationship to Psychological and General Medicine :—

Part I. (*a*) Anatomy and Physiology of the Nervous System.
(*b*) Psychology.

Part II. (*a*) Neurology, including Clinical and Pathological Neurology.
(*b*) Psychological Medicine, including its legal relationship.

III. The Examination will be written and oral in Part I. (*a*) and (*b*), written, oral, and clinical in Part II. (*a*) and (*b*).

IV. Candidates may enter for Part I. of the Examination at any time after a registrable qualification in Medicine, Surgery, and Midwifery has been obtained, and the divisions may be taken separately or together. (No special certificates of study will be required for this part, but evidence of holding a registrable qualification, with the date, must be produced.) Candidates must present themselves for the whole of Part II. In the event of failure in one division only, candidates may be allowed at the discretion of the examiners to present themselves for re-examination in that division alone.

V. Candidates may enter for Part II. of the Examination on the completion of a year of special study of Psychological Medicine after a registrable Medical Qualification in Medicine, Surgery, and Midwifery has been obtained, provided that Part I. has been previously passed, and on production of the following certificates :—

(*a*) Of having attended Clinical Instruction for at least two months at a recognized Hospital for Nervous Diseases, or in the Department for Nervous Diseases of a recognized General Hospital.

(*b*) Of having held a resident or whole-time appointment at an Institution for Mental Diseases where Clinical Instruction is given, recognized for the purpose, for a period of six months,

or

of having attended Clinical Instruction in Psychological Medicine at a recognized Institution during twelve months.

VI. The fee for admission or re-admission to each part of the Examination is £6 6s.

VII. Candidates must give 14 days' notice in writing of their intention to present themselves for examination, to the Secretary at the Examination Hall, 8-11 Queen Square, Bloomsbury, London, W.C. 1. They should state, in the case of Part I., whether they desire to enter for both divisions of that Part, and, in the case of Part II., the necessary certificates of study must be produced with the notice.

VIII. Graduates in Medicine or Surgery of Indian, Colonial, and Foreign Universities recognized by the Examining Board in England, but whose degrees are not registrable in this country, may enter for the Examination for the Diploma in Psychological Medicine on fulfilling the same conditions in regard to study.

IX. The above conditions of study may be modified at the discretion of the Committee of Management in the case of a Candidate (a) who has carried out original investigations, or has written a thesis on Psychology or Neurology in relation to Psychological Medicine, (b) whose studies have extended over a prolonged period of time without fulfilling the exact conditions; but exemption will not be granted from any part of the Examination.

Books of Questions set at the Examinations for the Diploma in Psychological Medicine during the years 1920 and 1921 may be obtained on application to Messrs. Taylor and Francis, Red Lion Court, Fleet Street, E.C. 4. Price 9d. each, post-free 10d.

Regulations for obtaining the Diploma in Laryngology and Otology of the Royal College of Physicians of London and the Royal College of Surgeons of England.

(D.L.O., R.C.P. & S. Eng.)

I. Both Parts of the Examination will be held in the months of June and December,

II. The Examination shall comprise :—

Part 1. (*a*) The anatomy, embryology, and physiology of the ear, nose, pharynx, and larynx. (Candidates will be expected to be acquainted with the vascular, lymphatic, and nervous connections of these parts and with the central nervous system in so far as it relates to the special regions concerned.)

(*b*) Elementary acoustics.

Part II. (*a*) The recognition and use of special instruments and appliances.

(*b*) The Medicine, Surgery, and Pathology of the ear, nose, pharynx, and larynx.

III. The Examination will be written, oral, and practical in Part I. and written, oral, practical, and clinical in Part II.

IV. Candidates may enter for Part I. of the Examination at any time after a registrable qualification in Medicine, Surgery, and Midwifery has been obtained. (Candidates must present themselves for the whole of Part I. In the event of failure in one division only, candidates will be allowed to present themselves for re-examination in that division.)

V. Candidates may enter for Part II. of the Examination on the completion of one year of special study of diseases of the ear, nose, pharynx, and larynx, after a registrable qualification in Medicine, Surgery, and Midwifery has been obtained, provided that Part I. has been previously passed, and on production of the following certificates :—

(*a*) Of having attended the Laryngological and Aural Clinical practice of a recognized hospital or of the Laryngological and Otological Departments of a recognized General Hospital for twelve months.

(The conditions of this certificate (*a*) will be fulfilled by holding the appointment as House Surgeon or House Physician or as Clinical Assistant at one of the above Hospitals or Departments, provided that in the case of a Clinical Assistant the certificate shows that he has attended for at least three hours a day on two days of the week.)

(*b*) Of having attended operations to the satisfaction of the Surgeons in charge.

(*c*) Of having received instruction in pathology and bacteriology with special reference to Laryngological and Otological Medicine and Surgery.

VI. The fee for admission or re-admission to each part of the Examination is £6 6s.

VII. Candidates must give fourteen days' notice in writing of their intention to present themselves for Examination, to the Secretary at the Examination Hall, 8–11 Queen Square, Bloomsbury, London, W.C. 1. In the case of Part II., the necessary certificates of study must be produced with the notice.

VIII. Graduates in Medicine or Surgery of Indian, Colonial, and Foreign Universities recognized by the Examining Board in England, but whose degrees are not registrable in this country, may enter for the Examination for the Diploma in Laryngology and Otology on fulfilling the same conditions in regard to study.

IX. The above conditions of study may be modified at the discretion of the Committee of Management in the case of a Candidate (a) who has carried out original investigations, or has written a thesis on some subject in Laryngology or Otology, (b) whose studies have extended over a prolonged period of time without fulfilling the exact conditions; but exemption will not be granted from any part of the Examination.

SYLLABUS OF THE EXAMINATION.

THE EAR.

Congenital deformities.
Wounds and injuries.
Foreign bodies and parasites.
Acute and chronic inflammations and their complications.
Otosclerosis. Tuberculosis. Syphilis.
Simple and malignant new growths.
Varieties of deafness, including deaf mutism—Vertigo—Tinnitus,
Tumours of the auditory nerve.
Malingering.

THE NOSE AND PHARYNX.

Congenital deformities.
Injuries and foreign bodies.
Acute and chronic inflammation. Vaso-motor rhinitis. Retro-pharyngeal abscess.
Nasal obstruction. Adenoid growths.
Acute and chronic inflammation of the nasal sinuses.
Diseases of the tonsils.
Tuberculosis. Syphilis.
Simple and malignant new growths.

THE LARYNX.

Congenital deformities.
Injuries and foreign bodies.
Acute and chronic inflammation.
Disorders of innervation, sensory and motor.
Tuberculosis. Syphilis.
Simple and malignant growths.

Note to Syllabus.—Candidates will be examined on Radiograms; and also will be expected to recognize under the microscope, and growing in or on nutrient media, the organisms common to infections of the above regions.

The following are the Hospitals and Schools of Surgery and Medicine from which Certificates of the Professional Education of Candidates for the Membership and Fellowship will be received by this College, for the year commencing the first of August, 1923.

I. Medical Schools and Hospitals at which the curriculum of professional education may be completed.

ENGLAND AND WALES.

LONDON.—St. Bartholomew's, Charing Cross, St. George's. Guy's, King's College, London, St. Mary's, Middlesex, St. Thomas', University College, Westminster, Royal Free Hospital and London School of Medicine for Women.

Provincial.

BIRMINGHAM.—The University, with General Hospital or Queen's Hospital.
BRISTOL.—The University, with Royal Infirmary or General Hospital.
CAMBRIDGE.—The University, with Addenbrooke's Hospital.
CARDIFF.—The Welsh National School of Medicine, with King Edward VII. Hospital, Cardiff.
DURHAM.—The University, with Newcastle-upon-Tyne Royal Infirmary.
LEEDS.—The University, with General Infirmary.
LIVERPOOL.—The University, with Royal Infirmary, Royal Southern Hospital, David Lewis Northern Hospital, Stanley Hospital, or United Hospitals Clinical School.
MANCHESTER.—The Victoria University, with Royal Infirmary.
NEWCASTLE-UPON-TYNE (*see* Durham).
SHEFFIELD.—The University, with Royal Infirmary or Royal Hospital.

SCOTLAND.

EDINBURGH.—The University, with Royal Infirmary; The School of Medicine, with Royal Infirmary; School of Medicine for Women, with Royal Infirmary.

Provincial.

GLASGOW.—The University, Anderson's College, and St. Mungo's College, with the Royal Infirmary, Western Infirmary, and Victoria Infirmary.
ABERDEEN.—The University, with Royal Infirmary.
ST. ANDREWS.—The University, with the Dundee Royal Infirmary.

IRELAND.

DUBLIN.—Medical Schools : The Royal College of Surgeons, including Carmichael College and Ledwich School; Trinity College ; Catholic University.— Hospitals : Dr. Steevens', Richmond, City of Dublin, Mercer's, Meath, Jervis Street, St. Vincent's, Adelaide, Mater Misericordiæ, Sir Patrick Dun's.

Provincial.

BELFAST.—Queen's University, with Royal Hospital, or Mater Infirmorum Hospital.

CORK.—Queen's College, with North and South Infirmaries.

GALWAY.—Queen's College, with County Infirmary and Town Hospital.

MALTA.
The University.

INDIA.

CALCUTTA.—The Medical College.
MADRAS.—The Medical College.
BOMBAY.—The Grant Medical College.
LAHORE.—Punjab University.
ALLAHABAD.—The University.
CEYLON (Colombo).—The Medical College.

CANADA.

TORONTO.—The University.
MONTREAL.—The University of McGill College ; Bishop's College.
KINGSTON.—Queen's University.
QUEBEC.—Laval University.
WINNIPEG.—The University of Manitoba.
LONDON, ONTARIO.—The Western University.

NOVA SCOTIA.

HALIFAX.—Dalhousie College and University.

AUSTRALIA.

MELBOURNE.—The University of Melbourne, with the Melbourne Hospital and Alfred Hospital.

SYDNEY.—The University of Sydney, with the Sydney Infirmary and Prince Alfred Hospital.

ADELAIDE.—The University of Adelaide, with Adelaide Infirmary.

NEW ZEALAND.

DUNEDIN.—The University of New Zealand, with the Dunedin Hospital.

HONG KONG.
The University.

SINGAPORE.
King Edward VII. Medical School and Hospital.

SOUTH AFRICA.

CAPE TOWN.—The University of Cape Town.
JOHANNESBURG.—The University of Witwatersrand.

FOREIGN COUNTRIES.

FRANCE.

PARIS.—The Medical Faculties of Alger, Bordeaux, Lille, Lyon, Montpellier, Nancy, Paris, Strasbourg, and Toulouse, and the Medical Schools of Marseilles, Nantes, and Rennes.

BELGIUM.

The Universities of BRUSSELS, LIÉGE, and LOUVAIN.

HOLLAND.

The Universities of AMSTERDAM, LEYDEN, GRONINGEN, and UTRECHT.

SWITZERLAND.

The Universities of BERN, BASLE, GENEVA, LAUSANNE, and ZURICH.

ITALY.

The Universities of ROME, BOLOGNA, FLORENCE, GENOA, MILAN, NAPLES, PAVIA, PISA, and TURIN.

RUSSIA.

The Universities of PETROGRAD, KHARKOV, MOSCOW, and WARSAW.

NORWAY.

CHRISTIANIA.—The University.

SWEDEN.

STOCKHOLM.—Royal Caroline Institute.
UPSALA.—The University.

DENMARK.

COPENHAGEN.—The University.

SPAIN.

The Universities of MADRID, SALAMANCA, and SEVILLE.

PORTUGAL.

The Universities of LISBON, COIMBRA, and OPORTO.

JAPAN.

TOKYO.—Imperial University.

UNITED STATES OF AMERICA.

ALBANY.—Union University.
ANN ARBOR.—The University of Michigan.
ATLANTA.—The Emory University.
BALTIMORE.—Johns Hopkins University; University of Maryland
BOSTON.—Harvard University.

BROOKLYN.—Long Island College Hospital.
BUFFALO.—The University.
BURLINGTON.—University of Vermont.
CHARLESTON.—Medical College of the State of South Carolina.
CHARLOTTESVILLE.—The University of Virginia.
CHICAGO.—University of Chicago (Rush Medical College); North-Western University; University of Illinois.
CINCINNATI.—University of Cincinnati.
CLEVELAND.—Western Reserve University.
COLUMBUS.—Ohio State University College of Medicine.
GALVESTON.—University of Texas.
GRAND FORKS.—University of North Dakota School of Medicine.
IOWA.—State University.
LAWRENCE-ROSEDALE.—University of Kansas School of Medicine.
LOUISVILLE.—The University.
MINNEAPOLIS.—University of Minnesota.
MOBILE.—University of Alabama.
NEW HAVEN.—Yale University.
NEW ORLEANS.—Tulane University.
NEW YORK.—The University of New York and Bellevue Hospital Medical College; Columbia University (The College of Physicians and Surgeons); Cornell University.
OMAHA.—Creighton University; University of Nebraska College of Medicine.
PHILADELPHIA.—The University of Pennsylvania; Jefferson Medical College; Women's Medical College of Pennsylvania.
PITTSBURG.—The University.
ROSEDALE.—University of Kansas School of Medicine.
ST. LOUIS.—Washington University; St. Louis University School of Medicine.
SAN FRANCISCO.—Leland Stanford Junior University; The University of California.
SYRACUSE.—The University.
WASHINGTON.—George Washington University; Howard University; Georgetown University.

II. Hospitals recognized for a part of the required attendance on Medical and Surgical Practice, for Medical Clinical Clerkship, and for Surgical Dressership.

ENGLAND AND WALES.

BATH.—Royal United Hospital.
BEDFORD.—County Hospital.
BRADFORD.—Royal Infirmary.
BRIGHTON.—Sussex County Hospital.
CANTERBURY.—Kent and Canterbury Hospital.
CARDIFF.—King Edward VII. Hospital.
COVENTRY.—Coventry and Warwickshire Hospital.
DERBY.—Derbyshire Royal Infirmary.

EXETER.—Royal Devon and Exeter Hospital.
GLOUCESTER.—General Infirmary.
HARTSHILL.—North Staffordshire Infirmary.
HULL.—Royal Infirmary.
LEICESTER.—Royal Infirmary.
NORTHAMPTON.—General Hospital.
NORWICH.—Norfolk and Norwich Hospital.
NOTTINGHAM.—General Hospital.
OXFORD.—Radcliffe Infirmary.
PLYMOUTH.—South Devon and East Cornwall Hospital.
PORTSMOUTH.—Royal Hospital.
READING.—Royal Berkshire Hospital.
SALFORD.—Royal Hospital.
SALISBURY.—General Infirmary.
SHREWSBURY.—Royal Salop Infirmary.
SOUTHAMPTON.—Royal South Hants and Southampton Hospital.
STAFFORD.—Staffordshire General Infirmary.
SWANSEA.—General and Eye Hospital.
WINCHESTER.—Royal Hampshire County Hospital.
WOLVERHAMPTON.—Wolverhampton and Staffordshire General Hospital.
WORCESTER.—General Infirmary.
YORK.—County Hospital.

TASMANIA.

HOBART TOWN.—The General Hospital.
LAUNCESTON.—The General Hospital.

III. Recognized Lunatic Asylums.

BANSTEAD.—London County Asylum.
BEXLEY.—London County Asylum.
BIRMINGHAM.—Borough Asylum.
BRISTOL.—City and County Asylum, Fishponds.
CANE HILL.—London County Asylum.
CLAYBURY.—London County Asylum.
COLNEY HATCH.—London County Asylum.
DARTFORD.—City of London Asylum.
EPSOM.—The Manor Asylum ; The Long Grove Asylum.
HANWELL.—London County Asylum.
HORTON.—London County Asylum.
LONDON.—Bethlem Royal Hospital; Camberwell House Asylum (Dr. W. H.
    B. Stoddart); Bethnal (Dr. J. Kennedy Will); Peckham House
    (Dr. E. D. Macnamara).
MANCHESTER.—Manchester Royal Asylum, Cheadle.
MORPETH.—Northumberland County Asylum.
RAINHILL.—Lancashire County Asylum.
WADSLEY, near Sheffield.—South Yorkshire Lunatic Asylum.
WAKEFIELD.—West Riding Asylum.

IV. Recognized Fever Hospitals.

BARKING.—Isolation Hospital.
BARNSLEY.—The Kendral Hospital for Infectious Diseases.
BIRMINGHAM.—Corporation Fever Hospital.
BOMBAY.—Municipal Infectious Diseases Hospital.
BRIGHTON.—Borough Fever Hospital.
BRISTOL.—Public Health Department Hospitals ; Corporation Fever Hospital.
CAMBRIDGE.—Infectious Diseases Hospital.
CAPE TOWN.—Fever Hospital.
CARDIFF.—Hospital for Infectious Diseases (The Sanatorium).
CHATHAM.—Royal Naval Hospital.
COLCHESTER.—Borough Isolation Hospital.
CROYDON.—Borough Fever Hospital.
DEVONPORT.—Small Pox and Fever Hospitals.
GREAT YARMOUTH.—Fever Hospitals.
LEEDS.—Corporation Fever Hospitals.
LIVERPOOL.—Corporation Fever Hospitals.
LONDON.—Metropolitan Fever Hospitals ; West Ham Fever Hospitals (Plaistow
    and Dagenham); Hornsey Borough Isolation Hospital ; East Ham
    Borough Isolation Hospital.
MANCHESTER.—Corporation Fever Hospital.
NEWCASTLE-UPON-TYNE.—Fever Hospitals.
PORTSMOUTH.—Fever Hospital.
SHEFFIELD.—City Hospitals.
SOUTHAMPTON.—Fever Hospital.
SWANSEA.—Borough Fever Hospital.
WILLESDEN.—District Isolation Hospital.

V. Recognized Ophthalmic Hospitals.

BIRMINGHAM.—Birmingham and Midland Eye Hospital.
LIVERPOOL.—The Eye and Ear Hospital ; St. Paul's Eye and Ear Hospital.
LONDON.—Royal London Ophthalmic Hospital, Moorfields ; Royal Westminster
    Ophthalmic Hospital ; Royal Eye Hospital, Southwark ; Central London
    Ophthalmic Hospital.
SOUTHAMPTON.—The Eye and Ear Hospital.

VI. Laboratories recognized for instruction in Public Health for the Diploma in Public Health.

LONDON.—St. Bartholomew's, Guy's, University College, King's College,
    Charing Cross, St. George's, St. Mary's, Westminster, St. Thomas's,
    Middlesex, Royal Institute of Public Health ; Royal Naval College,
    Greenwich ; Royal Army Medical College, Millbank.
BIRMINGHAM.—The University.

BOMBAY.—The University.
BRADFORD.—The Technical College.
BRIGHTON.—Technical School.
BRISTOL.—University College.
CAMBRIDGE.—The University.
CAPE TOWN.—The University.
CARDIFF.—University College.
EDINBURGH.—School of Medicine of the Royal Colleges of Physicians and Surgeons.
GIBRALTAR.—Sanitary Commissioners' Laboratory.
HONGKONG.—Government Laboratory.
LEEDS.—The University.
LIVERPOOL.—The University School of Science and Technology.
MANCHESTER.—Victoria University.
NEWCASTLE-UPON-TYNE.—University of Durham College of Medicine.
NOTTINGHAM.—University College.
PORTSMOUTH.—The Municipal College.
SHEFFIELD.—The University.

VII. Hospitals recognized for instruction for the Diploma in Ophthalmic Medicine and Surgery.

The Bristol Eye Hospital, Lower Maudlin Street, Bristol.
The Birmingham and Midland Counties Eye Hospital, Church Street, Birmingham.
The Oxford Eye Hospital, Walton Street, Oxford.
Liverpool Eye and Ear Infirmary, Myrtle Street, Liverpool.
The Manchester Eye Hospital.
Government Ophthalmic Hospital, Madras.

FOR PARTIAL COURSES.

Wolverhampton and Midland Counties Eye Infirmary, Wolverhampton. Under V. (*a*), (*b*) and (*c*).
Western Ophthalmic Hospital, Marylebone Road, N.W. 1. Under V. (*b*) and (*d*).

FOR COMPLETE COURSES. (Paragraph V. (*a*) (*b*) (*c*) (*d*) (*e*) of Regulations.)
Royal London Ophthalmic Hospital, City Road, E.C. 1.
Central London Ophthalmic Hospital, Judd Street, W.C. 1.
Royal Eye Hospital, St. George's Circus, Southwark, S.E. 1.
Royal Westminster Ophthalmic Hospital, King William Street, Strand, W.C. 2.

VIII. Institutions recognized for instruction for the Diploma in Psychological Medicine.

FOR CLINICAL INSTRUCTION IN NERVOUS DISEASES. (Paragraph V. (*a*) of Regulations.)

National Hospital for the Paralysed and Epileptic, Queen Square, W.C. 1.
Hospital for Epilepsy and Paralysis and other Diseases of the Nervous System, Maida Vale, W. 9.
Maudsley Hospital.

FOR RESIDENTIAL APPOINTMENT FOR 6 MONTHS OR CLINICAL INSTRUCTION IN PSYCHOLOGICAL MEDICINE FOR 12 MONTHS. (Paragraph V. (*b*) of Regulations.)

(*a*) District, County, Borough, City or Royal Asylums in the United Kingdom.

(*b*) Manchester Royal Lunatic Hospital, Cheadle, Manchester.
Wonford House, Exeter, Devon.
Barnwood House, Gloucester.
Lincoln Lunatic Hospital, The Lawn, Lincoln.
Bethel Hospital, Norwich, Norfolk.
St. Andrew's Hospital, Northampton.
Nottingham Lunatic Hospital, Nottingham.
Warneford Asylum, Headington Hill, Oxford.
Coton Hill Lunatic Hospital, Stafford.
Bethlem Royal Hospital, Lambeth Road, S.E. 1.
Holloway Sanatorium, St. Anne's Heath, Virginia Water, Surrey.
Bootham Park, York.
The Retreat, York.

(*c*) Northumberland Home, Finsbury Park, N. 4, whilst Dr. Bernard Hart is Medical Superintendent.
Haydock Lodge, Ashton, Newton-le-Willows, Lancs., whilst Dr. H. Langdale is Medical Superintendent.

FOR RESIDENTIAL APPOINTMENT FOR 6 MONTHS.

Camberwell House, Peckham Road, S.E. 5.	Heigham Hall, Norwich.
Brooke House, Upper Clapton, E. 5.	Bridlington House, Bristol.
Peckham House, Peckham, S.E. 15.	Ticehurst House, East Sussex.
The Priory, Roehampton, S.W. 15.	Fisherton House, Salisbury.

HONORARY FELLOWS.

HIS MAJESTY KING GEORGE V.
Elected 11th February, 1909, when Prince of Wales

HIS ROYAL HIGHNESS THE PRINCE OF WALES, K.G.
Elected 24th July, 1919.

HIS ROYAL HIGHNESS THE DUKE OF CONNAUGHT, K.G.
Elected 24th July, 1919.

Elected 12th July, 1900.

THE EARL OF ROSEBERY, K.G., K.T. 38 Berkeley-square, W.1.

Elected 25th July, 1900.

BASSINI, EDOARDO, M.D.; Professor of Clinical Surgery, Royal University of Padua. Clinica Chirurgica, Padua.

BERG, JOHN WILHELM, M.D.; Professor of Surgery, Royal Caroline Institute of Medicine and Surgery, Stockholm. Stockholm.

BLOCH, OSCAR THORVALD, M.D.; Professor of Clinical Surgery, University of Copenhagen. Kongl. Frederiks Hospital, Copenhagen.

CAMERON, IRVING HEWARD, M.B.; Professor of Surgery and Clinical Surgery, University of Toronto. 307 Sherbourne-street, Toronto, Ontario, Canada.

CARDENAL FERNANDEZ, SALVADOR, M.D.; Vice-President of the Royal Academy of Medicine and Surgery of Barcelona. Pasaje de Mercader 7 y 9, Barcelona.

D'ANTONA, ANTONINO, M.D.; Professor of Surgery, Royal University of Naples. Via Salvator Rosa 315, Naples.

DURANTE, FRANCESCO, M.D.; Professor of Clinical Surgery, Royal University of Rome. Real Istituto Chirurgico, Rome.

KEEN, WILLIAM WILLIAMS, M.D., LL.D.; Emeritus Professor of Surgery, Jefferson Medical College, Philadelphia. 1520 Spruce-street, Philadelphia, Pa., U.S.A.

KOSINSKY, JULIAN, M.D.; Professor of Clinical Surgery, Imperial University of Warsaw. 41 Królewska, Warsaw.

KÜSTER, ERNST GEORG FERDINAND, M.D., Geh. Med. Rath; Professor of Surgery, University of Marburg. Marburg in Hessen, Germany.

MACEWEN, Sir WILLIAM, C.B., M.D., LL.D., F.R.S.; Regius Professor of Surgery, University of Glasgow. 3 Woodside-crescent, Charing Cross, Glasgow.

NORBURY, Sir HENRY FREDERICK, K.C.B., M.D., R.N. Eltham, Kent.

RAYE, Colonel DANIEL CHARLES O'CONNELL, M.D., I.M.S. 44 Roland Gardens, London, S.W. 7.
1923.

WARREN, JOHN COLLINS, M.D., LL.D.; Moseley Professor of Surgery (Emeritus), Harvard University. 58 *Beacon-street, Boston, Mass., U.S.A.*
WEIR, ROBERT FULTON, M.D.; Professor of Surgery, College of Physicians and Surgeons, Columbia University, New York. 30 *West Fiftieth-street, New York, U.S.A.*

Elected 11th October, 1900.

MACCORMICK, Sir ALEXANDER, M.D.; Lecturer on Surgery, University of Sydney, N.S.W. 185 *Macquarie-street, Sydney, N.S.W.*

Elected 11th March, 1909.

WELIAMINOFF, His Excellency NICOLAS, Privy Councillor; Professor of Surgery, Imperial Military Academy of Medicine, Petrograd. *Fontonsca 33, Petrograd, Russia.*

Elected 31st July, 1913.

BASTIANELLI, RAFFAELE; Professor of Clinical Surgery, Royal University of Rome. *Rue delle Terme 83, Rome.*
BIER, AUGUST; Professor of Surgery, University of Berlin. *Lessingstrasse 1, Berlin N.W. 23, Germany.*
BIRD, FREDERIC DOUGAN, C.B., M.B., B.S.; Lecturer in Surgery, University of Melbourne, 43 *Spring-street, Melbourne, Victoria, Australia.*
CRILE, GEORGE WASHINGTON, M.A., M.D.; Professor of Surgery, Western Reserve University, Cleveland, U.S.A. *Euclid-avenue, at 93rd-street, Cleveland, Ohio, U.S.A.*
CUSHING, HARVEY, M.D.; Professor of Surgery, Harvard University. *Peter Bent Brigham Hospital, Boston, Mass., U.S.A.*
VON EISELSBERG, ANTON FREIBERR, LL.D., M.D.; Professor of Clinical Surgery, University of Vienna. *I Mölkerbastei 5, Vienna, Austria.*
FUCHS, ERNST, M.D.; Professor of Ophthalmology, University of Vienna. *VIII Skodagasse 16, Vienna, Austria.*
HARTMANN, HENRI, M.D.; Professor of Clinical Surgery, University of Paris. 4 *Place Malesherbes XVII, Paris.*
KÖRTE, WERNER, Geheimer Sanitäts-Rath; Director of the Surgical Division of the Urban Municipal Hospital, Berlin. *Kurfurstenstrasse 114, Berlin, W. 62, Germany.*
MAYO, WILLIAM JAMES, M.D., A M., D.Sc., LL.D.; Surgeon, St. Mary's Hospital, Rochester. 427 *West College-street, Rochester, Minn., U.S.A.*
MONPROFIT, AMBROISE, M.D.; Professor of Clinical Surgery, School of Medicine of Angers, University of Paris. 7 *Rue de la Préfecture, Angers, France.*
NICOLAYSEN, JOHAN, M.D.; Professor of Surgery, Royal Fredericks University, Kristiania. *Oscarsgate 43, Kristiania, Norway.*
OPPEL, WLADIMIR ANDREJEVIC: Professor of Surgery, Imperial Academy of Medicine, Petrograd; 23 *Kirotshnaia, Apart. 11, Petrograd, Russia.*
SHEPHERD, FRANCIS JOHN, M.D., C.M., LL D.; Emeritus Professor, Medical Faculty of McGill University. 152 *Mansfield-street, Montreal, Quebec, Canada.*
TUFFIER, Sir THEODORE, K.B.E.: Professeur agrégé de chirurgie à l'Université de Paris. 42 *Avenue Gabriel, Paris.*

Elected 26th July, 1917.

KEOGH, Lieut.-General Sir ALFRED HENRY, G.C.B., G.C.V.O., A.M.S. *Imperial College of Science, South Kensington, S.W. 7.*

Elected 12th February, 1920.

DEPAGE, ANTOINE; Professeur de Pathologie Chirurgicale, Université de Bruxelles.

DUVAL, PIERRE; Professeur à la Faculté de Médicine, Université de Paris. 119 *Rue de Lille, Paris.*

FINNEY, JOHN MILLER TURPIN, M.D.; Professor of Clinical Surgery, Johns Hopkins University. 1300 *Eutaw-place, Baltimore, Maryland, U.S.A.*

MAYO, CHARLES HORACE, M.D., A.M., D.Sc., LL.D.; Surgeon, St. Mary's Hospital, Rochester. *Rochester, Minn., U.S.A.*

DECEASED HONORARY FELLOWS.

Elected 14th June, 1900.

KING EDWARD VII., elected when *Prince of Wales*; died 6th May, 1910.

Elected 12th July, 1900.

ROBERT ARTHUR TALBOT GASCOYNE-CECIL, K.G., 3rd *Marquess of Salisbury*; died 22nd *August*, 1903.

Elected 25th July, 1900.

ALBERT, EDUARD, of *Vienna*; died 26th September, 1900.
BALL, Sir CHARLES BENT, Bart., M.D., M.Ch., of *Dublin*; died 17th March, 1916.
BENNETT, EDWARD HALLARAN, of *Dublin*; died 21st June, 1907.
VON BERGMANN, ERNST, Geh. Med. Rath., of *Berlin*; died 25th March, 1907.
HALSTED, WILLIAM STEWART, M.D., of *Baltimore*, died 7th September, 1922.
HINGSTON, Hon. Sir WILLIAM HALES, M.D., of *Montreal*; died 19th February, 1907.
JAMESON, Surgeon-General JAMES, C.B, M.D., LL.D.; died 13th September, 1904.
KOCHER, THEODOR, of *Bern*; died 27th July, 1917.
KÖNIG, FRANZ, Geh. Med. Rath., of *Berlin*; died 12th December, 1910.
LAMBOTTE, ELIE D. H., of *Brussels*; died 20th April, 1912.
LANNELONGUE, ODILON MARC, of *Paris*; died 22nd December. 1911.
LENNANDER, KARL GUSTAF, of *Upsala, Sweden*; died 15th March, 1908.
MACLEOD, Colonel KENNETH, I.M.S., M.D., LL.D.; died 19th December, 1922.
NICOLAYSEN, JULIUS, of *Christiania*; died 25th December, 1909.
OLLIER, LÉOPOLD, of *Lyons*; died 25th November, 1900.

I 2

PACHOUTINE, VICTOR, of Petrograd; died 2nd February, 1901.
POZZI, SAMUEL, of Paris; died 13th June, 1918.
RODDICK, Sir THOMAS GEORGE, M.D., LL.D., of Montreal; died 20th February, 1923.
RUBIO Y GALI, FEDERICO, of Madrid; died 31st August, 1902.
TILLAUX, PAUL, of Paris; died 20th October, 1904.

Elected 10th January, 1901.

FIELD-MARSHAL EARL ROBERTS, K.G., K.P., V.C.; died 14th November, 1914.

Elected 5th April, 1906.

LUCAS-CHAMPIONNIÈRE, JUST, of Paris; died 22nd October, 1913.

Elected 31st July, 1913.

MURPHY, JOHN BENJAMIN, of Chicago; died 11th August, 1916.

117

REGISTER OF FELLOWS IN CHRONOLOGICAL ORDER.

¶ Fellows elected as Members of 20 years' standing ...   28
§ Fellows by examination, under the Medical Act, 1876   11
* Fellow by examination (with Ophthalmology).........   1
Fellows by examination (*unmarked*) 1,696

Total..............   1,736

1857.
May 23. Teale, Thomas Pridgin.

1861.
Dec. 19. Cooke, John.

1862.
Dec. 11. Brown, Robert Charles (Kt.).

1863.
Dec. 10. Greenhill, Joseph Ridge.

1865.
June 8. Holland, Edmund.

1867.
Dec. 12. Cooper, Clarence.
Cowell, George.

1868.
June 11. Pollock, Edward James
(Kt. 1922).
Dec. 10. Arnott, Henry (Rev.).

9

1869.
June 10. Woodcock, John Rostron.
Tay, Waren.
Bush, John Dearden.
Dec. 9. Mackenzie, George Wellan.

1870.
June 9. Mackenzie, John Thomas.
Edye, Stonard.
Rundle, Henry.
Dec. 8. Stanger, William.

1871.
June 8. Bloxam, John Astley.
Dec. 14. Page, Herbert William.

1872.
June 13. Harvey, William.
Elliott, Arthur Bowes.
Joubert de la Ferté, Charles Henry.
Durham, Frederick.
Cumberbatch, Alphonso Elkin.
Dec. 12. Parker, Rushton.
Pritchard, Urban.

26

1873.
June 19. Lowne, Benjamin Thompson.
Morris, Henry (Bart. 1909).
McCarthy, Jeremiah.
Wiseman, John Greaves.
Warner, Francis.
Dec. 11. Saunders, Henry William.

1874.
June 11. Adams, Josiah Oake.
Cant, William Edmund.
Yate, Edward.
Golding-Bird, Cuthbert Hilton.
Dec. 10. Jessett, Frederic Bowreman.
Hartridge, Gustavus.

1875.
June 10. Ley, John William.
Lowe, Walter George.
Doran, Alban Henry Griffith.
Chicken, Rupert Cecil.
Eastes, Thomas.
Cripps, William Harrison.
Dec. 20. Mackenzie, Lewis.
Jacobson, Walter Hamilton
Acland.
Winterbottom, Augustus.
Barrow, Albert Boyce.

1876.
June 8. May, Bennett.
Lediard, Henry Ambrose.
Osborn, Samuel.
Tweedy, John (Knight 1906).
Morgan, John Hammond.
Godlee, Rickman John (Bart.
1912).
Webber, William Littleton.
Pepper, Augustus Joseph.
Dec. 14. Jackson, George.
Fisher, Frederick Richard.
Odell, William.
Verdon, Henry Walter.
Tyson, William Joseph.
Davies, Francis Joseph.

1877.
June 14. Colgate, Henry.
Harries, Thomas Davies.

1877.
June 14. Bennett, William Henry
(K.C.V.O. 1901).
Rendall, John.
Edmunds, Walter.
Hobson, Lewis John.
Southam, Frederick Armitage.
Dec. 13. Harsant, William Henry.
Verco, Joseph Cook (Kt.).
Cantlie, James (Kt.).

1878.
June 13. Cross, Francis Richardson.
Paul, Frank Thomas.
Firth, Charles.
Harrison, Charles Edward.
Frost, William Adams.
Manders, Horace.
Edwards, Frederick Swinford.
Dec. 12. Cumming, Hugh Gordon.
Treves, Frederick (Bart.1902).
Makins, George Henry
(G.C.M.G. 1918).
Moullin, Charles William
Mansell.
Brown, John.

1879.
June 12. Wherry, George Edward.
Lang, William.
Footner, John Bulkley.
Andrews, William Stratford.
Cheyne, William Watson
(Bart. 1908).
Cathcart, Charles Walker.
Dec. 11. Andrew, George.
Robson, Arthur Wm. Mayo
(Kt. 1918).

1880.
June 10. Pickering, Charles Frederick.
Howlett, Edmund Henry.
Battle, William Henry.
Takaki, Kanehiro.
Paddle, James Isaac.
Dec. 9. Newby, Charles Henry.
Black, James.
Clippingdale, Samuel Dodd.
Dunn, Hugh Percy.

1880.
Dec. 9. Turner, George Robertson.
Whitehead, Hayward Reader.

1881.
June 9. Symonds, Charters James
(K.B.E. 1919).
Carter, Frederick Heales.
Burton, Samuel Herbert.
Turner, Edward Beaden.
Williams, William Roger.
Bowlby, Anthony Alfred (Bt.
1923).
Pollard, Bilton.
Reid, Robert William.
Dec. 8. Haslam, William Frederic.
Shattock, Samuel George.
Uhthoff, John Caldwell.
Griffith, Walter Spencer
Anderson.
Barling, Harry Gilbert.
Gill, Richard.

1882.
June 8. Collier, Mark Purcell Mayo.
Hopkins, John.
Lane, William Arbuthnot
(Bart. 1913).
Poland, John.
Ballance, Charles Alfred
(K.C.M.G. 1918).
Bond, Charles John.
Aug. 3. Fenwick, Edwin Hurry.
Dec. 14. Firth, Robert Hammill
(K.B.E. 1919).
Prowse, Arthur Bancks.
Smith, Thomas Frederick
Hugh.
Dingley, Allen.
Walters, Fredk. Rufenacht.
Lane, James Ernest.

1883.
Mar. 8. Brown, John Macdonald.
June 14. Elam, William Henry.
Dec. 13. Day, Donald Douglas.
Marsh, Frank.
Morrison, James Thomas
Jackman.
Platt, Walter Brewster.

1883.
Dec. 13. Square, James Elliott.
Power, D'Arcy (K.B.E. 1919).
Rand, Richard Frank.

1884.
Feb. 14. Atkin, Charles.
June 12. Collins, William Job (Kt.
1902).
Briggs, Henry.
Evans, William George.
Bull, George Coulson Robins.
Bullar, John Follett.
Holthouse, Edwin Hermus.
Keser, Jean Samuel.
Jennings, Charles Egerton.
Perks, Robert Howell.
Bland-Sutton, John (Kt.
1912).
Knaggs, Robert Lawford.
Nov. 13. Hutchinson, Jonathan.
Dec. 11. Anderson, Alexander Richard
Johnson, George Lindsay.
White, Edwin Francis.
Tait, Henry Brewer.
Colville, Ernest George.
Hewer, Joseph Langton.
Watson, Archibald.
Bull, William Charles.
Wilson, James.

1885.
Mar. 12. Berry, James.
June 11. Barlow, John.
Galpin, George Luck.
Newland-Pedley, Frederick.
Thring, Edward Thomas.
Voss, Francis Henry Vivian.
Worthington, Sidney.
Sancyoshi, Yasuzumi.
Pigeon, Henry Walter.
Wynter, Walter Essex.
Paget, Stephen.
Steedman, John Francis.
Muspratt, Charles Drummond.
Dec. 10. Farnell, Henry Dawson.
Lawford, John Bowring.
Batterham, John Williams.
Hind, Alfred Ernest.

136

178

1885.
Dec. 10. Armstrong-Jones Robert (Kt.).
Plowman, Sidney.
Woolbert, Henry Robert.
Syme, George Adlington.
Garmany, Jasper Jewett.

1886.
May 13. Paterson, Wm. Bromfield.
June 10. Trott, Dudley Cox.
Sinclair, Thomas.
Buckell, William Robert.
Blaxland, Walter.
Heath, Charles Joseph.
Pearson, Charles Yelverton.
Dec. 9. Sylvester, George Holden.
Dodd, John Richard.
Vinrace, Felix Coulson.
Little, Ernest Muirhead.
Openshaw, Thomas Horrocks.
Harrison, Edward.
French, Geo. William Henry.
Campbell, Ernest Kenneth.
Tanner, Charles Edward.
Page, Harry Marmaduke.

1887.
Mar. 10. Barrett, James William.
June 9. Braddon, William Leonard.
Hare, Evan Herring.
Hatch, William Keith.
Hewkley, Frank.
Hadley, Wilfred James.
Lawrence, Laurie Asher.
Hughes, Edgar Alfred.
Tubby, Alfred Herbert.
Carr, John Walter.
Heatherley, Francis.
Lund, Herbert.
Spencer, Walter George.
Dec. 8. Taylor, Henry Herbert.
Waldy, John.
Thomas, David.
Murray, George Alfred Everett.
Roberts, James Reid.
Cropley, Henry.
Shadbolt, Lionel Pierrepoint.

220

1888.
Apr. 12. Carless, Albert.
Newbolt, George Palmerston.
June 14. Fox, Herbert.
Lloyd, Perceval Allen.
Adams, James.
Morton, Andrew Stanford.
Mackern, John.
Morris, Charles Arthur.
Willett, Edgar William.
Arnold, Ernest Charles.
Brock, James Harry Ernest.
Drew, Arthur John.
Beddoes, Thomas Pugh.
Hart-Smith, Franke Chamberlain.
Armstrong, Hugh.
Walker, Henry Secker.
Jowers, Reginald Francis.
Tonks, Henry.
Totsuka Kankai.
Solly, Ernest.
Taylor, Frederick Howard.
July 12. Kidd, Hugh Cameron.
Oct. 11. De Santi, Philip Robert William.
Dec. 13. Adams, John.
Douglas, Claude.
Brodie, Charles Gordon.
Spicer, Wm. Thomas Holmes.
Kinsey-Taylor, Alfred Ernest.
Johnson, Raymond.
Gooddy, Edward Samuel.
Lucy, Reginald Horace.
Coombe, Russell.
Stabb, Ewen Carthew.

1889.
Mar. 14. Burghard, Frédéric François.
Brook, William Henry Breffit.
June 13. Blakesley, Henry John.
Russell, Robert Hamilton.
Gunn, Donald Stilwell.
Gray, John Power William.
Spong, Charles Stuart.
Leech, Priestley.
Flemming, Percy.
Edge, Frederick.
Parsons, Frederick Gymer.
Redmayne, Thomas.

265

1889.
June 13. Drew, Henry William.
Thompson, James Edwin.
Jones, Sydney Harold.
Smith, Hugh.
Brown, Herbert Henry.
Crook, Herbert Evelyn.
Balgarnie, Wilfred.
Brook, William Frederick.
Davenport, Cecil John.
Gilford, Hastings.
Street, Ashton.
Oct. 17. Dean, Henry Percy.
Ward, Arthur Henry.
Dec. 12. Perry, Francis Frederic.
Morton, Charles Alexander.
Mortimer, John Desmond
Ernest.
Swain, James.
Crowle, Thomas Henry
Rickard.
Murray, Robert William.
McLachlan, John.
Larkin, Frederic Charles.
Permewan, William.
Pennell, George Herbert.
Ashworth, Percy.

1890.
Feb. 13. Thomas, William Thelwall.
Vernon, Arthur Heygate.
June 12. Parkin, Alfred.
Grant, James Dundas (Kt.).
James, Herbert Ellison
Rhodes.
Andrews, Arch. George.
Drew, Hedley Vicars.
Wilson, Alexander.
Lewis, Edward John.
Napier, Francis Horatio.
Lake, Richard.
Francis, Alfred George.
Smith, John William.
Crouch, Charles Percival.
Lawrence, Thomas William
Pelham.
Richardson, William George.
Solly, Reginald Vaughan.
Waterhouse, Herbert Furni-
vall.
307

1890.
June 12. Trechmann, Maximilian Lin-
coln.
Turney, Horace George.
Barnett, Louis Edward.
Smith, Guy Bellingham.
July 10. Parry, Albert Alexander.
Oct. 9. Moynihan, Berkeley George
Andrew (Bt. 1922).
Dec. 11. Coumbe, John Batten.
Collins, Edward Treacher.
Evans, Willmott Henderson.
Blight, William Lyne.
Barendt, Frank Hugh.
White, Frank Faulder.
Clarke, James Jackson.
Murray, John.
Braine, Charles Carter.
Cheatle, George Lenthal.
Collier, Horace Stansfield.
da Costa, Francis Xavier.
Mothersole, Robert Devereux.
Parkinson, John Porter.
Beale, Peyton Todd Bowman.
Barratt, John Oglethorpe
Wakelin.
Morison, James Rutherford.

1891.
Feb. 12. Deanesly, Edward.
Mar. 12. Caddy, Arnold.
Apr. 9. White, Gilbert Benjamin
Mower.
May 4. Thompson, Walter.
June 11. Pronger, Charles Ernest.
Morley, Edward John.
Nance, Henry Chester.
Turton, James.
Herbert, Herbert.
Stocks, William Percy.
Heaton, George.
Lucas, Albert.
Teichelman, Ebenezer.
Roberts, John Lloyd.
Housman, Basil Williams.
Campbell, John.
Cobbett, Louis.
Blacker, George Francis.
Johnstone, James.
349

1891.
June 11. Ross, Daniel McClure.
Dyall, Thomas James.
July 30. Forward, Francis Edward.
Oct. 15. Caiger, Herbert.
Waring, Holburt Jacob. ˙
Dec. 10. Woollett, Charles Jerome.
Voisey, Clement Bernard.
Jones, David Llewellyn.
Nairn, Robert.
Nash, Walter Gifford.
Vickery, William Henry.
Duer, Charles.
Falkner, Edgar Ashley.
Cook, Herbert George Graham.
Fowler, Charles Edward Percy.
Bickersteth, Robert Alexander.
Jordan, John Furneaux.
Langlands, Francis Henry.
Martin, Christopher.
Rouillard, Laurent Antoine
John.

1892.
Jan. 14. Wilkinson, Edmund.
Masterman, Ernest William
Gurney.
June 9. Abbott, Francis Charles.
Pickard, Ransom.
Anderson, George Reinhardt.
Pringle, James Hogarth.
White, Edgar Ramsay.
Cheatle, Arthur Henry.
Roberts, Charles Hubert.
Elliot, Robert Henry.
Cargill, Lionel Vernon.
Fawcett, John.
Griffiths, Joseph.
Shearer, Donald Francis.
Ashe, Evelyn Oliver.
Laws, William George.
Welsford, Arthur Gerald.
Aug. 1. Drew, Douglas.
Oct. 13. Eccles, William McAdam.
Dec. 8. Robinson, William.
Childe, Charles Plumley.
Lynn-Thomas, John (K.B.E.
1919).

1892.
Dec. 8. Edridge-Green, Frederic
William.
Olive, Eustace John Parke.
Foster, William James.
Grey, Thomas Campbell.
Hallidie, AndrewHallidieSmith
Thomas, John Llewellyn.
Preston, Charles Henry.

1893.
Feb. 10. Bailey, Robert Cozens.
Rogers, Leonard.
Maidlow, William Harvey.
May 11. Gibbs, Charles.
June 8. Roughton, Walter.
Smith, Ferdinand Clarence
Whitelocke, Richard Henry
Anglin.
Walker, Cyril Hutchinson.
Powell, William Wyndham.
Firth, John Lacy.
Fripp, Alfred Downing (Kt.
1903).
Griffiths, Cornelius Albert.
Marshall, Charles Frederic.
Musgrove, James.
Sequeira, James Harry.
Lack, Harry Lambert.
Box, Charles Richard.
Johnson, Frederick.
Lawson, Arnold.
Banks, Alfred.
Michels, Ernst.
Fisher, John Herbert.
Wallace, Cuthbert Sidney
(K.B.E. 1919).
Burden, Henry.
Hepburn, Malcolm Langton.
July 7. Gamgee, Leonard Parker.
Oct. 12. Jones, Martin Llewellyn.
Taylor, Tom Robinson.
Dec. 14. Thomson, St. Clair (Kt. 1912).
Wilson, Thomas.
Kelson, William Henry.
Pollard, Charles.
Roxburgh, Alexander Bruce.
Spurrell, Charles.
Yearsley, Percival Macleod.

1893.

Dec. 14. Ionides, Theodore Henry.
Leedham-Green, Charles Albert.
Low, Vincent Warren.
Salter, Charles Edward.
Rochfort-Brown, Herbert.

1894.

Feb. 8. Miles, William Ernest.
Clegg, John Gray.
Mar. 8. Rake, Alfred Theodore.
Turner, Joseph George.
Apr. 12. Blackwell, Arthur Seal.
May 10. Sheen, Alfred William.
June 14. Clarke, Ernest.
Cadman, Arthur Wellesley.
Green, Charles David.
Westmacott, Frederic Hibbert.
Littler, Robert Meredith.
Mahood, Allan Edward.
Hall, John Moore.
Hogarth, Robert George.
Rutter, Hubert Llewellyn.
Adams, Edmund Weaver.
Armstead, Hugh Wells.
Rutter, Francis Burchett.
Sichel, Gerald Theodore Silvester.
Henry, Edwin.
Jones, George David Edwardes.
Lister, Thomas David.
Belben, Frank.
Boyd, Thomas Hugh.
Buchanan, James Spittal.
Wilkinson, George.
Grimsdale, Harold Barr.
Keith, Arthur (Kt. 1921).
Leathes, John Beresford.
Barrington, Fournes.
July 30. Daldy, Arthur Mantell.
Scotson, Frederick Charles.
Durham, Herbert Edward.
Oct. 11. Griffin, William Watson.
Dec. 13. Hall, Geoffry Craythorne.
Counsell, Herbert Edward.
Evans, Evan.
Hughes, Samuel Henry.
Farmer, Gabriel Wm. Stabel.

477

1894.

Dec. 13. Mills, Yarnold Hubert.
Brownlow, Harry Lurgan.
Newby, Gervase Edward.
Carwardine, Thomas.
Selby, Edmond Wallace.
Cresswell, Frank Pearson Skeffington.
Pantin, Charles Satchell.
Luce, Richard Harman (K.C.M.G. 1919).
Baldwin, Gerald Robert.
Douglas-Crawford, Douglas.
Barrett, John Edward.

1895.

April 4. Smith, John Stanley Kellett.
June 13. Green, Chas. Robert Mortimer.
Bennett, William Edward.
Stevens, Thomas George.
Levick, Harry Driffield.
Ingall, Frank Ernest.
MacLeod, Charles Edward Alexander.
Warner, Thomas.
Spencer, Charles George.
Furnivall, Percy.
Marson, Francis Herbert.
Webb, James Ramsay.
Wightman, Cecil Frank.
Harris, William James.
Sloane, John Stretton.
Walton, Herbert James.
Cooper, Percy Robert.
Cuff, Archibald William.
Shillitoe, Arthur.
Gordon, John.
Lister, William Tindall (K.C.M.G. 1919).
Lockett, George Vernon.
Oct. 10. Wilson, Norman Octavius.
Nov. 14. Senior, Harold Dickinson.
Dec. 12. Foulerton, Alexander Grant Russell.
Tanner, Herbert.
Pisani, Lionel John.
Ridley, Nicholas Charles.
Lace, Frederick.
Curtis, Henry Jones.
Addison, Christopher.

519

1895.
Dec. 12. Ballance, Hamilton Ashley
(K.B.E. 1919).
Hainworth, Edward Marrack.
Randall, Martin.
Sutcliffe, William Greenwood.
Smith, Thomas Rudolf Hampden.
Turner, William.
Elworthy, Henry Stuart.
Arnold, Gilbert James.
Colby, Francis Edward Albert.
Brown, Ralph Charles.

1896.
Mar. 12. Edgecombe, Wilfrid.
June 11. Macnab, Allan James.
Wood, John Forrester.
Waddelow, John Joseph.
Paling, Albert.
Rayner, David Charles.
Smith, William Robert.
Coaker, Francis Wm. John.
Baldwin, Aslett.
Scrase, Frank Edward.
Maingay, Henry Bertram.
Taylor, Edwin Claude.
Adams, Evelyn Geo. Beadon.
Dick, John Lawson.
Parry, Leonard Arthur.
White, Charles Powell.
Lockyer, Cuthbert Henry Jones.
Ray, John Howson.
Stone, William Gream.
Bryant, Charles Hilary.
Moffat, Henry Alford.
O'Hea, James Patrick.
Cavanagh-Mainwaring, Wentworth Rowland.
Woods, William James.
Mahon, Ralph Bodkin.
July 9. Richardson, Sidney William Franklin.
Dec. 10. Harris, Herbert Elwin.
James, George Thomas Brooksbank.
Nall, John Frederick.
Riley, Frederick Radcliffe.
Gladstone, Reginald John.

1896.
Dec. 10. Howat, Robert King.
Davies, Hugh.
Hall, Charles Beauchamp.
Scott, James Andrew Neptune.
Pendred, Vaughan.
Grace, John Johnston.
Pinch, Albert Edwin Hayward.
Fraser, Forbes.
Hewer, Cecil Mackenzie.
Every-Clayton, Leopold Ernest Valentine.
Giles, Leonard Thomason.
Shaw, Harold Batty.
Savage, Ernest Smallwood.
Bruce, Herbert Alexander.
Melsome, William Stanley.

1897.
Mar. 11. Linington, William Webb.
Sprawson, Frederick Charles.
April 8. Cowen, George Hebb.
June 10. Howse, Neville Reginald (K.C.B.).
Luard, Hugh Bixby.
Watkins-Pitchford, Wilfred.
Paterson, Herbert John.
Hulke, Sydney Backhouse.
Wace, Cyril.
Crowley, John Henry Joseph.
Duffett, Henry Allcroft.
Fox, George Raymond.
Lee, William Edward.
Drake, Courtenay Henry.
Gullan, Archibald Gordon.
Handley, William Sampson.
Thomas, Thomas Morrell.
Legg, Thomas Percy.
Cook, John Howard.
Going, Robert Marshal.
Dec. 9. Freeland, Ernest Harding.
Blair, Charles Samuel.
Barnett, John Edward Sewell.
Cholmeley, William Frederick.
Martin, Albert Edward.
Bowring, Walter Andrew.
Strange, Arthur.
Hayes, George Constable.

1897.
Dec. 9. Phillips, Llewellyn Caractacus Powell.
Dickinson, Harold Bertie.
Miskin, Leonard John.
Pearson, Maurice Grey.
Ashdowne, Wallace Charles George.
Evans, Arthur Henry.
Dyball, Brennan.
Maxwell, John Preston.
Smith, James.
Christopherson, John Brian.
Pendlebury, Herbert String-fellow.

1898.
Jan. 12. Steward, Francis James.
Mar. 10. Madden, Frank Cole.
Apr. 14. Thurston, Edward Owen.
Fagge, Charles Herbert.
¶Tomes, Charles Sissmore (Kt. 1919).
June 9. Roll, Graham Winfield.
Wright, Dudley D'Auvergne.
Tilley, Herbert.
Frazer, John Ernest Sullivan.
Clarkson, George Aylwin.
Cochrane, Archer William Ross.
Collard, Frederick Stuartson.
Prain, John Leay.
Toye, Edwin Josiah.
Cooke, Arthur.
Benson, John Robinson.
Briggs, John Arthur Oswald.
Leicester, John Cyril Holdick.
Price, Henry James.
Godson, Alfred Henry.
Másiná, Hormasji Manekji.
Oct. 13. Nuthall, Alex. Wathen.
Russell, John Dill.
Dec. 8. Worth, Claud Alley.
Ince, Arthur Godfrey.
Sowry, George Herbert.
Harman, Nathaniel Bishop.
Bell, Hugh Thomas Symes.
Ormond, Arthur William.

643

1898.
Dec. 8. Sikes, Alfred Walter.
Stuart-Low, William.
Bonnin, James Atkinson.

1899.
Feb. 9. Heath, Arthur.
Burgess, Arthur Henry.
Apr. 13. ¶Dennis, Frederic Shepard.
June 8. Robinson, Frederick William.
Gaskell, Arthur.
Wood, William Charrington.
Cookson, Frederick Nesfield.
Shirley, Herbert John.
Copley, Stanley.
Carter, Felix Bolton.
Sanders, Alfred William.
Douglas, Archibald Robert John.
Crabtree, Angelo Matteo.
Hewetson, John Thomas.
Tucker, Alexander Benjamin.
Fox, Edward Joseph.
Watson, George Trustram.
Evans, John Jameson.
Newland, Henry Simpson.
Dee, Maurice Vincent.
Battersby, James.
Daniel, Peter Lewis.
Williams, Henry Thomas Hadley.
Rodocanachi, Ambrose John.
July 27. Modi, Shapurji Hormasji.
Nov. 2. Roberts, Charles.
Dec. 14. Playfair, Hugh James Moore.
Carson, Herbert William.
Evans, Evan Laming.
Lelean, Percy Samuel.
Howell, John.
Bonney, William Francis Victor.
Trotter, Wilfred Batten Lewis.
Stawell, Rodolph de Salis.
Walker, John William Thomson.
Cudmore, Arthur Murray.
Mundy, Herbert.
Ralston, Robert Gow.
Mannington, Frank.

685

1899.
Dec. 14. Skevington, Joseph Oliver.
Corner, Edred Moss.
Adam, John Law.
MacCallan, Arthur Ferguson.
Smith, Gilbert.

1900.
May 10. Smith, Edward Archibald.
Hine, Hugh FitzNeville.
May 31. Mulroney, Thomas Richard.
Rigby, Hugh Mallinson.
Fairbairn, John Shields.
Rawling, Louis Bathe.
Lynch, Stephen Frederick.
Armour, Donald John(C.M G.).
Harmer, William Douglas.
Hislop, Walter John Henry.
Clogg, Herbert Sherwell.
McGavin, Lawrie Hugh.
Middlebro, Thomas Holmes.
Lockhart - Mummery, John
Percy.
Dec. 13. Carpenter, Edgar Godfrey.
Parsons, John Herbert (Kt.).
Brewerton, Elmore Wright.
Wilson, Alexander Gordon.
Hewer, Edward Septimus
Earnshaw.
Hunter, Irwin Walter William.
Sargent, Percy William George.
Mayo, Thomas Alfred.
Sherren, James.
Johnstone, Robert James.

1901.
Apr. 11.¶Smith, Joseph Priestley.
¶Ross, Ronald (K.C.B. 1911).
June 20. Byles, John Beuzeville.
Newton, Robert Earle.
Banting, Cecil.
Vellacott, Philip Northcott.
Gibson, William Robert.
Rowlands, Robert Pugh.
Batchelor, Ferdinand Stanley.
Dent, Howard Henry
Congreve.
Dobson, Joseph Faulkner.

725

1901.
June 20. Tyrrell, Francis Astley Cooper.
Greg, Arthur Hyde.
Gask, George Ernest.
Unwin, William Howard.
Barwell, Harold Shuttleworth.
Pryce, Harold Vaughan.
Burrows, Harold.
Simpson, Graham Scales.
Tymms, Herbert George.
Lowman, William Henville.
Aitken, Robert Young.
Cunning, Joseph.
McMullen, William Halli-
burton.
Dec. 12. Steward, Edward Simmons.
Mayou, Marmaduke Stephen.
Turner, Philip.
Evans, John Howell.
Fairbank, Harold Arthur
Thomas.
Acland, Hugh Thomas Dyke.
Trotter, Edward.
Wilson, Alexander Garrick.
Nichols, William Robson.
Wright, William.
Billington, William.
McLachlan, Arthur Ronald.
Wilkin, Lancelot.
McCann, Frederick John.
Edwards, Thomas Henry.
Paul, Samuel Chelliah.
Secretan, Walter Bernard.
Edmunds, Arthur.
Greene, William Henry
Clayton.
Thompson, George William.
Tweedie, Alexander Robert.
Bruce, Harold Wilson.
Harbison, David Thomas.
Sawrey, Ernest Edward
Robert.

1902.
Jan. 16. Nutt, Harold Rothery.
June 12. Lewis, Herbert Wolseley.
Jones, Edmund Benjamin.
Pardoe, John George.
Dun, Robert Craig.

767

1902.
Juno 12. Wareham, Sidney James.
Marriage, Herbert James.
Mackie, Frederic Percival.
Greaves, Francis Ley Augustus.
Jones, Thomas Caldwell Litler.
Barnes, Frank.
Gordon-Watson, Charles Gordon (K.B.E. 1919).
Henderson, John Hunter.
Nitch, Cyril Alfred Pankin.
Soltau, Alfred Bertram.
Ward-Smith, Ward.
Newman, John Campin.
West, Charles Ernest.
Compton, Alwyne Theodore.
Curtis, Frederick.
Lett, Hugh.
Robinson, James Frederick.
Griffiths, William Layard.
O'Meara, Eugene John.
Paton, Leslie Johnston.
Henderson, Edward Erskine.
Richards, William Hunter.
July 10. Hartley, John Dawson.
Oct. 16. Lister, Alfred Ernest John.
Nov. 13. Connor, Frank Powell.
Dec. 11. Angus, Henry Brunton.
Wood, Cyril George Russ.
Greenyer, Vivian Tudor.
Hicks, Henry Thomas.
McClure, James.
Craig, James Andrew.
Smith, Sidney Maynard.
Morley, Arthur Solomon.
Scott, Sydney Richard.
Warren, Richard.
Longridge, Charles John Nepean.
Broomhall, Benjamin Charles.
Jones, Lawrence.
Wessels, François Henry.
Cross, Francis George.
Thompson, Arthur Ralph.
Ticehurst, Norman Frederic.
Shuttleworth, Charles Buckingham.
Jenkins, George John.
Dodds-Parker, Arthur Percy.
Swan, Russell Henry Jocelyn.

813

1903.
Mar. 12. Greenfield, Dudley George.
June 11. Lyle, Herbert Willoughby.
Peters, Edwin Arthur.
Mumford, Wilfred George.
Fremantle, Francis Edward.
Roberts, George Augustus.
Martin-Leake, Arthur, V.C.
Moorshead, Robert Fletcher.
Nicol, Burton Alexander.
Lilley, Ernest Lewis.
Wigman, Charles Wynn.
Collinson, Harold.
Cruise, Richard Robert.
Gough, William.
Camps, Percy William Leopold.
Dickie, William Stewart.
Hunt, Edmund Henderson.
Jaques, Robert.
Telford, Evelyn Davison.
Maclaren, Norman.
Atkins, John.
Fairlie-Clarke, Allan Johnston.
Jones, Bertrand Seymour.
Pitts, Arthur Gentry.
Stusser, Israel.
Odgers, Paul Norman Blake.
Marlow, Frederick William.
Formby, Henry Harper.
Howard, Russell John.
Aug. 4. Bowen, William Henry.
Oct. 15. English, Thomas Crisp.
Dec. 10. Myler, John William.
Molesworth, Theodore Henderson.
Taylor, Frank Edward.
Rose, Frank Atcherley.
Slater, Benjamin Holroyd.
Turner, George Grey.
Brawn, Harry Ellis.
Maxwell, William Henry.
Jennings, John Frederick.
Marshall, James Cole.
Phillips, Miles Harris.
Doble, Henry Tregellas.
Horsford, Cyril Arthur Bennett.
Wilson, William Carlyle.
Wylie, David Storer.

859

1904.
Jan. 14. Fedden, Walter Fedde.
Caddy, Adrian.
Apr. 14. Whitaker, Roy Henry Rollinson.
June 9. Watson, John Harry.
Heath, Philip Maynard.
Ridout, Charles Archibald Scott.
Jones, William Warner.
Addison, Oswald Lacy.
Fisher, Edward Fow.
Parkin, Alfred.
Scott, Wallace Arthur.
Thompson, Harold Theodore.
Beckett-Overy, Harry.
Roberts, James Alexander.
Hartley, Harold.
Oct. 13. Nesfield, Vincent Blumhardt.
Robertson, Carrick Hey.
Nov. 10. Greenwood, Charles Henry.
Dec. 8. Hayward, John Arthur.
Marriott, Cecil Edward.
Hasslacher, Francis Joseph.
Clay, John.
Pollard, Herbert Dean.
McGavin, Donald Johnstone.
Walters, Charles Ferrier.
Elmslie, Reginald Cheyne.
Waugh, George Ernest.
Coke, William Francis Harriott.
Carling, Ernest Rock.
Hastings, Somerville.
Davies-Colley, Hugh.
Upcott, Harold.
Adams, Joseph Ebenezer.
Lyth, Harold Ashton.
Rees, William Arthur.
Brailey, Arthur Robertson.
Harnett, Walter Lidwell.
Moon, Archibald Trevor.
Black, Kenneth.
Faulder, Thomas Jefferson.
Goulden, Charles Bernard.
Spriggs, Neville Ivens.
Ferguson, Robert James.
Tawse, Herbert Bell.

903

1905.
Jan. 12. Waterfield, Noël Everard.
Mar. 9. Rowntree, Cecil William.
June 1. Spreat, Frank Arthur.
Norman, Frederick.
Perrin, Thomas.
Taunton, Edgar.
Thomson, Charles Bertram.
Walker, Robert Alexander.
Graham, Cecil Irving.
Lakin, Charles Ernest.
Dolbey, Robert Valentine.
Smith, George Frederick Darwall.
Richards, Owen William.
Pierpoint, Harry William.
Ward, Bernard Joseph.
Williams, Moses Thomas.
James, William Warwick.
Atkey, Oliver Francis Haynes.
Goldie, Walter Leigh Mackinnon.
Guthrie, Thomas.
Hamilton, Arthur Francis.
Mylváganam, Henry Bailey.
Kidd, Francis Seymour.
Cooke, James Douglas.
Hudson, Arthur Cyril.
Daniels, Frederic William.
Bates, Tom.
Allen, Sydney Chalmers.
Dundon, John.
Ellis, Frederick William.
Pilcher, Edgar Montagu, D.S.O.
Nov. 9. Barling, Seymour Gilbert.
Dec. 14. Howse, Cyril Beresford.
Home, Alfred Lucette.
Groves, Ernest William Hey.
Hadley, Frederick Augustus.
Cunningham, John Francis.
Wrigley, Philip Roscoe.
Walker, Harold.
Bayley, Eric.
Boyd, Sidney Arthur.
Fitzmaurice-Kelly, Maurice Anthony Miller.
Hughes, Gerald Stephen.

946

1905.
Dec. 14. Balme, Harold.
Burfield, Joseph.
Holland, Eardley Lancelot.
Pye-Smith, Charles Derwent.
Wilson, Harold William.
Adams, Philip Edward
Homer.
Talbot, Leonard Smith.
Choyce, Charles Coley.
Kelly, Robert Ernest.
Patterson, Norman.
Stephenson, John.
Wright, Garnett.

1906.
June 14. Hugo, Edward Victor.
Mortimer. William Graddon.
Noall, William Paynter.
Hayden, Arthur Falconer.
Ridewood, Harold Edward.
Ward, Ernest.
Webber, Alexander Moxon.
Cole, Percival Pasley.
Footner, George Rammell.
Mollison, William Mayhew.
Coupland, James Alane.
Bennett, Vivian Boase.
Farquhar, George Greig.
Fitzwilliams, Duncan Camp-
bell Lloyd.
Oct. 11. James, Robert Rutson.
Dec. 13. Richards, William Jones.
Davies, Hugh Morriston.
de Silva, Arthur Marcellus.
Webb-Johnson, Alfred
Edward.
Williams, Gwynne Evan
Owen.
Gordon-Taylor, Gordon.
Riviere, Bernard Beryl.
Gilbert, Henry.
Gibb, Harold Pace.
Moore, Robert Foster.
Hughes, Ernest Cranmer.
Mant, Harold Turley.
Milne, Robert.
Moore, Walter William.
Greeves, Reginald Affleck.

988

1923.

1907.
Mar. 14. Robinson, Gerald Charles
Frederick.
Norbury, Lionel Edward Close.
Apr. 18. ¶Hill, Alex.
¶Thomson, Arthur.
June 13. Turner, Reginald George.
Denyer, Stanley Edward,
C.M.G.
Paramore, Richard Horace.
Arkle, James Vere.
Hepworth, Frank Arthur.
Cripps, William Lawrence.
Goyder, Francis Willoughby.
Cumberlidge, William Isaac.
Jeans, Frank Alexander
Gallon.
Ball, William Girling.
Perkins, Herbert Wilberforce.
Walton, Albert James.
Back, Ivor Gordon.
Mead, John Clarke.
Faulkner, Ebenezer Ross.
Giuseppi, Paul Leon.
Birks, Melville.
Forbes, Robert Dow.
McKenty, Francis Edmund.
Barry, David Thomas.
Goodwin, Arthur Charles.
Joly, John Swift.
Rayner, Henry Herbert.
Nov. 14. Bott, Robert Henry.
Dec. 12. Ainsworth, Hugh.
Maynard, Edwin.
Stock, William Stuart Vernon.
Fisher, Welby Earle.
Couzens, Alfred John.
Bain, Edward Walter.
French, John Gay.
Culpin, Millais.
Appleyard, William.
Hayman, Samuel Clifford.
Chitty, Hubert.
Hardwick-Smith, Henry.
Brierley, Wilfrid Edward.
Clarke, Colin.
Gray, Harry Tyrrell.
McPherson, Thomas.
Talbot, Philip.
Jamison, Reginald.

1034

1907.
Dec. 12. Braithwaite, Leonard Ralph.
Duncan, Kenneth McKenzie.
Falconer, James Law.
Gillespie, Edward.
Ligat, David.
Shorney, Herbert Frank.

1908.
Apr. 9. Dawson, Joseph Bernard.
¶Keatinge, Henry Pottinger.
June 18. Urwin, John Johnson.
Gray, Archibald Montague
Henry.
Hett, Geoffrey Seccombe.
Moore, Clifford Arthur.
Rischbieth, Harold.
Irving, Hamilton.
Hine, Montague Leonard.
Page, Charles Max.
Davies-Colley, Robert.
Roy, Donald Whatley.
Daw, Samuel Wilfrid.
Kinder, Alexander.
Unwin, Harold Arthur Robert
Edmond.
Frankau, Claud Howard
Stanley.
Wilson, George Ewart.
Simpson, George Charles
Edward.
Watkinson, Wilfred.
Short, Arthur Rendle.
July 9. Smith, Charles Harold.
July 30. Mills, George Percival.
Dec. 10. Balean, Hermann.
Macmillan, John McCallum
Anderson.
Ross, Robert Ainslie.
Hamilton, William Hay-
wood.
Blaxland, Athelstan Jasper.
Colt, George Herbert.
Coventon, Albert William
Duncan.
Hey, Wilson Harold.
Hope, Charles William
Menelaus.
Welchman, Walter.

1908.
Dec. 10. Davis, Haldinstein David.
Whitehouse, Harold Beck-
with.
Evans, John Jackson Whatley.
Fenwick, William Stephen.
Huggins, Godfrey Martin.
Walker, Kenneth Macfarlane.
Carswell, William Elliott.
Nightingale, Henry John.
Crawford, Andrew John.
Willan, Robert Joseph.
Pooley, George Henry.
Aitken, David McCrae.
Crymble, Percival Templeton.
Glendining, Bryden.
Killen, Thomas.
Payne, John Ernest.
Slinger, Robert Townley.

1909.
Jan. 14. Rutherford, Norman Cecil.
Mar. 11. Barrington, Frederick James
Fitzmaurice.
Apr. 1. ¶Thane, George Dancer (Kt.).
June 10. James, Charles Henry.
Oldfield, Carlton.
Dorrell, Edmund Arthur.
Smith, Percy Montague.
Battye, Walter Rothney.
Letchworth, Thomas Wilfrid.
Forshaw, William Herbert.
Levy, Aaron.
Rainforth, John Jekyll.
Woolfenden, Herbert Francis.
White, Clifford Sidney.
Worthington, Robert Alfred.
Juler, Frank Anderson.
Clare, Thomas Charles.
Barris, John Davis.
Layton, Thomas Bramley.
McDonagh, James Eustace
Radclyffe.
McDonald, Sydney Gray.
Quick, Hamilton Ernest.
Fleming, Alexander.
Joyce, James Leonard.
Leipoldt, Christian Frederic
Louis.

1909.
June 10. Neil, William Fulton.
Martin, Edward Kenneth.
Ollerenshaw, Robert.
Poate, Hugh Raymond Guy.
Pybus, Frederick Charles.
Cope, Vincent Zachary.
Devereux, Arthur Cecil.
Munby, William Maxwell.
Panting, Laurence Christopher.
Oct. 14. Woolf, Albert Edward Mortimer.
Nov. 11. Woodman, Edward Musgrave.
Dec. 9. Grant, John William Geary.
Davies, David Leighton.
Smith, Hugh Bernard Willoughby.
Edmond, William Square.
Howarth, Walter Goldie.
Griffith, Arthur Donald.
Hotop, Francis Rudolph.
Bankart, Arthur Sydney Blundell.
Roberts, James Ernest Helme.
Souttar, Henry Sessions.
Hedley, John Prescott.
Bristow, Walter Rowley.
Coorlawala, Rustom Nusserwan.
Rooke, Alfred Basil.
Bacha, Ardeshir Pestonji.
Spittel, Richard Lionel.
Gilder,MancershaDhanjibhai Dorabji.
Deshmukh, Gopal Vinayak.
Abraham, James Johnston.
Aitken, Andrew Blair.
Anderson, Henry Graeme.
Gough, Alfred.
Muecke, Francis Frederick.
Scott, Malcolm Leslie.
Spong, Ambrose.
Thompson, Hubert Gordon.
Worton, Albert Samuel.

1910.
Apr. 14.¶Lunn, John Reuben.
May 12. Daniels, Davis Woodcock.
1154

1910.
June 9. Novis, Thomas Shepherd.
Evans, Thomas John Carey.
Oram, Evelyn Henry Bardens.
Wright, Andrew John Metford.
Austin, Lorimer John.
Lang, Basil Thorn.
Digby, Kenelm Hutchinson.
Griffin, Walter Bristow.
Vellacott, Harold Fitz.
Campbell, William Archibald.
Davies, David.
Douglas, William Robert.
Vickerman, Philip Seston.
Dick, Alan MacDonald.
Guevara-Bojas, Felipe.
Joll, Cecil Augustus.
Buck, Howard.
Campbell, Robert Harold.
Eadie, James.
Jamison, Robert.
Ussher, George Herbert.
Dec. 8. Fenton, Thomas Gerald.
Pardhy, Krishna Moreshwar.
Ainger, William Bradshaw.
Maples, Ernest Edgar.
Fenwick, George Ernest Oswald.
Thomas, Gordon Wilson.
Wyatt, James Montagu.
Davies, Edwin Thomas Harries.
Wilson, John Black Ferguson.
Bryan, Charles Walter Gordon.
Macalpine, James Barlow.
Verrall, Paul Jenner.
Richardson, Alfred.
Gillies, Harold Delf.
Lobb, Edward Leslie Martyn.
Chapple, Harold.
Kumarasamy, Murugesem Muthu.
O'Malley, John Francis.
Mapother, Edward.
Pannett, Charles Aubrey.
Quick, Balcombe.
Roth, Paul Bernard.
1197

K 2

1911.
Jan. 12. Johnson, Walter Burford.
Feb. 9. Webb, Charles Henry Shorney.
Mar. 9. Cowell, Ernest Marshall.
Bharucha,Phirozshah Byramji.
June 8. Reid, John Buchanan.
Talbot, Francis Theodore.
Bevers, Edmund Cecil.
Sladen, Reginald John Lambart.
Loosley, Alfred Edward Arthur.
Adeney, George Cuthbert.
Kisch, Harold Albert.
Greene, Charles Williams.
Thompson, George Stanley.
Kennedy, Charles Matheson.
Miller, William Henry.
Buckley, John Philip.
Gauntlett, Eric Gerald.
Báriá, Dinshá Dáráshá.
Wilks, Washington Everitt.
Crook, Arthur Henry.
Haigh, William Edwin.
Hughes, Basil.
Jefferson, Geoffrey.
Roy, Bidham Chandra.
Bazett, Henry Cuthbert.
Morley John.
Fearnley, Harold.
Finch, Ernest Frederick.
Gray, George Munn.
Jordan, Anson Robertson.
Mouat, Thomas Bernard.
Wilson, Hugh Cameron.
Woodward, Alfred Chad Turner.
Yorke, Courtenay.
Oct. 12. Dalal, Anandrai Keshavlal.
Sampson, Herbert Henry.
Dec. 14. Robinson, Harry.
Smith, Thomas Waddelow.
Hull, Alfred John.
Haslam, Arthur Charles.
Jeremy, Harold Rowe.
Reckless, Philip Alfred.
Morgan, Henry Lewis.
Turton, James Richard Henry.
Girdlestone, Gathorne Robert.
McCaw, Alexander Todd.
1243

1911.
Dec. 14. Lloyd, Bertram Arthur.
Rankin, David.
Colledge, Lionel.
Townrow, Vincent.
Goodwin, Bernard Grainger.
Lee, Harry.
Parkinson, William Robert.
Pink, Wilfrid Langrish.
Moorhead, Andrew Samuel.
Bourne, Aleck William.
Bullock, Howard.
Aickin, Casement Gordon.
Johnston, Henry Mulrea.
Maclure, Alfred Fay.
MacWatt, Robert Charles.
Shaw, Charles Gordon.
Todd, Thomas Wingate.
§Davies-Colley, Eleanor.

1912.
Mar. 14. Harkness, Robert Coltart.
Apr. 11. ¶Pratt, James John.
June 13. Wilson, Roger Parker.
Cook, Lewis.
Carter, Robert Markham.
Whale, George Harold Lawson.
Davis, Edward David.
Strickland, Harold Foster.
Flint, Ethelbert Rest.
Lees, Kenneth Arthur.
Everidge, John.
Rix, Rowland Waters.
Holman, Charles Colgate.
Candler, Arthur Laurence.
Alderson, Gerald Graham.
Wood, Duncan.
Stanley, Ernest Gerald.
Cleminson, Frederick John.
Stout, Thomas Duncan Macgregor.
Stowell, Thomas Edmund Alexander.
Richardson, Alfred Henry.
Harty, John Percy Ingham.
Hughes, Ernest Ethelbert.
Phillips, Walter.
Walker, Albert Latimer.
Warburton, Gilbert Bertram.
1287

1912.
Oct. 10. Robinson, Arthur Leyland.
Nov. 14. Lovell, Arthur Gordon
Haynes.
Dec. 12. Higgins, Thomas Twisting-
ton.
Gowland, William Percy.
Finn, Allen Rigaen.
Graham, Samuel Lewis.
O'Brien, Arthur Boniface.
Morson, Albert Clifford.
Trethowan, William Henry.
Wilson, Ivan Stuart.
Gilliatt, William.
Viner, Geoffrey.
Mackenzie, Colin.
Vick, Reginald Martin.
Pearse, Robin.
Alles, Emmanuel Caetan.
Bromley, Lancelot.
Attwater, Harry Lawrence.
Lindsay, Ernest Charles.
Wildman, William Stanley.
Gardner, Arthur Duncan.
Gould, Eric Lush Pearce.
Smith, Wilburn.
Wade, James Owen David.
Fahmy-el-Minyawi, Ibrahim.
Platt, Harry.
Sauer, John Godfrey.
Hewitt, David Walker.
Mackenzie, Kenneth.
Barrington-Ward, Lancelot
Edward.

1913.
Jan. 9. MacWatters, Matthew Robert
Cecil.
Feb. 13. Maybury, Bernard Constable.
Apr. 10. Quine, Albert Edward.
June 12. Broome, Harold Holkar.
Taylor, Douglas Compton.
Iles, Arthur Ernest.
Darling, Harry Cecil Ruther-
ford.
Mawhood, Reginald Hawks-
worth.
Shattock, Clement Edward.
Hoyte, Stanley.

1913.
June 12. Palmer, Alexander Croydon.
Grange, Charles D'Oyly.
Neame, Humphrey.
Pinnock, Dudley Denham.
Todd, Alan Herapath.
Watts, John Ernest Price.
Anderson, Charles Vernon.
Davis, Kenneth James Acton.
Lock, Norman Francis.
Ritson, Stanley.
Vlasto, Michael Ernest Theo-
dore Demetrius.
Chubb, Gilbert Charles.
Jackson, Charles Eric Sweet-
ing.
Oakden, William Marshall.
Perrin, Walter Sidney.
Gemmill, William.
Kennedy, John.
Saint, Charles Frederick
Morris.
Stephens, Frederick Glover
Neason.
Thompson, John.
July 10. Foster, Philip Stanley.
Mitchener, Philip Henry.
Oct. 9. Martyn, Henry Linnington.
Hammond, Thomas Edwin.
Dec. 11. Rowe, Robert Morison.
Franklin, Philip Julius.
Benians, Thomas Herbert
Cecil.
Davies, Trevor Berwyn.
Bates, Mark.
Archer, Charles William.
Rainey, Edward Holmes.
Ritchie, John Lichtenstein.
Diggle, Frank Holt.
Jobson, James Stanley.
Brown, Stanley Eric Vincent.
Moreton, Adrian Leonard.
Neve, Clement Treves.
Ramsay, Robert Anstruther.
Slesinger, Edward Gustave.
Duggan, Norman.
Radley, Sidney Bertram.
Bell, Francis Gordon.
Lake, Norman Claudius.
Morrison, John Tertius.

1327
1371

1913.

Dec. 11. Bookless, John Smeed.
Gibson, Alexander.
Gow, John.
MacQueen, Ronald Chesney.
Stewart, Joseph Collingwood.

1914.

Feb. 12. Taylor, Julian.
Apr. 2.¶May, ArthurWilliam (K.C.B.).
June 11. Prynne, Harold Vernon.
Leonard, William Hugh.
Hughes, David Morgan.
Batten, Herbert Ernest.
Oliver, Matthew William
Baillie.
Donaldson, Malcolm.
Maxted, George.
Neligan, George Ernest.
Alexander, Harold George.
Wagstaffe, William Warwick.
Glendining, Vincent.
Griffith, Harold Kinder.
Jefferson, John Cecil.
Shafeek, Ahmad.
Tonks, John Wilson.
Ewart, George Arthur.
Graves, Thomas Chivers.
Pendered, John Hawker.
Curry, Wilfred Alan.
Loughnane, Farquhar
McGillivray.
O'Sullivan, Richard Francis.
Petty, Michael Joseph.
Redding, John Magnus.
Gabriel, Vraspillai.
Gardiner, Harold.
Mullally, Gerald Thomas.
Cook, Frank.
Wallace, Robert Allez
Rotherham.
Bearn, Andrew Russell.
Forsyth, John Andrew
Cairns.
Holmes, Thomas Sydney
Shaw.
Knox, Robert Welland.
Lincoln, William Ayer.
McKerrow,William Alexander
Hogg.

1412

1914.

June 11. Smerdon, Edgar Wilmot.
Storey, John Colvin.
Wickens, George Henry.
Nov. 12. Horton, Robert Lister.
Dec. 10. Geach, Robert Neville.
Hume, Douglas Walter.
Noon, Charles.
Beresford, Gerald Wadding-
ton.
Barclay, John Hamilton.
Howell, Bernard Whit-
church.
Doyne, Philip Geoffry.
de Mowbray, Ralph Marsh.
Green, Douglas.

1915.

Mar. 11. Moolgavker,Shamrao Ramrao.
Apr. 8.¶Larkin, Frederick George.
¶Symington, Johnson.
June 10. Gadgil, Shridhar Bheekajee.
Collins, Robert Edward.
Rivett, Louis Carnac.
Gray, Arthur Oliver.
White, James Renfrew.
Banerji, Lalit Mohan.
Marshall, Charles Jennings.
Edge, Benjamin Thomas.
Oct. 14. Driberg, James Douglas.
Dec. 9. Harries, David John.
Edwards, Arthur Tudor.
Southam, Arthur Hughes.
Chance, Arthur.
Romanis, William Hugh
Cowie.
Bridge, Reginald Harold.
O'Malley, Michael George.

1916.

Apr. 13 ¶Bassett-Smith, Percy William.
¶Colyer, James Frank (Kt.).
June 8. Saner, Francis Donaldson.
Littlejohn, Charles William
Berry.
Lawson, Robert Sharp.
Dec. 14. Walker, Harry Bertram.
Tanner, William Edward.
Cobbe, Thomas Jacob.
Woodall, Ambrose Edgar.

1453

1917.
Apr. 12. ¶Sloggett, Sir Arthur Thomas (K.C.B.).
June 14. Zamora, Alberto Medardo.
Cameron, Lyle John.
Oliver, John Dudgeon.
Dec. 13. Griffiths, Hugh Ernest.

1918.
Apr. 11. ¶Manby, Sir Alan Reeve.
¶Jones, Sir Robert, C.B.
June 13. Murray, Ernest Farquhar.
Wilkie, David Percival Dalbreck.
Dec. 12. Gabriel, William Bashall.
Gallie, William Edward.

1919.
Feb. 13. Martin, Frank Beauchamp.
Apr. 10. Morford, Arthur.
¶Adami, John George.
¶Goodwin, Sir Thomas Herbert John Chapman, K.C.B.
June 12. Greenwood, Henry Harold.
Just, Theodore Hartmann.
Baird, John Bruce.
Russell, Harrolde Bedford George.
Ward, Ronald Ogier.
Hindmarsh, Thomas Albert.
Bird, Martin Wright Kidman.
Phillips, Leonard George.
Molesworth, Hickman Walter Lancelot.
§Lewis, Emily Catherine.
Hurley, Thomas Ernest Victor.
Moore, Arthur Eisdell.
Newton, Hibbert Alan Stephen.
Tatlow, Robert Evelyn Tissington.
Upjohn, William George Dismore.
July 12. Keen, John Asarja.
Dec. 11. Ockwell, Charles Melton.
Fisher Alfred George Timbrell, M.C.

1486

1919.
Dec. 11. Kennon, Robert, M.C.
Smith, Alfred Bernard Pavey, M.C.
Pocock, William Agard.
§Basden, Margaret Mary.
Shah, Tribhovandas Oghaddas.
Jones, Rhys Trevor.
Adams, Arthur Wilfrid.
Shirwalkar, Raghunáth Dadoba.
Oldershaw, Martin Herbert.
Shaw, Simeon Cyril.
Anderson, Gerald Victor Wright.
Cooper, Rustam Nusserwanji.
Hailes, William Allan.
Julian, Thaddeus.
McCarter, Frederick Buick.
Maguire, Frederick Arthur.
Milligan, Edward Thomas Campbell.
Radford, Aubrey.
Trinca, Alfred John.

1920.
Apr. 8. ¶Thomson, Henry Alexis.
¶Grenfell, Wilfred Thomason.
June 10. Clark, Wilfred Edward Le Gros.
Forsdike, Sidney.
Sinclair, Neil Frederick.
Adams, James Wilmot.
Gushue-Taylor, George.
Simmonds, Bernard Sangster.
Reece, Leslie Norman.
Ogilvie, William Heneage.
Hooper, Arthur Norman.
Roberts, Cedric Sydney Lane.
McMillan, Kenneth Holl.
*Williamson-Noble, Frederick Arnold.
Perry, Alan Cecil.
Wright, Henry Wardel Snarey.
Griffith, John Richard.
Warwick, William Turner.
Wigram, Nathan Judah.
Mason, Francis Courtenay.
Hume, John Basil.

1526

1920.
June 10. Higgins, Lionel George.
§Landau, Muriel Elsie.
Joffe, Jack.
Whittingdale, John.
Gilmour, John.
Wardill, William Edward Mandall.
Mooro, Mohammed Abdel Wahhab.
Handfield - Jones, Ranald Montagu.
Buchanan, August Lyle.
Cantlie, Neil.
Cobb, John Henry.
Dew, Harold Robert.
Fowler, Robert.
Gill, John Frederic.
Hartley, James Norman Jackson.
Kerr, Robert Andrew.
Noble, Thomas Paterson.
Smith, Clive Nigel.
Sandes, Thomas Lewis Lindsay.
Whiting, Maurice Henry.
Dec. 9. Standage, Robert Frazer.
Stanley, John Brentnall.
Lindsay,Edwin Algernon.
Gilroy, Paul Knighton.
Dunmere, Henzell Howard.
Reader, Norbert Leo Maxwell.
Dingley, Lionel Alfred.
Brockman, Ralph St. Leger.
Mathias, Henry Hugh.
Morgan, Oswald Gayer.
Keynes, Geoffrey Langdon.
Crawshaw, Charles Harold.
Pennell, Vernon Charles.
Stretton, John Weston.
Bizarro, Alberto Henrique Ferreira.
Love, Robert John McNeill.
Marsh, Frank Douglas.
Elkington, George Ernest.
Costobadie, Lionel Paliser.
Jones, Samuel Walter Maslen.
Gerard-Pearse, John Ernest.
1567

1920.
Dec. 9. Somervell, Theodore Howard.
Beyers, Christian Frederick.
Maingot, Rodney Honor.
McEvedy, Peter George.
Tasker, Douglas George Clutsam.
§Claremont, Hetty Ethelberta.
Atkinson, Eric Miles.
Bailey, Henry Hamilton.
Churcher, Duncan Gillard.
Abel, Arthur Lawrence.
Cokkinis, Apollo John.
§Shufflebotham, Hilda Nora.
Maitland, Charles Dundas.
Chapman, Clement Lorne.
Debono, Peter Paul.
Dickson, William Muir.
Fleming, Robert Hood.
Hayman, Frank Keith.
Rea, Robert Lindsay.
Spedding, Leslie Alan.
Stephens, Horace Elliot Rose.
Watson, Donald.

1921.
Mar. 10. Andrews, John Alban.
Smythe, Henry James Drew.
Richardson, Geoffrey Bower.
Wilson, John St. George.
Wakeley, Cecil Pembrey Grey.
Huddy, George Philip Buckingham.
Perkins, George.
Evers, Henry.
Broster, Lennox Ross.
Coppleson, Victor Marcus.
Jenkins, James Alfred.
Kerr, Roy Russell.
Kneebone, John Le Messurier.
MacAuley, Charles John.
MacCormick, Kenneth.
Raison, Cyril Alban.
Smalpage, Edward Stanley.
Swan, James.
Trumble, Hugh Compson.
Apr. 14. ¶Sherrington, Charles Scott (G.B.E.).
¶Sprigge, Sir Samuel Squire.
1610

1921.
June 9. Nuttall, Henry Clarence
Wardleworth.
Pandalai, Krishen Gopinath.
Brandon, Gordon Normanby.
Carte, Geoffrey William.
Jones, Cecil Meredyth.
Bowden, Ellis Campbell.
Hunter, John Bowman.
Lambrinudi, Constantine.
Bellwood, Kenneth Benson.
Mason, Robert Paul Scott.
Dunn, Spencer Graeme.
Newell, Robert Leech.
Coyte, Ralph.
§Ghosh, Satapriya.
Kilner, Thomas Pomfret.
Corsi, Henry.
Hayes, Sydney Nuttall.
Robinson, Ronald Henry Otti-
well Betham.
Hillman, Oscar Stanley.
Ebden, John Alfred Wylde.
Haycraft, John Berry.
Kelly, Oswald Robert Michael.
Livingston, Herbert Max.
Watkyn-Thomas, Frederic
William.
Wookey, Harold William.
Dec. 8. McNair, Arthur James.
Negus, Victor Ewings.
Treston, Maurice Lawrence.
Buxton, Noel St. John Grey
Dudley.
Williams, Leslie Herbert
Worthy.
Davenport, Robert Cecil.
Evans, Griffith Ifor.
Norris, Donald Craig.
Lloyd, Eric Ivan.
Goldschmidt, Lionel Bernard.
§Bostock, Marian Noel.
§Partridge, Eleanor Joyce.
Green, Ronald Benjamin.
Wall, Austin Darley.
Reid, Hugh.
Watkins, Alfred Basil Keith.
Paton, Robert Young.
Appleby, Lyon Henry.
Bruce, George Gordon.

1054

1921.
Dec. 8. Bleaden, Wilfred Harry.
Brookes, George Arthur.
Cairns, Hugh William Bell.
Finny, Charles Morgan.
Heslop, Alfred Herbert.
Strachan, Gilbert Innes.
Sutherland, Donald McKay.

1922.
Apr. 6.¶Brook, Charles.
¶Coates, William.
June 8. Anderson, Frederick Jaspar.
Foley, Walter Barham.
Neilson, Drevor Frederick
Acton.
Medlock, Charles Harold.
Jones, James Gaymer.
Rose, Baron Theodore.
Wharry, Harry Mortimer.
Wilson, William Etherington.
Braine, John Francis Carter.
Pidcock, Bertram Henzell.
Dingley, Allen Roy.
Ross, James Paterson.
Corbett, Rupert Shelton.
Higgs, Sidney Limbrey.
Victory, Jose.
Crook, Eric Ashley.
Yates, Harold Blacow.
§Bloomfield, Alice.
Massie, Grant.
Parker, Spencer Tauria.
Browne, Denis John.
Corkey, Isaac Whitla.
Hewitson, William Andrew.
McCullagh, William McKim
Herbert.
Dec. 14. Goodwin, Aubrey.
Lumb, Norman Peace Lacy.
Gimblett, Charles Leonard.
Davies, John Llewellyn.
Stallman, John Frank Herbert.
Ainsley, Alan Colpitts.
Lodge, Samuel Durham.
Woods, Reginald Salisbury.
Halliwell, Arthur Clare.
Davies, Charles Owen.
Lindon, Leonard Charles
Edward.

1698

1922.
Dec. 14. Wilkinson, Valentine.
Sackett, Herbert Leyland.
§Ward, Mildred.
Wright, Arthur Dickson.
Chandrachud, Raghunath
Balkrishna.
Fulton, Roland Arthur
Hertslet.
Jose, Ivan Bede.
Judah, Nathanael Joseph.
Wellish, Gilbert Charrington.
Whitaker, John Grieve.
White, Horace Powell Winsbury.
Whyte, David.

1923.
Apr. 12.¶Mummery, John Howard.
¶Hill, Sir Robert, K.C.B.
June 14. Wheeler, Edwin Robert.
Syms, Gilbert Francis.
Salisbury, Walter.

1715

1923.
June 14. Scott, Rupert Strathmore.
Colquhoun, Gideon Robert
Ernest.
Phillips, John William
Glanmor.
Rhind, Sydney Devenish.
Williams, Roger Lester.
Makar, Naguib.
Shaw, Wilfred.
Currie, Donald Irvine.
Smith, Norman Ross.
Anderson, William.
Brookes, Herbert Adrian.
Bryce, Alexander Graham.
Carlton, Charles Hope.
Fouché, François Petrus.
Gillam, George Joshua.
Lytle, William James.
Moir, Percival John.
Pinkerton, John McLean.
Purves, James Ewart.
Wheeler, Donald Reid.
Woods, Samuel Henry.

1736

REGISTER OF FELLOWS IN ALPHABETICAL ORDER WITH THEIR ADDRESSES.

¶ Fellows elected as Members of 20 years' standing 28
§ Fellows by examination, under Medical Act, 1876 11
* Fellow by examination (with Ophthalmology) 1
Fellows by examination (*unmarked*) 1,696

Total 1,736

Name and Residence.	Fellow.	Member.
Abbott, Francis C., C.B.E., "*Hermitage,*" *White Hill, Bletchingley.*	June 9, 1892	Aug. 2, 1888
Abel, Arthur Lawrence, 48 *Harley-street,* W.	Dec. 9, 1920	July 26, 1917
Abraham, James Johnston, C.B.E., D.S.O., 38 *Harley-street,* W.	Dec. 9, 1909	Dec. 9, 1909
Acland, Hugh T. D., C.M.G., C.B.E., *North Belt, Christchurch, N.Z.*	Dec. 12, 1901	Nov. 10, 1898
Adam, John Law, *Blackwater, Hants*	Dec. 14, 1899	Nov. 10, 1898
¶ Adami, John George, C.B.E., *University of Liverpool, Liverpool.*	Apr. 10, 1919	June 27, 1887
Adams, Arthur Wilfrid, 9 *Mortimer-road, Clifton, Bristol*	Dec. 11, 1919	Feb. 10, 1916
Adams, Edmund Weaver, *Church-street, Slough*	June 14, 1894	Feb. 11, 1892
Adams, Evelyn Geo. Beadon, "*Oakdene,*" *Andover-rd., Newbury*	June 11, 1896	May 10, 1894
Adams, James, 4 *Chiswick-place, Eastbourne*	June 14, 1888	July 26, 1873
Adams, James Wilmot, *Penang, Straits Settlements*	June 10, 1920	Nov. 12, 1908
Adams, John, 180 *Aldersgate-street,* E.C.	Dec. 13, 1888	July 25, 1872
Adams, Joseph Ebenezer, 19 *Harley-street,* W.	Dec. 8, 1904	July 31, 1902
Adams, Josiah Oake, 117 *Cazenove-road, Stamford-hill,* N.	June 11, 1874	Apr. 28, 1865
Adams, Philip Edward Homer, 6 *Holywell, Oxford.*	Dec. 14, 1905	Feb. 11, 1904
Addison, Rt. Hon. C., *Murley Grange, Bishopsteignton, S. Devon*	Dec. 12, 1895	Nov. 12, 1891
Addison, Oswald Lacy, 125 *Harley-street,* W.	June 9, 1904	May 9, 1901
Adeney, George Cuthbert, *Broad Chalke, Salisbury*	June 8, 1911	Aug. 4, 1903
Aickin, Casement Gordon, *Auckland, N.Z.*	Dec. 14, 1911	Dec. 14, 1911
Ainger, William Bradshaw, 96 *Sloane-street,* S.W.	Dec. 8, 1910	Nov. 13, 1902
Ainsley, Alan Colpitts, M.C., *Greylands, West Hartlepool, Durham*	Dec. 14, 1922	May 13, 1915
Ainsworth, H., *Lt.-Col. I.M.S., Medical-college, Lahore*	Dec. 12, 1907	Nov. 9, 1893
Aitken, Andrew B., *P.O. Box 437, Lagos, S. Nigeria, B. W. Africa*	Dec. 9, 1909	Dec. 9, 1909
Aitken, David McCrae, 116 *Park-street,* W.	Dec. 10, 1908	Dec. 10, 1908
Aitken, Robert Young, O.B.E., 53 *Preston-new-road, Blackburn*	June 20, 1901	Feb. 7, 1901
Alderson, Gerald Graham, *Dudley-house, Kenilworth*	June 13, 1912	July 29, 1909
Alexander, Harold George, *Capt. I.M.S.*	June 11, 1914	May 11, 1911
Allen, Sydney Chalmers, 15 *Market-road, Remuera, N.Z.*	June 1, 1905	May 11, 1905
Alles, Emmanuel C., 13 *Kynsey-rd, Cinnamon-gds., Colombo, Ceylon*	Dec. 12, 1912	July 29, 1909
Anderson, Alex. Richard, C.B.E., 5 *East Circus-street, Nottingham*	Dec. 11, 1884	Jan. 24, 1877
Anderson, Charles Vernon, 39/40 *Chudleigh-bdgs., Johannesburg.*	June 12, 1913	May 11, 1911
Anderson, Fdk. J., *Capt. I.M.S., c/o Grindlay & Co., 54 Parliament-st.*	June 8, 1922	May 11, 1911
Anderson, George Reinhardt, M.B.E., 36 *Hoghton-st., Southport.*	June 9, 1892	Nov. 10, 1887
Anderson, G. V. W., *Standard-bldgs., 6th Avenue, Nairobi, B.E. Afr.*	Dec. 11, 1919	Feb. 12, 1918
Anderson, Henry Graeme, M.B.E., 75 *Harley Street,* W.......	Dec. 9, 1909	Dec. 9, 1909

Name and Residence.	Fellow.	Member.
Anderson, William, O.B.E., 5 *Albyn-terrace, Aberdeen*	June 14, 1923	June 14, 1923
Andrew, George, 5 *Montpelier-crescent, Brighton*	Dec. 11, 1879	Jan. 21, 1874
Andrews, Archibald George, 33 *Dover-rd., Birkdale, Southport*	June 12, 1890	Nov. 19, 1881
Andrews, J. A., M.C., *St. Peter's-hosp., Covent-garden,* W.C...	Mar. 10, 1921	May 9, 1912
Andrews, W. S., *St. Mary's-lawn, Leckhampton-rd., Cheltenham*	June 12, 1879	May 23, 1878
Angus, Henry Brunton, 5 *Eslington-road, Newcastle-on-Tyne*	Dec. 11, 1902	July 30, 1891
Appleby, Lyon Henry, 2224 *Larch-st., Vancouver, B.C., Canada.*	Dec. 8, 1921	May 12, 1921
Appleyard, William, 7 *Spring Bank-pl , Manningham, Bradford*	Dec. 12, 1907	Aug. 4, 1903
Archer, Charles William, 29 *Albion-street, Hull*	Dec. 11, 1913	July 29, 1909
Arkle, James Vere, *Dugan-street, Kalgoorlie, Western Australia*	June 13, 1907	May 8, 1902
Armour, Donald John, C.M.G., 89 *Harley-street,* W.	May 31, 1900	July 8, 1897
Armstead, Hugh Wells, 4 *Queen's-gardens,* W.	June 14, 1894	Feb. 11, 1892
Armstrong, Hugh, 139 *Macquarie-street, Hobart, Tasmania* ..	June 14, 1888	Apr. 28, 1885
Armstrong-Jones, Sir Robert, C.B.E., 9 *Bramham-gardens,* S.W.	Dec. 10, 1885	May 18, 1883
Arnold, Ernest Charles, 28 *Westbourne-road, Forest-hill,* S.E..	June 14, 1888	July 23, 1883
Arnold, Gilbert J., *c/o Messrs. Holt & Co.,*3 *Whitehall-place,*S.W.	Dec. 12, 1895	Nov. 9, 1893
Arnott, Rev. Henry, *The Precinct, Rochester, Kent*	Dec. 10, 1868	July 29, 1864
Ashdowne, Wallace Chas. Geo., 39 *Devonshire-street,* W.	Dec. 9, 1897	July 29, 1895
Ashe, Evelyn Oliver, 58 *Currey-street, Kimberley, Cape, S. Afr.*	June 9, 1892	June 9, 1892
Ashworth, Percy, *Durham-lodge,* 26 *Albert-road, Southport.*...	Dec. 12, 1889	Aug. 4, 1887
Atkey, Oliver Francis Haynes, *Khartoum, Sudan*	June 1, 1905	Feb. 12, 1903
Atkin, Charles, *Endcliffe Croft, Sheffield*..................	Feb. 14, 1884	Jan. 23, 1880
Atkins, Sir John, K.C.M.G., 3 *Grosvenor-crescent,* S.W.	June 11, 1903	May 9, 1901
Atkinson, Eric Miles, 47 *Queen Anne-street,* W.	Dec. 9, 1920	Feb. 8, 1917
Attwater, Harry L., 48 *Regent's-park-road,* N.W.	Dec. 12, 1912	Nov. 11, 1909
Austin, Lorimer John, *Queen's Univ., Kingston, Ontario, Canada.*	June 9, 1910	July 26, 1906
Bacha, Ardeshir Pestonji, *Bottlewala-villas, Sleator-rd., Bombay.*	Dec. 9, 1909	May 14, 1908
Back, Ivor Gordon, 14 *Queen Anne-street,* W.	June 13, 1907	May 11, 1905
Bailey, Henry Hamilton, 12 *Brunswick-road, Hove*	Dec. 9, 1920	Feb. 8, 1917
Bailey, Robert Cozens, *"Hazelwood," East Cowes, I.W.*	Feb. 10, 1893	Feb. 13, 1890
Bain, Edward Walter, 45 *Park-square, Leeds*	Dec. 12, 1907	Feb. 13, 1902
Baird, John Bruce, M.C., *Hokitika, Westland, N.Z.*..........	June 12, 1919	Oct. 12, 1911
Baldwin, Aslett, 6 *Manchester-square,* W.	June 11, 1896	July 27, 1893
Baldwin, G. R., 232 *Burke-rd., Up. Hawthorn, Melbourne, Vict.*	Dec. 13, 1894	Nov. 9, 1893
Balean, Hermann, *Hotel-mansions, Hong Kong, China*	Dec. 10, 1908	Feb. 7, 1901
Balgarnie, Wilfred, O.B.E., *The Dutch House, Winchfield*	June 13, 1889	Jan. 29, 1887
Ball, William Girling, 77 *Wimpole-street,* W. 1	June 13, 1907	Feb. 9, 1905
Ballance, Sir Chas. A., K.C.M.G.,C.B.,M.V.O.,106*Harley-st.,*W.	June 8, 1882	July 23, 1879
Ballance, Sir Hamilton A.,K.B.E.,C.B.,*All Saint's-green,Norwich*	Dec. 12, 1895	Aug. 1, 1892
Balme, Harold, 4 *Ribblesdale-road, Hornsey,* N.	Dec. 14, 1905	Aug. 4, 1903
Banerji,LalitMohan,*c/oCook& Son,*9*Old Court-house-st., Calcutta*	June 10, 1915	Nov. 12, 1914
Bankart, Arthur Sydney Blundell, 58 *Harley-street,* W.......	Dec. 9, 1909	May 10, 1906
Banks, Alfred, *St. Nicholas, Cheam-road, Sutton, Surrey*	June 8, 1893	July 30, 1891
Banting, Cecil, 57 *Harley-street,* W.	June 20, 1901	Feb. 13, 1896
Barclay, John Hamilton, 4 *Jesmond-road, Newcastle-on-Tyne* ..	Dec. 10, 1914	Nov. 9, 1911
Barendt, Frank Hugh, 65 *Rodney-street, Liverpool*	Dec. 11, 1890	Apr. 23, 1885

Name and Residence.	Fellow.	Member.
Báriá, Dinshá Dúráshá, 17 *Wodehouse-rd., MiddleColábá, Bombay*	June 8, 1911	May 14, 1908
Barling, Sir H. Gilbert, Bt., C.B., C.B.E., 87 *Cornwall-st., Birm.*	Dec. 8, 1881	July 25, 1879
Barling, Seymour Gilbert, C.M.G., 85 *Newhall-st., Birmingham.*	Nov. 9, 1905	Nov. 12, 1903
Barlow, John, 4 *Somerset-place, Glasgow*	June 11, 1885	Nov. 17, 1874
Barnes, Frank, 41 *Newhall-street, Birmingham*	June 12, 1902	May 4, 1898
Barnett, John Edw. Sewell, 49 *Queen's-rd., Kingston-hill, Surrey.*	Dec. 9, 1897	Aug. 2, 1888
Barnett, Louis Edward, C.M.G., 83 *Stafford-st., Dunedin, N.Z.*	June 12, 1890	May 9, 1889
Barratt, J. O. Wakelin, 56 *Alfriston-rd., Clapham-common, S.W.*	Dec. 11, 1890	Dec. 11, 1890
Barrett, John Edward	Dec. 13, 1894	Dec. 13, 1894
Barrett,SirJas.W.,K.B.E.,C.B.,C.M.G.,105 *Collins-st.,Melb.,Vict.*	Mar. 10, 1887	Jan. 25, 1884
Barrington, Fourness, 213 *Macquarie-street, Sydney, N.S.W.* ..	June 14, 1894	June 14, 1894
Barrington. Fredk. Jas. Fitzmaurice,10 *Chandos-street, W.*	Mar. 11, 1909	July 25, 1907
Barrington-Ward, Lancelot Edward, 85 *Harley-street, W.*	Dec. 12, 1912	Dec. 12, 1912
Barris, John Davis, 50 *Welbeck-street, W.*	June 10, 1909	Nov. 9, 1905
Barrow, Albert Boyce, 8 *Upper Wimpole-street, W.*	Dec. 20, 1875	Jan. 24, 1873
Barry, David Thomas, *Alexander-place, Cork*	June 13, 1907	June 13, 1907
Barwell, Harold Shuttleworth, 39 *Queen Anne-street, W.*	June 20, 1901	Feb. 9, 1899
§ Basden, Margaret Mary, 26 *Thurlow-road, Hampstead, N.W.* ..	Dec. 11, 1919	July 31, 1913
¶ Bassett-Smith,Sir P.W., K.C.B.,C.M.G., 18 *Queen Anne-str., W.*	Apr. 13, 1916	July 25, 1883
Batchelor, Ferdinand Stanley, 19 *London-street, Dunedin, N.Z.*	June 20, 1901	July 29, 1897
Bates, Mark, O.B.E., 33 *The Tything, Worcester*	Dec. 11, 1913	May 13, 1909
Bates, Tom, 44 *Foregate-street, Worcester*	June 1, 1905	Nov. 10, 1904
Batten, Herbert Ernest, 1 *Park-crescent, W.*	June 11, 1914	Feb. 12, 1904
Batterham, John Williams, "*Beechfields," Northiam, Sussex* ..	Dec. 10, 1885	July 23, 1880
Battersby, James, 616 *Great Eastern-road, Glasgow*	June 8, 1899	May 4, 1898
Battle, William Henry, 49 *Harley-street, W.*	June 10, 1880	July 31, 1877
Battye,W.R.,D.S.O.,Lt.-Col.I.M.S.,"*TheNest," Withingt'n,Glos.*	June 10, 1909	July 29, 1897
Bayley, Eric, 21 *Finsbury-square, E.C.*	Dec. 14, 1905	May 8, 1902
Bazett, H. C., O.B.E., M.C., *Univ.of Pennsyl.,Philadelphia, U.S.A.*	June 8, 1911	Feb. 9, 1911
Beale, Peyton T. B., *Lymore End, Everton, Lymington, Hants.*	Dec. 11, 1890	Feb. 12, 1889
Bearn, Andrew Russell, 29 *Amhurst-rd., Withington, Lancs* ..	June 11, 1914	June 11, 1914
Beckett-Overy, Harry, 19 *Lowndes-street, S.W.*	June 9, 1904	Aug. 4, 1903
Beddoes, Thomas Pugh, 19 *Harley-street, W.*	June 14, 1888	Aug. 6, 1884
Belben,Frank,O.B.E., "*Redlands," 25 Knyveton-rd.,Bournemouth*	June 14, 1894	May 11, 1893
Bell, Francis Gordon, M.C., *Dept. of Surgery, Univ. of Edinb'gh*	Dec. 11, 1913	Nov. 13, 1913
Bell, Hugh Thomas Symes, *Snoggwa-camp, Brisbane, Queensland*	Dec. 8, 1898	Feb. 13, 1896
Bellwood, Kenneth B., O.B.E., 8 *Harpur-place, Bedford*	June 9, 1921	Sept.24, 1914
Benians, Thomas Herbert Cecil, 7 *Cavendish-place, W.*	Dec. 11, 1913	July 25, 1907
Bennett,V.B., Col.I.M.S., c/o *Cook & Son, Esplanade-rd., Bombay*	June 14, 1906	June 14, 1906
Bennett, William Edward, 22 *Broad-street, Birmingham....* .	June 13, 1895	July 28, 1890
Bennett, Sir William Henry, K.C.V.O., 3 *Hyde-pk.-place, W.* ..	June 14, 1877	July 21, 1873
Benson, John Robinson, *Fiddington-house, Market Lavington* ..	June 9, 1898	May 14, 1896
Beresford, Gerald W.,O.B.E., 11 *Adelaide-cres., Hove, Brighton.*	Dec. 10, 1914	July 25, 1910
Berry, James, 21 *Wimpole-street, W.*	Mar. 12, 1885	July 21, 1882
Bevers, Edmund Cecil, 28 *Beaumont-street, Oxford*	June 8, 1911	May 9, 1901
Beyers, Christian Fdk , 10 *Geranium-st., Rosetteville,Johannesb'g.*	Dec. 9, 1920	Nov. 11, 1915
Bharucha, Phirozshah Byramji, O.B.E., D.S.O., *Maj.I.M.S.* ..	Mar. 9, 1911	May 13, 1909

Name and Residence.	Fellow.	Member.
Bickersteth, Robert Alexander, *Borwick Lodge, Outgate, Ambleside*	Dec. 10, 1891	Feb. 13, 1890
Billington, William, 47 *Newhall-street, Birmingham*	Dec. 12, 1901	July 27, 1899
Bird, Martin W. K., *Cooksditch, East-street, Faversham*	June 12, 1919	July 30, 1914
Birks, Melville, *Broken-hill-hospital, Broken-hill, N.S.W.*	June 13, 1907	Nov. 8, 1906
Bizarro, Alberto H. F., *Faculty of Medicine, Oporto*	Dec. 9, 1920	Feb. 12, 1914
Black, James, " *Hillcroft," Rotherfield, Sussex*	Dec. 9, 1880	Jan. 26, 1875
Black, K., *Maj., c/o Principal Med. Off., Singapore, Straits Settlemts.*	Dec. 8, 1904	Aug. 4, 1903
Blacker, Sir George Francis, C.B.E., 45 *Wimpole-street, W.*	June 11, 1891	July 28, 1890
Blackwell, Arth. Seal, *c/o Dr. Sealy, Aycliffe, Paddock-woods, Kent.*	Apr. 12, 1894	Feb. 11, 1892
Blair, Charles Samuel, *Matson-lodge, Richmond, Surrey*	Dec. 9, 1897	Oct. 24, 1884
Blakesley, Henry John, 16 *Severn-street, Leicester*	June 13, 1889	Nov. 16, 1880
Bland-Sutton, Sir John, 47 *Brook-street, W.*	June 12, 1884	Apr. 20, 1882
Blaxland, Athelstan Jasper, *St. Ethelbert's-ho., Tombland, Norwich*	Dec. 10, 1908	Feb. 11, 1904
Blaxland, Walter, *Freemantle, W. Australia*	June 10, 1886	Nov. 13, 1883
Bleaden, Wilfred Harry, 14 *Buckingham-gate, S.W.*	Dec. 8, 1921	Dec. 8, 1921
Blight, William Lyne, 47 *Newport-road, Cardiff*	Dec. 11, 1890	July 31, 1884
§ Bloomfield, Alice, 153 *Elm-park-mansions, Park-walk, S.W.*	June 8, 1922	Nov. 13, 1919
Bloxam, John Astley, *The Old Malt House, Bourne End, Bucks.*	June 8, 1871	Nov. 15, 1864
Bond, Charles John, C.M.G., " *Fernshaw," Springfield-rd, Leicester*	June 8, 1882	July 28, 1879
Bonney, William Francis Victor, 15 *Devonshire-place, W.*	Dec. 14, 1899	May 14, 1896
Bonnin, James A, " *St. Helen's," Mill-terr., N. Adelaide, S. Austr.*	Dec. 8, 1898	July 29, 1897
Bookless, John Smeed, 75 *Park-lane, Croydon*	Dec. 11, 1913	Dec. 11, 1913
§ Bostock, Marian Noel, *Monte Creek, B.C., Canada*	Dec. 8, 1921	May 10, 1917
Bott, Robert Henry, *Major I.M.S., Lahore, India*	Nov. 14, 1907	Feb. 9, 1905
Bourne, Aleck Wm., 27 *Harley-street, W.*	Dec. 14, 1911	Nov. 10, 1910
Bowden, Ellis Campbell, M.C., 108 *Christchurch-rd., Boscombe.*	June 9, 1921	Feb. 13, 1913
Bowen, William Henry, 24 *Lensfield-road, Cambridge*	Aug. 4, 1903	Nov. 14, 1901
Bowlby, Sir A.A., Bt., K.C.B., K.C.M.G., K.C.V.O., 25 *M'nch't'r-sq.*	June 9, 1881	July 29, 1879
Bowring, Walter Andrew, " *The Pines," Furze-hill, Brighton..*	Dec. 9, 1897	May 12, 1892
Box, Charles Richard, 2 *Devonshire-place, W.*	June 8, 1893	May 14, 1891
Boyd, Sidney Arthur, 144 *Harley-street, W.*	Dec. 14, 1905	Nov. 13, 1902
Boyd, Thomas Hugh, 183 *Hoddle-street, Richmond, Victoria*	June 14, 1894	July 27, 1893
Braddon, Wm. Leonard, *Sports-club, St. James's-square, S.W.*	June 9, 1887	Apr. 23, 1884
Brailey, Arthur Robertson, 24 *Harley-street, W.*	Dec. 8, 1904	Feb. 12, 1903
Braine, Charles Carter, 55 *Wimpole-street, W.*	Dec. 11, 1890	Nov. 10, 1887
Braine, John Francis Carter, 55 *Wimpole-street, W.*	June 8, 1922	Nov. 9, 1916
Braithwaite, Leonard Ralph, 45 *Park-square, Leeds*	Dec. 12, 1907	Dec. 12, 1907
Brandon, Gordon Normanby, 2/2 *Harington-st., Calcutta, India.*	June 9, 1921	May 11, 1911
Brawn, Harry Ellis, *Uitenhage, Cape Province, South Africa..*	Dec. 10, 1903	Nov. 2, 1899
Brewerton, Elmore Wright, 73 *Harley-street, W.*	Dec. 13, 1900	Feb. 7, 1895
Bridge, Regd. Harold, 235 *Macquarie-street, Sydney, N.S.W...*	Dec. 9, 1915	June 9, 1915
Brierley, Wilfrid E., *Maj. I.M.S., c/o Grindlay & Co., Bombay.*	Dec. 9, 1907	Jan. 12, 1905
Briggs, Henry, O.B.E., 3 *Rodney-street, Liverpool*	June 12, 1884	July 24, 1877
Briggs, J. A. Oswald, *Premier-house, Gregory Boulevard, Notts.*	June 9, 1898	May 14, 1896
Bristow, Walter Rowley, 102 *Harley-street, W.*	Dec. 9, 1909	Feb. 7, 1907
Brock, James Harry Ernest, 40 *Steeles-road, S. Hampstead, N.W.*	June 14, 1888	July 28, 1884
Brockman, Ralph St. Leger, 79 *Upper Hanover-st., Sheffield* ..	Dec. 9, 1920	Nov. 14, 1912

Name and Residence.	Fellow.	Member.
Brodie, Charles Gordon, M.C., *Fernhill, Wootton, Isle of Wight.*	Dec. 13, 1888	Jan. 24, 1883
Bromley, Lancelot, 35 *Harley-street,* W.	Dec. 12, 1912	Oct. 14, 1909
¶ Brook, Charles, *The Minster Yard, Lincoln*	Apr. 6, 1922	Apr. 19, 1861
Brook, William Frederick, *Longlands-house, Swansea*	June 13, 1889	May 5, 1887
Brook, William Henry Breffit, 8 *Eastgate, Lincoln*	Mar. 14, 1889	Jan. 21, 1887
Brookes, George Arthur, *Macquarie-street, Sydney, N.S.W.* ..	Dec. 8, 1921	Dec. 8, 1921
Brookes, Herbert Adrian, 29 *Christchurch-road, Winchester....*	June 14, 1923	June 14, 1923
Broome, Harold H., *Lt.-Col.I.M.S., Medical Coll., Lahore, India.*	June 12, 1913	May 10, 1901
Broomhall, Benjamin C., *Mission-hosp., Sianfu, Shensi, China.*	Dec. 11, 1902	July 25, 1900
Broster, Lennox Ross, O.B.E., 2 F *Morpeth-terrace,* S.W.	Mar. 10, 1921	Mar. 10, 1921
Brown, Herbert Henry, O.B.E., 3 *Museum-street, Ipswich*	June 13, 1889	Jan. 19, 1887
Brown, John, *Mowbray, Cape of Good Hope*	Dec. 12, 1878	Dec. 12, 1878
Brown, John Macdonald, 64 *Upper Berkeley-street,* W.	Mar. 8, 1883	Mar. 8, 1883
Brown, Ralph Charles, 116 *Wellington-st., St. Kilda, Melbourne*	Dec. 12, 1895	Nov. 14, 1895
Brown, Sir Robert Charles, 27 *Winckley-square, Preston*	Dec. 11, 1862	Nov. 5, 1858
Brown, Stanley Eric Vincent, 69 *Don-street, Invereargill, N.Z...*	Dec. 11, 1913	July 25, 1910
Browne, Denis John, 45 A *Arundel-gardens,* W.	June 8, 1922	June 8, 1922
Brownlow, Harry Lurgan, " *Shirley,*" *Henley-on-Thames*	Dec. 13, 1894	Feb. 11, 1892
Bruce, George Gordon, 5 *Rubislaw-place, Aberdeen*	Dec. 8, 1921	July 28, 1921
Bruce, Harold Wilson, 72 A *East Dulwich-grove,* S.E.	Dec. 12, 1901	Dec. 12, 1901
Bruce, Herbert Alex., 64 *Bloor-st.East, Toronto, Ontario,Canada*	Dec. 10, 1896	Aug. 4, 1896
Bryan, Charles W. Gordon, M.C., 118 *Harley-street,* W.	Dec. 8, 1910	May 9, 1907
Bryant, Charles Hilary, 68 *Brunswick-place, Hove*	June 11, 1896	Feb. 7, 1895
Bryce, Alex. Graham, 16 *Pilkington-road, Southport, Lancs....*	June 14, 1923	June 14, 1923
Buchanan, A. L., 231 *Macquarie-street, Sydney, N.S.W.*	June 10, 1920	June 10, 1920
Buchanan, James Spittal, 37 *Collins-st., Melbourne, Victoria* ..	June 14, 1894	July 27, 1893
Buck, Howard, 9 *Brighton-grove, Rusholme, Manchester*	June 9, 1910	June 9, 1910
Buckell, William Robert, *Salmon Arm, British Columbia, Canada*	June 10, 1886	May 16, 1882
Buckley, John Philip, " *Broadhurst,*" *Bury Old-rd., Manchester*	June 8 1911	Feb. 13, 1908
Bull, Geo.Coulson Robins, *Memel House, West Cliff-rd., Ramsgate*	June 12, 1884	July 21, 1880
Bull, William Charles, 5 *Clarges-street, Mayfair,* W.	Dec. 11, 1884	Apr. 19, 1882
Bullar, John Follett, *Houmet du Nord, L'Islet, Guernsey*	June 12, 1884	July 30, 1880
Bullock, Howard, 235 *Macquarie-street, Sydney, N.S.W.*	Dec. 14, 1911	Nov. 9, 1911
Burden, Henry, C.I.E., *Col.I.M.S.,*"*Heatherland,*"*BudleighSalt'n.*	June 8, 1893	Feb. 11, 1892
Burfield, Joseph, 8 *Earlham-road, Norwich*	Dec. 14, 1905	Aug. 4, 1903
Burgess, Arthur Henry, 17 *St. John-street, Manchester*	Feb. 9, 1899	Aug. 4, 1896
Burghard, F. F., C.B., *Craythorne, Rolleston, Burton-on-Trent*	Mar. 14, 1889	Jan. 25, 1886
Burrows, Harold, C.B.E., 1 "*The Cams,*" *Grove-road, Southsea.*	June 20, 1901	May 11, 1899
Burton, Samuel Herbert, 49 *St. Giles-street, Norwich*	June 9, 1881	Jan. 28, 1876
Bush, John Dearden, 5 *Uxbridge-rd., Stoke Poges*	June 10, 1869	May 10, 1866
Buxton, Noel St. J.(G.D., 13 *Upper Wimpole-street,* W.	Dec. 8, 1921	Nov. 13, 1913
Byles, John Beuzeville, *Brook Hospital, Shooter's-hill, Woolwich*	June 20, 1901	Nov. 13, 1891
Caddy, Adrian, 2/2 *Harington-street, Calcutta*	Jan. 14, 1904	Nov. 8, 1900
Caddy, Arnold, " *Chandpara,*" *Tylden, Victoria, Australia*	Mar. 12, 1891	Aug. 4, 1887
Cadman, Arthur Wellesley, 2 *Linden-gdns., Notting-hill-gate,* W.	June 14, 1894	May 15, 1882

Name and Residence.	Fellow.	Member.
Caiger, Herbert, 79 *Upper Hanover-street, Sheffield*	Oct. 15, 1891	Feb. 13, 1890
Cairns, Hugh M. B.," *Woodcroft," Baldwyn's-hill,Loughton,Essex.*	Dec. 8, 1921	Dec. 8, 1921
Cameron, Lyle John, 87 *Wimpole-street, W.*	June 14, 1917	Sept.24, 1914
Campbell, E. Kenneth, *Military-hosp., Tidworth, Hants*	Dec. 9, 1886	July 21, 1884
Campbell, John, *Crescent House, University-road, Belfast*	June 11, 1891	Nov. 8, 1888
Campbell, Robert Harold, 132 *Harley-street, W.*	June 9, 1910	June 9, 1910
Campbell, William Archibald, 23 *Woodside-place, Glasgow, W.*	June 9, 1910	July 30, 1908
Camps, Percy William Leopold, *Old Udney-cottage, Teddington.*	June 11, 1903	Nov. 8, 1900
Candler, Arthur Laurence, " *Shenley," Bamfield-road, Exeter..*	June 13, 1912	Nov. 12, 1908
Cant, Wm. Edmund, M.B.E., *The Mill-house, Lexden, Colchester*	June 11, 1874	May 9, 1867
Cantlie, Sir James, K.B.E., 37 *Harley-street, W.*	Dec. 13, 1877	May 24, 1877
Cantlie, Neil, M.C., *Capt. R.A.M.C.,* 37 *Harley-street, W.* ..	June 10, 1920	June 10, 1920
Cargill, Lionel Vernon, 35 *Cavendish-square, W.*	June 9, 1892	May 8, 1890
Carless, Albert, C.B.E., 38 *Enys-road, Eastbourne*	Apr. 12, 1888	July 30, 1885
Carling, Ernest Rock, 99 *Harley-street, W.*	Dec. 8, 1904	Nov. 14, 1901
Carlton, Charles Hope, 3 *Talbot-house, Upper Westbourne-terr.*	June 14, 1923	June 14, 1923
Carpenter, Edgar Godfrey, *Sallymount, Stroud, Glos.*	Dec. 13, 1900	Aug. 1, 1889
Carr, John Walter, C.B.E., 19 *Cavendish-place, W.*	June 9, 1887	Oct. 24, 1884
Carson, Herbert William, 111 *Harley-street, W.*	Dec. 14, 1899	July 29, 1895
Carswell, William Elliott	Dec. 10, 1908	Nov. 8, 1906
Carte, Geoffrey Wm., 18 *Upper Wimpole-street, W.*	June 9, 1921	July 25, 1912
Carter, Felix Bolton, " *Glenavon," London-road, Leicester* .. .	June 8, 1899	July 29, 1895
Carter, Frederick Heales, 117 *Upper Richmond-rd., Putney,* S.W.	June 9, 1881	July 23, 1875
Carter, R. Markham, C.B., *Lt.-Col. I.M.S.,*6*Briardale-gds.,*N.W.	June 13, 1912	Feb. 7, 1901
Carwardine, Thomas, 16 *Victoria-square, Clifton, Bristol*	Dec. 13, 1894	Aug. 1, 1892
Cathcart, Charles Walker, C.B.E., 3 *Tipperlinn-road, Edinburgh*	June 12, 1879	June 12, 1879
Cavenagh-Mainwaring, W. R., 103 *North-terr.,Adelaide,S. Aus.*	June 11, 1896	Feb. 13, 1896
Chance, Arthur, 90 *Merrion-square, Dublin*	Dec. 9, 1915	May 14, 1914
Chandrachud, Raghunath B., *Budhwar Peth, Poona City, India.*	Dec. 14, 1922	Apr. 6, 1922
Chapman, C. L., " *Panorama," Longueville, Sydney, N.S.W.* ..	Dec. 9, 1920	Dec. 9, 1920
Chapple, Harold, 18 *Devonshire-street, W.*	Dec. 8, 1910	July 30, 1908
Cheatle, Arthur Henry, C.B.E., 18 *Savile-row, W.*	June 9, 1892	Nov. 8, 1888
Cheatle, Sir George Lenthal, K.C.B., C.V O., 117 *Harley-st.,* W.	Dec. 11, 1890	Nov. 10, 1887
Cheyne, Sir W. Watson, Bt., K.C.M.G., C.B., *Fetlar, Shetland.*	June 12, 1879	June 12, 1879
Chicken, Rupert Cecil, *Upper Folkestone-rd., Sandgate, Kent..*	June 10, 1875	Apr. 30, 1872
Childe, Charles Plumley, "*Cranleigh," Kent-road, Southsea....*	Dec. 8, 1892	July 19, 1883
Chitty, Hubert, 46 *Pembroke-road, Bristol*	Dec. 12, 1907	Nov. 10, 1904
Cholmeley, Wm. Frederick, 31 *Waterloo-road, Wolverhampton* .	Dec. 9, 1897	Nov. 8, 1888
Choyce,C.C.,C.M.G.,C.B E.,*U.C.Hosp.Med.Sch.,Univ.-st.,*W.C.	Dec. 14, 1905	Dec. 14, 1905
Christopherson, John Brian, C.B.E., 29 *Devonshire-place, W....*	Dec. 9, 1897	Mar. 12, 1896
Chubb, Gilbert Charles, 4 *Devonshire-place, W.*	June 12, 1913	July 27, 1911
Churcher, D. G., 15 *Brodrick-rd., Wandsworth-comm.,* S.W. ..	Dec. 9, 1920	Feb. 8, 1917
Clare, Thomas Charles, 162 *London-road, Leicester*	June 10, 1909	July 27, 1905
§Claremont, Hetty E., 7 *West-heath-av., Hampstead,* N.W. ..	Dec. 9, 1920	Nov. 9, 1916
Clark, Wilfred E. Le Gros, *Kuching, Sarawak, Borneo*	June 10, 1920	July 26, 1917
Clarke, Colin, D.S.O., *Maj. R A.M.C., Holt & Co.,*3 *Whitehall-pl.*	Dec. 12, 1907	July 27, 1905
Clarke, Ernest, 3 *Chandos-street, W.*.......................	June 14, 1894	July 27, 1880

Name and Residence.	Fellow.	Member.
Clarke, James Jackson, 18 *Portland-place*, W................	Dec. 11, 1890	Oct. 20, 1886
Clarkson, George Aylwin, " *St. Agnes*," *Caterham-hill, Surrey*..	June 9, 1898	Feb. 8, 1894
Clay, John, C.B.E., 6 *Victoria-square, Newcastle-on-Tyne*......	Dec. 8, 1904	May 4, 1898
Clegg, John Gray, 22 *St. John-street, Manchester*	Feb. 8, 1894	Nov. 12, 1891
Cleminson, Frederick John, 32 *Harley-street*, W.............	June 13, 1912	May 12, 1910
Clippingdale, Samuel Dodd, 17 *Malvern-road, Hornsey*, N. 8 ..	Dec. 9, 1880	July 20, 1875
Clogg, Herbert Sherwell, 41 *Devonshire-street*, W.	May 31, 1900	Nov. 10, 1898
Coaker, Francis Wm. John, " *Sunnymead*," *New-rd., Bromsgrove*	June 11, 1896	Feb. 9, 1893
¶Coates, Wm., C.B., C.B.E., *Ingleside, Whalley Range, Manchr.*	Apr. 6, 1922	July 25, 1881
Cobb, John Henry, 281 *Glossop-road, Sheffield*	June 10, 1920	June 10, 1920
Cobbe, Thos. J., " *Garnavilla*," *Stillorgan, Co. Dublin*........	Dec. 14, 1916	Dec. 14, 1916
Cobbett, Louis. " *Inch-ma-home*," *Adams-road, Cambridge*....	June 11, 1891	Feb. 13, 1890
Cochrane, Archer William Ross, *Lt.-Col.I.M.S., Bhowali, India.*	June 9, 1898	Nov. 8, 1894
Coke, Wm. Francis Harriott, 90 *Harley-street*, W. 1	Dec. 8, 1904	Oct. 7, 1901
Cokkinis, Apollo John, 292 *Cranbrook-road, Ilford*	Dec. 9, 1920	July 26, 1917
Colby, Francis Edward Albert, *Hill View, Woking*	Dec. 12, 1895	Feb. 8, 1894
Cole, Percival Pasley, 15 *Harley-street*, W.	June 14, 1906	Feb. 11, 1904
Colgate, Henry, 2 *Seaside-road, Eastbourne*	June 14, 1877	July 23, 1872
Collard, Fred. Stuartson, *Haling-pk.-cott., Brighton-rd.,Croydon.*	June 9, 1898	Nov. 8, 1894
Colledge, Lionel, 22 *Queen Anne-street*, W.	Dec. 14, 1911	July 30, 1908
Collier, Horace Stansfield, 30 *Wimpole-street*, W............	Dec. 11, 1890	Feb. 9, 1888
Collier, Mark Purcell Mayo, *Kearnsey Abbey, Kent*	June 8, 1882	Jan. 24, 1879
Collins, Edward Treacher, 17 *Queen-Anne-street*, W.	Dec. 11, 1890	May 18, 1883
Collins, Robt. Edward, *Sittang, Burma*	June 10, 1915	July 14, 1910
Collins, Sir William Job, K.C.V.O., 1 *Albert-Terrace*, N.W. ..	June 12, 1884	July 28, 1880
Collinson, Harold, C.B., C.M.G., 38 *Clarendon-rd., Leeds*	June 11, 1903	Nov. 2, 1899
Colquhoun, Giden Robert Ernest, 6 *Gloucester-terrace*, W.....	June 14, 1923	May 14, 1914
Colt, George Herbert, 12 *Bon Accord-square, Aberdeen*	Dec. 10, 1908	July 28, 1904
Colville, Ernest George, *Ashford, Kent*	Dec. 11, 1884	Nov. 18, 1881
¶Colyer, Sir James Frank, K.B.E., 11 *Queen Anne-street*, W. ..	Apr. 13, 1916	Aug. 1, 1889
Compton, Alwyne Theodore, 42 *Welbeck-street*, W.	June 12, 1902	Feb. 7, 1901
Connor, F. P., D.S.O., *Lt.-Col. I.M.S.*, 2 *Upper Wood-st.,Calcutta.*	Nov. 13, 1902	Aug. 1, 1901
Cook, Frank, 14 *St. Thomas's-street*, S.E. 1..................	June 11, 1914	Nov. 13, 1913
Cook, Herbert George Graham, 22 *Newport-road, Cardiff*	Dec. 10, 1891	Feb. 12, 1889
Cook, John Howard, 31 *Narcissus-rd., West Hampstead,*N.W.6	June 10, 1897	July 29, 1895
Cook, Lewis, *Lt.-Col. I.M.S.*, c/o *King & Co.*, 9 *Pall Mall*, S.W.	June 13, 1912	July 27, 1899
Cooke, Arthur, *Grove-lodge, Cambridge*	June 9, 1898	Nov. 14, 1895
Cooke, James Douglas, *Clodiagh, Stanmore, Middlesex*	June 1, 1905	Nov. 12, 1903
Cooke, John, " *Holmleigh*," *Bishop's-road, Sutton Coldfield*	Dec. 19, 1861	Feb. 29, 1856
Cookson, Frederick Nesfield, " *Taggscroft*," *Stafford*..........	June 8, 1899	May 10, 1894
Coombe, Russell, 5 *Barnfield-crescent, Exeter*	Dec. 13, 1888	July 23, 1886
Cooper, Clarence, *I.M.S.*, 3 *Warminster-road, South Norwood.*.	Dec. 12, 1867	Dec. 17, 1852
Cooper, Percy Robert, *Glenthorn, The Downs, Bowdon, Cheshire*	June 13, 1895	July 27, 1893
Cooper, Rustam N., *Marshall-lodge, Cumballa-hill, Bombay*....	Dec. 11, 1919	May 8, 1918
Coorlawala, Rustom N., *Station-rd., Hyderabad, Deccan, India*	Dec. 9, 1909	July 25, 1907
Cope, Vincent Zachary, 40 *Wimpole-street*, W...............	June 10, 1909	June 10, 1909
Copley, Stanley, 116 *Innes-road, Durban, Natal, S. Africa*	June 8, 1899	Nov. 8, 1894

Name and Residence.	Fellow.	Member.
Coppleson, V. M., 225 *Macquarie-street, Sydney, N.S.W.*	Mar. 10, 1921	Mar. 10, 1921
Corbett, R. S., *Standard Bank of S. Afr.*, 10 *Clements-lane,* E.C.	June 8, 1922	May 10, 1917
Corkey, Isaac Whitla, M.C., *"Beechwood," Epsom, Surrey*	June 8, 1922	June 8, 1922
Corner, Edred Moss, *Woodlands-park, Gt. Missenden, Bucks* ..	Dec. 14, 1899	May 4, 1898
Corsi, Henry, 12 *Bernard-mansions, Russell-square,* W.C.	June 9, 1921	May 10, 1918
Costobadie, Lionel Paliser, *Overdale, Mottram, Manchester*	Dec. 9, 1920	Sept. 24, 1914
Coumbe, John Batten, *Elvin-house, Andover, Hants*	Dec. 11, 1890	July 30, 1877
Counsell, Herbert Edward, 37 *Broad-street, Oxford*	Dec. 13, 1894	Oct. 22, 1884
Coupland, James Alane, 25 *Park-square, Leeds*	June 14, 1906	Apr. 5, 1906
Couzens, Alfred John, 221 *Romford-road,* E.	Dec. 12, 1907	May 9, 1901
Coventon, Albert Wm. D., 61 *Buckingham-road, Aylesbury* ..	Dec. 10, 1908	Nov. 10, 1904
Cowell, Ernest Marshall, D.S.O., 84 *Park-lane, Croydon*	Mar. 9, 1911	July 25, 1907
Cowell, George, 24 *Harrington-gardens,* S.W.	Dec. 12. 1867	July 9, 1858
Cowen, George Hebb, *" Maycroft," Hulse-road, Southampton..*	Apr. 8, 1897	Nov. 9, 1893
Coyte, Ralph, 17 *Duke-street, Manchester-square,* W.	June 9, 1921	May 10. 1917
Crabtree, Angelo M., *Surrey Cott., Oatlands Drive, Weybridge.*	June 8, 1899	Aug. 4, 1896
Craig, James Andrew, 11 *University Square, Belfast*	Dec. 11, 1902	Aug. 2, 1898
Crawford, Andrew John, *Wanganui, New Zealand*	Dec. 10, 1908	July 25, 1907
Crawshaw, Charles Harold, *Chester-square, Ashton-under-Lyne*	Dec. 9, 1920	Nov. 13, 1913
Cresswell, Frank Pearson Skeffington, 24 *Windsor-pl., Cardiff.*	Dec. 13, 1894	Nov. 10, 1892
Cripps, William Harrison, 19 *Bentinck-street,* W.	June 10, 1875	July 23, 1872
Cripps, William Lawrence, 53 *Albany-street,* N.W.	June 13, 1907	Nov. 12, 1903
Crook, Arthur Henry, 2 *Chiswick-place, Eastbourne*	June 8, 1911	Nov. 12, 1908
Crook, Eric Ashley, 15 *Earl's-terrace,* W. 8	June 8, 1922	Nov. 14, 1918
Crook, Herbert E.,*c/o Lond.County & Westm.Bank,E.Twickenham*	June 13, 1889	Jan. 19, 1887
Cropley, Henry, 5 *East-park-parade, Northampton*	Dec. 8, 1887	Aug. 6, 1884
Cross, Francis Geo.,*c/o Bank of Br. W.Africa,Leadenhall-st.,*E.C.	Dec. 11, 1902	Feb. 7, 1901
Cross, Francis Richardson, *Worcester-house, Clifton, Bristol* ..	June 13, 1878	Jan. 25, 1871
Crouch, Charles Percival, *Penquarry, Weston-super-Mare* ..:.	June 12, 1890	Jan. 21, 1887
Crowle, Thomas Henry Rickard, 37 *St. James'-place,* S.W. ..	Dec. 12, 1889	Jan. 24, 1884
Crowley, John Henry Joseph, *Ashmead, Chertsey, Surrey*	June 10, 1897	Feb. 8, 1894
Cruise, Sir Richard Robert, K.C.V.O., 34 *Wimpole-street,* W. .	June 11, 1903	July 25, 1900
Crymble, Percival Templeton, 7 *Upper Crescent, Belfast*	Dec. 10, 1908	Dec. 10, 1908
Cudmore, Arthur Murray, *North-terr., Adelaide, S. Australia* .	Dec. 14, 1899	Nov. 12, 1896
Cuff, Archibald William, 285 *Glossop-road, Sheffield*	June 13, 1895	July 27, 1893
Culpin, Millais, 59 *Queen Anne-street,* W.	Dec. 12, 1907	Nov. 13, 1902
Cumberbatch, Alphonso Elkin, 11 *Park-crescent,* W.	June 13, 1872	June 2, 1870
Cumberlidge, William Isaac, 159 *London-road, Leicester*	June 13, 1907	July 28, 1904
Cumming, Hugh Gordon, *Walton Lodge, Torquay*	Dec. 12, 1878	Jan. 28, 1875
Cunning, Joseph, 3 *Upper Wimpole-street,* W.	June 20, 1901	June 20, 1901
Cunningham, John Francis, O.B.E, 27 *Weymouth-street,* W. ..	Dec. 14, 1905	Feb. 8, 1900
Currie, Donald Irvine, 87 *Clarendon-road, Leeds*	June 14, 1923	May 11, 1922
Curry, Wilfred Alan, 18 *Summer-street, Halifax, Nova Scotia..*	June 11, 1914	May 9, 1912
Curtis, Frederick, O.B.E , *Alton-house, Redhill, Surrey*	June 12, 1902	Feb. 7, 1901
Curtis, Henry Jones, 2 *Richmond-terrace, Whitehall,* S.W. ...	Dec. 12, 1895	Feb. 12, 1891

Name and Residence.	Fellow.	Member.
da Costa Francis Xavier, 5 *Infantry-road, Bangalore, India* ..	Dec. 11, 1890	Feb. · 8, 1888
Dalal, Anandrai Keshavlal, *Parekh-house, New Queen's-rd, Bombay*	Oct. 12, 1911	Feb. 10, 1910
Daldy, Arthur Mantell, 14 *Palmeira-avenue, Hove*	July 30, 1894	Nov. 12, 1891
Daniel, Peter Lewis, 1 A *Upper Wimpole-street*, W.	June 8, 1899	May 4, 1898
Daniels, Davis Woodcock, 74 *Nottingham-road, Mansfield, Notts*	May 12, 1910	July 25, 1907
Daniels, Frederic William, 19 *Cardiff-road, Newport, Mon*.....	June 1, 1905	July 28, 1904
Darling, Harry C. R., 229 *Macquarie-street, Sydney, N.S.W.* .	June 12, 1913	Nov. 12, 1908
Davenport, Cecil John, *London-mission, Shanghai, China*	June 13, 1889	May 5, 1887
Davenport, Robert Cecil, *St. Bartholomew's-hospital, E.C.*	Dec. 8, 1921	May 11, 1916
Davies, Charles Owen, 4 *Maryland-st., Rodney-st., Liverpool* ..	Dec. 14, 1922	Feb. 12, 1920
Davies, David, M.C., *Birchill, Llangeitho, Cardiganshire*	June 9, 1910	July 30, 1908
Davies, David Leighton, 31 *Newport-road, Cardiff*	Dec. 9, 1909	May 10, 1900
Davies, Edwin Thomas Harries, " *The Grove," Tredegar, Mon.*.	Dec. 8, 1910	May 10, 1906
Davies, Francis Joseph, *Hurtmore Croft, Godalming*	Dec. 14, 1876	Apr. 18, 1876
Davies, Hugh, 129 *Harley-street*, W.	Dec. 10, 1896	July 27, 1893
Davies, Hugh Morriston, *Vale of Clwyd-sanat., Ruthin, N. Wales*	Dec. 13, 1906	Aug. 4, 1903
Davies, Trevor Berwyn, 81 *Wimpole-street*, W.	Dec. 11, 1913	July 30, 1908
§ Davies-Colley, Eleanor, 16 *Harley-street*, W. ;	Dec. 14, 1911	Dec. 14, 1911
Davies-Colley, Hugh, *Moon-hill-cottage, Frensham, Farnham* ..	Dec. 8, 1904	May 8, 1902
Davies-Colley, Robert, C.M.G., 10 *Devonshire-place*, W.	June 18, 1908	May 10, 1906
Davis, Edward David, 46 *Harley-street*, W.	June 13, 1912	Apr. 21, 1903
Davis, Haldinstein David, 17 *Cavendish-place*, W.	Dec. 10, 1908	Nov. 9, 1905
Davis, John Llewellyn, 217 *Woodborough-road, Nottingham* ..	Dec. 14, 1922	Nov. 12, 1914
Davis, Kenneth James Acton, 24 *Upper Berkeley-street*, W. ..	June 12, 1913	May 11, 1911
Daw, Samuel Wilfrid, 24 *Park-square, Leeds*...............	June 18, 1908	July 26, 1906
Dawson, J. Bernard, *Durham-st., Glenelg, nr. Adelaide, S. Austr.*	Apr. 9, 1908	July 27, 1905
Day, Donald Douglas, 3 *Surrey-street, Norwich*	Dec. 13, 1883	May 20, 1880
Dean, Henry Percy. 11 *Abinger-road, Bedford Park*, W.......	Oct. 17, 1889	June 9, 1887
Deanesly, Edward, " *Claremont," Wolverhampton*	Feb. 12, 1891	June 24, 1887
Debono, Peter Paul, 35 *Sda. Mezzodi, Valetta, Malta*	Dec. 9, 1920	Dec. 9, 1920
Dee, Maurice V., *Chudleigh-bldgs., Johannesburg, Transvaal, S. Afr.*	June 8, 1899	Feb. 10, 1898
de Mowbray, Ralph Marsh. *Grosvenor-house, Lymington, Hants.*	Dec. 10, 1914	Feb. 12, 1914
¶ Dennis, Frederic S., 62 *East 55th St., New York City, U.S.A.*.	Apr. 13, 1899	July 25, 1877
Dent, Howard Henry, *Bilbrook, Wolverhampton*	June 20, 1901	July 29, 1897
Denyer, Stanley Edward, C.M.G., 16 *Albion-street, Hull*......	June 13, 1907	Feb. 10, 1898
Deshmukh, Gopal V., *Lamington-road, Bombay, India*........	Dec. 9, 1909	July 29, 1909
de Silva, Arthur M., *Laurel-cottage, Borella, Colombo, Ceylon* ..	Dec. 13, 1906	Aug. 4, 1903
Devereux, Arthur Cecil, *Howard-lodge, Avenue-road, Malvern*..	June 10, 1909	June 10, 1909
Dew, Harold Robert, 127 *Collins-street, Melbourne, Australia*..	June 10, 1920	June 10, 1920
Dick, Alan MacDonald, O.B.E., *Maj. I.M.S.*	June 9, 1910	July 29, 1909
Dick, John Lawson, 42 *Cholmeley-park, Highgate*, N.	June 11, 1896	May 10, 1894
Dickie, W. S ,O.B.E.," *Ardencaple," Southfield-rd., Middlesbrough*	June 11, 1903	Nov. 8, 1900
Dickinson, Harold Bertie, *Greyfriars, Hereford*.............	Dec. 9, 1897	Nov. 8, 1894
Dickson, William Muir, c/o *Holt & Co.*, 3 *Whitehall-place*, S.W.	Dec. 9, 1920	Dec. 9, 1920
Digby, Kenelm Hutchinson, *The University, Hong Kong*......	June 9, 1910	Feb. 7, 1907
Diggle, Frank Holt, O.B.E., 26 *St. John-street, Manchester* ..	Dec. 11, 1913	Feb. 10, 1910
Dingley, Allen, *St. Norberts, Cheam-road, Sutton, Surrey*......	Dec. 14, 1882	July 30, 1878

Name and Residence.	Fellow.	Member.
Dingley, Allen Roy, *St. Norbert's, Cheam-road, Sutton, Surrey.*	June 8, 1922	Feb. 8, 1917
Dingley, Lionel A., *Brunswick-house, Holyhead-rd., Wednesbury.*	Dec. 9, 1920	July 25, 1912
Doble, Henry Tregellas, *Dunoon, Yelverton, Devon*	Dec. 10, 1903	Feb. 13, 1902
Dobson, Joseph Faulkner, " *Longfield*," *Headingley, Leeds*	June 20, 1901	July 29, 1897
Dodd, J. R., *Col. A.M.S.*, 140 *Richmond-pk.-rd., Bournemouth.*.	Dec. 9, 1886	July 21, 1879
Dodds-Parker, Arthur Percy, 2 *Holywell-street, Oxford*	Dec. 11, 1902	Dec. 11, 1902
Dolbey, Robert Valentine, *Kasr-el-Aini-hosp., Cairo*	June 1, 1905	Feb. 13, 1902
Donaldson, Malcolm, 145 *Harley-street*, W.	June 11, 1914	May 13, 1909
Doran, Alban Henry Griffith, 6 *Palace-mansions, Kensington*, W.	June 10, 1875	Jan. 24, 1871
Dorrell, Edmund Arthur, 21 *Bolton-street, Mayfair*, W.......	June 10, 1909	Nov. 8, 1894
Douglas, Archibald Robt. John, *Burma Railway, Rangoon, India*	June 8, 1899	May 14, 1896
Douglas, Claude, " *Silchester*," *East Cowes, Isle of Wight*	Dec. 13, 1888	Nov. 19, 1873
Douglas, Wm. Rob., M.C., 10 *St. John-street, Manchester*	June 9, 1910	July 30, 1908
Douglas-Crawford, Douglas, 75 *Rodney-street, Liverpool*	Dec. 13, 1894	Dec. 13, 1894
Doyne, Philip Geoffry, 8 *Harley-street*, W.	Dec. 10, 1914	Feb. 13. 1913
Drake, Courtenay Henry, *Harlequin-lane, Crowborough*	June 10, 1897	Nov. 8, 1894
Drew, Arthur John, *Water Hall, St: Aldate's, Oxford*	June 14, 1888	July 31, 1884
Drew, Douglas, 6 *Wimpole-street*, W. .....:...............	Aug. 1, 1892	July 28, 1890
Drew, Hedley Vicars, *Timaru, New Zealand*	June 12, 1890	July 19, 1882
Drew, Henry William, *Westfield, Wing, near Oakham*	June 13, 1889	July 23, 1886
Driberg, Jas. Douglas, M.C., O.B.E., 46 *Queen-Anne-street*, W.	Oct. 14, 1915	May 8, 1913
Duer, C., *Lt.-Col. I.M.S., c/o Brown, Shipley & Co.*, 123 *Pall Mall*, S. W.	Dec. 10, 1891	Apr. 2, 1888
Duffett, Henry Allcroft, " *Withey Holt*," *Hatherley-road, Sidcup*	June 10, 1897	Feb. 8, 1894
Duggan, Norman, *College-gates, Worcester*	Dec. 11, 1913	Feb. 1, 1912
Dummere, Henzell Howard, M.C., 13 *Valinger's-rd., King's Lynn*	Dec. 9, 1920	May 12, 1920
Dun, Robert Craig, 41 *Rodney-street, Liverpool*	June 12, 1902	Nov. 14, 1895
Duncan, Kenneth McKenzie, 1 *Stanley-place, Preston, Lancs.* ...	Dec. 12, 1907	Dec. 12, 1907
Dundas-Grant, Sir James, K.B.E., 148 *Harley-street*, W. ...	June 12, 1890	Nov. 13, 1876
Dundon, John, 16 *St. Patrick's-place, Cork*	June 1, 1905	June 1, 1905
Dunn, Hugh Percy, 54 *Wimpole-street*, W.	Dec. 9, 1880	Aug. 1, 1876
Dunn, Spencer Graeme, *The Hospital, St. Brides, Pembrokeshire*	June 9, 1921	May 11, 1916
Durham, Frederic, 34 *Dover-street*, W.	June 13, 1872	Nov. 16, 1869
Durham, Herbert Edward, " *Dunelm*," *Hampton Park, Hereford.*	July 30, 1894	July 30, 1894
Dyall, Thomas James, 58 *Creffield-road, West Acton*, W.	June 11, 1891	June 11, 1891
Dyball, Brennan, 37 *Southernhay West, Exeter*	Dec. 9, 1897	Nov. 14, 1895
Eadie, James, 3 *Bentinck-mansions, Bentinck-street*, W.	June 9, 1910	June 9, 1910
Eastes, Thomas, 18 *Manor-road, Folkestone*	June 10, 1875	July 22, 1872
Ebden, J. A. W., *Capt. R.A.M.C.*, 21 *Jenner-h'se, Hunter-st.*, W.C.	June 9, 1921	June 9, 1921
Eccles, William Mc'Adam, 124 *Harley-street*, W.	Oct. 13, 1892	Feb. 13, 1890
Edge, Frederick, *Granville-house, Wolverhampton*	June 13, 1889	Oct. 22, 1885
Edgecombe, Wilfrid, 17 *Victoria-avenue, Harrogate*	Mar. 12, 1896	Feb. 9, 1893
Edmond, William Square, 26 *St. John's-hill, Shrewsbury*	Dec. 9, 1909	July 28, 1904
Edmunds, Arthur, C.B., 57 *Queen Anne-street*, W.	Dec. 12, 1901	Nov. 8, 1900
Edmunds, Walter, 5 *Carlton-road, Putney-hill*, S.W.	June 14, 1877	Jan. 27, 1875
Edridge-Green, F. W., C.B.E., 99 *Walm-lane, Willesden-gn.*, N.W.	Dec. 8, 1892	June 27, 1887
Edwards, Arthur Tudor, 58 *Harley-street*, W.	Dec. 9, 1915	Nov. 13, 1915

Name and Residence.	Fellow.	Member.
Edwards, Frederick Swinford, 68 *Grosvenor-street*, W.	June 13, 1878	Nov. 17, 1875
Edwards, Thomas Henry, 8 *New North-road, Huddersfield*	Dec. 12, 1901	July 25, 1900
Edye, Benjamin Thomas, *The University, Sydney, N.S.W.*	June 10, 1915	June 10, 1915
Edye, Stonard, *Monte Video, Uruguay, S. America*	June 9, 1870	Dec. 2, 1859
Elam, William Henry, *New Barnet*, N.	June 14, 1883	Nov. 13, 1877
Elkington, George Ernest, M.C., *Newport, Shropshire*	Dec. 9, 1920	July 30, 1914
Elliot, Robert Henry, *Lt.-Col. I.M.S.*, 54 *Welbeck-street*, W...	June 9, 1892	Nov. 14, 1889
Elliott, Arthur Bowes, 11 *South-parade, Pensarn, Abergele*	June 13, 1872	Apr. 25, 1867
Ellis, Frederick Wm., 68 *Hagley-road, Edgbaston, Birmingham.*	June 1, 1905	June 1, 1905
Elmslie, Reginald Cheyne, O.B.E., 1 A *Portland-place*, W.	Dec. 8, 1901	May 9, 1901
Elworthy, Henry Stuart, *Treve Cottage, Ebbw Vale, Mon.......*	Dec. 12, 1895	July 27, 1893
English, Sir Thomas Crisp, K.C.M.G., 82 *Brook-street*, W.....	Oct. 15, 1903	Feb. 8, 1900
Evans, Arthur Henry, O B.E., 86 *Brook-street*, W.	Dec. 9, 1897	July 29, 1895
Evans, Evan, 1 *Goring-place, Llanelly*	Dec. 13, 1894	Jan. 27, 1886
Evans, Evan Laming, C.B.E., 50 *Seymour-street*, W.	Dec. 14, 1899	Nov. 14, 1895
Evans, Griffith Ifor, 36 *Castle-square, Carnarvon*	Dec. 8, 1921	May 11, 1916
Evans, John Howell, 25 *Berkeley-square*, W.................	Dec. 12, 1901	Nov. 11, 1897
Evans, John Jackson W., *Osborne-house, St. Aubin's, Jersey* ..	Dec. 10, 1908	May 10, 1906
Evans, John Jameson, 41 *Newhall-street, Birmingham*	June 8, 1899	May 13, 1897
Evans, T.J.C.,M.C.,*Maj. I.M.S.,Grindlay&Co.,54Parl't-st.,S.W.*	June 9, 1910	Nov. 9, 1905
Evans,William Geo.,56*Holyhead-rd., Handsworth, Birmingham.*	June 12, 1884	Nov. 20, 1880
Evans, Willmott Henderson, 121 *Harley-street*, W.	Dec. 11, 1890	July 25, 1883
Everidge, John, O.B.E., 24 *Cavendish-square*, W............	June 13, 1912	Feb. 13, 1908
Evers, Henry, 73 *Shortridge terr., Jesmond, Newcastle-on-Tyne.*	Mar. 10, 1921	Nov. 11, 1920
Every-Clayton, L. E. V., *The Old School-house, Tetbury*	Dec. 10, 1896	Feb. 7, 1895
Ewart, George Arthur, 31 *Upper Brook-street*, W.	June 11, 1914	Feb. 1, 1912
Fagge, Charles Herbert, 3 *Devonshire-place*, W...............	Apr. 14, 1898	Aug. 4, 1896
Fahmy-el-Minyawi, Ibrahim, *Kasr El Aini-hosp., Cairo, Egypt.*	Dec. 12, 1912	Feb. 1, 1912
Fairbairn, John Shields, 42 *Wimpole-street*, W...............	May 31, 1900	Nov. 14, 1895
Fairbank, Harold A. T., O.B.E., D.S.O., 84 *Harley-street*, W...	Dec. 12, 1901	Aug. 2, 1898
Fairlie-Clarke, Allan Johnston, 11 *Waterloo-crescent, Dover* ..	June 11, 1903	Aug. 1, 1901
Falconer, James Law, *Parkfield-house, Chorley New-rd., Bolton.*	Dec. 12, 1907	Dec. 12, 1907
Falkner, Edgar Ashley, *Colstoun, Toowoomba, Queensland*	Dec. 10, 1891	Aug. 2, 1888
Farmer,G.W.S.,*Camden-ho,Lennox-st,Maryborough,Queensland*	Dec. 13, 1894	May 2, 1890
Farnell, Henry D., O B.E., "*Grasmere," Mead's-rd., Eastbourne.*	Dec. 10, 1885	May 20, 1874
Farquhar, George Greig, 24 *Stanhope-road, Darlington*	June 14, 1906	June 14, 1906
Faulder, Thomas Jefferson, 11 *Tenby-mansions*, W.	Dec. 8, 1904	Aug. 4, 1903
Faulkner, Ebenezer R., 101 *East 58th-st., New York City, U.S.A.*	June 13, 1907	Nov. 9, 1905
Fawcett, John, 66 *Wimpole-street*, W.	June 9, 1892	May 8, 1890
Fearnley, Harold, 147 *Bow-road*, E.	June 8, 1911	June 8, 1911
Fedden, Walter Fedde, 95 *Cromwell-road*, S.W.	Jan. 14, 1904	July 25, 1900
Fenton, Thomas Gerald, "*Rialto," Higher Erith-rd., Torquay.*.	Dec. 8, 1910	May 11, 1899
Fenwick, E. Hurry, C.B.E., 53 *Bedford-gardens, Kensington,* W.	Aug. 3, 1882	May 19, 1880
Fenwick, George E. O., O.B.E., *Northern Club, Auckland, N.Z.*	Dec. 8, 1910	Nov. 12, 1903
Fenwick, Wm. S., *Earldom's Lodge, Whiteparish, nr. Salisbury*	Dec. 10, 1908	July 20, 1906

Name and Residence.	Fellow.	Member.
Ferguson, Robert James, 10 *St. George's-place, Canterbury* ..	Dec. 8, 1904	Dec. 8, 1904
Finch, Ernest Frederick, 53 *Wilkinson-street, Sheffield*	June 8, 1911	June 8, 1911
Finn, Allan Rigden, *Thornhills, Speen, Newbury*	Dec. 12, 1912	Nov. 10, 1904
Finny, C. M., *Capt. R.A.M.C., c/o Holt &Co.,* 3 *Whitehall-pl.,*S.W.	Dec. 8, 1921	Dec. 8, 1921
Firth, Charles, *Cromer-house, Gravesend*	June 13, 1878	Nov. 18, 1873
Firth, John Lacy, 8 *Victoria-square, Clifton, Bristol*	June 8, 1893	Nov. 8, 1888
Firth, Sir Robert H., K.B.E., C.B., 4 *Finchley-road,* N.W.....	Dec. 14, 1882	Nov. 19, 1879
Fisher, Alfred George Timbrell, M.C., 86 *Harley-street,* W. ..	Dec. 11, 1919	July 27, 1911
Fisher, Edward Fow, 7 *Buckingham-terrace, Edinburgh*	June 9, 1904	Feb. 13, 1902
Fisher, Frederic Richard, 95 *Crane-street, Salisbury*	Dec. 14, 1876	Apr. 26, 1867
Fisher, John Herbert, 83 *Wimpole-street,* W.................	June 8, 1893	Nov. 12, 1891
Fisher, Welby Earle, 48 *Harley-street,* W.	Dec. 12, 1907	Nov. 8, 1900
Fitzmaurice-Kelly, Maurice A. M., 35 *Brunswick-square, Hove.*	Dec. 14, 1905	Nov. 13, 1902
Fitzwilliams, Duncan C. Lloyd, C.M.G., 31 *Grosvenor-street,* W.	June 14, 1906	June 14, 1906
Fleming, Alexander, 2 D *Bickenhall Mansions,* W.	June 10, 1909	July 26, 1906
Fleming, Robert Hood, 10 *Ladbroke-square,* W.1.............	Dec. 9, 1920	Dec. 9, 1920
Flemming, Percy, 70 *Harley-street,* W.	June 13, 1889	Jan. 27, 1885
Flint, Ethelbert Rest, 30 *Park-square, Leeds*................	Jan. 13, 1912	Nov. 9, 1905
Foley, Walter Barham, O.B.E., 106 *Ebury-street,* S.W.	June 8, 1922	Nov. 14, 1912
Footner, George Rammell, *Khartoum, Sudan*................	June 14, 1906	May 12, 1904
Footner, John Bulkley, 1 *The Priory, Tunbridge Wells*	June 12, 1879	Jan. 28, 1875
Forbes, Robert Dow, 908 *Cobb-bldys,Seattle, Washington,U.S.A.*	June 13, 1907	Nov. 8, 1906
Formby, Henry Harper, *Strathalbyn, S. Australia*	June 11, 1903	May 14, 1903
Forsdike, Sidney, 82 *Harley-street,* W.	June 10, 1920	Aug. 1, 1901
Forshaw, Wm. H., *Curuzu Cuatia,Provincia Corrientes,Arg.Rep.*	June 10, 1909	Feb. 7, 1901
Forsyth, John Andrew Cairns, 56 *Harley-street,* W.	June 11, 1914	June 11, 1914
Forward, Francis Edward, "*Eversley,*" *Boxley-road, Maidstone.*	July 30, 1891	Aug. 1, 1889
Foster, Philip Stanley, *Dalgety's-buildings, Christchurch, N.Z.* ..	July 10, 1913	Nov. 9, 1911
Foster, William James, 11 *Bath-road, Reading*..............	Dec. 8, 1892	Feb. 13, 1890
Fouché, François Petrus, 9 *Minet-avenue, Harlesden,* N.W. ..	June 14, 1923	June 14, 1923
Foulerton, Alex. Grant Russell, O.B.E., *Wealdside, Lewes*	Dec. 12, 1895	July 30, 1884
Fowler, Chas. E. P., *Col. A.M.S., Orient-house, Budge-row,* E.C.	Dec. 10, 1891	Feb. 12, 1889
Fowler, Robert, *c/o Bank of Victoria, Collins-street, Melbourne.*	June 10, 1920	June 10, 1920
Fox, Edward Joseph, 12 *Rylands-street, Warrington*	June 8, 1899	Feb. 11, 1897
Fox, George Raymond, 91 *Amhurst-park, Stamford-hill,* N. ..	June 10, 1897	May 10, 1894
Fox, Herbert	June 14, 1888	Oct. 21, 1884
Francis, Alfred George, O.B E, 101 *Beverley-road, Hull*	June 12, 1890	Oct. 23, 1885
Frankau, Claude H. S., C.B.E., D.S.O., 57A *Wimpole-street,* W.	June 18, 1908	May 9, 1907
Franklin, Philip Julius, 27 *Wimpole-street,* W...............	Dec. 11, 1913	Feb. 7, 1907
Fraser, Forbes, C.B E., 5 *The Circus, Bath*	Dec. 10, 1896	May 10, 1894
Frazer, John Ernest Sullivan, 2 *Pembridge-crescent,* W.	June 9, 1898	July 30, 1891
Freeland, Ernest Harding, "*Ivy Dene," East Cliff, Herne Bay.*	Dec. 9, 1897	Apr. 28, 1884
Fremantle, Francis E., O.B.E.,M.P., *Bedwell-pk., Hatfield, Herts*	June 11, 1903	Nov. 11, 1897
French, George William Henry, 42 *Church-lane, Hornsey,* N..	Dec. 9, 1886	Apr. 23, 1884
French, John Gay, 135 *Harley-street,* W.	Dec. 12, 1907	Feb. 13, 1902
Fripp, Sir Alfred Downing, K.C.V.O., C.B., 19 *Portland-pl.,* W.	June 8, 1893	Feb. 12, 1889
Frost, Wm. Adams, *c/o L. C. W. & P. Bank,* 21 *Hanover-sq.,*W.	June 13, 1878	July 22, 1874

Name and Residence.	Fellow.	Member.
Fulton, Roland A. H., 2 *Pitt-street, Dunedin, N.Z.*	Dec. 14, 1922	Dec. 14, 1922
Furnivall, Percy, " *Fernvale*," *Northam, N. Devon*	June 13, 1895	Nov. 10, 1892

Gabriel, Vraspillai, " *Blossholme*," *Greenpath, Colpetly, Colombo*	June 11, 1914	Nov. 14, 1912
Gabriel, William Bashall, 69 *Wimpole-street*, W.	Dec. 12, 1918	July 27, 1916
Gadgil, Shridhar Bheekajee, *Islington-infirmary, Highgate-hill.*	June 10, 1915	May 10, 1900
Gallie, William Edward, 143 *College-street, Toronto, Canada* ..	Dec. 12, 1918	Dec. 12, 1918
Galpin, Geo. L., *Box* 411, *Port Elizabeth, Cape Prov., S. Africa.*	June 11, 1885	Nov. 18, 1880
Gamgee, Leonard Parker, 95 *Cornwall-street, Birmingham*	July 7, 1893	Feb. 12, 1891
Gardiner, Harold, 12 *Aberdare-gardens, Hampstead,* N.W.	June 11, 1914	Apr. 10, 1913
Gardner, Arth. Duncan, *The Pathological Dpt., The Museum, Oxford*	Dec. 12, 1912	Feb. 9, 1911
Garmany, Jasper Jewett, 33 *W. 42nd-street, New York, U.S.A.*	Dec. 10, 1885	Apr. 28, 1881
Gask, George Ernest, C.M.G., D.S.O., 4 *York-gate,* N.W.	June 20, 1901	Aug. 2, 1898
Gaskell, A., C.B., M B.E., *Surg.-Capt., R. Naval-coll., Greenwich*	June 8, 1899	Aug. 1, 1892
Gauntlett, Eric Gerald, C.B.E., D.S.O., 14 *Kiukiang-rd., Shanghai*	June 8, 1911	Feb. 13, 1908
Geach, Robert Neville, 52 *Eaton-terrace,* S.W.	Dec. 10, 1914	Feb. 10, 1898
Gemmill, William, 54 *Newhall-street, Birmingham*	June 12, 1913	June 12, 1913
Gerard-Pearse, John Ernest, 11 *Royal-terrace, Weymouth*	Dec. 9, 1920	Sept. 24, 1914
§Ghosh, Satapriya, 51/1 *Raju Dinendra-street, Calcutta, India.* .	June 9, 1921	Nov. 8, 1917
Gibb, Harold Pace, 91 *Harley-street,* W.	Dec. 13, 1906	May 12, 1904
Gibbs, Charles, 23 *Upper Wimpole-street,* W.	May 11, 1893	July 20, 1890
Gibson, Alexander, 661 *Broadway, Winnipeg, Canada*	Dec. 11, 1913	Dec. 11, 1913
Gibson, Wm. R., 37 *Amherst-road, Ealing,* W.	June 20, 1901	Aug. 4. 1896
Gilbert, Henry, 172 *North-terrace, Adelaide*	Dec. 13, 1906	Apr. 14, 1904
Gilder, M. D. D., *Central Bank-bldg., Hornby-rd., Fort, Bombay*	Dec. 9, 1909	Dec. 9, 1909
Giles, Leonard Thomason, *Maveys, Brockenhurst*	Dec. 10, 1896	Feb. 7, 1895
Gilford, Hastings, *Norwood-house, Kings-road, Reading*	June 13, 1889	Nov. 10, 1887
Gill, John Frederic, 21 *Albion-street, Hull*	June 10, 1920	June 10, 1920
Gill. Richard, 17 *Albert Hall-mansions,* W.	Dec. 8, 1881	Dec. 8, 1881
Gillam, George Joshua, 14 *Prince's-square, Bayswater,* W.	June 14, 1923	June 14, 1923
Gillespie, Edward, 24 *Weymouth-street,* W.	Dec. 12, 1907	Dec. 12, 1907
Gilliatt, William, 58 A *Wimpole-street,* W.	Dec. 12, 1912	Feb. 13, 1908
Gillies, Harold Delf. C.B.E., 7 *Portland-place,* W.	Dec. 8, 1910	Feb. 13, 1908
Gilmour, John, 38 *Jesmond-rd., Newcastle*	June 10, 1920	May 8, 1919
Gilroy, P. K., M.C., *Maj. I.M.S., c/o Grindlay & Co., 54 Parliament-st*	Dec. 9, 1920	May 13, 1909
Gimblett, Charles Leonard, 26 *Welbeck-street,* W.	Dec. 14, 1922	May 4, 1914
Girdlestone, Gathorne R., *The Red-house, Headington, Oxford*	Dec. 14, 1911	Feb 13, 1908
Giuseppi, Paul Leon, *Trevise, Felixstowe*	June 13, 1907	Nov. 9, 1905
Gladstone, Reginald John, 22 *Regent's-park-terrace,* N.W.	Dec. 10, 1896	Aug. 1, 1892
Glendining, Bryden, " *Woodcote*," *Aspley Guise, Beds*	Dec. 10, 1908	Dec. 10. 1908
Glendining, Vincent, 1 *Mildred-avenue, Watford*	June 11, 1914	July 27, 1911
Godlee, Sir R J, Bt., K.C.V.O., *Coombe End Farm, Whitchurch, Oxf.*	June 8, 1871	July 24, 1872
Godson, Alfred Henry, *Oak Bank, Oldham*	June 8, 1898	May 4, 1898
Going, Robert Marshal, 3 *Granville-road, Littlehampton*	June 10, 1897	Aug. 4, 1896
Goldie, W. L. M., O.B.E., *Public Health Offices, Leamington Spa.*	June 1, 1905	Feb. 12, 1903
Golding-Bird, Cuthbert Hilton, *Pitfield-cottage, Meopham, Kent.*	June 11, 1874	Apr. 16, 1872

Name and Residence.	Fellow.	Member.
Goldschmidt, Lionel Bernard, *Queenstown, S. Africa*	Dec. 8, 1921	Feb. 8, 1917
Gooddy, Edward Samuel, *The Croft, Alsager, Cheshire*	Dec. 13, 1888	Oct. 30, 1885
Goodwin, Arthur Charles, *Toronto-house, West Bromwich*	June 13, 1907	June 13, 1907
Goodwin, Aubrey, O.B.E., 72 *Wimpole-street*, W.............	Dec. 14, 1922	May 8, 1913
Goodwin, Bernard G., 91 *Cornwall-steet, Birmingham*	Dec. 14, 1911	Feb. 11, 1909
¶Goodwin, Sir T. H. J. C., K.C.B., C.M G., D.S.O., *D.G.A.M.S.*	Apr. 10, 1919	Aug. 1, 1892
Gordon, John	June 13, 1895	May 10, 1894
Gordon-Taylor, Gordon, O.B.E., 80 *Harley-street*, W.........	Dec. 13, 1906	Nov. 12, 1903
Gordon-Watson, Sir Chas. G., K.B.E., C.M.G., 82 *Harley-st.*, W.	June 12, 1902	May 4, 1898
Gough, Alfred, 41 *Park-square, Leeds*.....................	Dec. 9, 1909	Dec. 9, 1909
Gough, William, 5 *Park-square, Leeds*	June 11, 1903	July 25, 1900
Gould, Eric Lush Pearce, 16 *Queen Anne-street*, W.	Dec. 12, 1912	May 11, 1911
Goulden, Charles Bernard, O.B.E., 42 *Welbeck-street*, W.	Dec. 8, 1904	Aug. 4, 1903
Gow, John, 28 *St. John-street, Manchester*.................	Dec. 11, 1913	Dec. 11, 1913
Gowland, William Percy, *University of Otago, Dunedin, N.Z.*..	Dec. 12, 1912	Nov. 14, 1901
Goyder, Francis W., 101 *Manningham-lane, Bradford, Yorks*..	June 13, 1907	Nov. 12, 1903
Grace, John Johnston, 61 *Welbeck-street*, W...............	Dec. 10, 1896	May 10, 1894
Graham, Cecil Irving, 17 *Upper Wimpole-street*, W.	June 1, 1905	Nov. 14, 1901
Graham, Samuel Lewis, 83 *Newhall-street, Birmingham*......	Dec. 12, 1912	May 11, 1905
Grange, Charles D'Oyly, 104 *Station-parade, Harrogate*	June 12, 1913	July 25, 1910
Grant, John William Geary, 19 *Windsor-place, Cardiff*	Dec. 9, 1909	Feb. 13, 1890
Graves, Thos. Chivers, *The Asylum, Rubery-hill, nr. Birmingham*	June 11, 1914	Feb. 1, 1912
Gray, Archibald Montague Hy., C B.E., 30 *New Cavendish-st.*, W.	June 18, 1908	Feb. 12, 1903
Gray, Arthur Oliver, 34 *Weymouth-street*, W..............	June 10, 1915	May 8. 1913
Gray, George Munn, P.O. 444, *Lagos, Nigeria*	June 8, 1911	June 8. 1911
Gray, Harry Tyrrell, 28 *Harley-street*, W.	Dec. 12, 1907	July 27, 1905
Gray, John Power William, 40 *The Ropewalk, Nottingham* ..	June 13, 1889	Aug. 5, 1884
Greaves, Francis Ley Augustus, O B.E., 83 *Friar-gate, Derby*..	June 12, 1902	Nov. 11, 1897
Green, Charles David, *Larry House, Main-road, Romford* ....*	June 14, 1894	July 20, 1883
Green, C. R. M., *Col. I.M.S., Cook & Son, Ludgate-circus*, E.C.	June 13, 1895	May 27, 1885
Green, Douglas, 2 *Comping-lane, Woodseats, Sheffield*	Dec. 10, 1914	Dec. 10, 1914
Green, Ronald Benjamin, 9 *Sherborne-gardens, Ealing*, W. ..	Dec. 8, 1921	Feb. 14, 1918
Greene, Charles William, *The Esplanade, Rochester, Kent*	June 8, 1911	May 10, 1906
Greene, Wm. Henry Clayton, C.B.E., 86 *Brook-st.*, W.	Dec. 12, 1901	Nov. 8, 1900
Greenfield, Dudley George, *Rushden, Northants*	Mar. 12, 1903	May 9, 1902
Greenhill, J. R., *Lt.-Col. A.M.S., Stone-house, Rose-hill, Dorking*	Dec. 10, 1863	Apr. 13, 1800
Greenwood, Charles Henry, 7 *Park-street, Ripon*	Nov. 10, 1904	Nov. 10, 1904
Greenwood, Henry Harold, 34 *Victoria-road, Swindon, Wilts.* ..	June 12, 1919	Feb. 11, 1897
Greenyer, Vivian Tudor, 45 *New Church-road, Hove, Sussex* ..	Dec. 11, 1902	Feb. 9, 1893 .
Greeves, Reginald Affleck, 23 *Wimpole-street*, W.	Dec. 13, 1906	May 10, 1906
Greg, Arthur Hyde, O.B.E., 19 *St. George's-court*, S.W.	June 20, 1901	Feb. 10, 1898
¶Grenfell, Wilfred T., C.M.G., c/o 181 *Queen Victoria-st.*, E.C. ..	Apr. 8, 1920	Feb 9, 1888
Grey, Thomas C., 17 *Alexandra-terrace, Newcastle-on-Tyne* ..	Dec. 8, 1892	May 8, 1890
Griffin, Walter Bristow, 1 *Pavilion-terrace, Scarboro'*	June 9, 1910	July 25, 1907
Griffin, Wm. Watson, c/o *Lloyds Bank, Weston-super-mare*....	Oct. 11, 1894	Nov. 15, 1893
Griffith, Arthur Donald, 39 *Hertford-street, Mayfair*, W.	Dec. 9, 1909	July 27, 1905
Griffith, Harold Kinder, *Roydon, Torquay*..................	June 11, 1914	July 27, 1911

Name and Residence.	Fellow.	Member.
Griffith, John Richard, 13 *Brunswick-square, Hove*	June 10, 1920	May 13, 1915
Griffith, Walter S Anderson, C.B.E., 19 *Cheyne-walk*, S.W. ..	Dec. 8, 1881	Apr. 16, 1878
Griffiths, Cornelius Albert, 35 *Newport-road, Cardiff*	June 8, 1893	May 9, 1889
Griffiths, Hugh Ernest, 90 *Harley-street*, W.	Dec. 13, 1917	Feb. 10, 1916
Griffiths, Joseph, C.M.G., 1 *St. Peter's-terrace, Cambridge*	June 9, 1892	July 30, 1891
Griffiths, William Layard, " *Melrose*," *St. James-cres., Swansea.*	June 12, 1902	Aug. 1, 1901
Grimsdale, Harold Barr, 3 *Harley-place, Harley-street*, N.W. ...	June 14, 1894	May 10, 1894
Groves, Ernest William Hey, 25 *Victoria-square, Clifton, Bristol*	Dec. 14, 1905	May 9, 1895
Guevara-Rojas, Felipe, *Caracas, Venezuela*	June 9 1910	Feb. 10, 1910
Gullan, Archibald Gordon, 37 *Rodney-street, Liverpool*	June 10, 1897	Nov. 9, 1894
Gunn, Donald Stilwell	June 13, 1889	July 27, 1883
Gushue-Taylor, G., 94 *St. Andrew's-road, Ilford, Essex*	June 10, 1920	Feb. 10, 1910
Guthrie, Thomas, 5 *Rodney-street, Liverpool*	June 1, 1905	Feb. 12, 1903
Hadley, Fk. A.,*Maj.R A.M.C.,Adelaide-ho ,Perth,Westn.Austr.*	Dec. 14, 1905	Feb. 9, 1899
Hadley, Wilfred James, 33 *Queen Anne-street*, W.	June 9, 1887	Nov. 16, 1883
Haigh, William Edwin, *Hodge Memor.-hosp., Hankow, China .*	June 8, 1911	Feb. 11, 1909
Hailes, W. A., *London Hosp., Students'-hostel, 62 Philpot-st.*, E.	Dec. 11, 1919	Dec. 11, 1919
Hainworth, Edward Marrack, M.B.E , 14 *Albion-street, Hull* ..	Dec. 12, 1895	Aug. 1, 1892
Hall, Charles Beauchamp, *St. Denys, Bellevue-rd., Exmouth* ..	Dec. 10, 1896	July 27, 1893
Hall, Geoffry Craythorne, *Col. I.M.S., Ulidia, Bexhill*	Dec. 13, 1894	May 2, 1871
Hall. John Moore, 8 *Grand-av., West Southbourne, Bournemouth*	June 14, 1894	May 14, 1891
Hallidie, A. H. S., 7 *Grosvenor-crescent, St. Leonards-on-Sea.* .	Dec. 8, 1892	May 8, 1890
Halliwell,ArthurC.,*County Bank House,St Anne's-on-sea,Lancs.*	Dec. 14, 1922	Feb. 13, 1919
Hamilton, Arthur Francis, *Maj.I.M.S., Grindlay & Co.,Bombay*	June 1, 1905	Feb. 12, 1903
Hamilton,Wm.H.,C.I.E. D S.O.,*Lt. Col.I.M.S.,Amritsar,Punjab*	Dec. 10, 1908	May 14, 1903
Hammond, Thomas Edwin, 6 *Windsor-place, Cardiff*	Oct. 9, 1913	July 25, 1912
Handfield-Jones, Ranald M., M.C., 27 *Harley-street*, W.......	June 10, 1920	May 13, 1920
Handley, William Sampson, 36 *Harley-street*, W.	June 10, 1897	Feb. 7, 1895
Harbison, David Thomas, *Bowral, N S. W.*...	Dec. 12, 1901	Dec. 12, 1901
Hardwick-Smith, Henry, *The Hospital. Wellington, New Zealand.*	Dec. 12, 1907	Nov. 10, 1904
Hare, Evan Herring, *Alresford-lodge, Tottenham-lane,Hornsey,N.*	June 9, 1887	Aug. 2, 1876
Harkness,R C.,*Bermondsey&Rotherhithe-hosp..Lower-rd.,Ro'ithe*	Mar. 14, 1912	Oct. 12, 1911
Harman, Nathaniel Bishop, 108 *Harley-street* W.	Dec. 8, 1898	July 9, 1895
Harmer, William Douglas, 9 *Park-crescent*, W.	May 31, 1900	Aug. 2, 1898
Harnett, Walter Lidwell, *Maj. I.M S., Belvedere-house, Barnet.*	Dec. 8, 1904	Feb. 12, 1903
Harries, David John, 106 *Newport-road, Cardiff*	Dec. 9, 1915	May 13, 1915
Harries, Thomas Davies, *Grosvenor-house, Aberystwyth*	June 14, 1877	May 24, 1873
Harris, Herbert Elwin, 15 *Lansdown-place, Clifton, Bristol*	Dec. 10, 1896	Oct. 28, 1885
Harris, William James, *Avishays, Shaftesbury, Dorset*	June 13, 1895	May 11, 1893
Harrison, Charles Edwd , C M.G., C.V.O., 19 *Westgate-ter.*,S.W.	June 13, 1878	Jan. 21, 1874
Harrison, Edward, 19 *John-street, Hull*	Dec. 9, 1886	May 17, 1883
Harsant, William Henry, *Tower-house, Clifton, Bristol*	Dec. 13, 1877	July 27, 1874
Hartley, Harold, " *Hillesden*," *Lancaster-rd., Newcastle, Staffs.* .	June 9, 1904	June 9, 1904
Hartley,Jas.Norman Jackson, O.B.E., 10 *Ainslie-pl., Edinburgh.*	June 10, 1920	June 10, 1920
Hartley, John Dawson, " *Cliveden*," *Pelham-road, Gravesend* ..	July 10, 1902	July 27, 1899

Name and Residence.	Fellow.	Member.
Hartridge, Gustavus, 12 *Wimpole-street*, W.	Dec 10. 1874	July 22, 1872
Hart-Smith, Franke Chamberlain, *West-lodge, Leominster*	June 14, 1888	Apr. 23, 1885
Harty, Jn. P.Ingham, *West-view,Clifton-down-rd.,Cliftn.,Bristol.*	June 13, 1912	June 13, 1912
Harvey, William, *I.M.S.*, " *St. Eweste*," *Newton Abbot*	June 13, 1872	Jan. 29, 1862
Haslam, Arthur Charles, 5 *London-road, Bromley, Kent*	Dec. 14, 1911	May 10, 1900
Haslam, Wm. Frederic, 8 *Vicarage-rd., Edgbaston, Birmingham.*	Dec. 8, 1881	May 22, 1878
Hasslacher, Francis Joseph M., *Parklands, Lustleigh, S. Devon.*	Dec. 8, 1904	Feb. 11, 1898
Hastings, Somerville, 43 *Devonshire-street*, W.	Dec. 8, 1904	Feb. 13, 1902
Hatch, Wm. Keith, *Col. I.M.S., Cleeve Cloud, Prestbury, Glos.*	June 9, 1887	Aug. 3, 1876
Haycraft, John Berry, M.C., 21 *The Parade, Cardiff.*	June 9, 1921	June 9, 1921
Hayden, Arthur Falconer, *Capt. I.M.S., St. Mary's Hospital*, W.	June 14, 1906	July 25, 1900
Hayes, George Constable, 6 *Park-square, Leeds*	Dec. 9, 1897	Nov. 10, 1892
Hayes, Sydney Nuttall, *L. J. C. & M. Bank*, 196 *Oxford-st.*, W.	June 9, 1921	July 25, 1918
Hayman, Frank Keith, 52 *Caister-road, Great Yarmouth*	Dec. 9, 1920	Dec. 9, 1920
Hayman, Samuel Clifford	Dec. 12, 1907	Oct. 18, 1904
Hayward, John Arthur, 23 *The Grange, Wimbledon*	Dec. 8, 1904	Feb. 12, 1889
Heath, Arthur, 29 *Ebers-road, Nottingham*	Feb. 9, 1899	Feb. 13, 1896
Heath, Charles Joseph, 34 *Devonshire-place*, W.	June 10, 1886	July 31, 1884
Heath, Philip Maynard, 12 *Upper Wimpole-street*, W.	June 9, 1904	July 27, 1899
Heatherley, Francis, " *Ashville*," *Andenshaw, Manchester*	June 9, 1887	Jan. 28, 1885
Heaton, George, 47 *Newhall-street, Birmingham*	June 11, 1891	Feb. 9, 1888
Hedley, John Prescott, 65 *Harley-street*, W.	Dec. 9, 1909	Dec. 13, 1906
Henderson, Edward Erskine, *Redrigg, Felixstowe*	June 12, 1902	June 12, 1902
Henderson, J. H., *Warnambool, Victoria*	June 12. 1902	Nov. 10 1898
Henry, Edwin, *Klerksdorp, Transvaal, South Africa*	June 14, 1894	Nov. 10, 1892
Hepburn, Malcolm Langton, 111 *Harley-street*, W.	June 8, 1893	Aug. 1, 1892
Hepworth, Frank Arthur, O.B.E., 71 *High-street,Saffron Walden*	June 13, 1907	Aug. 4, 1903
Herbert, Herbert, *Lt.-Col. I.M.S..* 19 *Brunswick-place, Hove*	June 11, 1891	Apr. 10, 1886
Heslop, A. H.,D.S.O., *Maj.R.A.M.C.,c/oHolt&Co.,Whitehall-pl*	Dec. 8, 1921	Dec. 8, 1921
Hett, Geoffrey Seccombe, 8 *Wimpole-street,* W.	June 18, 1908	Feb. 12, 1903
Hewer, Cecil Mackenzie. O.B E., *Glenthorne, Tarporley, Cheshire*	Dec. 10, 1896	July 30, 1894
Hewer, Edward S. E., O B.E., 6 *Church-st., Stratford-on-Avon.*	Dec. 13, 1906	Feb. 10, 1898
Hewer, Joseph Langton, 18 *York-terrace, Regent's-park*, N.W.	Dec. 11, 1884	Jan. 19, 1882
Hewetson, John Thomas, 89 *Cornwall-street, Birmingham*	June 8, 1899	Aug. 4, 1896
Hewitson, Wm. Andrew, " *Thorncliffe*," *Easington, Co. Durham.*	June 8, 1922	June 8, 1922
Hewitt, D.W.,C.B.,C.M.G.,R.N.,*Med.Dep.,TheAdmiralty,*S.W.	Dec. 12, 1912	Dec. 12, 1912
Hewkley, Frank, 37 *Walbrook*, E.C.	June 9, 1887	Nov. 21, 1881
Hey, Wilson Harold, 16 *St. John-street, Manchester*	Dec. 10, 1908	May 11, 1905
Hicks, Henry Thomas, 56 *Friars Gate, Derby*	Dec. 11, 1902	Nov. 10, 1896
Higgins, Lionel George, *Furze Down, Harpenden, Herts*	June 10, 1920	July 26, 1917
Higgins, T. Twistington, O.B.E., 27 *Harley-street*, W.	Dec. 12, 1912	Nov. 11, 1909
Higgs, Sidney Limbrey, 17 *Duke-street, Manchester-square,* W.	June 8, 1922	May 10, 1917
¶ Hill, Alex, O.B.E., *Highfield-house, Southampton*	Apr. 11, 1907	Apr. 21, 1880
¶ Hill, Sir R., K.C.B., K.C.M.G., C.V.O., 68 *Victoria-street*, S.W.	Apr. 12, 1923	Aug. 2, 1888
Hillman, Oscar Stanley, *Middlesex-hosp.*, W.	June 9, 1921	July 24, 1919
Hind, Alfred Ernest, *Portland-house, Midvale-road, Jersey*	Dec. 10, 1885	Apr. 19, 1883
Hindmarsh, Thos. A., "*Millfield,*" *Eldon-pl., Newcastle-on-Tyne*	June 12, 1919	Nov. 13, 1913

Name and Residence.	Fellow.	Member.
Hine, Hugh FitzNeville, *I'le Ives, Newark-on-Trent*	May 10, 1900	Nov. 11, 1897
Hine, Montague Leonaid, 30 *Weymouth-street*, W.	June 18, 1908	July 27, 1905
Hislop, Walter John Henry, 190 *Willis-street, Wellington, N.Z.*	May 31, 1900	Aug. 2, 1898
Hobson, Lewis John, 6 *Queen-parade, Harrogate*	June 14, 1877	July 21, 1875
Hogarth, Robert George, C.B.E., 60 *Ropewalk, Nottingham* ..	June 14, 1894	July 30, 1891
Holland, Eardley Lancelot, 55 *Queen-Anne-street*, W.........	Dec. 14, 1905	Aug. 4, 1903
Holland, Edmund, *Lark-fields, Halleswell-road, Hendon, N.W..*	June 8, 1865	Apr. 19, 1860
Holman, Charles Colgate, 21 *Billing-road, Northampton*	June 13, 1912	July 30, 1908
Holmes, Thomas Sydney Shaw, 5 *College-gardens, Belfast*	June 11, 1914	June 11, 1914
Holthouse, Edwin Hermus, 1 *Park-crescent*, W.	June 12, 1884	Jan. 21, 1881
Home, Alfred Lucette, 29 *Winchester-avenue, Pen-y-lan, Cardiff.*	Dec. 14, 1905	Feb. 7, 1895
Hooper, Arth. Normau, 2 *Priory-avenue, Caversham, nr. Reading.*	June 10, 1920	Oct. 9, 1913
Hope, Chas. Wm. Menelaus, O.B.E., *Queen Anne-street*, W.....	Dec. 10, 1908	May 11, 1905
Hopkins, John, *" Hamercot," Esher-avenue, Walton-on-Thames.*	June 8, 1882	July 28, 1875
Horsford, Cyril Arthur Bennett, 24 *Harley-street*, W........	Dec. 10, 1903	Dec. 10, 1903
Horton, Robert Lister, *" Morven," Westerhall-road, Weymouth.*	Nov. 12, 1914	Nov. 14, 1912
Hotop, Francis Rudolph, 86 *Queen-st., Dunedin, New Zealand*	Dec. 9, 1909	Feb. 8, 1906
Housman, Basil Williams, *The Lower House, Tardebigge, Bromsgr've*	June 11, 1891	Aug. 2, 1888
Howard, Russell John, C.B.E., 40 *Devonshire-street*, W......	June 11, 1903	June 11, 1903
Howarth, Walter Goldie, 21 *Devonshire-place*, W.	Dec. 9, 1909	Feb. 9, 1905
Howat, Robert King, 92 *Borough-road, Middlesburgh*	Dec. 10, 1896	Feb. 9, 1893
Howell, Bernard Whitchurch, 35 *Weymouth-street*, W.	Dec. 10, 1914	Feb. 1, 1912
Howell, John, C.B.E., 7 *Imperial-square, Cheltenham*	Dec. 14, 1899	Feb. 13, 1896
Howlett, Edmund Henry, C.B.E., 4 *Wright-street, Hull*	June 10, 1880	Jan. 24, 1877
Howse, Cyril Beresford, *" Nareena," Anson-st., Orange, N.S.W.*	Dec. 14, 1905	July 30, 1894
Howbe, Sir N. R., V.C., K.C.B., K.C.M.G., *Orange, N.S.W.* ..	June 10, 1897	July 23, 1886
Hoyte, Stanley, *China Inland Mission Hospital, Shansi, China.*	June 12, 1913	May 12, 1910
Huddy, Geo. Philip Buckingham, 7 *York-place-mansions*, W. 1..	Mar. 10, 1921	May 11, 1916
Hudson, Arthur Cyril, 50 *Queen Anne-street*, W.	June 1, 1905	May 12, 1904
Huggins, Godfrey Martin, *P.O. Box 21, Salisbury, Rhodesia* ..	Dec. 10, 1908	July 26, 1906
Hughes, B., D.S.O., 3 *Clifton-villas, Manningham-l, Bradfd, Yorks*	June 8, 1911	Feb. 11, 1909
Hughes, David Morgan, 150 *Harley-street*, W.	June 11, 1914	July 31, 1902
Hughes, Edgar Alfred, *Beechlands, Horeham Road, Sussex*	June 9, 1887	Jan. 24, 1884
Hughes, Ernest Cranmer, O.B.E., 16 *Harley-street*, W.	Dec. 3, 1906	July 28, 1904
Hughes, Ernest Ethelbert, 20 *St. John-street, Manchester*......	June 13, 1912	June 13, 1912
Hughes, Gerald Stephen, 6 *St. Leonards, York*	Dec. 14, 1905	Nov. 13, 1902
Hughes, Samuel Henry, 173 *Macquarie-street, Sydney, N.S.W.*.	Dec. 13, 1894	Aug. 2, 1888
Hugo, F.V., C.M.G., L.-Col. I.M.S., c/o Lloyds Bk., 9 Pall Mall, S.W.	June 14, 1906	Nov. 14, 1889
Hulke, Sydney Backhouse, *The Croft, Walmer, Kent*	June 10, 1897	Feb. 9, 1893
Hull, Alfred John, Lt.-Col. R.A.M.C.	Dec. 14, 1911	July 29, 1897
Hume, Douglas Walter, *Menaifron, Upper Bangor, N. Wales* .	Dec. 10, 1914	Nov. 8, 1906
Hume, John Basil, 47 *Queen Anne-street*, W.	June 10, 1920	July 27, 1916
Hunt, Edmund Henderson, *Secunderabad, India*	June 11, 1903	Nov. 8, 1900
Hunter, Irwin Walter Wm.	Dec. 13, 1900	May 4, 1898
Hunter, John Bowman, M.C., 103 *Harley-street*, W.	June 9, 1921	July 30, 1914
Hurley, Thos. Ernest Victor, 69 *Talgarth-rd., West Kensington*.	June 12, 1919	June 12, 1919
Hutchinson, Jonathan, 1 *Park-crescent*, W.	Nov. 13, 1884	July 21, 1880

Name and Residence.	Fellow.	Member.
Iles, Arthur E., O.B.E , 17 *Victoria-square, Clifton, Bristol* ..	June 12,1913	July 25,1907
Ince, Arthur Godfrey, *Sturry, Canterbury, Kent*	Dec. 8,1898	May 10,1894
Ingall, Frank Ernest, *Health Office, Clarence-st., Southend-on-Sea*	June 13,1895	July 30,1891
Ionides, Theodore Henry, 25 *First Avenue, Brighton*	Dec. 14,1893	July 28,1890
Irving, Hamilton, 72 *Wimpole-Street, W*.................	June 18,1908	July 28,1904

Jackson, Charles E. S., *Burnham House, Nelson-st., King's Lynn.*	June 12,1913	July 27,1911
Jackson, George, 10 *Portland-villas, Plymouth* ....:.	Dec. 14,1876	Nov. 15,1864
Jacobson, Walter H. A., *Lordine-court, Ewhurst, Hawkhurst* ..	Dec. 20,1875	Nov. 13,1872
James,C.H.,C.I E.,L.-*Cl.I M.S.,Douynys-p.,Linkfield-l ,Redhill.*	June 10,1909	Nov. 10,1887
James, George Thomas *Brooksbank*, 5 *Harley-street, W*.......	Dec. 10,1896	Feb. 13,1890
James,H.E.R ,C.B.,C.M.G.,O.B.E.,*Lt.-Col.*,5 *Wilbr'h'm-pl*,S.W.	June 12,1890	May 21,1879
James, Robert Rutson, 46 *Wimpole-street, W*.	Oct. 11, 1906	Feb. 8, 1906
James, William Warwick, O.B.E., 2 *Park-crescent, W*.	June 1,1905	Nov. 13,1902
Jamison,Reginald,*Lancaster-house,Green Point,CapeTown,S.Afr.*	Dec. 12,1907	Oct. 10,1907
Jamison, Robert, *Mbabane, Swaziland, South Africa*	June 9,1910	June 9,1910
Jaques, Robert, 20 *Athenæum-street, Plymouth*.............	June 11,1903	Nov. 8,1900
Jeans, Frank Alex. Gallon, 30 *Rodney-street, Liverpool*	June 13,1907	Nov.10,1904
Jefferson, Geoffrey, 264 *Oxford-road, Manchester*	June 8,1911	July 27,1909
Jefferson, John Cecil, 2 *West-street, Rochdale, Lancs*	June 11,1914	July 27,1911
Jenkins, George John, O B.E., 48 *Wimpole-street, W*.	Dec. 11,1902	Nov. 13,1902
Jenkins, James Alfred, 223 *High-street, Dunedin, New Zealand.*	Mar. 10,1921	Mar. 10,1921
Jennings, Charles Egerton, *Filands, Malmesbury, Wilts*	June 12,1884	Apr. 19,1881
Jennings, John Frederick, 13 *John-street, Mayfair, W*........	Dec. 10,1903	July 25.1900
Jeremy, Harold Rowe, 66 *Harley-street, W*.	Dec. 14,1911	Nov. 14,1901
Jessett, Frederic Bowreman, *Elvetham, Hartley Wintney, Hants*	Dec. 10,1874	Dec. 28,1859
Jobson, James Stanley, " *Beechwood*," *Church-street, Epsom* ..	Dec. 11,1913	Feb. 10,1910
Joffe, Jack, *Guy's-hospital, S.E.*	June 10,1920	July 25,1918
Johnson, Fdk., *Church Missionary Soc., Baghdad, Mesopotamia*	June 8,1893	May 14,1891
Johnson, G. Lindsay, *Britannia-bldgs.,West-st., Durban, Natal*	Dec. 11,1884	Jan. 24,1881
Johnson, Raymond, O.B.E., *Chobham Farm, Chobham, Surrey.*	Dec. 13,1888	July 31,1885
Johnson, Walter Burford, *Kaduna, Nigeria*	Jan. 12,1911	Nov.12,1908
Johnston, Henry Mulrea, 36 *Jesmond-road, Newcastle-on-Tyne* .	Dec. 14,1911	Dec. 14,1911
Johnstone, James, *Tudor-house, King's-road, Richmond, Surrey.*	June 11,1891	July 28,1890
Johnstone, Robert James, 14 *University-square, Belfast*	Dec. 13,1900	Dec. 13,1900
Joll, Cecil Augustus, 23 *New Cavendish-street, W*.	June 9,1910	May 12,1910
Joly, John Swift, 80 *Harley-street, W*.	June 13,1907	June13,1907
Jones, Bertrand Seymour, 93 *Cornwall-street, Birmingham*	June 11,1903	Nov. 14,1901
Jones, Cecil Meredyth, 96 *Lower Addiscombe-road, Croydon* ..	June 9,1921	July 15,1912
Jones, David Llewellyn, 231 *King-street, Hammersmith, W*. ..	Dec. 10,1891	July 19,1882
Jones,EdmundB.,"*Chatsworth*,"*NorthEnd-rd.,Golders-gn.,N.W.*	June 12,1902	May 10,1894
Jones, George David Edwards, *c/o N. P. & U. Bank, Cardigan.*	June 14,1894	Nov. 10,1892
Jones, James Gaymer, M.C., 2 *Morley-road, Lewisham*	June 8,1922	Feb. 11,1916
Jones, Lawrence, *Little Seeleys, Beaconsfield*	Dec. 11,1902	July 25,1900
Jones, Martin Llewelyn, 2 *Victoria-square, Aberdare, S. Wales.*	Oct. 12,1893	Feb. 13,1890
Jones, Rhys Trevor, *Rupert-house, Edgware, Middlesex*	Dec. 11,1919	July 30,1914

Name and Residence.	Fellow.	Member.
¶Jones, Sir Robert, K.B.E., O.B , 11 *Nelson-street, Liverpool* ..	Apr. 11, 1918	July 23, 1878
Jones, S. W. Maslen, 20 *Waterloo-road, Wolverhampton*	Dec. 9, 1920	Sept. 24, 1914
Jones, Sydney Harold, 23 *Matlock-lane, Ealing*, W.	June 13, 1889	July 29, 1886
Jones, Thomas Caldwell Litler, 48 *Rodney-street, Liverpool*...	June 12, 1902	Nov. 11, 1897
Jones, Wm. Warner, 41 *Avenue-road. Toronto, Ontario, Canada*	June 9, 1904	July 25, 1900
Jordan, Anson Robertson, 6 *Effingham-crescent, Dover*........	June 8, 1911	June 8, 1911
Jordan. John Furneaux, 9 *Newhall-street, Birmingham*........	Dec. 10, 1891	May 14, 1891
Jose, Ivan Bede, *Palmer-pl., North Adelaide, South Australia*..	Dec. 14, 1922	Dec. 14, 1922
Joubert de la Ferté, Chas. H., *Col. I.M.S., The Ferns, Weybridge*	June 12, 1872	May 5, 1868
Jowers, Reginald Francis, 55 *Brunswick-square, Brighton*	June 14, 1888	Jan. 19, 1886
Joyce, James Leonard, 126 *Castle-hill, Reading*.............	June 10, 1909	July 25, 1907
Judah, Nathaniel Joseph, *St. George's-hospital, S.W.*	Dec. 14, 1922	Dec. 14, 1922
Juler, Frank Anderson, 14 *Portland-place*, W.	June 10, 1909	May 11, 1905
Julian, Thaddeus, *Wairau-hospital, Blenheim, N.Z.*	Dec. 11, 1919	Dec. 11, 1919
Just, Theodore Hartmann, 9 *Park-crescent*, W.	June 12, 1919	Nov. 10, 1910
¶Keatinge, Hy. Pottinger, C.M.G., 21 *Regent-rd , St. Helier, Jersey*	Apr. 9, 1908	Jan. 24, 1883
Keen, John Asarja, 121 *London-road, Leicester*..............	July 12, 1919	May 10, 1917
Keith, Sir Arthur, 17 *Aubert-park, Highbury*, N.	June 14, 1894	May 10, 1894
Kelly, Oswald Robert M., 72 *Wimpole-street*, W.	June 9, 1921	June 9, 1921
Kelly, Robert Ernest, C.B., 80 *Rodney-street, Liverpool*	Dec. 14, 1905	Dec. 14, 1905
Kelson, William Henry, 17 *Cavendish-place*, W.	Dec. 14, 1893	Jan. 30, 1885
Kennedy, Charles Matheson, M.B.E., 19 *Lockyer-street, Plymouth.*	June 8, 1911	July 26, 1906
Kennedy, John, 16 *Collins-street, Melbourne, Victoria, Australia*	June 12, 1913	June 12, 1913
Kennon, Robert, M.C., 72 A *Rodney-street, Liverpool*	Dec. 11, 1919	Nov. 9, 1911
Kerr, Robert Andrew, M.C., 33 *Nottingham-place*, W........	June 10, 1920	June 10, 1920
Kerr, Roy Russell, 30 *Ann-street, Manchester*	Mar. 10, 1921	Mar. 10, 1921
Keser, Jean Samuel, *Grand Boissière, 60 Route de Chêne, Geneva*	June 12, 1884	Apr. 14, 1881
Keynes, Geoffrey Langdon, 10 *Boundary-rd., St. John's Wood*, N.W.	Dec. 9, 1920	July 31, 1913
Kidd, Francis Seymour, 55 *Harley-street*, W................	June 1, 1905	May 14, 1903
Kidd, Hugh Cameron, *Bromsgrove, Worcestershire*	July 12, 1888	June 1, 1885
Killen, Thomas, *Main-street, Larne, Ireland*	Dec. 10, 1908	Dec. 10, 1908
Kilner, Thomas Pomfret, 25 *Manor-road, Sidcup, Kent*	June 9, 1921	Dec. 13, 1917
Kinder, Alexander, 1 *St. George's Bay-rd., Parnell, Auckland, N.Z.*	June 18, 1908	July 26, 1906
Kinsey-Taylor, A.E., *The Old Orchard-house, Farnh'm Royal, Bucks*	Dec. 13, 1888	July 20, 1884
Kisch, Harold Albert, 15 *Wimpole-street*, W.	June 8, 1911	July 28, 1904
Knaggs, Robert Lawford, 84 *Hazlewell-road, Putney*, S.W. ..	June 12, 1884	Nov. 14, 1883
Kneebone, J. Le M., *Jamestown, South Australia*	Mar. 10, 1921	Mar. 10, 1921
Knox, Robert W., D.S.O., *Lt.-Col I.M.S.*	June 11, 1914	June 11, 1914
Kumarasamy, Murugesem M., *Sandiruppay, Jaffna, Ceylon*....	Dec. 8, 1910	July 30, 1908
Lace, Frederick, 5 *Gay-street, Bath*......................	Dec. 12, 1895	May 9, 1889
Lack, Harry Lambert, 16 *Devonshire-place*, W..............	June 8, 1893	Feb. 13, 1890
Lake, Norman Claudius, 51 *Welbeck-street*, W.............	Dec. 11, 1913	Nov. 13, 1913
Lake, Richard, 41 *Wimpole-street*, W.	June 12, 1890	Jan. 29, 1885
Lakin, Charles Ernest, 105 *Harley-street*, W..............	June 1, 1905	Nov. 14, 1901

Name and Residence.	Fellow.	Member.
Lambrinudi, Constantine, 2 *Hyde-park-square*, W.	June 9, 1921	July 30, 1914
§Landau, Muriel Elsie, 53 *Welbeck-street*, W.................	June 10, 1920	May 10, 1918
Lane, James Ernest, 47 *Queen Anne-street*, W..............	Dec. 14, 1882	May 18, 1880
Lane, Sir Wm. Arbuthnot. Bt., C.B., 21 *Cavendish-square*, W.	June 8, 1882	Nov. 13, 1877
Lang, Basil Thorn, 22 *Cavendish-square*, W.................	June 9, 1910	July 26, 1906
Lang, William, 22 *Cavendish-square*, W.	June 12, 1879	Jan. 23, 1874
Langlands, Francis Henry, 31 *Collins-st., Melbourne, Victoria.* .	Dec. 10, 1891	Nov. 12, 1891
Larkin, Frederic Charles, 18 *Rodney-street, Liverpool*	Dec. 12, 1889	Oct. 23, 1885
¶Larkin, Frederick George, *Craven-house, Grove-park, Lee*, S.E..	Apr. 8, 1915	Nov. 16, 1870
Lawford, John Bowring, 27 *Weymouth-street*, W.............	Dec. 10, 1885	Nov. 18, 1879
Lawrence, Laurie Asher, 44 *Belsize-square*, N.W.	June 9, 1887	Jan. 22, 1884
Lawrence, Thomas W. Pelham, *"Fairholme," Rickmansworth.* .	June 12, 1890	May 5, 1887
Laws, William George, 3 *East-circus-street, Nottingham*	June 9, 1892	June 9, 1892
Lawson, Sir Arnold, K.B.E , 12 *Harley-street*, W.	June 8, 1893	May 14, 1891
Lawson, Robert Sharp, *Rockleigh*, 160 *London-road, Leicester.* .	June 8, 1916	June 8, 1916
Layton, Thomas Bramley, D.S.O., 10 *Welbeck-street*, W.......	June 10, 1909	Feb. 8, 1906
Leathes, John Beresford, 2 *Manchester-road, Sheffield*	June 14, 1894	May 10, 1894
Lediard, Henry Ambrose, 26 *Lowther-street, Carlisle*	June 8, 1876	July 27, 1870
Lee, Harry, 45 *Park-square, Leeds*	Dec. 14, 1911	Feb. 11, 1909
Lee, William Edward, 17 *Princes-avenue, Muswell-hill*, N.	June 10, 1897	May 10, 1894
Leech, Priestley, *King Cross, Halifax, Yorkshire*	June 13, 1889	Jan. 22, 1885
Leedham-Green, Chas. Albert, 17 *Carpenter-rd., Edgbaston, Birm.*	Dec. 14, 1893	Feb. 12, 1891
Lees, Kenneth Arthur, O.B.E., 48 *Harley-street*, W.	June 13, 1912	Nov. 14, 1907
Legg, Thomas Percy, C.M.G., 139 *Harley-street*, W.	June 10, 1897	May 9, 1895
Leicester, J. C. H., *Lt.-Col. I.M.S.*, 6 *Harington-st., Calcutta.* .	June 9, 1898	May 14, 1896
Leipoldt, Christian F. L., *Education Dept., Pretoria, Transvaal*	June 10, 1909	July 25, 1907
Lelean, P. S., C.B., C.M.G., *Lt.-Col. R.A.M.C.*	Dec. 14, 1899	Nov. 14, 1895
Leonard, Wm. Hugh, *Lt.-Col. I.M.S., c/o Cook & Son, Bombay.*	June 11, 1914	May 11, 1899
Letchworth, Thomas Wilfrid, 68 *Claremont-rd., Surbiton*	June 10, 1909	Nov. 10, 1898
Lett, Hugh, C.B.E., 8 *Lower Berkeley-street*, W.	June 12, 1902	Feb. 7, 1901
Levick, Harry Driffield, " *Willerby," Cambridge-rd., Middlesboro'*	June 13, 1895	Feb. 12, 1891
Levy, Aaron, 67 *Wimpole-street*, W.	June 10, 1909	May 8, 1902
Lewis, Edward John, 74 *Hamilton-terrace*, N.W.	June 12, 1890	Jan. 28, 1884
§Lewis, Emily Catherine, 2 *Harley-place, Harley-street*, W. ..	June 12, 1919	Nov. 8, 1917
Lewis, H. Wolseley, *County Asylum, Barming Heath, Maidstone*	June 12, 1902	Feb. 11, 1892
Ley, John William, *Belmont, Newton Abbot*	June 10, 1875	Nov. 17, 1869
Ligat, David, 43 *Eversfield-place, St. Leonards-on-Sea*	Dec. 12, 1907	Dec. 12, 1907
Lilley, Ernest Lewis, *Waterloo-gates, New-walk, Leicester*	June 11, 1903	July 27, 1899
Lincoln, Wm. Ayer, 1701 *College-lane, Calgary, Alberta, Canada*	June 11, 1914	June 11, 1914
Lindon, Leonard Charles Edward, *North Adelaide, South Austr.*	Dec. 14, 1922	July 8, 1920
Lindsay, Edwin Algernon, 503 *Centre-st., Calgary, Alta., Canada.*	Dec. 9, 1920	Nov. 12, 1908
Lindsay, Ernest Charles, C.B.E., 46 *Queen Anne-street*, W. ..	Dec. 12, 1912	Nov. 11, 1909
Linington, William West, 1 *Radnor-park-avenue, Folkestone* ..	Mar. 11, 1897	July 27, 1893
Lister, A. E. J., *Lt.-Col. I.M.S.*, 88 *Harley-street*, W.	Oct. 16, 1902	July 25, 1900
Lister, Thomas David, C.B.E., 1 *Vicarage-road, Henley-on-Thames.*	June 14, 1894	Nov. 10, 1892
Lister, Sir William Tindall, K.C.M.G., 24 *Devonshire-place*, W.	June 13, 1895	May 9, 1895
Little, Ernest Muirhead, 40 *Seymour-street*, W...............	Dec. 9, 1886	Jan. 21, 1880

Name and Residence.	Fellow.	Member.
Littler, Robert Meredith, 54 *Hoghton-street, Southport*........	June 14, 1894	Nov. 13, 1890
Littlejohn, C. W. B., M.C., *Scotch College, Melbourne, Australia.*	June 8, 1916	Apr. 13, 1916
Livingston, Herbert Max, 21 *Sandringham-gardens, Ealing, W.*	June 9, 1921	June 9, 1921
Lloyd, Bertram Arthur, 25 *Hallewell-rd., Edgbaston, Birm.* ..	Dec. 14, 1911	Mar. 12, 1908
Lloyd, Eric Ivan, *Elybaston-grove, Birmingham*	Dec. 8, 1921	Nov. 9, 1916
Lloyd, Perceval Allen, *Chalfont-house, Haverfordwest*	June 14, 1888	Aug. 5, 1885
Lobb, Edw. Leslie Martyn, 11 *King-street, Maidstone*	Dec. 8, 1910	Feb. 13, 1908
Lock, Norman Francis, 5 *Barnfield-crescent, Exeter*	June 12, 1913	May 11, 1911
Lockett, George Vernon, 5 *Bedford-av., Kingston, Jamaica, W.I.*	June 13, 1895	May 9, 1895
Lockhart-Mummery, John Percy, 9 *Hyde-park-place, W.*	May 31, 1900	Nov. 2, 1899
Lockyer, Cuthbert Henry Jones, 117 *a Harley-street, W.*	June 11, 1896	July 30, 1894
Lodge, Samuel Durham, O.B.E., 28 *Manor-row, Bradford, Yorks.*	Dec. 14, 1922	June 29, 1915
Longridge, Charles J. Nepean, 24 *Lansdowne-place, Cheltenham.*	Dec. 11, 1902	May 10, 1900
Loosely, Alfred Edw. Arthur, 25 *New Cavendish-street, W.*.....	June 8, 1911	May 8, 1902
Loughnane, F. McGillivray, 33 *Weymouth-street, W.*	June 11, 1914	July 23, 1912
Love, Robert John McNeill, " *Outlanas*," *Devonport*	Dec. 9, 1920	Feb. 12, 1914
Lovell, Arthur Gordon Haynes	Nov. 14, 1912	Nov. 11, 1909
Low, Vincent Warren, C.B., 76 *Harley-street, W.*	Dec. 14, 1893	Feb. 12, 1891
Lowe, Walter George, " *Clarehaven*," *Birchington-on-Sea*......	June 10, 1875	Jan. 27, 1870
Lowman, William Henville, *Norton-house, White-st., Coventry*..	June 20, 1901	May 10, 1900
Lowne, Benjamin Thompson, 34 *Portland-road, Hove, Sussex*..	June 19, 1873	May 2, 1861
Luard, H. B., " *Woodlands*," *Little Baddow, Chelmsford*	June 10, 1897	Aug. 4, 1887
Lucas, Albert, 141 *Great Charles-street, Birmingham*	June 11, 1891	Feb. 9, 1887
Luce, Sir Richard Harman, K.C.M.G., C.B., 42 *Friargate, Derby*	Dec. 13, 1894	May 11, 1893
Lucy, Reginald Horace, " *Sunnymead*," *Abbotswood, Guildford.*	Dec. 13, 1888	May 4, 1886
Lumb, Norman P. L., O.B.E., 97 *Thurleigh-rd., Balham, S.W.*	Dec. 14, 1922	Feb. 12, 1914
Lund, Herbert, 22 *St. John-street, Manchester*................	June 9, 1887	July 30, 1885
¶ Lunn, John Reuben, O.B.E., *The Cottage, Chaucer-rd., Worthing.*	Apr. 14, 1910	Nov. 13, 1878
Lyle, Herbt. Willoughby, " *Speldhurst*," *Elmfield-road, Bromley*	June 11, 1903	July 27, 1893
Lynch, Stephen Fredk., *Belmore-rd , Randwick, Sydney, N.S.W.*	May 31, 1900	Feb. 11, 1897
Lynn-Thomas, Sir J., K.B.E., *Llwyndyrys, Llechryd, Cardig'nsh're*	Dec. 8, 1892	Jan. 20, 1886
Lyth, Harold Ashton, 2 *Queen-street, Newcastle, Staffs.*	Dec. 8, 1904	July 31, 1902
Lytle, William James, *Hampden-club, N.W*................	June 14, 1923	June 14, 1923
Macalpine, James Barlow, 21 *St. John-street, Manchester*	Dec. 8, 1910	May 9, 1907
MacAuley, Charles John, 22 *Lower Fitzwilliam-street, Dublin*..	Mar. 10, 1921	Mar. 10, 1921
MacCallan, Arthur F., O.B.E., *Public Health Dept., Cairo, Egypt*	Dec. 14, 1899	Nov. 10, 1898
McCann, Frederick John, 14 *Wimpole-street, W.*	Dec. 12, 1901	May 10, 1900
McCarter, F. B., " *Hughenden*," *Earlsfield-rd., Wandsworth, S.W.*	Dec. 11, 1919	Dec. 11, 1919
McCarthy, Jeremiah, 1 *Cambridge-place, Victoria-road, W.*.....	June 19, 1873	May 10, 1866
McCaw, Alexander Tod, 32 *Don-street, Invercargill, N.Z.*	Dec. 14, 1911	Feb. 13, 1908
McClure, James, 1 *Harley-place, Harley-street, W.*	Dec. 11, 1902	July 29, 1897
MacCormick, K., D.S.O., *Nat. Bank of N.Z* , 17 *Moorgate-st., E.C.*	Mar. 10, 1921	Mar. 10, 1921
McCullagh, W.McK. H., D.S.O., M.C., *SamaritanFree-hosp., N.W.*	June 8, 1922	June 8, 1922
McDonagh, James Eustace Radclyffe, 4 *Wimpole-street, W.* ..	June 10, 1909	Feb. 8, 1906
MacDonald, Sydney Gray, 51 *Queen Anne-street, W.*	June 10, 1909	Feb. 8, 1906
McEvedy, Peter George, 1 *Harewood-place, Marylebone, N.W.*..	Dec. 9, 1920	May 11, 1916

Name and Residence.	Fellow.	Member.
McGavin, Sir D.J., C.M.G., D S.O., 141 *Willis-st., Wellington, N.Z.*	Dec. 8, 1904	Nov. 2, 1899
McGavin, Lawrie Hugh, C.B , 1 *Moon's Mill, Blackboys, Sussex*	May 31, 1900	Nov. 10, 1898
McKenty, Francis Edmund, *Montreal, Canada*	June 13, 1907	Feb. 7, 1907
Mackenzie, C., O.B.E., 1 *Camden-ter., Manningham-lane, Bradford*	Dec. 12, 1912	July 30, 1908
Mackenzie, George Welland, 13 *William-st., Lowndes-sq.*, S.W.	Dec. 9, 1869	Apr. 28, 1864
Mackenzie, John T., *Maj. I.M.S.*, 356 *Stewart-st., Ottawa, Ontario*	June 9, 1870	Feb. 6, 1857
Mackenzie, Kenneth, 27 *Princes-street, Auckland, New Zealand.*	Dec. 12, 1912	Dec. 12, 1912
Mackenzie, Lewis, " *Avenel*," *Tiverton, Devon*	Dec. 20, 1875	Nov. 15, 1871
Mackern, John, *Newick, Sussex*	June 14, 1888	July 26, 1877
McKerrow, Wm. Alex. Hogg, 200 *Newhall-lane, Preston, Lancs.*	June 11, 1914	June 11, 1914
Mackie, F. P., O.B E., *Lt.-Col.I.M.S.*, 6 *Upp. Belgrave-rd., Bristol*	June 12, 1902	July 29, 1897
McLachlan, Arthur Ronald, 89 *Kloop-street, Cape Town, S.A.*	Dec. 12, 1901	July 27, 1899
McLachlan, John, 3 *Keble-road, Oxford*	Dec. 12, 1889	July 24, 1885
Maclaren, Norman, 23 *Portland-square, Carlisle*	June 11, 1903	Feb. 7, 1901
MacLeod, Charles Edwd. Alexander, 70 B *Ladbroke-grove*, W. .	June 13, 1895	July 30, 1891
Maclure, Alfred Fay, 127 *Collins-st., Melbourne, Victoria, Austr.*	Dec. 14, 1911	Dec. 14, 1911
Macmillan, John McC. A., *Maj.I.M.S., Grindlay & Co., Bombay*	Dec. 10, 1908	Aug. 1, 1901
McMillan, Kenneth Holl, *Dudley-road Hosp., Birmingham*	June 10, 1920	Feb. 12, 1914
McMullen, William Halliburton, O.B.E., 86 *Brook-street*, W...	June 20, 1901	Nov. 10, 1898
Macnab, A. J., C.B., C M.G., *Col.I.M.S.*, 16 *Gordon-rd., Camberley*	June 11, 1896	Jan. 27, 1887
McNair, Arthur Jas., 13 *Court-lane-gdns., Dulwich-village*, S.E.	Dec. 8, 1921	May 11, 1911
McPherson, Thomas, *Centre-st., Stratford, Ontario, Canada* ..	Dec. 12, 1907	July 27, 1905
MacQueen, Ronald Chesney, *Bolton-house, Bolton-rd., Eastbourne*	Dec. 11, 1913	Dec. 11, 1913
MacWatt, R.C., C.I.E., *Col. I.M.S., H. S. King & Co.*, 9 *Pall Mall*	Dec. 14, 1911	Dec. 14, 1911
MacWatters, M.R.C., *Maj.I.M.S.*, 82 *nd Punjabis, Nowshera, India*	Jan. 9, 1913	Feb. 13, 1902
Madden, F.C., O.B.E., *St.David's-bldgs., Sharia-el-Maghraby, Cairo*	Mar. 10, 1898	Nov. 12, 1896
Maguire, F. A., D.S.O., 231 *Macquarie-street, Sydney, N.S. W.*	Dec. 11, 1919	Dec. 11, 1919
Mahon, Ralph Bodkin, *Nile-lodge, Galway*	June 11, 1896	June 11, 1896
Mahood, Allan Edward, 2 *Morley-terrace, Tiverton, Devon*	June 14, 1894	Nov. 13, 1890
Maidlow, William Harvey, *The Ridge, Ilminster*	Feb. 10, 1893	July 30, 1891
Maingay, Henry Bertram, 34 *Queen-street, Scarborough*	June 11, 1896	Nov. 9, 1893
Maingot, Rodney Honor, 16 *Holland-park*, W...............	Dec. 9, 1920	Feb. 11, 1916
Maitland, C. Dundas, " *Winton*," *London-road, Guildford* ...	Dec. 9, 1920	Feb. 13, 1919
Makar, Naguib, *Kasr-el-Ainy-hospital, Cairo, Egypt*	June 14, 1923	May 13, 1920
Makins, Sir George Henry, G.C.M.G., C.B., 33 *Wilton-place*, S.W.	Dec. 12, 1878	July 22, 1875
¶ Manby, Sir Alan Reeve, K.C.V.O., *East Rudham, Norfolk* ..	Apr. 11, 1918	Apr. 19, 1870
Manders, H., *c/o Federal Steam Nav. Co.*, 2 *Fenchurch-av.*, E.C.	June 13, 1878	Nov. 16, 1875
Mannington, Frank, *Belmont, Muswell-hill-road*, N.	Dec. 14, 1899	July 29, 1897
Mant, Harold Turley, 39 *Devonshire-place*, W.	Dec. 13, 1906	July 28, 1904
Maples, Ernest Edgar, *The Warren, Calabar, Southern Nigeria*	Dec. 8, 1910	Aug. 4, 1903
Mapother, Edward, *Maudsley-hospital, Denmark-hill*, S.E.	Dec. 8, 1910	Dec. 8, 1910
Marlow, Fredk. Wm., 417 *Bloor-st.-west, Toronto, Ont., Canada.*	June 11, 1903	May 8, 1902
Marriage, Herbert James, 109 *Harley-street*, W.	June 12, 1902	Feb. 11, 1897
Marriott, Cecil Edward, 11 *Welford-road, Leicester*	Dec. 8, 1904	Feb. 13, 1896
Marsh, Frank, C.B.E., 93 *Cornwall-street, Birmingham*	Dec. 13, 1883	Apr. 24, 1877
Marsh, Frank D., M.C., *Quarry House, Northfield, Birmingham.*	Dec. 9, 1920	Feb. 12, 1914
Marshall, Charles Frederic, 37 *Welbeck-street*, W.	June 8, 1893	May 9, 1889

Name and Residence.	Fellow.	Member.
Marshall, Charles Jennings, 46 *Weymouth-street*, W.	June 10, 1915	May 13, 1915
Marshall, James Cole, 126 *Harley-street*, W.	Dec. 10, 1903	Nov. 8, 1900
Marson, Francis Herbert, *Eastgate*, *Stafford*	June 13, 1895	Nov. 10, 1892
Martin, Albert Edward, *Surrey-chambers. Perth, W. Australia*.	Dec. 9, 1897	Nov. 14, 1889
Martin, Christopher, *Cleveland-house, George-road, Edgbaston*..	Dec. 10, 1891	Nov. 12, 1891
Martin, Edward Kenneth, *Univ. College-hosp., Gower-st.*, W.C.	June 10, 1909	May 14, 1908
Martin, Frank Beauchamp, *Melbourne, Victoria, Australia*....	Feb. 13, 1919	Feb. 13, 1919
Martin·Leake, Arthur, V.C., " *Marshalls*," *Ware, Herts*	June 11, 1903	Nov. 10, 1898
Martyn, Henry Linnington, 124 A *High-street, Eton*..........	Oct. 9, 1913	July 25, 1910
Másiná, Hormasji Manekji, *Clare-road, Byculla, Bombay*	June 9, 1898	June 9, 1898
Mason, Francis Courtenay, 34 *Weymouth-street*, W............	June 10, 1920	May 11, 1916
Mason, R. P. S., M.C., " *Tolcarn*," *The Drive, Wembley-park* ..	June 9, 1921	May 13, 1915
Massie, Grant, 197 *Southwark-bridge-road*, S.E.	June 8, 1922	Feb. 12, 1920
Masterman, E. Wm. G , *Camberwell-infirm'y, Brunswick-sq.*, S.E.	Jan. 14, 1892	Feb. 12, 1891
Mathias, Henry Hugh, *Fern House, Penally, Pembrokeshire* ..	Dec. 9, 1920	Feb. 13, 1913
Mawhood, Reginald Hawksworth, *Green Meadows, Ascot, Berks*	June 12, 1913	May 13, 1906
Maxted, George, 14 *Thorpe-mansions, Norwich*	June 11, 1914	May 12, 1910
Maxwell, John Preston, *Union Medical College, Peking, China* .	Dec. 9, 1897	Feb. 13, 1899
Maxwell, Wm. Henry, *P.O. Box 473, Johannesburg, Transvaal.*	Dec. 10, 1903	Nov. 2, 1899
¶May, Sir Arthur W., K.C.B., *R.N., Tremeir, St. Tudy, Cornwall*	Apr. 2, 1914	July 27, 1876
May, Bennett, C.B.E., 50 *Frederick-rd., Edgbaston, Birmingham*	June 8, 1876	Jan. 23, 1868
Maybury, Bernard Constable, 42 *Wimpole-street*, W.	Feb. 13, 1913	July 29, 1909
Maynard, Edwin, 81 *Oxford-terrace, Hyde-park*, W.	Dec. 12, 1907	Feb. 13, 1896
Mayo, Thomas Alfred, *Clifton-house, Cowes, Isle of Wight*	Dec. 13, 1900	Nov. 10, 1898
Mayou, Marmaduke Stephen, 59 *Harley-street*, W.	Dec. 12, 1901	July 29, 1897
Mead, John Clarke, *Bryn-y-môr, Yarmouth-road, Lowestoft* ..	June 13, 1907	May 11, 1905
Medlock, Charles Harold, 110 *Haverstock-hill*, N.W.	June 8, 1922	July 29, 1915
Melsome, William Stanley, 29 *Circus, Bath*	Dec. 10, 1896	Dec. 10, 1896
Michels, Ernst, 48 *Wimpole-street*, W·	June 8, 1893	July 30, 1891
Middlebro, Thomas Holmes, *Owen Sound, Ontario, Canada*....	May 31, 1900	Nov. 2, 1899
Miles, William Ernest, 16 *Upper Wimpole-street*, W.	Feb. 8, 1894	July 30, 1891
Miller, William Henry, 4 *De Parys-avenue, Bedford*	June 8, 1911	July 26, 1906
Milligan, Edward Thomas Campbell, O.B.E., 13 *Harley-st.*, W.	Dec. 11, 1919	Dec. 11, 1919
Mills, George Percival, 61 *Newhall-street, Birmingham*	July 30, 1908	May 10, 1906
Mills, Yarnold Hubert, 27 *Hill-street, Haverfordwest*	Dec. 13, 1894	Feb. 12, 1891
Milne, Robert, 21 *Park-crescent, Portland-place*, W.	Dec. 13, 1906	July 28, 1904
Miskin, Leonard John, 2 *West-hill, Dartford*................	Dec. 9, 1897	May 9, 1895
Mitchener, Philip Henry, 8 *Harley-street*, W.	July 10, 1913	Feb. 1, 1912
Modi, Shapurj Hormasji, *I.M.S., Apollo Hotel, Bombay*	July 27, 1899	Nov. 11, 1897
Moffat, Henry Alford, D.S.O., 13 *Welyemeend-street, Cape T.*..	June 11, 1896	May 9, 1895
Moir, Percival John, 3 *Moorland-terrace, Leeds*	June 14, 1923	June 14, 1923
Molesworth, Hickman W. Lancelot, 51 *Cheriton-rd., Folkestone*	June 12, 1919	May 11, 1916
Molesworth, Theodore Henderson, *St Margaret's-at-Cliffe, Kent.*	Dec. 10, 1903	Nov. 12, 1896
Mollison, William Mayhew, C.B.E., 23 *Devonshire-place*, W. ...	June 14, 1906	Nov. 10, 1904
Moolgavkar, Shamrao R., *Bikaner, Rajputana, India*	Mar. 11, 1915	Feb. 11, 1909
Moon, Archibald Trevor, *Beddington-house, Wallington*	Dec. 8, 1904	Feb. 12, 1903
Moore, Arthur Eisdell, 43 *Symonds-st., Auckland, New Zealand*	June 12, 1919	June 12, 1919

Name and Residence.	Fellow.	Member.
Moore, Clifford Arthur, 56 *St. Paul's-road, Clifton, Bristol*	June 18, 1908	May 14, 1903
Moore, Robert Foster, O.B.E., 91 *Harley-street*, W...........	Dec. 13, 1906	May 12, 1904
Moore, Walter William, *Tennyson-street, Napier, New Zealand.*	Dec. 13, 1906	Nov. 9, 1905
Moorhead, Andrew Samuel, 146 *Bloor-street*, W., *Toronto, Canada*	Dec. 14, 1911	Apr. 14, 1910
Mooro, Mohammed Abdel Wahhab, *Kobba-bridge, Egypt*	June 10, 1920	Feb. 12, 1920
Moorshead, Robert Fletcher, 50 *Lanercost-rd., Tulse-hill*, S.W.	June 11, 1903	May 11, 1899
Moreton, Adrian Leonard, *The Gore-cottage, Burnham, Bucks.*.	Dec. 11, 1913	July 25, 1910
Morford, Arthur, 61 *Park-lane, Croydon*..................	Apr. 10, 1919	Nov. 9, 1916
Morgan, Henry Lewis, 6 *Huddleston-road*, N.	Dec. 14, 1911	May 9, 1907
Morgan, John Hammond, C.V.O., 3 *Connaught-square*, W.....	June 8, 1876	July 23, 1872
Morgan, Oswald Gayer, 7 *Devonshire-place*.................	Dec. 9, 1920	Feb. 13, 1913
Morison, James Rutherford, 1 *Claremont-pl., Newcastle-on-Tyne*	Dec. 11, 1890	Dec. 11, 1890
Morley, Arthur Solomon, 52 *Gordon-square*, W.C.	Dec. 11, 1902	July 27, 1889
Morley, Edward John, *R.N., Junior United Service Club*, S.W.	June 11, 1891	Jan. 21, 1879
Morley, John, 2 *St. Peter's-square, Manchester*	June 8, 1911	Feb. 9, 1911
Morris, Charles Arthur, C.V.O., 22 *Chester-square*, S.W......	June 14, 1888	July 19, 1882
Morris, Sir Henry, Bart., 42 *Connaught-square*, W.	June 19, 1873	Apr. 25, 1866
Morrison, Jas. Thos. Jackman, 54 *Newhall-street, Birmingham*.	Dec. 13, 1883	Jan. 24, 1879
Morrison, Jn. T., O.B.E., 33 A *Rodney-street, Liverpool*	Dec. 11, 1913	Nov. 13, 1913
Morson, Albert Clifford, O.B.E., 22 *Welbeck-street*, W.	Dec. 12, 1912	July 26, 1906
Mortimer, John Desmond E., 48 *Fairhazel-gdns., Kilburn*, N.W.	Dec. 12, 1889	Jan. 20, 1882
Mortimer, Wm. Graddon, *Duke-street, South Molton, N. Devon*	June 14, 1906	July 29, 1895
Morton, Andrew Stanford, 64 *Pembroke-rd., Clifton, Bristol* ..	June 14, 1888	July 23, 1874
Morton, Charles A., O.B.E., 14 *Vyvyan-terrace, Clifton, Bristol.*	Dec. 12, 1889	Nov. 17, 1881
Mothersole, Robert Devereux, 128 *St. George's-road, Bolton* ..	Dec. 11, 1890	Feb. 9, 1888
Mouat, Thomas Bernard, 305 *Glossop-road, Sheffield*.........	June 8, 1911	June 8, 1911
Moullin, Charles W. M., C.B.E., 28 *Victoria-road, Kensington*, W.	Dec. 12, 1878	Aug. 2, 1876
Moynihan, Sir Berkeley, Bt., K.C.M.G., C.B., 33 *Park-sq., Leeds.*	Oct. 9, 1890	Nov. 10, 1887
Muecke, Francis Frederick, C.B.E., 36 *Cavendish-square*, W...	Dec. 9, 1909	Dec. 9, 1909
Mullally, Gerald Thomas, M.C., 10 *Welbeck-street*, W. 1	June 11, 1914	July 31, 1913
Mulroney, Thos. Richard, *Lt.-Col. I.M.S.*, 14 *Hillgrove-rd.*, N.W.	May 31, 1900	Jan. 18, 1880
Mumford, Wilfred George, O.B.E., 18 *The Circus, Bath*	June 11, 1903	May 9, 1895
¶ Mummery, J. Howard, C.B.E., 79 *Albert-bridge-road*, S.W. ..	Apr. 12, 1923	Nov. 15, 1870
Munby, William Maxwell, 6 *Park-square, Leeds*	June 10, 1909	June 10, 1909
Mundy, Herbert, 102 *Florida-road, Durban, Natal*	Dec. 14, 1899	May 13, 1897
Murray, E. F., 52 *Jesmond-road, Newcastle-on-Tyne*	June 13, 1918	June 13, 1918
Murray, Geo. A. Everitt, 24 *Plein-st., Johannesburg, S. Africa* .	Dec. 8, 1887	Apr. 28, 1884
Murray, John, 110 *Harley-street*, W.	Dec. 11, 1890	Jan. 17, 1887
Murray, R. W., O.B.E., " *Brierfield*," *Churchdown, Gloucester*..	Dec. 12, 1889	Apr. 28, 1884
Musgrove, James, " *The Swallowgate*," *St. Andrews, N.B.*	June 8, 1893	May 9, 1889
Muspratt, Charles Drummond, 11 *Madeira-road, Bournemouth*..	June 11, 1885	July 30, 1884
Myler, John William, " *Trealaw*," *Rhondda, Glamorganshire* ..	Dec. 10, 1903	July 29, 1895
Mylvaganam, Henry Bailey, 6 *Infantry-rd., Bangalore, India*..	June 1, 1905	Feb. 12, 1903
Nairn, Robert, *Hastings, Napier, New Zealand*	Dec. 10, 1891	Apr. 22, 1886
Nall, John Frederick, " *Kalinga*," *Ellesmere-road, Torquay*	Dec. 10, 1896	July 28, 1890

Name and Residence.	Fellow.	Member.
Nance, Henry Chester, 59 *St. Giles'-plain, Norwich*	June 11, 1891	May 8, 1880
Napier, Francis H., *Adderley-ho., Kirk & Eloff-sts., Johannesburg.*	June 12, 1890	Jan. 26, 1885
Nash, Walter Gifford, *Clavering-house, De Pary's-avenue, Bedford*	Dec. 10, 1891	Aug. 4, 1887
Neame, Humphrey, 248 *Temple-chambers, Temple-avenue, E.C.*	June 12, 1913	July 25, 1910
Negus, Victor Ewings, " *The Lawn," Walton-on-Thames*......	Dec. 8, 1921	Feb. 13, 1913
Neil, William Fulton, 9 *College-street, Nottingham*	June 10, 1909	Nov. 14, 1907
Neilson, Drevor F. A., *Shandon, St. George's-hill, Weybridge* ..	June 8, 1922	Feb. 11, 1915
Neligan, Geo. Ernest, M.C., 46 *Queen Anne-street, W*........	June 11, 1914	May 12, 1910
Nesfield, Vincent B., *Maj. I.M.S., Sandhurst, Kent*..........	Oct. 13, 1904	Aug. 1, 1901
Neve, Clement Treves, 49 *Addiscombe-road, Croydon*	Dec. 11, 1913	July 27, 1913
Newbolt, George Palmerston, C.B.E., 5 *Gambier-terr., Liverpool*	Apr. 12, 1888	Jan. 22, 1885
Newby, Charles Henry, 14 *Broad-park-avenue, Ilfracombe*	Dec. 9, 1880	Jan. 22, 1873
Newby, Gervase Edward, O.B.E., 12 *Addiscombe-road, Croydon.*	Dec. 13, 1894	Feb. 11, 1892
Newell, R. L., "*Arnewood," Bennett-rd., Hr.Crumpsall, M'chester*	June 9, 1921	July 27, 1916
Newland, H. Simpson, C.B.E., D.S.O., 3 *N.-terrace, Adelaide..*	June 8, 1899	July 29, 1897
Newland-Pedley, Frederick, 22 *Willow-rd., Hampstead, N.W...*	June 11, 1885	Apr. 21, 1881
Newman, John Campin, O.B.E., " *Foxley," Bishop's Stortford..*	June 12, 1902	Nov. 8, 1900
Newton, Hibbert Alan Stephen, *Melbourne-club, Collins-st.,Melb.*	June 12, 1919	June 12, 1919
Newton, Robert Earle, 10 *Cavendish-place, Bath*	June 20, 1901	July 29, 1895
Nichols, William Robson, 83 *Carlton-st., Winnipeg, Canada* ..	Dec. 12, 1901	May 11, 1899
Nicol, Burton Alexander, 230 *Musgrave-road, Durban, Natal..*	June 11, 1903	May 11, 1899
Nightingale, Henry John, 13 *Cumberland-place, Southampton* ..	Dec. 10, 1908	Nov. 8, 1906
Nitch, Cyril Alfred Rankin, 69 *Harley-street, W*............	June 12, 1902	May 10, 1901
Noall, Wm. Paynter, *Bootham-lodge, York*	June 14, 1906	Nov. 2, 1899
Noble, Thomas Paterson, *Shropshire Orthopædic-hosp., Oswestry*	June 10, 1920	June 10, 1920
Noon, Charles, O.B.E., 25 *Thorpe-road, Norwich*	Dec. 10, 1914	May 12, 1910
Norbury, Lionel Edward Close, O.B.E., 25 *Harley-street, W...*	Mar. 14, 1907	Nov. 10, 1904
Norman, Frederick, *Wiltshire-house, Wiltshire-rd., Brixton, S.W.*	June 1, 1905	Apr. 28, 1886
Norris, Donald Craig, 13 *Vanbrugh-park-road, Blackheath, S.E.*	Dec. 8, 1921	May 11, 1916
Novis, T. S ,*Lt.-Col.I.M.S.,*12*Rocky-h'l-flats,Malabar-h'l,Bomb'y*	June 9, 1910	Nov. 11, 1897
Nuthall, Alexander Wathen, 89 *Cornwall-street, Birmingham..*	Oct. 13, 1898	Nov. 14, 1895
Nutt, Harold Rothery, *Lt.-Col. I.M.S.*	Jan. 16, 1902	Feb. 8, 1900
Nuttall, Henry C. Wardleworth, 78 *Rodney-street, Liverpool* ..	June 9, 1921	Nov. 10, 1910
Oakden, William M., *St. Luke's-hospital, Lowestoft*............	June 12, 1913	Nov. 9, 1911
O'Brien, Arthur Boniface, 70 *Papanui-road, Christchurch, N.Z.*	Dec. 12, 1912	May 11, 1905
Ockwell, Charles Melton, *Whitehill-house, Crayford, Kent*	Dec. 11, 1919	July 26, 1906
Odell, William, *Ferndale, Torquay*	Dec. 14, 1876	Nov. 13, 1872
Odgers, Paul Norman Blake, 16 *Castelian-street, Northampton..*	June 11, 1903	Feb. 13, 1902
Ogilvie, William Heneage, 27 *Hamilton-terrace, N.W.*	June 10, 1920	May 8, 1913
O'Hea, James Patrick, " *Longueil," Hook-hill, Sanderstead*	June 11, 1896	July 29, 1895
Oldershaw, Martin Herbert, 46 *Wimpole-street, W.*	Dec. 11, 1919	July 26, 1917
Oldfield, Carlton, 25 A *Park-square, Leeds*	June 10, 1909	July 27, 1893
Olive, E. J. P., O.B.E., "*Avon Royd," Kenilworth-rd., Leamington.*	Dec. 8, 1892	Nov. 14, 1889
Oliver, John Dudgeon, 21 *Upper Wimpole-street, W.*	June 14, 1917	July 27, 1916
Oliver, Matthew Wm. Baillie, O.B.E., 128 *Harley-street, W...*	June 11, 1914	Nov. 8, 1906
Ollerenshaw, Robert, 21 *St. John-street, Manchester*	June 10, 1909	July 30, 1908

Name and Residence.	Fellow.	Member.
O'Malley, John Francis, 6 *Upper Wimpole-street*, W.	Dec. 8, 1910	Feb. 10, 1910
O'Malley, Michael George, *University College, Galway, Ireland.*	Dec. 9, 1915	Dec. 9, 1915
O'Meara, E. J., O.B.E., *Lt.-Col. I.M.S., Drayton-wood, Norwich.*	June 12, 1902	Nov. 14, 1901
Openshaw, Thomas Horrocks, C.B., C.M.G., 16 *Wimpole-st.*, W.	Dec. 9, 1886	Jan. 17, 1882
Oram, Evelyn Henry Bardens, 43 *Lee-terrace, Blackheath*, S.E...	June 9, 1910	Nov. 9, 1905
Ormond, Arthur William, C.B.E., 9 *Devonshire-place*, W.	Dec. 8, 1898	Aug. 4, 1896
Osborn, Samuel, *Datchet, near Windsor*	June 8, 1876	Jan. 26, 1871
O'Sullivan, Richard Francis, 70 *Collins-street, Melbourne, Aust.*	June 11, 1914	July 25, 1912
Paddle, James Isaac, *Rose Hill, Mauritius* ....:	June 10, 1880	Apr. 24, 1880
Page, Charles Max, D.S.O., 134 *Harley-street*, W.	June 18, 1908	Feb. 8, 1906
Page, Harry Marmaduke, 53 *Welbeck-street*, W.	Dec. 9, 1886	Jan. 27, 1885
Page, Herbt. Wm., *Sedgecombe-house, The Bourne, Farnham* ..	Dec. 14, 1871	Nov. 16, 1869
Paget, Stephen, *Furzedown, Limpsfield-common, Surrey*	June 11, 1885	July 23, 1883
Paling, Albert, 19 *Duke-street, St. James's*, S.W.	June 11, 1896	May 12, 1892
Palmer, Alex. Croydon, O.B.E., 40 *Devonshire-street*, W.	June 12, 1913	May 12, 1910
Pandalai, K. G., *Maj.I.M.S.,Grindlay & Co.,Bombay,P.O.Box* 93	June 9, 1921	Feb. 9, 1911
Pannett, Charles A., 10 *Marlborough-pl., St. John's Wood*, N.W	Dec. 8, 1910	Dec. 8, 1910
Pantin, Chas. Satchell, *Finch Hill-house, Douglas, Isle of Man* .	Dec. 13, 1894	Feb. 9, 1893
Panting, Laurence Christopher, *Gwendroc, Truro*	June 10, 1909	June 10, 1909
Paramore, Richard Horace, 33 *Bilton-road, Rugby*	June 13, 1907	July 25, 1900
Pardhy, Krishna M., 60 *Newhall-street, Birmingham*	Dec. 8, 1910	Aug. 1, 1901
Pardoe, John George, *The Red-house, Port Errol, Aberdeenshire*	June 12, 1902	May 9, 1895
Parker, Rushton, 59 *Rodney-street, Liverpool*	Dec. 12, 1872	Apr. 20, 1869
Parker, Spencer Taurin, *Royal Lond. Ophthalmic-hospital*, E.C.	June 8. 1922	Feb. 12, 1920
Perkin, Alfred, *Carnaby Chalet, Bridlington, E. Yorks*........	June 12, 1890	Aug. 2, 1888
Parkin, Alfred, 56 *Jesmond-road, Newcastle-on-Tyne*..........	June 9, 1904	Oct. 16, 1902
Parkinson, John Porter, 15 *Upper Wimpole-street*, W.	Dec. 11, 1890	May 10, 1888
Parkinson, W. R., *"Lentholm," Branksome-rd.,St.Leon'rds-on-Sea*	Dec. 14, 1911	July 29, 1909
Parry, Albert Alexander, *Rockhampton, Queensland*	July 10, 1890	June 14, 1888
Parry, Leonard Arthur, 5 *The Drive, Hove*	June 11, 1896	May 10, 1894
Parsons, Frederick Gymer, *St. Thomas's-hospital*, S.E.	June 13, 1889	Jan. 27, 1886
Parsons, Sir John Herbert, C.B.E., 54 *Queen Anne-street*, W. .	Dec. 13, 1900	Nov. 12, 1891
§Partridge, Eleanor Joyce, 39 *Weymouth-street*, W.	Dec. 8, 1921	June 14, 1917
Paterson, Herbert John, C.B.E., 9 *Upper Wimpole-street*, W...	June 10, 1897	Nov. 10, 1892
Paterson, William Bromfield, 7A *Manchester-square*, W.......	May 13, 1886	Apr. 19, 1882
Paton, Leslie Johnston, 29 *Harley-street*, W.	June 12, 1902	May 8, 1900
Paton, Robert Young, 2 *Atholl-place, Perth, Scotland*	Dec. 8, 1921	July 29, 1920
Patterson, Norman, 16 *Devonshire-place*, W.	Dec. 14, 1905	Dec. 14, 1902
Paul, Frank Thomas, 31 *Rodney-street, Liverpool*	June 13, 1878	July 22, 1873
Paul, Samuel Chelliah, *Rao Mahal, Ward-place, Colombo, Ceylon*	Dec. 12, 1901	July 25, 1900
Payne, John Ernest, 57 *Carlisle-road, Eastbourne*............	Dec. 10, 1908	Dec. 10, 1908
Pearse, Robin, 206 *Bloor-street, West Toronto, Canada*.......	Dec. 12, 1912	May 13, 1909
Pearson, Charles Yelverton, 1 *Sidney-place, Cork*	June 10, 1886	June 10, 1886
Pearson, Maurice G., O.B.E., *Musgrave-rd., Durban, Natal*....	Dec. 9, 1897	May 9, 1895
Pendered, J.H.,M.C., *Capt.R.A M.C.,c/o Holt & Co.,3 Whitehall-pl.*	June 11, 1914	Feb. 1, 1912
Pendlebury, Herbert Stringfellow, 44 *Brook-street*, W. i	Dec. 9, 1897	Nov. 12, 1896

Name and Residence.	Fellow.	Member.
Pendred, Vaughan, 326 *Upper Richmond-road, East Sheen*	Dec. 10, 1896	Nov. 9, 1893
Pennell, George Herbert, *Edenbridge, Kent*	Dec. 12, 1889	Aug. 2, 1888
Pennell, Vernon Charles, *Pembroke-college, Cambridge*	Dec. 9, 1920	Nov. 13, 1913
Pepper, Augustus Joseph, *"Bracknell," Foots Cray-lane, Sidcup*	June 8, 1876	May 19, 1875
Perkins, George, M.C., *Thorpe Lee, Egham, Surrey*	Mar. 10, 1921	Dec. 11, 1919
Perkins, Herbert W., *" Llanberis," Haslemere-rd., Crouch-end, N.*	June 13, 1907	Feb. 9, 1904
Perks, Robert Howell, *Ferndale, Paignton, Devon*	June 12, 1884	July 26, 1881
Permewan, William, 31 *Rodney-street, Liverpool*	Dec. 12, 1889	July 22, 1886
Perrin, Thomas, *Gt. Western-street, Aylesbury*	June 1, 1905	Feb. 9, 1899
Perrin, Walter Sydney, 43 *Regent's-park-road, N.W.*	June 12, 1913	Feb. 1, 1912
Perry, Alan Cecil, *London-hospital, E.*	June 10, 1920	Nov. 12, 1914
Perry, Francis F., C.M.G., C.I.E., *Lt.-C. I.M.S., Headley, Hants.*	Dec. 12, 1889	Aug. 1, 1876
Peters, Edwin Arthur, 41 *Wimpole-street, W.*	June 11, 1903	Nov. 8, 1894
Petty, Michael Joseph, *Calle Juncal 790, Buenos Aires, S. Am.*	June 11, 1914	July 25, 1912
Phillips, John Wm. Glanmore, *London-hosp.-med.-coll., E.*	June 14, 1923	July 27, 1916
Phillips, Leonard George, 69 *Wimpole-street, W.*	June 12, 1919	July 29, 1915
Phillips, Llewellyn C. Powell, 8 *Sharia Suliman Pasha, Cairo* .	Dec. 9, 1897	July 30, 1894
Phillips, Miles Harris, 420 *Glossop-road, Sheffield*	Dec. 10, 1903	Nov. 8, 1900
Phillips, Walter, *Newchang, North China*	June 13, 1912	June 13, 1912
Pickard, Ransom, C.B., C.M G., 31 *East Southernhay, Exeter.*.	June 9, 1892	Feb. 12, 1889
Pickering, Charles Frederick, 13 *Berkeley-square, Bristol*......	June 10, 1880	May 18, 1876
Pidcock, Bertram Henzell, 17 *The Park, Golder's-green, N.W.*.	June 8, 1922	Nov. 9, 1916
Pierpoint, Harry William, O.B.E., *Major I.M.S.*	June 1, 1905	July 31, 1902
Pigeon, Henry Walter, *Ebor-lodge, Felbridge, East Grinstead.*.	June 11, 1885	Jan. 25, 1883
Pilcher, E. M., C.B , D.S.O., *Col. R.A.M.C.,* 17 *Eccleston-sq.,* S.W.	June 1, 1905	June 1, 1905
Pinch, A. E. Hayward, *Capt. I.M.S.,* 16 *Riding-house-street,* W.	Dec. 10, 1896	May 10, 1894
Pink, Wilfred Langrish, 4 *Blinmans-bldgs.,Eloff-st.,Johannesburg*	Dec. 14, 1911	Feb. 10, 1910
Pinkerton, John Maclean, 18 *Somerset-terr., Duke's-road, W.C.*	June 14, 1923	June 14, 1923
Pinnock, Dudley Denham, 15 *Cavendish-place, W.*	June 12, 1913	Feb. 9, 1911
Pisani, Lionel John, *Lt.-Col. I.M.S.,* 49 *Wimpole-street, W.*....	Dec. 12, 1895	Jan. 21, 1886
Pitts, Arthur Gentry, *Waimate, New Zealand*	June 11, 1903	Nov. 14, 1901
Platt, Harry, 26 *St. John-street, Manchester*	Dec. 12, 1912	May 9, 1912
Platt, Walter Brewster, 802 *Cathedral-st., Baltimore, U.S.A.*...	Dec. 13, 1883	Apr. 19, 1881
Playfair, Hugh James Moore, 7 *Upper Brook-street, W.*	Dec. 14, 1899	July 31, 1890
Plowman, Sidney, *The Tofts, Frankston, Victoria*	Dec. 10, 1885	Apr. 21, 1884
Poate, Hugh R. G., *Lt.-Col.,* 225 *Macquarie-st., Sydney, N.S.W.*	June 10, 1909	July 30, 1908
Pocock, Wm. Agard, 37 *Chudleigh-bldgs., Eloff-st., Johannesbury*	Dec. 11, 1919	May 8, 1913
Poland, John, *Home-cottage, Seal, Kent*	June 8, 1882	May 20, 1879
Pollard, Bilton, 7 *St. Winifred's-road, Bournemouth*	June 9, 1881	Nov. 19, 1879
Pollard, Charles, 23 *Foregate-street, Worcester*	Dec. 14, 1893	Jan. 22, 1886
Pollard, Herbert Dean, 6 *Harpur-place, Bedford*	Dec. 8, 1904	July 27, 1899
Pollock, Sir Edward James, 20 *York-terr., Regent's-park, N.W.*	June 11, 1868	July 30, 1863
Pooley, George Henry, 304 *Glossop-road, Sheffield*	Dec. 10, 1908	May 14, 1908
Powell, William Wyndham, 75 *Wimpole-street, W.*	June 8, 1893	Aug. 2, 1888
Power, Sir D'Arcy, K.B.E., 10 A *Chandos-street, W.*	Dec. 13, 1883	Jan. 18, 1882
Prain, John Leay, *Casilla* 1213, *Valparaiso, Chile, S. America.*.	June 9, 1898	Nov. 8, 1894
¶ Pratt, J. J., *Lt.-Col. I.M.S.,* 63 *Addison-road, Kensington, W.* ...	Apr. 11, 1912	July 22, 1881

Name and Residence.	Fellow.	Member.
Preston, Chas. H., 16 *Lynwood-grove, Broad-rd., Sale, Cheshire*..	Dec. 8, 1892	July 28, 1890
Price, Henry James, *Maldon, Essex*	June 9, 1898	May 14, 1896
Pringle, James Hogarth, 172 *Bath-street, Glasgow*	June 9, 1892	Aug. 2, 1888
Pritchard, Urban, 55 *Wimpole-street*, W.....................	Dec. 12, 1872	July 20, 1869
Pronger, Charles Ernest, " *Litchdow,"·East Parade, Harrogate*..	June 11, 1891	Jan. 27, 1876
Prowse, Arthur Bancks, 5 *Lansdown-place, Clifton, Bristol*	Dec. 14, 1882	July 25, 1877
Pryce, Harold Vaughan, 104 *Bethune-rd., Stamford-hill*, N.....	June 20, 1901	Feb. 9, 1899
Prynne, H. V.,C.B.E.,D.S.O.,*Col.A.M.S ,Holt&Co., Whitehall-pl.*	June 11, 1914	Feb. 11, 1892
Purves, James Ewart, " *Sundial," Gilmerton, Midlothian*......	June 14, 1923	June 14, 1923
Pybus, Fredk. C., *Windsor-house,Jesmond-rd., Newcastle-on-Tyne*	June 10, 1909	Jan. 28, 1909
Pye-Smith, Chas. D., D.S.O., M.C., *Vernon-house, Huddersfield.*	Dec. 14, 1905	Aug. 4, 1903
Quick, Balcombe D.S.O., 352 *Collins-street, Melbourne, Victoria*	Dec. 8, 1910	Dec. 8, 1910
Quick, Hamilton Ernest, 130 *Easton-crescent, Swansea*........	June 10, 1909	Feb. 8, 1906
Quine, Albert Edward, *Ministry of Health, Whitehall*, S.W. ...	Apr. 10, 1913	Apr. 10, 1913
Radford, A., M.C.,*National-bank-ch'mb'rs, West-st.,Durban,Nat'l*	Dec. 11, 1919	Dec. 11, 1919
Radley, Sidney Bertram, 11 *Castlegate, Newark, Notts*	Dec. 11, 1913	Feb. 13, 1913
Rainey, Edward Holmes, *Wakefield-house,Compton-st.,Eastb'rne.*	Dec. 11, 1913	Nov. 11, 1909
Rainforth, John Jekyll, 2 *Lindum-road, Lincoln*..............	June 10, 1909	Feb. 11, 1904
Raison, Cyril Alban, 93 *Cornwall-street, Birmingham*	Mar. 10, 1921	Mar. 10, 1921
Rake, Alfred Theodore, 23 *Lawn-crescent, Kew-gardens, Surrey*	Mar. 8, 1894	May 14, 1891
Ralston, Robert G , *Chudleigh's-bldgs., Johannesburg, Transvaal* .	Dec. 14, 1899	May 13, 1897
Ramsay, Robert Anstruther, 4 *Bryanston-st , Portman-sq.*, W.	Dec. 11, 1913	July 27, 1911
Rand, Richard Frank, *Vogies, Transvaal*	Dec. 13, 1883	Dec. 13, 1883
Randall, Martin, *The Lodge, Leopold-road, Wimbledon*	Dec. 12, 1895	Aug. 1, 1892
Ranken, David, c/o Messrs. *Holt & Co.*, 3 *Whitehall-place*, S.W.	Dec. 14, 1911	Mar. 12, 1908
Rawling, Louis Bathe, 16 *Montagu-street, Portman sq.*, W··...	May 31, 1900	Aug. 4, 1896
Ray, John Howson, 11 *St. John-street, Manchester*	June 11, 1896	July 30, 1894
Rayner, David Chas , 9 *Lansdowne-pl., Victoria-sq ,Clifton,Bristol*	June 11, 1896	May 12, 1892
Rayner, Henry Herbert, 14 *St. John-street, Manchester*	June 13, 1907	June 13, 1907
Rea, Robert Lindsay, 125 *Harley-street*, W.	Dec. 9, 1920	Dec. 9, 1920
Reader,Norbert L.M.,*Brunswick House,10High-st.,Bromley,Kent*	Dec. 9, 1920	May 12, 1910
Reckless, Philip Alfred, 13 *Westbourne-road, Sheffield*	Dec. 14, 1911	May 10, 1906
Redding, John Magnus, 9 *Cavendish-square*, W.	June 11, 1914	July 25, 1912
Redmayne, Thomas, *Droxford-house, St. Leonards-on-Sea*	June 13, 1889	Apr. 22, 1886
Reece, Leslie Norman, *St. Thomas's Hospital*, S.E.	June 10, 1920	Feb. 13, 1913
Rees, William Arthur, O.B.E., 1 *The Parade, Swanage, Dorset*..	Dec. 8, 1904	July 31, 1902
Reid, Hugh, 50 *High-street, Liverpool*	Dec. 8, 1921	July 24, 1919
Reid, John Buchanan, *Tillsonburg, Ontario, Canada*	June 8, 1911	Nov. 9, 1893
Reid, Robert William, 37 *Albyn-place, Aberdeen*	June 9, 1881	June 9, 1881
Rendall, John, *Forest-side, Lymington, Hants*	June 14, 1877	Apr. 20, 1874
Rhind, Sydney Devenish, *St. George's-hospital*, S.W.	June 14, 1923	July 27, 1916
Richards, Owen Wm., C.M.G., D.S.O., *Kasr-el-Ainy-hosp.,Cairo*	June 1, 1905	May 8, 1902
Richards, William Hunter, *Kemeys, nr. Usk, Mon.*	June 12, 1902	June 12, 1902

Name and Residence.	Fellow.	Member.
Richards, William Jones, *Brynhyfryd, Aberavon*	Dec. 13, 1906	Feb. 11, 1897
Richardson, Alfred, 37 *Park-square, Leeds*	Dec. 8, 1910	Nov. 14, 1907
Richardson, Alfred Henry, 15 *Queen Anne-street, W.*	June 13, 1912	July 25, 1910
Richardson, Geoffrey Bower, " *Dilkhusha," Newquay, Cornwall*	Mar. 10, 1921	May 14, 1914
Richardson, S. Wm. F., 2 *Vine-street, The Gardens, Cape Town*	July 9, 1896	July 27, 1893
Richardson, Wm. George, " *Braithwaite," Keswick*	June 12, 1890	Aug. 4, 1887
Ridewood, Harold Ed., 422 *St. Charles-st., Victoria, B. Columbia.*	June 14, 1906	Nov. 14, 1901
Ridley, Nicholas Charles, 27 *Horse-fair-street, Leicester*	Dec. 12, 1895	May 10, 1888
Ridout, Chas. Arch. Scott, " *St. Elmo," Clarendon-rd., Southsea*	June 9, 1904	Nov. 2, 1899
Rigby, Sir Hugh Mallinson, K.C.V.O., 24 *Queen Anne-street, W.*	May 31, 1900	Feb. 7, 1895
Riley, Frederick Ratcliffe, *Dunedin, New Zealand*	Dec. 10, 1896	July 28, 1890
Rischbieth, Harold, 8 *King William-st., Adelaide, S. Australia* .	June 18, 1908	May 14, 1903
Ritchie, J. L., *Maj.,* 12/13 *St. Mary's-buildings, Johannesberg* .	Dec. 11, 1913	Nov. 11, 1909
Ritson, Stanley, 3 *Grange-crescent, Sunderland*	June 12, 1913	May 11, 1911
Rivett, Louis Carnac, 118 *Harley-street, W.*	June 10, 1915	May 9, 1912
Riviere, Bernard Beryl, *St. Giles Plain, Norwich*	Dec. 13, 1906	Feb. 11, 1904
Rix, Rowland Waters, 51 *Friars-street, Sudbury, Suffolk*	June 13, 1912	Feb. 13, 1908
Roberts, Cedric Sydney Lane, *Upper-park-rd., Hampstead,* N.W.	June 10, 1920	Nov. 13, 1913
Roberts, Charles, 15 *St. John-street, Manchester*	Nov. 2, 1899	Aug. 4, 1896
Roberts, Charles Hubert, 48 *Harley-street, W.*	June 9, 1892	Feb. 12, 1889
Roberts, George Augustus, C.B.E., *Walcote, Winchester*	June 11, 1903	Aug. 2, 1898
Roberts, Jas. Alex., C.B., 19 *Bloor-st. West, Toronto, Ont., Canada*	June 9, 1904	Feb. 11, 1904
Roberts, James Ernest Helme, 26 *Harley-street, W.*	Dec. 9, 1909	May 10, 1906
Roberts, Sir J.R., *L.-Col. I.M.S., C.I.E.,* c/o *Lloyds Bk.,* 9 *Pall Mall.*	Dec. 8, 1887	July 28, 1884
Roberts, John Lloyd, 68 *Rodney-street, Liverpool*	June 11, 1891	May 10, 1888
Robertson, Carrick Hey, 1 *Alfred-st., Auckland, New Zealand* .	Oct. 13, 1904	July 31, 1902
Robinson, Arthur Leyland, 57 *Rodney-street, Liverpool*	Oct. 10, 1912	Feb. 10, 1910
Robinson, Frederick William, 7 *Spencer-road, Buxton*	June 8, 1899	Aug. 4, 1887
Robinson, Gerald Chas. Fredk., 7 *The Crescent, Plymouth*	Mar. 14, 1907	July 28, 1904
Robinson, Harry, O.B.E., 25 *Welbeck-street, W.*	Dec. 14, 1911	May 9, 1889
Robinson, James Frederick, 27 *Beaumont-street, Oxford*	June 12, 1902	Feb. 7, 1901
Robinson, Ronald H. O. B., 8 н *Bickenhall-mans., Baker-st., W.*	June 9, 1921	Nov. 14, 1918
Robinson, William, *Carlton-house, Sunderland*	Dec. 8, 1892	July 20, 1881
Robson, Sir A. W. Mayo, K.B.E., C.B., *Broadoak, Seale, Surrey.*	Dec. 11, 1879	July 21, 1874
Rochfort-Brown, Herbert, *West Koppies, Pretoria, Transvaal* ..	Dec. 14, 1893	Nov. 12, 1891
Rodocanachi, Ambrose John, " *Aingarth," Stalybridge*	June 8, 1899	July 25, 1895
Rogers, Sir Leonard, C.I.E., *Lt.-Col. I.M.S.,* 24 *Carendish-sq.,* W.	Feb. 10, 1893	Feb. 12, 1891
Roll, Grahame Winfield, 7 *Upper Wimpole-street, W.*	June 9, 1898	Oct. 26, 1886
Romanis, William Hugh Cowie, 31 *Harley-street, W.*	Dec. 9, 1915	Nov. 12, 1914
Rooke, Alfred Basil, *Boscombe-cottage, Bournemouth*	Dec. 9, 1909	July 25, 1907
Rose, Baron Theodore, 29 *Poplar-av., Edgbaston, Birmingham.*	June 8, 1922	May 11, 1916
Rose, Frank Atcherley, 68 *Wimpole-street, W.*	Dec. 10, 1903	Feb. 9, 1899
Ross, Daniel McClure, 69 *Portchester-rd., Bournemouth*	June 11, 1891	June 11, 1891
Ross, James Paterson, 14 *Coolhurst-road, Crouch End, N.*	June 8, 1922	Feb. 8, 1917
Ross, Robert Ainslie, *Bedford, Cape Province, South Africa* ..	Dec. 10, 1908	Nov. 14, 1901
¶ Ross, Sir R., K.C.B., K.C.M.G., 41 *Buckingham-palace-mans.,* S.W.	Apr. 11, 1901	July 30, 1879
Roth, Paul Bernard, 51 *Harley-street, W.*	Dec. 8, 1910	Dec. 8, 1910

Name and Residence.	Fellow.	Member.
Roughton, Walter, "*Goldstone,*" *Dyke-road, Brighton*	June 8, 1893	July 23, 1875
Rouillard, Laurent Antoine John, *Balgowan, Natal*	Dec. 10, 1891	Dec. 10, 1891
Rowe, Robert Morison, 88 *Harley-street*, W.	Dec. 11, 1913	Oct. 13, 1904
Rowlands, Robert Pugh, O.B.E., 12 *Queen Anne-street*, W. ..	June 20, 1901	Aug. 4, 1896
Rowntree, Cecil William, 9 *Upper Brook-street*, W	Mar. 9, 1905	May 8, 1902
Roxburgh, Alex. Bruce, 3 *Manchester-square*, W.	Dec. 14, 1893	Nov. 10, 1887
Roy, Bidhan Chandra, 36 *Wellington-street, Calcutta*	June 8, 1911	Feb. 10, 1910
Roy, Donald Whatley, 10 *Chandos-street*, W.	June 18, 1908	May 10, 1906
Rundle, Henry, 13 *Clarence-parade, Southsea*	June 9, 1870	Apr. 26, 1865
Russell, Harold George Bedford, 85 *Harley-street*, W	June 12, 1919	Nov. 9, 1911
Russell, John Dill, "*Blackmoor,*" *Londn-lane, Bromley, Kent* .	Oct. 13, 1898	Aug. 4, 1896
Russell, R. Hamilton, 85 *Spring-st., Melbourne, Vict., Australia.*	June 13, 1889	July 30, 1882
Rutherford, Norman Cecil, D.S.O.	Jan. 14, 1909	Jan. 14, 1909
Rutter, Francis Burchett, *Dewes-house, Mere, Wilts*	June 14, 1894	Feb. 11, 1892
Rutter, Hubert Llewellyn, M.B.E., 2 *Wentworth-pl., Newcastle.*	June 14, 1894	Nov. 12, 1891
Sackett, Herbert Leyland, 37 *Hillcroft-crescent, Ealing*, W. ..	Dec. 14, 1922	Feb. 10, 1921
Saint, C. F. Morris, C B.E., *Univ of Cape Town, Cape Town, S.A.*	June 12, 1913	June 12, 1913
Salisbury, Walter, "*Glanford,*" *Oswald-rd. Scunthorpe, Lincs...*	June 14, 1923	May 8, 1913
Salter, Charles Edward, 34 *Prince of Wales-terrace. Scarborough*	Dec. 14, 1893	July 30, 1891
Sampson, Herbert H.,O.B E.,M.C.,47*Newhall-street,Birmingham*	Oct. 12, 1911	Nov. 10, 1910
Sanders, Alfred Wm., 832 *Schoeman-st., Arcadia, Pretoria* ..	June 8, 1899	July 29, 1895
Sandes, T.L.L.,O.B.E.,"*Bellair,*"*Paradise-st., Claremont, CapeTn.*	June 10, 1920	June 10, 1920
Saner, Francis Donaldson, 35 *Harley-street*, W.	June 8, 1916	May 12, 1910
Saner, John Godfrey, 19 *Ansteys-bldgs., Kerk-st., Johannesburg.*	Dec. 12, 1912	Oct. 10, 1912
Saneyoshi, (Viscount) Yasuzumi, 9 *Toriyaka, Azabu, Tokio, Japan*	June 11, 1885	Jan. 24, 1883
Santi, Philip Robert William de, 18 *Wimpole-street*, W.......	Oct. 11, 1888	Nov. 24, 1884
Sargent, Percy Wm. Geo., C.M.G., D.S.O., 20 *Harley-street*, W·	Dec. 13, 1900	May 4, 1898
Saunders, Henry William, 18 *Silverdale-road, Eastbourne*	Dec. 11, 1873	Apr. 20, 1869
Savage, Ernest Smallwood, 133 *Edmund-street, Birmingham* ..	Dec. 10, 1896	May 14, 1896
Sawrey, Ernest Edwd. Robt., 90 *Collins-st., Melbourne, Australia*	Dec. 12, 1901	Dec. 12, 1901
Scotson, Frederick C., 9 *Plymouth-grove- West, Manchester*	July 30, 1894	Aug. 1, 1893
Scott, James A. N., *Lister-ho.-priv.-hosp , Rowan-st.,Bendigo,Vict.*	Dec. 10, 1896	July 27, 1893
Scott, Malcolm Leslie, *North-terrace, Adelaide, S. Australia* ..	Dec. 9, 1909	Dec. 9, 1909
Scott, Rupert Strathmore, 9 *Drayton-court, Drayton-gdns.,* S.W.	June 14, 1923	May 8, 1913
Scott, Sydney Richard, 130 *Harley-street*, W.	Dec. 11. 1902	July 27, 1899
Scott, Wallace A., C.M.G., 627 *Sherbourne-st., Toronto, Ont., Can.*	June 9, 1904	Nov. 13, 1902
Scrase, Frank Edward, 6 *Woodchurch-rd., West-end-lane*, N.W.	June 11, 1896	July 27, 1883
Secretan, Walter Bernard, 11 *Craven-road, Reading*	Dec. 12, 1901	July 25, 1900
Selby, Edmond Wallace, *Crescent House, Hillary-place, Leeds* .	Dec. 13, 1894	Aug. 1, 1892
Senior, Harold D., 338 *East 26th Street, New York City, U.S.A.*	Nov. 14, 1895	Feb. 11, 1892
Sequeira, James Harry, 10 *Queen Anne-street*, W.	June 8, 1893	May 9, 1889
Shadbolt, L. Pierrepoint, *The Old Farm-house,Bushey,nr. Watford*	Dec. 8, 1887	Aug. 5, 1885
Shafeek, Ahmad, 4 *Sharia Radwar, Shutsi, Abassieh, Cairo....*	June 11, 1914	Nov. 9, 1911
Shah, Tribhovandas Oghaddas, *Wadhwan City, Kathiawar, India*	Dec. 11, 1919	Dec. 11, 1913
Shattock, Clement Edward, 15 *Harley-street*, W.	June 12, 1913	Nov. 11, 1909
Shattock, Samuel Geo., 4 *Crescent-rd., The Downs, Wimbledon* .	Dec. 8, 1881	Jan. 25, 1876

Name and Residence.	Fellow.	Member.
Shaw, C. Gordon, D.S.O., 108 *Wellington-par., F. Melbourne, Vict.*	Dec. 14, 1911	Dec. 14, 1911
Shaw, Harold Batty, 122 *Harley-street*, W.	Dec. 10, 1896	July 29, 1895
Shaw, Simeon Cyril, 1 *Coronation-street, Barnstaple, N. Devon*	Dec. 11, 1919	Nov. 8, 1917
Shaw, Wilfred, *Ivydene, Birchfields, Birmingham*............	June 14, 1923	July 28, 1921
Shearer, Donald Francis, *The Hollies, Kidlington, Oxon*	June 9, 1892	May 12, 1892
Sheen, Alfred William, C.B.E., 69 *Wimpole-street*, W	May 10, 1894	May 12, 1892
Sherren, James, C.B.E., 6 *Devonshire-place*, W.	Dec. 13, 1900	July 27, 1899
¶Sherrington, Sir Chas. Scott, G.B.E., 9 *Chadlington-rd., Oxford*	Apr. 14, 1921	Aug. 4, 1884
Shillitoe, Arthur, 2 *Frederick-place*, E.C.	June 13, 1895	Nov. 9, 1893
Shirley, Herbert John, C.M.G., 19 *York-terrace*, N.W.	June 8, 1899	July 30, 1894
Shirwalkar, Raghunath D., *Tembavali, Devgad, Ratnagiri, Bombay*	Dec. 11, 1919	Feb. 8, 1917
Shorney, Herbert Frank, 8 *King William-st., Adelaide, S. Aust.*	Dec. 12, 1907	Dec. 12, 1907
Short, Arthur Rendle, 69 *Pembroke-road, Clifton, Bristol*......	June 18, 1908	June 18, 1908
§Shufflebotham, Hilda Nora, " *The Firs," Moor-gn., Birmingham.*	Dec. 9, 1920	Nov. 14, 1918
Shuttleworth, C. Buckingham, 478 *Huron-st., Toronto, Canada.*	Dec. 11, 1902	Feb. 13, 1902
Sichel, Gerald T. Sylvester, *Vine-house, Sevenoaks*	June 14, 1894	May 12, 1892
Sikes, Alfred Walter, *Moat-house, Langley, Buckinghamshire..*	Dec. 8, 1898	Aug. 4, 1896
Sim nonds, Bernard Sangster, 58 *Wimpole-street*, W.	June 10, 1920	Feb. 10, 1910
Simpson, George Charles E I., O.B.E. 15 *Rodney-street, Liverpool.*	June 18, 1908	Apr. 9, 1908
Simpson, Graham Scales, 342 *Glossop-road, Sheffield*	June 20, 1901	July 27, 1899
Sinclair, Neil Frederick, 72 *Wimpole-street*, W.	June 10, 1920	July 30, 1908
Sinclair, Thomas, C.B., 22 *University-square, Belfast*	June 10, 1886	Apr. 18, 1882
Skevington, Sir Joseph Oliver, K.C.V.O., " *Belmont," Windsor.*	Dec. 14, 1899	Feb. 10, 1898
Sladen, Reginald John Lambert, G.I.P. *Rly., Jhansi, U.P., India*	June 8, 1911	Aug. 1, 1901
Slater, Benj. H., *Holme Top-house, Little Horton-lane, Bradford*	Dec. 10, 1903	May 11, 1899
Slesinger, Edward G., O.B.E., 69 *Wimpole-street*, W.	Dec. 11, 1913	July 27, 1911
Slinger, Robert T., 42 *Foregate-street, Worcester*	Dec. 10, 1908	Dec. 10, 1908
Sloane, John Stretton, 82 *London-road, Leicester*	June 13, 1895	May 11, 1893
¶Sloggett,SirA.T.,K.C.B.,K.C.M.G.,K.C.V.O.,6*Bickenh'll-ms.*,W	Apr. 12, 1917	Apr. 21, 1880
Smalpage, Edward Stanley, *Macquarie-street, Sydney, N.S.W..*	Mar. 10, 1921	Mar. 10, 1921
Smerdon, Edgar Wilmot, 38 *Cornwall-road, Dorchester*	June 11, 1914	June 11, 1914
Smith, Alfred Bernard Pavey, M.C., 9 *Victoria-av., Harrogate.*	Dec. 11, 1919	Dec. 11, 1919
Smith, C. H., O.B.E., *Maj. I.M.S., Grindlay & Co., Parliament-st.*	July 9, 1908	Jan. 16, 1908
Smith, Clive Nigel, *Manly, Sydney, N.S.W.*	June 10, 1920	June 10, 1920
Smith, Ed. Archibald, 312–314 *Vancouver-blk., Vancouver, B.C.*	May 10, 1900	May 14, 1896
Smith, Ferdinand Clarence, 84 *St. Alban's-road, Watford*......	June 8, 1893	Apr. 24, 1877
Smith, George Frederick Darwall, 8 *Grosvenor-street*, W.	June 1, 1905	Feb. 13, 1902
Smith, Gilbert, *The Chalet, Hindhead, Surrey*...............	Dec. 14, 1899	Aug. 4, 1896
Smith, Guy Bellingham, 10 *Devonshire-place*, W.	June 12, 1890	June 12, 1890
Smith, Hugh, *Derwent-ho., Hof-street, Cape Town, South Africa*	June 13, 1889	Oct. 20, 1886
Smith, Hugh Bernard W., 113 *Morton-terrace, Gainsborough..*	Dec. 9, 1909	July 31, 1902
Smith, James, 16 *St. John's-road, Putney-hill*, S.W.	Dec. 9, 1897	Feb. 13, 1896
Smith, John William, *Richmond-road-house, Ingleton, Yorks ..*	June 12, 1890	July 19, 1886
¶Smith, Joseph Priestley,52 *Frederick-rd., Edgbaston, Birmingham*	Apr. 11, 1901	Nov. 16, 1871
Smith, J. S. K., *Craig-y-Don, Everard-rd., Rhos-on-Sea, N. Wales*	Apr. 4, 1895	Nov. 12, 1891
Smith, Norman Ross, *Nat. Bank of Australasia, 7 Lothbury*, E.C.	June 14, 1913	May 10, 1923
Smith, Percy Montague, 31 *Rosary-gardens, S. Kensington*, S.W.	June 10, 1909	May 9, 1895

Name and Residence.	Fellow.	Member.
Smith, Sidney Maynard, C.B., 49 *Wimpole-street*, W.	May 12, 1902	Jan. 22, 1898
Smith, Thomas Frederick Hugh, *Farningham, Dartford*	Dec. 14, 1882	Aug. 1, 1877
Smith, Sir Thos. R. H., Bt., C.B.E., 9 *Higher-terrace, Torquay.*	Dec. 12, 1895	Nov. 10, 1892
Smith, Thomas Waddelow, *City Asylum, Nottingham*	Dec. 14, 1911	July 27, 1893
Smith, Wilburn, 1012 *Brockman-bldg., Los Angeles, California.*	Dec. 12, 1912	May 11, 1911
Smith, William Robert, " *The Willows," Beeston, Nottingham.* .	June 11, 1896	Aug. 1, 1892
Smythe, Henry J. D., M.C., 72 *St. Paul's-rd., Clifton, Bristol.* .	Mar. 10, 1921	Nov. 13, 1913
Solly, Ernest, *Strathlea, Harrogate*	June 14, 1888	Aug. 4, 1886
Solly, Reginald Vaughan, 40 *West Southernhay, Exeter*	June 12, 1890	Aug. 4, 1887
Soltau, Alfred Bertram, C.M.G., C.B E., 1 *The Crescent, Plymouth*	June 12, 1902	May 10, 1900
Somervell, Theodore Howard, *Brantfield, Kendal.*	Dec. 9, 1920	May 13, 1915
Southam, Arthur Hughes, " *Oak-lawn," Rusholme, Manchester.*	Dec. 9, 1915	Feb. 12, 1914
Southam, Frederick Armitage, 13 *St. John-street, Manchester* . .	June 14, 1877	Apr. 18, 1876
Souttar, Henry Sessions, C.B.E., 58 *Queen Anne-street*, W. . .	Dec. 9, 1909	May 10, 1906
Sowry, George Herbert, 9 *King-street, Newcastle, Staffs*	Dec. 8, 1898	May 9, 1895
Spedding, Leslie Alan, *Remuera, Auckland, N.Z.*	Dec. 9, 1920	Dec. 9, 1920
Spencer, C. G., *Lt.-Col. R.A.M.C., Trotterscliffe, W.Malling,Kent*	June 13, 1895	Aug. 1, 1892
Spencer, Walter George, O.B.E., 2 *Portland-place*, W.	June 9, 1887	Aug. 3, 1885
Spicer, William Thomas Holmes, 5 *Manchester-square*, W.	Dec. 13, 1888	Jan. 24, 1884
Spittel, Richard Lionel, *Ward-place, Colombo, Ceylon*	Dec. 9, 1909	July 30, 1908
Spong, Ambrose, " *Five Ways," Torquay*	Dec. 9, 1909	Dec. 9, 1909
Spong, Charles Stuart, D.S.O., Maj., *Ghezireh, Cairo, Egypt.* . .	June 13, 1889	Aug. 7, 1884
Sprawson, F. Charles, 7 *Imperial-ter., Claremont-pk., Blackpool.*	Mar. 11, 1897	May 10, 1894
Spreat, Frank Arthur, "*Burrington," Oakleigh-pk., Whetstone,N.*	June 1, 1905	July 30, 1884
¶Sprigge, Sir S. Squire, *Stoke-green, Slough, Bucks.*	Apr. 14, 1921	Apr. 27 1886
Spriggs, Neville Ivens, 105 *Princess-road, Leicester*	Dec. 8, 1904	Aug. 4, 1903
Spurrell, Charles, *St. Andrew's-hospital, Bow*, E.	Dec. 14, 1893	Feb. 13, 1890
Square, James Elliot, 22 *Portland-square, Plymouth*	Dec. 13, 1883	Nov. 15, 1881
Stabb, Ewen Carthew, c/o *L.C. W.& P.Bank,* 21 *Hanover-sq.*, W.	Dec. 13, 1888	July 28, 1886
Stallmann, John F. H., 8 *Kinfauns-rd., Tulse-hill-park*, S.W. . .	Dec. 14, 1922	Nov. 12, 1914
Standage, Robert Frazer, C.I.E.,*Lt.-Col.I.M.S., Bangalore,India*	Dec. 9, 1920	Nov. 14, 1889
Stanger, William, *Haddon-hall, Hinton-rd., Bournemouth*	Dec. 8, 1870	Jan. 23, 1867
Stanley, Ernest Gerald, 51 *rue des Belles Feuilles, Paris*	June 13, 1912	Feb. 10, 1910
Stanley, John Brentnall, 181 *Horninglow-st., Burton-on-Trent* .	Dec. 9, 1920	July 27, 1899
Stawell, Rodolph de Salis, O.B E., " *Ayan Trigva," Falmouth* .	Dec. 14, 1899	Aug. 4, 1896
Steedman, John Francis, "*Arcall," Prentis-rd., Streatham*, S.W.	June 11, 1885	Nov. 13, 1883
Stephens, F. G. N., 13 *Dover-road, Rose Bay, Sydney, N.S.W.*	June 12, 1913	June 12, 1913
Stephens, H. E. R., *Surg.-Com. R.N.*, c/o *Admiralty, S.W.*	Dec. 9, 1920	Dec. 9, 1920
Stephenson, J., C.I.E., *Lt.-Col. I.M.S.,* 2 *Oxford-terr., Edinburgh*	Dec. 14, 1905	Dec. 14, 1905
Stevens, Thomas George, 20 *Queen Anne-street*, W.	June 13, 1895	July 28, 1890
Steward, Edward Simmons, 2 *South Park-road, Harrogate* . .	Dec. 12, 1901	Nov. 9, 1893
Steward, Francis James, 98 *Portland-place.* W.	June 12, 1898	July 29, 1895
Stewart, Joseph O., *Conrod-ho., Bentinck-rd., Newcastle-on-Tyne.*	Dec. 11, 1913	Dec. 11, 1913
Stock, Wm. Stuart V., 1 *Mortimer-road, Bristol*	Dec. 12, 1907	Feb. 10, 1898
Stocks, Wm. Percy, 59 *Wilmslow-road, Withington, Manchester*	June 11, 1891	Nov. 10, 1887
Stone, William Gream, " *Hillside," Champion-hill*, S.E.	June 11, 1896	Nov. 8, 1894
Storey, John Colvin, 185 *Macquarie-street, Sydney, N.S.W.* . .	June 11, 1914	June 11, 1914

Name and Residence.	Fellow.	Member.
Stout,Thos. D. M.,D.S.O.,O.B.E ,281 *TheTerrace,Wellington,N.Z.*	June 13, 1912	May 12, 1910
Stowell, Thomas Edmund Alex., *Fir Grove, Northwich, Chester*	June 13, 1912	May 12, 1910
Strachan, Gilbert Innes, 20 *Windsor-place, Cardiff*	Dec. 8, 1921	Dec. 8, 1921
Strange, Arthur, *Lydenburg, Transvaal Province, S.A.*........	Dec. 9, 1897	July 28, 1892
Street, Ashton, *Lt.-Col. I M.S., c/o Grindlay & Co., Parliament-st.*	June 13, 1889	July 30, 1888
Stretton, John Weston, 27 *Church-street, Kidderminster*	Dec. 9, 1920	Nov. 13, 1913
Strickland, Harold F., *"Margam," Wickham-road, Beckenham*.	June 13, 1912	Feb. 9, 1905
Stuart-Low, William. 49 *Wimpole-street, W.*	Dec. 8, 1898	May 13, 1897
Stusser, Israel, *Paula-house, Church-st., Oudtshoorn, Cape Prov.*.	June 11, 1903	Nov. 14, 1901
Sutcliffe, William Greenwood, O.B.E., 30 *Dalby-sq., Margate*..	Dec. 12, 1895	Aug. 12, 1892
Sutherland, Donald McKay, *Royal Infirmary, Manchester*	Dec. 8, 1921	Dec. 8, 1921
Swain, James, C.B., C.B.E., 4 *Victoria-square, Clifton, Bristol*.	Dec. 12, 1889	Nov. 14, 1883
Swan, James, M.C., *c/o Holt & Co.*, 3 *Whitehall-place, S.W.*...	Mar. 10, 1921	Mar. 10, 1921
Swan, Russell Henry Jocelyn, O.B.E., 75 *Wimpole-street, W.*...	Dec. 11, 1902	Dec. 11, 1902
Sylvester, Geo H., *c/o L. C. W. & P. Bank, Tunbridge, Kent*..	Dec. 9, 1886	Apr. 16, 1878
Syme, Geo. Adlington, 19 *Collins-street, Melbourne, Victoria* ..	Dec. 10, 1885	Apr. 26, 1884
¶Symington, Johnson, 4 *Montague-street, W.C.*	Apr. 8, 1915	July 24, 1877
Symonds, Sir Charters James, K.B.E., C.B., 14 *Portland-pl.*, W.	June 9, 1881	July 21, 1875
Syms, Gilbert Francis, *Surg.-Com.R.N., c/o Admiralty, S.W.*...	June 14, 1923	Feb. 13, 1908
Tait, Henry Brewer, *"Ashmount," Hornsey-lane, N.*..........	Dec. 11, 1884	July 21, 1881
Takaki (Baron), K., 13 *Higashi Toriizaka, Azaba, Tokio, Japan*	June 10, 1880	Apr. 16, 1878
Talbot, Francis Theodore, 25 *Bridge-road, Stockton-on-Tees* ..	June 8, 1911	May 4, 1898
Talbot, Leonard Smith, 53 *Church-street, Timaru, N.Z.*	Dec. 14, 1905	Feb. 9, 1905
Talbot, Philip, *"Early-bank," Stalybridge, Cheshire*	Dec. 12, 1907	Nov. 9, 1905
Tanner, Charles Edward, 4 *Downing-street, Farnham, Surrey*..	Dec. 9, 1886	Oct. 22, 1884
Tanner, Herbert. *Hamilton-house*, 152 *Westbourne-grove, W.* ..	Dec. 12, 1895	Apr. 28, 1885
Tanner, William Edward, 7 *Cavendish-place, W.* 1	Dec. 14, 1916	Nov. 13, 1913
Tasker, Douglas G. C., 16 *All Saints-road, Clifton, Bristol*	Dec. 9, 1920	May 11, 1916
Tatlow, Robert Evelyn Tissington, *The Oaks, Porlock, Somerset*	June 12, 1919	June 12, 1919
Taunton, Edgar, *Thora-house, Bethersden, Kent*..............	June 1, 1905	July 27, 1899
Tawse, Herbert Bell, 16 *Regent-street, Nottingham*	Dec. 8, 1904	Dec. 8, 1904
Tay, Waren, 61 *Oakfield-road, West Croydon*	June 10, 1869	Apr. 25, 1866
Taylor, Douglas C., M.C., O.B.E., *Lewisham-hospital, Lewisham*.	June 12, 1913	Nov. 8, 1906
Taylor, Edwin C., *Twenty-nine, Rosslyn-hill, Hampstead, N.W.*	June 11, 1896	Feb. 8, 1866
Taylor, Frank Edward, 43 *West Heath-drive, Hampstead, N.W.*	Dec. 10, 1903	Feb. 11, 1897
Taylor, F. Howard, *China Inland Mission, Newington-green, N.*	June 14, 1888	Jan. 20, 1887
Taylor, Henry Herbert, 36 *Brunswick-square, Hove, Sussex*....	Dec. 8, 1887	July 22, 1880
Taylor, Julian, O.B.E., 30 *Clifton-hill, St. John's-wood, N.W.*...	Feb. 12, 1914	Nov. 9, 1911
Taylor, Tom Robinson, 5 *Park-square, Leeds*..............	Oct. 12, 1893	Nov. 13, 1891
Teale, Thomas Pridgin, *North Grange, Headingley, Leeds*	May 23, 1857	Mar. 28, 1855
Teichelmann, Ebenezer, *Hamilton-street, Hokitika, New Zealand*	June 11, 1891	Feb. 9, 1888
Telford, Evelyn Davison, 8 A *St. John-street, Manchester*......	June 11, 1903	Nov. 8, 1900
¶Thane, Sir George Dancer, *"Hemmet," St.-John's-road, Harrow*	Apr. 1, 1909	Nov. 15, 1871
Thomas, David, *Elsmere, Manley, Sydney, N.S.W.*	Dec. 8, 1887	Apr. 23, 1884
Thomas, Gordon Wilson, *The Elms, Wakefield, Yorks*........	Dec. 8, 1910	Feb. 9, 1905
Thomas, John Llewellyn, 10 *Christchurch-road, Clifton, Bristol.*	Dec. 8, 1892	May 8, 1890

Name and Residence.	Fellow.	Member.
Thomas, Thomas Morrell, 12 *Clytha-park-road, Newport, Mon.*	June 10, 1897	Feb. 7, 1895
Thomas, William Thelwall, M.B.E., 84 *Rodney-street, Liverpool*	Feb. 13, 1890	Apr. 20, 1886
Thompson, Arthur Ralph, 45 *Queen Anne-street,* W.	Dec. 11, 1902	Aug. 1, 1901
Thompson, Geo. Stanley, *c/o B.M.A., Sydney, N.S.W.*	June 8, 1911	May 10, 1906
Thompson, George Willia n, 80 *Harley-street,* W.	Dec. 12, 1901	Nov. 8, 1900
Thompson, Harold Theodore, 94 *Portland-place,* W..........	June 9, 1904	May 14, 1903
Thompson, Hubert Gordon, 35 *Sydenham-av., Sefton-pk., Liv'pool*	Dec. 9, 1909	Dec. 9, 1909
Thompson, J. Edwin, 3224 *Broadway, Galveston, Texas, U.S.A.*	June 13, 1889	July 23, 1886
Thompson, John, " *Sunnycroft,*" *Paignton, S. Devon*	June 12, 1913	June 12, 1913
Thompson, Walter, 30 *Park-square, Leeds*	May 14, 1891	Nov. 10, 1887
¶Thomson, Arthur, 163 *Woodstock-road, Oxford*	Apr. 11, 1907	July 19, 1880
Thomson, Charles Bertram, " *Romansleigh,*' *Wimborne, Dorset* .	June 1, 1905	July 27, 1899
¶ Thomson, H. Alexis, C.M.G., 39 *Drumsheugh-gdns., Edinburgh*	Apr. 8, 1920	July 23, 1885
Thomson, Sir St. Clair, 64 *Wimpole-street,* W.	Dec. 14, 1893	Nov. 16, 1881
Thring, Edward Thomas, 185 *Macquarie-street, Sydney, N.S.W.*	June 11, 1885	July 20, 1882
Thurston, Edward Owen, *Lt.- Col.I.M.S.,11 Hastings-st., Calcutta*	Apr. 14, 1898	Nov. 8, 1894
Ticehurst, N. F., O.B.E., 24 *Pevensey-rd., St. Leonards-on-Sea.*.	Dec. 11, 1902	May 9, 1901
Tilley, Herbert, 72 *Harley-street,* W.	June 9, 1898	July 28, 1890
Todd, Alan Herapath, 6 *St. Thomas'-street, S.E.*	June 12, 1913	Feb. 9, 1911
Todd, T. Wingate, *Anat. Lab., W. Reserve Univ., Cleveland, O., U.S.*	Dec. 14, 1911	Dec. 14, 1911
¶Tomes, Sir Charles Sissmore, *Mannington-hall, Aylsham*......	Apr. 14, 1898	July 20, 1869
Tonks, Henry, *Slade School of Fine Art, Univ. Coll.,* W.C.	June 14, 1888	Jan. 22, 1886
Tonks, John Wilson, " *Lowgates,*" *Staveley, Chesterfield*	June 11, 1914	Nov. 9, 1911
Totsuka, Kankai, *Imperial Naval Hospital, Tokio, Japan*	June 14, 1888	Jan. 26, 1886
Townrow, Vincent, " *Leamhurst,*" *Ivy-park-road, Sheffield*	Dec. 14, 1911	Nov. 12, 1908
Toye, Edwin Josiah, " *Stanhope,*" *Bideford, N. Devon*	June 9, 1898	May 9, 1895
Trechmann, Max Lincoln, 88 *Eccleston-square,* S.W.	June 12, 1890	Nov. 10, 1887
Treston, Maurice L., *Capt.I.M.S., c/o Messrs. King & Co., Bombay*	Dec. 8, 1921	Feb. 13, 1913
Trethowan, William Henry, 8 *St. Thomas-street, S.E.*........	Dec. 12, 1912	Nov. 8, 1906
Treves, SirF., Bt., G.C.V.O., C.B., *Marlborough Club, PallMall, S.W*	Dec. 12, 1878	Apr. 21, 1875
Trinca, Alfred J., " *Intra,*" *Lisson-gr., Hawthorn, Melbourne* ..	Dec. 11, 1919	Dec. 11, 1919
Trott, Dudley Cox, *Hamilton, Bermuda, West Indies*	June 10, 1886	Nov. 17, 1880
Trotter, Edward, " *Netherfield,*" *Scholes, Huddersfield*	Dec. 12, 1901	Nov. 10, 1898
Trotter, Wilfred Batten Lewis, 119 *Harley-street,* W.	Dec. 14, 1899	Aug. 4, 1886
Trumble, Hugh C., *c/o Bank of Victoria, 69 King-William-st.,* E.C.	Mar. 10, 1921	Mar. 10, 1921
Tubby, Alfred Herbert, C.B., C.M.G., 68 *Harley-street,* W.....	June 9, 1887	July 29, 1884
Tucker, Alexander Benjamin, *Mayfair, Johannesburg, Transvaal.*	June 8, 1899	Aug. 4, 1896
Turner, Edward Beadon, 21 *Westbourne-terrace,* W..........	June 9, 1881	July 28, 1876
Turner, G. Grey, " *The Hawthorns,*" *Osborne-rd, Newcastle-on-Tyne*	Dec. 10, 1903	Oct. 12, 1899
Turner, Sir G. R., K.B.E., C.B., 49 *Oxford-mans., Oxford-cir.,* W.	Dec. 9, 1880	July 25, 1877
Turner, Joseph George, 59 *Wimpole-street,* W.	Mar. 8, 1894	Feb. 11, 1892
Turner, Philip, 73 *Wimpole-street,* W......................	Dec. 12, 1901	July 29, 1897
Turner, Reginald George, C.M.G., D.S.O., *Col. I.M.S.*........	June 13, 1907	Nov. 12, 1901
Turner, William, 92 *Harley-street,* W......................	Dec. 12, 1895	May 11, 1883
Turney, Horace George, O.B.E., 7 *Park-square-west,* N.W. ..	June 12, 1890	Aug. 2, 1888
Turton, James, " *Hatherley,*" *Preston-park, Brighton*	June 11, 1890	July 29, 1880
Turton, Jas. Richard Henry, 21 *Brunswick-place, Hove*	Dec. 14, 1911	July 25, 1907

Name and Residence.	Fellow.	Member.
Walters, Charles Ferrier, 5 *Mortimer-road, Clifton, Bristol* ..	Dec. 8, 1904	July 25, 1900
Walters, Fredk. R., *Pinecroft, Farnham, Surrey*	Dec. 14, 1882	Apr. 20, 1880
Walton, Albert James, 5 *Devonshire-street, W.*	June 13, 1907	Feb. 9, 1905
Walton, H. J., *Lt.-Col. I.M.S.*, c/o *King, King & Co., Bombay* .	June 13, 1895	May 11, 1893
Warburton, G. B., 33 *Parsonage-road, Withington, Manchester.*	June 13, 1912	June 13, 1912
Ward, Arthur Henry, 40 *Dover Street, W.*	Oct. 17, 1889	Nov. 10, 1887
Ward, Bernard Joseph, 141 A *Great Charles-street, Birmingham*	June 1, 1905	July 31, 1902
Ward, Ernest, *Withycombe-lodge, Torquay-road, Paignton*	June 14, 1906	Aug. 4, 1903
Ward, Ronald Ogier, D.S.O., M C., 86 *Harley-street, W.*	June 12, 1919	May 9, 1912
§Warde, Mildred, 23 *Hook-road, Surbiton*	Dec. 14, 1922	May 12, 1921
Wardill, Wm. Edw. Mandall, 64 *Jesmond-rd., Newcastle-on-Tyne.*	June 10, 1920	Nov. 13, 1919
Ward-Smith, Ward, *Victoria-park, Shipley, Yorks*	June 12, 1902	July 25, 1900
Wareham, Sidney James, 9 *Treborough-ho., Gt. Woodstock-st.,*W.	June 12, 1902	Nov. 12, 1896
Waring, Holburt Jacob, 37 *Wimpole-street, W.*	Oct. 15, 1891	May 8, 1890
Warner, Francis, *Whitbourne, Warlingham, Surrey*	June 19, 1873	Nov. 17, 1870
Warner, Thomas, 98 *Upper Cliff-road, Gorleston*	June 13, 1895	Feb. 11, 1892
Warren, Richard, 1 *Royal-terrace, Weston-super-Mare*	Dec. 11, 1902	Feb. 8, 1900
Warwick, William Turner, 18 *Great Ormond-street, W.C.*....	June 10, 1920	July 29, 1915
Waterfield, Noël Everard, *Port Sudan, Red Sea, Sudan*	Jan. 12, 1905	Nov. 13, 1902
Waterhouse, Sir Herbert Furnivall, 7 *Wimpole-street, W.*	June 12, 1890	Aug. 4, 1887
Watkins, Alfred B. K., 20 *Valkyrie-rd., Westcliff-on-Sea*	Dec. 8, 1921	July 24, 1919
Watkins-Pitchford, W., *S.A.Inst. for Med. Research, Johannesburg.*	June 10, 1897	Nov. 12, 1891
Watkinson, Wilfred, *Clipsey Lodge, Haydock, Lancs.*	June 18, 1908	June 18, 1908
Watkyn-Thomas, Frederic William, 14 *Welbeck Street, W.*....	June 9, 1921	June 9, 1921
Watson, Archibald, *Adelaide Club, Adelaide, S. Australia*	Dec. 11, 1884	Jan. 23, 1882
Watson, Donald, 10 *Walmer-villas, Bradford*	Dec. 9, 1920	Dec. 9, 1920
Watson, Geo. T., O.B.E., *Heathside, Mt.Ephraim, Tunbridge Wells*	June 8, 1899	Feb. 11, 1897
Watson, John Harry, 68 *Bank-parade, Burnley*	June 9, 1904	July 29, 1897
Watts, John Ernest Price, 136 *High-rd., Ilford.*	June 19, 1913	Feb. 9, 1911
Waugh, George Ernest, 77 *Portland-place, W.*	Dec. 8, 1904	Aug. 1, 1901
Webb, Charles Henry Shorney, 16 *Queen Anne-street, W.*	Feb. 9, 1911	May 14, 1908
Webb, James Ramsay, 179 *Power-street, Hawthorn*	June 13, 1895	Nov. 10, 1892
Webb-Johnson, Alf. Edw., C.B.E., D.S.O., 35 *Grosvenor-st.,* W.	Dec. 13, 1906	Aug. 4, 1903
Webber, Alexander Moxon, 2 *The Ropewalk, Nottingham*	June 14, 1906	Nov. 12, 1903
Webber, William Littleton, *Turleigh-house, Bradford-on-Avon* .	June 8, 1876	Jan. 22, 1873
Welchman, Walter, 30 *Fortescue-road, Yeoville, Johannesburg, S.A.*	Dec. 10, 1908	July 27, 1905
Wellish, Gilbert Charrington, 179 *Mount-view-rd., Stroud-green.*	Dec. 14, 1922	Dec. 14, 1922
Welsford, Arthur Gerald, *Hemingfold, Battle, Sussex*	June 9, 1892	June 9, 1892
Wessels, François Henry, *Box 1523, Cape Town, South Africa..*	Dec. 11, 1902	July 25, 1900
West, Charles Ernest, *Newquay-house, Flushing, Falmouth....*	June 12, 1902	Nov. 8, 1900
Westmacott, F.H., C.B.E., *Lt.-Col. R.A.M.C.*, 8 *St.John-st.,Manch.*	June 14, 1894	Feb. 13, 1890
Whale, George Harold Lawson, 84 *Wimpole-street, W.*	June 13, 1912	Feb. 13, 1902
Wharry, Harry Mortimer, 136 *Harley-street, W.*	June 8, 1922	July 27, 1916
Wheeler, D. R., *Shantung Christian Univ., Tsinan, Shant., China*	June 14, 1923	June 14, 1923
Wheeler, Edwin Robert, *Market-hill, Calne, Wilts.*	June 14, 1923	Aug. 4, 1903
Wherry, George Edward, 5 *St. Peter's-terrace, Cambridge*	June 12, 1879	July 23, 1873
Whitaker, John Grieve, " *Ericstone," Canterbury, Victoria, Aust*	Dec. 14, 1922	Dec. 14, 1922

Name and Residence.	Fellow.	Member.
Whitaker, Roy Henry R., *Toowoomba, Queensland*	Apr. 14, 1904	May 9, 1901
White, Chas. Powell, 1 *Albemarle-rd., Withington, Manchester*	June 11, 1896	May 10, 1894
White, Clifford Sidney, 62 *Harley-street, W.*	June 10, 1909	July 28, 1904
White, Edgar Ramsey, 1 *Victoria-road, Deal*	June 9, 1892	Aug. 2, 1888
White, Edwin Francis, 388 *Upper Richmond-rd., Putney, S.W.*	Dec. 11, 1884	Apr. 21, 1881
White, Frank Faulder, *The Close, Saffron Walden*	Dec. 11, 1890	Aug. 3, 1885
White, Gilbert Benjamin Mower, 112 *Harley-street, W.*	Apr. 9, 1891	Aug. 2, 1888
White, Horace Powell Winsbury, 1 *Bentinck-street, W.*	Dec. 14, 1922	Dec. 14, 1922
White, James Renfrew, 456 *George-street, Dunedin, N.Z.*	June 10, 1915	Feb. 12, 1914
Whitehead,SirH.R.,K.C.B.,*Maj.-Gen, Whinfield,Cobh'm,Surrey*	Dec. 9, 1880	Nov. 3, 1877
Whitehouse, H. B., 62 *Hagley-rd., Edgbaston, Birmingham* ..	Dec. 10, 1608	Feb. 8, 1906
Whitelocke, Richard Henry Anglin, 6 *Banbury-road, Oxford.*.	June 8, 1893	July 22, 1884
Whiting, Maurice Henry, O B.E., 9 *Welbeck-street, W.*	June 10, 1920	June 10, 1920
Whittingdale, John, " *Wharton," Sherborne Dorset*	June 10, 1920	July 25, 1918
Whyte, David, 269 *High-street, Dunedin, N.Z.*	Dec. 14, 1922	Dec. 14, 1922
Wickens, George Henry	June 11, 1914	June 11, 1914
Wightman, Cecil Frank, *Melbourn-street, Royston, Herts*	June 13, 1895	Feb. 9, 1893
Wigram, NathanGraham, 2 *Carter Knowle-rd., Sheffield*	June 10, 1920	July 29, 1915
Wildman, Wm. S., " *Hazlemount," Kimberworth-rd., Rotherham*	Dec. 12, 1912	July 25, 1910
Wilkie, David Percival D., O.B.E., 56 *Manor-place, Edinburgh.*	June 13, 1918	June 13, 1918
Wilkin, Lancelot, 46 *London-road, Gloucester*	Dec. 12, 1901	Nov. 2, 1899
Wilkinson, Edmund, *Lt.-Col.I.M.S.*, 4 *Helena-road, Ealing, W.*	Jan. 14, 1892	Aug. 2, 1888
Wilkinson, George, 387 *Glossop-road, Sheffield*	June 14, 1894	Feb. 8, 1894
Wilkinson, Valentine, *Strathmore. Ifield, Crawley*	Dec. 14, 1922	Nov. 11, 1920
Wilks, Washington Everitt, 314 *Vancouver Block, Vancouver.*.	June 8, 1911	July 30, 1908
Willan, R. J.,M.V.O.,O.B.E.,6*Kensington-terr.,Newc'tle-on-Tyne*	Dec. 10, 1908	July 25, 1907
Willett, Edgar Wm., *Spyways, Hartfield, Sussex*	June 14, 1888	July 16, 1883
Williams, Gwynne Evan Owen, 9 *Park-square-west, N.W.*...	Dec 13, 1906	Aug. 4, 1903
Williams, H. T. Hadley, 441 *Park-av., London, Ontario, Canada*	June 8, 1899	Aug. 2, 1898
Williams, Leslie H. W., " *The Caerau," Newport, Mon.*	Dec. 8, 1921	Sep. 24, 1914
Williams, Moses Thomas, 24 *St. George's-place, Canterbury*....	June 1, 1905	July 31, 1902
Williams, Roger Lester, 36 *Spilman-street, Carmarthen*	June 14, 1923	Feb. 13, 1919
Williams, Wm. Roger, " *Morven," Walton-by-Clevedon, Somerset*	June 9, 1881	Apr. 24, 1877
*Williamson-Noble, Frederick Arnold, 27 *Harley-street, W.* ..	June 10, 1920	July 30, 1914
Wilson, Alexander, 13 *Anson-road, Victoria-park, Manchester* .	June 12, 1890	Jan. 23, 1883
Wilson, Alex. Garrick,D.S.O., *Riverdale-croft,Ranmoor,Sheffield*	Dec. 12, 1901	Feb. 3, 1899
Wilson, Alexander Gordon, 1 *Philbeach-gardens, S.W.*	Dec. 13, 1900	May 13, 1897
Wilson, George Ewart, 205 *Bloor-street East, Toronto, Canada*	June 18, 1908	Nov. 14, 1907
Wilson, Harold William, 91 *Harley-street, W.*	Dec. 14, 1905	Nov. 12, 1903
Wilson, Hugh Cameron, " *Oaklands," Maidenhead* ..	June 8, 1911	June 8, 1911
Wilson, Ivan S., M.C., *c/o H.Comm.for N.Z.,Strand, W.C.*	Dec. 12, 1912	July 25, 1907
Wilson, James, 36 *High-street, Haverfordwest* ..	Dec. 11, 1884	May 14, 1883
Wilson, John Black Ferguson, 392 *Glossop-road,Sheffield*	June 8, 1910	July 26, 1906
Wilson, John St. George, M.C., 31 *Rodney-street, Liverpool* ..	Mar. 10, 1921	July 14, 1914
Wilson,N.O.,*Eve-villa,Station-rd.,Observatory,CapeProv.,S.Afr.*	Oct. 10, 1895	Nov. 10, 1892
Wilson, Roger Parker, *Lt.-Col. I.M.S*, 10 *Wood-st., Calcutta* .	June 13, 1912	July 27, 1893
Wilson, Thomas, 87 *Cornwall-street, Birmingham*	Dec. 14, 1893	Apr. 19, 1883

* Fellow by examination (with Ophthalmology)

Name and Residence.	Fellow.	Member.
Wilson, William Carlyle, *Harris-street, Gisborne, New Zealand*	Dec. 10, 1903	Dec. 10, 1903
Wilson, William Etherington, *St. Bartholomew's Hosp.*, E.C...	June 8, 1922	July 27, 1916
Winterbottom, Augustus, 16 *Sloane-street*, S.W.	Dec. 20, 1875	Nov. 13, 1872
Wirgman, Charles Wynn, 11 *Birchin-lane*, E.C.	June 11, 1903	July 27, 1899
Wiseman, J. Greaves, *St. Peter's-rd, St. Margarets, Twickenham*	June 19, 1873	May 8, 1867
Wood, Cyril George Russ, O.B.E., *Hardwick-house, Shrewsbury*	Dec. 11, 1902	Feb. 11, 1892
Wood, Duncan, 5 *Eaton-crescent, Clifton, Bristol*	June 13, 1912	Nov. 11, 1909
Wood, John Forrester, *Beaver-grove. Bettys-y-coed, N. Wales* .	June 11, 1896	May 9, 1889
Wood, William Charrington, *The Moat, Penshurst, Kent*......	June 8, 1899	Feb. 8, 1894
Woodall, A. Edgar, *Manor-house-hospital, Golders Green*, N.W.	Dec. 14, 1916	Dec. 14, 1916
Woodcock, John Rostron, " *Inglewood*," *Fulshaw-pk., Wilmslow*	June 10, 1869	July 28, 1864
Woodman, Edward Musgrave, 22 *Newhall-street, Birmingham* .	Nov. 11, 1909	Nov. 8, 1906
Woods, Reginald Salisbury, 60 *St. Andrew's-street, Cambridge*.	Dec. 14, 1922	May 11, 1916
Woods, Samuel Henry, *Naval & Military Club*, 94 *Piccadilly*,W.	June 14, 1923	June 14, 1923
Woods, William James, 191 *Chapel-st., Pietermaritzburg, Natal*	June 11, 1896	May 14, 1896
Woodward, Alfred Chad Turner, *Arley Castle, Bewdley*	June 8, 1911	June 8, 1911
Wookey, Harold William, 4 *Percival-terrace, Brighton*	June 9, 1921	June 9, 1921
Woolbert, Henry Robert, *Lt.-Col. I.M.S. Deoli, Rajputana* ..	Dec. 10, 1885	Apr. 24, 1884
Woolf, Albert Edward Mortimer, 81 *Wimpole-street*, W.	Oct. 14, 1909	Nov. 12, 1908
Woolfenden, Herbert Francis, 36 *Rodney-street, Liverpool*	June 10, 1909	May 12, 1904
Woollett, Charles Jerome, " *Ambleside*," *Streatham*, S.W.	Dec. 10, 1891	July 27, 1875
Worth, Claud Alley, 34 *Harley-street*, W.	Dec. 8, 1898	Mar 11, 1893
Worthington, Robt. Alfred, O.B.E., 30 *East Southernhay, Exeter*	June 10, 1909	Nov. 10, 1904
Worthington, Sidney, 23 *Jury-street, Warwick*	June 11, 1885	Nov. 16, 1882
Worton, Albert Samuel, 7 *Manchester-square*, W.	Dec. 9, 1909	Dec. 9, 1909
Wright, Andrew John Metford, 14 *Victoria-sq., Clifton, Bristol.*	June 9, 1910	Nov. 9, 1905
Wright, Arthur Dickson, 7 *Warwick-avenue*, W.	Dec. 14, 1922	Feb. 9, 1922
Wright, Dudley D'Auvergne, *Kittetoe, Parracombe, N. Devon.*.	June 9, 1898	Aug. 2, 1888
Wright, Garnett, 14 *St. John-street, Manchester*	Dec. 14, 1905	Dec. 14, 1905
Wright, H.W.S.,*Shantung Christn. Univ.,S.of Med.,Tsinan,China*	June 10, 1920	Feb. 12, 1915
Wright, William, *Villa Candens, Gerrard's-cross, Bucks*	Dec. 12, 1901	May 11, 1899
Wrigley, Philip Roscoe, 11 *St. John-street, Manchester*	Dec. 14, 1905	July 25, 1900
Wyatt, James Montagu, 15 *Queen Anne-street*, W.	Dec. 8, 1910	July 27, 1905
Wylie, D. S., C.M.G.,C.B.E.,77 *Broad-st.,Palmerston North,N.Z.*	Dec. 10, 1903	Dec. 10, 1903
Wynter, Walter Essex, 27 *Wimpole-street*, W.	June 11, 1885	Jan. 26, 1883
Yate, Edward	June 11, 1874	Nov. 16, 1871
Yates, Harold Blacow, 24 *Havelock-street, Preston, Lancs*	June 8, 1922	Feb. 13, 1919
Yearsley, Percival Macleod, 14 *Welbeck-street*, W.	Dec. 14, 1893	May 8, 1890
Yorke, Courtenay, 82 *Rodney-street, Liverpool*	June 8, 1911	June 8, 1911
Zamora, Alberto Medardo, 4 *Devonshire-place*, W.	June 14, 1917	Nov. 14, 1912

MEMBERS.

§ Members admitted under the Medical Act, 1876.

A.

1899. Abadjian, Alexander Tateosian.
1922.§Abbott, Edith, I. L., *Highgate.*
1888. Abbott, Frederic William, *Balham.*
1869. Abbott, George, *Tunbridge Wells.*
1897. Abbott, Horatio White, *Holloway.*
1895. Abbott, James Edward, *Leeds.*
1905. Abbott, Saml. Franklin, *Lond., Can.*
1886. Abbott, William Louis.
1923. Abbu, Conjeeveram, *Madras.*
1894. Abcarius, Jos. John, *Torrington-sq.*
1914. Abdelal, Ahmed, *Egypt.*
1922. Abdel, Razik, Abd-l Razik, *Cairo.*
1920. Abdel, Khalik Mohamed Khalil.
1919. Abd-El-Said, Iskander M., *Cairo.*
1920. Abdullah, Fauzi Fareed.
1860. A'Beckett,Wm.Goldsmid,*Melbourne.*
1893. Abel, Horace Marshall, *Hampstead.*
1918. Abelson, Abraham, *Brondesbury.*
1900. Abercrombie,Rodolph Geo.,*Holt&Co.*
1858. Ablett, Edward, *Whitehaven.*
1912. Abraham, Edward Smith, *Devizes.*
1909. Abraham,Richard Bernard,*Charlbury*
1909. Abrahams, Adolphe, O.B.E., *Fulham.*
1891. Abram, Sir George Stewart, *Reading.*
1887. Abram, John Hill, *Liverpool.*
1912. Acharya, B. G. S., *Bangalore.*
1923. Acheson, Patrick M., *Crystal-pal.-rd.*
1901. Ackery, Edward F., *Roy. Dent.-hosp.*
1897. Ackland, Chas. Herbt., *Bournemouth.*
1885. Ackland, Charles Kingsley, *Bideford.*
1899. Ackland, Donald, *Bath.*
1915. Ackland, John Gordon, *Exeter.*
1885. Ackland, John McKno, *Exeter.*
1890. Ackland, Rbt., C.B.E., *Brook-st.,W.*
1886. Ackland, William Robert, *Clifton.*
1922. Ackroyd, Stanley, *Halifax.*
1896. Acland, Jn. Musgrave, *New Swindon.*
1880. Acland,Theodore Dyke,*Bryanston-sq.*
1902. Acomb, John, *York.*
1906. Acomb, Leonard Ernest, *Newport.*
1903. Acres,Geo. Chas. Johnston,*Clapham.*
1888. Acton, Charles James, *Wangford.*
1905. Acton, Hugh William, *I.M.S.*
1900. Acton, Thomas, *Bournemouth.*
1907. Adam, George Henry, *West Malling.*
1909. Adam,Stanley Denovan,*Fernhead-rd.*
1901. Adam, Thomas, *Stirling*
1892. Adams, Alfred, *West Love.*
1923. 48

1897. Adams, Arth. Reg., *West Australia.*
1884. Adams, Chas. Edmund, *W. Croydon.*
1894. Adams, Edward Coker, *W. Africa.*
1866. Adams, Edward John, *Sheffield.*
1906. Adams, Eustace Henry, *Stockport.*
1893. Adams, Evelyn Lancelot,*E. Croydon.*
1910. Adams, Frank Shirley, *Clitheroe.*
1903. Adams,Geo. Basil Doyne, *Clifton-gds.*
1885. Adams, Gofton Gee, *A.M.S.*
1899. Adams, Harold Cotterell, O.B.E.
1889. Adams, Harry, *Wellington, N.Z.*
1900. Adams, Henry Cyril, *Sydney.*
1918. Adams, James Franklin, *Canada.*
1911. Adams, John Wroth, *Aldersgate-st.*
1909. Adams, Melville Mortimer, *Pretoria.*
1895. Adams, Percy Edward, *Ealing.*
1887. Adams, Percy Targett, *Bloemfontein.*
1912. Adams, Rupert Blake, *Gosport.*
1923. Adams, Wilfrid Fras. T., *Weymouth.*
1881. Adams, Wm. Coode, *Eton-av., N.W.*
1892. Adams, William Francis, *Rayleigh.*
1919. Adams, William Stirk, *Birmingham.*
1888. Adamson,HoratioGeo.,*Devonshire-pl.*
1902. Adamson,Jas.Weeden W.,*Ch.Strett'n.*
1910. Adamson, Oswald J. Wm., *Brighton.*
1893. Adcock, George Robert, *Bembridge.*
1878. Adcock, Harold, *Market Harboro.*
1896. Addenbrooke, Bertr., *Kidderminster.*
1919. Addenbrooke, R. G., *Kidderminster.*
1899. Addey, William Fielding, *Croydon.*
1901. Addinsell, John Howard, *Holt & Co.*
1894. Addison, Eldred Arth., *Ipswich.*
1914. Addison, Hallowes Lloyd, *Durban.*
1890. Addison, Hugh Cecil, *Eastbourne.*
1898. Addison, Joseph Bartlett, M.B.E.
1891. Addison, William Blagg, *Scilly Is.*
1879. Addison,Wm. Henry, *Durban, Natal.*
1923. Adeney, Noel Fredk., *Crowborough.*
1917. Adhya, Jugul Kisnor.
1890. Adkins, Albert James, *Beckenham.*
1921.§Adkins, Dulcie Stapleton, *Sevenoaks.*
1882. Adkins, George, *Exeter.*
1922. Adler, Samuel, *Manchester.*
1886. Adye,Wm.Jn. Alex. *Bradford-on-A.*
1922. Afifi, Mahmud Ahmed, *Egypt.*
1911. Afifh, Mohammed, *Cairo.*
1892. Agar, Morley Fredk.,*Wimpole-st., W.*
1834. Agar, Samuel H , *Henley-in-Arden.*
96
N

1916. Agar, Willoughby, *Henley-in-Arden*.
1916. Agarwala, Girdhar Clement, *India*.
1899. Agate, Henry St. Arnaud, M.C.
1899. Agnew, Colville Smith, *Ibstock*.
1886. Agnew, Edwd. D., *Bishop's Stortford*.
1897. Ahlswede, Oscar Jacob L, *Hambury*.
1916. Ahmad, Abdul Majid, *Punjab, India*.
1922. Ahmad, Mumtazuddin, *Woking*.
1917. Ahmed, Esawy, *Butanour, Egypt*.
1921. Ahmed, Mohammed Tewfik, *Cairo*.
1899. Ahrens, Henry Aug., *Basingstoke*.
1922. Aiengar, Nuggchatti Ananthram.
1884. Aikin, Wm. Arthur, *Bedf'rd-gdns.,W*.
1884. Aikins, Henry Wilberforce, *Toronto*.
1858. Aikins, Moses Henry, *Canada*.
1913. Aikman, Kenneth Blackie, *Glasgow*.
1899. Ainscow, James, *Wigan*.
1877. Ainsley, Thomas George, *Hartlepool*.
1915. Ainsworth, Cyrus G., *Elton, Bury*.
1922. Ainsworth, Douglas R., *Gt. Harwood*.
1888. Ainsworth, Herbert Pearson, *Marden*.
1899. Ainsworth, R. B., D.S.O., *R.A.M.C.*
1899. Ainsworth, Richard, *Kirkby*.
1867. Air, Alex. Cummings, *S. Norwood*.
1907. Air, Saml. Hy. Cummings, *S. Norwood*.
1883. Aird, Thomas Wilson, *Wallington*.
1920. Aitken, Arthur Noble, *Leatherhead*.
1922.§Aitken, Janet Kerr, *Hyde-pk. Mans*.
1898. Akers, William Dutton, *Transvaal*.
1916. Alabaster, Edw. Beric, *Moseley*.
1913. Alabaster, Geo. Herbert, *Dartmouth*.
1906. Alban, Edgar, *Steyning*.
1916.§Albuquerque, Mary Clara, *Goa*.
1902. Albury, Joseph Baird, *Bahamas*.
1904. Alcock, Frank, *Lincoln*.
1897. Alcock, George Herbert, *Taunton*.
1916. Alcock, Jn. A. Molony, *L. & P. Bank*.
1884. Alcock, Samuel King, *Burslem*.
1923. Alden, John Wenham, *Oxford*.
1900. Alderman, Harry Cole, *Halifax*.
1890. Alderson, Fdk. Hbt., *Queen's-g'te-terr*.
1900. Alderson, Percy Francis, *R.N.*
1907. Alderson, William Seaforth, *Silsden*.
1881. Alderton, Herbt. Chas., *Barnoldswick*.
1914. Alderton, Wilfred Herbert, M.C.
1912. Aldis, Carlyle, *Fontenoy-road*.
1885. Aldous, George Fredk., *Plymouth*.
1903. Aldred, Wilfrid Ashwell, *Wroxham*.
1900. Aldren, Bertr. Cecil Rbt., *Birmingh'm*.
1897. Aldridge, Arthur Wm., *Northfield*.
1890. Aldridge, Augustus Hy., *Br. Columbia*.
1906. Aldridge, Chas. B. M., *Bournemouth*.
1889. Aldridge, Edw. A., M.C., *Hannington*.
1909. Aldridge, Fredk. James, *Glastonbury*.
1896. Alexander, Alfred, *Tadley*.
1913. Alexander, Chas. Beresford, *Southport*.
1915. Alexander, Douglas Reid, M.C.

1902. Alexander, Fdk. Hugh, *Littlehampton*.
1881. Alexander, Fredk. Wm., *Teddington*.
1906. Alexander, Gervase D., *Halifax*.
1921. Alexander, Horace Edward.
1880. Alexander, John, *Trinity-square, S.E*.
1915. Alexander, John Struan, *Moor-lane*.
1898. Alexander, Kenneth Bush, *S. Africa*.
1886. Alexander, Sidney Robt., *Faversham*.
1909. Alexander, Wm. Arthur, *Boston*.
1896. Alford, Cyril Wolrige, *Chelmsford*.
1904. Alford, Ernest Francis R., M.C.
1858. Alford, Henry James, *Taunton*.
1897. Alford, Herbt. T. M., *Weston-s.-Mare*.
1908. Alguire, Alexander Ross, *Canada*.
1892. Ali, Subhan, *Agra*.
1891. Allan, Alexander William, *Skegness*.
1909. Allan, Douglas, *Sunderland*.
1891. Allan, Edward Buller, *Victoria*.
1923. Allan, Francis Glenn, *Wallington*.
1897. Allan, Herbert Wm., O.B.E., *Wells*.
1887. Allan, James Hugh Brodie.
1919. Allan, John Harrison, *Liverpool*.
1919. Allan, Wm. Jas. McBain, *Wandsworth*.
1916. Allchin, Frank Macdonald, *Fowey*.
1874. Allden, John Horatio, *Earl's-court*.
1892. Alldridge, Wm. Edwd., *Birmingham*.
1913. Allen, Charles H. Powell, *I.M.S.*
1897. Allen, Charles Percival, *Gillingham*.
1893. Allen, Charles Wm., *W. Hampstead*.
1880. Allen, Francis Edward, *Bedford-pk*.
1882. Allen, Frank James, *Cambridge*.
1919. Allen, Frederick Thos., *Brixton-rd*.
1923. Allen, Harold Sandeman, *Liverpool*.
1897. Allen, James Lynn, *Brentwood*.
1886. Allen, Norman, *Toronto*.
1907. Allen, Richard Clayton, *Belper*.
1884. Allen, Sydney Glenn, *A.M.S.*
1912. Allen, Thomas Stevens, *Forest-hill*.
1896. Allen, Walter Henry, *Hurst-hill*.
1915. Allen, Wm. Guy Embleton, *B'yswater*.
1894. Allen, William Herbert, *Derby*.
1909. Alleyne, Evelyn A. W., *Emmet & Co.*
1890. Allford, Hy. G. Lynwood, *St. Leonards*.
1898. Allfrey, Frederic Henry, *Southwick*.
1903. Allin, Edgar Wm., *Edmonton, Can.*
1922. Allin, Jhn. V. Dennis, *Sutton Coldfd*.
1907. Allin, Norman Geo., *Edmonton, Can.*
1914. Allingham, C. P. Sidney, *Stockwell*.
1904. Allingham, Harry Reginald, *Totnes*.
1896. Allingham, Walter, *Orsett*.
1914. Allinson, Bertrand Pater, *Dorset-sq*.
1919. Allison, Reginald John, *Redcar*.
1909. Allnutt, Edward Bruce, M.C.
1879. Allnutt, John, *Wrentham*.
1870. Allnutt, William, *Queensland*.
1909. Allott, Harold W. Leach, *R.A.M C.*
1891. Allott, John Ernest Cecil, *Richmond*.

1876. Allott, Wordsworth Leach, *Barnsley.*
1894. Allport, Alfred, *Chai les-st.*, S.W.
1902. Allport, Evett Gordon, *Tasmania.*
1899. Allport, Roland Harrison, *LeewardIsl.*
1896. Allport, Wilfrid, *Birmingham.*
1893. Allworth, Alfred Leigh, *Peckham.*
1902. Alment, Edw.Whyte, *Abbot'sLangley.*
1921. Almeyda, George Wilfred, *Bombay.*
1922.§Almond, Charlotte, K. J., *King's Coll.*
1881. Alpin, Wm. Geo. P., O.B.E., *Ealing.*
1892. Alston, Hugh, *Birkenhead.*
1896. Alston, John Averell, *Cape Town.*
1874. Alsop, Thos. Osmond Fabian, *Victoria.*
1889. Altmann, Chas. August, *Victoria.*
1910. Alton, Francis Cooke, O.B.E., *R.N.*
1916.§Alton, Hannah Katherine, *Hunter-st.*
1915. Altounyan, Ernest H. R., M.C.
1905. Ambler, Francis Barlow, *G.I.P. Rly.*
1900. Ambrose, Alfred Parker, *Clapham.*
1898. Ambrose, Wm. Cole, *Barnt-green.*
1897. Amenabar, Julio Daniel, *Santiago.*
1921. Amos, Samuel Edward, *Frimley.*
1869. Amsden, George, *Staines.*
1901. Amsden, Walter, *Roy. Soc. Club.*
1902. Amsler, Albert Maurice, *Eton.*
1885. Anderson, Adam R. Steele, *I.M.S.*
1914. Anderson, Alan D., *Christchurch, N.Z.*
1882. Anderson, Alfred Jasper, *Cape Town.*
1901. Anderson, Arthur, *Warrington.*
1900. Anderson, Arth. P. Moore, *Cape Prov.*
1902. Anderson, Cauldwell H., *Australia.*
1903. Anderson, Charles Alex., *Sandwich.*
1908. Anderson, Charles Ernest, *Woodford.*
1876. Anderson, Charles Morton, *New Zeal.*
1892. Anderson, Charles M., *Kensington.*
1896. Anderson, Chas. Thompson, *Cape T.*
1882. Anderson, Daniel Elie, *Harley-st.*
1923. Anderson, Donald D., *North-grove.*
1917. Anderson, Ewart Gordon, *New Zeal.*
1884. Anderson, Fitzgerald U., *Halifax,N.S.*
1899. Anderson, Harry Bertram, *Toronto.*
1899. Anderson, Hry. Geo.Sidley, *Bramhall.*
1889. Anderson, James Robert, *N.S.W.*
1892. Anderson, John Buckle, *R.A.M.C.*
1896. Anderson, John Sewell, *Willerby.*
1902. Anderson, Kenneth, *Banwell.*
1899. Anderson, Maurice Clare B., *Winfrith.*
1886. Anderson, Reginald Bean, *Bodmin.*
1890. Anderson, Richard Walker, *New Zeal.*
1890. Anderson, William Arthur, *Belfast.*
1884. Anderson, W. Dunlop, O.B E ,*Keswick*
1897. Anderson, W. Maurice, C.I.E , *I M.S.*
1887. Anderson, Sir Wm. M.A., M.V.O.
1881. Anderton, J. E , M.B E., *New Mills.*
1898. Anderton, Wm. Bury, *W. Didsbury.*
1891. André, Jas. Edwd. Felix, *Chichester.*
1922. André, Joseph Hermann, *Mauritius.*
267

1917. Andreæ, Eric Burn, *Fenchurch-st.*
1905. Andreæ, Harry, *Brisbane.*
1899. Andrew, Alfred John, *Cardiff.*
1888. Andrew, Bennet H., M.B.E., *Thame.*
1901. Andrew, Edwyn Gaved, *St. Austell.*
1890. Andrew, Francis William, *Hendon.*
1913. Andrew, G. W. Macbeath, *Bakewell.*
1890. Andrew, Henry, *Exeter.*
1916. Andrew, John, *Barkston-gdns.*, S.W.
1878. Andrew, John Edward, *Melbourne.*
1913. Andrew, John Vere Orlebar, *Brighton.*
1923.§Andrew, Katharine M., *Croydon.*
1915. Andrew, Percy Wm. Lavers, *Brighton.*
1896. Andrew, Philip Oswald, O.B.E., *N.Z.*
1921. Andrewes, Chris. Howard, *Highgate*
1887. Andrewes, Sir Fredk. Wm., O.B.E.
1884. Andrews, Alex Gordon, *R. Navy.*
1869. Andrews, Arthur, *Albury, N.S.W.*
1884. Andrews, Charles, *W. Kensington.*
1915. Andrews, David Wm. J., *Portsmouth*
1885. Andrews, Edward C., *Hampstead.*
1921. Andrews, Harold Newton, *Harrow.*
1895. Andrews, Henry Arthur, *Tonbridge.*
1894. Andrews, Henry Russell, *Wimpole-st.*
1901. Andrews, James Alford, *Corran.*
1919. Andrews, James C., *Hampstead.*
1918.§Andrews, Mary, *Totley-rise.*
1916.§Andrews, Mary Neville, *Ealing.*
1888. Andrews, Octavius Wm., C.B.E., *R.N.*
1885. Andrews, Richard, *Kingswear.*
1919.§Andrews. Sarah Helen, *Harley-st.*
1889. Angear, Frederick Chas., *Formosa.*
1909. Angior, Fredk. Leigh, O.B.E., *Wigan.*
1885. Angior, Thomas Matthews, *Wigan.*
1884. Anglin, Wm. Gardiner, *Ontario.*
1867. Angove, Edward Scudamore, *Harby.*
1910. Angus, W. Brodie Gurney, M.C., O.B.E
1918. Anklesaria, Kaiku Ardeshir.
1908. Anklesaria, Kekobad C., *Bombay.*
1907. Anklesaria, Manekjee D., *India.*
1902. Anley, Frederick Eustace, *Roy. Navy.*
1885. Annacker, Ernest, *Manchester.*
1903. Annand, William Fraser, *Coventry.*
1921. Annecke, Siegfried.
1914. Annesley, Francis Dighton, M.C.
1882. Anness, Fredk. Richd., *Barclay & Co.*
1923. Anning, Chas. Clifford Paul, *Leeds.*
1897. Anning, George Paul, *Leeds.*
1875. Anningson, Thirkell, *Great Grimsby.*
1894. Annis, Ernest George, *Greenwich*
1910. Annison, Richard Wm., *Bowes-rd.*
1909. Ansari, Mukhtar Ahmed, *Delhi.*
1880. Anson, Geo. Edward, *New Zealand.*
1916. Anson, Geo. Fredk Vernon, *St.Geo.-sq.*
1896. Anstey-Chave, Thomas, *Redhill.*
1914. Anthonisz, Carl Frederick, *Richmond.*
1903. Anthonisz, Edward Guy, *R.A.M.C.*
324
N 2

1856. Anthonisz, Peter D., C.M.G., *Ceylon.*
1914. Anthony, Arthur Lawr., *Gravesend.*
1915. Anthony, Christie M., *Lambeth-rd.*
1916. Anthony, Douglas Harris, *Kidwelly.*
1919. Anthony, WilfredM., *Queensu ood-av.*
1915. Anwyl-Davies, Thomas, *Southsea.*
1917. Apergis, Hector D, *Upo Norwood.*
1915. Apperly, Frank Longstaffe, *Tralee.*
1918. Apperly, Herbert Claude, *Chandos-st.*
1907. Apperly, Raymond Eben., *Tenby-nns.*
1830. Appleford,Stephen Herb., *Hoddesdon.*
1913. Applegate, Geo. Stanley, *Lydbrook.*
1838. Applegate, John Wm., *Dewsbury.*
1914. Appleton, Arthur B., *Cambridge.*
1923 §Appleton, Constance E., *Wallington.*
1884. Appleton, Harry, *Lizard, Cornwall.*
1888 Appleton, Jas. Enderby, *Bournem'th.*
1904. Appleton, Roy, *Beverley.*
1878. Appleton, Thomas Alfred, *Fulham.*
1894. Appleyard, Francis Edwd., *Rhodesia.*
1907. Appleyard, James, *Fontmell Magna.*
1913. Appleyard, John, *Bradford.*
1910. Appleyard,Syd.Vere, D.S.O., *N.S. W.*
1923. Apsey, George R. M., *Purley.*
1878. Apthorp, Fredk. Wm., *Burgess-hill.*
1900. Araugó, Miguel, *Colombia.*
1892. Arathoon, Hilary Chas., *Royal Navy.*
1900. Arbuthnot, T. S., *Pittsburgh, U.S.A.*
1904. Arch, Arthur James, *Coventry.*
1913. Archer, Chas. Sydney, *Long Eaton.*
1873. Archer, Edmond Lewis, *Lit leham.*
1881. Archer, Henry Edward, *Upton-park.*
1920. Archer, Henry Edwards.
1894. Archer,S'muel A ,C M.G.,*R.A.M.C.*
1892. Archer, Stafford Lewis, *Hampstead.*
1869. Archer, Thomas Brittin, *St. Pancras.*
1909. Archer,Tom Chamney R., *R.A.M.C.*
1918. Archer-Hall, Herbert Wm , *Moseley.*
1905. Archibald, Richard Jas , *Ramsgate.*
1921.§Ardell, Kathleen.
1914. Argles, Edgar Bernard, *Oxford-terr.*
1903. Argles, ErnestEdwd.,*Oxford-ter ,W.*
1892. Argyle, Stanley Seymour, *Victoria.*
1917. Arias, Adolfo, *Westgate-terrace.*
1907. Aris, Fredk. Wm , *Jamaica, W.I.*
1890. Arkle, Alex. Septimus, *Liverpool.*
1913. Arkle,JohnStanley,O.B.E.,*Gosforth.*
1889. Arkwright, Joseph Arthur, *Chelsea.*
1922.§Arkwright, Ruth M., *Regent's-park.*
1894. Armer, Alfred, *Barmouth.*
1894. Armit, Henry William, *N.S.W.*
1918. Armitage, Bernard F. Wm., *Ealing.*
1905. Armitage, Charles E. A., *Harlesden.*
1921. Armitage, George, *Rothwell.*
1903. Armitage, John James, *Salisbury.*
1922. Armour,JamesLaughland,*Wallasey.*
1896. Armson, Charles James, *Foxall.*

381

1885. Armson, Frank Greasley, *Foxall.*
1883. Armstrong, Arth. Jas. M., *Southgate.*
1913. Armstrong, Basil Wm , M.C., *Boston.*
1917. Armstrong, Cedric Whitfield, *Eye.*
1918. Armstrong, Chas. Walter W., *Guy's.*
1877. Armstrong, Geo Richd., *Foxrock, Ir.*
1896. Armstrong, Harry Fdk.Wm., *Pulney.*
1864. Armstrong, Henry Edwd., *Newcastle.*
1874. Armstrong,Hry.Geo., *Wellington Coll.*
1913 §Armstrong. Kathleen J., *Hampstead.*
1885. Armstrong, Leonard Hy., *Harrogate.*
1909. Armstrong,Richd. Robins.*Lewisham.*
1872. Armstrong, Robt. Stow, *Maida-hill.*
1889. Armstrong, Wilfrid Ernest A., *I.M.S.*
1877. Armstrong, William, *Buxton.*
1907. Armstrong-Dash, Chas.Jas.,*Chertsey.*
1923. Arndt, Edward Wilford, *Ceylon.*
1887. Arnison, Wm. Drewett, *Newcastle.*
1894. Arnold, Edwin Gilbert Emerson, *Fiji.*
1886. Arnold, Francis Sorell, *Berkhamsted.*
1907. Arnold, Frederick Octavias, *Hale.*
1885. Arnold, William, *Melton Mowbray.*
1885. Arnold-Wallinger, Robt. N., *Writtle.*
1905. Arnott, William, *Barnoldswick.*
1919. Aronsohn, Maurice, *Up. Clapton-rd*
1912. Aroor, Frank, *Portmadoc.*
1912. Arthur, David Greg, *R.N.*
1891. Arthur, Francis, *Bethnal-green-road.*
1921. Arthur, George Kilpatrick, *Langley.*
1861. Arthur, James, *Shrewley.*
1897. Arthur, Joseph Hugh, *Shadwell.*
1914. Arthur, William Daniel, *Llandaff.*
1907. Ascough, Matthew Thos., M C.
1913. Aserappa, Christian Victor, *Ceylon.*
1890. Ash, Alfred Edwin, *Honiton.*
1905. Ash, Berkeley Noel, *Hampstead.*
1917. Ash, Edwin Baylis, *Moseley.*
1904. Ash, Edwin Lancelot, *Harley-street.*
1914. Ash, Harry Arnold, *Birmingham.*
1898. Ashby, Edgar, *York.*
1907. Ashby, Hugh Tuke, *Manchester.*
1914. Ashby, Joe Edward, *Leeds.*
1917. Ashcroft, Philip Ardern, *Manch.*
1923. Asherson, Nehemiah, *Brighton.*
1898. Ashe, Frank, *R.A.M.C.*
1911. Ashe, Henry Park, *Wimbledon.*
1888. Ashford, Claude Henry, *Plymouth.*
1897. Ashford, William, Q.B.E., *Topsham.*
1900. Ashley, Hbt. Ernest, *Chobham-rd.,E.*
1893. Ashley, Martin, *Cirencester.*
1885. Ashley, Sydney Dukes, *Brixton.*
1911. Ashley, Thomas Ewart, *N.S.W.*
1912. Ashmore, Arthur. *Hedon.*
1881. Ashton, Charles Ernest, *Seine.*
1896. Ashton, George, *Manchester.*
1921.§Ashton,Hl-lenRosaline,*Montagu-Sq.*
1902. Ashton, John Hilton, *Southport.*

438

1895. Ashton, Joseph, *St. John's-hill*, S.W.
1915.§Ashton, Mary Elizabeth, *Calcutta*.
1856. Ashurst, Wm. Robert, *Farningham*.
1880. Ashwell,Herbt.G.,O.B.E.,*Nottingh'm*
1895. Ashwin, Richd.H.,*Market Weighton*
1877. Ashworth,John Wallwork,*Stockport*.
1913. Askey, Stephen Grange, *Highgate*.
1905. Askham, Hugh Lowrie,*Pershore*.
1882. Aslaniau, Bedros, *Tauris, Persia*.
1882. Aslett, George Stratton, *Tiverton*.
1897. Aslett, W. Stacey, M.B.E., *Leicester*.
1914. Aspinall, George Stivàla *Hampstead*.
1835. Aspinall, John, *Hindley, Wigan*.
1916. Aspinall, Robert Stivala, *M idstone*.
1890. Aspinwall, John Fullerton, *Marsden*.
1896. Aspland,Wm.HaroldG , *Westminst'r*.
1909. Asplen, Wm. Reg. W., *Kenilworth*.
1895. Astbury, Thomas, *Aberamon*.
1919. Astley-Weston, Bernard A., *Bristol*.
1801. Aston, Richard Henry, *Westcliff*.
1836. Aston, William, *Leamington*.
1892. Atcherley, John, *Vancouver*.
1892. Atchley,Edwd.Godfrey C. F.,*Clifton*.
1891. Atkey, Percy James, *Southampton*.
1913. Atkin, Charles Sydney, *St. Bart.'s-h*.
1861. Atkins, Charles Alfred, *A.M.S.*
1883. Atkins, Ernest, *Plumstead*.
1873. Atkins, Francis Thos., *Bournemouth*.
1908. Atkins,FrankRobt. Lowth,*Handley*.
1905. Atkins, Fredk. Durnford, *S. Norwood*.
1895. Atkins, George Ernest, *Wombwell*.
1891. Atkins, John Francis, *Birmingham*.
1923. Atkins, William Arnold, *Bloxwich*.
1890. Atkinson, Arthur Edw., *Russell-sq*.
1908. Atkinson, Arth. G.,M.B.E., *Norwood*.
1923. Atkinson, Cecil Hewitt, *Stainer-st*
1906. Atkinson, Edward Leicester, *R.N.*
1911. Atkinson, Edw.Wm.,*Isleworth-on-T*.
1909. Atkinson, Enoch Turner, *Canada*.
1874. Atkinson, Francis Edward, *Settle*.
1902. Atkinson, Geo. Jas. Smith, *Bampton*.
1837. Atkinson,Guy C. B.,*Melton Mowbray*.
1892. Atkinson, Hugh N. C.,*Upp. Norwood*.
1892. Atkinson, Jackson Arthur, *Elton*.
1909. Atkinson, John Lee, *Victoria, Aust*.
1893. Atkinson,J. P.,M.B.E ,*Saffron W'ldn*.
1922. Atkinson, Philip Bernard,*Bridgu'th*.
1869. Atkinson, Robert, *Smethwick*.
1901. Atkinson, Samuel Ernest, *Loughbro'*.
1881. Atkinson,Thos. Reuell, *St. Leonards*.
1910. Atkinson, W. P. Tindal, *Eaton-terr*.
1911. Atlee, Charles Nelson, *Ealing*
1922. Attaoullah, Hawah Khairul Nisa.
1911. Attenborough,Cuthbert H., *Frimley*.
1918. Attenborough,KeithEdw.,*St.Mary's*.
1905. Attenborough, Wilfrid G., *Frimley*.
1881. Atterbury, Walter, *Finchley*.

1916. Atteridge,KevinDoyle,*Ladbroke-gve*.
1921. Atteridge, T. J. D., *Ladbroke-grove*.
1850. Attfield, George Cooke, *Hove*.
1900. Atthill, Frank, *Colchester*.
1906. Attlee,Cecil K iight,*Brompton-hosp*.
1892. Attlee, John, *Grosvenor-st*., W.
1900. Attlee, Wilfrid Henry Waller, *Eton*
1915. Attwater,Geoff. Lewis, *W. Norwood*.
1922. Attwater, Wilfred F., *Lincoln's-inn*.
1912. Attwood, Herbt. Clifton, *S th'mpt'n*.
1901. Attwood, Richard Denton, *Royston*.
1865. Attygalle, John, *Ceylon*.
1895. Aubin, Emile Dupont, *New Zealand*.
1885. Aubrey,Alfd.Reub., *Weston-s.-Mare*.
1906. Aubrey, Cyril John Roby, *Cowes*.
1917. Aubrey, George, *Cowes*.
1903. Aubrey, George Ernest, *Hong Kong*.
1907. Aubrey, Harold Percivall, *Cwrzon-st*.
1916. Aubrey, Ivor, M.C., *Carmarthen*.
1897. Aubrey, Sydney Ernest, *Durban*.
1899. Aubrey, Thomas, *Bristol*.
1896. Auden, George Augustus, *Birm'ham*
1922.§Auden, Marjorie H S., *Bayswater*.
1832. Audland, William Edward, M.B.E.
1919. Aufranc, Doug. A. R.,*Tuffnell-pk.-rd*.
1921. Austen, Alfred Walter, *Shanklin*.
1911. Austen, Cecil Crees, *Old Kent-rd*.
1890. Austen, Harold Wm. C., *Ealing*.
1881. Austen, Henry Hinds, *Rye*.
1885. Austin, Herbert Ward, *R.A.M.C.*
1906. Austin, John Staines, *R.N.*
1898. Austin, Neville Henry, *Lingfield*.
1891. Austin, Reg. F. Edmund, *R.A.M C*.
1868. Austin. Sydney Charles, *Lingf'eld*.
1906. Austin-Smith, Herbert, *Hollinwood*.
1892. Auty. Charles Harley, *Harlesden*.
1914. Avarne, Claude H. B , *Maida-vale*.
1887. Aveline, Henry T. Sidney, *Catford*.
1908. Aveling, Charles James, *R.N.*
1909. Aveling, Kenneth John, *Watford*.
1902. Aveling, Leslie Baldwin, *Royton*.
1913. Avent, Mark, *Southsea*.
1884. Avenill, Charles, *Macclesfield*.
1904. Avery, John, *Forest-gate*.
1906. Avery, John Stanley, *Bournemouth*.
1896. Avery, Leonard Avery, D S.O.
1923. Axon, George Frederick, *Keswick*.
1916. Aydon, John, *St. Barth'.s-hospital*.
1901. Aylen, Ernest V., D.S.O., *R.A.M.C*.
1904. Aylen, John, *Halesworth*.
1917. Aylward, Roy Douglas, *London-hosp*.
1889. Aylward,Walt.Chas.,*Tunb'dge Wells*.
1888. Aymard, John Law, *Transvaal*.
1921.§Ayrton, Mary Joyce, *Wrexham*.
1912. Aznvr, Soliman. *Cairo*.
1922. Azurdia, José Roberto, *Liverpool*.

B.

1914. Ballingall, David C. G., *R.A.M.C.*
1888. Ballingall, Geo. A., *St. Leonard's.*
1916. Balmain, Aug. Rolls, *Birmingham.*
1907. Balsara, Jehangir C., *Bombay.*
1923. Balter, David Nesanel, *Finsbury-pk.*
1906. Balthasar, Ewald, *Fareham.*
1906. Baly, Arthur Lionel, *Lambeth.*
1894. Baly, Chas. Francis Peyton, *Harley-st.*
1878. Bamber, Chas. James, C.V.O., *I.M.S.*
1916. Bamber, Herbert Edward, c/o *T. Cook.*
1900. Bamber, William Edward, *Bolton.*
1893. Bamfield, Harold Jn. K., D.S O., *I.M.S.*
1882. Bamford, Chas. Robert, *Uttoxeter.*
1891. Bamford, Thomas, *Uttoxeter.*
1911. Bamforth, Joseph, *Warrington.*
1914. Bana, Framji Dossabhoy, *Bombay.*
1882. Banatvala, Sir H. E, C.S.I., *I.M.S.*
1919. Banbury, Percy, *Denmark-hill.*
1913. Banbury, Rich. Albert, *Denmark-hill.*
1905. Banda, Kobbekaduwé Tikiri, *Ceylon.*
1888. Banerji, Umadas, *Calcutta.*
1882. Banerjia, Mahendra Nath., *Calcutta.*
1915. Bangay, James Dorrington, *Chesham.*
1862. Bangay, Richard, *New Tredegar.*
1892. Banham, Cecil Walt. R., *Denby Dale.*
1902. Banham, Sidney Marshall, *Ealing.*
1882. Banham, Wm. Wilfred, *Sheffield.*
1912. Banister, Thurston Edmund, *Preston.*
1904. Bankes, John Herbert, *Cromby-place.*
1893. Bankes-Price, Hugh, *Lampeter.*
1918.§Banks, Annie Hardy, *Puddington.*
1916. Banks, James Reid, *Barnes.*
1868. Banks, John Alexander Percival.
1920. Banks, Wm. Eric Hallamore, *Falmouth*
1894. Bannerman, Geo. D. K., *High Wyc'mbe.*
1900. Bannerman, Walter Biggar, *New Zeal.*
1887. Bannister, Marmaduke, *Blackburn.*
1918. Banting, Fredk. Grant, M.C., *Canada.*
1918. Baranov, Monty, *Johannesburg.*
1919. Barbash, Hezekiah, *Grayling-rd.*
1906. Barber, Alec, *Sandown, I. of W.*
1902. Barber, Chas. Harrison, D.S.O., *I.M.S.*
1884. Barber, Fredc. Samuel, *Streatham.*
1890. Barber, Geo. T. Congreve, *Birmingh'm.*
1891. Barber, Geo. W., C.B, C.M.G., D.S.O.
1902. Barber, Hugh, *Derby.*
1904. Barber, John Watson, *Ilkeston.*
1895. Barber, Maurice Charles, *Bristol.*
1872. Barber, Oliver, *Hastings.*
1886. Barber, Percival Ellison, *Sheffield.*
1889. Barber, Sidney Frederick, *Sheffield.*
1892. Barberi, José Ignacio.
1904. Barclay, Alf E, O.B.E., *Manchester.*
1896. Barclay, Herbt. Clifford, *New Zeal.*
1911. Barclay, Isaac Bernard, *Lydbrook.*
1908. Bardsley, Henry, *Southport.*
1899. Bardswell, Noel Dean, *Midhurst.*
720

1922.§Barfield, Margarita S., *Finchley.*
1888. Barford, Arthur Morton, *Chichester.*
1905. Barford, James Leslie, *R.N.*
1895. Barford, Percy Crompe, *Selsey-on-S.*
1901. Barham, Guy Foster, *Epsom.*
1900. Barham, Percy Cornelius, *Dulwich.*
1901. Bark, Ernest Gilbert, *Liscard.*
1876. Bark, John, *Liverpool.*
1915. Barkan, Otto, *San Francisco.*
1918.§Barkas, Mary R., *N.Z. L. & M. Bank.*
1923. Barker, Alan, *Cardiff.*
1887. Barker, Alleyne Hayward, *Lindfield.*
1892. Barker, Chesman, *Finchley.*
1915. Barker, Eric Gordon, *Watford.*
1896. Barker, Ernest Marriott, *St. Leonards.*
1903. Barker, Frederic, *Japan.*
1889. Barker, Geo. Henry, *Clifton, Bristol.*
1893. Barker, George Laycock, *Rippingale.*
1908. Barker, Henry Lewis, *I.M.S.*
1885. Barker, John Collier, *Watford.*
1913. Barker, Malcolm, *Streatham.*
1896. Barker, Percy D., *Kensington-pk.-rd.*
1894. Barker, Toft, *Battersea.*
1923. Barker, Valentine H., *Muswell-hill.*
1875. Barker, Walter Herbert, *Victoria.*
1884. Barker, Wm. Jas. Townsend, *Fulham.*
1889. Barkworth, Hy. S., *Jun. Athenæ'm-Cl'b.*
1901. Barlet, Jehan Meredith, *Shaftesb'ry-av.*
1883. Barley, David Henry.
1886. Barling, Arthur Stanley, *Lancaster.*
1911. Barlow, Albert Malcolm, *Dalston.*
1890. Barlow, George, *Lytham.*
1898. Barlow, Herbert Cecil, *Lincoln.*
1898. Barlow, Hbt. Wm. Leyland, *Urmston.*
1914. Barlow, Launcelot White, *London.*
1917. Barlow, Noel Arthur Hamilton, *R N.*
1871. Barlow, Sir Thomas, Bart., K.C.V.O.
1896. Barlow, Thos. W.N., O.B.E., *Egremont*
1911. Barlow, William Rawson, *Ealing.*
1873. Barnard, Charles Edward, *Victoria.*
1878. Barnard, J. H., O.B.E., *Addison-gdns.*
1920. Barnard, William George, *Bath.*
1915. Barnden, Percy Wm., *Thornton-heath.*
1894. Barnes, Arthur.
1899. Barnes, Arthur Stanley, *Birmingham.*
1915. Barnes, Edgar Broughton, *Fernhurst.*
1870. Barnes, Edgar George, *Jersey.*
1905. Barnes, Ernest Chas. E., *Barnsbury.*
1907. Barnes, Ernest C. P., *Ponder's End.*
1921. Barnes, Fras. Gregory Lawson, *Bec les.*
1914. Barnes, Frank M., M.C., *Heckington.*
1904. Barnes, Frederick, *Sheffield.*
1901. Barnes, George, *Hammersmith.*
1919. Barnes, Geo. Arthur E., *Mauritius.*
1906. Barnes, Geo. Charles, *Hoylake.*
1880. Barnes, George Frederick, *Weymouth.*
1903. Barnes, Henry Edgar, *Eye.*
777

1879. Barnes, Henry John, *R.A.M.C.*
1911. Barnes, Howell Wood, *Lincoln.*
1918. Barnes, Hugh Woodward, *Linton.*
1898. Barnes, John Alfred, *Leicester.*
1899. Barnes, Jn. Arth. Percival, *Tottenham.*
1875. Barnes, John James, *Bury.*
1891. Barnes, Leonard S., O.B.E., *Welwyn.*
1862. Barnes, Thos. Henry, *Lavender-hill.*
1882. Barnes, Walter Stanley, *Br. Guiana.*
1921. Barnes, William Edward, *Highbury.*
1915. Barnett, Burgess, *Hastings.*
1907. Barnett, Ernest Cuthbert, *New Zeal.*
1885. Barnett, Frank Septimus, *Lewisham.*
1921. Barnett, Geoffrey Michael Fulton.
1888. Barnett, Horatio, *Church Stretton.*
1918. Barnett, John Binford, *Birmingham.*
1885. Barnett, Lawrence, S. *Hampstead.*
1923. Barnett, Maxwell Key, *Moseley.*
1921. Barnett, Sydney Herbert.
1923. Barnie-Adshead,Wm. Ewart,*Dudley.*
1879. Barns, John Gay, *Wheatley.*
1912. Barnsley,RobertEric,M.C.,*R.A.M.C.*
1905. Baron, Alfred Edwd., *Dunedin, Z.N.*
1888. Baron, Horatio Nelson, *Orford.*
1887. Barr, Horace Carlos, *Rotherham.*
1894. Barr, Valentine Herbt., *New Zealand.*
1865. Barraclough, Robt. W. S., *Par k-pl.*
1912. Barratt, Grantley, *Rhodesia.*
1880. Barratt, Herbert J., C.I.E., *R.A.M.C.*
1887. Barret, Edward Ernest, *Paris.*
1801. Barrett, Alfd. Keppel, *Kensington.*
1869. Barrett,AshleyWm , *Cavendish-place.*
1899. Barrett, Edmund Howard, *Harley-st.*
1886. Barrett, Ernest, *Market Deeping.*
1904. Barrett, Henry Edwd., *Holland-pk.*
1885. Barrett, Robert Hasbv. *Wisbech.*
1886. Barrett, Sidney E., *Tillingham.*
1920. Barrett, Sydney Thomas.
1893. Barrett, Walt. Russell, *Harley-st.*, W.
1914. Barrett, Wm. Claude P., *Folkestone.*
1885. Barrett, Wm Peard, *Folkestone.*
1867. Barrick, Eli James, *Toronto.*
1913. Barrie, Howard Greene, *China.*
1857. Barrington,Nicholas W.,*Margaret-st.*
1905. Barrionuevo, José Maria, *Costa Rica.*
1895. Barritt, John Thomas, *Patricroft.*
1921.§Barritt, Martha Florence, *Colne.*
1898. Barron, Henry Thompson, *Balham.*
1906. Barron, Richard Dunlop, *New Zeal.*
1900. Barron, Robt. M., D.S O., *I.M.S.*
1895. Barron, Thomas Ashbv, D.S.O.
1896. Barron, Willie N., M.V.O., *Ascot.*
1871. Barrow, Frank Edward, *A.M.S.*
1873. Barrow, Frederick, *Rothbury.*
1894. Barrow, Geo. Augustus, *Manchester.*
1898. Barrow, H. P. W., C.M.G., D.S.O.
1871. Barrow, Henry Jn.Waller, *R.A.M.C.*

1877. Barrow, Lancelot Andrews, *Charlton.*
1880. Barrow, Roger William, *Southport.*
1863. Barrow, Thos. Samuel, *Weymouth.*
1893. Barrow, Wm. Dodgson, *Lancaster.*
1913. Barrow-Clough, John R., *Wimbledon.*
1876. Barrs, Alfred George, *Leeds.*
1891. Barry, Cecil Chas. Stuart, *I.M.S.*
1921.§Barry, Frances Sophia.
1921.§Barry, Geraldine Mary.
1903. Barry, Thomas St. John, *Liscard.*
1883. Barry, Thos. David Collis, *I.M.S.*
1908. Bartholomew, Ernest U , *Conduit-st.*
1900. Bartlett, Basil S., D.S.O., *R A.M.C.*
1883. Bartlett. Benjamin Pope, *Bourton.*
1909. Bartlett,BertramF.,M.C.,*Onslow-gds.*
1904. Bartlett, Charles Eastty, *Tintern.*
1872. Bartlett, Edward, *Connaught-square.*
1903. Bartlett, Edwd. Leslie, *Connaught-sq.*
1901. Bartlett, Ernest Jn. Reeve, *Ipswich.*
1877. Bartlett, Felix Paul. *Ottery St. Mary.*
1891. Bartlett, Frank Whinfield, *Romsey.*
1906. Bartlett, George Bertram, *Lond.-hosp.*
1906. Bartlett, George Norton, *Horton.*
1886. Bartlett, Hedley C., *Saffron Walden.*
1875. Bartlett, Henry.
1868. Bartlett, James Prime, *Onslow-gdns.*
1900. Bartlett, Lionel Jasper, *Banbury.*
1921.§Bartlett, Marj. M. S., *Saffron Walden.*
1891. Bartlett, Ralph Clarke, *Romsey.*
1873. Bartlett, William, *Eketahuna, N.Z.*
1862. Bartley, Acheson Geo., *A.M.D.*
1906. Barton,Bertram Henry,M C.,*Harrow.*
1897. Barton, Chas. Nath., S. *Kensington.*
1887. Barton, Edwin Alfred, *Kensington.*
1897. Barton, Eustace Robt., *Portugal.*
1903. Barton, Francis, *Liverpool.*
1887. Barton, Francis Alex., *Beckenham.*
1889. Barton, Frederic Wm., *Stockwell.*
1888. Barton, Geo. A. Heaton,*Westb'rne-pk.*
1878. Barton, Geo. Henry, *Market-Rasen.*
1902. Barton, Guy Douglas, *Weybridge.*
1875. Barton,JamesKingston,*Courtfield-rd.*
1897. Barton, John, *Blackburn.*
1914. Barton, Maurice H., *R.A.M.C.*
1896. Barton, Percy Fredc., *Wimbledon.*
1880. Barton, Wm. Edwin, *Streatham.*
1918. Bartram, Lewis Henry, *Bulwell.*
1900. Barwell,FrancisReinagle,*Mildenhall.*
1907. Barwick, R. Lavington, *Yeadon.*
1885. Barwise, Sidney, *Duffield.*
1898. Bascombe, Edwin C. D., *Colchester.*
1895. Basden,HaroldStevens,*Crowborough.*
1893. Bashall, Chas. Edward, *W. Bushey.*
1904. Bashford, Henry Howard, *G.P.O.*
1891. Baskett, Bertr. Geo. M., *Rayleigh.*
1899. Bassano, Harold Fredc., *Ventnor.*
1885. Basset, Walter, *Newport, Mon.*

1911. Beatty,CyrilC.,M.C ,*Stockt'n-on-Tees.*
1899. Beatty, Henry Albert, *Toronto.*
1923. Beauchamp, Arthur, *Tipton.*
1904. Beaumont, Arthur Reg., *Uppingham.*
1917. Beaumont, Douglas Chas., *East Ham.*
1912. Beaumont, George Ernest, *Oxford.*
1901. Beaumont, Noel Chailes, *Staniland.*
1914.§Beaumont, Norah, *Bedford-park.*
1915. Beaumont, Owen Albert, M.C.
1922. Beaumont, William, *Highbury.*
1875. Beaumont, Wm. Mardon, *Bath.*
1919.§Beaven, Grace Mary, *Warminster.*
1888. Beaver,R.A.,O.B.E, *Wotton-u.-Edge*
1897. Beavis, John Douglas Wilson, *Assam.*
1893. Beazeley, Tom William, *Stechford.*
1897. Bebb, Richard, *Upp. Edmonton.*
1921.§Bebbington, Evelyn Francis, *Anfield.*
1923. Beccle, Harold Charles.
1906. Beck, William, *Cotham.*
1904. Beckett, Hugh George Wm., *Prees.*
1892. Beckitt, James Clay, *Leigh, Lancs.*
1909. Beckton, John James H., *R.A..M.C.*
1897. Beckton, William, *Bradford.*
1912. Bedale, Frederick Stanley, M.C.
1895. Beddard,Arthur Philip,*Gloucester-pl.*
1898. Beddard, William Oliver, *Cornhill.*
1907. Beddow, Harold Josiah, *Rugby.*
1885. Beddow, Josiah, *Thorverton.*
1911. Beddows,Edward Charles,*R.A.M.C.*
1893. Beddy, Thos. Alfred, *Jagersfontein.*
1874. Bedford, Chas. Fredk., *New Sleaford.*
1888. Bedford, Sir Chas. Henry, *I.M.S.*
1921. Badford, Davis Evan, *Boston.*
1900. Bedford, Douglas James, *Derby.*
1873. Bedford, Robert, *Auckland, N.Z.*
1906. Beeley, Arthur, *Keighley.*
1890. Beesley, Albert James, *Bunbury.*
1896. Beesley, Robert William, *Bolton.*
1901. Beet, William Ashley, *Brisbane.*
1900. Beetham, Herbert Arthur, *Leeds.*
1882. Beevor, Sir Hugh R., Bt., *Hargham.*
1880. Beevor,W.C.,C.B.,C.M.G.,*R.A..M.C.*
1911. Begg, Robert Campbell, M.C.
1920. Behman, Benj. Faltas, *Univ. Coll.*
1896. Behramjee, Dinshah B.
1897. Beit, Francis Victor Owen, *I.M.S.*
1922. Bekenn, Alexis Oswald,*Birmingham.*
1895. Bekenn,Geo. Hy.Ernest,*Birmingh'm.*
1901. Bekenn, Justin James, *Birmingham.*
1922. Bekker, FransW., *Standerton, S. Af.*
1895. Belcher, Geo. Clement, *Birmingham.*
1883. Belcher, Henry Edward,*Nottingham.*
1895. Belcher, James Arthur, *Herne-hill.*
1898. Belding, Davy Turner, *E Dereham.*
1899. Beley, George, *Sheffield.*
1898. Belfrage, Sydney H., *Gloucester-pl.*
1891. Bell, Arth. Sydney Gordon, *R.N.*
1062

1902. Bell, Charles Cameron, *Canada.*
1875. Bell, Chas. Edward Wallace, *Exeter.*
1884. Bell, George Craigie, *Finton-on-Sea.*
1889. Bell,Geo.Lawaluk, *Waverley.N.S.W*
1914. Bell, Howard Alexander, *Rodean.*
1892. Bell, James Adamson, *Gloucester.*
1884. Bell, John, *Hyde-park-mansions.*
1868. Bell, John Albert, *Parkstone.*
1904. Bell, John Arthur. M.C., *Sheffield.*
1920.§Bell, Julia, *St. John's-road.*
1904. Bell, Kenelm Digby, *Royal Navy.*
1898. Bell, Kenneth de Risley, *Lambourn.*
1895. Bell, Thomas Dobson, *Leeds.*
1897. Bell, Thomas Herbt., M.C., *Winnipeg.*
1899. Bell, Victor Samuel Alex., *Bedford.*
1914. Bell, Wm. A. H. Noel, *Clapham-rd.*
1896. Bell, William Blair, *Liverpool.*
1890. Bell, William Ker, *Meaford, Canada.*
1903. Bellamy, Gerald Eade, *Eythorne.*
1899. Bellamy, John Henry, *Ashby.*
1911. Bellew, Thos. Mulholland, *Liverpool.*
1916. Benbow,Thos.Alex.Palmer,*Victoria.*
1885. Bencraft, Hy. Wm. R., *Southampton.*
1923. Bendit, Lawrence John.
1917. Bendix, Fredk. Ernest, *Forest-gate.*
1904. Benett, Arthur Morris, *R.A.M.C.*
1918. Beney, Charles Clement, *Beckenham.*
1877. Benham, Fredk. Lucas, *S. Austr.*
1872. Benham, Henry James, *Boulogne.*
1909. Benjatield, Jos. Dudley, *Wimpole-st.*
1922. Benjamin,Francis Joseph, *Linthorpe.*
1916. Benner, Frank Aubrey, *Canada.*
1916. Bennett, Alex. Wm. Chas., *Putney.*
1877. Bennett, Arthur, *Hamilton, Victoria.*
1923. Bennett, Arthur Henry, *Derby.*
1906. Bennett, Cecil, *Shanghai.*
1868. Bennett, Chas. John, *Aberystwyth.*
1919. Bennett, Chas Wm., *St. Bart.'s-hosp.*
1889. Bennett, Chris. Hy. W., *Sandbach.*
1906. Bennett, Claude J. F., *Melksham.*
1889. Bennett, Colin E. Wilmot, *Forest-hill.*
1890. Bennett, Francis Dillon, *Saxile-row.*
1906. Bennett, Frank Cyril Harvie, *Walton.*
1914. Bennett, Frank Percy, *Maida-hill.*
1918. Bennett, Frederic James, *Stockport.*
1879. Bennett, Fredk. Joseph,*George-st.*,W.
1883. Bennett, Fredk. William, *Leicester.*
1887. Bennett, George Herbert, *Ealing.*
1906. Bennett, Harold G., *Billingshurst.*
1897. Bennett, Harry Chas. Plant, *New Z.*
1878. Bennett, Hy. Jas. Lee, *Newton Abbot.*
1874. Bennett, Henry Selfe, *Up. Berkeley-st.*
1903. Bennett, Henry Stagg, *Ipswich.*
1897. Bennett, James, *Warrington.*
1894. Bennett, James Henry, *Beckenham.*
1908. Bennett, Jas Wodderspoon, *Ilkley.*
1923. Bennett, John Cyril, *Moonta, S..A.*
1119

1913. Bennett, John Henry, *Vict., Austr.*
1900. Bennett, Kenneth Hugh, *Penzance.*
1922. Bennett, Louis Amos, *Bank of N.Z.*
1897. Bennett, Norman Godfrey, *Brook-st.*
1912. Bennett, Percy L. T., M.C., *Brentford.*
1896. Bennett, Robert Allan, *Torquay.*
1913. Bennett, Richard S. de C., *Malacca.*
1912. Bennett, Thomas Izod, *New Zealand.*
1896. Bennett, Wm. Boase, *Liverpool.*
1873. Bennett, Wm. Edward, *Royal Navy.*
1899. Bennett, Wm. Fay, *Bury-St-Edmunds.*
1896. Bennett, Wm. George, *Worcester.*
1919. Bennett, William Henry, *Bolton.*
1896. Bennetts, Frederick, *Edmonton.*
1902. Bennion, Jn. Menlove, *St. Mary Cray.*
1893. Bensley, Clement Henry, *I.M.S.*
1893 Bensley, Edwin Edwd., *Northampton.*
1893. Bensley, Geo. Egbert, *Kelfield-gdns.*
1898. Bensley, Vernon Cyril, *Cape Colony.*
1904. Benson, Alex. Vigors, *S. Australia.*
1880. Benson, Alfred, *Maida-vale, W.*
1908. Benson, Chas. Thornton V., *R.A.M.C.*
1884. Benson, Chris. Richmond, *Lew Down.*
1893. Benson, George Vere, *Lewes.*
1886. Benson, Matthew, *Wigan.*
1873. Benson, Percy Hugh, *I.M.S.*
1914. Benstead-Smith, W. F., *Middlx.-hosp.*
1916. Bensted, Harold J., M.C., *New Cross.*
1896. Bensted, Lewin, *Muswell-hill.*
1892. Bensusan, Arth. Daniel, *Transvaal.*
1903. Bent, Percy Claude Vincent, *Putney.*
1901. Bent, Sidney Chas. Hy., *Balham.*
1899. Bent, Vincent Thos. Clare, *Streatham.*
1876. Benthall, Albert, *Adelaide-rd.*
1889. Bentham, Andrew Occleshaw, *Wigan.*
1902. Bentley, Harold, *Mitcham.*
1883. Bentlif, Philip Barnett, *Jersey.*
1902. Benton, William, *East Ham.*
1880. Beresford, Chas. Wm., *Narborough.*
1893. Beresford, Edwyn H., *M.A.B., Tooting*
1873. Beresford, William Hugh, *Esher.*
1915. Berg, George Charles, *St. Thos.-hosp.*
1905. Bergin, Frank Gower, *Bristol.*
1897. Bergin, Wm. Marmaduke, *Walbrook.*
1913. Bergouignan, Paul T. G., *Evian.*
1898. Beringer, Fritz John A., *Highgate.*
1891. Berkeley, Geo. H. A. C., *Wimpole-st.*
1914. Berkeley-Cole, Geo. Albert, *Gosforth.*
1905. Berkeley-Hill, Owen, A. R., *I.M.S.*
1883. Berkley, E. J. Gibson. M.B.E.
1922. Berlie, Herbert Claye, c/o *Cook & Son.*
1893. Berlyn, John Aaron, *Birmingham.*
1892. Bernard, Claude, *Fishponds, Bristol.*
1893. Bernard, Robt. Spence, *Royal Navy.*
1923.§Bernard, Susanna May, *George-st.*
1890. Bernau, Henry Ferd., O.B.E., *N.Z.*
1883. Bernays, Adolphus Vaughan, *Solihull.*
1176

1877. Bernays, Aug. Chas., *St. Louis, U.S.*
1899. Berncastle, H. Melbourne, *Warlingh'm*
1897. Bernhardt, Dudley Richd., *Bell-st.*
1910. Bernstein, Benjamin, *Cape Town.*
1923. Bernstien, Jack, *Leeds.*
1876. Berridge, William Alfred, *Folkestone.*
1923. Berridge, Wm. C. Morpott, *Enderby.*
1892. Berridge, Wm. Rbt. Morpott, *Enderby.*
1886. Berrill, Alfred, *Woodford.*
1890. Berry, Albt. Edward, *Walkden.*
1906. Berry, Arthur William, *Edgeley.*
1904. Berry, Charles Harold, *Chagford.*
1923. Berry, Douglas Haycraft, *Watford.*
1910. Berry, Fleetwood S D., *Johannesburg*
1897. Berry, Herbert George, *Reepham.*
1907. Berry, Horace Simeon, *Totnes.*
1916. Berry, James Allen, *Guy's-hosp.*
1882. Berry, John Bourne, *Penn.*
1910. Berry, Noel William, *Bridgnorth.*
1893. Berry, Robert Sewers, *Queensland.*
1898. Berry, Thos. Percival, *Swindon.*
1918. Berry, William Leslie, *Cheam.*
1889. Berryman, Henry Arthur, *R.A.M.C.*
1907. Berryman, Richard C. P., *Guildford.*
1881. Bertram, Benjamin. *Pretoria.*
1923. Beshara, Fayek, *Mit Bera, Egypt.*
1895. Best, Fdk. Hy. de G., *Waltham Cross.*
1921.§Best, Margaret Gladys, *Sandon.*
1894. Best, Palemon, *St. Ives.*
1884. Best, William James, *Dover.*
1917. Beswick, Wilfred Thomas, *Buxton.*
1888. Betenson, Wm. Betenson, *Newhaven.*
1893. Betenson, Woodley Daniel, *Kew.*
1903. Bethell, Hugh Wood, *Basingstoke.*
1902. Bett, Douglas Horne Blackader, *New Z.*
1907. Bett, Francis Arnot Blackader, *New Z.*
1886. Bett, William, M.V.O., *Royal Navy.*
1897. Betteridge, Thomas, *Sutton Coldfield*
1899. Betts, Alfred John Vernon, *I.M.S.*
1896. Betts, Leonard Bowring, *Bradworthy.*
1899. Bevan, Arthur, *Gloucester-place.*
1881. Bevan, Henry Crook, *Rumney, Mon.*
1923. Bevan-Jones, John, *Ealing.*
1876. Bevan, Richard, *W. Kensington.*
1889. Bevan, Tom Webb, *Nantyglo.*
1913. Bevan-Brown, Frederick Vivian, *N.Z.*
1868. Bevan-Lewis, William, *Brighton.*
1915. Beven, John Junius O., *Middlx.-hosp.*
1895. Beven, Octavius, *Lee.*
1903. Beverley, Kenneth Harold, *Barnsley.*
1863. Beverley, Michael, *Scole.*
1890. Beville, Frederick Wells, *Bath.*
1899. Beville, Herbert George, *Brighton.*
1902. Bevir, George, *Timsbury.*
1909. Bevis, Alfred William, *R.A.M.C.*
1906. Bevis, Harold, *Portsmouth.*
1883. Bewes, Edwd. Anstis, *Otahuhu, N.Z.*
1233

1914.§Bishopp, Mabel Kate, *Tonbridge.*
1885. Bisshopp,FrancisR.B.,*Tunb'dye Wells.*
1905. Bisson, Albert Ogier, *Guernsey.*
1915. Biswas, Satish Chandra, *Bengal.*
1918.§Bjorkegren, Margaret E., *Hampstead.*
1896. Blaber, Percy Leonard, *Brondesbury.*
1888. Blachford, James Vincent, *Norwood.*
1895. Blachford, Jem, *Totnes.*
1891. Black,Arth.Campbell, *Paddock Wood.*
1897. Black, Charles, *Sheffield.*
1888. Black, George, *Hailsham.*
1911. Black, James Jamison, *Carlton, Vict.*
1868. Black, John Gordon *Harrogate.*
1896. Black, Lewis Potter, *Exeter.*
1906. Black, Patrick, *Kingston.*
1876. Blackader, Alex. Dougall, *Montreal.*
1903. Blackall, Wm. Edwd., *W. Australia.*
1904. Blackburn, Albert Edw., *Hartlepool.*
1872. Blackburn, Chas. W. A., *Mauritius.*
1895. Blackburn, Ernest W., *Barnsley.*
1922. Blackburn, John T., *Roundhay-mt.*
1898. Blackburn, Vernon Kent, *Barnsley.*
1916. Blackburn, Wm. Howard, *Liverpool.*
1895. Blackett, E. J., O.B.E., *Grosvenor-sq.*
1886. Blackler, Henry John, *Redhill.*
1923. Blacklidge, Thomas S , *Fleetwood.*
1911. Blackman. Hy. Geo. B , *Norwich.*
1877. Blackman, Josiah Geo., *Portsmouth.*
1901. Blackman,SidneySpencer F.,*Croydon.*
1920. Blackman, Sydney, *South Hackney.*
1909. Blackmore,Fredk.John C.,*Plumstead.*
1911. Blackmore, Herb. Stuart, *R A.M.C.*
1857. Blackmore, Humphrey P , *Salisbury.*
1917. Blackmore, Leslie G., *Gloucester-gds.*
1917. Blackstock, Anthony, *Birkenhead.*
1902. Blackstone Chas. Edgar, *Ringwood.*
1906. Blackstone, Leonard C , *Westcliff.*
1899. Blackstone,Willoughby A.,*Rgnts.-pk.*
1919 §Blackwell, Ursula P., *Lincoln's-inn.*
1911. Blackwood, Bertie, *Harrogate.*
1884. Blackwood, Fdk. Martindale, *N.S. W.*
1897. Blackwood, John, *Southsea.*
1896. Blagden, John James, *Chester.*
1882. Blagg, Arthur Frederick, *Clifton.*
1887. Blaikie, Arth. Babington, *Oswestry.*
1909 Blaikie, Cuthbert Jas., *R.A.M.C.*
1921. Blain, Israel, *Cheetham.*
1879. Blair, Archibald, *Newport, Mon.*
1917. Blair,Chas.Jas.Longworth,*St.Barts.*
1921. Blair, James Harold, *Tavistock-sq.*
1900. Blake, Anthony Fewster, *Grays.*
1913. Blake, Eliot Watson, *Gosport.*
1920. Blake, Frank.
1874. Blake, Geo. Farncombe, *Birmingham.*
1911 Blake, Gilbert Alan, *R.A.M.C.*
1918. Blake, John Churchill, *W. Wickham.*
1903. Blake, Matthew Robt., *Winnipeg.*
1404

1873. Blake, Samuel Hahnemann, *Bolton.*
1860. Blake, Thos. William, *Bournemouth.*
1908. Blake,TobiasR.H.,M.C.,*Cromwell-rd.*
1895. Blake, Victor John, *Portsmouth.*
1887. Blake, Wm. Henry, *West Wickham.*
1876. Blake, William Henry, *Harpenden.*
1891. Blakeman, Charles John, *Southport.*
1885. Blakemore, Benjamin, *Tyldesley.*
1900. Blakemore, Herbert, *Atherton.*
1914. Blakemore, Wm. Herbert, *Tyldesley.*
1886. Blakeney, John Henry, *Cheltenham.*
1898. Blaker, Percy Stanley, *Ealing.*
1876. Blaker, Thos. F. Isaacson, *Brighton.*
1922 §Blakeston. Mary H. Y., *Driffield.*
1903. Blakie, James Landells, *Melbourne.*
1877. Blamey, James, *Penryn.*
1886. Blamey, John Henwood, *Beer.*
1917. Blampied, Harold John, *Jersey.*
1901. Blanc, Antonio.
1923. Bland, Herbert Wm., *Moseley.*
1906. Blandford, Harry Oliver, *Highgate.*
1893. Blandford, Jos. Jn. G., *Whittingham.*
1913. Blandford, Walter F., *Gunterstone-rd.*
1914.§Blandy, Majorie Ada, *Hunter-street.*
1902. Blandy,WilfridBoothby,*Nottingham.*
1902. Blatchford, William Nichols, *R.N.*
1881. Blatherwick, Henry, *Walton-street.*
1902. Blathwayt, Arth. de Visme, *Bath.*
1888. Blaxall, Frank Richardson, *Hendon.*
1886. Blaxland, Ernest Gregory, *Sydney.*
1909. Blaydes, Wilfred, *Temple, E.C.*
1916. Bleasdell, John Tyldesley, *Leeds.*
1901. Blease,Arth. Torkington,*Altrincham.*
1910. Blechschmidt,Julius Gottlob,*Guy's-h.*
1887. Blenkinsop, Alfred P.,C.B.,*R.A.M.C.*
1867. Blenkinsop, Fredk. Henry, *I.M.S.*
1897. Bletchly, George Playne, *Nailsworth.*
1904. Bletsoe, John Henry, *Upminster.*
1894. Blewitt, Wm. Francis, *N. Walsham.*
1897. Blieden, Max, *Transvaal.*
1892. Bligh, William, *Caterham Valley.*
1885. Blight, John Henry, *Chesterfield.*
1892. Bliss, Ernest Wm., C.M.G., D.S.O.
1913. Bliss,Maurice Frederic,M.C., *Ealing.*
1893. Blomfield, Alfred Bealy, *Peckham.*
1923.§Blomfield, K athleen N., *Pontefract.*
1886. Blomfield, Geo. Wills, *Pontefract.*
1922. Bloom, Solomon, *Merthyr Tydfil.*
1859. Bloomenthal, Theodore, *Clapton-pk.*
1891. Bloomer, Fredk Wm., *Long Eaton.*
1895. Bloomfield,IIbt.W.G.,*Johannesburg*
1878. Blott, Herbert, *Beaumont-street.*
1915. Blount, Douglas Arthur, *Preston-pk.*
1909. Bloxsome, Harold Ernest, *Fairford.*
1891. Blucke, Harry Fdk. S., *Shaftesbury.*
1917. Bluemel, Charles Sidney, *Rugby.*
1919. Bluett, Cecil, *Tamworth, N.S. W.*
1401

1884. Bluett, Geo. Mallack, *Kensington*.
1917. Bluett-Duncan, Duncan C., *St. Thos.-h*.
1888. Blunt, Arthur Henry, *Leicester*.
1915. Blunt, Arthur Leslie, *Leicester*.
1903. Blunt, Thomas Edward, *Royal Navy*.
1918. Blurton, Gilbert, *West Bridgford*.
1887. Blurton, John Fredk., *Nottingham*.
1891. Boake, Basil, *Great Yarmouth*.
1859. Board, Edmund Comer, *Clifton*.
1889. Boase, Wm. George, *Brit. Guiana*.
1918. Bochenek, Moshek Zelmanovitch.
1904. Boclet, Faustin Marcel, *Eaton-sq*.
1875. Boddy, Evan Marlett, *Birmingham*.
1868. Boddy, Hugh Walter, *Manchester*.
1894. Boden, John S., O.B.E., *Muswell-hill*.
1905. Bodkin, Herbt. Alfred, *Chelmsford*.
1915. Bodley, Alf. Lang, M.C., *Newcastle*.
1918. Bodman, Alan Gabriel, *Clifton*.
1899. Bodman, Chris. Osmond, *Bristol*.
1871. Bodman, Francis Henry, *Bristol*.
1922. Bodman, Francis Hervey, *Bristol*.
1895. Bodman, John Hervey, *Bristol*.
1903. Bodvel-Roberts, Hugh F., *Napsbury*.
1865. Body, Henry Martin, *Wimborne*.
1901. Body, Thomas Howard, *Leigh-on-S*.
1902. Body, Thomas Munn, *Middlesbrough*.
1919. Boe, Max Richard, *Canada*.
1901. Boeddicker, Hans F.W., *Birmingham*.
1922. Boger, Hugo, *Maida Vale*.
1886. Boger, William Henry, *Fowey*.
1923. §Bohtlingk, Nina Olga, *Brixton*.
1879. Boissier, Arthur Henry, *Banbury*.
1900. Boissière, Felix Anthony, *Fortess-rd*.
1896. Bokenham, Thos. B., *Wokingham*.
1889. Bokenham, Thos. J., *Devonshire-st*.
1915. Boland, Chas. Vincent, *St. Barts.-hosp*.
1923. Boland, Edward Rowan, *Kensington*.
1915. Boldero, Harold E. A., *Mark Cross*.
1911. Bolt, Richard Frank, *Bristol*.
1917. Bolton, Alfred Octavius, *Enstone*.
1896. Bolton, Charles, *Queen Anne-street*.
1902. Bolton, Frank Elliott, *Royal Navy*.
1884. Bolton, Geo. Aug., *Piccadilly*.
1869. Bolton, Jn. Geo. Elliot, *Mauritius*.
1904. Bolton, Jn. Hry. Doug., *Univ. Coll*.
1882. Bolton, Jos. Shepherd, *Nottingham*.
1892. Bolus, Harry Boulcott, *Beckenham*.
1903. Bolus, Percy Reg., *Devonport*.
1909. Bomford, Trevor Lawrence, *I.M.S.*
1919. Bonar, Thos. Geo. Doughty, *Hull*.
1920. Bonar, Thos. Lonsdale, *Cavendish-pl*.
1917. Bonard, Numa Sylla, *Westbourne-ter*.
1905. Bond, Arthur Herbert, *R.A.M.C.*
1886. Bond, Barnabas Mayston, *Ha'mersmt'h*.
1893. Bond, Bertram Wm., *Godalming*.
1916. Bond, Charles Eric, *Leicester*.
1884. Bond, Chas. Knox, *Gt. Pulteney-st*.

1894. Bond, Charles Shaw, *Liphook*.
1899. Bond, Frank Fouracre, *Trowbridge*.
1898. Bond, Jas. Hy. R., C.B.E., D.S.O.
1878. Bond, Jas. William, *Harley-st.*, W.
1881. Bond, Richard Pratt, *R.A.M.C.*
1892. Bond, William Ernest, *Ashover*.
1909. Boney, Thos. Knowles, *Woodside-pk*.
1920. Bonfield, John Patrick.
1886. Bonnetin, Fernand Hry., *Leytonstone*.
1911. Bonner, Wm. Percy, *Peterborough*.
1898. Bonnet, Saint René, *France*.
1918. Bonnett, Eric John S., *Hounslow*.
1900. Bonney, Ernest Henry, *Church-st.*, W.
1888. Bontor, Sidney A., *Berkhamsted*.
1881. Boobbyer, Philip, *Nottingham*.
1922. Boobbyer, Philip Watson, *Nott'gham*.
1876. Boodle, Geo. Adolphus, *Gloucester*.
1873. Boodle, Rbt. Maxwell, *Reading*.
1897. Booker Charles Wm., *Witley*.
1917. Boon, Alfred Henry, *Chicago*.
1891. Boon, Ernest Gerald, *Italy*.
1923. Boone, William Brooke, *Newport*.
1904. Booth, Charles Herbert, M.C., *Leeds*.
1912. Booth, Claude Hebden B., *N. Univ. Club*
1887. Booth, Daniel, *Heaton Chapel*.
1882. Booth, Edwd. Hargrave, *Brighton*.
1881. Booth, George, *Chesterfield*.
1882. Booth, John Henry, *Chesterfield*.
1903. Booth, Lawr. Twemlow, *Manchester*.
1862. Booth, Lionel, *Worthing*.
1906. Booth, Lionel Hethorn, *Worthing*.
1873. Booth, Philip L., *Barrow-in-Furness*.
1879. Booth, Thos. Carter, *P.§ O.S. N. Co.*
1885. Booth, Wm. Henry, *Stamford-hill*.
1923. Booth, William George, *Lewisham*.
1886. Booth-Milner, Oscar M., *N. Cleethorpes*.
1910. Boothman, Wm. Stanley, *Manchester*.
1894. Borcherds, Walt. Meent, *C. Province*.
1889. Borrett, George Goss, *Royal Navy*.
1910. Borrie, David Forbes, O.B.E.
1902. Borrie, Fredk. John, *New Zealand*.
1918. Boruchowitz, Jules Saml., *Antwerp*.
1923. Bose, Jogesh Chandra, *Birmingham*.
1920. Bosman, Hubertus A. M., *Finchley-rd*.
1902. Bosson, George Archibald, *Alford*.
1900. Bostock, Arthur Hastings, *Chichester*.
1864. Bostock, Edwd. Ingram, *Horsham*.
1895. Bostock, Eustace Bernard, *Guernsey*.
1882. Bostock, John, *Loughborough*.
1913. Bostock, John, *Norton*, *Malton*.
1883. Bostock, John Yates.
1876. Boswell, Alexander, *Ashbourne*.
1881. Boswell, Jn. Irvine, *Newport Pagnell*.
1909. Boswell, Norman Alex., *Runcorn*.
1914. Boswell, Philip R., M.C., *Hartlepool*.
1900. Botham, Richard Henry, *Skelton*.
1874. Bott, Henry, O.B.E., *Brentford*.

1882. Bott, Joseph, *Richmond.*
1915 §Bott, Margaret Stote Glen, *Bolton.*
1901. Bott, Percival Geo. Alb., *Norfolk-sq.*
1905. Bott, Robert Henry, *I.M.S.*
1905. Bott, Stanley, *Caistor.*
1908. Bott, William, *Willenhall.*
1874. Bott, Wm. Gibson, *Brixton-road.*
1897. Bottomley,F.C.,O.B.E.,*Bournemouth.*
1897. Bottomley,Thos.Abbey,*Huddersfield.*
1917. Boucaud, Joseph Erwin A., *Trinidad.*
1918. Boucaud, Martin Vincent, *St. Bart's.*
1914. Bouchage, Ambroise, *Chambéry.*
1908. Boucher, Frank Treadwell, *Bristol.*
1873. Boulger, Isaac, *A.M.S.*
1880. Boulter, Walter Ernest, *Plumstead.*
1890. Boulton, Arthur, *Horncastle.*
1897. Boulton, Harold, *I.M.S.*
1923. Bounalie, Fredk. E. Graham, *Chester.*
1888. Bour, Edward François, *Mauritius.*
1899. Bourdas, Ernest Clarkson, *Balham.*
1905. Bourdas, John, *R.N.*
1912. Bourdillon, L. G.. D.S.O., M.C.
1914. Bourgault-Ducondray,A.R.,*Mauritius*
1923. Bourke, Bernard, *Castlebar, Ireland.*
1901. Bourke, Isidore MacWm., *N.S.W.*
1917. Bourne, Geoffrey, *Highgate.*
1879. Bourns, Newcome W., *S. Kensington.*
1895. Bousfield, Arthur, *Hornsey.*
1916. Bousfield, Edw. Geo. Paul, *Hendon.*
1902. Bousfield, Leonard, *R.A.M.C.*
1897. Bousfield, Stanley, *Bayswater.*
1868. Boutflower, Andrew, *Manchester.*
1915. Bouwer, Johannes William, *Cape.*
1905. Bowater, William,M.C.,*Birmingham.*
1887. Bowden, Ernest Edwd., *Warrington.*
1884. Bowden, Reg. Treacher, *Buscombe.*
1901. Bowdler, Archibald P., *Chiswick.*
1882. Bowe, Arthur, *St. Neots.*
1879. Bowe, Francis, *Fairlie, N.Z.*
1917. Bowell, Ernest Wm., *S. Norwood.*
1923. Bowen, Charles Glynne, *Guy's-hosp.*
1876. Bowen, Edward, *Upper Tooting.*
1913. Bowen, George James, *Newport.*
1877. Bowen, Owen, *Liverpool.*
1909. Bowen, Owen Henry, *Croydon.*
1911. Bowen, Thomas Rufus, *Penygroes.*
1913. Bowen, Tudor David John, *Cardiff.*
1904. Bowen-Jones, John, *Cardiff.*
1877. Bowen-Jones, Lloyd M., *Carmarthen.*
1875. Bower, Ernest Dykes, *Gloucester.*
1913. Bower, Harold James, *Knowle.*
1872. Bower, Reginald, *Knowle.*
1887. Bower, William George.
1916. Bowes, Edgar Scott, *Rusthall.*
1915. Bowes, Gerald Kessick, *Herne-bay.*
1872. Bowes, John Ireland, *Devizes.*
1910. Bowes, Richd. Fredk.Butlin,*Devizes.*

1895. Bowes, Tom Armstrong, *Herne-bay.*
1883. Bowhay, Albert, *Tavistock.*
1885. Bowie, Robert Forbes, C.B., *R.N.*
1891. Bowker, Chas. Stanser, *N.S.W.*
1883. Bowker, Robt. Steer, *Sydney, N.S.W.*
1906. Bowkett. Leon. Howard, *Queensland.*
1906. Bowle, Chas. William, *R.A.M.C.*
1903. Bowle, Sidney Clement, *R.A.M.C.*
1893. Bowle-Evans, Chas. Harford, *I.M.S.*
1920. Bowler, Walter, *Liverpool.*
1899. Bowles, Alfred, *Eastbourne.*
1888. Bowman,R.Oxley,M.B.E., *Ulverston.*
1882. Bown, Arthur Thomas, *I.M.S.*
1909. Bowring, Harold, *Liverpool.*
1919.§Bowser, Hilda C., *Long Buckley.*
1893. Bowtell, Hbt. Richmond, *Ealing.*
1896. Box, Stanley Longhurst, *Ealing.*
1903. Box, Wm.Fredk.,*Stratford-on-Avon.*
1886. Boxall, Frank, *Rudgwick.*
1912. Boyall, Arthur Vincent, *Porlock.*
1896. Boyan, John, *Royal Navy.*
1898. Boycott, Arthur Norman, *St. Albans.*
1892. Boyd, Alex. Brooke, *Godalming.*
1913. Boyd, Edgar James, *Wimbledon.*
1910. Boyd Edmund, *Toronto.*
1901. Boyd, Ezekiel Alexander,*Seymour-pl.*
1896. Boyd, Geo. Samuel Jas., *Birmingham.*
1893. Boyd, James, *New Zealand.*
1906. Boyd, Jn. Errol Moritz, *R.A.M.C.*
1905. Boyd, John Francis, *I.M.S.*
1919.§Boyd-MacKay, Sarah A. F., *Judd-st.*
1906. Boyd, Samuel John, *Ontario.*
1914. Boyd, W. Houston,*Up. Gloucester-pl.*
1889. Boyd, William Robert, *Victoria.*
1892. Boyes, William Isaac, *Victoria.*
1901. Boyle,Henry EdmundGaskin,O B.E.
1876. Boys, Arthur Henry, *St. Albans.*
1904. Boys, Leonard Hbt.H., *Woodhall Spa.*
1895. Boyton, Arthur Jas. Hry., *Penarth.*
1871. Brabant,Thos.Hughes.,*St.George's-rd.*
1905. Brabazon, Edward, *W. Afr. M.S.*
1921. Bracewell, Charles H., *Old Broad-st.*
1892. Bracewell, Walt. Hansford, *N.S.W.*
1919. Bracey, Wm. Edelsten, *Wedmore.*
1916. Brachman,David Simon,*Philadelphia.*
1916. Bracken, John Prichard, *Wimbledon.*
1887. Brackenbury, Hry.Britten, *Stroud-gr.*
1884. Bradbrook,William,*Fenny Stratford.*
1900. Bradbury, Charles Henry, *Salford.*
1885. Bradbury,HarveyKinnersley,*Burton.*
1886. Bradbury, John Augustus, *Wigan.*
1904. Bradbury, John Cecil O., *Sandgate.*
1903. Braddock, William, *Oldham.*
1917. Braddock, Wm. Hallock, *Cardiff.*
1917.§Brade-Birks,Hilda Kathleen,*Darwen.*
1894. Bradford, Andrew.
1902. Bradford,Anthony B.,*Henrietta-st.,*W

1877. Bradford, Cordley, *Birmingham*.
1914. Bradford,Ernest Cordley,*Birmingham*
1900. Bradford, John, *Exeter*.
1886. Bradford,SirJ.,K.C.M.G.,C.B.,C.B.E.
1903. Bradley, Alwyn Hewett, *Leicester*.
1877. Bradley, Chas. Aug., *Macclesfield*.
1908. Bradley, Clem. Hy. Burton, *Sydney*.
1913. Bradley, Edwin John, M.C., *Dover*.
1911. Bradley, George Francis, *Halstead*.
1899. Bradley, John, *Coventry*.
1919. Bradnack, Gerald A. A., *Morton*.
1857. Bradshaw,SirA.Fredk.,K.C.B.,*Oxf'd*
1905. Bradshaw, Gerald Arthur, *China*.
1884. Bradshaw, Thos. Robert, *Liverpool*.
1923. Bradsworth, Colin C., *Birmingham*.
1899. Braidwood, Thos. Lithgow, *Epsom*.
1901. Brailey, Wm. Herbert, *Hove*.
1923. Brail ford, Jas. Fredk., *Bearwood*.
1916. Brainbridge, C. V., *Kidderminster*.
1883. Braine-Hartnell, Geo. M. P., *Porwick*.
1896. Braine-Hartnell,Jas.C.R,*Cheltenham*.
1912. Braithwaite,Edward Wrigley, *Leeds*
1909. Braithwaite, Eldred Curwen, *Benton*.
1919. Braithwaite, John, V. C., *Chingford*.
1876. Braithwaite, Samuel, *Bournemouth*.
1895. Brakenridge, F. J., C.M.G., *R.A.M.C.*
1902. Bramhall, Charles, O.B.E., *R.A.M.C.*
1890. Bramwell, Herbert, *Nunney*.
1880. Bramwell, Hugh R., *Twickenham*.
1911. Brandenburgh, Leon Fras., *I.M.S.*
1901. Brandon, Arth. Jn. Spiller, *Sydney*.
1900. Brangwin, Charles Harold, *Swatow*.
1900. Bransbury,II.A.B., D.S.O.,*R.A.M.C.*
1895. Branson, Clement W., *Bournemouth*.
1886. Branson, Herbert Wm. Archer.
1900. Branson, W. Philip Sutcliffe, C B.E.
1881. Brauthwaite,Rbt.W.,C.B., *Whitehall*.
1896. Branwell, Charles, *Penzance*.
1913. Brash, Edw. John Yelverton, *Exeter*.
1917. Brash, James Bassett, *Exeter*.
1896. Brash, John Birdsley, *Birmingham*.
1917. Brash, John Walker, *St. Mary's*.
1892. Brasher, Chas. Wm. James, *Bristol*.
1921. Brass, John George Beadle, *Saltburn*.
1920. Bratton, Allen B., *Westbourne-pk.-rd*.
1917. Braun, Loswell Israel B., *Palliser-rd*.
1889. Braund, Arthur Mather, *Bude*.
1900. Braund, Henry, *King-street*, E.C.
1881. Bray, Ernest Edward, *Royal Navy*.
1907. Bray, Fredk. Richard, *Sheffield*.
1888. Bray, Geo. Arth. T.,D.S.O.,*R.A.M.C.*
1888. Bray, Hubert A., C.B., C.M.G.
1885. Bray, Percy Dean, *Blaymey, N.S.W.*
1888. Braye, Reginald James, *Leicester*.
1920. Brayshaw, Harold C., *Johannesburg*.
1886. Brazil, Walt. Henry, *Coventry*.
1900. Brée, Sidney, *Manningtree*.

1894. Breen, Adrian Louis, *Canada*.
1918. Breese, Henry Walter, *Brixton*.
1918. Breese, Maurice Charles, *Westm.*
1900. Brehm, Robt. Almon, *Newfoundland*.
1888. Bremner, Ramsay Allan, *Canterbury*.
1905. Bremner, W.lt Chas P hner,*Clapton*.
1897. Bremr dge, R.H.,O.B E., *Trowbridge*.
1901. Brenan, Alex. Richd. M., *Chislehurst*.
1875. Brenchley, A. Dutton, *Denmark-hill*.
1902. Brend, William Alfied, *Temple*.
1894. Brennan, Josh. Rchd. Mary,*Stockport*.
1923. Brenner, Oscar, *Handsworth*.
1911. Brentnall, Thos. Creswell, *Gorton*.
1894. Brereton, Fredk. Sadleir, C.B.E.
1900. Breton, Hewlett, *Victoria, Aust*.
1895. Breton,Lancelot Moyle,*Southampton*.
1902. Bieton, Wm. Kenneth Dudoit, *R.N.*
1917. Brett, Arthur Granville, *Cranleigh*.
1897. Brett, Harry Clarence M., *Cranbrook*.
1876. Brett, John, *Melbourne, Victoria*.
1919. Brett, Percy Croad, *Hampstead*.
1891. Brett, William George, *Barnstaple*.
1896. Breuer, Adam August, *Finsbury-cir*.
1923. Brew, John Arthur, *Compton-street*.
1899. Brewer, Alex. Hampton, *Woking*.
1897. Brewer, Dunstan, *Ilkley*.
1904. Brewer, Henry Jeaffreson, *Dulston*.
1893. Brewer, Wm. Kenneth, *Hampstead*.
1837. Brewis,AndrewSeymour,O.B.E.,*N.Z.*
1915. Brewis, Charles Carrick, *Crouch End*.
1913. Brewitt, Bertram James, *R.N.*
1881. Brewitt, James Bunney, *Natal*.
1909. Brewster, Rex Carrington, M.C.
1886. Briant, Arthur John, *Helsby*.
1900. Brice, Henry Doyle, *Dukinfield*.
1850. Brice, John Fouiness, *Ruthin*.
1921. Brice-Smith,Harold F.,*AlderleyEdge*.
1897. Brickwell, Frank, *Stowmarket*.
1902. Bridge, John C., *Alderley Edge*.
1879. Bridgeford, Walter A. S., *W. Aust*.
1901. Bridger, Jas. Fdk. Edmd., *Barbados*.
1903. Bridger, John Dell, *Cricklewood*.
1905. Bridger, Robt. Daniel, *Biggleswade*.
1895. Bridger, Sydney, *Southend*.
1912. Bridges,Arth.B.H.,O.B.E,*R.A.M.C.*
1903. Bridges, David, *Malay Straits*.
1891. Bridges, Ernest C., *Courtfield-rd*.
1910. Bridges, Robert Francis, *R A.M.C.*
1891. Bridgman, Harry M. Weaver, *Sicily*.
1871. Bridgman, Henry Edwd., *Budleigh*.
1912. Bridgman, Roger Orme, *Queensland*.
1901. Brierley, Chas. Isherwood, *I.M.S.*
1881. Briggs, Chris. Duffield, *Leicester*.
1898. Briggs, George Fredeick, *Hull*.
1922. Briggs, Harold William, *Bude*.
1914. Briggs, Norman, *Willerby*.
1920. Briggs, Percy James, *Keston*.

1894. Briggs, Robt. Warden, *Birmingham.*
1923. Briggs, Thomas Fielden, *Putney.*
1873. Brigham, Henry Geo., *Boston Spa.*
1887. Bright, Archibald Leonard, *Brighton.*
1889. Brightman, F., O.B.E, *Broadstairs.*
1865. Brigstocke, Chas. A, *Haverfordwest.*
1896. Brigstocke, Percy Ward, *Baghdad.*
1892. Brimacombe, R. W., *Tunbridge Wells.*
1908. Brimblecombe,StanleyL.,*Burlesc'mbe*
1898. Brincker, Jn. August H., *Savoy-hill.*
1893. Brind, Harry Hauslow, *Byfleet.*
1901. Brinton, Arthur Green , *Transvaal.*
1882. Brinton, Roland Danvers, *Queen's-gte.*
1921.§Briscoe, Hylda C., *Gloucester-terr.*
1905. Briscoe, James Rynd, *Chippenham.*
1898. Briscoe, John Charlton, *Harley-st.*
1888. Briscoe, John Edward, M.C., D.S.O.
1880. Briscoe, John Frederick, *Alton.*
1913. Briscoe, Ralph Cay, *Hawkchurch.*
1907. Briscoe, Wm. Thomas, *Chippenham.*
1892. Brisley, Charles Walker.
1884. Bristow, William Moss, *Christchurch.*
1888. Bristowe,HubertCarpenter,*Wington*
1885. Brito, Philip Sebastian, *Ceylon.*
1909. Brito-Salazar, Jn. Manuel, *Trinidad.*
1919 §Britten, Ella M., *Grahamstown.*
1872. Brittin, Fredk. Geo. Morris, *N.Z.*
1918. Britton. Reginald Bertram, *Bristol.*
1923. Broadbent, Bernard, *Tottenham.*
1891. Broadbent, John F. H., *Seymour-st.*
1923.§Broadbent, Marjorie, *Hebden Bridge.*
1893. Broadbent, Walter, *Brighton.*
1916. Broadbridge, Harold G., *Finsbury-pk.*
1891. Broadhurst, Wm Jas., *Cape Colony.*
1875. Brock, Charles de Lisle, *Tooting.*
1913. Brock, Edwd. Albt. Parry, *St. Bart's.*
1923 §Brock, Enid Agnes, *Liverpool.*
1886. Brock, Ernest Henry, *Streatham.*
1923. Brockington, Frank, *Cardiff.*
1922. Brocklehurst, Geo. Lawton, *Ashford.*
1884. Brockliss, Edward Lumley, *Banbury.*
1919. Brockman, Edward P., *Liverpool.*
1887. Brockway, Archibald Birt, *Brisbane.*
1900. Brockwell, Jn. B. Chambers, *Walton.*
1905. Broderick, Fredk.Wm.,*Bournemouth.*
1903. Brodie, Desborough, *Tetbury.*
1869. Brodie,Edwd.Fitzger., *Wickham-mkt.*
1887. Brodie, Frederick Carden, *Shoreham.*
1919. Brodie, Wm., *Stamford-hill.*
1906. Brodrecht,Jn.Hy.Richd., *Washington*
1897. Brodribb, Arthur Hubert, *Guildford.*
1905. Brodribb, Arth.W'mson ,*St.Leonards.*
1900. Brodribb, Chas. Hildred, *I.M.S.*
1896. Brodribb, Ernest, *R A.M.C.*
1904. Brodribb, Francis Arth., *Yattendon.*
1886. Brodrick, Harry Edward.
1889. Brohier, Louis Cyrus, *Colombo.*
1923. 1860

1908. Brohier, Saml. Lindsay, *Gambia.*
1919.§Broman, Anna Bridget, *Sussex-pl.*
1923. Broman, Benjamin, *Manchester.*
1895. Bromet, Edward, *Rufforth.*
1883. Bromhead, Frank Hodson,*Streatham.*
1904. Bromley, James, *Castle Hedingham.*
1860. Bromley, Jn. Bourne, *C. Hedingham.*
1885. Bronner, Adolf, *Bradford.*
1861. Brook, Charles, *Lincoln.*
1899. Brook, Francis William, *Harley-st.*
1887. Brook, Henry Darvill, *Fareham.*
1909. Brook, Samuel Stanley,*Walworth-rd.*
1891. Brook, Tom Stanbury, *Chingford.*
1922. Brooke, Eric Barrington, *Croydon.*
1894. Brooke, Baron, *Melbourne.*
1923. Brooke, Ralph, *Lee.*
1880. Brookes, Fredk. Wm., *Westminster.*
1881. Brookes, Robert, *Debrugah, Bengal.*
1871. Brookfield, John Storrs, *Upminster.*
1868. Brookhouse, Chas. Turing, *Bromley.*
1919. Brookman, Hubert,*Woodside-pk -rd.*
1915.§Brooks, Alice D., *Park-road,* S.W.
1890. Brooks, Charles, *Chalfont St. Peter.*
1888. Brooks, Francis Aug., *Bedford-park.*
1885. Brooks, Jabez Pratt, *Brownswood-pk.*
1881. Brooks, James, *Blackburn.*
1916. Brooks, James, *Blackburn.*
1887. Brooks, Richard Philip, *Welbeck-st.*
1882. Brooks, Walter Tyrrell, *Oxford.*
1895. Brooks, William Patrick.
1865. Broom, Charles, *Victoria.*
1914. Broome,Fredk.C.Sedgwick,*Woodf'd.*
1915. Brophy, Cyril Mary, M.C., *R.A.M.C.*
1919. Brossy, Jean, *Vevey.*
1917. Broster,Edw.Davenport,*Wirksworth.*
1901. Brough, Daniel, *Battle.*
1892. Broughton,HaroldJulius,*Holland-pk.*
1905. Broughton, John Frederick, M.C.
1913. Broughton,Wm. Hackett, *Stockport.*
1911. Broughton-Alcock,Wm.,*Eastbourne.*
1922. Brown, Alan Wood, *Kilmacolm.*
1898. Brown, Alex., *Kentish Town.*
1890. Brown,Alfred, *Masham.*
1900. Brown, Allen Bathurst, *Salisbury.*
1904. Brown, Arthur C., *Sevenoaks.*
1913. Brown, Arthur Edward, *Colac, Vict.*
1909. Brown,ArthurJas.,D.S.O.,*R.A M.C.*
1881. Brown, ClarenceW. Haig, *Godalming.*
1880. Brown, Daniel Dorward, *Harrogate.*
1884. Brown, David Matthews.
1921.§Brown, Doris Kathleen, *Hampstead.*
1901. Brown, EdwardArcher,*Johannesburg.*
1904. Brown, Edwd. M., *Stony Stratford.*
1886. Brown, Edward Vipont, *Manchester.*
1893. Brown, Elijah, *Fulham.*
1920. Brown, Elliott Fraser, *Birmingham.*

1917   o

1898. Brown, Evelyn Kempson, *Salisbury.*
1888. Brown, Francis Joseph, *R.A.M.C.*
1860. Brown, Frederick Gordon, *Chigwell.*
1891. Brown, Frederick James, *Newark.*
1886. Brown, Fredk. Nathaniel, *Reigate.*
1896. Brown, Geo.Walter, *Hoopstad,S.Afr.*
1922.§Brown, Gwendolen Mary.
1892. Brown, Harold Corser, *Tipton.*
1919. Brown,HaroldMallows,*Johannesburg*
1896. Brown,HarryMewb.,*Market Drayton.*
1913. Brown, Herbert Horan, *Leeds.*
1914. Brown, Jas. Jackson, *King Edw.-rd.*
1898. Brown, Jas. Warburton, *Wimpole-st.*
1881. Brown, James Wm. Henry, *Leeds.*
1899. Brown, John, *Flixton.*
1918. Brown, John Clifford, *Rugby.*
1914. Brown, John E. Kelly, *Oamaru, N.Z.*
1921. Brown, John L. M., *Blackhorse-rd.*
1920. Brown, John Piercy, *Wallasey.*
1872. Brown, Joseph L'Oste, *Shifnal.*
1894. Brown, Jos. Norwood, *Hampstead.*
1915. Brown, LeonardG.,M.C.,*Bk. N.S.W.*
1837. Brown, Lewis Henry.
1921.§Brown, Lorna Phoebe, *Purley.*
1923.§Brown, Mary Grace, *Goring.*
1920. Brown, Osmond Hayman, *Teignm'th.*
1891. Brown, Reginald, *Rectory-road, N.*
1912. Brown, Robert Graham, *Brisbane.*
1896. Brown, Robert Tilbury, C.M.G.
1922. Brown, Robson Christie, *Sunderland.*
1892. Brown, Stanley Mewburn, *Birkdale.*
1875. Brown, Thomas, *Kennington-pk.-rd.*
1885. Brown,ThomasAlex.,*SuttonColdfield.*
1920. Brown, Thomas Anderson, *Plymouth.*
1909. Brown, Thomas Frederick, *Victoria.*
1875. Brown, Thomas Lloyd, *Hoxton.*
1900. Brown, Thomas Warren, *Wallington.*
1923.§Brown, Violet Woods, *Wallington.*
1888. Brown,WalterG.Stephens,*Wadworth*
1888. Brown, Walter Sigismund, *N.S.W.*
1923. Brown, William Aelred, *Newcastle.*
1883. Brown, William Henry, *Victoria.*
1920. Brown, William Mark, *Bank of N.Z.*
1916. Brown, Wm. Wallace K.,*Asylum-rd.*
1922. Browne, Anthony Mark Francis.
1905. Browne, Cuthbert G., C.M.G., D.S.O.
1887. Browne, Edwd. Granville,*Cambridge.*
1909. Browne, Edw. Moxon, *R.N.*
1900. Browne, Edward Wemyss, *I.M.S.*
1874. Browne, Geo. Buckston, *Wimpole-st.*
1885. Browne, Harold Elliott, *N.S.W.*
1902. Browne,HarrieSpencerD.,*Winchester.*
1870. Browne,HenryW.J..,O.B.E.,*Langley.*
1878. Browne, Horace Ximenes, *R.N.*
1877. Browne, James Wm., *Holland-pk.-av.*
1892. Browne, John James, *Murton.*
1867. Browne, John Walton, *Belfast.*

1907. Browne, Josiah, *Bromyard.*
1887. Browne, Robley Hy.Jn., O.B.E.,*R.N.*
1923. Browne, Samuel Noel, *Albrighton.*
1899. Browne, Thomas Walker S.
1902. Browne, William Walker, *R.A.M.C.*
1883. Browne-Carthew, R. H., *Ashley-pl.*
1896. Browne-Mason, H. O. B., D.S.O.
1887. Brownfield, Harry M., *Petersfield.*
1914. Brownfield, Owen D., O.B.E.
1887. Browning, Edgar, *Canada.*
1898. Browning, Paul Ransome, *Totton.*
1909. Browning, Sidv. Howard, *Harley-st.*
1922.§Brownstone, Margaret M., *Hackney.*
1899. Browse, George, D.S.O., *I.M.S.*
1906. Bruce, Olliver, *East Ham.*
1883. Bruce, Robert Marston, *Fulham.*
1858. Bruce, Samuel Nobie, *Holland-park.*
1893. Bruce, Wm. James, *Milford-on-S.*
1888. Bruce-Bays, James, *Grahamstown.*
1893. Bruce-Porter, Sir H. E. B., K.B.E.
1876. Brumell, Arthur, *Morpeth.*
1874. Brummitt, Robert, *S. Australia.*
1867. Brumwell, Geo. William, *Kendal.*
1916. Brumwell. John, *Gosforth.*
1881. Brunton, Chas. Edwd , *Walthamstow.*
1901. Brunton. John, *Endsleigh-gardens.*
1889. Brunton, Walt. Revner, *Birchington.*
1897. Brushfield, Arch. Nadauld, *Halifax.*
1886. Brushfield, Thomas, *Battersea.*
1898. Bruzaud, Alfd.Sigismund,*Greenfield.*
1920. Bryan, Charles Gourt, *Sheffield.*
1900. Bryan,Clem. Arth. Douglas,*Leicester.*
1864. Bryan, Edward, *R. Societies Club.*
1899. Bryan, Herbert James, *Chatham.*
1918. Bryan, Hugh Stanford, *Ampthill.*
1905. Bryan, John, *Liverpool.*
1865. Bryan, John Morgan, *Northampton.*
1912. Bryan-Brown, Douglas S., *China.*
1917. Bryant, Ernest H., *Tunbridge Wells..*
1888. Bryden,Francis W. Aug.,*Godalming.*
1905. Bryden, Ronald A., D.S.O.,*R.A.M.C.*
1900. Brydone,JamesM ,O.B.E.,*Charles-st.*
1918. Brydson, John Maurice, *Forest-gate*
1888 Bryett, Lewis T. Fraser, *Canonbury. .*
1893. Bryett, William Robert, *Drury-lane*
1921. Bryning, Frank Alfred, *Bromley.*
1893. Bryson, Leonard Horner, *St. Andrews.*
1919. Bubb, C. H , O.B.E., *Burlington-gds.*
1893. Buchanan, Archibald G., *Harley-st.*
1886. Buchanan, John, *Vauxhall.*
1905. Buchanan, Norman Duncan, *Ontario.*
1888. Buchanan, Rbt. J. M'Lean, *Liverpool.*
1892. Buck, Arthur Herbert.
1875. Buck, Charles William, *Settle.*
1919. Buck, Harold, *St. Thomas, Canada.*
1878. Buck, John Stirling, *Bromley.*
1883. Buck, Lewis Archer, *Farnworth.*

1866. Buck, Thos. Alpheus, *Ryde, I. of W.*
1886. Buckell, Edward, *Brit. Columbia.*
1911. Buckell, Ernest Fred. W., *Chichester.*
1911. Buckell, Monamy A. C., *Chichester.*
1903. Buckeridge, Guy Leslie, *Roy. Navy.*
1886. Buckland, Sydney Chas., *Wimbledon.*
1916 §Buckle, Isabel F., *Sherborne-lane.*
1915. Buckler, Eric Francis, *Willenhall.*
1890. Buckley, Charles Herbert, *Manchester.*
1912. Buckley, George Bent, *Greenfield.*
1922.§Buckley, Gladys Lieba.
1891. Buckley, Joseph Richard, *Redditch.*
1910. Buckley, Leonard, *R.A.M.C.*
1883. Buckley, Thos. William, *Thrapstone.*
1894. Buckley, Wm. Hv., *Poulton-le-Fylde.*
1913.§Buckley, Winifred F, *O.B.E.*
1923.§Buckmaster, Dorothy E. B., *Clifton.*
1883. Buckmaster. George Alfd., *Hampstead.*
1894. Budd, Wm. Hindshaw, *Cape Town.*
1899. Budd-Budd, Edwd. Jn., *Brighton.*
1893. Budden, Tice Fisher, *Crouch End.*
1921. Buddle, Roger, *Bank of N.Z.*
1923. Budge, Corydon Henry, *St. Budeaux.*
1917. Buendia, Nicolas, *Bogota, Columbia.*
1917. Buer, Wm. Barnes, *Whittlesford-bdge.*
1920. Bulcock, Carl Henderson.
1920. Bulcock, Joseph H., *Thornton-heath.*
1888. Bulger, Alfd. James, *Wolverhampton.*
1922. Bull, Arthur Gilbert, *Clapham.*
1906. Bull, Douglas Wm. A ,*Stony Stratford.*
1914. Bull, Frank Bocquet, *Herne-hill.*
1899. Bull, George Vernon, *Hoddesdon.*
1895. Bull, Harry Ashworth, *Gt. Haywood.*
1918. Bull, Henry Cecil H., *Stony Stratford.*
1876. Bull, James Weston, *Wimbledon.*
1916. Bull, Leslie Jas. Forman, *Stanwell.*
1892. Bull, Stanley Arthur, M.C , *N.Z.*
1914. Bull, William Edw. Hugh, M.C.
1917. Bulleid, Arthur, *Torquay.*
1900. Bullen, Charles Henry, *Stillington.*
1917. Bullen, Horace Braithwaite, *Ealing.*
1887. Bullivant, Samuel.
1898. Bullmore, Edwd. Augustus, *Wisbech.*
1896. Bullmore, Fredk. Guy, *Golder's-green.*
1888. Bullock, Charles Penry, *Oswestry.*
1887. Bullock, Roger, *Warwick.*
1922. Bulman, Michael W. B., *Oakhill-rd.*
1902. Bulstrode, Chris. Victor, *Shrewsbury.*
1901. Bulteel, Cecil Edward, *I.M.S.*
1879. Bulteel, Marcus Henry, *Guernsey.*
1923 §Bumstead, Helen, *Hastings.*
1896. Bumsted, Henry James, *Streatham.*
1898. Bunbury, Edwin Garrett, *Mullion.*
1893. Bunch, John Le Mare, *Park-street.*
1876. Buncombe, John Dobrie, *Cape Col.*
1890. Buncombe, Wm. Dewey, *Clifden-rd.*
1877. Bunny, Jos. Brice, *Weston-s.-Mare.*
2088

1905. Bunting, Edwd. Lancelot, *Worcester.*
1902. Bunting, Geo. Lantsbery, *Tonbridge.*
1893. Burch, Henry Edwin, *Portsmouth.*
1888. Burchell, Ernest, *Brighton.*
1898. Burch,Cyril Prichard, *Upton-on-Severn.*
1878. Burd, Geo. Vauhouse, *Okehampton.*
1900. Burd, Reginald Shirley, *Oaken.*
1908. Burdett, John Head, *Ealing.*
1894. Burditt, Ralph Austin, *Manchester.*
1921.§Burfield, Mary, *Hailsham.*
1900. Burfield, Thomas, *Hailsham.*
1920. Burford, Harold George, *Q. Anne-st.*
1896. Burges, Fdk. Aug. L'E., M.B.E.
1903. Burges, Richard, *Hartley Wintney.*
1906. Burgess, Arthur Savell, *W.Af.M.S.*
1872. Burgess, Edwd. Arthur, *Manchester.*
1906. Burgess, Robert, D.S.O., M.C.
1894. Burgess, Thos. Wm. W., *N.S.W.*
1870. Burgess, W. F. R., O.B.E., *Streatham.*
1877. Burgess, William Milner, *Frinton.*
1907. Burke, Gerald Tyler, *I M.S.*
1914. Burke, Noel Hawley Michael.
1918. Burkitt, Frederick Thomas, *Ealing.*
1905. Burman, Hugh Westley, *Transvaal.*
1897. Burn, Alfred, *Crawley.*
1873. Burn, Geo. Wilson, *Cromer.*
1910. Burn, John Southerden, *Richmond.*
1912. Burn, Ronald E. Russell, *Crewkerne.*
1913. Burn, Stacey Archer, *Richmond.*
1878. Burn, Stacey Southerden, *Richmond.*
1885. Burn, Thos. Wm. Barnett, *Cambridge.*
1920. Burnell, George Frederic, *Weybridge.*
1905. Burner, Laur. Henry, *Gillingham.*
1904. Burnett, Arthur Hill, *Southampton.*
1918.§Burnett, Ellinor M., *Southampton.*
1895. Burnett, Frank Marsden, *Sevenoaks.*
1891. Burnett, John Ridley, *Keswick.*
1895. Burnett, Leslie Burton, *New Zealand.*
1902. Burnett, Philip, D.S.O., *Montreal.*
1886. Burnett, Reuben, *Leek.*
1897. Burney, Chas. Dudley F., *New Cross.*
1906. Burney, Walter Hry. S., *R.A.M.C.*
1901. Burnford, Julius Meyer, *Q. Anne-st.*
1878. Burnie, Wm. Gilchrist, *Bradford.*
1921. Burnier, Edmond E. L., *Switzerland.*
1919. Burnier, Michel Henri, *French-hosp.*
1893. Burniston, Hugh S., C.M.G., *R.N.*
1921. Burns, Charles L. C., *Wimbledon.*
1887. Burns, Theo. Gilbt. Alex., *Welbeck-st.*
1895. Burns, William Thomas, *Carlisle.*
1895. Burnshaw, M. M., *Commercial-rd.*
1914. Burnside, Bruce, *Guy's-hosp.*
1886. Burnside, Eustace Aug., *R.A.M.C.*
1904. Burpitt, Harry Reginald, *Newport.*
1906. Burr, Wilfrid Buchanan, *Harrow.*
1908. Burr, Wm. Alex., *Fergus, Canada.*
1905. Burra, Launcelot Toke, *Aylesbury.*
2145 o 2

1885. Burrell, Arthur William, *Fareham*.
1915. Burrell, Charles Milwyn, *Brondesbury*.
1864. Burrell, Edwin, *Doughty-street*, W.C.
1921. Burrell, Ellis Morgan, *Brondesbury*.
1923. Burrell, John Trevor, *Winchester-av*.
1908. Burrell, Lancelot S. T., *Wimbledon*.
18J5. Burrell, Lionel Cottingham, *Kew*.
1895. Burridge, Henry Alfred, *Battersea*.
1904. Burridge, Jn. Harold, M.B E., *Slough*.
1903. Burroughes, Henry N., D.S.O.
1870. Burroughs, Jn. Edwd. Buckland, *Lee*.
1892. Burroughs, John Herbert, *Albion-rd*.
1894. Burroughs, Wm. John, *Oakley-sq*.
1894. Burrow, Thomas, *Lancaster*.
1896. Barrow, Vincent, *Bath*.
1907. Burrows, Arthur, *Manchester*.
1901. Burrows, Cresswell, *Cambridge*.
1888. Burrows, Walt. Horncastle, *Dulwich*.
1878. Barry, Henry Burry Pullen, *Oregon*.
1897. Burt, Albert Hamilton, *Hove*.
1887. Burt, Cyril C. Barrow, *Stratford-o.-A*.
1902. Burt, Joseph Barnes, *Burton*.
1916 §Burt, Margaret Stuart, *Eastbourne*.
1914. Burt, William, *Wimborne*.
1894. Burton, Arthur, *Cromer*.
1913. Burton, Chas. Frank, M C., *Norwood*.
1886. Burton, Charles Frederick, *Whitby*.
1896. Burton, Chas. George, *L. Edmonton*.
1806. Burton, Edwd. Theodore, *R. Navy*.
1880. Burton, F. Hy. M., *Lt.-Col. R A.M.C*.
1916. Burton, Gordon Ernest, *St. Bart's*.
1875. Burton, Hbt. Campbell, *Blackheath*.
1893. Burton, James Cecil, *Calne*.
1895. Burton, Leonard Lamning, *Canada*.
1898. Burton, Percy, *Newcast'e, Staffs*.
1891. Burton, Wm· Edward, *Frodsham*.
1885. Burton-Fanning, Fdk. Wm , *Norwich*.
1877. Bury, Judson Sykes, *Manchester*.
1920. Bury, Kenneth Entwisle, *Weybridge*.
1892. Bury, Reg. Frederick, *Leamington*.
1891. Bushfield, James, *Enfield*.
1878. Bush, Erasmus, *Highweek*.
1881. Bush, James Paul, C.M.G., C B.E.
1890. Bushnell, Frank George, *Plymouth*.
1905. Bushnell, Percy Charles, *Plymouth*.
1887. Buswell, F. R., C.M G., *R.A.M.C*.
1905. Butcher, Chas. Bazett D., *Queensland*.
1902. Butcher, Harry Hendy, *Chiswick*.
1923. Butcher, Thomas Bertram, *India*.
1918. Butcher, Trevor Aveling, *Battersea*.
1915. Butcher, Walt. Herb., *Wark-on-Tyne*.
1900. Butcher, Wm· James, *Worthing*.
1893. Butement, Wm., *Waverley, N.S.W*.
1896. Butler, Arthur George, *Penge*.
1890. Butler, Charles, *East Budleigh*.
1911. Butler, Cuthbert John, *Wealdstone*.
1912. Butler, Eustace N.,M B.E.,*Lynmouth*.
2202

1907. Butler, Frank, *Finsbury-square*.
1906. Butler, George G.,M.B.E., *W.Af.M.S.*
1882. Butler, Gilbert Edward, *Tasmania*.
1901. Butler, Harold B., M.B.E., *Guildford*.
1900. Butler, James Alfred, *Goldhawk-rd*.
1906. Butler, Percival, *Bulwell*.
1913. Butler, Percy Patrick. *Univ. Coll -hosp.*
1897. Butler, Sydney Geo., D.S O., *R.A.M.C*.
1912. But'er, Terence Campbell, *Tasmania*.
1895. Butler, Thomas Harrison, *Leamington*.
1901. Butler, Thomas Langton, *R.A.M.C.*
1894. Butler, William Barber, *Hereford*.
1909. Butler, William Harold, *Barnsley*.
1870. Butler, William John, *I.M.S.*
1877. Butler-Smythe, Albt. Chas., M.B.E.'
1908 Butt, Harold Thos. H., *Transvaal*.
1892. Buttar, Charles, *Inverness-terrace*.
1890. Butterfield, Nath. Aug., *Cape Town*.
1906. Butterworth, John, *Middleton*.
1882. Butterworth, Samuel, *R.A.M.C*.
1917. Battery, Harold Robert, *Finchley*.
1870. Button, Horace Gooch, *N.S.W*.
1907. Button, Martin Binns Studer, *Rye*.
1913. Button, Philip Norman, O.B.E.
1881. Buxton, Dudley W., *New Cavendish-st*.
1885. Buxton, Edward, *Great Crosby*.
1917. Buxton, Patrick Alfred, *Tonbridge*.
1904. Byam, William, O.B.E., *R.A.M.C.*
1891. Byass, Thomas Sprv, *Northampton*.
1906. Bye, Norman H., *Buckhurst-hill*.
1895. Byford, William Francis, *Ruthin*.
1893. Byles, Jas. Beuzeville, *Sackville-st*.
1922. Byrd, Colin Bostock, *Stafford*.
1918. Byrd, John Dutton, *Tarporley*.
1915. Byrne, Chas. Hugh C., *Kingston*.
1867. Byrne, James Peter.
1899. Byrne, John Scott, *Dublin*.
1913. Byrne, Joseph, *New York*.
1895. Byrne, Peter Kevin, *Clarence-gate-gds*.
1911. Byrne, Thomas Wafer, *Liverpool*.
1915. Bywater, Harold George, *Wigan*.

C.

1918. Cade, Charles Reginald, *Exeter*.
1897. Cade, Harry Mills, *Ecclesfield*.
1892. Cade, Henry Lowless, *Wallington*.
1875. Cadge, Wm. Hotson, O.B.E., *I.M.S.*
1896. Cæsar, Richd. T., D.S.O.. M.C.
1895. Caglieri, Guido Enrico, *San Francisco*.
1882 Caiger, Frederick Foord, *Stockwell*.
1923. Caiger, George Herbert, *Ropley*.
1907. Cairn, Myles Denton, *N. Finchley*.
1884. Caldecott, Charles, *Redhill*.
1918. Caldecott, Francis, *Redhill*.
1877. Calder, Aug. Barclay, *Northwood*.
2255

1888. Calder, Frank, *Darlington, N.S.W.*
1895. Caldicott, Chas. H., M.B.E., *Chobham.*
1923. Caldwell, William Alex., *Streatham.*
1915. Caldwell-Smith, Eric L., *Putney.*
1884. Caleb, Clement Cornelius, *Lahore.*
1909. Caley, Fredk. Goodman, *Wandsworth.*
1890. Caley, Henry Albert, *Ealing.*
1897. Caley, Thomas Aloysius, *Rotherham.*
1895. Caley, Wm. Birch, J. *Athenæum-club.*
1886. Callender, Eustace M., C.B.E.
1879. Callender, John Hawkes, N. *Shields.*
1885. Calrow, Thomas, *Mealsgate.*
1867. Calthrop, Christopher Wm., *I.M.S.*
1918. Calthrop, Gordon T , *Carlyle Club.*
1888. Calthrop, Lionel C. E., *Woodhall Spa.*
1894. Calverley, J. E. G., C.M.G., *Folkestone.*
1912. Calvert, Edward. *I.M.S.*
1885. Calvert, James, C.B.E., *Harley-st.*
1887. Calvert, John Telfer, C.I.E., *I.M.S.*
1887. Calvert, Wm. Dobree, *Sooke, B.C.*
1918. Calvo, Ricardo, *St. Thomas's Hosp.*
1909. Cam, Walter Holcroft, *Towcester.*
1879. Cama Rastamji Hormasji, *I.M.S.*
1907. Camacho, Angel, *Mexico City.*
1907. Camacho, Martin.
1876. Cambridge, Thos. Arth., *Crouch-hill.*
1902. Cameron, Alexander, *I.M.S.*
1891. Cameron, Allan Gordon R., *Durham.*
1883. Cameron, Chas. Ernest, *Montreal.*
1876. Cameron, Chas. H. Hone, *Eastbourne.*
1917. Cameron, Donald, *Hampton-hill.*
1889. Cameron, Ewan G., *Lossiemouth.*
1917. Cameron, Finlay, *Delny, N.B.*
1905. Cameron, Hector Chas., *Devonshire-pl.*
1900. Cameron, John, *Halifax, N.S.*
1908. Cameron. John Joseph. *Jamaica.*
1896. Cameron, Malcolm, *Royal Navy.*
1903. Cameron, Rbt. Miles F., *W. Austr.*
1923 §Cameron, Viola C., *Westbourne-terr.*
1898. Cammidge, PercyJohn, *Nott'gham-pl.*
1911. Campain, Joseph Henry, *Guy's-hosp.*
1921. Campbell, Albert Vincent, *Shelton*
1919 Campbell, Alexander Rae, N. *Scotia.*
1897. Campbell, Alfred, *Adelong, N.S.W.*
1895. Campbell, Archibald Jn., *Ross.*
1892. Campbell, Arthur Minton.
1904. Campbell, Chris. Addison, *Toronto.*
1904. Campbell, Colin Alex., *Toronto.*
1912. Campbell, Collin G. Hurst, *Southport.*
1918. Campbell, Duncan.
1912. Campbell, Fredk. Wm , *Cardiff.*
1914. Campbell, George Maclean, M.C.
1881. Campbell, Harry, *Wimpole-street,* W.
1887. Campbell, HenryJohnstone, *Bradford.*
1880. Campbell, Henry Wm., *Queensland.*
1890. Campbell, Jas. Tweedie, *Canada.*
1892. Campbell, John Alex. L ,O.B.E.,R.N.
2312

1894. Campbell, John Hay, D.S.O., C.B.E·
1882. Campbell, Samuel George, *Durban.*
1874. Campbell, Wm. Macfie, *Parkgate.*
1903. Campbell, Wm. Wellesley, B. *Guiana.*
1923.§Campbell-Meiklejohn, D.M., *Ken's'tn.*
1920. Campey, Gordon Nowell, *Liverpool.*
1903. Campiche, Paul, *San Francisco.*
1917. Campion, Oliver St. L., *Shortlands.*
1915. Campion, Rowland B., *Bank of Aust.*
1883. Camps, Samuel, *Trinidad.*
1895. Candler, George, *Black Torrington.*
1886. Candler. Wallace Harry Chas., *Stone.*
1908. Candy, George Spence, *Gordon-sq.*
1910. Candy, Ronald Herbert, *I.M.S.*
1909. Cane, Arth. Skelding, D.S.O.. O.B.E.
1910. Cane, Edw. G. S., D.S.O., R.A.M.C.
1908. Cane, Howard Jas. Barrell, *Belvedere.*
1907. Cane, Leonard Buckell, *Peterboro'.*
1911. Cane, Lionel Chas. Wm., *Reading.*
1915. Cane, Maurice Hereward, *Eastbourne.*
1896. Cann, Francis Jn. Hughtrede, *Dawlish.*
1860. Cann, Francis Mark, *Putney.*
1884. Cann, Ralph Thomas, *Fowey.*
1898. Cannan, David. *Forest-gate,* E.
1887. Canney, Hy. Edwd. Leigh, *Harley-st.*
1907. Canney, Jas. Robertson C., *Cambridge.*
1923. Canning, H. G. Richmond, *Onslow-sq.*
1863. Canny, Dennis Joseph, S. *Australia.*
1895. Cant, Arthur, *Coleshill.*
1888. Cant, Frederick, *Woodley.*
1915. Cant, Frederick Vaudrey, *Woodley.*
1911. Canti, Robert George, *Hampstead.*
1921. Cantin, Antoine Yves, *Mauritius.*
1910. Capell, John, *R.A.M.C.*
1922. Capener, Norman Leslie, *Crouch-hill.*
1887. Capes, Robert, *Denmark-hill, S.E.*
1914. Caplan, Samuel, *Cambridge-gardens.*
1876. Capon, Herbt. James, *Up. George-st.*
1899. Capper, Harold Selwyn, *Sydney.*
1921. Capps, Fdk. Cecil Wray, *Brondesbury.*
1875. Carcenac, Edward, *Mauritius.*
1894. Card, Alfred Herbert, *Muswell-hill.*
1893. Cardell, Edward Stewart, *Tonbridge.*
1919. Cardell, John D. M., *Victoria-street.*
1922.§Carden, Gertrude B. G., *Radlett.*
1895. Carden, Wm. Alfred, *Bothaville, S.A.*
1912. Cardew, Arthur B , M.C., *Cheltenham.*
1877. Cardew, Geo. A.. O.B.E., *Cheltenham.*
1903. Cardew, Hy. Jameson, *Chorley-wood.*
1897. Cardin, Herbert, *Ingatestone.*
1893. Cardinall, Charles Daking, *Willesden.*
1846. Cardozo, Frederick Vinay.
1882. Cardwell, Thomas, *Andover.*
1874. Carey, John Thomas, *R.A.M.C.*
1909. Carey, Richard Stocker, O.B.E.
1900. Carlé, Frederick Charles, *Byfleet.*
1922. Carleton, Alan William.
2369

1907. Carlill, Hildred Bertram, *Harley-st.*
1873. Carline, William Arthur, *Lincoln.*
1891. Carling, Albert, *Bristol.*
1922. Carling, William Russell, *Southsea.*
1904. Carlisle, Geoffrey, *R.N.*
1882. Carlyon, Edwd. Trewbody, *I. of W.*
1877. Carlyon, Thomas Baxter, *Corentry.*
1903. Carmalt-Jones, D. Wm., *Wimpole-st.*
1914. Carmichael, Duncan A., *Canada.*
1908. Carmody,ErnestP.,M.B.E.,*Tulehurst.*
1897. Carnes, William, *Leeds.*
1872. Carolan, Jas. Fredk., *New Zealand.*
1891. Carolin, George, *Bournemouth.*
1898. Carpenter, Geoffrey D. Hale, M.B.E.
1918. Carpenter, Hayward, *Highbury.*
1917. Carpenter, Jas. Edwin, *Bethnal-grn.*
1890. Carpenter, Wm. Stanley, *Deptford.*
1894. Carpmael, Cecil Edward, *Dulwich.*
1880. Carr, Alfred Alexander, *Cannes.*
1914. Carr, George d'R., M.C., *R.A.M.C.*
1908. Carr, George Francis, *Leyburn.*
1882. Carr, Thomas, *Blackpool.*
1908. Carr, Wm. Jas., *Roy. Austr. Navy.*
1915. Carrasco, Milton, *India.*
1903. Carr-Harris, Ferguson F., D.S.O.
1892. Carré, Louis Jn. Gerard, *Cape Col.*
1891. Carre-Smith, Hbt. Lovell,*Holland-pk.*
1889. Carrell,Geo.Northern Piccaver,*Ilford.*
1916. Carrier, Caro P. L., *Kentish-town.*
1885. Carrington, George Hedwig, *Birtley.*
1917. Carroll, Charles Herbert, *Southsea.*
1884. Carroll, Edw. Richd. Wm.C., *I.M.S.*
1901. Carroll, Francis Radcliffe, *Caterham.*
1920. Carroll, Louis E. R., *Ennis, Co. Clare.*
1898. Carron, Fredk. Burke, *Ontario.*
1911. Carruthers, Norman Stuart, *Reedham.*
1905. Carruthers, Walter Donald, *Derby.*
1898. Carsberg, Alfred Ernest, *Bruton.*
1922. Carson, Charles Oliver, *Canada.*
1897. Carter, Arthur Burnell, *Dartford.*
1899. Carter,Arth. Hunton, *Wolverhampton.*
1916. Carter, Arthur Stanley, *Elland.*
1916. Carter, Charles Noel, *Stoke-on-Trent.*
1919. Carter, Ernest Edwin, *Plumstead.*
1883. Carter, Eustace Geo., O.B E.. *Leeds.*
1894. Carter, Frederick John, *I. of Wight.*
1901. Carter, George Archibald, *Tunstall.*
1880. Carter, Godfrey, *Sheffield.*
1892. Carter, Hugh Ronald *Kensington.*
1893. Carter, John George, *New-Kent-rd.*
1917. Carter, Octavius Cyril, *Bournemouth.*
1923. Carter, Ralph Harlan, *Nova Scotia.*
1907. Carter, Sydney, *Snodland.*
1863. Carter, Thomas, *Richmond. Yorks.*
1881. Carter, Thomas Edward, *Yelverton.*
1891. Carter,Thos.Moravian,O.B.E ,*Bristol*
1887. Carter, Tyler Pleydell, *Chippenham.*

1888. Carter, Weldon Cragg, *Southport.*
1910. Carter, William Edgar, *St. Leonards.*
1888. Carter, Wm. Jeffrys Becher, *C. Col.*
1890. Carter, William Robson.
1923.§Cartledge, Marjorie F., *Richmond.*
1922. Cartledge, Norman E. D., *Hertford.*
1874. Cartwright, Alex., *Old Burlington-st.*
1892. Cartwright, Ernest Henry, *Ticehurst.*
1908. Carver, Alf. Edw. Arthur, *Birm'ham.*
1900. Carver, Arthur Edmund, *Torquay.*
1904. Carver, Norman Clifton, *Surbiton.*
1914. Cascaden, John Harold, *Toronto.*
1897. Case, Hugh Martin, *Fareham.*
1873. Cash, Alfred Midgley, *Torquay.*
1876. Cash, John Theodore, *Aberdeen.*
1918. Casper, Walter Mattocks,*Finchley-rd.*
1917.§Cass, Kathleen Lydia, *Preston.*
1871. Cass, Stafford Thos.. *Avonmore-rd.*
1914. Cassidi, Francis Laird, *Derby.*
1906. Cassidy, Colin, M.C., *R.A.M C.*
1905. Cassidy, Maurice Alan, *Q. Anne-st.*
1866. Casson, John Hornsey, *Brighton.*
1881. Castañeda, Tiburcio Perez, *Madrid.*
1887. Castel, Adolphus Leo, *Mauritius.*
1918. Castell, Samuel Percy, *Liverpool.*
1906. Castellain, Jn. Graham, *Bagshot.*
1916. Castle, Henry H., *Newport, I. of W.*
1878. Castle, Hutton, *Newport, I. of Wight.*
1886. Castle, Richard Field, *Barnsley.*
1920.§Catchpool, Dorothy Maud, *Enfield.*
1914. Catford, Eric, *Crouch End.*
1901. Cathcart, Geo. E , O.B.E., *R.A.M.C.*
1908. Cathcart, Samuel Earle, *Highgate.*
1922. Cathrall, Thomas Hope, *Wrexham.*
1905. Catling, Henry, *R.A M.C.*
1921.§Catmur, Linda, *S. Hackney.*
1889. Cato, Alexander McLean, *Forest-hill.*
1899. Cato, Charles Stanley, *R.A.M.C.*
1885. Cattell, George Trew, *Cromwell-rd.*
1899. Catterall, Cuthbert Geo , *Finchley.*
1876. Cattle, Charles Henry, *Nottingham.*
1910. Catto, Henry William, *Jamaica.*
1887. Caudwell, Eber, *Clapham-common.*
1888. Caudwell, Francis B. IIv., *Coggeshall.*
1902. Causton,Edwd.P.G.,O.B.F.., *Boxford.*
1888. Cautlev, Edmund, *Park-street.*
1923. Cave, Edw. Henry Paul, *Norwood.*
1883. Cave, Edward John, *Bath.*
1895. Cave, Francis William, *Victoria.*
1886. Cave, Frank Evans, *St. Leonards.*
1920 §Cave, Joan Katherine S., *Woking.*
1912. Cave, Percy Norman, *Mitcham.*
1886. Cavell, Herbert Bertram, *Fleet.*
1915. Cavenagh, John Bernard, M.C.
1918. Cavers, Francis, *Islington.*
1895. Cawley, George, *Natal.*
1901. Cawston, Albt. Edwd., *Wantage.*

1909. Cawston, Fredk. Gordon, *Natal.*
1892. Cazalet, Grenville Wm., *Sutton.*
1898. Cazaly, William Henry, *I.M.S.*
1915. Célestin, Louis Abel, M.C.
1916. Célestin, Louis Arthur, *Mauritius.*
1902. Cerswell, William Alfred, *Toronto.*
1915. Chacin-Itriago, L. G., *Venezuela.*
1898. Chadborn, Chas. Nugent, *Hove.*
1874. Chadwick, Alfred, *Stockport.*
1832. Chadwick, C. Montague, *Easingwold.*
1873. Chadwick, Geo. James, *Cape Col.*
1917. Chadwick, Harold, *Brooklands.*
1880. Chadwick, Jas. Morley, *Stockport.*
1883. Chadwick, John, *Rochdale.*
1920. Chadwick, John William, *Hindley.*
1915. Chadwick, Morley, *King's Lynn.*
1923. Chadwick, Norman Ellis, *Parkstone.*
1922. Chadwick, Samuel A. R., *Croydon.*
1904. Chaff, Thos. W., M.B.E , *Manchester.*
1879. Chaffey, Wayland Charles, *Hove.*
1906. Chaikin, George, *Norton Folgate.*
1900. Chalk, Charles Launder, *Essex.*
1901. Challans, Frank, *Upton Manor.*
1890. Challenor, Harry Sept , *Abingdon.*
1912. Challenor, Lionel Thos., *Manchester.*
1899. Challice, John Scott, *Southampton.*
1889. Challis, Harry T., *Walthamstow.*
1896. Challis, Oswald, O.B.E., *R.A.M.C.*
1922. Chamberlain, Digby, *Knaresborough.*
1921.§Chamberlain, Dorothy S., *Cautley-av.*
1905. Chamberlain, Durie A., *E. Sheen.*
1893. Chamberlain, Edwd. B., *Lostwithiel.*
1876. Chamberlain, Edwd. T., *Billingshurst*
1920. Chamberlain, Fredk Wyndham, *Lee.*
1891. Chambers, Alex. Jasper. *R.A.M C.*
1913. Chambers, Ennis Ratcliff, *Surbiton.*
1908. Chambers, Ernest James, *Doncaster.*
1922.§Chambers, Grace Dorothy, *Croydon.*
1909. Chambers, Guy O., M.C., *R.A.M.C.*
1884. Chambers, Hbt. Wm., *Goldhawk-rd.*
1897. Chambers, John Miles, *Aberdeen.*
1921. Chambers, S. B., *Sutton-in-Ashfield.*
1891. Chambers, Wm. Francis, *Folkestone.*
1915. Chambry, J. K. J., *The Hague.*
1918. Champney, John D'Arcy, *Bristol.*
1875. Champneys, Sir Francis Henry, Bart.
1914. Chand, Hari, c/o *Grindlay & Co.*
1863. Chandler, Edward, *A.M.S.*
1911. Chandler, Frederick G., *Lond.-hosp.*
1899. Chaplin, Clem. W., *Angmering.*
1896. Chapman, Algernon Vivian, *Croydon.*
1897. Chapman, Chas. L. G., *Grimsby.*
1867. Chapman, Chas. Wm., *Harley-street.*
1901. Chapman, Donald Poyntz, *R.N.*
1922. Chapman, Edw. Fredk., *Freshford.*
1906. Chapman, Fdk. Hercy M., *R.A.M.C.*
1866. Chapman, George, *Birmingham.*

1877. Chapman, Herbt. Fredk., *Richmond.*
1901. Chapman, John Ellis, *Loc. Gov. Bd.*
1875. Chapman, Paul M.,M.B.E.,*Hereford.*
1916. Chapman, Percival D. H., *Mill-hill.*
1895. Chapman, Walter, O.B.E., *Totnes.*
1899. Chapman, Wm. Daniel, *Windermere.*
1907. Chapman, William James, *Canada.*
1919.§Chappel, Marjorie C., *Coventry.*
1885. Chapple, Aubrey Durant, *Weybridge.*
1895. Chapple, R bt. Llewellyn, *Barnsley*
1897. Chapple, William Allan, M.P.
1893. Charles, Blackwell.
1907. Charles, Clifford Pendrill, *Hitchin.*
1898. Charles, Godfrey Eustace, *I.M.S.*
1906. Charles, Herbert, *Cricklewood.*
1897. Charles, John Roger, *Clifton.*
1921.§Charlesworth,Christbl.L.M.,*Woking*
1873. Charlesworth,Henry,C.M.G., *A.M.S.*
1890. Charlton,FrederickJohn,*Spennymoor*
1913. Charnock, Fredk. Sutton,*Manchester*
1895. Charsley, Gilbert Wm., *Sydenham.*
1888. Charsley, Robert Stephen, *Slough.*
1907. Chase, Robt. Godwin, *Chesterfield.*
1909. Chasker, Keshev S., *Indore City.*
1903. Chatelain, Victor Albert, *Goodmayes.*
1898. Chater, Harold John, *Royal Navy.*
1895. Chater, John Samuel, *Yeovil.*
1905. Chater, Thomas Andrew, *Natal.*
1897. Chatterton, Edgar, *Bishop's-road.*
1896. Chatterton, Harold, *Maida-vale.*
1917. Chaudhri, Bodh Raj, *India.*
1922. Chaudhri, Jhangi Ram.
1899. Chaudhuri, Subrid Nath., *Calcutta.*
1904. Chauncy, Jas. Hornidge, *N. S. Wales.*
1915. Chavasse, Francis Bernard, *Liverpool.*
1894. Chavasse,Howard Sidney,*S.Coldfield.*
1915. Cheal, Percival, *Crawley.*
1886. Cheale, Montague, *Uckfield.*
1920. Cheater, Geo. Wm., *Shaftesbury.*
1903. Cheatle, Cyril Thomas, *Burford.*
1904. Cheatle, William George, *Hanwell.*
1902. Cheese, Frederick Wm., *Harpenden.*
1899. Cheese, John Wm., *Northwood.*
1909. Cheesman, Alg. Edg. Percy, *R.N.*
1897. Cheesman, Herbt. Hilton, *New Zeal.*
1878. Cheetham, Walter Henry, *Leeds.*
1904. Chell, Geo. Russell Haines, *E. Africa.*
1914. Chellappah, S. Francis, *Ceylon.*
1897. Chenery, Arthur, *New South Wales.*
1898. Chennells, Ernest P., *Thornton-heath.*
1889. Chepmell,Chas. Wm. J., *Whitstable.*
1912. Cherrington, Douglas G., *Winchelsea.*
1879. Chesshire, Arth. E., *Wolverhampton.*
1894. Chesson, Herbert, *New Zealand*
1917. Chesterman, Clement C., O.B.E.
1900. Chetwood, Thomas, *Sheffield.*
1873. Chetwood, Wm., *Christopher-st.*, E.C.

1919. Cheua, Nai, *Bangkok, Siam.*
1913. Cheune, Nai, *Bangkuk.*
1897. Chevallier, Claude Lionel, *E. Africa.*
1921. Chevens, Leslie Chas. Fredk., *Lee.*
1884. Cheves. James Trelawny, *Plymouth.*
1914. Chevreau, Paulin Roger, *Redcliffe-sq.*
1871. Cheyne, George Edward, *Jamaica.*
1913. Cheyne, Wm. H. Watson, *Harley-st.*
1905. Cheyney, G. Hammond, *Caversham.*
1922. Chiappa-Sinclair, Alfd. J., *Southgate.*
1891. Chichester, Edward, *Colchester.*
1885. Chick-Lucas, Jas. R.G., *Brading, I. W.*
1891. Chidell, Claude Churchill, *Reading.*
1887. Chilcott,Arth. Edwd.,*Highg'teInfirm.*
1906. Chilcott, William W. D., *R.N.*
1901. Child, Francis Joseph, *Winchester.*
1895. Child,GeraldA.,O.B.E.,*Southampton.*
1900. Child, Harry Norman Rix.
1884. Child, Herbert, *Bordon, Hants.*
1903. Child, Stanley, *Horsham.*
1909. Child, Wm. Noel, *Hayward's-heath.*
1879. Childs, Christopher, *Looe.*
1879. Chillingworth, Andrew, *Bedford.*
1914. Chillingworth, Andrew J., *Bedford.*
1914. Chiplonkar, T. I., *c/o Cook & Son.*
1912. Chipp, Eric Edmund, *Highgate.*
1880. Chipperfield, T. J. B. P., *Epsom.*
1860. Chisholm, Edwin, *Sydney, N.S. W.*
1880. Chisholm, William, *Sydney, N.S. W.*
1907. Chissell, Percy John, *Ceylon.*
1881. Chittenden, Thos. Hillier, *Oakfield.*
1886. Cholmeley, Hy. Patrick, *Forest Row.*
1897. Cholmeley, Montague Adye, *Truro.*
1896. Chopping, Arthur, C.B., C.M.G.
1907. Chopra, Ram. Nath., *I.M.S.*
1889. Chowry Muthu, David J. A., *Wells.*
1890. Christal, Thomas Forster.
1921. Christian. Francis, *Bangkok.*
1900. Christian, John Beresford, *I.M.S.*
1869. Christian, John Griffith, *Rock Ferry.*
1922. §Christie, Anaple Frances M., *Ealing.*
1919. Christmas, Benj. Y. H., *Hilldrop-rd.*
1895. Christmas, Robert Wm. S., *Aldridge.*
1914. Christoffelsz, Edwin L., *Ceylon.*
1912. Christofferson, Per Emil, *Clifton.*
1886. Christopherson, Cecil, *St. Leonards.*
1918. Christopherson,Wilfr'd B.,*Swaffham.*
1877. Chubb, Wm. Lindsay, *Farnborough.*
1912. Chun, John Wing Hon.
1916.§Church,HesterMary,*Cartwright-gds.*
1921. Churcher, James Chas.. *Wandsworth.*
1884. Churcher, Rev. Thos. G., *Tunisia.*
1919.§Churchill, Alix Jeanné, *Kensington.*
1902. Churchill, Geo. Brooke F., *R A M.C.*
1917. Churchill, Henry Joseph C., *Havre.*
1903 Churchill, Herbt. Melville, *Brighton.*
1864. Churchill, John Foot, *Chesham.*

1897. Churchill, Jos. Henry, *Wembley.*
1907. Churchill, Spencer, *Ryde.*
1917.§Churchill, Stella, *Hampstead.*
1915. Churchouse, William King, M.C.
1874. Churchward, Albert,*Selhurst-rd,S.F.*
1898 Churton, John Gaitskell, *R.A.M.C.*
1862. Churton, Thomas, *Leeds.*
1870. Chute, Hy. Macready, *Cape C.,S. Afr.*
1915. Cieb, Ying-Jue, *Chinese Legation.*
1862. Clapham, Edward, *Wimbledon.*
1899. Clapham, Edward Wm., *Cavendish-pl.*
1903. Clapham, Harold, *Peterborough.*
1909. Clapham,HowardDennis,*Letchworth.*
1888. Clapham, John Thurlow, *R A.M.C.*
1904. Clapham, Roderic Arthur, *Hove.*
1808. Clapham, Stanley Cornell, *Martock.*
1881. Clapp, George Tucker, *Exeter.*
1876. Clapp, Robert, *Tavistock.*
1882. Claremont, Louis B., *Haverstock-hill.*
1921. Claremont, Louis E., *Golder's-green.*
1902. Claridge, Wm. Walton, *Gold Coast.*
1910. Clark, Alf. Ern. Dagnall. *N. S. Wales.*
1909. Clark, AlfredJoseph,M.C.,*R.A.M.C.*
1888. Clark, Brown, *Hornsey.*
1896. Clark, Francis Wm., *Wokingham.*
1876. Clark, Frederick, *Somers Town.*
1806. Clark, Henry Colbatch, *Hereford.*
1894. Clark, Henry James, *Wareham.*
1907. Clark, James Aitken, *R.A.M.C.*
1878. Clark,Sir Jas. R. A., Bt.,C.M.G.,C B.
1915. Clark, John Edward,*Stoke-on-Trent.*
1916.§Clark, Mabel Campbell, *Huntingdon.*
1888. Clark, Percy John, *Spital-sq.,* E.C.
1897. Clark, Reginald Wm., *Maida-vale.*
1895. Clark, Richd. Foster,*Roy. Navy.*
1891. Clark, William Adams, *Penge.*
1904. Clark-Hall, Jas. Richd. Alex., *R.N.*
1906. Clark-Jones, Edwin, *Streatham.*
1918. Clark-Kennedy.Arch.Edm.,*Ewhurst.*
1916. Clarke,Ailwyn Herbt.,M.C.,*Norwich.*
1912. Clarke, Albert James, *Streatham.*
1861. Clarke, Arthur, *Ingatestone.*
1904. Clarke, Arth. Allen F., *Bayswater.*
1887. Clarke, Arthur Edward, *Leeds.*
1899. Clarke, A. E.,M.B.E.,*Rickmansworth.*
1894. Clarke, Arthur Hopkins, *Hobart.*
1896. Clarke, Astley Vavasour, *Leicester.*
1908. Clarke, Cecil. *Bristol.*
1918. Clarke, Cecil Belfield
1884. Clarke, Chas. Frederick, *Plumstead.*
1900. Clarke, Edward, *Beaconsfield.*
1900. Clarke, Edward Revely, *Plymouth.*
1894. Clarke, Fielding, *Reading.*
1897. Clarke, Fredk. A. H., *R.A.M.C.*
1891. Clarke, Geo. Gilbert, *Wakefield.*
1873. Clarke, Geo. Mouat Keith, *Soho.*
1888. Clarke,Geo Saunder, *Or. River Prov.*

1896. Clarke, Harold W., *N. Kensington.*
1891. Clarke, Harry Ward, *Dorking.*
1899. Clarke, Hry. Hugh Rose, *Stourbridge.*
1878. Clarke, Henry Joy, *Doncaster.*
1893. Clarke, Hy. Rbt. S., *Wolverhampton.*
1896. Clarke, James, *Walthamstow.*
1884. Clarke, Jas. McFarlane, *Tobermore.*
1906. Clarke, John, *Rotherham.*
1923. Clarke, J. H. Kempe, *W. Bromwich.*
1912. Clarke, John Joseph, *Balloyherdin.*
1923. Clarke, John Maxwell.
1909. Clarke, John Peter, *Crosby.*
1901. Clarke, John Stephenson, M.C.
1889. Clarke, John Tertius, *Malay States.*
1912. Clarke, Jos. Douglas, *Sutton-Coldf'd.*
1870. Clarke, Joseph Hirst, *Transvaal.*
1912. Clarke, Kenneth Bleckly, *Fowey.*
1923. Clarke, Leslie Thomas Griffith, *Birm.*
1922 §Clarke, Madeleine Harvey, *Harpenden*
1921.§Clarke, Marion Constance V., *Scalby.*
1910. Clarke, Noel Leicester, *Singapore.*
1910. Clarke, Richd. Christ., O.B.E., *Clifton.*
1919. Clarke, Roger Heine, *Trevorin-rd.*
1886. Clarke, Samuel Arathoon, *Horley.*
1904. Clarke, Sidney Herbert, *St. Albans.*
1912. Clarke, Thomas, *Burnley.*
1906. Clarke, Thos. Alex, *Bolingbroke-gr.*
1889. Clarke, Thos. Henry, *Poplar.*
1896. Clarke, Walter Travers, *Leeds.*
1886. Clarke, Wm. Frederick, *Toronto.*
1880. Clarke, William Jenner, *Exmouth.*
1897. Clarkson, Colin Campbell, *Watford.*
1911. Clarkson, Ernest R. T., *Cambridge.*
1885. Clarkson, Frank Cecil, *I.M.S.*
1885. Clarkson, Thos. H. Fredk., *R.A.M.C.*
1881. Clatworthy, Herbert, *N.S Wales.*
1920. Clavier, G. H. A. P., *Stamford-hill.*
1905. Clay, Cecil Ernest, *Dewsbury.*
1870. Clay, Charles, *Dewsbury.*
1895. Clay, David Lloyd, *New Zealand.*
1902. Clay, Ernest Langsford, *Birmingham.*
1895. Clay, Francis Edmund, *Brixton.*
1867. Clay, Geo. Langsford, *Birmingham.*
1902. Clay, James Duncan, *Brockley.*
1912. Clay, R. Challoner Cobbe. *Gillingham.*
1886. Clay, Wm. Rudolph, *Sydney, N.S.W.*
1919. Clayre, Oscar T 1. C. de H.
1905. Clayton, Arthur Ross. D S.O., *S. Aust.*
1888. Clayton, Chas. H , *Hampstead.*
1912. Clayton, Cyril J. Weston, *Blenheim-cr.*
1907. Clayton, Edwd Bellis, *Devonshire-pl.*
1898. Clayton, Ernest Tomlinson, *Kimberley.*
1907. Clayton, Frank, *Leamington.*
1884. Clayton, Geoffrey Sherborne, *New Z.*
1901. Clayton, John Cecil, *Cricklewood.*
1890. Clayton, Jn. Hazlewood, *Birmingham.*
1875. Clayton, Joseph Everett, *S. Africa.*
2768

1915. Clayton, Jos. W., *Edwardstown, S.A.*
1923. Clayton, Thos. Jones, *Stamford-hill.*
1896. Cleary, Augustine P. D.
1881. Cleaver, William Fidler, *Trinidad.*
1918. Clegg, Edwin Alfred, *Douglas.*
1923. Clegg, John Edward, *Pre twich.*
1914. Clegg, Marcus Thomas, *St. But's.*
1891. Clegg, Richard, *Accrington.*
1901. Clemens, Jas. Ross, *St. Louis, U.S.A.*
1917. Clément, Antonio Mario, *Panama.*
1906. Clementi-Smith, Herbt. D , *Sloane-st.*
1901. Clements, Edwd. Cecil, *Lincoln.*
1920. Clements, Gilbert Leedham, *Moseley.*
1917. Clements, William Arnold, *Moseley.*
1893. Clemesha, John Craig.
1895. Clemesha, W. Wesley, C.I.E., *I.M.S.*
1891. C.emmey, Wm. Newlands, *Bootle.*
1894. Clendinnen, Wm. McEntive, *Cannock.*
1865. Cleve, Richd. Plowman. *Lincoln's-inn.*
1897. Cleveland, Arth. John, *Norwich.*
1914. Cleveland, Francis Howard, *Bedford.*
1888. Cleveland, Henry Francis, *I.M.S.*
1904. Cleveland, John Wheeler, *St. Albans.*
1889. Cleveland, Robert Achilles, *Cyprus.*
1907. Cleverton, Thos. Chas. Albt , *Saltash.*
1896. Clifford, Frank Chas. W., *Swansea.*
1897. Clifford, Harold, *Manchester.*
1872. Clifford-Eskell, M. M., *Maida-vale.*
1910. Clifford, Reg. Charles, D.S.O., *I.M.S.*
1887. Clifford. Thomas, *Stalybridge.*
1891. Clift, Hugh, O.B.E., *Royal Navy.*
1881. Clifton, Frederick William, *Sheffield.*
'914 Clifton, George Frederick, *Sheffield.*
1894. Clindening, Fredk. Talbot D., *China.*
1915. Cline, Eric Clarence, *Weymouth-st.*
1901. Clitherow, Herbert George, *Peckham.*
1878. Clitherow, Robt. Edward, *Dulwich.*
1921. Cloake, Cecil Stedman, *Rochester.*
.1915. Cloake, Philip Cyril P., *Rochester.*
1906. Close, John Basil, *Canada.*
1897. Cloud, Frank H. L., *New Buckingham.*
1906. Clough, Alfred Hollier, *Esher.*
1913. Clough, Irene Nancy, *Bristol.*
1889 §Clough, Joseph, *Hunslet.*
1923. Clouston, Eric Crosby T., *Arlesey.*
1923.§Clouston, Olive G., *Arlesey.*
1900. Clover, Martin, *Cambridge.*
1897. Clowes, Ernest Francis, *Colchester.*
1856. Clowes, Francis, *Stalham.*
1879 Clowes, Herbt. Alfred, *Bayswater.*
1877. Clowes, Joseph Smith, *Queensland.*
1890. Clowes, Norton Burroughs, *Reading.*
1889. Clowes, Wm. Fdk. Albert, *Colchester.*
1876 Clubbe. Chas. Percy Barlee, *Sydney.*
1920 §Clulow, Florence R., *Haverstock-hill.*
1908 Cond, Claude Norman. M.C. *Walton.*
1886. Coad, John Edwin, *Royal Navy.*
2825

1893. Coad, Stanley Allan, *Farnham.*
1921. Coad, Wm. Elwin Raymond,*Canada.*
1907. Coalbmk, Robt. Malcolm,*Teddington.*
1899. Coates, Frederick Arthur, *Whitchurch.*
1878. Coates, George, *Rugby.*
1864. Coates, Geo. Alex. Augustus.
1894. Coates, Richard, *Gt. Barford.*
1915. Coates,VincentMiddleton,M.C.,*Bath*
1881. Coates,W., C.B., C.B.E., *Manchester.*
1872. Coates, Wm. H., *Hucknall Torkard.*
1889. Coates, William Henry, *Patrington.*
1859. Coathupe, Edwin Weise, *Oxford.*
1918. Cobb, Charles Eric, *Shortlands.*
1919.§Cobb, Enid M. M , *W. Kensington.*
1917. Cobb, Geoffrey Francis, *Rochester.*
1910. Cobb, Ivo Geikie, *Seymour-street.*
1862. Cobb, John Fredc., *Fitzroy, Vict.*
1891. Cobb, Wm. Ernest Stanley, *Tooting.*
1897. Cobbledick, Arth.Stanbury,*Bolton-st.*
1874. Cobbold, Chas. Spencer Waller, *Bath.*
1920. Coburn, Maurice, *West Hampstead.*
1894. Cock, Chas. Jas. Edwd., *Royal Navy.*
1903. Cock, Frederick, *Royal Navy.*
1883. Cock, Frederick Wm., *Randolph-rd.*
1896. Cock, George Herbert, *Rhodesia.*
1914. Cock, Gerald, *Plymouth.*
1907. Cock, Jas. Lyall, *Truro, Nova Scotia.*
1879. Cock, John, *Exmouth.*
1878. Cock, Morris Fisher, *Ashford.*
1910. Cock, Reginald, *Bethnal-green.*
1911. Cock, Thomas, *Royal Navy.*
1875. Cock, Williams, *Salcombe.*
1917. Cockayne, Alan Andreas, D.S.O.
1871. Cockburn, Sir John Alex., K.C M.G.
1882. Cockburn,LestockWeatherley,*C'nada*
1893. Cockburn, Robt. Pitcairn, *Ealing.*
1905. Cockcroft, George, *Middleham.*
1911. Cockcroft, Herbert Edw., *Southport.*
1860. Cockcroft, John, *Middleham.*
1915. Cockcroft, Wm. Lonsdale, *R.A.M.C.*
1880. Cockell, Edward Senton, *Grantham.*
1877. Cockell, Frederick Edgar, *Dalston.*
1917. Cocker, Albert Benj , *Palmer's-green.*
1887. Cockerton, Herbert, *Transvaal.*
1891. Cockill, Thomas Treffry, *Midhurst.*
1887. Cockill, William Baron, *Kendal.*
1918. Cocking, Alf. Wilkinson, *Torquay.*
1910. Cockrem, Guy Barton, *Royal Navy.*
1922. Cockshut, Rowland Wm., *Ormskirk.*
1885. Codd, Henry Robinson, *Ontario*
1867. Codrington,Jn.Fredc.,*Orange,N.S.W.*
1921. Cody, William Ernest, *Goldhawk-rd.*
1884. Coe, Henry Clark, *New York.*
1915. Coffin, Stephen Walter, *Hendon.*
1918.§Cogan, Kathleen Mary, *Bristol.*
1870. Cogan, Lee Fyson, *Northampton.*
1920. Coghlan, John Joseph, *Stamford-hill.*
2882

1898. Cogswell, Philip Darc, *Bromley.*
1880. Cohen, Alg. Aaron, *Sydney.*
1908. Cohen, Bertram, *Sidmouth.*
1918. Cohen,Charles Benjamin, *Limpsfield.*
1923. Cohen, Emmanuel, *Leeds.*
1919. Cohen, Harris, *Cardiff.*
1916. Cohen, Hyman Maurice, *Withington.*
1920. Cohen, Hyman S , *Doornfontein, S.A.*
1922. Cohen, Jacob, *Manchester.*
1896. Cohen, Joseph, *Aldershot.*
1922. Cohen, Julius, *Priory-road.*
1913. Cohen, Louis David, *Gracechurch-st.*
1922. Cohen, Morris Joshua, *Liverpool.*
1914. Cohen, Sam Nathaniel, *Leeds.*
1919. Cohen, Simeon Moses, *Cardiff.*
1892. Coke, Edmund P. Isaacs, *Sinclair-rd.*
1904. Coker, Alfred Philip, *New Zealand.*
1888. Colborne, George, *Bungay.*
1886. Colborne, Wm. John, C.B., *R.N.*
1916. Colborne, Wm. John, *Royal Navy.*
1892. Colclough, Wm. Frank, *Sidmouth.*
1894. Coldicott,Wm Rimell,*Hammersmith.*
1922. Coldrey, Eric Arthur, *Purley.*
1923. Coldrey, Ronald Shearsmith. *Purley.*
1916. Coldwell, Walter Herbert, *Harrow.*
1903. Cole, Arthur Frederick, *China.*
1920. Cole, Bernard Hedley, *Whitchurch.*
1921.§Cole, Doris Elizabeth, *Mansfield.*
1887. Cole, Francis, *Deloraine, Tasmania.*
1895. Cole, George, *Nottingham.*
1906. Cole, Horace Godden, *Liverpool.*
1897. Cole, John Wm. Edwd., *Wishford.*
1922. Cole, Leslie Barrett, *Beckenham.*
1912. Cole, Percival Courtney, *Whitchurch.*
1889. Cole, Robt. Henry, *Upp. Berkeley-st.*
1887. Cole, Samuel John, *Bideford.*
1900. Cole, Thos. Edwin Cecil, *Leamington.*
1915.§Colebrook, Dora Challis, *Compton-st.*
1886. Coleclough, John Arthur,*Winchester.*
1890. Coleman, Alfd. Thomas, *Leicester.*
1897. Coleman, Edwd. H., *Wolverhampton.*
1895. Coleman, Ernest, *Ilford.*
1900. Coleman, Frank, *Harley-street.*
1923. Coleman, Frank Stuart, *Downs-pk -rd*
1894. Coleman,James George Blyth,*Derby.*
1895. Coleman, James Jordan, *Bridlington.*
1896. Coleman, Maurice Were, *Reading.*
1890. Coleman, Percy, *Clacton-on-Sea.*
1885. Coleman, Wm. Edwaid, *Wednesbury.*
1871. Coleman, Wm. Franklin, *Chicago.*
1878. Colenso, Robt. John, *Southwell-gdns.*
1901. Coleridge, Alfd.,*Moreton Hampstead.*
1890. Coles, Charles, *Oxford.*
1881. Coles, William James, *Croydon.*
1876. Coley,Fredc. Collins,*Newcastle-on-T.*
1913. Collar, Frank, *E. Africa M. S.*
1906. Collard,BerullMolesworth,*Dorchester.*
2939

1894. Collcutt, Arthur Maurice, *Brighton.*
1880. Colledge, Lesley Robert, *Steyning.*
1875. Collenette, F. de B., *I. of Barra.*
1907. Collet, Gilbert Golding, *R.A.M.C.*
1918. Colley, Thomas, *Lytham.*
1920.§Collie, Alison Margaret, *Balcombe.*
1914. Collie, Jn.Robt.Mitchell, *Torr'yton-sq.*
1911.§Collie, Mavsie A.M., *Wellington, N.Z.*
1888. Collier, *Charles.*
1922.§Collier, Doris Bell, *Headley.*
1922 §Collier, Dorothy J., *Grove End,* W.
1895. Collier, Henry William, *Hampstead.*
1920.§Collier, Isabel Martha, *Liverpool.*
1921.§Collier, Ivy, *Oxford.*
1894. Collier, Jas. Stansfield, *Wimpole-st.*
1894. Collier, Walter Edgar, *Maidstone.*
1880. Collier, William, *Oxford.*
1914. Collier, Wm. Tregonwell, M.C.
1906. Collingham, David H, *Gerrard'sCross.*
1877. Collingridge, William, *Goudhurst.*
1905. Collingridge, Wm. Rex, *Goudhurst.*
1917. Collings, Bernard Stanley, *Guernsey.*
1881. Collings, Chas. d'Auvergne, *Guernsey.*
1895. Collings, Dudley Willis, *Southwold.*
1891. Collings, Edwd. Beresford, *Barnsley.*
1888. Collington, Frank Arnott, *Coventry.*
1879. Collington, John Wheler, *Kibwoith.*
1886. Collingwood, Fdk. Wm., *Park-place.*
1889. Collins, Algernon Boniface, *Yapton.*
1884. Collins, Arthur Ward, *Ulverston.*
1914. Collins, Barry K. Tenison, *Cardiff.*
1920.§Collins, Beatrice L., *Trebovir-rd.*
1890. Collins, Edward Tenison, *Cardiff.*
1909. Collins, Eric Abdy, *Yoxford.*
1890. Collins, Ethelbert, *Sawbridgeworth.*
1907. Collins, Francis Garland, *Plaistow.*
1922. Collins, Frederick Michael.
1878. Collins, George Duppa, *Broseley.*
1885. Collins, Geo. Fletcher, *Sutton Bridge.*
1881. Collins, Geo. Wm., *Wanstead, N.E.*
1875. Collins, Henry Abdy, *Saxmundham.*
1919. Collins, Henry N. W., *Up Tooting.*
1915. Collins, Hugh Michael, *S. India.*
1894. Collins, John Boniface, *Burnham.*
1890. Collins, John Norton, *Peterborough.*
1917. Collins, Joseph Clinton, *Chingford.*
1923. Collins, Leon, *Silksworth.*
1901. Collins, M. Abdy, O.B.E., *R A.M.C.*
1882. Collins, Octavius Aug. Glasier, *Bath.*
1891. Collins, Richard Hawtrey, *E. Ham.*
1884. Collins, William C. Glasier, *Brewham.*
1918. Collins, William, *Sutton-in-Ashfield.*
1876. Collins,W.E.,C.M G., *Wlington,N.Z.*
1899. Collinson, Francis Chas., *Rotherham.*
1885. Collinson, Fredk. William, *Preston.*
1894. Collis, Arthur John, *Newcastle-on-T.*
1896. Collis, Edgar Leigh, *HomeOffice,* S.W.

1898. Colls, Percy Cooper, *Cranbrook.*
1898. Collum, Rowland, *Nottingham.*
1893. Collyer, Brice, *Croydon.*
1884. Collyer, James Ralph, *Playden.*
1900. Collyns, John Moore, *Uganda.*
1919. Collyns, Percival Charles, *Dulverton.*
1882. Collyns, Robert John, *Dulverton.*
1881. Colman, Geo. Maurice H., *R.A.M.C.*
1886. Colman, Walt. Stacy, *Wimpole-st.*
1904. Colmer, Cecil, *Crewkerne.*
1892. Colmer, Ptolemy Augustus, *Yeovil.*
1905. Colmer, Vyvian, *Crewkerne.*
1877. Colquhoun, Daniel, *Dunedin, N.Z.*
1886. Colquhoun,Wm.Brooks, *Bloomsbury.*
1868. Colson, Edward, *I. M. S., Southsea.*
1879. Colt, Thos. Archer, O.B.E., *Portsea.*
1898 Coltart, Guy Hemming, *Fulham.*
1872. Coltart, William Wilson, *Epsom.*
1890. Colvin-Smith, Rbt. C. M., *Cromer.*
1900. Colwell,Hector Alfd.,*Middlesex-hosp.*
1891. Colyer, Arthur Reg., *Beckenham.*
1912. Colyer, Claude Gray, O.B.E., *Reigate.*
1907. Colyer, Horace Charles, *Guildford.*
1898. Colyer, Stanley Wm. R., *Cape Town.*
1884. Comber, Arthur W., *Oxford.*
1886. Comber,Chas.Thos.T.,O.B.E.,*Catf'rd*
1887. Comerford,BeaumontH.,*Chester-terr.*
1863. Compson, Jn. Chas., *Bridge of Allan.*
1913. Compston, George Dean, *Hastings.*
1913. Compton, A. G. W., *R.A.M.C.*
1896. Compton, Thomas, *Harefield.*
1864. Compton, Thomas A., *Parkstone.*
1907. Comyn, Arthur Fitzwilliam, *Hythe.*
1912. Comyn, Harold F., *Surbiton.*
1900. Comyn, Kenneth, *R.A.M.C.*
1893. Conder, Alfred Hartwell, *Bognor.*
1895. Conford, Geo. James, *Felixstowe.*
1923.§Connan, Annie Eveline, *N. Malden.*
1913. Connan, Donald Murray, *Old-street.*
1923. Connan, Peter, *Camberwell.*
1895. Connell Arthur Mayers, *Sheffield.*
1895. Connell, Walt. T., *Kingston, Canada*
1908. Connellan, Edmund Victor, *Newport*
1907. Connellan, Percival Sandys, *I M.S.*
1870. Connolly, Benjamin B , C.B., *A.M.S.*
1914. Connolly,Edwd.Worthingt'n,*Canada.*
1887. Connolly, Frank Glynn, *Brisbane.*
1896. Connor, Geo. Washington, *Newry.*
1918. Conoley, Oliver Francis,*Forest-gate.*
1885. Conolly, Charles Hamilton.
1907. Conran, Philip Crawford,*Nyasaland.*
1895. Constable, John Cecil, *Brixton.*
1912. Constant, Charles Fredk., *Grave-end.*
1856. Constant, Fredk. George, *I.M.S.*
1891. Constant, Thomas Edward, *York.*
1917. Constantin, Julien David, *Greenwich.*
1910. Contractor, Ardeshir K., *Univ. Coll.*

1889. Conway, Aubrey, *Stockport.*
1889. Conway, Basil Wiseman, *Longsight.*
1902. Coode, Claude Lionel, *Strond.*
1881. Cook, Augustus Henry, *Hampstead.*
1908. Cook, Ernest Neville, *Uganda.*
1893. Cook,HarryFr'uklyn,*Mudgee,N.S W.*
1854. Cook, Henry, *I M.S., Lee-on-Solent.*
1906. Cook, Isaac Reginald, *Woodford.*
1904. Cook, John, M.C , *Newport, Mon.*
1902. Cook, Joseph Basil, *Marloes-road.*
1876. Cook, Jos. Belcher, *Great Missenden.*
1881. Cook, Philip Inkerman, *Bromley.*
1916. Cook, Philip Nield, *Ealing.*
1887. Cook, Saml. Bird, *Askam-in-Furness.*
1914. Cook,William John,*Sudbury,Canada.*
1907. Cook,WilliamWarner, *W. Hartlepool.*
1887. Cooke, Albert Wm., *Northampton.*
1887. Cooke, Cecil Whitehall, *Cricklewood.*
1890. Cooke, Charles Michael.
1917. Cooke, Cyril J. Chesterfield, *Derby.*
1874. Cooke, Sir Edward Marriott, K.B.E.
1913. Cooke,EdwardR Cecil,M.C.,*Sheffield.*
1915. Cooke, Ernest James, *New Zealand.*
1903. Cooke, Francis Gerald H., *Westcliffe.*
1889. Cooke, Francis Henry, *Birch.*
1894. Cooke,FrederickArthur,*Haddenham.*
1923. Cooke, George Gervase, *Oldbury.*
1890. Cooke, George Harry, *St. Helen's.*
1917. Cooke, Gunaratnum F., *Highbury.*
1913. Cooke, Herbert W.. *Weston-s.-Mare.*
1889. Cooke, John Ambrose, *Hereford.*
1899. Cooke, John George, *Walsall.*
1895. Cooke,Martin Alfd ,O.B.E.,*Norwood.*
1923. Cooke, Norman Broadbent,*St Helen's.*
1906. Cooke, Owen C. P., *R.A M.C.*
1901. Cooke, Reginald Torriano, *Ventnor.*
1919. Cooke, Richard Alphonso, *Aspull.*
1922. Cooke, Robert Hunt, *Hendon.*
1915. Cooke,RonaldCampbell,M.C.,D.S.C.
1914. Cooke, Stephen Harold, *Prahran, V.*
1888. Cooke, Thomas Alfred B., *Hove.*
1912. Cooke, Wm. Albert, *Muswell-hill.*
1875. Cooke, William Conway, *Baynor.*
1892. Cooke, William Henry, *Bath.*
1894. Cooley, Alfred Glover, *N.S. W.*
1915. Coomaraswamy, Eleyathamby, *Ceyt.*
1881. Coombe,Albt.Townsend,*Notting-hill.*
1882. Coombe, Charles Frederick, *Sheffield.*
1917. Coombe, Ernest James, *Thorverton.*
1891. Coombe, Thomas Sandby, *Hoo.*
1907. Coomber, Arth. B'champ. *Shoreditch.*
1917. Coombes, George Wilfred, *Wigan.*
1904. Coombes, Percival Chas., *Merstham.*
1918. Coombs, Cyril George, *Radstock.*
1909. Coombs,HaroldMartinMcC.,*Bedford.*
1866. Coombs, Rowland Hill, *Bedford.*
1852. Coombs, Savill James.

1913. Coope, George Malcolm, *Farnworth.*
1889. Cooper, Ardaseer D., *Bombay.*
1870. Cooper, Arthur, *Harrogate.*
1892. Cooper, Arth. Tanner,*Gt. Portland-st.*
1900. Cooper, Charles Miner,*San Francisco.*
1892. Cooper, Dossabhoy Nowrojee.
1888. Cooper, Edward. *R.N., Bournemonth.*
1896. Cooper, Edward Harold, *Radlett.*
1875. Cooper, Ernest Fredk., *Belsize-rd.*
1894. Cooper, Francis Bastow, *Ramsgate.*
1898. Cooper, Frank, *Birmingham.*
1831. Cooper, George Fredk., *Loughton.*
1911. Cooper,HaroldAlex., *Wellington,N.Z.*
1896. Cooper, Harold M., O.B.E.,*Hampton.*
1893. Cooper, Harry, *Surbiton.*
1897. Cooper, Harry Gordon, M.B.E.
1890. Cooper, Harry Joseph, *Lyme Regis.*
1904. Cooper, Henry, D.S.O., *Royal Navy.*
1900. Cooper,HenryCreemer,*Gloucester-rd.*
1890. Cooper, Hy. Spencer, *Peterborough.*
1920.§Cooper, Joan, *Char. X.-hosp.*
1903. Cooper, John Sephton, *Clitheroe.*
1890. Cooper, Ludford, *Rochester.*
1916. Cooper, Mervyn Clement, M.C.
1918. Cooper, Norman C., *Winscombe.*
1876. Cooper, Peter, *Blackheath.*
1895. Cooper, Rbt. M. Le H., *Wimpole-st.*
1881. Cooper,Walter, *Barnstaple.*
1909. Cooper, Walter Edward, *E. Harling.*
1917. Cooper, Walter Tyrell, *Abergavenny.*
1905. Cooper, Wilbye, *Leeds.*
1923. Cooper, William Francis, *Watford.*
1910. Cooper, William Russell, *Bristol.*
1912. Cooray, Denis Clarence, *Ceylon.*
1909. Coorey, Edward Abraham, *Ceylon.*
1900. Cope, Gilbert Edgar, *Vauxhall.*
1901. Cope, Ricardo, *Bingham.*
1917. Copeland, Alex. John, *St. Bart's.*
1888. Copeland, Wm. H. L , *S. Kensington*
1873. Copeland, William Lowry, *Chicago.*
1894. Copeman, Alfd. Heathcote, *Brighton.*
1887. Copeman,SydneyArth.M.,*Whitehall.*
1893. Copland, Geo. Anderson, *Gore, N.Z.*
1907. Copland, Jas. Ebenezer, *Grenada.*
1913. Coplans, Eliezer, *Elgin-avenue.*
1899. Copp, Charles Joseph, *Toronto, Can.*
1893. Corben, Charles, *Cheam.*
1905. Corbett, Geo. Holmes U., *Steyning.*
1921. Corbett, Ivor Joseph. *Plymouth.*
1900. Corbett,Sidney d'Alton,*Cavendish-pl.*
1909. Corbett, Wm. Victor, *R.A M.C.*
1873. Corbin, Edwd. Kinnersly, *Guernsey.*
1902. Corbin, John, *Adelaide, S A.*
1894. Corbould,V. A. L. E.,*Victoria-rd.,W.*
1887. Cordiner, Richard, *Douglas, I.ofMan.*
1903. Cordner, Robt. Harry L., *R.A.M.C.*
1894. Corfe, Robert, *Greenwich.*

1902. Corfield, Charles, *Bristol.*
1897. Corfield, Edwd. Carruthers, *Tooting.*
1904. Corfield, Walt. Francis, *Colchester.*
1884. Corkhill, Jos. G. Garibaldi, *Southport.*
1899. Cornaby,EdgarEdw.,*Ravenscourt-pk.*
1915. Cornelius,StephenAndrew,*Highbury.*
1914. Cornelius,William Hern,*Teignmouth.*
1888. Corner, Frank, *Poplar,* E.
1888. Corner, Harry, *Southgate,* N.
1874. Corney, Bolton Glanvill, *I.S.O., Fiji.*
1890. Cornilliac, Joseph.
1881. Cornish, Chas. Newton, *Southwick-pl.*
1900. Cornish, Charles Vivian, *Kew.*
1857. Cornish, Kenneth Henry.
1894. Cornish, Sydney,*Dorking.*
1880. Coronado, Daniel Enrique, *Colombia.*
1884. Coronel,Julius,*Paramaribo,Surinam.*
1872. Corrie, Alfred Thomas, *Royal Navy.*
1922. Corry, Daryll Cedric, *Sidcup.*
1918. Corry, Eric Vere, *Sidcup.*
1907. Corry, Harry Barrett, *Liss.*
1887. Cort, John Giles Denison, *Whitburn.*
1893. Cory, Evan James Trevor, O.B.E.
1889. Cory, Frank Gillett, *Dorset.*
1875. Cory, Fredk. William, *Leeds.*
1901. Cory, Harold Myrie, *Chesterfield.*
1885. Cory, Isaac Rising, *Guildford.*
1910. Cory, Rob Fias. Preston, *R.N.*
1881. Cory, William Howard, *Bristol.*
1889. Coryn, Hbt. Alfd. Wm., *California.*
1886. Cosens, Chas. H. Champion, *Hitchin.*
1894. Cosens,FrancisRbt.Seppings,*Oakh'm.*
1887. Cosens, Wm. Burrough, *Dorchester.*
1874. Cossham, Wm. Raymond,*Cirencester.*
1862. Costin, Jn.Quick,*Market Harborough.*
1890. Costine, Wm. Courter, *Liverpool.*
1905. Costobadie, Vincent A. P., *Leicester.*
1887. Cotes, Digby Francis Baynes, *Burton.*
1879. Cottell, Arthur Bowditch, *R.A.M.C.*
1886. Cottell. Reg. James Cope, C.B.E.
1897. Cotterill, Albt. Ernest, *Manchester.*
1879. Cotton, Charles, O.B.E., *Canterbury.*
1899. Cotton, Fredk. Wm., *R.A.M.C.*
1922.§Cotton, Gwendolen Coode, *Bude.*
1894. Cotton,Hv.Hugh Powell,*Westerham.*
1889. Cotton, John, *St. Helen's.*
1905. Cotton, Robert Hugh, *Reading.*
1923. Cotton-Cornwall, Victor, *Wallasey.*
1921. Couacaud, Philippe, *Mauritius.*
1888. Couch,Jas.Kynaston,*Perth, W.Aust.*
1912. Couchman, Hugh John, *Edgbaston.*
1903. Couldrey, Thos. Reg., *Scunthorpe.*
1893. Coulson, James Edmund, *Fulham.*
1888. Coulton, John James, *Cape, S Africa.*
1909. Councell, Edw. Leslie, *Liverpool.*
1892. Councell,RichardW.,*Walworth-road.*
1906. Couper, James, *Golder's-green.*

3224

1906. Couper, Sam Barrett, *Blaby.*
1871. Coupland, Sidney, *Hampstead.*
1889. Court, Arthur, *Chesterfield.*
1899. Court, Edward Percy, *Cosham.*
1863. Court, Sir Josiah, *Chesterfield.*
1916. Courtis, Alan Osborne, *Llandaff.*
1889. Courtney, Guy Budd, *Bracknell.*
1905. Courtney, Harold Geo. S., *Burton.*
1916. Courtney, Jos. Moulas, *Bracknell.*
1895. Coutts, Francis James, *Leytonstone.*
1921.§Coutts, Nancy M., *Hampstead.*
1894. Couzens, Albert Ebenezer, *New Zeal.*
1891. Coventon, Charles Arthur, *Oxford.*
1896. Coventry, Charles, *Perth, W. Aust.*
1891. Coverton, Hugh Selby, *S. Aust.*
1894. Cowan, Frank, *Strood.*
1879. Cowan, Geo. Hoyle, *Canada.*
1923. Cowan, Isadore Henry, *Leeds.*
1910. Cowan, James, *Farnworth.*
1921. Cowan, Richard D., *Galt, Canada.*
1906. Cowan, Wm. Joshua, *Bolton.*
1911. Cowardin, Wm. Lewis, *Roy. Navy.*
1909. Cowasjee, Maneckjee Merwanjee.
1897. Cowburn,Arth Doug., *Barkston-gdns.*
1891. Cowell, Alfred Rodgers, *Hoxton-st.*
1915. Cowell, Stuart Jasper, *Steyning.*
1910. Cowen, Edw.Geo. Huxley, *R.A.M.C.*
1902. Cowen, Marcus Woolf, *Amhurst-pk.*
1864. Cowen, Philip, *Balham.*
1889. Cowen, Thos. Philip, *Rainhill.*
1894. Cowes, Adam, *St. Leonards.*
1904. Cowie, James Alexander, *N. Zealand.*
1896. Cowin, Doug. Hy. Fawcett, *I.M.S.*
1871. Cowley, John Selwyn, *Upton-on-Sev.*
1923.§Cowlin, Florence E., *Redcliffe-road.*
1904. Cowper, Claude M.L.,*Leighton Buzz'd.*
1913. Cowper,Hy.Dalziel,*Owen Sound,Can.*
1920.§Cowperthwaite,Elsie E.,*St.John's-wd.*
1912. Cowtan, Frank C., *R.A.M.C.*
1888. Cox, AlfredEdward, *Grange-o-Sands.*
1919. Cox, Alfred Innes, *Old Cavendish-st.*
1890. Cox, Arthur Brooks, *Sydney, N.S.W.*
1903. Cox, Clement Harlow, *Edgbaston.*
1910. Cox, Donald Maxwell, *Clifton.*
1902. Cox, Ernest Alfred, *Long Buckby.*
1910. Cox, Frank Elton, *Melbourne.*
1899. Cox, Franklin, *Reading.*
1906. Cox, George Lissant, *Preston.*
1901. Cox, George Ralph, *Winchcombe.*
1918. Cox, Hedley Chave, *Hornsey.*
1895. Cox, Henry Procter, *Vancouver.*
1883. Cox, John Henry, *Nottingham.*
1922. Cox, John Leigh, *Glamorgan.*
1918. Cox, John Rudolph, *Nottingham.*
1901. Cox, Joseph Bethel, *Seven Kings.*
1879. Cox, Llewelyn Frederick, *Llanbedr.*
1908. Cox, Ralph, *Cricklewood.*

3281

1905. Cox, Reg. John Hands, *Bannu.*
1919. Cox, Ursula Beatrice, *Harerstock-hill.*
1887. Cox, Walter John Roalfe, *Mortimer.*
1893. Cox, Walt.Mundy,M C., *Birmingham.*
1915. Cox, Wilfred Leigh, *Ealing.*
1888. Cox, Wm. Alfred Spencer, *Kensington.*
1880. Cox, William Laird, *Tunbridge Wells.*
1922. Cox, Wm. Leigh Spencer, *Kensington.*
1920. Coxon, Arth. Cedric M., *King's Lynn.*
1881. Coxwell, Chas. Fillingham, *Dulwich.*
1887. Coy, Wm. Filmer, *Vancouver, B.C.*
1921. Cozens, Frederick Cyril, *Walsall.*
1909. Crabb, Robert Lawson, *Esher.*
1901. Crabtree, Emilio F., *Buntingford.*
1910. Craddock. Francis John, *Bath.*
1856. Craddock, Samuel, *Bath.*
1899. Cragg, Edward Henry, *Billingboro.*
1918.§Craggs, Joyce Emily, *London-wall.*
1883. Crago, Wm. Henry, *Sydney, N.S.W.*
1833. Craig, James, *Congleton.*
1921. Craig, Joseph Murison, *St. Andrews.*
1891. Craig, Sir Maurice,C.B.E., *Harley-st.*
1922. Craig, Norman McLeod.
1918. Craig, Roy Neville, *Torquay.*
1890. Craig, Wm. Wallace, *Bridgnorth.*
1863. Craister, Thomas Lawson.
1877. Crallan, George Edw. James, *Jersey.*
1917. Cramer, William, *Hampstead.*
1906. Crampton, Harold Percy, *Finchley.*
1905. Crampton, Walter, *Birkenhead.*
1903. Cran, Hugh Rose, *New Malden.*
1895. Cran, Robert David, *Salford.*
1913. Cran, William James.
1887. Cranstoun, George, *Clunbury.*
1914. Cranstoun, Gordon, *Long Compton.*
1899. Crapper, Harold Sugden, *Poole.*
1896. Craven, Walter, *Rhodesia.*
1911. Crawford, Arthur H., *Ottawa, Can.*
1893. Crawford, Cyril Rodney H., *Pembury.*
1920. Crawford, David, *St. Bart's.-hosp.*
1912. Crawford, Hugh Gregan,M.C., *Clunes.*
1911. Crawford, Jas. Garfield, M.C., *N.Z.*
1907. Crawford, Robert, *Leicester.*
1905. Crawford, Stephen Estridge,*NewZeal.*
1904. Crawford, Thos.Wm. Walt.,*Hackney.*
1899. Crawford,VincentJ.,D.S.O.,*R.A.M.C.*
1902. Crawford,Wm.Thomson,*Nottingham.*
1918. Crawhall, Thos. Lionel, *Newcastle.*
1900. Crawley,HerbertEdwd.,*Portsmouth.*
1901. Crawshaw,ErnestJn.,*High Wycombe.*
1905. Crawshaw, James Henry, *New Zeal.*
1920. Crawshaw, Jas. Wardle, *Ramsbottom.*
1883. Crawshaw, Samuel, *Ashton-u.-Lyne.*
1894. Creak, Alex. Brodie, *Birmingham.*
1922.§Creak, Eleanor Mildred, *Highgate.*
1895. Creasy. Lawrence E., *Weymouth-st.*
1885. Creasy, Rolf, *Windlesham.*
3338

1913. Creasy, Rolf, *Windlesham.*
1885. Cree,Gerald, C.B., C.M.G., *R.A.M.C.*
1883. Cree, Herbert Eustace, *R.A.M.C.*
1888. Cree, James Douglas, *Hampstead.*
1874. Cree, William Edward, *Tavistock.*
1866. Creed, John Mildred, *Sydney.*
1923. Creed, Richard Stephen, *Brockley.*
1916. Crellin, Dougl.,M.C.,*Douglas,I.ofM.*
1866. Cresswell, Richard, *Portishead.*
1893. Cresswell,Stuart Cornwallis,*Dowlais.*
1914. Cresswell, Thomas H., *Cheltenham.*
1887. Cressy, Arth. Z. Claydon,*Wallington.*
1888. Cressy, Charles James, *Ringwood.*
1913. Creswell, Harry Edmund, M.C.
1889. Creswell,John Edwards,M.B.E.,*Suez.*
1917. Crétin, Jean, *Acton.*
1907. Creux, Paul Alfred, *Cape, S. Africa.*
1905. Crew, Fredk. Denys,*Higham Ferrers.*
1895. Cribb, Harry Gifford, *Winterton.*
1919. Crichlow, Egbert A. L., *Trinidad.*
1878. Crick, Samuel Arthur, *Leicester.*
1882. Crick, Wm. Throne, *Leicester.*
1898. Cridland, Arth. B., *Wolverhampton.*
1905. Crinks, Victor Adolphus, *Newport.*
1916. Crinsoz de Cottens, François, *Geneva.*
1877. Cripps, Chas. Couper, *Camberwell-gr.*
1920. Crisp, Eric John.
1887. Crisp, Ernest Hy., *Old Burlington-st.*
1897. Crisp, Geo. Bedford, *R.A.M.C.*
1884. Crisp, James Ellis, *Corsham.*
1886. Crisp, John, *Market Harborough.*
1898. Crispin, Edw. Smyth, *Khartoum.*
1872. Critchett, Sir G. A. Bart., K.C.V.O.
1922. Critchley, Macdonald, *Bristol.*
1875. Crocker, Henry Lawrence, *Roy.Navy.*
1890. Crocker, James Meadmore, *Bingley.*
1884. Crocker, John Hedley, *Richmond.*
1922. Crockford, Allen Lepard, *Brighton.*
1883. Croft, Edward Octavius, *Leeds.*
1892. Croft, John Thos. Herbt., *Edgwick.*
1907. Croft, Lawrence, *Tarleton.*
1908. Crofton, J. Hutchinson, *Oswestry.*
1905. Crofts, Arthur Douglas, *Windsor.*
1892. Crofts, George Harry, *Leicester.*
1902. Croly, Henry Pennington, *Charlbury.*
1923. Crombie, David Weisbrod, *Canada.*
1904. Cromie, Mortimer John, *R.A.M.C.*
1889. Crompton, Ernest, *Newmarket.*
1905. Crompton, Ralph, *Ramsbottom.*
1901. Crompton, Richard Hy., *Manchester.*
1895. Croneen, Sydney, *Royal Navy.*
1913. Cronin,MichaelJoseph,*Stamford-hill.*
1879. Cronk, Herbert George, *Repton.*
1913. Cronk, Herbert Leslie, *Repton.*
1880. Crook, Arthur, *Norwich.*
1923. Crook, Bertram Austin, *Bristol.*
1920. Crook, Francis William, *Shanklin.*
3305

1877. Crook, Herbt. David, *Canada.*
1891. Crooke, William, *New Brighton.*
1881. Crookshank, Edgar March, *Grinstead.*
1894. Crookshank, Francis G., *Wimpole-st.*
1885. Cropley, Alfred, *Northampton.*
1892. Cropp, Edward Lycett, *Reading.*
1923 §Cropper, Dorothy A. D., *Grove-lane.*
1909. Cropper, John Westray, *Sutton.*
1895. Crosby, Arth. Hy. Pascal, *New Z.*
1890. Crosby, Herbt. Thomas, *Gordon-sq.*
1885. Crosby. Robert, *South Shields.*
1905. Cross, Claude Harold, *I.M.S.*
1888. Cross, Edward John, *St. Neots.*
1893. Cross, Ernest William, *Leytonstone.*
1892. Cross, Geoffrey, *Cape Province.*
1902. Cross, Gerald Conybeare, *Roy. Navy.*
1886. Cross, Robert George, *Petersfield.*
1880. Cross, Thomas Brown.
1896. Cross, Wm. Foster, *New Cavendish-st.*
1889. Crosse, Reg. Edward, *Balham.*
1912. Crosse,SpencerStawell,M.C.,*Reigate.*
1923.§Crosskey, Cecily D., *Edgbaston.*
1886. Crossley, Ely Wilkinson, *Halifax.*
1897. Crossley, Hy. Jos., C.I.E., *R.A.M.C.*
1895. Crossley, Samuel, *Leeds.*
1894. Crossman, FrancisW.,O.B.E.,*Bristol.*
1875. Crouch, Ernest John, *Hobart.*
1914. Crouch, Harold A , M.C.
1895. Crouch, Herbert Challice, *Ascot.*
1885. Crowdy, Franc. Demainbray, *Torquay.*
1906. Crowe, Henry Neville, *Worcester.*
1901. Crowe, Henry Warren, *Yelverton.*
1893. Crowley, Ralph Henry, *Letchworth.*
1920. Crown, Saul, *Leicester.*
1874. Crowther, Arthur Bingham, *Hobart.*
1893. Crowther, Charles Keith, *Queensbury.*
1866. Crowther, Edwd. Lodewyk, *Hobart.*
19:?1. Crowther, Herbert Arnold, *Burley.*
1885. Crowther, Jn. W., *West Bromwich.*
1912. Crowther, Wm. Edmund, *Howden.*
1896. Crowther-Smith, Stanley F., *Headley.*
1903. Crozier, Geo. Rowland H., *Transvaal.*
1923. Crozier, John Edwin Digby.
1919. Cruchley, Ignatius Joseph, *Jamaica.*
1897. Cruddas, Hamilton Maxwell, *I.M.S.*
1888. Cruickshank, John David, *Horsham.*
1920.§Cruickshank, M. Ombler, *Norwood.*
1909. Crump, Colin Harold,*Auckland,N.Z.*
1893. Crump, James Arthur, *Welshpool.*
1904. Crump, Stanley Trefusis,*I.M.S.*
1889. Crump, Thos. Greenwood, *Yelverton.*
1896. Cryer, Joseph, *Manchester.*
1918. Cubbon, Henry Thomas,*Letchworth.*
1900. Cubley, Arthur, *W. Hampstead.*
1899. Cuddon-Fletcher,A.J.McN.,*Leicester.*
1921. Cuérel, Emmanuel, *Switzerland.*
1918. Cuff,Cyril Charles Herbert,*Mitcham.*
3452

1882. Cuff, Robert, *Scarborough.*
1868. Cuffe, Alfred Gordon, *Chester.*
1879. Cuffe, Edward Meade, *Wonford.*
1880. Cuffe, Robert E. Gillhurst.
1882. Culhane, Francis Jn. Fitzg., *Marlow.*
1908. Cullen, Alfred Edgar, *W. Australia.*
1921. Cullen, Carl Knight,*E.Ind. Dock-rd.*
1899. Cullen, Jas. Alfd. Patrick, *Bedford.*
1880. Culling, John Chislet, C.B., *A.M.S.*
1896. Culmer,John James, *Nassau, W.I.*
1896. Culmer, Joseph William, *Saltley.*
1902. Cuming, Richard Ingram. *Racton-rd.*
1908. Cumming,Chas. Reginald, *Galt, Can.*
1879. Cumming, Geo. Wm. H., *Torquay.*
1919. Cumming, Herbert E., *Montreal.*
1911. Cumming, John Hamilton, *Torquay.*
1921. Cumming, Patrick Grant,*Manch'st'r.*
1903. Cumming, William Allan, *Quebec.*
1895. Cummings, Arth. Pollard, *Stratford.*
1917. Cummings.Eust'ce H.T.,*SierraLeone.*
1884. Cummings,Harold Lytton, *Tasmania.*
1892. Cummings, Henry Joseph.
1902. Cundell, Harold Juler, *Liverpool.*
1888. Cundell, Wm. Hatch, *Somerset.*
1908. Cunningham, Arth. Jn.W.,*Liverpool.*
1914. Cunningham,F.H.L.,M.C.,*St.Bart's.*
1903. Cunningham,Herbert H.B.,*Palestine.*
1916. Cunningham, Leslie, *Hutton.*
1906. Cunningham, Norman R., *Transvaal.*
1883. Cunningham, Cecil Wm., *Hampstead.*
1916.§Cunnington, Phillis E., *Finchley.*
1917. Cunnington,Thos.Morley, *WestEnd-l.*
1883. Cuolahan, John Herbt., *Bermondsey.*
1879. Curd, Charles, *Bath.*
1913. Curé, Jules Maurice, *Mauritius.*
1885. Curgenven, Jn. Sadler, *Craven-h'll.*
1890. Curgenven, Wm. Brendon, *Victoria.*
1906. Curl, Henley Frank, *Ely.*
1899. Curl, Sydney Walter, *Colchester.*
1915. Curle, Reginald, *Leamington.*
1861. Curme, Decimus, *Blandford.*
1898. Curme, Duncan, Edwd. *R.A.M.C.*
1917. Curnock, Dennis Reginald, *Epping.*
1895. Currey, Edmond Fr. Neville, *Lismore.*
1884. Currey, Robert Henry, *Liverpool.*
1874. Currie, Andrew Stark, *Oxford-terr.*
1894. Currie, John, *Lagos.*
1923. Currie,John Alex.,*Claremont, S. Afr.*
1914. Currie, John Duncan Legge, *Bungay.*
1922. Currie, John Gavin Drummond.
1881. Currie, Oswald James, *Cape Town.*
1911. Cursetjee, H. J. M., D.S.O., *I.M S.*
1923. Curson. Gerald C. W., *Cricklewood.*
1881. Curtayne, Herbert Maxwell.
1899. Curties,Arthur Wm.Statter,*Burwas.*
1904. Curtis, Arthur Humphry, *New Zeal.*
1865. Curtis, Chas. Edwin, *Bath.*
3509

1908. Curtis,George Herbert, *Devonshire-st.*
1901. Curtis, Geo. Wm , *Wick St. Mary.*
1893. Curtis,Montague Wm.W.,*Kensington.*
1899. Curtis, Percy James, *Beckenham.*
1858. Curtis, William, *Alton.*
1880. Curwen, Eliot, *Hove.*
1921. Curwen, Eliot Cecil, *Hove.*
1877. Cusack, Robert Oriel, *R A.M.C.*
1884. Cusse, Ernest, *Broughton.*
1892. Cutcliffe, Montagu, *Dawlish.*
1879. Cuthbert, Chas. Firmin, *Gloucester.*
1915. Cuthbert,Edm.Sheppard,*Southwark.*
1909. Cutler, Fredk. John, *Pembroke-dock.*
1902. Cutler, Horace Arthur, *Walton.*
1891. Cutler, Lennard, *Kensington.*
1919. Cutts, George Lambert, *Boynor.*
1908. Cyriax, Richd. Julias, *Welleck-st.*

D.

1917. Dabbons, Ahmed Tayel, *Egypt.*
1883. Dabbs, Charles John, *Manchester.*
1923. Dabbs, William, *Coventry.*
1914 §D'Abreu,DelphineGertrude,*Lucknow*
1882. Dacre, John, *Clifton.*
1914. Dacre, Richard Irving, *Clifton.*
1910 §Dadabhoy, Dossibai J. R., *Bombay.*
1907. Dadachanji, Kaikhosru K., *I.M.S.*
1910. Dadachanji, Rustom K., *I.M.S.*
1907. Daft, Hedley Gascoyne, *Manchester.*
1921. daGamaMachado,JoséJ.,*Pembroke-sq*
1922. Dagger, Richard Leslie, *Heaton*
1890. Daggett,Hy.Ingledew,*Boroughbridge.*
1883. D'Aguiar, João Gomes, *Demerara.*
1893. Dain, Harry Guy, *Birmingham.*
1917.§Daintree, Dorothy Trevor, *Croydon.*
1910. Dainty, Ralph George, *Slough.*
1908. Dakeyne, Daniel Irving, *Cheadle.*
1897. Dak n, Thomas Burns, *Henley.*
1882. Dakin, Wm. R., *Moreton-in-Marsh.*
1913. Dakin-Smith, Wm. Hy., *R.A.M.C.*
1895. Dalál, Ratanshá Dinshaw, *India.*
1894. Dalby, Jn. L. J. Bennett, *Brighton.*
1909. Dale, Aston Ridley, *Chiswick.*
1909. Dale, Benjamin, *Birmingham.*
1879. Dale, Benjamin Hague, *Ashford.*
1891. Dale, Cuthbert Bracey, *Edgbaston.*
1908. Dale, John, O.B.E , *Coleshill.*
1882. Dale, Walter Fred., *Upp. Parkstone.*
1913 Dale, William, *Ashford.*
1910. Dale, William Chalmers, *China.*
1898. Dalebrook, John, *Spain.*
1898. Dalgado, Patrick, *Ceylon.*
1906. Dalgliesh, Frank Bell, *R.A M.C.*
1887. Dalgliesh, John Wm., *Sutton.*
2561

1862. Dalgliesh, Jonathan, *Newcastle-on-T.*
1878. Dallaway,Jos.Wm.D., *Windh'mCl'b.*
1883. Dallewy, John, *Wem.*
1901. Dally, Jn. Fredk. H., *Up. Wimpole-st.*
1856. Dalton, Frederick George, *N.S. W.*
1891 Dalton, Fredk. Jas. A., C.M.G.,*R.N.*
1904. Dalton. G. F., *Kingston, Canada.*
1922. Dalton, Patrick Philip, *Marlow.*
1864. Dalton, Thomas, *Llandudno.*
1923. D'Alwis, David Basil.
1905. Daly, Ashley Skeffington, *Seaford-crt*
1899. Daly, Fredk. Jas. Purcell, *P & O. Co.*
1922. Daly, Harold Patrick, *Whitchurch.*
1909. Daly, James Thomas, *Bombay.*
1896. Daly, Nolan, *Bramley.*
1879. Damant, Arthur Johnson, *Cowes.*
1908. D'Amico, Guido de Piro,*W.Af.M.S.*
1895. Dampier-Bennett, A. G , *Kingstown.*
1896. Danaher, Edwd. Harry J., *Rainham.*
1909. Danaher, Harry Wms. B., *Luton.*
1913. Danby, Alfred Beuthin, *N. Zealand.*
1914. Dancy, John Horace, *Ramsgate.*
1920. Dando,GeoffreyWright,*Birmingham.*
1920.§Dando, Kathleen Mary, *Bexley.*
1887. Dane, Robert, *Straits Settlements.*
1916. Dani, Raghunall Ganesh, *Sholapoor.*
1898. Daniel, Alfred Wilson, *Hanwell.*
1895. Daniel, EdgarGeorgeClement,*Epsom.*
1887. Daniel, Ernest C. S., *Orange Rio. Col.*
1886. Daniel, Fredc. E., *Barrow-in-Furness.*
1915. Daniel, Herbert McW., *Dublin.*
1867. Daniel,Jn.Waterhouse,*N.Brunswick.*
1892 Daniel, Robt. Napier, *Nevern-square.*
1858. Daniel, Thos. Palmer, *Beaminster.*
1891. Daniel, Wm. P. Taylour, *Cable-st.*
1888. Daniell, Edgar Percy, *Thorpe Bay.*
1888. Daniell, Geo. W. B., *Capetown.*
1889. Daniell, Henry Pywell.
1886. Daniels, Charles W., *Harley-street.*
1899. Danks, Walter Seymour, *Sutton.*
1915. Dannatt,RobertMalcolm,*Blackheath.*
1892. Dausey-Browning, George, C.B.E.
1920.§Dansie, Ada M., *Mecklenburgh-sq.*
1921. Dausie, Charles Brandon.
1919. Dansie, Redgewell G., *Denmark-hill.*
1897. Dantes, Augustus Paul, *Bombay.*
1901. Danvers-Atkinson,F.C.E.,*Seymour-st.*
1893. Darabseth, Navroji Beramji, *India.*
1898. Darby, William Sydney, *Harrow.*
1898. Darbyshire, Douglas Edwd., *Lincoln.*
1903. Darbyshire, Harold S. C., *Ealing.*
1916. Dargan,Patrick Arthur,*Grove-end-rd.*
1913. d'Arifat, André C. de L., *Paris.*
1892. Darker, George Fitzjames, *Temple.*
1886. Darlow, Alfred. *Plaistow,* E.
1883. Darroll, Wm. Burwell. *Leintwardine.*
1896. Dartnell, Louis Edward, *Roy. Navy.*
3618

1922. Darukhanawala, Kaikhosru A., *India.*
1917. Das, Hari, *Lahore.*
1913 Das, Manindranath, M.C., *I.M.S.*
1906. Daser, Peter Paul, *Finsbury-pavement.*
1896. Dashwood, CharlesEwart,*Rodney-rd.*
1922. Date,WilliamAdlington,*Colville-terr.*
1888. Date, William Horton, *Exeter.*
1918. Datta, Jatindra Kumar, *Mexborough.*
1918. Datta, Pares Chandra.
1905. Daukes, Sidney H., O.B.E., *Norwich.*
1913. Daunt, Francis Eldon, *Clapham-rd.*
1885. Davenport, Arthur Fredk., *Victoria.*
1896. Davenport, Edwd. Chas., *China.*
1874. Davey, Charles James, *Natal.*
1896. Davey, Ernest Llewellyn, *Walmer.*
1900. Davey, James, *Rhodesia.*
1899. Davey, John Bernard, *Nyasaland.*
1888. Davey, Samuel, *Caterham.*
1887. Davey, Thomas George.
1910. Davey, Thomas Ronald, *Bampton.*
1900. David, Archbd. Sinclair, *Fyfield.*
1923. David, Cecil Kenyon, *Llanelly.*
1884. David, Evan Thomas.
1914. David, Thomas Wm., *Abergavenny.*
1880. David, Wm.Washington,*Pontypridd.*
1904. Davidson, Alan, *Vermont, U.S.A.*
1878. Davidson, Alexander, *Toronto.*
1920. Davidson, Andrew N. M. *Ilkley.*
1922. Davidson, Donald, *Worple-road.*
1908. Davidson, Archibald,*Norwich.*
1906. Davidson, Duncan, M.C., *Coventry.*
1895. Davidson, Guilford, *Queensland.*
1886. Davidson, Harold, *Teddington.*
1883. Davidson, Hugh M., *Queensberry-pl.*
1879. Davidson, John, *Uxbridge.*
1909. Davidson, Maurice, *Southsea.*
1921. Davidson, Percy T., *Seven Kings.*
1901. Davidson, Wm. Henry, *China.*
1893. Davies, Alban Davy, *Yarmouth.*
1887. Davies, Albert Barnes, *Stroud.*
1917. Davies, Albert Victor S.,*Carmarthen.*
1916. Davies, Albert Wm. Abell, *Leicester.*
1923. Davies, Alfred Bentley,*Harborne.*
1888. Davies, Alfred Owen, *Machynlleth.*
1908 Davies, Arthur, *Greenwich.*
1912. Davies, Arthur A. M., *R.A.M.C.*
1913. Davies, Arthur Lewis, *Llanmwehllyn.*
1880. Davies, Arthur Mercer, *R.A.M.C.*
1900. Davies, Aubrey Hugh, *Vancouver.*
1902. Davies, Charles Woolmer, *Southport.*
1922. Davies, Daniel Alexander, *Tondu.*
1898. Davies, David, *Tunbridge Wells.*
1871. Davies, David Arthur, *Swansea.*
1912. Davies, David Arwyn, *Llandilo.*
1912. Davies, David Henry, *Wattstown.*
1920. Davies, David Justin, *Middx.-hosp.*
1914. Davies, David Lloyd, *Boncath.*
1923. 3675

1905. Davies, David Morgan, *Aberayron.*
1879. Davies, David Samuel, *Bristol.*
1921.§Davies, Edith M. P., *Judd-street.*
1915. Davies, Eric David D., *Clifton.*
1915. Davies, Ernest Ivon, *Barry.*
1918. Davies, Evan Sherrah. *Westm.*
1922. Davies, Francis, *Mythyr-Tydfil.*
1905. Davies, Fredk.Spencer,*B ickhurst-hill.*
1917. Davies, George Vincent, *Llanelly.*
1922. Davies, Harold Spencer, *Vauxhall.*
1913. Davies, Hector Wynne, *Colwyn Bay.*
1883. Davies, Hry. Arth. Bluett, *Levin, N.Z.*
1908. Davies, Herbert Rees, *Kingston.*
1884. Davies, Howard, *Pontypridd.*
1891. Davies, Howard Owen, *Ealing.*
1809. Davies, Howell, *Transvaal.*
1919. Davies, Idris, *Ynysybwl.*
1879. Davies, James David, O.B.E., *Ryde.*
1919. Davies, Jenner Conway, *Hampstead.*
1882. Davies, John Charles, *Ruabon.*
1914. Davies, John Christopher, *Bristol.*
1914. Davies, John Edgar, M.C., *Cardiff.*
1891. Davies, John Edward,*Liscard.*
1894. Davies, Jn. Edwd. Henry, *Wrexham.*
1895. Davies, Jn. Edgar Philip, *Llanelly.*
1915. Davies, John Kenyon, *Outram-rd.*
1893. Davies, John Lloyd, *Newport, Mon.*
1911. Davies, John Lloyd, *Llandyssul.*
1879. Davies, Jn. M. Lloyd, *Haverfordwest.*
1910. Davies, John Philip Hy., *Ton-Pentre.*
1905. Davies, John Rees, *Long Ditton.*
1914. Davies, John Rhys, *Cardigan.*
1883. Davies, John Thomas, *Leicester.*
1899. Davies, Jos. Trower, *Grahamstown.*
1922.§Davies, Kathleen Fawckner.
1916. Davies, Lionel Meredith, *Carmarthen.*
1916. Davies, Llywelyn ApIvan, M.C.
1923.§Davies, Mary Ll., *Campden-hill-rd.*
1921.§Davies, Muriel Alice M., *Stroud.*
1914. Davies, Percy Vernon, *Talgarth.*
1892. Davies, Richard, *Cheltenham.*
1913. Davies, Richard William, *Bonn.*
1894. Davies, Samuel Hugh R., *Worthing.*
1881. Davies, Sidney, *Woolwich.*
1918. Davies, Sidney R. E., *Shooter's-h.-rd.*
1908. Davies, Sidney Trevor, *Westminster.*
1884. Davies, Sievewright Arth.,*Blackburn.*
1923. Davies, Simon John, *Pontardawe.*
1875. Davies, Thomas, *West Kensington.*
1908. Davies, Thomas, *Pencader.*
1917. Davies, Thomas, *Hampstead.*
1902. Davies, Thomas Ashton, *Ruislip.*
1908. Davies, Thomas Bonnor, *Tonypandy.*
1922. Davies, Thos. Hy. R., *Old Southgate.*
1898. Davies, Thos. John, *Rhondda Valley.*
1918. Davies, Thomas Morris, *Ilford.*
1915. Davies, Thomas Reginald, *Llanelly.*
3732 P

1904. Davies, Thomas Sidney, *Pretoria.*
1907. Davies, Timothy Howell, *Swansea.*
1901. Davies, Walter Ernest L., *Llanidloes.*
1918. Davies, William, *Cardiff.*
1869. Davies, Wm. Henry, *Frome.*
1902. Davies, Wm. James, *Aberayron.*
1898. Davies, Wm. John Edwin, *Japan.*
1896. Davies, Wm. Lloyd B., *Harley-st.*
1913. Davies, William Ll. Gwyn, *Garthe.*
1882. Davies, Wm.Thos.F.,D.S.O.,*S.Africa.*
1885. Davis, Arth. Holdsworth, *Bournem'th.*
1907. Davis, Arth. Hubert Treby, *R.A.M.C.*
1880. Davis, Arthur Randall, *Hythe.*
1881. Davis, Charles Daniel, *Kenley.*
1903. Davis, Charles Noël, *Shanghai.*
1888. Davis, Cyril Stephen, *New Zealand.*
1881. Davis, Edward, *R.A.M.C.*
1885. Davis, Edw. Sandom Stone, *St.Blazey.*
1900. Davis, Everard Inseal, *Worthing.*
1889. Davis, Fredk. Lionel, *Br. Honduras.*
1904. Davis, Rev. George B., *Cambridge.*
1886. Davis, George William, *Eastbourne.*
1888. Davis, Harry, *Callington.*
1911. Davis, Henry Harvard, M.C.
1895. Davis, Hy. John Banks, *Portman-st.*
1904. Davis, John James, *Ontario.*
1882. Davis, John Warren, *Dorset-square.*
1917. Davis, Peter Gerald S., *Barnes.*
1887. Davis, William, *Whitstable.*
1880. Davis, William George.
1899. Davis, William Herbert, *Devonport.*
1899. Davison, Henry Edward,*Golder's-gr.*
1912. Davison, Kaye F. R., *New Malden.*
1874. Davison,RashellThomas,*NewMalden.*
1915. d'Avray, Alexander Decimus.
1893. Davson,Jas.Benj.Hoghton,*W.Africa.*
1907. Davy, Gerald H., O B.E., *R.A.M.C.*
1903. Davy, Philip C.T.,C.M.G.,*R.A.M.C.*
1913. Davy,Richard Denis, M.C.,*R.A.M.C.*
1904. Davy, Wm. Bradshaw, *Hampstead.*
1911. Daw, Hubert, *Stratford-place.*
1895. Daw, William Henry, *R.N.*
1903. Dawe, Charles Henry, *R.N.*
1899. Dawe, Frank Sherwill, *Chiswick.*
1895. Dawes, Christopher Dering, *I.M.S.*
1890. Dawes, George Harry, *Sheffield.*
1907. Dawes, Herb. Edwin T., *Huddersfield.*
1893. Dawkin, George Mansell, *Pontypridd.*
1890. Dawson, of Penn, Rt. Hon. Lord.
1891. Dawson, Cecil Lacy, *Berry, N.S.W.*
1916. Dawson, Fredk. G. Leslie, *Plymouth.*
1911. Dawson, Guy de H., D.S.O., M.C.
1913. Dawson, Hugh Pudsey, *Harston.*
1911. Dawson, Lionel Montrose, M.C.
1908. Dawson,Reginald Branch, *Willenhall.*
1899. Dawson,Thomas Denman, *W. Austr.*
1919. Dawson, Wm. Siegfried, *Beckenham.*
3789

1906. Day, Arthur Percival, *Ceylon.*
1908. Day, Bernard, *Fed. Malay States.*
1903. Day, Charles Frederick, *Leigh-on-Sea.*
1874. Day, Edward Joseph, *Dorchester.*
1916. Day, George, *Norwich.*
1902. Day, Harold Benjamin, M.C., *Cairo.*
1896. Day, James John, O.B.E., *Sandwich.*
1882. Day, John Roberson, *Devonshire-pl.*
1892. Day, Joseph Henry, *Oxford-street.*
1913. Day, Sidney Alfred, *Kingston.*
1880. Day, Thomas Montagu, *Harlow.*
1880. Day, William Aloysius, *Bath.*
1903. Day, Wm. Frank Lydstone, *Roydon.*
1902. Day, Wm. L. M., O.B.E., *Colchester.*
1919. Day-Lewis, Alfred Kay, *Guy's.*
1911. De, Jyotish Chandra, *I.M.S.*
1917. de Abrew,Leslie Perkins,*Balcombe-st.*
1917. de Almeida, Milanius, *Ceylon.*
1886. Deacon, George Edward, *Norwich.*
1897. Deakin, Frank Newstead, *Walsall.*
1913. Deakin, Howard Vipond, *Parkend.*
1920. Deakin, Kenneth Vincent,*Northwich.*
1914. Dean, Christopher, M.C., *Markbeech.*
1899. Dean, Edmund Clapperton, *W. Aust.*
1904. Dean, Henry Roy, *Manchester.*
1908. Dean, Lawrence Thompson, *Spilsby.*
1879. Deane, Arthur Dorman, *W. Aust.*
1886. Deane, Edward, *Reading.*
1915. Deane, George Stanley, *Scothorne.*
1881. Deane, Herbt. Edward. *Weymouth-st.*
1920. Deane,KennethHamilton,*Forest-gte.*
1907. Deane, William, *Wrayby.*
1862. Deans, John, *Victoria.*
1911. Dearden, Harold, *Lowndes-street.*
1882. Dearden, John Walter, *Castleford.*
1885. Dearden, Wm. Francis, *Manchester.*
1915. Dearden, Wm. John, *Manchester.*
1889. Deare, Benjamin Hobbs, *I.M.S.*
1895. Deas, Frank, *Merton.*
1887. Debenham, Horace Allan, *Presteigne.*
1918. Debenham, Leonard Snowden, *Acton.*
1890. Debenham, Robt. Barsham, *Poplar.*
1923. de Boissiè e,V.R.J.,*Dartmth.-pk-hill.*
1913. de Boer, Henry S., M.C., *Ceylon.*
1920. Deboo, Sorabji Navroji, *India.*
1904. de Brent, Harold John, M.C.
1921. de Caux, Francis P., *Chancery-lane.*
1920. de Chaumont, John J. P., *Streatham.*
1886. de Chazal, Edmd. Lucien,*Mauritius.*
1896. Deck, Edward James, *New Zealand.*
1906. Deck, Horace Leigh, *Sydney.*
1862. Deck, John Feild, *Sydney.*
1914. de Costa, Marcelline, *Ceylon.*
1906. de Coteau, Joseph Taaffe, *Grenada.*
1911. Deer, Alexander Arnitt, *Bebington.*
1914. de Fonseka, Duncan C., *Blackheath.*
1899. de Freitas, Quirino B., *Brit. Guiana.*
3846

1898. de Gannes, Jos. Louis F., *Trinidad.*
1896. de Gébert, Louis Jean Adam,*Hornsey.*
1914. de Glanville, L. R. G., *Bexhill.*
1885. de Gruchy, Chas. William, *Caerleon.*
1922. Deif, Ahmed Mahmoud, *Bernard-st.*
1883. Deighton, Frederick, *Cambridge.*
1922. Déjani, Fuad Daudi, *Brentwood.*
1894. de Jong, Edward Meyer, *Lymm.*
1893. de Korté, Wm. Edmond, *Cape Town.*
1894. de Kretser, Edward William, *Ceylon.*
1904. De la Cour, George, O.B.E.,*R.A.M.C.*
1866. De la Cour, Geo. Francis, *Camden-rd.*
1909. Delafield,Max Everard,M.C.,*Ebury-st.*
1877. DeLautour, BertrandEdgar,*NewZeal.*
1896. Delbruck, Raoul E., *Chelsea.*
1916. de Lemos, Martin Jos., *Brixton.*
1861. De Leon, John,*Montego Bay,Jamaica.*
1911. Delmege, James Anthony, O.B.E.
1831. DeLom, Henry Anthony, *Pimlico.*
1917. Demerdash,MahomoudA.B.,*Barnsley*
1909 de Miranda, Pedro Joaquim, *Goa.*
1912. De Morgan, C. Wm., *Rotherhithe.*
1917. De Morgan, Harold A., *Weybridge.*
1896. Dempster, Wm. T., M.B.E., *Croydon.*
1922. Denham, H. K., *Gloucester-cres.*
1923. Denman, Morris, *Stoke Newington.*
1907. Denholm, George, *Brandon.*
1895. Denne, Francis Vincent, *Brook-green.*
1863. Denne, Henry, *Birmingham.*
1908. Denning, Arth. F. Wm., *Long Eaton.*
1905. Denning, Geo. Fanning, *Blackfriars.*
1906. Denning, William Frederic, *Elland.*
1914. Dennis, Arthur Wesley, *Battersea.*
1889. Dennison, Rev. Tom S., *Birmingham.*
1894. Denny, Arthur William, *Soham.*
1915. Denny, Cedric Roland, *Walton.*
1864. Denny, Charles John, *Southsea.*
1890. Denny, Herbert Reg. Harry,*R.N.*
1878. Dennys, Geo. Wm. P., C.I.E., *I.M.S.*
1907. Densham, Arnold Thos., *Stratford-pl.*
1893. Densham, Ashley B., *Stratford-pl.*
1883. Dent, Harry Lord Richd., *Kensington.*
1884. Dent, Herbert Crowley, *R.A.M.C.*
1922. Denton, George, *Normanton.*
1904. Denyer,Clarence H.,M.C.,*R.A.M.C.*
1885. de Nyssen, Petrus Joh., *Halesworth.*
1921. De Penning, Herbert C., *Bombay.*
1905. de Pinna, Herbert Alfred, *N.S.W.*
1918. Depla, Charles, *Gower-street.*
1911. Depree,HubertTempler,*Portland-crt.*
1913. Depree, Sidney Barron, *Blackpool.*
1905. Derham-Reid, Jas., M.C., *Bolton.*
1914. Dermer, Edmund Rupert, *W. Aust.*
1896. Dermer, Wm. Thos., *W. Australia.*
1908. Dermott, Edward James, *Paraguay.*
1916. de Robillard, Jos. Ed. E., *Mauritius.*
1917. Derry, Bartholomew Gidley,*Bodmin.*
3903

1915. Derry, David Hamilton, *Radford.*
1920. de Rynck, Godfried L.J. A.,*Belgium.*
1920. Desai, Purshottamrai M., *Bombay.*
1923. de Saram, Gerald Sam. Wm.,*Ceylon.*
1909. Deshmukh, Gopal Vinayak, *Bombay.*
1891. De Silva, Charles Edward, *Ceylon.*
1911. De Silva, Hinton, *Ceylon.*
1919. de Silva, John Paul, *Stamford-hill.*
1917. de Silva, Wilton Lionel, *Ceylon.*
1916. de Smidt, Frank P. G., *Limpsfield.*
1914 D'Souza, Alex. John, M.C., *I.M.S.*
1922. De Souza, Alex C., *Secunderabad.*
1903. de Souza, David H., *Hampstead.*
1915. de Souza, Edward V.,*Wool Exchange;*
1923.§de Souza,Gert.*Magdalen,Caroline-pl.*
1880. Dester, Wm. Parker, *Turriff.*
1893. d'Esterre, Jn. Norcott, *Fawcett-st.*
1893. d Esterre, Wm. Hry. D. P., *Norwood:*
1883. DesVœux,HaroldA.,*Buckingham-gte.*
1909. Deuntzer, Canut, *Middlesex-hosp.*
1907. Devas, Horace Charlton, *Royal Navy*
1921. Devegney, Fernand E. C., *Geneva.*
1889. Devenish-Meares, A. Lewis, *N.S.W.*
1895. Devereux, Norman, *Tewkesbury.*
1890. Devereux, Wm. Charles, *Tewkesbury*
1907. de Verteuil, Eric Joseph, *Trinidad.*
1877. de Verteuil, Ferd. Aimé, *Trinidad*
1906. de Villiers, Carel Chris. A., *Tonbridge;*
1896. de Villiers, Jas. Henry, *Cape Town.*
1902. Devine, Henry, O.B.E , *Portsmouth.*
1922. Devine, John Bernard, *Middlesbrough*
1888. Devis, Harry François, *Bristol.*
1901. Devitt, Herbt. Pye Smith, *Rochester.*
1912. Devonald, Alfred Evan L.,*Bridgnorth.*
1912. Dew, John Wescott, M.C.
1910. Dewar, Allan, *Tuxford.*
1911. Dewar, John Evan, *Minneapolis.*
1902. D'Ewart, John Thos., *Manchester.*
1876. De Watteville, Armand, *Rolle.*
1886. Dewes, Frederick Joseph, *I.M.S.*
1891. de Wet, Peter Christian, *Cape.*
1902. Dewey, Edwd. Wm. *Portsmouth.*
1889. Dewhurst,J.H.,M.B.E.,*C'g. Campden*
1888. Deyns, Chas. John, *Bletchley.*
1921. De Zilva, Irving Gerald.
1923. de Zoysa, Vincent Ploris, *Hampstead.*
1895. Dhingra, Behari Lal, *Punjab.*
1914. Dia, Mostafa, *Egypt.*
1909. Dias, Anthony, *Karachi.*
1915. Dias, Charles Wilmot, *Ceylon.*
1914. Diay, Ismail Fahmy, *Egypt.*
1914. Dick, Carl Keating Graeme, M.C.
1910. Dick, Frederick Adolph, *Tadworth.*
1855. Dick, Henry.
1909. Dick, James Reid, *Scarborough.*
1894. Dick, Maxwell, *I.M.S.*
1899. Dick, Walter, *Gt. Massingham.*
3900   P 2

1894. Dickens, Chas. Henry, *Leeds.*
1907. Dickey, Wm. C. McNaghten, *N.S.W.*
1895. Dickin, Edwd.Percival, *Brightlingsea.*
1896. Dickins, Sidney Jn. Oldacres, *Cowfold.*
1904. Dickinson, Chas. Marshall, *Maldon.*
1890. Dickinson, Geo. Frank, *Warwick.*
1884. Dickinson, Jos. Jewitt, *Tenbury.*
1923. Dickinson, Kenneth S., *Newcastle.*
1894. Dickinson, Robert Lumley, *R.N.*
1879. Dickinson, T. Vincent, *Cadogan-mns.*
1903. Dickinson, W. H., O.B.E., *Kensington.*
1916. Dickinson, Wm. Robinson, *St. Bart's.*
1906. Dickson, Arth. Norman, *I.M.S.*
1915. Dickson, David McM., M.C.
1905. Dickson, Harold Stewart, *R.A.M.C.*
1912. Dickson, Ivan Wanless, *Toronto.*
1890. Dickson, John William, *Wilton-cr.*
1913. Dickson, Kenneth Bruce, *Newbury.*
1901. Dickson, Louis Edington, *Bridgnorth.*
1905. Dickson, Wm. Leonard, *Brighton.*
1912. Digby, Wm. E. Sheraid, *Westward Ho.*
1914. Dikshit, Kashinath J., *c/o Cook & Son.*
1884. Dill, John Fdk. G., O.B E., *Brighton.*
1895. Dillon, Rupert W., *Uxbridge.*
1886. Dimmock, Aug. Fredk., *Harrogate.*
1917. Dimock, James Douglas, *Retford.*
1883. Dimsey, Edgar Ralph, D.S.O., *R.N.*
1919. Dina, Ahmad R. K., *Guy's-hosp.*
1905. Dingle, Percival Alfred, *N. Borneo.*
1877. Dingle, Wm. Alfred, *Ilfracombe.*
1885. Dingley, Arthur Wm., *Argyle-sq.*
1882. Dingley, Edwd. Alfred, *Wednesbury.*
1915. Dingley, Eric Gordon, *Tufnell-park.*
1917. Dingley, John Ralph, *Wednesbury.*
1910. Dinnick, Oswald Tilson, *Hamilton-gds.*
1906. Dinnis, Alfred, *Hoddesdon.*
1905. Dismorr, Cecil Jas. S., *Gravesend.*
1870. Dismorr, Henry, *Hastings.*
1900. Dismorr, Henry Bertram, *Swindon.*
1923. Distaso, Michele Arcangelo, *Naples.*
1890. Distin, Howard, *Enfield.*
1906. Dive, Gilbert H., D.S.O., *R.A.M.C.*
1913. Dive, Hubert Roy, M.C., *N. Zealand.*
1890. Diver, Ebenezer William, *Alberta.*
1902. Dix, Charles, *Bruton.*
1914. Dix, Richard Henry, *Sunderland.*
1885. Dixey, Fredk. Augustus, *Oxford.*
1908. Dixon, Alban, *Kingsland-road.*
1891. Dixon, Arthur, *Preston.*
1904. Dixon, Austin Clarence, *Walsall.*
1887. Dixon, Charles Harvey, M.P.
1923 §Dixon, Enid Marcella, *Bow.*
1881. Dixon, George Frederick, *Potton.*
1901. Dixon, Godfrey Brookes, *Birm'gham.*
1882. Dixon, Henry Charles, *Transvaal.*
1897. Dixon, Henry Cuthbert, *Hackney.*
1870. Dixon, Henry Edward, *Buntingford.*

1873. Dixon, Henry George, *City-road.*
1884. Dixon, Jacob Robert Lucas.
1854. Dixon, John, *Jamaica-road,* S.E.
1899. Dixon, Montague, *Melton Mowbray.*
1917.§Dixon, Phyllis Decima, *Rothwell.*
1899. Dixon, Robert Halstead, *Ealing.*
1892. Dixon, Thomas, *Eccleshall.*
1875. Dixon, Thomas Arthur, *R.A.M.C.*
1909. Dixon, Thomas Benjamin, *Bath.*
1895. Dixon, Walter E, O B E., *Cambridge.*
1919. Dixon, William Herbert, *Stroud-gn.*
1901. Dixon, Wm. John, *Trong, Perak.*
1886. Dixson, Chas. Fdk. Lyne, *Acton.*
1906. Dobbin, Wilfrid Arthur E., *Holloway.*
1891. Dobbs, Matthew, *Folkestone.*
1894. Dobell, Clarence Brian, *Cheltenham.*
1894. Dobie, Edward Cyril, *Chester.*
1890. Dobie, Herbert, M B.E.. *Chester.*
1897. Dobie, Robert Douglas, *Aldwych.*
1882. Dobie, William Henry, *Chester.*
1906. Doble, Francis Carmnow, *Uganda.*
1912. Dobrashian, George R., *Harlesden.*
1919. Dobrashian, Theodore H, *Harlesden.*
1894. Dobson, Arthur, *Ilkeston.*
1913. Dobson, Eric L., *Holland-pk.-avenue.*
1873. Dobson, Joseph, *Leeds.*
1909. Dobson, Josiah Rowland B., *Staunton.*
1885. Dobson, Leonard C. T., *Kensington.*
1908. Dobson, Maurice Rowland, O.B.E.
1862. Dobson, Thomas, *Windermere.*
1912. Dobson, Wm. Townsend, *Cardiff.*
1895. Dockray, John S, *Bishop's Stortford.*
1883. Dodd, Anthony, *R.A.M.C.*
1884. Dodd, Arthur Herbert, *Hove.*
1899. Dodd, Arthur Timothy M., *Liverpool.*
1896. Dodd, Ernest Jas. Aubeion, *Leeds.*
1914. Dodd, Fredk. Henry, *Blackheath.*
1895. Dodd, Fredk. Lawson, *Devonshire-st.*
1887. Dodd, Percy Vernon, *Folkestone.*
1902. Dodd, Stanley, *Wimpole-st.*
1921. Dodds, Edwd. Chas., *Cambridge-gds.*
1897. Dodgson, Geo. Stanley, *Wolsingham.*
1895. Dodgson, Robt. Wm., *Maida-vale.*
1897. Dodson, George Everard, *Persia.*
1917. Dodwell, Howard Branson, *Battersea.*
1889. Dodwell, Philip Rashleigh, *Battersea.*
1914.§Doherty, Mary Agatha, *Toronto.*
1920. Doherty, William David, *Streatham.*
1922. Doggart, Jas. Hamilton, *Darlington.*
1883. Doidge, Maurice John, *Glastonbury.*
1904. Doig, Kenneth Alin C., *R.A.M.C.*
1892. Dolamore, Wm. Henry, *Harley-st.*
1906. Dolan, Edmund Michael, *Wigton.*
1914. Dolan, Stephen Ormond, *Wigton.*
1910. Doll, Henry Wm, *Hampton-hill.*
1901. Dolman, Edgar Winn Fox, *Queensland.*
1923. Dolman, Gerrit A., *Lincoln's-inn-fields*

1898. Domela-Nieuwenhuis, Theo, *Tunis*.
1915. Dominick, G. M., *Lansdowne-place*.
1899. Dominy, Geo. Herbert, *Milton Abbas*.
1871. Domville,Edw Jas.,O.B.E.,*Chelwood*.
1883. Donald, Archibald, *Manchester*.
1903. Donald Robert, *Dunedin, N. Zealand*.
1903. Donaldson, Alex. Henry, *Holsworthy*.
1910. Donaldson, Arthur Wm.,*B.Columbia*.
1914. Donaldson, Eric, *Melbury-road*.
1901. Donaldson, Samuel, *Transvaal*.
1901. Donaldson-Sim, Ernest A., *Balham*.
1922. Donelan, Conor John, *Harrow*.
1873. Donkin, Sir Horatio B, *Hyde-park-st*.
1918. Donne, Cecil Lucas, *Hampstead*.
1919. Donovan, Hugh, *Birmingham*.
1882. Donnet, Jas. Jn. Conway, *R.A.M.C.*
1913. Doorly, Arthur Rawdon C., *Lee*.
1912. Doraisamy, Subramanya, *I.M.S.*
1909. Doran, Robert Sydney, *Stockwell-rd*.
1898. Dore, Saml. Ernest, *NewCavendish-st*.
1903 Dorman, Oscar Chipman, *Manitoba*.
1911. Dorner,Georg,*Koenigsberg-i.-Prussen*.
1893. Dornford, Arth. Clifford, *Bow*, E.
1885. Dornford, Chas. T., *Lytham*.
1914. Dotto, John Baptist G., *Gibraltar*.
1910. Dottridge, Cecil Alfred, *Godalming*.
1900. Doubble, Meredith S , *Perranporth*.
1912. Doubleday, Frederic Nicklin, *Boro'*.
1870. Doudney, Edwin, *New South Wales*.
1885. Doudney, Geo. Herbert, *Wainfleet*.
1912. Douglas, Harold A., *Newcastle, Staff*.
1917. Douglas, Howard Lexster, *Chingford*.
1905. Douglas, Jas. Sholto C., *Sheffield*.
1898. Douglas, Kenneth H., *Walthamstow*
1904. Douglas, Reginald Inglis, *Dulwich*
1896. Douglas, Stewart Rankeu, *I.M.S.*
1868. Douglas, William, *Goudhurst*.
1870. Douglas,Wm. Thos. Parker, *Lee-on-S.*
1900. Douglass, Percy Clarence, *R.A M.C.*
1900. Douglass, Wm. Claughton, *M.C.*
1903. Douse, John Freeman, *Farnborough*.
1921. Douthwaite, Arth. Hy., *Guy's-hosp*.
1889. Douthwaite, Geo. H., *Stockton-on-T.*
1912. Douty, Rbt. Joel Cazalet, *Eastbourne*.
1883. Dovaston, Milward Edmund.
1916. Dove,Arthur Farrell R., *Sierra Leone*.
1922.§Dove, Alice Elizabeth, *Crouch-hill*
1890. Dove. Percy Wm.,O.B.E.,*Crouch-hill*.
1897. Dove.William Bathurst, *Leatherhead*.
1891. Dow, John Hardman, *St. Helen's*.
1921. Dow, John Roy, *Hornsey-road*.
1892. Dow, William Alexander, *Lewes*.
1905. Dowdall,Arth.Melville, *W. Af. M.S.*
1888. Dowdell, Chas. Seymour,*Gold Coast*.
1808. Dowding, Ernest Fdk. C., *Hove*.
1898. Dowding,Wm.Fdk.Chas.,*Wimbledon*.
1893. Dowler, Herbt. Matthew, *India*.
4131

1888. Dowling, Ed. Alfd. Griffiths, *Clifton*.
1919. Dowling, Geoffrey Barrow, *Guy's-h.*
1890. Dowling, Geo. Wm., *Alderley Edge*.
1891. Dowling, Norman, *New S. Wales*.
1905. Dowling, Stanislaus Marcus, *Woodford*
1921. Down, Alfred Henry Gerald, *Exeter*.
1895. Down, Elgar, *Plymouth*.
1907. Downer, Reg. Lionel E., *Matlock*.
1881. Downes, Chas. Hagger.
1897. Downes, Godkin, *Wealdstone*.
1883. Downes, Howard, *Hornsey*.
1862. Downes, James Badger, *New Zeal*.
1901. Downes, Thos.W.Hardwicke,*Ludlow*.
1918. Downing, Chas. Cottrell R., *Cardiff*.
1882. Downman, Chas. F., *Wellington, B.C.*
1890. Downing, William, *Birmingham*.
1902. Downton,Arthur Sydney, *Crouch-end*.
1898. Dowse, Thos. Alex., *W. Af. M.S.*
1865. Dowse, Thos. Stretch, *Exmouth*.
1899. Dowsett, Ernest B., *D.S.O., R.A.M.C.*
1883. Dowsing, Hbt. Leopold,M.B.E.,*Hull*.
1878. Dowsley, David Henry, *Ottawa*.
1881. Dowson, John, *Royal Navy*.
1918. Doyle, Austin Roland.
1883. Doyle, Edward Angel G., *Trinidad.*
1886. Doyle, Henry Martin, *N.S.W.*
1912. Drabble, Edward Percy, *Bloxwich*.
1921. Drabble, Horace Silva, *Sheffield*.
1907. Drake, Arth. W. Courtney, *Rochester*.
1871. Drake, Cecil, *Royal Navy*.
1896. Drake, Dennys John, *Suva, Fiji*.
1891. Drake, Ernest Charles, *Shanklin*.
1916. Drake,Herbert Mervyn,*Bournemouth*.
1903. Drake, Hugh Basil, *I.M.S.*
1902. Drake, John Alexander, *Tenby*.
1894. Drake, William, *Canterbury*.
1900. Drake-Brockman,Hy.G.,*Middlesbro'*.
1887. Drake-Brockmann,Hbt.Edwd.,*I.M.S.*
1899. Drake-Brockman, Ralph E., *D.S.O.*
1891. Drake-Brockman, Vivien G., *I.M.S.*
1881. Draper, Jas. William, *Huddersfield*.
1896. Draper, Robert Athelstan, *York*.
1920. Draper, Thomas, *Uppingham*.
1890. Draper, Thomas Makin, *Watlington*.
1866. Draper, William,*Lancaster-gate*.
1904. Drapes, Thos. L., M.B.E , *Chepstow*.
1904. Drawbridge, Wilfd. R. L., *Ellesmere*.
1915. Dresing, Herman Gerald, M.C.
1894. Drew, Albt. John Knigman,*Sydham*.
1894. Drew, Edward Hatherell, *Balham*.
1871. Drew, Henry Wm., *Ballyduff*.
1905. Drew, John Harmer, *Poole*.
1902. Drew, Robert Stanbanks, *Egham*.
1871. Drew, William Thomas, *Egham*.
1918. Drewe,Frank Swinburne, *Wimbledon*.
1876. Drewitt, Fdk. George D., *Kensington*.
1876. Dring, Wm. Ernest, *Tenterden*.
4188

1901. Drinkwater, Frédk. A. W.,*Llangollen.*
1877. Drinkwater, Harry, *Wrexham.*
1902. Driver, Henry Lloyd, *Southsea.*
1921. Drobig, Casper T.J. N., *Hampton-hill.*
1905. Droop, Chas. Edward, *Minsterley.*
1896. Druitt, Arthur Edward, *Torquay.*
1896. Druitt, Claud Francis, *Alvaston.*
1909. Druitt, Daniel Cuthb.,*Saffron Walden.*
1916. Drummond, Gerald G., *Teignmouth.*
1910. Drummond, Robert, *Nyasaland.*
1916. Drury, Alan Nigel, *Northwood.*
1896. Drury, Edwd. Guy Dru, *Cape.*
1904. Drury, Godfrey Dru, *Corfe Castle.*
1919. Dıyerre, Henry, *Lasswade.*
1907. Dryland, Gilbert Winter, *Kington.*
1891. Dryland, Leslie Winter, *Kettering.*
1889. Drysdale, Jn. Hannah, *Devonshire-pl.*
1904. Drysdale, Theodore, *Sloane-street.*
1919. Dublé, Lucien, *Héverlé, Belgium.*
1885. Du Boulay, Hubert H., *Weymouth.*
1885. Du Buisson, Edwd. Wm., *Hereford.*
1923.§Du Buisson, Helen M., *Hurst-green.*
1894. Ducat,ArthurDavid,D.S.O.,*Chiswick.*
1912. Duck, Wm Agar S., O.B E., *R.N.*
1862. Duckworth,SirD.,Bart ,*Grosvenor-pl.*
1900. Dudding, John Scarbrough, *R.N.*
1902. Dudding.Thos.Scarbrough,*R.A.M.C.*
1885. Dudfield, Reg. Saml. O., O.B.E.
1912. Dudgeon, Chris. Robson, *R.A.M.C.*
1896. Dudgeon, Heibert Wm., *Cairo.*
1899. Dudgeon, L. Stan., C.M.G., C.B.E.
1895. Dudley, Arth. Dudley Parr, *Temple.*
1901. Dudley, Bernard John, *New Zealand.*
1904. Dudley, Edwd. Percy H., *Caxton.*
1923. Dudley, Geoffrey, *Stourbridge.*
1890. Dudley, Geo.Jas.,O.B.E.,*Stourbridge.*
1906. Dudley, Sheldon F , O.B.E.,*R. Navy.*
1883. Dudley, William, *Canada.*
1891. Duer, Sidengham Unwin.
1881. Duff, Chas. Henry, *East Bridgford.*
1919. Duff, Keith M. K., *Hendon.*
1920. Duff, Thos. Alex. Jamieson, *Toronto.*
1895. Duffield, Ernest Alph., *Treherbert.*
1920. Duffy, Arthur, *Westhoughton.*
1891. Duffy, Patrick Joseph, *Forest-gate.*
1876. Duggan, M., M.B E., *Altrincham.*
1888. Dugon, Francis, *Ilderton-road.*
1900. Dugon,Thos. Henderson, *W.Af.M.S.*
1901. Duigan, Victor John, *E. Dereham.*
1889. Duigan, William, *Oxford.*
1892. Duka,Albt.Theo.,*D.S.O.,Southbourne*
1867. Duke, Benjamin, *Clapham-com.,S.W.*
1872. Duke, David, *Leicester.*
1904. Duke, Harold Denny, *Brondesbury.*
1873. Duke, Maurice Smelt, *Kennington.*
1857. Duke, Roger, *Hastings.*
1867. Dukes, Clement, *Rugby.*
4245

1894. Dukes, Edmund Sprague, *New Zeal.*
1890. Dukes, Thomas Archibald, *Croydon.*
1922. Dulake, Lawrence, *Ridgway-gardens.*
1916. Dummere, Alf. Beresford, *Brasted.*
1880. Dummere, Howaid Howse, *Sevenoaks.*
1916. Dumphy, Frederick, *L. & S. W. Bank.*
1882. Dun, Walter Angus.
1876. Dunbar,Jn.Jas. Macwhirter,*Clapham.*
1921. Duncan, Archibald Glen, *Ilford.*
1909. Duncan, Archibald W., *I.M.S.*
1880. Duncan, Duncan, *Eccleston-street.*
1897. Duncan, Geo. Ernest, M.B.E., *R.N.*
1922.§Duncan, Helen Winifred, *Southpoit.*
1887. Duncan, Horace, *Bolton-street,* W.
1907. Duncan, John, *Toronto.*
1838. Duncan, Percy James, *Bournemouth.*
1887. Duncker, Wm. Reinhold, *Portslade.*
1910. Dunderdale, Geoffrey, *E. Af. M.S.*
1892. Dunderdale,R.H.W.,M.B.E.,*Bl'kpool*
1903. Dunkerton,NormanEdwin,*R.A.M.C.*
1899. Dunkin, Silas Ethelbert, *Clapham.*
1887. Dunlop, James Craufurd, *Edinburgh.*
1901. Dunlop, John Beattie, *Bradford.*
1909. Dunn, George Hunter, *Farnborough.*
1866. Dunn, George Newman, *Kinsale.*
1885. Dunn, Philip Henry, *Regent-street.*
1890. Dunn, Robert Ayton, *Hertford.*
1905. Dunn, Thos Wm. Newton, *Bath.*
1879. Dunn, Walter, *Roxburgh, N.Z.*
1910. Dunn, Wm. Alex., *Wellington, N.Z.*
1864. Dunn, William Daniel, *Clifton.*
1895. Dunn, Wm. Edwd. N., *Brondesbury.*
1901. Dunne, Arthur Briggs, *Doncaster.*
1908. Dunning,Jn.Beatson,M.C.,*Cricklew'd.*
1919. Dunscombe, Clement, *Maida-vale.*
1921. Dunscombe,T. Wm. King, *Stratford.*
1872. Dunstan, Robert, *Paignton.*
1900. Dunstan, Robert, *Paignton.*
1900. Dunstan, Walter Robt., *Lewes.*
1877. Dunstan, William, *Plymouth.*
1899. Dunston, John Thos., *Transvaal.*
1917 §Du Pré, Fiances Jane, *Char. Cr.-hosp.*
1911. Dupré, William Henry, *Buxton.*
1893. Duprey, Albert Joseph B., *Trinidad.*
1902. Dupiey, Geo. Perry, *Cairo.*
1899. Durance,Wm.Arth.,*Sutton-in-Ashf'ld*
1882. Durant,Robt Jas.Anderson,*R.A.M.C.*
1914. Durante, James Angel, *Gibraltar.*
1900. Durbridge, Henry, *Matlock Bath.*
1896. Durrant, Chas. Edwin, *Malay States.*
1888. Durrant, Thomas A., *Stanhope-terr.*
1893. Durston, John Christopher, *R.N.*
1916. Duské, Herbert James, *Paris.*
1871. Dustan, Henry, *Jersey.*
1897. Dutch, Henry Asher, *Berkeley-street.*
1919. Dutt, Dwijendra Nath.
1885. Dutt, Upendra Krishna, *Cambridge.*
4302

1892. Dutton, Arthur Stayt, *Oxford.*
1918. Dutton, Francis B., *St. Petersburg-pl.*
1902. Dutton, Hugh Reginald, *I.M.S.*
1909. Duvivier, Marc Antoine E.,*Mauritius.*
1914. Dvorkovitz, Paul, *Kensington.*
1886. Dwyer, Hubt. de Burgh, *Banbury.*
1916. Dwyer, Maurice, M.C., *Dewsbury.*
1912. Dwyer, W. Jas.Ignatius,*Mildmay-pk.*
1912. Dyas, George Eldridge, *R.A.M.C.*
1916. Dye, William Hood, *Balham.*
1898. Dyer, Harold, *Vancouver.*
1888. Dyer, John Edward, *Pretoria.*
1883. Dyer, Sidney Reginald, *Brixton.*
1867. Dyer, Thomas Birch, *Norwich.*
1899. Dyer, Walter Percy, *R.N.*
1897. Dykes, Charles Reg., *Buckhurst-hill.*
1897. Dykes, Percy Armstrong, *Cambridge.*
1893. Dymoke, Frederick, *Bristol.*
1878. Dymott, Donald Fred., *Croydon.*
1923. Dyson, Alex. Dacre, *Heighington.*
1918. Dyson, Charles Bertram,*Heighington.*
1909. Dyson, Ernest Andrews, *Sheffield.*
1904. Dyson, Harold Edward, *Wembley.*
1916. Dyson, James Daniel, *Highgate.*
1901. Dyson, John Newton, *Eastbourne.*
1909. Dyson, Percy Albt.Stanley, *Ackworth.*
1873. Dyson, William, *Sheffield.*

E.

1913. Eacrett, Edwin John, *Newfoundland.*
1915. Eades, Reginald Oliver, *Ipswich.*
1872. Eady, George John, *S. Kensington.*
1906. Eager, Gurth, *Hertford.*
1903. Eager, Mervyn, *Watford.*
1870. Eager, Thomas Cawley, *Acton.*
1913. Eagleton, Arthur Joseph, *Goring.*
1922.§Ealand, Winifred, *Highgate.*
1885. Eales, George Young, *Torquay.*
1910. Eales, Wm. Harold Fulford, *Birm.*
1917.§Eames, Alethea Josephine.
1895. Eames, Charles Wm., D.S.O.,*Shipley.*
1896. Eames, Edwd. Shairp B., *Uffculme.*
1892. Eames, Edwd.Thos. Philip,*Roy.Navy.*
1875. Eames, Jas. Crompton, *Stonedough.*
1881. Eames, William, *Royal Navy.*
1897. Eardley, William, *Goole.*
1871. Eardley-Wilmot, Robert, *Petworth.*
1906. Earl, Guy Stanley, *Plymouth.*
1923. Earlam, Francis, *Frodsham.*
1884. Earle, Cyril Somerset, *Blackpool.*
1890. Earle, Edward Robert Chas.,*Jamaica.*
1866. Earle, Frederick, *Edgware.*
1890. Earle, Hubert Malins, *I.M.S.*
1893. Earle, John Rolleston, *Oxford.*
1907. Earle, Maurice Mason, *New Zealand.*
4355

1864. Earle, Robt. Chas., *Wanganui, N.Z.*
1912. Early, Philip Vanner, *Canton.*
1917. Earp, John Rosslyn, *Birchington.*
1912. Easmon,MacormackC.F.,*SierraLeone*
1898. Eason, Herbert L., C.B., C.M.G.
1921. East, Charles Frederick Terence.
1886. East, Charles Harry, *Gt. Malvern.*
1910. East, Edwin Chas., *Gawler, S. Aust.*
1897. East, William Norwood, *Manchester.*
1894. Eastes, George Leslie, *Harley-street.*
1898. Eastman, Julio Daniel.
1921. Eastman-Nagle, Ernest R. D.
1898. Eastment, Alan Grant, *Royal Navy.*
1900. Eastment, Gerald Meade.*Royal Navy.*
1902. Eastmond, Reg. Anthony, *Mansfield.*
1892. Easton, Frank Edward, *Hyde-pk.-sq.*
1902. Easton, Harold Aug.,*Thornton-heath.*
1901. Easton, Philip George,C.B.E.,D.S.O.
1915. Easton, Wilfred Angel, *Wimbledon.*
1916. Easton,Wm.Cochrane C.,*Manchester.*
1881. Eastwick-Field, Charles, *Midhurst.*
1888. Eaton, Oliver, *Bingham.*
1922.§Ebden, Beatrice Emily, *Exmouth.*
1916. Eberle, Wm. Felix, *Luton.*
1905. Eccles, Bertram Joseph, *Transvaal.*
1888. Eccles, Charles Henry, *Nafferton.*
1916. Eccles, Charles Yarrow, *Nafferton.*
1877. Eccles, Friend Richard, *Ontario.*
1913. Eccles, Geo Dunluce, M.C.,*Plymouth.*
1891. Eccles, Herbert Annesley, *Croydon.*
1898. Eccles, Oreste, *Kensington.*
1892. Eccles, Robert Burton, *Driffield.*
1921. Eccles, Thomas Annesley, *Croydon.*
1912. Ecclestone,Wilfred Marlow, *Toronto.*
1906. Eckenstein, Kenneth Ed.,*Kensington.*
1908. Eckstein, John McDougall, *I.M S.*
1898. Eddison, Francis Ryalls, *Bedale.*
1917. Eddison, Herbert Wilfred, *Epsom.*
1864. Eddison, John Edwin, *Adel, Yorks.*
1907. Eddlestone, Neville A., *Whitley Bay.*
1861. Eddowes, William, *Shrewsbury.*
1897. Eddy, James, *Leicester.*
1889. Edelsten, Ernest Alfred, *Streatham.*
1893. Eden, Wm. Annesley, *Birmingham.*
1895. Eder, Montague David, *Welbeck-st.*
1915. Edey, Thomas Hugh, *Loughton.*
1911. Edgar, William James, *Caerwys.*
1893. Edge, Arthur James, *Maidenhead.*
1895. Edge, Bruce Edgar, *Doncaster.*
1920. Edge, William, *Blackley.*
1884. Edgelow, Herbert, *Delagoa Bay.*
1883. Edgelow, Percy, *Devonshire-place.*
1877. Edgelow, Samuel Henry, *Melbourne.*
1871. Edginton, Robert Wm., *Clevedon.*
1899. Edington, Ernest A., *Huddersfield.*
1896. Edington, George Henry, *Glasgow.*
1909. Edis, Isaac Marcus, *Liverpool.*
4412

1871. Edis, John Butler, *Liverpool.*
1897. Edleston, Richd. S.Chambers, *Baslow.*
1884. Edlin, Herbt. Ebenezer, *Manchester.*
1875. Edmond, Wm. Richardson, *Totnes.*
1916. Edmonds, Arth.Wm. Foster, *Balham.*
1902. Edmonds, Chas. Jn. E., *Streatham.*
1903. Edmonds, Frank Rowe, *Br. Guiana.*
1889. Edmonds, George, *Mayfield.*
1889. Edmonds, Henry Aug., *New Zealand.*
1905. Edmondson, Watts, *Lancaster.*
1905. Edmunds, Clive T., D.S.O.,*R A.M.C.*
1883. Edmunds, Daniel Taylor, *New Sth. W.*
1893. Edmunds, Flavell,M.B. E.,*Chesterfield*
1923. Edmunds, Henry Tudor.
1894. Edmunds, Percy Jas.,*Gt.Mar lboro.-st.*
1905. Edridge, Ray, *Bath.*
1888. Edward, Charles Stanstay.
1922. Edwards, Alun Myfenydd, *Llandre.*
1881. Edwards, Arthur Rea, *I.M.S.*
1899. Edwards, Augustus Lea, *Upavon.*
1900. Edwards, Charles, *Bridport.*
1884. Edwards, Charles Reginald, *Jamaica.*
1888. Edwards, Charles Wright, *Wincanton.*
1917.§Edwards, Constance Maude, *L'pool.*
1923. Edwards, D. Glyn M., *St. Kilda's-rd.*
1899. Edwards, David Richard, *Corwen.*
1899. Edwards, Edgar Steele, *Stamford.*
1917.§Edwards, Flor. Marjory, *Regent's-pk.*
1893· Edwards, Francis Hy., *Camberwell.*
1920. Edwards, Francis Henry, *Liverpool.*
1900. Edwards, Frank Payne, *Victoria.*
1900. Edwards, Fred. Geo. Hy.,*R. Col.Inst.*
1892. Edwards, Fredc.William, *Forest-hill.*
1906. Edwards, Geo. B., D.S.O.,*R.A.M.C.*
1889· Edwards, Harford Norman,*Dunstable.*
1923. Edwards, Harold C., *Newport, Mon.*
1918. Edwards, Harpur Vernon, *Harrow.*
1908. Edwards, Harry Rumsey, *R.A.M.C.*
1877. Edwards, John, *Manchester.*
·1900· Edwards, John Maltby, *Bromley.*
1921.§Edwards, Keridwen St.V.,*Highbury.*
1917. Edwards, Monte, *Kingston-on-Thms.*
1886. Edwards, Percy, O.B.E.; *Liverpool.*
1893. Edwards, Philip Hugh, *Devoran.*
1885. Edwards, Richard, *Liverpool.*
1921. Edwards, Richard Tudor, *Oswestry.*
1893. Edwards, Robert, *Hawkhurst.*
1910. Edwards, RogerBellis, M B E.,*Mold.*
1923. Edwards, William, *Norbury*
1884. Edwards, Sir Wm. R., K C.B.,C.M.G.
1895. Eedle, Edward John, *Bristol.*
1912. Eggar, William Halley, *Hassocks.*
·1889· Ehrmann, Albert, O.B.E.,*Camden-rd.*
1918. Eidinow, Albert, *Lond.-hosp.*
1917. Eidinow, William, *S. Hackney.*
1916. Ekanayake, Hector E., *Hampstead.*
1900. Ekins, Charles Maxwell, *Cairo.*
4409

1921. Eksteen, Hendrick Oostenwald.
1889. Elam, George, *Sheffield.*
1923. Eland, Arthur John C., *Kensington.*
1913. el Arculli, Hassan, *Hong Kong.*
1914. El Bakry, Mohammed, *Cairo.*
1922. El-Biblawi, Mohammed A., *Egypt.*
1918. El Daab, Snad-el-Din Ahmed.
1911. El-Dabâ, Garas Girgis.
1904. Elder, Armin Gascoigne V., D.S.O.
1901. Elder, Geo. Tatham D., *Mansfield.*
1899. Eldred, Arthur G.,O.B.E.,*Nyasaland.*
1884. Elevatamby Mudalitamby, *Colombo.*
1915. El Gawly, Nassry Gobran, *Cairo.*
1882. Elgood, Charles Reginald, *Windsor.*
1915. El Hakim, Ahmed Fahmi, *Egypt.*
1916. Elias, Mikhail, *Banha, Egypt.*
1914. Elkholy, Mohamed Kamil, *Egypt.*
1910. Elkin, Samuel James, *Winnipeg.*
1871. Elkington, Ernest Alfred, *Newport.*
1863. Elkington, George, *Llwyngwril.*
1921. Elkington, Guy Waterman.
1855. Elkington, John.
1920. El Kirdany, Aly Mohammad, *Egypt.*
1896. Ellacombe, Gilbt. Hy. W., *Rhodesia.*
1907. Ellcombe, John Edwin, *R.A.M.C.*
·1894. Ellerton, Henry Byam, *Brisbane.*
1862. Ellerton, John, *Middlesbrough.*
1874. Ellerton, Jn. Fdk. Heise, *Leamington.*
1898. Ellery, Ernest Edwd., *R.A M.C.*
1880. Elliot, Edmund Arth. S., *Kingsbridge.*
1894. Elliot, Ernest Edward, *Dover.*
1879. Elliot, Henry, *Burton.*
1915. Elliot, Henry Hawes, M.C.
1886. Elliot, Wm Hy. W., D.S.O., *I.M.S.*
1892. Elliot-Blake, Hubert, *Beer.*
1892. Elliott, Chas. Caldwell, *Cape Town.*
1922. Elliott, Charles C., *Coventry.*
1905. Elliott, Christopher, *Tunbridge Wells.*
1881. Elliott, Edgar, *Herne Bay.*
1910. Elliott, Edgar Lionel, *Sevenoaks.*
1900. Elliott, Harold St. Clair, *Oxford-st.*
1892. Elliott, Harry Scott, *Southsea.*
1907. Elliott,Howard Robinson,*Rotherham.*
1922.§Elliott, Mary Catherine, *Bingham.*
1880. Elliott, Nich. Phillipps, *N.S. Wales.*
1915. Ellint, Stanley E. Y., *Londonderry.*
1907. Ellis, Carlton Atkinson, *Clapham.*
1903. Ellis, Edgar Severn, *Gloucester.*
1903. Ellis, Ernest Alfred, *Ashburton.*
1901. Ellis, Ernest Fitzgerald, *Roy. Navy.*
1899. Ellis, Francis Hamilton, *Shirley.*
1902. Ellis, Francis Heygate,M.C.,*Rhodesia.*
1892. Ellis, Fred, M.C., *Parkstone.*
1912 Ellis, Gordon Ernest D.,O.B.E.,*R.N.*
1915. Ellis, Harold, *Radyr.*
1896. Ellis, Henry Reginald, *W.Af.M.S.*
1872. Ellis, Hyacinth D'Arcy, *Stourbridge.*
4526

1911. Ellis, John Chute, *S. Australia.*
1891. Ellis, John Constable, *Highcliffe.*
1883. Ellis, John Lloyd.
1917. Ellis, John Stanley.
1876. Ellis, Joseph Watson, *Cambridge.*
1903. Ellis, Leonard Erasmus, *Transvaal.*
1923. Ellis, Rhys Salter, *Edybaston.*
1910. Ellis, Robert, *Swansey.*
1914. Ellis, Robert, *Alsager.*
1895. Ellis, Robert Mackav, *Chudleigh.*
1883. Ellis, Sidney, *Salisbury.*
1912. Ellis, Thomas Leslie, *Radyr.*
1861. Ellis, Thomas Smith, *Gloucester.*
1901. Ellis, Wm. Francis, O.B.E., *R.A.M.C.*
1886. Ellis, Wm. McDonagh, *Woldingham.*
1893. Ellison, Arthur, *Leeds.*
1887. Ellison, Ernest Henry, *Syston.*
1908. Ellison, Harold Blades, *Frodsham.*
·1915· Ellison, Hubert Henry L., *Liston.*
1916. Ellison, Philip Oswald, *Wood-green.*
1897. Ellwood, Thos. A., *Tollington-pk.*
1919 §Elman, Sylvia Victoria. *Amhurst-rd.*
1917. Eloff, Johan Sarel, *Transvaal.*
1911. Elphick,Geo. Jas. Frank, *Carlton-hill.*
1923. Elphick, H. Noel Keyes,*Hereford-rd.*
·1915· Elphick, Sidney Ernest, *Carlton-hill.*
1921. El-Ramli, Aly Hassan, *Cairo.*
1893. Elrington, Nicolas, *Wethersfield.*
1915. Elsaved, Ahmed Yuki, *Egypt.*
1877. Elsmere, Edward, *Alderney-street.*
·1923.§Elsom, Lucy Margaret, *Rowditch.*
1920. Elson, William Cyril, *Bradford.*
1920. Elt, Edward Ernest. *N. Finchley.*
1908. Elton, Hy. Brown,O B.E ,*Llandovery.*
1893. Elvy, Frank, *Fowlesburg, S Africa.*
1898. Elwes,Frederick Fenn,O.I.E.,*I.M.S.*
1896. Elwin, Geo. Richd.. *Blackfrias-rd..*
1904. Elworthy, Henry H., *Westminster-h.*
1906. Elworthy, Reg. Robt., *W Lond -hosp.*
1918. El-Zeneinv, Abdel Aziz Hassan.
1896. Emanuel, Joseph George, *Edgbaston.*
1906. Embleton, Dennis, *Weymouth-street.*
1894. Emerson, Herbt. Biec, *Pershore.*
1879. Emerson, Peter Henry, *Christchurch.*
1892. Emery, Arthur, *Ludlow.*
1885. Emery, Frederick William, *Totnes.*
1918. Eminson, Clarence Franklin, *Scotter.*
1881. Eminson, Thos. B Franklin. *Scotter.*
1890. Emlyn, Chas. Willmore, *Banbury.*
1915. Emmerson, Cuthbert L., *St. Bart's.*
1904. Emmerson, Herbt. Harry, *Sheffield.*
1891. Emmet, John William, *Eastbourne.*
1920. Emmett, Roger Henry, *Portsmouth.*
1885. Emmett, Richard, *Portsmouth.*
1920. Empey, Cecil Weldon, *Lewisham.*
1910. Endean, Fredk. Chas., *Guy's-hosp.*
1901. Enderby, Chas. Dawber, *Grimsby.*
4583

1912. Engels, Wladimir Gerhard, *Munich.*
1868. England, George, *Hove.*
1887. England,Geo.F.Ashbridge,*Winchester*
1897. England, Humphrey, *Chesham Bois.*
1909. English, Arthur Oxley, *Knightwick.*
1881. English, Edgar, *Doncaster.*
1892. English, Thos. Harks, *Sleights.*
1898. Ennion,·Octavius Roberts, *Burwell.*
1923. Enoch, Robert Henry, *Harrow.*
1889. Enraght, William, *Anerley.*
1895. Ensor, Cecil Arthur, *Tisbury.*
1888. Ensor, Charles William, *Ealing.*
1899. Ensor, John William, *Golder's-green.*
1878. Ensor, Theodore Francis, *Swanage.*
1922. Epstein, Alchonan, *Birmingham.*
1917. Erfan, Mahmond, *Cairo.*
1914. Errington, Roger, M.C., *R.A.M.C.*
1905. Erskine-Collins, Jas. Edw.,*East Ham.*
1913. Erulkar, Abraham Solomon.
1895. Escombe, William, *Grimsby.*
1918. Escritt, Fredk. Knowles, *Streatham.*
1910. Eskell, Bertie Cecil, *Clifton.*
1885. Eskrigge. Richd. Bertram, *Barnsley.*
1913. Esler, Alex. Rentoul, *Peckham.*
1912. Esler, Maberly Squire, *Peckham.*
1900. Esser, Saml. Jonath. David, *Transvaal.*
1887. Essery,Wm. Joseph, C.V.O., *Southsea.*
·1876. Essex, James Rowlands, *Pontypool.*
1883. Etches, Wm. Robert, *Warlingham.*
1899. Etheridge, Chas. Edward, *Whitstable.*
1923·§Eva, Ursula Elizabeth, *Chiswick.*
1912. Evans, Abel, *Charing Cross-hospital.*
1907. Evans, Albert Edward,*Golder's-green*
1899. Evans, Alexander, *Market Weyghton.*
1870. Evans, Alfd. Henry, *Sutton Coldfield.*
1864. Evans, Alfred Paget, *Erdington.*
·1912. Evans,Arthur Geoffrey,*Longridge-rd.*
1899. Evans, Arthur John, *Liverpool.*
1893. Evans, Arthur Vernon, *Weybridge.*
1916. Evans, Charles A. Lovatt, *Hendon.*
1899. Evans, Chas. Edwd., *Lower Clapton.*
1897. Evans, Chas. Robt.,D.S.O.,*R.A M.C.*
1876. Evans, Charles Walter, *Bakewell.*
1911. Evans, Daniel Charles. *Llanrenog.*
1916. Evans, Daniel Davies, M.C., *Llanelly.*
1894 Evans, Daniel Edward, *Swansea.*
1898. Evans, David, *Cardiff.*
1912. Evans, David Benjamin, *Llangybyth.*
1897. Evans, David Edward, *Pontypridd.*
1902. Evans, David Haydn, *Sheffield.*
1913. Evans, David John, *Bournville.*
1916. Evans, David John, *Cowbridge.*
1900. Evans, David Rbt.Powell,*Wimbledon.*
1915. Evans, David Trevor, *Tonypandy.*
1918. Evans,DavidWashington,*Sydenham.*
1880. Evans, Ebenezer Daniel, *Wrexham.*
1898. Evans, Edward, *Holbeach.*
4640

218 MEMBERS.

1899. Evans, Edward Alban, *Swansea.*
1889. Evans, Ernest William, *Mark-lane.*
1890. Evans, Evan, *Felinfach.*
1899. Evans, Evan, M.C., *Lampeter.*
1907. Evans, Evan Parry, *Llanwit Vardre.*
1903. Evans, Evan Robert, *Mostyn.*
1921. Evans, Ewart William, *Smethwick.*
1921. Evans, Frankis Tilney, *Woodford-gn.*
1919. Evans, Frederick Augustus, *Anglesey.*
1897. Evans, Frederick Hudson, *Lewisham.*
1888. Evans, Geo. Edward Alfred, *Chard.*
1923. Evans, George Morgan, *Pontypridd.*
1919. Evans, Gwilym P., *Westbourne-gds.*
1923.§Evans, Gwladys, *Aberdare.*
1889. Evans, Harold Muir, *Lowestoft.*
1905. Evans, Harry Loft, M.B.E., *Hull.*
1913. Evans, Henry William, M.C., *Bedford.*
1860. Evans, Herbert Norman, *Seaford.*
1923. Evans, Herman.
1887. Evans, Howell Thomas, *Blackwood.*
1905. Evans, Hugh Roker, *Folkestone.*
1916. Evans, Humphrey Silvester, *Balham.*
1892. Evans, John, *Carnarvon.*
1902. Evans, John, *Neath.*
1906. Evans, John, *Brockenhurst.*
1921. Evans, John Cardoc, *Southwark.*
1881. Evans, John Durance, *Ebbw Vale.*
1886. Evans, Jn Morgan,*Llandindrod Wells.*
1893. Evans, John Morton, *Bristol.*
1923. Evans, John Morton, *Bristol.*
1916. Evans, Leonard Wynne, *Gipsy-hill.*
1909. Evans, Leslie Wilson, M.C.
1923. Evans, Mortimer W. H.,*Brondesbury.*
1886. Evans, Oliver C. P., *Kidder minster.*
1891. Evans, Percy, *R.A.M.C.*
1894. Evans, Richard, *Wrexham.*
1908. Evans, Robt. Cecil Turle, *Herne-bay.*
1896. Evans, Robert Jones *Pwllheli.*
1923. Evans, Rowland H., *Newport, Mon.*
1874. Evans, Thos. D. Fabian, *Birmingham.*
1909. Evans, Thomas Garfield, *Port Talbot.*
1881. Evans, Thos. G. C., *Kyogle, N.S.W.*
1916. Evans, Tom Stenner, *Dowlais.*
1907. Evans, Trevor, *Swansea.*
1919. Evans, Tyrrell George, *Bath.*
1913. Evans, Walter Stuart, *Carmarthen.*
1886. Evans, William, *Johannesburg.*
1893. Evans, William, *Pimlico-road.*
1897. Evans, William, *New Zealand.*
1883. Evans, William Arnold, *Sheffield.*
1886. Evans, William Edward, *Torquay.*
1882. Evans, William Henry, *Colyton.*
1887. Evans, William Norman, *Hampstead.*
1902. Evans, William Thomas, *Treharris.*
1887. Evelyn, William Arthur, *York.*
1900. Everard,Arth.George,*Stockwell.*
1892. Everett, Ernest William, *Norwich.*
4697

1899. Everington,Herbt.Devas,*Sanderstead.*
1894. Evers, Charles Henry, *North Seaton.*
1884. Evers, Charles John, *Faversham.*
1893. Eves, Percy Stanhope, *Brighton.*
1886. Evill, Frederick Claude, *Barnet.*
1894. Evison, Frank Arthur, *March.*
1871. Ewart, William, *Upper Brook-st.*
1887. Ewbank, Wm. Withers, *S. Aust.*
1902. Ewen, Gerald Sidney, *Twickenham.*
1877. Ewen, Harry Walter, *Cowes.*
1918. Ewen, John Harold, *Clifton-hill.*
1912. Ewens, Bernard Creasy, *Guernsey.*
1889. Ewens, Henry Luther, *Maldon.*
1908. Ewing, Alfred Washington, *Ware.*
1888. Ewing, Andrew Melville, *U.S.A.*
1894. Ewing, Samuel Arthur, *Victoria.*
1854. Ewington, C. H. Thomas.
1888. Exley, John, *Leeds.*
1904. Eyre, Chas. Roland B., *Brondesbury.*
1893. Eyre, John Wm. Henry, *Guy's-hosp.*

F.

1902. Faber,Hamilton Stanley, *Cricklewood.*
1876. Fabien, Lewis, *Trinidad.*
1923. Facey, Reginald Vaughan,*S.Kens'gt'n*
1897. Facey, Samuel Henry, *Royal Navy.*
1886. Facey, William Edwin, *Southbourne.*
1889. Fagan, Arth. R. St. Leger, *Holloway.*
1906. Fagan, Charles Horace, Jn., O.B.E.
1914. Fagan, Richard Feltrim, *Beaconsfield.*
1894. Fagge, Robt.Hilton,*Melt'n-Mowbray.*
1915. Fahmy, Moustafa, *Folkestone.*
1915. Fahmy, Nashed, *Egypt.*
1890. Faichnie, Frederick, *R.A.M.C.*
1885. Failes, Fredk. Geo., *New South Wales.*
1922. Fairbairn, Donald C., *Kensington.*
1915. Fairbairn, Robert C.,*St. Bart.'s-hosp.*
1901. Fairbairn, SidneyHerbert,*Bolton-gds.*
1898. Fairbank, Christian Beverley, *R.N.*
1867. Fairbank, John, *George-street, W.*
1903. Fairbank, John Gerald A., O B.E.
1873. Fairbank, Wm , M.V.O., O.B.E.
1917. Fairburn, James, *Hove.*
1914. Fairchild, Geo. C., *Bishop's Stortford.*
1877. Fairclough,John James Kent,*Buxton.*
1907. Fairclough,Wm. Aiken, *New Zealand.*
1901. Fairfax, Edward Wilfred, *N.S.W.*
1921. Fairfax, Ralph Wilfrid, *Goodmayes.*
1900. Fairhall, Geo. Victor H., *Lewisham.*
1898. Fairweather,Wm.Ernest,*Manchester.*
1903. Falk, Herman, *I.M.S.*
1895. Falkener, Lyon, *East Molesey.*
1910. Falkner, Sandbrook, *Fulham.*
1884. Fall, Edwin Armstrong.
4749

1879. Falla, Walter, *Jersey*.
1922. Fallis, Laurence Sydney.
1897. Falwasser, Arthur Thos., *Maidstone*.
1919. Fanning, James, *Leytonstone*.
1897. Fanning, Wm. Joseph, *Norwich*.
1922. Fanous, Riad Akhnookh, *Manchester*.
1915. Fanstone, James, *Hassocks*.
1918. Faraci, Paul.
1915. Farag, Mounir, *Alexandria*.
1920. Faraker, Erskine Claud, *Brockley*.
1883. Faraker, John Joseph, *Brockley*.
1876. Farbstein, Henry, *Hull*.
1906. Fardon, Albert Henry, *Redhill*.
1905. Fardon, Harold Joseph, *Redhill*.
1889. Fardon, John H., M.B.E., *Birkenhead*.
1906. Farebrother, Harold Wm., *R.A.M.C.*
1850. Farish, Henry Greggs, *Nora Scotia*.
1874. Farley, John Jay, *Belleville, Canada*.
1880. Farmer, Ernest W.m. White, *Lewisham*.
1883. Farmer, Fredk. Reginald, *Gravesend*.
1880. Farmer, Septimus, *Ferryhill*.
1895. Farmer, William Henry, *Ludlow*.
1905. Farncombe, Harry, *Southsea*.
1851. Farncombe, Thos. Beard, *I.M.S.*
1893. Farncombe, Thos. Stone, *Trenton, Can.*
1890. Farncombe, Wm. Turberville, *Birm'gh.*
1896. Farndale, John William, *Rhodesia*.
1906. Farnfield, John Stewart, *Hastings*.
1896. Farnfield, William Walter, *Mere*.
1894. Farnum, Chas. M. Stone, *Trinidad*.
1918. Farquharson, Donald Charles.
1889. Farquharson, Geo. S., *Southampton*.
1918.§Farquharson, Loveday S., *South'mpt'n*
1916. Farquharson, William, *Acton*.
1891. Farquharson, Wm. Geo. R., *Jamaica*.
1897. Farr, Arthur, *Pembroke-road*.
1866. Farr, Arthur John, *Ferryhill*.
1895. Farr, Conrad Chailes Jas., *Watlington*.
1885. Farr, Ernest, *Ealing*.
1885. Farr, Ernest Augustus, *Andover*.
1887. Farr, Jos. Jas. Wm., *Warwick-gdns*.
1912. Farr, Montague Albert, *Kensington*.
1923. Farr, Valentine Francis, *Woodville-y's*.
1896. Farrant, Charles, D.S.O., *R.A.M.C.*
1889. Farrar, John Frederick, *Putney*.
1911. Farrer, Robert Noel, *Clayton West*.
1879. Farrer, Robt. Thompson, *Brighouse*.
1921. Farris, Sadik.
1886. Farrow, Frederick, *Manchester*.
1889. Fasnacht, Reymond Edwd., *Bedford*.
1911. Faulkner, Cyril Douglas, *Stanford*.
1916. Faulkner, Henry Andrew, *Melbourne*.
1923. Faull, John Langdon, *Honor-oak*.
1922. Faull, William Collins, *St. Ives*.
1882. Faunce, Charles Edmund, *R.A.M.C.*
1906. Favell, Richard Vernon, *Sheffield*.
1914. Fawcett, Hugh Alderson, *Chalfont*.
4806

1903. Fawcett, Hugh Hbt. Jas., *R.A.M.C.*
1907. Fawkes, M., O.B.E., *Midhurst*.
1902. Fawley, Tom Bower, *Hull*.
1912. Fawn, George Frederick, *Bristol*.
1867. Fawsitt, Thomas, *Oldham*.
1899. Fawssett, Basil, *Birmingham*.
1903. Fawssett, Francis Wm., *Edmonton*.
1887. Fawssett, Frank, M.B.E., *Lewes*.
1920. Fawssett, Richard Shirley.
1905. Fawssett, Wilfrid, *Fulham*.
1896. Fayrer, Fdk. Durand Stirling, *I.M.S.*
1889. Fazan, Chas. Herbert, *Wadhurst*.
1913. Fazan, Eric A. Chas., M.C., *R.A.M.C.*
1890. Fearnhead, Thomas, *Lytham*.
1892. Fearnley, Jonathan, *Bow*.
1891. Featherstone, Geo. Wm. B., *Vict., Aust.*
1916. Featherstone, Hy. Walter, *Erdington*.
1885. Featherstone, Wm. B., *Birmingham*.
1893. Feaver, Lewis, *Truro*.
1898. Fegan, Jn. Herbt. Crangle, *E Grinstead*.
1897. Fegan, Richard Ardra, *Forest Row*.
1885. Fegen, Charles Milton, *Croydon*.
1901. Fehrsen, Alex. Oloff M., *Transvaal*.
1888. Fehrsen, Frederic John, *Cape*.
1916. Fehrsen, Frederick Oloff, *Cape*.
1914. Feilden, Fredk. Ernest, *S. Shields*.
1909. Feiling, Anthony, *Devonshire-street*.
1915. Feldman, Israel (Junr.), *Church-lane*.
1915. Feldman, Israel (Senr.), *Osborne-st.*
1915. Feldman, Victor, *Osborne-street*.
1921. Feldman, Vivian, *Gt. Alie-street*.
1918. Feldman, William, *Gt. Alie-street*.
1904. Feldman, Wm. Moses, *Whitechapel-rd.*
1886. Felix, Edward, *Elgin-avenue*.
1904. Félix, Jean Jos. T. R., *Mauritius*.
1898. Fell, M. H. Gregson, C.B., C.M.G.
1900. Fell, Robert, *York*.
1881. Fell, Walter, *Strand*.
1900. Felton, Edgar Hall, M.B.E., *Grimsby*.
1904. Felton, Richard, M.C., *Vancouver*.
1920. Fenn, Arthur James, *Southampton-st.*
1898. Fenn, Charles Edward, *Streatham*.
1897. Fenn, Jos. Hiorns, *Southport*.
1900. Fennell, Chas. Henry, *Reform-club*.
1865. Fennell, Theodore, *Knutsford*.
1882. Fenner, Robt. Nath., *Spanish-place*.
1917. Fenning, Reg. John Keith, *Worthing*.
1892. Fennings, Arthur Allen, *Brighton*.
1922. Fenton, Charles Edmund, *Barking*.
1886. Fenton, Charles Francis, *Barking*.
1880. Fenton, Herbert A. H, *Fulham*.
1919. Fenton, Victor Norman, *Salcombe*.
1880. Fenton, Wm. Hugh, *George-street*, W.
1877. Fenwick, Bedford, *Upper Wimpole-st.*
1922.§Fenwick, Claude, *Gosforth*.
1923.§Fenwick, Emmie Dor'thy, *S. Nutfield*.
4863

1894. Fenwick, Percival C., C.M.G., *New Z.*
1896. Fenwick, Saml. Chas. C., *Norbury.*
1888. Fenwick, Wm. Soltau, *Harley-st.*
1880. Féré, Gregory Arthur, *Toronto.*
1912. Ferguson, Archibald, *Stepney.*
1893. Ferguson, Arnold Saml., *Jersey.*
1905. Ferguson, Geo. Edward, *R A..M.C.*
1916. Ferguson, Jacob Young, *Japan.*
1884. Ferguson, James Haig, *Edinburgh.*
1896. Ferguson, James Henry, *Keighley.*
1876. Ferguson, John, *Manchester.*
1904. Ferguson, John, *Cheam.*
1904. Ferguson, Lionel Cecil, *Bedford-park.*
1890. Ferguson, Robt. Bruce, *New Southgate.*
1897. Ferguson, Wm Alexander, *Douglas.*
1923. Fergusson, Alec Everett, *Southend.*
1911. Fergusson, George D. G., *R.N.*
1897. Fergusson, James Herbert, *R.N.*
1905. Fergusson, Jn. Newbury F., *Plymouth.*
1908. Fernandes, Caétano José, *Calcutta.*
1919. Fernaudez, Thomas, *Guy's-hospital.*
1922. Fernan lo, Andrew C., *Negombo, Ceyl.*
1917. Fernando, Edwin Francis, *Kalburn.*
1918. Fernando, Huxley, *Ceylon.*
1910. Fernando, Walter Andrew, *Ceylon.*
1906. Fernia, Charles Henry, *Greenwich*
1893. Fernie, Francis Edward, *Stone, Staffs.*
1896. Fernie, John Firth, *Stone, Staffs.*
1888. Ferraby, Geo. Arthur, *Nottingham.*
1874. Ferrier, John Christian, *Norwood.*
1904. Ferrière, Jos. Anthony, *Mauritius.*
1872. Ferris, John Edward Charnock, *I.M.S.*
1885. Fetherstonhaugh, Rbt. T., *Victoria.*
1913. Ffoulkes, Meredvdd, *Llanberis.*
1906. Fiaschi, Piero, *New York.*
1913. Fickling, Edwin L. Zenas, *Brook-st.*
1903. Fiddian, Arthur Edwin, *Cardiff.*
1900. Fiddian, Benj. Gregory, *Cardiff.*
1916. Fiddian, Eric Alfred, *St. Bart's-hosp.*
1912. Fiddi m, James Victor, *Brentford.*
1893. Fido, Herbert Adamson, *Brixton,*
1884. Field, Adolphus Theodore, *Hastings.*
1868. Field, Albert Frederick, *Falmouth.*
1883. Field, Edgar Alfred, *Darwen.*
1801. Field, Frederick Arthur, *Knutsford.*
1894. Field, Geo. Hammond, *Rickm'nsworth.*
1880. Field, James William.
1919.§Field, Kathleen, *Bedford.*
1887. Field, Oliver, *Capham.*
1909. Field, Philip Charles, *R.A.M.C.*
1908. Field, Wm. V., O.B.E., *Transvaal.*
1881. Fielden, Wm. Eckett, *Burgess-hill.*
1893. Fielder, Fredk. John, *Brixton.*
1905. Fielding, Charles Henry, *I.M.S.*
1921. Fifield, Lionel Richard, *Clapton.*
1806. Finch, Alex. Henry, *Shepton Mallet.*
1891. Finch, Ernest James, *R.N.*

1895. Finch, Herbert Jonathan, *Purton.*
1916.§Finch, Susan Alfreda, *Ladbroke-gr.*
1897. Finch, Wm. Stanley, *Pontefract.*
1889. Findlay, Harry, *Rangoon.*
1923.§Findlay, Margaret, *South Africa.*
1923. Finiefs, L. A., *Lancaster-gate-terr.*
1901. Finigau, Danl.C.O'Conn., *Fordingb'dge*
1883. Fink, Geo. Herbert, *I.M.S.*
1902. Finlay, Douglas Edward, *Gloucester.*
1903. Finlayson, Walter Taylor, *I.M.S.*
1886. Finley, Fredk. Gault, C.B., *Montreal.*
1892. Finley, Harry, *Malvern.*
1893. Finnie, John Ellison, *Birkdale.*
1837. Finucane, Morgan Ignatius, *Ashley-pl.*
1904. Finzel, Harry, *Bristol.*
1903. Finzi, Neville Saml., *Harley-street.*
1917. Firman-Edwards, L. P. L., *Croydon.*
1907. Firth, Arth.Chas.Douglas, *Wimpole-st.*
1894. Firth, Edwin Gore, *Shipley.*
1902. Fish, William Ambrose, *Toronto.*
1906. Fisher, Arthur Roland, *R.N.*
1877. Fisher, Frederic Bazley, *Tiverton.*
1911. Fisher, Frederick Thomas, *Cardiff.*
1907. Fisher, Fredk. Pearson, M.C.
1867. Fisher, George, *Donking.*
1918. Fisher, George Annesley, *Russell-sq.*
1923. Fisher, George Edward, *S. Norwood.*
1884. Fisher, Henry Holdrich, *Sittingbourne.*
1903. Fisher, Henry Richmond, *Atherstone.*
1900. Fisher, Herbert W., *Cowes.*
1896. Fisher, John Cecil, *Lytham.*
1918 §Fisher, Lilian Mabel, *Cartwright-gds.*
1909. Fisher, Reginald, *King's Langley.*
1894. Fisher, Reginald Willis, *Westbury.*
1896. Fisher, Richard Deuington, *Natal.*
1909. Fisher, Robt. Hankinson W., *Garstang.*
1914. Fisher, Robert Ovens, *Canada.*
1886. Fisher, Theodore, *Sidcup.*
1890. Fisher, Thos. E. Hervarre, *Hornsey.*
1887. Fisher, Walter, *Rhodesia.*
1902. Fisher, Walter H., O.B E., *Grimsby.*
1896. Fisk, Edward, *Ramsgate.*
1915. F.sk, Harry Hope, *Southsea.*
1916. Fisk, Sidney William, *Watford.*
1895. Fison, Edmund T., O.B E , *Salisbury.*
1917. Fitch, Arthur Alfred, *Liverpool.*
1886. Fitch, Chas. Dennis, *Kidderminster.*
1881. Fitch, Richd. Aubrey, *Royal Navy.*
1870. Fitzgerald, Conrad, *Newfoundland.*
1889. Fitz-Gerald, Ed. Desmond, *Folkestone.*
1887. Fitzgerald, Gerald C., *Canterbury.*
1923. FitzGerald, Gerald H.; *Weymouth-st.*
1876. Fitzgerald, Jas. Gubbins, *Beddington.*
1886. FitzHenry, Geo. Wm., *E. Dulwich-rd.*
1916. Flamer-Caldera Justin B., *Ceylon.*
1920. Flanagan, Joseph, *Bootle.*
1896. Flavelle, John Mason, *J.Athenæum Cl.*

1909. Flaxman, Sam Chris. Reeve, *Peckham*.
1911. Fiecker, Hugo, *Neutral Bay, N.S.W.*
1905. Fleetwood, Wm. Hardy, *Hoylake.*
1894. Flegg, Fredk. Arth. Martin, *Woodford.*
1869. Fleming, David Gibb, *Chatham, Ont.*
1920. Fleming, Gerald W. T. H., *Durham.*
1898. Fleming, Jas. K. S., O.B.E., *I.M.S.*
1895. Fleming, Wilf Louis Remi, *Pirbright*
1894. Flemming, Arth. Launcelot, *Bristol.*
1885. Flemming, Chas. E.S, *Bradford-on-A.*
1886. Fletcher, Arthur Aug., *Kington.*
1922.§Fletcher, Betty, *Queen's-road.*
1906. Fletcher, Cavendish, *N. Cavendish-st.*
1877. Fletcher, Chas. Wm. Corrie, *Derby.*
1893. Fletcher, Frederick James, *Stoke-on-T.*
1872. Fletcher, George, *Highgate, N.*
1886. Fletcher, Rev. Geo. Rory Jn., *Streatham*
1920. Fletcher, James O'Farrell, *Trinidad.*
1883. Fletcher, John, *Fulham.*
1898. Fletcher, John Howard, *Wigan.*
1893. Fletcher, Leslie, *Kempsey.*
1923.§Fletcher, Mary Dorothy, *Highgate.*
1904. Fletcher, Nigel Corbet, *Haverstock-hill*
1895. Fletcher, Roland Hry., *Bournemouth.*
1886. Fletcher, Thomas Johnson, *Derby.*
1862. Fletcher, Wm. Bainbrigge, *Roy. Navy.*
1923. Fletcher-Barrett, K., *Gray's-inn-rd.*
1900. Flewitt, Chas. York, *Sutton Coldfield.*
1881. Fligg, William, *Weston-super-Mare.*
1877. Flint, Arthur, *Westgate-on-Sea.*
1907. Flint, Harold Edwards, *Norwood.*
1895. Flint, Thomas Buxton, *Buxton.*
1904. Flintoff, Charles Ashley, *Pocklington.*
1878. Flood, Francis Pulteney, *Cefn.*
1901. Flook, Hubert Sydney, *Natal.*
1896. Flory, Cyril Hobson, *Assam.*
1895. Flower, Arth. Fdk. Ashbrook, *Derby.*
1907. Flower, Norman, *Yeovil.*
1892. Floyd, Stephen George, *Grays.*
1872. Floyer, Blaise Bernard, *N.S.W.*
1918. Flynn, Walter Alan, *Dulwich.*
1907. Foerster, Arthur Edwin, *Gloucester-pl.*
1897. Fogarty, Daniel, *Harringay.*
1884. Foley, Chas. Nicholas, *Tollington-pk.*
1914. Foley, John Edward, c/o *Holt & Co.*
1915. Folinsbee, Francis John, *Alberta.*
1889· Folker, Hbt. Henry, O.B.E., *Shelton.*
1920. Folliet, Louis, F.R.C.L., *Aix-les-Bains*
1896. Follott, Edwin, *Royal Navy.*
1908. Follit, Harold Harry Baily, *Bedford.*
1923.§Foner, Annie, *Swansea.*
1919. Fonseka, Frederic Lionel, *King-st.*
1899. Fookes, Ernest Faber, *N. Zealand.*
1894. Fcoks, Edwd. Verdon Russell, *S. Aust.*
1879· Fooks, George Ernest, *I.M.S.*
1885. Fooks, Henry, *I.M.S.*
1891. Fooks, Walt. Pemberton, *Birmingham.*
5034

1884. Foot, Ernest George, *Pulborough.*
1908. Foot, Thomas James, *Crawley-down.*
1907. Foote, Edmund George, *Sedbergh.*
1909. Foote, Percy Leslie, *New Zealand.*
1923. Foote, Robert Rowden, *Beckenham.*
1897. Foote, Vivian Percival, *Hailsham.*
1904. Footner, Bertram M., M.B.E., *Walsall.*
1923. Forbes, Hugh Scott.
1918. Forbes, John Turnbull Thompson, *N.Z.*
1914. Forbes, Septimus Alex., *Muswell-hill.*
1914. Ford, Alma Percy, *New Barnet.*
1891. Ford, Frank Chubb, *Wimbledon.*
1916. Ford, Maurice Rolfe V., *Chesterfield.*
1879. Ford, Sir R.W., K C M G., C.B, D.S O.
1915. Ford, Ronald Kelson, *Up Tooting.*
1887. Ford, Theodore Albt. Vores, *Hertford.*
1907. Forde, Cecil Ledward, *Birkenhead.*
1891. Forde, Thos. Arth. Munro, *Southsea.*
1885. Fordin, George, *Berkeley.*
1897. Fordham, John William, *Leicester.*
1904. Fordham, William John, *Selby.*
1921. Foreman, Edw. Cyril Henry, *Esher.*
1874. Foreman, Joseph, *Sydney, N.S.W.*
1923. Forman, Louis, *Portsmouth.*
1897. Forge, George Baynton, *Windlesham.*
1863. Forman, Elizha Baxter, *Chalfont.*
1883. Forrest, James Rocheid, *R.A.M.C.*
1876. Forrest, Jn. Geoorge S., *Winchester.*
1919. Forrest, Wm. Devereux, *S. Shields.*
1901. Forrest, Wm. Duff. *Halifax, N.S.*
1906. Forrester, Arch. T. Wm., *Narborough.*
1895. Forrester, William, *Sitapur, India.*
1915. Forrester-Paton, Ernest, *Alloa.*
1879. Forsbrook, Wm. Hy. Russell, *Eaton-sq.*
1915§Forster, Annie Mary C., *Newcastle.*
1850. Forster, Arthur.
1912. Forster, Charles Michael, *Badminton.*
1864. Forster, Edward Wood, *Felixstowe.*
1899. Forster, Fredk. Cecil, *Southbourne.*
1888. Forster, John Erwood, *Brockley.*
1884. Forster, Thos. Fdk., *Dalton-in-Furness.*
1902. Forsyth, Charles Wesley, *Sutton.*
1900. Forsyth, David, *Wimpole-street.*
1903. Forsyth, Lennard Wm., *Harley-st.*
1902. Fort, Charles Leyland.
1915. Fort, Charles Wainwright, M.C.
1896. Fort, Henry R. Trecothick.
1909. Fortin, Claude Edw. Freer, *Winnipeg.*
1919. Forty, Arthur Alan, *Leeds.*
1899. Forward, Ernest Lionel, *Nottingham.*
1894. Fosbery, Francis Clifford, *Bath.*
1872. Fosbroke, George Haynes, *Worcester.*
1898. Foss, Alwin Vincent, *Bristol.*
1919. Foss, Reginald Stafford, *Dulwich.*
1868. Foster, Anthony Clarence, *Leeds.*
1900. Foster, Arthur Herbert, *Hitchin.*
1908. Foster, Arthur Leslie, *R.A.M.C.*
5091

1902. Foster, Edward Cecil, *Oxford.*
1913. Foster, Edwin James, *Canada.*
1922.§Foster, Ena Dorothy, *Reading.*
1915. Foster, George Muir, *Cricklewood.*
1876. Foster, Henry, *York.*
1900. Foster, Henry Bertram, *I.M.S.*
1896. Foster, John Joseph, *Cheltenham.*
1892. Foster, MichaelBernard,*Harrogate.*
1888. Foster, Michael G.,O.B.E.,*Harrogate.*
1867. Foster, Oswald Henry, *Hitchin.*
1899. Foster, Percy, *Assam.*
1861. Foster, Philip, *Leeds.*
1901. Foster, RaymondLeslie V.,*R.A.M.C.*
1873. Foster, Reginald Henry, *Porlock.*
1879. Foster, William, *Shipley, Yorks.*
1911. Foster-Smith, Geoffrey T., *Cairo.*
1906. Fothergill, Claud F., *Chorley Wood.*
1899. Foulds, Francis Henry, *Droitwich.*
1900. Foulds, Matthias Fredk., *R.A.M.C.*
1897. Foulerton,HarryPercival,*Crowthorne.*
1921.§Foulkes, Mary Gwendolen, *Exeter.*
1903. Foulkes, Peter Gifford, *Purfleet.*
1920. Foulkes, RichardKenrick,c/o*Cox&Co.*
1902. Foulkes, Samuel Newall, *Amlwch.*
1914. Fountain, Edward Dance, *Ruislip.*
1885. Fountain, Edward Osborne, *Ruislip.*
1867. Fountaine, David Owen, *Muswell-hill.*
1909. Fowell,PatrickHarveyC.,*Welshpool.*
1884. Fowler, Alfred Henderson, *Tilbury.*
1890. Fowler, Chappell H., *Eccleston-street.*
1882. Fowler, Chas. Owen, *Thornton-heath.*
1901. Fowler, Edwin Samuel Geo., *Leeds.*
1874. Fowler, Sir Jas. K.,K.C.V.O.,C.M.G.
1892. Fowler, James Stewart, *Edinburgh.*
1856. Fowler, Rev. Jos. Thos , *Durham.*
1904. Fowler, Trevor Hayman, *Redhill.*
1907. Fowler,Wm.E. Lindsey, *Carlshalton.*
1922. Fox, Albert Robert, *Clapton.*
1901. Fox, Campbell Tilbury, *Ashford.*
1873. Fox, Charles Allen, *Bridgwater.*
1910. Fox, Charles Joshua, *Blidworth.*
1915.§Fox, Charlotte Iris, *Devonshire-pl.*
1922.§Fox, Dora Janet, *Isleworth.*
1897. Fox, Edwd. Hamilton B., *Yealmpton.*
1885. Fox, Edward Lawrence, *Plymouth.*
1863. Fox, Francis, *Arundel-gardens*, W.
1887. Fox, Fdk. Geo. Townsend,*O. Riv.Col.*
1881. Fox, George, *Swansea, Tasmania.*
1887. Fox, George Martin, *Walsall.*
1905. Fox, Henry Edward, *Accrington.*
1898. Fox, Hereward Evelyn C., *Weymouth.*
1900. Fox, Hugh Watson, *Bettws-y-Coed.*
1888. Fox, James Stanislaus, *St. Helen's.*
1903. Fox, John William, *Rotherham.*
1878. Fox,Joseph Tregelles, *Oregon,U.S.A.*
1910. Fox, Joseph Tylor, *Tufnell-park.*
1923.§Fox, Mary Elizabeth, *Woodford-green*

1874. Fox,Richard Hingston,*Devonshire-pl.*
1882. Fox, Robert Fortescue, *Devonshire-pl.*
1887. Fox, Stephen Chas. Gundry, *Perak.*
1910. Fox, Walter Egbert, *Gloucester.*
1902. Fox, Wilfrid Stephen, *Grosvenor-st.*
1914. Foxell,Humphrey L. G.,*Muswell-hill.*
1887. Foxton, Edward, *Ottawa.*
1870. Frakes, Henry Sowter, *Haslemere.*
1884. Frames, Alfred Cromwell, *Cape.*
1883. Frampton, Fredk. Thos, *Paignton.*
1880. Frampton,TomHenryT.,*Twickenham.*
1893. France, Charles Frederic, *Wigan.*
1884. France, Edward, *Sheffield.*
1920. France, James Hassall. *Wandsworth.*
1903. France,Wm. Henry, *Tierra delFuego.*
1899. Francis, Arthur Edward, *Khargpur.*
1922.§Francis, Christine Phyllis, *Streatham*
1892. Francis, Ernest Edward, *Bengal.*
1886. Francis, Harry Arthur, *Canada.*
1891. Francis, Harvey, O.B.E., *Arnold.*
1890. Francis, HenryAlex.,*Henrietta-st.*,W.
1902. Francis, Jas. Bernard C., *Dockhead.*
1886. Francis, John Arth., *Tufnell-park.*
1900. Francis, John Edmund, *Northam.*
1923. Francis, Kenneth Victor, *Uxbridge.*
1880. Francis, Lloyd, *Stourbridge.*
1891. Francis, Louis Arthur, *Uxbridge.*
1909. Francis, Reg. Cyril Herbt., *Brecon.*
1896. Francis. Sylvestre A., *Demerara.*
1922. Francis, Wilfrid Frederick,*Uxbridge.*
1884. Francis, William Henry, *Chili.*
1900. Francis, Wm. Vare C., *Los Angeles.*
1900. Francis-Williams, C. H., *Dowlais.*
1858. Franey,'Edward, *Banbury.*
1876. Frankish, Wm. John, *Cadogan-gdns.*
1923. Franklin, Charles A. H., *Blackheath.*
1923.§Franklin, Emily Lorna, *Devonport.*
1902. Franklin, Geo. Denne,O.B.E., *I.M.S.*
1888. Franklin, Lawrence, *Southwick.*
1916.§Franklin,Marjorie E.,*Porchester-terr.*
1908. Franklin, Reginald, *Newington-green.*
1898. Frankling, Hbt. G.,C.B.E.,*Harrogate*
1921. Franklyn, Harold, *New Eltham.*
1921. Franks, Jacob, *Amhurst-road.*
1907. Fraser,Alex. Edw.Gordon,*R.A.M.C.*
1903. Fraser, Chas. Frederick. M.C.,*I.M.S.*
1894. Fraser, David Henry, *Pendleton.*
1901. Fraser, Ernest Albert,*Delamere-cres.*
1889. Fraser, Herbert, *Slough.*
1892. Fraser, Herbert St. John, *I.M.S.*
1882. Fraser, James Alexander, *Romford.*
1880. Fraser, James William, *Hull.*
1899. Fraser, Jn. Henry P., D.S.O., M.C.
1886. Fraser,NuttingStuart,*Newfoundland.*
1886. Fraser, Paul Wilkes, *Victoria.*
1886. Fraser, Robt. Nelson, *Ontario, Can.*
1892. Frazer, Ernest Edward, *Jersey.*

1898. Frazer, Ewan Richards, *E. Grinstead.*
1902. Frazer, James Hogg, *Stratford.*
1919. Frazer, Lionel E., *Eastbourne.*
1895. Frazer, William Dyer, *Shanklin.*
1896. Frederick, Edwd. Gurdon, *Woolwich.*
1905. Frederick, Ernest Victor, *Canada.*
1899. Freear, Alexander, *Chatham.*
1882. Freeborn, John Chas. Richd., *Oxford.*
1923.§Freeborough, Margery, *Sheffield.*
1923. Freedman, Sidney L., *Pontycymmer.*
1891. Freeland, Reg. S., *Brockenhurst.*
1886. Freeman, Chas. Delamark, *Trinity-rd.*
1912. Freeman, Claude Emery, *Sheffield.*
1886. Freeman, Ernest C., C.M.G., *R.A.M.C.*
1921. Freeman, Harry, *Dalston.*
1891. Freeman, John, *Bristol.*
1886. Freeman, Richd. Austin, *Gravesend.*
1877. Freer, Edward Luke, *Natal.*
1888. Freer, Gerald Dudley, *Thurlestone.*
1900. Freer, Horace Wilberforce, *Stourb'dge.*
1899. Freer, Wm. Leacroft, *Blackheath.*
1919. Freilich, Joseph Pinkus.
1888. Fremlin, Heaver Stuart, *Hendon.*
1874. French, Alex. Martin, *R.N., Kingston.*
1909. French, Arthur Gordon Valpy, *R.N.*
1910. French, Frank Austin, *Herne-bay.*
1898. French, Gilbert Edwin, *Chiswick.*
1910. French, Gilbert James, *Fairfield.*
1922. French, Leslie, *Hornsea.*
1897. French, Louis Alex. W., *Portland.*
1917. French, Robert, *Carlisle.*
1894. Frend, Eustace Clifford, *H'rstpierpoint*
1903. Freshwater, John D. H., *Welbeck-st.*
1907. Frew, Wm. Doug., M.C., *Kilmarnock.*
1893. Freyberger, Ludwig, *Regent's-park.*
1900. Friedlander, Arth. Jonas, *Chingford.*
1914. Friedlander, Hugo Rudolph, *Mark-l.*
1875. Friend, Fredk. Worrell, *Brighton.*
1905. Friend, Gerald Edward, *Horsham.*
1877. Friend, Herbt. Edwd., *Westbourne-pk.*
1917. Frith, Fred. Chris. Ashley, *Bristol.*
1903. Frizzell, William Thomas, *Canada.*
1877. Frobisher, William Martin, *Leeds.*
1889. Frossard, Emilien Edward, *Taunton.*
1917. Frossard, Phil. Edw. Fraser, *Taunton.*
1887. Frost, Francis Turner, *Derby.*
1882. Frost, George, *Bournemouth.*
1920. Frost, Isaac, *Mortimer-street.*
1888. Frost, John Kingdon, *Exeter.*
1899. Frost, Joseph Reginald, *New Cross.*
1870. Frost, Richard Russell, *S. Australia.*
1863. Frost, Walter, *Hove.*
1885. Frowen, Fraser, *Burton.*
1896. Fry, Arthur B., C.I.E., D.S.O., *I.M.S.*
1895. Fry, Augustine Cradock, *Stone.*
1911. Fry, Hubert Jn. Burgess, *St. Thos.-h.*
1863. Fry, John Blount, *Beahill.*
5262

1874. Fry, John Farrant, *Budleigh Salterton.*
1915. Fry, Lewis Salisbury, *Limpsfield.*
1896. Fry, Percy Victor, *Sowerby Bridge.*
1922. Fry, Rowdon Marrian, *Willesden.*
1893. Fry, Walter Ernest, *Hammersmith.*
1894. Fry, William Herbert, *Malay States.*
1912. Fry, William Kelsey, M.C., *R.A.M.C.*
1888. Fryer, Geo. Ernest, O.B.E., *Urmston.*
1881. Fryer, John, *Dewsbury.*
1888. Fullard, John, *Manchester.*
1895. Fuller, Alfred Leonard, *Bath.*
1882. Fuller, Andrew, *Loc. Govt. Board.*
1916. Fuller, Andrew Radburne, *Weybridge.*
1908. Fuller, Ashbury Jos. S., *Aberystwyth.*
1892. Fuller, Charles Arthur, *Cawnpore.*
1922. Fuller, Charles Basil Sabine.
1889. Fuller, Courtenay James, *Woolwich.*
1908. Fuller, Fredk. Holcombe, *Bournem'uth*
1884. Fuller, Geo. Harry Hingston, *O.R.C.*
1880. Fuller, Hy. Roxburgh, M.V.O., *Mayf'ir*
1891. Fuller, John Reginald, *Tollington-pk.*
1878. Fuller, Leedham Henry, *Streatham.*
1898. Fuller, Laurence Otway, *Arlesey.*
1905. Fuller, Ralph A., M.C., *Long Ashton.*
1898. Fuller, Wm. Anderson, *Milnthorp.*
1922 §Fuller-Maitland, Lydia S., *Brighton.*
1892. Fullerton, Alex. Young, *N.S.W.*
1893. Fullerton, Francis William, *New Zeal.*
1897. Fulton, Henry, D.S.O., *Sevenoaks.*
1918. Fuoss, Armin F. M., *Wolverhampton*
1888. Furber, Edward Price, *Welbeck-st.*
1908. Furness, Harold Sid., *Melton Mowbray.*
1922.§Furniss, Ada, *Manchester.*
1923. Furniss, Frank Webster, *Sheffield.*
1882. Furnival, Francis Henry, *N.S. W.*
1898. Furnivall, Charles Hilton, C.M.G.
1869. Furnivall, Henry Wallace, *Exeter.*
1886. Furrer, Edward, *Kamloops, B.C.*
1912. Fyffe, Andrew Alexander, *Sheffield.*
1908. Fyffe, Eric Leigh, *R.A.M.C.*
1874. Fyson, Edmund, *St. Leonards-on-S.*
1905. Fyzee, Ali Azhar H., *Bombay.*

G.

1878. Gabb, Claude Baker, *Hastings.*
1873. Gabb, James Edward, *Wellingborough.*
1877. Gabb, Jas. Percy Alwyne, *Guildford.*
1918. Gabb, Harold Percy, *Guildford.*
1909. Gabe, Howell Woodwell, *Morriston.*
1913. Gabe, Ivor Stanley, *Royal Navy.*
1906. Gabe, William, *Morriston.*
1917. Gabe, William Vincent, *Morriston.*
1895. Gabell, Doug. Phillimore, *Portland-pl.*
1880. Gabriel, Joshua Samuel, *Ceylon.*
5314

1885. Gabriel, Leon. Maurice, *Penbridge-v.*
1884. Gabriel, Wm. Maurice, *Wardrobe-pl.*
1899. Gadsden, Arthur Horace, *Newquay.*
1899. Gaff, James, *Hammersmith.*
1919. Gaffney, Edward James, *Streatham.*
1919. Gaha, John Francis, *Sydney.*
1921. Gainer, Eric St. Clair. *Thrapston.*
1892. Gains, John Edwin, *South Cave.*
1917. Gainsborough, Hugh, *Bi ondeshury.*
1918. Gainsborough, Richard, *Bryanston-st.*
1918.§Gainsford, Lucie, *Charing-cross-hosp.*
1875. Gairdner, John, *Tasmania.*
1897. Gairdner, Jn. Francis Rbt., *Transvaal.*
1902. Gaitskell, Chas. Edward, *Lympstone.*
1869. Gaitskell, Edwd. Forbes, *Beckenham.*
1904. Galbraith, Colin James, *Chingford.*
1916. Galbraith, Douglas Hugh Aird, M.C.
1889. Gale, Arthur, *Kingston-on-Thames.*
1881. Gale, Arthur Knight, *Sheffield.*
1908. Gall, Herbert, *R.A.M.C.*
1922. Gallant, Israel Wolf, *Hazlett-road.*
1922. Gallant, Nahum, *Grove-road.*
1921. Gallegos, Octavio Pacifico.
1921. Gallop, Edward, *Willesden-lane.*
1908. Galloway, Hugh, *Southall.*
1922. Galloway, Rbt. Menzies, *Birkenhead.*
1914. Galloway, Wm. Dawson, *Stourwood.*
1898. Galloway, Wm. Hearfield, *Leeds.*
1870. Galpin, Richard, *Sutton.*
1918. Galstaun, Shanasar G., *St. Bart's.*
1898. Galt, William James, *Minories.*
1870. Gamble, Charles Edward, *Elland.*
1910. Game, Lennard, *New Barnet.*
1921 §Gamgee, Katherine M. L., *Dorset-sq.*
1910. Gamlin, Raymond, *Liverpool.*
1883. Gandevia, Navroji Bamanji, *Victoria.*
1906. Gandhi, Nadir H. S., *Stoke-on-Trent.*
1921. Gandhy, P.P., *H'kong & Shanghai Bk.*
1908. Gandy, Eric W., *O B.E., Norwood.*
1899. Gandy, Thomas Hall, *Peppard.*
1890. Gane, Edwd. Palmer Steward, *York.*
1923. Gane, Noel Gerald Carleton, *Lambeth*
1891. Gange, Fdk. Whitchurch, *Faversham.*
1923. Gann, John Hurndall. *Peterborough.*
1890. Gann, Thos. Wm. Francis, *Hayling.*
1895. Ganner, Joseph, *Acocks Green.*
1905. Gans, Friedrich, *Welbeck-street.*
1915. Garcés, Luis Hernando, *Colombia.*
1922. Garden, Mark, *Hove,*
1891. Gardener, Wm. Fredk., *Sydenham.*
1921. Gardham, Arthur John, *Leytonstone.*
1896. Gardiner, Geoffrey Edwd., *New Zeal.*
1896. Gardiner, John, *Oxford.*
1896. Gardiner, Joseph Napier, *Dunmow.*
1915. Gardiner-Hill, Clive, *Wimbledon.*
1915. Gardiner-Hill, Harold, *Wimbledon.*
1876. Gardner, Arthur John, *Darlington.*

1920 §Gardner, Blanche S., *Cheltenham.*
1904. Gardner, Eric, *Weybridge.*
1886. Gardner, Frank Gower, *Oxford.*
1892. Gardner, Harold Bellamy, *Harley-st.*
1902. Gardner, Harry, *Streatham.*
1885. Gardner, Hv. Willoughby, *Shrewsbury.*
1916. Gardner, Humphrey Douglas, *Finchley*
1809. Gardner, John, *Mexborough.*
1921. Gardner, Jonathan Earl, *Singapore.*
1881. Gardner, Percy Herbert, *Ilfracombe.*
1897. Gardner, Thomas Hudson, *Streatham.*
1895. Gardner, William, *Steeple Ashton.*
1886. Gardner, Wm. Thos., *Bournemouth.*
1903. Gardner-Medwin, Frank M., *Liverpool.*
1922. Garfield, Montagu, *Hackney.*
1874. Garland, Albert Isaac, *New Zealand.*
1913. Garland, Geoffrey, *Saltash.*
1901. Garle, Robt. Hubert Wm., *Purley.*
1912 Garlick, George Herbert, *Thakeham.*
1887. Garman, Edwin Cornelius, *Hailsham.*
1892. Garman, John Bernard, *Great Barr.*
1900. Garman, Joseph Marcus, *Ashford.*
1859. Garman, Wm. Chancellor, *Worcester.*
1896 Garner, Wm. Langham, *Ampthill.*
1923. Garnham, Percy C. C., *Bethune-road.*
1920. Garnett, Donald Godd., *Windermere.*
1894. Garrad, Francis Wm., *Harrogate.*
1881. Garrard, Chas. Roland O., *Pendleton.*
1909. Garrard, Edw. Brown, *Leeward Is.*
1891. Garrard, George, *St. Leonards-on-Sea.*
1913. Garrard, Norman, *Thrybergh.*
1911. Garratt, Frank, *Malay States.*
1916. Garraway, Gloster Tyndell, *Univ -coll.*
1907. Garrett, Percy Charles, *Dursley.*
1890. Garrett, Philip Gell, *Hinckley.*
1904. Garrett, Raymond R., *Eastleigh.*
1884. Garrod, Sir Archibald E., K.C.M.G.
1922. Garrod, Herb. Jn. Jos., *Guildford-st.*
1920. Garrod, Lawrence Paul, *Queen's-gds.*
1921.§Garrod, Marjorie, *Queen's-gardens.*
1914. Garson, Herbert Leslie, M.C., O.B.E.
1878. Garstang, Thos. Walt. H, *Altrincham.*
1903. Garton, Wilfrid, *Rugby.*
1923.§Garvin, Una Christina, *Weymouth-st.*
1902. Gask, Charles Herbert, *Upton-park.*
1897. Gaskell, Len. Sadgrove, *Birkenhead.*
1881. Gaskin, Thos. Law, *Barbadoes.*
1916. Gasperine. John Jones, *St. Bart's.*
1916. Gaspey, Ernest Thomas, *Univ.-coll,*
1914. Gassmann, Georg Arnold, *Enfield,*
1899. Gaster, Sidney, *Quetta.*
1886. Gaston, Harry Percival, *Southall.*
1902. Gater, Arthur William, *R.A.M.C.*
1898. Gates, Edward Alfred, O.B E.
1916. Gathergood, Leslie S., *Sydenham.*
1899. Gatt, Joseph, *R.A.M.C.*
1883. Gaudin, George Charles, *Jersey.*

1873. Gaunt, John Penn, *Hythe.*
1909. Gauntlett, Harry Leon, *Bloxham.*
1884. Gaussen, David Peter, *Dunmurry.*
1923. Gautier-Smith, C. E., *York-mans.*
1906. Gauvain, Henry John, *Alton.*
1911. Gavronsky, Jacob, *Regent's-park.*
1918. Gawne, Edwin Stowell, *Liverpool.*
1876. Gay, Charles Wm. Ebenezer, *India.*
1884. Gay, John, *Putney.*
1922. Gaydon, Frank Alfd., *Hampton Wick.*
1923.§Gayer, Lena Bella, *Edith-road.*
1896. Gayer, Reg. Courtenay, *Stanhope-gds.*
1903. Gayer-Anderson, Robt.G.,*R.A..M.C.*
1905. Gayner, Francis, *Redhill.*
1900. Gayner. John Stansfield, *Carswick.*
1879. Gayton Fras Carteret,*MuchHadham.*
1922. Gaze, John Edwin, *Cheshunt.*
1878. Gaze, Wm. Henry, *Victoria, Aust.*
1886. Gedge, Arthur Johnson, *Havant.*
1892. Gedge Arthur Sydney, *Pewsey.*
1899. Gee, Claude Alfred Heath, *Evercreech.*
1886. Gee, Frederick William, *I.M.S.*
1919. Geffen, Dennis Herbert, *Dawson-pl.*
1917. Geffen, Maximilian W., *Dawson-pl.*
1923.§Geldard, Joan O., *Ridgmount-gdns.*
1923. Geldart, Richard Morton, *Worthing.*
1915. Gell, George Cowley, *Douglas.*
1885. Gell, Hy. W., O.B.E., *Woolhampton.*
1884. Gemmel,Arch. Burns,C.B.E.,*Liverp'l.*
1911. Gemmell, Alan Cecil, *Brighton.*
1922. Gemmell, Arthur Alex, *Liverpool.*
1895. Genge, Geo. Fredk. S., *Bournemouth.*
1894. Genge, George Gilbert, *Croydon.*
1912. Genge-Andrews, Geo. Edw., *O.B.E.*
1889. George, Alfd. Walter, *Brondesbury.*
1910. George, Archibald Louis, *Trinidad.*
1857. George, Chas.Fdk.,*Kirton-in-Lindsey.*
1887. George, Henry, *Alberta, Canada.*
1904. George, Howard Trevelyan, *Cardiff.*
1893. George, Isaac, *West Australia.*
1912. George, Wm. Stanley, *Hampstead.*
1886. Georges, Absolom.
1902. Geraty, Laur.Unthank,M.C.,*Ingham.*
1874. Geraty, Thomas, *Ingham.*
1920.§Gere, Dorothy Bellows, *Kensington.*
1892. German, Arthur William, *Liverpool.*
1894. Gerrard, Alfred Henry, *Wimbledon.*
1906. Gerrard, Robert Francis, *Chester.*
1895. Gerrish, Daniel Smith, *Bristol.*
1919. Gerson, Herman Meyer, *Clapton.*
1891. Gervis, Arthur Fredk., *Hampstead.*
1897. Gervis, Charles Berkeley, *Seaford.*
1858. Gervis, Henry, *Bath.*
1889. Gervis, Henry, *Brighton.*
1908. Gerzabek, Boleslaw, *Winnipeg.*
1911.§Gethen, Rachel, *Harlesden.*
1904. Gettings, Cuthbert Keay, *Chasetown.*
1923. 5485

1923. Ghabrial, Labib, *Grove-park.*
1910. Ghadiali, Erach Pestonji.
1893. Ghany, Mohomed Abdul, *Hyderabad.*
1916. Ghose, Suresh Chandra, *Bengal.*
1914. Ghosh, Sourendra Mohon, *Calcutta.*
1915. Gibb, Alex Terris, *St. Anne's-on-Sea.*
1914. Gibb, Cassidy de Wet, *S. Africa.*
1917. Gibb, Edward Austin, *Wimbledon.*
1836. Gibbard, Thomas W., C.B., C.B E.
1887. Gibbens, Frank Edward, *Barking.*
1923. Gibberd, Geo. Fredk.. *Gipsy-hill.*
1865. Gibbes, John Murray, *Sydney.*
1895. Gibbes, Lewes Nicholas, *Kensington.*
1899. Gibbins, Herbert Bowly, *Davies-st.*
1888. Gibbon, Ernest Henry, *S. Shields.*
1922.§Gibbon, Laura Phœbe, *Oxford.*
1895. Gibbons, Arth. Philip, *Finsbury-circ.*
1897. Gibbons,Chas.Jas. P.T.,*KentishTown.*
1914. Gibbons, Gerald F. P., O.B.E.
1911. Gibbous, Lister, *Hove.*
1874. Gibbons, Robert Alex., *Cadogan-pl.*
1879. Gibbs, Alfd. Napier Godby, *Bristol.*
1904. Gibbs, Herbert Jennings, *Singapore.*
1922.§Gibbs, Nancy Kathleen, *Cardiff.*
1873. Gibbs, Robert, *Yardley-Hastings.*
1889. Gibbs, Seymour Farrage, *Girdler's-rd.*
1905. Gibbs,Stanley Rider,M.C.,*Barnstaple.*
1895. Giblin, Wilfrid Wanostrocht, C.B.
1910. Gibson, Alfred John, *Brentwood.*
1922. Gibson, Cecil Percy R., *Croydon.*
1910. Gibson, Charles, *Harrogate.*
1906. Gibson, Charles Walter, *Wareham.*
1915. Gibson, Colin Chas. Gordon, *Tooting.*
1922.§Gibson, Dorothy, *Forest-gate.*
1912. Gibson, Douglas Medlicott,*Parkstone.*
1900. Gibson, Fredk. Goulburn, *New Zeal.*
1873. Gibson, Hy. Christ. Mends,*Chalkwell.*
1891. Gibson, Henry Wilkes, *Hampstead.*
1913. Gibson, Hubert, *Leeds.*
1882. Gibson, John Hutchinson, *Aldershot.*
1885. Gibson, John Lockhart, *Brisbane.*
1912. Gibson, John Torbet Smith, *Acton.*
1905. Gibson, Lawrence George, *R.A.M.C.*
1889. Gibson, Louis Percival, *Cowes.*
1915. Gibson, Paul Currey, *Cranham.*
1911. Gibson, Percy Lempriere, *R.N.*
1919. Gibson, Ralph Byron, *Sheffield.*
1910. Gibson,Robert Wm.Beor,*Transvaal.*
1904. Gibson, Sydney Herbert, *Temple.*
1902. Gibson, Thomas, *Shipdham.*
1908. Gibson, Thomas Sidney, *Edgware.*
1903. Gibson, Wm. Edmund, *New Zealand.*
1907. Gibson, William Stonier, *Hampstead.*
1887. Giddings, George Thomas,*Beckenham.*
1883. Giddings, Robt. Ritchie,*Nottingham.*
1910. Gideon, Cyril Searle, *Jamaica.*
1908. Gideon,Eugene de Montevin,*Jamaica.*
5542 Q

1892. Gideon, Geo. V. Minchin, *New Cross.*
1886. Gidley, Gusta\us, *Cullompton.*
1918. Gidlow Jackson, Geoff. H., *Chorley.*
1917. Gie, Johan Coenraad, *Guy's.*
1906. Giesen, Ernest Wm., *New Zealand.*
1871. Giffard, Douglas Wm., *Bournemouth.*
1889. Giffard,Gerald Godfray,C.S.I.,*I.M.S.*
1877. Giffard, Henry Edward, *Eyham.*
1908. Gifford, Alexahder Harold, *Natal.*
1886. Gifford, George Taylor, *Crowthorne.*
1900. Gilbart-Smith, T. Bewley, *Notting'm.*
1892. Gilbert, Charles William, *Purley.*
1886. Gilbert, Clarence Edwin Lloyd,*I.M.S.*
1915. Gilbert, John Wesley, *Bi istol.*
1897. Gilbert, Leonard, C.I.E., *I.M.S.*
1912. Gilbertson, Herbert M., *Hitchin.*
1883. Gilbertson, James Henry, *Hitchin.*
1897. Gilbertson, William, *Onslow-sq.*
1910. Gilchrist, Arch. J., O.B E., *R.A.M.C.*
1887. Gilchrist, Thomas Caspar, *Baltimore.*
1904. Gilder, Dhanjibhai R , *Warrington.*
1888. Giles, Arth. Edwd., *Up. Wimpole-st.*
1920.§Giles, Madeline, *Barnet.*
1881. Giles, Oswald, *New Sleaford.*
1871. Giles, Peter Broome, C.B., *Bletchley.*
1917.§Gilford, Dorothy, *Letchworth.*
1914. Gilhespy, Frank Brayshaw, *Saltash.*
1886. Gilkes, Ernest Osmond, *Brighton.*
1880. Gilkes, Malin D'Oyley, *Ludlow.*
1904. Gilks, John Langton, *E.Af.M.S.*
1920. Gill, Aubrey Dudley, *W. Bromwich.*
1901. Gill, Clifford Allchin, *I.M.S.*
1920. Gill, Cyril, I. C., *Oldham.*
1898. Gill, Francis Philip, *Bristol.*
1903. Gill, George Brittan, *Belper.*
1902. Gill, Geo. Frederick, *Jamaica.*
1890. Gill, Jas. MacDonald, *Sydney.*
1878. Gill, John Wallis, *St. Germans.*
1888. Gill, Joseph William. *Callington.*
1917. Gill, Lawrence, *Hatch End.*
1893. Gill, Samuel Ernest. *Victoria-street.*
1871. Gill, Stanley Augustine, *Formby.*
1805. Gill, Sutton Dudley, *West Bromwich.*
1918. Gill-Carev, Chapple, *Q. Victoria-st.*
1877. Gillam, Thomas Henry, *Tenbury.*
1877. Gillard,Clarence Richard, *Wimbledon.*
1892. Gillbard, Richard, *Willesden-green.*
1900. Gillespie, Thomas, *Southampton.*
1911. Gillett, Aubrey Scott, *Torquay.*
1891. Gillett, George Edward, *Brooke.*
1895. Gillett, Henry Tregelles, *Oxford.*
1904. Gillies, John Wnn Ford, *Wimbledon.*
1907. Gillies, Robert Gray, *Finchley.*
1895. Gillies, Sinclair, *Sydney, N.S.W.*
1870. Gillingham, Alfred, *Chiswick.*
1902. Gillitt, William, C.I.E., *I.M.S.*
1917. Gilmour, Charles Hawkins, *Toronto.*

1903. Gilmour, Harry Morgan, *Hornsey.*
1873. Gilmour, John Henry, *Andover.*
1888. Gilmour, Percy Graham, *Gorleston.*
1895. Gilmour, Richd. Withers, *West Meon.*
1905. Gilmour, Robert Thomas, *R.N.*
1887. Gilpin, Wm. John, M.B.E., *Bourne.*
1914. Gimlette, Charles Hart M., *Chatham.*
1877. Gimlette, Geo. Hart D., C.I.E ,*I.M.S.*
1915. Gimlette, George Turner, *Epsom.*
1890. Gimlette,John Desmond,*Malay States.*
1879. Gimlette, Sir Thos. Desmond, K.C.B.
1887. Gimson, Wm. Douglas, *Chelmsford.*
1878. Gipps, Alex. Geo. P., D.S.O., *R.N.*
1917. Girgis, Aziz, *Finsbury-park-rd.*
1922. Girgis, Wahba, *Kolossne, Egypt.*
1889. Girling, Charles John, *Salisbury.*
1886. Girling, John, *Clacton-on-Sea.*
1906. Gittens, Carleton Wyndham, *Clapton.*
1894. Gittins, Alfred Benjamin, *Madeley.*
1922. Gittins, Thomas John E., *Dudley.*
1923. Gladish, Albert Denis, *Retford.*
1906. Glaister, John Norman, *Islington.*
1886. Glanville, Mark, *Balham.*
1900. Glasgow, John George, *Brixton-rd.*
1898. Glasier, Howard, *Mildenhall.*
1909. Glass, Robert Lionel, *Simla.*
1922. Glass, Samuel, *Birmingham.*
1902. Glassford, Ian Canute Gordon, M.C.
1886. Gledden, Alfd. Maitland, *Sydney.*
1907. Gleed, Seymour Richard, *Finchley.*
1915. Gleeson, Olaf, *Westminster-hospital.*
1910. Glen, Alex Kennedy, *Glasgow.*
1910. Glenister, Wilf. Mont., *St. Leonard's.*
1906. Glenny,-Elliott Thornton, *Grimsby.*
1885. Glinn, Cornelius Fredk., *Plymouth.*
1889. Glinn, George Frederick, *Camden-sq.*
1898. Glover, John Abel, *Burgess Hill.*
1892. Glover,Lewis Gladst'ne,*Fitzjohn's-av.*
1917. Gluckman, Henry, *Transvaal.*
1922.§Glyn-Jones, Kate, *Palmer's-green.*
1898. Glynn, Ernest Edward, *Liverpool.*
1864. Glynn, Thomas Robinson, *Liverpool.*
1918.§Glynne, Eryl, *Judd-street.*
1900. Goadby, Sir Kenneth W., K.B.E.
1896. Goard, Thomas Arthur, *Exeter.*
1900. Goble, Edwin Wallace,*Winchmore-h.*
1904. Goble, Fredk. George, *Roy. Navy.*
1883. Goddard, Charles Ernest, O.B.E.
1912. Goddard, Cyril E.Ambrose, *Wembley.*
1898. Goddard, Eugene Gilbert, *Cape.*
1895. Goddard,Gerald H ,D S.O.,*R.A.M.C.*
1872. Godding, Chas. Cane, C.B., *R.N.*
1913. Godding, Harold Cane, *R.A.M.C.*
1889. Godding, James, *Wanstead.*
1885. Godfrey, Albert Edward, *Finchley.*
1875. Godfrey, Benj. Geo., *Washington.*
1891. Godfrey, Clarence George, *Victoria.*

1884. Godfrey, Hry. John C., *Bridlington.*
1923.§Godfrey, Marjorie A., *Wilbraham-pl.*
1887. Godfrey, Thomas Henry, *Finchley.*
1904. Godson, Chas. Aubrey, M.C., *1 M.S.*
1880. Godson, Edwin, *Kenmore, N.S.W.*
1897. Godson, Francis Arth., *W. Didsbury*
1893. Godson, Leonard Jos., *Shrewsbury.*
1897. Godwin,Herb.Jas.,O.B.E., *Winch'st't*
1922.§Goetze, Marie Louise l'auline.
1897. Goffe,ErnestGeo. Leopold, *N.E.-hosp.*
1901. Gofton, Edward, *North Shields.*
1878. Gofton, Joseph Edward, *Paignton.*
1908. Gokhale, Vinayak Balvant, *Bombay.*
1923. Golden, Stanley John, *Highfield.*
1918. Goldhurst, Stuart Victor, *Swansea.*
1912. Goldie, Edw. Alex. M. J., M.C.
1903. Goldie, Ellis Gordon, *Bermondsey.*
1897. Goldie-Scot, Thomas, *Pilmuir.*
1922.§Golding, Irene Mary, *Eastbourne.*
1922.§Goldman, Alice M. F., *Cape Town.*
1888. Goldney, Arth. Geo. N., *Loughboro.*
1893. Goldney, Thos. William, *Richmond.*
1918. Goldschmidt,Wm.N ,*Phillimore-gds.*
1894. Goldsmith, Arthur Fredk., *Bedford.*
1910. Goldsmith, Bernard, *Llandudno.*
1916. Goldsmith, Edm. Onslow,*Cambridge.*
1892. Goldsmith, Geo. Harvey, *Bedford.*
1872. Goldsmith, Sept. Jesse, *I.M.S.*
1903. Goldstein, Herbert Myer, M.C.
1903. Goldstein, John Leopold, *Tangier.*
1900. Gollan, Lachlan, *Tasmania.*
1877. Golland, Alfred, *Altrincham.*
1867. Gomes,AntonioSimplicio.*HongKong.*
1902. Gomess,Alfd.Fra cis B.,*Drayton-gns.*
1900. Gomez, Francis Joseph, *S. Petherton.*
1900. Gomez, Guillermo, *Bogota.*
1904. Gompertz,Richd.H.C.,*Berkhampsted.*
1902. Gonin, Bertram Winter, *Greenford.*
1906. Gooch, Horace, *Brentwood*
1900. Good, Arnold Saxty, *Umberleigh.*
1919. Good, Chris. Frank. *Herne-hill.*
1905. Good, Edgar Hubert, *Worthing.*
1919. Good, Frederick John, *Brighton.*
1897. Good, Hardman Allgood, *New Zeal.*
1922.§Good, Janet Vera.
1888. Good, John, *Tenbury.*
1893. Good, Thomas S., O.B E , *Littlemore.*
1878. Good, William Ernest, *Dorchester.*
1886. Goodale, Henry, *Ebury-st.*
1916. Goodall, Charles Cunliffe, *High-lane.*
1920 §Goodall, Doris E. F., *Birmingham.*
1885. Goodall, Edwin, *Cardiff.*
1890 Goodbody, Cecil M., D.S.O., *I.M.S.*
1904. Goodchild, John Fleming, *Toronto.*
1887. Goodchild, Nath. Jn., *Highgate-rd.*
1900. Goode, George Ernest, *Shanghai.*
1897. Goode, Henry Norman, M.C., *York.*

5713

1888. Goodfellow, T. A., C.B.E., *Didsbury.*
1894. Goodhue, Fdk. Wm. J., *Ashley-gdns.*
1894. Gooding, Angelo, *Adelaide, Cape.*
1884. Gooding, Charles Ernest, *Barbados.*
1899. Goodman, Harold, *Wakefield.*
1919. Goodman, Harold Hyman, *Leeds.*
1894. Goodman, Henry Cyril,C B.E.,*Cairo.*
1923. Goodman, Neville M., *Kingston-hill.*
1887. Goodman, Roger Neville, *Kingston.*
1923. Goodman, Roy, *Haverhill.*
1886. Goodman, Thomas Herbt., *Haverhill.*
1896. Goodridge, Walt. Lisle Taylor,*Erith.*
1893. Goodson, Wm. Henry, *Leytonstone.*
1892. Goodwin, Edwd. Knox, *Oxford.*
1910. Goodwin, Ernest St G. Sagar, *R.N.*
1887. Goodwin, Frederick Charles, *Oxford.*
1899. Goodwin, Fredk. Wm., *Nova Scotia.*
1900. Goodwin,W. R.P., D.S.O.,*R.A.M.C.*
1918. Goolden,(George Anthony, *Cookham.*
1904. Goonetilleke, Fredk.Wm., *Singapore.*
1905. Goonewardene, Andrew S. S.,*Ceylon.*
1923. Gordon, Arthur, *Finchley-road.*
1890. Gordon,ArthurWm.,*Auburn,N.S.W.*
1919. Gordon, Boris, *New Tredegar.*
1923. Gordon, Brian Wilson B., *Willesden.*
1881. Gordon, Bryce.
1882. Gordon, Edward, *Bembridge.*
1917. Gordon, Edw.Fras.Strathearn,*Edinb.*
1909. Gordon, Francis Jervis, *Frome.*
1884. Gordon, Fredk. Wm., *Auckland, N.Z.*
1891. Gordon, Harry, *Natal.*
1894. Gordon, James E., O.B.E., *Salisbury.*
1905. Gordon, Kenneth F., M.C., *N.Z.*
1923.§Gordon, Louisa Patricia, *Newport.*
1922. Gordon. Samuel, *Battersea.*
1909. Gordon, Stephen, *I.M.S.*
1884. Gordon, Thomas Elisha, *Debenham.*
1888. Gordon, William, *Exeter.*
1889. Gordon-Green, H. W., M.B.E., *R.N.*
1886. Gore, Alfred Joseph, *Folkestone.*
1890. Gore, Henry Bushell, *Bordon.*
1888. Gornall, John Pegge J., *Blackpool.*
1923. Gornall, William Arthur, *Bristol.*
1919. Gorst, Philip Eldon, *Liverpool.*
1922. Gorton, Leslie Donovan, *Leamington.*
1876. Gosling, Charles Edward, *Moseley.*
1907. Goss, Edward Slade, M.C., *I.M.S.*
1903. Goss, John, *Gloucester.*
1877. Goss, Samuel, *Southsea.*
1890. Gossage, Alfred M., C.B.E.
1893. Gossage, Wm. Herbt., *Chertsey.*
1910. Gosse, Alfred Hope, *Nevern-square.*
1880. Gosse, Hope Wilkes, *Eccleshall.*
1907. Gosse, Philip Hy. Geo., *Beaulieu.*
1886. Gosse, William, *Parkstone.*
1920. Gosset, Arthur C. V., *Watlington.*
1875. Gosset, George. Sumner, *N.Z.*

5770 Q 2

1384. Gostling, John Harry, *York.*
1883. Gostling, Thos. P., O.B.E, *Worthing.*
1883. Gostling, Wm. Ayton, *Worthing*
1905. Gotelee, Hugh Evelyn, *Kingsteignton.*
1921. Gothe, Werner, *Wimpole-street.*
1923. Gott, Arthur William, *Leeds.*
1888. Gott, Henry, *Dulwich.*
1905. Gough, Harold Oscar, *Brentwood.*
1886. Gough, Henry Edward, *Northwich.*
1884. Gough, John Harley, *Torquay.*
1922. Gough, John Henry Harley, *Torquay.*
1921. Gould, Baruett, *Hackney.*
1913. Gould, C. Hamilton, *Basinghall-st.*
1916. Gould, Cyril, *Lamb's Conduit-street.*
1885. Gould, Ernest Edward, *Hailsham.*
1902. Gould, Harold Utterton, *Shaftesbury.*
1868. Gould, Henry, *Margate.*
1887. Gould, John Edwin, *Bolton.*
1873. Gould, Thomas, *Birmingham.*
1896. Goulden, Herbert Edward, *Exeter.*
1909. Gouldesbrough, Claude, *Welbeck-st.*
1886. Goullet, Chas. Arthur, *Finchley-rd.*
1888. Goulston, Arthur, *Exeter.*
1917. Goument, Lionel Charles, *Ealing.*
1917. Gourevitch, Mendel, *Balham.*
1878. Gover, Henry John, *Saffron Walden.*
1900. Gover, John Maxwell, *Gosforth.*
1908 Gow, Alex. Edward, *Welbeck-street.*
1885. Gow, William John, *Finchley-road.*
1887. Gowan, Bowie Campbell, *Marnhull.*
1919.§Gowers, Dorothy W., *Watford.*
1892. Gowring, Benj.Wm. N., *Dorchester.*
1908. Grabham, Henry Leatham, *Tonb'dge.*
1891. Grabham, Michael, *Jamaica.*
1861. Grabham, Michael Comport, *Madeira.*
1913. Grace, Edgar Mervyn, *Thornbury.*
1900. Grace, Nathaniel, *Tunbridge Wells.*
1918. Grace, Walter Henry, *Guy's.*
1884. Graham, Albert Wilfiam, *Tasmania.*
1899. Graham, Allan Gordon, *Brighton.*
1892. Graham, Chas. Hunter, *Southampton.*
1889. Graham, Charles Nicol.
1878. Graham, Charles Robert, *Wigan.*
1901. Graham, Edwd. Naggiar, *Malacca.*
1907. Graham, George, *Ladbroke-gardens.*
1872. Graham, Geo. Wm., *Bournemouth.*
1905. Graham, Harold Ernest, *Cirencester.*
1898. Graham, Howard William.
1884. Graham, Hugh Henry, *Ontario.*
1899. Graham, Jn. Chas. Wm., *Cambridge.*
1891. Graham, Jn. Hy. Porteus, *Wallasey.*
1875. Graham, John Thomas, *Perth.*
1905. Graham, Jos. Sutherland A., *Toronto*
1918. Graham, Lorne Benjamin.
1912. Graham, Richard Sydney.
1896. Graham, Vyner, *Doncaster.*
1899. Graham, Walter, *Vancouver.*
5827

1901. Graham, William Ezra, *Canada.*
1886. Graham, Wm. Perceval Gore, *A.M.S.*
1908. Graham-Jones, John L., *Sanderstead.*
1901. Graham-Smith, Geo. Stuart, *Camb.*
1912. Grauge, Frank Arthur, M.C., *Tring.*
1878. Granger, Edgar Bridden, *Wallingford.*
1915. Granger, Edmund Douglas. *Wimb'don.*
1914. Granger,Edw.HaroldH.,M.C.,*Ealing.*
1874. Granger, Farington Marsden, *Chester.*
1907. Granger, Henry, *Bournemouth.*
1896. Grant, Alex. Smeaton, *Brondesbury.*
1897. Grant, Alfred Jas., *W. Kensington.*
1869. Grant, Frederick, *Queen's-gate*, S.W.
1916. Grant, Harry Goudge, *Nova Scotia.*
1864. Grant,SirJas.Alex.,K.C.M.G.,*Ottawa.*
1900. Grant, John Prescott.
1904. Grant, Montagu Fredk., *R.A.M.C.*
1852. Grant, Nathaniel James, *I.M.S.*
1923. Grant, Sydney Alex., *West Mersea.*
1903. Grant, William Prince, *Rochdale.*
1911. Grant, Willoughby Gordon, *Madras.*
1898. Grant-Johnston, Joseph, *Brackwell.*
1895. Grant-Wilson, Chas. W., *Sidmouth.*
1918. Grantham-Hill, C., *Lexham-gdns.*
1900. Grantham-Hill,Wilfd.St.G.,*Chiswick.*
1897. Granville, Alexander.
1898. Grapel, Francis Gaspar, *Croydon.*
1875. Grasett, Fredk. Le Maitre, *Toronto.*
1894. Grattan, Henry William, *R.A.M.C.*
1920. Gravelle, Arthur Edwards, *Pembrey.*
1887. Gravely, Harry, *Uckfield.*
1879. Gravely, John Gabbitas, *Bedford.*
1874. Gravely, Wm. Homewood, *Horsham.*
1915. Graves, Basil, M.C., *Barnes.*
1888. Graves, Charles, *Southsea.*
1909. Graves, Harman John H., *Hoxton.*
1904. Graves, Robert, K. G., *Cleredon.*
1879. Graves, Thomas William, *Knighton.*
1901. Gray,A.ClayponH.,O.B.E,*R.A.M.C.*
1870. Gray, Clement Fredk., *Newmarket.*
1902. Gray, Douglas, *Bolton.*
1920. Gray, E. Emile Delisle, *Drayton-gds,*
1914. Gray, Egerton, *Peterborough.*
1919. Gray, Frank, *Gt. Shelford.*
1909. Gray, Gilbert Clement, *Newmarket.*
1909. Gray, Henry, *West Malling.*
1901. Gray, Henry Albert, *Fulham.*
1898. Gray, Herbert Edward.
1894. Gray, J. A. W. Pereira, *Exeter.*
1882. Gray, John Alfred, *Ealing.*
1905. Gray, Leonard, *Stafford.*
1914. Gray, Norman, *Newmarket.*
1904. Gray,RonaldEvelynGordon,*Hindhead*
1919. Gray, St. George B. D , *Drayton-gdns.*
1884. Gray, Thomas Underwood, *Essex-rd.*
1880. Gray, Walter, *Holsworthy.*
1896. Gray, Wm. Henry, *Mansfield.*
5884

1892. Graydon, Archibald, *Argentina.*
1880. Grayling, Arthur, *Forest-hill.*
1896. Grazebrook, Edwyn Robert, *R.N.*
1896. Great Rex, Jas. Burnell, *Plumstead.*
1892. Greaves, Edward Harrison, *Penrith.*
1872. Greaves, Frank, *Junction-road,* N.
1909. Greaves, Geo. Aldon, *Kingston, Can.*
1891. Greaves, Henry.
1908. Greaves, Horatio Norman, *Demerara.*
1923.§Greaves, Marion, *Ilkley.*
1914. Greaves, Samuel S., D.S.O., M.C.
1893. Grech, John, D.S.O., *R.A.M.C.*
1914. Green, Alan Renata, *St. John's,* S.E.
1885. Green, Albert, *Chesterfield.*
1918. Green, Algernon Sanders, *Rushden.*
1915. Green, Alex. Percival, *Fitzjohn's-av.*
1877. Green, Alfd. Withers, *Wardrobe-pl.*
1904. Green, Arth. Aug. Russell, *Aldridge.*
1902. Green, Arthur Llew. Baldwin, *Ross.*
1891. Green, Arthur Robert, *Ledbury.*
1887. Green, Conrad Theodore, *Birkenhead.*
1901. Green, Edward, *Ludlow.*
1915. Green, Edwin Allan Thos., M.C.
1916. Green, Edwin Augustus, *Highgate.*
1881. Green, Edwin Collier, O.B.E., *Derby.*
1887. Green, Geo. Sydney, *Weston-s.-Mare.*
1906. Green, Gilbert Egerton, *Prescot.*
1886. Green, Henry Lee, *Muscatine, Ohio.*
1892. Green, Joseph.
1891. Green, Percy Andrew, *Transvaal.*
1902. Green, Philip Anthony Mark.
1912. Green, Philip Withers, *Wardrobe-pl.*
1887. Green, Robert Walter, *Leeds.*
1914. Green, Samuel Lionel, *Lincoln.*
1899. Green, Samuel Morris, *Prescot.*
1892. Green, Sebert F.St.D.,C.B.E.,*A.M.S.*
1915. Green,StanleyWilloughby,*Harrog'te.*
1901. Green, Sydney Balch, *Bristol.*
1864. Green, Thomas Henry, *St. Albans.*
1906. Green-Armytage, Vivian B., *I.M.S.*
1916. Greenaway, Thomas S., *Westm.-hosp.*
1896. Greene, Arnold James, *Wigan.*
1883. Greene, Edward Ferdinand,*Brighton.*
1902. Greene, George Watters, *Fulmer-way.*
1887. Greene, Hry. Bertr. B., *Wandsworth.*
1912. Greene, John, D.S.O., M.C., *Shifnal.*
1915. Greene, John Alan C., M C.
1921.§Greene, Marjorie Pearl Christine.
1896. Greene, Wm. Adams, *Cheshunt.*
1892. Greenhalgh, Arthur, *Accrington.*
1907. Greening, Wm. Robert, *Transvaal.*
1916. Greenish, Fredk. H. S., *Warlingham.*
1915. Greensill, Bernard H., *Bollington.*
1873. Greensill, Edwd. Samuel, *Minehead.*
1918. Greenstreet,NormanB.deM.,*Lamb'th.*
1894. Greenway,CharlesMelville,*Plumstead.*
1877. Greenwood, Arthur, *Highgate.*

1909. Greenwood, Arth.Atkins, *Crouch End.*
1897. Greenwood,Arth. Rowland,*R.A.M.C.*
1895. Greenwood, Aug. Chas., *Grantham.*
1883. Greenwood, Cecil Danforth, *N.S.W.*
1886. Greenwood,E.C ,O.B.E.,*St.John's-wd*
1893. Greenwood, Frank Redm., *Edgbaston.*
1881. Greenwood, George, *Goswell-road.*
1904. Greenwood, Major, Junr., *Loughton.*
1891. Greenwood, Richard E.
1875. Greenwood, Thos. Porter, *Stamford.*
1888. Greeves, Thomas Neville, *Willesden.*
1892. Gregerson, William Jens, *S. Aust.*
1894. Gregor, Edmund Wm., *Melbourne.*
1921. Gregor, John Beaumont, *Penryn.*
1836. Gregory, Alf. J., O.B.E., *Cape Town.*
1902. Gregory, Arnold, *Manchester.*
1902. Gregory, Chas. Hebden, *Aylesford.*
1896. Gregory, Edwd. Thos., *Redcliffe-gdns.*
1918. Gregory, H.A.Chodak,*Gordon-mans.*
1897. Gregory, Henry Lonsdale, *Highgate.*
1836. Gregory, Seth.
1896. Gregory, Thomas, *Manchester.*
1901. Greig, Alex. William, I.M.S.
1919.§Greig, Dorothy M., *Cartwright-gdns.*
1887. Greig,Duncan McBean,Q.-*Anne-gate.*
1910. Greig, Frank Cyril, M.C., *N.Z.*
1906. Grell, Jesse Mitchinson P., *Trinidad.*
1913. Grellier, Bernard, *R.A.M.C.*
1911. Grellier, Ernest Franz W., *Putney.*
1915. Grellier, Norman, M.C., *Epsom.*
1886. Grenfell, Henry Osborne, *Saltash.*
1899. Grenfell, Pascoe Bevil, *Cape.*
1883. Gresswell Albert, *Louth.*
1914. Greville, Ernest Richard G., *Kew.*
1920. Grey, Egerton Charles, *Paris.*
1908. Grey,HarryMartin,*Camberwell-green.*
1888. Grey, J. Temperley, O.B.E., *Lenham.*
1916. Grey, Llewellyn, *Gorseinon.*
1900. Gribbell, William Ernest, *R N.*
1908. Grice, John William, *Guy's-hospital.*
1917. Grice,JohnWm.Hawksley, *Tonb'dge.*
1893. Grieves, James Percy, *Portishead.*
1889. Grieves, Thomas Arthur, *N.S.W.*
1883. Griffin, Albt. Watson, *Crowborough.*
1873. Griffin, Chas. Thomas, *Crylon.*
1913. Griffin, Cyril J. Anthony, D.S.O.
1923. Griffin, E. Harrison, *Up. Berkeley-st.*
1907. Griffin, Fredc. Wm.Wandby,*Fulham.*
1902. Griffin, Gerald, *Limerick.*
1886. Griffin, John Hubert, *Randolph-cres.*
1883. Griffin,Saml.Nashumil R.P.,*Padstow.*
1886. Griffith, Christopher Arth., *Victoria.*
1914. Griffith, David Wm., *Raglan.*
1922. Griffith, Edward Fyffe, *Guildford.*
1918.§Griffith, Elsie Maud, *Rosslyn-hill.*
1914. Griffith, Evan Williams, *Raglan.*
1917.§Griffith, Grace M. G., *Holloway.*

1865. Griffith, Griffith, *I.M.S.*
1915. Griffith, Herbert Stuart, *Herne-hill.*
1858. Griffith, Hugh, *I.M.S.*
1901. Griffith, John Richard, *Argoed.*
1923.§Griffith, Ma tha, *Pwllheli.*
1902. Griffith, Richard, *Portmadoc.*
1872. Griffith, Richd. Glyn, *Bath.*
1892. Griffith, Robt. Const., *Kingston, Can.*
1919. Griffith-Jones, Cyril, *Bradford.*
1913 Griffitn-Williams, A , *E. Dereham.*
1883. Griffiths, Alfd. Philip Henry, *A.M.S.*
1918.§Griffiths, Alice Muriel, *Cardiff.*
1882. Griffiths, Chas.Thomas, *Birmingham.*
1906. Griffiths, Cyril Verity, *D.S O , R.N.*
1912. Griffiths, David Henry, *Lletty, Carn.*
1903. Griffiths, Edward Reginald, *B ory.*
1916.§Griffiths, Ethel Rosaline, *Hampstead.*
1880. Griffiths, Ernest Edward, *N.S. W.*
1892. Griffiths, George Batho, *King's-av.*
1891. Griffiths, Gilb. Henderson, *Degantry.*
1912. Griffiths, Gilbert H. C. St.G., *Clifton.*
1876. Griffiths, Gilbert Saunder, *Bristol.*
1921. Griffiths, Griffith Idwal, *Bangor.*
1919.§Griffiths, Gwenvron M., *Broadesbury.*
1910. Griffiths, Henry Edwar es, *Newport.*
1911. Griffiths, Henry Leroy, *Malpas.*
1890. Griffiths, John, *Llandindrod Wells.*
1911. Griffiths, John, *Lampeter.*
1922. Griffiths, John, *Newcastle Emyln.* •
1895. Griffiths, John Alban K , *Knighton.*
1895. Griffiths, John Crisp, *Kidderminster.*
1893. Griffiths, John Howell, *Dartford.*
1891. Griffiths, John Samuel, *Bristol*
1867. Griffiths, Lemuel Matthews, *Clifton.*
1917.§Griffiths, Lilian Maud, *Newport.*
1892. Griffiths,Saml.Albt.Ernest,*Meopham.*
1909. Griffiths,Sydney Harold, *Hampstead.*
1883. Griggs, William Alfred, *Brighton.*
1884. Grimmer, Charles George, *Victoria.*
1920.§Grimmer, Mary Isabel A., *Batham.*
1879. Grimoldby, George Henry, *Grimsby.*
1881. Grimsdale,Thos.Babington,*Liverpool*
1891. Grimshaw, John, *Birkenhead.*
1901. Grimwade, Alfd. Sheppard, *Victoria.*
1906. Grimwade, Sidney W , O B.E . *R.N.*
1881. Grindon, Francis James, *Olney.*
1881. Grinling, John Campion, *N. Zeal.*
1915. Gripper, Geoffrey D., *Wallington.*
1881. Gripper, Walter, *Wallington.*
1902. Grigono, Eric Walter, *Stratford.*
1906. Grogono, Jonathan, *Camberwell-road.*
1906. Grogono, Raby Montague,*Herne Bay.*
1883. Groom, Harry, *Wisbech.*
1880. Groom, Henry Thomas, *Garston.*
1881. Groom, William, *Wisbech.*
1878. Groome, Wm. Wollaston, *Surbiton.*
1887. Grose, John Sobey, *Bideford.*
6055

1881. Gross, Asher, *Clapham.*
1896. Gross,Chas. Fredk., *WickhamMarket.*
1913. Gross, Malcolm, *Clapham.*
1896. Gross, Solomon, *Finchley-road.*
1918. Gross, William Stovell, *Holden-rd.*
1921. Grossman, Simon, *Bayswater.*
1891. Grosvenor, Alfred Aug , *Stevenage.*
1896. Grosvenor, Randolph Lea, *Chelsea.*
1888. Grosvenor,Wilshaw Wm.,*Gloucester.*
1903. Grote, Robert George Ernest.
1913. Grout, John Lewis A., *M.C.*
1897. Grove, Ernest George, *York.*
1901. Grove, Fredrick Pierce, *Taunton.*
1893. Grove, Wm. Reginald, *St. Ives.*
1915. Groves, Harold Stanley, *Forest-hill.*
1877. Groves, Henry Edward, *Hornsey.*
1899. Gruber, Rudolph, *Harley-street.*
1893. Gruffydd, John, *Bethesda.*
1897. Grummitt, Charles Chris, *Bognor.*
1905. Grundy, Morris, *Blackpool.*
1901. Gruner, Oskar Cameron, *Leeds.*
1920. Grylls, Ed. Anthony Hawke,*Redruth.*
1884. Gubb, Alfred Samuel,*Algiers.*
1880. Gubbin, Geo. Frederick, *R.A.M.C.*
1866. Guest, John, *North Woolwich.*
1900. Guest,LeslieHaden,M.C.,*Wimpole-st*
1884. Guilding, Lansdown Murray, *Reading.*
1918 Guilfoyle, Denis Paul, *Shepperton.*
1878. Guillemard,BernardJas.,O.B.E.,*Cape*
1891. Gunnand, Paul, *Victoria.*
1889. Guinane, Joachim, *Toronto.*
1915. Guiness, Alexander F. G., *Sydenham.*
1888. Guiselm, Frentz Wm., *Jamaica.*
1923. Guiver, Frank, *Ponder's End.*
1904. Gully, Percy, *Shanklin.* •
1890. Gummow,Jas.Freeman,*Birmingham.*
1916. Gunasekara, Alfred Barnes, *Ceylon.*
1920. Gunasekara, Churchill H., *Ceylon.*
1908. Gunasekara, Sept.Theodosius, *Ceylon.*
1913. Gunasekara, Frank Arnold, *Ceylon.*
1919. Gunewardene, Hubert Oliver.
1916. Gunewardene, Theodore H , *Ceylon.*
1889. Gunn, Frank Walter, *Widdrington.*
1903. Gunn, John Nisbet, D.S.O , *Ontario.*
1906. Gunne, J hn Robert, *Winnipeg.*
1904. Gunning,Chas. J. Hope,*Grosvenor-sq.*
1896 Gunson, John Bernard,*Adelaide.*
1896. Gunther, Hermann Arth., *Hampton.*
1914. Guppy, Francis Hy ,M C.,*Blandford.*
1899. Gurd, Charles Cowen, *Montreal.*
1875. Gurdon, Edwin John, *Sydney.*
1907. Gurley, John H., O.B E., *R A.M.C.*
1894. Gurney, Alexander Cecil, *Eastbourne.*
1909. Gurney-Dixon, Samuel, *Lyndhurst.*
1897. Gutch, John, *Ipswich*
1897. Guthrie, Thos.Clem.,*Tunbridge Wells.*
1880. Gutierrez-Ponce, Ignacio.
6112

1914. Gutteridge,BernardGeo.,*South'mpt'n.*
1883. Gutteridge, Matthew W., *Victo1ia.*
1914. Guy, Ernest Frederick, *Penarth.*
1874. Gwatkin, Owen, *Grange-over-Sands.*
1921. Gwillim, Calvert Merton, *Holloway.*
1879. Gwillim, Richd. D. H., *Southampton.*
1879. Gw)nn, Chas. Henry, *Whitchurch.*
1896. Gwynn, Wm. Purnell, C.M.G.
1893. Gwynne, Neville Claude, *Belstone.*
1914. Gwynne-Jones, H., *Gerrard's-cross.*
1915. Gwynne-Jones,Wm.T., *Gerrard's-cr.*
1891. Gyton, Walter Geo., *Lavender-hill.*

H.

1908. Habgood, Arthur Henry, *Coltishall.*
1915. Habgood, George, *London-hospital.*
1875. Habgood, Henry, *Eastbourne.*
1884. Habgood, William, *Sutton.*
1911. Habich, Leopold S. M., *Transvaal.*
1923. Hack, Philip, *Irene, Transvaal.*
1914. Hacker, Alfred Risdon, *S. India.*
1911. Hacker, Henry James, *Barnsbury.*
1921. Hacking, Alan Ba-il, *Phillimore-gds.*
1885. Hacking, John Herbert, *Wilmslow.*
1896. Hackney, Alfd. Clifford J. H., *Hythe.*
1901. Hackney,GordonHerbt.,*Birmingh'm.*
1902. Hackney, William, *Calgary, Canada.*
1921. Hackwood, John Fereday, *Balham.*
1893. Hacquoil, Philip Homfray, *Penarth.*
1904. Hadfield, C. F., M.B E., *Up. Clapton.*
1908. Hadfield, Rowland Hurst, *Preston.*
1871. Hadley, Clement, *Marlborough.*
1900. Hadley, Ernest Cutcliffe. *Leicester.*
1923.§Hadley,Margaret C.N., *QueenAnne-st*
1859. Hadlow, Henry, *Royal Navy.*
1893 Hadwen, Walt. Robert, *Gloucester.*
1912. Haffey, Matthew Joseph *Toronto.*
1903. Haggard,Thos. BarkerA.,*Hampstead.*
1920 §Haggett, Hilda T., *Bridgwater.*
1892. Hague, John, *Northwich.*
1916. Hahr,CarlGustaveW.,*Courtfield-gds.*
1879. Haig,Alexander, *Upper Brook-street.*
1885. Haig, Francis Murray, *Woking.*
1904. Haig, Harold Axel, *Aberdeen.*
1891. Haig, Patrick Balfour, *I.M.S.*
1908. Haigh, Bernard, *Winchester.*
1916.§Haigh, Ethne. *Muswell-hill.*
1896. Haigh, Harold, *Chorlton-cum-Hardy.*
1908. Haigh,Kenneth George,*Up. Brook-st.*
1921. Haight, Walter R. W., *Clapton.*
1907. Hailstone, John Edward, *Uganda.*
1894. Haines, Arthur, *Melbourne.*
1897. Haines, Aubrey Wheeler, *Llanbedr.*
1895. Haines, Edward, *Rochdale.*
1889. Haines, Fdk. Haselfoot, *Dorchester.*

1915. Haines, Geo. Harris, M.C., *Highgate.*
1908. Haines, Rupert Lawrence,*Gloucester.*
1886. Hains,Wm.Rbt Hall,*Shepherd's-bush*
1896. Hair, Allan, *Hounslow.*
1911. Haji, Haji Sulaiman G.,M.C., *I.M.S.*
1884. Hale, Geo. Ernest, O.M.G., D.S.O.
1917. Hale, John, *Kensington-court.*
1907. Hale,Rbt.EugeneVaughan,*Camb.-sq.*
1922. Hale-White, Reginald, *Wimpole-st.*
1915. Hales, Henry Waid, *Holt.*
1875. Hales, Robert Turner, *Holt.*
1922. Hall, Albert William, *Taunton.*
1902. Hall,Alex Ritchie,*Minnesota,U.S.A.*
1882. Hall, Alfred, *Ashbourne.*
1921. Hall, Arthur Harrison, *Solihull.*
1902. Hall, Arthur James, *Dunedin, N.Z.*
1889. Hall, Arthur John, *Sheffield.*
1880. Hall, Ben, *Colchester.*
1877. Hall, Charles Ross, *Hatfield.*
1905. Hall, Charlton Rbt. Fdk., *Shrewton.*
1910. Hall, Clifford, *Ashbourne.*
1900. Hall, Donald George, *Hove.*
1920.§Hall, Edith Mav, *Upper Woburn-pl.*
1898. Hall, Edmund Stokes, *Southampton.*
1911. Hall, Edward Wilson, *Eastbourne.*
1890. Hall, Elias George, *Bristol.*
1868. Hall,FrancisdeHavilland, *Wimpole-st.*
1922. Hall, Fredk. Jas. Simkin, *Reading.*
1920. Hall, Frederick Richard, *Clapham.*
1890. Hall, Fdk. William, *Sydney, N.S.W.*
1903. Hall, George, *Newcastle-on-Tyne.*
1921. Hall, Giles Arthur M., *Newcastle.*
1885. Hall, Gilbert Capel, *I.M.S., Barnes.*
1896. Hall, Henry Acton, *Rotherfield.*
1922. Hall, Herbert Glynn, *Watford.*
1885. Hall, Herbert Strange, *Leigh.*
1872. Hall, James Thomas, *Alton.*
1896. Hall, John Arthur, *Edgbaston.*
1890. Hall, John Basil, *Bradford.*
1897. Hall, John Spencer, *Farnham.*
1895. Hall, Joseph Percy, *Liverpool.*
1921. Hall, Maxwell, *Bournemouth.*
1908. Hall, Percy, *Hull.*
1900. Hall,Richd.Chas.Baker,*Burton-on-T.*
1900. Hall, Robert Wm. Basil, *Royal Navy.*
1863. Hall, Samuel.
1915. Hall, Stanley Allman, *W. Mersea.*
1880. Hall, Thomas Lambert, *Dilwyn.*
1853. Hall, Thomas Prior.
1889. Hall, Walter, *Hodnet.*
1855. Hall, William, *Leeds.*
1885. Hall, Wm. Hamilton,*Tunbridge Wells*
1875. Hall, William Henry, *Woking.*
1889. Hall. Wm. Winslow, *Bournemouth.*
1869. Hallam, Arthur, *Scarborough.*
1896. Hallam, Herbert, *Sheffield.*
1909. Hallam, Martin, *Burbage.*

1874. Hallam, Walter, *Scarborough*.
1912. Hallett, Dennis B. I., *Lincoln's-inn*.
1888. Halley, William, *Fulham*.
1883. Halliburton, Wm. D., *Marylebone-rd*.
1916. §Halliday, Hilda Mary, *Blackheath*.
1900. Hallilay, Herbert, *I.M.S.*
1913. Hallinan, Alfred Ernest, M.C. .
1912. Hallinan, John Cecil, *Clapham-com*.
1908. Hallinan, Thomas John, *R.A M.C.*
1913. Hallinan, Wm. Edw., M.C., *Clapham*.
1889. Halliwell, John, O B.E., *Winchcombe*.
1886. Halliwell, Thomas, *Forest-hill*.
1894. Halliwell, Thomas Oates, *Dewsbury*.
1866. Hallows, Adolph. Hv B, *Maidstone*.
1921. Hallows, Brabazon James.
1876. Hallsworth, Francis Arth., *Bierley-h*.
1867. Hallwright, Matthew, *Edgbaston*.
1895. Hallwright, Matthew L. G., *Birm*.
1904. Halsall, Cuthbert Murray, *Liversedge*.
1920. Halsall, Reginald Rowley, *Eccles*.
1917. Halstead, Douglas Vernon, *Ramsgate*.
1886. Halstead, George Ezra, *Ramsgate*.
1891. Halsted, Denis Gratwicke, *Sutton*.
1885. Halsted, Harold Cecil, *Selsey*.
1900. Halsted, Wm. Wilfrid, *Waltham-cross*.
1896. Ham, Bertie Burnett, *Hampstead*.
1918.§Hamel, Magdalena A.H., *Stratford-pl*.
1886. Hamer, Wm.Heaton, *Dartm'th-pk.-hill*
1899. Hamerton, Albt. E., C.M.G , D.S.O.
1923. Hamerton, Jas. Rowland, *Forest-hill*.
1904. Hamill, John Molyneux, O.B.E.
1910. Hamill, Philip, *Welbeck-street*.
1910. Hamilton, Alex. Keith, *Deganwy*.
1908. Hamilton, Archibald, *Bradford*.
1901. Hamilton, Arch. Douglas, *Chester*.
1878. Hamilton, Benjamin F., *Wimbledon*.
1889. Hamilton, Bruce, *W. Hampstead*.
1914. Hamilton, C. S. P., D.S.O., *R.A.M.C.*
1889. Hamilton, Charles Dai.
1920. Hamilton, Charles Keith J., *Lambeth*.
1923. Hamilton, Geoffrey Edw. Roper.
1900. Hamilton, George, *Bath*.
1905. Hamilton, George, *Bosham*.
1889. Hamilton, Henry, *Brighton*.
1898. Hamilton, John James Cecil, *Surbiton*.
1916. Hamilton, Melville St. C., *Deganwy*.
1912. Hamilton, Percy D., *Transraal*.
1890. Hamilton, Richard, *Birmingham*.
1896. Hamilton, Roger Kerr, *Rothley*.
1899. Hamilton, Wm. Gavin, *I.M.S.*
1903. Hamilton, Wm. Thompson, *Toronto*.
1916. Hamlin, Alfred Edward, *Stroud-grn*.
1923. Hammond, Alfred George, *Harrow*.
1850. Hammond, Charles William.
1922.§Hammond, Doris M., *Masham*.
1894. Hammond, Fredk.Arth. Lucas, *I.M.S.*
1921. Hammond, Harry W., *Harrow*.

1901. Hammond, Jn. A. Balding, *Shanklin*.
1919 §Hammond, Margaret, *Judd-st*.
1858. Hammond, Samuel, *Queensland*.
1870. Hammond, William, *W. Kensington*.
1914. Hammonda, Moustafa, *Egypt*.
1903. Hamond, Philip Wm , *Thornton-heath*.
1923 Hamp, Leslie Walton, *Wolverh'mpton*
1878. Hampson, Joseph, *Atherton*.
1914. Hanafy, John Zaky, O.B.E , *Jarrow*.
1907. Hanau, Alfred, *Cape, S. Africa*.
1903. Hanbury, Reg Janson, *Plough-court*.
1901. Hanbury, Saville Waldron, *Sutton*. .
1894. Hanbury, William Reader, *Goodmayes*.
1911. Hance, James Bennett, *I.M.S.*
1913. Hancock, Allen Coulter, M.C.
1897. Hancock, Arthur Ernest, *Birmingham*
1922. Hancock, Basil John, *Hurst-green*.
1922. Hancock, Bernard Oswald, *Birm'gham*.
1898. Hancock, Edwd. Dawbney, *Guildford*.
1908. Hancock, Frank Thompson, *Bentley*.
1895. Hancock, George Chas.. O.B.E.
1888. Hancock, Jn. Edwin, *Hurst Green*.
1914. Hancock, Thomas Watson. O.B.E.
1890. Hancock, Wm. John, *Stalybridge*.
1888. Handcock, George, *Scarborough*.
1920. Handel, Theodore, *Balham*.
1890. Handfield-Jones, Chas.R., *Leamington*.
1878. Handford, Henry, *Southwell*.
1872. Hands, Arthur, *Wolverhampton*.
1887. Hands, Charles Hubert, *Freshwater*.
1898. Handson, Lionel E. Chas., *Polegate*.
1918. Handy, Lawrence, *St. Bart's*.
1892. Hanham, Leonard Leighton, *Devonp'rt*.
1912. Hanington, John W. B., *W.Af.M.S.*
1879. Hann, Henry Fred, *Southsea*.
1893. Hann, Reginald George, *Leeds*.
1913. Hanna, Edw. Chas., *Thorold, Canada*.
1911. Hannah, Beverley, *Toronto*.
1900. Hannay, Maurice Gilbert, *Roffey*.
1868. Hanne, Jn. Jas. Arundell, *Peckham*.
1885. Hannen, John Jabboor, *Beyrout*.
1907. Hanschell. Hother McC., D.S.O., *R.N*.
1884. Hanson, Alfred, *Swansea*.
1913. Hanson, David Marcus, *Belfast*.
1896 Hanwell. Gerald Lucas. *Shanghai*.
1915.§Hanworth, Honoria J., *Russell-sq*.
1901. Harbinson, Robert James, *Fishburn*.
1879. Harbord, Edwd. Augustus, *Q.Anne-st*.
1921.§Harbord, Katherine M., *Englefield-gn*.
1892. Harcourt, Chas. Harold, *Birmingham*.
1894. Harcourt, George Robert. *Leyton*.
1896. Harcourt. John Charles, *Stratford*.
1885. Harcourt, Vincent X., *CastleDonington*.
1906. Hardcastle, Alfred Herbert, *Nelson*.
1915. Hardcastle, D. N., *Hayward's-heath*.
1895. Hardcastle. Wm.. *Newcastle-on-Tyne*.
1901. Hardenberg, Emile Jn. F., *Changford*.

1902. Hardie, Charles Frederick, *Barnet*.
1919. Hardiman, Benjamin Charles.
1870. Harding, Alfred Wm., *Bournemouth*.
1894. Harding, Charles Headley, *Whittlesea*.
1883. Harding, Sir Chas. O'Brien, *Eastbourne*.
1921. Harding, Geo. Henry C., *Nantwich*.
1892. Harding, Harold Wm. Litton, *New Z*.
1894. Harding, Henry Wm, *Walthamstow*.
1923. §Harding, Kathleen M D., *Dulwich*.
1895. Harding, Lionel Nicholson, *Nutfield*.
1894. Hardman, Richard Smith, *Stockport*.
1914. Hardwick, Arth. G.P., M.C., *Newquay*.
1896. Hardwick, Harold George Cook.
1904. Hardwick, Reginald Hy., *Headcorn*.
1911. Hardwicke, Edwin C., *Bury-St.-Ed*.
1897. Hardwicke, George, *Snainton*.
1886. Hardy, Albt. Edward, *Huddersfield*.
1906 Hardy, Edward William Dacre, M.C.
1922. Hardy, Eric. *Redhill*.
1919. Hardy, Erne t Alphonse, *Barnes*.
1895. Hardy, Frank Samuel, *Sheffield*.
1905. Hardy, G. Francis, M.C., *Champion-hill*.
1906. Hardy, George Wilfrid.
1919. Hardy, Herbert William, *Carrer-rd*.
1879. Hardy, Hy. Louis Preston, *Stroud*.
1867. Hardy, Horatio Nelson, *Croydon*.
1903. Haidy, Percy, *Nottingham*.
1923. §Hardy, Tatiana Ivanovna, *Weymouth*.
1912. Hardy, Thomas L., *Tunbridge Wells*.
1888. Hardy, William Edmund, *R.A.M.C.*
1886. Hare, Arthur William, *Newquay*.
1886. Hare, Edward Christian, *I.M.S.*
1912. Hare, Francis F. T., *Durham*.
1879. Hare, Francis W. E., *Beckenham-pk*.
1915. Hare, Wm. Theo., M.C., *Cheltenham*.
1889. Harford, Charles Forbes. *Leyton*.
1886. Harger, Frank Arnold, *Transvaal*.
1911. Hargreaves, Alfred Ridley, *Cairo*.
1915. Hargreaves, Robert, *Sheffield*.
1922. Hargreaves, T.H.J., *Up. Tollington-pk*.
1894. Hargreaves, Walter Hbt., *N. Zealand*.
1921. Hargreaves, Wm. Bertram, *Urmston*.
1888. Haring, Nathan Charles, *Manchester*.
1903. Harke, Sydney Lawrence, *New Zeal*.
1880. Harker, Thomas.
1903. Harker, Thomas Henry, *Southport*.
1914. Harkness, Arthur Herbert, *Natal*.
1902. Harkness, Geo. Fras. Innes, *I.M.S.*
1903. Harland, William Chas. Fredk., *Hull*.
1913. Harley-Mason. Robert John, *Sutton*.
1892. Harman, Albert Brice, *Southampton*.
1894. Harman, Leonard, *Lewisham*.
1911. Harmar, Cuthbert Izon, *Luton*.
1875. Harmar, James Raffles. *Birmingham*.
1909. Harmens. Wyger, *Addlestone*.
1901. Harneis, Theop. Wm. Morcom, *Clapton*.
1898. Harness, Henri Nelson, *Kensington*.

1884. Harper, Alexander, *Eastbourne*.
1874. Harper, Gerald Samuel, *Mayfair*.
1890. Harper, Henry Cecil, *Stowmarket*.
1900. Harper, James Eder, *Oldbury*.
1893. Harper, John, *Victoria, B.C.*
1886. Harper, John Maurice, *Bath*.
1890. Harper, John Robinson, C.B.E.
1908. Harper, Philip Thomas, *Fiji*.
1906. Harper, Raymond Sydney, *Faversham*.
1875. Harper, Robt. Russell, *Haverstock-hill*.
1893. Harper, Thos. Edwd., *Virginia Water*.
1892. Harper, Walter Joseph, *Braunton*.
1904. Harper-Smith, Geo. Hastie, *Stamford*.
1899. Harper, Thos. Tomkinson, *Rye*.
1920. §Harre, Gertrude Eleanor, *Binsted*.
1906. Harries, Eric Henry Rhys, *Newport*.
1882. Harries, Henry Jones, *Royal Navy*.
1900. Harries-Jones, Evan H., *Northampton*.
1890. Harrington, Andrew Jerome, *Toronto*.
1918. Harrington, Frank Tandy, *Newport*.
1887. Harrington, Saml. Hy. N., *Birkenhead*.
1857. Harris, Arthur Ben, *Falmouth*.
1870. Harris, Arthur George Rawson, *Looe*.
1885. Harris, Arthur Wellesley, *Catford*.
1923. Harris, Charles Felix, *Reigate*.
1884. Harris, Chas. Joshua Jos., *Whitehaven*.
1893. Harris, Charles Poulett, *Croydon*.
1885. Harris, Clayton Campbell, *Kensington*.
1881. Harris, David.
1904. Harris, Dudley Raymond, *Falmouth*.
1917. Harris, Edwin Gabriel, *London-hosp*.
1889. Harris, Frederick, *Cape Town*.
1904. Harris, Fredc. Rosenberg, *Otterbourne*.
1890. Harris, Fredk. Stuart, *Kentish-town*.
1877. Harris, Geo. Frank A., C.S.I., *I.M.S.*
1880. Harris, George James, *Leicester*.
1922. Harris, Harold Augustus Henry.
1920. Harris, Henry Albert, *Highgate*.
1899. Harris, Hy. Arth. Clifton, *Brighton*.
1898. Harris, Herbert George, *Southampton*.
1901. Harris, Herbert Stocker, *Esher*.
1869. Harris, James Alfred, *Chorley*.
1892. Harris, James Edward.
1898. Harris, John, *Sydney, N.S.W.*
1859. Harris, John Charles, *Ramsgate*.
1916. Harris, John Charles Neville, *Ealing*.
1884. Harris, John Henry, *Dartmouth*.
1917. Harris, Jn. Richd., O.B.E., *R.A.M.C.*
1912. Harris, Leslie Price, M.C.
1922. §Harris, Muriel Minnie, *Streatham*.
1923. Harris, Noel Gordon, *Wandsworth*.
1897. Harris, Noel Hugh, *Royal Navy*.
1895. Harris, Norman McLeod, *Toronto*.
1886. Harris, Percy Reeves Traer, *Harley-st*.
1899. Harris, Robt. James, *Rochdale*.
1888. Harris, Sampson G. V., *Walthamstow*.
1916. Harris, Spencer Frederick, *Ely*.

1881. Harris, Underwood A. C.
1874. Harris, Vincent Dormer, *Mitford-on-S.*
1868. Harris, William, *Wadebridge.*
1908. Harris, Wm. Roberts, *Stamford-hill.*
1919. Harris, Wm. Rufus Geo., *L'nd.-hosp.*
1887. Harris-Liston, Llewellyn, *Darlington.*
1858. Harrison, Alfred James, *Clifton.*
1879. Harrison, Arthur, *Bridport.*
1890. Harrison, Arthur Wm., *Merton.*
1916. Harrison, Cecil C., *Kensington.*
1883. Harrison, Charles, *Keynsham.*
1893. Harrison, C. Alan, *Chelsea.*
1893. Harrison, Chas. Joseph, *Chelsea.*
1915. Harrison, Cyril Edward, *Golders-gn.*
1905. Harrison, Edwd. M., *Huddersfield.*
1917. Harrison, Geoff. A., *Cheadle Hulme.*
1901. Harrison, Gerald Woodforde, M.C.
1900. Harrison, Harold Chas., *R.M.S.P.Co.*
1872. Harrison, Henry Baskcomb, *Exeter.*
1887. Harrison, Henry Leeds, *Worthing.*
1896. Harrison, Herbert, *Deal.*
1895. Harrison, Hbt.Meredith, *Malay States.*
1879. Harrison, James, *Garstang.*
1916. Harrison,JamesMaurice,D.S.C.,R.N.
1882. Harrison, John, *Braintree.*
1896. Harrison, Louis Kenneth, C.B.E.
1916. Harrison, Newcome H., *Adversane.*
1906. Harrison, Percy Booth, *Dalston.*
1901. Harrison, Reginald Temple, *Cape.*
1908. Harrison, Samuel Richard, *Canada.*
1922. Harrison, Sidney Gilbert, *Highgate.*
1900. Harrison, Sydney George, *Rugby.*
1909. Harrison, Thomas, *New Zealand.*
1906. Harrison, Thomas Smith, *Evesham.*
1890. Harrison, Tom Henry, *Betley.*
1911. Harrison, Walter Parker, *Hove.*
1905. Harrison, William, *Stockport.*
1902. Harrison,Wm. John, *Newcastle-on-T.*
1916. Harrison, Wm. Ll. A., M.C.
1902. Harrison, Wm. Rhodes, O.B.E., *R.N.*
1893. Harriss, Stanley Arthur, *I.M.S.*
1898. Harrisson, Alfred Everson, *Daventry.*
1886. Harrop, George Burton, *Cleckheaton.*
1903. Harry, Normau George, *Evesham.*
1916. Harsant, Arnold Guy, *Muswell-hill.*
1921.§Harse, Eleanor, *Golders-green.*
1898. Harston,George Montagu, *Hong Kong.*
1886. Harston, Lionel de C. E., *Kingsbridge.*
1880. Hart, Alfred Paul, M.C., *R.A.M.C.*
1883. Hart, Arthur Herbert, *Southall.*
1903. Hart, Bernard, *Wimpole-street.*
1911. Hart, Charles Herbert, *Bristol.*
1915 §Hart, Constance, *Darlington.*
1912. Hart, Ernest R., *Derby.*
1899. Hart, Frederick James, *Winnipeg.*
1875. Hart, George Henry, *Birmingham.*
1902. Hart, John Hamilton, *Walton.*
6507

1912. Hart, William John, *Doncaster.*
1898. Hart-Smith, Humphry M.,*Southwold.*
1894. Hartford, William, *Bloomsbury.*
1914. Hartgill, Wm. Clavering, M.C., *N.Z.*
1835. Harthan, Herbt. Dunville, *Stretford.*
1893. Hartley, Francis William, *Heywood.*
1920. Hartley,Geo.Cleverdon,*Gravelly-hill.*
1883. Hartley, Isaac.
1897. Hartley, James Victor, *Cape.*
1917. Hartley, Leslie Briggs, *Hull.*
1893. Hartley, Sir P. H. S., C.V.O.
1907. Hartley, Robert Norman, *Wigan.*
1921. Hartley, Sydney, *Southampton.*
1905. Hartley, Walter Dixon, *Castleford.*
1878. Hartley, Wm. Darley, *Cape Town.*
1885. Hartzhorne, Bernard F., *London-rd.*
1914. Harty, Arthur Harry, *Jamaica.*
1892. Harvey, Arthur George,*New Zealand.*
1903. Harvey, Arthur George, *Wirksworth.*
1890. Harvey, Charles Edward, *Jamaica.*
1857. Harvey, Charles Hamilton, *A.M.S.*
1905. Harvey,Chas.W.Cowell,*Abergavenny.*
1881. Harvey, Eldon, *Hamilton, Bermuda.*
1888. Harvey, Frank, *Padstow.*
1902. Harvey, Frank, *Rotherham.*
1909. Harvey, Frank Melville, *Montevideo.*
1897. Harvey, Frederic, *R.A.M.C.*
1875. Harvey, Fdk. George, *Harley-street.*
1917. Harvey, Fredk. John, *Bromsgrove.*
1912. Harvey, Harold, *Bradford.*
1896. Harvey, Henry, *Llandindrod Wells.*
1875. Harvey, Hy. Fredk., *W. Australia.*
1922. Harvey, HenryWilkes, *Broad Haven.*
1865. Harvey, Jas. D'Arcy, *R.N.,Plymouth.*
1892. Harvey, John Owen, *Kensington.*
1899. Harvey, John Owen, *Wolverton.*
1899. Harvey, Joseph Fredk., *Manchester.*
1892. Harvey,JoshuaH.,O.B.E., *WykeRegis.*
1902. Harvey, Percival George, *Monmouth.*
1923. Harvey, Peter Gush, *Paarl, S. Afr.*
1921. Harvey, Sidney Estridge, *Cranby-pl.*
1880. Harvey, Sidney Fredc , *Queen's-gate.*
1909. Harvey, Thomas Reginald, *Avebury.*
1898. Harvey,Wm. J.S.,D.S.O.,*R.A.M.C.*
1918 §Harvey-Kelly, Sybil M., *Walton.*
1915. Harvey-Williams, Robert, *Hitchin.*
1905. Harwood,ClaudSeb.van R., *Maida-v.*
1894. Harwood, Elias Francis.
1911. Harwood, Leonard Austin, *Sloane-st.*
1917.§Harwood, Lily Fanny,*New Kent-rd.*
1902. Harwood-Yarred,W. H.,*H. Wycombe.*
1885. Hasell, Edwd.Suter,*British Columbia.*
1921. Hashish, Mahdy Sayed, *Egypt.*
1916. Haskins, Basil, *Golders-green.*
1880. Haslam, Geo. Jas., *Nebraska, U.S.A.*
1896. Haslam, Hy. Cobden, *Cambridge.*
1872. Haslam, Wm. Doidge, *Croydon.*
6564

1922. Hasler, John Kenneth, *Bristol.*
1889. Haslett, Wm. Jn. Handfield, *Sunbury.*
1887. Haslip, George Ernest, *St. James-sq.*
1879. Hassan, Syed, *Gloucester-terr.*
1886. Hassard, Edward Moresby, *R.A.M.C.*
1887. Hastings, Edwin Birchall, *Mile-end.*
1875. Hastings, Sir George, *Bruton-street.*
1907. Hastings, John Patrick, *New Zealand.*
1905. Hastings. Wm. Howitt, *Roy. Navy.*
1890. Haswell, John Francis, *Penrith.*
1892. Hatch, Herbt. Lincoln, *Pinner.*
1861. Hatchett, Joseph, *Ashby-de-la-Zouch.*
1904. Hatfield, Henry Francis, *Forest-hill.*
1873. Hatfield, Wm. Henry, *Forest-hill.*
1883. Hathaway, Harold G., C.B., *R.A.M.C.*
1894. Hatherell, Robert Ratcliffe, *N.S.W.*
1896. Hatherley, Sidney Oldall, *Swinton.*
1864. Hatherly, Henry Reg., *New Zealand.*
1912. Hatter-ley, Sidney Martin, M.C.
1881. Hatton, Edwin Fullarton, *Canada.*
1855. Haughton, Edward, *Upper Norwood.*
1911. Havard, Arthur Wm., *Newport, Mon.*
1879. Havell, Chas. Graham, *Felixstowe.*
1918. Havers, Geoffrey Gordon, *Norwich.*
1888. Haviland, Frank P., *St. Leonards.*
1885. Haviland, Hy. Alfred, *Rusper.*
1884. Haw, Walter Herbert, *Knysna, Cape.*
1894. Haward, Hy Horace, *Northwich.*
1904. Haward, Walter, *W. Hampstead*
1891. Hawarden, Sa i uel, *Transvaal.*
1923. Hawe, Albert Joseph, *Liverpool.*
1922. Hawe, Philip Reginald, *Liverpool.*
1923. Hawes, John Stanley, *Wanstead.*
1916. Hawes, Richard Brunel, *Surbiton.*
1918. Hawes, Walter Anley, *Malden.*
1891. Hawke, Edward D. Hay, O.B.E.
1923. Hawke, Montague, *Southend.*
1874. Hawken, Giles L. Lang, *Hurstpierpoint*
1904. Hawkes, Alfred Ernest U., *Liscard.*
1897. Hawkesworth, T Avscough, *Watungt'n*
1906. Hawkins, Arthur, *Reigate.*
1899. Hawkins, Charles Louis, *Bromsgrove.*
1908. Hawkins, Charles Thomas, *Garnant.*
1892. Hawkins, Edward James, *Bristol.*
1880. Hawkins, Fdk Daly Cæsar, *I.M.S.*
1886. Hawkins, Herbt. Cæsar, *Cheltenham.*
1887. Hawkins, Herbert Pennell, C.B.E.
1921.§Hawkins, Marjorie C., *Tonypandy.*
1862. Hawkins, Robert Richards.
1904. Hawkins, Wm. Lawrence, *Roy. Navy.*
1889. Hawkins-Ambler, Geo. Arthur, *U.S.A.*
1881. Hawksworth, Hbt. B., *Littleham-cross.*
1891. Hawley, Arthur, O.B.E., *Coventry.*
1910. Hawley, Arthur Thomas, *Coventry.*
1892. Hawley, Fredk. Hulme, *Blythe Bridge.*
1916. Haworth. Arthur Noel, *Oswaldtwistle.*
1922. Haworth, Edwin.

1895. Hawthorn, Frank, D.S.O., *Newcastle.*
1903. Hawthorn, Hy. Wm. John, *Wellington.*
1921. Hawthorne, Charles B., *Coventry.*
1922.§Hawthornthwaite, H.M., *Kgs. Langley.*
1873. Hawton, Jas. Wm. Humbly, *R.N.*
1904. Hay, Arthur Edgar, *Cowes.*
1914. Hay, Horace William, *Sheffield.*
1895. Hay, John, *Liverpool.*
1876. Hay, John Home, *Alloa, N.B.*
1898. Hay, Kenneth R., O.B.E., *St. James's-pl.*
1901. Hay, Malcolm Bell, *W. Af. M.S.*
1913. Hay, Sydney Hartley, *R.A.M.C.*
1919. Hay, Wm. Geo., *Queenstown, S. Afr.*
1898. Hay, William Leslie, *Walmer.*
1909. Haycraft, Guy Fleetwood, *New Cross-r.*
1914. Haydon, Arth. Dodsworth, *Shrewsbury*
1892. Haydon, Arth. Geo., *Henrietta-st.*, W.
1902. Haydon, Maurice Willoughby, *R.N.*
1891. Haydon, Thos. Horatio, *Marlborough.*
1902. Haydon, Walter Turner, *R.N.*
1809. Hayes, Arthur Herbert, *R.A.M.C.*
1904. Hayes, Edwin Claude, C.B.E., *N.Z.*
1876. Hayes, Francis George, *Dunster.*
1902. Hayes, Geo. Sullivan C., *R.A.M.C.*
1888. Hayes, Horace Frederick, *Victoria.*
1881. Hayes, James, *Leigh.*
1893. Hayes, Joseph, D.S.O., *N. Brunswick.*
1885. Hayes, Juliar P. Swindell, *R.A.M.C.*
1907. Hayes, Lionel Chattock, *R.A.M.C.*
1895. Hayes, Reginald Hewlett, *Queen's-gte.*
1921. Hayes, William Edward, *Oxford.*
1894. Hayles, Alfred Wm., *Pontnewydd.*
1898. Haylock, Sydney John, *Southbourne.*
1875. Hayman, Frederick Dell, *Victoria.*
1906. Hayman, George Atkin, *Taunton.*
1911. Hayman, John Rollo, *Washford.*
1890. Hayman, William Speed, *Bournem'uth.*
1902. Hayne, Percy Alfred, *Mandalay.*
1888. Haynes, Edmund Lyall, *Harrogate.*
1886. Haynes, Edwin Jas. Ambrose, *W. Aust.*
1866. Haynes, Fredc. Harry, *Leamington.*
1897. Haynes, Geo. Secretan, *Cambridge.*
1869. Haynes, Horace Eyre, *Brentwood.*
1903. Haynes, Horace Guy L., *Markfield.*
1867. Haynes, James Robert, *Cathcart-rd.*
1916. Haynes, John Frederic, *Leamington.*
1877. Haynes, Percy Octavius, *Birmingham*
1916. Haysom, Nathan Norris, *Shirley.*
1884. Hayward, Arthur Ernest, *Brisbane.*
1907. Hayward, Arthur Wm., *Bournemouth.*
1888. Hayward, Chas. Williams, *Hatch-end.*
1920. Hayward, George Eyes, *Leigh.*
1888. Hayward, Gerald Cobden, *Adelaide.*
1880. Hayward, John Davey, *Liverpool.*
1864. Hayward, John William, *Whitstable.*
1897. Hayward, Wm. Curling, *Port Said.*
1912. Haywood, Alf Kimball, M.C., *Toronto,*

1921.§Haywood, Margaret, *Duke's-road.*
1871. Hazel, Wm. Francis, *Oakley-square.*
1895. Head, Ernest Edward, *Bulawayo.*
1890. Head, Henry, *Montagu-square.*
1884. Head, Philip Alex. Dewar, *Sandgate.*
1888. Head, Timothy John, *Crawford-place.*
1918. Heaf, Fredk. Roland Geo., *Cambridge.*
1909. Heald, Charles Brehmer, *Whitehall.*
1883. Heald, Hugh, *Ormskirk.*
1910. Heale, Arthur S., M.C., *R.A.M.C.*
1900. Heanley, Chas. Montague, *Hong Kong.*
1901. Heap, Edward F. Geo. T., *St. Asaph.*
1922. Heap, Ellis Clifford, *Rochdale.*
1902. Heapy, Harold Ernest, *Small Heath.*
1896. Heard, John, *East Dulwich.*
1903. Hearn, Edward Michael Wm., *R.N.*
1888. Hearnden, Ernest Morgan, *Sutton.*
1895. Hearnden, Hamilton, *St. Ives.*
1888. Heasman, Frank, *Bournemouth.*
1909. Heasman, Herbert Wilks, *Walton.*
1888. Heasman, Wm. Gratwicke, *Woking h'm*
1892. Heath, Arthur Douglas, *Birmingham.*
1898. Heath, Francis Harold R., *Weymouth.*
1916. Heath, George Edwin, *Derby.*
1890. Heath, Jas. Glover, *Ladybrand, O R.P.*
1911. Heath, John Rippiner, *Barmouth.*
1917. Heath, Thos. Lowthian, *Winchmore-h.*
1918. Heath, Walter Ernest, *St. Bart's.*
1882. Heathcote, Ralph George, *nr. Didsbury.*
1922.§Heather, Evelyn Nora, *Catford.*
1892. Heaton, Arth. Frederick, *Malmesbury.*
1890. Heaton, Charles James, *Westgate-on-S.*
1912. Heaton, Edwd. Howard, *Brightlingsea.*
1880. Heaven, John Cookesley, *Bristol.*
1879. Hebb, Frederick Theodore, *Chelsea.*
1880. Hebbert, Charles Alfred, *Montreal.*
1891. Hebblethwaite, Alfd. George, *Keighley.*
1887. Hebblethwaite, Harold, *Burley.*
1885. Hebblethwaite, Sept. M., *Cheltenham.*
1920. Heber, Frank, *New Barnet.*
1880. Heberden, Wm. Stanley, *Transvaal.*
1916. Heckels, Graham Wm., *Lewisham.*
1922. Hector, Francis John, *Bristol.*
1896. Hedden, Richard, *Honiton.*
1874. Heddy, William Jackson, *Walton.*
1914. Heddy, Wm. Regt. Huleatt, *Walton.*
1895. Hedges, Charles Edwd., *Mayfield.*
1864. Hedley, John, *Middlesbrough.*
1863. Hedley, Wm. Snowdon, *Wimbledon.*
1906. Heekes, John William, *Barnes.*
1912. Heelas, Harold J. Beresford, *Sydenh'm.*
1882. Heelis, Robert, *Nottingham.*
1920. Hefferman, Leslie Wm., *Ilchester-mns.*
1922. Hegab, Mohamed M., *Cairo.*
1885. Hehir, Patrick, C.B., C.M.G., C.I.E.
1919. Heimann, Henry Lewis, *Johannesburg.*
1912. Heiron, George Murray, *Stroud-green.*
6735

1904. Heiser, Arthur Lewis, *Eastbourne.*
1904. Hele, John Warwick, *Carlisle.*
1906. Hele, Thomas Shirley, O.B E.
1875. Hellier, John Benjamin, *Leeds.*
1907. Hellyer, Wm. Woodman, *Aberavon.*
1912. Helm, Cyril, D.S.O., *R.A.M.C.*
1885. Helps, George Crawford, *Frome.*
1912. Helsby, William George, *Porth.*
1919. Helsham, Chris. Thomas, *Beccles.*
1887. Helsham, Hugh Paul, *Beccles.*
1888. Helsham, Wm. Macdonald, *N.S.W.*
1914.§Hemingway-Rees, Mary I., *Harley-st.*
1891. Hemming, Chas. Harold, *Brighton.*
1887. Hemming, Claude P., *Bishop's Walth'm*
1887. Hemming, John Joseph, *Margate.*
1915. Hempson, Geoffrey Oliver, *Blackheath.*
1892. Hemsted, Edmd. Spencer, *Kintbury.*
1899. Hemsted, Heury, *Whitchurch.*
1893. Hemsted, Rustat Henry, *West. Aust.*
1911. Henderson, Alan Ashton, *Hendon.*
1914. Henderson, David Alex., *Toronto.*
1902. Henderson, Fredc. Louis, *E. Af. M.S.*
1907. Henderson, Henry John, M C.
1886. Henderson, Jas. Threapland, *Bradford.*
1895. Henderson, Robert, *Canada.*
1863. Henderson, Roderick W., *Rickm'nsw'th*
1899. Henderson, William Savile, *Liverpool.*
1887. Hendley, Arthur Gervase, *I.M.S.*
1882. Hendley, Harold, *I.M.S.*
1921. Hendley, Harold Jas. H , *Caxton.*
1880. Hendley, John Lupton, *Wallingford.*
1882. Hendriks, Cecil M., O.B.E., *Bicester.*
1923. Hendy, Bernard Drummond.
1893. Henley, Walt. Farrar, *Heckmondwike.*
1896. Henly, Albert William, *Bromley.*
1923. Henly, Gilbert Starkey, *Willenhall.*
1906. Hennessy, Pat. Howard, *Malay States.*
1890. Henning, Thomas Irwin, *Newry.*
1913. Henry, Arthur Martin, *Royal Navy.*
1919. Henry, Cyril Bowdler, *Westm.-hosp.*
1880. Henry, George McWilliams, *Halifax.*
1893. Henry, Gordon Geo. Wm., *Minehead.*
1892. Henry, Robert, *Southampton.*
1905. Henry, Sydney Alex., *Rochdale.*
1897. Henshaw, Harry Williams, *Bromley.*
1909. Henshaw, Wm. Alfred, *Northampton.*
1890. Henshaw, Wm. Henry, *Manchester.*
1916. Hensley, Egerton, Henry V., *Frome.*
1887. Hensley, Philip Henry, *Jersey.*
1915. Hensman, Henry Saumarez, *Madras.*
1896. Henson, William Warner, *Natal.*
1890. Henstock, John Lea, *Chili.*
1905. Henton, Albert Ernest, *Ashford.*
1886. Hentsch, George Fredk., *Brixton.*
1880. Henty, Sydney Haviland.
1878. Hepburn, Alfred. *Hartley Wintney.*
1921. Hepburn, Aglionby D., K. *Henry's-rd.*
6792

1884. Hepburn, David, C.M.G., *Card,ff.*
1900. Hepper, Evelyn Charles, *I.M.S.*
1911. Hepper, John Eric, *R.A.M.C.*
1892. Hepton, John Cussons, *Liverpool.*
1884. Hepworth, Aithur.
1894. Hepworth, John, *Beaumaris.*
1910. Herald, Benjamin, *Manchester.*
1907. Herapath, Chas. Edwd. K., M.C.
1890. Herbeit, Arthur Stanley,O.B.E.,*N.Z.*
1889. Herbeit, Chailes Henry, *Natal.*
1883. Herbert, George, *Honolulu.*
1898. Herbert, George Heywood, *Uttoxeter.*
1889. Herbert, Sidney, *Beer.*
1901. Herbert, Solomon, *Manchester.*
1905. Hereford,Chas.Francis Alex.,*Bristol.*
1918. Herington,Cecil Edw. E., *Chichester.*
1914. Herga,Ernest Eugène.M.C.,*Brisbane.*
1914. Herklots, Charles Lyon, *Hampstead.*
1899. Herklots, Gerard Andreas, *Glasgow.*
1911. Herman, Ashley Ernest,O.B.E.,*Cam.*
1882. Herman,Christian Lawr.,*Cape Town.*
1918. Herman,WalterSebastian,*Cambridge.*
1891. Hern, George, *Stratford-place*, W.
1881. Hern, John, *Darlington.*
1882. Hern, Wm., O.B.E., *Stratford-place.*
1904. Heron, Geo. W., D.S.O., O.B.E.
1896. Herring, Edward Ken, *Victoria.*
1887. Herring, Herbt. T., O B E., *Harley-st.*
1881. Herringham, Sir W., K.C.M.G.,C.B.
1897. Herrington,EdmundWm.,*Kennington*
1901. Hertslet, Lewis Eccles, *Transvaal.*
1904. Heseltine, Vernon George, *Adelaide.*
1903. Heslop, James Willie, *Newcastle.*
1892. Hessey, James Dodson, *Hastings.*
1904. Hetherington, Vernon, *Wokingham.*
1887. Hewan, John, *Upper Assam.*
1902. Héwavitárna, Chas. Alwis, *Colombo.*
1918. Hewer, Austin George, *Burford.*
1918. Hewer, Chris. Langton, *St. Albans.*
1866. Hewer, Edward, *North Kensington.*
1900. Hewetson, Alfred, *Scarborough.*
1895. Hewetson, Henry, D.S.O., *R.A.M.C.*
1876. Hewett, Augustus, *R.A.M.C.*
1905. Hewett, Sir F. S., *Cleveland-row.*
1893. Hewett, Julius Winch, *China.*
1884. Hewish, Edgar Milne, *Phil., U.S.A.*
1891. Hewitson, Jn. Geo., *Newcastle-on-T.*
1880. Hewitson, Wm. Andrew, *CastleEden.*
1897. Hewitt, Harry Edward, *G.P.O., E.C.*
1917. Hewitt,Norman Sinclair,*London-hsp.*
1915. Hewitt, Rupert Conrad, *Queen's-gdns.*
1921. Hewitt,Strafford Smith,*Tichborne-st.*
1889. Hewlett, Richd. Tanner, *Putney.*
1891. Hey,Chas.Edwd Milnes,*Royal-cresc.*
1892. Iley, Harold Darwin, *Sutherland-av.*
1900. Hey, Samuel, *Ripon.*
1832. Heyd, Herman Emile, *Canada.*
6849

1880. Heygate, Fdk. Nicholas, *Billingshn st*
1906. Heygate,Reg.Beaumont,*Billingshurst*
1871. Heygate, William Harris, *Belvedere.*
1890. Heywood, Chas. Chris., *Manchester.*
1892. Heywood, Thomas, *Chile.*
1885. Heywood, T. Walmsley, *Blackburn.*
1896. Heywood, Wm. Benjamin, *Newbury.*
1916. Heywood-Waddington,W.B.,*D'vnpt.*
1907. Heyworth, Geo. Alex. Fredk., *Belper.*
1920. Hiam, Frank, *Northampton.*
1862. Hibberd, Edward, *Elgin-avenue.*
1870. Hibberd, Henry Jukes, *Brockenhurst.*
1880. Hibbert, Chailes Alfred.
1894. Hibbert, Joseph Coote, *Blackburn.*
1909. Hibbert, Wilf. Lawrence, *Ipswich.*
1884. Hichens, Frank, *Redruth.*
1896. Hichens,PeverellSymthe,*North'mpton*
1875. Hick, Henry, *New Romney.*
1923.§Hick, Katharine Maud, *Leeds.*
1909. Hick,Reg.Heber Prowde, *Eaglescliffe.*
1916. Hick, R. Bannatyne, *Delamere-terr.*
1910. Hickey, Augustus Joseph, M.C.
1906. Hickey, Carl Cornelius, *Kilkee.*
1885. Hickey, Evan Lewis, *Stourbridge.*
1893. Hickinbotham,Jas.Ryland,*Colchester.*
1889. Hickley, Arth. Mack., *S. Lambeth-rd.*
1918.§Hickley, Edith Mary P., *Hampstead.*
1911. Hickley, Thomas Brooke, *Ealing.*
1894. Hickman, Henry Richd. B., *Chesham.*
1893. Hickman,JohnEdwin, *Orange Riv. P.*
1870. Hickman, Richard, *Newbury.*
1900. Hicks, Charles Edwd., *Huntingdon.*
1860. Hicks, Edward Buller, *Easingwold.*
1887. Hicks, Edward Harman, *Wymesuold.*
1889. Hicks, Edward James, *Amhurst-rd.*
1919. Hicks, Eric Perrin, *Temple.*
1879. Hicks, Fredk. John,*Buckingham-gate.*
1883. Hicks, George Beaman, *Hackney.*
1889. Hicks, Robert Grieve, *Ramsgate.*
1893. Hicks, Thos. Roper H. C., *Colchester.*
1892. Hicks, Thos. Wm., M.B.E., *Finchley.*
1916. Hickson, Eric Blanford, *Swanage.*
1920.§Hickson, Sylvia Kema, *Withington.*
1884. Hiddingh, William Henry.
1910. Higgin, Robert Francis,*NewtonAbbot.*
1899. Higgin, AlexanderGeorge.*Mortimer.*
1915. Higgins, Frank Edmund, *Cheltenham.*
1876. Higgins, George Hodgson, *Bradford.*
1888. Higgins, Hubert, *Warlingham.*
1902. Higgins, James Gilkison, *Jersey.*
1914. Higgins, John, *Ealing.*
1903. Higgins, Patrick Charles, *R.A.M.C.*
1910. Higgins, Sydney James, *R.A.M.C.*
1918. Higgins,Thos.Cornelius,*Napier,N.Z.*
1907. Higgins, Tom Shadick, *St. Pancras.*
1904. Higgins, William Robert, *Louth.*
1896. Higginson, Chas. Gaskell, *Edgbaston.*
6906

1895. Higginson, George, *Church Stretton.*
1889. Higginson, John Wigmore, *Hayes.*
1918. Higginton, John Martin, *Croydon.*
1878. Higgs, Alfred, *Leicester.*
1913. Higgs, James Stanley, *Chelsea.*
1892. Higgs, Walt. Alpheus, *Chippenham.*
1903. Higham, Bernard, *I.M.S.*
1923. Highmoor, Richard A., *Litcham.*
1892. Hignett, Lionel Watson, *Northwood.*
1900. Higson, Thomas, *Blackburn.*
1886. Hildyard, Robert Loxham, *Paris.*
1911. Hiley, Harold Howard, *Norwood.*
1910. Hiley, Reginald Melville, *Cardiff.*
1886. Hill, Alfred Wm., *Adelaide, S. Austr.*
1899. Hill, Arthur Croft, *Cromwell-road.*
1910. Hill, Arthur Hilary Clifton, *I.M.S.*
1919. Hill, Arthur Robert, *Hitchin.*
1887. Hill, Edward Brereton, *Chiswick.*
1900. Hill, Edward Falkner, *Manchester.*
1892. Hill, Ernest, M C., *Cape Province.*
1895. Hill, Ernest Gardiner, *Wymondham.*
1913. Hill, Fdk. Theophilus, M.C., *Sydenham*
1888. Hill, George Leonard, *Birmingham.*
1923.§Hill, Gladys, *Harrington-gardens.*
1918. Hill, Harold Awberry, *Edgbaston.*
1888. Hill, Hedley, *Bristol.*
1904. Hill, Horace Bryden, *R.N.*
1879. Hill, Hugh Gardiner, *Wimbledon.*
1922. Hill, Humphrey Cheetham, *Roby.*
1916. Hill, John Anderson, *Woolwich.*
1910. Hill, John Percival, *Stowmarket.*
1917. Hill, Kenneth Reed, *Ipswich.*
1889. Hill, Leonard Erskine, *Loughton.*
1904. Hill, Ludovic, *Hull.*
1904. Hill, Nelson Wood, *Tiverton.*
1923 Hill, Norman Gray, *Stockbridge.*
1915. Hill, Norman Hammond, *Bradford.*
1864. Hill, Philip Edward, *Crickhowell.*
1910. Hill, Philip Keith, *Hankow.*
1896. Hill, Reg. Aug. Lowder, *Wimbledon.*
1906. Hill, Richard Athelstane P., *Peking.*
1906. Hill, Richd. C., *Montana, U.S.A.*
1871. Hill, Thomas Wood, *Battersea.*
1907. Hill, Walter de Marchot, *C.B.E.*
1902. Hill, Walter Henry Philip, *Montreal.*
1881. Hill, William John, *Lincoln's Inn.*
1886. Hill-Wilson, A. Edw., *Ravenscourt-pk.*
1883. Hillaby, Arthur, *Pontefract.*
1896. Hilliard, Harvey, *Wilton-place.*
1918. Hilliard, Richard, *S. Hackney.*
1891. Hillier, Robert John, *Sheffield.*
1885. Hillier, Thos. Ernest, *W. Hampstead.*
1919. Hillier, Thomas Lucas, *Wimbledon.*
1920. Hillier, Tom R. E., *W. Hampstead.*
1899. Hillier, William Thomas, *Bromley.*
1912. Hills, Harold William, *Epsom.*
1894. Hills, Wm. Chas. Dillon, *Maidstone.*

1896 Hills, William Ernest, *Hampstead.*
1884. Hillstead, Herbert John, *Putney.*
1887. Hillyer, Wm. Henry, *E. Grinstead.*
1917. Hilmy, Abdel Halim, *St. Thos.-hosp.*
1911. Hind, Guy Reginald, *Stoke.*
1870. Hind, Henry, *Harrogate.*
1875. Hind, Henry Joseph, *Twickenham.*
1858. Hind, John Marriott, *Bleasby.*
1886. Hinde, Alfred B., O B E., *R.A.M.C.*
1917.§Hinde, Bertha, *Croydon.*
1917. Hinde, Eric Clark, *Croydon.*
1907. Hinde, Ernest Bertram, *Norwich.*
1887. Hinde, Francis Richard B., *Hythe.*
1897. Hindley, Godfrey Jn. Doug., M.C.
1884. Hinds, Frank, *Worthing.*
1895. Hinds, Herbert Austen, *Chilham.*
1889. Hinds, Thomas Walter, *Bexley.*
1864. Hinds, Wm. Richard Gore, *A.M.S.*
1892. Hine, Alfd. Ernest Barratt, *Charmouth.*
1878. Hine, Alfred Leonard, *Harpenden.*
1861. Hine, William Conway, *Poole.*
1918. Hines, Cyril Patrick, *Ealing.*
1891. Hinge, Hy. Alex., C.M.G., *R.A.M.C.*
1901. Hingston, Clayton A.F., O.B.E., *I.M.S.*
1904. Hingston, Donald Alex., *Montreal.*
1904. Hingston, Jas. Clar. Ledeatt, *R.A.M.C.*
1881. Hingston, Richard, *Liskeard.*
1903. Hingston, Wm. Perceval, *Royal Navy.*
1878. Hinings, John William, *Leeds.*
1891. Hinks, Alfred Grosvenor, *Southend.*
1887. Hinnell, J.S., O B E., *Bury St. Edm'ds.*
1921. Hipshon, Isaac, *Leeds.*
1899. Hipwell, Harry, *Banbury.*
1908. Hird, Alfred Ernest Wilson, *Coventry.*
1891. Hird, Frederick Robert, *Wimbledon.*
1903. Hird, Robert Beaison Dennis, *Birm.*
1891. Hirsch, Chas. T. W., *Hyde-park-gate.*
1901. Hirsch, Leonard, C.I.E., *I.M.S.*
1916. Hirsch, Valentine Rbt., *Stamford-hill.*
1903. Hirst, Geoffrey Gratrix, *I.M.S.*
1921. Hirst, Joseph Walker, *Aspley.*
1905. Hirst, Leonard Fabian, *Colombo.*
1907. Hitch, Frederick George, *R.N.*
1883. Hitchcock, Alfred John, *Jersey.*
1916. Hitchcock, Charles Guy, *London-hsp.*
1896. Hitchfield, Alfd. Reg., *Newcastle-on-T.*
1923 Hitchings, Douglas B., *Golder's-gr'n.*
1887. Hitchings, Robert, *Oxford.*
1889. Hitchon, H. Hardacre Irving, *Heywood.*
1882. Hoar, Charles de Sambler, *Dover.*
1869. Hoar, Charles Edward, *Maidstone.*
1905. Hoar, James Edward, *R.A.M.C.*
1880. Hoare, Alfred, *Fleet-street, E.C.*
1894. Hoare, Edwin Stanley, *Lupus-street.*
1911. Hoare, James Frank, *Holloway-rd.*
1893. Hoare, William Wallis, *Queensland.*
1893. Hobart, Nathaniel Henry, *Cork.*

1874. Hobbes, Charles Edward, *Bidford.*
1901. Hobbs, Albt. Remington, *Hawkhurst.*
1909. Hobbs, Edward Coomber, *Leicester.*
1919. Hobbs, Frank Bedo, *Chiswick.*
1908. Hobbs, Fredk. Wm., *High Wycombe.*
1912. Hobbs, Gordon Victor, *Royal Navy.*
1890. Hobhouse, Edmund, *Brighton.*
1913. Hobhouse, Edm. W. N., *Gloucester.*
1919. Hobson, Fredk. Greig, *St. Thos.-hosp.*
1907. Hobson, Hugh George, M.C., *China.*
1875. Hobson, Jn. Morrison, *Hammersmith*
1912. Hoby, Harry James, *Chatham.*
1892. Hocken, James Preston, *N.S.W.*
1880. Huckridge, Thos. Granville, *Lloyd-sq.*
1908. Hodder-Williams, Frank G., *India.*
1895. Hodge, Albert, *Bolton.*
1881. Hodge, Arthur.
1908. Hodge, Edw. Humfrey Vere, *I.M.S.*
1904. Hodge, Reg. Felix Vere, *Woodford.*
1913. Hodge, Wm. Hy. Stewart, *Torquay.*
1884. Hodge, Wm. Theodore, *West Aust.*
1910. Hodges, Arthur Noel, *Bedford.*
1889. Hodges, Aubrey D.P., C.M.G., *Uganda.*
1906. Hodges, G. Mont. Wms., *Deddington.*
1896. Hodges, Geo. Wm. Cecil, *Bridgnorth.*
1912. Hodges, Robert Hamer, M.C.
1909. Hodges, Wm. Cliff, *E. Bridgford-hill.*
1908. Hodgins, Emerson Le Roy, *Canada.*
1892. Hodgins, Walt. Wm., *Bloemfontein.*
1898. Hodgkins, Albert Edwd., *California.*
1921. Hodgkinson, Robert John, *Guys.*
1893. Hodgson, Charles, *Streatham.*
1897. Hodgson, Cortis Rawsthorne, *Sydney.*
1902. Hodgson, Ernest Chas., D.S.O., *I.M S.*
1914. Hodgson, Gordon Alex., *Bradford.*
1890. Hodgson, Harold, *Alresford.*
1900. Hodgson, Harold West, M.C.
1882. Hodgson, Jos. Willoughby, O.B.E.
1914. Hodgson, Norman, *Sunderland.*
1901. Hodgson, Robert Edward, *Frankley.*
1900. Hodgson, Stanley, *Salford.*
1921. Hodgson, Thomas B., *Beverley.*
1890. Hodgson, Victor James, *Westcliff.*
1907. Hodgson, Wm. Hammond, *Blackpool.*
1915. Hodgson-Jones, Russell W., *Kersal.*
1907. Hodson, John Ernest, *S. Australia.*
1912. Hodson, Ronald, M.C., *Temple.*
1861. Hodson, Thomas, *Waltham-cross.*
1871. Hodson, Wm. Edwd., *Bishops Stortford*
1920. Hoey, John Trevor S., *Penzance.*
1890. Hoffmann, Aug. Wm. W., *Brook-st.*
1910. Hoffmann, Geoffrey, *St. Thos.-hosp.*
1874. Hoffmeister, John Bates, *Cowes.*
1900. Hogan, Cyril Evelyn, *Hammersmith.*
1900. Hogan, Edwd. V., C.B.E., *Nova Scotia.*
1898. Hogan, James Josiah.
1911. Hogan, John Wm. Wynne, *Sheffield.*
7077

1890. Hogarth, Bertram Whewell, *Morec'mbe*
1887. Hogarth, Chris. Whewell, *Greenwich.*
1908. Hogarth, Frdk. Whewell, *Morecambe.*
1922. Hogben, George Hamilton, *Southsea.*
1867. Hogg, Chris. H. Jenner, *Birmingham.*
1900. Hogg, Ernest Henry, *Bridgwater.*
1888. Hogg, Fdk. S. Dickey, *Rickmansworth.*
1922. Hogg, Hector Stuart, *Clapham.*
1809. Hogg, Rich. Bowen, *Timaru, N.Z.*
1892. Hogg, Robt. Hy., *Invercargill, N.Z.*
1902. Hogg, William John, *Belfast.*
1917. Hoidge, Edward Thomas, *Toronto.*
1879. Holbeche, Arthur Oliver, *Malvern.*
1881. Holberton, Henry Nelson, *E. Molesey.*
1908. Holburn, Claud Anthony, *Leeds.*
1918. Holden, Eric Geo. Theodore, *Birm.*
1880. Holden, George Herbt. Rose, *Reading.*
1873. Holden, Lonsdale Andrew, *Lostwithiel.*
1908. Holder, Sidney Ernest, *Adelaide.*
1886. Holderness, Jn. Cautley, *Huddersfield.*
1866. Holderness, Wm. Brown, *Windsor.*
1881. Holdsworth, Arth. Thos., *Birmingham.*
1904. Holdsworth, Charles D., *Wakefield.*
1908. Hole, Kenneth Hill, *R N.*
1902. Holford, Chris. T., *Burton-on-Trent.*
1888. Holford, Walter Stanley, *Sutton.*
1921.§Holgate, Janet Katherine, *Bradford.*
1907. Holgate, Maurice Jas., O.B.E., *I.M.S.*
1907. Holl, Francis Harold, *R.N.*
1888. Holland, Chas. Thurstan, *Liverpool.*
1905. Holland, Edwd. Torriano, *Chelsea.*
1907. Holland, Hy. Houwink, *Pahiatua, N.Z.*
1904. Holland, Wm. Alg. Louis, *Erdington.*
1898. Hollander, Bernard, *Wimpole-street.*
1901. Hollick, Bernd. Sept., *Sturminster Newt*
1899. Hollick, Hubert Harry, *Ashbourne.*
1893. Hollick, John Orton, *Knowle.*
1896. Holliday, William Henry, *Leeds.*
1892. Hollings, Edwin Thomas, *Bermondsey.*
1898. Hollings, Guy Bertram, *Gordon-st.*
1877. Hollingworth, John, *Hull.*
1905. Hollis, Herbert Stanley, *Hove.*
1923 §Holloway, Nancy Winifred, *Bromley.*
1887. Holloway, Samuel Frederick, *Chiswick.*
1914. Holman, Alec George, *Bristol.*
1888. Holman, Frank Kay, *S. Hampstead.*
1909. Holman, George, *Putney.*
1889. Holman, Henry James, *Eastbourne.*
1895. Holme, Crampton W., *Eastbourne.*
1896. Holmes, Bernard Willoughby, *Bengal.*
1891. Holmes, Chas. Denton, *Victoria, B.C.*
1918. Holmes, Edward Arthur, *Porlock.*
1865. Holmes, Frank, *Manchester.*
1917. Holmes, Harold W. H., *Cheltenham.*
1897. Holmes, John, *Goldington.*
1912. Holmes, Joseph Francis, *I.M.S.*
1915. Holmes, Richard Annesley, *Kent.*
7134

1914.§Holmes, Rosalie, *Wimpole-street.*
1901. Holmes, Willmot, *Newcastle-on-T.*
1916. Holmwood, Lionel Snowdon, *Epsom.*
1901. Holroyd, Benjamin, *Pannal.*
1905. Holroyd, Gilbert, *I.M.S.*
1923. Holroyd, James, *Manchester.*
1910. Holroyd,Jn.BrookHenderson,*Shef'ld.*
1912. Holroyd, Thos. Herbert, *Birmingh'm.*
1907. Holroyde, Gerald, M.C., *Windermere.*
1884. Holroyde, John, *Chatham.*
1891. Holst, Otto Leonard, *Eastbourne.*
1917. Holst, Wilh· lm Otto, *Eastbourne.*
1888. Holt, Arthur Knight, *Henfield.*
1893. Holt, Geo. Fredk., *Minchinhampton.*
1892. Holt, Henry Mainwaring, *Malton.*
1900. Holt, John Lupton, *Hull.*
1886. Holt,SirMaurice P.,K.C.M.G.,D.S.O.
1831. Holt, William.
1906. Holtby, Richard, *Musbury.*
1908. Holthusen, Alan Wm., *Forest-gate.*
1885. Holtom, Charles John.
1908. Holtom, Ernest Charles, O.B.E., *R.N.*
1885. Holton,FrancisWm.Parke,*Cunning T.*
1891. Holton, George Waddington, *Elland.*
1883. Holton, Richard, *Hednesford.*
1900. Holyoak, Ernest Wm., *Leicester.*
1886. Holyoake, Hubert, *Royal Navy.*
1922. Homa, Bernard, *Sandringham-road.*
1873. Homan, George William, *Lichfield.*
1901. Home,Fred.ChristianHy.,*Tarrington.*
1917. Homi, Cawas.
1906. Honeybourne, VictorCyril,*R.A.M.C.*
1880. Honeyburne, Richard, *Idle.*
1876. Honeywill, Silas, *Bildeston.*
1923. Honigsberger, Max, *Avonmore-road.*
1882. Honman, Andrew, *Victoria.*
1903. Hood, Basil, *Marylebone-infirmary.*
1869. Hood,Don'ldWm.C.,C.V.O.,*Green-st.*
1905. Hood, Eric Crichton, *Ilkley.*
1896. Hood, Thomas, *Gambia.*
1860. Hood, William, *York.*
1855. Hooke, Benjamin.
1905. Hooker, Alfred Wyatt, *Putney.*
1923. Hooker, Reginald James, *Brighton.*
1876. Hookham, Paul, *Clapham.*
1881. Hooley, Arthur, *Cobham.*
1874. Hooper, Alfred, *Stiffkey.* [*C.*
1895. Hooper,A.W.,C.M.G.,D.S.O.,*R.A.M.*
1892. Hooper, Geo. H. J., O B.E., *Sutton.*
1914. Hooper, Henry Sydney C., *Blackhill.*
1883. Hooper, Henry Walpole, *Sevenoaks.*
1903. Hooper, Lionel Swinton, *Blackheath.*
1893. Hooton, Alfred, *I.M.S.*
1911. Hooton, George Ashby, *Natal.*
1889. Hooton, Wm. Arthur, *Manchester.*
1910. Hooton, William Henry, *Bradford.*
1896. Hope, Edwd. Culbertson, *Queensland.*

7191

1836. Hope, George, *Hanwell.*
1891. Hope,Hubt.Linds.Curling,*Guildford.*
1918. Hope, John, *Worsley.*
1895. Hope,Jn.Lamplugh Allen,*Addlestone.*
1899. Hope, Percy Lake, *Grosvenor-st.*
1899. Hope, Walter Bayard, *Reading.*
1900. Hopewell, Samuel Prince, *Brixton* .
1891. Hopewell-Smith, Arth., *Philadelphia*
1875. Hopgood, Wm. Chas., *St. Leonards.*
1892. Hopkin, Richard, *Llangadock.*
1896. Hopkins, Charles Hensley.*R.A.M.C.*
1916. Hopkins, Edwin Lancelot, M.C.
1894. Hopkins, Fredk. Gowland, *Cambridge.*
1869. Hopkins, John, *Westcliff-on-Sea.*
1882. Hopkins, John Walter, *Leeds.*
1908. Hopkins, Walter Donald, *Hayes.*
1896. Hopkins, Walter Kempson, *R.N.*
1902. Hopkins, Wm. George, *Gt. Cent. Ry.*
1896. Hopkinson,E.,C.M.G.,D.S.O.,*Gambia*
1919. Hopkinson. Harry C., *Cambridge.*
1895. Hopton, Ralph, *Leeds.*
1916. Hopwood, Charles Ewart, *Barrow.*
1909. Hopwood,Joseph Stanley,*Cornholme.*
1895. Hora, Julian, *Cambridge-road.*
1896. Horder,Si .Thos.Jeeves,Bt.*Harley-st.*
1921. Horden, Cecil Arthur, *Penton-place.*
1859. Hore, Ernest Wickham, *I.M.S.*
1885. Hore,HarrySt.G.Standish,*R.A.M.C.*
1922. Hore, Wm. Geo. Robins, *Bodmin.*
1900. Horley, Richard Rothwell, *R.N.*
1889. Hormusji, Sorab Cowasji, *Bombay.*
1897. Hornabrook, Rupert Walt.,*Melbourne.*
1902. Horn, Andrew Ferguson, M.C.
1899. Horn,Arthur Edwin,C.M.G.,*Gambia.*
1884. Hornby, Thomas Edmund.
1904. Horne, Harold Forster, *Barnsley.* ·
1899. Horne, Maynard, *Nottingham-place.*
1886. Horner, Charles Julian, *Walthamstow.*
1906. Horner,NormanGerald,*Philbeach-gds.*
1895. Horner, Wm. Ernest L., *Stoke-on-T.*
1918. Hornibrook,H'nryN.,*Gerrard's-cross.*
1920. Horrocks, Frank Sutcliffe, *Darwen.*
1914. Horrocks, George B., *Darwen.*
1890. Horrocks, Herbert, *Italy.*
1882. Horrocks, Sir W. H., K.C.M.G., C.B.
1917. Horsburgh, Percy G., *Muswell-hill.*
1895. Horseman, Frederick, *Whitley Bay.*
1890. Horsfield, William, *Newcastle-on-T.*
1915. Horsley, Lancelot, *Croydon.*
1902. Hort, Fred. Aylmer, *Aix-les-Baines.*
1923.§Horton, Mary Dorothy, *Edgbaston.*
1923.§Horton, Phyllis Mary, *Buxton.*
1894. Horton, Thomas, *Torquay.*
1895. Horton, Walt. Hartland, *Walsall.*
1895. Horwich,David,O.B.E.,*Johannesburg.*
1919. Horwitz,Charles H. S.,*Johannesburg.*
1913. Horwood, Oswald Ryle, *Tunstall.*

7248

1905. Hosford, Alfred Stroud, *Birmingham.*
1894. Hosford, Arth. Holloway, *Leeds.*
1922. Hosford, John Percival, *Hornsey-lane.*
1895. Hosford, John Stroud, *St. James's-pl.*
1921. Hosford, Reg. W. P., *Hornsey-lane.*
1869. Hosford, Thos. Stroud, *Eastbourne.*
1898. Hosken, Jas. Gerald Fayrer, *Brazil.*
1882. Hosker, James Atkinson, *Boscombe.*
1914. Hoskin,Theo. Jenner H., *Amhurst-pk.*
1888. Hosking, Jn. Edwd. Francis, *N.S.W.*
1923. Hoskins, William David, *Newport.*
1907. Hoskyn, Charles Reginald, *Rugby.*
1879. Hoskyn, Donald Templeton, *R.N.*
1891. Hotchkis, Robert Dunmore, *Paisley.*
1916. Hotson, Wm. Andrew, *Harringay.*
1893. Houfton, Ernest Henry, *Mansfield.*
1878. Hough, Charles Hen J, *Ambleside.*
1881. Houghton, Frank E. C., *Dorrington.*
1893. Houghton, Leonard F., *Br. Columbia.*
1893. Houghton, Murtaugh James, *Ilford.*
1902. Houghton,NorrisNorman A.,*Croydon.*
1887. Houghton, Philip Arth., *Aldeburgh.*
1901. Houlbrook, Wm. Edwd., *Bradwell.*
1879. Houlgrave, Augustine, *Harrogate.*
1908. Houlton, José Leighton, *Cape Town.*
1886. Hounsell, Fdk. Claude W., *Dover.*
1916.§Hounsfield,M.Isabelle,*Endsleigh-gds.*
1895. Hounsfield, S. Coupland, *Stowmarket.*
1922. Housden, Edgar Gerard, *Tooting.*
1923. Housden, Leslie George, *Sydenham.*
1838. House, Fredk. Maurice, *West Austr.*
1875. Hovell, Thos. Mark, *Harley-street.*
1893. Hovenden, Arthur Cecil, *East Sheen.*
1894. Hovenden, Gerald Stanley, *Barnes.*
1893. Howard, Arth. Dashwood, *Hampton.*
1909. Howard, Arthur H.Howard, *Sheffield.*
1891. Howard, Arth. Walters, *Maidenhead.*
1903. Howard, Ernest Henry, *Nelson, N.Z.*
1879. Howard, Henry, *Victoria.*
1867.Howard, James, *Richmond, NewZeal.*
1903. Howard, James, *Hyde.*
1893. Howard, Jn. Alexander, *Up.Norwood.*
1902. Howard, Joseph Louis, *California.*
1880. Howard, Robt. Nesbit, *Cape Prov.*
1894. Howard, Vincent, *Holt & Co.*
1883. Howard, Wilfred, *New Buckenham.*
1904. Howard, Wm. Henry, *Hornsey.*
1908. Howden, Chas. Ernest, *New Zealand.*
1910. Howden, Ernest, *Wakefield.*
1892. Howe, Geo. Bradley, *Stalybridge.*
1917. Howe, Joseph Chris. C., *Preston.*
1885. Howe, Joseph Duncan, *Preston.*
1873. Howe, Lucien, *Buffalo, U.S.A.*
1896. Howell, Alfred, *Cardiff.*
1903. Howell, Conrad M. H.,*Queen Anne-st.*
1916. Howell, Ernest Gwyn,*Lletai Pencoed.*
1900. Howell, Francis Musgrave.
1923. 7305

1905. Howell,Fr.DukeG.,*D.S.O.,R.A.M.C.*
1905. Howell,H.L.,*O.B.E,M.C.,R.A.M.C.*
1905. Howell, Jas. Bonnell, *Hammersmith.*
1832. Howell, Jas. Bromley, *Wandsworth.*
1921.§Howell, Margaret Olwen, *Llanelly.*
1890. Howell, Robert Edward, *Middlesbro'.*
1892. Howell, Stephen Yates, *Buffalo.*
1879. Howell, Thomas Arth. Ives, *Putney.*
1902. Howell, Trevor, M.C., *Barnsley.*
1922. Howell, Wilfrid Eric, *Croydon.*
1922. Howells, Gilbert H., *Newport, Mon.*
1908. Howells, Howell Tylford, *Bargoed.*
1899. Howels, Jenkin, *Bridgend.*
1898. Howells, John, *Swansea.*
1909. Howey, Richard, *Owen Sound, Can.*
1905. Howitt, Alfd. Bakewell, *Chesham-st.*
1907. Howitt, Hy. Orton, *Guelph, Canada.*
1906. Howitt, Joseph Henry, *Chester.*
1896. Howitt, Wm. Adlington, *Nottingham.*
1901. Howkins, Cyril H., *C.B.E., D S O.*
1902. Howland, Goldwin Wm., *Toronto.*
1899. Howlett, Ber. Featherstone, *Kingston*
1920. Howorth, Geo. F.W., *Palmer's-green.*
1893. Howorth, Wilfred, *West Didsbury.*
1893. Howse, Alfred Oswald, *Sydney.*
1889. Howse, Arthur Edward, *Nunney.*
1878. Howse, Francis Robert, *Derby.*
1910. Howson, Frank, *Darwin, Australia.*
1882. Hoyland, Stanley Stenton, *Ipswich.*
1900. Hoyle, John, *Brierfield.*
1880. Hoyle, William Evans, *Llandaff.*
1886. Hoysted, Lionel Norton. *Victoria.*
1894. Hoyten, Wm. James, *Wimbledon.*
1902. Hubbard, Adrian Russell F., *Quebec.*
1883. Hubbard, Arthur John, *Newnham.*
1917. Hubbard, Geo. Raymond,*Guy's-hosp.*
1886. Hubbard, James Punter, *Bloxwich.*
1869. Hubbard, Walt. Lovett, *Edenbridge.*
1885. Hubbersty,Robt.Stephen,*Sunderland.*
1923. Hubbs, Donald Henry, *Canada.*
1921.§Hubert, Marjorie B., *Maida Vale.*
1895. Hubert,William Arth., *Berkhamsted.*
1895. Huckle,Arth. Hy. Headley, *Hastings.*
1916. Huddleston,Geo.J.Procter,*Ulverston.*
1916.§Hudgell, Edith Caroline, *Witney.*
1911. Hudleston, Ivor Robert, *D.S O.*
1893. Hudleston,W. Ed.,*D.S.O.,R.A.M.C.*
1893. Hudson, Arthur, *Dawlish.*
1801. Hudson, Arthur Byrn, *Victoria, B.C.*
1904. Hudson, Augustine Henry, *Hendon.*
1903. Hudson, Bernard, *Davos-Platz.*
1888. Hudson, Charles Tilson, *I.M.S.*
1919. Hudson, Claude Osborne, *Sheffield.*
1897. Hudson, Corrie, *D.S.O., I.M.S.*
1900 Hudson, Edmund, *Chelsea.*
1922. Hudson, Frank, *Sutton.*
1888. Hudson, Frank Horace, *Lavenham.*
7362 R

1887. Hudson, Henry, *Deal.*
1909. Hudson, Henry, *Manchester.*
1914.§Hudson, Irene Bastow, *Canada.*
1872. Hudson, John, *Southport.*
1894. Hudson, John Saml., *Mytholmroyd.*
1922. Hudson, John Spink, *Wellington,N.Z.*
1883. Hudson, Osborne Henderson, *Sheffield.*
1915. Hudson, Philip, *Sutton.*
1922. Hudson, Rupert Vaughan, *Cowes.*
1904. Huelin, Lewis William, *Jersey.*
1889. Hues, Frank, *Handsworth.*
1918. Huggett, A. St.G.J. McC., *Wimbledon.*
1915. Huggins, George William, *Toulouse.*
1870. Huggins, Saml. Tillcott, *Finchley.*
1896. Huggins,SydneyPenrose,H.*Wycombe*
1914. Hughes, Alf. Morgan, M.C., *Croydon.*
1923.§Hughes, Audrey Margaret, *Ashford.*
1922. Hughes, Benjamin David, *Loughor.*
1903. Hughes, Cecil Hugh M., O.B.E.
1891. Hughes, David Arth., *Ammanford.*
1902. Hughes, Edmund Octavius, *Liverpool.*
1909. Hughes, Edwd. P. Llewellyn, *Derby.*
1923. Hughes,Ed. Richard,*Stoke Newington.*
1906. Hughes,ErnestTheodoreC.,*Kings-gds.*
1893. Hughes, Ernest Wm. Shaw, *Halifax.*
1922. Hughes, Evan Nicholas,*NewBrighton.*
1912. Hughes, Frank Mainwaring, *Deal.*
1904. Hughes, Frank Percival, *Pinner.*
1911. Hughes, Geoffrey R., *Barnet.*
1902. Hughes,Geoff.W.G.,D.S O.,*R.A.M.C.*
1884. Hughes, Hy. Milner, *Stockton-on-T.*
1894. Hughes, HenrySpencer,*Birmingham.*
1900. Hughes, Hugh, *Penrhyn Deudraeth.*
1915. Hughes, Hugh L. G., D.S.O., M.C.
1899. Hughes, James Bradley. *Bethesda.*
1897. Hughes, Jno. Brierley, *Macclesfield.*
1885. Hughes, John Douglas, *Royal Navy*
1918. Hughes, John Morgan, *Rhyl.*
1922. Hughes, Kenneth,E.A.,*Bournemouth.*
1902. Hughes, Leslie E., M.C., *Cirencester.*
1886. Hughes, Morgan, *Croydon.*
1900. Hughes, Norman Alex. A., *Calverley.*
1902. Hughes,Reg.Hug.St.BernardE.,*R.N.*
1895. Hughes, Robert, *Stoke-on-Trent.*
1898. Hughes, Robert, *Royal Navy.*
1872. Hughes, Robert Harry, *Tavistock.*
1895. Hughes, Robert Thomas, *Birkenhead.*
1885. Hughes, Samuel, *New Milton.*
1897. Hughes, Sidney, *Clapham-park,* S.W.
1893. Hughes, Thomas Clarke, *Stockwell.*
1905. Hughes, Thomas Martin, *Hale.*
1879. Hughes, ThomasMont., *Handsworth.*
1890. Hughes, Wilfrid Kent, *Melbourne.*
1903. Hughes, Wm. Stanley, *Shrewsbury.*
1920.Hughes, William Vincent, *Swansea.*
1884. Hugill, George Frederick, *Balham.*
1895. Hugo, James Henry, D.S.O., *I.M.S.*

1890. Hulbert, Ernest Beddoe, *Highbury.*
1889. Hulbert, Henry Harper, *Queen's-gdns.*
1901. Hulbert, Hy. Louis Powell,*Brixworth.*
1891. Hulbert, Joseph George, *I.M.S.*
1886. Hulke, Fredk. Backhouse, *Deal.*
1913. Hulke, Fredk. M. Stirling, *Deal.*
1919. Hull, Gilbert Rashleigh, *Streatham.*
1893. Hull, Henry Woolcott, *Southend.*
1910. Hull, Herbert Rich. Barnes, *R.N.*
1882. Hull, Walter, *Sydney, N.S.W.*
1922. Hulme, John Walter, *Eccles.*
1903. Humby, Daniel Morgan, *Newgate-st.*
1898. Humby, William John. *Bloemfontein.*
1919. Hume, Graydon Oscar.
1905. Hume, Norman Haliburton, *I.M.S.*
1880. Hume, Walter Augustus, *Clapton.*
1913.§Humpherson, Elsie Mary, *Coventry.*
1881. Humphery, Francis Wm., *Newbury.*
1921. Humphrey, Stuart H. G., *Banbury.*
1884. Humphreys, Charles Evan, *Llanfair.*
1883. Humphreys, Charles Style, *Acton.*
1920.§Humphreys, Florence Janetta.
1884. Humphreys, Francis R., *Hampstead.*
1888. Humphreys,Geo. Herbert, *Gray's Inn.*
1881. Humphreys, William Can. *Swansea.*
1895. Humphris, Francis Howard,*Mayfair.*
1913. Humphry, Alex. M., *Thaxted.*
1893. Humphry, Edward Scott, *W. Aust.*
1885. Humphry, Ernest, *Queensland.*
1909. Humphry,Gilbert Perry,*Abergavenny.*
1898. Humphry, L , C.M.G , *R.A.M.C.*
1904. Humphry, Philip Reg., *Chichester.*
1904. Humphry, Robt. Ernest, *Northwood.*
1909. Humphrys, Herbert Edward,*Retford.*
1894. Hunnard, Arthur, *Mansfield.*
1913. Hunot, Frank Cornwall. *Royal Navy.*
1889. Hunt, Arthur Henry Wm , M.B.E.
1897. Hunt, Ed. Lewis, *Upp. Montagu-st.*
1883. Hunt, Edwin Guy, *Charlwood-street.*
1893. Hunt, Ernest, *Auckland, New Zeal.*
1898. Hunt, Ernest Rivaz, *Hove.*
1922. Hunt, Fred Cecil, *Ilkeston.*
1907. Hunt, George Henry, *Ascot.*
1881. Hunt, HowardWraugham. *Ramsgate.*
1875. Hunt, John Aspinall, *Borrowash.*
1900. Hunt, John William, *Fiji.*
1921. Hunt, Joseph William, *Toronto.*
1902. Hunt, Lawrence Chas., *R.N.*
1873. Hunt, Richard, *Leeds.*
1897. Hunt, Spencer, *I.M.S.*
1900. Hunt, Sydney, *Spondon*
1867. Hunt, William Alfred, *Yeovil.*
1877. Hunter, Christian Bernard, *I.M.S.*
1896. Hunter, Clem Harris,*Swansea.*
1920. Hunter, Donald, *Manor-park.*
1885. Hunter, George Holbrey, *Haughley.*
1890. Hunter, George Yeates Cobb, *I.M.S.*

1905. Hunter, Mark Oliver, *Hatch End.*
1902. Hunter, Percy Douglas, *Arlesey.*
1917 Hunter, Reginald, *Sunderland.*
1884. Hunter, Rbt. Rankin, *Birmingham.*
1914. Hunter,RonaldNelson,*Buckhurst-hill.*
1883. Hunter, William, C.B., *Harley-street.*
1883. Huntington, William, *S. Andrew's.*
1893. Huntley, Edgar, *Sudbury.*
1885. Hunton, Alfred W., O.B.E., *Birkdale.*
1885. Hurlbutt, Spencer, *Collingham-road.*
1882. Hurry, Jamieson Boyd, *Reading.*
1912. Hurst, Reuben Levi, *Canada.*
1866. Husband, Henry Aubrey, *Jamaica.*
1881. Husband,John Chas. Radclyffe,*Ripon.*
1877. Husband, Walter Edward, *Clevedon.*
1894. Husband-Clutton, Frank, *Crowland.*
1915. Husbands, Harold R. W., *Taunton.*
1887. Husbands, Harold Wessen, *Taunton.*
1894. Huskinson, Harold, *Royal Navy.*
1900. Hussey, Bertram Fowler, *W. Austr.*
1896. Hussey, James, *Farnham.*
1923. Hussey, Leonard D. A., *Dulwich.*
1914. Hutchence, Byron Levick, *Saltburn.*
1899. Hutchens,Harold Jn.,*D.S.O.,N'castle.*
1897. Hutcheson, George, *I.M.S.*
1886. Hutcheson, James.
1874. Hutchings,Edwd.Jn.,*Tunb'dge Wells.*
1920. Hutchison, Chas. Arundel, *Ealing.*
1891. Hutchinson,Cyril George,*East Ham.*
1922. Hutchinson, Donald M., *Sheffield.*
1895. Hutchinson, Fredk. A. Stewart, *Hove.*
1898. Hutchinson, Fredk. Ernest, *Victoria.*
1899. Hutchinson, Geo. Arnold, M.B.E.
1861. Hutchinson, John Hanley, *Catterick.*
1883. Hutchinson, Joseph A.,*Northallerton.*
1909. Hutchinson, Robt. Hilton, *Heathfield.*
1889. Hutchinson, Roger Jacks.,*Haslemere.*
1916. Hutchinson, Samuel, *Bournemouth.*
1902. Hutchinson, Thomas. *Cannock.*
1909. Hutchison, Victor P., *R.A.M.C.*
1906. Hutchison, Cyril Bertram, *Brixton.*
1911. Huth, Sydney Francis, *Culmstock.*
1893. Huthwaite, Wm. Hy. Jos., *New Zeal.*
1894. Hutley, Wm. Charles, *Walthamstow.*
1905. Hutt, Cecil William, *Brighton.*
1899. Hutt, Herbert Augustus, *Tottenham.*
1896. Hutton, Albert Edward, *Leeds.*
1899. Hutton, Eustace, *Rhyl.*
1888. Hutton, James Alfred, *Scarborough.*
1892. Hutton, James William, *Leeds.*
1887. Hutton, John, *Aldersgate.*
1910. Hutton-Attenborough,E.A., *Stamf'd.*
1879. Huxley, Frank Earle, *Birmingham.*
1888. Huxley, Henry, *Porchester-terrace.*
1914. Huxtable, Arthur Edward, M.C.
1891. Huxtable, Arth. Edwin, *St. Leonard's.*
1905. Huxtable,Richard R.,*Bishop'sStortf'd*
7533

1908. Huÿssen, Charles William, *Spain.*
1873. Hyatt, James Taylor, *Shepton Mallet.*
1916. Hyatt, James Wynn, *Shepton Mallet.*
1902. Hyde, Edwin, *Southampton.*
1896. Hyde, Harry Feeney, *Worthing.*
1917. Hyde, John Wilkinson D., *Bloxham.*
1897. Hyde, Reginald Henry, *Kingston.*
1917. Hyman, Oscar Hyam, *St. Thos.-hosp.*
1876. Hyne, Fredk. Alexander, *St. Maues.*
1873. Hynes, Alfred Mortimer, *Galway.*
1896. Hynes, Ernest Jermyn, *Shipton.*

I.

1903. Ibbotson, William, *Royal Navy.*
1921. Ibrahim, Aziz Yousif, *Egypt.*
1887. Iddon, Thos. Whittaker, *Southport.*
1913. Idris, Arthur Ernest W., *Highgate.*
1902. Ievers, Osburne, D.S.O., *R.A.M.C.*
1907. Iles, Alfd. John Hopkinson, *Taunton.*
1875. Iles, Alfred Robert, *Taunton.*
1905. Iles, Charles Edward, *Moseley.*
1883. Iliewicz, Henry Frederick, *R. Nary.*
1907. Illesinghe, Rchd. de Silva, *Colombo.*
1892. Illington, Edmond Moritz, *I.M.S.*
1900. Illus, Henry Warwick, *I.M.S.*
1900. Illus, John Warwick, *I.M.S.*
1906. Ilott, Cyril Herbert Thos., *Bromley.*
1874. Ilott, Herbert James, *Bromley.*
1904. imThurn,Robt.Mackenzie,*Whetstone.*
1900. Inchley, Orlando, *Cambridge.*
1902. Ind, Charles Uncles, *Sittingbourne.*
1896. Infield, Stephen, *Kippax.*
1909. Ingersoll,Rbt.Stephenson,*Washingt'n*
1885. Ingle, Arnold Clarkson. *Harpenden.*
1899. Ingle, Charles Durban, *Somerton.*
1914. Ingle,LawrenceMansfield,*Harpenden.*
1916.§Ingleby, Helen, *Sedgford.*
1886. Ingleby-Mackenzie,K.W., *Ryde,I.W.*
1912. Ingoldby, Chris. Martin, *R.A.M.C.*
1881. Ingoldby, Fredk. John, *W. Australia.*
1904. Ingouville, John Geo., *Inverness-terr.*
1893. Ingram, Alexander, *W. Af. M.S.*
1900. Ingram, Arthur Charles, *I.M.S.*
1923. Ingram, John Thornton, *Exeter.*
1919.§Ingram, Mabel Marian, *Wimbledon.*
1899. Ingram, Percy Cecil Parker, *Newport.*
1898. Inkson, Edgar Thos., V.C , D.S.O.
1906. Inman, Harold Mundee. *I.M.S.*
1877. Inman, Robt. Edward, *Higham.*
1884. Innes, Chas. Barclay, *Wellington, N.Z.*
1880. Innes,HenryJas.Dempster,*Colville-sq.*
1896. Innes, Hubert, *I.M.S.*
1903. Inness,Wm. Jas. Deacon, *W. Af. M.S.*
1885. Inniss, Benjamin James, *R.A.M.C.*
1901. Instone, Bradney, *Addison-road.*
7586   R 2

1893. Instone, Noel, *Addison-road*, W.
1915. Iredale, Syd C. Warneford,*St. Bart's.*
1903. Iredell, Alfred William, *R.N.*
1903. Iredell, Charles Edward, *Guy's-hosp.*
1871. Iredell, Chas. Lesingham M., *Victoria.*
1905. Ireland, James Aubrey, *Shoreham.*
1908. Ironside, Arthur E., M.C., *R.A.M.C.*
1906. Ironside, Reg. William, *Gledhow-gds.*
1884. Irvin, Frederic David, *Preston.*
1890. Irvine, Arth. Gerard, *Birmingham.*
1875. Irvine, Delaware Lewis, *R.A.M.C.*
1911. Irvine, Leonard C. Dundas, *Chesham.*
1908. Irvine, Maurice Lionel C., *I.M.S.*
1883. Irving, Duncan Bell, *Brit. Colombia.*
1917. Irving, John Bruce, *Chingford.*
1895. Irving, William, *Christchurch, N.Z.*
1905. Irwin, John Robert, *Coburg,Ont.,Can.*
1904. Isaac, Charles Leonard, *Swansea.*
1908. Isaac, E. Emrys, M.C., *N. Southgate.*
1917. Isard, Clifford Venning, *Tonbridge.*
1911. Ismail, Abd El Aziz.
1923. Ismail, Mahmond Fahmy, *Herne-hill.*
1910. Iswariah, John Anderson, *Madras.*
1890. Ivatts, Edgar Reginald, *Putney.*
1915. Ivens, Eric Llewelyn, *Ealing.*
1907. Ivers, John Gladstone, *Birkdale.*
1920.§Iyer. Teresa Jadwiga, *Russell-square.*
1900. Izard, Arnold Woodford. O.B.E.
1896. Izard, Herbert Edward, *Birmingham.*

J.

1917. Jabir, Seka Maribar M., *Guy's-hosp.*
1916. Jack, George Gerald, M.C., *Barnes.*
1907. Jack, Wm. Andrew Morton, *I.M.S.*
1878. Jackman, Geo. Fredk , *Brockenhurst.*
1918. Jackman, William Austin, *Bath.*
1912. Jackson, Albert, *R.A.M.C.*
1884. Jackson, Allan Heslop, *Cape Town.*
1889. Jackson,BasilFdc. Forrester,*Brighton.*
1868. Jackson, Edward, *Folkestone.*
1876. Jackson, Edwin, *Manchester.*
1895. Jackson, Francis Seymour, *Aberdovey.*
1902. Jackson, Francis Willan, *Denbigh.*
1902. Jackson, Fredk. Douglas S., *Harley-st.*
1866. Jackson, Fredk. William, *Newbury.*
1878. Jackson, George Henry, *Eastbourne.*
1915. Jackson, George Maudslay, *Bristol.*
1901. Jackson,HaroldEdgarAthel., *Victoria.*
1923. Jackson, Harvey. *Herne-hill.*
1918. Jackson, Henry B., *Thornton-heath.*
1897. Jackson, H. Hart, *Newbiggen-by-Sea.*
1920. Jackson, Herbert Vivian, *Bristol.*
1896. Jackson, Herbt. William, *Middlesbro.*
1909. Jackson, James Eustace, *Barnsbury.*
1922. Jackson, John, *Bickenhall-mansions.*
1882. Jackson, John Charles, *Fulham.*

7640

1880. Jackson, Mark, *Purley.*
1918. Jackson, Marshall, *St. Albans.*
1923. Jackson, Monté, *Brockley.*
1884. Jackson, Percy Vaughan, *R. Navy.*
1884. Jackson,Richd.Arth.,*KirkbyMoorside.*
1892. Jackson, Richd. Houlton, *Bakewell.*
1923. Jackson, Robert, *Nelson.*
1910. Jackson, Robert Ashton, *Oldham.*
1910. Jackson, Roderick, *Lydiate.*
1915. Jackson,Rupert Wm. P.,M.C.,*Guy's.*
1916. Jackson, Thomas Henry, *Finchley.*
1896. Jackson, Thomas Leonard, *Cheadle.*
1893. Jackson, Thomas Sparks, *Eastbourne.*
1897. Jackson, Wilfrid Anth.L., *Smethwick.*
1899. Jackson, Wm. Ferriday, *Manchester.*
1868. Jackson, Wm.Fdk. Marsh, *Smethwick.*
1901. Jackson, William Taylor, *Hayduck.*
1904. Jackson-Taylor,BasilJn. F.,*Hucknall.*
1905. Jacob, Arth. Hildebrand, *R.A.M.C.*
1895. Jacob, Frank Harwood, *Nottingham.*
1915. Jacob, Lancelot George, *Radlett.*
1904. Jacob, Norman Bremer Vicars, *R.N.*
1889. Jacobsen, George Oscar, *Alford.*
1904. Jacobson, Sidney Dattner, *Vienna.*
1884. Jacomb-Hood, Chas. Jn., *Brighton.*
1921. Jagger, Edwin Rayner, *Manchester.*
1892. Jago, Ashley Tilsed, *St. Buryan.*
1883. Jago, Charles Sprague, *Latchford.*
1916. Jago, Frank Bernard, *Ashton.*
1871. Jago, Thomas, *Finsbury-park.*
1897. Jago, Thomas Dinnen, *Liverpool-rd.*
1907. Jago, William John, *Muswell-hill.*
1917. Jaidka, Karam Chand, *Peterborough.*
1878. Jakins, Percy Septimus, *Harley-st.*
1858. Jakins, William Vosper, *Victoria.*
1911. James, Alfred Herbert, *Lutterworth.*
1905. James,AlgernonMeyrickA.,*Hampst'd.*
1887. James, Arthur Wm., *Gloucester-terr.*
1880. James, Chas. Alfred, *Up Clapton-rd.*
1903. James,Chas.WilmotWanklyn,*Clifton*
1887. James, Coram L. Stuart, *Cricklewood.*
1892. James, Ernest Wm., *Attleborough.*
1920. James, Frederick, *Finchley.*
1895. James, Frederick Charles, *Harleston.*
1899. James, Frederick William, *Ealing.*
1911. James, Gwilym, *Aberystwyth.*
1894. James,GwilymP.W.,O.B.E.,*Penarth*
1911. James, Harold Llewellyn, *Purley.*
1884. James, Henry Daniel, *R.A.M.C.*
1903. James, Henry Walter, *Bedworth.*
1915. James, Ifan Septimus, *Aberystwyth.*
1884. James, John, *Glandyfi.*
1887. James, John Angell, *Bristol.*
1891. James, Leo Edward.
1878. James, Philip, *Senghenydd.*
1897. James, Philip William, *Croydon.*
1892. James, Robert Blake, *Littlehampton.*

7697

1906. James, Robert Rutson, *St. Geo.-hosp.*
1891. James, Rupert, *Johannesburg.*
1899. James, Samuel, *Gwaun-Caegurwen.*
1893. James, Stanlake, *Putney.*
1895. James, Sydney Price, *I.M.S.*
1877. James, Thomas, *Moonta, S. Australia.*
1923. James, Thomas, *Westcliff.*
1917. James, Thomas Glyn, *Rogerstone.*
1913. James, Thomas Hitchings, *Dorbuch.*
1916. James, Vincent Coram, *Cricklewood.*
1876. James, Walter Culver, *Marloes-road.*
1890. James, Walter Evelyn, *Bradsford.*
1906. James, William Abel, *Cwmbran.*
1900. James, William Morgan, *Newport.*
1900. Jameson, Archibald Douglas, *R.A.M.C*
1913. Jameson, George Battersby, *Hale.*
1913. Jameson, George Dearden, *Warwick.*
1875. Jameson, George Herbert, *Warwick.*
1896. Jameson, Robert William, *Transvaal.*
1897. Jamieson, Harold Hry., *Sheffield.*
1911. Jamieson, Heber Carss, *Guelph, Can.*
1898. Jamieson, Robert, *Brodick, N.B.*
1889. Jamieson, Sydney, *Sydney, N.S.W.*
1903. Janion, Har. Garnett, *M.C., R.A.M.C.*
1911. Jap, Ah Chit, *Singapore.*
1887. Jaques, John Warren.
1876. Jaquet, John Lewis, *Tonbridge.*
1912. Jardine, Edmund Basil, *M.C.*
1886. Jardine, Robert, *Glasgow.*
1916. Jareja, Bhoputsinhji B., *Kathiawar.*
1923. Jarratt, Wm. Otley Chas., *Bridlington*
1874. Jarrett, Michael Lewis, *Sierra Leone.*
1907. Jarvis, Charles George, *C.M.G., Paris.*
1885. Jarvis, John, *Bath.*
1887. Jarvis, Joseph Hy. Ernest, *Ashford.*
1887. Jarvis, Wm. Chas., *Southampton-st.*
1914. Jatar, Nilkanth S., *D.S.O., I.M.S.*
1920. Jauch, Francis Joselin, *Middlx.-hosp.*
1912. Jay, Drue Drury Butler, *Chippenham.*
1867. Jay, Henry Mason, *Chippenham.*
1922. Jay, Maurice Bernard, *Fashion-st.*
1923. Jayaker, Mansoor, *Hampstead.*
1911. Jayaramulu, Tiruvallur K., *Madras.*
1915. Jayewardene, Frederic N., *Ceylon.*
1885. Jaynes, Frederick John.
1877. Jaynes, Victor Alexander, *Jamaica-rd.*
1904. Jays, Tom, *Kingston-on-Thames.*
1921. Jeaffreson, Bryan Leslie, *Enfield.*
1892. Jeaffreson, Geo. Cordy, *Framlingham.*
1887. Jeaffreson, John Leslie, *Tudworth.*
1905. Jeans, Alfred Norman, *Transvaal.*
1877. Jeans, Francis Austen, *Royal Navy.*
1893. Jeans, Thos. Tendron, *C.M.G., R.N.*
1921 §Jebens, Erna Henrietta, *Tulse-hill.*
1889. Jeeves, John, *Sheffield.*
1900. Jefferiss, Fredk. Burroughs, *Chatham.*
1909. Jefferiss, Iain Mackinnon., *Gillingham.*

1912.§Jefferson, Gertrude May, *Hove.*
1920.§Jeffers on, Marjorie Mary, *Rochdale.*
1884. Jefferson, Robert P., *Manchester.*
1862. Jefferson, Thos. Jewison, *M. Weighton.*
1877. Jefferson, William Dixon, *Ripon.*
1923. Jeffery, Arch. L. P., *Seven Sisters-rd.*
1903. Jeffery, Thos. Walter, *O.B E., R.N.*
1884. Jeffree, Frank, *Merstham.*
1891. Jeffreys, Alfred, *Briton Ferry.*
1909. Jeffreys, Harold Edwd., *Porirua, N.Z.*
1898. Jeffreys, Hbt. Castelman, *W.Af.M.S.*
1912. Jeffreys, Howel Gabriel G., *Kensington*
1907. Jeffreys, Walt. Marmaduke, *South'mt n*
1891. Jeffreys-Powell, Jn. Powell, *Brecon.*
1923. Jeger, Santo Weisberg, *Stoke Newi'gt'n*
1889. Jekyll, Lewis Nugent, *Leytonstone.*
1901. Jellicoe, Stanley Coleman, *Totnes.*
1896. Jelly, George Aubrey, *Bury.*
1923. Jemson, James, *Preston.*
1908. Jenkin, Nelson West, *Hindhead.*
1918. Jenkins, Aneurin E., *Stamford-h'll.*
1922. Jenkins, Arthur Edgar, *Pontypridd.*
1894. Jenkins, Arthur Wm., *Hinckley.*
1914. Jenkins, Charles Evans, *Dowlais.*
1882. Jenkins, Edwd. Johnstone, *Sydney.*
1916.§Jenkins, Elizabeth Ethel, *Croydon.*
1901. Jenkins, Evan Llewellyn, *Linton.*
1904. Jenkins, Henry Hollis, *Sidcup.*
1894. Jenkins, Herbt. Thos., *Penmaenmawr.*
1884. Jenkins, John, *Royal Navy.*
1902. Jenkins, John, *Hammersmith-infirm.*
1803. Jenkins, John David, *Rhondda.*
1892. Jenkins, Jn. Elystan Morris, *Wimbledon*
1918. Jenkins, John Powell J., *Pontypridd.*
1917. Jenkins, Naunton Reginald, *Porthcawl*
1907. Jenkins, Richard Sydney, *East Sheen.*
1906. Jenkins, Thomas Jones, *Henllan.*
1921. Jenkins, William David, *Abercanaid.*
1922.§Jenkins, Winifred M., *Chelsea.*
1907. Jenner, Arthur Gordon, *Liverpool.*
1919. Jenner-Clarke, Reginald, *Hale-end.*
1916. Jennings, Arthur Richard, *Stonehouse.*
1886. Jennings, Edgar, *I.M.S.*
1878. Jennings, Edward, *Christchurch, N.Z.*
1915. Jennings, Henry Cecil, *Brixton.*
1921. Jennings, Leslie Middlemiss, *S.Barts.*
1897. Jennings, Richd. E.W., *Bournemouth.*
1883. Jennings, Robert.
1901. Jensen, Ernest Thomas, *Harley-st.*
1923. Jensen, Julius, *Fentiman-road.*
1923. Jephcott, Alexander, *Enfield.*
1896. Jephcott, Charles, *Chester.*
1913. Jeppe, Theodor Julius Juta, *S. Africa.*
1901. Jepson, Victor Brodie, *Palliser-rd.*
1915. Jepson, William Balv, *M.C., Brockley.*
1888. Jermaine-Lulham, Fdk. Sydney, *Vict.*
1896. Jerman, Arthur Edward, *Belvedere.*

1892. Jerome, Geo. Percy, *Su'ton Coldfield.*
1885. Jervis, Arthur, *Dorset-street.*
1916. Jerwood, Bernard Ellery, *Cambridge.*
1923. Jessop, Harold Vernon, *Brownhills.*
1877. Jewell, Charles Coleman, *Victoria.*
1891. Jeweil, John Wm. Frank, *Balham.*
1893. Jewell. Wm. Hy., O.B.E., *Q. Anne-st.*
1905. Jewesbury, Reg. Chas., *Wimpole-st.*
1894. Jiménez, Gerardo.
1902. Jiménez, Ricardo Luis, *Costa Rica.*
1894. Job, Henry Percy, *Newark-on-Trent.*
1885. Joberns, William, *Wolverhampton.*
1901. Jobson, Fdk. Cuthbert, *Wapping.*
1919. Joglekar, Shankar Ramchandra.
1916. Joekes, Theodorus, *Alexandra-park.*
1901. John, Ambrose Hilton, *Stoke-on-T.*
1882. John, David, *New York, U.S.A.*
1913. John, David Wm., M.C., *Cowbridge.*
1916. John, John Robert, *Treorchy.*
1910. John, Jordan C., O.B.E , *I M.S.*
1915. John, Rhys Bevan, *Hirwain.*
1902. Johns, Chas. Percival, *Thornhill, Ont.*
1889. Johns, Henry Douglas, *Hornsea.*
1888. Johns, John Francis, *Cheltenham.*
1916. Johns, Llewellyn Price,*Billingshurst.*
1916. Johns, Samuel Hy. M., *Kensington.*
1921. Johnson, Albert V., *Birmingham.*
1897. Johnson, Alfred, *Liscard.*
1911. Johnson, Arthur Carreth, *Norwood.*
1900. Johnson, Edward Angas, *Adelaide.*
1867. Johnson, Edward Reg., *I.M.S.*
1921.§Johnson, Eva May, *Highgate-road.*
1920. Johnson, Evelyn Hope, *Pendleton.*
1913. Johnson, Frank Edwin, *Lordship-pk.*
1871. Johnson, Frederick Philipps.
1883. Johnson, George Arthur, *Cambridge.*
1918. Johnson, George Henry, *Streatham.*
1887. Johnson. HaroldJossé,O.B E., *Byfleet.*
1896. Johnson,Hy.Heath Pochin,*Manchest'r*
1914.§Johnson, Hilda Grace, *Finchley.*
1874. Johnson, John James, *Norwich.*
1887. Johnson, John Mountfort, *Leek.*
1907. Johnson,John Piatt.*Stoke Newington.*
1895. Johnson, John Robert, *Richmond.*
1892. Johnson, Lawrence Alfd.,*Normanton.*
1900. Johnson, Lionel Capper, *Leeds.*
1896. Johnson,M.Beauchamp,*Henrietta-st.*
1898. Johnson,Rance Dreweatt,*Hampstead.*
1913. Johnson, Richard Bertram, *Yatton.*
1900. Johnson, Robt. Geo.,*Stoke Newingt'n.*
1903. Johnson, Smeeton, *Kidderminster.*
1911. Johnson, Stanley Gower, *Southsea.*
1911. Johnson, Thos.Wm. Jas., *Napier, N.Z.*
1905. Johnson, Valentine Goode, *R.A.M.C.*
1908. Johnson, William, M.C., *Wrexham.*
1901. Johnson,Wm.JeroldGreaves,*Bedford.*
1893. Johnson, William John, *Shefford.*

7868

1871. Johnson, Wm. Murray, *Valparaiso.*
1877. Johnston, Alex. John James, *R.N.*
1887. Johnston, Arth. Hammersley, O.B.E.
1884. Johnston, Benjamin Rigby,*Grasmere.*
1888. Johnston,Chas.S.,M.B.E.,*Gloucester.*
1900. Johnston, Duncan M., *Maidstone.*
1883. Johnston, Geo. David, *Br. Columbia.*
1908. Johnston,Geo. Lawson H.,*Allahabad.*
1890. Johnston, Geo. Saint, *Birmingham.*
1871. Johnston, John, *Maidstone.*
1908. Johnston, John M., *Winchmore-hill.*
1901. Johnston, Lambert A. W.,*Bir m'gham.*
1917.§Johnston, Loiza Elwell, *Compton-st.*
1883. Johnston, Matthew, *Bewdley.*
1913. Johnston, Robert Edmund, *Toronto.*
1895. Johnston, Robt. Mache, *St. Leonards.*
1916. Johnston,Stewart Russell,*Maidstone.*
1917.§Johnston, Theodora, *Blessington-rd.*
1881. Johnston, Thomas, *Hove.*
1909. Johnston, Thomas James, *Ontario.*
1897. Johnston, William, *Cape Town.*
1916. Johnston, Wm. George, *M C.*
1912. Johnston, Wm. Philip, *New Zealand.*
1921. Johnstone, John Gordon, *Bromley.*
1889. Johnstone, John Lloyd.
1878. Jolliffe, Walter John, *Isle of Wight.*
1918. Jolliffe,Wm. Anthony,*Bournemouth.*
1920.§Jolly, Doris Eleanor Parker, *Ipswich.*
1908. Jolly,Robt. Henry Hatten,*Carshalton.*
1883. Jollye,Arth.Dixon, *Hemel Hempstead.*
1885. Jollye, Francis William, *Alresford.*
1887. Joly, Antoine Maurice, *Mauritius.*
1912. Joly, James Moncrieff, *Assam.*
1897. Jonas, Herbert Charlton, *Barnstaple.*
1876. Jones, Abraham Emrys, *Manchester.*
1879. Jones, Albert Edward, *Crickhowell.*
1900. Jones, Alfred, *Rhondda.*
1900. Jones, Alfred Ernest, *Harley-street.*
1918. Jones, Alfred Kenneth Ince, *Ilford.*
1906. Jones, Alfred Lancelot, *Brynmawr.*
1891. Jones, Alfred Stanley.
1883. Jones, Arthur, *Northallerton.*
1896. Jones, Arthur Bassett,*Aberystwyth.*
1880. Jones, Arth. Crosby Brett, *Chatham.*
1922. Jones, Arthur David William.
1879. Jones, Arthur Lloyd, *Oystermouth.*
1916. Jones, Arthur Maddock, *Festiniog.*
1922. Jones, Arthur Owen, *Holywell.*
1897. Jones, Arthur Reg., *Leigh.*
1910. Jones, Arthur Rocyn, *Rhymney.*
1895. Jones, Arthur Thos . *Mountain Ash.*
1889. Jones, Rev. A. W., *Buckland Ripers.*
1889. Jones, Benjamin, *Bournemouth.*
1902. Jones, Bernard Watson, *Small Heath.*
1923. Jones, Bertram H., *Stoke Newington.*
1893. Jones,Bevington Sydney,*Up. Tooting.*
1893. Jones, Cecil Herbert, *W. Australia.*

7925

1918. Jones, Ceri McColm, *Liverpool.*
1894. Jones, Charles Albert, *Penarth.*
1907. Jones, Chas. Edwd. Mellersh, *Alton.*
1903. Jones, Charles Owen, *New Brighton.*
1877. Jones, Cyril Lloyd, *Blackfriars-rd.*
1876. Jones, David, *Sutherland-avenue.*
1917. Jones, David Bruce Stewart, *Sut'erl'nd*
1891. Jones, David Egryn, *Melbourne, Vict.*
1921. Jones, David Ellis, *Aberdare.*
1921. Jones, David John, *Cardiff.*
1877. Jones, David Johnston, *Sutton.*
1917. Jones, David Jos. Her tage, *Penygraes.*
1895. Jones, David Lewis, *Neath.*
1905. Jones, David Morgan, *Trinsaran*
1918. Jones, David Morris, *Llanon.*
1915. Jones, David Rees, *Chester.*
1915. Jones, David S., *Llandrindod-wells.*
1890. Jones, David Thomas, *Sheffield.*
1914. Jones, David William, *Osborne-terr.*
1921.§Jones, Dilys Menai, *Llanrwst.*
1873. Jones, Edgar Averay, *Fownhope.*
1922. Jones, Edmund Mervyn, *Cardiff.*
1902. Jones, Edward Alfred, *Winnipeg.*
1897. Jones, Edward Shirley, *Hoylake.*
1918. Jones, Eric Shirley, *Droitwich.*
1858. Jones, Evan, *Aberdare.*
1891. Jones, Evan, *Goswell-road,* E.C.
1901. Jones, Evan, *Llanybyther.*
1910. Jones, Evan Hugh, *Llanberis.*
1908. Jones, Evan Rhys, *Menai Bridge.*
1906. Jones, Francis Samuel, *Natal.*
1920. Jones, Frank Carlton, *Birkdale.*
1904. Jones, Frederic Wood, *Adelaide.*
1879. Jones, Frederick Felix, *Bath.*
1884. Jones, Fdk. Wm. C., C.B., *R.A.M.C.*
1891. Jones, George, Lee, S.E.
1913. Jones, George Basil Henry, *Alton.*
1886. Jones, Geo. Burnett Mander, *Sydney.*
1904. Jones, George Francis, *Stourbridge.*
1879. Jones, Geo. Henry West, *E Langton.*
1898. Jones, George Horatio, *Doddington.*
1889. Jones, George Mellersh, *Alton.*
1892. Jones, George Reginald, *Manchester.*
1921.§Jones, Gladys H.E.H.J., *Gt.Missenden*
1905. Jones, Grenville Parry, *Norwood.*
1914. Jones, Griffith Lewis, *Aberporth.*
1887. Jones, Guy Carleton, C.M.G., *N.Scotia.*
1923. Jones, Harry Victor M , *Herne-hill.*
1903 Jones, Hector, *Maesteg.*
1922. Jones, Henry Benjamin, *Llanelly.*
1892. Jones, Hy. H. Averay, *Ocean S S. Co.*
1906. Jones, Henry Travers, *Woking.*
1893. Jones, Hy. Macnaughton, *Hampstead.*
1912. Jones, Henry Wallace, *Liverpool.*
1903. Jones, Herbert Stanley, *Bournemouth.*
1885. Jones, Hugh Edward, *Liverpool.*
1882. Jones, Isaiah Henry, *Maida-vale.*
7982

1903. Jones, Ivor Davenport, *I.M.S.*
1914. Jones, James Dennistoun, *Winnipeg.*
1915. Jones, James Phillips, M.C., *Pontypool.*
1921. Jones, James Trevelyan, *Aberkenfig.*
1918. Jones, Jeffrey Woodward, *Belsize-pk.*
1877. Jones, James Thoresby, *Sutherland-av.*
1904. Jones, John, *Shantung, China.*
1887. Jones, John Arnallt, *Aberavon.*
1914. Jones, John Chris., *Birmingham.*
1876. Jones, John Day, *Vauxhall.*
1907. Jones, John Elington, *Bristol.*
1899. Jones, John Henry, *Toowoomba.*
1883. Jones, John Hervey, *Reading.*
1896. Jones, John Howard, *Goswell-road.*
1897. Jones, John Llewelyn, *Gerrard's-cr.*
1885. Jones, John Lloyd Thomas, *I.M.S.*
1900. Jones, John Pugh, *Barmouth.*
1864. Jones, John William, *Coleshill.*
1916. Jones, Leslie William, *Anglesey.*
1899. Jones, Lewis, *Hornsey.*
1892. Jones,Llew.G. Dwaffydd, *Swanscombe.*
1921.§Jones, Margaret Gray, *Anerley.*
1895. Jones, Murray Parry, *R N.*
1904. Jones, Oswal Wynn, *Ashton.*
1882. Jones, Owen Clayton, *Silverton.*
1910. Jones, Pendrill Chas. Verrier, *Hereford*
1916. Jones, Percy Tudor, *St. Clears.*
1893. Jones, Philip Napier, *Crowthorne.*
1896. Jones, Philip Theodosius, *Coleford.*
1896. Jones, Rees Gabe, *Rhondda.*
1880. Jones, Rees Rowland, *Bangor.*
1894. Jones, Richard, *Llandilo.*
1912. Jones, Richard Arthur, *Liverpool.*
1868. Jones, Richard Mansell.
1884. Jones, Rd. Nelson, O.B.E , *Swansea.*
1921. Jones, Richard Owen, *Anglesey.*
1913. Jones, Richard O. H., M.C., *Harlech.*
1911. Jones, Robert Francis, *Mysore.*
1909. Jones, Roger Percival, *Goncerton.*
1890. Jones, Rowland Francis H, *Walthstow.*
1885. Jones, Samuel Cromwell, *Methyr Tydfil.*
1896. Jones, S. Lloyd, *Radcliffe-on-Trent.*
1903. Jones, Seymour W., O.B E., *I.M.S.*
1920. Jones, Silas Glynne, *Anglesey.*
1896. Jones, Thomas, *Amlwch.*
1914. Jones, Thomas Arthur, *Walton.*
1908. Jones, Thomas Burnell, *Lewisham.*
1922. Jones, Thomas Evans, *Llanrhystid.*
1886. Jones, Thomas Joseph, *Ross.*
1861. Jones, Thos. Ridge, *Chesham-place.*
1908. Jones, Thomas Robert Lloyd, *R.N.*
1885. Jones, Thos. Slater, *Wood-green, N.*
1920. Jones, Thomas Trefor, *Corwen.*
1916. Jones, Tom, *Blackburn.*
1919. Jones, Tom Aubrey, *Horsehay.*
1875. Jones,Valentine H Watson. *St. Clears.*
1872. Jones, Vaughan Daniel W., *Llanbidy.*
8639

1880. Jones,Vincent Alexander, *Erdington*.
1910. Jones, Walter Foulkes, *Anglesey*.
1916. Jones, Walter Hewitt,*Pembridge-gds*.
1896. Jones, Walter Paul, *Walton-pl*.
1892. Jones, Wm. Black, *Llangammarch*.
1920. Jones, Wm. Britain, *Middlesbrough*.
1894. Jones, Wi liam David, *Gloucester*.
1898. Jones, William Edmund, *Blackburn*.
1890. Jones, Wm. Ernest, *Melbourne, Vict*.
1907. Jones, William Forsyth, *Formby*.
1907. Jones, Wm. Griffith. *Newport, Mon*.
1910. Jones, Wm. Hy. Tulford, *Harlesden*.
1906. Jones, Wm. Howard, *Cambridge-st*.
1898. Jones,Wm. James Bennett, *Liverpool*
1896. Jones, William Meredith, *Aberdare*.
1861. Jones, William Owen, *Bowdon*.
1903. Jones, William Phillips, *Sheffield*.
1881. Jones, Wm. Wansbrough, *B. Columb*.
1921. Jones-Evans, Eric J. L., *Winchester*.
1896. Jones-Phillipson, Cecil Ernest, *Cape*.
1898. Jordan, Alfred Charles, O.B.E.
1914. Jordan, John Herbert, *Clough, Irel*.
1910. Jordan, Joseph Bagnall, *B nei ley-hill*.
1910. Jordan, Norman T. K., *Heaton Moor*.
1883. Jordan, Thomas Luckman.
1923. Jory, Norman Adams, *Titchfield-terr*.
1889. Joscelyne, Arthur Edwin, *Taunton*.
1887. Joseph, Arthur Hill, *Bexhill*.
1919. Joseph,Edw.Gordon,*Wellington,N.Z*.
1874. Joseph, Geo. William, *Warrington*.
1903. Joseph, Henry M., M.C., *Guernsey*.
1911. Joseph, Hugh Percival, *Colombo*.
1881. Joseph, Jn. Baptiste Edgar, *Trinidad*.
1913. Joshi, Manishankar K., *Linden-gds*.
1922. Joshi, Shankar P., *Baroda*.
1912.§Joshi, Vagubai Moreshwar, *Berat*.
1888. Joslen, Hubert, *Jamaica*.
1883. Josling, Charles Langford, *R.A.M.C.*
1923. Joule, John Wilfrid, *Pinner*.
1888. Jowers.LancelotEmilius,*St.Leonards*.
1921. Joy, Henry Charles Victor, *Ealing*.
1898. Joy, Norman Humbert, *Bradfield*.
1917. Joyce, Henry Cyril Conwy, *Cai diff*.
1895. Joyce, Robert Dwyer, *Dublin*.
1858. Joyce, Thomas, *Marfield*.
1862. Joyce, Thomas, *Cranbrook*.
1897. Joynes,FrancisWm., *Wolverhampton*.
1893. Joynson, Harold Mead.
1917. Joynt, Malcolm Cyril, *Blackheath*.
1923. Joyston-Bechal, E., *W. Ind Dock-rd*.
1905. Jubb, Archie Vivian, *Lytham*.
1888. Jubb, Frank, *Peckham*.
1897. Judd,Walter Rossell,*Ashton-u.-Lyne*.
1903. Judson, James Douglas, *Folkestone*.
1900. Judson, Jos. Edwd , *Ashton-under-L*.
1876. Judson, Thomas Robert, *Reigate*.
1869. Jukes, Andrew, *Salisbury-square*.

1885. Julian, O. R. A.,C.B., C.M.G., C.B.E.
1917. Jupe, Montagu Horace, *Reigate*.
1905. Jupp, Edgar Norman, *Chard*.

K.

1917. Kadinsky,Salomon, *Westminster-h'sp*.
1910. Kahlenberg, Fritz, *Gisbon ne, N.Z*.
1885. Kaka, Sorabji Manekji, *Karachi*.
1901. Kalomiris, Nicholas John, *Egypt*.
1915. Kalyanvala, Dadabhai N., *Chelsea*.
1919. Kamal, Hassan, *Cairo*.
1917. Kamchorn, Nai, *Ashburn-place*.
1916. Kameneff, Vladimir, *Moscow*.
1921. Kamil, Mohammed, *Helwan, Egypt*.
1916. Kan, Ten Liang, *Wimbledon*.
1923.§Kane, Winifred Alma, *Rhodesia*.
1909. Kanga,Hormusji Dorabji,*Hampstead*.
1909. Kantawala, Chhaganlal H., *Baroda*.
1909. Kapadia, Rustom Darashaw, *Bombay*.
1911. Kapur, Nawin Chand, *I.M.S.*
1903. Karanjia,KhursedjiNasserw.,*Bombay*
1881. Karanjia,Menw.Dhunjibhai,*Bombay*.
1922. Kark, Charles Lazar.
1922. Karn, Reginald George, *Hampstead*.
1875. Karop, George Charles, *Herne Bay*.
1921. Karunaratna, Geo. Wilfred, *Ceylon*.
1922. Kassem, Abdel Hamid, *Streatham*.
1885. Kauffmann,OttoJackson,*Birmingham*
1911. Kaufman, Victor Stanley, *Toronto*.
1899. Kaufmann. Geo. Bernard, *Mincing-l*.
1913. Kauntze, W. Hy., M.B.E.,*W.Af.M.S*.
1899. Kav, Alfred Reginald, *Cley*.
1871. Kay, Hildreth, *Mablethorpe*.
1897. Kay, Richard, *Nelson, Lancs*.
1883. Kay, Walter Smith, *Sheffield*.
1901. Kaye, Ernest George, *Wootton Bassett*.
1884. Kaye, Joe Nicholson, *Hull*.
1919. Kazim, Aga Mohamed, *Bangalore*.
1915. Keane,Chas.G. Gordon,*Ladbroke-gr*.
1915. Kearney,C.S.J.,*Bartholomew's-close*.
1890. Keats, Wm. John Chas., *Camberwell*.
1909. Kebbell. Chas. Fredk. Vivian, *Ealing*.
1860. Keele, Chas. Ferdinand, *Langford-pl*.
1892. Keele, David, *Highbury*.
1898. Keeling, Geo. Sydnev, *Attleborough*.
1902. Keeling, Hugh Nevill, *Nuneaton*.
1866. Keen, William, *Chelsea*.
1923. Keene, Reginald, *Muswell-hill*.
1882. Keep, Arthur Corrie, *Gloucester-pl*.
1877. Keer, Jn. Cordy, *Wickham Market*.
1913. Keer, Kenneth J. T., *Wickam Market*.
1883. Keess, Arthur, *Madras*.
1916.§Keess, Ivy, *Gordon-square*.
1922. Keevil, Arthur James, *Bristol*.
1893. Keevil, George Mulready.

1889. Keiffenheim-Trubridge,L.Walt.,*Hoo.*
1893. Keighley, Herbert, *Batley.*
1906. Keith,Darwin Mills,*Rockford,U.S.A.*
1912. Keith, Thomas Skene, *Penge.*
1896. Keith, Wm. Dow, *Brit. Columbia.*
1894. Kekwick, John, *Carlisle.*
1889. Kelbe, Walt. Edward, *B.E. Africa.*
1919. Kelf, Henry David, *Greenwich.*
1894. Keller, Hermann L. A.,*Br. Columbia.*
1904. Kellett, Orme Stirling, *Br. Honduras.*
1906. Kellgren, Ernst Gregor, *Eaton-sq.*
1876. Kellie, George Jerome, *I.M.S.*
1903. Kellond-Knight, Hy. Arthur, *R.N.*
1896. Kelly, Bruce Curtis, *Burnham.*
1913. Kelly, Francis Henry, *Hampstead.*
1922. Kelly, Robert Wm. Creighton.
1919. Kelly, Simon, *Manchester.*
1881. Kelly, Thomas, *Ontario.*
1902. Kelly, Thomas Thelwell, *Ropsley.*
1886. Kelly, Thos. William, *Nottingham.*
1872. Kelly, William, *Worthing.*
1911. Kelman, Geo. Arth. E., *Charlwood-st.*
1886. Kelsall, Chas. Jas. Seddon, *R N.*
1886. Kelsall, Hry.Truman, *Perth, W. Aust.*
1918. Kemm,Noel Edw.Ffarnewell,*Clifton.*
1858. Kemp, Benjamin, *Wakefield.*
1907. Kemp,Chas.Gordon,M.C.,*St.Albans.*
1919. Kemp, Francis William, *Putney.*
1905. Kemp, Frederick Wm., M.C., *N.Z.*
1888. Kemp, George Lajus, *Worksop.*
1918. Kemp, Geo. Spencer Lajus, *Worksop.*
1906. Kemp,Jas. Reginald, M.C., *Newbury.*
1899. Kemp, John Harold, *New Zealand.*
1913. Kemp, J. Wallace, *Coldharbour-lane.*
1893. Kempe,Chas.G Burrington,*Salisbury.*
1896. Kempster, Chris. Richd., *Clapton.*
1886. Kempster, Felix Charles, *Battersea.*
1902. Kempthorne, Gerard A., *R.A.M.C.*
1884. Kendal, Arthur Saml., *Nova Scotia.*
1863. Kendal, Cuthbert Robert, *Hexham.*
1883. Kendali, George, *Battle.*
1916. Kendall, Guy Melville, *Cashely.*
1885. Kendall,Hy.Wm.Martindale,*N.Zeal.*
1915. Kendall, Nicholas Edward, *Cashel.*
1892. Kendall, Nicholas F., *Chiddingfold.*
1871. Kendall, Walter Benger, *Llandogo.*
1923. Kenderdine, Eric C K., *Bristol.*
1903. Kenderdine, Ernest Hy., *Coventry.*
1884. Kendle, Fredk. Wellesley, *Bengal.*
1907. Kendrew, Alex. John, *Barnstaple.*
1892. Kendrick, Horace Herbt., *Coventry.*
1906. Kenion, Thomas Lloyd, *Ceylon.*
1886. Kennard, Chas. Poole, *Brit. Guiana.*
1896. Kennard, David Gerald, *Faringdon.*
1893. Kennedy, Angus Endicott, *Plaistow.*
1911. Kennedy, Anthony, *I.M.S.*
1912. Kennedy, Cornelius, *New Brighton.*

1909. Kennedy, David, *Geelong, Victoria.*
1923.§Kennedy, Hilda Mary, *Jersey.*
1893. Kennedy, Jas.BuckleyM.,*Birmingh'm*
1893. Kennedy, John, *Camberwell.*
1915. Kennedy, John Scott, *Glasgow.*
1921.§Kennedy, Mary Elisabeth, *Plaistow.*
1920. Kennedy, Oswald Edward, *Ottawa.*
1902. Kennedy, Robt. Pettigrew, *York-st.*
1874. Kennedy, Wm. Adam, *West Aust.*
1891. Kennedy, Wm. Willoughby, *Calcutta.*
1894. Kennington, Edgar, *P. & O. S. N. Co.*
1882. Kenny, Fredk. Hamilton, *Queensland.*
1911. Kenny, Randal Young, *Canada.*
1895. Kenrick, William Hamilton, *I.M.S.*
1889. Kent, Charles Arthur, *Dover.*
1908. Kent, Hugh Brand, *China.*
1895. Kent, Percy Wheeler, *Barry, Glam.*
1892. Kent, Sydney, *Bexhill.*
1919.§Kenworthy, Muriel M., *Southport.*
1914. Kenworthy, Tom Ramsden, M.C.
1917. Kenyon, James Douglas, *Accrington.*
1868. Kenyon, Jn. Edward, *Twickenham.*
1907. Keogh,Fdk.EdwinHubt.N.K'nsingt'n
1893. Keppel-Compton,Jn.H ,*Southampton.*
1902. Ker, Wm. Perceval, *Berkhamsted.*
1912. Kerby, Clement Carlyon, *Truro.*
1918. Kerby, Ernest Francis, *West-end-lane.*
1916. Kerby, Theo. Rosser Fred., *Allesley.*
1922.§Keresztes, Mary Anne, *Hungary.*
1919. Kerfoot, Herbert W., *Canada.*
1900. Kerfoot, Stanley James, *Bedminster*
1908. Kernahan, Joseph Arth. A., *I.M.S.*
1889. Kerr, Alex. Livingstone, *N.S.W.*
1904. Kerr, Arthur Edgar, *Petworth.*
1889. Kerr, George Douglas, *Brighton.*
1922. Kerr, John Norman, *Ealing.*
1890. Kerr, William James, *Rochdale.*
1918.§Kerruish, Florence M., *Douglas.*
1873. Kershaw, Alfred, *Bolton.*
1881. Kershaw, Hugh, *Leeds.*
1894. Kerswill, Harry, *Sandwich.*
1865. Kerswill, John Bedford, *Norbury.*
1922. Kessel, Barney, *Johannesburg.*
1873. Kesteven, Leighton, *Sydney, N.S.W.*
1869. Kesteven, Wm. Henry, *Norbiton.*
1896. Ketchen, Arthur Dickson, *Cape Town.*
1918.§Kettle, M. H., *Nottingham-pl.*
1895. Kettlewell, Geo. Douglas,*Ilfracombe.*
1893. Kevern, Grahame Travers, *Rowhedge.*
1881. Keys, Elias, *Cape.*
1914. Keys, Sydney Hudson, *Hunter-st.*
1873. Keyworth, George Hawson, *Wem.*
1922. Khaleel, Ahmed M., *Maida-vale.*
1908. Khambata, Ratanshaw B., *Bombay.*
1907. Khambata,SohrabManeckji,*Cook&Sn.*
1907. Khan, Abdus Sattar. *I.M.S.*
1917. Khan, Haji Hyderali, *Guy's-hosp.*

1909. Khan, Latafat Husain, *I. M.S.*
1914. Khan, Mahomed Musa, *Bombay.*
1889. Khan, Masha Allah, *Agra.*
1910. Khan, Mirza Mohammed, *Dorset-sq.*
1912. Khanna, Bhagat Ram.
1919. Khanolkar, Vasant R., *West-end-lane.*
1914. Kharegat, Rustam Merwan.
1891. Kidd, Archibald, *Gravesend.*
1881. Kidd, Arthur.
1914. Kidd, Gerald Patrick, *Bromsgrove.*
1889. Kidd, Harold Andrew, *Chichester.*
1884. Kidd, Leonard Joseph, *Hampstead.*
1878. Kidd, Percy, *Montagu-street.*
1875. Kidd, Walter Aubrey, *Blackheath.*
1909. Kidd, Walter Shirley, *Harrogate.*
1902. Kiddle, Horace Harvard, *R.A.M.C.*
1916. Kidman, George Edwin, *Hitchin.*
1903. Kidner, Henry Ratcliff, *Shortlands.*
1923. Kies, Jean Pierre.
1876. KilBride, James, *Athy.*
1906. Kilgour, Wm. Robert, *Cromwell-rd.*
1923. Killard-Leavey, M. E. J , *Southend.*
1910. Killard-Leavey, Tim. Jos., *Southend.*
1892. Killery, St. Jn. Browne, *R.A M.C.*
1922. Killingback, Harry C., *Hampstead.*
1910. Killpack, Ch. Dones, *Haywards H'th.*
1909. Kilner, Henry Goff, *Bury St. Edmunds.*
1903. Kilner, John Newport, *Bengal.*
1914. Kilner, Strangman D., *Bury-St.-Edm.*
1893. Kilroy, Lancelot, *Royal Navy.*
1898. Kilvert, John Ellis, *Derby.*
1912. Kimber, Wm. Jos. Teil, *Brighton.*
1902. Kincaid, Frederick, *Matlock.*
1916. Kindersley, Charles Edward, *Eton.*
1922. Kindness, John, *Cheriton.*
1890. King, Arthur, *Bow, Devon.*
1894. King, Arthur Frederick Wm., *I.M.S.*
1905. King, Colin, O.B.E., *Cuckfield.*
1854. King, Edwyn John, *Bickleighscombe.*
1896. King, Frank Raymond, *Peckham.*
1890. King, Fdk. Wm. Rbt. Jn., *New Zealand.*
1914. King, Geoffrey William, *Reigate.*
1912. King, Gordon Burnham, *Cape.*
1892. King, John Charles, O.B.E., *Barry.*
1923.§King, Kathleen Helena Beatrice.
1908 King, Leslie Reg , *Chipping Norton.*
1922.§King, Lorna Susan, *Bramham-gdns.*
1897. King, Nevill Pearce, *Monmouth.*
1887. King, Preston, *Bath.*
1907. King, Ralph De Veil, *Inverness-terr.*
1888. King, Richard Henry, *Banstead.*
1899. King, Thomas Arthur, *Bude.*
1915. King, Thos. Harold V., *College-hill.*
1862. King, T. William, *Horsham.*
1904. King, Wm. Athol Desmond, *Paignton.*
1906. King, William Herbert, *Royal Navy.*
1906. King, William Wiltr.d, *Sheffield.*

8320

1922. Kingdon, Alfred Thos. Lock, *Torquay.*
1889. Kingdon, Edwd. Owen, *Holsworthy.*
1890. Kingdon, Ernest Cory, *Twehurst.*
1896. Kingdon, Jas. Renorden, *King's Lynn.*
1913. Kingdon, William Edward, *Buxton.*
1921. Kingsbury, Alan Neave, *Ealing.*
1904. Kingsbury, Wm. Neave, *Lee.*
1889. Kingsford, Arth. Beresford, *Up. Geo.-st.*
1873. Kingsford, Percival, *Queensberry-pl.*
1913.§Kingsley, Merlin, *Moulmein, Burma.*
1902. Kingsmill, Hry. Ardagh, *Canada.*
1903. Kingston, Chas. Samuel, *Trowbridge.*
1913. Kingston, Claude, *Bristol.*
1910. Kingston, Stuart Hardy, *Bristol.*
1900. Kinloch, Robert Blair, *St. Albans.*
1881. Kinneir, Francis Wm. Edw., *Horsham.*
1921. Kinneir, Guy, *Horsham.*
1894. Kinnersly, Geo. E., M.B.E., *Guernsey.*
1884. Kirby, Ernest Dormer, *Birmingham.*
1902. Kirby, Guy Hannah, *Smethwick.*
1916. Kirby, Paul Rustat Ellis, *Norwood.*
1893. Kirby, Rowland Arthur, *Letchworth.*
1906. Kirby, Thos. Wm., *Maple, Canada.*
1897. Kirk, John Lamplugh, *Pickering.*
1893. Kirkby, Robert Casement, *Solva.*
1920. Kirkham, Arthur Welsby, *Bolton.*
1899. Kirkman, A.H. Beaumont, *Staplehurst st.*
1904. Kirkness, Wm. Ronald, *Portsmouth.*
1911. Kirkpatrick, Chas. Gordon, *Canada.*
1887. Kirkpatrick, R'ndolph, *Mus. Nat. Hist.*
1881. Kirkpatrick, R., C.B., C.M.G. *R A M.C*
1893. Kirkpatrick-Picard, A.W , *B'ndary-r.*
1920. Kirton, Charles Ainger, *Univ. Coll.*
1890. Kirton, Chas. Imray, *Honor Oak.*
1894. Kirton, Reginald Gower, *Cairo.*
1890. Kirton, Martin Ainger, *Ealing.*
1865. Kisch, Albert, *Gloucester-pl.*
1906. Kitchen, Harold Ernest, *Douglas.*
1901. Kitchin, Ernest Hugh, *Parkstone.*
1889. Kitchin, Hy. Brunton, *Brockley-rd.*
1902. Kitchin, Percy, *Gerrard's Cross.*
1892. Kitching, Charles Atkinson, *Cape.*
1883. Kitching, Jn. Lea Walton, *Cobham.*
1884. Kite, Edwin Whitf. Dawson, *St Albans.*
1894. Kitson, John Pole, *Falmouth.*
1919. Kittell, Paul Bruno, *Hampstead.*
1923. Klionsky, Georges, *Antwerp.*
1891. Knaggs, George John, *Dublin.*
1881. Knaggs, Hry. Valentine, *Camden-rd.*
1890. Knapp, Geo. Harvey, D S.O , *S. Af.*
1892. Knapp, Montague Henry, *R.N.*
1894. Knapton, Hy. Alfd. Forbes, *I.M.S.*
1897. Knechtel, Robert, *Brussels, Ontario.*
1891. Knevitt, Herbert, *Ealing.*
1881. Knight, Alfd. Osborne, *Auckland, N.Z.*
1919. Knight, Allan Osborne, *Hampstead.*
1903. Knight, Aubrey Harvey D., *Vict.-st.*

8377

1864. Knight, Chas. Fredk., *Letchworth.*
1898. Knight, Chas. Voughton, *Gloucester.*
1889. Knight, Edward, *Handel-st.*
1893. Knight, E., O.B.E., *St. Anne's-on-Sea.*
1895. Knight, Henry Bury, *Bude.*
1889. Knight, Henry Ernest, *Rotherham.*
1905. Knight, Herbert Stanley, *Brockley.*
1913. Knight, John Iles Francis, *Windsor.*
1875. Knight, John Tomlinson, *Carlton.*
1920.§Knight, Margaret H., *Q'ns-gate-terr.*
1880. Knight, William, *Gravesend.*
1892. Knightley, Walt. Randall, *Tulse-hill.*
1901. Knobel, Wm. Bernard, *Bourne Castle.*
1895. Knocker, William Douglas, *Temple.*
1891. Knott, Edwd. Milward, *Sutton Coldfield.*
1915. Knott, Frank Alex., *W. Wickham.*
1910. Knowles, Charles Haley, *Garforth.*
1920.§Knowles, Doris Gertrude, *Chesham.*
1885. Knowles, Frederic Joseph, *St. Helens.*
1896. Knowles, Ralph, *Preston.*
1907. Knowles, Robert, *Elgin-avenue.*
1881. Knowling, Ernest Mansford, *Tenby.*
1899. Knowlton, Alexr. John, *Bitterne.*
1874. Knox, Charles Fredk., *Trinidad.*
1893. Knox, Robert, *Harley-street.*
1897. Knox, Robert George, *Freshford.*
1877. Knox-Shaw, Chas. Thos., *Harley-st.*
1901. Kœnig, René Paul, *Geneva.*
1923. Kohnstam, Geoffroy L. S., *Frognal.*
1908. Kolapore, Framroze J., *I.M.S.*
1907. Kolapore, Phiroze J., *Bombay.*
1920. Kooy, Frans Hieronvmus, *Barnsbury.*
1921. Korn, Morris, *Canfield-gardens.*
1923 Kostich, Dushan, *Serbia.*
1923.§Krause, Emilia B. M., *Judd-street.*
1922. Krestin, David, *Whitechapel-rd.*
1907. Krestin, Solomon, *Sidney-street.*
1922. Kretchmar, Arthur H., *Muswell-hill.*
1915. Krupenia, Yankel, *Slonim, Russia.*
1910. Krupp, *Weston.*
1901. Kunhardt, Jn. Conrad Gie, *I.M.S.*
1909. Kureishi, MozafferDinA.. *RawalPindi.*
1914. Kusumbeker, Gajanan Chintaman.
1876. Kyan, John Howard, *Preston.*
1893. Kyffin, John, *Gosport.*
1918. Kyle, James, *Hampstead.*
1885. Kynaston. John William, *Coseley.*
1874. Kyngdon, Fredk. Hy., *Bank of N S. W.*

L.

1887. Labey, Julius, *Jersey.*
1922. Labieb, Fouad Ibrahim, *Highbury.*
1915.. Laborda, Felix E. R., *Stroud-green.*
1883. Lace, Wm. Francis, *Sutton-at-Home.*
1892. Lacey, Allan Ramsey, *Natal.*
8430

1905. Lacey, Bernard Warner, *Woolwich.*
1911. Lacey, George EricWarner, *Woolw ch.*
1901. Lacey, Hugh Kirbeli, *Torquay.*
1898. Lacey, William Walter.
1923. Lachlan, Kenneth H., *Hampstead.*
1869. Lack, Thomas Lambert, *Attleboro'.*
1918. Lack, Victor John Fredk., *Streatham.*
1875. Lacy, Alex. Gairdner, *Ascot.*
1900. Ladell, Ernest Wm. Julius, *Cape, S.Af.*
1909. Laidlaw, F. Fortescue, *Tffculme.*
1881. Laimbeer, Frederick James.
1910. Laing, Clifford Yule, *Manchester.*
1920. Laing, James Niven, *Manchester.*
1922. Laing, Wallace, *Manchester.*
1911. Laird, William Balfour, *R.A.M C.*
1913. Lake, Herbert Arnold, *Stockwell-rd.*
1903. Lakin. Cecil Lionel, *Redhill.*
1900. Lakshmanan, Peter N.
1912. Lal, Sohan, *Punjab.*
1918. Lâlâ, Daulat Maughirmal, *Hyderabad.*
1897. Lamb, Archibald Walt., *Albrighton.*
1918. Lamb, FrancisWm. M., *Birmingham.*
1911. Lamb, Harold Victor, *Bath.*
1884. Lamb, Hugh, *Wood-green.*
1901. Lamb, Ralph, *Liverpool.*
1895. Lambe, Thomas, *Hornchurch.*
1886. Lambert, Frederick Samuel, *Newland.*
1896. Lambert, Hugh Llewelyn, *Barnes.*
1904. Lambert, John. O.B.E., *Shoreham.*
1878. Lambert, John Speare, *R. Navy.*
1894. Lambert, Percv, *Finsbury-pk.*
1920. Lambert, Wright, *Leeds.*
1899. Lamburn, Wm· Alf. Stedwell, *Lagos.*
1922.§Lambourne,GladysM., *Golder's-green.*
1885. Lamont, John Chas., C.I.E., *I.M.S.*
1895. Lamplough, Charles, *Alverstoke.*
1903. Lamplough, Wharram Hy., *Alverstoke.*
1890. Lancashire, Geo. Herbt., *Manchester.*
1887. Lancaster, ErnestLeCronier, *Swansea.*
1875. Lancaster, Hy. Francis, *Gloucester-ter.*
1910. Land, John Murgatroyd, *Bradford.*
1920. Landau, Joseph Victor, *Highbury.*
1898. Lander, Chas. Llewellyn, D.S.O., M.C.
1911. Lander, Harold Drew, *Burnham.*
1892. Landon, Ernest Edwd. B., *Kidderm'ster*
1880. Lane, Alexander, *Weymouth.*
1893. Lane, Clayton Arbuthnot, *I.M.S.*
1922. Lane, Cvril Rickword, *Camberwell.*
1884. Lane, Frederick Herbert, *Brixton.*
1914. Lane, Harold Dunmore, M.C.
1891. Lane, Harry Augell, *Mile End.*
1881. Lane, James Oswald, *Hereford.*
1923. Lane, Ronald Epev, *Canterbury.*
1888. Lane, Wm. B, C.B.E., C.I.E., *I.M.S.*
1894. Lane, Arthur Joseph, *Cape Province.*
1919. Lang, Charles Albert, *New York.*
1871. Lang, John Messiter, *Gloucester-rd.*
8487

1886. Lang, Walter Scott.
1905. Langdale, Harry Marmaduke, *R.N.*
1888. Langdale, Henry, *Warrington.*
1872. Langdale, Hry. Marmaduke, *Uckfield.*
1915. Langdale-Kelham, Roy D., *Brighton.*
1897. Langdon, Hy. Chas. Theo., *Chiswick.*
1860. Langdon, John, *A.M.S.*
1911. Langdon, Wm. Morgan, *N. Tawton.*
1889. Lange, André Philip, *Trinidad.*
1897. Lange, Massilon Henri Jn., *Trinidad.*
1893. Langford, Charles Harris, *Highgate.*
1896. Langford, Fdk. C., M.B.E., *Dulwich.*
1892. Langford, Morris Charles, *R.N.*
1916. Langford-Jones, Robert P., *Bangor.*
1898. Langley, John Edwd., *Fulham.*
1898. Langley, John Inman, *Coventry.*
1865. Langley, John Thomas, *Exmouth.*
1902. Langmead, Fredk. Saml., *Q.-Anne-st.*
1893. Langmore, Hbt. Richd., *Wallingford.*
1920. Langridge, Frank F., *Ilfracombe.*
1888. Langridge,FrankWash't'n,*Ilfracombe*
1871. Langridge, George Thomas,*R.A.M.C.*
1863. Langston, Thomas, *Sandown, I. of W.*
1891. Langston,Thos. Alfd. Ollivant,*I.M.S.*
1917. Langton, Edw. Athol C., *Brighton.*
1911. Langton, Peregrine S. B., *Poole.*
1893. Langworthy,W.Southmead,*Torcross.*
1890. Lankester, Arth. Colborne, *Peshawar.*
1884. Lankester,Alfd.Owen,*Up. Wimpole-st.*
1897. Lankester, Cecil P., *Guildford.*
1887. Lankester, Francis John, *Leicester.*
1884. Lankester, Herbt. Hy., *C. M. Socy.*
1898. Lankester, Ralph Albt. R., *Bradford.*
1886. Lansdale, William, *Grove Park.*
1891. Lansdown, C. E., O.B.E , *Cheltenham.*
1895. Lansdown, Gilbert Harry, *Winnipeg.*
1919. Lansdown, Robert Blake P., *Clifton.*
1890. Lansdown, Robt. Guth. Poole,*Clifton.*
1896. Lanyon, Edgar Temple, *Redruth.*
1898. Lanyon-Owen, L. Edw., *J. Carlton-c.*
1876. Lapage, Charles Clement, *Nantwich.*
1914. Lapage, Francis Claud, *Walmer.*
1888. Larcombe, George Garmany.
1887. Larcombe, Samuel Slee.
1888. Larkam, Edward Thomas, *Birm.*
1903. Larkin, Reginald, *Grove-park.*
1883. Larking, Arthur Ernest, *Buckingham.*
1905. Lascelles, John Eaton, *Thrapston.*
1907. Lash, Henry Andrew,*Brit. Columbia.*
1895. Laslett, Maurice Howard,*Gillingham.*
1884. Laslett, Thomas George, *Bolton.*
1900. Last, Cecil Edwd., *Littlehampton.*
1920. Last, Geo. Valentine C., *Liverpool.*
1898. Last, Thomas Clifford, *Burnham.*
1896. Latchmore, Arthur Thos , *New Zeal.*
1903. Latham, Charles Hugh, *Derby.*
1897. Latham, Denyer Wm. F., *Barnsbury.*
8544

1921. Latham, F. G., *Ashton-in-Makerfield.*
1903. Latham, Godfrey Holland, *Derby.*
1913. Latham, Harold William, *Barnsbury.*
1923. Latham, Thomas, *Sandbach.*
1911. Latham,WmE,*Ashton-in-Makerfield.*
1891. Lathbury,Arth.Edwd.A.,*Eastbourne.*
1904. Lathbury,ErnestB.,O.B.E.,*R.A.M.C.*
1916. Latif, Moh. Elwan Abdel, *Middlx.-h.*
1871. Latimer, Henry Arth.,*Tunb'dge-wells.*
1875. Latour, George Lewis, *Grenada.*
1870. Lattey, Arthur, *Bournemouth.*
1918. Lau, Edward Ek Dun, *Penang.*
1923. Lauder, H.V.R. T.,*Marlborough-gate.*
1913. Lauder, James Lafayette,D.S.O.,M.C.
1909. Lauderdale, Edw. Maitland,*Grimsby.*
1897. Laurence,BertramEustace.*Teddingt'n*
1904. Laurence, George, *Chippenham.*
1913. Laurence, Gerald, *Wellington.*
1881. Laurent,EugeneArth.Oscar,*Mauritius*
1918. Laurent, Louis Jacques Maurice.
1923. Lautre, Max Apthorp.
1922. Laver, Basil L.,c/o *Lloyd's Bank,*E.C.
1917. Laver, Chas. Hardiman, *Cox & Co.*
1893. Laver, Philip Guyon, *Colchester.*
1896. Lavers, Norman, *Bath.*
1884. Lavie, Tudor Germaine, *R.A.M.C.*
1885. Lavies,Harry Brandreth,*Belgrace-rd.*
1919. Lavine, Louis, *Guy's-hospital.*
1877. Law, Edward, *Harley-street.*
1917. Law, Francis Reginald, *Leeds.*
1918. Lawn, John Gunson, *Golders-green.*
1923. Lawn, Lawrence, *Chalk Farm.*
1909. Lawrance, Milo Chas. S., *Earlestown.*
1905. Lawrence, Alan Arthur Hinds, *Cape.*
1911. Lawrence, Alex. C. C., *Darlington.*
1884. Lawrence, Alfred, *Kutbery, Cape.*
1857. Lawrence, Arth. Garnous, *Chepstow.*
1923. Lawrence, Frank.
1896. Lawrence, Hy. Gwynne, *Green-st.*
1891. Lawrence, John, *Crewe.*
1883. Lawrence,SidneyCameron,*B'rnem'th.*
1903. Lawrence,Stephen March, *Gravesend.*
1874. Lawrence, Thomas George, *Cape.*
1904. Lawry, James Littleton, *Calstock.*
1902. Lawry, Richard Coger, *Penzance.*
1885. Laws,CuthbertUmfreville,*Newcastle.*
1905. Laws, Harold Lionel, *W. Australia.*
1918. Lawson, Alex. Smirle, *Basingstoke.*
1868. Lawson, Archibald, *Halifax,N.Scotia.*
1890. Lawson, Douglas, *R.A.M.C.*
1898. Lawson, Frank Howard, *Steyning.*
1914. Lawson, Frank Winter, *Brighton.*
1901. Lawson, Fredk. James, *Ovington-gds.*
1882. Lawson, Geo. L. Leathes, *Forest-hill.*
1922. Lawson, Henry Dillon, *Leytonstone.*
1886. Lawson, Hugh, *Chislehurst.*
1895. Lawson, Richard, *Balham.*
8601

1872. Lawson, Thomas Cornelius, *Oulton.*
1893. Lawton, Walt. Chaplin, *Cambridge.*
1902. Laycock, Albert Penard, *Highgate.*
1894. Layton, Frank George, *Walsall.*
1879. Layton, Henry Albert, *Bedford.*
1916. Lazanas, Elias P., *Taviton-st.*
1917.§Lazarus, Hilda Mary, *Waltair, S. I.*
1912. Lea, Edmund Thos.Howard,*Dulwich.*
1882. Lea, Francis James, *Holland-pk.-av.*
1874. Lea, Julian Augustus, *Grahamstown.*
1911. Lea-Wilson, Basil H. C.
1901. Leach, Edgar, *Eccles.*
1904. Leach, Harold, *Halifax.*
1901. Leach, Herbert, *Rhodesia.*
1902. Leach, Richard E. H.,O.B.E.,*Bungay.*
1899. Leader, Harold, *Sheffield.*
1898. Leah, Thomas Noy, *Plymouth.*
1878. Leak, Hector, *Winsford.*
1923.§Leak, Ruth A. M., *Denmark-park.*
1915. Leak, Walter Norman, *Winsford.*
1870. Leake, Geo. DaltonNugent,*R.A.M C.*
1897. Leake,Jonas Wm.,C.M.G., *R.A.M.C.*
1898. Leaning,Robert Craske,*Gunnersbury.*
1905. Leapingwell, Arthur Edward, *Derby.*
1870. Leapingwell, Wm. T. G., *Frogmore.*
1915. Learoyd, Cyril George, *Debden.*
1879. Leatham, HenryBlackburn,*New Zeal.*
1917. Leatham, Hugh Wm., *Wentbridge.*
1903. Leathart, Percival Wilson, *Norwood.*
1902. Leathem,Alfd. Newman, *Beckenham.*
1915. Leather,James Bertram,*Handsworth.*
1901. Leathes, Hill Mussenden, *Godalming.*
1903. Le Bas, Dumaresq, *R.A.M.C.*
1917. Leblanc, Felix Raoul, *Herne-hill.*
1914. Le Blanc, Louis Gaston, *Mauritius.*
1906. Lebon, Camille, *Saargemund.*
1921. Le Brasseur,John Henry, *Wimbledon.*
1905. Le Brocq, Charles Noble, *Jersey.*
1887. Leche, Arthur, *Axbridge.*
1869. Leckie, Walt. James, *Grosvenor Club.*
1918. Le Clézio. Eugene Henri Leon.
1900. Leclézio, Geo. Jos. Alexis, *Mauritius.*
1897. Leclézio, Gustave Ernest.
1878. Le Cronier, Hardwick, *Jersey.*
1889. Le Cronier, Maxwell, *Jersey.*
1908. Ledger, Alfred Vernon, *Leicester.*
1917. Ledger, Lloyd Kirwood, *Hereford.*
1919. Ledlie, Reg. Cyril Bell, *Guy's.*
1909. Ledlie, William, *Croydon.*
1923. Ledward, Colin Prentice, *Epsom.*
1902. Ledward,HughDavenport,*Letchworth*
1906. Lee,CrichtonStirling, *Wolverh'mpton.*
1873. Lee, Edmund, *Manchester.*
1875. Lee, Edwin, *Dewsbury.*
1898. Lee, Frederick William, *Hindhead.*
1910. Lee, Jas Arth. Richard, *Mexborough.*
1920. Lee, Richard Thomas, *Swinton.*
8658

1902. Lee, Robert Hammersley, *Campden-h.*
1903. Lee, Ronald Outram, *Thame.*
1892. Lee, Sidney Herbert, *Teddington.*
1904. Lee, William Emerson, *Worksop.*
1897. Lee, William Howe, *Chesterfield.*
1921. Lee-Michell, Robert, *Wellington.*
1901. Leech, Ernest Bosdin, *Manchester.*
1900. Leech, Frederick Samuel, *Gateshead.*
1891. Leeder,Forrest Bertram, *B. Columbia.*
1923. Leekam, Felix Hiram, *Trinidad.*
1914. Leembruggen, Robert A.. *Ceylon.*
1904. Leeming, Arnold, *Sudbury.*
1907. Leeming, Arthur Norman, *Colwyn.*
1883. Leeming, Robert Whinerey. *Kendal.*
1915. Lees, Alec Anthony, M.C., *Moseley.*
1909. Lees, Alfred Everard, *Knutsford.*
1894. Lees, Charles Arch., C.B.E., *Ealing.*
1900. Lees, Charlie, *Tunbridge Wells.*
1916. Lees, Douglas Leonard, *Clifton.*
1885. Lees, Edwin Leonard, *Bristol.*
1915. Lees, Francis Charles, M.C ,*Walsall.*
1904. Lees, Harold Cruickshank, *Darwen.*
1885. Lees, William, *Chester.*
1907. Leeson, Harold H., M.C., *R.A.M.C.*
1875. Leeson, John Rudd, *Twickenham.*
1917. Leete, Harold Mason, *South Shields.*
1888. Le Feuvre, Wm. Philip, *Bulawayo.*
1904. Le Fevre, John Speechly, *N.S.W.*
1898. Le Fleming, Ernest Kaye,*Wimborne.*
1923. Leftwich, Philip, *South Africa.*
1904. Legassick, Wm. Kingdon, *Plympton.*
1897. Le Geyt, Daniel Edward, *Jersey.*
1890. Legg, Cyrus, *Upper Tooting.*
1885. Leggatt, Gerard Stedman,*Harpenden.*
1894. Legge, Sydney Colen, *Worcester.*
1910. Legge, Tam, *Singapore.*
1923. Leggett, Bernard John, *Forest-gate.*
1889. Legh, Harry Legh de, *Redcar.*
1901. Lehmann, Julius Eduard, *Winnipeg.*
1907. Leicester, William Saml., *Singapore.*
1893. Leigh, Albert, *Malpas.*
1920. Leigh, Arthur, *Manchester.*
1913 Leigh, Hubert Vere, *Treharris.*
1886. Leigh, Randle, *Liverpool.*
1870. Leigh, Richmond, *Orange River Prov.*
1865. Leigh, Thomas Drake, *Liverpool.*
1907. Leigh, William Hamer, *Bolton.*
1878. Leigh, William Watkin, *Cowbridge.*
1919. Leitch, John Neil, *Sutton.*
1912. le Maistre, Edw. Aleck,*Greenwich-rd.*
1888. Leman,Thos.Curtis, *Chipping Sodbury*
1844. Le Marchant, Rev. Robt., *Rhisington.*
1918. Le Marquand, Horace Sharman.
1914. Le Mesurier, Arthur Baker, *Toronto.*
1889. Lemon, Edwd. Henry, *Bournemouth.*
1878. Lendon, Alfred Austin, *Adelaide.*
1874. Lendon, Edwin Harding, *Holland-pk.*
8715

1922§Lendrum, Catherine Emma Lilian.
1909. Leney, Ronald John B., *Godalming*.
1902. Lennane, Alf. Jas. Andrew, *Clapham*.
1895. Leon, George Alexander, *Torquay*.
1922. Leon, Kenneth W., *Montagu-mans*.
1905. Leonard, Leonard Gascoyne, *Manchr*.
1902. Leonard, Napoleon, *Westcliff-on-Sea*.
1894. Leonard, Robert Cecil, *Bristol*.
1912. Leopold, Gustav A. M., *Dalston*.
1836. Le Quesne, F. Simeon, V.C., *R A.M.C*.
1889. Le Riche, Philip John, *Worthing*.
1895. Lermitte, Edward Aug., *Sydney*.
1913. Lescher, Frank G., M.C., *Palace-court*.
1915. Leslie, James Stuart, *Norbury*.
1898. Leslie, Lewis F., O.B.E., *Evesham*.
1907. Lessel, John Fredk., *Halifax, N.S.*
1882. Lessey, Sandford Scobell, *Birmingham*
1904. Lester, Geo. Mackenzie Lester, *N.Z.*
1893. Lesur, Marie Paul Aimé.
1914. L'Etang, Joseph Georges, *Bethnal-grn*.
1914. Letchworth, George H.S., *Canterbury*.
1868. Lett, Francis, *Hastings*.
1912. Levene, Leon, *Blackpool*.
1904. Leverton-Spry, Edward, *St. Keverne*.
1922. Levi, David, *Portsdown-road*.
1883. Levi, Reuben, *Montreal*.
1890. Levick, George David Baker, *Pinner*.
1896. Levick, George Kenny, *Hatant*.
1902. Levick, George Murray, *R.N.*
1919. Le Vieux, Henri T., *Johannesburg*.
1921.§Levin, Bessie, *Clapton*.
1919. Levin, Gdal Leizer, *Maida-vale*.
1911. Levinson, Wilfred Edgar, *Luton*.
1860. Levis, John Sampson, *R.N.*
1916. Leviseur, Ernest Alfred, *Bloemfontein*.
1918. Leviseur, Herbert John.
1892. Levy, Alfd. Goodman, *Manchester-sq*.
1919. Levy, Hyman Jacob, *Dowlais*.
1895. Levy, Oscar Ludwig, *Russell-square*.
1922. Levy, Simon Isaac, *Dowlais*.
1892. Lewarne, Frank, *Cricklade*.
1902. Lewellyn, John Woodruff, *Bristol*.
1858. Lewer, Alfred, *A.M.S.*
1883. Lewers, Arthur H. N., *Southwick-st*.
1881. Lewers, Thos. Ross, *Berry, N.S.W.*
1901. Lewin, George, *Croydon*.
1923. Lewin, Meyer Maxwell, *Lambeth*.
1890. Lewis, Albt. Cornewalle, *Pontyberem*.
1918. Lewis, Allan Wellesley, *Grenada*.
1921.§Lewis, Anna G. Mary, *Llandyssul*.
1901. Lewis, Arthur Cedric, *Rochford*.
1899. Lewis, Arth. Daniel, *Stoke Newington*.
1888. Lewis, Benj. Morgan, *Pontypridd*.
1897. Lewis, Cecil Ernest M., *Bickley*.
1921. Lewis, Charles Gordon, *Ealing*.
1865. Lewis, Charles Gray M., *Goudhurst*.
1885. Lewis, Charles James, *Birmingham*.

8772

1921. Lewis, Charles John, *Moseley*.
1879. Lewis, Chris. John, *Birmingham*.
1917. Lewis, David John Adams, *Mydrim*.
1906. Lewis, David Thomas, *Pontypridd*.
1921. Lewis, Edmund Oliver, *Brynmawr*.
1922. Lewis, Edward Gordon, *Finsbury*.
1887. Lewis, Ernest Edward, *Weymouth-st*.
1893. Lewis, Ernest Wooi, *Saltash*.
1898. Lewis. Frank Charles, *Hill-street*.
1891. Lewis, Frederick, *Henfield*.
1921. Lewis, Frederick Charles, *Liverpool*.
1894. Lewis, Frederick Wm., *Lowestoft*.
1896. Lewis, George Williams, *Sydenham*.
1920. Lewis, Glyndwr Morison.
1895. Lewis, Gwilym, *Sidcup*.
1917. Lewis, Harold Warburton, *Scorrier*.
1916. Lewis, Herman, *Stamford-hill*.
1920. Lewis, Ivor, *Llandilo*.
1885. Lewis, James King, *Westbury*.
1885. Lewis, Jenkyn, *Llanon*.
1917. Lewis, John Biddulph S., *Norwich*.
1913. Lewis, John Ll. David, *Aberystwyth*.
1914. Lewis, Kingsley Wassell, *Pontypridd*.
1871. Lewis, Lewis, *St. Margaret's-on-T*.
1911. Lewis, Lewis F. G., *Merthyr Tydfil*.
1889. Lewis, Llewelyn, O.B.E., *Neath*.
1916. Lewis, Naunton Morgan, *Cardiff*.
1886. Lewis, Percy George, *Folkestone*.
1887. Lewis, Philip King, *Bromyard*.
1916. Lewis, Rhys Thomas, *Trevine*.
1903. Lewis, Robert Robinson, *R.A.M C*.
1905. Lewis, Rowland P., D.S.O., *R.A.M.C.*
1904. Lewis, Thomas, *Queen Anne-street*.
1912. Lewis, Thomas Percy, O.B.E.
1921. Lewis, Wm. Basil Aylmer, *Oswestry*.
1903. Lewis, William Collins, *Swansea*.
1901. Lewis, William Edwd. V., *Sheffield*.
1889. Lewis, William Edwd. V., *Forest-gate*.
1919. Lewtas, Fredk. Geo., *St. George's-hosp*.
1923. Lewthwaite, John L., *Isle of Man*.
1897. Lewys-Lloyd, Evan, *Towyn*.
1893. Ley, Bernard, *Longridge-road*.
1884. Ley, Henry James, *Southbourne*.
1907. Ley, Richard Leonard, *Gt. Yarmouth*.
1920. Liang, Pao Tsang, *Hampstead*.
1915. Liang, Pow Kan, *Hove*.
1900. Libby, Harold Samuel, *Falmouth*.
1923. Libert, Carlos E. M. J., *Camberwell*.
1911. Liddell, John Rhodes, *Dronfield*.
1898. Lidderdale, Fras. John, M.C.
1872. Lidderdale, James, *Cheltenham*.
1890. Liddle, Percy Herbert, *Victoria*.
1915. Liebson, Stephen Abraham, *S. Africa*.
1923. Liebster, Lionel Bertram, *Park-l., N.*
1893. Ligertwood, Walter Hood, *Wells*.
1901. Light, Leonard Wm., *Southminster*.
1889. Lightbody, John H., *Budd'h Salterton*.

8829

1899. Li htfoot, John Henry, *Royal Navy*.
1916. Lightwood, Edw. Eric, *Sanderstead*.
1921. Lightwood, Reginald C., *Sanderstead*.
1914. Liley, Jas. Arthur, M.C., *Highbury*.
1884. Lilley, James Harris, *Hereford*.
1908. Lillie, Charles Ogilvie, *Dunedin, N.Z.*
1879. Lillies, Herbert, *Victoria*.
1884. Lilly, Alfd. Thos. Irvine, *R.A.M.C.*
1882. Lilly, Frederick John, *Royal Navy*.
1913. Lilly, Geo. Aus en, M.C., *Canterbury*.
1915. Linder, Geoffry Challen, *Thornton-hth*.
1900. Lindop, Llewellyn, *Royal Navy*.
1886. Lindow, Albert, *Plumstead*.
1915. Lindow, Eric Delafield, *Plumstead*.
1910. Lindsay, Andrew Bonar, *Dunedin, N.Z*
1920. Lindsay, Gordon Parmiter, *Forest-hill*.
1923. Lindsay, Lewis Oswald, *Caterham*.
1918. Lindsay, Sidney Simon, *Hampstead*.
1894. Lindsey, Colin Dunrod, *Plymouth*.
1900. Lindsey, Edw. Vaughan, *Burton-on-T*
1903. Lindsey, Eric Craigie, *Chelsea*.
1911. Lindsey, Mark, *Southbourne*.
1921. Lindup Charles Arthur, *Sutton*.
1881. Line, William Henry, *Birmingham*.
1923. Linfoot, Ernest, *Halifax*.
1913. Ling, Charles Cooper, *March*.
1904. Ling, Harold Charles, *Keighley*.
1873. Lingard, Alfred, *Naini-Tal*.
1923. Lingford, Chas George, *Hampstead*.
1923. Linklater, James Thomas, *Aberdeen*.
1883. Linnell, Alfred, *Towcester*.
1911. Linton, Edward Claude, *Salisbury*.
1915. Linzee, Neville Hood, *Hampton-wick*.
1917. Lipkin, Isaac Jacob, *Oudtshoorn*.
1882. Lipscomb, Arth. Augustus, *Wrotham*.
1886. Lipscomb, Eustace Henry, *St. Albans*.
1912. Lipscomb, Fredk. Martin, *Farningh'm*.
1883. Liptrot, Alfred Bailey, *Crowle*.
1883. Lisboa, Patrocinio
1912. Liscombe, Robert Hy., *Finchley*.
1923. Lissack, Philip Marcus, *Johannesburg*.
1888. Lissaman, Thomas, *Bolton*.
1923. Lister, Arthur Reg., *Devonshire-pl*.
1905. Lister, Frederick Spencer, *Transvaal*.
1901. Lister, Herbert Shaw, *Bath*.
1882. Lister, Joseph Herbert.
1886. Lister, Joseph Jackson.
1916.§Lister, Louisa Margaret, *Clifton*.
1892. Lister, Sept. Rayner, *King's Lynn*.
1904. Lister, Walter, *Leeds*.
1923. Lister, Wm Alex., *Devonshire-pl*.
1922. Liston, Edward, *Warrington*.
1883. Liston, Walt. Lawrence, *Tewkesbury*.
1915. Litchfield, Eldon Munro, *N. Zealand*.
1906. Litchfield, Percy Collins, M.C., *Purley*.
1904. Lithgow, Ernest Geo Robt., *R.A.M.C.*
1901. Litteljohn, Edwd Salterne, *Coulsdon*.
8886

1887. Littig, Lawrence William.
1914. Little, Andrew Hunter, *Aylsham*.
1896. Little, Arthur Edwin, *Leeds*.
1893. Little, Ernest Gord. Grah., *Wimpole-st*.
1885. Little, Francis Ernest, *Teignmouth*.
1362. Little, Frederick, *Aylsham*.
1907. Little, Harold Norman, *Strood*.
1908. Little, Joseph Pearson, *Boundary-rd*.
1918. Little, Neville Hall, *Ont., Canada*.
1897. Littlehales, Arthur G., *Queen's-rd*.
1897. Littlejohn, Thos. Plested, *Southbourne*.
1904. Littlejohns, Arch.S., D.S.O., *R.A.M.C*
1910. Littlewood, Martin W., *Bideford*.
1884. Livermore, William L., *Stroud-green*.
1897. Liversidge, William, *Skipton*.
1911. Livesey, Ernest M., *Wellington, N.Z.*
1919. Livingston, David, *Newcastle*.
1919. Livingston, Philip C., *Fitzjames-av*.
1889. Livingstone, David Wm, *Brighton*.
1922. Livingstone, James L.
1889. Livsey, Wm. Edward, *Liverpool*.
1923. Llewellyn, Basil Stanley, *Roger stone*.
1883. Llewellyn, Dvd. Wm. Hy., *Eastbourne*.
1917. Llewellyn, Evan Edwards, *Rhondda*.
1922. Llewellyn, Henry Davies, *Lyme-st*.
1882. Llewellyn, James Davies, *Victoria*.
1885. Llewellyn, John, *St. Mawes*.
1895. Llewellyn, Richard L. Jones, *Bath*.
1901. Llewellyn, Thomas Lister, *Trentham*.
1894. Llewellyn, Thos. Richard, *Penygraig*.
1918. Llewellyn, Tudor David, *Ogmore-vale*.
1905. Llewelyn, Llewelyn, *Bridgend*.
1870. Lloyd, Albert Eyton, *Alanwood*.
1917.§Lloyd, Annie, *Weneth*.
1900. Lloyd, Brinley Richd, *Merthyr Tydfil*.
1911. Lloyd, David Charles, *Llanybyther*.
1904. Lloyd, David Geo., *Newcastle Emlyn*.
1898. Lloyd, Edmund Eyre, *Southend*.
1877. Lloyd, Edward James, *Bangor*.
1921. Lloyd, Evan Thomas.
1898. Lloyd, Francis S., O.B.E., *Luton*.
1911. Lloyd, Frederic George, *Forest-hill*.
1892. Lloyd, Fredk. George, *Addison-rd*.
1905. Lloyd, George William, *Alsager*.
1884. Lloyd, Henry, *St. Asaph*.
1900. Lloyd, John Allden, *Natal*.
1905. Lloyd, John Daniel Stuart, *Chirk*.
1923. Lloyd, John Harrop M., *Towyn*.
1907. Lloyd, John Ross, *R.A.M.C.*
1909. Lloyd, John Thomas, *Tregaron*.
1904. Lloyd, John Trweryn, M.C.
1889. Lloyd, John Wesley, *Liverpool*.
1914. Lloyd, Joseph, *Killay*.
1898. Lloyd, L.N., C.M.G., D.S.O., *R.A.M.C.*
1897. Lloyd, Lewis Jones, *Tasmania*.
1873. Lloyd, Morgan, *Llanarthney*.
1923. Lloyd, Neville Langdon, *Bridgend*.
8943

1900. Lloyd, Richard Ernest, *I.M.S.*
1898. Lloyd, Richard Harte, *R.A.M.C.*
1880. Lloyd, Rickard Wm, *Addison-rd.*
1908. Lloyd, Robert, *Burnham-on-Crouch.*
1900. Lloyd, Robert Archer, D.S.O.,*I.M.S.*
1891. Lloyd, Thomas Edward, *Abergavenny*
1917. Lloyd, Thomas P., *Newcastle Emlyn.*
1915. Lloyd, Vernon Edmund, M.C.
1921. Lloyd, William Ernest, *Swansea.*
1893. Lloyd, Wm. Frederick, *Windsor.*
1918. Lloyd-Davies,AllanW., *Wolverhp'ton*
1921. Lloyd-Jones, David M., *Regency-st.*
1917.§Lloyd-Williams,Alice L.,*E.Grinst'd.*
1914. Lloyd-Williams, I. Hubert, M.C.
1919. Lloyd-Williams. Peirce, *Cricklewood.*
1866. Loane, Joseph, *Gt. Alie-st.*
1893. Lock, George Haylett, *Uxbridge-st.*
1900. Lock, John Lewis, *Uxbridge.*
1899. Lock, Lyonel John, *Old Charlton.*
1903. Lock, PercyGonville, *Tunbridge Wells*
1886. Locke, George, *Hastings.*
1855. Locke, Thos. Wm. Spink, *Coatham.*
1892. Lockhart, Alfred, *Canada.*
1923. Lockhart, Len. Phipps, *Highbury-rd.*
1875. Lockwood, John Parker, *Faringdon.*
1858. Lockwood, Joseph, *Huddersfield.*
1888. Lockyer, Conrad Wm., *Birchington.*
1893. Lockyer,Gerard Edw.,*Much Wenlock.*
1907. Loddiges, Conrad, M C., *Bedford-pk.*
1889. Lodwidge, Wm. Charrott, *Langport.*
1922. Logan, Alfred Q uentin, *Clifton.*
1916. Logan, Harold Bishop, *Bristol.*
1883. Logan, Robert.
1890. Logan,RoderickR.W.,*Ashby-de-la-Z.*
1916. Loganadan, Arcot D., *Lansdowne-pl.*
1920. Lomax, Harold Aloysius,*Manchester.*
1883. Lomax, Montagu, *Colville-rd.*
1921.§Lombard, Eva, *S. Canara, India.*
1883. London, John Edward, *Brit. Guiana.*
1923.§Lones, Marian, *Harlesden.*
1889. Long, Edward Charles, *Basutoland.*
1880. Long, Edwin Walter, *New Zealand.*
1863. Long, Frederick, *Norwich.*
1915. Long,Geo.Sam Bousfield,*Guy's-hosp.*
1918. Long, Harold Octavius.
1893. Long, Herbert Birch, *Bicester.*
1898. Long, James Ernest, *Bath.*
1897. Long, John Reginald, *Dover.*
1894. Long, Thomas Freeman, *Chesham.*
1899. Long, Wm. Christopher, *I.M.S.*
1871. Longhurst, Alex. Keene, *Ealing.*
1853. Longhurst, Arth. E. T.,*Chandlersford.*
1891. Longhurst, Bell Wilmott, *R.A.M.C.*
1901. Longhurst,ErnestA.,*OldBurlingt'n-st.*
1900. Longhurst, Frederic Wm., *Hobart-pl.*
1900. Longhurst,Percv A.,*OldBurlington-st.*
1894. Longinotto, Michael Jos., *Russell-sq.*

1900. Longley, Jn. Augustus Noel, *Bristol.*
1883. Longman, Arthur, *Salisbury.*
1917. Longstaff, Eadbert Ralph, *Surbiton.*
1919. Longton, Eric Shaw, *Frome.*
1922. Longton,NormanH.II.,*NewBrighton.*
1892. Loos, William Christopher, *Natal.*
1907. Loosely, Charles James, *Hampstead.*
1917. Lopes, Albert Victor, *Demerara.*
1897. Lord, Cyril Courtenay, *Orpington.*
1839. Lord, Robert Ellis, *Colwyn Bay.*
1893. Lord, Samuel Thomas, *Manchester.*
1900. Lord, William James, *Kew.*
1922. Lorenzen, Albert Ernest,*Bishop's-av.*
1922. Loring,John Nigel,*St.Thomas's-hosp.*
1884. Loring, Jonathan Brown, *Montreal.*
1878. Lory, William Manley, *R.N.*
1887. Lotz, Henry John, *W. Australia.*
1895. Loud, Frank, *Lewes.*
1908. Loudon, Julian Derwent. *Toronto.*
1921.§Lough, Muriel Jessie, *S. Woodford.*
1913. Loughborough, Geoffrey T., *Dorking.*
1905. Loughborough,Walt.Gerald,*Lee-on-S*
1908. Loughlin, Dermot, *R.N.*
1916. Loughlin, Douglas, *Neasden.*
1922. Louis, Francis, *Dollis-hill.*
1904. Louisson, Maurice Geo., *New Zealand.*
1889. Lourensz, Charles Ball.
1907. Louwrens, Jas. Johnson, *Lady Grey.*
1902. Love, Herbert, *Burnham-market.*
1902. Loveday, George Edwd., *Manchester.*
1892. Loveday, Wm. Dunmore, O.B.E.
1898. Lovegrove, Fdc. Thos. Alex., *W.Aust.*
1867. Lovegrove, Thos. Henry, *W. Aust.*
1915. Loveless, Maynard L., *Stockbridge.*
1915. Loveless,Wm.Bird,M.C.,*Stockbridge.*
1914. Lovell, Edward Richardson, *Lynton.*
1878. Lovell, Robert Haynes, *Hans-cresc.*
1873. Lovell, Walter Fredk., *Hastings.*
1907. Lovell, William, *Cricklewood.*
1874. Low, Charles Arthur, *St. Leonards.*
1902. Low, George Harvey, *Woolwich.*
1890. Low, Harold, *S. Kensington.*
1903. Low, Nelson, D.S.O., *R.A.M.C.*
1906. Low, R bert Bruce, *Borneo.*
1920. Low, William Alexander, *Surbiton.*
1877. Lowdell, Chas. Geo. Walton, *I.M.S.*
1914. Lowe, Charles Eric, *Chester.*
1873. Lowe, Chas. Henry,*Burton-on-Trent.*
1920. Lowe, Ernest, *West Bromwich.*
1900. Lowe, Francis Henry, *Peckham.*
1907. Lowe, Fredk. Boulton, *Grays.*
1918. Lowe, Geoffrey Burman, *Barnt-grn.*
1894. Lowe, Godfrey Jn. Ralph, *Lincoln.*
1896. Lowe, Henry, *Tycroes.*
1912. Lowe, John Burman, *Barnt Green.*
1894. Lowe, Lockhart, *Darlaston.*
1905. Lowe, Otto Wm. Axel, *Birkdale.*

1882. Lowe, Thos. Pagan, *Bath*.
1918.§Lowenfeld, M. F. J., *Gt. Cumb-pl.*
1919.§Lowenstein, Lillian, *Cape*.
1901. Lowenthal,LouisLawrence,*H'mpst'd.*
1897. Lower,Nyman Yeo, *Presteign*.
1907. Lowry, Ernest Ward, *Brentford*.
1905. Lowry, William Herbert, *Toronto*.
1890. Lowsley, Lionel Dewe, *Uganda*.
1896. Lowsley,Mont. Marmion, D.S.O.
1872. Lubbock,Montagu, *Mount-st.*, W.
1896. Lubeck, Wilfred Joseph, *India*.
1875. Lucas, Arthur, *Buckingham*.
1890. Lucas, Arthur, *Bury*.
1923 §Lucas, Bar)ara V., *Brunswick-sq.*
1879. Lucas, Charles, *Burwell*.
1894. Lucas,ClaudeRobinson,*H'mmersmith*
1866. Lucas, George, *Uckfield*.
1897. Lucas, George Humphrey, *Wisbech*.
1914. Lucas,Harry Audley, *Bury-St.-Edm.*
1897. Lucas, Joseph John Scammell,*Bristol.*
1913. Lucas, Reg. Hutchinson,M.C.,O.B.E.
1869. Lucas,Robt.Harry,*Bury St.Edmunds.*
1898. Lucas, Stanley Arthur, *N. Zealand.*
1903. Lucas, Travis Clay, *R.A.,M.C.*
1909. Lucey, Herbert Cubitt, *Haslemere.*
1908. Luciani, Julius Caesar, *Caracas.*
1885. Luckham,Levi Stephenson,*Salisbury.*
1872. Lucus, Thomas D'Arcy.
1891. Lucy, Sidy. Hbt. Reg , *Malay States.*
1915. Ludolf, Henry Guy, M.C., *Leeds.*
1836. Luff, A. P., C.B.E., *Queen Anne-st.*
1891. Lukmani, B. Abdulkarim, *Bombay.*
1896. Lulham, Edwin Percy H., *Brighton*
1907. Lumb,Thomas Fletcher, *E. Af. M. S.*
1887. Lumley, Charles Armstrong, *Cape.*
1892. Lumley, Fredk. Davidson, *R.N.*
1912. Luna, Victor Alfred, *Lima, Peru.*
1922. Lund, Guy Sefton, *Milnthorpe.*
1902. Lund, John Knowles, *Manchester.*
1921. Lund,JohnRushworth,*Clapham-com.*
1892. Lunn, Cyril Reginald, *Olton.*
1890. Lunn, Percy Trenavin, *Kaitaia, N.Z.*
1917. Lunnon, Leslie G., *Bourne End.*
1922. Lupprian, Ernest Victor, *c/oCox&Co.*
1923. Lupton, Charles Athelstane, *Leeds.*
1910. Lupton, James Parkinson, *Cape.*
1913. Lupton, Wm. Mawhood, *Yarmouth.*
1876. Lush, John Selfe, *Devizes.*
1917. Lush, Ronald William, *Hampstead.*
1873. Lush, William Henry, *Devizes.*
1888. Luson, Thomas, *Norbiton.*
1903. Luxmoore, Evelyn Jn H., *R A.,M.C.*
1871. Lycett, John Allan, *Tettenhall.*
1895. Lydall,WykehamTracy.*Birmingham.*
1887. Lyle, Chas. Conway Vacey,*Zululand.*
1913. Lyle, James Duncan, *Margaret-st.*
1863. Lyle, Thomas, *Maida-vale.*
1923. 9114

1911. Lyn-Jones, Rupert L., *Forest-gate.*
1908. Lynch, Arthur Alfred, M.P.
1885. Lynch, Geo. Wm. Aug., *Suva, Fiji.*
1864. Lynch, Jordan Roche. *Holland-park.*
1922.§Lynch, Mary C., *Gloucester-terr.*
1901. Lynch, William Warren, *Quebec.*
1886. Lyndon, Arnold, O.B.E., *Hindhead.*
1914. Lyne, Chas. Virgil N.,*E.I.U.S.Club.*
1919. Lyne, Leslie, *Dulwich-park.*
1858. Lynes, Edward, *Coventry.*
1885. Lynes, John, *Argyll-road,* W.
1878. Lynn, Edward, *Woolwich.*
1908. Lyon, Edwin James, *Winnipeg.*
1918. Lyon-Smith, Geo. Lyon, *Bentinck-st.*
1923. Lyons, James Isaac, *Hyde-road.*
1890. Lys, George, *Bere Regis.*
1886. Lys, Henry Grabham, *Bournemouth.*
1886. Lyster, Arth. Edward, *Chelmsford.*
1914. Lyster, R. G., C.B.E., *Chelmsford.*
1902. Lyth, Chas. Ernest W., *New Zealand.*
1888. Lyth, Edgar Roe, *Shepherd's-bush.*
1910. Lyttle, George Gibson, *Belfast.*

M.

1910. Maaz, Mahmoud Foad, *Egypt.*
1885. Maberly, Ernest, *Finchampstead.*
1871. Maberiy, Fdk. Herbert, *Handsworth.*
1879. Maberly, Henry Edward, *Ealing.*
1888. Maberly, John, *Cape.*
1918. MacAlevey, Gerald Esmond, M.C.
1905. Macalister, Geo. Hugh Kidd, *Chelsea.*
1918. McAlister, Hector Clive.
1912. McAllister, Andrew Carey, *Croydon.*
1904. McAllum, John Henry, *Milford.*
1892. McAnally,Archibald Acheson, *Dover.*
1897. McAnally,Edw.Arth.,*N'wingt'n,K'nt*
1919. McAusland,Stuart Douglas,*Hoylake.*
1890. Macann, Arth. Chas. Jos., *Manitoba.*
1917. McArthur, Alex. G. F., *Linden-gds*
1894. McArthur, Arthur Norman, *Victoria.*
1800. McArthur, Duncan Campbell, *Cape.*
1904. Macarthur, John, *Molesey.*
1921.§McArthur, K. M. B., *Linden-gdns.*
1906. McAsh, John, *Varna, Canada.*
1916. Macaulay, Hugh M. C., *Brixton.*
1903. Macaulay, Wm. Cameron, *Herne-hill.*
1923.§Macbeth-Morland,A.N.,*Tavistock-sq.*
1917.§McBirnie, Ruby Eva, *Liverpool.*
1920. McCabe, Richard Alger, *Edenbridge.*
1915. McCall, Henry Dundas, *Blackheath.*
1901. McCallum, Hugh A., *London, Ont.*
1906. McCandlish,Alex.Heury,*New Ferry.*
1921. McCann, Ivan Bailey, *Golder's-green.*
1917. McCann,JamesGalway,*Wandsworth.*
9166   S

1894. McCardie, Wm. Joseph, *Birmingham*.
1876. McCarthy, Geo. Francis, *Westminster*.
1887. McCarthy, Ibar Ansbert O., *R.A.M.C.*
1857. M‘Carthy, James Joseph, *A.M.S.*
1876. McCarthy, Justin McC., *St. Geo., Salop*.
1899. McCarthy, Thomas, *Sherborne*.
1903. McCaskie, Harry Bertram, *Sydney-pl.*
1899. McCaskie, Norman James, *Onslow-sq*
1878. McCausland, Albt. Staaley, *Swanage*.
1921. McClean, Douglas. ·
1897. McClean, Jn. Francis, *Constantinople*.
1893. McCleland, Hugh Augustus, *N.Z.*
1901. M‘Clintock, Joseph Andrew, *Toronto*.
1923. McClure, Chas. R., *Up. Clapton*.
1906. McClure, Walt. St. Clair, *Manchester*.
1847. M‘Clure, William George, *N.S.W.*
1915. McClymont, Cecil G., *Edgware-rd.*
1906. McCollum, John Alex., *Toronto*.
1901. McCombe, John, *Quebec*.
1912. McCombie, Frederick Champ, *Assam*.
1894. McCone, Jas. Francis, *San Francisco*.
1884. McConnel, H. Wilson.
1891. M‘Connell, James, *Battersea*.
1899. McConnell, James, *Tynemouth*.
1902. McCord, James Bennett, *Natal*.
1892. McCormack, Chas. Vincent, *Bootle*.
1881. McCormick, Sir Alex., *Sydney, N.S.W.*
1902. McCowen, William Thomas, *I.M.S.*
1903. McCoy, Samuel Harvey, *Toronto*.
1899. McCoy, William John, *I.M.S.*
1900. McCrae, Thomas, *Guelph, Canada*.
1874. McCreery, John Alex., *New York*.
1888. M‘Cullagh, Richd. Cheveley, *Belfast*.
1876. McCullagh, Thos. A., *Bsh'p Auckland*.
1921.§McCulloch, Elizabeth E., *Prenton*.
1880. McCulloch, James, *Bexhill-on-Sea*.
1907. McCulloch, Robert Jno. P., *Canada*.
1894. McCullough, Hugh Allan, *Ontario*.
1885. McCully, Oscar James, *Montreal*.
1915. McCurrich, Hugh James, *Chelsea*.
1912. McDermott, Bryen, *Bexley*.
1880. McDonagh, James Saml., *Forest-gate*.
1905. Macdonald, Arthur II., *Warminster*.
1908. McDonald, Charles E. W., *Ilford*.
1900. MacDonald, Chas John, *Isle of Skye*.
1909. MacDonald, Daniel Robert, *Nova Scotia*.
1904. McDonald, Edgar Jn. Cecil, *I M.S.*
1919. Macdonald, Ernest K., *Wimbledon*.
1884. Macdonald, Geo. Childs, *California*.
1879. MacDonald, Greville M., *Harley-st.*
1913.§McDonald, Jessie, *Glasgow*.
1904. Macdonald, John George, *New Zealand*.
1897. Macdonald, John Norman, *Queen-st.*
1909. McDonald, Niel, *Preston*.
1919. Macdonald, Norman J., *Cheddington*.
1883. Macdonald, William Hector, *Toronto*.
1896. McDonald, Wm Maclachlan, *W. Indies*

9223

1915. McDonnell, Alex. Jos. V., *Stamf'd-hill*.
1915. McDonnell, Jas., M.C., *Stamford-hill*.
1919. MacDonnell, John J. M., *Wimbledon*.
1884. McDonnell, Wm. C., *Stoke Newington*.
1884. McDouall, Herbert Crichton, *N.S.W.*
1903. McDouall, Jn. Crichton S., *Gold Coast*.
1896. McDougal, Ernest Duncan, *Park-st.*
1893. McDougall, Alan, *Manchester*.
1882. McDougall, Hbt. Alan. Hosier, *Farnbro'*
1884. McDougall, Jas. Edlington, *Liverpool*.
1899. McDougall, Jno. Tiley M., *Southampton*.
1907. McDowall, Colin Fras. Fk., *Ticehurst*.
1901. MacDowall, Wm. McD., *R.A.M.C.*
1913.§McEnery, Margaret J., *Sherborne*.
1900. McEnery, Wm. Aug., *San Francisco*.
1906. McEvedy, Patrick Francis, *New Zeal.*
1886. Macevoy, Henry John, *Brondesbury*.
1910. MacEwan, Ernest, *R.N.*
1906. McEwen, Owen Reginald, *R.A.M.C.*
1910. Macewen, William, O.B.E., *Glasgow*.
1917. McFadyean, Kenneth, *Gt. College-st.*
1902. Mac'adyen, Norman, *Letchworth*.
1915. McFarland, John Beattie, *M C.*
1891. McFarlane, Alex. Rastrick, *Milner-st.*
1913. McGeagh, G. R. D., M.C., *I. of Man.*
1878. McGeagh, Thos. E. Foster, *Hadlow*.
1914. MacGibbon, Francis Oreti, *New Zeal.*
1916. McGibbon, Peter, *Canada*.
1905. MacGill, Donald Grey, *Rochdale*.
1918.§McGill, Janet McAllister, *Tufnell-pk.*
1914. MacGill, Roderic, M.C., *Littleborough*.
1900. McGillivray, Donald, *Toronto*.
1912. McGillycuddy, A. R. N., *Bournem'th*.
1885. MacGillycuddy, Niell, *Bournemouth*.
1889. McGowan, James Sinclair, *Oldham*.
1892. MacGrath, Edmund John, *Norwood*.
1907. McGreer, Charles Grange, *Winnipeg*.
1896. MacGregor, Arthur Rbt., *Weymouth*.
1890. McGregor, George, *Portsmouth*.
1885. MacGregor, John, *Duke-st.*, W.
1922.§McHardy, Caroline G. L., *Aberdeen*.
1905. Machin, Frank Smith, *Hereford*.
1920.§McHugh, Mary Alice, *Liverpool*.
1917. McIlroy, Howard Douglas, *Havant*.
1904. McIlroy, James Archibald, *Moseley*.
1888. McIlroy, Jn. Black, *Balmain, N.S.W.*
1903. McIlroy, Jn. Morrison, *Roehampton*.
1920. McIlroy, Patrick Thos., *Kingston, Ont.*
1915. McInnis, Archibald, *Canada*.
1902. Macintosh, Arch. Malcolm, *Natal*.
1922. McIntosh, Duncan Cameron, *Acton*.
1905. McIntyre, Ernest, *Mitcham*.
1910. McIver, Colin, *Grindlay & Co.*, S.W.
1889. Mack, Cyril Gordon, *Highbury*.
1921. Mackay, Arthur George, *Edinburgh*.
1922. McKay, Donald Walter, *Canada*.
1897. Mackay, Duncan Matheson, *Hull*.

9280

1922.§Mackay, Elizabeth K., *Tollington-ph.*
1901. Mackay, Ernest Chas., *St. Leonards.*
1883. Mackay, George, *Edinburgh.*
1914.§Mackay, Helen M. M., *Manchester.*
1873. McKay,H.Kellock,C.B.,C.I.E.,*I.M.S.*
1894. McKay, John Gilbert, *N.S.W.*
1884. Mackay, Norman Eben., *Halifax, N.S.*
1910. MacKay,PatrickAndrew,*Dumbarton.*
1838. Mackay, Percy Barnard, *Doncaster.*
1898. McKay, Robert, *Chandos-street.*
1885. Mackay,Wm.Bertie,C.M.G.,*Berwick.*
1923. Mackay Ross, John A., *Chelsea.*
1902. McK-an, George Birtley, *Ledbury.*
1902. McKee, Joseph Fennel, *Indianopolis.*
1895. Mackenzie, Alexander, *Leeds.*
1909. McKenzie, Alex. Ernest, *Appleton.*
1883. McKenzie, Archibald, *Natal.*
1866. Mackenzie, Fdc. Morell, *Hans-place.*
1921. McKenzie, H., *Dungannon, Canada.*
1834. Mackenzie,Hect.Wm. G , *U.Brook-st.*
1919. Mackenzie, John Alex., *Winnipeg.*
1880. Mackenzie, John F. Edward.
1917. Mackenzie, Kenneth A. I., *Ryde.*
1892. Mackenzie, Kenneth Morell.
1907. Mackenzie,Louis Hope Lovat,*I.M.S.*
1922. Mackenzie, Murdo, *Guy's-hosp.*
1923.§Mackenzie, Phyllis Child, *Cardiff.*
1904. Mackenzie, Stephen Morton,*Dorking.*
1903. Mackenzie, Stuart Donald, *Ontario.*
1920. McKenzie,Thos. Clyde,*Birmingham.*
1915. McKenzie, William George, *Bristol.*
1878. McKeough, George Thomas, *Canada.*
1918.§McKeown, Kathleen McC., *Enfield.*
1890. McKeown, P. Walt. Hughes, *Toronto.*
1922 §McKerrow, Elizabeth, *Tavistock-sq.*
1892. Mackeson, Guy.
1907. Mackey,LeonardGeo.Jos.,*B'mingh'm.*
1897. McKie,Gordon McKenzie,*Rotherhithe.*
1902. McKinney, Hugh Giffen, *W. Af. M. S.*
1894. Mackinnon, John Alexander.
1895. Mackintosh, Jn. Stewart, *Hampstead.*
1921. Machlin, Christopher Hugh, *Sandy.*
1890. Macknight, Conway Montg., *N.S.W.*
1910. Mackwood, John Charsley, M C.
1904. McLaren, George Hagarty, *Toronto.*
1885. MacLaren, M., C.M.G., *N. Brunswick.*
1917. Maclean, Bruce, *Mincing-lane.*
1919. MacLean,Charles Fergus,*Hollington.*
1877. Maclean, Fitzroy Beresford,*R.A.M.C.*
1920. Maclean, Francis Sydney.
1909. McLean, Hugh, *Richmond.*
1906. Maclean, Neil John, *Winnipeg.*
1904. McLeay, Charles Wm , *W. Af.M. S.*
1906. McLellan, Wilbert Ernest, *Ontario.*
1898. MacLellan, William, *Cricklewood.*
1896. Maclennan, Duncan Neil, *Toronto.*
1881. McLennan, Warwick Guy.
9337

1888. Macleod,David Thos., *Holland-ph.-av.*
1891. MacLeod, Ewan Cameron, *I.M.S.*
1889. MacLeod, Harold Hay Brodie,M.B.E.
1901. McLeod, James Alex., *Buffalo, N.Y.*
1922. Macleod, Loudoun H. B , *Sidmouth.*
1898. MacLeod, Rodk. Alex., *Charlwood-st.*
1917. McLeod, Thomas Hawks, *Richmond.*
1887. McLurg, John, *Michigan, U.S.A.*
1869. McMahon, John James.
1906. McMune, Charles, *Donegal, Canada.*
1914. MacManus, Desmond M., *Kiltimagh.*
1910. McMaster, Albert Victor, *Bangor.*
1901. MacMaster,DonaldA.Dunlop,*N.S.W.*
1892. McMichael,Arth.William, *Powch'rch.*
1920. McMichael, Gerald J.W , *Alvechurch.*
1917. McMillan,Arthur Niel, *Middle.x.-hosp.*
1919. Macmillan, Edgar Duncan, *York.*
1882. McMillan, John Furse, *Sandown.*
1907. McMurtry,Walter Campbell,*Canada.*
1905. Macnab, John Theodore, *Balham.*
1886. McNabb,SirD.J.P.,K.B.E.,C.B.,*R.N.*
1921.§McNair, Dorothy, *Dulwich.*
1897. Macnair, Norman, *Glasgow.*
1897. McNally, Geo Johnston, *Canada.*
1909. MacNalty, Arthur Salusbury, *L.G.B.*
1897. Macnamara,Eric Danvers, *Harley-st.*
1880. Macnamara, Hugh Winckworth,*R.N.*
1902. McNutt,Wm.Fletcher,*SanFrancisco.*
1922. Maconie, Alan Cameron, *Hastings.*
1889. McOscar, John, *Buxton.*
1910. Macoun,John, *Campbellford, Canada.*
1922. McOustra, Oswald E. J , *St. Albans.*
1889. Macphail, John Andrew, *Montreal.*
1918. Macpherson, Donald Gregory.
1922. Macpherson, Nor. S., *Chepstow-villas.*
1891. Macpherson, Wm. Hugh, *Topsham.*
1888. McQueen,Chas. Alex.S.,*Nova Scotia.*
1903. McQueen, Robert Martin, *Eaton-terr.*
1914. McRae, David Gair, M.C., *Bow-road.*
1910. McRae, John Roy, *Canada.*
1920. McRae, Richard Turner, *Bow-road.*
1877. McReddie, Geo. Dougal, *Greenhithe.*
1913. McRitchie, Philip, M.C., *Canada.*
1908. McSheehy,O.Wm.,D.S.O.,*R.A.M.C.*
1904. McTavish, Frank, *Vancouver.*
1904. McVail, John Borland, *Assam.*
1884. McVitie, John William, *Hove.*
1896. MacWatters, Jn. Courtenay, M.B.E.
1886. Madden, Francis Brian, *Blythe.*
1923.§Madders, Kate, *Hampstead.*
1879. Maddick,Edmund D ,O.B.E.,*Brixton.*
1905. Maddison, Thos. Wm., *Stamford-hill.*
1881. Maddison, Wm. Thomas, *Bristol.*
1887. Maddox, Ralph Henry,C.I.E.,*I.M.S.*
1887. Mader, Pieter Johannes, *Cape.*
1919.§Madgavkar, Malati, *Hampstead.*
1891. Madge, Arthur Ernest.
9394 s 2

1896. Madge, Edward Douglas, *Mayfair*.
1911. Madge, Quintus, O.B E., *Liverpool*.
1916. Madgwick, George Alex. S., *Ilford*.
1920. Madgwick, Rupert Alex., *Ilford*.
1917. Maelzer, Noel H. S., c/o L. & S. W.-bk.
1888. Magauran, James, *Cavan*.
1901. Magee, Charles Crozier Tandy, *Vict*.
1885. Maggs, Wm. Adolphus, *Northam*.
1871. Magill, Sir James, K.C.B., R.A.M.C.
1906. Magowan, Peter Donald Fraser. *Larne*.
1923. Maguire, Cyril Chas Wm., *Edgbaston*.
1914. Mahabir, Frank, *Trinidad*.
1884. Maher, Chas. Henry, *Sydney*, N.S. W.
1904. Maher, Mahmoud, *Egypt*.
1899. Maher, Michael Robert, *Liverpool*.
1881. Mahomed, Arth.Geo.S., *Bournemouth*.
1913. Mahon, Edw. McMahon, *Dulwich*.
1923. Mahoney, Cyril Clare, *Bayswater*.
1911. Mahrus, Nagib, *Fayoum, Egypt*.
1910. Maidment, Fredk. N. H., *Harleston*.
1879. Maile, Charles Edm. Drayson, *Const. Cl*.
1912. Maile, Wm. Chas. Drayson, *Barnet*.
1921.§Main, Henrietta A. C., *Hampstead*.
1897. Mainprise,Cecil W., D.S.O., R.A.M.C.
1888. Maisey, Charles Thos. Boodle, N.S. W.
1896. Maitland, Charles Robt., *Dulwich*.
1917. Maitland, Chas. Titterton, *Highgate*.
1919. Maitland, Hugh Bethune, *Toronto*.
1884. Maitland, Percy Edmund, R. N.
1904. Maitland, Vivian Gray, *Nuneaton*.
1914. Maitland-Jones, A. G., M.C., O.B.E.
1922.§Maitland-Jones, Elizabeth.
1920. Maizels, Montague, *Willesden*.
1889. Major, Arthur Cundell, *Hungerford*.
1903. Major, Hugh Marcus. *Jersey*.
1866. Major, Napoleon Bisdee, R.A.M.C.
1892. Makalua, Matth.Manuia, St. Leonards.
1920. Makar, Tadros Ibrahim, *Egypt*.
1875. Makeig-Jones, William, *Torquay*.
1893. Malabre, Herbert Frederic, *Jamaica*.
1914. Malcolm, Alan S Lack, *Holloway*, N.
1899. Malcolm, Alex. John, *Bedford-park*.
1883. Malcolm, John David, *Wimpole-st*.
1915. Malden, Edm. Claud, *Cambridge*.
1885. Malden, Frank James, *Malvern*.
1886. Male, Herbert Christopher, *Croydon*.
1916. Malik, Labib Abdul, *Dudley-place*.
1865. Malim, George Warcup, *Rochdale*.
1915. Maling, Geo. Allan, V.C , R A.M.C.
1883. Maling, Wm. Haygarth, *Sunderland*.
1916. Malkani, Showkiram S., *Hyderabad*.
1923. Malkin, Harold Jordan, *Longport*.
1915. Malkin, Sydney Alan S., *Longport*.
1913. Mallam, Dalton, *Wantage*.
1896 Mallam, Harry Guy, *Brighton*.
1891 Mallam, William Andrew, *Naples*.
1869. Mallam, William Prior, *Acton*.
9451

1889. Mallard, Frank Reg., *Hammersmith*.
1906. Malleson, Herbert Cecil, *Hampstead*.
1915. Mallinick, Samuel, *Oudtshoorn*.
1915. Mallya, Ganapathy, *Cromwell-road*.
1877. Malpas, Douglas Dent, *Biarritz*.
1913. Malpas, Douglas Duncan, *Boscombe*.
1887. Malpas, James, *Southsea*.
1914. Maltby, Henry Wingate,M.C., *Boston*.
1901. Maltby, Wm. Ernest Geo., *Brighton*.
1877. Malvin, Mark, *Scarborough*.
1905. Maulock, Harold Charles, *Paris*.
1897. Manasseh, Antonius Joseph, *Beyrout*.
1886. Manby,Edwd.Petronell,Loc.Gov.Brd.
1895. Manby, Walter Edward, *Bridport*.
1904. Manchester, John Wm., N. *Brunswick*.
1908. Mandel,EliasLeop.Woolt,Guy's-hosp.
1884. Mander, Percy Robert, *Pentonville*.
1901. Mandy, Percy Stephen, *Hythe*.
1915. Manfield, Alwyne H., *Northampton*.
1901. Manfield,Geo.Ilbt.H.,M.C.,Lichfield.
1866. Manisty, Francis Steuart, *Chester*.
1891. Manknell, Arthur, *Bradford*.
1899. Manlove,Jas.Ernest,St.Leonards-o.-S.
1895. Mann, Fairman Rackham, *Roy. Navy*.
1895. Mann,Fredk. Wm. Slingsby,Revesby.
1903. Mann, Harold Chas. Corry,O.B.E.
1910. Mann, Horace Lloyd, *Folkingham*.
1920.§Mann, Ida Caroline, *Cricklewood*.
1922. Manners, Robert, *Sunderland*.
1900. Manning, Ernest John, *Southall*.
1889. Manning, Hy. Paul Owen, *Faversham*.
1897. Manning,Herbt.Campbell,Dorchester.
1886. Manning, Philip Percy, *Kendal*.
1896 Manning, Richd. Beattie, *Wells, Som*.
1893. Manning, Thomas Davys, *Weymouth*.
1889. Mansbridge, Josiah, *Harley-street*, W.
1877. Mansell, Edward Rosser, *Hastings*.
1891. Mansell, Harry Rosser, *Hastings*.
1864. Manser, Frederick, *Tunbridge Wells*.
1901. Mauser.Fredk.Bailey,Tunb'dge Wells.
1913. Mansfield, Harold Young, *Cambridge*.
1904. Mansfield, Perceval Aub., *Sevenoaks*.
1922.§Manson,PhyllisMargaret,Hampstead
1907.Manson-Bahr,P.H.,D.S.O.,Wym'th-st
1919. Mansour, Aziz Abd El Sayed.
1879. Mantle, Alfred, *Harrogate*.
1905. Manuel, Alexander, *Harley-street*.
1891. Manwaring, Edwd. Ernest, *Worthing*.
1874 Maples, Reginald, *Kingsclere*.
1892. March, Edwd. Gerald, *Reading*.
1894. March, Jos. Ogdin,M.B.E.,Amesbury.
1907. Marchant, Eric Lachlan, O.B.E.
1922.§Marchant, Gladys H., c/o Cox & Co.
1919. Marcus, Maurice, *Forest-gate*.
1913. Marcus, S. Hugo, *Northumberland-av*.
1884. Marder, Edward Swan, *Lyme Regis*.
1904. Marett, Philip Jauvrin, R..A.M.C.
9508

1922.§Margerison, Fran. M., *Up. Woburn-pl.*
1914. Maiguat, Jean E., *Vichy.*
1879. Mark, Leonard Portal, *Oxford-terr.*
1897. Markby, Herbert, *Morley.*
1923. Markiles, Maurice, *Johannesburg.*
1909. Marklove, John Carrington, *Stroud.*
1875. Marks, Charles Ferdinand, *Brisbane.*
1895. Marks, Herbt. Wm. Jas., *N.S.W.*
1896. Marks, Leonard Freeman, *Mumbles.*
1886. Marks, Robert John, *I.M.S.*
1905. Maiks, Urban, *Swansea.*
1903. Markus, Charles, *Wimpole-street.*
1872. Marlatt, Chas. Wm, *Ontario.*
1911. Marle, Samuel, *Buckfastleigh.*
1923. Marley, James, *New Brighton.*
1880. Marlow, Fiank Wm., *Syracuse, U.S.A.*
1898. Marrack, George Comyns, *Woolston.*
1902. Marrett, Henry Norman, *Sandon.*
1919. Marriner, Humphrey I., *Bournemouth.*
1910. Marriner, Kenneth D., *Keighley.*
1884. Marriner, Wm. Hbt.L., *Bournemouth.*
1895. Marriott, Arthur, *Aldeburgh.*
1915. Marriott, Francis Keene, *Brinton.*
1887. Marriott, Henry Tancred, *Brighton.*
1888. Marriott, Horace Bruce, C.B.E.,*R.N.*
1884. Marriott, Hyde, *Stockport.*
1900. Marriott, Oswald, *Hong Kong.*
1917. Marriott, William, *St. Thos.-hosp.*
1904. Marris, Henry Fairley, *Bourne End.*
1894. Marris, Wm. Arthur, *Birmingham.*
1922. Marrison, Arthur Wilson, *Castleton.*
1922. Marsden, Heibert Harold, *Liverpool.*
1884. Marsden, Herbert Harrison, M.B.E.
1883. Marsden, James Aspinall, *Lightcliffe.*
1879. Marsden, James Cort, *I.M.S.*
1891. Marsden, Richd. Walter, *Manchester.*
1919. Marsh, Alfred, *St. Helens.*
1901. Marsh, Charles Alfred, *Bath.*
1879. Marsh, Charles James, *Yeovil.*
1894. Marsh, Edward Henry, *Long Preston.*
1897. Marsh, Henry Rupert, *Anerley.*
1894. Marsh, John Hedley, *Macclesfield.*
1911. Marsh, Octavius de Burgh, O.B.E.
1876. Marsh, Octavius E. Bulwer, *Newport.*
1879. Marsh, Wm. Aspinall, *Skelmersdale.*
1887. Marshall, Arth. Lumsden, *Up. Clapton.*
1902. Marshall, Arthur Thomson, *Bideford.*
1903. Marshall,Chas.deZouche, *Thorverton.*
1915. Marshall, Chas. Jennings,*Char.Cr.-h.*
1908. Marshall, Claude Herbert, *Uganda.*
1912. Marshall, Crawford C., *Vict., Aust.*
1923.§Marshall, Edith Treliving, *Brighton.*
1923 §Marshall, Edith W. W., *Endsleigh-st.*
1914. Marshall, Edward Hillis, *Hampstead.*
1889. Marshall, Edwd. Williams, *Mitcham.*
1906. Marshall, Eric Stewart, M.C.
1911. Marshall,Geoffrev,O.B.E.,*Kensingt'n.*

1915. Marshall, GeraldS.,O.B.E.,*R.A.M.C.*
1905. Marshall,Herbert Frank,*Macclesfield.*
1906. Marshall, Jn. Dodds, D.S.O., *Bolton.*
1881. Marshall, John Grissell.
1923. Marshall, LesliePhillips, *Staplehurst.*
1870. Marshall, Lewis Walt., *Nottingham.*
1916. Marshall, Philip Sydney, *Barnham.*
1901. Marshall, Reg. Prynne, *Bermondsey.*
1909. Marshall, Russell Hardy Sidney, *Ely.*
1900. Marshall, Thomas Bingham, *Oxford.*
1906. Marshall, William Burton, *Norwich.*
1890. Marshall, William Ernest, *R.N.*
1914. Marshall, William Henry, *Bath.*
1884. Marshall,W.L.,W.,C.M.G.,*Lympstone*
1891. Marson, Cyril Darby, *Stafford.*
1915. Marston, Arch. Daniel, *Clapham.*
1881. Marston, Francis Ernest, *Berriew.*
1887. Marston, Henry John, *Willesden.*
1923. Marston, Wilfrid Harvey, *Willenhall.*
1901. Mart, Wm. Thos. Dakin, *Sheffield.*
1883. Marten, Robt. Humphrey, *Adelaide.*
1883. Martin, Albert, *Wellington, N.Z.*
1899. Martin, Alfred Eugene, *Elstree.*
1867. Martin, Anthony Herbert, *Evesham.*
1893. Martin, Antony Alex., *Eastbourne.*
1893. Martin, Arth. James, *Bloxwich.*
1923. Martin, Charles Andrew, *Wandsworth*
1921. Martin, Charles Gutherless.
1889. Martin,Chas. Jas.,C.M G.,*Lister Inst.*
1879. Martin,Edwd.Fuller,*Weston-s.-Mare.*
1902. Martin, Edward Lister, *Hull.*
1911. Martin, Ernest Percy.
1898. Martin,FrancisJn.Hensley,*Bottesford.*
1897. Martin, Francis Raynes, *Transvaal.*
1893. Martin, Frederic William, *Brighouse.*
1887. Martin, Fredk. Geo. S.G., *Darlington.*
1913. Martin, Gerald Noel, *Sheffield.*
1905. Martin, Harold Philip, *Toronto.*
1870. Martin, Hy. Charrington,*Reform Club.*
1885. Martin, Hy. Jos. Walklate, *Mill Hill.*
1903. Martin, James Ernest, *Epsom.*
1864. Martin, Jas. Hamilton, D.S.O., *R.N.*
1883. Martin, James Pirie, *Box.*
1897. Martin, John, *Royal Navy.*
1917. Martin, John Aston, *Norwood.*
1908. Martin, John Birch, *Felsted.*
1860. Martin,Jn. Hy.C.Erridge,*Portsmouth.*
1893. Martin, Jn.Newton,M.B E.,*Tavist'ck.*
1916. Martin, Louis Charles, *Hounslow.*
1916. Martin, Owen Sidney, *Wimpole-st.*
1864. Martin, Paulin, *Abingdon.*
1909. Martin, Paulin John, *Abingdon.*
1909. Martin, Philip Sidney, M.C.
1913. Martin, Reginald Victor, *I.M.S.*
1899. Martin, Robert Collins, *Clifton.*
1910. Martin, Robert Telford, *Sheffield.*
1875. Martin, Samuel Edgar, *Newry.*

1882. Martin, Sidney H. Cox, *Wilpole-st.*
1879. Martin, Theodore, *Temple Cloud.*
1897. Martin, Thomas, *Thatcham.*
1907. Martin, William Beare, *Barrasford.*
1914 §Martland, Edith Marjorie, *Oldham.*
1877. Martland, Edward William, *Oldham.*
1886. Martland, Thomas, *Bournemouth.*
1890. Martley, Francis Charles, *Bayswater.*
1912. Martyn, Avenell F. Cleeve, *R.A.M.C.*
1881. Martyn, Ernest, *Mansfield.*
1902. Martyn, Frank D., *Sutton-in-Ashfield.*
1893. Martyn, George, *Los Angeles.*
1887. Martyn, Reginald, *Exmouth.*
1911. Martyn, Valentine Cleeve, M C.
1920. Marwood, Sydney Francis, *Exminster*
1876. Masáni, Hormasji Dadábhói, *I.M.S.*
1906. Mascarenhas, Eugene A., *Bombay.*
1911. Masefield, Wm. Gordon, *Trentham.*
1906. Masina, Dinshaw Manekji, *Bombay.*
1914. Másiná, Pestanji Manekji.
1896. Maskell, John William, *Hobart.*
1883. Mason, Arth. Henry, *Walton-on-Th.*
1920.§Mason, Dora, *Bexley-heath.*
1923.§Mason, Dorothy E., *Gt. Portland-st.*
1885. Mason,Francis J.Gorringe,*Cheltenh'm.*
1890. Mason, Frank, *Bournemouth.*
1894. Mason, Frank William, *Boston.*
1896. Mason, Gerald Bovell, *Baldock.*
1890. Mason, Harold, *Leamington.*
1884. Mason, Henry, *Leicester.*
1912. Mason, Henry Sinclair, *Pontypool.*
1900. Mason, Herbert Alfred, *Duffield.*
1881. Mason, John, *Windermere.*
1898. Mason, John Harold, *Northampton.*
1875. Mason, Jn. Wallis B., *Osnaburgh-terr.*
1875. Mason, John Wright, M B.E., *Hull.*
1910. Mason, Maurice Charles, *Newton-rd.*
1922. Mason, Philip de Roos, *Paddington.*
1900. Mason, Samuel, O.B.E , *S. Africa.*
1893. Mason, Wm. Blaikie, *Southsea.*
1879. Mason, William Harrap, *Leeds.*
1868. Mason, William Inglis, *Sudbury.*
1889. Masser, Edwd. Chas., *Hampden-club.*
1917. Masson, Keith, *St. Bart.'s.*
1919. Massonda, Alfred Yaphet, *Cairo.*
1893. Master, Alfred Edmund, *R.A.M.C.*
1892. Master, George, *Bury St. Edmunds.*
1907. Master, Jehangir Ardeshir, *Holloway.*
1876. Masters, John Alfred, *Knightsbridge.*
1918. Masters, Walter Edgar, *Hassocks.*
1872. Matcham, Alfred, *St. George's-rd.*
1913. Mather, Edw. Elton, *Tunbridge-wells.*
1922. Mather, Frank Henry, *Stamford.*
1913. Mather, George S., *Ceylon.*
1913. Mather, Horace, *Cheltenham.*
1914 Mather, Joseph Henry, *Southport.*
1923. Mather, Leonard, *Whalley Range.*
9679

1903. Matheson, Farquhar M., *Harrow.*
1893. Mathew, Chas. Montague, *I.M.S.*
1883. Mathew, Chas. Pynsent, *Thorncombe.*
1894. Mathew, Geo. Porter, *Port Elizabeth.*
1907. Mathew, Philip Walter, *Colombo.*
1895. Mathews, Charles, *Hove.*
1885. Mathews, Frank Edwd., *Nantwich.*
1880. Mathews,SidneyRobt.Harvey,*Buckley*
1907. Mathews, Wm. L'Estrange, *Bradley.*
1892. Mathews, Wm. Robert, *Transvaal.*
1905. Mathias, Charles David, *Tenby.*
1922 §Mathias, Clara Edith, *Putney.*
1916. Mathie, George Cecil, *Bilston.*
1908. Mathieson, William, *R.A.M.C.*
1896. Mathison, Arthur John, *Hornsey.*
1911. Mathur, Kalka Prasad, *Bareilly.*
1916.§Matland, Adeline Mabel, *Loughton.*
1904. Matson, Horace Sidney, *I.M.S.*
1915. Matson, Robert Charles, *Kensington.*
1882. Mattei, Edward.
1921.§Matthai, Elizabeth.
1913. Matthew, A. Wellington, *Chingford.*
1894. Matthews,Arth.Kenward,*Nottting-hill*
1887. Matthews,Chas. Edwd.,*North'n-hosp.*
1906. Matthews, Edgar Wm., *Kingston.*
1912. Matthews,GeorgeWilliam,*Dewsbury.*
1918.§Matthews, Gladys, *Cheltenham.*
1910. Matthews, Guy, *Suffolk-street.*
1884. Matthews, Harry E. H., *Whetstone.*
1923. Matthews, Hugh R , *Burton.*
1899. Matthews, John, *R.A.M.C.*
1914. Matthews, John Burnett, M C.
1901. Matthews, John Cuthbert, *Liverpool.*
1917. Matthews, Joseph S., *Hoppers-road.*
1923.§Matthews, Kathleen F., *Poplar.*
1919.§Matthews, K. H , *L. Margaret-rd.*
1896. Matthews, Saml. Ryder R , *Deptford.*
1890. Matthews, Sidney Philip, *Crawley.*
1901. Matthews,ThomasArnold, *Richmond.*
1922. Matthews, Vivian Matthew.
1920. Matthews, Walter Frank, *Torquay.*
1896 Maturin, Francis Hv., *Lymington.*
1921. Maude, Alexander, *Luddendenfoot.*
1882. Maude, Arthur, *Forest Row.*
1922. Maude,Cecily Marg't E., *Farringdm.*
1917. Maudling, Walter Harry, *Wallington.*
1880. Maudsley,SirHenry,K C.M.G ,C.B.E.
1897. Maugham, Wm. Somerset, *Dover-st.*
1883. Maughan, James, *Albany-street.*
1890. Maund, John Hansby, *Newmarket.*
1897. Maunsell, Debonnaire Fdk , *Earl's-ct.*
1916. Maunsell.Fdk. W , *Gt. Winchester-st.*
1890. Maurice,Geo.T. K ,C M G.,*R A.M.C.*
1910. Maurice.Godfrey K.,M.C., *Marlboro'.*
1896. Maurice,W.B ,M.B.E , *Marlborough.*
1883. Maurice, William James, *Reading.*
1923.§Mautner, Margarethe, *Dartmouth-rd.*
9736

1874. Mayor, Rev. Wm. Samuel, *Brentwood.*
1902. Mavrogordato, Anthony, *Oxford.*
1902. Maw, George, *Shortlands.*
1914. Maw, Gerald Woffinden, *Bedford.*
1892. Maw, Henry Trentham, *Westcott.*
1915. Mawe, Eric Spanton, *Chislehurst.*
1914. Mawer, Percy Uvedale, *St. Bart's.*
1899. Mawson, Joseph Arthur, *Liverpool.*
1914. Mawson, Owen David B., *Hampstead.*
1890. Mawson, Samuel Francis, *Bolton.*
1872. Mawson, Wm. Arthur, *I.M.S.*
1922. Maxim s, Yunanis, *Egypt.*
1895. Maxwell, Ernest Jas., *South Shields.*
1906. Maxwell, Herbt. Bowen, *B. Columb.*
1923. Maxwell, James, *Muswell-hill.*
1896. Maxwell, Jas. Laidlaw, *Formosa.*
1920. Maxwell, Leslie Blyth, *Lambeth.*
1910 Maxwell,Thos Clarkson,*SierraLeone.*
1900. Maxwell,Wm.Walker,*ThamesDitton.*
1877. May, Albt. Edward, *S. Hayling.*
1864. May, Augustus Square, *Forest Hill.*
1901. May,Chas. MontagueNeale,*Kimberley*
1886. May, Chichester Gould, *Cadoyan-pl.*
1914. May, Claude Jocelyn Delabère, *Bath.*
1893. May, George Ernest, *Ware.*
1896. May, Henry James, *Southampton.*
1859. May, John Henry Square, *Plymouth.*
1892. May, Percival Marshall, *R.N.*
1877. May, Percy, *Endsleigh-gdns.*
1897. May, Sydney William, *Burton-on-Tr.*
1870. May, Thomas, *Bicester.*
1898. May, Walter John, *Up. Wimpole-st.*
1874. May, William Allan, C.B., *R.A.M.C.*
1904. May, Wm. Norman, *Sonning.*
1872. Maybury, Aurelius Victor, *Landport.*
1905. Maybury,AureliusVictor,*Portsmouth.*
1877. Maybury, Lysander, *Southsea.*
1870. Maybury, Wm. Augustus, *Colchester.*
1882. Maye, John, *Manila.*
1906. Mayer, Clifford Antony Leo, *Baroda.*
1909. Mayer, Ernest, *Ealing.*
1902. Mayer, Thos. Fdk. Gisborne, *Gambia.*
1871. Mayer, William Lewin, *Benenden.*
1911. Mayers, Lewis Mendel, *Cape.*
1901. Mayes, Fred. James Alex., *Bristol.*
1898. Mayhew, Christopher Jn., *Southsea.*
1905. Mayhew, Evelyn Hill, *St. Albans.*
1882. Maynard, Edward Charles.
1898. Maynard, George Darell, *Transvaal.*
1918.§Maynard, Joyce Baron, *Wimbledon.*
1895. Mayne, Bertie James, *Carn Brea.*
1913. Mayne, Cyril Frederick, C.B.E.
1890. Mayne, James O'Neil, *Brisbane.*
1877. Mayne, Walt. Furlong, *Urmston.*
1899. Mayne, William Boxer, *Swindon.*
1895. Mayne, Wm. Sidney, *Lydney.*
1870. Mayo, Alfd. Charles, *Gt. Yarmouth.*
9793

1897. Mayo, Edmond Godfrey, *Corsham.*
1882. Mayo, Frank Herbert, *Headingley.*
1899. Mayo, Herbt. Reginald, *Yarmouth.*
1891. Mayo, Walter Cyril, *Headingley.*
1907. Mayston, John Henry, *Up. Clapton-rd.*
1897. Mayston, Robt. Wm., *Erith.*
1899. Meachen, George Norman, *Durham.*
1897. Meacock, Henry Chas., *Wisbech.*
1880. Mead, Charles.
1885. Mead, Francis Henry, *California.*
1908. Mead, Guy Harvey, *Sheffield.*
1883. Mead, Ravis, *Quirindi, N.S.W.*
1880. Mead, Robert William, *Whitby.*
1888. Mead, Theophilus Wm., *Portsmouth.*
1861. Meade, Edward, *Royal Navy.*
1860. Meade, Harry,*Bradford.*
1897. Meade, Norman Gerald,*Manningham.*
1899. Meade, Warren, *P. & O. Co.*
1892. Meade-King,Richd. Liddon, *Taunton.*
1904. Meade-King,Wm.Thos. P., *Minehead.*
1902. Meaden, Alban A.,D.S.O., *R.A.M.C.*
1909. Meaden, Charles Anderson, *Finchley.*
1886. Meaden, Edwd. Henry, C.M.G., *R.N.*
1891. Meadows, Arth.Hamilton,*Yarmouth.*
1858. Meadows, Chas. Jas. Barr, *Clapham.*
1918. Meadows, Guy, *Luton.*
1901. Meadows, Syd. Manvers W.,*R.A.M.C.*
1891. Meagher, Edwd. Thomas, *R.N.*
1919. Meaker, Sam. Raynor, *Boston, U.S.A.*
1909. Meakin, Leslie, *Newcastle, Staffs.*
1872. Measures, Jn.Wm., *St. Leonards-on-S.*
1922. Meathrel, Hubert Charles.
1877. Meek, John William, *Barrow-road.*
1889. Meerwald, Osmond S., *Maida-vale.*
1894. Meggs, Theo. Hugh Egbert, *Slough.*
1912. Mehta, Jivraj Narayan, *Bombay.*
1912. Mehta, Nanalal Maganlal, *Bombay.*
1903. Meiklejohn, Norman S., D.S.O , *R.N.*
1902. Melhuish, Hbt. M. Hy.,D.S.O.,*I.M S.*
1915. Melhuish, Thos.Walter, *Middlesex-h.*
1886. Meiland, Brian, *Bowdon.*
1894. Melland, Chas. Herbert, *Manchester.*
1883. Meller, Charles Booth, *Cowbridge.*
1912. Meller, Robert William, *Ipswich.*
1897. Mellish, John Stafford, *Tetbury.*
1916. Mellon, Bagenal Harvey, *Dublin.*
1901. Mellor, Alfred Shaw, *Westbourne-st.*
1892. Mellor, George Mullins, *Wood-green.*
1909. Mellor, John, *Bury.*
1879. Mellor, Thomas, *Bury.*
1911. Melrose, Malcolm Milton. *R.N.*
1885. Melson, George Hyde, *Birmingham.*
1893. Melville, Stanley, *Devonshire-place.*
1918. Menage, Henry Marie A.,*Kensington.*
1913. Menagé, Louis M.Jacques,*Mauritius.*
1917. Mence, Harold G. Victor, *Birm.*
1911. Mendis, Jas. Wm. Edwin,*Chalk-farm.*
9850

1882. Mends, Bowen Stilou, *Hove.*
1908. Mennell, Jas. Beaver, *Royal-cresc.*
1900. Mennell, Zebulon, *Hyde-pk.-terr.*
1917. Menon,Ambadi Krishua,*T. Cook's Son.*
1919. Menon, Anakara V. R., *Golder's-gn.*
1908. Menon, Chittayil R., *Cochin, Indiu.*
1917. Menon,Putkiyaveettil N.*Malab'r,Ind.*
1914. Menon, Tottakat Krishua, *Trichur.*
1920. Mensa-Annan, Tete, *Accra.*
1911. Menzies, James, *Dorset-square.*
1884. Menzies, Jas. Herbert, *Wetherby-pl.*
1898. Mercer, Alexander, *Southwark-st.*
1858. Mercer,Arth.Wyatt,*Stanford-le-Hpe*
1913. Mercer, James Dennis, *Eccles.*
1876. Mercer, Robert, *Bournemouth.*
1892. Mercer, Wm. Biacewell, *Kaes, N.Z.*
1893. Mercer,Wm. Staintou, *Wolverh'mpt'n.*
1901. Mercier,Chas. Jerome A.N.,*Upton-pk.*
1900. Meredith, Richd.Wm. H., *Wellington.*
1883. Merrifield, Sydney Sargent, *N.S.W.*
1899. Merry, Edward, *Brighton.*
1903. Merryweather,Roy Chas.,*Perth,W.A.*
1914. Merson, Ronald Kelburne, *Willerby.*
1914. Messenger,H.Leslie,M.C.,*Hampstead*
1922. Messinier, Edwin Bunkall.
1885. Messiter, Arth. Fredk., *Doncaster.*
1913. Messiter, Cyril Casson, *Dudley.*
1878. Messum, Gordou B. Willie, *Pretoria.*
1890. Metcalfe, Alfred Waugh, *York.*
1907. Metcalfe, Brian Bentley, *Lee.*
1888. Metcalfe, Geo. Herbert, *Clare.*
1909. Methven,Ju.CecilWilson,*South'mpt'n*
1914. Métivier. Vivian Mercer, *Trinidad.*
1883. Meyer, Charles Hartvig Louw.
1889. Meyers, Donald Campbell, *Toronto.*
1881. Meyers, Herbert Henry, *Tasmania.*
1914. Meynell, Jos. Leopold, *Dovercourt.*
1893. Meyrick-Jones,H.Meyrick,*Cheltenh'm*
1894. Miall, Charles L'Oste. *Paulton.*
1916.§Miall-Smith, Gladys Mary, *Highgate.*
1897. Michael, Cyril Eden, *Sydenham.*
1918.§Michael, Daisy K. F., *Byng-place.*
1922 §Michael, Mary.
1902. Michel, Arthur George Hav, *Cape.*
1922. Michell, George Ghiddon, *Dei onnort.*
1876. Michell, Henry Slyman, *Liverpool.*
1886. Michell, John Charles, *Seaton.*
1899. Michell, Ralph, *Leicester.*
1886. Michelmore, George, *Torquay.*
1915. Michelmore,Relph God'rev. *Topsham.*
1897. Michôd, Fred.Aich Hope,*Queensland.*
1902. Micklethwait, Geo. Whitley, *York.*
1907. Middlemiss, James Ernest, *Leeds.*
1894. Middlemist, Robt. Chas, *Stevenage.*
1922.§Middlemore, Merell P., *Worcester.*
1906. Middleton, E. M.,O.B.E., *R.A.M.C.*
1899. Middleton, Percy Ellwand, *Scarboro'.*

1888. Midelton, William Ju., *Bournemouth.*
1921. Miedema,Sytze Edw.J,*Bloemfontein.*
1903 Miéville,Geo.Christian B,*Maidstone.*
1921. Mikhail Arnin, *Hor, Egypt.*
1922. Mikhail, Rizk, *Alexandria.*
1899. Milbanke, Wm. Byron, *Sunderland.*
1896. Milbank-Smith,HarryJ.M.,*Worthing.*
1908. Milburn, Fredk. Valentine, *Desford.*
1900. Milburn, Leslie, *Winchester.*
1906. Milburn,Oscar Le Fevre,*Biggleswade.*
1908. Miles, Alfred, O.B E., *Dinas Powis.*
1894. Miles, Henry Pode, *Modbury.*
1915. Miles, Stanley Howard, *Shortlands.*
1896. Miles, Usher Wm. Newton,*Bewdley.*
1902. Miles, Peter, *Gerrard's Cross.*
1887. Miley, Miles, *St. Mary Bourne.*
1882. Mill, William, *Wigan.*
1898. Millar, Alex. Fleming, *Fulham.*
1918. Millar, Gordon, *Tottenham.*
1918. Millar, Reginald Stanley, *Brockley.*
1913. Millard, John, *Dolgelly.*
1898. Millen, Seymour Alfred, *Bridgend.*
1894. Miller, Alfred, *I.M.S.*
1899. Miller, Arthur Alan, *Westminster.*
1916. Miller, Arthur Alfonce, *Stratford.*
1888. Miller, Arthur Dixon, *Birmingham.*
1905. Miller, Arthur Hallowes, *Manchester.*
1901. Miller, Charles Hewitt, C.B.E.
1918. Miller, Emanuel, *Stamford-hill.*
1900. Miller, Ernest Alfred, *Putney.*
1922. Miller,Fredk.Rich.L.,*Ashworth-mns.*
1895. Miller, George, *Bothwell, Lanarksh.*
1899. Miller, Geo. Valentine, *Rock Ferry.*
1902. Miller, Guy Witton, *N. Thoresby.*
1879. Miller, Hbt. Percy, *Stoke Newington.*
1892. Miller, John, *Wolverhampton.*
1904. Miller, Reginald Hy., *Harley-street.*
1912. Miller, Robert Hamilton, *Gambia.*
1909. Miller, Robt. M., D.S.O., *Wimbledon.*
1901. Miller, Thos. Davidson, *Sidcup.*
1908. Miller, Thomas Mackinlay, *R.A.M.C.*
1894. Miller, Walter Frederick, *Wainfleet.*
1896. Miller,Walt. Richd Saml., *N.Nigeria.*
1884. Miller, Wm. Francis, *Victoria.*
1918. Millett, Harry, *Oakley-square.*
1909. Milligan, James Knowles, *Guildford.*
1881. Milligan, R. A.,O.B.E., *Northampton.*
1868. Milligan, William, *Birmingham.*
1914. Milligan, William Hubert, *Lytham.*
1876. Millman,Thomas, *Toronto, Ontario.*
1894. Mills, Andrew McFarlane, *Jamaica.*
1882. Mills, Bernard Largley, *Sheffield.*
1910. Mills, Charles, *Northampton.*
1909. Mills, Claude Harry, *Parkstone.*
1905. Mills, Henry, *Ebbw-vale.*
1895. Mills, Henry William, *California.*
1892. Mills, Herbert Henry, *Kensington.*

1923 §Mills, Margaret Sophie, *Gordon-sq.*
1902. Mills, Oswald, *Royal Navy.*
1905. Mills, Percy Strickland, *I.M.S.*
1884. Mills, Robert.
1876. Mills, Robert James, *Norwich.*
1894. Mills, Thomas Ingham, *Easingwold.*
1870. Millson, George, *Brixton.*
1887. Mills-Roberts,R.H.,C.M.G.,*Llanberis.*
1904. Milne, James Alexander, *Forest-gate.*
1914. Milne, John Daniel, *Canada.*
1892. Milner, Arth. Edwd., *R.A.M.C.*
1911. Milner, Charles Edward H., *Reigate.*
1893. Milner, Cyril William, *Nottingham.*
1884. Milner, James, *Bournemouth.*
1898. Milner, Norton, *Sheffield.*
1883. Milner. Samuel George.
1906. Milner, Sydney Wood, *Malton.*
1906. Milner, William Arnold, *Southsea.*
1903. Milner-Moore, Edwd. Hy , *R.A.M.C.*
1884. Milnes, John George, *Eye.*
1909. Milroy, Thos. Alex., *Manaia, N.Z.*
1903. Milsom, Edwin Hy. Britton,*NewZeal.*
1905. Milsom, Ernleigh Guy Durham,*I.M.S.*
1896. Milsome, Harry Blunt, *Chertsey.*
1902. Milson, Ernest Henry,*J.Conserv.Club.*
1892. Milton, Arth. Reg. Octavius, *Ceylon.*
1889. Milton,Francis Ralph Sept.,*Llanberis.*
1898. Milton, John Penn, *Yelverton.*
1912. Milton, Leonard, M.C., *Penzance.*
1899. Milton, William Tayler, *Eltham.*
1922.Milward,J.K.,c/o *Pacific Cable-bd.*,S.W
1922. Minasian, Caro Owen, *Lancaster-rd.*
1907. Minett, Edward Pigott, *B. Guiana.*
1903. Minkley, Hy. Richmond, *Reading.*
1894. Minnes, Rbt. Stanley, *Ottawa.*
1884. Minns, Allan Glaisyer, *Thetford.*
1892. Minshall, A. Gladstone,*Mass., U.S.A.*
1899. Minshull, Hbt. Barford, *Birmingham.*
1893. Minter, Leonard Jn., *Brighton.*
1892. Minton, Alfred Hugh, *Woolwich.*
1914. Mirajkar,VamanRaghunath,*Bombay.*
1903. Miskin, Albert Francis, *Kennington.*
1893. Miskin, Ernest, *Brighton.*
1863. Miskin, George Albert, *Brighton.*
1920. Misquith, Oscar Gerald.,*St. Geo.-hosp.*
1889. Mitchell, Albert W., *Wandsworth.*
1922. Mitchell, Alfred, *Duluich.*
1900. Mitchell,Arth.Hy.McNeill,*R.A M.C.*
1910. Mitchell, Arth. Oscar, *Camberwell.*
1899. Mitchell, Charles Martin, *Stafford.*
1909. Mitchell, Douglas Ashley, *R.N.*
1890. Mitchell,ErnestJu.Green,*M'rylebone.*
1921. Mitchell, George Stanley, *Herne-hill.*
1912. Mitchell, Godfrey Wm., *Elgin-av.*
1909. Mitchell, Howard E. H., *Carshalton.*
1906. Mitchell, Howard Vincent, *Clacton.*
1879. Mitchell, James Thos., *Victoria.*

10021

1920. Mitchell, John Roderick, *Malvern.*
1869. Mitchell, Rev. Joseph, *Kew-gardens.*
1887. Mitchell, Richard Pryce,*Monte Carlo.*
1900. Mitchell, Talbot Carter, *Thirsk.*
1922. Mitchell.Wm.EricMarcus,c/o *Cox§Co*
1906. Mitchell, Wm. Steele, *Grenada.*
1923. Mitman, Maurice.
1915. Mitra, Bireswar, *Calcutta.*
1914. Mitra, Khamini Mohon, *Calcutta.*
1912. Mitterstiller, Josef, *Innsbruck.*
1881. Mivart, Fredk. St. Geo., *Russell-rd.*
1923. Mizen, Grace Emily, *Mitcham.*
1913. Moberley, Alan Vivian, *Ditton-hill.*
1888. Moberly,Sydney C. Hillyard,*Winslow*
1921.§Mocatta,Sybil Grace, *Westbourne-ter.*
1919. Mody, Girdharlal Tejpal, *Jamnagar.*
1923. Mody, Manek Sorabji H., *Poona.*
1910. Mody, Rustom Dhunjibhoy, *Bombay.*
1919. Moffat, Charles, *Sutton.*
1923.§Moffat, Elspeth Bruce, *Cape Town.*
1896. Moffitt,Alfd. Arth. Paget, *Blackburn.*
1904. Moffatt, Chris. Wm. Paget, *Bolton.*
1896. Moffitt, Charles Gordon, *N. S. Wales.*
1915. Moftah, Sadek Girgis, *Cairo.*
1917. Mohamed, Farid, *Cairo.*
1919. Mohile, Vasant Ganesh, *Leytonstone.*
1910. Moir, Archiba d, *Dunnville, Canada.*
1904. Moiser, Bernard, *York.*
1902. Moiser, Lionel Henry, *Coventry.*
1908. Mold, Geo. Hy. Chavasse, *Erdington*
1884. Molesworth, Rbt. Everard, *R.A.M C.*
1889. Molesworth,W.,C.I.E.,C.B.E..*I.M.S*
1915. Molina, Ferdinand, *Mexico.*
1886. Mollison, Crawford Henry, *Victoria.*
1920. Molloy, Bernard, *Birmingham.*
1922.§Molony, Iva C. M., *Tunbridge Wells.*
1890. Molson, John Elsdale, *Worthing.*
1875. Molson, Wm. Alexander, *Montreal.*
1905. Molyneux,Echlin Storry,*Leamington.*
1889. Molyneux, Edward, *Southport.*
1883. Moiyneux, Jn. F., *Thatched-ho.-club.*
1911. Monaghan, Patrick John.
1857. Moncton, Francis Alex., *New Zeal.*
1903. Monckton, Rbt.V.G., *Emperor's-gate.*
1922. Moncrieff, Alan Aird, *Caterham.*
1899. Mondy, Saml. Lee Craigie,*Tottenham.*
1883. Money, Percy Frederick.
1923. Monie, Victor Stephen, *Ilford.*
1890. Monier-Williams,M.S.F.,*Onslow-gar.*
1885. Monk, Henry Geo. Hawkins, *New Z.*
1884. Monks, Geo. Howard, *Boston, U S.A.*
1910. Monod, Gustave Jean Philippe,*Vichy.*
1913. Monrad-Krohn,GeorgH.,*Christiania.*
1896. Montague, Aubrey Alfred, *Fiji.*
1909. Monteith, Hugh G., D.S.O., O.B.E.
1923. Monteith, Wm. Black R , *Edinburgh.*
1907. Montesole,Max H.Edwd.R.,*Hornsey.*

10078

1882. Montford, James, *Upton-on-Severn*.
1907. Montgomery, Colonel Harry, *Canada*.
1896. Montgomery, EdwinCecil,*Maidenh'd*.
1923. Montgomery, Geoffrey Owen.
1907. Montgomery, Gordon Nevil, *Bicester*.
1914. Montgomery, James Allen, M.C.
1910. Montgomery, Raymond, *Halifax*.
1883. Montgomery,Wm.A.Dawson,*Toronto*
1895. Montgomery-Smith,E.,C.M.G.,D.S.O
1911. Moody, Harold Arundel, *Peckham*.
1918. Moody, Ludlow Murcott, *Peckham*.
1896. Moon, Edwd. Gibson, *Broadstairs*.
1903. Moon, Harold Joseph, *St. Anne's*.
1894. Moon, Robert Henry, *Norwood-road*.
1896. Moon, Robert Oswald, *Montagu-sq*.
1919. Moor, Frewen, *Lexham-gds*.
1910. Moore, Albert Ernest, *Punjab*.
1913. Moore, Alex. Geo. Hains, *Lewisham*.
1905. Moore,A.W.,O.B.E.,*StoneyStratford*.
1855. Moore, Arthur William.
1904. Moore, Athol Raymoud, M.B.E.
1876. Moore, Charles Arthur, *Leicester*.
1910. Moore,Chs.Gdon Holland,*Hampstead*
1905. Moore, Charles William, *St. Anne's*.
1920. Moore, Desmond G. F., *Bedford*.
1901. Moore, Edwd. Bertr. Leslie,*Hw lesden*
1889. Moore, Edward James, *Blackheath*.
1891. Moore, Edwd. J. Fleetwood, *Hackney*.
1921.§Moore,Enid Marjorie,*Cartwright-gns*.
1902. Moore, Geoffrey S., *Raglan, N.Z.*
1850. Moore, George, *St. Kilda, Victoria*.
1874. Moore, George Edward, *Maidenhead*.
1890. Moore, George Ogle, *Victoria*.
1910. Moore, Gilbert, M.C., *Maidenhead*.
1913. Moore,Jas. York,O B. E., *Blackheath*.
1919. Moore, John Stephen, *Epsom*.
1897. Moore, Joseph, *Amersham*.
1897. Moore, Julius, *Enfield*.
1900. Moore, Leonard Augustine, *Bristol*.
1917. Moore, Leslie Clifford, *Chester*.
1863. Moore, Milner Montgomery,*Coventry*.
1895. Moore, Percy Lyndon, *Rhodesia*.
1808. Moore, Percy Wm , *Buckhurst-hill*.
1908. Moore, Reginald Mark, *Exeter*.
1910. Moore, Sydenham Frederick, *Egypt*.
1866. Moore, Walter, *Stourport*.
1885. Moore,Walt.Hy B., *StraitsSettlements*
1883. Moore, Wm. Hodgson,*Kidderminster*.
1882. Moore, York Thos. Gray, *Blackheath*.
1888. Moores,Saml. G ,C B.,C.M.G.,*A.M S*.
1883. Moorhouse, Benj Michael, *New Zeal*.
1896. Moorshead, Chas. Woollven. *Manch*.
1922.§Moos-Schwabacher, H , *Willesden-gr*.
1908. Mora, Chas. Bernabé, *Westminster-h*.
1909. Morcom, Alfred Farr, *Dunstable*.
1919. Morcos, Farid, *Gerrard-st*.
1890. More, John, *Kettering*.

1894. Moreton, Frederick, *Victoria*.
1882. Moreton, John Smith, *Crewe*.
1895. Moreton, Reginald, *Overton*.
1890. Moreton, Thos. Wm Earl, *Tarvin*.
1917. Morford, Arthur, *The Chase, S.W.*
1910. Morgan, Arthur, *Staveley*.
1879. Morgan, Aug. Kinsey, *Bournemouth*.
1905. Morgan, Conwy Llewellyn, *Hastings*.
1901. Morgan,Daniel Leigh, *Pembroke-dock*.
1890. Morgan, David Naunton, *Bridgend*.
1893. Morgan, Edgar John, *I.M.S.*
1906. Morgan, Edward, *Shetty*.
1885. Morgan, Edwd. Hume, *Tasmania*.
1871. Morgan,EdwardRice,*Llanwrtyd Wels*
1901. Morgan, Edwin, *Pontypridd*.
1916. Morgan, Ernest Cecil de M., *Guy's-h*.
1902. Morgan, Frank, *West Norwood*.
1909. Morgan, Frank Cyril, *Malay States*.
1886. Morgan, Fred. Jas., C.M.G., C.B.E.
1899. Morgan, Frederick Charles, *Elgin-av*.
1884. Morgan, George, *Brighton*.
1886. Morgan, Geo. Fdk. Elliot, *Hartlepool*.
1923. Morgan, George Sydney, *Shrewsbury*.
1920. Morgan, Gwilym Evan, *Bow*.
1892. Morgan, Harry de Riemer, *Elstree*.
1915. Morgan, Henry Naunton, *Bridgend*.
1904. Morgan, Idris Naunton, *Tonypandy*.
1894. Morgan, James Arthur, *Builth-wells*.
1877. Morgan, John. *Aberystweith*.
1921. Morgan, John Clifford R., *Pontypridd*.
1909. Morgan, John Frederick Hy., *I.M.S.*
1908. Morgan, John Griffiths, *Nyasaland*.
1921. Morgan, Leslie Stuart, *Avenue-rd*.
1883. Morgan, Llewellyn Arth., *Liverpool*.
1889. Morgan, Morgan John, *Aberystwyth*.
1915. Morgan, Richard Glyn, M.C.
1916. Morgan, Telford David, *Cardiff*.
1902. Morgan, Thomas, *Garnant*.
1897. Morgan,Walt Harmon, *Westcliff-on-S*.
1876. Morgan, William, *Swansea*.
1898. Morgan, Wm. Ellis, *Peckham*.
1913. Morgan, Wm Frank, *Beaconsfield*.
1892. Morgan, William Holmes, *Longtown*.
1904. Morgan, William Parry, *Cardiff*.
1923. Morgenstern, Louis, *Salford*.
1892. Morice, Chas. Geo. Fredk., *New Zeal*.
1886. Morison, Albt. E.,O B.E.,*Sunderland*.
1885. Morison, Fredk. William, *Cadogan-pl*.
1923. Morland, Andrew John, *Glastonbury*.
1897. Morland, Egbert Coleby, *Switzerland*.
1915.§Morland, Hannah Grace, *Bishopsgate*.
1923. Morledge,John Walker, *Durban*.
1915. Morley, Allan Hawkins, *Barton*.
1913. Morley,DonaldE.,*Barton-on-Humber*
1909. Morley,Edwin B.,*Barton-on-Humber*
1895. Morley, Frank. *Harley-street*.
1893. Morley, Hy. Webster, *Portsmouth*.

1874. Morley, Thos. Simmons, *Barton.*
1923. Morlock, Herbert Victor, *Beulah-hill.*
1896. Mornement, Robert Harry, *R.N.*
1890. Morphew, Edwd. M., C.M.G., D.S O.
1908. Morrell, Reg. Arthur, *Hailey-street.*
1910. Morres, Frederick, *Cane-hill.*
1905. Morris, Arnold, *Leamington.*
1915. Morris, Arthur Daniel, *Treorchy.*
1916. Morris, Arthur Geoffrey, *Clifton.*
1917. Morris, Arthur Harry, *Bristol.*
1894. Morris, Arthur Hugh, *R.A.M.C.*
1895. Morris, Charles Edward, *Holywell.*
1904. Morris, Charles S., *Park-street.*
1910. Morris, Claude W., O.B.E.
1893. Morris, Cyril George, *Bath.*
1886. Morris, Edward, *Croydon.*
1907. Morris, Edward, *Spalding.*
1884. Morris,Edwd.Griffith Freeman,*Dover.*
1915. Morris, Edward Hugh, *Croydon.*
1887. Morris, Edwd. Walter, *Port Adelaide.*
1891. Morris, Edwin Haigh G., *Rockcliffe.*
1898. Morris, Frank Mayo, *Cape Town.*
1892. Morris, Frederick Temple, *Cardiff.*
1905. Morris,George Edwd.V.,*Wednesbury.*
1905. Morris, Gerald Hamilton, *Park-st.*
1922. Morris, Haydn Jones, *Wembley.*
1800. Morris, Henry Cecil Low, *Bognor.*
1890. Morris, Henry Gibbins, *Warwick.*
1898. Morris, Isaac Llywelyn, *Abercynon.*
1891. Morris, Jas. Jn. Nixon, *Devonport.*
1921. Morris, James Nixon, *Devonport.*
1912. Morris, John, *Purley.*
1898. Morris, John Ignatius Worgan, *Holt.*
1905. Morris, Jonas, *Buenos Ayres.*
1905. Morris, Leonard Newsom, *Bristol.*
1901. Morris, Leslie Miles, O.B.E , *R.N.*
1870. Morris, Sir Malcolm Alex., K.C.V.O.
1900. Morris, Richard John, *Harrogate.*
1923. Morris, Richard John.
1894. Morris, Robert Alex., *Bedlington.*
1894. Morris, Thos. Harold Pryce.*Newcastle.*
1913. Morris, William, *Bedford-place.*
1882. Morris, Wm. David Joseph, *Cardiff.*
1913. Morris, William John, *Carmarthen.*
1917. Morris-Jones, Hugh G., *Colwyn-bay.*
1902. Morrish, Wm John, *Streatham.*
1895. Morrison, Alexander, *Opunake, N.Z.*
1895. Morrison, David, *Gisborne, N.Z.*
1921. Morrison, Edward Oliver, *Bookham.*
1923. Morrison, R. G., *Up.-Richmond-rd.*
1918. Morrison, Henry, *Knaresborough.*
1911. Morrison, Michael W., *St. Vincent.*
1906. Morrison, Wm. Cecil, *Ontario.*
1903. Morrow, David, *Palmer's-green.*
1911. Morse, Chas. Geo. *Norwich.*
1887. Morse, Fredk. Batho, *Finsbury-pk.*
1879. Morse, Richd. E. Ricketts, *R.A.M.C.*
10249

1882. Morse, Thos. R., O.B.E., *Hungerford.*
1911. Morshead, Reg. Sperling, M.C.
1898. Mort, James Henry, *Manchester.*
1909. Mort, Samuel Parker, *Derby.*
1915. Mortada, Ismail, *Golder's-green.*
1891. Mortimer, Edgar Fairbank, *R.N.*
1914. Mortimer,Leonard W.,*Kingskerswell.*
1891. Mortimore,Jas. Anning,*NewCross-rd.*
1886. Mortlock, Charles, *Woodhall-spa.*
1877. Morton, Augustus Chas , *Aylsham.*
1920.§Morton, Eva, *Kenton-street.*
1912. Morton, Harold J. S., *Blackheath-pk.*
1913. Morton, Herbert H. P., *Bournemouth*
1922. Morton, James Aird, *Southminster.*
1890. Morton, James Douglas, *Stockwell.*
1900. Morton, James Robert, *Bournemouth.*
1919. Morton,John Edw.Blackburn,*Oxford*
1892. Morton, Jn. Leyden, *W. Hampstead.*
1863. Morton, Samuel, *Sheffield.*
1893. Morton, Samuel Ernest, *Sheffield.*
1878. Morton, Shadforth, *Hove.*
1890. Morton, Wm. Britain, *Exeter.*
1909. Morton, Wm. John, *Inverell, N.S.W.*
1917.§Mosalt, Marie M. Alice, *Westcliff.*
1909. Moseley, Charles Albert, *Jamaica.*
1892. Moseley, Chas. Kingdon, *Ipswich.*
1917. Moseley, Fredk. Maurice, *Barnet.*
1911. Moseley, John Grimson, *Jamaica.*
1915. Moser, Herbert Guy, *Kendal.*
1916. Moser, Richard, *Kendal.*
1907. Moses, David Assur Hy., M.C.
1838. Moss, Arthur James, *Kingston.*
1905. Moss, Basil Eustace, *Blandford.*
1900. Moss, Bertram Wilmore,*Luttelworth.*
1904. Moss, Edw. Lawton, C.M.G., M.C.
1888. Moss, Enoch, O.B.E., *Wrexham.*
1922.§Moss, Lily, *Leeds.*
1920. Moss, Louis, *Leeds.*
1922.§Moss, Rose, *Bancroft-road.*
1899. Moss-Blundell, C. B , *Huntingdon.*
1902. Mosscrop, Gilbert Phillips, *Stockport.*
1915. Mosse, Cotton Grimley T., *Harrow.*
1913. Mosse, Francis Henry, *Henrietta-st.*
1882. Mosse, Herbt. Ryding, *Twickenham.*
1880. Mossop, Arthur George, *Maldon.*
1897. Mossop,Charles Henry, *New Romney.*
1905. Mossop, Ernest Edward, *Cape Town.*
1902. Mostyn, Sydney G., *Darlington.*
1895. Mott, Clarence Harry, *Burslem.*
1880. Mott,Sir F.W.,K B.E.,*Nottingh'm-pl.*
1904. Mott, Raymond Culver, *Lee.*
1892. Motteram,Henry Prince,*Birmingham.*
1893. Mottram, Guy Nasmith, *Preston.*
1903. Mottram, Jas. Cecil, *Regent's-pk -rd.*
1904. Mottram, Maurice John, *Banbury.*
1884. Mount-Biggs,Chas. E.F.,*Babbacombe.*
1894. Mould, Gilbert Edwd., *Sheffield.*
10306

1923. Mould, Herman, *Go'der's Green*.
1896. Mould, Philip Geo., *Manchester*.
1906. Mould, Richard John, *Somerby*.
1887. Mould, William Thomas, *C.M.G.*
1916. Moulson, Geoffrey, *Sidmouth*.
1899. Mounsey, Ridley Ewart, *Camberley*.
1916. Mountain, Bernard, *Grimsby*.
1885. Mourilyan, Edward Pain, *R.N.*
1862. Mowat, George, *Ipswich*.
1923. Mowle, Alf. Chas., *King Henry's-rd*.
1917. Mowll, Chris. Kilvington, *Dover*.
1891. Moxey, Vincent, *Finchley*.
1887. Moxham, Marcus Camplin, *Boston*.
1886. Moxon, Alban Henry, *Catford*.
1891. Moxon, Chas. Carter, *Pontefract*.
1909. Moxon, Harold Richard, *Park-cresc*.
1906. Moxon, Herbt. Wm., *Matlock*.
1907. Moyle, Henley Hamlyn, *Henstridge*.
1916. Moyle, Robert Davies, M.C., *Toronto*
1911. Mozumder, Satyen, *Worthen*.
1923.§Mucadam, Naja R., *Newton-rd*.
1897. Mudd, Frank Burnand, *Transvaal*.
1917. Mudge, Jn. Branwell, *Winchmore-hill*.
1881. Mudge, Thomas, *Hayle*.
1885. Mudge, Zachary Belling, *Hayle*.
1906. Muelberger, Arthur, *Wurttemberg*.
1886. Mugford, Sidney Arthur, *Park-st*.
1895. Muggleton, Ferdinand C. H.,*Southsea*.
1908. Mugliston, Reginald, *W. Af. M. S.*
1875. Mugliston, Thos. Crichton, *Penang*.
1920 §Muir, Annie Agnes, *West Kirby*.
1890. Muir, Arthur, *Bushey-heath*.
1914. Muir, Arthur Rennie, *Abertillery*.
1903. Muir, Berthold, *Buckhurst-hill*.
1922. Muir, David Clark, *Brynteg*.
1918. Muir, David Miller, *Castledon-rd*.
1899. Muir, David Wm. Stevens,*Manchester*.
1921. Muir, John B. G., *Middlesex-hospital*.
1915. Muir, John Keer, *Brynteg*.
1897. Muir, Joseph Corbett, *Leytonstone*.
1904. Muirhead, James, *North Shields*.
1883. Mukerji, Upendra Nath, *I.M.S.*
1909. Mulder, William, *Durban*.
1918 §Mules, Annie Shortridge, *Kenton*.
1912. Mulla-Feroze, Kavasji C., *Clapham*.
1914. Mullan, Hy. F., M.B.E.,*Dalston-lane*.
1918. Mullen, Kenneth, *Up. Tollington-pk*.
1895. Mulligan, Fredk. Wm., *Ontario*.
1918. Mullins, Geo. Edw., *Birmingham*.
1909. Mullins, Hy. R.,O.B.E.,*Grahamstown*.
1900. Mullins, Reg. Cuthbert,*Grahamstown*.
1891. Mulvany, John, *I.M.S.*
1905. Mulvany, Joseph Archie, *Cape*.
1891. Mulvany, Thos. Edwd., *Muswell-hill*.
1885. Mumford,Alfd.Alexander,*Manchester*
1902. Mummery, Norman Howard, *N.S.W.*

1903. Mummery,StanleyParkes,*Crendish-p*.
1889. Munday,Richd Cleveland,C.B.,*R.N.*
1867. Munden, Charles, *Ilminster*.
1911. Munde n,Marwood Mintern,*Ilminster*.
1907. Munden,Wm.PooleHenley,*Ilminster*.
1899. Munro, Donald John, *Portland*.
1894. Munro, Henry Acland, *Catford*.
1900. Munro, John May Herbert, *Bath*.
1893. Murdoch, Alan, *Paignton*.
1905. Murdoch, Alex., *Brucefield, Canada*.
1882. Muriel, Cecil Jeffery, *Norwich*.
1896. Muriel, George Bertram, *Whitehaven*.
1886. Muriel, John, *Hadleigh*.
1901. Murison, Alexander Logan, *Cyprus*
1904. Murphy,BasilN.,M.C.,*NewBrighton*.
1873. Murphy, George, *Carlisle*.
1876. Murphy, Hy. Howard, *Twickenham*.
1904. Murphy, John Findon, *Pickering*.
1916. Murphy, John James, *London-hosp*.
1913.§Murphy, Margaret Clare, *India*.
1904. Murray, Charles Molteno, *Cape Town*.
1903. Murray, Frederick Wm., *Liverpool*.
1889. Murray,George,QueenAnne's*ns*.
1888. Murray, G. Redmayne, *Manchester*.
1879. Murray, Henry Walker, *R.A.M.C.*
1882. Murray, Horace Herc. Chr., *Hornsey*.
1923. Murray, John Douglas R , *Harley-st*.
1895. Murray, John Hanna, C.I.E., *I.M.S.*
1898. Murray, Richd. Galway, *Sussex-gds*.
1921. Murray, Robert Edmund, *Lahore*.
1904. Murray, Stuart, O.B.E., *Didsbury*.
1896. Murray, William Berkeley, *Perak*.
1889. Murray-Aynsley,Jn.Henry,*Montrose*.
1923. Murrell, E. Bartram, *Gt. Ormond-st*.
1896. Mursell, Henry Temple,O.B.E.,*S.Afr*.
1892. Musgrave, Cecil Benj. Thos., *Lifton*.
1882. Musgrave, Frank Ernest, *Leeds*.
1923. Mushin, Louis, *Stepney-green*.
1903. Muspratt,Percy Knowles,*W.Drayton*.
1897. Mussellwhite, William, *Spennymoor*.
1863. Mussen, Arthur, *Glenary, co. Antrim*.
1906. Musson, John Orrett, *Leicester*.
1889. Musson,Wm.Edwd.C.,*Hammersmith*
1911. Mutch, Nathan, *Guy's-hospital*.
1872. Mutch, Robt. Samuel, *Lancaster-gate*.
1916. Muttiah, S., *Brompton-hospital*.
1916. Muttukumaru, Kathira Velu, *Ceylon*.
1906. Myer, Leonard, *Cambridge-circus*.
1902. Myers, Albert Angelo, *Leeward Is*
1898. Myers,BernardE .C.M.G.,*Bloomsbury*
1897. Myers, Chas. Samuel, *Cambridge*.
1884. Myles, George Thomas, *Bristol*.
1905. Myott, Edgar Coningsby, *Newcastle*.
1895. Myrtle, George Yule, *Harrogate*.

N.

1897. Nabarro, David Nunes, *Harley-st.*
1891. Naden, John Bassett, *Warrington.*
1917. Nagamuttu, Canapathy P., *Colombo.*
1909. Naik, Naranji Ranchhodji, *Bulsar.*
1896. Naish, Albert Ernest, *Sheffield.*
1868. Naish, Fdk. James, *Bexhill.*
1879. Nall, Samuel, *Furness-vale.*
1916. Nalliah, Nava Ratnam, *Ceylon.*
1920. Nanavati, Bapuji Phiroyshaw.
1882. Nance, Sir A. S., K.B.E.,C.B., *R.N.*
1902. Nanji, Ratanji Maucherji, *Durban.*
1907. Nankivell, Austin Threlfall, *Poole.*
1892. Nankivell, B. Wright, *Bournemouth.*
1875. Nankivell, Frank, *Upp. Norwood.*
1914. Napier, Lionel Everard, *Windsor.*
1866. Napper, Albert Arthur, *Cranleigh.*
1902. Nash, Arthur Charles, *B. Columb.*
1886. Nash, Charles, *Horndean.*
1896. Nash,Elwin HarralThos., *Wimbledon.*
1882. Nash, John Brady, *Sydney, N.S.W.*
1902. Nash, Lorimer Gifford, *Turvey.*
1874. Nash, Wm. Gunner, *Wokingham.*
1912. Nash-Wortham, F. Leslie,*Haslemere.*
1886. Nason, Edward Noel, *Nuneaton.*
1923. Nathan, Albert, *N. Kensington.*
1891. Nathan, Edward Albert,*New Zealand.*
1922. Nathan, Horace Abe, *N. Kensington.*
1902. Nattle,HaroldRundleFitz,*Basutol'nd.*
1894. Nattle, William Robert, *Basutoland.*
1914. Nattrass, Frederick John, *Lincoln.*
1923. Naudé, Alfred L te Water, *S. Africa*
1908. Nauth, Bhola,C.I.E., *I.M.S.*
1900. Navarra, Norman, *Dartford.*
1916. Navine, Noel Spencer, *Baldock.*
1876. Naylor, Chas. Geo. R., *Bangalore.*
1922.§Naylor, Olga Mary, *Keighley.*
1890. Naylor, Wm. Roebuck, *Nelson.*
1899. Naz,JeanBaptisteChas.O.,*Mauritius.*
1904. Neal, Frank, *Ontario.*
1891. Neal, James, *Golder's-green.*
1891. Neale, Benjamin Gabriel, *Bristol.*
1879. Neale, Wm. Henry, *Loudoun-road.*
1905. Nealor, Wm. Steward, *I.M.S.*
1880. Neatby, Edwin Awdas, *Wimpole-st.*
1904. Neatby, Thomas Miller, *Leytonstone.*
1906. Neave, Lionel Digby, *Colchester.*
1900. Neave, S. Hv. Morier, *Ingatestone.*
1918. Neckles, Arthur Richard, *Grenada.*
1902. Nedwill, Courtney Llewellyn, *N.Z.*
1858. Needham, Sir Fredk., *Victoria-st.*
1923. Needham, Hubt.Wm.,*Bounds-gr.-rd.*
1902. Needham, Richard A., C.I.E., D.S.O.
1915. Neely, Wilfred Guy Stuart, *Bromley.*
1918. Neighbour, Philip Morgan, *Shiplake.*
1902. Neil, James Hardie, D.S.O., *N.Z.*

10471

1905. Neil, Reginald Cavan, *Brentford.*
1902. Neil, William Herbert, *Acton.*
1906. Neild, Frederic Miller, *Shanghai.*
1897. Neild, Newman, *Bristol.*
1889. Neill, Balfour, *Egerton-terrace.*
1919. Nel, Jacobus Gideon, *Theale.*
1903. Neligan, Anthony Richd., *Persia.*
1922. Nelken, George J. V., *Denmark-hill.*
1904. Nell, Audreas, *Colombo.*
1802. Nellen, Geo. Marshall Fdk., *Brighton.*
1862. Nelson, Charles Eugene.
1914. Nelson,Frank Andrew M.,*Highbury.*
1912. Nelson, George, *New Cross-rd.*
1890. Nelson, Harry Aug. deB., *Barking-rd.*
1915. Nelson, Kenneth Montague, M.C.
1908. Nelson, Malcolmson Knox, *Belfast.*
1920. Nelson, Thomas Sidney, *Goring.*
1888. Nelson, Wm. Bremner, *Wallingford.*
1900. Nelson,Wm. Ernest,*Henley-in-Arden.*
1922. Ness Walker, John, *Danby.*
1922. Nettlefield, Wm. Hbt., *Stroud-green.*
1870. Nettle, William, *Liskeard.*
1882. Neve, Ernest Fredc., *Kashmir.*
1901. Neville, Thomas Crofts, *Putney.*
1886. Nevins, John Ernest, *Liverpool.*
1903. New, John Sherwood, *Amersham.*
1913. New, Way Ling, *London-hosp.*
1895 Newbald,Clement Arth.,*Macclesfield.*
1909. Newcomb, Clive, *I.M.S.*
1914. Newcomb,WilfridDavison,*Herne-bay*
1881. Newcombe, Frank, *Thame, Oxon.*
1916. Newey, Frank, O.B.E., *Birmingham.*
1893. Newey, William Edward, *Dudley.*
1923. Newfield, Maurice, *Chelsea.*
1898. Newham, Hugh Basil G., C.M.G.
1895. Newington,C.Wilmott II.,*Edenb'dge.*
1878. Newington, Theodore, *Ticehurst.*
1875. Newland, Chas. Francis, *Royal Navy.*
1915. Newland, William Douglas, M.C.
1900. Newling, Harry Tudor, *Shirley.*
1872. Newman, Alfd. Kingcome, *New Zeal.*
1878. Newman, Arthur Joshua, *Godalming.*
1919. Newman, Charles Fredk., *Moseley.*
1890. Newman,Ernest A. R.,C.I.E.,*I.M.S.*
1912. Newman, Frank C., *Littlehampton.*
1920. Newman, Geo. Geoffrey, *Lond.-hosp.*
1898. Newman,Herb.R. Cambridge,*Clifton.*
1921. Newman, Maurice, *Liverpool.*
1921. Newman, Wm. Phillip, *Sydenham.*
1877. Newmarch,BernardJ.,C.M.G.,*Sydney*
1910. Newmarch, John Hy., *Campden-hill.*
1880. Newman, Christopher, *Bristol.*
1893. Newnham-Davis, Rbt, *Greville-rd.*
1902. Newport, Alex. Chas. Wm., *R.N.*
1905. Newport, HarryMac G., *W.Af.M.S.*
1879. Newsholme, Sir Arthur, K.C.B.
1901. Newton,Arth.Chas.Duncan,*Southsea.*

10528

1921. North,ThomasStanley,*NewSouthyate*
1893. Northcote, Percy, *Jei myn-st.*
1899. Northcott, John Ford, *Hither-gi een.*
1855. Norton, Algernon C. W., *Chepstow-v.*
1907. Norton,EdgarLionelR.,*BuresS.Mary.*
1889. Norton, Eveiitt Edwd., *Isleworth.*
1908. Norton, Frank Arthur, *Jamaica.*
1887. Norton, Henry Harvey, *Kennington.*
1887. Norton, John, *Queen Anne's-gate.*
1900. Norton, Jn. Chalmers, *Birminyham.*
1877. Norton, Thomas Chalmers, *Bristol.*
1881. Norvill, Fred. Harvey,*St.John's-wood.*
1903. Nothwanger, Robt. Geo., *Newcastle.*
1895. Nott, Herbert Walter, *Chester.*
1893. Nourse. Stuart Chris. Myngs, *Rugby.*
1918.§Novinsky, Esther, *Regent-square.*
1908. Novis, Rupert Stanley, *Turford.*
1897. Nowell, Walt. Salmon, *Kingsdown.*
1886. Noyes, Alex. Wellesley F., *Victoria.*
1901. Noyes, Frederick, *Newmarket.*
1904. Nunn, Gerald, O.B.E., *Royal Navy*
1896. Nunn, Jas. Henry Francis, *Tooting.*
1900. Nunn, John Wilfred, *Barnet.*
1883. Nunnerley, Philip Jebb, *R.A.M.C.*
1922. Nurick, Max, *Willesden.*
1907. Nuthall, Ernest Edwin T., *Weymouth*
1890. Nuthall, Rbt. L. S., *Orpington.*
1893. Nuttall, Arthur Peel, *Bury.*
1910. Nuttall, Ernest, *Blackpool.*
1892. Nuttall, Walt. Wingfield, *Folkestone.*
1885. Nutting, Philip Henry, *Victoria.*
1891. Nyulasy, Arthur John, *W. Australia.*

O.

1914. Oakden, George Marshall, *Retford.*
1905. Oakeley, Arthur Eckley, *Kimberley.*
1853. Oakes, Arthur, *Bi minyham.*
1896. Oakley, George Gardner, *Halifax.*
1909. Oakley, Philip Douglas, *Accra.*
1885. Oakley, Wm. Donald, *Ontario.*
1888. Oakman, Joseph John, *Battersea.*
1900. Oates, James Christopher, *Leek.*
1918. Oats, Wilfred, *Penzance.*
1891. Obasa, Orisadipe, *Lagos, W. Africa.*
1923. Obermer, Edgar, *Stoi e-street.*
1904. O'Brien, Chas. William, *R.A.M.C.*
1921.§O'Brien, Helen, *Abbey-rd.-mans.*
1902. O'Brien, Jas. Matthew, *W. Af. M. S.*
1885. O'Brien, Patrick Moriarty, *Bradford.*
1907. O'Connor, Francis Wm., *Paddington.*
1878. O'Connor, James, *Clonmellon.*
1885. O'Connor, William Patrick, *India.*
1916. Odam, Charles Leslie, *Dai tmouth.*
1896. Oddin-Taylor, Gordon Ernest, *Natal.*
10604

1916. Oddy, Hubert Musgrave, *Bradford.*
1890. Odell, Robert, *Hertford.*
1917. Odling,Francis Crawford,*Golder's-yn.*
1919. O'Donovan, Daniel, *Richmond.*
1909. O'Donovan, Wm. J., O.B E., *Bow.*
1898. O'Dowd, John Austin, *Dudley.*
1904. Ofenheim, E. R. von, *Weymouth-st.*
1901. O'Flaherty,AustinRomuald,*R.A.M.C*
1894. O'Flanagan, Martin Jos., *Manchester*
1919. O'Flyn, James Lucius Camillo.
1917.§O'Flynn, Elizabeth, *Nevern-place.*
1867. Ogden, Charles, *Southport.*
1895. Ogden,OgdenWatson,*Newc'stle-on-T.*
1915. Ogilvie, Duncan C., M.C., *Bedford.*
1897. Ogilvie, James, *Moffat.*
1879. Ogle, Charles John, *Cavendish-place.*
1888. Ogle, Cyril, *Gloucester-place.*
1906. Ogle-Skan, Henry Wm., *Hendon.*
1883. Oglesby, Hy. Newsome, *Gaisford-st.*
1899. O'Hea, John, *R.N.*
1888. O'Heffernan,HaroldHilton,*Kempsey.*
1885. O'Heffernan, W. Hilton, *Wimbledon.*
1890. Ohlmus, Walt. Theodore, *Ceylon.*
1915. Okell, Charles C., M.C., *Tichfield-tei r.*
1890. Okell, Edwin Thomas.
1888. O'Kinealy, Frederick, *I.M.S.*
1922. Olafsson, Kjaitan, *Leith.*
1896. Old, Jos. Edgar Sydney, *Nyasaland.*
1885. Oldacres, Chas. Everard, *Daventry.*
1891. Oldershaw, George, *Liverpool.*
1923. Oldershaw, Herbert Leslie, *Lincoln.*
1897. Oldfield, Josiah, *Bromley.*
1889. Oldham, Geo.Fredk.,*Tunbridge Wells.*
1889. O'Leary, Arth. Pryce Evelyn,*S.Austr.*
1894. O'Leary, Elystan G. Evelyn, *R.N.*
1870. O'Leaiy, Morgan Philip, *S. Austr.*
1909. O'Leaiy, Ralph Daniel, *Gi eenwich.*
1922. Oliva, Guillermo Bustillo, *Liverpool.*
1908. Oliver, Arthur Caidell, *W. Australia.*
1887. Oliver, Chas. Pye, C.M.G.,*Maidstone.*
1922. Oliver, Charles Pye, *Maidstone.*
1921. Oliver, Francis Robert, *Battenhall.*
1885. Oliver, George Henry, *Bradford.*
1919. Oliver, Geo.Younger,*Ridymount-gds.*
1914. Oliver, Harold Gordon, M.C.
1891. Oliver, John Percy, *Penarth.*
1894. Oliver, Leonard Wm., *Alresford.*
1906. Oliver, Norman Henry, *Ham Com.*
1922. Oliver, Thomas Chailes, *Bow.*
1883. Oliver, Vere Langford, *Sunninghill.*
1916.§Olivera, May, *Bombay.*
1900. Olivey, Jn. Michael Abraham, *Poole.*
1891. Olivey, Wm. James, *N.S.W.*
1907. Ollerhead, Henry Sandford, *Minehead.*
1902. Ollerhead, Thos. Hamilton, *Minehead.*
1918. Olphert, Robert Alan, *Dublin.*
1901. Olsen, Alfred Berthier, *Caterham.*
10751

1895. Olver, Richd. Sobey, *St. Austell.*
1892. Olver, Thomas, *Crown Hill.*
1895. O'Malley, Edwd. Dominic Jos., *R.N.*
1916. Omar, Mustafa A., *Char. Cross-hosp.*
1920. O'Meara, Daniel Joseph Patrick.
1907. O'Neill, Arthur, O.B.E., *St. Albans.*
1901. O'Neill, Bernard Price, *Chiswick.*
1903. O'Neill, Eugene Jos., C.M.G., D.S.O
1898. O'Neill, Gordon, *N. China.*
1884. Opie, Edward Augustus, *Darwen.*
1879. Oppenheim, Michael, *Theobald's-rd.*
1899. Oppenheimer,Heinrich,*Finsb'ry-pav't*
1899. Opzoomer, William, *Montreal.*
1912. Oram, Richard Goodhart, *Wandsw'th.*
1876. Oram, Richd. R. Wm., *Wandsworth.*
1881. Orchard, Alfred, *Ashby-de-la-Zouch.*
1907. Orchard, Harry Percival, *Brixton-rd.*
1921. Orchard, Stuart, *Regent's-park-road.*
1912. Orchard, Wilfred G,, *East Hoathly.*
1919. Ord, Arthur Gordon, *Stoke.*
1893. Ord, Reginald Whistler, *Dover.*
1888. Ord, Wm. Theophilus, *Bournemouth.*
1887. Ord, Wm. Wallis, O.B.E , *Salisbury.*
1891. Ord-Mackenzie, S. A., *Reading.*
1916.§Oreilly, Alice, *Mecklenburgh-street.*
1909. O'Reilly, Bert. Chas. Noble, *Coventry.*
1904. O'Reilly, B. Rolph, O.B.E., *Toronto.*
1920. O'Reilly, Francis Ambrose, *Canada.*
1886. O'Reilly, Geo. Hartley, *Bermondsey.*
1894. Orella, Fermin Ralph, *California.*
1916. Orenstein,A. Jeremiah,*Johannesburg.*
1866. Orfeur, Charles Howard, *Torquay.*
1900. Orford, H. John, O.B.E., *Transvaal.*
1883. Orford, John, M.B.E., *Pontefract.*
1890. Orford, Robt. James, *New S. Wales.*
1900. Orford, Thomas Christian, *Grenada.*
1905. Orlebar,JeffreyAlex.Amerst,*Bright'n.*
1917. Orme, Edmund Stuart, *Derby.*
1899. Orme, Gilbert Edward, *Clitheroe.*
1894. Orme, William Bryce, *Borneo.*
1896. Ormerod, Arth. Latham, *Oxford.*
1888. Ormerod, Charles Evelyn, *Epsom.*
1887. Ormerod, Edw. Booth, *Queensland.*
1919. Ormerod, Edwin Ronald, *Pendleton.*
1894. Ormerod, Ernest Wm., *Wimborne.*
1895. Ormerod, Ernest Wm., *Southam.*
1916. Ormerod, Frank Cunliffe, *Chorley.*
1889. Ormerod, Hy. Lawrence, *Bristol.*
1875. Ormerod,Jos.Arderne,*Up.Wimpole-st.*
1923.§Ormerod, Judith E. M., *Bromsgrove*
1921. Ormerod, Thomas L., *U. Wimpole-st.*
1898. Ormond, James Service, *Victoria.*
1901. Ormond, Sidney James, *Leatherhead.*
1890. Orr, Frederick Layton, *Norbury.*
1863. Orr, Gawin, *Ballylesson, Lisburn.*
1891. Orr, John, *Edinburgh.*
1900. Orr, Vivian Bernard, *Lowndes-street.*

1881. Orr, William Young, *Putney.*
1913. Orr-Ewing, Hugh J., *Weston-s.-Mare.*
1923. Orsmond, Edwin, *Brockley-rise.*
1892. Ortlepp, Albert James, *Transvaal.*
1905. Orton, Douglas Catterell L.,*St.Helens.*
1886. Orton, Francis Jos. J., *Birmingham.*
1901. Orton, Geo. Harrison, *Up. Berkeley-st.*
1893. Orton, John, *Coventry.*
1900. Orton, Lionel Edward, *Bedworth.*
1860. Orton, Theodore.
1906. Orton, Wm. Hunt, *Campden-hill-rd.*
1906. Orton, William Stewart, *Chailey.*
1892. Osborn, Francis Arthur, *Dover.*
1921. Osborn, Henry Alex., *Camberwell.*
1898. Osborne, Albert, M.B.E., *Ilfracombe.*
1889. Osborne, Frank, *Bexhill-on-Sea.*
1898. Osborne, Harry, *Southport.*
1898. Osborne, Richard Sidney, *R.N.*
1902. Osburn, Arthur C., D.S.O., *R.A.M.C.*
1922. O'Shaughnessy, Laurence F.,*S.Shields*
1919. Osman, Arthur Arnold, *S. Norwood.*
1923.§Osmond,Carrie Hooper,*BurntAsh-hill*
1887. Osmond, Edwd. Bartrum, *Pontefract.*
1910. Osmond, Thomas Edward,*R.A.M.C*
1900. Ostheimer, Alfred James, *Paris.*
1921. Ostrowick, Montague Max, *Edin.*
1895 O'Sullivan, Daniel, *Kinsale.*
1913. O'Sullivan, Michael B., *Melbourne.*
1881. Oswald, Rbt. Jas. Wm., O.B.E.
1920. Othman, Ahmed, *Egypt.*
1880. Otway, Alfred Carrol, *Barnes.*
1907. Oulton, Ernest Vivian, *Cairo.*
1905. Ouranofski, Vladimir N., *Liverpool.*
1917. Ouseley-Smith, Edw. Ernest, *Hyde.*
1923. Ousep,Chattupuzhankaren L.,*Trichur*
1899. Outred, Charles Deane, *Gravesend.*
1913. Overend, Hubert Fredk., *Bacup.*
1920. Overend, Thomas Dallas,*St.Leonards.*
1922. Overton, Reginald Ernest, *Birkdale.*
1910. Overton, Robert Sydney, *Sutton.*
1919.§Overton, Sibyl Gertrude, *Brighton.*
1908. Owen, Albert Harold, *Uganda.*
1921.§Owen, Alice, *West Bridgford.*
1885. Owen, Arthur Deaker, *Hampton.*
1895. Owen, Rev. Arthur Dunley, *Cape.*
1889. Owen, Charles Arthur, *Lahore.*
1880. Owen, Charles Richard, *Rushden.*
1865. Owen,David Chas.Lloyd,*Birmingh'm.*
1919. Owen, David Richard, *Liverpool.*
1923. Owen, Emrys Daniel, *Ebbw Vale.*
1883. Owen, Herbert, *Ebury-st.*
1875. Owen, Sir H. Isambard, *Bristol.*
1909. Owen, John George, *Henllan.*
1888. Owen, John Lewis, *Holyhead.*
1881. Owen, John Morgan, *Fishguard.*
1886. Owen, John Vaughan, *Llanidloes.*
1913. Owen, Joseph, *Hendon.*

1904. Owen, Sydney Arthur, Q. Anne-st.
1915. Owen, Thomas, Amhurst-park.
1912. Owen, William David, Whitland.
1919. Owen, William Griffith, Holloway.
1866. Owens, Edwd. Matthews, Vict., Aust.
1893. Owens, Isaac Edwd., Liverpool.
1911. Owens, John Herbt., Long Stratton.
1862. Owles, Jas. Allden, W. Kensington.
1898. Owsley, Geo. Chetwode, Blackheath.
1877. Oxley, Sir Alfred Jas. Rice, C.B.E.
1888. Oxley, Frederick John, O.B.E.
1899. Oxley, Jas. Chas. Stewart, I.M.S.
1897. Oxley, Wm. Hy. Francis, Poplar.
1886. Ozzard, Albert Tronson, Br. Guiana.
1888. Ozzard, Fairlie Russell, I.M.S.

P.

1893. Pace, Harold Everett, Leyton.
1923. Pacheco, Julian N. J., Bangalore.
1894. Packer, Harry Dixon, R.A.M.C.
1876. Packer, Wm. Herbert, Shrewsbury.
1917. Packham, Arthur Leslie, Wimbledon.
1886. Packman, Alfd. C. Aug., Rochester.
1888. Padbury, George John, Axminster.
1877. Paddison, Edmund Howard, Hove.
1911. Paddon, Henry Locke, Weybridge.
1893. Padmore, Gordon, Blackpool.
1896. Padwick, John Cayley, Bridgnorth.
1886. Pagden, Trayton Charles, Horley.
1898. Page, Algernon Fountain, Handcross.
1904. Page, Cecil Hbt. Winter, N. Walsham.
1913. Page, Dennis Salmon, Blakeney.
1899. Page, Edward Ferdinand, Solihull.
1923. Page, Erichsen Sutton, Solihull.
1897. Page, Fredk. Wm. Tudor, Queensland.
1909. Page, George Frank, Aldershot.
1922.§Page, Hilda Winifred, Brondesbury.
1903. Page, Jn. Howard Le Bouverie, R.N.
1913. Page, Lionel, Bristol.
1917. Page, Sydney Watson, Highfield.
1893. Page, Walt. Thomas, Stoke Newington.
1900. Page, William Sidney, Brisbane.
1882. Paget, Chas. Edward, Northampton.
1889. Paget, Peter, Hove.
1890. Paget, Tom Lakin, Stratford, N.Z.
1901. Paget, Walter Gray, Croydon.
1909. Paget-Tomlinson, E.E., K'by Lonsdale.
1870. Paget-Tomlinson, W., Kirkby Lonsdale
1914. Pailthorpe, Duncan W., M.C.
1877. Pain, Alfred, New Kent-road.
1921. Pain, Alfred, New Kent-road.
1894. Pain, Arthur, Durham.
1903. Pain, Basil Hewitt, Leatherhead.
1886. Pain, Francis, Allora, Queensland.
1923.

1906. Paine, Ernest Wm. Mynall, R.A.M.C.
1904. Paine, Frederick, Woodford Bridge.
1886. Paine, Wm. Henry, Green-lanes.
1904. Painton, George Richard, R.A.M.C.
1909. Paira Mall, Amritsar, India.
1901. Pakes, Alb. Ern. Hardman, Transvaal.
1895. Pakes. Walter Charles, Transvaal.
1910. Paley, Chas. Edw. Hewitt, Stockwell.
1883. Paley, Frederick John, Hove.
1908. Paley, Wm. Norman A., Fiji.
1897. Palgrave, Edwd. Francis, Ealing.
1895. Palin, Edwd. Watson, Fakenham.
1906. Pallant, Hubert A., M.C., D.S.O.
1902. Pallant, S. Luis, D.S.O., R.A.M.C.
1910. Palmar, Georg Natanael, Sweden.
1899. Palmer, Arthur Aubrey, Sydney.
1872. Palmer, Ambrose Myrie, Chesterfield.
1907. Palmer, Basil Henry, Ramsgate.
1904. Palmer, Cadwallader Edwds, I.M.S.
1901. Palmer, Charles Ambrose, Yeovil.
1898. Palmer, Chas. John Linton, Gosport.
1892. Palmer, Chas. Spencer, Dawlish.
1873. Palmer, Fdk. Jn. Morton, Worthing.
1869. Palmer, Fdk. Stephen, Wimpole-st.
1893. Palmer, George Edward, Dublin.
1902. Palmer, Harold Thornbury, Gold Coast.
1918. Palmer, Harry, St. John's Wood.
1922. Palmer, Harry Mark, c/o Bank of N.Z.
1870. Palmer, Henry Drake, Alassio, Italy.
1897. Palmer, Horace Kemp, R.A.M.C.
1881. Palmer, J.I., O.B.E., New Cavendish-st.
1896. Palmer, Percy Allan, Battersea.
1903. Palmer, Russell Edwards, Rochester
1884. Palmer, Sydney J., M.B.E., Liverpool.
1892. Palmer, William Mortlock, Linton.
1897. Palser, John Edwin Ford, Southsea.
1918.§Pam, Mary Millicent, Transvaal.
1900. Panckridge, W. P., O.B.E., Petersfield.
1911. Pande, Chandrashekhar D., India.
1918. Pandit, Vijaya Shankar Rao.
1915. Pandithesekere, Cuthbert F.O., Ceylon
1902. Pauk, Harold William, Market Rasen.
1916. Pank, Philip E. D., Chandler's Ford.
1918. Panniker, Aerath N. N., S. India.
1913. Panter, Arthur Edward, R.N.
1918. Panthaky, Maneck J., Bombay.
1922.§Pantin, Dorothy, Douglas, I. of M.
1894. Panting, Charles Henry, Leyton.
1890. Panting, John, Watton.
1917. Panton, David Forsyth, Forest-hill.
1917. Panton, John Allison, Bolton.
1908. Panton, Kenneth Douglas, Canada.
1903. Panton, Philip Noel, Queen Anne-st.
1912. Papadopoulos, Stylianos G., Cyprus.
1918. Papenfus, Edmund Jacobsz, S. Africa.
1883. Papillon, Jas. William, Bridgwater.
1873. Paradise, Thos. Decimus, Kingston.

1911. Patel, Jorabhai Bhaibabhai, *Hampst'd.*
1912. Patel Purushottam Tulsidass.
1910. Paterson, Adrian Charles, *R.N.*
1897. Paterson, Archibald Richd., *Dorset.*
1923.§Paterson, Emily C. N., *Hartlebury.*
1890. Paterson, Geo. Wm., *Grenada, W.I.*
1892. Paterson, Hugh Gordon, *Sheffield.*
1906. Paterson, Jas. Jenkins, *Maidenhead.*
1923.§Paterson, Louise Olivia.
1894. Paterson, Marcus Sinclair, *Newtown.*
1914.§Paterson, Margaret Russell, *Judd-st.*
1913. Paterson, Matthew W., M.C., O.B.E.
1893. Paterson, Peter, *Glasgow.*
1908. Paterson, Robert Kerr, *Canada.*
1901. Paterson,T.W.Staniforth,*Holland-pk.*
1902. Paterson, Wm. Fergus, *New Zealand.*
1922. Patey, David Howard, *Abertillery.*
1913. Patey, Percy Edw. Hughes, *Derby.*
1907. Patey, Walter, *Wimbledon.*
1875. Patmore, Tennyson D., *Notting-hill.*
1901. Paton, James Scott, *Lismore, Vict.*
1868. Paton, John Wilson, *Bath.*
1922. Patrick, Conrad Vincent, *Leicester.*
1834. Patrick, Jos. Henry, *Birmingham.*
1908. Patrick, Norman Colum, *Glarryford.*
1901. Patten, Stephen Kerr, *Boston, U.S.A.*
1891. Patterson, Chas. Sumner, *Lambourn.*
1882. Patterson, Geo. de J., *Lechlade.*
1879. Patterson, Geo. Henry, *Ulverston.*
1920. Patterson, Roney Moore.
1889. Pattin, Harry Cooper, *Norwich.*
1900. Pattison, Albert John, *Ilford.*
1912. Pattison, Cresswell Lee, *Sheffield.*
1879. Pattison,Edwd.S.,*Atl. TransportLine.*
1916.§Paul, Edith Winifred, *Lucknow.*
1884. Paul, Edmund William, *Nottingham.*
1886. Paul, Geo. Wm. Frederic, *Brisbane.*
1916. Paul, Gilbert Eugene, *S. India.*
1900. Paul, John Frederick, *Finsbury-pk.*
1889. Paul, Maurice Eden, *Parkstone.*
1876. Paul, Reginald, *Loughborough.*
1915. Paul, Sachchidananda H., *Moradpur.*
1893. Pauli, Edwin Hry. Churton, *Bristol.*
1907. Paulin, Stanley, D.S.O., *Kansas City.*
1892. Pauling, Wm. Tennant, *Bulawayo.*
1877. Paulley, Job Nath. Legge,*Cheltenh'm.*
1906. Paulley, John, *Harleston.*
1921. Pauw, Daniel B., *Stellenbosch.*
1919. Pauw, Jacobus C., *Stellenbosch,S.Af.*
1900. Pavillet, Leonard John.
1902. Pavitt, Percy George, *Wimpole-st*
1890. Pawlett, Thomas Lawr., *N.S.W.*
1897. Payne, Alfred Ernest, *Leicester.*
1877. Payne, Algernon Archibald, *Sheffield.*
1902. Payne, Archibald Gates, *Egypt.*
1879. Payne, Charles Alex., *Hobart.*
1900. Payne,Edwd. M.Bruce,*Shepherdswell.*
11145

1893. Payne, Ernest Le Fevre, *Kew.*
1882. Payne, Frank Cobham, *Witham.*
1879. Payne, Henry, *Southport.*
1883. Payne, James Rowland, *Coleford.*
1915. Payne, John Fredk. M., *Tasmania.*
1913. Payne, John Rowland, *Penarth.*
1899. Payne, J. Lewin, O.B.E., *Portland-pl.*
1923. Payne, Reginald T., *Gt. Ormond-st.*
1917. Payne, Reuben Woodland, *Ealing.*
1918. Payne, Thomas Melville, *Penarth.*
1919. Payne, Wilfrid Walter, *Brighton.*
1868. Payne, William Hele, *Hampstead.*
1893. Payne, Wm. Henry, *Brockley.*
1900. Payne, William Pitt.
1869. Peacan, Luke, *Buenos Ayres.*
1903. Peace, Percy Clift, *Tylorstown.*
1921.§Peacey, Winifred, *Victoria-grove.*
1904. Peach, Wm Frank, *Putney-park.*
1903. Peachell, George Ernest, *Chichester.*
1922. Peacock,Gerald Eust., *Denmark-hill.*
1870. Peacock, Hry. George, *Torquay.*
1912. Peacock, Wm. Baly, *Leatherhead.*
1909. Peacock, William Henry, *W.Af.M.S.*
1894. Pead, John Hunter, *Royal Navy.*
1898. Peake, Arthur Edward, *Henley.*
1893. Peake, Arthur Walton, *Bristol.*
1894. Peake, Frederic Ernest, *Bristol.*
1892. Peake, George Arthur, *Cheltenham.*
1886. Peake, Solomon, *Goldhawk-road.*
1900. Peake, Sydney John, *Tembuland.*
1887. Peake, Wm. Pemberton, *Leicester.*
1909. Peall, Guy Harcourt, *Rhodesia.*
1903. Peall, Percy Alfred, *Rhodesia.*
1917. Pearce, Andrew Harman, *Denbigh-st.*
1867. Pearce, Arthur, *Salcombe.*
1923. Pearce, Cyril Morgan, *Blackheath.*
1896. Pearce,Francis Henry,*Madeley Court.*
1887. Pearce, Frank, *Brighton.*
1889. Pearce, Fredk. William, *Brighton.*
1878. Pearce, Henry, *Brighton.*
1923. Pearce, John, *Market Drayton.*
1867. Pearce, Joseph Chaning, *Ramsgate.*
1905. Pearce, Percival Leslie, *Manchester.*
1900. Pearce, Thomas Massey, *Gillingham.*
1923. Pearce, Thomas Vibert, *Streatham.*
1876. Pearless, Walter Relf, *New Zealand.*
1887. Pearman, Thos. Ed.Allaway,*Hornsey.*
1916. Pearman, Walter D., *Jamaica.*
1907. Pearn,OscarPhillipsN.,*Thornton-h'th.*
1888. Pearse, Albert, *R.A.M.C.*
1896. Pearse, Athol Stewart Jos., *Cardiff.*
1899. Pearse,Edward Mountjoy, *B. Columb.*
1884. Pearse, Frank, *Transvaal.*
1883. Pearse, Frederick Edward, *Ripley.*
1891. Pearse, Herbert Henry, *Royal Navy.*
1895. Pearse, Joseph Steele, *Plymouth.*
1889. Pearse, Robert Edwd. F., *Buxted.*
11202 T 2

1870. Perigal, Arthur, *New Barnet.*
1923. Perkins, Alan C. Temple, *Dean's-yd.*
1867. Perkins, Alfred Robts. Steele, *Exeter.*
1869. Perkins, Edward, *Manchester.*
1902. Perkins, Eric McLeod, *Westminster.*
1895. Perkins, George, *Transvaal.*
1880. Perkins, Geo. C. Steele, *Weymouth-st.*
1873. Perkins, Hy. Alleine, *Tunbridge Wells.*
1890. Perkins, Henry Bowen, *Tilbury.*
1893. Perkins, Henry Campbell, *India.*
1908. Perkins, Herbt. Edwd., *Royal Navy.*
1923. Perkins, John William, *Maida-vale.*
1891. Perkins, Jos. John, *Harley-street.*
1900. Perkins, Philip Mesler, *Tunb'dge Wells.*
1918. Perkins, Rowland John, *Bedford.*
1910. Perlman, Archie, *Leeds.*
1910. Pern, Alfred Spearman, *Botley.*
1895. Pern, Edgar Courtney, *Droxford.*
1895. Pern, Horace, *Victoria.*
1901. Pern, Lionel, *Whitby.*
1900. Pern, Norman, *Victoria.*
1900. Pern, Sydney, *Victoria.*
1891. Pernet, George, *Devonshire-pl.*
1904. Perodeau, Edwd Geo., *Twickenham.*
1893. Perram, Charles Herbt., *Bedford.*
1892. Perram, Edwd. Arth, *Whitchurch.*
1891. Perrine, Edmund Kirby.
1884. Perry, Sir Allan, *Colombo.*
1877. Perry, Charles Edward, *Folkestone.*
1908. Perry, Dallas Gordon, *Vancouver.*
1895. Perry, Edmund Ludlow, D.S.O., *I.M.S.*
1876. Perry, Edw Verdon, O.B E, *Reepham.*
1885. Perry, Sir Edwin Cooper, *Guy's-hosp.*
1906. Perry, George Downing, *Tiverton.*
1919. Perry, Hugh Hamilton.
1909. Perry, Lionel Banks, *Lowestoft.*
1892. Perry, Saml. Herbert, *Spalding.*
1891. Perry, Sidney Herbert, *Birmingham.*
1898. Pershouse, Frank, *Southsea.*
1893. Pershouse, Frederick, *Transvaal.*
1898. Pestonjee, Rustom, *Galle, Ceylon.*
1910. Pestonji, Ardeshir B., *Bombay.*
1907. Patch, Chas. Hy. Lambert, *Royal Navy.*
1869. Petch, Richard, *Harrogate.*
1918. Peter, John, *Westbourne-park.*
1891. Peters, Albt. Edwd D. R'lph, *Pet'rsfield*
1900. Peters, Charles Ayre, *Montreal.*
1918. Peters, Gordon Frank, *Streatham.*
1915. Peters, Haydn, *Swansea.*
1920. Petersen, Fredk. Ferd, *Cape Town.*
1911. Peterson, Geo Reynolds, *Canada.*
1880. Petherick, Wallace, M.B E, *Thetford.*
1890. Pethick, Chas. Stuart, *Liverpool.*
1914. Petley, Cyril Eaton, M.C, *Charlton.*
1918. Petrie, George Arthur, *Hastings.*
1910. Pettigrew, Arch. Bruce, *Sheffield.*
1875. Pettigrew, Aug. Jos. W., *Victoria.*

11373

1902. Pettigrew, Daniel, *Sheffield.*
1914. Pettigrew, Michael G, M.C., *Sheffield.*
1908. Petty, Wm. Joseph, *Cardiff.*
1911. Pfeiffer, Albert, *Wimpole-street.*
1916.§Pfeil, Enid Maud, *Sussex-pl.*
1910. Pfister, Friedrich O. M., *Heidelberg.*
1913. Phatak, V. Damodar, *Poona, C. India.*
1857. Phelps, Arthur Martin, *Plymouth.*
1906. Phelps, Arthur Robert, *Highbury.*
1922.§Phelps, Edith Cecily, *Audley-sq.*
1899. Phelps, Jn. Hy. Dixon, *Scorton.*
1876. Phelps, William, *Victoria.*
1921. Philbin, Edmund, *Chorlton-c.-Hardy.*
1914. Philip, B. Don Hugo, *Ceylon.*
1919. Philip, Geo. Stuart Bain, *Powis-sq.*
1917. Philippe, Victor F. C. J.
1895. Philipps, Arthur Edward, *Fulham.*
1921. Phillipps, Frederick Alfd., *Battersea.*
1909. Phillipps, Richd. Biddulph, *A.M.S.*
1878. Phillipps, Wm. Alfred, *Dover-street.*
1876. Phillips, Alfred, *Petherton-road, N.*
1910. Phillips, Alfred Percy, *Walsall.*
1892. Phillips, Alfred Stanbury, *Bedford.*
1896. Phillips, Chas. Alleyne, *Cape Prov.*
1876. Phillips, Charles Henry, *Hanley.*
1893. Phillips, Chas. Morley, *Bristol.*
1858. Phillips, Daniel Weld, *Steeple Claydon.*
1895. Phillips, David, *Llandilo.*
1902. Phillips, David Jonathan, *Jamaica.*
1888. Phillips, Edgar Vaughan, *Kibworth.*
1885. Phillips, Edward, *Coventry.*
1913. Phillips, E., D S.O., M.C., *R.A.M.C.*
1865. Phillips, Edward England l, *Bath.*
1916. Phillips, Edwin Seymour, *Sydenham.*
1918. Phillips, Evan Albert Idris.
1883. Phillips, Francis B Willmer, *Bedford.*
1907. Phillips, Fred. Eust L., *St. George's-rd.*
1894. Phillips, George, *New Zealand.*
1871. Phillips, George Arthur, *Walsall.*
1887. Phillips, Geo. Gordon Owen, *Queens'nd*
1906. Phillips, George Ramsey, *Walsall.*
1913. Phillips, George Stanley, *Carmarthen.*
1893. Phillips, Harry Harding, *Penge.*
1895. Phillips, Henry Arthur, *York.*
1881. Phillips, Henry Whitby, *E. Croydon.*
1887. Phillips, Hubert Chas., *Gloucester-terr.*
1854. Phillips, James, *New York.*
1898. Phillips, James, *Bradford.*
1879. Phillips, Sir John, *Brook-street.*
1895. Phillips, John, *St. Clear's.*
1893. Phillips, Jn. Elphinstone Hood, *R.N*
1907. Phillips, Jn. G. Porter, *Bethlem-hosp.*
1896. Phillips, John Robt. Parry, O B E.
1923. Phillips, Leslie Penhall, *Aberdeen-pk.*
1907. Phillips, Lionel Lewis, *Redruth.*
1915. Phillips, Lloyd Desbat, *Highgate.*
1907. Phillips, Montagu, *Preston.*

11430

1902. Phillips, Nathaniel R., *Abergavenny*
1901. Phillips,NormanRouth,*Northampton*.
1892. Phillips, Percy Cranston, *Abridge*.
1916. Phillips, Percy R.O'Rourke,*Norwood*.
1894. Phillips, Richd. Edwd.G., *Wimpole-st*.
1877. Phillips, Sidney Philip, *Up. Brook-st*.
1887. Phillips, Thomas, *Harley-street*.
1912. Phillips, Thos. Harold, *Pontypridd*.
1887. Phillips,Wm.Edwd P.,*Egerton-gdns*.
1907. Phillips-Jones,Benj.J.,*Pen hincceiber*.
1866. Philpot, Chas. William, *Croydon*.
1906. Philpot, Henry Austin, *Chester-sq*.
1872. Philpot, Jos. Hy , M.B.E.,*Chester-sq*.
1894. Philps,Fdk.Geo.Meynell,*Earl's-court*.
1906. Phippen, H. Garnet, *Newbridge*.
1902. Phipps, Chas. Arth. Gayer, *R.N*.
1880. Phipps, Edgar Vivian Ayre,*Bedford*.
1888. Phipps, Henry Hostache, *Manchester*.
1897. Phipps, J. Hare, D.S.O., *M*., *N.S.W*.
1909. Phipps, MichaelW.,*Barraba,N.S.W*.
1907. Phipson,EdwardSelby, D.S.O.,*I.M.S*.
1903. Pick, Arthur, *Kissingen*.
1904. Pick, Bryan Pickering, *Royal Navy*.
1902. Pick, Lawrence, *Barry, Glam*.
1890. Pickels, Joseph Arthur, *W.Af.M.S*.
1913. Pickering, Dennison Veitch, *Banff*.
1892. Pickering,Rowl.N.U., *U.-Berkeley-st*.
1904. Pickering,Wm. Cowper, *Wellingboro'*.
1880. Pickersgill, EdwinPulleine, *Sherburn*.
1916. Pickett, Alfred C., O B.E., *Ealing*.
1919. Pickett, Francis Lionel, *Manchester*.
1914. Pickett, Leonard Rbt.,*Tunbdge-wells*.
1892. Pickford, James Shaw, *Bolton*.
1915. Pickles, Harold Dobson, M.C., *Leeds*.
1873. Pickles, John Jagger, *Leeds*.
1892. Pickthorn, Edward Butler, *R.N*.
1917. Pickup, Arthur M'Lean, *Regent's-pk*.
1876. Pickup, Wm. Jas., O.B.E., *Coventry*.
1921. Pickworth, Fredk. Alfred, *Brandon*.
1900. Picton, Lionel James, *Holmes Chapel*.
1923. Piddock, John Hurley, *Birmingham*.
1888. Pierce, Bedford, *York*.
1903. Pierce, Frederick James, *Enfield*.
1898. Pierce, George Oliver, *Barking*.
1911. Pierce, Hugh, *Liverpool*.
1898. Pierce, Robt.Wynne Chas., *Guildford*.
1885. Pietersen, James. *Kingsunford*.
1919. Pigeon, Hugh Walter, *New Zealand*.
1896. Pigg-Strangeways, T. S., *Cambridge*.
1903. Piggot, Allen Pledger, *Sleaford*.
1914. Piggott,Fredk.Stanley L.,*Teignmouth*
1920 §Piggott, Winifred K.. *Lambeth*.
1874. Pike, Joseph Balm, *Loughborough*.
1896. Pike. Norman Howard, *Cheltenham*.
1899. Pilcher, Cecil W., M B E., *Boston*.
1856. Pilcher, Edwd Wm. Humphery.
1922.§Pilgrim,RuthEmerita, *Barlston-gds*.

1880. Pilkington, Fredk. Wm., *Lechlade*.
1877. Pilkington, John Edgar, *Salford*.
1915. Pill,Stanley Victor Percy,*Ladb'ke-gr*.
1923. Pillai, Mangalam K. G., *Travancore*.
1922.§Pilley, Evelyn Violet,*C'mb'rw'll-gr*.
1912. Pimm, Allan, *Guildford*.
1903. Pinches, Henry Irving,*Nevern-square*.
1900. Pinches, Horace George, *R.A.M.C*.
1834. Pinches, William Hooper, *R.A.M.C*.
1906. Pinchin,Arth.John Scott, *Wimpole-st*.
1902. Pinching,Chas. J.,O.B.E.,*Gravesend*.
1883. Pinching, Sir Horace H., K.C.M.G.
1908. Pinching, Wm. Guy, *Frampton-on-S*.
1905. Pinder, Alan Hargrave, *Stoneycroft*.
1870. Pinder, George Holtby, *Manchester*.
1914. Pinder, John, M.C., *Horsforth*.
1870. Pinder, John William, *Leeds*.
1896. Pineo, Ernest Geo. Douglas, *Bristol*.
1918. Piney, Alfred, *Birmingham*.
1835. Pinhorn, Richard, *Dover*.
1917. Pink, Cyril Valentine, *Winchester*.
1875. Pink, Thomas, *Liddington*.
1900. Pinker, Henry Geo., *Mutley*.
1919.§Pinkerton, Norah Dorothy.
1901. Pinniger,Albert E.,O.B.E.,*Broadst'rs*.
1902. Pinniger, Francis Baldwin, *Brighton*.
1919. Pinniger, Thos. Hy. Alg., *Boscombe*.
1894. Pinniger Walt. Augustus, *Brighton*.
1911. Pinnock,Vivian St.Leger,*Maida-vale*.
1914. Pinson, Kenneth Barnard, *Codsall*.
1919.§Pinson, Lillie Mary, *Manchester*.
1915. Pinson,RaymondFearle,*Birmingham*.
1908. Pinto-Leite, Hubert, S. *Hampstead*.
1922. Piotrowski, Georges, *Geneva*.
1893. Piper, Francis Parris. *Whitstable*.
1889. Pires, George, *Karachi, India*.
1871. Pires, Jos. Octaviano, *Bangalore*.
1921.§Pires, Tressila Laura, *Clapham*.
1915. Pirie, George Robinson, *Calgary*.
1913 §Pirrie, Evelyn, *Sunderland*.
1896. Pisani, Orestes Victoriano, *Clapham*.
1887. Pitcairn, John James, *Wandsworth*.
1905. Pitcairn, Stephen Hugh, *Rothwell*.
1906. Pitkin, Mont. Claud Melville, *Ascot*.
1901. Pitman, Geo. John Edward, *Cape Col*.
1881. Pitt, G. Newton,O.B.E., *Portland-pl*.
1872. Pitt, Isaac, *West Smethwick*.
1923.§Pitt, Mary Florence R., *Portland-pl*.
1913. Pitt, Oswald, *Barry Island*.
1902. Pitt, Robert Cecil, *Malmesbury*.
1921.§Pitt-Lewis,MaryW.,*Cartwright-gds*.
1881. Pittard, Marmaduke, *Cardiff*.
1912. Pittard, Reg. Arthur, S. *Petherton*.
1911. Pitts. Arthur Thomas, D.S.O.
1905. Pitts, Robert Elliot,M C , *Chelmsford*.
1873. Place, Modesto, *Trinidad*.
1865. Place, Thomas Lloyd, *Oxford-terr*.

1866. Plaister, Wm. Henry, *Tottenham.*
1892. Planck, Charles, *Hayward's-heath.*
1913. Plant, Arth.S.,M C.,*Poulton-le-Fylde.*
1903. Plant, Henry Wilham, *Pensnett.*
1908. Platt, Arthur Hardwicke, *W. Ealing.*
1893. Platt, John Noble, *Wilmslow.*
1914. Platts, David John, *York.*
1911. Platts, Harry, *Plumstead.*
1912. Platts, Sydney Goodman, *Wimbledon.*
1895. Playfair, Ernest, *Gloucester-terr.*
1915. Playfair, Kenneth, *Kelvedon.*
1910. Playne, Basil Alfred, D.S.O.,*Torquay.*
1903. Plews, John Mackay, *Mitcham-lane.*
1921.§Plimsoll, Ruth Wade, *Judd-street.*
1895. Plowman,T. A. Barrett,*Wiveliscombe.*
1903. Plowright,Chas.T. MacL.,*King's Lynn*
1923. Plowright, Herbert John, *Durban.*
1893. Plumbo, Arthur, *Sydney, N.S. W.*
1898. Plumley, Arth. Geo. Grant,*Wakefield.*
1880. Plummer, Chas. Joseph.
1901. Plummer, Edgar Curnow, *Bath.*
1896. Plummer, Wm. Edwin, *Oromocto.*
1909. Plumptre, Cyril M., *I.M.S.*
1913. Pochin, Courtney Hy. G., *Guy's-h.*
1880. Pockett, Lewis Walter, *Grimsby.*
1884. Pockley, Francis Antill, *Sydney.*
1881. Pocock, Alfd. Geo. C., *Shotley-bridge.*
1899. Pocock, Arth. Rbt. Geo., *Beaconsfield.*
1886. Pocock, Herbert I., C.M.G., *A.M.S.*
1905. Pocock, Theodore Charles, *Hove.*
1913. Poh, Lao Htin.
1904. Poignaud, R. N., *Walsham-le-Willows.*
1918. Polhill, Montagu Cecil, *Renhold.*
1906. Pollard, Alex. Morton, *Holt & Co.*
1886. Pollard, Geo. Fredk., *Hanwell.*
1882. Pollard,Geo.Saml.,*Midsomer-Norton.*
1920. Pollard, Harold J. A., *Southport.*
1912. Pollard, J. McFarlane W., *W.Af.M.S.*
1881. Pollard, Joseph, *Queen-Anne-street.*
1898. Pollard,SidneyPochin,*Hebden Bridge.*
1894. Pollard, Walt. Henry, *Birmingham.*
1902. Pollock, Aubrey, Keatinge H., *India.*
1891. Pollock, Chas. Edw., C.B.E., D.S.O.
1914. Pollock,Humphrey Rivers, *Welb'k-st.*
1892. Pollock, Jn. Robt. Russell, *Tiverton.*
1890. Pollock, Richd. Gordon, *Warlingham.*
1883. Polson, James Ronald, *Highcliffe.*
1894. Pomeroy, Wallace, *Cape Province.*
1892. Pond, Francis Aloysius, *Liverpool.*
1906. Ponder, Constant Wells, *Maidstone.*
1915. Pool, Garnet Wolseley, *Hayle.*
1897. Poole, Cyril Cecil, *Pontefract.*
1900. Poole, Edwd A. Bodenham, *Taunton.*
1923.§Poole, Ethel Beatrice, *Dumbarton.*
1910. Poole, Francis Stedman, *Yate, Glos.*
1923. Poole, Jeffrey Wm . *Caren Arms.*
1894. Poole,John Copeland,*Hampton Wick.*
11601

1889. Poole, Kenneth Worsley, *Kensington.*
1896. Poole, Thos. Brice, *Westcliff-on-Sea.*
1890. Pooler, Harry William, *Stonebroom.*
1903. Pooley, John Milnes, *Nettlebed.*
1914. Pooley, John Sandys, *Chew Magna.*
1887. Poolman, Arth. Edwd., *Weymouth-st.*
1877. Pope, Chas. Ernest, *Griqualand E.*
1907. Pope, Edw. Campbell,*Gnowangerup.*
1903. Pope, Egerton Llewellyn, *Winnipeg.*
1903. Pope, Fredk. Samuel,*Victoria,Brit. C.*
1885. Pope, Henry, *Leeds.*
1879. Pope,Hy.FrancisMontagu, *W.Malling*
1912. Pope, Herbert Barrett, *Leeds.*
1913. Pope, Herbert Montagu, *W. Malling.*
1881. Pope, Percy, *Kensington-park-road.*
1896. Pope, William Henry, *Royal Navy.*
1880. Pope,Wm.Wippell,C.M.G.,*R.A.M.C.*
1876. Popert, Adolphe Joseph, *Southport.*
1886. Popert, Alfred William, *Br. Colombia.*
1879. Porritt, Norman, *Bettws-y-Coed.*
1911. Porritt, Reginald Norman, *Bettws.*
1892. Porritt, William, *Natal.*
1893. Port, Arthur William, *Bournemouth.*
1917. Portas, Frank, *Windsor.*
1918. Porteous, Leonard D., *Huddersfield.*
1920. Porter, Arthur Digby, *St.George's-sq.*
1897. Porter Arthur Edwd , *Reigate.*
1891. Porter, Charles, O.B.E., *Transvaal.*
1900. Porter,Chas. Robertson,*Berkhamsted.*
1892. Porter, Frank Constable, *Nottingham.*
1890. Porter,Fdk.J.Wm.,D.S.O.,*R A.M.C.*
1882. Porter, Guy David, *Frensham.*
1903. Porter, James Houston, *Dalston.*
1921. Porter, John Herbert, *Preston.*
1872. Porter, Jos.Francis, O.B.E.,*Helmsley.*
1901. Porter, Robert Laugley.
1879. Porter, Thos. Morrison, *Albert-street.*
1885. Porter, Wm. Ernest, *Wood-green.*
1899. Porter, William Geo., *New Malden.*
1878. Porter, William Smith, *Sheffield.*
1915. Porter-Smith, Frederick, *Denmark-h.*
1916. Portway, Robert Louis,*Walthamstow.*
1920. Posner, Joseph, *Manchester.*
1892. Posnett, Edward, *Grimsby.*
1885. Postlethwaite, Frank, *Tavistock.*
1906. Postlethwaite,Jos.Marshall, *Whalley.*
1885. Pott, Francis Henry, *Argyll-place.*
1914. Potter, Alex. Frederic. *Croydon.*
1896. Potter, Bernard Elwell, *Park-street.*
1920. Potter, George Harold, *Aintree.*
1900. Potter, Godfrey Russell, *Barnsley.*
1911. Potter, James, M.C., *Bow, E.*
1882. Potter, John Hope, *Bayswater.*
1921.§Potter, Olive Gwendoline, *Croydon.*
1888. Potter, Paul de Cresse,*Leicester.*
1893. Potts, Horace, *Yarmouth.*
1877. Potts, Laurence, *Leatherhead.*
11658

1923. Potts, Tho uas Hy. Ingram, *Baker-st.*
1886. Potts, Walter Alfd. Beevor, *Victoria.*
1899. Potts, Wm. Alexander, *Birmingham.*
1904. Pou, William Oscar, *Pahang, Malay S.*
1838. Poulter, Arther Reg., *Addle-street.*
1910. Poulton, Edward Palmer, *Borough.*
1905. Pounds, Gordon Chris., *Bexley-heath*
1923. Powell, Abraham T. W., *Aberystwyth*
1891. Powell, Charles Marten, *Reading.*
1908. Powell, Dan Arthur, *Bedlinog.*
1887. Powell, Edgar Elkins, *R A.M.C.*
1914.§Powell, Edna Mary, *Sutton.*
1921§Powell, Enid Mary, *Trebovir-road.*
1873. Powell, Evan, *Nottingham.*
1880. Powell, Henry Albert, *St. Swithin's-l.*
1920. Powell, Henry Christoffers.
1800. Powell, Herbt. Andrews, *Guildford.*
1883. Powell, Hbt. Edward, *Dunchurch.*
1904. Powell,Hugh F., M.B E., *Cheltenham.*
1911. Powell, James, *Aberdare.*
1902. Powell, Jas. Farquharson, *Caterham.*
1898. Powell,John Edw., D.S.O , *R.A.M. C.*
1883. Powell, John Joseph, *Bristol.*
1883. Powell, Jos. Harry, *S. Hayling Isld.*
1806. Powell, Josiah Cecil, *Alfred-place.*
1910. Powell, Leslie, *Reading.*
1889. Powell, Llewelyn Wm., *Lympstone.*
1921. Powell, Rhys Vaughan, *Warwick-av.*
1865. Powell, Sir Richd. D., B irt.,K C.V.O.
1916. Powell, Ronald Rees, *Barry.*
1891. Powell, Thos. Morgan Jones, *Swansea.*
1912. Powell, Thos. Wm. W., *Heathfield.*
1892. Powell, Walt. Augustus, *Brighton.*
1917. Powell, Walter Erichsen, *Brighton.*
1917. Powell, Wm. I. Fitz-G., *London-hosp.*
1914. Power, D'Arcy, *Chandos-street*
1884. Power, Edwd Thomas, *Atherstone.*
1895. Power, Jno. Hugh, *Spalding.*
1908. Power, Jn. Wardell, *Harrington-gns.*
1889. Powers, Charles Henry, *Southampton.*
1898. Powers, Richard Henry, *Southend.*
1885. Powne, Leslie, M.B.E , *Crediton.*
1892. Powrie,PercyChamberlain,*Transvaal.*
1912. Poynder, Ernest G. Thornton, *Egypt.*
1894. Poynder, Fredk. Cecil, *E. Grinstead.*
1874. Poynder, George Frederick, *Bedford.*
1877. Poynder, John Leopold, *I.M.S.*
1893. Poynton, Fredk. Jn.,*Devonshire-place.*
1908. Poyser, Arth. Vernon, *Wisbech.*
1913. Poyser,Richard Cruikshank,*Charlton.*
1916. Pracy, Douglas Sherrin, *Crouch End.*
1892. Prada, Enrique, *Trinidad.*
1911. Prall, Edward, *Newcastle-on-Tyne.*
1885. Prall, Samuel Esmond, *I.M S.*
1915. Prall, S muel Reginald, *Hythe.*
1897. Prance,Chas.H.Gouldsmith,*St.Austell*
1921. Prance, Cyril Seymour C., *St. Barts.*

11715

1871. Prankerd, Orlando Reeves, *Hornsey.*
1877. Pratt, Alfred, *Bletchingley.*
1921.§Pratt, Cassie Ethel, *Newcastle, Staffs.*
1896. Pratt, Eldon, *Whitehaven.*
1921. Pratt,Fdk.Wm.Markham,*Charges-st.*
1915. Pratt, Guy Algernon, *Bletchingley*
1902. Pratt, John Isaac, *Ontario.*
1868. Pratt, John Wyatt, *Otley.*
1915. Pratt, Oliver Beakley, *Leicester.*
1880. Pratt, Reginald, *Leicester.*
1918.§Pratt, Sybil Madeline G., *Tonbridge.*
1918. Pratt, Thomas Dawson, *Bradford.*
1911. Pratt, Walter Woodall, *R.A.M.C.*
1887. Pratt, Wm. S., *Plymouth Constl.-club.*
1907. Prausnitz, Otto Carl Willy,*Breslau.*
1913. Precope, John, *Larissa.*
1902. Prell John Philip, *Aberdulais.*
1884. Prendergast, James Jos., *Tasmania.*
1906. Prentice, Hugh Ridley, *Welbeck-st.*
1907. Prentis John Edward, *Westcliff.*
1914. Preston, Arthur Bennet, *St. Mawes.*
1896. Preston, Chas. Chichester, *Earl's-ct.*
1891. Preston, Frederick, *Norwich.*
1912. Preston, George Lionel, *Saltash.*
1920. Preston, Gosford J., *Lancaster-gate.*
1885. Preston, Henry Octavius, *Canterbury.*
1891. Preston, John Robert, *Fleetwood.*
1897. Preston,LionelLitchfield, *Ryde,I.of W*
1911. Preston-Hillary, CecilW., *Upminster.*
1914. Prestwich, Frank G., *Lytham.*
1900 Pretty, Harold Cooper, *Kettering.*
1908. Pretty, Kenneth, *Grantham.*
1885. Price, Alfred Edward, *Bromley.*
1898. Price, Archibald Ainslie, *Romford-rd.*
1878. Price, Arthur, *Liverpool.*
1891. Price, Arthur Edward.
1908. Price, Charles Edwin, *Orpington.*
1901. Price, Clifford, *Abertillery.*
1897. Price, David, *Saddleworth.*
1904. Price,Edwin Edgar M , *Birmingham.*
1903. Price, Ernest Aubrey, *Kettering.*
1901. Price, Ernest Walters, *Narbreth.*
1896. Price, Francis Edward,*Mutley.*
1907. Price, Geoffrey, *Kineton, Warwick.*
1895. Price, Geo. Basil, C.M.G., *Welbeck-st.*
1887. Price, George Elliott, *Redhill.*
1915. Price, Hoel Parry, *Reading.*
1908. Price,HoraceJn.D'ArcyG.,*Gt.Bridge.*
1872. Price, Hugh Pugh Jones, *Clynderwen.*
1923. Price, Ivor Noble Orpwood,*Reading.*
1882. Price, John Alfred Parry, *Reading.*
1880. Price, John Dodds, *Assam, India.*
1882. Price, John Dudley, *Dudley*
1904. Price, Lawrence Edwin, *Nuneaton.*
1923. Price, Leslie R. W., *Barking ide.*
1907. Price, Maurice Dyball, *Busrah.*
1908. Price, Philip Seymour, *Sloane-gdns.*

11772

1920. Price, Regina'd Francis, *Forest-hill.*
1908. Price, Robert Bernard, *D.S.O.*
1876. Price, Sir Robert John, *M.P.*
1912. Price, Thos. B. Bourne, *M.C.*
1915. Price, Thomas Lord, *Grange.*
1917. Prichard, A. Abercrombie, *Cardiff.*
1874. Prichard, Arthur William, *Clifton.*
1921. Prichard, John Augustin, *Bristol.*
1903. Prichard, John Llewelyn, *Aberdare.*
1915. Prichard-Evans, Edw. A., *Cardiff.*
1877. Prickett, Marmaduke, *Bridlington.*
1899. Priddle, Alfred Ernest, *Llanrwst.*
1908. Prideaux, Jas. Fras. E., *Fiji, M.S.*
1920.§Prideaux, Mary C , *Enfield.*
1891. Pridham, Chas. Fortescue, *Wittersh'm*
1909. Pridham, Fredk. Chas., *Darlington.*
1908. Pridham, Gerald Henry, *Woolston.*
1918. Pridham, Hubert L., *Melrose-ter.*
1914. Pridham, Jn.Alex., M.C., *Melrose-ter.*
1887. Pridham, Wm. Fredk., *Bloxham.*
1922. Pridie, Eric Denholm, *Southport.*
1890. Pridmore, Eric L.Norman, *Folkestone.*
1896. Pridmore, John Walter, *Ryde, I.W.*
1886. Pridmore, W. George, C.M.G., *I.M.S.*
1879. Priest, J. D , M.B.E., *Walthnm Abbey.*
1908. Priest, Robert Cecil, *R. A.M.C.*
1874. Priestley, C. Edward, *Norwich.*
1919 §Priestley, Dorothy P., *Leeds.*
1905. Priestley,HaroldE.,C.M.G.,*R.A.M. C.*
1882. Priestley, John, *Stafford.*
1883. Priestley, Joseph, *Brixton-hill.*
1920. Priestley, Norah K., *Muswell-hill.*
1908. Priestley, Reg. Fawcett, *Muswell-hill.*
1885. Priestley, Rbt. C., O.B.E.,*Linden-gns.*
1888. Primrose, Alexander, C.B., *Toronto.*
1898. Primrose, William, *Glasgow.*
1893. Prince, Hugh Tennant, *Boston Spa.*
1875. Prince, Jas. Perrot, *Durban.*
1890. Prince,Jn.WoolnoughGeo.,*Hartfield.*
1897. Prince, Peregrine Charles, *Reigate.*
1894. Pring, Horace Reg., *Highbury-pl.*
1890. Pringle, Arthur Y., O.B.E., *Ipswich.*
1902. Pringle, Ernst George, *Anerley*
1908. Pringle, Kenneth Douglas, *Wimborne.*
1907. Prins, Hy. Mallock, *West Australia.*
1877. Prior, Edward Thurlow, *Loddon.*
1906. Prior, Edw. Symes, *Wandsworth.*
1898. Prior, Guy P. Underdown, *N.S.W.*
1894. Prior, James, *Heclmonduike.*
1896. Prior, John Ralph, *Finchley.*
1914. Priston, Julian Lionel, *Royal Navy.*
1890. Pritchard,Edwd.Josiah,*Hampsnorth.*
1891. Pritchard, Eric Law, *S. Hampstead.*
1914. Pritchard, Geo Brentnall, *Richmond.*
1901. Pritchard, Harold, *Harley-street.*
1895. Pritchard, Harry W., *Manchester.*
1885. Pritchard, Jos Jas. Cauier, *Dewsbury.*
11829

1913. Pritchard, Norman Pallister, M.C.
1881. Pritchard, Owen, *Southwick-street.*
1899. Pritchard, Robert Jn., *W. Australia.*
1917. Pritchard, S. Hy. de G., *New Romney.*
1898. Pritchard, Wm. Clowes, *St. Leonards.*
1901. Pritchett,Geo.Wm.Morris,*Callington.*
1917. Pritchett, Hy. Norman, *Kensington.*
1890. Pritchett, Sidney Isaac, *Rochester.*
1920. Probert, Cyril M., *Mountain Ash.*
1893. Probyn, Percy Jn., D.S.O., *R.A.M.C.*
1890. Probyn-Williams,Rbt.Jas.,*Welbeck-st.*
1900. Procter, Geo. Woodyatt, *Garston.*
1915. Procter, Rbt. A. W.,.M.C., *Guildford.*
1862. Proctor, Peter, *Birkenhead.*
1877. Proctor, Samuel Fitzgerald, *Trinidad.*
1896. Proctor-Sims, FrankRichd., *Essex-rd.*
1920. Pronj,anskv, Joseph, *Listria-park.*
1894. Propert, Walt. Archib., *Gloucester-pl.*
1888. Prosser, Astley Bennett, *Birmingham.*
1877. Prosser, Thos. G., O.B.E., *Monmouth.*
1892. Prosser-Evans, Jehosophat,*Dagenham*
1885. Proud, Frederick, *Maryport.*
1898. Provis, Francis Lionel, *Brook-st.*
1900. Prowse, Wm. Barrington, *Brighton.*
1877. Prowse, William Byass, *Oxford.*
1883. Pruen, Sept. Tristram, *Cheltenham.*
1878. Pryce, Evan William, *Stonehouse.*
1882. Pryce, Thomas Davies, *Nottingham.*
1911. Pryce-Davies, John, *Chester.*
1916. Pryn, Richard Harold C., *Plymouth.*
1880. Pryn, SirWm.W., K.B.E.,C.B., *R.N.*
1918. Prys-Jones,IlywelTegid,*Pontypridd.*
1906. Pryse, Albert Edward, *New Cross.*
1900. Prytherch, Jno. Rowlands, *Llanyefni.*
1887. Puddicombe,Edw.Leonard,*Sydenh'm.*
1904. Puddicombe, Thos. Phare, *D.S.O.*
1880. Puddicombe, W. Noble, *St. Albans.*
1899. Pugh, Arthur Bailey, *Bream.*
1898. Pugh, Chas. Grant, *Southend.*
1908. Pugh, John, *E. Af.Protectorate, M S.*
1877. Pugh, John Hopkins, *Buckhurst-hill.*
1894. Pugh,Wm. Thos. Gordon, *Carshalton.*
1921.§Pughe,PhilippaParry.,*BankofN.S.W.*
1923 §Pugmire, Gertrude Elsie, *Liverpool.*
1893. Pullen, Ralph S. McDougall, *Stoke.*
1884. Pullin, Bingley Gibbes, *Sidmouth.*
1883. Pulling, Herbert John, *Brighton.*
1910. Pulling, John Bernard, *Fav ingdon.*
1915. Punch, Arthur Lisle, *Hendon.*
1914. Purcell, Nicholas.
1884. Purchas, Arthur Challinor, *New Zeal.*
1914. Purchase, William Bentley, M.C.
1916. Puri, Jagan Nath, *Punjab.*
1915. Purkis, Kenneth Noel, M.C.
1879. Purkiss, Arthur, *Teignmouth*
1889. Purnell, Purnell, *Streatham-hill.*
1884. Purslow, Chas. Edwin, *Birmingham.*
11886

1888. Purvis, Alfred, *Blackheath.*
1863. Purvis, John Prior, *Greenwich.*
1918. Putnam, Philip Wm., *Thornton-heath.*
1905. Puttock, Reginald, *Billingshurst.*
1888. Pym, Chas. Brownlow, *N.S.W.*
1908. Pywell, Ernest Alfred, *Stilton.*

Q.

1916. Quackenbos, Harrie M., *Woburn-pl.*
1895. Quait, Alex.Wortley, *Mundesley.*
1886. Quarty-Papafio,Benj.Wm.,*GoldCoast*
1893. Quay, Fdk. Aiken Wm., *Sunbury.* ·
1893. Quayle, Edwin, M.B.E., *Urmston.*
1892. Quennell, Arthur, *Brentwood.*
1884. Quennell, Rbt.W.,O.B.E..*Brentwood.*
1896. Querney, Thos. Mather, *Pondoland.*
1866. Quick, John, *Torquay.*
1877. Quieke, Wm. Jenkins, *Brixham.*
1912. Quigley, Joseph Paterson, *Canada.*
1887. Quiller, Chas. Turner, *Clapham.*
1891. Quinby,Edwd.Melville,*Boston,U.S.A*
1903. Quinby, Frank Gray, *Shrewsbury.*
1916.§Quinby, Katharine, *Church Stretton.*
1923.§Quine, Margaret A.
1909. Quinlan, William Thomas, *Cardiff.*
1918. Quinton, Percival G., *Newport, I.W*
1874. Quinton, Richd. Frith, *Winchester.*
1913. Quinton, Richard Frith, *Royal Navy.*
1908. Quirk,Edw.J.J.,M.B.E., *W.Af.M S.*
1901. Quirke, Herbert Chas., *Handsworth.*
1893. Quirke, John Joseph, *Fulham.*
1918. Quitmann,Walter Ernst Karl Adolf.

R.

1918. Rabey, Ernest Frank, *Highbury.*
1887. Raby, Leonard, *Devizes.*
1900. Race,John Percy,*Durham Co.Asylm.*
1904. Racker, Eugene C., *Westhoughton.*
1913. Rackham, Arthur L. H., *Elmham.*
1881. Rackham, Arth. Richard, *Elmham.*
1912. Radford, Maitland, *Gt. Ormond-st.*
1890. Radford, William John, *Plymouth.*
1912. Rae, Arthur Joseph, *Fownhope.*
1899. Rae, Francis Lionel, *London-wall.*
1915. Raffle, Wilfrid, *S. Shields.*
1904. Rahilly, Jn.MauriceBisdee, *R.A.M.C.*
1903. Rahim,Bakhshi Isaac, *Commercial-rd.*
1914. Rahman, Ibrahim I. Abdel, *Cairo.*
1907. Rahman, Mohamed Abdur. *I.M.S.*
1917. Rahman, Walter M. A., *Hampstead.*
1913. Rail, William Arthur, *Cape Town*
1908. Raiment, Percy Chas., *Hammersmith.*
1915. Rame, Reginald Thompson, M.C.
11935

1917. Rainer, Charles Farrell, *Norwood.*
1898. Raines, Robert, *Hull.*
1893. Rainier, Norman R. Jones, *I.M.S.*
1911. Rajan,Thillustanum S.S.,*Trichinopoly*
1886. Rake, Hbt. Vaughan, *Fordingbridge.*
1892. Ralph, Chas. Hugh D., *W.Af.M.S.*
1918. Ralph, Ronald Seton, *Richmond.*
1915. Rammell, John Wootton, M.C.
1917. Rampling, Ronald Eric, *Malden.*
1907. Ramsay, Jeffrey, O.B.E., *Blackburn.*
1917.§Ramsay, Marianne O., *Bournemouth.*
1903. Ramsav, Palmer Devoy, *R.N.*
1906. Ramsbottom, Edgar Nelson,*Horwich.*
1881. Ramsden, Albert.
1910. Ramsden, Ernest Arthur, *Dobcross.*
1889. Ramsden, Herbert, *Dobcross.*
1922. Ramsden, Wa't Maur., *Loftus,Yorks*
1920. Ramzy, Abdel Magid, *Cairo.*
1920. Rana, Manchershaw Rustomji.
1918.§Randall,ConstanceA.,*Christchurch-pl*
1888. Randall, Ernest Bidgood,*Romford-rd.*
1908. Randall, George Fredk., *Bolton.*
1922.§Randall, Gladys H , *Crickhowell.*
1915. Randell, Griffith James, *Barry.*
1884. Randell R.M.H.,M.B.E.,*Beckenham.*
1906. Randle,Alan,M.C.,*Mile-end-infirm'y.*
1875. Randle, James Mayne, *Helston.*
1871. Randolph, Charles, *Milverton.*
1899. Randolph, William H., *Wiveliscombe.*
1906. Rankin, Allan Coats, C.M.G., *Siam.*
1907. Rankine, John Lawson, *Kirklinton.*
1909. Rankine, Roger Aiken, *Royal Navy.*
1907. Ranking,G.Lancaster, *Whitley Cross.*
1874. Ranking,Geo.SpeirsA.,C.M.G.,*I.M.S*
1902. Ranking, Rbt. Maurice, *Tunb. Wells.*
1902. Ransford, A'an C., *Ingatestone.*
1893. Ransford, John Ernest, *Birkdale.*
1898. Ransford, S. Teast G., *Westbourne-st.*
1912. Ransom, Peter Warwick, *Winscombe.*
1895. Ransome, Arthur Cyril, *Birkenhead.*
1897. Ransome, Gilbert Holland, *Bungay*
1916. Ranson,Jn.Sturges,*Needham Market.*
1883. Ranson,Wm.Edwd.,*Needham Market*
1922. Rao, Appa Babu, *S. India.*
1913. Rao, Kotz Venkata Ramana, *Madras.*
1910. Rao, Srikantia Subba, *Mysore, India.*
1894. Raper,MatthewHenry, *Shoeburyness.*
1913. Rasbrook, Stanley Owen, *Devonport.*
1911. Rashbrook, Henry Martin, *Devonport.*
1902. Rasleigh, Hugh George, *Chatham.*
1922. Rast, Hugo, *Stamford-hill.*
1901. Rastrick, Robt. Jos., *King William-st.*
1916. Ratcliffe, Cecil Nuttall, *Liverpool.*
1914. Rathier du Vergé,P.J.F.L.,*Mauritius.*
1917. Ratnarajah, Hallock, *Ceylon.*
1921. Ratnavale, Wm. Setravale, *Ceylon.*
1921. Rattray, Ian Maxwell, *Blairgowrie.*
11992

1907. Rattray, Malcolm John,*Malay States.*
1920. Rau, Bantwal Narasinga.
1923. Rau, Chernagiri K., *Bagalore.*
1916. Rau, Keshava Narayana, *Mysore.*
1916. Rau-Damodar, R , *Ernaknlam, India.*
1901. Raven, Hugh Milville, *Broadstairs.*
1913. Raven,Martin O.,*St.Peters-in-Thanet.*
1901. Raw, Herbert Harland, *Whitby.*
1891. Rawes, Charles Kinsman, *Harlesden.*
1905. Rawes, Leslie, *Hampstead.*
1905. Rawlence, Harold Ernest, *Kashmir.*
1889. Rawlings, Horatio Edwd., *Swansea.*
1869. Rawlings, John Adams, *Swansea.*
1886. Rawusley, Gerald T., C.B., *A M.S.*
1878. Rawson,Ernest, *Wellingt'n,N.Zealand.*
1914. Rawson, Herbert Jack, *Bank of N.Z.*
1914. Rawson,Philip H.,M.C. *Wetheringh'm*
1895. Rawson, William Foster, *Bradford.*
1898. Rawsthorne, Hubert, *Bukdale.*
1896. Ray, Walt. Jno. Orbell, *Wimborne.*
1909. Raymond, Cuthbert, *Withypool.*
1905. Raymond, George, *Newport, I. of W.*
1873. Rayne, Charles Alfred, *Lancaster.*
1910. Rayner,Arthur E.,O.B E,*Hampstead.*
1918. Rayner, Clifford Geo. J., *St. Barts.*
1912. Rayner, Edwin Cromwell,*Hampstead.*
1922. Rayner, Francis Louis, *Shanklin.*
1864. Rayner, Henry, *Queen Anne-st.*
1921. Rayner, Howard L., *Myatts-park.*
1881. Rayner, Hugh, *Army.*
1862. Rayner, William, *Cambridge-terr.*
1904. Rayner, William Hartree, *Stockport.*
1892. Rayson,Herb. Knights,*Cape Province.*
1911. Razzak, Ibrahim Abdel, *Damietta.*
1892. Read, Arth. William, *Gloucester-rd.*
1896. Read, Charles Stanford, *Salisbury.*
1893. Read, Clarence, *Chatswood, N.S.W.*
1914. Read, Grantly Dick, *Eaton Norwich.*
1905. Read,Harold William,*Newport,I.W.*
1879. Read, Mabyn, *Worcester.*
1890. Read, Richd. Henry, *Han'ey.*
1903. Read, Walter Woolfe, *Lewisham.*
1902. Read, Walton Rix, *Portland-pl.*
1905. Reade, A. G. L., O.B.E., *Hampstead.*
1915.§Reade, Violet, *Hampstead*
1906 Reader, Stanislaus, *Wakefield.*
1887. Reading, Richd. Fairfax, *Sydney.*
1916. Reckitt, Charles Reginald, M C.
1883. Reckitt. Jn. Dennis Thorpe, *Barnes.*
1886. Reddall, Osborne Henry, *N S.W.*
1920. Redelinghuys, Johanner J., *Cape.*
1908. Redman, Charles Edward, *Ealing.*
1886. Redman, Wm Edward, *New Zealand.*
1879. Redmayne, Hugh, *Ambleside.*
1903 Redmond, Robert Clark, *Toronto.*
1892. Redpath, William, *Woodbridge.*
1903. Redwood, Rbt. V. de A., *Rhymney.*
12049

1919.§Reece,Eleanor Margaret,*Addison-gns.*
1918. Reece, Richard Harold, *Addison-gns.*
1885. Reece, Richard Jas., C.B., *Whitehall.*
1902. Reed, Geo. A. Keppel Hart, *R.A.M.C.*
1885. Reed, Henry Albert, *Fenchurch-av.*
1896. Reed, John Chas. Groscort, *R N.*
1921. Reed, John Groscort, *Epsom.*
1888. Reed, John Sleeman, *Gorleston.*
1920. Reed, Thomas, *East Sheen.*
1876. Rees, Alfred, *Cardiff.*
1916. Rees, David, *Port Talbot, Glam.*
1893. Rees, Edward Davies, *Caersws.*
1905. Rees, Frederick John, *Pontypridd.*
1914. Rees, Frederick Tavinor, *Cardiff.*
1904. Rees, Griffith Henry, *R.A.M.C.*
1898. Rees, Harry Wm. Melville, *R.N.*
1870. Rees, Howell, C.B.E., *Cardiff.*
1889. Rees, Sir J. M., C.V.O., *Wimpole-st.*
1887. Rees, John Morgan, *Pontypridd.*
1914. Rees, John Rawlings, *Epping.*
1904. Rees, John Valentine, *Ammanford.*
1923. Rees, Rufus Price, *Brecon.*
1922.§Rees, Sybil Maglona, *Trebour-road.*
1923. Rees, Thomas Percy, *St. John's-pk.*
1922. Rees, Thomas Roger, *Cardiff.*
1893. Rees-Thomas,Wm. Hy., *Basingstoke.*
1912. Reeve, Edwd. Gordon, *Queen's Gate.*
1900. Reeve, Ernest Frederick, *Rainhill.*
1899. Reeve, Herbert Midgley, *Southend.*
1891. Reeve, Walter.
1905. Reeve, Walter, *New Zealand.*
1895. Reeves, Albert, *Streatham-hill.*
1920 Reeves,GuyKingham,*Upp.Tulse-hill.*
1888. Reeves, John Kingham, *Tulse-hill.*
1911. Reeves, Thomas Conrad, *Alfriston.*
1903. Regan, Thos. Edward, *Birkdale.*
1905. Reichwald, Max Balzar, *Ashtead.*
1900. Reid, Alfied, *Straits Settlements.*
1898. Reid, Allan George, M C., *Plaistow.*
1901. Reid, Sir A. D., K.B.E., *Welbeck-st.*
1921. Reid, Andrew McKie, *Birkenhead.*
1893. Reid, Arthur Lestock, *Watford.*
1854. Reid, Douglas Arthur, *Westminster.*
1894. Reid, Edgar. *Swansea.*
1909. Reid, Edwd. Douglas W., *Canterbury.*
1885. Reid, Edward Waymouth.
1896. Reid, Ernest Stewart, *R.N.*
1892. Reid, Matthew Alex., *Melbourne.*
1913 §Reid, Minerva Ellen, *Toronto.*
1880. Reid, Norman Macbeth,*Army.*
1890. Reid, Peter Macpherson, *Victoria.*
1903. Reid, Robert Watson, *Woking.*
1894. Reid, Sidney Thomas, *R.N.*
1919 Reikan, William, *Broughton.*
1884. Reily, Charles Cooper, C.B., *A.M.S.*
1890. Reilly, Fredk. Bradshaw, *Vict.-pk -rd.*
1905. Reilly, Percy George, *Globe-road.*
12106

1884. Reily, Alexander Yates, *R.A.M.C.*
1913. Reinhardt-Goodwin,C.G., *Barrasford*
1903. Reinhold, Carl Henry, *I.M.S.*
1921. Reith, John, *Gower-street.*
1918. Reitz, Francis William.
1899. Relph, Arthur Ernest, *Wimpole-st.*
1897. Relph, Herbert John, *Wimpole-street.*
1885. Relton, Bernard, *Rugby.*
1920. Remington, William, *West Dulwich.*
1920. Renall, Montague Henry, *Acton.*
1886. Rendall, P. J., O.B.E., *Moorgate-st.*
1906. Rendall, Rbt. Montgom., *Nottingham.*
1905. Rendall,Saml.Shuttleworth,*Salisbury*
1878. Rendall, Stanley Morton, *Mentone.*
1889. Rendel, Arth. Bowen, *Norfolk-cres.*
1918.§Rendel,Frances Elinor, *Courtfield-rd.*
1891. Rendle, Anstruther Cardew, *Uganda.*
1893. Rendle, Arthur Russel, *Chichester.*
1880. Renner, Charles, *Montrose-avenue.*
1918. Rennie, Dennis Charles, *Edgbaston.*
1887. Rennie, George Edward, *Sydney.*
1914. Rennie, Henry Chas. Cadell,*Adelaide.*
1878. Rennie, Saml. Jas.,C.I E., *R.A.M.C.*
1889. Rennie, William, *Birmingham.*
1892. Renny, Eustace George, *Colchester.*
1898. Renshaw, Graham, *Sale.*
1907. Renshaw, John Allister, *R.A.M.C.*
1862. Renshaw, Joshua Wm., *Stretford.*
1910. Renton,Harold Ferdinand,*Harrogate.*
1879. Rentoul, Robert Reid, *Liverpool.*
1893. Rentzsch, Sigism. Henry, *Launceston.*
1912. Retallack-Moloney, H. T., *Forest-gate.*
1923. Reuvid, Leslie, *Finchley-road.*
1881. Revell, George Toms, *Yelverton.*
1894. Revell, Hugh Stanley, *Wimbledon.*
1919. Revell Rowan Wm., *Elgin-avenue.*
1886. Revely, Jos. Smith, *Weston-s.-Mare.*
1904. Rew, George Russell, *Andover.*
1923.§Rex, Phyllis Marjorie, *Highgate.*
1904. Rey, Jules Frederick, *Bognor.*
1912. Reynell, Walter Rupert, *S. Australia.*
1891. Reynolds,Austin E.,*Finsbury-ch'mb'rs*
1919. Reynolds, Benn Roland, *Cardiff.*
1894. Reynolds,Bernard Gore,*Montgomery.*
1899. Reynolds, Bryan Ellis, *Horusey.*
1904. Reynolds, Cecil Edward, *Norfolk-st.*
1908. Reynolds, Douglas, *R.A M.C.*
1888. Reynolds, Ernest Jas., *Barry-road.*
1883. Reynolds, Ernest Sept., *Manchester.*
1895. Reynolds, Frank Ernest, *Watford.*
1917. Reynolds, Frank Neon, *Sutton.*
1922. Reynolds, Harry Edwd. King, *York.*
1880. Reynolds, Harry Williams, *York.*
1922 §Reynolds, Hilda Elizabeth, *Bristol.*
1869. Reynolds, John, *Brixton-hill.*
1901. Reynolds, Leethem, *I.M.S.*
1897. Reynolds, Leonard Grugeon, *Balham.*

1908. Reynolds, Lewis L. C., D.S.O.
1878. Reynolds, Lewis Wm.,*High Wycombe*
1907. Reynolds, Russell John, *Streatham.*
1912. Reynolds, Walter Alex., *Gillygate.*
1912. Reynolds, Walter Graham, *China.*
1910. Reynolds, William, *Great Crosby.*
1911. Reynolds, William Alfred, *Poole.*
1915. Reynolds, William L. E., M.C.
1876. Reynolds, William Percy, *Malvern.*
1894. Rhind, Thomas, *Hawkesbury Upton.*
1909. Rhodes, Arthur, *Bingley.*
1909. Rhodes, Edw. Ll. Noott, *Bridgnorth.*
1918.§Rhodes, Florence Mildred, *Grange.*
1900. Rhodes, Fred Schofield, *Thornton-*
1917. Rhodes, Herbert Eyton, *St. Albans.*
1880. Rhodes, James H. Alex., *R.A.M.C.*
1881. Rhodes, Thomas, *Dudley.*
1909. Rhodes, Wm. Frederick, *Bridgnorth.*
1919. Rhys, Rupert Idris, *Whitchurch.*
1916. Rhys, Trefor Hughes, *Kidwelly.*
1923. Riad, Mohammed M., *Golder's-green.*
1881. Rice, Bernard, O B E., *Leamington.*
1898. Rice, David, *Hellesdon.*
1879. Rice, Edward, *Allesley.*
1905. Rice, Frank Melville P., *W.Af.M.S.*
1879. Rice, George, *Bideford.*
1911. Rice, Henry Goulding, *Bideford.*
1899. Rice,Hubert Richd , *Bank of Adelaide.*
1921. Rice, Lewis Melville, *Vancouver.*
1882. Rice, Richard, *Stevenston.*
1902. Rice, Thos. Harper, *Colorado, U.S.A*
1909. Rice-Oxley, Douglas G., M.C.
1880. Rich, Evelyn Arthur, *Marlow.*
1903. Richard, George Herbert, *R.A. M.C.*
1919. Richards, Arthur Hywel, *Bargoed.*
1922. Richards, Beresford Tom, *Burton.*
1905. Richards, David Harold, *Ditchling.*
1915. Richards, Douglas Oliver, *Richmond.*
1922. Richards,Edward Horace, *Streatham*
1912. Richards, Evan David, *Cardiff.*
1899. Richards, Geo. Maurice Oswald, *R.N.*
1888. Richards, George Oliver.
1885. Richards, Geo. William, *Camberwell.*
1891. Richards, Harold Meredith, *Cardiff.*
1922. Richards, Harry, *Maida-vale.*
1913. Richards,HughAugustine, *Llangollen.*
1900. Richards,JohnEvans,*Stoke Newington.*
1912. Richards, John F. G., *Guy's-hospital*
1890. Richards, Joseph Stewart, *Croydon*
1917.§Richards, Noel Olivier, *Caroline-pl.*
1890. Richards, Norman Lloyd, *Lyme Regis*
1898. Richards, Ramsey Martyn, *R.N.*
1890. Richards, Richd. Walt., *Llandudno.*
1886. Richards, Thomas, *Cardiff.*
1893. Richards, Walter Guyon, *Burgess-h.*
1919. Richards, Wm. Arthur, *Llanelly.*
1915. Richards, Wm K. A., M.C., *Clifton.*

1916. Richardson, Alan Harvey, O.B.E.
1887. Richardson, Alfd. Ernest, Tamworth.
1875. Richardson, Arthur, West Australia.
1902. Richardson, Arthur Hy. Sims, R.N.
1910. Richardson, Cecil Geo ,Loughborough.
1867. Richardson, Charles, Leeds.
1880. Richardson, Charles Board, Hove.
1917. Richard-on,D. Wm.R.,Saxmundham.
1916. Richardson, Edm. Douglas, Brockley.
1891. Richardson, Horace, Commercial-rd.
1899. Richardson, Irwin Browne, Grinshll.
1911. Richardson, James Freer, Upper-st.
1880. Richardson, James Nowell, Ilkley.
1914. Richardson, James Wilson, Alberta.
1919. Richardson, John C. R., Lond.-hosp.
1921. Richardson, Philip L , Norwood.
1900. Richardson, Reg. Percy, Wellingboro'.
1909. Richardson, Robert Samuel, Toronto.
1861. Richardson, Timothy, Bournemouth.
1876. Richardson,Thos.Arth.,CombeMartin.
1898. Richardson, Walter S., Boscombe.
1889. Richardson,Wm., Union Mills, I.ofM.
1909. Riches, Reginald George, Catfield.
1902. Richmond, Arthur, M.C., Liverpool.
1915. Richmond, Arthur Eaton, O B.E.
1896. Richmond, Benj. Arth., Rotherhithe.
1897. Richmond, Reginald Thos., Seascale.
1863. Richmond, Sylvester, Greenhithe.
1900. Rickard, Cecil Rodney, R.N.
1923.§Rickard, Esther M. E , Croydon.
1922.§Rickards, Esther, St. Mary's-hosp.
1899. Ricketts, Arthur, C.M.G., Gordon-sq.
1906. Rickman, Hubert Geo., Blandford.
1902. Riddell, James, S. Australia.
1896. Riddett, Albert John, Leicester.
1914. Riddett, Stanley Alf., M.C., Redhill.
1894. Riddick, Geo. Bushman, R A.M.C.
1917. Riddiough, Sidney, Bingley.
1905. Ridewood,VivianErn.,Bethnal-gn.-rd.
1905. Ridge, Robert Leslie, Enfield.
1912. Ridge-Jones, Ivor, Chesham-place.
1896. Ridgeway-Macauley, W. G.
1923. Riding, Douglas, Ormskirk.
1922.§Ridout, Constance E., Hanover-sq.
1894. Ridsdale,Arth.Errington,Rottingdean.
1922. Rieley,Stan. Desmond, Lanark-villas.
1907. Rigby, Claude Mallinson, R.A.M.C.
1881. Rigby, John, Preston.
1922. Rigby, John Wilfred, Barnsley.
1885. Rigby, John William, Chorley.
1894. Rigby, Morris Notley Jn., Brighton.
1879. Rigden, Brian, Canterbury.
1912. Rigden, Geo. FitzPatrick, M.C.
1870. Rigden, Walter, Thanloe-place.
1910. Rigg, Ern E.AndrewT ,Kentish Town.
1913. Rigg, Henry Charles, Richmond.
1895. Rigg, Samuel Edward, Carlisle.
12277

1887. Rigg, Vincent John, Eastbourne.
1916. Riggall, Paul Rigauld, Sutton-on-Sea
1915. Riggall, Robert M., Royal Navy.
1906. Rigoulet, Marie Jos. Jean R., Pau.
1915. Rihan, Alex. Iskander, St. Bart's-h.
1897. Riley, Arthur, Sale.
1879. Riley, Jas. Woodward, Pontesbury.
1886. Riley, Roland John, Kenilworth.
1923. Riley, R nald, Brook-green.
1388. Rilot, Chas. Fredk., Wimpole-street.
1890. Ringrose, Ernest, Newark.
1881. Riordan, Daniel, Walsall.
1911. Rippon, Thos. Stanley, O.B.E., Leeds.
1886. Risdon, Wm. Elliot, Finchley.
1922. Rishworth,Henry Richd.,Hampstead.
1880. Risk, Edmund Jn. Erskine, R.A.M.C.
1877. Risk, Reg. Rodd Tudor, Pall Mall.
1872. Ritchie, James, Edinburgh.
1875. Ritchie, John Lichenstein, R.A.M. C.
1904. Ritchie, Russell Ian, New Zealand.
1870. Ritchie, William, Barnsley.
1885. Ritson, Robert, Reading.
1913. Rivera, José Eduardo, Peru.
1906. Rivers, Arthur Tunna, Royal Navy.
1898. Rivers, Charles Henry.
1915. Rivers,Stanley,Capital & Counties Bk.
1898. Rivers,WalterCourtenay,Barrasford.
1898. Riviere, Clive, Queen Anne-street.
1906. Rivington, Chas. Sangster, China.
1916.§Rivington, Ev-leen B. G., Epping.
1891. Rix, Francis Wm., W. Hampstead.
1911. Rixon, Chris. Hugh Leete, Lowestoft.
1886. Roach, G. Ernest.
1897. Roach, Sidney, Royal Navy.
1923. Roach-Smith, C. E., Sawbridgeworth.
1896. Roache, William Henry, Ilkeston.
1904. Roaf, Herbert Eldon, St. Mary's-hosp.
1912. Robbins, Frank Hubert, M.C.
1904. Robbins, Reginald Hy., Kensington.
1888. Robbins, Tom Wiltshire, Ipswich.
1900. Robbs.Chas HaldaneDenny,Grantham
1913. Robbs, Francis Charles, M.C.
1872. Roberson, Edward, Tewkesbury.
1920. Robert, Earl Leslie, Camden-road.
1909. Robert, Joseph Xavier, Toronto, Can.
1885. Roberton, Ernest, Auckland, N.Z.
1923. Roberton, John Arthur Wilkie.
1893. Roberts, Alfred Dean, Shrewsbury.
1887. Roberts, Alfd. Ernest, I.M.S.
1885. Roberts, Arthur, Reading.
1883. Roberts, Arthur Henry, W. Malling.
1888. Roberts, Astley C., Eastbourne.
1900. Roberts, Bernard H. St. Clair, Dudley.
1895. Roberts, Cecil David Dale, Dursley.
1909. Roberts, Chas. Dudley, Cape Colony.
1916. Roberts, Charles Young, Westminster.
1883. Roberts, Edward, Aberystwyth.
12334

1889. Roberts, Edwd.Augustus,*Lowndes-rd.*
1919. Roberts, Edwd. Doug. T.,*Lowndes-st.*
1898. Roberts, Edward Hugh, *Battersea.*
1863. Roberts, Edwin, *Queensland.*
1884. Roberts, Edwin, *Leeds.*
1896. Roberts, Edwin Shelton, *Pen-y-groes.*
1905. Roberts, Ellis James, *Chiswick.*
1904. Roberts, Emmanuel, *Ceylon.*
1903. Roberts, Ernest, *Peckham-rye.*
1917. Roberts,Ernest Digby,*King Geo.-hosp.*
1912. Roberts, Ffrangcon, *Cambridge.*
1890. Roberts, Francis Hry., *Forest-hill.*
1891. Roberts, Frank Allan, *Brighouse.*
1904. Roberts, Fred. E., D.S.O., *R.A.M.C.*
1885. Roberts,Geo. Aug. Edward,*Twyford.*
1890. Roberts, George Edwin.
1912. Roberts, George Henry, *Hurlingham.*
1913. Roberts,George Marsden, *Winchester.*
1921. Roberts, Gordon Hussey, *Croydon.*
1877. Roberts, Henry William, *St. Johns.*
1893. Roberts, Hugh Corrall,*M'lton Mowb'y.*
1885. Roberts, Hugh Jones, *Pen-y-groes.*
1923. Roberts, Jas. Arnold Lanson, *Pilning.*
1923. Roberts, John, *Aigburth.*
1905. Roberts, Jn. Chambers L., *Ruabon.*
1869. Roberts, John Dungey, *Ealing.*
1899. Roberts, John Haselwood, *Cambridge.*
1884. Roberts,John Saund.Hughes,*Swansea.*
1918. Robetts,John Saund Lewis.*Swansea.*
1888. Roberts, John William, *Thirsk.*
1889. Roberts, Kilham, *Shillington.*
1920. Roberts, Leon. Ignatius, *Mangalose.*
1897. Roberts,Llewellyn W.,*Cowra,N.S.W.*
1890. Roberts, Llewelyn, *Pontypridd.*
1880. Roberts, Oswald, *Harlesden.*
1921. Roberts, Owen A. Ll., *Cambridge-gds.*
1884. Roberts,OwenWm.,*Cambridge-g'd'ns.*
1920. Roberts, Owen Wm., *Thornton-heath.*
1906. Roberts,PhilipMeredith,*NetleyAbbey.*
1880. Roberts, Reginald, *Napton, Rugby.*
1906. Roberts, R. Cadwaladr, *Wymeswold.*
1888. Roberts, Richd. Lewis, *Highbury.*
1892. Roberts, Sidney John,*Shaftesbury-av.*
1884. Roberts, S. M. Pearson, *Bloomsbury.*
1918. Roberts, Theodore Ernest, *Glasgow.*
1912. Roberts, Theodore Essex, *Reigate.*
1904. Roberts,Thos. Howard Fdk.,*Dulwich.*
1908. Roberts,Wm.Edgar,*Roy.Aust.Navy.*
1921. Roberts, Wm. Goodacre.*Liverpool.*
1876. Roberts, Wm. Stewart W., *New Zeal.*
1912. Robertson, Alex. Roche.
1921. Robertson, Angus, *Sydenham.*
1890. Robertson, Christopher, *Cape Colony.*
1881. Robertson, C. A. James.
1922. Robertson, Douglas, *Leeds.*
1895. Robertson, Fredk. Wm., *Bletchingly.*
1888. Robertson, Geo. Arbuth., *Holmwood.*

1902. Robertson, George Struan, *Dulwich.*
1893. Robertson, Geo. Watson, *Cape Town*
1914. Robertson, Granville D., *Bray.*
1911. Robertson, Hermann M., C.B.E.
1920.§ Robertson, Isab Ila McD., *Glasgow.*
1882. Robertson, James.
1896. Robertson, James, *Tulse-hill.*
1901. Robertson, Jas. Fenwick, *Doncaster.*
1884. Robertson, Jas. Sprent, *Kensington.*
1909. Robertson,Jas.Stauley,*Winchmore-h.*
1888. Robertson. John, *Streatham-hill.*
1903. Robertson, Lorne Forbes, *Ontario.*
1916. Robertson, Miles Kenneth, *Ventnor.*
1885. Robertson, Robert Smith, *Bolton.*
1899. Robertson, William, *New Zealand.*
1904. Robertson, William E., *Milton, Ont.*
1905. Robertson,Wm.Graeme,*Abch'rch-lane*
1894. Robertson, William John, *Clapham.*
1872. Robey, Ralph Pryme, *Wandsworth.*
1903. Robins, John Norman, *Rochester.*
1888. Robinson, Abraham H., *Bradford.*
1882. Robinson, Alfred, *Rotherham.*
1896. Robinson, Arthur, *Edinburgh.*
1898. Robinson, Arthur Cecil, *Brixton-rd.*
1858. Robinson, Augustus, *Nova Scotia.*
1901. Robinson, Benj. J. Adolph., *Jamaica.*
1886. Robinson, Bernard, *Stafford.*
1914. Robinson, Cecil Arthur, *Ludlow.*
1896. Robinson, Chas. Allen, *Leominster.*
1895. Robinson, Chas. Henry James, *R.N.*
1902. Robinson, Christian Cathcart, *Rugby.*
1867. Robinson, Edmund. *Leeds.*
1888. Robinson, Edwd. Stanley, *Stourport.*
1876. Robinson, Ernest Laurie, *Guernsey.*
1908. Robinson, Fras. Harry, *Transvaal.*
1893. Robinson, Frederick Cecil, *Sutton.*
1903. Robinson, Frederick Cecil, *R.N.*
1914. Robinson, Geoffrey S., *Sunderland.*
1861. Robinson, George, *Bedford.*
1892. Robinson, George Burton, *Liverpool.*
1916. Robinson, Geo. Cuthbert, *R.A.M.C.*
1896. Robinson, Geo. Edward J. A., M.C.
1889. Robinson,Geo.HenkellD.,*Seymour-st.*
1879. Robinson, Geo. Somerville, *A.M.S.*
1923. Robinson, G. Twernlow,*W.Didsbury.*
1876. Robinson, George W.,*C.B.,R.A.M.C.*
1903. Robinson, Harold Joseph, *Kirkoswald.*
1919. Robinson, Harold Shillito, *Epsom*
1861. Robinson, Haynes Sparrow, *Norwich.*
1893. Robinson, Henry James, *Burnley.*
1881. Robinson, Hugh Shapter,*Peckham-rd.*
1873. Robinson, James, *Bolton.*
1915. Robinson, James Albert, *Nelson.*
1899. Robinson, Jas. Herbt., *R.A.M.C.*
1920. Robinson, James Scott, *Dover.*
1898. Robinson, John Elliott, *Dorchester.*
1899. Robinson, Jn. Hugh R.,*Birmingham*

1883. Robinson, Louis, *Streatham.*
1923. Robinson, Morris, *Commercial-road.*
1890. Robinson, Oliver Long, C.M G.
1917. Robinson, Ralph Leslie, *Kensington.*
1878. Robinson,S.ChapmanBates,*R.A.M.C.*
1888. Robinson, Thomas, *Leicester.*
1892. Robinson, Waring, *Peckham.*
1881. Robinson,WilfordVidal,*Cambridge-st*
1894. Robinson, Wm. Edward, *Hertford-st.*
1902. Robson, Hy.Naunton,*Nat.Prov.Bank.*
1885. Robson, Herbert John, *Leeds.*
1908. Robson,HubertAlanH.,*Grindlay&Co.*
1895. Robson, Thos. Stretton, *Waterbeach.*
1901. Robson, Wm. Morton, *Northampton.*
1883. Robson, Wm. Waller C., *Chiswick.*
1899. Roch, Horace S., C.M.G., D.S.O.
1922. Roche, Alex. Ernest, *Fernshaw-rd.*
1900. Roche, A. Reginald, M.C.,*Queen's-cr.*
1870. Roche, Eleazer Birch, *Norwich.*
1906. Roche, Ivan Joseph, *Coulsdon.*
1915. Roche,LaurenceS.C.,M.C.,*R.A.M.C.*
1899. Roche, Nelson Joseph, *R.N.*
1894. Roche, Redmond John, *Eccleston-sq.*
1892. Rock, Cecil Howard, *Royal Navy.*
1893. Rock, Ernest Albert, *Leeds.*
1876. Rockliffe, William Craven, *Hull.*
1891. Rockstro, Frank Braine, *Wimbledon.*
1902. Rockwood, David Pratt, *Ceylon.*
1916. Rodd, Arthur, *Yelverton.*
1891. Rodd, Mont. Louis B., O.B.E., *R.N.*
1898. Roderick, Hy. B., O.B.E., *Cambridge.*
1891. Rodgers, Rbt. Isaac Craig, *Burnley.*
1882. Rodley, John, *Rochdale.*
1883. Rodman, George Hook,*Putney-heath.*
1902. Rodrigo, William Paul, *Ceylon.*
1913. Rodrigues, Gabriel Fras.,*Bishopsgate.*
1899. Rodriguez, J. D.
1882. Roe, Arthur Dumville, *Putney.*
1910. Roe, Arthur Stanley, *Brisbane, Aust.*
1914. Roe, Clive Watney, M.C., *Gipsy-hill.*
1894. Roe, Edwin Ernest Wm., *Hambledon.*
1862. Roe, Edwin Hodgson, *Wandsworth.*
1884. Roe, Montagu Walter, *Penryn.*
1881. Roe, Robert Bradley, *Ipsden, Oxon.*
1912. Roe, Robert Bradley. *Ispden, Oxon.*
1923. Roffey, Bernard Wilson, *Gillingham.*
1891. Roger-Smith, Hugh R., *College-cres.*
1921. Rogers, Alfred Talbot, *Chudleigh-rd.*
1895. Rogers, Arth. Anderson, *Woolston.*
1889. Rogers, Bertram Mitford H., *Bristol.*
1857. Rogers, Braithwaite, *Piccadilly.*
1871. Rogers, Chas. Claude, *Harley-street.*
1873. Rogers, Edward Coulton, *Ivybridge.*
1900. Rogers, E. Norman Tilly, *Mullion.*
1900. Rogers, Frederick Colin, *I.M.S.*
1895. Rogers, Fredk. Edwd., *Bethnal-green*
1865. Rogers, Henry Cripps, *Lympstone.*

12505

1919. Rogers, John Southmead, *Modbury.*
1893. Rogers, Kenneth, O.B.E., *Bromley.*
1920. Rogers, Lambert C., *Cambridge-st.*
1897. Rogers, Reginald James, *Bath.*
1891. Rogers, Wm. Gusterson, *Transvaal.*
1909. Rogerson, Cecil John, M.C., *Lewes.*
1904. Rogerson, Frederick, *Morley, Leeds.*
1881. Rogerson, Jn. Thomas, *I. of Man.*
1914. Rogerson, Wm. Albert, *Preston.*
1918.§Rolfe, Gwendolen Mary, *Bowes-park.*
1890. Rollason, Abel, *Heidelberg, Victoria.*
1909. Rolleston, Christopher.
1893. Rolleston, L.Wm., C.B.E., D S.O.
1909. Rollinson, Harry Dudley, O.B.E.
1908. Rolls, Allison Mont, *Toronto, Ont.*
1910. Rolph, Albert Hill, *Toronto.*
1879. Rolston, Jn. Restarick, *Plymouth.*
1897. Roman, Alphonse Hy., *Berlin.*
1875. Romano, F. W. Richard, *Brazil.*
1894. Romer, Frank, *Seymour-street.*
1894. Romer, Harry, *St. Leonards-on-Sea.*
1892. Romer, Rbt. L.,O.B.E.,*Gt. Stanmore.*
1890. Ronald, Arthur Edwin, *Leadenhall-st.*
1910. Ronaldson, Jas. Bruce, *Beaconsfield.*
1891. Ronaldson, Rbt. Miller, *Edinburgh.*
1880. Roocroft, Wm. Mitchell, *Wigan.*
1906. Rood, Felix Stephens, *Canonbury.*
1915. Rook, Alan Filmer, *Streatham.*
1883. Rook, Albert Edward, *Eastbourne.*
1912. Rook, Henry Colwell, *Streatham.*
1921 §Rooke, Edith Marjorie, *Whetstone.*
1892. Rooke, Ernest Morley, *Piccadilly.*
1900. Rooke, Fdk. Jas. Faulkland,*Newbury.*
1901. Rooke, Wm. Stanley, *North Finchley.*
1906. Roome, Alfred Martin, *Gt. Grimsby.*
1921.§Roope, Mary Frances, *Hampstead.*
1901. Rooth, Jas. Augustus, *Brighton.*
1874. Roots, Wm. Henry, *Kingston-on-Th.*
1909. Rope, Arthur Denys, *Shrewsbury.*
1880. Roper, Arthur Charles, *Exeter.*
1909. Roper, Frank Arthur, *Exeter.*
1887. Roper, Herbert John, *Leeds.*
1901. Roper,Richd.S.,*British North Borneo.*
1919. Roper-Hall, Harry Thos., *Moseley.*
1901. Rorke, Robert Francis, *Canada.*
1922. Rose, Charles Vincent Douglas.
1918. Rose, Edward Snow, *Burnet.*
1898. Rose, Frank Herbert, *Bristol.*
1911. Rose, Frederic G., *Br. Guiana, M.S.*
1923. Rose, Harold Norman, *Hackney.*
1896. Rose, Horace, *Aylesbury.*
1923. Rose, Max, *Rotherham.*
1919. Rose, Samuel, *Guy's-hospital.*
1898. Rose, Samuel Frank.
1903. Rose, Thomas, *Bloomsbury-street.*
1920. Rose, William George, *Hanwell.*
1917. Rose-Innes, Arthur, *Acton.*

12562

1921. Rosenberg, Isaac.
1917.§Rosenberg, Sophie S., *King's Cross-rd.*
1909. Rosewarne, David Davey, *Bow, E.*
1913. Rosher, Arthur Burch, *Sheffield-terr.*
1904. Ross, Alexander, *Crediton.*
1898. Ross, Alexander Michael, *Mayfield*
1903. Ross, Donald Murray, *Victoria.*
1912. Ross, Douglas, *Brighton.*
1874. Ross, Douglas McKissock, *Brighton.*
1898. Ross, Edward Halford, *Cairo.*
1905. Ross, George William, *Toronto.*
1898. Ross, Hugh Campbell, *Curzon-street.*
1901. Ross, James MacBain, *N.S.W.*
1918.§Ross, Joan Margaret, *Paddington.*
1897. Ross, Murdoch Wm., *Petone, N.Z.*
1901. Ross, Percy Alexander, *Boscombe.*
1900. Ross, Philip Hedgeland, *Uganda.*
1911. Ross, William Dallas, *St Asaph.*
1872. Ross, William Grahame, *Watford.*
1917. Rossdale, Geo. H., *Pembridge-villas.*
1869. Rosser, Walter, *Horley.*
1921. Rossiter, Fredk. Magee, *Los Angeles.*
1908. Rossiter, Harold T., *St.Thomas's-hosp.*
1895. Rost, Ernest Reinhold, O.B E ,*I.M.S.*
1893. Rostant, André Arsène, *Tottenham.*
1905. Rosten, Leslie Martin, *Birmingham.*
1872. Rosten, Wm. Martin, *Birmingham.*
1917.§Roth, Helen, *Enfield.*
1881. Roth, ReuterEmerich, D.S.O.,*Sydney.*
1892. Roth, Walt. Edmund, *Queensland.*
1896. Rothwell, Thos. Andrew, *Hale.*
1886. Roughton, John Paul, *Kettering.*
1897. Rouillard, Jean Antoine Abel, *Natal.*
1891. Round, Jn. Cornwell, *Sydenham.*
1899. Rouse, Algernon Edward, *Worthing*
1890. Rouse, Eusebius Rouse, *Frant.*
1883. Rouse, Rolla Edward, *Harley-street.*
1921. Roushdy, Abdel R., *Denmark-hill.*
1910. Rousseau, Johannes Z. H.,*Middelburg.*
1880. Routh, Amand.J.McC.,*Manchester-sq.*
1887. Routh, Charles Frederick, *Southsea.*
1909. Routh, Laurence M., *Bryanston-sq.*
1890. Routh,RandolphH.Felix,*Bridgwater.*
1904. Routley, Edwin Walter, *Aldershot.*
1904. Routly, Ernest Sydney, *Woolwich*
1889. Rouw, Robert Wynne, *Wimpole-st.*
1913. Roux, Pierre, *Cape Province.*
1899. Row, Charles Martin, *Chipstead.*
1899. Row, Edward Reginald, *Queensland.*
1881. Row, Frederick Everard, *Salcombe.*
1917. Rowan, Henry, *St. Alban's.*
1876. Rowbotham, Arth. Jos , *Handsworth.*
1894. Rowbotham,Edgar Joseph, *Clapham.*
1915. Rowbotham,EdgarStanley,*Clapham.*
1891. Rowbotham,IIbt.Barnwell,*Birm'h'm.*
1914. Rowcroft,G. F.,D.S.O.,*Gundlay§ Co.*
1883. Rowe, Arthur Walton, *Margate.*
12619

1877. Rowe,Bernard Meredith,*Compton-ter*
1897. Rowe, William Trethowan, M.C.
1884. Rowell, George Ball, *California.*
1915. Rowell, Harold Arth, M.C., *Torquay.*
1882. Rowell, Herbert Ellis, *E. Rudham.*
1892. Rowell, John George, *Huddersfield.*
1918. Rowland, Charles Cecil.
1869. Rowland, Edwd. Roger, *Wodehouse.*
1899. Rowland,Edwd. W.Spencer,*Reading.*
1891. Rowland, Frank Mortimer, C.B.E.
1896. Rowland, Frederic Samuel, *Chester.*
1896. Rowland, Fredk. Wm., *Wroxham.*
1917. Rowland, John, M.C , *Richmond.*
1883. Rowland, John Jones, *Aberystwith.*
1898. Rowland,LewisThos.Arch.,*Lampeter.*
1898. Rowland, Perry Wm., *Colchester.*
1895. Rowland, Walter John, *Brighton.*
1880. Rowlands, Hugh Pugh, *Towyn.*
1921. **Rowlands**, John Jenkin, *Ladbroke-gr.*
1907. Rowlands, John Sydney, *Cardiff.*
1901. Rowlands, Moses John,*Knightsbridge.*
1911. Rowlands, R. Alun, O.B.E.,*Anglesey.*
1906. Rowlands,Rchd.Pugh,*QueenAnne-st.*
1896. Rowlands,Wm.Herbert, *Bromsgrove.*
1916. Rowlands, Wm. Richard, *Anglesey.*
1881. Rowley, Charles, *Otahuhu, N.Z.*
1893. Rowley, Oswald Francis, *Barnsley.*
1906. Rowntree, Sidney John, *Islington.*
1891. Rows, Richard Gundry, C.B.E.
1890. Rowse, Edward Leopold, *Putney.*
1893. Rowstron, N. Florentine, *Sunderland.*
1912. Roxburgh, Archibald C., *Hampstead.*
1886. Roxburgh, David, *Seymour-street.*
1882. Roy, Siva Prasad, *Calcutta.*
1893. Royden, William, *Gt. Yarmouth.*
1896. Rozelaar, AbrahamLevie,*Hampstead.*
1892. Rubra, Henry Homer, *Crouch-end.*
1883. Ruck, David Naunton, *Ealing.*
1884. Ruck,John Ernest,*Sandbach,Cheshire.*
1892. Rudall, James Ferdinand, *Victoria.*
1891. Rudd, Arthur, *Old Kent Road.*
1881. Rudd, Chas. Frederick, *Stalham.*
1888. Rudd, William Arthur, *Acton.*
1886. Ruddock, Wm. Jas., *Newcastle-on-T.*
1874. Rudduck, Jn. Burton, *West Mersea.*
1923.§Ruddy, May Kathleen, *Catford.*
1869. Rudge, Charles King, *Bristol.*
1904. Rudge, Fredk. Henry, *Lostwithiel.*
1905. Rudkin, Gerald F., D.S.O., *R.A.M.C.*
1915. Rudkin, Gordon W. R., M.C.
1921. Rudolf, G. R. A. de M., *Denmark-hill.*
1889. Rudyard, Henry Ashton, *Watford.*
1880. Ruel, Chas. Percival, *Southsea.*
1901. Rugg, Godfrey Faussett, *R.A.M.C.*
1874. Rugg, Harold, *Temuka, New Zealand.*
1882. Rumboll, Chas. Frederic, *Melksham.*
1918. Rumboll, Norman, *Leeds.*
12676

1907. Rumsey, Cecil Frank, *Cambridge*.
1895. Rundle, Claude, *Liverpool*.
1880. Runnalls, Harry Boyle.
1912. Runting, E. Arthur, *N.Burlington-st*.
1922. Rupasingha, Bane C. de S., *Ceylon*.
1908. Rupp, Karl, *Harley-street*.
1896. Rusby, Edwd.L.Macpherson,*Brixton*.
1885. Rushbrooke, Thomas, *Stamford-hill*.
1914. Rushworth,Arthur Norman, *Walton*.
1880. Rushworth, Frank, *South Hampstead*.
1880. Rushworth, Norman, *Walton-on-Th*.
1903. Russ, Charles, *Beaum mt-st*.
1889. Russel-Rendle, Chas.Edm.,*New Zeal*.
1893. Russell, Alfred Ernest, *Wimpole-st*.
1922.§Russell, Dorothy Stuart, *Royston*.
1872. Russell, Edgar Geer.
1908. Russell, Edm. Neptune, *Limerick*.
1912. Russell, Edmund Uniacke, M.C.
1918.§Russell, Elizabeth Dill, *Cape Town*.
1905. Russell, Francis John, *Greenwich*.
1912. Russell, George Andrew, *Oldbury*.
1879. Russell, Geo. Hannah, *Manchester*.
1836. Russell, George Herbert, *Upton-pk*.
1917. Russell, Henry Bret, *Twickenham*.
1876. Russell, James, *Sandhurst*.
1919. Russell, John Clement, *St. James's*.
1881. Russell, Jn. Hutchinson, *Romford-rd*.
1892. Russell, John Ronaldson,*Westerham*.
1882. Russell, Sir Michael Wm., K.C.M.G.
1916. Russell, Percy Gunn, *Acton*.
1916 §Russell, Violet Ione, *Twickenham*.
1911. Russell, Wilfred Alan,*Gt.Ormond-st*.
1887. Rust, John, M.B.E., *Manchester*.
1917. Rustomijee, Khurshedjee J.,*Colombo*.
1894. Rutherford,Alfd.Ernest Raif,*Kilburn*.
1891. Rutherford, George James, *Ceylon*.
1917. Rutherford, John D., *R.N*.
1887. Rutherford,Jn.V.W.,*Newcastle-on-T*.
1903. Rutherford,Randolph H. N.,*Devonp'rt*
1905. Rutherford, James Edmund, M.C.
1921. Rutnam, Alan Raja, *Middlesc.x-hosp*.
1900. Ruttledge, Wm. Edwd.,*Wandsworth*.
1860. Ruttledge, William Frederick.
1899. Ruzzak, Shaik Abdur, *I M.S*.
1893. Ryall, Edwd. Canny, *Harley-st*.
1917. Ryan, John Francis, *Brondesbury*.
1901. Ryan, Victor Fowell, *Coulsdon*.
1895. Ryan, W. Bonner.
1892. Ryde, Cyril Alexander, *Ostend*.
1898. Ryder, Claude Clifford, *Cuba*.
1897. Rygate,ArthurMontague, *Wellington*.
1874. Rygate, Broughnm R., *Cannon-st.-rd*
1889. Rygate,C.D.Hartley,*Beecroft,N.S.W*.
1881. Rygate, David John, *Hunstanton*.
1891. Rygate, Hy. Bertram, *Saxmundham*.
1895. Rykeit, Arthur Frederick.
1909. Ryland, Archer, *Wimpole-street*.
1923. 12733

1897. Ryland, Robert Felix.
1913. Ryle, John Alfred, *Brighton*.
1912. Ryley, Charles Meadows, *Yarmouth*.
1918. Rymer, Hugh Thornton.
1923. Ryves, Thomas Evan, *Brockley*.

S.

1910. Sabawala,Behram Pestonjee,*Bombay*.
1914. Sabri, Ahmed, *Egypt. Educ. Mission*.
1922. Sabry, Abd-El-Hakim M., *Egypt*.
1907. Sachs, Alfred Ludovicus, *Wimpole-st*.
1917. Sacks, Samuel, *Stoke Newington*.
1890. Sadler, Ernest Alfred, *Ashbourne*.
1855. Sadler, Michael Thos., *Hammersmith*.
1920. Sadler, Wilfrid Ralph.
1905. Sadler, Wm. Mackenzie, *Slough*.
1916. Sahai, Bishambhar, *Lucknow*.
1917. Sahib, Khan, *Cornwall-road*.
1914. Sai, Pinthu, *St. Thomas's-hospital*.
1909. Said, Ahmed, *Cairo*.
1879. Sainsbury, H.,*O.B.E., Wimpole-st.*
1915. Saint,Arthur Paul,M.C.,*Monkseaton*.
1908. St. John, Alfd. Hy.Valentine, *Sinaia*.
1919. St. John, Charles Herbert, *Guy's-h*.
1873. StJohn,Leonard,*StCatherine,Ontario*.
1898. St. John, Winstan St. Andrew, *Derby*.
1914. St.Johnston,Adrian,*Harrington-gdns*.
1906. St. Johnston, Thomas Reginald, *Fiji*.
1893. St. Stephens, Wm. T., *Golder's-green*.
1907. St. Vincent-Welch, Leslie, *N.S. W*.
1916. Sakoschansky, Ephraim, *Nottingham*.
1923. Salama, Anis, *Golder's-green*.
1900. Salaman, Redcliffe Nathan, *Barley*.
1896. Salaman, Selim Myer, *I.M.S*.
1909. Saldanha, Frederick Francis, *Poona*.
1901. Sale, Jn. Caruthers, D.S.O., M.C.
1923. Salib, Ragheb, *Mansourah, Egypt*.
1888. Salisbury, C. Ramsden, *Rochester*.
1906. Salisbury, Harold Kenneth, *Clifton*
1900. Sall, Ernest Frederick, *Canterbury*.
1906. Salmon, Albert, *Brighton*.
1882. Salmon, Arthur Guy, *Bodmin*.
1883. Salmon,Lawr. Ernest Albt.,*Tavistock*.
1909. Salmon, Norman G. Hawtry, *Bodmin*.
1922.§Salmon, Olive Metcalfe, *Sutton*.
1921.§Salmond, Elaine M. K., *Brunswick sq*.
1904. Salt, Arthur Philip, *Canterbury*.
1909. Salt,Chas. E. Fosbrooke, *Leytonstone*.
1922. Salt, James Samuel, *Richmond*.
1896. Salt, Thomas, *Birmingham*.
1895. Salter, Alfred, *Bermondsey*.
1882. Salter, George Herbert, *Victoria*.
1864. Salter, John Henry, *Witham*.
1893. Salter, Samuel Colley, *Manchester*.
12785 u

1883. Salvage, John Valentine, *Dulwich.*
1916. Samaraweera, Edward E., *Ceylon.*
1894. Sames, John William, *Acton.*
1921. Sami, Abd-el-Rahman, *Streatham.*
1888. Samman, Charles Thos., *R.A.M.C.*
1915. Sampson, Basil, M.C., *Grahamstown.*
1903. Sampson, Bernard Moore, *N.S.W.*
1875. Sampson, Henry Moore, *Cavendish-sq.*
1922.§Samter, Effie F. A., *Withington.*
1899. Samuel, David, *Neath.*
1907. Samuel, Henry Chas., *Walthamstow.*
1914. Samuel, Henry Christmas, *Perak.*
1903. Samuel, Henry Thos., D.S.O., *Cardiff.*
1912. Samuel, Samuel, *Leeds.*
1922. Samuel, Trist.Albt.Seton, *Lond.-hosp.*
1834. Samut, Richard Philip, *Malta.*
1891. Samways, Daniel West, *Mentone.*
1917. Samy, Ahmad Hussein, *St. Bart's.*
1893. Sandall, T. E., C.M.G., *Sutton-on-S.*
1880. Sanders, Charles, *Forest-gate.*
1923.§Sanders, Edna Mary, *Denmark-hill.*
1901. Sanders, Edwd. Arth., *Northampton.*
1868. Sanders, Edwin, *I.M.S., Bengal.*
1911. Sanders, Frederic, M.C., *Forest-gate.*
1900. Sanders, James Herbert, *Hong Kong.*
1907. Sanders, Louis Philip, *Transvaal.*
1904. Sanders, Thomas, *Barnard Castle.*
1909. Sanderson, Arthur F., *Hornchurch.*
1905. Sanderson, Geo. Meredith, *Nyasaland.*
1921.§Sanderson, Maud, *Sheffield.*
1881. Sanderson, Robert, *Brighton.*
1920. Sanderson, Roland E. R., *Bedford.*
1895. Sanderson-Wells, Thos. H., M.B.E.
1922.§Sandes, Gladys M , *Queen Alex. Mans.*
1901. Sandiland, Digby Sayer, *Fulham-rd.*
1905. Sandiland, Ernest L., *Southgate-rd.*
1897. Sandilands,J.Edwd.,M.C.,*Kensington*
1922. Sandler, Samuel, *Dalston.*
1896. Sandner, Adolph, *Bendigo, Victoria.*
1886. Sandoe, John Warden, *Exeter.*
1899. Sanger, Frederick, C.M.G, *Surbiton.*
1916.§Sanger-Davies, Enid E., *St. Leonards.*
1867. Sangster, Charles, *Lambeth-road,*S.E.
1876. Sangster, Jn. Ikin, *Kooringa, S. Aust.*
1897. Sanguinetti, Harold Hbt., *Kensington.*
1908. Sankey, Chas. Fox Octavius, *R.N.*
1886. Sankey, Julius Ivor, *Yarmouth.*
1867. Sankey, Julius Ottaway, *Oxford.*
1922.§Sankey, Norah B.A., *Queensboro-terr.*
1902. Sankey, Richard Harvey, *Oxford.*
1906. Sankey, William Octavius, *Ashburton.*
1902. Sansom, Bertram Eli, *Palmer's-green.*
1883. Sansom,Chas.Lane,C.M.G.,*Malay S.*
1914. Sansom, Eric Arthur L , *Hampstead.*
1923.§Sansom, Ena Mildred, *Hampstead.*
1897. Sansome, Thomas, *West Bromwich.*
1915. Sanyal, Saroz Kumar, *Birmingham.*

12842

1918. Sanzgiri, Vasant Ramrao.
1888. Sapp, John Geo. Victor, *Bedford-st.*
1901. Sapwell, Benj Beckham, *Aylsham.*
1923. Sarafian, Dirtad Haig, *Camden-road.*
1920. Saravanamuttu, Ernest T.
1912. Saravanamuttu, Ratnasothy, *Ceylon.*
1893. Sargant, Wm. Edward, *Chesham.*
1913 Sargent, Eric Lancelot K., *Bristol.*
1890. Sarjant, Frank Percy, *Manchester.*
1893. Sarjeant, John Fredk., *Parkhurst-rd.*
1919. Sarkies, Malcolm, *Ealing.*
1919. Sarra, Edwin Roland, *Redruth.*
1916. Sarra, William Henry, *Redruth.*
1900. Sass, Fredk. J. Wilfrid, *Dalmeney-av.*
1884. Satchell, Chas. George, *New Zealand.*
1911. Satow, Lawrence L.,M.C., *Fellows-rd.*
1922. Satyaraju, Chittoory.
1910. Saul, Alec Linford, *Pretoria.*
1907. Saul, Barnett, *Manchester.*
1923.§Saul, Margaret Vivian, *Withington.*
1889. Saul, Victor Salmon, *Manchester.*
1894. Saunders, Allan Lindsay, *Maida-vale.*
1876. Saunders, Edwd. Argent, *Pembroke.*
1912. Saunders, Edw. Argent, *Pembroke.*
1894. Saunders, Edwd. Arth., *Harley-st.*
1912. Saunders, Eric Graham, *Surbiton.*
1907. Saunders,ErnestAlbert,*Winchmore-h.*
1879. Saunders, Francis Henry, *Jamaica.*
1915. Saunders,Fredk.Josh.P.,*S.Farnboro'.*
1884. Saunders, James Frederick, *Derby.*
1801. Saunders, John Harry, *Sydney.*
1898. Saunders, Leonard Dimock, *Salisbury.*
1902. Saunders, Leonard D., *Tunbdge Wells.*
1905. Saunders, P. Whittington, *Queen-sq.*
1919. Saunders, Robert James, *Lavender-h.*
1907. Saunders,StuartMacKenzie,*R.A.M.C*
1913. Saunders, Wm. Eric R., *Newcastle.*
1923.§Saunders-Jacobs, E. V., *Regent's-pk.*
1914. Saunderson, Alex. Elder, *Liverpool.*
1867. Saundry, James Baynard, *Lewisham.*
1882. Saunt,Thos.Ernest,*Leighton Buzzard.*
1921. Savage, Edward, *Llandinam.*
1922. Savage, Horace Simkin, *Gt. Bridge.*
1917. Savage, John James, *Hampstead.*
1914. Savage, Philip, c/o *Grindlay & Co.*
1894. Savage, William Arthur.
1896. Savage, William Geo., *Weston-s.-M.*
1887. Savery, Frank, *Ealing.*
1918. Savery,Hy.Mearns,*Budleigh Saltert'n.*
1918. Savery,Walt.Manley,*BudleighS'lt rt'n*
1901. Savill, Philip, *Bexhill-on Sea.*
1885. Saville, Hy. Wm. Brooks, *Manchester.*
1923. Savin, Lewis Herbert, *Evesham.*
1915. Savory,Chas.Harley,*Bramham-gdns.*
1887. Savory, Wm. Harmsworth, *N. Kens.*
1885. Saw, Francis Albert, *Army.*
1898. Saward,Arth.Hy.Michael,*Richmond.*

12899

1919. Sawday, Albert Ernest, *Hastings.*
1898. Sawdy, Edward Charles, *Roy. Navy.*
1886. Sawel, Frank L. P., *W. Australia.*
1892. Sawers, Jn. Lorimer, *Margate.*
1908. Sawhney, Mulk Raj, *Grindlay & Co.*
1888. Sawhny, Bhagat Ram, *Lahore.*
1877. Sawyer, Henry, *Bradford.*
1903. Saxby, Charles James Izzard, *Rugby.*
1922.§Saxton, Eileen Margaret, *Ilkley.*
1914. Sayed, Farid Henein Abdel,*Chiswick.*
1878. Sayer, Thomas, *Ampthill-square.*
1913. Sayers,Bernard Edw. P.,*Royal Navy.*
1895. Sayers,Matthew Jas. Hazlitt,*Alsager.*
1871. Scale, George John, *Warwick.*
1880. Scale, Thomas William, *Aberdare.*
1918. Scales, Cedric Kennedy,*Earl's-court.*
1905. Scales, John Edwin, *Radstock.*
1878. Scallon, Ernest Oliver, *Romsey.*
1883. Scanlan, Arthur de Courcy, C.M.G.
1900. Scanlan, Henry, *Montreal.*
1916. Scanlan, James Ernest, *Linthorpe.*
1897. Scanlon, L. E., M.B.E., *Manchester.*
1898. Scaping, Harold Massey.
1905. Scarborough, Oswald Lowndes,*Leeds.*
1911. Scargill, Henry Edwin, *Royal Navy.*
1911. Scargill, Lionel W.K.,*Cambridge-st.*
1911. Scarisbrick, William, *Chester.*
1915. Scarr, Ellis Herbert S., *Littleborough.*
1916. Scarr, Ronald James, *Littleborough.*
1896. Scatchard, Jas. Percival, *Tadcaster.*
1882. Scatchard, Walter, *Brit. Colombia.*
1903. Scatliff, Harold H. Elboro., *Brighton.*
1885. Scatliff, Philip Melancthon, *Dulwich.*
1909. Scawin,Harold W.,O.B.E.,*Fairford.*
1881. Schacht, Frank Fredc., *Cromwell-rd.*
1885. Schade, Julius Hermann A.
1874. Schafer, Sir Edw. Alb. Sharpey,*Edin.*
1904. Schapiraff, Abraham, *Gt. Russell-st.*
1920. Schapiro, Harry N., *Golder's-green.*
1906. Schenck, Edward, *Frankfort.*
1892. Scheurer, Jan Gerrit, *Holland.*
1921. Schiff, Charles Isaac, *Amhurst-rd.*
1923. Schlesinger, Bernard E.,*Fitzjohn's-av*
1914. Schmidt, Paul Hans K. K., *Kew.*
1888. Schnehage, Caleb, *Orange Province.*
1895. Schnöller, Anton, *Switzerland.*
1883. Schofield, Alfd. Taylor, *Harley-st.*
1923. Schofield, Alfred Thompson.
1902. Schofield, Arthur Reginald, *R.N.*
1899. Schofield, Cusack Roney, *Southport.*
1920. Schofield, Frank Paul, *St. Barts.*
1885. Schofield, Gerald, *Chesham Bois.*
1923. Schofield, Jas. Mortimer, *Leinster-sq.*
1914.§Schofield, Mary, *Bow-road.*
1893. Schofield,Saml.Robt.,*Phillimore-g'ds.*
1913. Schokman, Arthur E., *Brompton-h.*
1898. Scholberg, Harold Arthur, *Cardiff.*
12956

1899. Scholberg,Peter Herb.,*Little Britain.*
1898. Scholefield, Ernest Hall, *Barnstaple.*
1914. Scholtz, Claude Justin, *Old Jewry.*
1921. Schonebrom, Carl Gustav, *Clapham.*
1919. Schroeter, Marco Ludwig, *Zurich.*
1909. Schulenburg, August Carl, *Transvaal.*
1902. Schumer, Jacob, *Golders-green.*
1915. Schurr, Christopher Geo , *Petersfield.*
1916 §Schwab, Elisabeth H , *Cricklewood.*
1916. Schwartz, Morris, *Johannesburg.*
1905. Schwarz, Emil, *Vienna.*
1888. Sclater, Nelson Cameron, *Liscard.*
1905. Scoones, Harold Edward, *Hythe.*
1893. Scorer, Frank, M.B.E., *Bournemouth.*
1870. Scoresby-Jackson,Thos.*Walthamstow.*
1895. Scot-Skirving, Arch. A., C.M.G.
1898. Scott, Aleck Lauriston, *R.A.M.C.*
1910. Scott, Alex. R. Prinski, *Edmonton.*
1875. Scott, Alex.T., M.B.E., *Parkhurst-rd.*
1879. Scott, Alfred, *Brighton.*
1888. Scott, Arnold, *Braintree.*
1908. Scott, Arthur Bodley, *Bournemouth.*
1896. Scott, Arthur Eldon, *Cairo.*
1884. Scott, Arthur Wm., *Sheffield.*
1881. Scott, Bernard, *Bournemouth.*
1882. Scott, Bernard Charles, *Doncaster.*
1885. Scott, Bertal H., C.M.G., *A.M.S.*
1899. Scott, Charles Walter, *S. Norwood.*
1912. Scott, David, *Staplehurst.*
1914. Scott, Donald C.,O.B.E., *Twickenham.*
1902. Scott, Edward Spencer, *Hampstead.*
1911. Scott, Emmanuel Prinski, *Tottenham.*
1915. Scott, Eric Arnold, *Finchley.*
1898. Scott, Ernest Harold, *W. Norwood.*
1913. Scott, Evelyn Dennis, O.B.E.,*R.N.*
1892. Scott, Francis Gilbert, *New Malden.*
1912. Scott, Frank Ramsay,*Beeton, Canada.*
1908. Scott, Frank S., *Penzance.*
1914. Scott, Fredk. Gilbert L., *Stafford.*
1885. Scott, George Henry, *Sheffield.*
1906. Scott, Gerald Claude, *Southport.*
1907. Scott, Gilbert Bodley, D.S.O., *R.N.*
1905. Scott, Harold Munro. *Gloucester-terr.*
1897. Scott, Henry Harold, *Jamaica.*
1911. Scott, Henry Wakeman, *Dorking.*
1904. Scott, Herbert Bodley, *I.M.S.*
1917. Scott, James Jules Avit, *Moseley.*
1884. Scott, John, *Edenbridge.*
1918. Scott,John Andrew A P.,*Fletcher-ho.*
1897. Scott,John Geddes, *Madeira.*
1872. Scott, John Walter, *Chelmsford.*
1905. Scott, John Walt. Lennox,*R.A.M.C.*
1876. Scott, John Wm., *Ashton-on-Mersey.*
1912. Scott, Maitland, *Sway, Brockenhurst.*
1901. Scott, Maitland B.,O.B.E.,*R.A M.C.*
1915. Scott, Noel Archibald, *Hampstead.*
1914. Scott, Philip Dennis, *Guy's-hospital.*
13013

1916. Scott, Ralph R., M C., *Tynemouth*.
1889. Scott, Sack Noy, *Plymstock*.
1904. Scott, Sebastian Gilbt., *Cavendish-st*.
1916. Scott, Steuart Noy, *Plymstock*.
1873. Scott, Thomas Bodley, *Bournemouth*.
1892. Scott, Thomas Graham, *Herne-hill*.
1901. Scott. Th mas Walter, *Victoria*.
1888. Scott, Thos. Wilfred, *Southbourne*.
1903. Scott, Walter Henderson, M.C.
1877. Scott, Wm. George, *Auckland, N.Z.*
1905. Scott, Wm. Lockhead, *Liss, Hants*.
1921.§Scott-Moncrieff. M., *Cheyne-walk*.
1911. Scott-Wilson, Hew Wm.,*Auchinleck*.
1876. Scovil, Francis Simonds, *Brighton*.
1897. Scowby, Edward Thos , *Worsley*.
1899. Scowcroft, Herbt. Edwin, *Bolton*.
1879. Scowcroft, Walter, *Cheadle*.
1901. Scrase, Jas. John Shent,*NewtonAbbot*.
1922.§Scrase, Margaret Charlotte,*Chatham*.
1914. Scripture, E. Wheeler, *Strand*, W.C.
1882. Scroggie, Wm. Reith, *Cook & Son*.
1901. Scroggie, Wm. Reith John, *I.M.S.*
1911. Scurlock, David, *West Ealing*.
1919.§Scutt, Ruth Mary, *Poole*.
1884. Scutt, Tom, *Maidenhead*.
1879. Seager, Herbt. West, *Southampton*.
1886. Seagrove, Hbt.Aylward,*Brondesbury*.
1896. Seal,FrancisMontgomery,*Wirksworth*
1904. Seal, Philip Henry, *South Molton*.
1886. Sealy, Francis M., *Paddock-Wood*.
1896. Sealy, Geoffrey Orr Fern, *I.M.S.*
1912. Sealy, Humfrey N., *R.A.M C.*
1865. Seaman, Albert Baird, *I.M.S.*
1880. Searancke, Niccoll Fdk., *Mitcheldean*.
1896. Sear, John Taylor, *Enfield*.
1906. Searle, A. C. H., M.C., *R.A.M.C.*
1909. Searle, Chas. Fredk ,M.C.,*Cambridge*.
1895. Sears, Alfred Ernest, *Blackheath*.
1902. Sears, Charles Newton, *Lee*.
1860. Seaton, Daniel, *Lymington*.
1907. Sebastian,Gerald Noel B.,*Kensington*.
1896. Seccombe, Charles Wm., *Tavistock*.
1908. Seccombe, Clovis Leopold, *Transvaal*.
1874. Seccombe, Geo. Samuel, *King & Co.*
1901. Seccombe, J. W. S., O B.E.,*R.A.M.C.*
1894. Seccombe,Philip Jn. Ambrose,*Oporto*.
1889. Seccombe, Samuel Hubt., *Queensland*.
1921. Sechachalam, Tirumalichey, *I.M.S.*
1914. Seddon, Allan, *c/o Cox & Co.*
1907. Sedgwick, Geo. Henry, *Rotherham*.
1862. Sedgwick, Hy. Nanton Murray, *R.N.*
1895. Sedgwick, Hubt. Redmayne, *Weeke*.
1923. Sedgwick, Philip Giles, *India*.
1893. Seed, Wm. Pope, *W. Australia*.
1923. Seelenfreund, Harry, *Clapton*.
1922. Seelenfreund, Jacob, *Clapton*.
1921. Segal, Louis, *Transvaal*.
13070

1891. Segundo,Chas. Sempill de,*Manch.-sq.*
1921. Selby, Edward Arthur, *Bradford*.
1914. Selby, Edw. J., O.B.E.,*Nottingham*.
1893. Selby, Jn. Saml. Ernest, *Wellingboro'*.
1887. Selby, Prideaux G ,O.B.E., *Teynham*.
1906. Seldon, George Elliott, *Canada*.
1907. Selfe, John, *Sutton*.
1896. Seligman, Chas. Gabriel, *Thane*.
1914. Selim, Abdel Khalek, *Tantah, Egypt*.
1889. Sellers, Arth. Edward, *Thornhill*.
1868. Sells, Charles John, *Guildford*.
1882. Sells, Hubert Thomas, *Northfleet*.
1915. Sells, Roland, *Northfleet*.
1916. Sellwood, Geo. Binford, *Cullompton*.
1900. Selous, C. Fennessy, *New Milton*.
1916. Selwyn-Clarke, Percy, M C.
1901. Semmence, Ernest Edwd., *Grays*.
1905. Semon, Hy. C. Gust., *Grindlay & Co.*
1877. Semple, Edward, *St. Ives*.
1886. Semple,HenryFdk.,*BudleighSalterton*.
1887. Sen, Chandi Charan, *Munich*.
1914. Sen, Jatindranath, *Kharajpur*.
1922. Senanayeke, Irving A., *Ceylon*.
1891. Senior, Arthur Wm., *Llanfairfechan*.
1918. Sennett, Stanley Nahum, *Stellenbosch*.
1882. Seon, Ewing Greville, *Folkestone*.
1867. Sephton, Robert, *Atherton*.
1905. Sephton, Robt. Poole, *Atherton*.
1889. Sequeira, Geo. William, *Jewry-street*.
1885. Sequeira, Henry James, *Jewry-street*.
1893. Sequeira, Walt. Scott Harcourt, *R.N.*
1922. Sergeant, Cecil F. H., *Liverpool*.
1919. Sergeant, E. Livingstone, *Highbury*.
1903. Sergeant, John Noel, *Tooting*.
1862. Serjeant, David Maurice, *Peckham-rd*.
1896. Serjeant, Robert, *Thornbury-rd*.
1903. Serpell, Hugh Hamilton, *Launceston*.
1897. Sessions, Fdk. Leonard, *Shaa-road*.
1913. Seth-Smith, Douglas N., *Biddeston*.
1891. Seton, Sir Bruce Gordon, C.B , *I.M.S.*
1918. Severn, Adolphe G. M., *Brighton*.
1893. Sevestre, Robert, *Leicester*.
1886. Seville, Chas. Frederick, *Leeds*.
1890. Sewaki, Hisao.
1914. Seward, John Hunter.
1903. Sewell, David Lindley, *Manchester*.
1899. Sewell, Ev. Pierce,C.M.G., D.S O.
1907. Sewell, Rbt. Beresford S., *I.M.S.*
1891. Sewill, Jos. Sefton, *Cavendish-sq*.
1902. Sexton, Henry William, *Rochester*.
1905. Sexton, Timothy Wm., *R.A.M.C.*
1902. Seymour, Chas. Gibbons, *I.M.S.*
1893. Seymour, Edgar Wm., M.V.O.,*Cowes*.
1909. Seymour, Edwd. Albert, *Putney*.
1901. Seymour, Harold Farley, *Worcester*.
1897. Seymour, Lionel Wm., *Oxford*.
1884. Shackel, George Arthur, *Mayfield*.
13127

1885. Shackleton, Herbert, *Bradford.*
1918. Shacklock,Geo.Aug.S.,*HonorOak-pk.*
1885. Shadwell, Harry W., *York.*
1904. Shadwell, LancelotWalt.,*Bedford-pk.*
1914. Shah, BagerZainulabedin,*Greenwich.*
1915. Shah, Jelal Moochool, c/o *King & Co.*
1923. Shaheed, Ibrahim I. A., *Biba, Egypt.*
1910. Shaheen, Hassan Ibrahim, *Cairo.*
1914. Shakespeare, William G., *Highgate.*
1902. Shand, Walter Moray, *New Zealand.*
1875. Shaun, Frederick, *York.*
1914. Shaun, Gerald D., *Stanhope-gardens.*
1879. Shann, Henry Charles, *Saltburn.*
1878. Shann, Wm. Arthur, *Eastbourne.*
1921. Shannon, Harry, *Maida-vale.*
1890. Shannon, Jas. Webster, *Cal., U.S.A.*
1902. Shannon, Stanley Saml. Howard,*R.N.*
1922. Shapland, Cyril Dee, *Brixton-hill.*
1914. Sharaf, Mohammad, *Cairo.*
1896. Shardlow, Joseph, *Brighton.*
1890. Sharman, Eric Harding, *I.M.S.*
1889. Sharman, Henry, *Hampstead, N.W.*
1887. Sharman, Jn.S.Wm. Edwd.,*Norwood.*
1860. Sharood, Edwd. Julian, *Royal Navy.*
1918. Sharp, Bryan Buckley, *Swallowbeck.*
1922. Sharp, Douglas Gordon, *Leeds.*
1915. Sharp, EverardWm.Lewen,*Brook-gr.*
1868. Sharp, John Adolphus, *Derby.*
1914. Sharp, John Edward, *Derby.*
1913. Sharp, Leonard E. S., *Wimbledon.*
1908. Sharp, Leonard Whittaker, *Preston.*
1910. Sharp,Neville Alex. Dyce, *W. Africa.*
1919.§Sharp, Olive Ballance, *Wimbledon.*
1922. Sharp, Percival Henry.
1891. Sharp, Percy, *Lincoln.*
1914. Sharpe, Herbert, *Rye.*
1888. Sharpe, Wm. Salisbury, *Wimpole-st.*
1915. Sharpe, W. W. Salisbury, *Cleveland.*
1889. Sharpin, Archdale Lloyd, *Maidstone.*
1882. Sharpin, Edward Colby, *Bedford.*
1895. Sharpin, Walter Archdale, *Bedford.*
1902. Sharples, Joseph Percival, *York.*
1903. Sharpley, Chris. Wilfred, *Ulceby.*
1883. Sharpley, Edward, *Louth.*
1890. Sharpley,Jn.Ernest,*Kirt'n-in-Lindsey*
1911. Sharpley, Thos. Stoney, *Ashby.*
1917.§Sharrard,WinifredHannah,*Gloucester*
1903. Shattock, Chas. Robert, *Chiswick.*
1889. Shave,Edwd Simpson, *Camden-road.*
1892. Shaw, Alfd. Eland, *Victoria.*
1893. Shaw, Arth. H. Plows, *Cranbrook.*
1894. Shaw, Arthur Priest, *Hull.*
1920. Shaw, Campbell, *Putney.*
1901. Shaw, David Chris. M., *Manchester.*
1916.§Shaw, Edith Annie, *Maidstone.*
1905. Shaw, Ernest Henry, *Camden-road.*
1881. Shaw, Frank Herbert, *St. Leonards.*

13184

1878. Shaw, George, *Hove.*
1923. Shaw, George Drury,*Pietermaritzburg*
1923. Shaw, Harold Bernard, *Reigate.*
1884. Shaw,HarryChas.Costello,*Queen sl'nd.*
1920. Shaw, John Arthur P., *Westminster.*
1888. Shaw, John Custance, *Goodmayes.*
1890. Shaw, John Hepworth, *Liverpool.*
1914. Shaw, John Patrick, M.C., *Harrow.*
1899. Shaw, John Porte Brockton, *Mass.*
1896. Shaw, Justus Martin, *Harlesden.*
1920.§Shaw, Katherine Jane, *St. Austell.*
1881. Shaw, Lauriston Elgie, *Park-sq.*, W.
1922. Shaw, Noel Francis, *Middlesex-hosp.*
1377. Shaw, Oliver Cromwell, *Hove.*
1922.§Shaw, Patricia Helen Simpson.
1921. Shaw,RichardG.V., *Bk. of Australia.*
1891. Shaw, Richard Holgate, M.B.E.
1900. Shaw, Robert Wesley, *London. Can.*
1920. Shaw, Ronald C., *Poulton-le-Fylde.*
1864. Shaw, Thomas Claye, *Harley-street.*
1917. Shaw, Thomas Wilson, *Ferryhill.*
1922.§Shaw, Vera Elizabeth, *Oxford.*
1879. Shaw, William, *Maidstone.*
1912. Shaw, Wm. Geoffrey, *Manitoba.*
1884. Shaw, William Ormerod.
1917. Shaw-Crisp, Cuthbert, *Ealing.*
1881. Shaw-Mackenzie,Jn. A ,*Bryanston-sq*
1897. Shea. Henry Francis, *R.A.M.C.*
1912. Sheard, Charles.
1879 Sheard, Charles, *Toronto.*
1911. Sheard, Robert Henry, *Toronto.*
1873. Sheard, William, *Bexhill.*
1879. Shears, Chas. H. Bedwell, *Liverpool.*
1893. Shears, William, *Catford.*
1898. Shedden,Arnold Ward, *Walsall.*
1920. Sheehan, Gerald, *Carlisle.*
1874. Sheehy,Wm.Hy.Patmore,*Totteridge.*
1900. Sheldon, Arthur Izod, *R.N.*
1900. Sheldon, Hugh Fredk., *Orange Prov.*
1918. Sheldon, Joseph H., *Wolverhampton.*
1888. Sheldon, Robert Garnett, *Liverpool.*
1877. Sheldon, Thomas Steele, *Chester.*
1915. Sheldon, Thomas William, *Chester.*
1898. Sheldon, Walter Sirr, *Notting-hill.*
1923. Sheldon, Wilfrid P. H., *Woodford.*
1884. Sheldrake, Edwd. Nodin, *St. Geo.-sq.*
1904. Shelley, Arnold, *Chatham.*
1914. Shelley, Lewis Wilton, *Chislehurst.*
1895. Shelley, Percy Wilfrid G., *Bermuda.*
1922. Shellshear,Ken.Eden,*Sydney,N.S.W.*
1879 Shelly, Charles Edward, *Hertford.*
1921. Shelswell, Arthur Hugh, *Mitcham.*
1884. Shelswell, Oscar B.,O B.E.,*Mitcham.*
1910. Shelton, Chas. Frank, *Maida-vale.*
1904. Shelton, Harvey Llewellyn, *Hove.*
1901. Shelton-Jones, Ernest, *Pwllheli.*
1909. Shenstone, Norman Strahan, *Toronto.*

13241

1901. Shenton, Edwd. W. Hine, *Harley-st.*
1921. Sheorey, Narayan Lakshman.
1880. Shepard, E. William, *Willes-rd.,N.W.*
1894. Shepard, Robt. Henry, *Cookham.*
1914. Shepard,Wm.Hopper,*Hammersmith.*
1895. Shepheard, Henry, *Hammersmith.*
1890. Shepheard, John, *North Walsham.*
1862. Shepheard, Philip Candler, *Aylsham.*
1909. Shepheard, Samuel, *Aylsham.*
1895. Shepherd, Alfd. Edwd., *Doncaster.*
1862. Shepherd, Charles Dunbar, *Arnside.*
1917. Shepherd, Charles E. A., *Coleherne-ct.*
1922 §Shepherd, Creina, *Calcutta.*
1898. Shepherd, Cyril, *Sydney.*
1922. Shepherd, Cyril, *Whitchurch.*
1906. Shepherd, Doug. Rbt.C.,*Midd'x-hosp.*
1874. Shepherd, F. John, *Montreal.*
1922. Shepherd, Harry Leslie, *Clevedon.*
1889. Shepherd, Henry Bowman, *Sheffield.*
1896. Shepherd, Hy. Brooks, *Portland-pl.*
1900. Shepherd, Thomas Scott,*Henstridge.*
1895. Sheppard, Arthur Murray.
1884. Sheppard,Hy.Anderson,*Southampton*
1915. Sheppard, Henry Richard, *Hove.*
1878. Sheppard, John, *Bottesford.*
1882. Sheppard, William John, *Putney.*
1914. Shera, Arthur Geoffrey, *Sheffield.*
1877. Sherburn, Sir John, *Brough.*
1914. Sherrard, Noel Sigismund, *Highgate.*
1914. Sherris, Cyril, *Sidcup.*
1913. Sherwood, Arthur Leonard.
1915.§Sherwood, Edith Grace, *Coventry.*
1913. Sherwood, Geo. Douglas, *Eastbourne.*
1903. Shettle, Francis Broughton, *I.M.S.*
1917 §Shields, Charlotte Annie, *Westcliff.*
1901. Shields, Wm. Thomas, *Longport.*
1883. Shillito, Henry, *Edgbaston.*
1917. Shimberg, Mandell, *London-hospital.*
1901. Shipman,Geo.Alfd.Cargil,*Grantham.*
1877. Shipton, Arthur, *Buxton.*
1888. Shipton, Herbert, *Buxton.*
1910. Shipton, William, *Buxton.*
1913. Shirgaokar, Jagannath V.
1801. Shirtliff, Edwd. Dickinson, *N.S.W.*
1907. Shirvell, Edgar Arthur, *Exeter.*
1883. Shone, William Vernon, *Victoria.*
1876. Shoolbred, Wm. Andrew, *Chepstow.*
1909. Shorbagi, Ibrahim, *Egypt.*
1911. Shore, Geo. Wm., O.B.E., *Streatham.*
1913. Shore, Lewis Rudall, *Norwood.*
1901. Shore, Richd.AllanAmbrose,*Toronto.*
1911. Shore, Thos. H. Gostwyck, *Norwood.*
1883. Shore, Thos. Wm., O.B.E., *Norwood.*
1864. Shorland, Edward Peter, *Westbury.*
1895. Shorland, Ernest Trevor, *Westbury.*
1922. Short, Clifton Max, *Brook-st.,* S.E.
1887. Short, James Joseph, *Clapham.*

1883. Short, Thomas Sydney, *Birmingham.*
1919. Showell-Rogers, Eric N., *Leicester.*
1921. Shri-Kent, Shamsher Singh.
1900. Shrubsall, Frank Chas., *Mull Hill-pk.*
1922. Shulman, Jack, *Sclater-st.*
1918. Shurlock, Arthur George, *Derby.*
1887. Shute, George Sidney, *Northfleet.*
1904. Shutte, Malcolm Winfrid, *Walton.*
1893. Shutte, Theodore, *St. Bart's.-hosp.*
1922.§Shuttleworth, Doris K., *Castleford.*
1864. Shuttleworth, Geo. Ed., *Cavendish-st.*
1921. Sibley, Osbert Lacon Carden, *Ealing.*
1896. Sibley, Reg. Oliver, *Caterham-valley.*
1886. Sibley,Walt. Knowsley, *Cavend.sh-pl.*
1896. Sibson, Arth. Bertram, *Cape Prov.*
1864. Siddall, Jos. Bower, *Gt. Malvern.*
1887. Sidebotham, Edward John, *Bowdon.*
1916. Sidebotham, Fras. Nasmyth, *Bowdon.*
1887. Sidebotham, Harold, *California.*
1887. Sidebottom, Ralph Bennett, *Glossop.*
1903. Sidgwick, Harry C.,O.B.E.,*R.A.M.C.*
1881. Sieveking,Herbt. Ed.,*Cambridge-gds.*
1919. Siggs, Cecil George Dougias, *Guy's.*
1898. Silas, Walt. Biscombe, *Southgate-rd.*
1914. Silcock, Ronald. *Maida-vale.*
1880. Silk, Jn. Fdk. Wm., *Nottingham-pl.*
1918. Silley, Herbert Henry, *Muswell-hill.*
1898. Sills, Clarence Ham, *Leeward Islands.*
1923 Silver, Aaron Gideon, *Clapton-com.*
1899. Silver, Hugh William, *Sydenham.*
1921. Silverman, Abraham I., *Wigmore-st.*
1921. Simaika, Sobhi Riskallah, *Abassich.*
1901. Simey, Athelstane Iliff, *Rugby.*
1896. Simmonds,Ernest Geo.,*Alta.,Canada.*
1874. Simmonds, Wm. Allason, *I.M.S.*
1893. Simmons, Edmund W., *Bishopstoke.*
1883. Simmons, Edward Walpole, O.B.E.
1889. Simmons, Fredk. Hero, *Transvaal.*
1907. Simmons, Geo. Alan, *Southwick-pl.*
1885. Simmons, Harold, *Bournemouth.*
1882. Simmons, Herbt. Chas., *Transvaal.*
1896. Simmons, Stewart Sept, S. *Norwood.*
1918. Simmons, William Henry, *Hore.*
1884. Simms, Henry, *Birmingham.*
1905. Simon, John Wellesley, *Buntingford.*
1916. Simons, Gordon Ernest L, *Sydenham.*
1893. Simons, Rbt. Jn. R.Cobden,*Bridgend.*
1915. Simons, Simon, *Aberdstery.*
1898. Simpson,Adam PearsonHope,*Liverp'l.*
1895. Simpson, Cecil Butler, *Filey.*
1887. Simpson, Chas. Shackleton, *Hore.*
1889. Simpson, Francis Odell, *Jamaica.*
1900. Simpson, Fred Algernon, *Winterton.*
1894. Simpson,Fredk.Hamps'n,*Birmingh'm*
1886. Simpson,Geo.Aug.Garry,*Cleveland-sq*
1900. Simpson, George Herbert, *Brighton.*
1907. Simpson,George Maxwell,*Bayswater.*

1889. Simpson, Godfrey Wm., *Wandsworth.*
1891. Simpson, Henry, *Brenchley.*
1909. Simpson, James Starr, *Ont., Canada.*
1919. Simpson, Jas. Victor Alex., *Bedford.*
1905. Simpson, Julius Benedict, *Weymouth.*
1917. Simpson, Maurice Oliver, *R.A.M.C.*
1914. Simpson, Reginald Hugh, *Southfleet.*
1865. Simpson, R. Palgrave, *Bournemouth.*
1916 Simpson, Robert Gordon, *Plymouth.*
1862. Simpson, Thomas, *Bukdale.*
1901. Simpson, Thos Young, *C.B.E ,Plym'th*
1895. Simpson, William, *Bury St. Edmunds.*
1913. Simpson, William, *Woodford.*
1910. Simpson, Wm. Faulkner V.,*Muswell-h.*
1909. Simpson, William Sidney, *Erith.*
1892. Sims, David, *Leeds.*
1918. Sims, George Harold, *Derby.*
1888. Sims, George Samuel, *Derby.*
1898. Simson, Colin Coape, M.C., *Papua.*
1898. Simson, Harold, *R.A.M.C.*
1909. Sinclair, Alexander, *Kilsyth, Canada.*
1901. Sinclair, Harold W., *Springfield.*
1904. Sinclair, James D., O.B.E., *Darlington.*
1922. Sinclair, James Ward, *Toronto.*
1882. Sinclair, John, *Dunoon.*
1916.§Sinclair, Stephanie, P.L.H.T., *Oldham*
1896. Sing, Wilfrid MacDonald, *Strand.*
1907. Singer, Arthur Leonard, *Gisborne, N.Z.*
1903. Singer, Charles Joseph, *Oxford.*
1898. Singer, Harold Douglas, *U.S.A.*
1917. Singer, Kildare Lawrence, *Norwood.*
1914. Singh, Bawa Harkishan, M.C., *I.M.S.*
1889. Singh, Bawa Jiwan, *I.M.S.*
1917.§Singh, Flora Nihal, *Cartwright-gdns.*
1905. Singh, Kanwar Shrumshere, *I.M.S.*
1905. Sington, Harold Sigis., *Hyde-park.*
1882. Sinha, Narendra Prasanna, *Ealing.*
1921. Sinnatamby, George Selvaratnam.
1893. Sinigar, Harry, *Southall.*
1908. Sircom, Edmund Ralph, *Romford-rd.*
1860. Sissons, Wm. Harling, *Scarboro'.*
1915. Sittampalam, Samuel A., *Ceylon.*
1893. Skeels, William, *Brighouse.*
1913. Skeet, Jack Garland, *Auckland, N.Z.*
1882. Skeete, F. de Courcy.
1917. Skeggs, Basil Lyndon, *Beckenham.*
1886. Skelding, Henry, *Bedford.*
1878. Skelding, Henry Jn., *Bridgnorth.*
1901. Skelton, Dudley S., D.S.O., *R.A.M.C.*
1923 §Skelton, Helen Octavia, *Tavistock-sq.*
1915. Skelton, John Devil G., *Gosport.*
1876. Skerman, Sidney, *Marton, N.Z.*
1900. Skerrett, F. Blenkinsopp, *Forest-gate.*
1896. Skey, Arth. Richd. Harrie, *R N.*
1879. Skinner, B.M., C.B., C.M G , M.V.O.
1906. Skinner, Edward Fretson, *Sheffield.*
1888. Skinner, George Henry, *Victoria.*

13412

1916. Skinner, John Adrian D., *Anerley.*
1873. Skinner, Robt. Alexander, *Tenterden.*
1907. Skinner, William Fretson, *Sheffield.*
1875. Skipworth, Herbert, *Loughborough.*
1894. Skipworth, P. Lyon elGrey, *Gravesend.*
1911. Skrimshire, Francis R. B., *R.A.M.C.*
1902. Skrimshire, Henry Finch, *Holt.*
1888. Skyrme, Henry Edward, *Cardiff.*
1902. Slade, Herbert James, *Newcastle.*
1903. Slade, John Godfrey, *Fleet.*
1907. Slade, Sidney, *Nayland.*
1906. Slaney, Chas. Newnham, *Parkhurst.*
1880. Slate, Alfred, *Canonbury.*
1899. Slater, Alan Butler, *Jun. Conserv.-club.*
1922. Slater, Alan Edward.
1918. Slater, Bertram Leslie, *Brighton.*
1884. Slater, Charles, *Tunbridge Wells.*
1894. Slater, Geo. Nathan O., *Brentwood.*
1890. Slater, Howard, *St. Budeaux.*
1881. Slater, William, *East Southsea.*
1887. Slater, William Arnison, *Haslemere.*
1876. Slatter, Oliver Thomas, *Kensington.*
1921. Slaughter, Henry Lawrence.
1871. Slaughter, William Budd, *A.M.S.*
1922. Slim, Charles John, *Edgbaston.*
1896. Slocock, Richard, *Spilsby.*
1890. Sloggett, Harry Paynter, *Victoria.*
1913. Sloper, John Smith, O.B.E., *Chelsea.*
1886. Sloman, Frederick, *Brighton.*
1876. Sloman, Herbert, *Bedford.*
1869. Sloman, Samuel George, *Farnham.*
1920. Slot, Gerald Maurice J., *Kensington.*
1896. Slowan, William John More, O.B.E.
1909. Smale, Herbert, *Cavendish-square.*
1891. Smale, John, *Darlington.*
1908. Smale, Oswald Ridley, *Lisheard.*
1903. Smales, W. Clayton, D.S.O., *R.A.M.C.*
1897. Small, Arthur Atwell, *Toronto.*
1901. Small, Robert, *East Africa.*
1911. Smalley, Arthur Ashton, M.C., *Cheadle.*
1875. Smalley, Sir Herbert, *Home Office.*
1906. Smalley, James, *I.M.S.*
1907. Smalley, Jas. Thornton, *Hong-Kong.*
1921. Smalley, Leonard, *Olvaston.*
1905. Smallhorn, Cyril Aubrey, *Knutsford.*
1883. Smallpiece, Wm. Donald, *Felsted.*
1902. Smallwood, Edward. *W. Norwood.*
1898. Smallwood, Mat. E., *Wheathampstead.*
1895. Smallwood, Robert Percy, *Chelmsford.*
1880. Smart, Alfred, *Marden.*
1918. Smart, Arthur Hbt. J., *Tamworth.*
1903. Smart, Herbert D , M.C., *Shelley.*
1920. Smart, Wm. Arthur M., *Golder's-gr.*
1898. Smeaton. Bronte, *S. Australia.*
1902. Smedley, Ralph Davies, *Worthing.*
1912. Smeed, Edward, *Southsea.*
1888. Smeeton, Charles Wm., O.B.E., *York.*

13469

1876. Smelt, Frank Hayes, *Newent*.
1906. Smillie, Alex. Buchanan, *Ontario*.
1923.§Smith, Agnes Bryce, *Glasgow*.
1901. Smith, Alan Ayre, *Sunderland*.
1889. Smith, Alfd. Alex., *Clare, S. Austr.*
1893. Smith, Alfd. Egerton M., *Retford*.
1923. Smith, AlfredWm. Lumsden, *Hulme*.
1913. Smith, Algernon Chas. S., M.C.
1905. Smith, Armstrong, *Ebury-street*.
1916. Smith, Arthur Cloudesley, *Highbury*.
1896. Smith, Arth. Grosart Lehman, *Crick*.
1887. Smith, Arthur Henry, *Manchester*.
1878. Smith, Arthur Lapthorn, *Montreal*.
1897. Smith, Arthur L. H., *Adelaide*.
1865. Smith, Charles, *Victoria*.
1898. Smith, Charles Charnock, *Woburn*.
1875. Smith, Charles Edwin, *Altrincham*.
1865. Smith, Charles James Hardy.
1860. Smith, Charles John, *W. Drayton*.
1923. Smith, Charles Newlyn,*Brondesbury*.
1917. Smith, Charles Rees.
1896. Smith, Daniel Lloyd, *Pontardawe*.
1902. Smith, Dansey, *Shanghai, China*.
1909. Smith, David Priestley, *Birmingham*.
1916. Smith, Denys Munro, *Clifton*.
1902. Smith, Edward Bertram, *Braintree*.
1894. Smith, Edward Hickson, *Brentford*.
1885. Smith, Edward John, *Beveley*.
1899. Smith, Edwd. Protheroe, *Redditch*.
1892. Smith, Edwin, *Balham High-road*.
1897. Smith, Edwin Chas. Temple, *Sydney*.
1879. Smith, Ernest Barratt, *Herne-hill.*
1922. Smith, Ernest Flavel, *Lee*.
1901. Smith, Ernest George, *Plymouth*.
1891. Smith, Ernest Newlyn, *Dollis-hill*.
1876. Smith, Ernest Sutton, *Broadstairs*.
1919. Smith, Francis Henry, *Cambridge*.
1907. Smith, Francis Maylett, *Twickenham*.
1895. Smith, Frank Addinsell, *I.M.S.*
1873. Smith, Fiank Jn. Shersby, *Plumstead*.
1895. Smith, Frank Laughton, *Louth*.
1909. Smith, Frank Lewis, *Royal Navy*.
1902. Smith, Frank Wybourn, *Plumstead*.
1912. Smith, Frederic Battinson, M.C.
1923. Smith, Frederick Elliott.
1902. Smith, Tdk. Morton Vincent, *R.N.*
1903. Smith,F. W. W.,*Newington-causeway*.
1902. Smith, Gayton Warwick, *Tooting*.
1872. Smith, Geo. Cockburn,*Newton Abbot*.
1885. Smith, Geo. Francis, *Watford*.
1914. Smith, George Holmes, *Brook-street*.
1901. Smith, Geo. Melville, *Buntingford*.
1901. Smith, George Percy, *Birmingham*.
1876. Smith, Gerald Hy., *St. John's-wood*.
1881. Smith, Gilbert Thomas,*New Zealand*.
1895. Smith, GrahamUdale,*Whatley & Son*.
1920. Smith, Harold Edward, *Bow*.
13526

1886. Smith, Henry Archbold, *Leeds*.
1889. Smith Henry Cleveland, *Southend*.
1909. Smith, Henry Gordon, *Putney*.
1872. Smith,Hy.Hammond,*St.Albans-mns.*
1886. Smith, Henry Sandford, *Eltham*.
1879. Smith, Henry Strode, *Axbridge*.
1889. Smith, Henry Walter, *Mansfield*.
1881. Smith, Herbert, *Jersey*.
1914. Smith, Herbert, *Castle Bromwich*.
1879. Smith, Herbeit Arthur, *Ealing*.
1890. Smith,Herbert Austen,*C.I.E.,I.M.S.*
1882. Smith, Howard Lyon, *Inkberrow*.
1906. Smith, Hoyland, *Armley*.
1914. Smith, Issachar Reuben, *Toronto*.
1873. Smith, James, *Newcastle-on-Tyne*.
1906. Smith, Jas. Edmund, *Chelsea*.
1902. Smith, Jas. Ernest Sutcliffe, *Bacup*.
1864. Smith, James William, *Bournemouth*.
1862. Smith, John, *I.M.S.*
1880. Smith, John, *Crouch-hill.*
1885. Smith, John, *Kirkcaldy, N.B.*
1836. Smith,JohnAnderson,*Willesden-lane*.
1889. Smith, John Arthur, *Wakefield*.
1916. Smith, John Forest, *Catford*.
1889. Smith, John Percy, *Caton-terrace*.
1900. Smith, John Salmon, *West Africa*.
1897. Smith, Julius Hodgetts, *Ilford*.
1878. Smith, Kenneth Rawlings, *Kew*.
1914. Smith, Kenneth V., *Knatchbull-rd.*
1914. Smith, Leslie Muir, *Eastbourne*.
1895. Smith, Lewis Albert, *Queen Anne-st.*
1898. Smith, Malcolm Arthur, *Siam*.
1903. Smith,MalcolmWm.S.,*NewSouthy'te.*
1896. Smith, Maurice Hamblin, *Portland*.
1897. Smith, Montague, *Clapton*.
1917. Smith, N. Hardcastle, *D.S.C., R.N.*
1917. Smith, Norman Fairbanks, *Hertford*.
1887. Smith, Percival, *Sirhowy, Mon.*
1914. Smith, Peter de Safforie, *Cannock*.
1912. Smith, Philip, M.C., *Bromley*.
1910. Smith, Ralph Gillespie, *Wrangle*.
1894. Smith, R. Nitch, *St. Andhew's-place*.
1909. Smith, Reginald R., *Cape Province*.
1889. Smith, Richard Arthur, *Islington*.
1869. Smith, Richd. Thos., *Haverstock-hill*.
1830. Smith, Richard Wagstaff, *Exmouth*.
1894. Smith, Robert Bramwell, *Manchester*.
1889. Smith, Robert Edward, *Busley*.
1902. Smith,Rbt.HowardNewby,*Lewisham*
1878. Smith, Robt. Percy, *Queen-Anne-st.*
1900. Smith, Robt. Wm. Innes, *Sheffield*.
1873. Smith, Roland Dunn, *Clapton*.
1923. Smith, Ronald Wylie, *Cambridge*.
1912. Smith, Sidney, *Feltham*.
1890. Smith, Sidney B, C.M.G., *I M.S.*
1896. Smith, Sidney Fredk., *Leicester*.
1898. Smith, Sidney Robert, *Plumstead*.
13583

1900. Smith, Stephen Francis, *Brentford.*
1910. Smith, Sumner Hugh, M.C.
1891. Smith, Sydney Calvin, *Muswell-hill.*
1864. Smith, Thomas Haywood, *Alcester.*
1902. Smith, Thos. Morland, *Bournemouth.*
1900. Smith, Thomas William.
1889. Smith, Thomas Wilson, *Bath.*
1917. Smith, Vincent Russell, *Kew.*
1906. Smith, Walter Heaton, *Wigan.*
1868. Smith, Walt. Hugh Mont., *Croydon.*
1897. Smith, Walt. Hugh Mont., *Norwood*
1880. Smith, William Alex., *Clifton.*
1882. Smith, Wm. Arthur W., *Torquay.*
1901. Smith, Wm Christian B., *R.N.*
1908. Smith,Wm.Fdk.,*Halifax,NovaScotia.*
1879. Smith, William Harvey, *Meriden.*
1877. Smith, William Henry, *Boston.*
1909. Smith, William John, *Canada.*
1896. Smith, Wm. Steele, *Chorlton.*
1901. Smith, Witney C. Palmer, *Burnham.*
1898. Smithson, Arthur Ernest, *R.A.M.C.*
1923. Smout, Chas. Fredk.Vict., *Harborne.*
1904. Smulian, Samuel, *Dalston.*
1917. Smuts, Phineas A , *Malmesbury, S.Af.*
1923. Smyth, Arthur John, *Wymeswold.*
1893. Smyth, Ernest Jackson, *Guildford.*
1914. Smyth, Fras.Gerald Aug., *Weymouth.*
1908. Smyth, Francis Radway.
1914. Smyth, Geo. Jn. C., *Ravenscourt-pk.*
1902. Smyth, James Arth.,*Melton Mowbray.*
1904. Smyth, John Cecil, M.B.E., *Malvern.*
1893. Smyth, Joshua Charles, *Benenden.*
1889. Smyth, Nugent Edward, *Malvern.*
1892. Smyth, R. Mander, *Richardson & Co.*
1879. Smyth, Sydney, *Cape Province.*
1912. Smyth, Wm. Jas. Dobson, *Bromley.*
1912. Smythe, Gerald Arthur, *Bath.*
1923. Snaith, Eric George, *Golder's-grn.*
1905. Snell, Doug. Mont. B., *Stapleford.*
1869. Snell, Enoch, *Nottingham.*
1889. Snell, Ernest Hugh, *Coventry.*
1918. Snell, Francis Rupert, *Nottingham.*
1874. Snell, George, *Bedford.*
1921. Snell, Harrie Kennard.
1908. Snell, Henry Cecil, *Sheffield.*
1915. Snell, John Aubrey B., *Sheffield.*
1922. Snell, Norman William, *Rye Lane.*
1890. Snell, Sidney Herbert, *Christchurch.*
1914. Snelling, Trevor Richard, *Wroxham.*
1907. Snoad, Francis George, *Leicester.*
1895. Snoad, Philip Ephraim, *Leicester.*
1890. Snook, Samuel Penny, *Mill-hill.*
1868. Snow, Herbert Lumley, *Mill-hill.*
1886. Snow, Lionel Mason, *N.S.W.*
1897. Snowden, Arthur de Winton, C B.E.
1911. Snowden,Ern.Nedwons,*Cavendish-st.*
1911. Snowdon, Alan Richmond,*Scotswood.*
13640

1894. Snowman, Jacob, *Brondesbury.*
1910. Soames, Ralph Martin, *Reigate.*
1872. Sobey, Arthur Lyne.
1892. Soden, Thomas A. Bourne, *Coventry.*
1893. Soden, Wilfred Newell, M.C.
1913. Soden, Wilfrid Scovil, *Conduit-st.*
1863. Soffe, Wm. Edward, *Bournemouth.*
1920. Sofi, Syed Sarwar Hussain.
1892. Soilleux, Garnet, *Camberwell, Vict.*
1922. Soliman, Yassa Sudki, *Lambeth.*
1912. Soltau, Henry Kenneth V., *Yatton.*
1920. Somasundram, Saravanamuttu.
1897. Somers,C.Dudley,O.B.E.,*Aldeburgh.*
1884. Somers, Edward O'Reilly, *Pendleton.*
1887. Somerset, Edward, *Newbury.*
1923. Somerset, Robert Masters, *Sheffield.*
1911. Somerset, Vere Edward, *Finchley.*
1914. Somervell, Leonard Colin, *Kendal.*
1901. Somerville, Henry, *Sharnbrook.*
1914. Somerville, Thos.V.,M.C., *R.A.M.C.*
1912. Sothill, Victor Farrar, *Harrogate.*
1901. Soper, Arthur Walrond, *Anerley.*
1919. Sophianopoulos, George John.
1913. Soutar, Alan Ker, *Gloucester.*
1906. South, Frank Montague W., *Peckham.*
1888. South, Frdk.Wm. B , *Perth, W.Aust.*
1885. South, Henry Erskine, *R.N.*
1890. South, Richd. Edwd. Ernest, *Boston.*
1868. Southam, John Binns, *Queensland.*
1883. Southcombe, Arth. Geo., *Homerton.*
1885. Southern, Francis Gerald, *Llandebie.*
1883. Southern, John Acton, O.B.E.,*Derby.*
1909. Southern, Walt. Duckett, *Wimpole-st.*
1895. Southey, Herbt. Watson, *Maidstone.*
1904. Southwick, Geo. Rinaldo, *U.S.A.*
1885. Soutter, James, *Hull.*
1913. Soutter, James Stewart, *Hull.*
1922. Soutter, Luther James, *Highbury.*
1891. Soutter, Mansfield Knox, *Highbury.*
1900. Sowden, George, *Gloucester-gate.*
1915. Sowerby, William.
1917. Spackman, Eric D , *Wolverhampton.*
1879. Spackman, Hy. Robt., *Wolverhampton.*
1913. Spackman,Wm.Collis,*Wolven'h'mpt'n*
1895. Spain, Chas. Milner, *Wolverhampton.*
1901. Spalding, Archibald Denize, *R.N.*
1914. Spalding, Fredk. Lionel, *Worcester.*
1896. Spark, Percy Charles. *Banstead.*
1896. Sparkes, Wm.M.B.,D.S.O.,*R.A.M.C.*
1914. Sparks, Clifford W., M.C., *Forest-hill.*
1921. Sparks. Ernest Algernon, *Staines.*
1923. Sparks, John Victor, *Surbiton.*
1907. Sparrow, Edwd.Cyril, *Wolverhampton.*
1912. Sparrow, Geoffrey, M C., *Portland-st.*
1875. Sparrow, Geo. Gordon, *Seaview, I. W.*
1895. Sparrow, George Randal, *Cardiff.*
1915. Sparrow, George Sydney.
13697

1880. Sparrow, Horatio S. Richd , *R. Navy.*
1887. Sparrow, Jn. E. Pennington,*Cosham.*
1894. Spaull, Percy William, *Stanwick-rd.*
1919. Spear, Frederick Gordon, *Bath.*
1896. Spear, John Augustus, *Brazil.*
1909. Spedding, Ivan Norman, *Dunedin.*
1903. Speechly, Alec. Jn. Lincoln, *Paisley.*
1839. Speechly,Harry Martindale, *Manitoba*
1876. Speed, Henry Andrews,*NewNorth-rd.*
1888. Speedy, Robert Geo. Dunell,*Bedford.*
1907. Speers, Charles, *Newbury.*
1904. Speers, Wm. Gordon, *Brazil.*
1893. Spence, Daniel Benham, *New York.*
1913. Spence, Douglas Benham, *Guildford*
1913. Spence, Douglas Leigh, *Bedford.*
1915. Spence, Harold D. L., *New York.*
1900. Spencer, Alfred Richard, *Battersea.*
1871. Spencer, Francis Henry, *Army.*
1920. Spencer, Frederic Downing,*Stratford.*
1900. Spencer, George Herbert, *Wallsend*
1912. Spencer,Gordon Winstanley, *Preston.*
1888. Spencer, Henry Alex., *Transvaal.*
1883. Spencer, Herbt. Ritchie, *Harley-st.*
1906. Spencer, John Heatly, *Seymour-st.*
1887. Spencer,MatthewHenry,*Oxford-gdns*
1903. Spencer, Sandy, *Ashton-u.-Lyne.*
1897. Spencer, Thomas, *Keighley.*
1918. Spencer-Payne, ArthurLl.,*Ramsgate.*
1908. Spencer-Phillips,Percy T.,*Gt.Baddow*
1921. Spibey, Harry, *Tottington.*
1896. Spicer, Arthur Herbert, M.C.
1884. Spicer, Frederick, *Harley-st.*
1915. Spicer, Gerald Evan, M.C ,*Dulwich.*
1894. Spicer, Harry, *Royal Navy.*
1882. Spicer, Rob. Hy. Scanes, *Eaton-sq.*
1918.§Spickett, Frances Minnie, *Sevenoaks.*
1895. Spillane, James Charles,*St.James's-st.*
1836. Spiller, Walter Charles.
1888. Spink, Chris. Peirson, *Cape Town.*
1918. Spira, Jacques, *Antwerp.*
1900. Spitta, Harold Robert Dacre,M.V.O.
1905. Spitteler, Alfred, *I.M.S.*
1876. Spofforth, John, *Cricklewood.*
1876. Spokes, Peter Sidney, *Portland-pl.*
1896. Spon, Harry James, *Harley-street.*
1883. Spong, John Fuller, *Tooting.*
1918. Spong,VictorAlex.Trevor,*Herne-hill·*
1920. Spoor,ArthurTwynham,*Wigmore-st.*
1886. Spoor, William Joseph, *Bristol.*
1904. Spotswood, Maurice, *Shaw.*
1909. Sprague, Cecil Gordon, *Roy. Navy.*
1899. Sprague, Francis Henry, *Gloucester.*
1880. Spranger, Francis Jefferies, *Southsea.*
1868. Spratt, Henry Howell, *N. Zealand.*
1898. Sprawson, Cuthbert Allan, C.I.E.
1905. Sprawson, Evelyn C., M.C.
1907. Sprawson, Fras. Edgar, *Highbury-pl.*
13754

1923. Spreadbury, H. J. H., *Bourne nouth.*
1892. Sproat,Jas. Hugh, *Gravelly-hill.*
1904. Sproat, Robert Douglass, *Toronto.*
1873. Sprod, John, *S. Australia.*
1916. Sprott,NormanArmitage,*Manchester.*
1879. Sprott, William John, *Manchester.*
1911.§Sproule, Pearl Jane, *Toronto.*
1861. Spurgin, Fdk. William, *Welbeck-st.*
1864. Spurgin,Hy.Bramwhite,*Northampton.*
1898. Spurgin, Percy Bertram, *Welbeck-st.*
1879. Spurgin, Thomas, *Bournemouth.*
1873. Spurgin, Wm.Henry,*Newcastle-on-T*
1891. Spurr, James, *Lyme Regis.*
1891. Spurrell, Wm. Dewing, *Norwich.*
1901. Spurrier, Harry, *Maidenhead.*
1907. Square, Wm. Russell, *Thurlestone.*
1892. Squibbs,Robt.Edwd. P.,*Nottingham*
1883. Squire, Edward Herbert, *Wivenhoe.*
1890. Squire, Frank Henry, *Pudsey.*
1918. Squire. Henry Fremlin, *Kenley.*
1895. Squire,MauriceFdk.,*Padd.Infirmary*
1884. Squire, Walter Perfect, *Hanover-sq.*
1874. Squire, William, *Transvaal.*
1920. Squires, Frederick Vaughan.
1905. Squires,Herbert Chavasse,*Khartoum.*
1889. Stabb, Arth. Francis, *Harley-street.*
1894. Stableford,Frank B. Gorton, *TyCroes.*
1884. Stables, Alexander, *A.M.S.*
1869. Stables, Walt. Wms.Godfrey,*Fair-st.*
1899. Stacey, Fredk. George, *Sheffield.*
1881. Stacey, Herbert Gleeson, *Leeds.*
1902. Stacy, Richd. Davis, *Crayford.*
1914. Staddon,CecilSpurling,M C.,*Ipswich.*
1913. Staddon, Eric John, *Ipswich.*
1892. Staddon, Henry Ernest, *R.A.M.C.*
1885. Staddon, John Richard, *Ipswich.*
1886. Staddon, Walter Joseph, *Ipswich.*
1914. Stafford, Harry Neville, M.C.
1859. Stafford, Patrick Walter, *Army.*
1913. Stafford, Thos. Sidney, *Birmingham.*
1883. Stafford, William, *Nottingham.*
1915. Staffurth, Alan Edward, *Boston.*
1906. Staley, Herbert McLean, *St. Ann's*
1917. Staley, Robert Cyril W., *Southsea*
1919. Staley, Robert James, *Bexhill.*
1889. Stalkartt, Chas. E. Grey, *R.A.M.C.*
1913. Stallard, Chas. Marshall, *Manchester.*
1893. Stallard, Harry, *Newark-on-Trent.*
1899. Stallard, Nigel Frampton, *Hastings.*
1907. Stallard, Philip Lechmere, *Bombay.*
1905. Stallybrass, Clare Oswald, *Liverpool*
1897. Stamford, Rbt. Basil, *Loughborough.*
1871. Stamford, William, *Tunbridge Wells.*
1863. Stamford, Wm. Ackrill, *Tibshelf.*
1923. Stammers, Francis A. R., *Dudley.*
1896. Stammers, Geo. Elliott F., O.B E.
1907. Stamp, Lionel Duncan, *Plympton.*
13811

1876. Stamp, Wm. Daniel, *Plympton.*
1919. Standing, David Fox, *Rugby.*
1907. Standish, Frank, *Nottingham.*
1893. Stanford, Wm. Bedell, *Ealing.*
1912. Stanger, Geoffrey, *Winterbourne-pk.*
1902. Stanger-Leathes, Hugh Ellis, *I.M.S.*
1887. Staniforth, John William, *Hinderwell.*
1894. Staniland, Meaburn Francis, *Bristol.*
1896. Stanistreet, Richd. Weld, *R.N.*
1894. Stanley, Arthur, *Shanghai.*
1899. Stanley, Arthur John, *Hinckley.*
1888. Stanley, Charles James, *Ealing.*
1900. Stanley,Edwd.HamiltonBlake,*I.M.S.*
1895. Stanley, Hubert, *St. Leonards.*
1906. Stanley-Clarke,Crispian,*Rickm'nsw'th*
1901. Stannus, Hugh Stannus, *Nyasaland.*
1916.§Stansfeld, Elsie, *Belsize-pk.-gardens.*
1897. Stansfeld, John Stedwell, *Oxford.*
1913. Stansfeld, Rex, M.C., *Hailsham.*
1902. Stansfield, Fredk Jos., *Ben Rhydding.*
1873. Stansfield, Geo. S., O B.E., *Birkenh'd.*
1905. Stanton,Ambrose Thos ,*Malay States.*
1892. Stanton, James Wm. Wilcocks, *R.N.*
1896. Stanton, Thomas Wm., *Folkingham.*
1893. Stanwell, St. John, *Johannesburg.*
1881. Stanwell, William, *Rochdale.*
1860. Staples, Francis Patrick, *A.M.S.*
1892. Star, Paul Hohling Mills,O.B.E ,*R.N.*
1896. Stares, Chas. Lindsay Baker, *Swanley.*
1909. Starkey, Hy. S. Crichton,.*St. Bart's.*
1894. Starkey, Thomas Albert, *Montreal.*
1892. Starkey-Smith, Reginald, *Wrexham.*
1907. Starkey-Smith, Thos. G.,*Hungerford.*
1914. Starkie, Richard P. A., *Gloucester-st.*
1910 Starkie, Richard Wm., *Oakley-sq.*
1881. Starling,EdwinAlfd.,*Tunbridge Wells.*
1914. Starling, Edwin C. W., M.C.
1888. Starling, Ernest Henry, C.M.G.
1897. Starling, Hubert John, *Norwich.*
1884. Starr, W. H., C.B., C.M.G., A.M.S.
1908. Startin, John, M.C., *R.A.M.C.*
1902. Statham, Hugh, *Lymington.*
1895. Statham,Jn.Chas. B.,C.M.G.,C.B.E.
1910. Statham, Reg. S. S., O.B E., *Cheddar.*
1882. Statham, Reg. Whiteside, *Cheddar.*
1879. Stathers, Geo. Nicholson, *Brackley.*
1911. Stathers, Gerald Nicholson,*Brackley.*
1890. Statter, Hy. Bellamy, *Bournemouth.*
1918. Staunton, Gilbert Patrick, *Hornsey.*
1893. Staunton, Henry Foster.
1922.§Staveley, Dulcie Cicely, *Tonbridge.*
1896. Stead, Chas. Clement, *Hawkhurst.*
1892. Stead, Dryden, *Sydney, N.S.W.*
1907. Steadman, Sid. F.St. J., *Cavendish-sq.*
1916. Steadman, William. M.C., *Mallwyd.*
1906. Stebbing, Geo. F., *Lambeth-infirm'ry.*
1885. Stedman, Fred. Osmund, *Honghong*
13868

1899. Stedman,PercyT.H.,*LeightonBuzzard*
1899. Stedman, Savignac Bell, *Ceylon.*
1914. Steedman,Mackenzie T.W., *Stoneh'se*
1877. Steedman, Percy Andrew, *Oxford.*
1898. Steele, Geo. Herbert, *Much Birch.*
1872. Steele,Hy.Francis Arth.,*Bloomsbury.*
1877. Steele, Henry Frederic, *Brandon.*
1911. Steele, Hy. L. Hugh,*Wellington, N.Z.*
1872. Steele, Sidney Thomas, *Leeds.*
1894. Steele, Wm. Kenneth, *Devizes.*
1900. Steele.Wm. Lawr.,C.M.G.,*R.A.M.C.*
1900. Steele-Perkins, John S. S., *Exeter.*
1916. Steell, John W. G., *Heaton Mersey.*
1900. Steen, Wilfred Alexander, *Ilford.*
1881. Steer, William, *Plymouth.*
1892. Steggall,Sept Leonard Jn.,*Costa Rica.*
1878. Stein, Charles Guthrie, *Hampstead.*
1911. Steinbach, Chas. Horace, *Knaresboro'.*
1920. Steinberg, Philip, *Commercial-rd.*
1888. Steinthal, Walt. Oliver, *Manchester.*
1874. Stelfox, John Brideoake, *Southport.*
1895. Stenhouse, James Wilson, M.B E.
1894. Stenhouse, John Robert, *Lewes.*
1893. Stepanian, Hovsep Der, *Roumania.*
1881. Stephen, Guy Neville, O.B.E.
1873. Stephens,Aug.Edwd.Richard,*I.M.S.*
1908. Stephens,Frank Harold,O.B.E.,*R.N.*
1912. Stephens,Harold Frieze, *Redhill.*
1891. Stephens, Henry Newport, *Malvern.*
1890. Stephens, Hy. Woolcott, *Cape Prov.*
1900. Stephens, Hy. Zouch, *Tasmania.*
1903. Stephens, James Batson, *Rangoon.*
1917. Stephens, James R. Wm.,*Withington.*
1921. Stephens, John Alcwyn,*Huddersfield.*
1911. Stephens,Jn.R.Cook,*Weston-s.-Mare.*
1882. Stephens,L.Edwd.Walker,*Emsworth.*
1883. Stephens, Samuel, *Walcha, N.S.W.*
1896. Stephens. Stanley, *Sherborne.*
1893. Stephens, Wm. John, *Newquay.*
1913. Stephenson, Humphrey M., M.C.
1890. Stephenson, Owen Taunton,*Woolston.*
1907. Stephenson, Robt. West, *Windermere.*
1894. Stephenson, Wm. Arth , *W. Haddon.*
1883. Stericker, Geo. Fdk., *Illinois, U.S.A.*
1915. Sterling. Robert Gee. *Highbury-pk.*
1916. Sterne-Howitt,Harold,*Clement's-l'ne.*
1894. Sterry. John, O.B.E., *Sevenoaks.*
1911. Steuart, William, *Transvaal.*
1868. Steven, Alexander, *Victoria.*
1853. Stevens, Alfred, *Tauranga, N.Z.*
1897. Stevens, Alfred Edward, *Horsham.*
1874. Stevens, Alfred Felix, *Seaford.*
1901. Stevens, Andrew Norris, *Yarmouth.*
1877. Stevens, Arthur Frederic, *Studley.*
1923. Stevens, Arthur L. B , *Wimbledon.*
1899. Stevens,Bertram Crossfield,*Mortlake.*
1888. Stevens, Charles Henry, *Plympton.*
13925

1883. Stevens, Francis Joseph, *Camberwell.*
1917. Stevens, John Greet, *Guy's-hosp.*
1871. Stevens, Mordaunt A. de B. C., *Nice.*
1907. Stevens, Richd. Hy. E., *Madeira.*
1888. Stevens,Wm.Edwd.,*N.Bright'n,N.Z.*
1891. Stevens, Wm. Mitchell, *Cardiff.*
1891. Stevenson,Arch. Campbell, *Univ.Coll.*
1904. Stevenson,ClaudeMaberley,*Camb'dge.*
1873. Stevenson,SirEdm Sinclair, *C. Town.*
1880. Stevenson, Henry W., C.S.I., *I.M S.*
1896. Stevenson,T.H.C.,C.B.E.,*Somers't-ho.*
1897. Stevenson, Walter Brodie, *Cape Prov.*
1835. Stevenson, Wm. Dymes, *Honiton.*
1904. Steward,Sidney J.,Ḋ S.O ,*Farncombe.*
1895. Stewart, Chas. Balfour, *Bridgwater.*
1894. Stewart, Chas. Howard, *Cricklade.*
1914. Stewart, Charles John, *Alta, Canada.*
1917. Stewart, David, *Heaton-moor.*
1921.§Stewart, Dorothy Mary, *Exmouth.*
1883. Stewart, Sir E., K B.E., *E. Grinstead.*
1877. Stewart,Howard Doug., *Redcliffe-gdns.*
1892. Stewart, Jas. Allan, *Normanton.*
1912. Stewart, James Lennox, D.S.O.,M.C.
1894. Stewart, Sir J. Purves,K.C.M G.,C.B.
1887. Stewart,Rbt Wray,*Pittsburg,U.S.A.*
1912. Stewart, Roger Papillon, *Manchester.*
1883. Stewart, Rothsay Charles, *Leicester.*
1899. Stewart, Walter G., M.B.E., *Ware.*
1913. Stewart, William Allan, *Tasmania.*
1902. Stewart, Wm. H. Edwin, M.C.
1903. Sthamer, Eduard Franz A., *Transvaal.*
1908. Stibbe, Edward Philip, *Jesmond.*
1906. Stidston, Chas. Algernon, D.S.O.
1914. Stiell, Gavin, M.C., *Clapham.*
1915. Stiell, William Fletcher, *Clapham.*
1901. Stiff,HaroldHenry,*Bury-st-Edmunds*
1884. Stiles, Arthur Jalland, *Spalding.*
1893. Still, Geo. Frederic, *Queen Anne-st.*
1891. Stilwell,Geo. Rbt.Fabris,*Beckenham.*
1899. Stilwell, Reginald John, *Hillingdon.*
1893. Stirk, Percy Herbert, *Exeter.*
1901. Stirling-Hamilton, John, M.B.E.
1909. Stiven, Harold Edwd. S., *Cairo.*
1911. Stobie, Harry, *Sutton.*
1900. Stock, Philip G., C.B.,C.B.E ,*S.Afr.*
1896. Stockdale, Ernest Malcolm, *Liverpool.*
1889. Stocken, Leslie Maury, *Ealing.*
1910. Stocker, Charles Jas., M.C., *I.M.S.*
1872. Stocker,Chas.Jos.,*Budleigh-Salterf'n.*
1889. Stocker, Edward Gaved, *CarnBrea.*
1889. Stocker, Walt. Woodley, *Willesden.*
1908. Stockert, Wilhelm, *Heidelberg.*
1919.§Stocks, Mary Sylvia, *Weybridge.*
1907. Stocks, Reg. Woolsey, *Clapham.*
1886. Stockton, Hubt. Saml., *Peckham-rd.*
1893. Stoddart, Wm. Hy. B, *Bethlem-hosp.*
1913.§Stogden,MildredBlanche,*Seymour-pl.*
13982

1882. Stoker, George, C.M.G., *Hertford-st.*
1922. Stoker, George Morris, *Beddington.*
1912. Stokes,Adrian,D.S.O.,O.B.E.,*Dublin.*
1881. Stokes, Arthur Samuel, *Kettering.*
1883. Stokes, Francis Alex., *Albemarle-st.*
1879. Stokes, Henry Fraser, *Highbury.*
1872. Stokes, Henry Haldane, *R.A.M.C.*
1846. Stokes, James, *Prahran, Victoria.*
1887. Stokes, John, *Sheffield.*
1907. Stokes, Kenneth Henry, *Bexhill.*
1881. Stokes, Lennard, *Blackheath.*
1860. Stokes, William, *Bedford.*
1911. Stokes, Wm. Albert, *Gloucester.*
1903. Stolterfoth, Charles S., *Wallingford.*
1909. Stone, Bertram Alfd. Wood, *Southsea.*
1923 §Stone, Doris May, *Up. Richmond-rd.*
1911. Stone, Dudley Macaulay, *Park-mans.*
1922.§Stone, Ele mor Charlotte E., *Acton.*
1909. Stone, Ernest Richard, *Hildenborough.*
1883. Stone, Fdk. Wm. Stanley, *Norbury.*
1902. Stone, Gerald William, *Brighton.*
1877. Stone, Herbert Stanley, *Reigate.*
1895. Stonehouse, Hry., *Loftus-in-Clevel'd.*
1895. Stoner, Harold Boniface, *Brighton.*
1907. Stones, Robt. Yelverton, M.C.
1910. Stones, Wm. Boys, *Garstang.*
1891. Stonham, Hy. Arch., *College-crescent.*
1880. Stonham,Thos.Geo.,*Broadhurst-gdns.*
1905. Stordy, Thomas, M.C., *Surbiton.*
1922.§Store, Emma Marjorie, *Gt. Sutton-st.*
1911. Storer, Elliott John, *Hampstead.*
1923. Storer, Robert V., *Glenelg, S. Aust.*
1894. Storey, Percy Arth., *Marylebone-rd.*
1922. Story, Arthur Gordon, *Wadham-gds.*
1916. Stormer, Harold Gane, *Wandsworth.*
1901. Stormont,James Henry,*Birmingham.*
1895. Storrs, Eric Gleadow, *N. Rhodesia.*
1890. Storrs, Wm. Hy.Townsend, *Rhodesia.*
1897. Storrs,Wm. Townsend,*Tunb'ge Wells.*
1909. Stott, Arnold Walmsley, *Addison-rd.*
1884. Stott, Hugh, *Lewes.*
1908. Stott, Hugh, O.B.E., *I. M.S.*
1890. Stott, William Atkinson, *Leeds.*
1910. Stout, Robert, *Wellington, New Zeal.*
1920. Stoute, Athelstan Da Costa.
1922. Stovin, George Horace T., *Westcliff.*
1896. Stowe, William Reginald, *N.Z.*
1873. Stowers, Jas. Herbert, *Harley-st.*
1915. Stowers, Raymond, M.C.
1919. Strachan, James Grant, *Toronto.*
1912. Strachan, Jas. Simpson, *Cardiff.*
1908 Strahan,StuartSéguin,*Ravensc'rt-pk.*
1908. Strahy, George Stewart, *Toronto.*
1894. Strand, Alick Condell, *Harley-st.*
1908. Strange, Chas. Frederick, *China.*
1920. Strange, Edward Howard, *Wanstead.*
1896. Strange, Robt. Gordon, *Belsize-av.*
14039

1919.§Straschun, Sonia, *Antwerp.*
1899. Stratford, Howard M. B., *Kensington.*
1904. Straton, Alex. Wa't. Keith, *Salisbury.*
1907. Straton, Arthur Arbuthnot, *Wilton.*
1893. Straton, Charles Henry, *R.A.M.C.*
1923 §Stratton, Ella Mary, *Blackheath.*
1898. Stratton,PercyHoughton,*Hanover-sq.*
1921. Strawbaun, Albert Edward.
1893. Streatfeild, Thomas, *Folkestone.*
1888. Streatfield,Percy W., *WalthamAbbey.*
1903. Streatfield, W. Hugh R., *Ovington-sq.*
1897. Street, Albt. Ernest, *Woburn Sands.*
1880. Street, Alfd. Francis, *Westgate-on-S.*
1883. Street, Chas. Tidbury. *Newton, Lancs.*
1890. Streeten, Ernest Rock, *Barnsbury.*
1881. Stretton, Jn. Lionel, *Kidderminster.*
1922. Stribling,Bertram Hooper, *Devonp'rt*
1886. Stickland. Perev Chas. H., *I.M.S.*
1912. Stringer, Louis Brace, *Guy's-hosp.*
1909. Strode, Thomas Wm. R, *Ealing.*
1919. Strong, Condren Maurice, *Winnipeg.*
1889. Strong, Edgar Hugh, *Buluwayo.*
1898. Strong, Robert Hy., O.B.E., *Vict.*
1903. Strong, Walter Mersh, *Papua.*
1890. Strouts, Sidney Robert, *Maidstone.*
1881. Stroyan, Frederick, *Aldershot.*
1873. Struguell, Fredk. Wm., *Highgate-rd.*
1915. Strugnell, Lionel Fdk., *Brixton-hill.*
1884. Strugnell, Walt. Thos., *Brixton-hill.*
1922. Struthers,James Arth.,*Portsdown-rd.*
1902. Struthers, Wm. Eugene, *Canada.*
1911. Stuart, Alan Murray, *Leamore.*
1900. Stuart, Frederick, *Knightsbridge.*
1896. Stuart,Fredk.J.,O.B.E.,*Northampton.*
1890. Stuart, Robert, *Durham.*
1900. Stuart, Wm· Lumsden, *Camberley.*
1905. Stubbs, Ismay Donald, *Wimpole-st.*
1886. Stubbs, Percy B. Travers, *Cape Town.*
1893. Stuck, Sidney Joseph, *Fairlop-road.*
1881. Studer, Benjamin.
1922. Studdy, Louis William, *South Shields.*
1886. Sturdee, Alfred Hobart, C.M.G.,*Vict.*
1910. Sturdee, Edwin Lawrence, O.B.E.
1896. Sturdee, Fdk. Herbert, *Walsingham.*
1899. Sturdy, Harry Carlisle, *Wandsworth.*
1880. Sturge, Henry Havelock, *Elgin-av.*
1891. Sturge, Wm. Howard, *Hoddesdon.*
1894. Sturges-Jones,Wilfred E., *Herne-hill.*
1874. Sturmer, Arthur James,c/o *King & Co.*
1915. Sturridge, Fredk. Reg.,M.C.,*Kendal.*
1881. Sturridge, Peter Frederick, *Kendal.*
1905. Sturrock, Wm. D., D.S.O., *Oxford.*
1922. Sturton, Clement, *Bournemouth.*
1920. Sturton, Stephen Douglas, *Cambridge.*
1918. Stuttaford, Frank Hugo, *Plymouth.*
1906. Stuttaford, Wm. Jos. Ed., M.C.
1884. Styan, Thomas George, *Ramsgate.*
14096

1901. Style, Arthur Hurrell, *Pembroke.*
1889. Style, Fdk. William, *S. Brent.*
1881. Style, Robert George, *Brady-st.*
1913. Styles, William Vere Taylor, *Lee.*
1879. Suckling,CorneliusWm.,*Birmingham*
1922. Sudbury. Francis Bennett, *Ilkstone.*
1920. Sudki, Awad, *Moseley.*
1906. Sudlow,GeorgeWray,*Stoke-on-Trent.*
1920. Suffern, Canning, *Lambeth.*
1886. Sugden, Edward Scott, *Aintree.*
1899. Sugden, Henry, *Ealing.*
1854. Sullivan, Jn. Bond, *Knock,* co. *Clare.*
1887. Sully, Albert Max, *Claygate.*
1921. Sumbul, Yousuf Ahmed, *Egypt.*
1891. Summerhaves, J. O , D.S.O., *Thame.*
1881. Summerhill, Thomas Henry, *Rhyl.*
1923. Summers, George D , *Wandsworth.*
1922. Summers, Hug , *Holford-road.*
1922. Summers, Maxwell H., *Hounslow.*
1891. Summers, Thomas Collyer, *Bow-rd.*
1915. Summers, Thomas Collyer, *Bow-rd.*
1888. Summerskill, William, *Manor-park.*
1885. Sumner, Benjamin, *Liverpool.*
1898. Sumner, Fred. William, *I.M.S.*
1881. Sumner, Jos. Hy. Surtees, *Russell-sq.*
1887. Sumpter, Berners Geo., *Hunstanton.*
1884. Sumpter, Walt. Jn. E., *Sheringham.*
1923. Sumption,Harold H., *Oxford-terrace.*
1906. Sundell, Charles Ernest. *S. Elmsall.*
1886. Sunder, Chas. Edward, *Grindlays Co.*
1916. Sunderland, Arthur, *Bexley Heath.*
1914. Sunderland,Edward Benj.,*Ringwood.*
1888. Sunderland, Oliver, *Berley-heath.*
1918. Sunderland, Regd. Henry, *Bradford.*
1902. Sunderland, Robert Arch. S., *Hull.*
1882. Sunderland, Sept., *Cavendish-square.*
1923. Surial, Hayim Atiya, *Assiout.*
1917. Surrage, Harold Jas. R., *Sydenham.*
1900. Susman, Walter James, *Henley.*
1912. Sutcliffe, Alan Lee, *Burley, Yorks.*
1907. Sutcliffe, Edward, *Wisbech.*
1874. Sutcliffe, E. Crossley T·, *India.*
1905. Sutcliffe, James Herbert, *Acomb.*
1879. Sutcliffe, John, *Cheadle Roy. Asylum.*
1922. Sutcliffe, Maurice Lister.
1883. Sutcliffe, Victor Eugene, *Chesterfield.*
1897. Sutcliffe, William, *West Bromwich.*
1909. Sutcliffe, William Francis, *Clapham.*
1921. Suter, Harold Edward, *Portsmouth.*
1886. Sutherland, Geo. Alex , C.B.E.
1907. Sutherland.Jos.Roderick,*Stonehouse.*
1853. Sutherland, Philip Warren, *I.M.S.*
1900. Sutherland, William.
1894. Sutter, Robert Ross. *Warboys.*
1885. Sutton, A., C.B..C.M.G., *Queensland.*
1885. Sutton, Alfred Martin, *California.*
1922. Sutton,Dick Brasnett,*Champion-hill.*
14153

1893. Sutton, Edward, C.M.G., *R.N.*
1914. Sutton, Evelyn Alex., M.C., *R.A.M.C.*
1922. Sutton, Harold John Vane, *Acacia-yds*
1883. Sutton, Henry Martin, *Truro.*
1921.§Sutton, Muriel Amy, *Brookfield-pk.*
1881. Sutton, Samuel Walter, *T'bridge Wells.*
1877. Sutton, Thos. Seagrave, *Bishop's Castle.*
1907. Sutton, Wm. Hubert R., *Cape Prov.*
1922. Suvanaa, Synn, *Ashbury-place.*
1923. Suzman, Samuel Sappy, *Finchley-rd.*
1887. Suzuki, Shigemichi, *Tokio.*
1908. Svensson, Robert, M.C., *Fed. Malay S.*
1879. Swabey, Louis William, *R.A.M.C.*
1892. Swabey, Maurice, *R.A.M.C.*
1921. Swaine, Richard Obank, *Bradford.*
1895. Swainson, Ed. A. C., *Stoke-on-Trent.*
1889. Swallow, Allan James, *Clapham.*
1890. Swan, Chas. Robert Jn. Atkin, O B.E
1923. Swan, George Ronald M., *Kenilworth.*
1918. Swan, George Seymour, *Rock Ferry.*
1870. Swan, Richd. Jocelyn, *Wallington.*
1917. Swann, Meredith B. R., *Beckenham.*
1916. Swanson, George Carson, *Glasgow.*
1874. Swanwick, Eustace M., *W.Hartlepool.*
1888. Swayne, Walter Carless, *Bristol.*
1896. Sweet, Edwd. Hoare, *Uckfield.*
1905. Sweet, Samuel Henry, *Dowlais.*
1905. Sweet, Wm. Sidney, *Perth, W. Aust.*
1893. Sweetnam, Stephen W., *R.A.M.C.*
1894. Swenden, Benj. Wood. *Bournemouth.*
1902. Swete-Evans, Wm. Benj., *Southport.*
1912. Swietochowski, G. de, *Clifton-hill.*
1882. Swift, Harry, *Adelaide, S. Australia.*
1889. Swift, Sidney Sampson, *Liverpool.*
1874. Swift, Wm. Jn. Cropley, *Gordon-sq.*
1920. Swinburne, Spearman Charles.
1904. Swindale, Hy. Vernon, *Southwick-pl.*
1922. Swindell, Ralph S., *Alexandra-pk.-rd.*
1893. Swinhoe, Geo. Rodway, *New Swindon.*
1855. Swinson, George Newton, *N.S. W.*
1891. Swinton, Francis Ed., C.I.E.. *I.M.S.*
1896. Sworder, Ernest George, *Streatham.*
1875. Sworder, Horace, *Luton.*
1904. Sworn, Alfred Geo., *Highbury-cres.*
1892. Sworn, Ernest Andrew, *Hanley.*
1884. Sworn, Henry George, *Highbury-cres.*
1887. Swyer, Robert, *Bethnal-green.*
1912. Swyer, Robert, *Bethnal-green.*
1885. Sydenham, Geo. Francis, *Dulverton.*
1890. Sykes, Arthur, *Nelson.*
1905. Sykes, Arthur Barry, *Formby.*
1914. Sykes, Frank, *Batley.*
1889. Sykes, John Herbert, *Birkdale.*
1897. Sykes, John Lewis, *Tottenham.*
1879. Sykes, Wm. Ainley, D.S.O., *I.M.S.*
1919. Sykes, William Stanley, *Morley.*
1917.§Sylk, Ellen, *Highgate.*
14210

1914. Sylvester, Clement K., *Trowbridge.*
1892. Sylvester, Hbt. Mayris, *Leiston.*
1902. Sylvester Bradley, Chas. R., *R.A.M.C.*
1892. Syme, Arthur Edward, *Victoria.*
1908. Symes, Arthur Jessop, *I.M.S.*
1898. Symes, Ernest, *Box.*
1891. Symes, John Odery, *Clifton.*
1921. Symes, Richard N. L., *Teddington.*
1890. Symes, Wm. Legge, *Univ. of London.*
1900. Symes-Thompson, Hy.E., *Cavendish-sq*
1911. Symns, James L. M., *Bungay.*
1915. Symonds, Chas. Putnam, *Portland-pl.*
1888. Symonds, Henry, *Kimberley, S. Afr.*
1901. Symons, Angelo Nelson, *Jersey.*
1918. Symons, Arthur Denis, *Bath.*
1911. Symons, Cecil Hearle, *R.N.*
1916. Symons, Godfrey Trehane, *Penzance.*
1916. Symons, Hy. John Hugh, *Penzance.*
1876. Symons, John, *Penzance.*
1922.§Symons, Mary Irene, *Bradford.*
1920. Symons, Percival W., *Bristol.*
1894. Symons, Sir Robert Fox, K.B.E.
1894. Symons, Thomas Henry, *I.M.S.*
1913. Symons, Wm. John Francis, *Scorrier.*
1904. Syms, John Kendall, *Birmingham.*
1915. Sy Quia, Ramon Romero, *Manila.*
1883. Syrée, Anton Hugh, *Walsall.*

T.

1879. Tabb, John Fredk., *Trafalgar-rd.*
1886. Tabor, Chas. James, *Bath.*
1906. Tacey, Dalton Wm., *Woodford.*
1921. Tagoe, Edward, *Lancaster-rd.*
1896. Tahmisian, Paul Baldasar, *Balham.*
1879. Tait, Edwd. Sabine, *Highbury-park.*
1923. Tait, Greville Brend.
1022. Tait, Joseph Gillison, *Edinburgh.*
1904. Takaki, Kenji, *Tokio, Japan.*
1899. Takaki, Yoshihiro, *Tokio, Japan.*
1896. Takayasu, Michisige, *Osaka, Japan.*
1921. Talaat, Abbass Hilmy, *Cairo.*
1895. Talbot, Alfred George, *Auckland, N.Z.*
1903. Talbot, Francis, *Highgate.*
1889. Talent, Jn. Wm., *Ashton-under-Lyne.*
1899. Tallent, John Henry, *Chislehurst.*
1921. Tallerman, Kenneth Harry.
1923. Tame, Ronald Granville, *Bournemo'th*
1875. Tamplin, Chas. Harris, *Ramsgate.*
1915. Tamplin, E. Cooper, M.C., *Farncombe.*
1910. Tamplin, Frank Stuart, *R.A.M.C.*
1905. Tangye, Claude Edward, *Leamington.*
1861. Tanner, Richard Canning, *Kempsey.*
1923. Tanner, Selwyn Edward, *Swansea.*
1893. Tarachand, Nowroji M., *Mansfield.*
14262

1906. Taraporwala, Pheroze K., *I.M.S.*
1923. Targett, Edgar James, *Hockley.*
1879. Tarleton,P., *Standard Bank of S Afr.*
1919. Tarring, Guy Barford, *Arkwright-rd.*
1909. Tasker, Harold Lindley, *U. Coll.-h.*
1917. Tasker, Ron dld Henry, *Bristol.*
1905. Tatam, Edwin Charles, *Westcliff.*
1900. Tatchell, Percy, *Holland-park.*
1904. Tatchell, Wm. Arthur, *Hankow.*
1882. Tate, Alan E., C.S.I., C.M.G., *A.M.S.*
1922. Tate, George, *Hampstead.*
1906. Tate, John, *Harrow.*
1894. Tatham, Arth. Leopold, *Abergavenny.*
1883. Tatham,Chas.Jn.W.,O.B.E.,*Scarbro'.*
1883. Tatham, Edward, *Glasgow.*
1886. Tatham, Ernest John, *Cheltenham.*
1887. Tattersall, Chas. Hermann, *Salford.*
1900. Tattersall, John, *Harnwell.*
1874. Tattersall, Lord, *Clayton-le-Moors.*
1919. Tattersall, Stanley Roy, *Rochdale.*
1916. Tatton, Glyde Philip, *Stroud-green.*
1898. Taunton, Jn. G. Cresswell, *Chatham.*
1915. Taunton, Thomas Joseph.
1913. Taves, Archibald Wm., *Swanage.*
1897. Taw, Moung Pha, *Up. Bedford-place.*
1903. Tayler, Fred. Ernest, *Trowbridge.*
1900. Tayler, Hy. Christopher, *Bradford.*
1900. Tayler, John Lionel, *Highbury.*
1906. Taylor,Alfd.K.B.R.Wm.,*Sittingb'rne.*
1912. Taylor, Arnold Rothwell, *Bacup.*
1920. Taylor, Arthur Walford, *Norwich.*
1894. Taylor, Ashby, *Sark.*
1881. Taylor, Benj. Robert Archer, *N.S. W.*
1911. Taylor, Berthold S., *Southwold.*
1922. Taylor, Cecil Geoffrey, *Cambridge.*
1912. Taylor, Cedric R., O.B.E., *Ealing.*
1909. Taylor,Chas.Hy.Shinglewood.*Jersey.*
1911. Taylor, Chas. Jos. G., *Glenlock-rd.*
1893. Taylor, Dudley Claude Palmer,*Sibsey.*
1901. Taylor, Edwd. Jas. Davis, *Southsea.*
1908. Taylor, Edwd. L., n., *Saffron Walden.*
1913. Taylor, Sir Eric S., Bt., O B.E.
1891. Taylor, Fdk. Hy. Arth., *S. Hackney.*
1889. Taylor, Fdk. R. Percival, *Hellingley.*
1901. Taylor, George Orissa, *Chittagong.*
1906. Taylor, Gerald Maberly, *Leeds.*
1917. Taylor, Harman, *Liverpool.*
1921. Taylor, Harold Bourne.
1922. Taylor, HaroldWestgarth,*Cambridge.*
1917. Taylor, Harold George, *Sutton.*
1923. Taylor, Harry Charles C., *Plymouth.*
1876. Taylor, Henry Edward, *Bradford.*
1898. Taylor, Henry James, *Preston.*
1866. Taylor, Hy. Shinglewood, *Ficksburg.*
1893. Taylor, Herbert, *Wakefield.*
1921. Taylor, Horace Wilfred, *Bolton.*
1916. Taylor, Hugh Watts, *Highbury.*
14319

1898. Taylor, Isaac, *Leeds.*
1876. Taylor, James, *Clifton.*
1899. Taylor, James George, *Chester.*
1920. Taylor, James McWilliam, *Chelsea.*
1884. Taylor,Jn.Cleasby,*Berwick-on-Tweed*
1887. Taylor, John Francis, *Leyton.*
1911. Taylor, John Frank, *Chiswick.*
1893. Taylor, John William, *Methley.*
1894. Taylor, John William,O.B.F.,*Bristol.*
1910. Taylor, Leonard Herbert, *Hart-st.*
1916.§Taylor, Lily Dorothea, *Victoria-st.*
1886. Taylor, Lot Albert, *Brierley-hill.*
1921.§Taylor,MarjoriePerrers,*Comeragh-rd.*
1894. Taylor, Mark Ronald, *Acton.*
1905. Taylor, Martin Bramley, *Hemsworth.*
1916. Taylor, Norman Burke, *Ramsgate.*
1870. Taylor, Reginald, *Gray's-inn-road.*
1906. Taylor, Reg. Thane,*Shepherdess-walk.*
1877. Taylor, Richd. Stanley, *Surbiton.*
1923. Taylor, Richard William, *Syston.*
1905. Taylor, Robt. Stanley, *Watchet, Som.*
1872. Taylor, Seymour, *Seymour-street.*
1863. Taylor, Shephard Thomas, *Norwich.*
1878. Taylor, Sidney Johnson, *Norwich.*
1880. Taylor, Thomas Percy.
1908. Taylor, Walter, *Dunmville, Canada.*
1908. Taylor, Wilfrid Reginald, *Rangoon.*
1900. Taylor,Wm.Benj.Batchelor,*Sevenoaks*
1870. Taylor, Wm. Bramley, *Weybridge.*
1879. Taylor, Wm. Chas. Everley, *Scarbro'.*
1867. Taylor, William Fredk., *Brisbane.*
1900. Taylor, William Irwin, *W. Africa.*
1916. Taymour, Aly Heidar, *Cairo.*
1896. Teale, Michael Aubrey, *Leeds.*
1905. Teasdale, John Camidge, *Retford.*
1889. Tebb, Albt. Edward, *Hampstead.*
1902. Tebbs, Basil Nelson, *Southampton.*
1896. Tebbs, Lionel Virtue, *S. Africa.*
1910. Teichmann, Gottfried Oram, *Bengal*
1906. Teichman, Oskar, D.S.O., M.C.
1898. Telling, Walt. Hy. Maxwell, *Leeds.*
1890. Tempest, Henry, *Thorner.*
1897. Tempest, James, *Manchester.*
1865. Temple, James Algernon, *Toronto.*
1897. Temple, Percy Geo., *Buro'-high-st.*
1909. Templeton, Henry Hercules S., *Peel.*
1902. Templeton, James, *Grafton-rd.,* N.
1890. Templeton, Percy, *Nat. Bank, Ltd.*
1888. Tench, Montague, *Dunmow.*
1895. Tench, Sidney Edward, *Frinton.*
1896. Tenison, Adolph, *Scalby, Yorks.*
1917. Tennekoon, Jn. Percy R.,*Balcombe-st.*
1916. Terry, Cecil Henry, *Bath.*
1915. Terry, Gordon Stuart, *Cheltenham.*
1880. Terry, Henry George, *Bath.*
1914. Terry, Leonard Hankinson, *Barnet.*
1899. Tetley,ThomasWalsh,*Kabymoorside.*
14367

1919. Teuten, Aubrey Clifford, *St. Mary's-h.*
1910. Te Water, Frans Karel, M.C.
1916. Tewfik, I-mail, *Cairo.*
1915. Tha, Richard R. Htoon Oo, *I.M.S.*
1914. Thackeray, Joseph Bulwer, M.C.
1900. Thackray, Christopher, *Pancras-rd.*
1918. §Thackwell, Mary, *Norwich.*
1876. Thain, Le-lie Lachlan, *Hereford.*
1910. Thakur, Keshav Sadashiv, *Bombay.*
1885. Thane, Edgar Herbt., *Sydney.*
1881. Thane, Philip Thornton, *N.S. W.*
1914. Thavara, Mom Chow, *Bangkok.*
1880. Theed, Stanley Vipan, *Transvaal.*
1922. Theiler, Max.
1920. Theobald, G. Wm., *Cartwright-gdns.*
1887. Theobalds, Owen Lemare, *Glenloch-rd.*
1917. Theron, Raymund, *Somerset W., S.Af.*
1880. Thistle, Fredk Thomas, *Torquay.*
1918. §Thom, Edith Marjorie, *Barry.*
1891. Thomas, Abraham, *Aberystwyth.*
1876. Thomas, Sir Abraham G., *Newport.*
1922. §Thomas, Agnes W. O'D., *Malvern.*
1901. Thomas, Albert Edward, *Cape Prov.*
1888. Thomas, Archibald, *Chandler's-ford.*
1905. Thomas, Arnold Newall, D.S.O.
1910. Thomas, Arth.Hy.Leop'ld, *Vincent-sq.*
1899. Thomas, Arthur Richd., O.B.E., *R.N.*
1917. Thomas, Benjamin, *Hirwain.*
1884. Thomas, Benj. Wilfred, *Welwyn.*
1919. Thomas, Beriah M. G., *Nantymoel.*
1923. §Thomas, Blanchette, *Aberdare.*
1901. Thomas, Cadogan, *Wandsworth.*
1914. Thomas, Charles Hamblen, *Ormesby.*
1898. Thomas, Charles James, *Epsom.*
1921. Thomas, Cleme it Price, *Abercarn.*
1920. Thomas, Cyril James, *Clapham.*
1917. Thomas, Daniel Jenkin, *Lampeter.*
1902. Thomas, Daniel Jenkins, *Bargoed.*
1893. Thomas, Daniel Lewis, *Bromley-st.*
1922. Thomas, David Cyril, *Cardiff.*
1880. Thomas, David John, *Bridgend.*
1899. Thomas, David Jones, *Acton.*
1891. Thomas, David Owen, *Minneapolis.*
1915. Thomas, David Page, *Aberystwyth.*
1915. Thomas, Donald C., c/o *Holt & Co.*
1906. Thomas, Edmund Fairfield, *Charlton.*
1902. Thomas, ElijahRichd. Lockwood, *R.N.*
1897. Thomas, Ellis Rae, *Gillingham.*
1921. Thomas, EricWaldoC iryl, *Carnarvon.*
1903. Thomas, Frank Leslie, *Barnstaple.*
1914. Thomas, Geo. R. S., *Bristol.*
1882. Thomas, Geo.TrevorHarley, *R.A.M.C*
1873. Thomas, George Tucker, *I.M.S.*
1918. Thomas, Graham McKim, *Swansea.*
1921. Thomas, Harold Edwin, *St. Clears.*
1899. Thomas, Harold Sebert, *Portsmouth.*
1908. Thomas, Harold Skarratt, *N.S.W.*

1889. Thomas, Harold Wynne, *Bromley.*
1907. Thomas, Henry Darby, *Melbourne.*
1874. Thomas, Herbt. Henry, *Hebden-b'dge.*
1897. Thomas, Herbert John, *Epsom.*
1921. Thomas, Horace Rees John, *Swansea.*
1914. Thomas, Horatio, *Cardiff.*
1923. Thomas, Hugh Arwel, *Rhos.*
1904. Thomas, Hugh Mortimer, *Goodwick.*
1905. Thomas, James Douglas, *Rotherithe.*
1915. Thomas, Jas.Wm.Tudor, *Breconshire.*
1876. Thomas, John Hannibal, *Barrow.*
1882. Thomas, John Henry, *Royal Navy.*
1917. Thomas, John Herbert, *Lampeter.*
1887. Thomas, John Lewis, *Newport.*
1892. Thomas, Jn.Morgan Mortimer, *Bristol.*
1914. Thomas, Jn O., M.C., *Westm.-hosp.*
1876. Thomas, John Raglan, *Exeter.*
1913. Thomas, John William, *Leeds.*
1921. Thomas, Joseph Stanley, *East Ham.*
1886. Thomas, Josiah Telfer, *Camborne.*
1896. Thomas, Leonard Kirkby, *Birmingh'm.*
1905. Thomas, Lewis, *Halifax, Nov. Scotia.*
1910. Thomas, Martin Phillips, *Llanelly.*
1918. Thomas, Norman Beattie, *Beaumaris.*
1896. Thomas, Rhys Tudor, *Cardiff.*
1887. Thomas, Richd. Francis, *Cwmaman.*
1905. Thomas, Robert Arthur, *Toronto.*
1906. Thomas, Robert Evans, *Bristol.*
1903. Thomas, Robert J. Percy, *Devonport.*
1892. Thomas, Robert Stanley, *Barrow.*
1915. Thomas, Rufus Clifford, *Pontypridd.*
1896. Thomas, Thomas, *Ferndale, Glam.*
1923. Thomas, Thomas Ben, *Swansea.*
1914. Thomas, Thomas Harold, *Laugharne.*
1903. Thomas, Thomas Jas. Bell, *Maesteg.*
1886. Thomas, Thos. Nash, *Pembrokeshire.*
1900. Thomas, Thomas Price, *Brecon.*
1885. Thomas, Thos. William, *Caerphilly.*
1922. Thomas, Trevor Meyrick, *Bangor.*
1877. Thomas, William, O.B.E., *Rhyl.*
1915. Thomas, William, *Clapham.*
1922. Thomas, William, *Anglesey.*
1879. Thomas, Wm.Fredk., *Nat. Bk.of India.*
1896. Thomas, Wm. George, *Birmingham.*
1916. Thomas, William Henry, *Gorseinon.*
1897. Thomas, William John, *Pengam.*
1915. Thomas, William Leslie, *Swansea.*
1900. Thomas, Wm. Murray, *Lostwithiel.*
1912. Thomas, William Rees, *Hellingly.*
1919. Thomas, Wm. Stanley Russell, *Hay.*
1899. Thompson, Arthur, *Newbury.*
1906. Thompson, Arth.Geo.Jas., *T'ick'nh'm.*
1876. Thompson, Arth. Hirst, *Knaresboro'.*
1891. Thompson, Arth. Hugh, *Weymouth-st.*
1921. Thompson, BernardWoolcott, *Cardiff.*
1899. Thompson, Cecil C. Brandon, *Tutshill.*
1891. Thompson, Charles, *Burton-on-Tr.*

1877. Tidswell, Herbt. Henry, *Torquay.*
1906. Tidy, Henry Letheby, *Devonshire-pl.*
1901. Tierney, Thomas, *Marple.*
1922. Tilander, Nils Filip, *Natal.*
1901. Tilbury, Robert, *Peckham.*
1902. Tilleke, Rbt. Edwin GooLe, *Bangkok.*
1919. Tilleke, Wm. Guna, *Shaftesbury-av.*
1913. Tilley, Jas. L. Octavius, *Welbeck-st.*
1910. Tilling, Harold Wm., *Queensland.*
1918. Tilsley, George Edwin, *Bristol.*
1910. Timberg, Richard Teodor, *Reading*
1922. Timings, Leslie James, *Handsworth.*
1903. Timothy, John Haydn, *Nantyaredig*
1907. Timpson, George Gilbert,'*Highgate.*
1866. Tindale, W. Raynes, *Hampton.*
1889. Tindall,ErnestEdw.Partridge,*Exeter.*
1913. Tingey, Aubrey Jn. Colby, *Reading.*
1911. Tinker, Frank Stanley, *Graubunden.*
1895. Tinley,Wm.E. Falkingbridge,*Whitby*
1902. Tinne, Philip Frederic, *Liverpool.*
1896. Tipper, Ernest Harry, *W. Africa.*
1916. Tippet, J. Aylmer, M.C., *Cleeve,Ross.*
1894. Tippett,SydneyGordon,*Huddersfield.*
1892. Tipping,Henry Hubert, *Birmingham.*
1876. Tirard, Sir Nestor I. Chas., *Harley-st.*
1883. Tireman, Arthur Lumley. *Hull.*
1917. Tisdall, Fredk. Fitz-Gerald, *Toronto.*
1909. Titlestad. Karl Johannes, *Zululand.*
1899. Titley, Frederick Lionel, *Plumstead.*
1911. Titmas, Jn. St. Andrew, *Hampstead.*
1902. Titterton, Herbert Chas.,*King'sCross.*
1907. Tiwary,SheoNandon, *Cawnpore,India*
1890. Tizard, Henry John, *New Zealand.*
1920. Tjon-A-Man, C J. A., *Amsterdam.*
1896. Todd, Arthur Rochefort, *Jamaica.*
1894. Todd, Charles, O.B.E., *Cairo.*
1896. Todd, David Bansall, *Chillington.*
1923 §Todd, Doris, *Linthorpe.*
1915. Todd, Edgar William, *Hull.*
1911. Todd, Francis Richd., *N. Petherton.*
1886. Todd, Frederick.
1880. Todd, George Dixon, *Selby.*
1887. Todd, Hy. Bansall, *Cheltenham.*
1876. Todd, Howard Jas. McC., C.B., *R.N.*
1865. Todd, John, *Mile-End-road.*
1907. Todd, John Lancelot, *Montreal.*
1923. Todd, Kenneth Waller, *Wallington.*
1907. Todd, Ronald Ernest, *R.A.M.C.*
1907. Todd, Wm. Fentham, *N. Malden.*
1907. Todd-White, Arth. Thos., *Leyton.*
1910. Todesco, Jas. Massimo, *Grenville-st.*
1911. Todhunter, Jn.Reg.A.D.,*Bedford-pk.*
1912. Toll, William Clair, *Alberta.*
1882. Toller, Chas. Wm.Edwd., *Ilfracombe.*
1898. Tolputt, Arnold George, *Kettering.*
1884. Tomalin,Wm. Jn. Clarkson,*Manitoba*
1873. Tomes, Arthur, *Exmouth.*

1861. Tomkins, Chas. Payne, *Epsom.*
1884. Tomkins, Harding Henbest, *Ealing.*
1893. Tomkys, Leonard Sydney, *Lichfield.*
1894. Tomlinson,Geo. Hedley,*Birmingham.*
1920. Tomlinson, Henry, *Hazel-grove.*
1891. Tomlinson, Henry Edward, *R.N.*
1897. Tomlinson,John Henry,M.C.,*Egham.*
1908. Tomlinson, Percy Stanley, D.S.O.
1890. Tompsett, Robert Henry.
1921.§Tompson Helen C., *Winchcombe.*
1918. Toms, Humphrey Woodland, *Jersey.*
1894. Toms, Philip Moysey, *Ham-street.*
1883. Tomson, Walter Bolton, *Luton.*
1902. Tong, Livsey, *Bolton.*
1900. Tongue, Edwin John, *Winterton.*
1920. Tonkin, Bertie Moorwood, *Natal.*
1886. Tonking, John Herbert, *Camborne.*
1895. Tonks, Arthur Edwin, *Newport.*
1915. Tonks, Myles Denison B., *Strood.*
1918. Toogood, Edward Sherman.
1886. Toogood, Fdk. Sherman, O.B.E.
1894. Toombs, Herbert Geo., *Trebovir-rd.*
1921. Toop, Howard Metherell, *Devonport.*
1914. Tooth, Frederick, *Nether Stowey.*
1880. Tooth, Howard Henry, C.B., C.M.G.
1901. Topham, Frederick Stocks, *Halifax.*
1914. Topham, Harold, *Halifax.*
1902. Topham, John Arthur, *Canterbury.*
1916. Topham, Richard Stanley, *Halifax.*
1909. Topley, Wm. W. C., *Harley-street.*
1887. Tordoff, Sargen, *Southport.*
1897. Torrance, James, *New Zealand.*
1905. Torrens. James Aubrey, *South-street.*
1903. Tosswill; Leonard R., O.B.E., *Exeter.*
1907. Totesau, Geo. Stiebel, *Jamaica.*
1918. Tothill, Alfred Robert, *Sydenham.*
1922. Tothill, Henry, *Staines.*
1905. Toulmin, Arthur, *Preston.*
1908. Toulmin, Ernest Wm., *Guildford.*
1901. Tovey, Arthur Hamilton, *New Zeal.*
1918.§Towers, Agnes Elizabeth, *Bolton.*
1880. Towlson, Harry Joseph, *Barrowden.*
1895. Towne, Hugh Rose Forster, *S.Africa,*
1895. Townend, Richd. Hamilton, *Brockley.*
1916. Townend, Rob. Ockleston, *Ealing.*
1903. Townroe,Eugene Dunbar,*Kensington.*
1890. Townsend, Arth. Allen D.,*Gloucester.*
1884. Townsend, Edwd. Bridges, *R. Navy.*
1907. Townsend,Reg.Stephen,M.C.,*I.M.S.*
1893. Townsend-Whitling, H. T. M.,*Rugby.*
1919. Townshend, Desmond V., *Yarmouth.*
1922. Townshend, Maurice A., *Hendon.*
1919.§Townshend, Ruth C., *Croydon.*
1912. Tozer, Ernest Alfred, *Boscombe.*
1921. Tozer, Fred H. Wickham, *Sheerness.*
1923. Tracey, Basil Martin, *Willand.*
1921. Tracy, George Dillon Croil,*Harrow.*

1906. Tracy,Horace E. H.,*Bury St.Edmunds.*
1902. Trail, David Herbert, *Falmouth.*
1916. Traill, Ralph Rbt., *Newport Pagnell.*
1906. Trapnell, Francis Cyril, *Beckenham.*
1882. Trapp, John Best.
1884. Tratman, Frank, *Perth, W. Australia.*
1887. Travers, Archibald Lindsay.
1885. Travers, ErnestAstonO.,*MalayStates.*
1904. Travers, Ernest Frank,*Phillimore-gns.*
1803. Travers, Fredk. Thos., O.B.E.
1882. Travers, Geoff. Frederic, *Victoria.*
1885. Travis, George Lewis, *Llandudno.*
1383. Travis, William Owen, *Hampton.*
1902. Traylen, Chas. Leonard, *Willesden.*
1921. Traylen, John Phillip, *Muswell-hill.*
1909. Treadgold, Hy. A., *Osterley-park.*
1881. Treadwell,Oliver F.Naylor,*Parkhurst.*
1883. Treasure, Wm. B. Crawford, *Cardiff.*
1899. Tredg ld, Alfred Frank, *Guildford.*
1886. Tredinnick, Albt. Stephen,*Melbourne.*
1875. Tredinnick, Ernest, *Craven Arms.*
1920. Tree, Mark, *Bethnal-green.*
1894. Tregaskis, Edwd. Paul Robins, *O.F.S.*
1923.§Trezelles, Olga Frances, *Blomfield-rd.*
1895. Tregenza, William, *Sheffield.*
1904. Trench, John Henry, *St. John's-wood.*
1890. Trenfield, George Hy., *Bristol.*
1905. Tresawna,Wm.Samson.,*Abergavenny*
1906. Tresidder, Alfred Geddes, *I.M.S.*
1882. Tresidder, Edwd. Stanley, *Milbrook.*
1883. Tresidder, Harry Innis, *New Zealand.*
1897. Tresidder, Morton Everard,*Blackheath*
1895. Tresidder, Percy Edgar, *Nottingham.*
1888. Tresidder, Wm. Elliot, *Paignton.*
1923.§Tresilian, Kathleen Edith, *Enfield.*
1911. Trevan, John William, *Plymouth.*
1906. Treves, Fredk. Boileau, *Margate.*
1886. Trevor, Edward Fitzg., *Pelsall.*
1881. Trevor, Henry Octavius, *R.A.M.C.*
1908. Trevor-Roper, B. W. E., *Bowdon.*
1897. Trewby, Henry Wm., *Hanover-sq.*
1906. Trewby, Joseph Fredc., *Brixton-hill.*
1914.§Tribe, Naomi, *Brondesbury.*
1895. Tribe,Paul Cuningham Edwd.,O.B.E.
1904. Tribe,Reginald Herman,M.C.,*Kell'm.*
1874. Triggs, Jn. Bellhouse Bowden, *R.N.*
1926.§Trimmer, Edith Helen, *Bromley.*
1902. Trimmer, Francis Inman, *Blyth.*
1883. Trinder, Alfred Probus, *Wadebridge.*
1850. Tripe, Decimus, *Wanganui, N.Z.*
1900. Tripp,Basil Hubt. Howard,*Southwold.*
1881. Tripp, Chas. Lllew. Howard, *Taunton.*
1919. Trist, George Marston, *Bayswater.*
1905. Trist, John Ronald Rigden, M.C.
1902. Tritsch, Robert, *Johann esburg.*
1881. Trotter, Walt Octavius, *Brandon.*
1914. Trounce, Thos. Reg.,*Waltham Abbey.*

14775

1918. Troup,Howard Branston,*Gloucester-pl*
1918.§Trouton, Norah Edith, *Rotherfield.*
1884. Trower, Arthur, *St. Leonards-on-Sea.*
1914. Trower, Geoffrey Say, *St. Leonards.*
1901. Trubshaw, Kenneth Vincent, *Mold.*
1900. Truman,Bernd.Rensh'wB.,*N'ttingh'm*
1875. Truman, Charles Edwin, *Slough.*
1912. Truman, Dudley Beckit, *Oxford.*
1899. Trumper, Wm. Arthur, *Torquay.*
1894. Trythall, Wm. Reynolds, *Roy. Navy.*
1913. Tsoi-A-Sue, Jos. Alex., *Trinidad.*
1894. Tuck, Ernest Sydney, *Roy. Navy.*
1919. Tucker, Donald Leslie, *Burnet.*
1895. Tucker, Ernest Fdk. Gordon, *I.M.S.*
1922. Tucker, Harold Keith, *Walthamstow.*
1830. Tucker, Joseph, *Chulmleigh.*
1876. Tucker, Milton Mallosey, *Ontario.*
1906. Tucker, Sydney Arthur, *Bromley.*
1899. Tucker, Wm. Eldon, *Bermuda.*
1899. Tucker, Wm. Hancock, *I.M.S.*
1898. Tuckett, Ivor Lloyd, *Cambridge.*
1884. Tuckett,Walter,R.,O.B.E.,*Loughbro'.*
1910. Tudge, Cecil Carrington, *Chipstead.*
1872. Tudge, Jas. McDougall, *Cricklewood.*
1923. Tughan,Norman Chas.,*Grosven'r-gds.*
1896. Tuke, Arthur William, *I.M.S.*
1914. Tuke, Bryan Montague, M.C.
1881. Tuke, Chas. Molesworth, *Chiswick.*
1876. Tuke, Geo. Montague, *Maidstone.*
1903. Tuke-Johnson, Wm., *Twickenham.*
1878. Tulk, Marmaduke James, *Parkstone.*
1897. Tulk-Hart, Thos. Jn. Aug., *Brighton.*
1923.§Tullidge, Gladys Mary, *Clapham.*
1910. Tumber, Henry Shemeld, *Sheffield.*
1918. Tunbridge,Wm.Stephen,*Leamington.*
1888. Tunnicliffe, F. Whittaker, *Harley-st.*
1874. Turle, Arthur, *Swanage.*
1903. Turle, James Evan, *Weeley.*
1900. Turnbull, Chas. Cuthbert I., *Hulme.*
1913. Turnbull, Fredk. Chas., *Queensland.*
1887. Turnbull, Geo. Lindsay, *Ladbroke-sq.*
1902. Turnbull,Hubt. Maitland,*Lond.-hosp.*
1897. Turnbull, Hugh Prideaux,*Roy. Navy.*
1900. Turnbull, Robt. Cyril, *Brentwood.*
1895. Turner,Alan Charles,D.S O ,*Sheffield.*
1884. Turner, Alfred Jefferis, *Brisbane.*
1904. Turner, Arthur Hewett, *Golborne.*
1907. Turner, Arthur John, *Bournemouth.*
1896. Turner, Arthur Scott, *Anerley-road.*
1890. Turner, Charles Byron, *Grimsby.*
1923. Turner, Chas. F., *King's Norton.*
1900. Turner, Charles H.,D.S.O.,*R.A.M.C*
1903. Turner, Charles William, *Leigh.*
1900. Turner, Douglas Duke, *Roy. Navy.*
1888. Turner, Edgar Olive, *Gt. Missenden.*
1922.§Turner, Eileen Maud, *Basingstoke.*
1899. Turner, Frank Douglas, *Colchester.*

14832   x 2

1884. Turner, Frederick Senior, *Horley.*
1907. Turner, Fredk. Thos., M.C.,*R.A.M.C.*
1897. Turner, Harry Fulham, *Muswell-hill.*
1899. Turner, Harry Stanley, *R.A.F.*
1904. Turner, Henry Strawson, M.C., *R.N.*
1886. Turner, Henry Swetnam.
1808. Turner, Henry Watson, *Wimpole-st.*
1898. Turner, Jas. William, *Saffron Walden.*
1883. Turner, Nathaniel Henry, *Highbury.*
1892. Turner, Olivier Polhill, *Hastings.*
1893. Turner, Percy Edward, *Crow h-hill.*
1884. Turner, Philip Dymock, O.B.E.,*Ryde.*
1918. Turner, Robert Hugh, *Bristol.*
1905. Turner, Sydney Booth, *Bargoed.*
1897. Turner, Sydney Duke, *Purley.*
1921. Turner, Terence Watson, *Southwark.*
1906. Turner, Thomas, *Eastbourne.*
1895. Turner, Thos. Wm., *Deddington.*
1920. Turner, Walter Aslatt, *Bournemouth.*
1900. Turner, Walter Edward, *Willesden.*
1876. Turner, Walter Pickett, *Balham.*
1905. Turner, Wm George, *Montreal.*
1905. Turnly, Jn. Edwd. L. Alex., *Glenarm.*
1893. Turnor, Philip Watson, *Canada.*
1887. Turtle, Fredk. Wenman, *Peckham.*
1902. Turtle, Godfrey de Bec, *Cambr.-terr.*
1904. Turtle, James, *S. Hackney*
1905. Turtle,Wm.Reg.Margetts, *Woodford.*
1919. Turton, Alfred Howard, *Droitwich.*
1898. Turton, Edward, *Hull.*
1899. Tuxford, Arthur Wren, *Boston.*
1897. Tuxford, Reginald, *Boston.*
1887. Tweed, Edwd. Reginald, *Honiton.*
1922.§Tweed, Lendal, *Cheyne-walk.*
1918. Tweed, Martin Baird Moore, *N.Z.*
1894. Twemlow, Wm. Albt. F., *Flint.*
1921. Tweedie, Francis J G., *Sutton, Notts.*
1914. Twigg,DonaldSargenson, *Wirksw'rth*
1907. Twigg, Garnet Wolsley, *Ventnor.*
1906. Twigg, Stuart Wm. Jackson, *Manch*
1911. Twining, Daniel Owen, *Salcombe.*
1913. Twining,Edw.Wing.*Univ -coll.-hosp.*
1900. Twort, Fredk. Wm., *Bagshot.*
1917. Twort, John Ferdinand, *Camberley.*
1874. Twort, William Henry, *Camberley.*
1880. Twynam, Geo. Edwd., *Wetherby-pl.*
1888. Tyacke. Nicholas, *R.A.M.C.*
1906. Tylor, Christopher, *Oxted.*
1901. Tylor, Max Forster, *Wisbech.*
1897. Tyndale,W. Fras.,C.M.G., *R.A.M.C.*
1886. Tyndall, Francis, *Liverpool.*
1881. Tyrrell, Charles Robert, C.B., C.B.E.
1915. Tyrrell, Edgar James, *Newcastle.*
1876. Tyrrell, Walter, *Petersfield.*
1895. Tyson, Wilson, *Lowestoft.*

U.

1881. Udale, Joseph James, *Brixton-road.*
1913. Udall, Edward Hugo, *Southborough.*
1914. Uloth, Alex. Wilmot, M.C., *Reigate.*
1907. Ulrich,Frank Ferd. A.,*Dunedin,N.Z.*
1890. Umney, Wm. Francis, *Sydenham.*
1921.§Umpleby, M. H. J., *Gt. Holland.*
1872. Underhill, Arthur Stopford, *Tipton.*
1915. Underhill, Eric, *R A.M.C.*
1865. Underhill, FrancisWm., *Maidenhead.*
1898. Underhill, Sydney V. H., *Newport.*
1910. Underwood, Arth. B. Guy, *Harley-st.*
1893. Underwood, Arth. Cressee, *Birm.*
1894. Underwood, Frank Louis, *Weedon.*
1882. Underwood. John Chas., *Putney.*
1915. Underwood. John E. A., *Blackheath.*
1915. Unger, Oscar Ramsay, *Merton-park.*
1883. Unitt, Jas. Arthur, *Loughborough.*
1900. Upcott-Gill, Geoffrey Allen, *Hatfield.*
1885. Upham, Charles Hazlitt, *New Zeal.*
1915. Upton, Algernon Randolph, *Hove.*
1866. Upton, Herbt. Chrippes, *Hove.*
1900. Upward, Harold Arthur, *Romford.*
1901. Urwick, Reg. Henry, *Shrewsbury.*
1921. Urwick, Wm. G.D.H., *Canfield-gdns.*
1922. Utidjian, Haigouni Dikran Absalom.
1899. Utting, Horace Ebbage, *Walsall.*
1874. Utting, John, *Liverpool.*
1909. Uttley, Wm. Wilkinson, *Bolton.*

V.

1877. Vachell, Herbert Redwood, *Cardiff.*
1914. Vaidya, Jagannath Balkrishna.
1915. Vaidya,ShankarlalKuuvaji,*Bomb'y.*
1913. Vaile, Thos. B., *Northumberland-st.*
1903. Vaile, Wm. Bartholomew, *Aldershot.*
1915. Vaisey, Cedric Norman, *Winslow.*
1879. Vaisey, Thomas Frederick, *Winslow.*
1908. Vakeel,Nusserwanjee H., *Bombay.*
1913. Vakil, Chunilal B., *Highgate.*
1916. Vakil, Rustom Navroji, *U. Coll-hosp.*
1917. Valentine, Dougl. Jas., M.C.,*Catford.*
1900. Valérie, Jn., O.B.E., *Hampton-court.*
1906. Valerio, Ismael, *Costa Rica.*
1890. Valintine, Thos. H. A., *New Zealand.*
1886. Vallance, Ernest, *Westcliff.*
1893. Vallance, Herbert, *Lewes.*
1885. Vallance, Hugh, *Redhill.*
1903. Van Buren, Asa Claude Ali, *Plym'th.*
1916. Vance, William John, *Whitehall-pl.*
1920. Van Coller,Fdk.Albertyn,*Manchester.*
1912. Van der Beken,Henri R. G.,*Evesham.*
1918. Van der Merwe, Jacob E. de V.,*Cape.*

1906. Vandermin, Hy. François, *E field*.
1916. Van Gehuchten, Paul M. J., *Camb'ge*.
1893. Van Geyzel, Colvin Thomasz, *Ceylon*.
1916§VanHeerden,AnnaP.,*Edinburg,S.Afr.*
1917. Van Heerd n,J.Aurèt,*St. Barts.-hosp.*
1883. Vann, Alfred Mason, *Durham*.
1920. van Roojen, Johan, *Amsterdam*.
1898. Van Rooyen, Charles Ellard.
1909. Van Schalkwijk,Jouannes,*Transvaal*.
1911. Van Someren Boyd, Stanley, *Fenton*.
1886. Varley, George, *Minehead*.
1904. Varughese,MangattuKuriyan,*Madras*
1907. Varvill, Bernard. M.C., *R.A.M.C.*
1877. Vasey, Samuel William, *Chudleigh*.
1899. Vaughan, Arthur Llewellyn, *Diss*.
1923. Vaughan, Frank Senior, *Hereford*.
1903. Vaughan, Jn. Courtney F.D.,*R.Navy*.
1909. Vaughan, Richard Grenville, *Bristol*.
1901. Vaughan, Walter Fdk. H., *R.A.M.C.*
1885. Vaughan-Jackson,Hbt.F.,*Potter'sBar*
1921.§Vaus, Nellie, *Surbiton*.
1873. Vawdrey,Theoph.Glascott,*Plymouth*.
1907. Vazildar, Sohrab Shapoorji, *Bombay*.
1921.§Veale, Doris Lyne, *Sidcup*.
1913. Veale, Henry de Paiva B , *Ilkley*.
1905. Veale, Rawdon Aug., *Leeds*.
1915. Veitch, Henry Cecil Craven, *R.N.*
1887. Venis, Walter, *Bombay*.
1903. Venniker, John Chas., *Cape, S.A.*
1907. Venning, Jas. Arthur, *Steeple Aston*.
1910. Vercoe,Richd. Herbt., *Loudoun-road*.
1896. Verdon, Edgar Sumner, *Morocco*.
1888. Verdon, Francis, *Wetherby-mansions*.
1912. Verdon, Philip, *Streatham-hill*.
1907. Verdon, Walter Geo. H. M., *Luton*.
1897. Verdon-Roe, Spencer, *Wandsworth*.
1898. Verley, Reginald Chas., *Jamaica*.
1900. Verling-Brown, Charles R., *Sutton*.
1889. Vermaak. Herman, *Transvaal*.
1911. Verner, Bernard Thomas.
1918. Verney, Ernest Basil, *Tonbridge*.
1913.§Verney, Sydney Jessie, *Kensington*.
1917. Verniquet. Wilfrd G., *Darjeeling*.
1898. Vernon, Alex Apfell, *Jamaica*.
1912. Vernon, Arthur Sidney, *Harley-st*.
1918. Vernon, Cecil Hevgate,*Bournemouth*.
1890. Vernon, Claude Martin, *Ashford*.
1884. Vernon, John James Dean, *Audley*.
1875. Vernon, Mark Hy. Hbt., *Horsham*.
1909. Vernon. Rupert John, *Shirley*
1915. Vernon-Taylor, Aubrey D., *Notts*.
1876. Verrall. Sir Thomas Jenner, *Bath*.
1906. Verry, Guy Tyrreil, *R.N.*
1886. Vertannes, Carr Aratoon, *Rangoon*.
1921. Verwey, Antony, *Rotterdam*.
1912. Vesselovsky, Victor, *Ealing*.
1915. Vevers, Geoffrey Marr, *Princes-sq*.
14994

1905. Vevers, Oswald Henry, *Norton*.
1914. Vey, David Chris. Leslie, M.C.
1916. Vey, Fras. Hamilton, *Blundellsands*.
1890. Vicars, Fredc. Geo., *Bilbao, Spain*.
1912. Vicary,Walter Palmer, *Newton Abbot*.
1915. Vickers, Harold, *Chiswick*.
1890. Vickers,Jn.Benj.Nicholson,*Yarmouth*
1893. Vickers, Kirsop B. Jas., *Wellington*.
1899. Vickers, Thomas Hedley, *Roy. Navy*.
1914. Vickers, Vernon C.W., *Finchampst'd*.
1922. Vickers, William John, *Birmingham*.
1916. Vidot, Samuel, M.C., *Seychelles*.
1917. Viehoff,HermanCrowther,*Gt. Crosby*.
1910. Vilrandré, Geo. Ernest, *Bromley*.
1884. Vince, John Foster, *Birmingham*.
1887. Vincent, Herbert Edmund, *Horley*.
1886. Vincent, John Francis, *Tooting*.
1881. Vincent, Philip, *Waltham, U.S.A.*
1892. Vincent, Thos. Swale, *Middlx.-hosp*.
1892. Vincent, Wm. Jas. Nath., O.B E.
1899. Vine, Alfred Bertram, M.B.E., *Bury*.
1920.§Vine, Kathleen Suzanne, *Chard*.
1888. Vines, Charles Stuart, *Newport*.
1919. Vines,Howard Wm.Copland,*Oxford*.
1913. Viney, Arnold, *Chertsey*.
1882. Viney, Josiah Ernest, *Chertsey*.
1883. Vinrace, Edwd. Dennis, *Gower-st*.
1918. Vint, Morley Dyson, *Idle*.
1894. Vinter, Ch. Hbt. Sawyer, *Framl'gh'm*.
1920. Vinter, Noël Syd. Bailey, *Torpoint*.
1887. Vinter, Sydney Garratt, *Torpoint*.
1890. Vintras, George C. Louis, *Brighton*.
1876. Vipan, Charles, D.S.O., *St. Leonards*.
1863. Vipan, William Henry, *Canterbury*.
1912. Visner, Adolf Lucas Jacob, *Basel*.
1889. Vise, Arthur Blithe, *Holbeach*.
1896. Vise, Jn. Neville Blithe, *Vict., Aust*.
1901. Visger, Charles, O.B.E., *Clevedon*.
1922. Visick, Arthur H. C., *Hampstead*.
1892. Visick, Chas. Hedley C., *Rosslyn-hill*.
1908. Vivian,Chas.St.Aubyn,*Winchmore-h.*
1906. Vivian, Harold Sugden,*Winchmore-h.*
1895. Vivian, Jn. Hy. Percival, *Herne Bay*.
1879. Vlieland, Charles James, *Exeter*.
1884. Voelcker, Arth. Francis, *Harley-st*.
1886. Volckman, Bernard, *New Zealand*.
1880. Volckmen. Ronald, *New Zealand*.
1901. Voller, Frank, *Battersea*.
1899. Von Bergen, Carl W., *Leatherhead*.
1912. Von Braun,Carl R. B.,*BorehamHolt*.
1899. Von Eberts, Edwd. Urquhart M.
1916. von Mengershausen, H. M., *Manch'r*.
1900. Von Rosen, Alfd. Dillop B., *Vict.-st*.
1895. Von Winckler, Wm. Jos., *Br. Guiana*.
1913. Von Wyss, W. Heinrich, *St. Jas.-st*.
1882. Vos, George Herklots, *Tottenham*.
1905. Vosper, Cecil, *Bannu, N. India*.
15051

1899. Vosper, Percy, *Regent's-pk.-road.*
1907. Vosper, Sydney, *Plymouth.*
1886. Vost, William, *I.M.S.*

W.

1871. Wacher, Frank, *Canterbury.*
1906. Wacher, Geoffrey, *Leigh-on-Sea.*
1901. Wacher, Harold, *Canterbury.*
1916. Wacher, Herbert Stewart, *Canterbury.*
1893. Wadd, Henry Randall, *Richmond.*
1913. Waddell, Ivan Lindley, *Lee.*
1913. Waddington, George O'Neill, *Natal.*
1870. Waddy, Henry Edward, *Gloucester.*
1876. Wade, Arth. Breedon, *Southampton.*
1888. Wade, Herbert, *Ponders End.*
1889. Wade, Newton, *Intake.*
1872. Wade, Reginald, *Highbridge.*
1922. Wade, Richard Herbert, *Ponders End.*
1906. Wade, Rubens, *Farnham.*
1910. Wade, Wallace Robert, *New Zeal.*
1915. Wade, William Ernest, *Llanelly.*
1888. Wadham, Frank Jesser, *Ryde, I. of W.*
1882. Wadia, Daneck Rustamji.
1906. Wadia, Maneckshaw D., *King & Co.*
1904. Wadmore, James Chris., *New Zealand.*
1920. Wadsworth, Norman Victor, *Catford.*
1890. Waggett, Ernest B., *Wimpole-st.*
1899. Wagstaff, Charles Bertraud, *Leigh.*
1890. Wagstaff, Frank Alex., *Northampton.*
1907. Wahby, Behdjet, *Cairo.*
1878. Wainewright, Rbt. Spencer, *Hove.*
1889. Wainman, Benjamin, *Leeds.*
1911. Wainwright, Chas. Barron, *Bermuda.*
1909. Wainwright, Donald, *Waterbeach.*
1909. Wainwright, G. Bertram, *St. Thos.'s-h.*
1890. Wainwright, Lennox, *Folkestone.*
1891. Wainwright, Wm. Longworth, *Henley*
1886. Waite, Davis Allan, *Golder's-green.*
1884. Waite, Henry, *Armley, Leeds.*
1895. Waite, Joseph Edwd., *Leicester.*
1894. Waithman, Jas. Clarkson, *Willesden.*
1890. Wake, Chas. Hereward, *New Zeal.*
1904. Wakefield, Arthur Wm., *Kendal.*
1896. Wakefield, Chris. Frank, *Charlwood.*
1889. Wakefield, Rbt. Clarke, *Brondesbury.*
1875. Wakefield, Thomas, *Northwood.*
1912. Wakeford, Victor D. C., *Fulham.*
1894. Wakeling, Thos. Geo., *O.B E., Cairo.*
1913. Wakely, Alfred Stewart, *M.C.*
1887. Walcott, Thomas, *Camberley.*
1907. Waldmeier, Fredk. Jn., *Chesterfield.*
1879. Waldo, Fredk. Joseph, *Holland-pk.*
1871. Waldo, Henry, *Clifton.*
1909. Waldo, Henry Cecil, *Bristol.*

1907. Waldron, Chas. Edwd., *London-hosp.*
1896. Waldron, Francis Thos., *Cape Prov.*
1880. Waldron, John.
1884. Wale, George, *Croydon.*
1890. Wale, Malcolm Edwd. Hy., *Bexhill.*
1901. Wales, Edwd. Garneys, *Downham.*
1907. Wales, Harry, *Hull.*
1902. Wales, Henry Charles, *Ontario.*
1855. Wales, Thos. Garneys, *Downham.*
1923. Walford, Alfred S. H., *Palace-court.*
1869. Walford, Edward, *Cardiff.*
1906. Walford, Harold Rosser S., *Porrick.*
1890. Walford, Reg. Manwood H., *Finchley.*
1861. Walford, Walter Gilson, *Finchley.*
1888. Walker, Alex. Hope, *Cranleigh.*
1887. Walker, Alfd. Wm. Hinsley, *Harrogate*
1870. Walker, Arch. Dunbar, *Pembd'ge-gns.*
1923. Walker, Arnold L., *Huddersfield.*
1894. Walker, Arthur, *Glossop.*
1906. Walker, Arthur, D.S.O., *Gillingham.*
1920. Walker, Arthur Robert, *Bushey.*
1901. Walker, Arthur West, *Cromer.*
1877. Walker, Basil Woodd, *Dawson-place.*
1887. Walker, Benjamin, *Natal.*
1909. Walker, Chas. Edwd., *Glasgow.*
1908. Walker, Cuthbert Ferguson, *Rochdale.*
1922 §Walker, Doreen G. C., *Bath.*
1920. §Walker, Edith M., *Waltham Cross.*
1923. Walker, Edward G. L., *Huddersfield.*
1884. Walker, Edw., M.B.E., *Huddersfield.*
1881. Walker, Ernest Geo. Agars, *Ightham.*
1914. Walker, Ernest Haines, *Ightham.*
1901. Walker, Ernest Ronald, *Bromley.*
1881. Walker, Francis John, *Spilsby.*
1894. Walker, Frederick, *Holbeach.*
1889. Walker, George, *Forest-hill.*
1860. Walker, George Charles, *Southport.*
1898. Walker, Geo. Chas., *Winchmore-hill.*
1896. Walker, Harold Albert, *Fortess-road.*
1904. Walker, Hy. Jas. Davey, *Dormansland.*
1895. Walker, Henry Roe, *Torquay.*
1912. Walker, Herbert, M.C., *Newcastle.*
1897. Walker, Herbert John, *Brighton.*
1876. Walker, Horace, *Hammersmith.*
1879. Walker, Horatio Edward, *Corwen.*
1867. Walker, James, *Hull.*
1922. Walker, James Alex., *Redhill.*
1887. Walker, James Pixton, *Ryde, I. W.*
1902. Walker, John, *Kalgoorlie.*
1899. Walker, John Fredk., *Southend.*
1921. Walker, John George, *Moyser-rd.*
1907. Walker, John Leeming.
1897. Walker, John Norman, *I.M.S.*
1906. Walker, John Philip, *Ryde.*
1868. Walker, John Robert, *Hamilton-ter.*
1886. Walker, John Thomas, *Hull.*
1882. Walker, John W., O.B.E., *Wakefield.*

1883. Walker, Joseph, *Liverpool.*
1884. Walker, Joseph Eagland, *Bexley.*
1908. Walker, Josiah, M.C., *Peterborough.*
1912. Walker, Lawrence Cecil, *Malton.*
1899. Walker, Lewis Aug., *Lee-on-Solent.*
1907. Walker, Norman Hamilton, *Natal.*
1888. Walker, Reginald F., M.B.E., *Esher*
1899. Walker, Robert, *Cardiff.*
1907. Walker, Ronald Ralph, *S. China.*
1910. Walker, Samuel Burns, *Manitoba.*
1906. Walker, Spencer Lewis, *E. Grinstead.*
1897. Walker, Sydney Robert, *Ripon.*
1899. Walker, Thos. Malcolm, *Hailsham.*
1867. Walker, Wm. Abraham, *Southwell.*
1921. Walker, Wm. John G., *Parkill-rd.*
1807. Walker, Wm. Percival, *Royal Navy.*
1905. Walker, Wm. Percy, *Victoria, B.C.*
1898. Walker, Wm. Walter, *Batley.*
1896. Walker, Wm. Watson, *Kilburn.*
1902. Wall, Alfd. Hbt. Edwin, *New Zeal.*
1920.§Wall, Doris Irene, *Coleshill.*
1892. Wall, Frank.
1908. Wall, Harold E. M.. *St. Stephen's-rd.*
1897. Wall, Jas. Bligh, *Broadstone, Dorset.*
1918. Wall, James Thomas, *Brit. Columb.*
1911. Wall, Maximilian Christian, *U.S.A.*
1920.§Wall, Nellie, *Liverpool.*
1866. Wall, Reginald Bligh, *Aylesbury.*
1897. Wall, Reg. Cecil Bligh, *Cavendish-pl.*
1902. Wall, Vivian Francis, *Welbeck-st.*
1882. Wallace, Alfred Cyprian, *Guernsey.*
1886. Wallace, Sir David, K.B.E., C.M.G.
1892. Wallace, Francis Gore, *Earl's Ct.-rd.*
1903. Wallace, Fredk. Herbert, *Uppingham.*
1907. Wallace, Gerald Doug. H , *Newtown.*
1922. Wallace,Herbt.Kelvin,*Hampton-wk.*
1923.§Wallace, Hygeia L. J., *Temple.*
1912. Wallace, James Montague, *Harrow.*
1899. Wallace, Jas. Williamson, *Bristol.*
1906. Wallace, John, *Cardiff.*
1894. Wallace, Lewis Alex. R., *Welbeck-st.*
1893. Wallace, Rbt. F. Stanley, *Skegness.*
1872. Wallace, Thomas, *Cardiff.*
1904. Wallace, William Thomas.
1889. Waller, Alfred Whalley, *Cromer.*
1902. Waller, Arthur Beaumont, *Kirkby.*
1909. Waller, Harold Kirk, *Hook.*
1898. Waller, Herbert Ewan, *Moseley.*
1914. Waller, Jocelyn Langton, *Ealing.*
1866. Waller, John, *Queen-street.*
1881. Waller, Theodore Harry, *Chelmsford.*
1881. Wallers, William, *Blackburn.*
1918. Wallice, Donald, *Plymouth.*
1915. Walliee, Percy, *Plymouth.*
1920. Wallington, K. T. K., *Wolverhampton.*
1860. Wallis, Albert William, *Folkestone.*
1894. Wallis, Chas. Edwd., *QueenAnne-st.*
15217

1886. Wallis, Charles George, *Pepys-road.*
1915. Wallis, Morris John Theo., *Croydon.*
1910. Wallis, Percy Boyd, *Royal Navy.*
1895. Wallis, Sid. Seymour, *E. Dulwich-rd.*
1903. Wallis, Vernon Montague, *Doncaster.*
1873. Wallis, William, *Groombridge.*
1897. Wallis, William, *Barnsley.*
1909. Wallis, Wm. Evershed, *Bexhill.*
1895. Walls, Edward Geoffrey, *Burgh.*
1914. Walls, Edward Sancton, *Ealing.*
1887. Walls, James, *New Zealand.*
1905. Walsh, Fred Newton, *Birmingham.*
1903. Walsh, George Delaval, *Roy. Navy.*
1881. Walsh, John Henry Tull, *I.M.S.*
1890. Walsh, Leslie Herbert, *Bath.*
1887. Walsh, Robt. William, *Manchester.*
1919. Walsham, William, *Hanwell.*
1904. Waltenberg, Theoph. R., *Manchester.*
1896. Walter, Albert Elijah, O.B E., *I.M.S.*
1893. Walter, Edwin Charles, *Wallingford.*
1878. Walter, Ernest Wm., *Landor-road.*
1892. Walter,Richd.Arth ,*Tunbridge Wells.*
1878. Walter, Wm. Henry, *Brentford.*
1892. Walters, Alex. Radclyffe, *Reigate.*
1907. Walters, Arthur Leslie, *Onslow-gdns.*
1889. Walters, Arth. Piercefield, *Caithness.*
1892. Walters, Frederick Wilfred.
1904. Walters, Henry B.,O.B.E.,*Chudleigh.*
1902. Walters, Joseph, *Neath, Glam.*
1917. Walters, William James, *Swansea.*
1892. Walthard, Robt. R. Max, *Manch.*
1883. Walton, Francis Fielder, *Hull.*
1897. Walton, Hy. Beckles Gall, *R.A.M.C.*
1896. Walton, Walter Rees, *Chester.*
1914. Wambeek,Wm.Godfried L.,*Colombo.*
1918. Wan, Yik Shing, *Univ.-coll.-hosp.*
1895. Wanhill, Chas. Fredk., *R.A.M.C.*
1893. Wanklyn, Wm. McC., *Harley-street.*
1920. Wanless, Robert Paulin, *Newcastle.*
1905. Warburton, John, *Wigan.*
1914. Warburton, John R. Noel, M.C.
1912. Warburton, Llewellyn Rnys, O.B.E.
1911. Warburton, Percival D.,*c/o Holt & Co.*
1883. Ward, Allan Ogier, *Onslow-square.*
1883. Ward, Anthony Arthur, *Peckham.*
1919. Ward, Arthur Elston, *Asylum-rd.*
1896. Ward,Arth. Blackwood,*Bloemfontein*
1875. Ward, Charles, *Pietermaritzburg.*
1897. Ward, Ellacott L., C.B.E., *I.M.S.*
1888. Ward, Ernest, M.B.E., *Wokingham.*
1904. Ward, Ernest Lewis, *Merthyr Tydfil.*
1865. Ward, Frederic Henry, *Ealing.*
1917. Ward, George H., *Scarborough.*
1902. Ward, George Stafford, *Wanstead.*
1909. Ward, Gordon Reg., W. *Kensington.*
1902. Ward, Herbt. Kingsley, M.C., *F.M.S.*
1921. Ward, Horace Smith, *Dewsbury.*
15274

1905. Ward, Horace Walsham, *Glos.*
1887. Ward, H. P., M.B.E., *Southampton.*
1891. Ward, Jas Philip Stephens, *Plymouth.*
1887. Ward, John Alfred, *Grays.*
1912. Ward, John Forbes, *Stockport.*
1866. Ward, Jn. Lewis Wm., *Merthyr Tydv.*
1886. Ward, John Oddy, *Ferrybridge.*
1872. Ward, Joseph, *Warwick.*
1904. Ward, Jos., C.M.G., D.S.O., *Sheffield.*
1922. Ward, Kenneth Leslie, *Wanstead.*
1874. Ward, Lloyd Brereton, *A.M.S.*
1900. Ward, Oswald Erasmus, *Chesterton.*
1917. Ward, Percival, *Sheffield*
1901. Ward, Percy Harold, *Rhodesia.*
1899. Ward, Ronald Francis C., *Harrogate.*
1911. Ward, Rowland, M.C., *Dewsbury.*
1909. Ward, Sidney Harland, *Stroud, Glos.*
1886. Ward, Stanley Edward, *Sevenoaks.*
1902. Ward, Vere Godsa've, *W. Byfleet.*
1872. Ward, Walter Alfred, *Richmond.*
1888. Ward, Walter Fisher, *Bautry.*
1868. Ward, Wm. Jn. Cuthbert, *Harrogate.*
1923. Ward, William Roy, *Mountain Ash.*
1869. Ward, William Simpson, *Hunslet.*
1872. Wardale, Jos. Aug. Wm., *Worthing.*
1915. Warde, A. H., O.B.E., *Bedford-pk.*
1886. Warde, Arthur W. Brougham.
1889. Warde, Wilfrid B., *Manchester.*
1915. Warden, Arthur Reg. S., *Felixstowe.*
1913. Warden, Horace Fdk. W., *Lerham-yns.*
1913. Wardrop, John Glen, *Ealing.*
1899. Ware, Arth. Maitland, *Gloucester-rd.*
1889. Ware, Ernest Edwin, *Cavendish-pl*
1886. Ware, George Stephen, *Barnstaple.*
1879. Ware, Jn. Wm. Langston, *Craven-terr.*
1917. Ware, Syd. Arthur T., *Stamford-hill.*
1895. Waring, A Henry, D S O., *R.A.M.C.*
1891. Waring, John Alfred, *Nottingham.*
1882. Waring, John Arkle, *Chichester.*
1894. Warke, Charles Lyle, *Alva., Canada.*
1877. Warliker, Damodar Purshotam, *I M.S.*
1892. Warneford, Stanley W. C., *New Zeal.*
1896. Warner, Allan, *Kirby Murloe.*
1917. Warner, Charles Horne, *Langport.*
1912. Warner, Cuthbert, *Woodford-green.*
1884. Warner, Fdk. Ashton, *Brechin-place.*
1911. Warner, Harold Percy, *Woodford-arn.*
1906. Warner, Howard Francis, *Fakenham.*
1914. Warner, Refna, *Fisherton*
1885. Warnock, Jn., C.M G , C B.E , *Cairo.*
1904. Warren, Alfred Castle, *Notting-hill*
1876. Warren, Chas. Edw. H., *Haywird's-h'th*
1894. Warren, Chas. Frank, *Sydney, N S. W.*
1872. Warren, George Milton, *Toronto.*
1918. Warren, Hugh Pennefather, *Enfield.*
1904 Warren, Leonard, O.B.E., *R.N.*
1923.§Warren, Marjory Winsome, *Highgate*
15331

1915. Warren, Philip P., *Enfield-highway.*
1905. Warren, Stanley Hbt., *Hampstead.*
1920. Warrick, Robert Walter, *Lambeth.*
1895. Warrington, Richd. James, *Manchester*
1913. Warrington, Thomas, *Waterbench.*
1884. Warwick, Francis Jas., *Finsbury-disp.*
1921 §Warwick, Joan M. R., *Limpsfield.*
1878. Warwick, Percy, *Halesworth.*
1884. Washbourn, Wm., C.B.E., *Gloucester.*
1892. Wason, Richd. Llewhellin, *Bath.*
1880. Wasse, Gervas Miles, *N. Zeal.*
1902. Waterhouse, Amyas Theo., *Oxford.*
1911. Waterhouse, Arch. Farrell, *Sheffield.*
1897. Waterhouse, Rupert, *Bath.*
1913. Watermeyer, H. Arnold, *St. Mary's-h.*
1901. Waters, Alfred Chas. Stanley, *March.*
1895. Waters, Fred Wm., *Adelaide, S. A.*
1892. Waters, Geo. Wm. B., *Mytholmroyd.*
1892. Waters, Harry George, *E. Ind.a Rly.*
1897. Waters, Jn. Frank Wm., *Wellingboro.*
1862. Waters, John Mangin, *A.M.S.*
1899. Waters, Walter Jas., O.B E , *R.A.M.C*
1897. Waters, Wm. Arth. Pernow, *Oxford.*
1906. Watkin, Arthur Chris., *Caer cinion.*
1908. Watkin, Paul Ieuan, *Barking-road.*
1913. Watkin, Philip J., M.C., *Guy's-hosp.*
1894. Watkin-Williams, Penrose L., *D.S O.*
1900. Watkins, Alan Percival, *Zanzibar.*
1875. Watkins, Arnold Hirst, *Kimberley.*
1884. Watkins, A. M., M.B.E., *Whitchurch.*
1896. Watkins, Bernard V., *Whitchurch.*
1892. Watkins, Devereux J. Gregory, *Lincoln.*
1887. Watkins, Frank Aug., *Denmark-hill.*
1905. Watkins, Gwilym David, D.S.O., M.C.
1889. Watkins, Harold E., *Newt'n-le- Willows*
1905. Watkins, Jn. Grandisson, *B. Salterton.*
1888. Watkins, Walter, *Westcliff-on-Sea.*
1914. Watkins, Watkin, *Tonypandy.*
1892. Watkins, William, *Crickhowell.*
1912. Watkins-Baker, L. C., *Natal.*
1917. Watkinson, Arthur Alward, *Grimsby.*
1905. Watney, Herbert Andrew, *Epping.*
1912. Watney, Martyn Herbert, *Buckhold.*
1922. Watson, Bernard Gretton, *Birm'gham.*
1896. Watson, Chas. Everard Sam., *W. Afr.*
1894. Watson, Charles Henry, D S.O..I.M.S.
1923 §Watson, Constance C. M ,*Selhurst-rd.*
1899. Watson, Douglas Percival, *D.S.O.*
1914. Watson, Francis Clark, *Doncaster.*
1917. Watson, Francis Eaton Gordon, *R.N.*
1895. Watson, Fredk. James, *New Zealand.*
1901. Watson, George William, *Leeds.*
1914. Watson, George William, *Leeds.*
1891. Watson, James, *Nott.ngham.*
1884. Watson, Jas. Russell, *Shantung, China.*
1862. Watson, John, *Manchester.*
1912. Watson, John Glegg, *Honduras, C.A.*
15388

1907. Watson, J. Nuthall, *Wootton Bassett*.
1897. Watson, John William, C.I.E.
1921. Watson, Lionel K., *W. Cromwell-rd.*
1900. Watson, Robert Nimmo, *Harrogate.*
1881. Watson, Solomon George, *Southsea.*
1915. Watson, Tertius T.Boswall,*Battersea.*
1912. Watson, Walter Geoffrey,*Forest-row.*
1899. Watson, Wm. Bertram, *Harrogate.*
1896. Watson, Wm. Douglas, *Leigh-on-Sea.*
1885. Watson, Wm. Ivens, *Wellinghoro'.*
1914. Watson-Williams, Eric,*Stockwell-rd.*
1917. Watt, Fdk. W. Arbuthnot, *Tavistock*
1906. Watt, John Alexander, *N.S.W.*
1907. Watt, Thos. Newlands, *New Zeal.*
1918. Watters, Henry George.
1894. Watts, Alexander Minter, *Ashford.*
1895. Watts, Brian, D.S.O., *R.A.M.C.*
1886. Watts, Harry J. Manning, *Tonbridge.*
1903. Watts, Hugh, *I.M.S.*
1892. Watts, Jas. Alexander Wood, *Hyde.*
1891. Watts, Thomas, *Hyde, Cheshire.*
1901. Watts-Silvester, Thos. Hy. E., *Dorset.*
1882. Waugh, Henry Dunn, *Onslow-gdns.*
1902. Waugh, Robert James, *Gt. James-st.*
1921 §Wauhope, Gladys M., *Loughton.*
1887. Wawn, Edward Russell, *Bramley.*
1898. Way, Arth. Orsborn, *Winchester.*
1896. Way,John Henry Frederick,*Southsea.*
1910. Way, Leslie Ferguson K., D.S.O.
1886. Way, Lewis, *R.A M.C.*
1897. Way, Montague Harold, *Southsea.*
1894. Way, William, *Bramley.*
1908. Waylen, Geo. Hy. Hitchcock, M.C.
1873. Waylen, Geo. Swithin Adee, *Devizes.*
1903. Wayne-Morgan, Lewis, *Whitchurch.*
1904. Wayte, Frank Edward, *Halifax.*
1888. Wayte, John, *Croydon.*
1915. Wayte. John Woollaston, M C.
1884. Weakley,AlfredJames,*Westcliff-on-S.*
1879. Woakley, Arthur, *Cane Prov.*
1908. Weakley,Arth. Leon., *St.George's-cir.*
1921. Weaklev, Joseph Fredk., *Westcliff.*
1875. Weakley, Saml. J. John, *Forest-gate.*
1873. Wear, Arth. Taylor,*Newcastle-on-T.*
1903. Weatherhead, Ernest, *Coulsdon.*
1872. Weatherhead, John F, *Los Angeles.*
1874. Weatherly,Lionel Alex.,*Bournem'th.*
1897. Weaver, Fredk Kearsley, *Guildford.*
1920. Weaver. Robert, *Merstham.*
1895. Webb,SirA.L.A.,K.B.E.,C.B.,C.M.G
1879. Webb, Charles Alfred, *A.M.S.*
1892. Webb, Cholmondeley, *Margate.*
1919. Webb, Eric Roland, *Edgbaston.*
1890. Webb, Frank, *Leigh.*
1894. Webb, Fdk. Edwd. Apthorpe, O.B.E.
1912. Webb, Harold, *Loughborough.*
1907. Webb, Harry Gordon, *Sheffield.*
15445

1884. Webb, Hugh, *Parson's Green.*
1901. Webb, Hugh Geo. Stiles, *I.M.S.*
1886. Webb. John Bartlett, *Bristol.*
1893. Webb, John Curtis, *Bina-gardens.*
1911. Webb, John Rbt. D., O.B.E., *I.M.S.*
1917. Webb, Ralph Edwin Stuart, *Southsea.*
1921. Webb, Robert Alexander, *Wembley.*
1912. Webb, William Leslie, *Uganda.*
1879. Webb, Wm. Simpson, *Queensland.*
1903. Webb, William Tudor, *Kingsbridge.*
1923. Webb-Peploe, M. H.. *Farnborough.*
1896. Webb-Ware, Hugh Robt., *Norwich.*
1881. Webber, Edwd. Samuel, *Southsea.*
1912. Webber, Harald Norris, *Putney.*
1890. Webber, Hy.Woolmington,*Plymouth.*
1909. Webber, Leonard Mortis, *Merstham.*
1898. Weber, Edward Albert, *Transvaal.*
1890. Weber, Fredk. Parkes, *Harley-st.*, W.
1908. Webley,Arth.Sydv.,*Pembridge-villas.*
1884. Webster, Alfred George, *Goleur.*
1912. Webster,Clement Arthur,*Manchester*
1893. Webster, Edwin, *Osberton-road.*
1915. Webster, Fredk. Langton, *Hoghton.*
1886. Webster, George Alex., *Tasmania.*
1899. Webster, Harold George, *Coventry.*
1920.§Webster, Helena Jane, *Cardiff.*
1870. Webster, Henry William, *Ventnor.*
1872. Webster, Joseph Henry, *Weedon.*
1891. Webster, Percy Lawrance, *Margate.*
1886. Webster, Percy Samuel, *Victoria.*
1879. Webster, Ridley Manning, *Ealing.*
1910. Webster, Vivian Thos. P., *Brynglas.*
1903. Wedd, Bernard Harry, *Portman-mns.*
1898. Wedd, Gilbert, *Wellington.*
1909. Weddell, John Murray, *R.A.M.C.*
1887. Wedgwood,W.Brack'b'y,*King'sLynn.*
1920. Weeden, Alfred Douglas, *Tufnell-pk.*
1897. Weekes,Charles Peterson,*South'mpt'n*
1893. Weekes, Hy. Holman, *Crowborough.*
1893. Weekes, Reg. Newton, *Modbury.*
1895. Woeks, Courtenay Charles, *Lincoln.*
1896. Weeks, Harold, *Tolago Bay, N.Z.*
1914. Weerasooria, Felix F., *Ceylon.*
1903. Weinberg, Solomon Jas., *Victoria*
1923. Weinbren, Maurice, *Honor-oak-pk.*
1903. Weir, Edmund G. Harrison,*Malacca.*
1907. Weir, Henry Bright, *St. Thos.-hosp.*
1901. Weir, Hugh Heywood, *Tufton-st.*
1908. Weir, Walter, *Merstham.*
1900. Welch, Charles Herbert, *Bath.*
1908. Welch Cuthbert Gerald, *Norwood.*
1908. Welch, Cyril Howard, *W. Norwood.*
1895. Welch, Edmund, *Leeds.*
1901. Welch, Frederick Day, *Wood-green.*
1880. Welch,SirGeo ,K.C.M.G.,C.B.,*R.N.*
1910. Welch,Harvey H. Vincent,*E.Africa.*
1873. Welch, Samuel, *W. Norwood.*
15502

1914. Welch, Thomas Burges, *Acton.*
1872. Welchman, Edward, *Cambridge.*
1902. Welchman, Frank Ernest, *Putney.*
1897. Weld, Alfred Edmond, *R.A.M.C.*
1873. Welford, Geo. Edwd., *Sunderland.*
1903. Welham,Geo.Sydney,*Charing Cross-h.*
1913. Weller, Charles Alex., *Torquay.*
1884. Weller, Charles Jos., *Stonehouse.*
1902. Wellington, Arth. Robartes, *F.M.S.*
1891. Wellington, Rchd.Henslowe,*Hitchin.*
1908. Wells, A. Geoffrey, D.S.O., *R.A.M.C.*
1881. Wells, Alfred Ernest, *Cuckfield.*
1878. Wells, Alfd. George, *W. Kensington.*
1905. Wells, Arthur Geo., *Winchmore-hill.*
1880. Wells, Arth.P. Lethbridge,*Harley-st.*
1917. Wells, Arthur Wm., *Chatsworth-rd.*
1881. Wells, Charles, *Maidenhead.*
1920. Wells, Clement J. L., *Belsize-sq.*
1911. Wells, Frank, *Tinnevelly, S. India.*
1888. Wells, Frank Barber, *Hampstead.*
1900. Wells, Hardy Vesey, *R.N., Bedford.*
1918. Wells, Jack Pascoe.
1903. Wells, John, *Bilston.*
1893. Wells, Jn. Edmd. Bishop, *Hoddesdon.*
1921. Wells, Leslie Ralph Aug., *Llanelly.*
1897. Wells, Lionel Thomas, *Wakefield.*
1915. Wells, Philip Hewer, M.C., *Belsize-sq.*
1905. Wells, Stanley Martin, *Valparaiso.*
1893. Wells,Sydney Russell,*Lr.Seymour-st.*
1914. Wells-Cole, Gervas Charles, *Lincoln.*
1884. Welpton, John.
1901. Welsh, John, *Chester.*
1884. Wenyon, Edwin James, *Dundee.*
1909. Werapermall, Arthur A. M., *Ceylon.*
1898. Wernet, August Joseph, *R.N.*
1892. Wesley, Frank William, O.B.E.
1899. Wessels,Cornelius Adrian, *Cape Prov.*
1885. West, Charles Jas., O.B.E.,*Newbury.*
1917.§West, Joan, *Stroud.*
1902. West, John Arthur, *Chancery-lane.*
1914. West, John Frankland, *Wimpole-st.*
1891. West, Lionel Frederick, *Handsworth.*
1891. West,Richd.Milbourne,D.S.O.,O.B.E
1907. West, Stephen Harold.
1880. Westcott, Sinclair, C.B., C.M.G.
1897. Westcott, Warron Guy, C.M.G.,*R.N.*
1870. Westcott, Wm. Wynn, *Holloway.*
1905. Western, Geo. Trench, *York-street.*
1918. Westlake, Aubrey T., *Fordingbridge.*
1915. Westman, Karl J. F., *Wimpole-st.*
1918. Westmorland, A. S., *Broadhurst-gds.*
1865. Westmorland, Joseph, *Stockport.*
1880. Weston, George Edward, *R.A.M.C.*
1884. Weston, George Henry, *Southampton.*
1900. Weston, Henry James, *St. Leonards.*
1879. Weston, Saml. T. Darby,*Handsworth.*
1908. Weston, Thomas Alex., *R.A.M.C.*
15559

1905. Weston,Walter Jn.,D.S.O.,*R.A.M.*C.
1894. Westrup, Jos. Perceval, *Salisbury.*
1921.§Westwood, Agnes Edie, *Cupar.*
1889. Westwood, John, *Birmingham.*
1892. Wetherall,PritzlerS.Batten,*Weym'th.*
1910. Wetherbee, Hugh, *Hampstead.*
1885. Wethered, Frank Joseph, *Harley-st.*
1902. Wetherell, Marmaduke C., *R.A.M.*C.
1884. Wetwan, Wm. Albt., *Bridlington.*
1893. Whait, Jn. Robt., *Finchley-road.*
1901. Whalley, Edgar, *Leeds.*
1879. Wharry,Arthur James,*Malvern Wells.*
1871. Wharry, Charles John, *Sutton.*
1875. Wharry, Robert, *Cambridge-gate.*
1919.§Wharton, Effie Adela, *Withyam.*
1902. Whatley, James Lawson, *Knowle.*
1908. Wheat, Ernest Godfrey, *Transvaal.*
1886. Wheatley, James, *Shrewsbury.*
1851. Wheatley, Thos. Delmaine, *U.S.A.*
1886. Wheaton, Samuel Walton, *Streatham.*
1887. Wheeldon, Fredk. John, *Middleton.*
1892. Wheeler, Chas. Edwin, *Q.-Anne-st.*
1909. Wheeler, Francis James, *Southport.*
1919. Wheeler, Frederic Francis, *Putney.*
1887. Wheeler,Hump'ryJn.,*High Wycombe.*
1887. Wheeler, James Atkin, *Queensland.*
1908. Wheeler, Jas. Norman, *Wimborne.*
1896. Wheeler, Malcolm, *Camden Town.*
1885. Wheeler,Percy C. E.D'Erf,*Worthing.*
1918. Wheeler, Thomas Digby, *C.A.M.C.*
1913. Wheeler-Bennett, C. W., *Keston.*
1902. Wheen, Charles, *Albion-street.*
1881. Whelan, George.
1912. Whelan, Hamlet Mark, *Royal Navy.*
1894. Whelpton, Edwd. Smith, *Beckenham.*
1912. Whetnam, George Jamieson, *Canada.*
1894. Whichello, Harold, *Heswall.*
1887. Whicher, Alex. Hastings, *Bristol.*
1913. Whigham, John R. M., *Wembley.*
1897. Whipham, Thos. Rowland C.,*Park-st.*
1887. Whiston, Philip Henry, *Irish Guards.*
1905. Whitaker, Alfd. Gurth, *Evershot.*
1888. Whitaker,Geo. Herbt., *S.Norwood-pl.*
1891. Whitaker,Jas.Smith,*Buckingh'm-g'te*
1899. Whitaker, Leonard Edgar, *N.Z.*
1889. Whitaker, Sydney Morgan, *Liverpool.*
1904. Whitamore,Vernon N.,O.B.E.,*I.M.S.*
1910. Whitby, Edwd. Vernon, *R.A.M* C.
1913. Whitby, Edwd. Vickers,*Birmingham.*
1923.§Whitby, Ethel, *Hampstead.*
1922. Whitby, Joseph, *Stoke Newington.*
1923. Whitby, Lionel E. H., *Mill-lane.*
1883. Whitcombe,PhilipPercival,*Queen's-g.*
1916. Whitcombe,RichardC.P.,*Queen's-gte*
1896. Whitcombe-Brown,Wm.H.,*Westcliff*
1880. White, Alfd. Thos. Oliver.
1918.§White, Alice, *Sheffield.*
15616

1911. White, Arthur, *Stratford-place.*
1903. White, Arthur Denham, *I. M.S.*
1908. White, Charles Fras. Orr, *Bexhill.*
1887. White, Charles Percival, *M.V.O.*
1900. White,CyrilChas.ColebyKirke, *Yorks*
1900. White, Edward, *Bath.*
1908. White, E. Barton Cartwright,*Cardiff.*
1903. White, Edward How, *Bournemouth.*
1915. White, Edward Scott, *Bath.*
1878. White,Edwd.W.Wood,*Birmingham.*
1912. White, Ernest, *Barnsley.*
1882. White, Ernest Alfred, *Leeds.*
1872. White, Ernest Wm ,O.B.E., *Brixton.*
1918.§White, Ethel, *Sheffield.*
1915.§White, Eva Muriel, *Stoke Newington.*
1897. White, Frank Harris, *Forest-gate.*
1901. White, Fdk. Norman, C.I.E., *I.M.S.*
1872. White, George Bentley, *Nottingham.*
1897. White, Harold Edwd., *Birmingham.*
1896. White, Henry, *Persia.*
1911. White, Herbert, *Royal Navy.*
1892. White, Herbt. George, *Swineshead.*
1892. White, Jas. Atkin Heuton, *Edgbaston.*
1893. White, John A. T., O B E., *Harlow.*
1867. White, John Campbell.
1904. White, Jn. Doug. Campbell, *Harrow.*
1920. White, John Stanley, *Champion-hill.*
1884. White, John William, *Nailsea.*
1906. White, Leonard, *Mossley.*
1914. White, Leslie Gordon. *Bradford.*
1897. White, Malcolm, *British Columbia.*
1923. White, Norman Lewis, *Adelaide-rd.*
1898. White, Percy Stanhope, *Baybrooke.*
1902. White, Percy Walter, *Bristol.*
1904. White, Ralph Kuper, D.S O., *I.M.S.*
1879. White, Richard Watts, *St. Ives.*
1870. White,Richd.Wentworth,*Lymington*
1880. White, Robert Prosser, *Wigan.*
1895. White, Sidney Hugh, *Cambridge.*
1914. White, Syer Barrington, *Lyndhurst.*
1907. White, Walt. Woodworth, *Canada.*
1880. White, Sir William Hale, K.B.E.
1917. White, William Harold, *N. P. Bank.*
1878. White, William Robert, *Wadhurst.*
1915. White-Cooper, Wm. R., *Cape Prov.*
1892. Whiteford,Chas.Hamilton,*Plymouth.*
1919. Whitehall-Cooke, E. C., *Cricklewood.*
1871. Whitehead, Alfred, *Baltimore,U.S.A.*
1904. Whitehead, Arthur, *Queen's-road.*
1892. Whitehead, Arthur Longley, *Leeds.*
1915. Whitehead, Brian, *Salisbury.*
1906. Whitehead, Chas. Ernest, *Battersea.*
1898. Whitehead,ClarenceBarns,*Richm'nd.*
1902. Whitehead, Eugene Chris., *R.A.M.C.*
1905. Whitehead, Francis Hy., *Lavender-h.*
1905. Whitehead, Frank Eldred, *W.Africa.*
1888. Whitehead,HenryEdward,*Holloway.*
15673

1863. Whitehead, John, *Ventnor.*
1893. Whitehead, John Herbert, D.S.O.
1912. Whitehead, Noel Tancred, M.C.
1912. Whitehead, Percy, *Lavender-hill.*
1903. Whitehouse, Alfd. L. W., *Hobart-pl.*
1893. Whitehouse, Edwin St.John, M.B.E.
1880. Whitehouse, John, *Dudley.*
1920. Whitelaw, Alan Dunlop, *Harrogate.*
1896. Whitelaw, Francis, *Wrexham.*
1876. Whitelegge,SirB.A.,K.C.B.,*Home-of.*
1885. Whiteley, Daniel Flockton, *Fulham.*
1879. Whiteley, Geo. William, *Downton.*
1915. Whitelocke, Hugh A. B , *Oxford.*
1923.§Whitelocke, Joan F., *Whitchurch.*
1911. Whiteman, John Wells, *Grenada.*
1898. Whiteside, Hy. Cadman, *Royal Navy.*
1872. Whitfeld, Wm. J. Clarke, *Hereford.*
1897. Whitfield, Allan, *Harpurhey.*
1891. Whitfield, Arthur, *Harley-street.*
1883. Whitfield, D. Wms., *Abbots Bromley.*
1922.§Whitfield,Hilda Margt.,*Beaconsfield.*
1913. Whiting, Edgar Wm., *Ilford.*
1901. Whiting,Rbt.Garden, *Stoke-by-Clare.*
1895. Whitley, Henry Walter, *Stroud.*
1923. Whitlock, Denis Banes, *Oxted.*
1889. Whitman, Royal, *New York, U.S.A.*
1903. Whitmore, Fielding Chas., *Plymouth.*
1869. Whitmore, Wm. Beach, *Thurloe-sq.*
1908. Whitnall, Samuel Ernest, *Oxford.*
1910. Whitney, Cyril U., *Wandsworth.*
1904. Whitney, Willis Norton, *Japan.*
1873. Whitsed, Jas. Longland, *Tilehurst.*
1908. Whittall, Harold Frederick.
1880. Whittick, Fallon Peicy, *Brook-st.*
1883. Whittingdale, John F. L.
1913. Whittington, Gerald, *Betchworth.*
1896. Whittington, Richard, *Brighton.*
1909. Whittington,Theo.Hy.,*King's-coll.-h.*
1920. Whittle, Claude Howard,*Harpenden.*
1877. Whittle, Ewing M. Glynn, *Liverpool.*
1919. Whitway-Wilkinson,A.C.S.,*T'nn'th*
1885. Whitwell, Alfd. Frank, *Shrewsbury.*
1913. Whitworth, Wm. Cuthbert, *Scorrier.*
1912. Whorlow, Cyril Guy, *Ealing.*
1919. Whyte, Angus Hedley, *S. Shields.*
1915. Whyte, Henderson, *Bromley.*
1890. Whyte, Herbt. William.
1883. Whyte, John Mackie, *Dundee.*
1916. Whyte-Venables, Harold, *A. Caran.*
1921. Whytock, Arthur Beaton, *Canada.*
1913. Wickenden, Stanley, *Tunbridge Wells.*
1912. Wickham, Frede. St.B., O.B E.,*R.N.*
1907. Wickham, Harrie Bruce, *Rufford.*
1886. Wickham, OnslowArthur,*Barnsbury.*
1922. Wickramasinghe, Sextus F., *Ceylon.*
1922. Wickremesinghe, Walter G., *Ceylon.*
1870. Wicks, Frederick, *Ilford.*
15730

1896. Wicks, Spencer, *Beaconsfield, Cape.*
1914. Widdowson, Hugh L., *Fulham.*
1909. Widegren,MathiasW.E.,*Knightsb'dge*
1922. Widgery, Fredk. Wm., *Exeter.*
1882. Wigan, Charles Arthur, *Portishead.*
1908. Wigan, William Cecil, *Nyasaland.*
1920.§Wigfield, Dorothea C., *Crouch End.*
1883. Wigg, Henry Higham, *Adelaide.*
1894. Wiggin, Hugh Peter Victor, *Torquay.*
1923. Wiggins, Alan Kingsley,*North'mpt'n*
1890. Wiggins, Charles, *East Sheen.*
1900. Wiggins, Clare Aveling, *Uganda.*
1894. Wiggins, Henry, *Worthing.*
1897. Wiggins, Wm. Denison, *Greenwich.*
1893. Wigginton,Albt.Edwd.,*Birmingham.*
1887. Wigglesworth, Sidney, *St. Albans.*
1885. Wigham, Wm. Harper, *Tattenhall.*
1906. Wight, Edward, *Brighton.*
1887. Wight, John Cam, *Victoria.*
1891. Wightman, John Prest, *York.*
1867. Wigin, George William, *Leeds.*
1892. Wiglesworth, Thos. Ridler, *Minster.*
1905. Wigmore, Alfred James, *Catford.*
1910. Wigmore, Arth. Jn. Ormsby, *Bath.*
1912. Wigmore, Jas. B. Aquilla, *R.A.M.C.*
1908. Wijegoonewardena, William, *Ceylon.*
1919. Wijewardene, Don Edmund.
1917. Wijeyeratne, Jas. de Silva, *Colombo.*
1919. Wijeyeratne, Simon Cyril de Silva.
1898. Wijeyesakere, William, *Colombo.*
1858. Wikeley, Charles Edward, *A.M.S.*
1886. Wilbe, Richd. H. Wiffin, *Finchley-rd.*
1920.§Wilberforce, Octavia M., *Henfield.*
1873. Wilcox, Henry, *Salcombe.*
1898. Wilcox, Richd. Loy,*Whitehall-court.*
1914. Wilcox, Stanley Mu ray, *Salcombe.*
1887. Wild, Charles Henry, *Prescott.*
1916. Wild, Granville Burnett, *Whitworth.*
1892. Wild, Henry Sydney, *Guernsey.*
1885. Wild, Robert Briggs, *Manchester.*
1895. Wilde, Alfd, Neville, *Barry.*
1882. Wildey, Alex. Gascoigne, C.B., *R.N.*
1890. Wilding, Walter Frederick William.
1879. Wiles, Fredk. Wm., *Bowes-park.*
1901. Wilkes,ErnestAlfd.Freear,*S'hampton*
1892. Wilkes, Geo. Arthur, *Birmingham.*
1901.Wilkes,Wm.Hy.Griffin,*Lac'nder-hill.*
1862. Wilkin, John Fredk., *North Devon.*
1893. Wilkin, Robt. Hugh, *Newmarket.*
1888. Wilkins, John, *Hampstead.*
1865. Wilkins, John Canning, *Water-lane.*
1895. Wilkins, Jn Claude Verity, *Sarisbury.*
1899. Wilkins, Thos. Halford, *Birmingham.*
1905. Wilkins, Trevor Hamilton, *Chiswick.*
1896. Wilkins, Walter, *Liverpool.*
1906. Wilkins, Wm. Douglas, *Winwick.*
1857. Wilkinson, Alfd. Geo., *Northampton.*
15787

1895. Wilkinson, Arthur Norris, *Victoria.*
1877. Wilkinson, Arth. Thos., *Manchester.*
1873. Wilkinson, Auburn, *Tynemouth.*
1884. Wilkinson, Clement John, *Windsor.*
1906. Wilkinson, Edmund, *Bordesley.*
1903. Wilkinson, Edw. A. G., C.B.E., *R.N.*
1923. Wilkinson, Ernest G., *Wednesbury.*
1915. Wilkinson, Geoffrey Legh, *Stechford.*
1922.§Wilkinson, Helen P., *Leicester.*
1892. Wilkinson, Henry Bacon, *Ivybridge.*
1889. Wilkinson, Jas. Howard, *Dudley.*
1877. Wilkinson, John Cooper, *Ashford.*
1915. Wilkinson, John Douglas, *Sutton.*
1911. Wilkinson, John Helby, *B. Columbia.*
1923. Wilkinson,Michael C.,*Ramsey,I.ofM.*
1890. Wilkinson, Robert, *Anerley.*
1913. Wilkinson,Russell Facey,*Hampstead.*
1892. Wilkinson, Sidney, *Liverpool.*
1914. Wilkinson, Sydney Arthur, *Ealing.*
1882. Wilkinson, Wm. Camac,*Wimpole st.*
1905. Wilkinson, William John, *Binbrook.*
1913. Wilks, Henry, *Middlesbro'.*
1891. Wilks, Joseph Henry, *Sheffield.*
1895. Wilks, Morris, *Sparkhill.*
1892. Wilks, Stephen L. B., *Colwyn Bay.*
1922.§Will, Ella Kennedy.
1898. Will, Henry Chis olm, *Sidcup.*
1901. Willan, Geo. T., D.S.O.,*Sittingbourne.*
1907. Willan, Reginald, *West Africa.*
1903. Willan, Richard, *Royal Navy.*
1911. Willans, Esmond Tetley, *Stockton.*
1910. Willans, Fredc. Jeune,*Much Hadham.*
1915. Willatt, Arthur, *Nottingham.*
1873. Willcocks, Alex. John, *I.M.S.*
1882. Willcocks, Arth. Durant, *Taunton.*
1912. Willcocks,Robt. Waller,*Roehampton.*
1907. Willcox, Jos. Wm. Jas., *Glastonbury.*
1867. Willcox, Robt. Lewis, *Warminster.*
1916. Willenberg, Richard W., *Ceylon.*
1909. Willes, Charles Fitzgerald, *R.N.*
1803. Willes, Joseph, *Penge.*
1878. Willes, William, *Bournemouth.*
1862. Willett, Edmund, *Eastbourne.*
1881. Willett, Geo Gilmore Drake, *Bristol.*
1899. Willett, John Abernethy, *Wimpo'e-st.*
1830. Willey, Charles Henry, *Sheffield.*
1921. Willey, Henry Lawrence, *Sheffield.*
1891. Willey, Thomas, *Swanage.*
1884. Williams, Alfred, *Pendleton.*
1901. Williams, Alfd. Carleton, *Albion-rd.*
1876. Williams, Alfd. Glover, *Brixton-hill.*
1872. Williams, Alfred Henry.
1910. Williams,Arth.Donald J.B.,*E.Africa.*
1906. Williams, Arth. Harold, *Worcester.*
1911. Williams, Arthur Tudor, *Bengal.*
1905. Williams, A. Scott, D.S.O.,*R.A.M.C.*
1921. Williams, Bernard Warren, *Westm.*
15844

1922.§Williams,CatherineM., *Cambridge-st.*
1914. Williams, Cecil Leonard, *Plymouth.*
1913. Williams, Charles Eustace, *Hendon.*
1876. Williams, Chas. Lewis, *Potter's Bar.*
1888. Williams, Charles Louis.
1895. Williams,Chas.Wellingham,*Norwich.*
1915. Williams, Cyril Mathias, *Barry Port.*
1908. Williams, Cyril Oswald O., *Clapham.*
1886. Williams, David, *Carmarthen.*
1921. Williams, David Charles.
1891. Williams, David John,*Jamaica.*
1883. Williams, David Lewis, *Ferryside.*
1909. Williams, David Phillips, *India.*
1878. Williams, Sir Dawson, C.B.E.
1889. Williams,EdgarMcKenzie, *R.A.M.C.*
1917. Williams, Edward, *Shillong, India.*
1871. Williams, Edward, *Aberayron.*
1901. Williams, Edwd. Colston, *Brecon.*
1904. Williams,Edwd. Kynaston, *Leicester.*
1885. Williams, Edwd.Lloyd,*B'ck'gh'm-gte.*
1882. Williams, E. R , M.B.E.,*Carmarthen.*
1914.§Williams, Emma Christine Pillman.
1922. Williams, Emrys, *Cwm-y-Glo.*
1889. Williams,ErnestGraham H.,*Malvern.*
1899. Williams, Ernest Harry, *New Zealand*
1892. Williams, Ernest M., *R.A.M.C.*
1903. Williams, Ernest Ulysses, O.B.E.
1895. Williams,FenwickD'ArcyM ,*C'pe Col.*
1874. Williams, Fredk. Mann, *Plymouth.*
1916. Williams, Geoffrey C., *Thornbury.*
1892. Williams, Geo. C. W., *Cavendish-st.*
1901. Williams,George Edwd., *Rhostryfan.*
1884. Williams, Geo. Herbert, *New York.*
1886. Williams,Geo.Rowland,*Sinclair-gns.*
1919.§Williams, Gladys M. T., *Builth Wells.*
1909. Williams, Gwilym A., *Gowerton.*
1913. Williams, Harold Austin, *Swansea.*
1891. Williams, Harry Bowen, *Brockley.*
1916. Williams,Harry G. Everard,*M'chester*
1892. Williams, Harry J. E. II., *Sheffield.*
1902. Williams, Henry Currer, *Alton.*
1923. Williams,Henry Wm.Miles,*Southsea*
1920. Williams, Herbert Edward.
1881. Williams, Herbt. Egerton, *Newport.*
1885. Williams, Herbt. Leader, *Tufnell-pk.*
1918. Williams, Howel Pennant, *Liverpool.*
1908. Williams, Howell Meyrick, *Liverpool.*
1872. Williams, Howell, *Richmond, Yorks.*
1923. Williams,Hubert C.,*Newcastle Emlyn.*
1922. Williams,HubertN.,*Cartwright-gdns.*
1886. Williams, Hugh Lloyd,*Harley-street.*
1907. Williams, Hugh Owen, *Abersoch.*
1866. Williams, Sir John. Bart., G.C.V.O.
1897. Williams,Jn.Daniel Evans,*Battersea.*
1890. Williams, John Edward, *Ilford.*
1881. Williams, Jn. Fredk., *Camberwell-rd.*
1883. Williams,Jn H.Hywell,*Hereford west*
15901

1893. Williams, John Owen, *Barmouth.*
1888. Williams, John Price, *Manchester.*
1917. Williams, John Pritchard, *Cardiff.*
1910. Williams, John Pryce, *Maida-hill.*
1890. Williams,John Robert,*Penmaenmawr*
1896. Williams, John Sydney, *Immingham.*
1867. Williams, Jn. Terrell, *Barrow.*
1910. Williams, John Wilson, *Pontypridd.*
1896. Williams, Joseph Wm., *Stourport.*
1895. Williams, Kenway Thos., *Grosmont.*
1878. Williams, Lemuel Edwd., *Liverpool.*
1895. Williams,LeonardAddams,*R.A.M.C.*
1923. Williams, Leslie Graeme,*Kensington.*
1886. Williams, Lionel Henry, *Thornbury:*
1919 §Williams,Margt. A.,*Church Stretton.*
1921.§Williams, Mary G., *Montpellier-sq.*
1878. Williams, Miles Melbourne, *Chorley.*
1883. Williams, Montagu Wm., *Leicester.*
1922.§Williams, Muriel B., *Westminster.*
1875. Williams, Neville, *Harrogate.*
1910. Williams, Neville Scott, *Uganda.*
1916. Williams, Oscar, *Llanelly.*
1911. Williams, Owen Elias, *Bloxwich.*
1834. Williams, Patrick Watson, *Bristol.*
1901. Williams,Percy Glyn Savours, *Cairo.*
1918. Williams, Peter Erbin.
1894. Williams,Philip Geo.,*Stoke Newington*
1908. Williams, Rajaiya Robert, *Ceylon.*
1896. Williams, Ralph Paul, *Whitehall.*
1884. Williams, Reg. Muzio, *Notting-h.-gte.*
1871. Williams, Richard, *Bangor.*
1873. Williams, Richd, M.B.E , *Wrexham.*
1914. Williams, Richard, *Wanstead.*
1904. Williams, Richd. Geoffrey, *Wrexham.*
1906. Williams, Richard Hugh, *Manchester.*
1907. Williams, Richard Tudor, *Caergwrle.*
1881. Williams, Robert, *Liverpool.*
1888. Williams, Robert Edwin, *Worthing.*
1883. Williams, Robert Richard.
1891. Williams, Samuel, *Llanelly.*
1896. Williams, Stanley Walter, O.B.E.
1910. Williams, Sydney, *Llanelly.*
1900. Williams, Sydney Rice,*Buckfastleigh.*
1911. Williams, Thomas Davies, *St. David's.*
1886. Williams, Thos. Henry, *Plymouth.*
1903. Williams, Thomas John, *Liverpool.*
1909. Williams, Thomas John, *S. Rhodesia.*
1916. Williams, Thomas Pearse, *Crapstone.*
1913. Williams, Trevor Owen, *Liverpool.*
1919. Williams, Tudor, *Kidwelly.*
1873. Williams, William, *Liverpool.*
1887. Williams, Wm. Griffith, *Liverpool.*
1876. Williams, William Henry, *Acton.*
1921. Williams, Wm. Hubert, *Liverpool.*
1907. Williams, Wm.Humphrey,*Wrexham.*
1905. Williams, Wm. Percival G., *I.M.S.*
1900. Williams,Wm.Reg Eyton,*Pembroke.*
15958

1920. Williams, Wm. Robert, *Warrington.*
1905. Williams, Wm. Wynne, *Middlesbro'.*
1886. Williams-Freeman,Jn.Peere,*Andover.*
1916. Williams-Walker,Alfred,*Birm'gh'm*
1900. Williamson, Arch. Rbt. B., *Ontario.*
1907. Williamson, Cecil Lennox, *Liverpool.*
1886. Williamson, Chas. Frederick, *Horley.*
1915. Williamson, Harold, *Streatham.*
1896. Williamson, Herbt., *Queen Anne-st.*
1883. Williamson, H. Holdrich, *Andover.*
1892. Williamson, John, *Epsom.*
1869. Williamson, John Gover, *A.M.S.*
1908. Williamson, John Samuel, *Swindon.*
1898. Williamson, Joshua, *Cleethorpes.*
1896. Williamson,Oliver Key,*Bryanston-st.*
1884. Williamson, Richd.Thos.,*Manchester.*
1906. Williamson. Wm. Sugden,*Bradford.*
1906. Williamson Wilson Trevor,*Hereford*
1881. Willis, Arthur Keith.
1921.§Willis, Constance Mur'el, *Chiswick.*
1893. Willis, Cyril Hamer, *Bournemouth.*
1913. Willis, Fredk. Edw. S., *Streatham.*
1897. Willis, Harry Alex. Legge. *N.S.W.*
1904. Willis, John Keith, *Cranleigh.*
1898. Willis, Jos. Darrington, *Nottingham.*
1899. Willis,Wm. Frederick, *Fielding, N.Z.*
1906. Willis-Bund, Hy. Dewi H., M.C.
1906. Willmore. James Graham, *Egypt.*
1895. Willmore, Wm. Southwick, *I.M.S.*
1863. Willmot, Robert, *Tasmania.*
1923. Willmott, Leslie Arthur, *Harpenden.*
1892. Willock, Edwd. Hulse, *Croydon.*
1879. Willoughby, Jas. Fdk. Digby, O.B.E.
1888. Willoughby, Wm. Geo., *Eastbourne.*
1914. Wills, Alfred, *Denmark-hill.*
1916. Wills, Arthur Gerald P., M.C.
1896. Wills, James Tremlett, *Felstead.*
1920.§Wills, Lucy, *Kensington.*
1903. Wills, Robert Glover, *Gt. Crosby.*
1898. Wills, Walter Kenneth, O.B.E.
1884. Wills, Wm. Alfred, *Midhurst.*
1864. Willson, Henry, *Weybridge.*
1892. Willson, Jn. Wherry, *Bradford.*
1894. Willway, Fred.Wm.,*DeepSeaMission.*
1894. Wilmot, Philip McK. C., *Plymouth.*
1902. Wilmot, Reg. Cameron, *R.A.M.C.*
1899. Wilmot,Rbt.EardleyByam,*Burnham.*
1877. Wilmot, Thomas, *Bradford.*
1912. Wilson, Alan, M.C., *Lothersdale.*
1916. Wilson, Alban, *Muswell-road.*
1885. Wilson, Albert, *Hull.*
1908. Wilson, Ambrose Cyril, *Oldham.*
1888. Wilson, Arch. Scarlyn, *St. Leonards.*
1875. Wilson,Arth.CobdenJordan,*Penistone*
1876. Wilson, Arth. Huelin, *G. Post-office.*
1892. Wilson, Arthur Marius, *Cape Town.*
1913. Wilson, Cecil William, *Fellows-rd.*
16015

1908. Wilson, C. McMoran, M.C., *Barrow.*
1922. Wilson, Charles Paul, *Stroud Green.*
1874. Wilson, Chas. W., *Bury St. Edmunds*
1890. Wilson, Chas. William, *Ontario.*
1906. Wilson, Chris. James, M.C., *E. Afr.*
1919. Wilson,Claude Bawden,*Bk.of S.Afr.*
1905. Wilson, David, *Huddersfield.*
1920. Wilson, Edric Frank, *Acton.*
1902. Wilson, Edward Allan, *Keighley.*
1886. Wilson, Foden, *Birkenhead.*
1902. Wilson, Fredk. Ernest, *Brockley.*
1893. Wilson, Frederick Wallace, M.B.E.
1902. Wilson, Geoff. Plumpton,*Langwathby*
1882. Wilson, George, *R.A.M.C.*
1922. Wilson, George, *Westcliffe.*
1880. Wilson, George John, *Plymouth.*
1915. Wilson,Gerald Richd.C., *E. Malling.*
1908. Wilson, Graham Lionel J.,*Sumner-pl.*
1916. Wilson, Graham S., *Charing-cross-h.*
1904. Wilson, Harry Theo. Minden, D.S.O.
1881. Wilson, Henry, *Manchester.*
1908. Wilson,Hy.AdrianFitzroy,*Ringwood.*
1903. Wilson, Henry Lydiard, *Gordon-sq.*
1895. Wilson, Horace Bagster,*Birmingham.*
1894. Wilson, Horace Richard, *Grove-lane.*
1909. Wilson, Humphrey B., O.B.E.
1861. Wilson, James, *Liverpool.*
1883. Wilson, John Grant, *Clevedon.*
1890. Wilson, John Gratton, *Victoria.*
1923. Wilson, John Greenwood, *Charlton.*
1867. Wilson,Jn.Hy.Parker,*Brondesb'y-rd.*
1873. Wilson, John Smith, *Bank of N.S.W.*
1907. Wilson, Lorton Alex., *Barrow.*
1914. Wilson, Maurice U., M.C., *Battersea.*
1882. Wilson,MervynSeppings,*Chippenham.*
1906. Wilson, Murray Richd. Osmond, *Bath.*
1904. Wilson. Norman Methven, *I.M.S.*
1912. Wilson, Oscar Reg. Lewis, *Croydon.*
1909. Wilson, Philip Fredk., *Letchworth.*
1882. Wilson, Reg. William, *Croydon.*
1923. Wilson, Robert Kenneth, *Evesham.*
1923. Wilson, Robert N. Price, *Leeds.*
1923. Wilson, Ronald E., *Much Wenlock.*
1873. Wilson, Samuel, *Mare-street.*
1915. Wilson, Samuel, *Mare-street.*
1883. Wilson,TheodoreStacey,*Birmingham*
1883. Wilson, Thomas, *West Australia.*
1916. Wilson, Thomas, *Burnley.*
1915. Wilson, William Bernard, *Mare-st.*
1873. Wilson,Wm.Teasdale,*Oregon,U.S.A.*
1898. Wilton, Stanley, *East Liss, Hants.*
1904. Wiltshire, Harold W., O.B.E., D.S.O.
1913. Wiltshire, H. Goodwill,*King'sColl.-h.*
1902. Wiltshire, Hbt. Pattison, *Emsworth.*
1896. Wimble, Herbert Chas., *Bushey.*
1909. Vince, Walter George.
1867. Winckworth, Chas. Trew, *Brighton.*
16072

1903. Winckworth,Harold Chas., *R.A.M. C.*
1893. Winckworth,WadhamBruce,*Taunton*
1922. Windemer, Don. Asbury, *Mevagissey*
1907. Winder, John, *Bedford-park.*
1900. Winder, MauriceG.,D.S.O.,*R.A.M. C.*
1901. Windeyer, John Cadell.
1891. Windle, Jabez Davenport, *Southall.*
1884. Windley, William, *Nottingham.*
1899. Windsor, Charles William, *Royston.*
1892. Windsor, Frank Needham, *I.M.S.*
1907. Windsor, James Frederick, *Henley.*
1885. Windsor-Aubrey, Hy. W., *Bristol.*
1861. Wine, Henry Charles, *New Zealand.*
1917. Winfield, Arthur, *Hoylake.*
1914. Winfield, Fredk. Butwell, O.B.E.
1899. Wingate, Basil F., D.S.O., *R.A.M.C.*
1902. Wingate,SaulW.Wingate,*Lancaster.*
1923.§Wingfield, Lina M. C., *W. Drayton.*
1885. Wingrave, Thomas, *Finsbury-circus.*
1885. Wingrave ,V. H. W., *Bloomsbury-sq.*
1909. Wink, Charles Stewart, *Wimbledon.*
1898. Winkfield, Chas. Franks, *Whetstone.*
1898. Winkfield, Wm. Bertram, *R.A.M.C.*
1920.§Winn, Grace Elizabeth, *Wimbledon.*
1889. Winn, Thomas Cromwell, *Chingford.*
1888. Winnett, Frederick, *Toronto.*
1920. Winnicott,Donald Woods, *Plymouth.*
1885. Winship, Wm. Algernon, *California.*
1878. Winskell, William Edwin, *Ontario.*
1891. Winslow, Walter, *North Stoke.*
1880. Winstanley,Rbt.Wyndh'm,*H'slemere*
1899. Winston, Gerald Denton, *Oxford-gns.*
1893. Winston, Wm. Bamford, *Bowes-pk.*
1914. Winter, Arthur Graham, *Penrith.*
1894. Winter, Edward Stuart, *Lincoln.*
1918. Winter, Geoffrey, *Wolverhampton.*
1890. Winter, G. Mitchell, O.B.E., *Torquay.*
1888. Winter, Herbt. Edmund, *R.A.M.C.*
1913. Winter, Herbert G., M.C., *Lewisham.*
1895. Winter, John Bradbury, *Brighton.*
1883. Winter, Thomas Bassell, *R.A.M.C.*
1879. Winter, Walt. Hy. T.,*W'lverh'mpt'n.*
1903. Winterbotham,LauristonL.,*Lambeth.*
1899. Winterbotham, Raynor, *Briaworth.*
1877. Winterbottom, Arth. Thos., *Stroud.*
1891. Wintle, Colston, *Bristol.*
1914. Wippell, Wm. Pridham, *St. Bart.'s.*
1903. Wisdom, Rbt. Horace C.O., *Sudbury.*
1876. Wise, Alfred Thos. Tucker, *Strete.*
1916. Wise, Cuthbert Edward, *Switzerland.*
1895. Wise, Harry Mortimer, *Plumstead.*
1888. Wise, Henry Wellsted, *Stockport.*
1904. Wise, Kenrick Stanton, *Br. Guiana.*
1910. Wise, Walter Fredk., *George-st.*
1921.§Wiseham, Beryl.
1895. Wiseman, David Wm., *Forest-hill.*
1917. Wiseman, James Harry, *Walkley.*
16129

1877. Wishart, John, *London, Ontario.*
1887. Wisken, Charles, *Heywood.*
1912. With, Percy Arthur, *R.A.M. C.*
1891. Witham, Ernest Wells, *Assam.*
1921. Witham, Henry Norman, *Kirton.*
1892. Withers, Fredk. Ernest, *Netley.*
1882. Withers, John Sheldon, *Sidmouth.*
1880. Withers, Oliver, *Sidmouth.*
1894. Withers,Percy,*Broadway, Worcester.*
1872. Withers, Robert, *Southsea.*
1918. Withers, Samuel Anthony, *Ewell.*
1903. Withrow, Oswald Charles, *Ontario.*
1908. Witney, Ernest Wm., *Whitstable.*
1910. Witts, Charles, M.C., *Hereford.*
1893. Woakes, Claud Edward, *Wimpole-st.*
1923. Wolf, Ioos Erhard, *Davos.*
1906 Wolfe, John Henry, *Hanwell.*
1909. Wolfeistan, Kenneth, *Salop.*
1905. Wolff, Ernest Douglas, *E. Dereham.*
1918. Wolff, Eugene, *Finchley-road.*
1918. Wolff, Robert, *Oudtshoorn, S.A.*
1919. Wolff, Sidney, *Guy's-hospital.*
1903. Wollaston, Alex. Fdk. R., *Bristol.*
1879. Wolrige,Herbt.E.Rhodes,*Melbourne.*
1880. Wolstenholme,Rchd. Hanson,*Salford*
1919. Wong, Man, *West Kensington.*
1919. Wong, Sik To, *Hythe.*
1894. Wonnacott,Rchd. Reg.H.,*Faversham*
1913. Woo, Arthur Wai-tak, *Highbury-pl.*
1880. Wood, Arthur George, *Corsham.*
1886. Wood, Arth. Thorley, *Ipswich.*
1878. Wood, Charles, *Folkestone.*
1908. Wood, Chas. Albert, M.C., *I.M.S.*
1902. Wood, Charles Herbert, *Langley.*
1899. Wood, Charles Rawdon, *Hove.*
1923.§Wood, Edith Victoria, *Uttoxeter.*
1885. Wood, Edward, *Enfield.*
1880. Wood, Edward Archer, *Dulwich.*
1876. Wood, Edward Joshua, *Maidstone.*
1870. Wood,EdwinBrownrigg,*Birmingham*
1904. Wood, Frank Herbert, *Bampton.*
1890. Wood, Frank Stanley, *Sheffield.*
1918. Wood, Franklin Garrett, *Southport.*
1886. Wood,Geo.Edwd.Cartwright,*Balham*
1907. Wood, George Ernest, *Doncaster.*
1854. Wood, George Jacob.
1890. Wood, Guy Edwd. Mills, *Charterh'se.*
1873. Wood, Henry Thorold, *Heathfield.*
1893. Wood, Henry Utting, *Brandon.*
1896. Wood, Horatio C. Wm.,*Birmingham.*
1887. Wood, Hubert Moody, *Dulwich.*
1880. Wood, James, *St. Anne's-on-Sea.*
1898. Wood, James, *Crosby, I. of Man.*
1920.§Wood, Jane Edith, *Lightcliffe.*
1893. Wood, John, *Walmer.*
1912. Wood, John Alfred, *Oxford.*
1890. Wood, John Askey, *Northampton.*
16186

1899. Wraith,Ernest Arnold,C.B.E.,D.S.O.
1894. Wrangham, John Marris, *Lincoln.*
1896. Wrangham, Wm., O.B.E., *Bradford.*
1894. Wray, William Thomas, *Hull.*
1901. Wreford, Heyman, *Exeter.*
1887. Wreford,Jn.,*Jun. Army & Navy Club.*
1902. Wrench, Guy Theodore, *Bath-club.*
1886. Wright, Alfred, *R.A.M.C.*
1896. Wright, Alfd. Bosworth, *Southsea.*
1887. Wright, Bernard Duncan Z., *St. John*
1922.§Wright, Caroline Isobel, *Harlesden.*
1886. Wright, Charles Franklin, *Rye.*
1908. Wright, Chas. Samuel E., *New Catton.*
1887. Wright, Edmund Hasell, *I.M.S.*
1921. Wright, Edwd. Taylor, *Warwick-av.*
1914. Wright, Ernest Jen er, *Sierra Leone.*
1906. Wright, Everard Lister, *S. Africa.*
1911. Wright, Frederick Cecil, *R.N.*
1904. Wright,Fdk. Rbt. Elliston,*Braunton.*
1834. Wright, Gaskoin Richd. M., *Thame.*
1886. Wright, Geo. Cornelius Wm., *G.P.O.*
·1906. Wright, Harold Nairne, *Farnham.*
1878. Wright, Harry Claude, *Cape Prov.*
1914.§Wright, Helena R., *Tsinan, China.*
1876. Wright, Henry, *New Zealand.*
1883. Wright,HollandHodgs'n,*Ospringe-rd.*
1921. Wright, James Roberts, *Chorley.*
1921. Wright, John Edward, *Luton.*
1834. Wright, John Lister, *Southsea.*
1920. Wright, Joseph M. McC, *Liverpool.*
1913. Wright, Leslie Doug., *Cavendish-pl.*
1907. Wright, Oswald Kentish, *Holt.*
1886. Wright, Robert W., C.M.G., *A.M.S.*
1920. Wright, Samson, *Clapton-common.*
1896. Wright, Samuel Reginald, *Romford.*
1892. Wright, Sydney Faulconer, *Lee.*
1900. Wright, Thomas James, *Norwich.*
1909. Wright, Thomas Strethill, *Thaxted.*
1894. Wright, Walter Southey, *Wool.*
1876. Wright, Wm. Henry, *Leamington.*
1834. Wright, William Henry, *Liverpool.*
1894. Wrinch, Edwin Percy, *Boston.*
1898. Wroughton,Arth.OliverB.,*R.A.M.C.*
1885. Wunderlich, Otto Fredk., *N.S.W.*
1917. Wyatt,Alfred Frank, *Ottery St.Mary.*
1892. Wyatt, Charles John, *Penycraig.*
1906. Wyatt, Harold Douglas, *Godalming.*
1919. Wyatt, Raymond B. H., *Bedford.*
1888. Wyatt, Walter Lionel, *Hornsea.*
1886. Wyatt-Smith, Frank, *Crofton.*
1882. Wyborn, Samuel, *Ross.*
1918. Wyborn, Vyvian Deane, *Windsor.*
1923. Wybourn, James Thomas, *Ynysddu.*
1893. Wyche, Ernest Morton, *Nottingham.*
1914. Wyer, John Fras. Wilcox, *Ringwood.*
1896. Wykes, Wm. Henry, *Hugglescote.*
1906. Wyler, Edwin Jos., M.C., *Coleman-st.*
1923. 16357

1901. Wylie, Angus, *Regent's-pk.-rd.*
1892. Wylie, Jas. Thompson Roy, *Sallins.*
1894. Wyllys, William, *Great Yarmouth.*
1901. Wynn, William Hy., *Birmingham.*
1887. Wynne, Edwd. Thomas, *Queensland.*
1901. Wynne,GrahamShawA.S.,*Amersham*
1888. Wynne, John Darley, *Clonmel.*
1888. Wynter, Andrew Ellis, *Bristol.*
1892. Wysard, Alex. Thomas, *Ashtead.*
1923. Wyse, Harry David, *Hampstead.*

X.

1923.§Xavier, Marguerite, A. M., *Bangkok.*

Y.

1917. Yale, Sidney, *Hampstead-rd.*
1923.§Yate, Mildred May E., *Tavistock-sq.*
1907. Yates, Arthur Lowndes, M.C.
1919. Yates, Harold Blacow, *Preston.*
1923. Yates, James, *Tyldesley.*
1900. Yates, Thomas Preston, *Manchester.*
1888. Yates, Wm. Bartlemore, *Oldham.*
1881. Yeatman,JohnWalt.,*Auburn,S.Aust.*
1889. Yeld, Walter Harry, *Welbeck-street.*
1893. Yelf, Jn. Burnet, *Shipston-on-Stour.*
1914. Yeo, Kenneth John, *Reigate.*
1921.§Yeoman, Greta Isabel, *Northallerton*
1923.§Yeoman, Joyce P., *Northallerton.*
1916. Yeoman, William, *Stokesley.*
1887. Yeoman, Wm. Metcalfe, *Stokesley.*
1903. Yetts,Walter Perceval, *Lloyds-bank.*
1904. Yin, Suat Chwan, *Singapore.*
1923. Yodh, Bhaskar Balvantro, *Putney.*
1886. Yolland, John H., C.B.E., *Bromley.*
1907. Yonge, Ambrose Pode, *Twickenham.*
1920. Yonge,FrancisBernard,*W. Norwood.*
1910. Yood, Raphael, *New Jersey, U.S.A.*
1896. Yorke-Davies, Jn. Wynne, *Harley-st.*
1877. Yoshida, Kenzo Hidenari, *Japan.*
1919. Young,Alfred Ernest, *Weston-s.-mare*
1902. Young, Alistair Cameron, *Ipswich.*
1895. Young, Archibald, *Sheffield.*
1898. Young, Bertram Michell, *Hassocks.*
1916. Young, Campbell, *Worthing.*
1921. Young, Chas. Florance, *Forest-hill.*
1884. Young, Charles Stewart, *Dundee.*
1886. Young,Chas.W.Forrest,*Westminster.*
1920. Young, Claude Railton, *Oxford.*
1885. Young, Edwd. Herbt., *Okehampton.*
1874. Young, Edward William, *I.M.S.*
1901. Young, Ernest Eric, *Stoke-on-Trent.*
1922.§Young, Eva, *Stamford-hill-mans.*
1902. Young, Fred. Armstrong, O.B E.
16406 y

1902. Young, George, *New York*.
1904. Young, Graham Pallister, *Birmingh'm*
1903. Young, Hy. Geo. Keith, *Braintree*.
1896. Young, Hy. Wm. Pennyfather, *N'rbury*
1872. Young, John, *Narborough*.
1891. Young, John, *Stamford-hill*.
1922. Young, John Alexander.
1899. Young, John Charles, *Lexham-gds*.
1892. Young, J. Claudius, *Cuba, New York*.
1919. Young, Maurice Lindsay, *Hove*.
1886. Young, Rchd. Weekes, *Botany, N.S.W*
1904. Young, Sam. LeggateO., *Yarm'th, I.W*
1901. Young, Thomas, *Woolacombe*.
1888. Young, Thomas Brett, *Halesowen*.
1872. Young, Thos. Frederic, *Liverpool*.
1910. Young, Walter Ansley, *Redmans-rd*.
1914. Young, William Arthur, *Blackheath*.
1922. Young, William Arthur, *Stourport*.
1906. Young, Wm. Arth. Bruce, *Blackburn*.
1900. Young, William John, *Cambridge*.
1879. Young, Wms. Hy. Frome, *Grantham*.
1916. Younger, Geo. C.N., *Mecklenburgh-sq*.
16428

1902. Yule, Bransby, *Highgate-rd*.
1887. Yunge-Bateman, M. Geo., *Folkestone*

Z.

1917. Zachariah, George, *Malabar, S. I*.
1921. Zaglama, Fuad Wanis, *Egypt*.
1890. Zeidan, Selim, *Cairo*.
1920. Zeitlin, Jacob Elias, *Colverston-cres*.
1916. Zeitline, Leiba, *Tavistock-place*.
1923. Zeitoun, Bishai, *Ladbroke-grove*.
1919. Zerolo, Thos. Fernando, *St. Bart's*.
1887. Ziemann, Hermann Peter, *Cricklewood*.
1923. Zimmerman, M. I., *Stoke Newington*.
1920. Zinn, Philip Richard, *Cape Town*.
1928. Zinober, L. S. V., *PortElizabeth, S. A*.
1906. Zorab, Arthur Batoum, *Southampton*.
1917. Zortman, Israel Hyman, *Leeds*.
1895. Zumbado, Federico, *Costa Rica*.
1896. Zum-Busch, Josef Paul, *Finsb'ry-pvmt*.
16445

LICENTIATES IN MIDWIFERY..

N.B. Licentiates marked † are not Fellows or Members of the College.

A.

1868. Adams, Edward John.
1872. Adams, John.
1869. Angove, Edward Scudamore.

B.

1862. Barnes, Thomas Henry.
1865. Barraclough, Rbt. Wooding Sutton.
1867. Barrick, Eli James.
1871. Bodman, Francis Henry.
1863. Brown, Frederick Gordon.
1867. Browne, John Walton.

C.

1873. Charlesworth, Henry, C.M.G.
1867. Coombs, Rowland Hill.
1853. Cooper, Clarence.
1858. Cowell, George.
1866. Creed, John Mildred.
1866. Cresswell, Richard.
1866. Crowther, Edward Lodewyk.

D.

1856. Dalton, Frederick George.
1854. Dixon, John.
1862. Dobson, Thomas.
1868. Douglas, William.
1867. Draper, William.

E.

1865. Earle, Robert Charles.
1863. Ellerton, John.
23

F.

1867. Fawsitt, Thomas.

G.

1857. George, Charles Frederick.
1866. Gibbes, John Murray.
1871. Giles, Peter Broome, C.B.
1867. Gomes, Antonio Simplicio.
1860. Greenhill, Joseph Ridge.
1858. Griffith, Hugh.

H.

1855. Hall, William.
1860. Harris, John Charles.
1867. Harvey, James D'Arcy.
1865. Hatherly, Henry Reginald.
1862. Hibberd, Edward.
1869. Hoar, Charles Edward.
1875. Hosford, Thomas Stroud.
1870. Huggins, Samuel Tilcott.

I.

†1875. Ievers, Eyre.

J.

1872. Jay, Henry Mason.
1858. Jones, Evan.
1865. Jones, William Owen.
1859. Joyce, Thomas.
43   Y 2

L.

1869. Lack, Thomas Lambert.
1863 Langston, Thomas.
1872. Lett, Francis.
1866. Loane, Joseph.
1871. Lycett, John Allan.
1858. Lynes, Edward.

N.

1868. Naish, Frederick James.
1858. Needham, Sir Frederick.

P.

1872. Parkes, William Edmund.
1871. Pires, Joseph Octaviano.

Q.

1866. Quick, John.
54

R.

1862. Robinson, George.

S.

1864. Salter, John Henry.
1863. Smith, Richard Wagstaff.

T.

1866. Thurston, William French.

W.

1873. Ward, Walter Alfred.
1862. Willett, Edmund.
1868. Winckworth, Charles Trew
1863. Wine, Henry Charles.
62

LICENTIATES IN DENTAL SURGERY.

The Prefix ‡ indicates a Fellow of the College.

The Prefix * indicates a Member of the College.

A.

1923. Aaranson, Godfrey Warren.
1923. Abercrombie, Angus McKay.
1912. Achner, Conrad Adolph.
*1890. Ackery, Edward Faulknor.
*1894. Ackland, Charles Herbert.
*1897. Ackland, Donald.
*1882. Ackland, John McKno.
*1887. Ackland, Robert.
*1884. Ackland, William Robert.
1890. Acton, George Harris.
1886. Acton, John Streets.
1918. Adams, Douglas William Smale.
1912. Adams, Robert Reginald.
1914. Adams, Sidney.
1912. Adderley, William.
1912. Adé, Marcel.
1921. Ainsworth, Norman John.
1904. Aitken, Frederick Watson.
1908. Alabaster, Stammers Henry.
1874. Alabone, Alfred.
1913. Alabone, Leslie.
1923. Albertijn, Pieter Kuijpers.
1918. Alcée, Jacques.
1897. Alder, James Urquhart.
1900. Aldis, Allan Walter.
1920. Aldred, Alexander Benjamin.
1878. Alexander, Adolphus Benjamin.
1913. Alexander, Henry John Farrow.
1906. Alexander, Matthew.
1922. Alexander, Victor St. John.
1921. Allen, Arthur George.
1906. Allen, Arthur Raymond Burnett.
1921. Allen, Dorothy Mary.
1916. Allen, Geoffrey Walter.
1916. Allen, Harold John.
1900. Allen, Robert Westmore.
1885. Allen-Smith, Charles Robert.
1901. Allenby, Ernest Waldegrave.
1891. Allin, Charles James.
1917. Allin, Hubert John Vere Raywood.
1922. Allin, John Freeman.
1910. Allison, Henry Kiver.
1921. Allwood, John Hulme.

43

1875. Allworth, Alfred.
*1894. Allworth, Alfred Leigh.
1892. Allworth, Frank Parnell.
1889. Ambrosoni, Francis Angelo.
1919. Amm, Richard Durban.
1881. Amoore, John Spencer.
1901. Amoore, Sydney Gordon.
1896. Amphlett, Donald.
1896. Anderson, Charles Frederick.
1903. Anderson, Harry Adams.
1902. Anderson, John Horace.
1896. Anderson, Jonathan Harrison
1902. Anderson, Lionel Bertram.
1906. Anderson, Oswald Harry.
1903. Anderson, Percy David.
1923. Anderton, Eric James.
1882. Andrew, John James.
1900. Andrew, Percy Nathaniel.
1920. Andrew, William Blair Spencer.
1923. Andrews, Donald James.
1921. Andrews, Freda Mary.
1902. Andrews, George Lancelot.
1922. Andrews, Robert Collingwood.
1905. Angell, Allan.
1866. Apperly, Ebenezer.
1899. Apperly, Henry David.
1884. Apperly, Herbert.
*1921. Apperly, Herbert Claude.
*1890. Appleton, James Enderby.
1900. Archer, Archibald.
1921. Ardouin, Herbert Charles.
1908. Armin, Frederick George Hayward.
1911. Armitage, Eric Bernard.
1891. Armitage, Frank Arthur.
1905. Armitage, John Joseph.
1923. Armytage, Geoffrey.
1897. Arnold, John Cressy.
1914. Ash, Gerald Beaumont.
1899. Ash, John Robert Slade.
1909. Ash, Richard Guy.
1897. Ashby, Cecil.
*1896. Ashby, Edgar.
1893. Ashby, Herbert Grimsdale.
1900. Ashby, Reginald Frank.
1908. Ashdown, William Percy Charles.

88

1920. Ashling, Harry.
1906. Astbury, Reginald Hudson.
1920. Atkinson, Cecil Graham.
1895. Atkinson, Frederick George.
1919. Attkins, Harry Edward.
1907. Attkins, Leonard Charles.
1922. Attwooll, Stanley.
1905. Aubrey, Francis Leonard.
1902. Aubrey, Frederick Edward.
*1903. Aubrey, Harold Percivall.
*1915. Aufrane, Douglas Albert Raoul.
*1897. Austen, Harold William Colmer.
1893. Austen, Leslie Gilmore.
1906. Austin, Albert Edward Stead.
1915. Austin, Arthur Bramston.
1911. Austin, Norman Arthur.
1884. Ayers, Arthur William Percy.
1900. Aylen, George Herbert.
1912. Ayien, Oswald Gelling.
1923. Ayliffe, Lawrence.
1920. Ayling, Albert Cecil.

B.

1911. Bacon, Ernest Walter.
1902. Bacon, Harold.
1922. Bacon, Hugh Dores.
1914. Bacon, Sidney Roland.
1899. Bacon, William Beadell.
1922. Bachrach, Fanny Henrietta.
1904. Badcock, Cecil Edgar.
1891. Badcock, Christopher Frampton.
1901. Badcock, George Wallace.
*1887. Badcock, John Henry.
1919. Badcock, Walter Frederic Edgar.
1893. Badgery, William.
*1911. Bailey, Edwin Randolph.
1902. Bailey, Frederick William.
1913. Bailey, Henry Leonard.
1909. Bailey, Reginald John.
1922. Bailey, William Oakley.
1923. Bailey-King, Caroline Winifred.
*1886. Baker, Arthur Ernest.
1922. Baker, Dudley James.
1909. Baker, Reginald Henry Christmas.
1900. Baker, Thomas Algernon.
1893. Baker, Wm. Henry Griffiths.
1895. Baker, William Herbert.
1891. Balding, Edmund.
1898. Balding, Leonard Montague.
*1884. Baldwin, Sir Harry.
1907. Balkwill, Alfred Newman.
1914. Ball, Alexander Douglas.
1922. Ball, Aubrey.
1904. Ball, John Bramley.
1904. Ball, Leonard Charles William.
141

1919. Ball, Victor Henry.
1913. Ballard, Reginald Willis.
1909. Balls, Herbert George.
1915. Balls, John Herbert.
*1892 Balv, Charles Francis Peyton.
1912. Bampton, Horace Edgar.
1910. Bangert, Albert Frederick.
1922. Bangert, Victor Richard.
1922. Banks, Hubert Kenyon.
1913. Barber, Arthur James.
1885. Bardet, Paul Charles Albert.
1917. Barfoot, Walter Pigot.
1908. Barfoot, Walter Pigott.
1911. Barge, Herbert Ferris.
1922. Barker, Douglas.
*1909. Barker, Malcolm.
1902. Barkshire, Frank.
1908. Barlow, Ernest William.
1902. Barlow, George William.
1904. Barlow, Stanley Harold.
1900. Barlow, Thomas Hinde.
1882. Barnard, Alfred George Wm.
1896. Barnard, Walter Burrows.
*1892. Barnes, Arthur.
1914. Barnes, James Millard.
1914. Barnett, Albert Edward.
1910. Barnett, Charles Holme.
1901. Barnett, George Samuel Hubert.
1907. Barnett, Thornton John.
1912. Barr, David Harold.
1921. Barrand, Herbert Joseph.
*1873. Barrett, Ashley William.
1894. Barrett, Charles.
*1890. Barrett, Walter Russell.
1912. Barritt, Alfred.
1901. Barron, James Bertrand.
1915. Barrows, Edward Doane.
1918. Bartle, Arthur Frederick.
1906. Bartle, Francis William.
1903. Bartlett, Alfred Cyril.
*1870. Bartlett, Edward.
1900. Bartlett, Mountjoy Henry.
1903. Bartlett, Owen Mortimer.
*1870. Bartlett, William.
1905. Barton, Edward Robert.
1923. Barton, Frederic William.
1904. Barton, Herbert Gray.
1898. Barton, Lewis Fryer.
1917. Barton, Theodore Boques.
*1895. Bascombe, Edwin Cecil Dare.
1896. Bascombe, Ernest Dare.
1892. Bascombe, Reginald Edward.
1922. Bason, Cyril Thomas.
1902. Bateman, George Stanley.
.1895. Bateman, Julius Barthroppe.
·1913. Bater, Carl William Reeves.
*1895. Bates, George Llewellyn.
198

1893. Bates, Herbert Astley.
1888. Bates, Reginald Henry.
1916. Bates, Reginald Naunton.
1918. Batsford, John Frederick.
1907. Batt, William Gordon.
1913. Batten, Kevern.
1837. Battersby, James.
1908. Battersby, John.
1882. Baudry-Mills, Alfred Felix.
1839. Baylis, George William.
1923. Baylis, Harold Paxton.
1906. Beadnell-Gill, Russell.
1922. Beamish, Gordon.
*1912. Beare, Stanley Samuel.
1920. Beauchamp, Walter Samuel.
*1904. Beaumont, Arthur Reginald.
1895. Beaumont, Frederick Charles.
1914. Bebb, Roland Harry.
1917. Becker, Cyril Charles.
1903. Beckett, Charles Stevenson.
1903. Beckett, John Holden.
1906. Beckley, Frederick Augustus.
1910. Beddoes, Ernest.
1901. Bell, Arthur Hastings.
1898. Bell, Arthur Osborne.
1923. Bell, Arthur William.
1877. Bell, Martin Luther.
1910. Bell, Robert Dudley.
1897. Bell, Robert John.
1910. Bell, Sydney Martin.
1916. Bell-Bonnett, Vernon Wilfred Ayres.
1895. Bellaby, Francis Montagu FitzWalter.
1907. Bellman, Stanley.
1898. Belsey, Herbert Henry.
1922. Bench, Alfred George Richard.
1902. Bendall, Frederick.
*1913. Bendix, Frederick Ernest.
1918. Benischowitz, Myer Isaac.
1923. Bennett, Clarence Alfred.
*1878. Bennett, Frederick Joseph.
1900. Bennett, John.
1899. Bennett, Liston Wheatley.
*1894. Bennett, Norman Godfrey.
1908. Bennett, Ralph Dougherty.
1899. Bennette, Horace Willie Paul.
1906. Bennette, William Ryding.
1911. Benson, John.
1903. Bentley, John Fielding.
1923. Bentley, Percy.
1911. Bergh, Victor Emanuel Dawson.
1915. Bernard, Philip Eric.
1905. Berwick, George Henry.
1922. Best, Gordon.
1898. Besford, Harry Newton
1895. Bettridge, Albert Edward.
1920. Betts, Evelyn Olive.
1897. Betts, George Owen.
255

1893. Beverley, Edgar Adolph.
1897. Bevington, Ernest.
1916. Bevis, Douglas Arthur.
1922. Bevis, Ernest Cecil.
1912. Bevis, Sidney William.
1911. Bevis, Walter Sydney.
1896. Bidlake, Luther.
1897. Billing, Fred.
1923. Bingay, John Vivian.
1902. Binns, Herbert Theodore.
1922. Binns, Ronald Francis.
1919. Birch, Cyril Chas. de Albuquerque.
1891. Birkett, William Rawes.
*1909. Birt, Guy Capper.
1907. Biscombe, Leonard Webster.
1919. Bishop, Cyril Arthur Duvall.
1922. Bishop, Cyril Ferguson.
1898. Bishop, Frank Russell.
1899. Biss, John Sydney.
1919. Bitar, Ibrahim.
1891. Blaaberg, Charles Jens.
*1901. Blachford, Jem.
1889. Black, Arthur.
1899. Black, John.
†1900. Black, Kenneth.
1900. Black, Norman.
1902. Black, Osborne.
1916. Blacklaws, Alec Stuart.
1921. Blackmore, Harry Charles.
1882. Blackmore, Herbert George.
*1910. Blackmore, Herbert Stuart.
1892. Blain, Edouard John.
*1922. Blain, Israel.
1918. Blairman, Samuel Isaac.
1914. Blake, Philip.
1923. Blakesley, Mabel Hatchett Blockley.
*1900. Blandy, Wilfrid Boothby.
1905. Blaxley, Thomas Tebbutt.
1921. Bleby, Charles Wendell.
1892. Blewitt, Frederick James.
1899. Blight, Frederick John.
1896. Blomfield, Edgar Athelstan.
1916. Blomfield, Frederick David.
1916. Bloom, Geo. Fredk. Harry Harrison.
1909. Blows, Charles Ernest.
1912. Blundell, Charles Cecil.
1923. Boetius, Frederick Richard.
1904. Bollard, Willie Julian.
1912. Bond, Harold Henry.
1923. Boness, Walter Leslie.
1897. Bonnalie, Stanley.
1909. Boorer, George Rowlands.
1885. Booth, Richard Baxter.
1912. Booth, Robert Leslie.
1923. Booth, Walter Richard Baxter.
1893. Bostock, Arthur Leigh.
1917. Bottomley, Eric.
312

1904. Boulter, William Ernest.
1900. Boulton, Arthur George.
*1903. Bourdas, John.
1912. Boutwood, Ralph.
*1903. Bowater, William.
1893. Bowden, Edwin.
1913. Bowen, Caswell Glynne.
1911. Bowen, John William.
1910. Bower, Harold Edgar.
1916. Bowes, Alfred Herbert.
1905. Bowes, John Arnold.
1899. Bowkley, Alfred Harold.
*1900. Bowle, Sidney Clement.
*1900. Bowler, Walter.
*1890. Bowtell, Herbert Richmond.
1895. Bowtell, Stewart Ross.
1908. Boxall, William Francis.
1915. Boyle, Patrick.
1888. Boyton, Ivan John Howard.
1919. Bradbeer, Leonard Harry.
*1901. Braddock, William.
1921. Bradfield, George Rowland Durston.
1897. Bradford, Sydney.
1923. Bradley, Eric Alfred James.
1913. Bradley, Reginald Gordon.
1903. Bradley-Watson, Cecil Hugh.
1909. Bradnam, Cecil Hastings.
1880. Bradshaw, Richard Giles.
1919. Brailsford, Francis Edward Stuart.
1879. Brameld, Clement Neville.
1921. Brampton, Duncan Norman.
1912. Brandon, William Reginald.
*1909. Brangwin, Charles Edward.
1923. Brattle, Claud Collingwood.
1921. Braun, Martin.
1921. Braun, Maurice Franklin.
1906. Brawn, James Essington Oswell.
1919. Brazilier, Francis.
1895. Breakell, John James.
1891. Breese, Frederick.
1915. Breese, Henry Walter.
1920. Bremner, Stanley.
1921. Brevetor, Thomas Ernest.
1905. Brewster, David.
1896. Briant, Wallace Watson.
1890. Briault, Ernest Henry Lewis.
1908. Bridges, Arthur Henry.
1909. Briggs, Harry Fielden.
1889. Bright, Stanley Charles.
1893. Brimmer, Arthur Vidler.
1900. Bristow, Herbert.
1894. Britten, Arthur.
1899. Britten, Robert Victor.
1922. Britz, Andries Johannes.
1921. Broadhead, John Heath.
*1903. Broderick, Frederick William.
1912. Broderick, Ralph Alexander.
369

1891. Bromley, Charles Edward.
1893. Bromley, Frank Charles.
1900. Bromley, Frederick William.
1897. Bromley, Thomas William.
1921. Broude, Isidore.
1917. Brough, Kenneth Charles.
1901. Broughtonhead, Leslie Charles.
1912. Brown, Allen.
1913. Brown, Allwright Alfred.
1909. Brown, Charles Edward.
1897. Brown, Charles Every.
1906. Brown, Charles Sydney.
1910. Brown, Ernest Benjamin.
1897. Brown, Ernest Chodwick.
1922. Brown, Frank.
*1897. Brown, James Warburton.
*1904. Brown, John Piercy.
1903. Brown, Joseph Stevenson.
1893. Brown, Leonard.
1920. Brown, Leonard Alfred,
1876. Brown, Richard.
1909. Brown, Thomas Percy.
1919. Browne, Ellis Gardner.
1914. Browne, Henry Montague.
1902. Bryan, Hermann.
*1920. Bryant, Ernest Horace.
1874. Bryant, Frank.
*1899. Bubb, Charles Henry, O.B.E.
1920. Buchan, Hubert Frederick.
1921. Buchan, Leonard Henry.
1912. Buck, Alan Darcy.
*1884. Buckland, Sydney Charles.
*1887. Buckley, Charles Herbert.
1905. Buckley, Samuel Milnes.
*1890. Buckley, William Henry.
*1902. Budden, Tice Fisher.
1893. Bulgin, Robert John.
1890. Bull, Ernest Rogers.
1909. Bull, Frank Bocquet.
1914. Bull, William Milton.
*1921. Bulleid, Arthur.
1913. Bulleid, William Allen.
1915. Bullock, Oscar.
1916. Bullpitt, Cyril Montague.
1911. Burch, Henry James.
1922. Burger, Maurice Fitzgerald Stewart.
1911. Burke, Thomas Benjamin.
1900. Burney, Stanley Douglas Francis.
1902. Burns, Percy Edwin.
1912. Burnside, David Cohen.
1904. Burpitt, Charles Augustus.
*1903. Burr, Wilfrid Buchanan.
1893. Burroughs, Joseph Henry.
1919. Burt, Aubrey Ernest.
1909. Burt, Victor Charles.
1878. Burt, Walter.
1900. Burton, Charles James.
426

1890. Burton, Francis.
1917. Burton, Malcolm Beverley.
1910. Burton, Percivale James.
*1895. Burton, Percy.
1909. Burton, Reginald John.
1902. Burton, Thomas.
1918. Busbridge, Chris. Egbert George.
1883. Butcher, John Oliver.
1923. Butler, Albert Edward.
*1904. Butler, Frank.
1912. Butler, Henry O'Neil.
1900. Butler, Henry Richard Codrington.
1897. Butler, Hubert Arnold George.
1914. Butler, Montague Kempston.
1922. Butler, Thomas Catling.
1893. Butler, William Reginald.
1903. Buttar, Edward James.
1894. Butterworth, John.
1923. Buttle, William John.
1907. Button, John.
1915. Buxton, John Levcester Dudley.
*1896. Byrne, Thomas Wafer.
1916. Bywaters, Rossiter Hodgson.

C.

*1920. Cade, Charles Reginald.
1895. Cahill, Alfred.
1918. Cairns, Arthur John.
1903. Calland, Alfred Oswald.
1902. Cameron, John.
1913. Camp, Alfred Fisher.
1902. Campbell, Charles Cecil.
1922. Campbell, Nigel Stuart.
1912. Campbell, Robert.
1916. Campbell, William Sutton.
1885. Campion, George Goring.
*1911. Campion, Rowland Burnell.
1899. Campkin, Hugh Titford.
1898. Campkin, Percival Sidney.
1894. Cannell, Charles.
1895. Cannell, Edward Kemp.
1897. Canning, Henry Albert Ellis.
*1920. Canning, Henry George Richmond.
1915. Canton, Howard.
1897. Canton, Loftus Henry.
1902. Capon, Jack Cecil.
1890. Cardell, Arthur John.
1898. Cardell, George Parminte.
1908. Cardell, Norman Sambell.
1898. Carden, Alfred Eastland.
1899. Cardwell, Edward.
1895. Cardwell, Ernest Edward.
1898. Cardwell, Harold.
1899. Carey, Frank Russell.
1900. Carpenter, Alexander Evan Clair.
479

1893. Carpenter, Frank Holly.
1905. Carpenter, Geo. Alfred Lonnon.
1893. Carpenter, Sidney Henry Mark.
1916. Carrington, Vincent Clifford.
1915. Carson, James Arthur Balfour.
1875. Carteighe, John.
*1914. Carter, Arthur Stanley.
1896. Carter, Charles Edward.
1889. Carter, Edward George.
1890. Carter, Henry Charles.
1914. Carter, Henry Claude.
1899. Carter, James Thornton.
1896. Carter, Stuart.
1876. Carter, Thomas Scales.
1914. Cartman, Herbert.
*1875. Cartwright, Alexander.
1892. Castellote, Bonaventura Alfred.
1887. Cater, Alfred Parker.
1918. Caute, Edward Honoré Clarence.
1920. Cavanagh, Henry James.
1894. Cave, Urban Edward.
1895. Chambers, Thomas Rubery.
1904. Chandler, Horace Stanley.
1899. Chandler, Percy Ernest.
1914. Chapman, Arnold John.
1903. Chapman, Harold.
1910. Chapman, Ralph.
1917. Chapple, Albert William Ewart.
1913. Charles, George Frederick.
1908. Charles, Stephen Wilson.
1917. Charlesworth, Reginald Geo. Joseph.
1905. Charlick, Alfred Braithwaite.
1909. Charlton, Pereie Chater.
1898. Charnock, Harry.
1896. Chatterton, Guy.
1900. Chaundy, Arthur Ernest.
1921. Chenoy, Jamshed Bejunjee.
1909. Chesters, Eric Horsfall.
1908. Chetwood, Sydney William.
1916. Chiappa, Joseph John Charles.
*1919. Chiappa-Sinclair, Alfred Joseph.
1902. Chignell, Thomas Alexander.
1912. Child, Cyril Holland.
1903. Chilton, Frank.
1902. Chinneck, Herbert Edward.
1923. Christian, Frank Reid.
1921. Christie-Anderson, John.
1921. Churchill, Harold Cordes.
1922. Churchyard, Arthur Rolf.
1900. Ciceri, Giovanni Battista.
1923. Cilliers, Barend Jacobus.
*1906. Clapham, Howard Dennis.
*1914. Claremont, Louis Edmund.
1892. Clarence, Thomas Herbert.
1870. Clark, Charles Lane.
1921. Clark, Edgar.
1906. Clark, Hugh Gordon.
536

1897. Clark, John Kenneth.
1923. Clark, Joseph William.
1921. Clark, Reginald John.
1913. Clarke, Alan Stafford.
1922. Clarke, Amilius.
1923. Clarke, Hubert Arthur.
1911. Clarke, James Fernandez Howard.
1905. Clarkson, Ernest Thomas.
1893. Clayton, Edward.
1902. Clegg, William.
1904. Clements, William Alexander.
1900. Clench, Bernard George William.
1914. Clewer, Donald.
1900. Clibborn, Frederic Hervey.
1875. Clifford, Herbert Hyeman.
1901. Clifford, Sydney.
1901. Clogg, Arthur Henry.
1922. Cloke, Ernest John.
1920. Close, Ralph Lea.
1919. Clothier, Basil.
*1897. Coates, Frederick Arthur.
1900. Cockburn, Joseph.
*1905. Cocker, Albert Benjamin.
1913. Cocker, James Percy.
1914. Cocker, William Lawton.
1906. Codner. Horace George.
1914. Coe, Walter Ernest.
1909. Cohen, Abraham.
1898. Cohen, Isaac.
1913. Cohen, Louis Charles.
1902. Coish, Henry John.
1901. Colbran, Coningsby Leslie.
1900. Cole, Archibald Bernard.
1914. Cole, Arthur Hedley.
1923. Cole, Harold.
1905. Cole, Herbert John.
†1899. Cole, Percival Pasley.
*1898. Coleman, Frank.
1895. Collett, Albert James.
1885. Collett, Edward Pyemont.
1914. Collett, Henry Robert Pyemont.
1903. Collett, Herbert Edgar.
1922. Colling-Baugh, Cecil Victor Thomas.
1904. Collis, Albert.
1900. Collis, Arthur.
1909. Collis, Cyril Allan.
1896. Coltman, Ernest.
*1889. Colyer, Arthur Reginald.
*1910. Colyer, Claude Grav.
*1905. Colyer, Horace Charles.
†1887. Colyer, Sir James Frank.
*1895. Colyer, Stanley William Randolph.
1923 Comber, Douglas George.
1896 Conder. Harold.
*1896. Connor, George Washington.
1909. Connor, Sydney Garfield.
1922. Constance, Albert James.

1894. Constant, Frederick Charles.
*1888. Constant. Thomas Edward.
1921. Conway-Jones, Powis Naranzo C.
1915. Cook, Charles Alfred Ernest.
1895. Cook, Horace.
1879. Cook, Stanley.
1905. Cook, William Edmund.
1921. Cooke, Cecil.
1907. Cooke, Ernest William.
1917. Cooke, Herbert Howard.
1880. Cooksey, Edward Thomas.
1912. Cooksey, George Basil.
1897. Cooper, Albert.
1921. Cooper, Arnett Temple.
*1901. Cooper, Henry Creemer.
1897. Cooper, Percy Henry Rogers.
1907. Cooper, Reginald William Clayton.
1906. Cooper, Samuel Sugden.
1912. Cooper, Thomas Percy.
*1914. Cooper, Walter Tyrrell.
1904. Cooper, Wilfred Francis.
1920. Cooper, William Henry.
1921. Coplans, Joseph Moses.
1919. Coplans, Samuel Hyman.
1875. Corbett, Joseph John Francis.
*1898. Corbett, Sidney d'Alton.
1900. Corfe, Ernest William.
1901. Corin, Herbert John.
1914. Corke, Henry Charles.
1915. Corke, Trafford Dudley.
1882. Cornelius, William Fryer.
*1910. Cornelius, William Hern.
1921. Cornwell, George Burrell.
1911. Cottam, Arthur Caspar Stevenson.
1911. Cotterell, Graham.
1900. Couchman, Ernest.
*1906. Councell, Edward Leslie.
1913. Coupe, Arthur.
1922. Course, Reginald Royston.
1915. Court, Arnold.
1919 Cousins, Bertram Poole.
1905. Cowden, William.
1915. Cowell, James Frank.
1913. Cowell, Richard Groves.
1909. Cowin, Daniel.
1896. Cowles, Hector Charles.
1916. Cowley, Richard Lawton.
1923. Cowper, Frederick William Henry.
1920. Cox, Alan Raymond.
*1917. Cox, Alfred Innes.
*1890. Cox, Arthur Brooks.
1922. Cox-Moore, Cicely May.
1910. Cox-Moore, Percy George Hastings.
1915. Cox-Moore, Sidney John Vaughan.
1921. Coysh, Harold Arthur.
1891. Coysh, Thomas Arthur.
1917. Crabb, Leslie Douglas.

1912. Craig, Gordon Robert.
1902. Craig, Robert Walter.
1913. Craine, Frederick Andrew.
1913. Crane, Walter Alexander.
1884. Crank, Peter.
1902. Cranston, Henry Selby.
1896. Crapper, Harold Sugden.
1889. Crasweller, Charles Walton.
1919. Crawford, James Douglas.
1911. Crawford, James Kenneth.
1922. Creasy, John Horace Reginald.
1896. Cribb, Harold Ernest.
1922. Crisp, Basil.
1914. Crocker, Cyril James.
*1884. Crocker, James Charles Vipond.
1908. Crockett, Leonard Marshall.
1913. Crofts, Arthur Douglas.
1921. Croke, Augustine Ethelbert.
1897. Crombie, James Melville Paterson.
1898. Crombie, Walter Paterson.
1923. Crone, Frank.
*1921. Crook, Francis William.
1902. Croot, Horace.
1907. Cross, Arthur Basil.
1915. Cross, Leopold Harold.
1903. Cross, Robert Wilfrid.
1904. Crouch, Richard Halford Winterly
1886. Croucher, Arthur Thomas.
1920. Croucher, Henry Valentine.
1920. Crowe, Arthur Alexander Robert.
1905. Crump, John Arthur.
1915. Cullen, Frank Briggs.
1915. Cullwick, Herbert Ronald.
1915. Culverwell, Wilfrid Arthur.
1882. Curle, Arthur Lister.
1916. Curle, Cyril Lister.
1922. Curle, Gerald.
1923. Curley, James William.
*1914. Curnock, Dennis Reginald.
1908. Curnock, George Leslie.
1911. Curnow, Reginald Northey.
1892. Curtis, Ernest Arthur.
*1905. Curtis, George Herbert.
1916. Curtis, Howard.
1921. Curtis, James Walter.
1903. Curtis, Lionel.
1915. Curtis, William John.
1900. Cuthbertson, Thomas Maitland.
1907. Cuttriss, William Allison.
1890. Cutts, Frederick Edward.
*1914. Cutts, George Lambert.
1899. Cutts, Henry Whitmore.

D.

1910. Dabbs, Arthur Josiah.
1905. Dagger, Henry.
1905. Dainty, Arthur John.
1879. Daish, William George.
1896. Dalby, Charles Burkitt.
1914. Dally, Arthur Thomas.
1891. Dalton, George.
1895. Dalton, John Willie.
*1903. Daly, James Thomas.
1904. Damon, Walter Milroy.
1914. Dancer, Ulysses James Garfield.
1922. Daneel, Alexander Berthin.
1922. Daniels, William George.
1917. Danks, George Harold.
1890. Davids, Ernest Cornils.
1923. Davies, Arthur Sidney.
1908. Davies, Arthur Walter.
1922. Davies, David Ewart.
1906. Davies, Gwilym Llewellyn.
1913. Davies, Gwilym Tremain.
*1912. Davies, John Edgar.
1911. Davies, Philip Percival.
1910. Davies, Richard Pittard.
1911. Davies, Thomas Clement.
1917. Davies, Thomas John.
1915. Davies, William Robert.
*1881. Davis, Charles Daniel.
‡1903. Davis, Edward David.
1901. Davis, Edwin Lawrence.
1879. Davis, Harry.
1910. Davis, Joseph Henry Creasy.
1862. Davis, Murray Joel.
1891. Davis, Neville Murray.
1920. Davis, Stanley Willoughby Augustus.
1903. Davy, Richard Humphry.
1912. Daw, Hubert.
1915. Dawson, Ernest Archibald.
1905. Dawson, Geoffrey.
1895. Dawson, William James Oliver.
1895. Day, Ernest Frank.
1901. Day, Frederick George.
1921. Day, Frederick Walter.
*1889. Day, Joseph Henry.
1896. Day, Kendrew James.
1914. Dean, Arthur Cyril.
1905. Dean, William Thomas.
1907. Dear, Harold John.
1902. Deck, Ernest Field.
1915. Dee, George.
1919. Deeks, Geoffrey.
1922. Deighton, Graham Stanley.
1921. de Kock, Joseph Louis.
1896. DeMierre, Albert.
1895. Denham, Norman.
1912. Denne, Francis Vincent.

1902. Dennis, James Hollis.
1915. Densham, Arnold Thomas.
*1893. Densham, Ashley Bloomfield.
1893. Densham, Walter Arnold.
1900. Dent, Harry Lambton.
1907. Denty, Frederic Leonard.
1922. De Pass, Kingsley.
*1903. de Pinna, Herbert Alfred.
1901. de Pinto, Ph'neas Abraham.
1903. Deravin, Norman Sydney.
1904. Derriman, Wm. Euart Alexander.
1890. Derwent, Arthur Holmes.
1920 Desai, Dhauvant Maneklal.
1915. Deverall, Edmund Percy.
1923. Deverell, Alan Clark.
1921. de Villiers, Jacob Isaac.
1899. Devonshire, Richard Kempe.
1916. Dewar, Robert Peter.
1879. Dewes, Hugh William.
1917. de Wet, Pieter Jacob Stephanus.
1922. Dick, John Speechly.
1920. Dickens, Donald Tom Gordon.
1914. Dickin, Eric Sutton.
1900. Dickin, Henry Ormrod.
1904. Dickins, Charles Francis.
1922. Dickinson, Richard.
1906. Dicks, Wilfrid James Parsons.
1888. Digby, Everard.
1895. Dimock, Edward Claude.
*1914. Dimock, James Douglas.
1923. Dingle, Hubert Ivor.
1923. Dingley, George Samuel.
*1904. Dinnis, Alfred.
1909. Dinnis, Leonard.
1906. Ditch, John Richard Doren.
1899. Dixon, Arthur Harvey.
1915. Dixon, Clifford Cedric.
1920. Dod, George Augustus Norman.
*1892. Dodd, Frederick Lawson.
1914. Dodd, William Edwin.
1901. Dodds, Arthur Wavell.
1894. Dodson, Arthur Ranken.
1907. Doherty, John William.
*1888. Dolamore, William Henry.
1923. Domb, Philip.
1902. Donald, John Alexander.
*1909. Donne, Cecil Lucas.
1917. Donovan, Francis Desmond.
1905. Doran, Francis Sydney.
1899. Doran, Samuel Sydney.
1897. Dorrell, Harry.
1921. Dorward, Cyril Dudley Melville.
1914. Doubleday, Ernest Francis.
*1908. Doubleday, Frederic Nicklin.
1904. Doubleday, John Lloyd.
1904. Dougan, William Bateman.
1920. Doughty, Leonard Allen.

1897. Douglas, James Carfrae.
1908. Douglas, Norman Malcolm McArthur.
1922. Douglas, William Thomas Lloyd.
1914. Doun, Robert Lester.
1905. Douthwaite, Harold Seymour.
*1898. Dowling, Edward Alfred Griffiths.
1920. Downing, Frederick John.
1922. Downs, William.
*1897. Dowsett, Ernest Blair.
1896. Doyle, Clement Needham.
1901. Drabble, Charles Clement.
1897. Drake, Arthur.
1899. Drake, George Herbert.
1913. Drake, Harry.
1921. Drayton, Ernest.
1907. Dredge, William Albert.
1907. Drew, William.
1900. Drewitt, Alfred.
1910. Drinkall, John Herbert.
1903. Driscoll, John Frederick.
1916. Drummond, Walter Edmund.
1923. Drury, George Belfit.
1921. Drury, John Beswick.
1921. du Buisson, David Izak.
1922. Duckworth, John Edwin Hardie.
1870. Dudley, Edmund Lewis.
1907. Dumayne, Harold Gordon.
1913. Dumayne, Henry Oswald.
1899. Duncalf, William John.
1897. Duncan, Frank Hubert.
1863. Duncan, Richard.
1923. Dunkin, Horace Frederick.
1893. Dunlop, David.
1896. Dunlop, Harry.
1889. Dunlop, James Nairn.
1889. Dunlop, John.
1923. du Plessis, Stephanus Johannes.
1923. du Preez, Johannes Urbanno Human.
*1901. Duprey, George Perry.
1922. Durant, Victor Edmund Bruce.
1922. du Toit, Izak Stephanus de Villiers.
1920. du Toit, Jacob Johannes.
*1912. Dye, William Hood.
1914. Dyke, Victor Robert.
1902. Dykes, Thomas.
1910. Dymott, George Vivian.
1903. Dymott, Gerald Lang.

E.

1916. Eady, Barrington.
1922. Eady, Kenneth Wilfred.
1912. Ealand, Philip Lewis.
1922. Eason, William John.
*1920. Easton, Wilfred Angel.
*1903. Eccles, Bertram Joseph.
1911. Edey, Frank Harold.

1896. Edey, George Russell.
1915. Edgar, John William.
1910. Edgar, Niel.
1921. Edmonds, David Mark.
1922. Edmonds, Hubert Alfred.
1911. Edmonds, William Henry.
1900. Edmondson, Hubert Henry.
1901. Edmondson, Thomas Asher.
1906. Edward, John Hutchison-Rodney.
1900. Edwards, Alfred Culmer.
1923. Edwards, George Allen.
1922. Edwards, G orge Henry Bennett.
1923. Edwards, Rex.
1914. Edwards, Herbert James.
*1882. Edwards, Richard.
1902. Edwards, Richard Burnell.
1901. Edy, Charles William.
1890. Efford, Charles Fursman.
1922. Eglington, Dudley Clarkes.
1911. Elliott, Harold Graham.
1906. Elliott, Sidney Gilbert.
1896. Ellis, George Garnett.
1914. Ellis, Gilbert George.
1916. Ellis, Richard John Spaull.
1922. Ellis, Thomas Ernest.
1921. Elmer, Lancelot William.
1889. Elphinstone, William Robb.
1903. Elstobb, Harry George.
1922. Elston, Lionel Frank.
1907. Elvy, Rupert Woodward.
1906. Elwood, Walter.
1903. Elwood, William Henry.
1904. Emery, Edmund Aloysius.
1899. English, Frederick.
1900. Entwisle, Edward.
1891. Eskell, Eustace Lewis.
1898. Etheridge, Frederic Ledger.
1893. Evans, Albert John Geal.
1922. Evans, Arthur Basil.
1921. Evans, Donald Farr.
1920. Evans, Herbert Reginald.
1922. Evans, Llewellyn.
1917. Evans, Morgan James.
1896. Evans, Sydney James.
1921. Evelyn, Alan.
1897. Everett, Charles.
1914. Everett, Francis Arthur.
1923. Evetts, Brian George Edgar.
1914. Eyetts, Raymond Cecil Thomas.

F.

‡1899. Fairbank, Harold Arthur Thomas.
*1905. Fairbank, John Gerald Atkinson.
1909. Falkner, Ernest William Frank.
1893. Farebrother, Aubrey Harry Burne.

1921. Farmer, Frederick John.
1898. Farnfield, John Stewart.
1889. Faro, Richard Sydney Newman.
1904. Farr, Frederick Harold.
1902. Farrant, Edward.
1908. Farrar, Llewellyn Saltonstall.
1911. Farrington, Reginald Gilbert.
1923. Farris, Cyril Douglas.
1902. Farwell, Edward.
1910. Faulkner, Charles Repton.
1922. Faure, Johannes Christoffel.
1922. Faure, Roland Hardy.
1917. Faustmann, George Frederick.
*1911. Fawn, George Frederick.
1906. Fenn, Roland Pitt.
1892. Fennings, Frank Joseph.
1907. Fernie, John George.
1923. Ferris, George Francis.
*1912. Fickling, Edwin Llewellyn Zenas.
1901. Fickling, Robert Marshall.
1910. Fiddick, Thomas Leonard.
1889. Field, Edgar Albert Hector.
1905. Fielder, Theodore James Gayton.
1902. Finch, Arthur George.
1902. Finigan, Percy O'Connell.
1919. Fishburn, John Eskdale.
1901. Fisher, Enoch Hughes.
1914. Fisher, Harold Mayston.
1921. Fisher, Hilton George.
1896. Fisher, Sydney Bailey.
1891. Fisher, William.
1877. Fisher, William Macpherson.
1888. Fisk, Edgar Charles.
1919. Fisk, Sidney William.
1905. Fitch, Claude Rawlingson.
1900. Fitch, Humbert Pearce.
1892. Fitter, Septimus.
1906. Fitzgerald, John Herbert Wilson.
1917. Flanders,Frederick George Pritchard.
1898. Fleetwood, Leonard Montague.
1923. Fletcher, Cyril.
1907. Fletcher, Edward Ernest.
1902. Fletcher, George William Morgan.
1923. Flotcher, Henry George Leslie.
1923. Fletcher, Jeffrey.
1894. Flintan, Francis Robert.
1917. Flinton, Francis Malcolm Timothy.
1913. Flook, Percy William.
1913. Flooks, William Trevor.
1897. Floyd, Walter.
1889. Fogg, Arthur.
1894. Fogg, Ernest.
1903. Fooks, Herbert Johnstone.
1905. Forbes, Augustus Harold.
1916. Forbes, Victor William Russell.
1913. Forrest, Arthur Gerald.
1912. Forster, Louis Edward Tracy.

1891. Forsyth, Harry Arthur.
*1900. Forsyth, Lennard William.
1897. Forsyth, William Frederic.
*1905. Forty, Arthur Alan.
1905. Foster, Tom Scott.
1878. Fothergill, Edward.
1915. Foulkes, Harold.
1918. Foulston, Edward Garratt.
1892. Fouraker, Frank.
1921. Fourakes, Leslie Frank.
1922. Fourie, Frederick Johann.
1884. Fox, Arthur Makinson.
1920. Fox, Frank Leslie Hooton.
1902. Fox, Frederic Neidhart.
1903. Fox, Herbert James.
1917. Fox, Hyman.
1912. Fox, Reginald.
1922. Fox, Thomas Frederick.
1875. Fox, Walter Henry.
1901. Francis, John Stanley.
1902. Frank, George Henry.
1910. Frank, James Mutrie.
1899. Frankish, Henry.
1907. Franks, Duncan Baron.
1922. Freedman, George.
1921. Freeman, Charles Henry.
1893. Freeman, John Robert.
1906. Freeman, William Edward.
1906. Freer, Cecil Charles.
1920. Freiberger, Israel.
1915. Freni-Sterrantino-Sante.
*1905. Frew, William Douglas.
1913. Fripp, Samuel Trude.
1906. Fritche, George Edward.
1920. Froggatt, George Henry.
1887. Frost, Abraham William.
1899. Frost, Emmanuel Bower Marshall.
1923. Frourie, Andries Theodorus Spies.
1909. Fruhauf, Lionel David.
*1913. Fry, William Kelsey, M.C.
1906. Fryer, Gordon.
*1905. Fuller, Frederick Holcombe.
1904. Fuller, Harry Wardlaw.
1910. Fullerton, Herbert Edward.
1900. Furnivall, Percy Harry.
1909. Furse, Frank Leonard.
1922. Fyffe, Albert Edward.
1920. Fyffe, Robert William.
1916. Fyson, Reginald.

G.

1907. Gabell, Alverstone Harold.
*1892. Gabell, Douglas Phillimore.
1904. Gabell, Reginald Hopgood.
1893. Gabell, Wilfrid William.

1900. Gabriel, Arnold Maurice.
*1885. Gabriel, William Maurice.
*1901. Gaffney, Edward James.
1923. Gaffyne, Henry Alexander Smith.
‡1878. Galpin, George Luck.
1907. Gant, Arthur William.
1922. Gardenner, Frederic Clifford.
1918. Gardiner, Iris Elizabeth.
*1917. Gardner, Blanche Sutton.
1908. Gardner, Charles Richard.
1892. Gardner, Charles Smith.
1891. Gardner, Ernest.
1913. Gardner, Stanley Maddox.
1923. Gardner, William.
*1918. Garfield, Montagu.
1922. Garland, Arthur Sherrington Talbot.
1899. Garman, Francis Wilberforce.
1898. Garne, Sydney William.
1915. Garrard, John Langley.
1894. Gartrell, John Herbert.
1891. Gask, Arthur Cecil.
1919. Gaskill, Dudley Keverne.
1913. Gaverick, Rae Haydn.
1912. Gawne, William Francis.
1906. Geake, George Burt.
1905. Geckie, George William.
1907. Gee, Percy.
1911. Geekie, Bernard John.
1874. Geldard, Richard Henry.
1913. Gell, George Cowley.
*1902. George, Archibald Louis.
1909. George, John Daniel.
1922. George, Violet Helena.
1920. Gerson, Nathaniel.
1907. Gibbings, Reginald John.
1906. Gibbon, Ernest.
1909. Gibbons, Henry Vincent.
1899. Gibbons, John Walton.
1862. Gibbons, Sills Clifford.
1923. Gibbs, Philip Norman.
1920. Gibson, George Paterson.
*1920. Gibson, Ralph Byron.
1898. Gibson, Zephaniah Job.
1904. Gilbert, Douglas.
1919. Gilbert, James Alan.
*1912. Gilbert, John Wesley.
1906. Giles, Frank.
1902. Giles, Walter.
1877. Gill, Christopher Lawrence.
1909. Gill, Frederic Edwin.
1875. Gill, Harry Beadnell.
1899. Gillemaud, Edward Joseph Fabian.
1910. Gillett, Guy Leroy.
1893. Gillett, Richard William.
1900. Gillies, John Blakeney.
*1905. Gillies, Robert Gray.
1915. Gillis, Julius.

1908. Gillis, Max David.
1892. Gilmour, William Henry.
1871. Gingell, George.
1918. Ginsberg, Myer.
1904. Glaisby, Leonard Anderson.
1921. Glassington, Charles.
1877. Glassington, John Henry.
1906. Glassington, John Perrino.
1907. Glindon, Reginald Algernon.
1913. Glover, Clementson.
1910. Glover, Frederick Simpson.
1910. Glover, Harold Harding.
1885. Goadby, Allan Lindsay.
*1896. Goadby, Sir Kenneth Weldon, K.B.E.
*1887. Goard, Thomas Arthur.
1911. Goddard, Arthur Raymond.
1902. Goddard, Henry Brokenshere.
1895. Goddard, John Wood.
1922. Godden, Leslie James.
1885. Goffe, Frank Hampton.
*1909. Goldsmith, Bernard.
1922. Gomes, Arthur Annesley.
1903. Goodey, Albert.
1917. Goodman, Florence.
1910. Goodman, Montague Nathaniel.
1896. Goodman, Thomas Dawson Edwin.
1892. Goodman, William Henry.
1903. Goodman, William John.
1892. Goodridge, Alan.
1922. Goodson, Albert Vernon.
*1900. Goodwin, Frederick William.
1903. Goodwin, Frederick William.
1922. Goonewardene, Chas. Arnold Rodrigo
1905. Gordon, Francis.
1923. Gosling, Alfred Stanley.
1895. Gosschalk, Meyer.
1918. Goudge, Alwyn Norman.
1910. Gow, John Ferguson.
1891. Gracey, Ralph Nelson.
1903. Grant, Charles Hamilton Russell.
1910. Grant, Henry David.
1921. Gratrix, Frank Dawson.
1899. Graves-Morris, Herbert William.
1922. Gray, Leslie George.
1921. Gray, William Marshall Kemp.
1923. Gray, William Richard.
1919. Grayson, Jack Kenneth.
1921. Greaves, Harold.
*1910. Green, Edwin Allan Thomas.
1903. Green, Herbert Frederick.
1916. Green, Philip.
1901. Green, Richard James.
1901. Green, Roland.
1903. Green, Thomas James.
1896. Green, Walter.
1917. Greenfield, Sidney Francis.
1904. Greenhalgh, James Taylor.
1145

1913. Greenish, Vivian Arthur Frederick.
1923. Greenwall, Edward Andrew.
1919. Greenwall, Joseph Walter.
1921. Greenwood, Alfred Walter.
1900. Greenwood, Percy.
1883. Greetham, Peter William.
1922. Gregory, Thomas Leslie Clarke.
1911. Gregg, Robert Daniel.
*1910. Grellier, Bernard.
1910. Grellier, Norman.
1900. Grenside, Claude Bolton.
1898. Grewcock, William James.
1920. Grieve, Allistair Hyland.
1919. Griffin, John Harvey Havers.
1908. Griffin, Leonard Beard.
1915. Griffin, Percy Gordon Barlow.
1899. Griffin, Robert William.
1902. Griffin, Thomas Harold.
1901. Griffin, Wilfred Ernest.
*1923. Griffith, David William.
1922. Griffith, Gwilym Wynne.
1921. Griffiths, Gwilym Ungoed.
1898. Griffiths, Hubert Malcolm.
1906. Griffiths, Trevor.
1922. Griffiths, William Cross.
1888. Grimsdale, Frank Gannon.
1917. Grobbelaar, Philippus Elisa.
1920. Grose, Doris Ada.
1904. Grubb, Duncan Henry.
1908. Guanziroli, Louis Francois.
1923. Gubb, Hélène Marie.
1897. Gudgeon, Henry Halliday.
1908. Guilding, William Edwin.
1899. Gwatkin, Archibald James.
1904. Gwynne, Robert Percy.
1903. Gwyther, Henry Wilton.

H.

*1914. Hacking, Alan Basil.
1904. Haddock, Arthur John.
1921. Hagen, Frederick James.
1913. Haine, Claude Frederick.
1923. Haines, Norman.
1921. Haines, Octavius Charles Moore.
1916. Halden, Richard John Gustavus.
1921. Hall, Alfred William.
1893. Hall, Edward Caleb Joseph.
1890. Hall, Frederick George.
1923. Hall, Harry Donald.
1908. Hall, Henry.
1903. Hall, John.
1913. Hall, John Wilfrid.
1908. Hall, Mark.
1904. Hallam, Samuel.
1919. Hallett, Leonard Richard Joseph.
1198

1896. Halliday, Alfred Reginald.
1894. Halliday, Harold David.
1916. Hallman, William Ewart.
1908. Halsall, Fred.
1893. Ham, Hedley Herefoot.
1921. Hambridge, Edward William.
1902. Hamilton, Frank Paxton.
1904. Hammond-Smith, Arthur.
1914. Hammond-Williams, Wm. Cecil.
1895. Handel, Franz Edward.
1911. Handford, Edwin Joseph.
1894. Hands, Francis William.
1922. Hankey, George Trevor.
1893. Hankey, John Trevor.
1895. Hankey, Stanley James.
1906. Hanna, John Ernest.
1913. Hanreck, Samuel.
1905. Hanson, Arthur Tidswell.
1911. Harborow, Gerald John.
1878. Hardie, Walter Jackson.
*1915. Harding, GeorgeHenryCharlesworth.
1894. Harding, Henry Paxton.
1909. Hardman, Ciaud Noel.
1921. Hardwicke, Clifford.
*1916. Hardy, Ernest Alphonse.
*1894. Hardy, Herbert William.
1920. Hardy, Oscar King.
1904. Hargreaves, James.
1907. Hargreaves, Joseph Knowles.
1899. Hargreaves, Samuel.
1921. Harley, Laurence.
1905. Harlock, Sidney.
1889. Harper, Henry Guy.
*1898. Harper, John.
1903. Harrington, Reginald George.
1904. Harris, Albert.
1897. Harris, Aubrey Hastings.
1888. Harris, Douglas Howard.
1896. Harris, Harold Octavius Whitfield.
1902. Harris, James.
1912. Harris, John Gordon.
1912. Harris, Leslie Price.
*1887. Harris, Percy Reeves Traer.
1888. Harris, Theodore William.
*1881. Harris, Underwood Arthur Carpenter
1915. Harris, Will Smith.
1895. Harrison, Edward.
1907. Harrison, Ernest.
1910. Harrison, Harold.
1910. Harrison, Laurence Edgar Crespin.
*1908. Harrison, Newcome Herbert.
1908. Harrison, Percy Samuel.
1892. Harrison, Philip.
1891. Harrison, Richd. Malcolm Crowther.
1897. Harrison, Sydney.
1882. Harrison, Walter.
*1909. Harrison, Walter Parker.
1255

1888. Harsant, Frank Arnold.
1875. Hart, Alfred Abraham.
1916. Hart, Herbert.
1921. Hart, Selim Laurence.
*1911. Harvey, Harold.
1892. Harwood, Edwin William.
*1908. Harwood, Leonard Austin.
1912. Harwood, Lily Fanny.
1904. Haskew, William Hunt.
1905. Hatt, Charles.
1918. Hatton, Wallace Duncan.
1921. Havenga, Andries.
1904. Hawkes, Arthur Barber.
1903. Hawkes, Richard John James.
1916. Hawkins, Charles Frederick.
1909. Hawksley, Arthur Rusby.
1919. Hawksworth, Ralph.
*1898. Hawthorn, Henry William John.
1923. Hay, Gordon Manley.
1902. Haycraft, Arthur Herbert.
1889. Haycroft, Frederic Theodore.
1913. Haydon, Lawrance Richards.
1923. Hayes, Esmonde Villis.
1911. Hayes, John Otway.
1888. Hayman, Albert Stephen.
1910. Hayman, Frank James.
1890. Hayman, Howard Little.
1891. Haynes, Frederick.
1922. Haynes, Gerald George Thomas.
1923. Hayns, Frederick Henry.
1892. Hayward, Savill Henry.
1915. Hazell, William Samuel.
1923. Head, Lionel Henry.
1891. Hendridge, David.
1894. Headridge, John Parsons.
1906. Heald, Oliver William.
1897. Heath, Arthur Reginald.
1920. Heath, John Samuel Robert.
1900. Heath, Robert Harold.
1881. Hedley, William Snowdon.
1896. Heesom, Edwin Ernest Dailey.
1923. Hegarty, John.
1922. Helder, Leonard Basil.
*1903. Hele, John Warwick.
1864. Hele, Warwick.
1908. Helliwell, John Percival.
1885. Helyar, Albert.
1909. Helyar, Philip Reginald.
1906. Helyar, William Alfred.
1922. Hemmings, Laurence Gower.
1896. Hemsted, Frederick.
1904. Hemsted, John Garnet.
*1893. Henly, Albert William.
1914. Henry, Albert Ernest.
*1908. Henry, Arthur Martin.
1910. Henry, Clement John.
*1915. Henry, Cyril Bowdler.
1312

1878. Henry, Martin.
1915. Henry, Maurice George.
1894. Henry, Percy Francklin.
1875. Henry, William Francklin.
1910. Herbert, Albert Henry.
1905. Herbei t, Frank William.
1919. Herbert, John.
1915. Herdman, Garvin.
*1915. Herman, Walter Sebastian.
*1890. Hern, George.
*1881. Hern, William, O.B.E.
1892. Herschell, Ridley.
1904. Heslop, Albert Oliver Macarius.
1898. Hessenauer, Hermann Charles.
1916. Hewer, Austin George.
1897. Hey, Stephen Daniel.
1900. Heydon, Arthur George.
*1921. Hiam, Frank.
1921. Hibbins, William Rowland.
1915. Hick, Godfiey Macdona.
1900. Hickes, Charles.
1916. Hickley, Gerald Mackenzie.
1904. Hickman, Percy Harold.
1904. Hicks, Alfred.
1914. Hicks, Charles Lewis.
1922. Hide, Walter James.
1903. Highton, Herbert Cragg.
1905. Higson, Alfred John.
1892. Hilder, Albert Thomas.
1922. Hill, Harold.
1919. Hill, Herbert William.
1915. Hill, Joseph James Sterling.
1900. Hillier, Henry Norman.
1912. Hills, William Arthur Sowden.
*1894. Hills, William Ernest.
1922. Hilton, Richard Byron.
1896. Hinchliff, Charles John.
1906. Hindle, John William.
1922. Hine, James Burnett.
1922. Hine, Sydney Thomas.
1908. Hinson, Harold.
1901. Hinton, John Henry.
1900. Hiorns, George Henry Maynard.
1921. Hirschfield, Solomon Marcus.
1897. Hislop, John William.
1908. Hoare, Ernest Alfred Sebastian.
1912. Hoare, Walter Stanley.
1912. Hobbs, George.
1902. Hobson, Alfred.
1910. Hoby, Kenneth George.
1907. Hochapfel, Adam Friedrich.
1903. Hoddy, Douglas Victor.
1901. Hodge, John Leslie.
1903. Hodgson, Algeon Sugden.
1908. Hodgson, William Archer.
1902. Hodson, William Francis.
*1890. Hoffman, Augst Wm. Wistinghausen.
1923. 1369

1923. Hofmeyer, Roland.
1921. Hogbin, Frank Roy.
1917. Hoggard, Hugh Donald.
1906. Holborn, Frank Maurice.
1910. Holburn, Clement Eugene.
1912. Holburn, Harold.
1894. Holden, Allen.
1898. Holding, Frank.
1904. Hole, Sidney Herbert.
1897. Holford, Sidney John.
1922. Holford, Stanley Arthur.
1902. Holford, Trafford Claudius.
*1890. Holford, Walter Stanley.
1915. Holgreaves, Francis William.
1904. Hollick, Edward Henry.
1922. Hollier, Francis Gillespie.
1919. Hollington, Joseph James Luckett.
1911. Holloway, Guy William Euston.
1903. Holman, Ambrose Edgar.
1918. Holmes, Herbert Oliver.
1897. Holmes, Robert Gabriel Stuart.
1918. Holmes-Siedle, Bertram Adolphe.
1916. Holmes-Siedle, Rosa Edwards.
1898. Holt, Reginald Crompton.
1923. Hooker, Martin Linton.
*1920. Hooker, Reginald James.
1883. Hooper, Gordon.
1903. Hooper, Herbert Prestbury.
1922. Hooper, Kenneth.
1900. Hooper, Robert.
*1888. Hooton, William Arthur.
1892. Hope, Arthur Curling.
*1888. Hope, Hubert Lindsay Curling.
1909. Hope, Robert.
1893. Hope, Vacey Linnington.
1916. Hope, William Kenneth Talbot.
*1887. Hopewell-Smith, Arthur.
1899. Hopkins, Alfred David.
1922. Hopkins, Roland.
1912. Hopkinson, Frederick.
1901. Hopkinson, Harry.
1905. Hopkinson, Seth Moore.
1891. Hopson, Montagu Frank.
1913. Hopson, Montagu Fred.
1890. Hordern, Joseph Brookhouse.
1915. Horniblow, Francis Walsh.
1899. Horrocks, Francis Walsh.
1921. Horton, Egbert Ernest Mugeridge.
1917. Horton, James Ernest.
1905. Horton, John Joseph.
1912 Horton, John Stanley Frank.
1904. Houchin, Victor Stanley.
1906. Houghton, Edgar.
1922. Houlton, John Victor.
1912. Housden, Charles Henry.
1923. House, Sidney Gerald.
1905. Houston, John Fulton.
1426

1888. Howard, Frederic Richard.
1903. Howard, George.
1906. Howard, Percy Edward.
1900. Howard, Robert.
1896. Howe, Albert Frederick Alonzo.
1919. Howe, George Hubert.
1923. Howe, Wilfred Fildes.
1894. Howitt, Herbert George.
*1899. Howkins, Cyril Henry.
1899. Howlett, Ernest Robert.
1902. Howorth, Frederick Arthur.
1922. Hubbard, John Bryan.
1912. Huckett, Ernest Sharman.
*1894. Huckle, Arthur Henry Headley.
1898. Huckle, Claud Hamilton.
1903. Huddart, Frederick Ernest Percival.
1921. Hudson, Charles Frederick.
1910. Hudson, Edward Palmer.
1922. Hudson, James Alfred.
1903. Huggins, Burnell Townsend.
1899. Huggins, Harold Samuel.
1911. Huggins, Samuel Carson.
*1912. Hughes, Alfred Morgan.
1899. Hughes, Arthur.
1892. Hughes, Geoffrey.
1909. Hughes, George Theodore Douglas.
1900. Hughes, John Taylor.
*1882. Hughes, Morgan.
1904. Hughes, Richard Bulkeley.
1922. Hughes, Royston.
*1903. Hughes, Thomas Martin.
1914. Hughes, Walter Owen.
1916. Hugo, Pierre Jean.
1922. Human, John Urban.
*1900. Humby, Daniel Morgan.
1903. Humby, Harry Robinson.
1899. Humby, John Daniel Dawson.
*1895. Humby, William John.
1880. Humby, William Robinson.
1912. Hume, Arnold Augustus.
1908. Hume, Frederic Oscar.
1921. Hume, William Henry.
1909. Humm, Percy Stanley.
1894. Humphreys, Harold Francis.
1909. Humphreys, Humphrey Francis.
1920. Humphreys, John Roland.
1912. Humphry, Hubert.
1896. Humphrys, Jack Edmund.
1922. Hunt, Albert Edward Thomas.
1907. Hunt, Graham.
1922. Hunt, Thomas.
1902. Hunter, Ranulph Brocas.
1905. Husbands, Frank Alfred.
1922. Hutchison. Francis Graham.
1894. Hutson, Edward.
1915. Hutson, Harry Austen.
1482

1909. Hylton, Doris Yvon.
1921. Hyslop, Albert Leslie.

I.

1921. Iago, Petronel.
1903. Ide, Harry.
1920. Ide, Horace Leonard.
1912. Iles, George Denis.
1920. Immerman, Maurice David.
1918. Inder, Mabel Frances.
1914. Inder, Reginald John.
1912. Ingram, Sidney William.
1917. Inman, Wallace.
1911. Ireland, Eric Greaves.
1907. Ireland, William Henry.
*1906. Ironside, Arthur Edmund.
1919. Irwin, Horace Oliver.
1913 Isaacs, Bernard.
1905. Isaacs, Samuel.

J.

*1912. Jack, George Gerald.
1911. Jackson, Arthur Carlyle.
1903. Jackson, Arthur Toase.
1916. Jackson, Bertrand Kemp.
1921. Jackson, Harvey.
1906. Jackson, Herbert Eyre.
1903. Jackson, Matthew.
1914. Jackson, Thomas Henry.
1910. Jackson, William Lowe.
1905. Jacob, Edmund David Reed.
1923. Jacob, Ida.
1920. Jacobs, Israel.
1897. Jacobs, Jacob Michael Cecil.
1895. James, Benjamin Edgar.
1907. James, Charles Edward.
1905. James, Herbert Henning.
1914. James, Howell Gwyn.
1918. James, John.
1896. James, John Joseph.
1919. James, Lionel Beresford.
1901. James, Needham.
1908. James, Newton.
1908. James, William Alfred.
‡1898. James, William Warwick.
1915. Jaques, Frederic Amos.
1900. Jarvis, William.
1896. Jeffery, Ernest.
1920. Jeffery, Violet Ruth.
1907. Jeffries, Thomas Neville.
1900. Jenkin, Arthur Edward.
1895. Jenkin, Thomas George.
1922. Jenkins, Roy Layton.
1916. Jennings, Edward Almond.
1532

1898. Jennings, George Frederick William.
1921. Jennings, George Kingsley.
1914. Jennings, Henry.
1913. Jensen, Carl Joseph Oldham.
1899. Jepson, Alfred de Betham.
1895. Jepson, Harold Ernest.
1898. Jessop, Charles Ferdinand.
1914. Jessop, Philip Everard.
1876. Jewers, Ernest Edwin.
1900. Jiménez, José Joaquin.
1922. Juels, Edwin James.
1917. John, Clifford Morley.
1903. Johnson, Alfred Adolf Harold.
1910. Johnson, Arthur Percy Livett.
1910. Johnson, Arthur William.
1913. Johnson, Benjamin Durrans.
1913. Johnson, Edward Eastaugh.
1911. Johnson, Gordon.
1892. Johnson, Horace William.
1917. Johnson, John Christopher.
1902. Johnson, Richard Hugh Cecil.
1914. Johnson, Sydney Emil.
1918. Johnson, William Trevor.
*1895. Johnston, William.
1913. Johnstone, William Sanders.
‡1907. Joll, Cecil Augustus.
1923. Jollye, Stanley Arthur.
1921. Jonas, Gerald John.
1905. Jones, Albert James.
1887. Jones, Albert Sidney.
1886. Jones, Alexander John.
*1885. Jones, Alfred Ernest.
*1916. Jones, Alfred Kenneth Ince.
1910. Jones, Bertram Howard.
1908. Jones, Charles Cabread.
1891. Jones, David Richard.
‡1891. Jones, Edmund Benjamin.
1900. Jones, Ernest Guy.
1911. Jones, Ernest Victor.
1895. Jones, Frederick Warner.
1894. Jones, George Silva.
1894. Jones, George Willcox.
1921. Jones, Gilbert Sidney.
1903. Jones, Harold Wightman.
1922. Jones, Harry Wilson.
1902. Jones, Henry Cadwaladr.
1907. Jones, Herbert Emlyn.
1917. Jones, Hugh Llywelyn.
1923. Jones, John Emrys.
1922. Jones, Llewelyn Thomas.
1903. Jones, Richard William.
1899. Jones, Sydney Herbert.
1913. Jones, Theodore Hesketh.
1923. Jones, Trevor Wynne.
1896. Jones, William.
1911. Jones, William Edward.
1588

1897. Jones, William Henry.
1898. Jones, William Henry.
1906. Jones, William John.
1922. Jones, William Leslie Cooper.
*1893. Jones, William Meredith.
1919. Jordan, James Joseph.
1893. Joscelyne, Harry Percy.
1897. Joseph, Edgar.
1911. Joseph, Michael Wm. Joseph Davis.
1917. Joyner, Eric William.

K.

1899. Kaye, Sydney Jones.
1895. Keall, Clarence Albert Harry.
1893. Keay, Colin.
1922. Keay, John Raymond.
1912. Keay, William Howard.
*1893. Keele, Stephen.
1918. Keet, Elisha Clemens.
*1890. Keevil, George Mulready.
1891. Kekwick, John.
1909. Kemp, Leonard John.
1897. Kempe, Arthur Marshall.
1922. Kempster, Gordon Beutley.
1887. Kendall, William Henry.
1897. Kendrew, Augustus.
1910. Kennealy, William Joseph.
1904. Kennedy, Marshall.
1922. Kenroy, Ronald Victor.
1901. Kenworthy, Frederick Clowes.
1908. Kenyou, Louis Edwin.
1923. Kerrison, Frederick Arthur.
1892. Kershaw, George.
1912. Kershaw, Reginald Charles.
1900. Kershaw, Samuel.
1913. Kettlewell, Leonard Stanley.
1913. Kettlewell, Norman Harold.
1921. Keyter, Bernard John Morkel.
1916. Kidner, Charles Henry.
1922. Kilvington, George.
1913. Kincaid-Smith, Aurelius Percy.
1883. King, Arthur.
1918. King, Frederick Laurence.
1895. King, Herbert Fawcett.
1908. King, Leonard Algernon Bertram.
1917. King, Percy.
1912. King, Reginald Manton.
1875. King, Thomas Edward.
1918. Kingham, Roy Victor.
1905. Kingsbury, Francis Joseph.
1911. Kinnersley, Leslie Gordon.
1883. Kirby, Alexander.
1905. Kirkman, Bertram Charles.
1908. Kirkman, Frederic Butcher.
1873. Kissack, Edward Thomas.
1641   z 2

1882. Kissack, Frank Hill.
1900. Kittow, William.
1896. Knaggs, Sydney Angelo.
1907. Knight, Arthur Thirlby.
1893. Knight, Ernest Vincent.
1900. Knight, Leonard Adolphus Charles.
1901. Knight, Reginald Douglas.
1905. Knott, John Robertson.
1910. Know-Davies,Edwd.AubreyClement
1917. Knowler, Felix Reginald.
1896. Knowles, Charles Heygate.
1900. Knowles, George Frederick.
1910. Knowles, John.
1922. Knowles, John Orrell.
1910. Knowling, Harold William.
1899. Kolesar, Thomas Henry Paul.
1921. Krause Otto Friedrich Albert.
1921. Krige, Johannes Albertus.
1921. Krige, Pieter.
1921. Krige, William Adolph.
1919. Kropman, Sholam Meerowitz.
1923. Kull, George René.

L.

1904. Lacey, Arthur George.
*1896. Lacey, William John Mark.
1891. Ladmore, Frederick Thackway.
1919. Lake, Carol Pinson.
1911. Lakeman, William Symons.
1902. Lamb, Charles John.
1900. Lamb, Frank Donald.
*1903. Lamb, Ralph.
1900. Lambert, Athol Lucien.
1894. Lambert, Francis Ernest Lewis.
1908. Lambert, John Vollans.
*1916. Lambert, Wright.
1921. Lanchester, John.
1921. Landsler, Arthur Samuel.
1900. Lane, Everard Foster.
1894. Lane, Keith Foster.
1910. Lang, William Stuart.
1912. Langley, Lionel Scott.
*1888. Lankester, Francis John.
1919. Lauer, Joseph.
1921. Laurence, Eric Herbert.
1900. Laurence, Hector Ernest.
1904. Law, John Jackson.
1900. Law, William Jackson.
1912. Lawrey, Andrew.
*1918. Lawrence, Frank.
1912. Lawrence, Frank Wentworth.
1911. Laws, Harold Lionel.
1910. Lawson, Stanley.
1916. Lean, Frank Cecil.
1920. Lean, John Leslie.
1805. Lean, Norman Henry.
1695

1911. Leatherby, Linthall Harry.
1920. Leathlean, Bartle.
1883. Lechmere, Edward.
1909. Leeming, James Pensam.
*1897. Lees, Charlie.
1894. Lees, James Adam.
1895. Lees, Tom.
1891. Leigh, Percival Tookey.
1894. Leigh, William Johnson.
1920. Leipoldt, Helmar August Friedrich.
1903. Lennox, William John.
1912. Lethaby-Morgan, Bernard.
1884. Levason, Peyton Grenville.
1922. Levien, Linds Saul.
1921. Levinson, Samuel.
1907. Levy, Isaac.
1921. Levy, Jack.
1904. Lewars, Joseph Henry.
1923. Lewin, Michael Solomon.
1901. Lewis, Edwin Henry.
1910. Lewis, Frederic Winbolt.
*1904. Lewis, Frederick William.
1922. Lewis, Maurice.
1923. Lewis, Sidney Ernest.
1887. Linnell, Percy Allison.
1923. Linnell, William Allison.
1875. Lipscombe, John Moore.
1897. Lishman, James.
1913. List, Roy William.
1908. Little, Edward Stephen William.
1895. Little, Frederick.
1901. Littleboy, Reginald Lindley.
1900. Livsey, Thomas Edward.
*1900. Llewellyn, Richard Llewellyn Jones.
1863. Lloyd, Augustus.
1906. Lloyd, Charles Evan.
1923. Lloyd, Edgar Allan.
1916. Lloyd, Oswald Octavius.
1923. Lloyd, Trevor Gwynne.
1914. Lloyd, William George.
*1922. Lloyd-Williams, Pierce.
1906. Lockett, Alfred Cookman.
1899. Lockett, Reginald Frederick.
1911. Lodge, Frank.
1890. Lombardi George.
1920. Long, Cecil Frank.
1903. Long, Edwin George.
*1901. Longhurst, Ernest Archibald.
1860. Longhurst, Sir Henry Bell, C.V.O.
*1891. Longhurst, Percy Augustus.
1899. Longhurst, Sidney Herbert.
1898. Loosely, William Henry.
1902. Lord, James Lewtas.
1920. Loretz, Margherita Maria.
1893. Love, Hugh.
1887. Lovitt, Robert James.
1901. Lowe, William Ernest.
1752

1915. Lowein, Arthur Edmund.
1910. Lucas, George Bertrand.
1904. Luce, Philip Edwin.
1921. Luck, Henry John.
1886. Ludbrook, Frederick Milner.
1895. Ludbrook, Stephen Percy.
1893. Lukyn, Herbert Edward.
1909. Lumley, Percy William.
*1916. Lunnon, Leslie Grantham.
1922. Lycett, Joseph Sambourne.
1861. Lyddon, George.
1902. Lyne, Wilfrid Courtney.
1893. Lyne, William Henry.
1918. Lyon, Harold James.
1920. Lyon, Leslie.
1910. Lyons, Harris Raphael.

M.

*1885. Maberly, John.
1916. Mabe, Harold Pembroke.
1899. McAlpin, John Gerdes.
1920. McAlpin, Kenneth Fergus.
1887. McAlpin, Kenneth Wade.
1912. McArd, Ewart.
1905. McBride, John.
1879. M'Call, John Henry.
1913. McCallin, Sidney.
1917. McCormack, Stephen Alphonsus.
1911. McDonald, Donald Henry.
1895. Macdonald, George Ernest.
1904. Macdonald, John Purvis.
1913. MacDonald, William Douglas.
1903. Mace, Harry Edward.
1906. Mace, Hugh Widenham.
1913. Mace, John Farnham.
1919. Mace, Stanley George.
1904. McFadden, Wilfrid Edgar Walter.
1913. McFarlane, Percy Scott.
*1904. Machin, Frank Smith.
1915. Machin, Launcelot.
*1895. McKay, Robert.
1899. Mackenzie, Frederick.
1922. Mackie, Edward Mark Duncanson.
1895. Mackley, Herbert Edwin.
1902. Mackley, Leopold Anderson.
1905. McMahon, George Edward.
1900. McMillan, William Henry.
1909. McNaught, James Norman.
1904. Maden, John Edward.
1922. Madgwick, Alva Alexander Robert.
1917. Madin, Aubrey Thompson.
1888. Madin, William Thompson.
1917. Maes, Georges.
*1879. Maggs, William Adolphus.
1923. Maguire, Amadeus Charles.

1805

1916. Maguire, Francis Vincent.
1915. Maguire, George Francis.
1907. Maguire, James Frederick.
1906. Maguire, Maurice John.
1918. Maher, Amin.
1893. Makepeace, Alfred Joseph.
*1903. Malleson, Herbert Cecil.
1889. Mallet, John Aubrey.
1905. Mallory, George Kennaway.
1896. Malone, Charles Albert.
1923. Mann, Isaac.
1897. Manning, Robert Harris.
*1886. Mansbridge, Josiah.
1891. Mansell, Edward Anson.
1888. Manton, Edward Alfred.
1893. Manton, George Sydney Frederick.
1920. Marais, Christoffel Albertus.
1915. Marais, Hendrik Christoffel.
1896. Mardon, Frederick William.
1905. Mardon, Percy Barrett.
1923. Maree, Johannes Bernardes.
1922. Margetts, George Duncan.
1906. Margolies, Ivor.
1920. Markham, Hubert Ransome.
1915. Markham, James Henry.
1900. Markham, Leonard Montgomery.
1914. Markham, Lionel Everett.
1898. Marks, Arthur Roberts.
1908. Marr, Douglas John.
1911. Marsh, Ainslie Palk.
1919. Marsh, Cyril Bernard.
1906. Marsh, Horace Edmund.
1923. Marsh, Leonard Russell.
1916. Marsh, Philip Henry.
1913. Marshall, Gerald Struan.
1897. Marshall, Graham.
*1903. Marshall, Herbert Frank.
*1890. Marson, Cyril Darby.
1902. Marson, Frederic James.
*1913. Marston, Archibald Daniel.
1921. Marston, Frederick Harold Edward.
1895. Marston, Walter.
1888. Marten, Alfred Ernest.
1904. Martin, Baunar Harry.
1915. Martin, Cyril Randell.
*1861. Martin, John Henry Charles Erridge.
1918. Martin, Percy Robert Cox.
1922. Masey, Sydney.
1881. Mason, Charles Browne.
1898. Mason, Edgar.
1898. Mason, Ernest Noel.
1923. Mason, Harry Keith.
1876. Mason, Henry Biging.
1909. Masselink, Benjamin Henry.
1895. Masters, Edwin Clarence Platt.
1908. Masters, Vivian.
1877. Matheson, Leonard.

1862

1903. Mathews, Arthur Llewelyn.
1895 Mathews, Harold Dewe.
1895. Mathews, John Hilditch.
1922. Matley-Moore, Malcolm John.
1882. Matthews, Arthur Alexander.
1912. Matthews, George.
1896. Matthews, George Frederick Cale.
1911. Matthews, Leonard Clive.
1907. Matthews, Lewis Trevor Bamford.
1913. Matthews, Wilfred Richard.
1881. Matthews, William.
1903. Matthews, William Arthur.
1913. Matthews, William Henry.
1922. Maudsley, Aubrey Granville.
1899. Maurice, Harold.
1904. Mawer, James William.
1913. Mawson, Harold Woodhead.
1902. Maxwell, Fred Martin.
1923 Maxwell, Reginald.
1923. May, Charles Bernard.
1922. May, Reginald William.
1885. May, Robert.
1923. May, Robert Cyril.
1900. May, Rowland Claude Gasson.
*1893. May, Walter John.
1890. May, William.
1908. May, William Edward Southcomb.
1912. Mayer, John William.
1919. Mayo, Helen Patri in Clara.
1906 Mays, Herbert Reginald.
1922. Meacock, Stanley Preece.
1906. Meadows, Joseph Wesley.
1900. Meads, William Edward.
*1912. Medlock, Charles Harold.
1900. Meek, George Herbert.
1908. Meek, Harold Matthews.
1921. Meldrum, Thomas Alfred.
1913. Melhuish, John Dudley.
1893. Mellersh, William Francis.
1922. Mellor, Sydney.
1911. Mendleson, Bertie.
1916. Mercer, William.
1923 Merrett, Ronald Norman.
*1911. Messenger, Henry Leslie.
1904. Messent, Rupert Josiah.
1905. Messer, Fritz Julian.
1914. Metcalf, Harold Frederick.
1922. Mew, Gordon Morrison.
1922. Meyer, Frederick Albert.
1911. Meyer, Harold Leonard.
1916. Micklethwait, Benjamin.
1923. Milburn, Romney.
1922. Miles, Herbert James.
1915. Miller, Alan Lawrence.
1905. Miller, Arthur.
1914. Miller, Arthur Helmuth John.
1906. Miller, Claude.

1892. Miller, Ernest Arthur.
1887. Miller, Frederick Tayler.
1897. Miller, Nathaniel.
1894. Miller, Quintin Herbert.
1910 Miller, Richard Gornall.
1897. Miller, Thomas Henry.
1909. Miller, William Coffyn.
*1917. Millett, Harry.
1916. Millican, Percy.
1900. Milligan, James.
1902 Mills, Arthur Henry.
1901. Mills, Charles.
1906. Mills, Randolph Henry.
1900 Mills, Thomas Charles.
1905. Mills, Victor Edwin.
1915. Milnes, Albert Victor.
1915. Milton, Wallis John.
1919. Milton, William Eric.
1920. Milton, William Grant.
1912. Miron, Wilfred Woolfe.
1921. Mist, Charles Priestley.
1898. Mitchell, Arthur.
1902. Mitchell, Richard David.
1900. Mitchell, Thomas.
1920. Mitchell, Thomas Wemyss.
1907. Modi, Jamshedji Jivanji.
1915. Moghé, Harihar Gangadhar.
1922. Monteiro, Valery Victor.
1907. Montuschi, Frederico.
1919. Moody, Charles Aston.
1890 Moon, William Draper.
1904. Moore, Alic.
1922. Moore, Brian Russell.
1914. Moore, George Douglas.
1921. Moore, George King.
1834 Moore, George Peirce.
1886. Moore, Henry John.
1921. Moore, Henry Summer Hyatt.
1896. Moore, Hubert William
1907. Moore, Lionel Alexander Burke.
1921. Moore, Reginald Arthur.
1897. Moore, Robert Henry.
1899. Moores, De la Hey.
1892. Mordaunt, Francis George.
1900. Mordaunt, Thomas.
1910. Morgan, Arthur Stanley.
1895. Morgan, Edwin
1921. Morgan, Evan Idrisvn.
1893. Morgan, Frederick John.
1909 Morgan, Reginald Charles.
1887. Morley, Charles Reginald.
*1893. Morley, Frank.
1912 Morley, Herbert Vincent.
1915. Morphy, Owen Colville.
1913. Moriell, Frederick Humble.
1902 Morrell, John George.
1899. Morrell, Richard James.

1919

1976

1910. Morrell, Robert William.
1909. Morris, Cecil Graves.
*1900. Morrie, Charles Sculthorpe.
1900 Morris, Frank.
*1901. Morris, Gerald Hamilton.
1922. Morris, Harold Alexander Leopold.
1897. Morris, Henry James.
1910. Morris, Hubert Stanley.
1894. Morris, Lionel Frederick.
1916. Morris, Llewellyn Arwyn.
1921. Morris, Ormond D'Ewes.
1921. Morris, Owain Gwym.
1910. Morris, Victor Mayfield.
1875. Morris, William Graves.
1912. Morris, William Reginald.
1899. Morrish, Jonathan Baron.
1919. Morrison, Peter John.
1892. Mosely, Edward.
1903. Mosely, Lewin Lewis Rose.
1905. Moser, Frederick Rudolph.
1901. Mosscrop. Harold Edwin.
1911. Motton, William Davies.
1903. Mountain, William.
1882. Mountford, Arthur Hambledon.
1895. Mountford, Edwin Henry.
1888. Mountford, James.
1898. Mountfort, Charles Ernest.·
1896. Mudie, Walter.
1885. Mugford, George Henry.
1915. Murford, John Lisle.
1895. Muhlenkamp, Fritz-Heinrich Arthur.
1920. Muir-Smith, Edgar Hamilton.
1914. Muirhead, Thomas Dickson.
1922. Muller, Ralph Harry.
1896. Mullord, Charles.
1913. Mulliner, Norman.
*1873. Mummery, John Howard, C.B.E.
*1902. Mummery, Stanley Parkes.
1884. Mundell, Stephen.
1904. Mundy, Alfred James.
1922. Murch, Alfred Henry.
1913. Murch, Charles Edward.
1914. Murch, Winifred Amelia.
*1901. Murphy, Basil Newman.
1897. Murphy, James Montague.
1877. Murphy, Octavias Brabazon.
1885. Murray, Harold.
1923. Murray, Herbert Shires.
1909. Murray, Walter Cecil.
1915. Murray-Shirreff, Cecil.
1894. Musgrave, Gilbert Mordaunt.
1897. Musgrove, Edward Hugh.
1914. Musson, Glenn Fowler.
·1898. Must, William Henry.
1923. Mutch, Stanley Robert.
1921. Myatt. James Harold Douglas
*1902. Myer, Leonard.

2033

1921. Myers, Francis John.
1907. Myers, Francis Richard Henry.
1893. Myers, Lancelot Brainard, M.B.E.
1896. Myers, Thomas Cyrill.

N.

1896. Naish, Godfrey.
1917. Nandé, Johann Lodewijk te Water.
1898. Narramore, Edward Giles.
1899. Nathan. Major Percival.
1921. Neal, Frank Douglas.
1913. Neal, Frederick James.
1906. Neal, George Kelsey Breward.
1912. Neale, Charles Douglas.
1920. Neame, Cyril Stanley.
*1913. Neely, Wilfrid Guy Stuart.
1911. Neft, Raphael.
1883. Nehmer, Ferdinand.
1900. Ness, Kenneth Carrington.
1899. New, George Herbert.
1921. Newbald, Leoni Harold.
1896. Newbery, Ernest Arthur.
1894. Newland, Herbert George.
†1880. Newland-Pedley, Frederick.
1915. Newman, Arthur Llewellyn.
1923. Newman, James.
1878. Newton, John Newton Peill.
1905. Newton, Sydney Bullen.
1922. Newton, Thomas Frederick.
1905. Nibbs, Norman McLeod.
1902. Nicholls, Arthur Ernest.
1923. Nicholls, Eric Carson.
1894. Nicholls, Reginald Edward.
*1906. Nichols, Frederick Cecil.
*1898. Nicholson, William.
1922. Nicolai, Frank Archibald.
*1896. Nixon, Arthur Percival.
1923. Nodine, Alonzo Milton.
1919. Norman, Edith Mynott.
1894. Norman, Harry William.
1905. Normandale, Harold George.
1884. Norris, Edward Lewington.
1880. Norris, John.
1897. North, Benjamin.
1923. Northheld, Douglas Wm. Claridge.
1892. Northcroft, George.
*1895. Nowell, Walter Salmon.
1918. Nunn, Ernest Albert.

O.

1901. Cades, Geoffry Smyth.
1911. Oakden, George Marshall.
1881. Oakley, Archibald Harold.
1904. Oates. John Arnold.
1912. O'Callaghan, Charles Justin.

2084

1904. Oddie, Arthur Brearley.
1897. Oddy, Alfred Ernest.
1916. Ogden, John Austen.
1913. O'Kane, William John.
1913. Oliver, Cyril Henry.
1866. Oliver, John Cardell.
*1890. Oliver, John Percy.
1896. Oliver, Norman Henry.
1906. Oliver, Reginald Joseph.
1908. Oliver, William Grant.
1918. Olivier, Cornelis Hermanus.
1921. Olivier, William Johannes.
1912. Ollis, Wilfrid Stephen.
1904. Olver, Julian Henry.
1899. Olver, Stephen Holloway.
1893. Oram, Charles Henry.
1919. Ordish, Fairinan John.
1909. Ormrod, James.
1896. Orridge, Alfred Edward Horton.
1911. Orozco-Casorla, Raul.
*1912. Orton, Douglas Catterall Leyland.
1909. Orton, Percy Hills.
1892. Osborn, Lewis James.
1912. Osborne, Claude Vernon.
1923. Osborne, Leslie Bartlet.
1921. Osmer, Edmund Boyd.
1911. Osmer, Thomas Spencer.
*1898. Outred, Charles Deane.
1911. Ovey, Henry Kinnear.
1907. Ovey, William Charles Augustus.
1899. Owen, Hugh Gwilym.
1900. Owen, Owen.
1901. Owen, Thorold.
1892. Owen, William Gladstone.

P.

*1909. Packe, George Garfield.
*1913. Packham, Arthur Leslie.
1921. Packham, Eric Charles.
1906. Packham, George.
1896. Padgett, Frank Joseph.
1904. Padley, Gillies.
1911. Paget, John Hayward.
*1922. Pain, Alfred.
1922. Pain, Margery Gav.
1921. Painter, Oswald Frederick Robert.
1923. Palfrey, Jack Reginald.
1906. Palk, William Charles.
1904. Pallant, Hubert Arnold, M.C.
*1899. Pallant, Santiago Luis, D.S.O.
1912. Pallett, Roy Harry Barkly.
1911. Palmer, Arthur Hugh Spencer.
1903. Palmer, Charles Lucey.
1901. Palmer, Frank Robert Edward.
1903. Palmer, Frederick Nelson.
2137

1908. Palmer, John Ramsey.
1899. Palmer, Perceval Henry Hayes.
1915. Pank, John Durrell.
1902. Pannell, Harry George.
1903. Parfitt, Felix William.
*1893. Parfitt, John Brodribb.
*1894. Park, William Hodgson.
1903. Parker, Albert Thomas.
1917. Parker, Edward Alfred Penney.
1921. Parker, George.
1922. Parker, Sidney Francis.
1903. Parker, William Richard.
1913. Parkes, Harold Robert.
1919. Parkes, Herbert Percy.
1923. Parkin, Arthur Reginald.
1917. Parkinson, Ernest George.
1905. Parkinson, George Herbert.
*1880. Parkinson, George William.
1884. Parkinson, Herbert Stephen.
1908. Parkinson, Samuel Stephenson.
1902. Parks, Norris John.
1899. Parlett, Frank.
1892. Parris, Richard Stanway.
1896. Parrot, Ernest Garner.
1897. Parrott, Arthur Hughes, O.B.E.
1905. Parrott, Arthur William.
1921. Parry, Reginald George Wolfe.
1912. Parry, William.
1914. Parsonage, Frank Henry.
1906. Parsonage, John Hodson.
1922. Parsons, Dudley Anthony.
1890. Parsons, Ernest.
1914. Parsons, Thomas Harold.
1898. Partridge, Alfred Mitchell.
1920. Partridge, Alfred Thomas.
*1894. Partridge, Walter Eriencus.
1912. Partridge, William Linnell.
1918. Pasmore, Charles Lindley Donald.
1912. Pasmore, Ivan Wallace.
1911. Patel, Jal Framji.
1898. Paterson, Howard James.
‡1883. Paterson, William Bromfield.
1922. Patlansky, Max.
1903. Patterson, Percy Montgomery.
1886. Pattinson, Charles Augustine.
1915. Paul, Arthur Norman.
*1911. Paul, Frederick William.
1922. Pauw, Carel Marthinus Arnold.
*1900. Pavitt, Percy George.
1921. Paxton, Harry Simmons.
*1898. Payne, Archibald Gates.
1923. Payne, Frederick Richmond.
*1895. Payne, Joseph Lewin, O B E.
1922. Payne, Ralph Richard Bedford.
1898. Peach, William Frank.
1923. Peacock, Basil.
1904. Peacock, Charles Nassau.
2194

*1904. Peacock, Henry Maurice.
*1901. Peacock, William Baly.
1894. Peake, George Arthur.
1885. Peall, Frederick Snell.
1899. Pearce, Frank James.
1905. Pearce, Henry Garfield.
1915. Pearce, Philip Thomas.
1922. Pearce, Raymond Marson.
1892. Pearse, Arthur Samuel.
1895. Pearse, Cecil Gilbert.
1896. Pearse, Francis Henry.
1900. Pearse, Walter Leslie.
1917. Pearson, Clarence Norman.
1917. Pearson, Maurice.
1911. Peatfield, Percy John.
1903. Peatfield, Sydney Herbert.
1901. Peatfield, William Henry.
1910. Peaty, Archie Ernest Frederick.
1907. Peaty, Charles Robert Mower.
1889. Peckover, Charles Edward.
1914 Peckover, Lancelot Eric Charles.
1904. Pedler, Septimus Edward.
*1895. Pedler, William Frederick.
1923. Pedley, Eric Wolsey.
*1884. Pedley, Richard Denison.
*1885. Pedley, Samuel Edward.
*1877. Pedley, Thomas Franklin.
*1906. Pedrick, Percy Vivian Giles.
1912. Pegler, Herbert James.
1904. Pellow, Charles James.
*1901. Penfold, Fred Bailey.
1898. Penfold, Oliver Crace.
1919. Penfold, William Douglas.
*1910. Penny, Charles Harry Greville.
*1901. Penrose, Arthur Wellesley.
*1921. Percy, Archibald Felix.
1912. Percy, Arthur John.
1909. Percy, Leopold Képler.
1899. Perkins, Harold Goodwin.
†1903. Perkins, Herbert Wilberforce.
1903. Perry, Frederick William.
1902. Perry, William Kerby.
*1916. Peter, John.
*1913. Peters, Haydn.
1883. Petherbridge, James.
1887. Petit, Charles Frederick Newton.
1897. Pettey, James Bertie.
1921. Pfaff, Edward Reinhold.
*1905. Pfeiffer, Albert.
1912. Phillips, Charles Joseph.
1901. Phillips, Edward.
1908. Phillips, Geoffrey Ayres.
1916. Phillips, George Evan Henry Holt.
1892. Phillips, Howard.
1922. Phillips, James Edward.
1902. Phillips, Richard Herbert.
1898. Phillips, William Herbert.
2251

1920. Phillips, Withiel Herbert Leslie.
1900. Philpots, Montague.
1903. Pickerill, Henry Percy.
1893. Pickering, Harold John.
1906. Pickett, Arthur Henry.
1921. Pickett, Henry Horton.
1912. Pickett, Leonard Robert.
1914. Pickett, Reginald Jack.
1897. Picnot, Ernest.
1894. Picton, Edwin.
1881. Pidgeon, William John.
1922. Pienaar, Pieter.
1906. Pierrepont, Edward Spencer.
1922. Pike, John Edridge.
1894. Pike, Walter James.
1904. Pilbeam, Edward Laurence.
1922. Pilbeam, John Frederick.
1915. Pilbeam, Leonard Stanley.
1894. Pilcher, John.
1894. Pilcher, William Henry.
1905. Piper, Stanley Arthur.
1899. Pitt, Charles Fox.
1919. Pitt, Edward.
1923. Pitt, Henry Leslie.
1906. Pitts, Arthur Thomas.
1909. Place, James Frederick.
1909. Plank, Alfred Bunce.
1906. Plowman, William Henry.
*1896. Plumley, Arthur George Grant.
1907. Plumley, Cuthbert Grant.
1905. Plummer, Edwin Noyes.
1921. Pocock, Claude Leslie Tory.
1923. Poland, Herbert Leonard.
1915. Pollitt, Eric Vincent.
1899. Pollitt, Gerald Paton.
1923. Pomeroy, Cyril Thomas.
1909. Pomeroy, John Morley.
1919. Pomeroy, Stanley Edwin.
1906. Ponder, Ronald Richard Bertram.
1910. Poock, Alfred Graham.
1920. Poole, Alfred Edward.
*1906. Pooley, Charles Cook.
1922. Porter, Andrew Ferdinand.
1889. Porter, Frank Constable.
1912. Potter, William Macqueen.
1908. Pounds, Roland Thomas.
1922. Pow, Harold Ernest.
1921. Power, Eric Maynard.
1922. Power, Ronald Victor.
1917. Powell, Harold John.
1900. Powell, John Woodward.
1897. Powell, Matthew Pearce.
1909. Powell, Reginald Wood.
1906. Power, Horatio Leonard.
1904. Poyton, Hérbert.
1911. Pradier, Felix Lambert.
1891. Prager, Arnold
2308

1923. Pratelli, Carlo.
1900. Prall, Sydney Lionel.
1890. Preedy, Edward John.
1903. Preston, Alfred Ernest.
‡1897. Preston, Charles Henry.
1902. Preston, James Rudge.
1920. Pretorius, Wessel Johannes.
1895. Price, George Herbert.
1922. Price, Gordon Edwards.
1921. Price, Harold King.
1881. Price, Rees.
1900. Prickett, George Frederick.
1903. Prideaux, Albert Edgar Dunkin.
1894. Prideaux, Charles Sydney.
1894. Prideaux, Harry Symes.
1899. Prideaux, William de Courcy.
1914. Pridham, Arthur George Drake.
1911. Pridham, Cyril James.
1900. Pridham, William Collier.
1902. Priestley, George William.
*1900. Pring, Horace Reginald.
1923. Pringle, Lawrence Frederick Irwin.
1888. Pritchard, Athol Cravnant.
1893. Pritchard, Francis Edwin.
*1911. Pritchard, George Brentnall.
1922. Pritchard, George Percival.
1903. Probyn, Frank Ernest.
1904. Procter, Alfred Heathcoat.
1915. Procter, Horace James.
1907. Proud, Percy James.
1908. Pugh, Henry Stanley.
1911. Pulford, Frederick Gordon.
1903. Pulford, Herbert.
1915. Pullan, William Greaves.
1913. Purdom, Harold Neish.
1909. Pusey, Arthur.
1916. Pywell, Christopher Hodgson.

Q.

1895. Quinby, Arthur Henry.
*1901. Quinby, Frank Gray.
1899. Quinton, Herbert.
1905. Quinton, Percy Julian.

R.

1921. Rabinowitz, Louis.
1922. Radin, Harry.
1903. Randall, Charles William.
1909. Randell, George Hubert Walter.
1921. Rands, Stanley Harry.
1892. Ranken, John George.
1903. Rankin, David Stevenson.
1904. Ransford, Leonard Urban.
2357

1903. Ransford, William Reginald.
1901. Rathbun, Charles John.
1921. Raubenheimer, Hendrik Jacobus.
1905. Rawsthorne, Felix.
1919. Ray, Arthur Douglas.
1914. Ray, Ernest Russell.
1900. Ray, George Wheatcroft.
1900. Raymont, James Martin.
1896. Read, Arthur.
1904. Read, Charles.
*1908. Read, Harold William.
1890. Read, Stanley.
1887. Read, Thomas George.
*1898. Read, Walton Rix.
1897. Reading, George Frederick.
1891. Reading, Philip Burdett.
*1888. Reading, Richard Fairfax.
1901. Reatchlous, Henry Arnold.
1907. Redpath, Ralph.
1897. Redpath, Stuart James.
1896. Reece, Thomas Cadarn.
1922. Reed, John Burrman.
1920. Rees, Albert Edward.
1916. Rees, David Maurice.
1894. Reeve, Alfred.
1922. Reeve, Edmund Arthur.
1910. Reeve, Harold Todd.
1894. Reeve, Harry George Cleave.
*1899. Regan, Thomas Edward.
1921. Reid, John Hanna.
1901. Reid, Percy John.
*1896. Relph, Arthur Ernest.
*1895. Relph, Herbert John.
1921. Remes, Leo.
1909. Renshaw, Arnold.
1906. Renton, Edmund Louis.
1904. Retallack, William Charles.
*1902. Rey, Jules Frederick.
1923. Reynolds, Alfred William.
1910. Reynolds, Augustus John.
*1902. Reynolds, William.
1923. Reynolds, William Newton.
1900. Rhodes, Edmund.
1913. Rhodes, John Hargrave.
1921. Rhodes, Walter Edmund.
1899. Rice, Arthur.
1910. Rice, Charleton Edmund.
1913. Rice, Francis Rupert.
1905. Rice, George Eugene.
*1917. Richards, Beresford Tom.
1883. Richards, Frederick William.
*1885. Richards, George Oliver.
1911. Richards, John Griffith.
1915. Richards, Louis Philip.
1904. Richards, Martin.
1881. Richardson, Francis.
1889. Richardson, Frank Victor.
2414

1896. Riches, Charles John Hurry.
1906. Riches, Norman Vaughan Hurry.
1907. Richter, Lewis.
*1908. Riddett, Stanley Alfred.
1878. Ridge, Walter Henry.
1916. Ridout, Leslie George.
1917. Rigg, Sydney Kilshaw.
1921. Rilot, Bernard Arthur.
*1886. Rilot, Charles Frederick.
1919. Ripley, Mary Jane.
1894. Rispin, William.
1913. Rivers-Cole, Harold Robert.
1913. Rix, Reginald Harry.
1880. Robbins, Cornelius.
*1918. Robert, Earl Leslie.
1910. Roberts, Alexander James.
1898. Roberts, Alfred William.
1884. Roberts, Charles Alfred.
1916. Roberts, Clair William.
1892. Roberts, Harry Trist.
1922. Roberts, Herbert Douglas.
1922. Roberts, Jack Desmond Percy.
1909. Roberts, John.
1923. Roberts, John Barnett.
1903. Roberts, Richard.
1923. Roberts, Victor Rhodes.
1913. Roberts, William Owen.
1897. Robertson, Arthur Edwin.
1895. Robertson, Harry Lennox.
1896. Robey, Arthur Malcolm.
1898. Robey, Harry Webb.
1885. Robinson, Arthur Bernard.
1887. Robinson, Charles Cecil.
1917. Robinson, David Erland.
*1894. Robinson, George Edw. Jas. Antoine
1904. Robinson, George Theodore.
1912. Robinson, Henry Clifford.
1911. Robinson, James Stacey.
1923. Robinson, John.
1900. Robinson, John Henry.
1897. Robinson, Robert Percy.
1903. Robinson, Sydney William.
1901. Robinson, Thomas.
1918. Roche, Richard Stanislaus.
1914. Rodda, Stephen Archibald.
1904. Rodgers, Percy Hartley.
1900. Rodway, Barron John, O.B.E.
1902. Rodway, James Henry.
1900. Roe, Samuel Henry.
*1870. Rogers, Charles Claude.
1894. Rogers, John Percival.
1921. Rohan, Peter Max.
1879. Rook, Eustace Henry.
*1894. Rooke, Frederick James Faulkland.
1906. Roots, Oscar John.
1897. Roper, John Langdon.
1899. Rose, Charles Frederic.

1881. Rose, Frederick.
1901. Rose, Frederick George.
1912. Rose, Gilbert John Stuart.
1912. Rose, Harry Edward Campbell.
1898. Rose, Henry.
1907. Rose, John Alfred.
1905. Rose, Robert.
*1895. Rose, Samuel Frank.
1906. Rose, Walter.
1904. Rose, Walter Sidney.
1900. Ross, Harry Bruce.
1917. Ross, William John.
1905. Rotelli, Raniero.
1904. Rothwell, John Clarkson.
1900. Round, Harold.
*1897. Round, John Cornwell.
*1885. Rouw, Robert Wynne.
1921. Rowat, Frederick Haddon.
1913. Rowe, Arthur Ridges.
1904. Rowe, Harold Ridges.
1893. Rowe, Henry Burbery.
1910. Rowe, Wilfrid Aubrey.
1897. Rowe, William Francis.
1899. Rowlett, Alfred Ernest.
1898. Rowley, Arthur Lewis.
1909. Rowley, George Henry.
1877. Rowney, Thomas Walter Farraday.
1904. Rowstron, Ronald Nathaniel Maclean.
1912. Royle, George Wesley.
1910. Royston, Gordon Evelyn.
1882. Royston, Jonathan.
1891. Royston, Joseph.
1919. Royston, Joseph Walter.
1922. Rubenstein, Myer.
1922. Rubinstein, Barney.
1910. Ruck, Charles Frederic Leyson.
1915. Rudd, Frank Edwin.
1907. Rudolf, Carl Robert.
1901. Rumball, Aubrey Tom.
*1903. Rumsey, Cecil Frank.
1904. Ruscoe, Alfred William.
1889. Rushton, William.
1920. Russell, Eveline Mary.
1913. Russell, George Herbert Heywood.
1899. Russell, Richard John.
1902. Rust, Arthur Bernard Wills.
1908. Rutter, William Stanley.
1899. Ryan, Thomas Francis.
1914. Rycroft, Alfred Thomas.
1914. Rycroft, Ernest Charles.
1922. Ryder, Harry Gorden.
1904. Ryder, John Francis.
1917. Ryland, Reginald Joseph.
1895. Ryle, Arthur Buxton.
1917. Ryss, Willem Gerrit.

S.

1897. Sadler, Bernard Frederick.
1911. Sadler, Robert Dendy.
1903. Saies, Charles Lochore.
1922. Saile, Dudley Gilbert.
1913. Sainsburv, Arthur Pomroy.
1916. Sainty, Valentine.
1916. Salsbury, Frederick Robert.
1913. Salsbury, Archibald Frank.
1914. Salt, Harold Osbert.
1909. Salter, Bertram Charles.
1921. Salter, Douglas Reginald.
1907. Salter, Frank Henry.
1908. Sampson, Edward Spenser.
1923. Sampson, Frank Ackland.
1912. Sampson, William Edwin Ackland.
1900. Sams, Virley Stevenson.
1923. Samson, Edward.
1907. Samuel, Bertram Barnett.
1922. Samuels, Edgar.
1922. Samuels, Elle.
1911. Samuels, Isidore.
1916. Sanders, Enoch.
1916. Sanders, Simon.
1907. Sansom, Wilfrid Tom.
1891. Sansom, William Bertram.
1922. Sargent, Charles Pearse Crodacott.
1904. Sargent, Vyvian FitzGerald.
1893. Satterthwaite, Robert.
*1908. Saul, Alec Linford.
1887. Saul, Barnett Bendet.
1913. Saul, Edward Royston.
1898. Saul, William Albert Hodgins.
1893. Saul, William Henry.
1899. Saunders, Arthur Harold.
1913. Saunders, George Vincent.
1884. Saunders, Herbert Sedgwick.
1902. Saunders, Stanley Jennings.
1899. Sawday, George Curnock.
1901. Sawday, Hairy Burt.
1904. Sawer, John Stewart.
1911. Saxton, Sidney.
1876. Sayles, Francis Austin.
1910. Scales, Walter Herman.
1910. Schaefer, Albert John.
1890. Schelling, Carl.
1897. Schlesinger, William Augustus.
1912. Schneider, Max.
1910. Scott, Alfred Gladstone.
1903. Scott, Frank.
1903. Scott, Philip.
1907. Scott, Robert Alexander.
1909. Scott, Theodore.
1923. Seal, Gladys Muriel.
1921. Seal, Harry Sydney Kempe.
1921. Searle, Alexis Francis.

1900. Searle, William Radley.
*1895. Seccombe, Clovis Leopold.
1901. Segar, Alfred John.
1883. Segar, Frank.
1922. Sellers, Henry Victor Russell.
1904. Senior, Martin Chas. Theodore Wm.
1922. Sennitt, Stanley Ebenezer.
*1892. Sewill, Joseph Sefton.
1885. Sexton, Louis Edwin.
1896. Sexton, Walter.
1887. Seymour, George.
1904. Seymour, James Alfred.
1904. Seymour, Louis Napoleon.
1900. Shapland, Hubert Raleigh.
1907. Sharp, Herbert Victor.
1910. Sharp, James Bennett.
1922. Sharp, John Trevor.
1923. Sharp, Percy Buckley.
1922. Sharvill, Kenneth Gordon.
*1900. Shattock, Charles Robert.
1918. Shaw, Ernest Findlay.
1904. Shaw, John Herbert Jones.
1922. Shearer, George Linden.
*1897. Shedden, Arnold Ward.
1912. Sherford, Alan Douglas Edward.
1899. Shelton, Frank Lyon.
*1900. Shelton, Harvey Llewellyn.
1913. Shepherd, Hubert Ernest.
1922. Sheppard, Ernest Alfred.
1901. Sheppard, George.
1903. Sherratt, Albert Edwin.
1898. Sherratt, Benjamin.
1891. Sherratt, Thomas Edward.
1897. Shields, Ernest Thompson.
1895. Shields, John Lewis.
1900. Shields, Joseph Harold.
1918. Shipway, William Holder.
1911. Shore, Hubert Dennis.
1898. Shorrock, John Isherwood.
1902. Shovelton, John Sydney.
1912. Shovelton, Leslie.
1907. Shovelton, Sydney.
1914. Shrimpton, Sydney Victor.
1899. Shrubsole, Ernest.
*1894. Sibson, Arthur Bertram.
1894. Sibson, Percival Reginald.
1899. Sidebottom, John Wilson.
1919. Sievers, Robert Ferdinand.
1902. Silver, Clifford Marking.
1921. Silver, Wilfrid Ernest.
*1900. Simmonds, Ernest George.
1906. Simms, Harold.
†1896. Simpson, Graham Scales.
*1915. Simpson. Maurice Oliver.
1913. Simpson, Sydney Frank.
1923. Sims, William Owen.
1912. Singleton, William Joseph.

1896. Skae, John Walter.
1909. Skerritt, John Henry.
1910. Skerritt, William.
1921. Skipper, Theodore George.
1912. Slade, Reginald Alfred.
*1882. Slate, Alfred.
1922. Slater, Harold.
1888. Smale, Charles Henry.
*1903. Smale, Herbert.
1922. Small, Clarence John Charles.
1879. Small, David Mann.
1923. Smallbone, Eric George.
1917. Smallbone, Norman Leslie.
1898. Smallwood, George Valentine.
1900. Smedley, Harold Charles.
1902. Smith, Alexander Alfred.
1900. Smith, Alfred Henry.
1907. Smith, Ashley Wetherhead
1896. Smith, Bernard.
1900. Smith, Charles William.
1919. Smith, Cyril Fryer.
1918. Smith, Dorothy Mary
1908. Smith, Edgar.
1892. Smith, Edward Frederick.
1901. Smith, Edward Gethen.
1897. Smith, Edward Percy.
1897. Smith, Edwin Wylde.
*1913. Smith, Francis Henry
1906. Smith, Frederick.
1914. Smith, Frederick Elliott.
1912. Smith, Frederick John.
1919. Smith, George Edward.
1922. Smith, George Harold.
*1905. Smith, George Holmes.
1922. Smith, George Richards.
1912. Smith, Grantley.
1901. Smith, Harold.
1913. Smith, Herbert Leslie.
1919. Smith, Hugh Muir.
1921. Smith, James Stuart.
1863. Smith, John Alexander.
*1886. Smith, John Percy.
1923. Smith, Joseph Edward Bernard.
1915. Smith, Leonard.
1888. Smith, Leonard Charles.
1913. Smith, Leslie Bacchus.
1898. Smith, Percy Lambert.
1896. Smith, Sidney.
1916. Smith, Stanley Gordon.
*1899. Smith, Sydney Calvin.
1922. Smith, Sydney George.
1909. Smith, Theodore Victor.
1907. Smith, Thomas Lionel.
*1897. Smith, Thomas William.
1897. Smith, Victor George.
1922. Smith, William Garraway.
1903. Smithard, Walter Reginald Norman.
2695

1923. Smitheringale, Charles Robert.
1923. Smuts, Louis.
*1905. Smyth, Francis Radway.
1923. Smyth, Kathleen Corisande.
1908. Solomon, Edgar Eaton.
1902. Solomon, William Harry.
1923. Somers, Maurice Raymond.
1894. Soper, Frank Arthur.
1904. Soper, George Edward.
1902. Soper, Norman Bowden.
*1906. Southern, Walter Duckett.
1916. Southwell, Cecil Stanley.
1920. Southwood, Stuart Walter.
1923. Soutter, Joseph Lister.
1916. Soutter, Mansfield John Knox.
1909. Spain, Harold Gordon.
1907. Spain, Ivan Scott.
1905. Spaven, Arthur Thomas.
1916. Speak, John.
1895. Spencer, George Ross.
*1920. Spencer-Payne, Arthur Llewellyn.
1919. Spendelow, Cyril Wells.
1911. Spill, Alfred Edmund Victor.
1901. Spiller, John Edmund.
1903. Spiridion-Kliszczewski, Clement
        Grant.
*1892. Spokes, Peter Sidney.
1917. Spong, Robert William.
1919. Spouse, Herbert Augustus.
*1902. Sprawson, Evelyn Charles.
*1904. Sprawson, Francis Edgar.
1906. Spray, Albert.
1889. Spray, George Goldfinch.
1923. Sprong, Ernest Lodewijk.
1909. Spurgeon, Eric Le Masurier.
1903. Spurgeon, Ernest Le Masurier.
1891. Spurr, Alfred Peter.
1894. Stabb, Edward William.
1903. Stacey, Attilio Regolo.
1910. Stacey, Claud.
1921. Stafford, Arthur.
1897. Stainer, Courtenay Biffin.
*1913. Staley, Robert Cyril Wilmer.
1917. Stamp, Sidney.
1905. Staniforth, Henry Edward.
1906. Stansfield, Greenwood.
1901. Staple, Arthur Hubert.
1913. Stark, Thomas William.
1905. Starr, Oran Edgar.
1896. Staton, Henry Hamilton.
1923. Stay, Frederic John.
*1902. Steadman, Sidney Fras. St. Jermain.
1915. Stebbings, Hedley Victor.
1916. Stebbings, John Morley.
1921. Steele, Richard Reginald.
1892. Steele, Tom Barton.
1898. Stelfox, Walter Edmund.
2751

1906. Stephen, Thomas Cowley.
1922. Stephens, Anne Myfanwy.
1903. Stephens, Bernard Maxwell.
1912. Stephens, Hugh Dynevor.
1896. Stephenson, John.
1900. Stephenson, Thomas.
1919. Sterwin. Rodney Fredk. Jarrett.
1900. Stevens, Alfred Montague Austin.
1922. Stevens, Charles Henry.
1895. Stevens, David Sydney.
1903. Stevens, Ernest Oxley.
1922. Stevens, Frank Burdett.
1903. Stevens, John.
*1871. Stevens, Mordaunt Augustus de
          Brouquens Capel.
1896. Stevens, Richard Henry.
1913. Stevens, Stanley.
1903. Stevens, William Stewart.
1901. Stewart, Cameron Robertson.
1916. Stewart, Samuel Ogden.
1901. Steweni, George Henshall.
1923. Steyn, Hermanus Christiaan.
1894. Steynor, Arnold William.
1900. Steynor, Herbert Steynor.
1921. Stiven, Frank Watson.
*1910. Stobie, Harry.
*1891. Stocken, Leslie Maury.
1889. Stoddart, Walter George.
1922. Stofberg, Daniel Jordaan.
1901. Stokes, Percy Southwell.
*1898. Stone, Frederick William Stanley.
*1892. Stoner, Harold Boniface.
1887. Stoner, Harry John.
1910. Stoner, Patrick Barry.
1914. Stones. Hubert Horace.
*1903. Stordy, Thomas.
1905. Storey, Christopher John.
1897. Storey, George William.
1909. Storey, Stanley Runton.
1913. Stradling, Frank Bedford.
1912. Stranack, Whalley Seath.
*1895. Strand, Alick Condell.
1922. Strange, Thomas Neville.
1896. Strangways, Ludlow.
1914. Straton, Norman David Swayne.
1903. Street, Elgernon George.
1922. Stretton, John William.
1916. Stretton, Thomas Charles.
1913. Strickland, Harold John.
1922. Strickland, John Newby.
1922. Strickland, Weatherill Abbott.
1915. Stride, William Henry Barton.
1898. Stringfellow, Ernest.
1902. Stroud, Alfred Charles.
1921. Stuart, George Murrell.
1909. Stuart. James Alfred Wyllys.
1881. Stuck, Thomas James.
          2807

1911. Sturdee, Frank Percival.
1899. Sturridge, Ernest.
1920. Sturridge, Frank Alexander Leslie.
1921. Sturridge, Montague Hylton Galway.
1916. Sturridge, Vera Elsie Marie.
1910. Sturton, Harry.
1897. Styer, Albert St. John.
*1912. Styles, William Vere Taylor.
1911. Suffield, William.
1903. Sugden, John.
1895. Sugden, Thomas Edward.
1893. Sumerling, Arthur Newton.
1897. Sumerling, Bertram James.
1897. Summers, Gilbert Hamilton.
1922. Sunderland, Verney Leo.
1923. Sutcliffe, Harold Percival.
1915. Sutcliffe, Joseph Gilbert Wade.
1907. Sutcliffe, Percy Sidney Charles.
1923. Sutherland, Janet Helen Muriel.
1923. Sutton, Denton Redvers.
1911. Sutton, Gordon Bower.
1907. Swan, William Marshall.
1900. Swannell, Richard Pancoast.
1863. Swanson, Andrew Isles.
1903. Sykes, Alfred.
*1915. Symons, Percival Washington.

T.

1891. Ta'Bois, Frederick William.
1893. Ta'Bois, Leopold.
1910. Tait, Ernest Sutton.
1908. Tait, Harold Pearson.
*1900. Talbot, Francis.
1894. Talintyre, Charles.
1892. Tanner, Frank Leopold.
1912. Tanner, Reginald Douglas.
1902. Targett, Frederick William.
1901. Tarry, Charles Robert James.
1896. Tasker, Benjamin George.
1908. Tasker, Dudley Bayzand.
1898. Tattersall, Harold.
1899. Tattersfield, William Henry.
1878. Taylor, Arthur.
1904. Taylor, Charles Lancelot Deslandes.
1921. Taylor, Charles Sidney.
1910. Taylor, Claude.
1906. Taylor, Cyprian Herbert.
1894 Taylor, Edwin Henry Pascal.
1905. Taylor, George Frederick.
1895. Taylor, Harry Percy.
1891. Taylor, Harry William.
1905. Taylor, Hedley Hargreaves.
1902. Taylor, John Hardy.
1899. Taylor, Lionel.
          2859

1922. Taylor, Rowland Cecil.
1912. Taylor, Sidney Thomas.
1898. Taylor, Wallace Atkinson.
1922. Taylor, William Henry.
1922. Taylour, Alec.
1896. Tebbitt, Ernest Reginald.
1905. Tebbutt, Edwin Spencer.
1901. Tessier, Charles Padgitt.
1906. Tessier, Norman York.
1882. Tester, Alfred Horace.
1902. Thacker, Harold.
1895. Theakston, Joseph.
1922. Theron, Louis Naude.
1908. Thew, Wilton.
1916. Thom, Michael Christian Vos.
1913. Thomas, Cecil Ernest.
1897. Thomas, Charles Browne.
1922. Thomas, Charles William Fowler.
1923. Thomas, David Egerton.
1913. Thomas, Eric Wesley.
*1915. Thomas, Graham McKim.
1898. Thomas, William Hendy.
1908. Thomason, Arthur Brookes.
1905. Thompson, Wilfred Boyd.
1912. Thompson, William Andrew.
1887. Thomson, Archibald Fredk. Charles.
1883. Thomson, George.
1903. Thomson, Harold.
1918. Thomson, Ian Murray.
1914. Thorman, Frederick Edward Alan.
1879. Thorman, Frederick James.
1915. Thorn, Harry Laurence.
1914. Thorne, Donald.
1909. Thornton, Herbert.
1894. Thornton, Robert.
1904. Throp, Frank.
1914. Thurston, Vernon John.
1908. Tibbalds, William Edgar Antonius.
1862. Tibbits, William.
1902. Tice, Ernest Harriman.
1895. Tice, Henry William.
1915. Tighe, John Alphonsus.
1897. Tilley, Edgar.
*1901. Tilley, James Leonard Octavius.
1889. Timms, Samuel Day.
1894. Timms, Walter Thomas Day.
*1905. Timpson, George Gilbert.
1895. Tindal, John.
1905. Tindall, Herbert John.
1912. Tipper, Francis Joseph.
1907. Tippet, Aubrey Collins.
1892. Tisdall, Charles James.
*1905. Titmas, John St. Andrew.
1913. Titmas, Oscar Henry.
*1888. Todd, Frederick.
‡1869. Tomes, Charles Sissmore.
1908. Tomes, Edgar Arthur.
2916

1903. Tomey, Edmund Vaughan.
1905. Tomlinson, Henry Harrison.
1893. Tomlinson, John William.
1890. Tomlyn, Louis Crowhurst.
*1921. Tonkin, Beltie Moorwood.
1900. Toogood, Albert Edward.
1894. Torpey, Herbert James.
1881. Tothill, Walter.
1892. Townend, Edmund Francis.
1917. Townley, Sydney Granville.
1906. Townsend. James Garfield.
1901. Townsend, Lewis William.
1911. Townshend, Oliver Beale.
1923. Trace, Lawrence Archibald.
1898. Tracy, Duncan Powerscourt.
*1904. Tracy, Horace Ernest Humphrey.
1922. Trafford, Philip George.
1922. Travis, Walter Geoffrey.
1913. Treleaven, Harold.
1908. Tressider, Samuel Lewis.
*1894. Trewby, Henry William.
1895. Trick, Walter Henry.
1909. Trott, Arthur George.
1892. Trott, Frederick Thomas.
1884. Trott, George William.
1903. Trotter, Arthur Oscar.
*1911. Trounce, Thomas Reginald.
1905. Trude, Henry John.
*1881. Truman, Charles Edwin.
1916. Truman, Frederick Charles.
1918. Trusscott, William Wallace Harold.
1905. Tuck, William Collingwood.
1923. Tucker, Percival Albert.
1905. Tuckett, Francis James.
1912. Tuit, Arthur Cyril.
1922. Tunstall, Arthur Folliott.
1922. Turley, Frederick Ernest.
1922. Turner, Charles Edgar.
1897. Turner, Edward Ernest.
1912. Turner, Ernest Victor Breen.
1892. Turner, Harold Arthur.
1896. Turner, Henry Watson.
1903. Turner, James Dewhurst.
1890. Turner, Joseph George.
1913. Turner, Robert Douglas Breen.
1918. Turner, Stanley Carlyle.
*1921. Turner, Walter Aslatt.
1918. Turner, William Henry.
1895. Turton, Arthur William.
1902. Turton, Charles Mitchinson.
1904. Turton, Ernest Henry.
1912. Tustian, Thomas Bernice.
1921. Tweney, Harold Christopher.
1899. Tweney, Sidney James St. Helier.
1919. Tweney, Stanley Ethelbert.
1894. Tyrrell, Albert John.
1911. Tyson, Basil William.
2973

U.

1898. Umney, Reginald.
*1913. Underwood, Arthur Bayford Guy.
1918. Underwood, Richard Murray.
1923. Urbani, Cyril Philip.
1923. Urquhart, John Leslie Thisdelton.
1922. Urwin, George Frederick.
1899. Uttley, Edgar Preston.

V.

1921. Valette, Charles Pierre Marie.
1922. Van der Hoven, Frederick Walter.
1923. Van der Merwe, Gert Michael R.
1888. van der Pant, Francis Henry Morgan.
1923. van der Pant, Francis Neville.
1894. Van der Pant, Horace William.
1919. Van der Pant, Leslie Horace.
1919. Van der Spuy, David Cornelius.
1923. van Dockum, Ingeborg Marie.
1922. Van Dyck, Edwin Albert.
1922. Van Geuns, Rudolf.
1922. van Niekerk, Arnold Klosser.
1915. Van Schalkwijk, Petrus Lafras.
1921. Van Zyl, Harold.
*1871. Vasey, Charles Lyon.
1922. Vaughan, Maldwyn.
1899. Vaughan, Thomas Herbert.
1905. Vaughan, William Westland.
1913. Veale, Reginald McKenzie.
1895. Veitch, William McGregor.
1912. Venning, George Lotan.
1899. Venning, Sidney Dunstan.
1922. Verheyden, Walravine Johanna.
1915. Vernon, Herbert.
1903. Vernon, Thomas.
1923. Vidler, John George Holdbrooke.
1923. Vignale, Otho Rudolf.
1915. Viljoen, Willem Jacobus Rousseau.
1899. Vincent, George Gray.
1919. Vincent, Ina Valentine.
1904. Vine, Frederick Stockman.
1922. Vinsen, Alec George.
1907. Visick, Hedley Clarence.
1901. Visick, Herbert Clarence.
1916. Vogt, Herbert Victor.
1904. Vosper, Frederick.
1920. Vowles, Edward Francis.

W.

1911. Wade, Walter Colin.
1911. Wain, Douglas.
1912. Wakley, Percy James.

3020

1915. Waldman, William Harold.
1896. Wale, Samuel Thomas.
1897. Walker, Alfred William.
1908. Walker, Andrew Robertson.
*1897. Walker, Arthur West.
1919. Walker, Enid.
1893. Walker, Frank.
1923. Walker, Frederick Aubrey.
1891. Walker, Frederick Vincent.
1912. Walker, Harold.
1908. Walker, Harold.
1922. Walker, Henry.
1923. Walker, Vernon Dudley.
1900. Walkington, Thomas.
1923. Wall, Redvers Percy.
1915. Wallace, Frederick Harry.
1895. Wallace, James Sim.
1891. Waller, Robert Edward.
1909. Wallis, Augustus Vallack.
1903. Wallis, Charles Doswell.
*1897. Wallis, Charles Edward.
1900. Wallis, David Henderson.
1897. Wallis, Elton George Whishaw.
1893. Wallis, Ferdinand Hammans.
1911. Wallis, Frank Roland.
1916. Wallis, Hampdon.
1903. Wallis, Harold Whishaw.
1895. Wallis, Herbert.
1903. Wallis, Ross.
*1923. Wallis, Vernon Montague.
1923. Walmsley, Eric Stanley.
1922. Walters, Hermanus Johannes.
1922. Walters, Philippus Jacobs.
1902. Walton, John Walker.
1907. Ward, Alexander Ivan.
1897. Ward, Frank.
1921. Ward, Herbert Read.
1912. Ward, John James.
1909. Ward, Reginald Wildblood.
1922. Warden, Sorab Byramji.
1912. Wardill, Harold.
1909. Wardill, Joseph Jackson.
1916. Waring, Maurice Harold.
1899. Warlow, Frank.
1913. Warner, Geoffrey Heegaard.
1914. Warner, Norman Steffan Heegaard.
1905. Warner, Reginald Geo. Heegaard.
1923. Warner, Richard Oliver.
1906. Warren, Gladstone.
1921. Warren, John William Ernest.
1869. Washbourn, Edward Norman.
1916. Waters, Robert Augustus.
1922. Watkins, Henry Herbert.
1904. Watkins, Howel Trevor.
1909. Watson, Alexander MacDonald.
*1891. Watson, Charles Henry.
1911. Watson, Clifford Toulson.

3077

1902. Watson, Frank.
1905. Watson, Ingram Ernest.
1900. Watson, Jacob Louis.
1916. Watson, Maurice Gustave.
1894. Watson, Robert.
1922. Watt, Frederick William.
1915. Watterson, Eleanor Cannell.
1893. Watts, George William.
1923. Watts, John Weldon.
1922. Wayman, Hector.
1901. Wayte, Walter Alexander.
*1903. Weakley, Alfred James.
*1921. Weakley, Joseph Frederick.
1906. Weaver, Bargrave Lancelot.
1903. Weaver, Edward Alfred.
1910. Weaver, Edward Algernon.
1906. Webb, Arthur Ernest.
1893. Webb, Gerald Bertram.
1900. Webb, Humfrey John.
1912. Webb, Stanley Joseph Frederick.
1908. Webb, William Thomas Clarkson.
1923. Webber, Arnold Richard.
1923. Webster, Horace James Veals.
*1888. Webster, Percy Lawrance.
1905. Webster, Reginald Cecil.
*1868. Webster, Ridley Manning.
1889. Wedgwood, Herbert Williamson.
1922. Weedon, Charles William.
1905. Weighell, Henry Johnson.
1876. Weiss, Felix Henri.
1879. Weiss, Willoughby Gaspard.
1891. Welham, George William.
*1914. Wells, Clement John Lethbridge.
1921. Wells, Norman Buist.
1914. Welton, Frank Edward.
1911. West, Charles Frederick Marling.
1898. West, Ernest William.
1905. Westmorland, Joseph Hindle.
1892. Weston, Ernest.
1897. Westron, Henry.
1922. Whateley, Leo Ferdinand Charles C.
1878. Whatford, Frederick Russell.
1875. Whatford, Jack Henry.
1896. Wheeler, Ernest Alfred.
1901. Wheeler, Sydney.
1916. Wheldon, George William.
1920. Whelpton, Leonard Gould.
1902. Whitaker, John Ambrose.
1905. Whitaker, Thomas.
1913. White, Arthur.
1914. White, Clarence Leslie Brunel.
*1903. White, Ernest.
1899. White, Eustace Beaumont Lathbury.
1919. White, Graham Arthur Osborne.
1915. White, Marjorie Jane.
1913. White, Reginald Wallace.
*1869. White, Richard Wentworth.
1923.   3134

1907. White, Robert Graham.
1912. White, Sidney.
1920. White, Stanley Vernon.
1900. White, William.
*1900. Whitehouse, Alfred Landon Walter.
1908. Whiteley, William Frederick.
1901. Whitlow, Herbert Leslie.
1922. Whittaker, Alfred Stanley.
1886. Whittaker, George Oldham.
1914. Whitten, Maurice George.
1899. Whittington, John Albert.
1909. Whittington, Walter William.
1896. Whittington, William Borrett.
1921. Whittle, James Andrew.
1892. Whittles, John Dencer.
1914. Whitworth, Arthur Stuart.
1903. Whitworth, James William.
1911. Whitworth, William Henry.
1919. Whybro, Ronald Harold Vivian.
1900. Widdowson, Thomas William.
1921. Wiggins, Alan Kingsley.
1920. Wight, Lauder Lylestone.
1909. Wild, George Kerry.
1911. Wiles, John Herbert.
1899. Wilkes, John Hamilton.
1911. Wilkinson, Alan Ayscough.
1914. Wilkinson, Geoffrey Legh.
1898. Wilkinson, Thomas Henry.
1901. Wilkinson, William Franklin.
1910. Wilkinson, William Jefferson.
1899. Willcox, Samuel Joseph.
1921. Wille, Thomas Daniel.
1902. Willey, Edgar Arthur.
1921. Williams, Alun Gruffydd.
1917. Williams, Alfred.
1905. Williams, Alfred Owen.
1921. Williams, Arthur Idwal.
1922. Williams, Cecil.
1911. Williams, Charles Eustace.
1895. Williams, Charles Henry Hughes.
1913. Williams, Edgar Roskelly.
*1877. Williams, Edward Lloyd.
1893. Williams, George.
1877. Williams, Harold.*
1836. Williams, Herbert.
1899. Williams, Herbert Gill.
*1885. Williams, Hugh Lloyd.
1909. Williams, Hugh Parry.
1902. Williams, Ivor Thomas.
1904. Williams, James Herbert.
1903. Williams, John.
1915. Williams, Leslie.
1913. Williams, Malcolm Lloyd.
1916. Williams, Percy.
1922. Williams, Philip Harding.
1897. Williams, Sidney Herbert.
1901. Williams, Sidney James.
                3191   2 A

1885. Williams, Tom Gill.
*1904. Williams, William Hubert.
1922. Williams, William James.
1914. Williams, William Thomas.
1909. Williamson, Douglas Herbert Walker.
1921. Willis, George Samuel William.
1920. Willis, William Herbert.
1910. Willows, Frederick Charles.
1910. Wills, Thomas Edwin.
1907. Willsher, William Hubert.
1897. Wilmore, Walter.
1917. Wilshere, George.
1915. Wilshere, Roger Gilbert.
1919. Wilson, Cecil Alexander.
1897. Wilson, Charles Albert.
1922. Wilson, Charles Bennett.
1911. Wilson, Charles Henry.
1905. Wilson, Francis Raymond.
1897. Wilson, George Edward.
1920. Wilson, George William.
1922. Wilson, Lindsay William.
1922. Wilson, Melmoth Blundell.
1919. Wilson, Thomas Alexander Moffat.
1922. Wilson, Wilfrid Hugh.
*1900. Winckworth, Harold Charles.
1913. Windemer, Leonard Duncan.
1898. Winder, Harry.
1900. Winder, Reuben Archibald.
1923. Windsor, Walter Astley.
1923. Winer, Samuel.
1897. Wing, John Clifford.
1922. Winn, Thomas Leith.
1914. Winstanley, Edgar Joseph.
1915. Winter, George Rodney.
1904. Winter, Percy Gibson Deslandes.
‡1878. Winterbottom, Augustus.
1899. Witcomb, Charles Frederick.
*1914. Withers, Samuel Anthony.
1921. Withers, Thomas Everett.
1922. Wolfendale, William Atkinson.
1905. Wolfenden, Albert Blagbrough.
1913. Wolfenden, Harold Vincent.
1913. Wolff, Herman.
*1917. Wolff, Robert.
1898. Wolter, Ernest Alfred.
1880. Wonfor, Thomas Walter Cropley.
1902. Wood, Arthur Exley.
1898. Wood, Bryan Jardine.
1897. Wood, Charles Carey.
1901. Wood, Colin Dawson.
1921. Wood, Cyril Blake.
1905. Wood, George Edmund.
*1895. Wood, James.
1916. Wood, James Thomson.
1889. Wood, Robert Ernest.
1907. Wood, Rowland Talbot.
*1893. Wood, Walter Robert.

1922. Woodbridge, Oswald Howard M.
1892. Woodcock, Richard Ernest.
1921. Woodford, Frank.
1909. Woodhouse, Henry Alfred.
*1886. Woodhouse, Joseph.
1920. Woodroffe, Bernard Charles.
1910. Woodruff, Charles Reynolds.
1876. Woodruff, William Herbert.
1902. Woods, Edward Cuthbert.
1894. Woods, Joseph Ainsworth, O.B.E.
1916. Woods, Samuel Hamilton.
1878. Woodward, Francis Herbert.
1919. Wookey, Eric Edgar.
1903. Wooldridge, Hubert John de Burgh.
1890. Woolf, Michael Yeatman.
1906. Woolford, George.
1922. Woolley, Frederick Henry.
1901. Wooster, Percy William.
1906. Wootton, Aubrey Geer.
*1908. Worboys, Thomas Sanders.
1905. Wordsworth, Howard.
1899. Workman, Joseph.
1908. Wormald, Ronald Martin.
1904. Wormald, William John.
1903. Worsley, John Gillins.
1919. Worth, Harry Mullins.
1916. Wotton, Walter Reginald.
1910. Wotton, William Hector.
1886. Wright, Charles Frederick.
1906. Wright, Ernest.
1900. Wright, Harold Simpson.
1916. Wright, James Alfred Snarey.
*1914. Wright, John Edward.
*1914. Wright, Leslie Douglas.
1906. Wright, Stephen John.
1918. Wright, Sydney Molero.
1901. Wright, William.
1923. Wyatt, Benjamin Thomas.
1922. Wyatt, Edward Leslie.
1901. Wyatt, Herbert John.

Y.

1905. Yates, Ralph Greatrex.
1915. Yeoman, John Clark.
1910. Yerbury, Edgar Olyve.
*1914. Yonge, Francis Bernard.
1911. Yonge, George Trevor.
*1915. Young, Alfred Ernest.
1894. Young, Ernest Edward.

Z.

1923. Zobel, William Edward.
1923. Zondagh, George.
1923. Zondagh, Ignatius Michael.

DIPLOMATES IN PUBLIC HEALTH.

The Diploma in Public Health is granted conjointly with the ROYAL COLLEGE OF PHYSICIANS OF LONDON.

Diplomates marked † are not Fellows or Members of the College.

A.

1891. Acton, Charles James.
†1911. Adam, Scott Campbell.
1894. Adams, Edmund Weaver.
1892. Adams, Percy Targett.
†1890. Adie, Alexander James.
†1912. Agrawal, Ram Swarup.
1921. Alderson, Percy Francis.
†1892. Aldridge, Arthur Russell.
†1890. Aldridge, Norman Elliott.
1888. Alexander, Frederick William.
1895. Allen, Sydney Glenn.
†1909. Allison, Andrew.
†1900. Allison, John.
1923. Allnutt, Edward Bruce.
†1920. Anderson, Lewis.
†1902. Armstrong, Pattison.
†1902. Arnold, Frank Arthur.
1893. Atkinson, Arthur Edward.
1912. Atkinson, Arthur George.
†1914. Atkinson, Estelle Irene Elgin.
1905. Atkinson, Jackson Arthur.
1914. Atlee, Charles Nelson.

B.

1889. Bailey, Charles Frederick.
1919. Bailey, Lionel Danyers.
1892. Bailey, William Henry.
†1911. Baillie, David Main.
1891. Bain, David Stuart Erskine.
†1921. Baker, Madeleine Stuart.
1918. Baker, Stephen Leonard.
1909. Ball, Alfred.
1913. Balme, Harold.
. 1913. Balthasar, Ewald Mouat.
†1905. Bankart, Arthur Reginald, M.V.O.
†1907. Banks, Alexander Gray.
1894. Banks, Alfred.
†1914. Bannister, William Jacob.
†1894. Barbeau, Louis Gabriel.
1910. Barber, Alec.

38

†1912. Barbour, Thomas.
†1922. Bardhan, Sarojini Nath.
1919. Barker, Malcolm.
1903. Barratt, Herbert James.
1910. Barry, Thomas David Collis.
†1923. Basa, Phanindra Nath.
1896. Bartlett, Felix Paul.
1896. Batchelor, George Arthur.
1921. Batchelor, Tremlett Brewer.
†1909. Beamish, James Aylmer.
1908. Beards, Clifford.
1917. Beaumont, George Ernest.
1918. Beaumont, Norah.
1912. Beet, William Ashley.
†1913. Bell, Arthur Francis.
1903. Bell, John.
†1914. Bell, Whiteford John Edward.
1911. Bennett, Claude John Eddowes.
1903. Bennett, James.
1902. Bennett, Kenneth Hugh.
†1907. Bennetts, Harold Graves.
†1921. Betenson, Wm. Francis Whitaker.
1907. Betenson, Woodley Daniel.
†1909. Bethune, Robert James.
†1913. Bethune, William.
1889. Bevan, Richard.
1913. Bharucha, Jamasp Cursetji.
†1920. Bharucha, Kaikhushroo Maneckji.
†1910. Bhúshan, Kul.
1923. Binning, William McHutchinson.
1920. Bird, Geoffrey Andrew.
1896. Birdwood, Gordon Travers.
†1919. Birnie, George Alexander.
1906. Birt, Amelius Cyril.
†1914. Biswas, Lalit Mohou.
†1905. Blackham, Robt. James.
†1907. Blacklock, Breadalbane.
1913. Blackmore, Herbert Stuart.
†1904. Blackwell, Charles Thomas.
1923. Blackwell, Ursula Ponsett.
1912. Blaker, Percy Stanley.
†1914. Bloom, Arthur.
1909. Bolus, Harry Boulcott.
1890. Bond, Charles Knox.

82   2 A 2

1896. Bond, Charles Shaw.
†1889. Bond, Frederick Fielding.
†1916. Bond, Reginald St. George.
†1917. Borland, Vynne.
†1923. Boul, William Thomas Gardthorpe.
1897. Boulton, Arthur.
1911. Boulton, Harold.
1923. Bourdillon, Lancelot Gerard.
1907. Bourke, Isidore McWilliam.
†1920. Bourne, Eleanor Elizabeth.
1921. Bowen, George James.
†1922. Bowen, John Edmund.
1896. Bowen-Jones, Lloyd Middleton.
1898. Box, Stanley Longhurst.
†1921. Boyce, William Wallace.
†1912. Bracey, Herbert Charles Horace.
1922. Brachman, David Simon.
†1914. Bradbury, Samuel.
1909. Bradley, Clement Henry Burton.
1921. Braine, John Francis Carter.
†1891. Braja, João Francisco.
1896. Branthwaite, Robert Welsh.
†1902. Bray, Ernest James.
†1923. Brereton, Maeve Cluna.
1904. Brewer, Dunstan.
1904. Bridger, James Frederick Edmund.
1902. Brincker, John Augustus Herman.
1897. Brind, Harry Hanslow.
†1923. Brodziak, Frank Adolphus James.
1911. Brohier, Samuel Lindsay.
1890. Brook, Henry Darvill.
1923. Brookman, Hubert.
†1903. Brown, Edwin Harold.
†1908. Brown, Henry Martyn.
†1911. Brown, Herbert Maughan.
†1894. Brown, Richard King.
1918. Brown, Thomas Frederick.
1892. Bryett, Lewis Thomas Fraser.
1920. Buckell, Monamy Aston Cornwall.
†1923. Burt, Alida Charlotte.
†1898. Butler, William.
1913. Butler, William Harold.
†1922. Butt, Abdul Hamid.

C.

1904. Caddy, Adrian.
†1906. Caird, Henry.
†1923. Cairney, Maude Cristine.
†1904. Caldwell, Alfred George.
1920. Calthrop, Gordon Thomas.
†1910. Cameron, Robert.
1921. Campbell, Duncan.
†1905. Campbell, Niel.
†1903. Candler, John Pycock.
1920. Cane, Arthur Skelding.
135

1923. Carleton, Alan William.
1923. Carpenter, Hayward.
†1912. Carrick, James.
1909. Carter, Arthur Burnell.
1898. Carter, Godfrey.
1898. Cartwright, Ernest Henry.
1920. Cass, Kathleen Lydia.
†1921. Caton, John Wilfrid.
1921. Catto, Henry William.
1911. Cave, Percy Norman.
1910. Cazaly, William Henry.
1917. Chacin-Itriago, Luis Gregorio.
1914. Chand, Hari.
†1915. Chandry, Kishori Lál.
†1902. Charpentier, Ambrose Edward Lea.
†1904. Chatterjee, Basanta Kumar.
1923. Cheater, George William.
1917. Chellappah, Seemampillai Francis.
†1922. Chenoy, Cali Feroze.
1906. Chesson, Herbert.
†1914. Child, Armando Dumas.
1895. Childs, Christopher.
†1899. Chitale, Vinazak Narayan.
†1915. Chohan, Noormahomed Kasembhai.
†1922. Choksy, Kaikushru Nusserwanjee.
†1895. Chown, Francis.
†1913. Chubb, Elsie Mary.
1911. Clapham, Roderic Arthur.
1904. Clapham, Stanley Cornell.
†1909. Clark, James.
†1910. Clark, John Thomson.
1903. Clark, Richard Foster.
1920. Clarke, Fredk. Adderley Howard.
†1910. Clarke, James Kilian.
†1912. Clayton, Robert Vickers.
†1904. Clements, John Matthewson.
†1923. Clyde, David.
†1921. Cochrane, George.
1923. Cockayne, Alan Andreas.
1904. Cole, John William Edward.
†1920. Cole, Thomas Philips.
1912. Collins, Francis Garland.
1914. Collins, Robert Edward.
1906. Collyns, John Moore.
1904. Comerford, Beaumont Harry.
1921. Comyn, Kenneth.
1922. Connan, Donald Murray.
1912. Cooke, Francis Gerrard Hamilton.
†1913. Cooke, William Edmund.
1890. Cooper, Ardaseer Dossabhoy.
1894. Cooper, Dossabhoy Nowrojee.
†1896. Cope, Albert Ernest.
1889. Copeman, Sydney Arthur Monckton.
†1906. Corcoran, Gerald.
†1923. Cotter, Edward.
1905. Courtauld, Louis.
1912. Cowasjee, Maneckjee Merwanjee.
192

1900. Cowburn, Arthur Douglas.
1922. Cowperthwaite, Elsie Eleanor.
1912. Cox, Frank Elton.
1923. Cox, Ursula Beatrice.
1891. Coxwell, Charles Fillingham.
†1910. Craig, James Crawford.
†1902. Crawford, George Morris.
1893. Cresswell, Richard.
†1923. Cronin, Archibald Joseph.
1891. Cropley, Alfred.
1891. Cropley, Henry.
1890. Cross, Robert George
1909. Cullen, James Alfred Patrick.
†1905. Cullen, John.
†1906. Cumpston, John Howard Lidgett.

D.

1920. D'Abreu, Delphine Gertrude.
1916. Dalal, Ratonjee Dinshaw.
†1914. Dalby, Marjorie Eva.
1892. Daniel, William Patrick Taylour.
†1888. Dantri, Sorabshaw Hormasji.
1898. Darabseth, Naoroji Beramji.
†1915. Das, Ram.
†1922. Dasgupta, Arunkumar.
†1922. Dasgupta, Bhupes Chandra.
1912. Daukes, Sidney Herbert.
†1889. Dávar, Framroz Shàvakshá.
1899. Davey, Samuel.
1904. David, Archibald Sinclair.
†1903. Davidson, Alexander Gordon.
†1917. Davies, Herbert.
1911. Davies, John Phillip Henry.
†1922. Davies, Purser.
1904. Davies, Walter Ernest Llewellyn.
†1914. Davy, Rose Lilian Humphry.
1922. Dawe, Charles Henry.
†1911. Dawson, Alexander.
†1922. Dawson, Frederick Walter Whitney.
†1919. Day, Cyril Douglas.
1902. Day, James John.
1913. Delmege, James Anthony.
1901. Denyer, Stanley Edward, C.M.G.
†1900. De Wytt, William Henry.
1921. de Zilva, Irving Gerald.
1917. Dia, Mostafa.
†1899. Dickson, John Rhodes.
†1903. Divine, Thomas.
†1920. Dobbie, John Nairn.
1899. Dodd, Frederick Lawson.
1899. Dodd, John Richard.
1918. Dominick, Gnanayndam M.
1896. Dorrell, Edmund Arthur.
1902. Douglas, Archibald Robert John.
1911. Douglas, Reginald Inglis.
245

†1900. Dove, Rolland Atkinson.
1894. Dow, William Alexander.
1904. Downton, Arthur Sydney.
1919. Drake, John Alexander.
1904. Dryland, Leslie Winter.
†1913. Dube, Hari Shankar.
†1911. Dube, Kali Charan.
1922. Duck, William Agar Scholefield.
1920. Dudley, Sheldon Francis.
†1920. Dukes, Cuthbert Esquire, O.B.E.
†1923. Duncan, John Alfred Alexander.
1914. Dunkerton, Norman Edwin.
†1914. Dunn, Cuthbert Lindsay.
1903. Dunne, Arthur Briggs.
1913. Dunstan, Walter Robert.
†1912. Dupont, George Henry.
†1892. Duthie, Robert Campbell.
1891. Dyer, Sidney Reginald.
†1913. Dykes, Andrew Leslie.
1898. Dymott, Donald Frederick.

E.

1920. Eades, Reginald Oliver.
†1907. Eckersley, Edwin.
1921. Edmonds, Arthur William Foster.
†1897. Edwards, Henry James.
1923. Edwards, Richard Tudor.
†1914. Egan, William.
†1902. Elkington, John Simeon Colebrook.
1922. El-Kirdany, Aly Mohammad.
†1892. Elliot, Andrew.
1911. Elliot, William Hy. Wilson, D.S.O.
1922. Ellis, Harold.
†1902. Ellis, William Charles.
†1914. Emerson, Henry Horace Andrews.
†1923. English, Geoffrey Dix.
†1914. Erlank, James.
†1897. Erskine, Alexander McConnell.
1893. Etches, William Robert.
1891. Evans, Evan.
†1920. Evans, Harry.
1897. Evans, John Morton.
1908. Evans, Robert Cecil Turle.
†1909. Evans, Thomas.

F.

1922. Fagan, Richard Feltrim.
†1904. Faichnie, Norman.
1906. Fairbairn, Sidney Herbert.
†1912. Fairfield, Josephine Letitia Denny.
†1909. Fairley, James.
†1912. Fairlie, William Miller.
†1904. Falconer, Alexander Robertson.
1919. Falk, Herman.
295

1900. Falkener, Lyon.
†1915. Fankhauser, Herbert William.
1891. Farmer, Septimus.
1920. Fawcett, Hugh Anderson.
†1893. Fawcett, William Herbert.
1907. Fell, Matthew Henry Gregson.
†1914. Féré, Maud Tresilian.
1913. Ferguson, Archibald.
1907. Ferguson, Robert Bruce.
1891. Field, Oliver.
1893. Fielden, William Eckett.
†1900. Finch, Hugh Earnshaw.
†1922. Findlay, Harry Taylor.
†1910. Findlay, John.
1891. Firth, Robert Hammil.
1894. Footner, John Bulkley.
1902. Foster, Henry Bertram.
1899. Foster, Michael Bernard.
1900. Foulerton, Harry Percival.
†1899. Fowler, George.
1905. Fox, John William.
1920. Fox, Walter Egbert.
†1907. Foy, Harry Andrew.
†1908. Francis, Thomas Evans.
1904. Freeman, Ernest Carrick.
1904. Freer, Gerald Dudley.
†1909. Freer, Robert Mylcraine.
1902. Fremantle, Francis Edward.
1895. Fremlin, Heaver Stuart.
†1901. Frengley, Joseph Patrick.
1891. Frost, Francis Turner.
1914. Fry, Arthur Brownfield.
1920. Fry, Hubert John Burgess.
1909. Fry, Walter Ernest.
1920. Fuller, Andrew Radburne.
†1921. Fuller, Thomas Arthur.

G.

1900. Gadgil, Shridhar Bheekajee.
1914. Galbraith, Colin James.
†1908. Galbraith, ErnestEdwd.ScottJoseph
1923. Gamgee, Katherine Mary Lovell.
†1921. Gândhi, Kaikhooshru Ardesheer.
†1897. Gardiner, Peter.
†1913. Garrow, Robert Philip.
1913. Gaskell, Arthur.
1921. Gasperine, John Jones.
1892. Gay, John.
1921. Geffen, Dennis Herbert.
1922. Geffen, Maximilian Walter.
1899. George, Isaac.
†1895. Gepp, Maurice.
†1914. Ghosh, Kiranendu.
1914. Ghosh, Saurendra Mohon.
†1901. Gibson, Thomas.
348

1912. Gibson, William Robert.
1913. Gill, Clifford Allchin.
1895. Gill, Joseph William.
1913. Gill, Samuel Ernest.
†1906. Gillies, James.
1912. Gillitt, William.
†1910. Giri, Devarayadovrg Venkata.
†1914. Given, David Hughes Charles.
†1908. Glass, Alexander Gibb.
†1905. Glover, James Alison.
†1908. Gloyne, Stephen Roodhouse.
1910. Goldie, Walter Leigh Mackinnon.
1913. Goode, Christina Love.
1902. Goode, Henry Norman.
1905. Goodridge, Walter Lisle Taylor.
1921. Goodwin, Ernest St. George Sagar.
†1921. Gore, Dinanath Narayan.
†1922. Govan, Robert.
1923. Gowers, Dorothy Winifred.
1919. Grace, Walter Henry.
†1897. Grandy, William Edward.
†1899. Grant, William Francis.
1904. Grattan, Henry William.
1890. Green, Charles David.
1891. Gregory, Alfred John.
†1921. Griffin, Austin Jewkes Barlow.
†1917. Griffin, Una.
†1902. Griffith, Arthur Stanley.
1914. Griffiths, John.
1899. Griffiths, John Howell.
1914. Griffiths, Sydney Harold.
1921. Gross, Malcolm.
1890. Gubbin, George Frederick.
†1912. Guinness, ErnestWhitmoreNewton.
1922. Gunasekara, Septimus Theodosius.
†1922. Gupta, Priyabar.
†1915. Gupta, Syama Prasauna.
1923. Gwillim, Calvert Merton.

H.

1920. Habgood, Arthur Henry.
1923. Habgood, George.
1893. Habgood, William.
†1912. Hagerty, John Andrew.
1908. Hague, John.
1921. Haig, Harold Axel.
1905. Haines, Edward.
1899. Haines, Frederick Haselfoot.
1892. Hall, John Moore.
1901. Halliwell, Thomas.
1916. Hamill, Philip.
1906. Hamill, John Molyneux.
†1905. Hamilton, Hermann Lander.
1921. Hancock, Allen Coulter.
1900. Hancock, George Charles, O.B.E.
401

1909. Harding, Henry William.
†1893. Hardwick, Arthur.
1897. Hardy, Henry Louis Preston.
†1922. Harold, Charles Henry Hasler.
1889. Harris, Arthur Wellesley.
1900. Harris, John.
1891. Hart, George Henry.
1916. Hart, William John.
1906. Harvey, Frederic.
†1920. Harvey, George Alfred Duncan.
1913. Harwood,ClaudeSebast.Van Renen
1891. Haslip, George Ernest.
1894. Hatch, Herbert Lincoln.
1922. Hawes, Walter Anley.
1910. Hayes, Arthur Herbert.
†1905. Hayes, Edwin Charles.
1922. Hayne, Percy Alfred.
†1921. Healy, John Weston.
1902. Heanley, Charles Montague.
1890. Heaven, John Cookesley.
1915. Heddy, William Reginald Huleatt.
1921. Hempson, Geoffrey Oliver.
1894. Henderson, James Threapland.
†1921. Henderson, Patrick Hagart.
1900. Henshaw, Harry Williams.
1923. Herington, Cecil Edward Eede.
1899. Herrington, Edmund William.
†1923. Hesterlow, Edward.
1903. Hewetson, Henry.
†1921. Hewitt, Eileen Mabel.
1896. Hewlett, Richard Tanner.
1903. Hibbert, Joseph Coote.
1891. Hichens, Frank.
†1901. Highet, Hugh Campbell.
1903. Hill, Ernest Gardiner.
1909. Hill, Richard Athelstane Parker.
1913. Hilliard, Harvey.
1901. Hillier, William Thomas.
1911. Hills, William Charles Dillon.
1908. Hillyer, William Henry.
1896. Hine, Alfred Ernest Barratt.
1909. Hirst, Leonard Fabian.
1897. Hoare, Edwin Stanley.
1922. Hobbs, Frank Bedo.
1891. Hobson, John Morrison.
†1922. Hogg, Cecil Beresford.
1889. Holberton, Henry Nelson.
1921. Holden, Eric Theodore.
†1919. Holmes, Mervyn John.
†1909. Holmes, Thomas Edward.
†1910. Holroyd, Henry.
1891. Holroyde, John.
†1905. Holt, Henry.
†1897. Home, George.
1889. Hope, George.
1921. Hopkins, Edwin Lancelot.
1891. Hormusji, Sorab Cowasji.

1897. Horrocks, Herbert.
†1905. Horrocks, Oswald.
1902. Horrocks, William Heaton.
1921. Horsburgh, Percy Gilbert.
1914. Howell, Frederick Duke Gwynne.
1911. Howell, James Bonnell.
†1922. Howells, William Muir.
1910. Huckle, Arthur Henry Headley.
1912. Hudson, Charles Tilson.
1904. Hughes, David Arthur.
†1899. Hughes, Percy Theodore.
1907. Hugo, James Henry, D.S.O.
1898. Hunter, George Holbrey.
1920. Hunter, Ronald Nelson.
1901. Hynes, Ernest Jermyn.

I.

1896. Ingall, Frank Ernest.
1922. Ironside, Arthur Edmund.
1891. Irvin, Frederick David.
†1918. Isaac, Hyman.
1913. Ismail, Abdel Aziz.
†1910. Iyengar, Kombur Ramaswamy Krishnaswamy.

J.

1898. Jackson, Herbert William.
1889. James, Arthur William.
1903. James, Frederick Charles.
1903. James, Gwilym Prosser Wozencroft.
1907. James, Sydney Price.
1920. Jameson, George Dearden.
†1914. Jameson, William Wilson.
†1919. Jamieson, Thomas Hill.
†1893. Jefferiss, Walter Robert Spencer.
†1904. Jenkins, Hugh Llewelyn.
1899. Jenkins, John David.
1920. Jennings, Henry Cecil.
†1911. Jervis, John Johnstone.
†1901. Jobson, Thomas Battersby.
1892. Johns, John Francis.
†1893. Johnson, Gilbert Petgrave.
1913. Johnson, Robert George.
†1896. Johnston, Charles Arthur.
1909. Johnston, Duncan Matheson.
1910. Johnston, John Macpherson.
1922. Jolly, Doris Eleanor Parker.
1911. Jolly, Robert Henry Hatten.
1890. Jollye, Francis William.
†1893. Jones, Benjamin.
1923. Jones, David Morris.
1893. Jones, Evan.
1893. Jones, Frederick Felix.
1895. Jones, George.
1911. Jones, John Henry.

1893. Jones, Martin Llewelyn.
1895. Jones, Rowland Francis Hugh.
1897. Jones, William Black.
1920. Jordan, John Herbert.
†1922. Joshi, Brij Lal.
1905. Julian.Oliver Richd. Arthur,C.M.G.

K.

†1910. Kabraji,ShiavaxKaikhosroNowroji.
1893. Kàká, Sorabji Manekji.
†1914. Kapur, Maharaj Krishna.
†1923. Karandikar, Dattatraya Gangadhar.
†1910. Karve, Jagannath Vasudev.
†1913. Keane, Percival Maurice.
1896. Keats, Wm. John Charles.
†1907. Keble, Alfred Ernest Conquer.
1921. Keith, Thomas Skene.
†1922. Kelly, Eleanor Heald.
1913. Kempthorne, Gerard Ainslie.
†1922. Kennedy, Thomas Fuller.
†1891. Kenwood, Harry Richard.
1900. Kidd, Archibald.
†1905. Kilkelly, Chas. Randolph, C.M.G.
†1911. King, Charlotte Alice.
1920. King, Ralph De Veil.
1923. Kingsbury, Allan Neave.
1899. Kirton, Martin Ainger.
1898. Kitching, John Lea Walton.
1903. Knocker, William Douglas.
1920. Knott, Frank Alexander.
†1921. Kotwall, Nariman Sorabji.
†1922. Kuriyan, Ampattu Thomas.

L.

1901. Lakshmanan, Peter Narainasawmi.
1908. Lamplough, Wharram Henry.
†1920. Langrishe, John du Plessis.
1899. Lausdale, William.
1895. Larkam, Edward Thomas.
†1921. Lawder, Trevor Abbott.
†1889. Lawless, Edmund James.
1897. Lawrence, Sidney Cameron.
1906. Leake, Jonas William.
1910. Leaning, Robert Craske.
1903. Leclezio, George Joseph Alexis.
1919. Legge, Tam.
1905. Lelean, Percy Samuel.
1806. Leon, George Alexander.
1923. Le Vieux, Henri Toussaint.
1902. Lewis, Frank Charles.
†1907. Lewis, Frederick William.
†1913. Leys, Norman Maclean.
†1913. Lilley, Charles Herbert.
1895. Lindow, Albert.
558

†1904. Linnell, John Everard.
1923. Linzee, Neville Hood.
1921. Liscombe, Robert Henry.
†1907. Liston, William Glen.
†1893. Lithgow, Thomas George.
†1909. Littledale, Herbert Edward.
1904. Lloyd, Brinley Richard.
1906. Lock, George Haylett.
1903. Lodwidge, William Charrott.
1919. Loganadan, Arcot Doraisawmy.
1923. Lough, Muriel Jessie.
1920. Lovell, Edward Richardson.
†1921. Low, John Bruce.
†1900. Low, John Spencer.
1914. Low, Nelson.
1920. Lucey, Herbert Cubitt.
†1921. Lynch, Gerald Roche.

M.

1909. McClure, Walter St. Clair.
†1923. McClurkur, Thomas.
1897. McCormack, Charles Vincent.
†1901. McDade, Charles Edmund.
1923. Macdonald, Ernest Kenneth.
1921. Mac Donnell, John Joseph.
†1906. Macewen, Hugh Allen.
†1891. McGachen, Frederic Wm. Dobson.
†1899. McGowan, Robert George.
†1922. McGregor, Evelyn C. McDonald.
†1914. McIntosh, Thomas Steven.
†1914. McIntyre, Donald.
1923. McKay, Donald Walter.
†1920. Mackenzie, Bessie Russell.
†1921. Mackenzie, Eric Francis Wallace.
1911. McKenzie, John.
†1914. McKinstry, William Henry.
†1920. Mackintosh, James Macalister.
1912. McLeay, Charles William.
†1900. Macleod, Herbert William George.
†1893. Macleod, Robert Lockhart Ross.
1921. Macnab, John Theodore.
1892. Macnamara, Hugh Winckworth.
1922. McMichael, Gerald Joseph Wyld.
†1903. McNaught, James Gibson.
†1921. McNeight, Arthur Anderson.
†1921. McNeill, Arthur Norman Roy.
†1909. McWhan, Andrew Alexander.
†1922. Madhok, Mohkam Chand.
1908. Mair, James.
1921. Maitland, Charles Titterton.
†1912. Maitra, Satyaranjan.
†1906. Malcolmson, Green Edmund.
†1901. Male, Maurice Taylor.
†1891. Mallins, Clement.
†1923. Mann, James Wallace.
†1897. Mapleton, Henry Banbury.
612

†1915. Marlin, Thomas.
1922. Marshall, Gerald Struan.
1899. Martin, Anthony Alexander.
†1911. Martin, James FitzGerald, C.M.G.
1900. Martin, John Newton.
†1921. Martin, Mary.
†1897. Martyn, Gilbert John King.
†1912. Mascarenhas, Joseph Victor.
†1920. Mason, Charles Arthur.
1912. Mathur, Kalka Prasad.
1891. Matthews, Charles Edward.
1920. Matthews, Edgar William.
1897. Maynard, Edwin.
†1895. Meadows, Robert Thornton.
†1921. Mearns, Alexander.
†1905. Meek, James.
1921. Mehta, Amolak Ram.
1913. Melhuish, Herbert Michael Henry.
†1901. Melville, Charles Henderson.
†1905. Menzies, Frederick Norton.
†1909. Mhaskar, Krishnaji Shripat.
1921. Miall-Smith, Gladys Mary.
1902. Michell, Ralph.
1903. Milburn, Leslie.
1910. Milne, James Alexander.
†1916. Minett, Ethel Mary.
†1922. Misquitta, Joseph.
†1922. Mitchell, James Robertson, M.C.
†1905. Mitchell, Robert Macfarlane.
†1912. Mitra, Maumatha Nath.
1901. Moffit, Charles Gordon.
†1920. Moir, William John.
1911. Moiser, Bernard.
1890. Monk, Henry George Hawkins.
†1914. Moore, Alan Hilary.
†1895. Moore, Samson George.
1898. Moores, Samuel Guise.
†1920. Moos, Framroz Nanabhoy.
†1908. Moran, Austin Joseph.
1889. Morgan, George Frederic Elliot.
†1914. Morgan, Hyacinth B. Wesceslaus.
1898. Morgan, Morgan John.
1921. Morgan, William Ellis.
†1889. Morgan, William Pringle.
†1923. Morphy, Edward Olave.
†1914. Morrell, Clayton Conyers.
1905. Morris, Arthur Hugh.
†1923. Morrison, William Watson.
†1914. Mozoomdar, Bidham Prosad.
1902. Mundy, Herbert.
1899. Murray, John Hanna.
†1903. Murray, William.
1889. Muspratt, Charles Drummond.
1906. Muspratt, Percy Knowles.
1898. Mussellwhite, William.
1905. Myler, John William.

N.

1901. Naharro, David Nunes.
†1923. Nain, Kanwal.
†1923. Naoleker, Gopal Gangadhar.
†1921. Narayan, Ram.
†1911. Newsholme, Henry Pratt.
1895. Newton, Henry William.
†1898. Nicol, Percy Wood.
†1902. Nicoll, James.
†1905. Nightingale, John.
1894. Nightingale, Samuel Shore.
1889. Norman, Frederick.
†1914. Norman, Vincent Philip.
†1895. Norris, William Perrin.
1906. Northcott, John Ford.
1893. Norton, Everitt Edward.
1891. Norton, John.

O.

1922. Oats, Wilfrid.
†1909. O'Brien, Richard Alfred.
†1893. O'Connor, Bernard.
1923. Okell, Charles Cyril.
1896. Oliver, Charles Pye.
1892. Orr, William Young.
1923. Osborn, Henry Alexander.
†1913. Otway, Alexander Loftus.
1912. Owen, John George.
1908. Ozzard, Fairlie Russell.

P.

1920. Page, Dennis Salmon.
1900. Page, Harry Marmaduke.
1889. Paget, Charles Edward.
†1895. Paine, Alexander.
1922. Painton, George Richard.
†1921. Pandit, Chintaman Govind.
†1922. Pandit, Nilkanth Vinayak.
†1920. Parker, Wyndham.
1914. Parkinson, George Singleton.
†1920. Parmanand.
†1919. Passey, Richard Douglas, M.C.
†1921. Patel, Amritlal Harjiman.
1908. Paterson, James Jenkins.
†1921. Patterson, Alexander John.
1896. Patterson, George Henry.
1917. Paul, Sachchidananda Hoshen.
†1923. Pawan, Joseph Lennox.
†1910. Payne, Helen Nora.
1912. Pearce, Thomas Massey.
1905. Pearse, Albert.
1921. Pearson, George Harold.
1923. Pearson, Sigrid Letitia Sharpe.

1909. Penny, Frederick Septimus.
1908. Penton, Richard Hugh, D.S.O.
1900. Perkins, George.
1910. Perkins, Herbert Wilberforce.
1892. Perry, Sir Allan.
†1903. Petrie, John Moir.
†1913. Phillips, John Alfred Steele.
†1920. Phillips, Rees.
1913. Phipson, Edward Selby.
1911. Pick, Lawrence.
1891. Pires, George.
1912. Pollard, John McFarlane William.
1922. Pollock, AubreyKeatinge Halliday.
†1920. Porkous, Arthur Borland.
†1920. Porteous, Arthur Borland.
1921. Portway Robert Louis.
1905. Powell, James Farquharson.
1913. Powell, Thomas William Watkin.
1899. Powell. Walter Augustus.
1904. Pratt, John Isaac.
1914. Pratt, Walter Woodall.
1901. Price, George Basil.
1914. Price, Robert Bernard.
1922. Priston, Julian Lionel.
1892. Priest, James Damer.
1902. Prior, John Ralph.
1904. Pritchett, Sidney Isaac.
1907. Probyn, Percy John, D.S.O.
†1922. Proctor, Ruth Elizabeth.
†1911. Pryce-Tannatt, Thomas Edwin.
1895. Pryn, William Wenmoth.
1906. Puddicombe, Thomas Phare.
†1913. Pugh, Laura Williams.
1920. Purchase, William Bentley.

Q.

†1912. Quin, Henry Christian Ernest.
1923. Quine, Albert Edward.

R.

1921. Rackham, Arthur Leslie Hanworth.
1920. Radford, Maitland.
†1917. Radford, Muriel Ann.
†1914. Rahman, Khwaja Abdul.
†1913. Rai, Balwant.
†1911. Rai, Jitendra Nath.
1899. Raines, Robert.
†1913. Ram, Shobha.
1923. Ranking, George Lancaster.
1921. Ranson, John Sturgess.
1903. Raper, Matthew Henry.
†1902. Rattray, Samuel.
†1914. Rau, Keshava Narayana.
†1921. Ray, Benoy Kumar.
766

†1923. Rebello, John Lawrence.
1923. Reece, Eleanor Margaret.
1888. Reece, Richard James.
1896. Rendle, Anstruther Cardew.
†1903. Rennie, Robert.
†1921. Renwick, Alexander Cameron.
1920. Revell, Rowan William.
1897. Richards, Joseph Stewart.
†1922. Richardson, Barbara.
1918. Richardson, Edmund Douglas.
†1901. Riddell, Robert George.
†1919. Roberts, Eva Louise Cairns.
1920. Roberts, Frederick Emilius.
1897. Roberts, George Augustus Edward.
1888. Roberts, John Lloyd.
†1923. Robinson, Francis Aidan.
†1902. Robinson, Frank.
1905. Robinson, John Elliott.
1907. Robinson, Oliver Long.
†1903. Robson, Neil.
†1922. Rodriquez, George Victor Sydney.
†1910. Rose, John.
†1913. Rose, Percy.
1920. Rosher, Arthur Burch.
†1922. Rosha, Joti Prasad.
†1898. Ross, Frederic William Forbes.
†1915. Ross, Lucy MacBean.
1888. Ross, Sir Ronald, K.C.B.
1888. Roughton, John Paul.
1891. Roughton, Walter.
†1898. Rowlands, David Richard.
†1914. Roy, Rajendra Coomar.
1922. Rudkin, Gordon Wilfrid Ritchie.
1922. Rudolf, G. R. Anderdon de Montjoie
1901. Rundle, Claude.
1922. Russell, Elizabeth Dill.
†1922. Ryles, Charles.

S.

†1908. Safford, Arthur Hunt.
†1911. Sahni, Bickrama Jit.
†1921. Sahni, Chuni Lal.
1903. Salisbury, Charles Ramsden.
1897. Salter, Alfred.
1902. Samman, Charles Thomas.
1912. Sandiland, Ernest Littleton.
1898. Sapp, John George Victor.
1910. Sass, Frederick Joseph Wilfred.
1915. Saunders, Ernest Albert Argent.
1897. Savage, William George.
1902. Saw, Francis Albert.
†1889. Scatliffe, Arthur William.
1888. Schofield, Gerald.
†1912. Schwabe, Dorothea Lenore.
†1890. Scott, Gavin Steel.
819

†1912. Scott, Jessie Anne.
†1911. Scott, Norman Emil Henry.
1923. Scott, Ralph Roylance.
1892. Scott, Sack Noy.
1905. Scrase, Frank Edward.
1910. Searle,AlfredChristopherHammond
1906. Seccombe, John William Smyth.
†1921. Sen, Lolitmohan.
†1921. Sen, Protap Chandra.
†1896. Senior, Arthur.
†1922. Seth, Pran Nath.
†1914. Sethna, Kaikhushroo Sorabjee.
1918. Shand, George Ernest.
1901. Sharpe, William Salisbury.
†1923. Shenai, Kaup Krishna.
†1902. Sherlock, Edward Birchall.
†1915. Shinnie, Andrew James.
1914. Shirgaokar, Jaganath Vishnu.
†1910. Shroff, ErachDinshaw.
†1895. Shrubshall, Wm. Wyatt.
1914. Sibley, Reginald Oliver.
1902. Sikes, Alfred Walter.
1895. Simmons, Harold.
†1919. Simon, Keith Myrie Benoit.
1904. Simpson, Godfrey William.
1920. Simpson, William.
†1920. Sims, Carrie.
1921. Simson, Henry John.
1905. Sinclair, Harold Weightman.
†1903. Sinclair, Thomas Walker.
†1923. Singh, Harnath.
†1923. Singh, Jaimal.
†1923. Singh, Kapur.
1902. Sinigar, Harry.
1908. Skelton, Dudley Sheridan.
1906. Skerrett, Frank Blenkinsopp.
1921. Sladen, Reginald John Lambert.
1923. Slot, Gerald Maurice Joseph.
1905. Small, Robert.
1922. Smith, Charles Rees.
1898. Smith, Daniel Lloyd.
†1920. Smith, Hector.
†1890. Smith, James.
1919. Smith, Philip.
1910. Smith, Sidney Browning.
1897. Smith, Sydney Calvin.
1900. Smith, William Steele.
1904. Smithson, Arthur Ernest.
1900. Smyth, Ernest Jackson.
1894. Snell, Sidney Herbert.
1922. Snell, John Aubrey Brooking.
1923. Soames, Ralph Martin.
†1922. Soares, Alexander Durante.
1893. Solly, Ernest.
1889. Southcombe, Arthur George.
1909. Spaull, Percy William.

1901. Spicer, Arthur Herbert.
1900. Spitteler, Alfred.
†1904. Spooner, Charles Augustus.
1896. Spreat, Frank Arthur.
1912. Squires, Herbert Chavasse.
1908. Stammers, George Elliott Frank.
1914. Standish, Frank.
1897. Stanley, Arthur.
1923. Stansfeld, Elsie.
1922. Stanton, Ambrose Thomas.
1902. Starkey, Thomas Albert.
1904. Statham, John Charles Baron.
†1891. Stawell, Richard Rawdon.
1911. Steadman,SidneyFrancisSt Jermain
1904. Stedman, Percy Taylor Humphrey.
1897. Steegmann, Edward John.
1904. Stenhouse, John Robert.
1902. Stephen, Guy Neville.
†1906. Stephen, Lessel Philip.
1898. Stephens, Henry Woolcott.
1908. Stephens, James Batson.
1891. Stevens, Francis Joseph.
†1913. Stevenson, George Henderson.
†1914. Stevenson,Wm. David Henderson.
1911. Steward, Sidney John, D.S.O.
†1920. Stewart, John.
1911. Stirk, Percy Herbert.
1891. Stirling, Alexander Williamson.
†1906. Stock, Philip Graham.
1894. Stonham, Henry Archibald.
1896. Storrs, Eric Gleadow.
1892. Stott, Hugh.
1920. Stott, Hugh.
†1902. Stovin, Cornelius Frederick.
1911. Straton, Charles Henry.
†1921. Stringer, Charles Herbert.
†1921. Subramanyam, Mysore.
†1923. Sullivan, John.
†1914. Sur, Sachindra Nath.
†1914. Sutherland, Charles Lindsay.
1921. Swyer, Robert.
1889. Sylvester, George Holden.
1894. Symes, John Odery.

T.

†1921. Tandy,OswaldCornwallis Stratford.
†1923. Talwar, Mukund Lal.
†1922. Tarr, William.
1923. Tate, George.
1908. Tate, John.
1894. Tatham, Charles John Willmer.
1901. Taunton, Edgar.
†1906. Taylor, Daniel Macpherson.
†1913. Taylor, John.

1906. Taylor, John Francis.
1889. Taylor, Lot Albert.
1920. Taylor, Wilfrid Reginald.
1921. Taylor, William Benjamin Batchelor.
1893. Tebb, Albert Edward.
†1902. Thomas, Albert Edward.
†1904. Thomas, Arthur Hitchings.
1901. Thomas, Charles James.
1921. Thomas, Daniel Jenkin.
1897. Thomas, Daniel Lewis.
1900. Thomas, David Jones.
1910. Thomas, Edmund Fairfield.
1923. Thomas, Eric Waldo Lange.
1921. Thomas, John Herbert.
1906. Thomas, William John.
1890. Thompson, Charles Herbert.
+1912. Thompson, Gustav Weber.
†1896. Thompson, James Arthur.
1912. Thompson, John.
1894. Thompson, Wilberforce.
†1910. Thomson, Alex. Butchart MacArthur.
†1907. Thomson, Alfred George Patrick.
†1893. Thomson, Frederic Holland.
†1906. Thomson, Jack Mowbray.
†1911. Thomson, May.
1904. Thornley, Robert Lewis.
1922. Thynne, Mildred Archer.
1896. Tibbetts, Thomas Major.
1900. Tilleke, Robert Edwin Goone.
†1921. Tiwari, Charan Das.
1914. Todesco, James Massimo.
1920. Todhunter, Jn. Reginald Arthur D.
1922. Toms, Humphrey.
1894. Toogood, Frederick Sherman.
1905. Townroe, Eugene Dunbar.
1922. Townshend, Ruth Catherine.
1892. Tratman, Frank.
†1910. Trivedi, Chandiprasad.
1911. Tucker, Sydney Arthur.
†1910. Turner, Alfred Charles Foster.
†1912. Turner, Frederick Meadows.
1911. Turtle, William Reginald Margetts.
1902. Tuxford, Arthur Wren.
1907. Tyndale, Wentworth Francis, C.M.G.

U.

1921. Underwood, John Ernest Alfred.
†1914. Urquhart, Alexander Lewis.

V.

1890. Valintine, Thos. Harcourt Ambrose.
1895. Vallance, Hugh.
†1910. Van Ingen, Alice Mauricia.
†1917. Van Ingen, Mary Alice.

†1922. Variava, Hormusji Edulji.
†1922. Varma, Nand Lal.
†1904. Vickers, Philip.
1921. Viney, Arnold.
†1911. Vining, Charles Wilfred.

W.

†1902. Waddy, Frederick Henry.
1921. Wakely, Alfred Stewart.
1890. Waldo, Frederick Joseph.
†1921. Walker, Elizabeth Stevenson.
1899. Walker, George Charles.
†1910. Walker, Joseph.
1909. Walker, Norman Hamilton.
†1917. Walker, Robert Septimus.
1908. Walker, William Percy.
†1904. Wallace, George Smith.
†1914. Wallace, Nariman Bejanji.
1906. Walton, Henry Beccles Gall.
1903. Wanhill, Charles Frederick.
1904. Wanklyn, William McConnel.
1908. Ward, Ellacott Leamon.
1901. Warner, Allan.
1908. Warren, Stanley Herbert.
†1914. Waterworth, Francis William.
1912. Watkin, Arthur Christopher.
†1902. Watt, James.
1907. Watts, Brian.
†1904. Watts, Edward Croft.
1907. Webb, Arthur Lisle Ambrose.
1906. Webb, Hugh George Stiles.
†1920. Webb, John Newton.
1922. Webb, John Robert Douglas.
1919. Webb, William Leslie.
†1914. Webster, John Sutton.
1907. Wedd, Bernard Harry.
1920. Wernet, Augustus Joseph.
†1916. West, Henry Owen.
1892. Westcott, William Wynn.
1889. Wheaton, Samuel Walton.
1891. Whiston, Philip Henry.
†1918. White, Edmund Leigh.
1900. White, Frank Harris.
1920. White, Frederick Norman.
†1894. White, Thomas Edward.
1890. Whitehead, Hayward Reader.
1888. Whittick, Fallon Percy.
†1919. Whittingham, Harold Edward.
†1910. Whittingham, Hilda Kate.
1901. Wiggins, William Denison.
†1895. Wigmore, Arthur William.
†1899. Wilkes, Edwin Montague.
1911. Wilkes, Ernest Alfred Freear.
·1895. Wilkes, George Arthur.
†1892. Wilkie, John.

†1898. Wilkinson, John.
†1901. Wilkinson, Percy John.
†1900. Willcox, William Henry.
 1910. Williams, Alfred Carleton.
†1895. Williams, Arnold Winkelried.
 1899. Williams, Ernest Graham Hamilton.
 1919. Williams, John Pryce.
 1900. Williams, Robert Edwin.
 1894. Williamson, John.
†1901. Willson, Howard Samuel.
†1902. Willson, Reginald John.
†1909. Wilson, Arthur Harold.
†1914. Wilson, Frederic Ernest.
 1920. Wilson, Graham Selby.
 1916. Wilson, Horace Richard.
†1907. Wilson, James Edwin.
†1914. Wilson, James Ingram Pirie.
†1902. Wilson, James Patterson.
†1915. Wilson, Norman Leslie Galloway
 1922. Wiltshire, Henry Goodwill.
 1914. Winston, William Bamford.
 1906. Winter, Thomas Bassell.
†1911. Wood, Charles Frederic.
 1907. Wood, Charles Rawdon.
1054

†1901. Wood, Frank Lomax.
 1914. Wood, John Hutchinson.
 1892. Wood, Louis Edmund.
†1891. Wood, William Atkinson.
 1899. Woodfield, Thomas Harold.
 1893. Woodhouse, Francis Decimus.
†1898. Woollacott, Francis James.
 1921. Woollcombe, Alfred.
†1919. Wotherspoon, John.
 1905. Wright, Frederick Robt. Elliston.
†1902. Wright, Thomas.
†1914. Writer, Jamsetji Hormusji.
 1888. Wunderlich, Otto Frederick.
 1899. Wyche, Ernest Morton.

Y.

†1909. Yenamandram, Subrahmanyam.
 1888. Young, Edward Herbert.
†1922. Young, Frederick Hugh.
†1901. Young, Ludovic Unwin.
†1902. Young, Meredith.
†1911. Young, William Allan.
1074

DIPLOMATES IN TROPICAL MEDICINE AND HYGIENE.

The Diploma in Tropical Medicine and Hygiene is granted conjointly with the ROYAL COLLEGE OF PHYSICIANS OF LONDON.

Diplomates marked † are not Fellows or Members of the College.

1920. Abdel-Khalik, Mohamed Khalil.
†1923. Albuquerque, Justin W. Francis.
†1921. Allan, William.
†1921. Allen, George Vance.
†1921. Anderson, John.
†1921. Anklesaria, Jehangir Ardeshir.
†1921. Antia, Pirojsha Merwanji.
1920. Armstrong, John Scaife.
1912. Arzmy, Soliman.
†1923. Baldwin, Alec Hutchison.
†1921. Bardhan, Sarojinnath.
1920. Basile, Carlo.
†1921. Basu, Sunil Chandra.
1922. Beatson, Basil Fraser.
†1923. Benson, Walter Tyrrell.
1922. Berlie, Herbert Claye.
1921. Beven, John Osmonde.
1922. Bharucha, Kaikhushroo Maneckji.
†1922. Bleakley, Nancy Ethel.
1922. Boland, Charles Vincent.
1923. Bomford, Trevor Laurence.
†1921. Bordon, William Benjamin.
†1923. Briercliffe, Rupert.
†1923. Brosius, Otto Tiemann.
†1921. Brown, Henry Robert.
1911. Bruce-Bays, James.
†1922. Butt, Abdul Hamid.
†1921. Caddick, Charles John.
†1923. Calder, Clarence Alexander.
†1922. Cameron, Donald Ian.
†1922. Cilento, Raphael West.
†1921. Clark, Edward James.
†1922. Cline, Charles.
1921. Comyn, Kenneth.
1913. Connor, Frank Powell.
1912. Contractor, Ardeshir Koyaji.
†1923. Cook, Cecil.
1920. Cosgrave, Alexander Kirkpatrick.
38

†1922. Cossery, George Naguib.
†1921. Costello, Francis Xavier.
†1923. Covell, Gordon.
†1921. Crawford, Andrew.
†1920. Croly, Robert George Gibbon.
†1914. Croley, Vivian St John.
†1921. Cullen, Wm.Barbour Alex.Kennedy.
†1921. Dasgupta, Arunkumar.
†1923. Dasgupta, Bhupes Chandra.
1923. de Boer, Henry Speldewinde.
†1921. Denham, Arthur Armstrong.
1921. de Silva, John Paul.
†1921. de Vos, Samuel Denis.
1923. Dhawan, Manohar Lal.
1920. Dive, Hubert Roy, M.C.
1922. Dimock, James Douglas.
†1923. Donald, John.
1921. Dudley, Sheldon Francis.
†1922. Dunham, George Clark.
†1922. Edmond, John James Balmanno.
1921. Ei-Kirdany, Aly Mohammad.
1920. El Daab, Saad el Din Ahmed.
†1922. el-Kattan,Mahmoud A.Mohammed.
†1922. English, Geoffrey Dix.
1920. Fanstone, James.
†1922. Fisher, Vicars Maddison.
†1921. Flowerdew, Richard Edward.
1920. Forrester-Paton, Ernest.
1920. Frendo, John Augustine.
†1922. Gale, Berkeley.
†1921. Gândha, Kaikhooshro Ardesheer.
†1922. Giglioli, Giorgio.
1913. Gill, Clifford Allchin.
†1922. Godlieb, Edward Samuel.
†1923. Gollerkeri, Ganesh Venkatrao.
1922. Grace, Walter Henry.
†1922. Gregg, Arthur Leslie.
†1923. Gregory Helen.
. 76

†1922. Griffiths, Mary Louise.
†1922. Gupta, Priyabar.
1923. Hamilton, William Haywood.
†1923. Han, Chung Hsin.
†1913. Harper, Frances Margaret.
1923. Harsant, Arnold Guy.
1920. Harvey, Alex. Wm. Montgomery.
1920. Hawes, Richard Brunel.
†1922. Hennessy, Joseph Martin Reeves.
†1921. Heppenstall, Clement Hoyle.
†1921. Hermicte, Louis Constant Daniel.
†1923. Hewat, Harry Aitken.
1922. Hicks, Eric Perrin.
†1922. Hingston, Henry Sandiford.
†1922. Hofmeyr, Harold Osmond.
†1920. Hogg, William Peat.
1923. Holgate, Maurice James.
†1921. Howells, William Muir.
1922. Hunt, Spencer.
†1921. Jacques, Frederick Viel.
†1920. Jamison, Robert.
1922. Joy, Henry Charles Victor.
†1914. Jolly, Gordon Gray.
†1914. Kapur, Maharaj Krishna.
1923. Keevill, Arthur James.
1920. Keith, Thomas Skene.
†1922. Kellersberger, Eugene Roland.
†1921. Khaled, Zaky.
1923. Kingsbury, Allan Neave.
†1922. Kirk, James Balfour.
†1922. Lal, Ram Bihari.
†1920. Lane, Thomas Joseph.
†1922. Lee, Chung Un.
1921. Liang, Pao Tsang.
†1921. Liat, Lee Ee.
1921. Liscombe, Robert Henry.
†1921. Litt, John Percy.
†1922. Luciaft, Harry Stephenson.
1923. McCallum, Frank.
1923. McIver, Colin.
†1921. Mackay, Annie Mark.
†1920. Mackenzie, Melville Douglas.
1920. Madgwick, George Alex. Sheridan.
†1922. Madhok, Mohkam Chand.
1921. Maitland, Charles Titterton.
1912. Marshall, Eric Stewart.
1922. Marshall, Gerald Struan.
†1923. Martin, Charles de Carteret.
†1921. Martin, Mary.
†1921. Mehta, Amolak Ram.
†1922. Mehta, Daulat Ram.
†1922. Mills, Everard Arnold.
†1922. Mody, Maneck Sorabji Hormusji.
1922. Moody, Ludlow Murcott.
1922. Moore, Desmond Garrett Fitzgerald.
†1920. Moos, Framroz Nanabhoy.
†1921. Morrison, Malcolm.

133

†1921. Morton, Terrace Charles St. Clessie.
†1914. Murphy, Andrew.
†1912. Murray, William Alfred.
†1923. Nain, Kanwal.
†1922. Naoleker, Gopal Gangadhar.
†1921. Nicolson, James Stuart.
1920. Nedergaard, Niels.
†1921. Nigam, Kali Sahai.
†1922. Noble, Alexander.
†1912. O'Donoghue, Denis J. FitzGerald.
†1920. O'Driscoll, Elizabeth Josephine.
†1912. Oxley, James Charles Stewart.
†1923. Pampana, Emilio Juvendis.
†1923. Pandit, Chiutaman, Govind.
1921. Paranjpé, Anand Shridhar.
1921. Parker, Henry Brice.
†1921. Parthasrarathy, Parasurama.
†1921. Patel, Amritlal Harjiman.
1922. Peacock, William Henry.
†1922. Pedris, James.
†1923. Peterson, Edwin.
†1923. Phillips, William James Ellery.
1920. Phipson, Edward Selby, D.S.O.
1921. Procter, Robert Arthur Welsford.
†1921. Ray, Benoy Kumar.
1921. Ratnavale, William Sitravale.
1922. Razik, Abdel Razik.
†1923. Rebello, Alfred Camillo.
†1923. Rebello, John Laurence.
†1922. Reubens, Adeline.
†1920. Reynolds, Francis Esmond.
†1921. Richards, Henry Edward Sutherland.
1921. Roach, Sidney.
†1921. Ross, Mona Margaret.
†1912. Roy, Satyendra, Nath.
†1921. Sahni, Chuni Lal.
1923. Salama, Anis.
†1921. Salter, Evelyn Bessie.
†1922. Samuel, Henry Pounampalam.
1922. Schwartz, Morris.
†1921. Scott, Douglas Somerville.
†1921. Ségal, Jacob.
†1921. Sen, Lolitmohan.
†1921. Seth, Pran Nath.
†1923. Sethi, Narinjan Singh.
†1922. Shaba, Brajaballar.
†1923. Sharp, Clive Justin Hicks.
†1921. Shaw, Alice Isabel.
1912. Sibley, Reginald Oliver.
1921. Silcock, Ronald.
1923. Simmons, William Henry.
1923. Simpson, Reginald Hugh.
1921. Simpson, Robert Gordon.
†1921. Sinderson, Harry Chapman.
1921. Smith, Herbert.
†1922. Soares, Alexander Durante.
1921. Somasundram, Saravanamuttu.

1915. Sokhey, Sahib Singh.
†1922. Spear, Frederick Gordon.
†1921. Stedeford, Edward Thomas Arnold.
1923. Tagoe, Edward.
1921. Taylor, Wilfrid Reginald.
1922. Theiler, Max.
†1921. Tough, William Milne.
1921. Turner, Harry Morton Stanley.
1923. Valentine, Douglas James.
†1922. Vassallo, Salvator Michael.
†1921. Walcott, Allan Moore.
201

1921. Welch, Thomas Burges.
1921. Westmorland, Arthur Stewart.
1920. Whittingham, Harold Edward.
1921. Wilson, Norman Methven.
1921. Wiltshire, Henry Goodwill.
1920. Wong, Man.
1920. Wood, Edward Jenner.
1922. Wood, Charles Albert.
†1922. Wynne, Thomas Gillis.
†1922. Yacob, Mahomed.
†1922. Young, Margaret Helen Rattray.
212

DIPLOMATES IN OPHTHALMIC MEDICINE AND SURGERY.

The Diploma in Ophthalmic Medicine and Surgery is granted conjointly with the ROYAL COLLEGE OF PHYSICIANS OF LONDON.

Diplomates marked †are not Fellows or Members of the College.

†1923. Abbu, Conjuvaram.
†1922. Ahmed, Tajammul.
†1922. Ajinkya, Ramrao Narayam.
†1921. Ali, Gulzar Mohammad.
†1921. Anderson, Joseph Ringland.
1921. Anklesaria, Maneksha Dhanjisha.
†1921. Athavale, Chintaman Ramkrishna.
1923. Baranov, Monty.
†1922. Beedham, Henry William.
†1923. Berge, Charles Gustav.
1922. Bhargava, Dwarka Prasad.
1922. Bharucha, Jamasp Cursetji.
1920. Bickerton, Herbert Richard.
†1923. Breen, Gerald Edward.
1923. Brookes, George Arthur.
†1923. Butler, Thomas.
†1921. Candlish, Robert Smith.
1921. Chambers, Ennis Ratcliff.
1921. Chavasse, Francis Bernard.
†1923. Colley, Richard.
1923. Colley, Thomas.
1922. Collins, Robert Edward.
†1921. Dickson, Robert Milne.
†1921. Dixon, Gerald Conroy.
†1920. East, Arthur Gerard.
†1923. El-Kattan, Mahmond A. Mohammed
1923. Evans, Daniel Davies.
1922. Eminson, Clarence Franklin.
†1920. Fleming, Norman Bell Beattie.
†1923. Gangriwala, Najmudin Kamrudin.
†1921. Gibson, John McCoy.
†1922. Glassford, Eric MacAllan Gordon.
†1922. Glynn, Robert McMahon.
†1922. Gregg, Norman McAlister.
1920. Gokhale, Vinayak Balvant.
1920. Haycraft, Guy Fleetwood.
†1923. Heal, James Gordon Freeman.
†1921. Ingle, Ernest Wilfred.
†1921. Kamdin, Rustom Dassabhoy.
†1922. Kapasi, Abdulhusen Jivajee.
†1923. Keyms, Joshua.
†1921. Koil Thampuran, Lakshmipuram Avittam Ravi Varma.
1922. Kolapore, Phiroze Jamshedji.
†1921. Labiebe, Kamil Maximus.
1923.

1923. Livingstone, Philip Clermont.
†1921. Lodge, William Oliver.
†1923. McGuinness, Edward John.
†1922. Madan, Kaikhushru Edulji.
1921. Mann, Ida Caroline.
1922. Marchant, Gladys Helen.
†1921. Mishra Raghunath Rai.
†1923. Mitchell, Brenda Aileen.
†1921. Mohamedi, Shakir Shamsudin.
†1923. Moher, Murray Joseph.
†1922. Monro, John Stuart.
†1920. Mukerjee, Susil Kumar.
1922. Navanati, Bapuji Phirojshaw.
†1922. North, Alan Lindsay.
†1921. North, Robert Bell.
†1922. O'Malley, Charles Conor.
†1921. Pesikaka, Behram Hormusji.
†1923. Pittar, Rowland J. Gore Armstrong.
†1921. Rahim, Syed Abdur.
†1920. Ratnakar, Ratanji Popat.
1923. Reid, Andrew McKie.
1921. Robinson, Francis Harry.
†1921. Rudd, Charles.
1922. St. John, Charles Herbert.
†1923. Schwartz, Zelman.
†1922. Scoular, Stuart.
1921. Shorey, Narayan Lakshman.
†1921. Shroff, Chimanlal Namchard.
†1920. Sichel, Alan William Stuart.
†1920. Simpson, William Henry.
1922. Skrimshire, Francis Robert Bradley.
†1923. Soudhi, Sundar Das.
†1922. Sykes, Stanley Parkinson.
†1921. Taggart, Hugh Joseph.
†1922. Twigg, Francis John Despard.
†1921. Tennent, James Nisbet.
†1923. Thakore, Mukundrai Dolatrai.
†1920. Vaidya, Jadavji Hansraj.
†1923. Varma, Nand Lal.
1922. Vickers, Thomas Hedley.
1922. Vivian, Harold Sugden.
1921. Whittington, Theodore Henry.
†1923. Woolworth, Joseph Deane.
1921. Zachariah, George.

DIPLOMATES IN PSYCHOLOGICAL MEDICINE.

The Diploma in Psychological Medicine is granted conjointly with the ROYAL COLLEGE OF PHYSICIANS OF LONDON.

Diplomates marked † are not Fellows or Members of the College.

†1922. Annandale, James Scott.	†1923. Markwell, Norman Walter.
1923. Barkas, Mary Rushton.	†1923. Martin, Frederick Robertson.
†1923. Barrada, Yousif Abul-Nasr.	1922. Martin, James Ernest.
†1923. Blanton, Smiley.	1920. Martin, Owen Sidney.
1922. Bostock, John.	†1922. Maudsley, Henry Fitzgerald.
1922. Cholmeley, Montague Adye.	1922. Morton, Herbert Henry Powys.
†1923. Clubwala, Nariman Hormusji.	1922. Navarra, Norman.
†1922. Connolly, Victor Lindley.	†1922. Noronha, Frank Xavier.
†1923. Davie, Thomas Macnaughton.	1922. Paine, Frederick.
1922. Dawson, Guy de Hoghton.	1920. Parnis, Henry William.
1921. Dawson, William Siegfried.	1922. Penson, John Frederick.
1920. Dia, Mostafa.	1922. Powell, James Farquharson.
†1923. Edwards, Thomas Lloyd.	1922. Rayner, Edwin Cromwell.
1923. El-Kholy, Mohamed Kamil.	1923. Rivington, Eveleen Blanche Gibson.
1921. Fox, Joseph Tylor.	1922. Rixon, Christopher Hugh Leete.
1922. Franklin, Marjorie Ellen.	†1923. Roberts, Norcliffe.
1922. Gasperine, John Jones.	†1922. Rodger, Kenneth Mann.
1923. Gifford, John.	1922. Rose, Edward Snow.
1923. Greene, George Watters.	†1923. Sammon, William Douglas.
1923. Guppy, Francis Henry.	1923. Shepherd, Charles Ernest Alan.
†1920. Hayes, Edmund Duncan Tranchell.	1923. Shore, George William.
1923. Hopkins, Edwin Lancelot.	†1923. Turnbull, Peter Mortimer.
1923. Hunter, Percy Douglas.	†1922. Walker, George Turnbull.
†1922. Laing, John Kidd Collier.	1921. Wilson, Alban.
1921. Macarthur, John.	†1922. Wilson, Marguerite.
†1921. McCowan, Peter Knight.	1921. Wootton, Leonard Henry.
†1922. MacInnes, John.	†1922. Yellowlees, Henry.
†1923. McLuskie, Peter.	
28	55

ROLL OF HONOUR.

List of Fellows, Members, and Licentiates in Dental Surgery
who have been killed in action or lost their lives from
wounds or disease contracted while on active service
abroad with H.M. Forces.

PRO PATRIA.

FELLOWS.

	Rank.	Fellow.	Member.
Barker, Arthur Edward James....	Col. A.M.S.	1880	1880
Chisnall, George Henry	Lt. R.A.M.C.	1913	1908
Connolly, James Harris	Capt. R.A.M.C.	1911	1911
Fairley, James Fairbairn	Capt. R.A.M.C.	1914	1914
Ferguson, Philip	Capt. R.A.M.C.	1913	1913
Gould, Alfred Leslie Pearce	Surg. R.N.	1916	1913
Horsley, Sir Victor Alexander Haden, C.B.	Col. A.M.S.	1883	1880
Jones, Arthur Webb	—	1900	1899
Marshall, Charles Devereux	Staff Surg. R.N.V.R.	1892	1890
McNab, Angus	Capt. R.A.M.C.	1904	1904
Michell, Robert Williams	Capt. R.A.M.C.	1895	1895
Miller, George Sefton	Capt. R.A.M.C.	1916	1912
Murphy, James Keogh	Staff Surg. R.N.V.R.	1901	1894
Porter, Robert Nuttall	Capt. R.A.M.C.	1910	1910
Rayner, Edward	Surg. R.N.	1913	1913
Ridge, Edwyn Manners	Sub. Lt. R.N.V.R.	1902	1900
Savage, Thomas Copeland	Maj. N.Z.A.M.C.	1901	1900
Selby, William, D.S.O.	Lt.-Col. I.M.S.	1894	1892
Smith, Douglas Wilberforce	Capt. R.A.M.C.	1911	1901
Sneath, Wilfred Archer, M.C.	Capt. R.A.M.C.	1913	1912
Stonham, Charles, C.M.G.	Col. A.M.S.	1884	1881
Sturdy, Arthur Carlile, M.C.	Capt. R.A.M.C.	1912	1909

22 Fellows.

† Combatant Forces.

MEMBERS.

	Rank.	Member.
Acland, John Henry Dyke	Capt. R.A.M.C.	1905
Almond, George Hely-Hutchinson	Capt. R.A.M.C.	1906
†Armitage, Frank Rhodes, D.S.O.	Capt. R.F.A.	1908
Armstrong, Arthur Keith	Lt. R.A.M.C.	1907
Armstrong, Walter Seymour	Capt. R.A.M.C.	1903
Arnould, Loris Arthur	Capt. R.A.M.C.	1904
Atal, Pandit Piaraylal	Maj. I.M.S.	1898
Atkin, Keyser	Capt. R.A.M.C.	1916
Atkinson, Ambrose	Lt. R.A.M.C.	1884
Atkinson, Charles Mason	Lt. R.A.M.C.	1896
Atkinson, George Louis	Capt. R.A.M.C.	1897
Austen, Thomas	Surg. Commander R.N.	1888
Austin, John Henry Edward	Col. A.M.S.	1892
Ayre, Frederick John	ex-Capt. R.A.M.C.	1907
Bailey, James Connor Maxwell, O.B.E.	Capt. R.A.M.C.	1901
Baird, Leonard Barron, M.C.	Capt. R.A.M.C.	1914
Ball, Malcolm Edward	Lt. R.A.M.C.	1908
Batchelor, Henry	Maj. R.A.M.C.	1912
Bearblock, Walter James	Fleet Surg. R.N.	1887
Bell, Edward Augustine	Capt. R.A.M.C., T.	1902
Bell, John Cunningham	Lt. R.A.M.C., T.	1900
Benham, Charles Henry	Maj. R.A.M.C., T.	1897
Benson, Alfred Hugh	Maj. R.A.M.C.	1887
Berry, Percy Haycraft	Lt. R.A.M.C.	1913
Bharucha, Rustom Hormasji	Capt. I.M.S.	1909
Bhat, Kalyanpur Harihar	Lt. I.M.S.	1916
†Bingham, Frank Miller	Capt. K. O. R. Lanc. Regt. ..	1900
†Birley, Hugh Kennedy	Capt. Manch. Regt.	1895
Blandy, Francis Dawson, M.C.	Lt.-Col. R.A.M.C., T.	1900
*Bond, Cecil William	Capt. R.A.M.C.	1901
Bond, Francis Spencer	Capt. R.A.M.C.	1891
Bonser, Geoffrey Alwyn Gershom	Capt. R.A.M.C.	1914
Bostock, Robert Ashton	Surg.-Capt. Scots Guards	1885
Bower, William Charles	Lt. R.A.M.C.	1900
Bowlby, George Herbert	Capt. C.A.M.C.	1880
Bradburn, Thomas Stratford	Surg. R.N.	1909
Bridges, Roland Harley, D.S.O.	Lt.-Col. R.A.M.C.	1902
Brodie, Thomas Grigor	Maj. C.A.M.C.	1890
Brogden, Ingram Richard Rhodes	Lt. R.A.M.C.	1916
Brooke, Frederick Arthur John Robertson..	Capt. R.A.M.C.	1894
Brotchie, Robert Traill	Surg. R.N.V.R.	1913
Brown, Ian Macdonald	Capt. R.A.M.C.	1914
Brown, Wilfred Stephenson	Capt. R.A.M.C.	1916
Brownson, Roger Dawson Dawson-Duffield .	Capt. R.A.M.C.	1908
Brunton, Edward Henry Pollock	Lt. R.A.M.C.	1913
Burgess, Harold Lynch	W. Af. M.S.	1903
Burnett, Maurice	Capt. R.A.M.C.	1911
Burrell, Stanley Walter	Lt. R.A.M.C.	1915
Burton, Percy Herbert	Capt. R.A.M C.	1914
Burke, John	Capt. R.A.M.C.	1917

* L.D.S. 1912.   † Combatant Forces.

MEMBERS (cont.)

	Rank.	Member.
Buxton, Gurney White	Capt. R.A.M.C.	1891
Byatt, Harry Vivian Byatt	Capt. R.A.M.C.	1907
Carrington, Edward Worrell, M.C.	Capt. R.A.M.C.	1913
Center, William Rudolph	Fleet Surg. R.N.	1896
Chaning-Pearce, Wilfrid Thomas, M.C.	Capt. R.A.M.C.	1911
Chaplin, Harold Garrett	Surg. R.N.	1914
Chapman, George Martin	Lt. R.A.M.C.	1912
Chavasse, Arthur Ryland	Capt. R.A.M.C.	1911
Chavasse, Noel Godfrey, V.C. (with clasp), M.C.	Capt. R.A.M.C.	1912
Chenoy, Ferozeshah Bapuji	Capt. I.M.S.	1913
Chiles-Evans, David Brynmor, D.S.O.	Lt.-Col. R.A.M.C., T.	1903
Chissell, George Edwin, M.C.	Capt. R.A.M.C.	1916
Clark, Sydney	Capt. R.A.M.C.	1896
Clark, William Brown	Capt. R.A.M.C.	1903
†Clifford, Anthony Clifford	2nd Lt. 3rd Dragoon Guards.	1913
Cocke, Robert Sturgeon	Capt. R.A.M.C.	1900
‡Cocks, John Stanley	Capt. R.A.M.C.	1914
Cohen, Aaron Simeon	Lt. R.A.M.C.	1913
Collins, Reginald Thomas, D.S.O.	Lt.-Col. R.A.M.C.	1902
Cowper, Geoffrey Moore	Capt. R.A.M.C.	1914
Cox, Edmund	Fleet Surg. R.N.	1899
Crombie, William Maurice	Lt. I.M.S.	1916
Crossman, Lionel Gordon	Capt. R.A.M.C.	1912
†Crowther, Sydney Nelson	Despatch Rider	1903
Cunnington, Edward Charles	Capt. R.A.M.C.	1915
Custance, Gustave William Musgrave	Surg. R.N.	1907
Dandridge, William Leslie	Lt. R.A.M.C.	1917
Dauber, John Henry	Lt.-Col. R.A.M.C., T.	1890
Davies, Frederick Charles	Capt. R.A.M.C.	1908
De Lautour, Harry Archibald	Lt.-Col. N.Z.M.C.	1874
†Dennys, Richard Molesworth	Capt. Loy. North Lancs. Regt.	1909
de Verteuil, Fernand Lewis	Surg. R.N.	1904
Downie, James Maitland	Capt. R.A.M.C.	1916
Dunkerley, Harold	Capt. R.A.M.C.	1914
Dunn, Arthur Gibson	Lt. R.A.M.C.	1906
East, Gordon Doulton	Capt. R.A.M.C.	1914
Eccles, Horace Dorset	Capt. R.A.M.C.	1893
Edmond, John Adamson	Capt. R.A.M.C.	1910
Edsell, George Alfred	Lt.-Col. R.A.M.C., T.	1886
Evans, William Jones	Capt. R.A.M.C.	1916
Evatt, James Millar	Capt. R.A.M.C.	1913
Faulks, Edgar	Lt. R.A.M.C.	1902
Fayle, Barcroft Joseph Leech	Capt. R.A.M.C.	1913
Field, Hassell Dyer	Capt. R.A M.C.	1914
Field, Stephen	Capt. R.A.M.C.	1906
Finch, George	Capt. R.A.M.C., T.	1905
Fisher, Edward Garlick	Surg.-Lt. R.N.	1912
Foreman, John Eugene	Lt. R.A.M.C.	1906
Forrest, Frank	Capt. R.A.M.C.	1904

† Combatant Forces.   ‡ L.D S. 1912.

MEMBERS (cont.)

	Rank.	Member.
Fox, Arthur Claude, D.S.O.	Lt.-Col. R.A.M.C.	1891
Fry, Walter Burgess	Maj. R.A.M.C.	1900
Gabbett, Pulteney Charles	Lt.-Col. I.M.S.	1891
Gardner, Alfred Linton	Capt. R.A.M.C.	1912
Garrod, Alfred Noel	Lt. R.A.M.C.	1914
German, Hugh Bernard, M.C. (with bar)	Maj. R.A.M.C.	1904
Gibson, Harold	Capt. R.A.M.C.	1907
Gibson, Howard Graeme	Maj. R.A.M.C.	1907
Glenny, Ernest Howard	Lt. R.A.M.C.	1917
Goodden, Henry Wyndham	Lt. R.A.M.C.	1912
Gough, Bernard Bradly	Lt. R.A.M.C.	1897
Gow, Charles Humphry	Surg. R.N.	1915
†Grandage, William Briggs	Lt.-Col. R.F.A.	1905
Grant, George Leonard	Capt. R.A.M.C.	1914
Grayfoot, Bleuman Buhôt, C.B.	Col. I.M.S.	1886
Green, John Leslie, V.C.	Capt. R.A.M.C.	1913
Greer, Morrice	Capt. R.A.M.C.	1907
Gregory, James Alfred	Lt. R.A.M.C.	1914
Gyllencreutz, James Randolph	Capt. R.A.M.C.	1908
Hadwen, John	Surg.-Lt.-Com. R.N.	1907
Hairsine, Owen, M.C.	Capt. R.A.M.C.	1914
Hammond, John Maximilian	Lt. R.A.M.C.	1909
†Hanbury, Langton Fuller	Pte. Sportsman Bn. Roy. Fus.	1902
Harris, Frederick William Henry Davie	Lt.-Col. R.A.M.C.	1880
Harris, Hubert Alfred	Capt. R.A.M.C.	1910
*Harris, Joseph Cecil	Capt. R.A.M.C.	1910
Harris, William Trengweath	Lt. R.A.M.C.	1903
‡Harrison, Frank Cecil	Capt. R.A.M.C.	1915
Harrison, Stanley Sextus Barrymore, M.C.	Maj. R.A.M.C.	1914
Hartnell, Edward Bush	Capt. R.A.M. , T.	1892
Harvey, Alfred Wallace	Capt. R.A.M.	1905
Hawes, Godfrey Charles Browne	Capt. R.A.M.C.	1894
Hayward, Milward Cecil	Capt. R.A.M.C., T	1898
Heald, William Margetson	Lt. R.A.M.C., S.A.	1918
Heard, Geoffrey Richard	Capt. R.A.M.C.	1909
Hebbert, Robert Francis	Capt. I.M.S.	1906
Hill, Reginald Gordon, M.C.	Lt. R.A.M.C.	1911
Hillbrook, Wallace	Capt. R.A.M.C.	1915
Hitchcock, Frank Norman Spurrell	Capt. N.Z.M.C.	1907
Hobbs, Roland Augustus	Surg.-Lt. R.N.	1908
Hodgson, John Edward	Lt.-Col. R.A.M.C.	1898
Hodson, Thomas George Smith	Capt. R.A.M.C.	1893
§Hopkins, Herbert Leslie	Lt. R.A.M.C.	—
Horton, James Henry, D.S.O.	Lt.-Col. I.M.S.	1895
Howard, Charles Reginald, O.B.E.	Capt. R.A.M.C.	1902
Howells, John Francis	Surg. R.N.	1917
†Hughes, Burroughs Maurice	Capt. 1/4th Norfolk Regt.	1895
Hughes, Oscar Cecil Laurence	Lt. R.A.M.C.	1916
Humphreys, Frederick James	Surg.-Lt. R.N.	1912

     * L.D.S. 1906.   † Combatant Forces.
     ‡ L.D.S. 1913.   § Qualified for Membership but not admitted.

MEMBERS (cont.)

	Rank.	Member.
Ingram, Thomas Lewis, D.S.O., M.C.	Capt. R.A.M.C.	1903
James, John	Capt. R.A.M.C.	1903
†Jessop, John William	Lt.-Col. 4th Bn. Lincs. Regt.	1889
Johnston, John Edward Lionel	W.Af.M.S.	1909
Jones, Alfred Gwilym	Capt R.A.M.C.	1905
Jones, Cyril Oscar Howe	Surgeon R.N.	1915
Jones, Henry John Rutherford	Capt. R.A.M.C.	1892
Jones, Myrddin Emrys	Surg.-Lt. R.N.	1918
Kellie, Kenneth Harrison Alloa	Capt. R.A.M.C.	1903
Kennedy, Ronald Sinclair, M.C. (with bar)	Capt. R.A.M.C.	1912
*Kidney, Thomas Clatworthy	Capt. R.A.M.C.	1914
Kimbell, Henry John Sullings	Lt. R.A.M.C.	1907
Knaggs, Francis Henry	Capt. R.A.M.C.	1885
Kynaston, Albert Evelyn Fairfax	Surg. R.N.	1904
‡Lacey, William Stocks	Lt. R.A.M.C.	1912
Lambert, Ernest Charles	Lt. R.A.M.C.	1898
Lambert, Francis Courtenay	Maj. R.A M.C.	1902
Langford, Martyn Henry, D.S.O.	Surg.-Lt.-Com. R.N.	1909
Latham, Thomas Jones	Lt. R.A.M.C.	1906
Leckie, Malcolm, D.S.O.	Capt. R.A.M.C.	1907
Leon, John Temple	Capt. R.A.M.C.	1895
Limbery, Kenneth Thomas, M.C.	Capt. R.A.M.C.	1916
Linnell, Robert McCheyne	—	1907
Lister, William Howard, D.S.O., M.C.	Capt. R.A.M.C.	1913
Little, John Wishart	Maj. I.M.S.	1900
Lloyd, Walter Everard	Surg.-Lt. R.N.	1908
Lloyd, Walter Henry	Capt. R.A.M.C.	1915
Lloyd-Jones, Percy Arnold, D.S.O.	Maj. R.A.M.C.	1904
Lobb, Francis Frederick	Fleet Surg. R.N.	1898
Lones, Percy East	Capt. R.A.M.C.	1915
Loy, Martin William	Lt. R.A.M.C.	1894
MacAevley, William Francis	Capt. R.A.M.C.	1915
McCrae, John	Lt.-Col. C.A.M.C.	1904
McGillycuddy, Richard Hugh, M.C.	Maj. R.A.M.C.	1911
Macgregor, Reginald Kinloch	Capt. R.A.M.C.	1911
Mackenzie, Maurice	Lt. R.A.M.C.	1912
McKerrow, Charles Kenneth	Capt. R.A.M.C.	1908
Mackinnon, Frank Irvine	Capt. R.A.M.C.	1883
Maclean, Ivan Clarkson, M.C.	Capt. R.A.M.C.	1906
MacMullen, Alfred Robinson, D.S.C. (with bar)	Surg. R.N.	1913
Maginness, Oscar Gladstone	Lt. R.A.M.C.	1913
Manders, Nevill	Col. R.A.M.C.	1883
Mann, John Bently	Col. R.A.M.C., T.	1885
Martin, Lionel Arthur	Surg. R.N.	1912
†Martineau, Alfred John	Maj. R.G.A	1895
Matthews, Vernon Lickford	Surg. R.N.	1906
Maule, Geoffrey Lamb	Capt. R.A.M.C.	1916
Mays, Charles Cecil Wildman	Lt. R.A.M.C., T.	1900
Maw, George Oliver	Capt. R.A.M.C.	1912
Meers, John Harry	Capt. R.A.M.C.	1910

* L.D.S. 1912.   † Combatant Forces.   ‡ L.D.S. 1908.

MEMBERS (cont.)

	Rank.	Member.
Miles, Maurice William Holt	Capt. R.A.M.C.	1917
Milligan, Donald Samuel Eccles	Lt. R.A.M.C.	1915
Mulkern, Hubert Cowell	Capt. R.A.M.C.	1906
Nangle, Edward Jocelyn	Capt. R.A.M.C.	1912
Naylor, Joseph.......................	Lt. R.A.M.C.	1889
Nesham, Robert Anderson	Surg.-Maj. R.F.A., T.	1896
Nicholls, William Howard	Capt. R.A.M.C.	1914
Norris, Hugh Leigh	Fleet Surg. R.N.:	1898
Noyes, Harry Francis Golding............	Capt. R.A.M.C.	1906
O'Connor, Richard Dominic	Capt. R.A.M.C.	1907
†Openshaw, Edward Hyde	Lt.-Col. Som. Lt. Inf.	1890
Pagen, Wilfred Robert	Capt. R.A.M.C.	1905
Palmer, Ambrose Henry	Surg.-Maj. Staffs. Yeom.	1899
Parker, Jeffery Wimperis................	Lt. R.A.M.C.	1906
Parker, Joseph Edmund.................	Surg. R.N.	1885
Parry-Jones, Owen Guy................	Capt. R.A.M.C.	1915
Parsons, Edward Daniell	Lt. R.A.M.C.	1903
Pern, Montagu	Lt. R.A.M.C.	1912
Peter, Alastair Gordon, M.C.	Capt. R.A.M.C.	1907
Pettinger, James Wilson	Capt. R.A.M.C.	1899
Philson, Samuel Cowell...............	Col. A.D.M.S., R.A.M.C.	1883
Pickles, Clifford Crawshaw	Capt. R.A.M.C.	1909
Pickup, William Howard...............	Surg.-Lt. R.N.	1915
Piggott, Frederick Cecil Holman.........	Capt. R.A.M.C.	1884
Plaister, Geoffrey Ratcliffe	Capt. R.A.M.C.	1905
Pocock, Frank Pearce, D.S.O., M.C. (with bar)	Surg. R.N.	1913
Pope, Charles Alfred Whiting	Capt. R.A.M.C.	1903
Porter, Reginald Edward	Lt. R.A.M.C.	1911
Preston, Richard Amyas, M.C.............	Capt. R.A.M.C.	1914
Priestley, Percival Thomas	Maj. R.A.M.C.	1912
Pritchard, William Bridgett	Lt.-Col. R.A.M.C., T.	1890
Pryn, William Reginald	Lt. R.A.M.C.	1914
Quirk, Frederick Whitly	Surg. R.N.	1908
Ramier, Lakshminaraynapuram Subramanier	Lt. I.M.S.	1916
Randall, John Beaufoy	Capt. R.A.M.C.	1914
Ransome, Herbert Fullarton.............	Lt. R.A.M.C.	1892
Rawlins, John Bromley.....	Capt. R.A.M.C.	1914
Reaney, Michael Foster................ ..	Capt. I.M.S....	1900
Rees, Morgan James	Capt. R.A.M.C.	1902
Richards, Francis Graham...............	Maj. R.A.M.C.	1899
Rielly, William Ernest	Capt. R.A.M.C., T..........	1891
Rix, John Cecil	Capt. R.A.M.C.	1902
Roberts, Walter Rowland Southall	Capt. R.A.M.C., T....	1912
Robinson, Henry Ellis	Capt. R.A.M.C.	1915
Robinson, Henry Harold, D.S.O., M C.	Capt. R.A.M.C.	1899
Robinson, Hugh Huntley, M.C.	Maj. R.A.F.M.S.............	1912
Robinson, Kenneth....................	Lt. R.A.M.C.	1907
Rock, Frank Ernest	Surg. R.N.	1893
Rowland, Sydney Domville	Maj. R.A.M.C.	1897
Rutherfoord, Thomas Corrie	Maj. I.M.S.	1902
Ryley, Charles	Maj. R.A.M.C.	1901
Sadler, Vyvyan Kendall..................	Capt. R.A.M.C.	1907

† Combatant Forces.

MEMBERS (cont.)

	Rank.	Member.
Sargent, Alfred George	Lt.-Col. I.M.S.	1896
Saw, Noel Humphry Wykeham, M.C.	Capt. R.A.M.C.	1915
Sayres, Alexander Ward Fortescue	Lt.-Col. R.A.M.C., T.	1890
Scudamore, Leonard George	Lt. R.A.M.C.	1891
Seabrooke, Alexander Stanger	Capt. R.A.M.C.	1912
Searle, Francis Charles	Surg. R.N.	1908
Selby, Gerald Prideaux	Capt. R.A.M.C.	1914
Sells, Clement Perronet, M.C.	Capt. R.A.M.C., T.	1916
Sherman, Reginald	Capt. R.A.M.C.	1912
Shields, Hugh John Sladen	Lt. R.A.M.C.	1912
Shorland, George	Surg. R.N.	1901
Sinha, Atul Krishna	Capt. I.M.S.	1913
Smith, Francis Shingleton	Capt. I.M.S.	1906
Smith, John Godfrey Bradley	Lt. R.A.M.C.	1915
Spence, Reginald Westmore	E.Af.Protect.M.S.	1913
Spensley, Frank Oswald	Capt. R.A.M.C.	1907
Spensley, James Richardson	Lt. R.A.M.C.	1891
Stainsby, John Addison	Lt. R.A.M.C.	1894
Stiebel, Charles	Lt. I.M.S	1902
Stokes, John Wilfred	Lt.-Col. R.A.M.C., T.	1895
Stratford, Ernest	Lt. R.A.M.C.	1908
Sutcliffe, Archibald Alfred	Capt. R.A.M.C.	1905
Symons, Vivian Hood	Maj. R.A.M.C.	1901
Taylor, Herbert Hampden	Capt. R.A.M.C.	1907
Thomas, Charles Ernest	Lt.-Col. N.Z.A.M.C.	1888
Thompson, William Frank	Lt. R.A.M.C.	1912
Thursfield, Richard Mortimer Rowland	Surg.-Lt. R.N.	1909
Tilbury, Arthur	Capt. R.A.M.C.	1913
Tolhurst, St. John Alexander Molesworth	Capt. N.Z.A.M.C.	1907
Townsend, Thomas Ainsworth, M.C.	Capt. R.A.M.C., T.	1914
Treherne, Claude William	Capt. R.A.M.C.	1912
†Treves, Harold Thomsett	Lt. R.N.D.	1907
Vaughan, Robert William Walter	Lt. R.A.M.C.	1908
Venables, Aubrey William	Capt. R.A.M.C.	1913
Waddy, John Raymond, M.C.	Lt. R.A.M.C.	1912
Walker, Arthur Nimmo	Lt.-Col. R.A.M.C.	1898
Walker, Godfrey Alan	Surg. R.N.D.	1912
Wallace, Joseph Stephen, M.C. (with bar)	Maj. R.A.M.C., T.	1915
Watson, George Henry	Capt. R.A.M.C., T.	1907
Waugh, Arthur John	Capt. R.A.M.C.	1912
Weaver, John James	Capt. R.A.M.C.	1886
Webb, George Harvey Duder	Capt. R.A.M.C., T.	1914
Wedd, Edward Parker Wallman	Capt. R.A.M.C.	1911
Welchman, Eliot William	Surg. R.N.	1883
Weller, Charles	Capt. R.A.M.C.	1910
Whincup, Frank	Lt. R.A.M.C.	1897
Whitaker, Frederick	Lt. R.A.M.C.	1903
Whitehorne-Cole, Arthur George	Capt. R.A.M.C.	1906
Whitworth, Henry Parks	Capt. R.A.M.C.	1914
Wight, Ernest Octavius	Col. R.A.M.C.	1881

† Combatant Forces.

MEMBERS (cont.).

	Rank.	Member.
Williams, Peury Garnons	Fleet Surg. R.N.	1899
Wilson, James Ernest Studholme, M.C.	Capt. R.A.M.C.	1911
Wilson, Walton Ronald	Lt. R.A.M.C.	1915
Winter, Laurence Amos	Capt. R.A.M.C.	1892
Wooderson, Douglas Henry David	Capt. R.A.M.C.	1914
Woodhouse, Bernard	Capt. R.A.M.C.	1913
Wood-Robinson, Thomas Mansergh	Surg. R.N.	1914
Wooster, Reginald Joseph	Capt. R.A.M.C.	1911
Wright, Eric Alfred	Lt. R.A.M.C.	1903

309 Members.

LICENTIATES IN DENTAL SURGERY.

	Rank.	
Arbery, Frederick James	—	1915
†Fennell, Linton Albert Ramsey	Artists' Rifles	1909
†Neeley, Hugh Bertram	2nd Lt. 1st Suffolk Regt.	1912
†Palmer, John Stanley	2nd Lt. & Adj. Durham L.I. .	1913
†Rail, Richard Angwin	Lt. Grenadier Guards	1911
†Snell, Herbert........................	2nd Lt.Lon.R.,attd.Lancs.Fus.	1905
†Snell, Norris	Capt. East Yorks. Regt.	1896
†Snow, Charles Foote	2nd Lt. R.F.A.	1910
Wearing, Douglas George	—	1905
†Wood, Paul Bernard	Lt. Royal Fusiliers..........	1913
†Wyand, Edward Herbert	Capt. 16th King's Royal Rifles	1901

11 Licentiates.

† Combatant Forces.

MEMBERS OF COLLEGE STAFF.

	Rank.
Brightwell, Henry	Corporal R.A.M.C.
Skinner, Albert A.	Gunner R.F.A.

RETURNS OF THE RESULTS OF THE SEVERAL EXAMINATIONS.

FELLOWSHIP.

First Examination.

	Number of Candidates.	Passed.	Referred.
December 1922	153	56	97
June 1923	133	42	91
	286	98	188

Second or Final Examination.

	Number of Candidates.	Passed.	Referred.
November 1922	93	24	69
May 1923	91	24	67
	184	48	136

CONJOINT EXAMINING BOARD IN ENGLAND.

FIRST EXAMINATION.

	Part I. Chemistry.			Part II. Physics.			Part III. Elementary Biology.		
	Number of Candidates.	Passed.	Referred.	Number of Candidates.	Passed.	Referred.	Number of Candidates	Passed.	Referred.
July 1922	121	75	46	128	61	67	89	52	37
Oct. 1922	53	31	22	72	33	39	42	24	18
Jan. 1923	63	38	25	77	45	32	65	32	33
Apr. 1923	57	42	15	65	46	19	147	98	49
Totals	294	186	108	342	185	157	343	206	137

SECOND EXAMINATION.

	PART I. Anatomy and Physiology.				PART II. Materia Medica and Pharmacology.		
	Number of Candidates.	Passed.	Referred.		Number of Candidates.	Passed.	Referred.
July 1922	187	93	94		100	71	29
Oct. 1922	172	88	84		98	75	23
Jan. 1923	166	72	94		117	85	32
Apr. 1923	175	95	80		86	62	24
Totals....	700	348	352		401	293	108

THIRD OR FINAL EXAMINATION.

	MEDICINE.			SURGERY.			MIDWIFERY.		
	Number of Candidates.	Passed.	Referred.	Number of Candidates.	Passed.	Referred.	Number of Candidates.	Passed.	Referred.
July 1922....	257	146	111	300	128	172	261	185	76
Oct. 1922....	212	123	89	257	144	113	242	189	53
Jan. 1923....	261	163	98	300	155	145	245	181	64
Apr. 1923....	317	200	117	335	207	128	289	216	73
Totals	1047	632	415	1292	634	558	1037	771	266

DIPLOMA IN PUBLIC HEALTH.

	PART I. OF EXAMINATION.			PART II. OF EXAMINATION.		
	Number of Candidates.	Passed.	Referred.	Number of Candidates.	Passed.	Referred.
July 1922	32	20	12	40	25	15
Jan. 1923	36	28	8	37	24	13
Apr. 1923	32	23	9	30	20	10
Totals....	100	71	29	107	69	38

DIPLOMA IN TROPICAL MEDICINE AND HYGIENE.

	Number of Candidates.		Passed.		Referred.
July 1922	29	....	17	....	12
Dec. 1922	31	....	13	....	18
Apr. 1923	26	....	10	....	16
Totals	86		40		46

DIPLOMA IN OPHTHALMIC MEDICINE AND SURGERY.

	Part I.			Part II.		
	Number of Candidates.	Passed.	Referred.	Number of Candidates.	Passed.	Referred.
July 1922	17	10	7	19	14	5
Jan. 1923	23	16	7	18	13	5
Totals	40	26	14	37	27	10

DIPLOMA IN PSYCHOLOGICAL MEDICINE.

	Part I.			Part II.		
	Number of Candidates.	Passed.	Referred.	Number of Candidates.	Passed.	Referred.
June 1922	19	15	4	13	9	4
Dec. 1922	16	12	4	13	13	0
Totals	35	27	8	26	22	4

LICENCE IN DENTAL SURGERY.

PRELIMINARY SCIENCE EXAMINATION.

	CHEMISTRY.			PHYSICS.		
	Number of Candidates.	Passed.	Referred.	Number of Candidates.	Passed.	Referred.
July 1922....	116	.. 73	.. 43	127	.. 84	.. 43
Sept. 1922....	38	.. 18	.. 20	43	.. 20	.. 23
Jan. 1923....	64	.. 31	.. 33	62	.. 28	.. 34
Apr. 1923....	76	.. 48	.. 28	82	.. 55	.. 27
Totals....	294	170	124	314	187	127

FIRST PROFESSIONAL EXAMINATION.

	DENTAL MECHANICS.			DENTAL METALLURGY.			GENERAL ANATOMY AND PHYSIOLOGY.			DENTAL ANATOMY AND PHYSIOLOGY.		
	Number of Candidates.	Passed.	Referred.	Number of Candidates.	Passed.	Referred.	Number of Candidates.	Passed.	Referred.	Number of Candidates.	Passed.	Referred.
Oct. 1922 ..	144	..106	.. 38	137	..116	.. 21	145	..108	.. 37	148	.. 89	.. 59
Jan. 1923 ..	91	.. 70	.. 21	88	.. 53	.. 35	136	..105	.. 1	169	.. 80	.. 89
Apr. 1923 ..	81	.. 60	.. 21	84	.. 69	.. 15	140	..108	.. 32	125	.. 87	.. 38
Totals....	316	236	80	309	238	71	421	321	100	442	256	186

SECOND PROFESSIONAL EXAMINATION.

	GENERAL SURGERY.			DENTAL SURGERY.		
	Number of Candidates.	Passed.	Referred.	Number of Candidates.	Passed.	Referred.
Nov. 1922	109	.. 78	.. 31	112	.. 85	.. 27
Feb. 1923	106	.. 76	.. 30	100	.. 73	.. 27
May 1923	103	.. 73	.. 30	107	.. 79	.. 28
Totals....	318	227	91	319	237	82

REPORT OF PROCEEDINGS OF COUNCIL.

CONTENTS OF THE REPORT.

I. Annual Meeting of Fellows and Members.

This meeting was held on Thursday, the 16th November, 1922, at 3 o'clock P.M.

The Chair was taken by the President, Sir Anthony Bowlby, and 8 other Members of the Council were present. Four Fellows (not on the Council) and 35 Members attended the meeting.

The President placed before the meeting the Report of the Council for the period from the 1st August, 1921, to the 31st July, 1922, copies of which had previously been circulated to 745 Fellows and Members, and referred to some of the subjects dealt with in the Report.

Sir John Bland-Sutton gave an account of the work in the Museum, and referred to the progress which was being made with the arrangement and housing of the Army Medical War Collection.

After some preliminary questions had been asked by Dr. Red-mond Roche and others and answered by the President, the following resolution was moved by Dr. Roche :—

That˜ this Thirty-fourth Annual Meeting of Fellows and Members again affirms the desirability of admitting Members to direct representation on the Council of the College, which (as now constituted) only represents those Members who also hold the Fellowship; and that it does so, in order that the constitution of the Council of the Royal College of Surgeons of England shall be in keeping with modern ideas of true representation; further that, as the Royal College of Surgeons is composed of about 18,000 persons, of whom over 16,000 are engaged in general practice, this Annual Meeting requests the President and Council to nominate at least two Members in general practice to represent the interests of general practitioners on the Council of the College.

Dr. Roche said that this resolution had been brought forward for twenty years and had been carried almost invariably by overwhelming majorities, only to be strangled by the Council and buried in the waste-paper basket. No reasons had ever been given for refusing the request of the Members. The government of the College was a mediæval anachronism, and the constitution of the electorate an unblushing usurpation. The result was a Council consisting exclusively of surgical specialists who had no right to speak for general practitioners, who formed the bulk of the Members.

The resolution was seconded by Dr. E. E. Ware, supported by Dr. F. G. Lloyd, Dr. Arthur Haydon and others, and carried by 26 votes to 2.

The following resolution was moved by Dr. M. I. Finucane, seconded by Dr. F. W. Collingwood, and carried:—

That this Meeting of Fellows and Members requests the President of the College to make a detailed statement HERE AND NOW as to all the reasons, legal and otherwise, for the Council's refusal to allow representation on the Council of the Members in general practice; and to state whether legal advice had been taken as to any possible means of overcoming any difficulties in the way of carrying out our wishes: and, if so, to declare what that advice was.

The President demurred to the terms of the resolution which referred to the Council's refusal to allow representation. That was a misstatement. The Council had power neither to refuse nor to grant. It was strictly limited by its charter, which conveyed no such powers. It was unfortunate also that Members should speak as though there was hostility between themselves and the Fellows; he did not admit there was any such hostility. In one breath they were told that the status of Members was grievously affected by the action of the Council; in the next, that the status of Members was extremely high. He himself had no hostility to the Members, nor had any Member of the Council. Many of the Members were their friends, and many had been their pupils. It was said that this was a matter for which all the Members were pressing. The first resolution spoke of the College as composed of 18,000 persons, of whom 16,000 were engaged in general practice. No indication had ever been given as to how many Members there were in the "Society of Members"; no list of names had ever been published, no figures had been furnished. In the past the Council had consulted the Fellows, who were the electorate, and their opinion on the proposal was adverse. The Council is naturally bound to attach weight to this opinion. In 1908 the "Society of Members" asked the opinion of Members of the College, but the result had never been published; it was not known what the result was. Under the circumstances the only way in which the Council could judge of the feeling of the Members was by means of the annual general meeting. There were 18,000 Fellows and Members of the College, and the number of votes cast that day for the main resolution was 26—something like 1·5 per 1000. He wished to ask the Secretary of the "Society of Members" what was its total membership.

Dr. S. C. Lawrence said that the Society represented the 16,000 Members; he had never yet met a Member who justified the Council's action. Two Members thereupon said that the Society of Members did not represent them. Although further pressed for an answer to the President's question, Dr. Lawrence failed to give any information as to how many Members of the College were members of his "Society."

The President, continuing, said that, in the absence of any more definite figures from the "Society of Members," the Council had no information as to the feeling of Members on this subject. He was intimately associated during the war with many hundreds of Members, and this subject was never raised. It was never raised at all except at the annual meeting, when it was often difficult even to get a quorum. He wished also to point out that the present electorate of Fellows was representative. It was constantly suggested that the Fellows were not in general practice; that was a misstatement. Hundreds of Fellows of the College to his own knowledge were in general practice, and every one of them was eligible for a seat on the Council. He was satisfied that the Council represented every part of the profession.

In conclusion, the President read the following reply approved by the Council on the 9th November, 1922:—

The chief reasons why the Council has not advised that application should be made for an amended Charter enabling Members to vote for and sit upon the Council of the College are :—

First. The Council believe that the present electorate of 1,700 Members who have taken the Fellowship is a thoroughly representative one. They know that a very large number of the Fellows of the College are in general practice in various parts of Great Britain, and it is consequently quite wrong to assume that the Fellows are all engaged in work as Consulting Surgeons. Many other Fellows, as well as Members, are serving in various appointments under the Government or Local Authorities.

1923. 2 c

Second. The Council are not prepared to advocate measures which are in direct opposition to the opinions of a large number of the present electorate. They are aware that many Fellows are opposed to the granting of such an amended Charter as would meet the approval of the Society of Members of the Royal College of Surgeons, and when, on two occasions, the Fellows have been invited to vote on the question of the extension of the franchise, a majority has voted against it. The present Council has been elected by the Fellows and is bound to give due weight to their opinions.

Third. There is no evidence before the Council of a widespread demand by the Members themselves for an amended Charter, and very few Members come to the annual meeting to support the Motions of the Society of Members.

II. Fellows by Election.

Surgeon Vice-Admiral Sir Robert Hill, K.C.B., K.C.M.G., and Mr. John Howard Mummery, C.B.E., have been elected Fellows of the College under Sect. 5 of the 15th Victoria relating to the admission to the Fellowship without examination of Members of twenty years' standing.

III. Jacksonian Prize.

The Jacksonian Prize for the year 1922 has been awarded to Mr. Sidney Forsdike, M.D., F.R.C.S., of Harley Street, for his essay on "The effects produced by Radium upon living tissues, with special reference to its use in the treatment of Malignant Disease."

The subject for the year 1924 is "The pathology, diagnosis and treatment of Œsophageal Obstruction."

IV. Streatfeild Scholar.

Mr. Kenneth Norman Grierson Bailey, M.B.Lond., M.R.C.S., has been appointed the second Streatfeild Scholar.

The subject of his research, to be carried out at St. Bartholomew's Hospital, is "Infection of the Urinary Tract by Coliform Bacilli."

V. Lister Medal.

Dies for the Lister Medal have now been made from a design by Mr. Charles L. Hartwell, A.R.A.

The medal in bronze is to be awarded triennially with an honorarium of £500 in recognition of distinguished contributions to surgical science, the recipient being required to give an Address in London under the auspices of the Royal College of Surgeons.

VI. Hunterian Oration.

The Hunterian Oration was delivered by Sir John Bland-Sutton on the 14th February, 1923, the anniversary of John Hunter's birth.

In accordance with the terms of the Deed of Trust for the endowment of the Oration, a dinner was given in the evening, at which a number of distinguished guests were present, including Mr. Rudyard Kipling, who made an eloquent speech in proposing the health of "The Hunterian Orator."

In connection with this occasion, an interesting addition to the collection of portraits was made through the presentation by Sir John Bland-Sutton of a copy by Mr. Dorofield Hardy of the portrait of John Hunter by his relative Robert Home.

VII. Lectures.

The following lectures have been delivered during the year :—

BRADSHAW LECTURE.

Sir William Thorburn .... On the Surgery of the Spinal Cord.

THOMAS VICARY LECTURE.

Mr. Walter G. Spencer............... On Vesalius and his delineation of the Framework of the Human Body.

HUNTERIAN LECTURES.

Sir Arthur Keith .... Six lectures on Man's Posture: its evolution and disorders.

Prof. R. Lawford Knaggs............ One lecture on Osteitis Fibrosa.

Prof. L. Bathe Rawling .... One lecture on Remote Effects of Gunshot Wounds of the Head.

Prof. E. M. Woodman............... One lecture on Malignant Disease of the Upper Jaw, with special reference to operative technique.

Prof. C. A. Joll .... One lecture on the Metastatic Tumours of Bone.

Prof. H. Ernest Griffiths .... One lecture on the relation of Diseases of the Gall Bladder to the secretory function of the Stomach and Pancreas.

Prof. Geoffrey L. Keynes .... One lecture on Chronic Mastitis.

ARRIS AND GALE LECTURES.

Mr. L. R. Braithwaite .... One lecture on the Flow of Lymph from the Ileo-Cæcal Angle and its possible bearing on (1) the formation of Gastric and Duodenal Ulcer, and (2) the cause of other types of Indigestion.

Mr. E. R. Flint......................... One lecture on Abnormalities of the Hepatic and Cystic Arteries and Bile Ducts.

VIII. Removal of Member.

The name of one Member has been removed from the list of Members of the College under Clause 2, Sect. XVI, of the Bye-Laws relating to Fellows and Members of the College whose names have been removed from the Medical Register by order of the General Medical Council.

The Member had been adjudged by the General Medical Council to have been guilty of infamous conduct in a professional respect (adultery with a patient).

IX. New Regulations—Conjoint Examining Board.

The Regulations of the Conjoint Examining Board for candidates for the diplomas of M.R.C.S. and L.R.C.P. have been revised, and the amended course of study and examination will apply to all candidates commencing professional study on or after the 1st January, 1923.

Under these Regulations, Chemistry and Physics become subjects of a Pre-Medical Examination to be passed before the commencement of the five years of professional study.

Biology will no longer be a subject of examination, but candidates will be required to take out a course of instruction in that subject in accordance with a revised syllabus which has been drawn up.

The subjects of the First Examination will be Anatomy and Physiology, and, whereas formerly candidates were required to pass in both subjects together, candidates under both the old and new regulations will in future be allowed to pass in one of these subjects, provided they obtain not less than half the number of marks required to pass in the other subject.

The subjects of the Second or Final Examination will be Medicine, Surgery, and Midwifery.

X. Licence in Dental Surgery.

The alterations in the Regulations for the diplomas of M.R.C.S. and L.R.C.P. have rendered necessary a revision of the Regulations for the Licence in Dental Surgery.

Amended Regulations have been drawn up by the Board of Examiners in Dental Surgery and approved by the Council. As in the case of Medical Students, for Dental Students also Chemistry and Physics become subjects of a Pre-Medical Examination.

There will be the same standard of Preliminary Examination in General Education for Dental Students as for Medical Students.

XI. Diploma in Laryngology and Otology.

In association with the Royal College of Physicians it has been decided to institute a Diploma in Laryngology and Otology on the lines of the recently instituted Diploma in Ophthalmic Medicine and Surgery.

Regulations have been drawn up and are available for intending candidates.

Examinations for the Diploma will be held in December 1923 and June 1924.

XII. Diploma in Public Health.

The Regulations for the Diploma in Public Health have been revised so as to bring them into conformity with new resolutions and rules issued by the General Medical Council, and will come into force on the 1st January, 1924.

Before the new resolutions were finally adopted by the General Medical Council, the Royal Colleges were invited to express their views in regard to the proposed alterations, and they pointed out what appeared to them to be defects in regard to the following particulars:—

In the new resolutions and rules no provision is made for candidates in the Army to receive instruction in the duties of a Medical Officer of Health under a Sanitary Staff Officer in the R. A. M. Corps having charge of an Army Corps, District, Command or Division, such as was formerly provided for in the regulations.

Further, it appears that under the new Regulations, the instruction under a Sanitary Officer in India, in the British Dominions and the Colonies will be no longer acceptable, because, according to the interpretation of the new rules by the General Medical Council, the whole course of training under a Medical Officer of Health must be given under one and the same Officer in one and the same area and must cover all the subjects mentioned in Section II. paragraph II. 4 (a) to (f), and it is improbable that these conditions can be fulfilled elsewhere than in this country.

In these respects the new Regulations cause a distinct hardship to Officers in the R. A. M. C. and to Indian and Colonial Doctors.

In spite of the representations of the Royal Colleges, the General Medical Council has failed to amend the new resolutions and rules in any of the ways suggested with a view to removing the hardships complained of.

XIII. Resolutions of Condolence.

Sir Charles Ryall, C.B.E., Member of the Council, died 5th September, 1922.

The President and Council of the Royal College of Surgeons beg to offer their sincere sympathy to Lady Ryall in the lamented and untimely death of her husband and their esteemed colleague Sir Charles Ryall. They recall the valuable services he rendered at all times, and in many ways to the College, as a Member of the Council, at whose deliberations his opinion was always listened to with attention and respect. Besides the loss of his co-operation in the business affairs of the College, his death has removed one whose winning personality endeared him to all his colleagues. Sir Charles gained the affection and esteem of others to a degree rarely attained, and his passing has left a void which will long be felt.

Sir William Thorburn, K.B.E., C.B., C.M.G., Member of the Council and Chairman of the Court of Examiners, died 18th March, 1923.

The Council of the Royal College of Surgeons beg to offer their sincere sympathy with the Misses Thorburn in the lamented death of their father, Sir William Thorburn. In doing so the Council desire also to express their deep sense of the loss they have sustained in the removal of a colleague who rendered service of signal value in the affairs of the College, both as a Member of the Council and as a Member of the Court of Examiners.

XIV. Issue of Diplomas.

The following is a record of the number of Diplomas issued during the period with which this Report deals, viz. :—

Qualification.	Number of Diplomas issued.
Membership	621 (including 137 women)
Fellowship	49 (including 1 woman)
Licence in Dental Surgery	238 (including 10 women)
*Diploma in Public Health	66 (including 12 women)
*Diploma in Tropical Medicine and Hygiene	39 (including 1 woman)
*Diploma in Ophthalmic Medicine and Surgery	24 (including 1 woman)
*Diploma in Psychological Medicine	21 (including 2 women)

* Granted jointly with the Royal College of Physicians.

XV. Financial Report.

INCOME.

The gross income of the College, exclusive of income from Trust Funds, amounts to £42,967, and is £3,152 more than in the previous year.

The gross receipts of this College from the Conjoint Examining Board are £3,664 higher, mainly due to the increase in the examination and diploma fees for the Membership.

In the fees for the Fellowship there is a decrease of £512, and in the fees for the Licence in Dental Surgery a decrease of £728.

In the dividends on investments there is an increase of £356 in the case of the general funds, and of £366 in the case of the Erasmus Wilson Bequest.

EXPENDITURE.

The total expenditure in respect of revenue amounts to £38,090, and exceeds the expediture of the previous year by £4,838.

The increase in the number of candidates examined is mainly responsible for an addition of £1,775 in the expenses of the Conjoint Examining Board payable by this College.

The cost of the Fellowship Examinations is £358 less, and of the Dental Examinations £145 less than in the previous year.

As regards the establishment charges, the General Working Expenses are £310 less than in the previous year, but in the special expenses of the Museum there is an increase of £75, and in the special expenses of the Library an increase of £108.

The extraordinary expenditure, which amounts to £3,948, is exceptionally heavy, and includes a sum of £3,044 for the installation of a new heating system and a sum of £680 for alterations in the basement providing additional lavatory accommodation.

GENERAL REMARKS.

The balance on the Revenue Account amounts to £4,877, a decrease of £1,686 on the sum realised in the previous year, when however, the extraordinary expenditure only amounted to £255. In the year just completed over £3,700 has been expended out of revenue on structural and other alterations in the nature of capital expenditure.

The value of investments at the 24th June, 1923, shows a further improvement, the decrease in depreciation on the general investments amounting to £11,071, thus reducing the depreciation to £62,640.

The investments under Trusts have appreciated in value during the year, with the exception of the Cline Trust invested in French 3 per cent. Rentes. Owing to the depreciation in the value of the Franc, the capital value of this Trust has fallen from £5,344 to £3,366.

XVI. Attendance of Members of the Council
during the year 1922-1923.

(11 Meetings of the Council in the year.)

Name.	Councils attended.	Committees attended.	
Sir Anthony A. Bowlby, Bt., *President*	11	31 out of 32	
Sir D'Arcy Power, *Vice-President*	11	27	„ 30
Sir Berkeley Moynihan, Bt , *Vice-President* ..	10	16	„ 30
Sir Charles A, Ballance	9	1	„ 1
Sir John Bland-Sutton	11	11	„ 11
Sir Charters J. Symonds..................	11	1	„ 1
Mr. William F. Haslam	8	0	„ 0
Mr. H. J. Waring	9	0	„ 1
*Sir William Thorburn	5	4	„ 10
†Sir Charles Ryall	2	0	„ 0
Mr. Walter G. Spencer	11	10	„ 10
Mr. F. F. Burghard	11	8	„ 9
Sir Herbert F. Waterhouse	10	6	„ 6
Mr. T. H. Openshaw	9	9	„ 12
Mr. Raymond Johnson	11	12	„ 13
Mr. V. Warren Low	11	18	„ 18
Mr. James Sherren	11	7	„ 8
Sir John Lynn-Thomas	8	0	„ 0
Mr. Ernest W. Hey Groves	11	2	„ 5
Sir Cuthbert S. Wallace..................	11	8	„ 9
Mr. F. J. Steward	10	10	„ 14
Mr. W. Thelwall Thomas	8	0	„ 1
Mr. C. H. Fagge.......................	10	2	„ 5
Mr. R. P. Rowlands	7	4	„ 5

* Died after 8th meeting.
† Died after 2nd meeting.

XVII. Election to the Council.

At a meeting of the Fellows on the 5th July, 1923, for the election of five Fellows into the Council in the vacancies occasioned by the retirement in rotation of Sir Charters J. Symonds and Sir Herbert F. Waterhouse, by the deaths of Sir William Thorburn and Sir Charles Ryall, and by the resignation of Mr. F. F. Burghard, Mr. James Berry of Wimpole Street, Mr. John Herbert Fisher of Wimpole Street, Mr. William Sampson Handley of Harley Street, Mr. Percy Sargent, C.M.G., D.S.O., of Harley Street, and Mr. George Ernest Gask, C.M.G., D.S.O., of York Gate, were elected into the Council.

Mr. Handley becomes substitute Member of Council for Mr. Burghard until July 1929, and Mr. Sargent becomes substitute Member of Council for the late Sir William Thorburn until July 1930.

In all 1052 Fellows voted, 1043 sending their ballot-papers through the post and 9 voting in person, and the result of the Poll was as follows:—

Candidates.	Votes.	Plumpers.
· JAMES BERRY	612	6
GEORGE ERNEST GASK, C.M.G., D.S.O...	466	28
JOHN HERBERT FISHER	445	53
PERCY SARGENT, C.M.G., D.S.O.......	445	3
WILLIAM SAMPSON HANDLEY	433	8
Sir Herbert Furnivall Waterhouse....	358	4
Herbert John Paterson, C.B.E.	342	11
George Grey Turner	332	13
Victor Bonney....................	304	3
Thomas Percy Legg, C.M.G.	177	4
Donald Armour, C.M.G............	111	5

(In addition 14 voting papers were received too late.)

S. FORREST COWELL,
1st August, 1923. *Secretary.*

THE MUSEUM.

The Hunterian Collection, which forms the basis, and still a large proportion, of the contents of the present Museum of the Royal College of Surgeons of England, was originally arranged in a building which its Founder, John Hunter, erected for it in 1784, behind his house in Leicester Square.

John Hunter died October 16th, 1793, aged 65. By his will he directed the Museum to be offered in the first instance to the British Government, on such terms as might be considered reasonable, and in case of refusal to be sold in one lot, either to some foreign state, or as his executors might think proper.

In the year 1799 Parliament voted the sum of £15,000 for the Museum, and an offer of it being made to the Corporation of Surgeons, it was accepted on the terms proposed by Government*.

In 1806 the sum of £15,000 was voted by Parliament in aid of the erection of an edifice for the display and arrangement of the Hunterian Collection; a second grant of £12,500 was subsequently voted, and upwards of £21,000 having been supplied from the funds of the College, the building was completed in Lincoln's-Inn-Fields, in which the Museum was opened for the inspection of visitors in the year 1813.

In consequence of the large number of additions, this building became too small for the adequate display and arrangement of its contents; and more space being at the same time required for the rapidly increasing Library, the greater portion of the present building was erected, wholly at the expense of the College, in 1835, at

---

* The following are the Terms and Conditions on which the Hunterian Collection, purchased by Parliament, was delivered to the late Corporation of Surgeons; which Corporation having become dissolved, the Members thereof were re-incorporated by Charter. dated the 22nd day of March, 1800, under the Title of The Royal College of Surgeons in London:—

1st. The Collection shall be open Four Hours in the Forenoon of two days every week for Inspection and Consultation of the Fellows of the College of Physicians. the Members of the Company of Surgeons and Persons properly introduced by them; a Catalogue of the Preparations, and a proper Person to explain it, being at those times always in the Room.

† 2nd. That one Course of Lectures, not less than twenty-four in number, on Comparative Anatomy and other subjects, illustrated by the preparations, shall be given every year by some Member of the Company.

3rd. That the Preparations shall be kept in a state of Preservation, and the Collection in as perfect a state as possible, at the Expense of the Corporation of Surgeons, subject to the annual Inspection and Superintendence of the Trustees.

4th. That there shall be a Board of Trustees, to consist of sixteen (increased to seventeen by the Lords of the Treasury in 1856) Members, by virtue of their Public Offices, and of fourteen others, to be appointed, in the first instance, by the Lords of the Treasury, and afterwards to be elected, as Vacancies may happen, by a Majority of the remaining Trustees.

5th. That the Museum shall always be open for the Inspection of all or any of the said Trustees, who are to take care that the Corporation of Surgeons perform their Engagements respecting the said Collection. That a day be appointed for the annual Inspection of the Museum, by the Trustees acting collectively as a Board; and that they are also to have quarterly Meetings. for the transacting of any Business relative to the Museum, and for the filling up of such Vacancies as may happen in the number of the Trustees; and that the Corporation of Surgeons shall engage some person to officiate as Secretary to the Board upon such occasions, and to issue previous Notice to the Members, in which he is to state particularly whether any Vacancies are to be filled up by new Elections.

† This Clause was altered by the Lords of the Treasury in 1894, to the following, viz.:—

2nd. That one Course of Lectures, not less than twelve in number, on Comparative Anatomy and other subjects, illustrated by preparations from the Hunterian Collection and the other contents of the Museum, shall be given every year by Fellows or Members of the College.

a cost of about £40,000, and the Hunterian and Collegiate Collections were re-arranged in what are now termed Rooms Nos. III. and IV., which were opened for the inspection of visitors in 1836.

Further enlargement of the building having become necessary by the continued increase of the Collection, the College, in 1847, purchased the extensive premises of Mr. Alderman Copeland, in Portugal Street, for the sum of £16,000, and in 1852 proceeded to the erection of Room No. V., at the expense of £25,000, Parliament granting £15,000 in aid thereof. The rearrangement of the specimens was completed, and the additional portion of the building opened to visitors in 1855. The Collection still continuing to increase and more space having again become necessary, the College in 1888 determined to erect, at a cost of £19,000, two new Museums on the western side of the old structure. These buildings, called Rooms Nos. I. and II., were completed in 1891. Besides giving greater accommodation for the Collection in general they have also provided space for the display of photographs and drawings illustrating Diseases.

The Hunterian Collection was estimated to consist of 13,682 specimens, distributed under the following heads :—

Physiological Department, or Normal Structures.

Physiological preparations in spirit		3745
Osteological preparations		965
Dry	do.	617
Zoological	do.	1968
Fossils :—		
Vertebrate		1215
Invertebrate		2202
Plants		292

Pathological Department, or Abnormal Structures.

Preparations in spirit	1084
Dry preparations (including bones)	625
Calculi and concretions	536
Monsters and Malformations	218
Microscopic preparations	215

Of the additions by which the size and value of the Collection have been so materially increased since it came into the possession of the College, very many have been presented by Fellows and Members of the College, and other persons interested in scientific pursuits. Among the largest contributions from this source have been the Collection, consisting of 847 specimens, presented in 1811 by Sir William Blizard; a valuable series of Pathological specimens presented in 1851 by Sir Stephen L. Hammick; and a Collection, presented in 1905 by Lt.-Colonel Sir Richard Havelock Charles, I.M.S., K.C.V.O., consisting of 248 skulls, and other specimens, representative of many of the Castes and Tribes of India. At the same time the Council of the College have availed themselves of various opportunities as they have occurred to purchase specimens of interest, especially at the dispersion of private anatomical and pathological museums, as that of Sir A. Lover in 1806, of Mr. Joshua Brookes in 1828, of Mr. Heaviside in 1829, Mr. Langstaff in 1835, Mr. South in the same year, Mr. Howship and Mr. Taunton in 1841, Mr. Liston in 1842, Mr. Walker in 1843, and, deserving of especial mention on account of the great number and value of the specimens acquired, those of Sir Astley Cooper in 1843 and Dr. Barnard Davis in 1880.

The Histological Collection, of which the 215 Hunterian specimens (prepared by Hewson) constitute the nucleus, was chiefly formed by the late Professor Quekett, with considerable additions by purchase from Dr. Tweedy J. Todd, Mr. Nasmyth, and Professor Lenhossek. It now contains upwards of 12,000 specimens, all arranged and catalogued so as to be readily available for reference.

In 1909 the Collection of the Odontological Section of the Royal Society of Medicine, consisting of about 5000 specimens, was transferred to the College under a Deed of Trust, and is now arranged with the other odontological specimens belonging to the College in a room specially prepared for its reception under Room II. of the Museum.

In 1913 an Agreement was entered into with the Royal Society of Medicine, under which the Society transferred to the College, as a loan, its Collection of Obstetrical and Gynæcological Instruments, formerly the property of the Obstetrical Society of London, and the College undertook to house and maintain the Collection without charge to the Society.

In 1921 a further important trust was undertaken by the College, and the Army Medical War Collection of Pathological and other Specimens is now entrusted to the care of the College under an Agreement, dated the 11th November, 1921, entered into with the Secretary of State for War *.

* The following are the Conditions on which the Army Medical War Collection of Pathological, Orthopædic, etc., specimens is entrusted to the care of the Royal College of Surgeons of England :—

1. His Majesty's Principal Secretary of State for the War Department (here'nafter called the Secretary of State) shall hand over for custody to the Royal College of Surgeons of England the Army Medical War Collection (hereinafter called the Collection) of specimens, including pathological preparations, models, drawings and photographs, at present kept at the Royal College of Surgeons, and of such other specimens as the Director General Army Medical Service may hereafter with the approval of the Royal College of Surgeons add thereto, also such orthopædic and facial exhibits as are judged by the representatives appointed by the Royal College of Surgeons and the Director General Army Medical Service respectively to be of permanent value, and the Royal College of Surgeons shall accept the custody of the same, subject to the terms and conditions hereinafter contained.

2. The Royal College of Surgeons shall distinguish the specimens comprised in the Collection by a special mark or letters on the label of each specimen or exhibit and by conspicuously displaying the title "Army Medical War Collection" at the entrance to the room or rooms in which the Collection is exhibited.

3. The Royal College of Surgeons shall suitably house, maintain, and exhibit the Collection in its Museum and shall provide such additional glass, preservatives, labels, catalogues, and other appliances and materials as may be required for the further preparation, exhibition, and maintenance of the Collection without any charge whatsoever.

4. The Royal College of Surgeons shall insure the Collection against fire in the same manner as the contents of the remainder of the Museum are insured.

5. The Collection shall be open at the times during which the rest of the Museum of the Royal College of Surgeons is open, and the Royal College of Surgeons shall, in addition, afford all reasonable facilities for officers of the Royal Army Medical Corps to visit the Collection at other times.

6. The Royal Army Medical College shall have power to select from the Collection type or duplicate specimens to be kept at Millbank for teaching purposes, and to exchange such specimens for others in the Collection from time to time.

7. The Royal College of Surgeons shall remount and maintain such specimens as may be sent to it for the purpose from the collection of type or duplicate specimens kept at Millbank.

8. The Secretary of State shall appoint in such manner as he shall think fit three to five Trustees, who shall be at liberty to inspect the Collection from time to time and confer with the

The superintendence of the Museum is confided by the Council of the College to a Committee of its Members, which Committee has held six meetings during the past year.

A summary of the progress made in the preservation, arrangement, and augmentation of the Collection will be found in the following Report.

CONSERVATOR'S REPORT.

In my report of last year it was announced that the War Office Collection of Medical Specimens—now known as the Army Medical War Collection—had been handed over to the custody of the College, and that steps were being taken to provide a special room in which this collection might be housed and exhibited. Early in the present year the new room was finished and the Collection, which has been placed in Room II of the Museum since 1917, was removed to its new quarters. Five teak-wood stands and two wall-cases were erected as the first instalment of stands and cases which will be required for the display of the Collection, which will comprise about 3000 specimens. Fourteen further stands—of glass and metal, similar to those now used in Room III for the Collection of General Pathology—have been placed on order, so that Mr. Cecil Beadles, who is now in charge of the Army Medical War Collection, will very soon be able to arrange it according to the scheme which has been approved by the Museum Committee. As in former years, Professors at the Royal Army Medical College at Millbank have been supplied with specimens to illustrate their lectures.

The removal of the Army Medical War Collection to its new quarters has set Room II free for its former use—the exhibition of dissections of the human body and the large and important collection which illustrates the various forms of human monster and human malformation.

The most noteworthy event concerning the history of the Museum is the completion of the series which illustrates the Principles of Pathology—the great series which is now exhibited on special stands on the Floor of Room III. In

Museum Committee of the Royal College of Surgeons in reference to matters concerning the Collection.

9. The Royal College of Surgeons shall exercise the same care and supervision over the Collection as over the rest of its Museum. The Conservator of the Museum of the Royal College of Surgeons shall be responsible for the maintenance and care of the Collection, and shall see that suitable assistance is provided for the purpose, subject to the supervision and control of the Museum Committee of the Royal College of Surgeons.

10. The Royal College of Surgeons shall complete the preparation and mounting of such specimens as have not yet been so dealt with and may be considered by the Conservator and Director General Army Medical Service to be suitable for exhibition, and shall care for, maintain, and arrange for the suitable display of the entire Collection for so long as the Secretary of State may desire, the Collection remaining the property of the Secretary of State

11. The Royal College of Surgeons shall carry out the several undertakings herein set forth to the satisfaction of the Trustees appointed under Clause 8 of this Agreement.

12 The Secretary of State shall have the right to remove the entire collection at any time should he consider this desirable for any reason whatsoever, but the Royal College of Surgeons shall not have the right to terminate the arrangement.

13. In consideration of the foregoing the Secretary of State shall pay to the Royal College of Surgeons the sum of £7,500, which sum shall be held to cover all future costs in connection with the housing, displaying, care, maintenance, preparation, mounting, etc., of the Collection and the provision and the payment of the necessary personnel so long as the Collection remains in the custody of the Royal College of Surgeons.

1910, Prof. Shattock and Mr. Cecil Beadles commenced to select, arrange, and catalogue specimens, thus laying the basis of the scheme which they have now brought to a most successful issue. For the first time a complete and systematic treatise on disease has been written, not in words, but in illustrative specimens. Their work was broken into by the War, and subsequently by the high prices charged for muscum materials. In the spring of the present year six further stands were obtained and interpolated, thus making it possible to exhibit all the specimens which are included in the Series of General Pathology. The scope of this section of the Museum is now fixed : if changes are made in the future they will have to be done by replacement rather than by addition.

The section of General Pathology having thus been completed, Prof. Shattock, assisted by Mr. Clement E. Shattock, has commenced the rearrangement, remounting, and re-cataloguing of that other great department of the Museum which illustrates disease of the various parts, organs, and systems of the human body. The sections of this department have not been revised since 1885, when Sir James Paget, Sir James Goodhart, and Mr. Alban Doran prepared the catalogue now in use. Since then many supplements have been printed, the greater number having been prepared by the late Sir Frederick Eve. New numbers are being given to the specimens, many new sections are being established, additional specimens incorporated, and the whole brought up to the present standard of knowledge. The preparation of the new catalogue represents a very great undertaking. Already the sections which illustrate disorders of the growth and nourishment of bone, fractures, imflammatory changes, etc., have been described, and new catalogue cards typed and placed so that they may be used by visitors. New "guide" cards have been fixed to each compartment of the galleries in which specimens are placed, so that students may quickly find those for which they are in search.

The new heating system for the Museum and workrooms, which was installed last autumn, has proved most effective, keeping the air in the Rooms of the Museum at an equable temperature throughout the winter months. At its meeting in March last the Council sanctioned a scheme which will give a direct and convenient access from the hall of the Museum to the proposed Whale-room. The new staircase, which leads down to this room and to new lavatories, was almost completed at the time this report was in preparation. The iron-gratings in Rooms I. and IL, needed in the old system of heating, have been replaced by teak-wood flooring, and it is hoped that the corresponding gratings in Room III. may also be dispensed with.

PATHOLOGICAL COLLECTION.

Since the last Annual Report, several specimens have been received. Such of these as were worth adding to the Museum have been prepared, mounted and catalogued, and distributed in the Collections of Special and General Pathology. Reference may be drawn especially to a specimen of adenomyomata beneath the mucosa of the rectum [Lockart Mummery, Esq.]; the breast of a negress from Nigeria, removed for scirrhous carcinoma [A. Sharp, Esq.]; an ivory-like osteoma, removed from the tonsil [Dr. H. Tilley]; a uterus and functioning ovary with Fallopian tube, excised from an inguinal hernia in a reputed male [Col. C. H. James]; a lobulated lipoma removed from the aryepiglottidean fold [J. M. Wright, Esq.]; a bilocular cyst of the larynx, part of which projects extra-laryngeally through the thyrohyoid membrane [E. D. D. Davis, Esq.]; malignant enlargement of the thymus gland compressing the air-passages [C. A. S. Ridout, Esq.]; portion of the shaft of a child's humerus affected with osteitis fibrosa, excised and replaced by bone-grafting [E. C. Shattock, Esq.].

In regard to the extensive Collection of Special Pathology contained in the Galleries of Rooms I., II., III., the following groups of specimens have been rearranged and re-catalogued, or the older descriptions modified: skin and sub-cutaneous tissue; muscle; tendons; bursæ; cartilage; bone, including Rickets; osteomalacia, osteitis fibrosa, osteitis deformans. Typed copies of these sections have been prepared in catalogue form and placed in the Collection ; and the different compartments have been provided with short lists affixed to the pilasters, and indicating the groups of specimens contained in them.

At present the work is being continued in Room II. to the groups illustrating caries and necrosis of bone, after which come Tumours of Bone ; Injuries and Diseases of Joints, etc.

Mr. Lawford Knaggs, Mr. A. G. T. Fisher, and Mr. C. Nicory have made use of the Pathological Collection for purposes of research.

ARMY MEDICAL WAR COLLECTION.

Mention has already been made of the new quarters provided for this collection and of its removal thereto. Certain points call for special mention. As was announced last year, Sir George Makins has kindly undertaken to arrange and catalogue the drawings which form an intrinsic and valuable part of this collection. A descriptive card catalogue is being prepared, and the drawings have been classified and mounted, and are grouped in a special cabinet placed in the new room. Duplicates of the excellent series of injured eyes which were collected in France during the War and prepared by Sir William T. Lister have now been added to the collection. These beautifully mounted preparations will be exhibited on a special stand.

A series of 50 drawings, prepared to illustrate injuries of the vascular system, mostly under the direction of Sir George Makins and others, to illustrate gunshot injuries of the spine, drawn for articles written by the late Sir William Thorburn, have been presented by Messrs. Wright, of Bristol, on behalf of the editors of the 'British Journal of Surgery.'

It was arranged by those in authority when the War Collection was made that the specimens left in store, when the central collection was completed, would be available for distribution. The President of the Royal College of Surgeons, Edinburgh, has applied for, and been given, leave to make a selection for the Museum of his College.

During the last twelve months 370 specimens have been mounted and added to the Army Medical War Collection. They include a considerable number of brains, and a further series illustrating dysentery and allied diseases, besides gunshot injuries of other parts.

There remain about 50 specimens (mainly limbs and joints) which have been selected from material in the stores ; their preparation, for the most part, has been completed, and it is hoped they will be in a condition to seal down before the end of the present year.

Most of the dry bones and about two-thirds of the glycerine-mounted specimens are now placed in the new room ; the rest, pending further shell accommodation, remain in the workrooms.

Considerable progress has been made with the cataloguing of this Collection. With the exception of about 150 of the wet preparations, a description has been drawn up, and an abstract added of the history of the case. The specimens have yet to be arranged in groups and numbered; this was not possible until all the specimens had been assembled. This grouping will now be proceeded with, and as the specimens receive a number, their descriptions will be typed and bound into book form.

TERATOLOGICAL SERIES.

Among the additions made to this section of the Museum during the past year, special attention is drawn to the remarkable heart of an ox presented by the Department of Physiology of the University of Aberdeen and described by Dr. Charles Reid in the 'Journal of Anatomy' of the current year. An opening from the left ventricle leads into the anterior coronary artery, and through this vessel the ventricle pumped blood into the aorta. A child's heart, showing an almost identical malformation, was presented by the late Mr. H. Blakeway in 1918. Noteworthy, too, is the remarkable malformation of the tricuspid region of the human heart presented by Dr. Alex. Blackhall-Morison. Another specimen of interest is the ileo-cæcal cyst presented by Dr. W. F. Macauley, of Dublin. Mr. Robert Ollerenshaw and Mr. R. C. Elmslie have added two specimens illustrating the anatomy of legs in which the tibia is congenitally absent. In Mr. Elmslie's case both right and left legs were affected; Mr. Ollerenshaw's specimens were obtained from the corresponding limbs of identical twins. The body of a child, obtained through Dr. Sydney Owen, showing absence of the urogenital system and rectum, is also a noteworthy addition.

The Onodi Collection.

The material for the formation of this Collection was obtained under the circumstances narrated in the Conservator's Report of 1921. Since the autumn of 1920 until the end of last year, the Prosector to the College, Mr. H. Wilson, has been engaged in dissecting and mounting preparations and in identifying the original sections shown in Prof. Onodi's published works. He has now completed the series of wet specimens, having set up about 50 preparations showing the condition of the accessory cavities of the nose as seen in children at various ages. There still remain many dried specimens to be prepared and mounted, which work is being carried out by H. George under the direction Mr. T. B. Layton.

Mr. Layton is proceeding with the numbering and arranging of the specimens in the upper gallery of Room III, and with the preparation of a descriptive catalogue for the entire series. The scheme of arrangement is not easy as so many preparations illustrate several points of anatomical and clinical interest. Mr. Layton is overcoming this difficulty by a free use of cross-references.

HUMAN OSTEOLOGY.

As in former years, some of the most interesting additions made to the Museum and some of the more important enquiries carried out in the workrooms, relate to the series of Human Osteology. Among the additions attention may be called to the cast of the tooth presented by the American Museum of Natural History, New York, which is held by Dr. H. F. Osborn to indicate the existence of a human genus, named *Hesperopithecus,* in North America during the

Pliocene period. Others regard it as the worn molar of a Pliocene bear. Also remarkable and instructive is the skeleton of the Eunuch, a negro, presented by Prof. Douglas Derry, of Cairo. A skeleton found in an ancient burial place, probably of Anglo-Saxon date, shows evidence of infantile paralysis, the earliest trace of this disorder in England. Dr. H. C. Sloman, of Copenhagen, presented a photograph, from a stella of the 18th Dynasty, showing a similar lesion in a priest of that date. The late Celtic remains presented by Mr. Reginald W. Hooley are valuable, as they represent the first definite discovery of Englishmen belonging to the pre-Roman period. Many valuable additions have been made to the British series of Roman and post-Roman dates. The donations made by Prof. Fred. D. Bird, Sir Hercules Read, and Mr. T. W. H. Migeod are of particular value. Most remarkable is the discovery of a skull and other bones of an Australian aborigine in a cachet of bones discovered by the police near Lowestoft. These bones, which were forwarded for report and afterwards presented by Dr. Wilson Tyson, probably represent a collection made by a sea captain or a medical student, and were got rid of by burial in the place where they were found. The negro skull presented by Mr. Howard Ross, to whom the College is already greatly indebted, shows extensive destruction in the occipital region, probably the result of a malignant growth.

Anthropological Research.

On October 1st, 1922, Miss M. L. Tildesley was reappointed by the Council of Scientific and Industrial Research for a third term of 12 months, to continue her task of preparing a new catalogue of the Human Remains preserved in the Museum of the Royal College of Surgeons of England.

At the present time Miss Tildesley has almost completed the new descriptions of the skulls and skeletons of British origin and those from France and Spain. An appeal to the Council of Scientific and Industrial Research to have Miss Tildesley's appointment renewed on Oct. 1st, 1923, for at least another year has not met with success.

Reports on Human Remains.

Human remains found in various caves and shelters in the Mendips have been sent for examination. Those found by Mr. H. E. Balch at Ebbor proved to be of late Celtic in date. The Conservator had an opportunity of examining three skulls found recently in Burrington cave and undoubtedly of palæolithic date. They show no feature which distinguishes them from skulls found in English graves of a neolithic date.

The National Museum of Wales has sent remains for examination from graves of various dates, ranging from neolithic to Roman. The skull of a child, from a dolmen grave, showed changes which Prof. Shattock assigned to Rickets—the earliest trace of this disorder so far found in England. Capt. C. E. Vulliamy sent fragmentary remains from a dolmen he excavated at Ffostill, Breconshire. Remains found in a megalithic tomb, Blanches Banques, Jersey, were sent for report by the Société Jersiaise. They proved to be remains of a people similar to those found in the megalithic tomb at Coldrum, Kent. This tomb has been reinvestigated by Mr. E. W. Filkins and many further fragmentary remains recovered. Further neolithic remains from Jersey were sent for examination by Major Rybot.

1923.   2 D

Especially important and complete are the skeletons found by Mr. Reg. W. Hooley in late Celtic graves, Wortley Down, Hampshire. They are of the same type as the Romano-British. Two further skulls have been received from the cemetery (4 Cent. A.D.) at Barnwood, Glos., through the kindness of Mrs. Clifford. Skulls and other bones of a mediæval date found in Romsey Abbey were presented by Col. Ashley, M.P. A skull of uncertain date was examined for the Darlington and Teesdale Field Naturalists' Club.

Several discoveries of human remains made in distant countries have been sent for examination. Near the site of Forbes Quarry, where the famous Gibraltar skull was found in 1846, Mr. A. Craven Greenwood, Colonial Secretary, Gibraltar, found remains of men and of animals, but all proved to be of the modern type. The remains were brought home by Commander F. G. Bowers of H.M.S. 'Cyclops.' Important finds of ancient and modern date have come from Malta, but the Conservator has not completed their examination. Dr. G. Arnold, Curator of the Rhodesian Museum, Bulawayo, sent for examination the remains of an individual found buried beneath a mass of débris at the bottom of an ancient gold-mine—the reputed mines of King Solomon. They were supposed to be the remains of an ancient miner, but proved to be those of a negro woman of the Matabele type and not of great antiquity.

Researches of an anthropological character have been carried out in the Museum by Prof. G. L. Sera, of Pavia, on Bushmen; by Mr. G. M. Morant, on skulls from Anglo-Saxon graves; by Mr. Sheldon Friel, of Dublin, on the normal articulation of the lower with the upper teeth. Miss Caton Thompson, Dr. Louis Reverdin, of Geneva, Mr. Gerald Dunning, and Mr. Mitchell Hedges have been supplied with help in their enquiries.

OTHER RESEARCHES.—Among those who have used the Museum and its work-room for the purpose of research, Mr. Lawford Knaggs deserves particular mention. He continues his investigations into the pathology of bone. Dr. Louis Gross has continued his research into the cause of Intestinal Stasis, and Mr. A. G. T. Fisher has made further progress in his enquiries concerning the nourishment and disorders of articular cartilage. The Conservator takes this opportunity to commend in the highest terms the very thorough investigation now being conducted by Mr. V. E. Negus on the comparative anatomy and mechanisms of the Larynx. Miss G. M. Duthie, of Manchester University, has carried out an examination of the vestigial structures of the broad ligament; Dr. J. N. McIntosh has searched for indications of rickets in certain cranial features; Mr. H. Tyrrell Gray has presented further specimens to illustrate the results which follow on different modes of intestinal suture; Sir Thomas Lewis has had the loan of material for investigations he is making on certain congenital malformations of the heart; Sir Jos. Skevington has been given assistance in studying the deformity which accompanies the presence of an omo-cervical bond; Dr. G. W. Nicholson has also been supplied with material for microscopic examination.

PHYSIOLOGICAL DEPARTMENT OF THE MUSEUM.

One or two points deserve notice here in connection with this important side of the Museum. It is particularly needful that the anatomy and physiology of those animals which are most nearly related to Man should be fully represented in the Physiological Series. Thanks to Miss Alyse Cunningham and Major Penny, the body of a young domesticated and intelligent gorilla, brought from the French Gaboon last year, was placed at our disposal. Unfortunately the viscera had been rendered useless for anatomical purposes by a rough post-mortem examination, but in the intestines Col. Clayton Lane found forms of intestinal worms which were new to science. The animal showed certain movements which were suggestive of a cerebellar lesion, and we found the fourth ventricle greatly distended with a red grumous fluid and the cerebellum itself largely destroyed. There was no sign of middle ear disease. The prosector, Mr. H. Wilson, has made several preparations from its body—of the pharynx, larynx, muscles of the face and facial mask. Preparations of the hernial regions are being made.

The specimens obtained by Mr. Burne, the Physiological Curator, to demonstrate the manner in which bones grow, the well-known method of feeding pigs with madder having been employed, are especially instructive. Emeritus-Professor Wm. McIntosh has used our collection for investigations he is making on whales, as also has Dr. Sharpus. Mr. R. T. Gunter, of Oxford, examined material in the Museum to elucidate certain features he had noted in the mandibles of bears. Prof. F. H. Edgeworth, Dr. A. E. Peake, Mr. C. J. Davies, Dr. C. F. Sonntag, Dr. H. C. Sloman, Mr. Mikelson, and Miss Knobel have had material put at their disposal for the purposes of research.

During the past year the collection has still required rather more than the normal amount of attention in remounting specimens that had either broken down or suffered through loss of spirit. This work, which in the case of more delicate Hunterian preparations requires great care and ingenuity, has been carried on with excellent results by S. Steward.

Progress has been made with the card catalogue of the section illustrating the " Process of Reproduction."

The work commenced last year on certain peculiarities in the vascular system of *Lamna* and certain species of Sharks has been continued, and the results are now ready for publication.

Collection of Surgical Instruments.

Mr. Alban Doran has almost completed the descriptive catalogue of the Collection of Surgical Instruments in the possession of the College—a task to which he has given twelve years of his life and an unrivalled fund of accurate scholarship. Mr. Doran, who is now in his 75th year, has been confined to his home during the winter owing to illness and failing sight, is now engaged on the last section of the Collection—the surgical instruments used by barbarous and semi-civilized peoples. He has written an introduction to the whole collection which will serve as a guide to those who visit this part of the Museum. He has also prepared a table of contents to guide students to the particular part of the Collection they may desire to study. In 1873, just 50 years ago, Mr. Doran became Anatomical Assistant in the Museum under Sir William Flower, afterwards becoming Pathological Assistant, and helping Sir James Paget to prepare the present edition of the Pathological Catalogue. Consulting practice then claimed him until 1910, when he returned to devote himself, as a voluntary worker, to the welfare of the Museum.

Odontological Collection.

During the year considerable progress has been made with the repair, cleaning, and numbering of the specimens. The catalogue has been completed, with the exception of the Series E. (Irregularities in position of the teeth). A few specimens have been added to the Collection. Especial mention may be made of two plaster casts—one of an angioma of the palate, and one of a large epithelial odontome involving the mandible.

The Collection is now in excellent order for the use of students, and it is gratifying to record that a large number of visitors have visited this part of the Museum during the past year.

Museum Demonstrations.

October Course, 1922.

Oct. 13.	Sir ARTHUR KEITH.	Specimens illustrating the effects of Castration in Man.
„ 16.	Prof. SHATTOCK.	Specimens illustrating the anatomical results of Inflammation.
„ 20.	Sir ARTHUR KEITH.	Hydrocephaly. Illustrative specimens shown, and recent investigation on the nature of the disorder discussed.
„ 23.	Prof. SHATTOCK.	Specimens illustrating Carcinoma.
„ 27.	Sir ARTHUR KEITH.	Results following resection of the bowel, illustrated by experimental work done by Mr. Tyrrell Gray on Cats.
„ 30.	Prof. SHATTOCK.	Specimens of Foreign Bodies.

April Course, 1923.

April 13.	Sir ARTHUR KEITH.	Madder-stained specimens illustrating the process of bone-growth.
„ 16.	Prof. SHATTOCK.	Demonstration of specimens illustrating repairs of fractures.
„ 20.	Sir ARTHUR KEITH.	The shape and relationships of the stomach.
„ 23.	Prof. SHATTOCK.	Syphilis.
„ 27.	Sir ARTHUR KEITH.	Surgical anatomy of the foot.
„ 30.	Prof. SHATTOCK.	Spina bifida, etc.

Visitors and Attendances.

On July 19th, 1922, the President gave a reception to the members of the Third International Congress of the History of Medicine.

The Association of Surgeons met in the Museum on Saturday, May 5th, 1923.

On June 6th, 1923, the delegates to the 800th anniversary of the foundation of St. Bartholomew's Hospital were received at the College.

The Certificated Midwives Association visited the Museum, Jan. 23rd, 1922.

The Cambridge University Medical Society, numbering 200 members, were received by the President and officers in the Museum, Oct. 21st, 1922.

Saturday Afternoon Classes.—Museum open on 34 Saturdays. Students attending 2643.

Students and Visitors using Museum during the past year 11,688.

The Conservator regrets to announce the death of Mr. William Pearson, in his 82nd year, at his home at Waddon, Croydon. He retired from his office of prosector in April 1914, having then served the College for 57½ years. His unrivalled dissections of the human body are familiar to all visitors to the Museum. Many of these preparations form the originals for illustrations in our standard works on human anatomy. Mr. Pearson kept up his interest in the welfare of the Museum and the College to the last. His grandfather and father also worked in the Museum, the collective service of the three—grandfather, father and son— amounting to 153 years. Appreciative biographical notices appeared in the *Lancet* and *British Medical Journal* in their issues of March 24th, and a fuller notice of his services to the Museum and College is given in the Conservator's Report of 1914.

The Conservator also regrets to report that he was absent from duty, on account of an illness, from Oct. 27th, 1922, until Feb. 26th, 1923. In his absence, his colleague, Mr. R. H. Burne, carried out the duties of Conservator. The Conservator would avail himself of this opportunity of thanking the President and Council for the great consideration they extended to him during his illness, and for the long leave given him to make a complete recovery.

ARTHUR KEITH,

1st August, 1923.   *Conservator.*

REGULATIONS RELATING TO ADMISSION TO THE MUSEUM.

1. The Museum is open on each week-day, except Saturday, from Ten to Five o'clock from the 1st of March to the 31st of August and during October, and from Ten to Four o'clock from the 1st of November to the last day of February, and on Saturdays from Ten to One o'clock. During the month of September the Museum is closed. It is also closed on Bank Holidays and on the Saturday before each Monday Bank Holiday.

2. The Museum is open, at the times stated, to Fellows, Members, and Licentiates in Dental Surgery of the College; to Trustees of the Hunterian Collection; to Peers and Members of Parliament; to duly qualified medical men and women; to Medical Students (men and women); to the Officers of the Public Service; to members of the learned and Scientific Bodies in the United Kingdom; to learned and scientific Foreigners; to persons introduced personally or by written orders from Fellows or Members of the College or Trustees of the Hunterian Collection; and to persons obtaining orders of admission from the Secretary or Conservator.

3. The Museum is also open on Fridays and Saturdays, at the times and with the exceptions mentioned in Clause 1, to nurses in uniform.

4. Persons desirous of devoting special study to particular departments of the Museum may have access for that purpose on Friday and Saturday on making written application to the Conservator.

Special facilities for making drawings of specimens may be obtained by artists on application to the Conservator.

Special leave for the inspection of the Histological Collection may be obtained on application to the Conservator.

5. Visitors are required to write their names and addresses in the book kept for the purpose in the Entrance Hall.

The several Parts of the Catalogue of the Collection may be obtained on application to the Secretary at the College or to Messrs. TAYLOR and FRANCIS, Red Lion Court, Fleet Street, E.C., at the following prices, viz.:—

A.—NORMAL ANATOMY AND NATURAL HISTORY.

	s.	d.
Descriptive and Illustrated Catalogue of the Physiological Series of Comparative Anatomy, comprising: (A) Endoskeleton, (B) Flexible Bonds of Union and Support—Vertebral Column—Joints, (C) Muscular and Allied Systems. Edited by Professor Charles Stewart, LL.D., F.R.S. 2nd edit., vol. i. 8vo, pp. 160, 14 plates: 1900	12	0
Descriptive and Illustrated Catalogue of the Physiological Series of Comparative Anatomy, comprising: (D) Nervous System—Invertebrata—Brain and Spinal Cord of Vertebrata. Edited by Professor Charles Stewart, LL.D., F.R.S. 2nd edit., vol. ii. 8vo, pp. 518, 254 text-figures: 1902	12	0
Descriptive and Illustrated Catalogue of the Physiological Series of Comparative Anatomy, comprising: (D) Nervous System of Vertebrata (continued), (E) Organs of Special Sense. Edited by Professor Charles Stewart, LL.D., F.R.S., assisted by Mr. R. H. Burne. 2nd edit., vol. iii. 8vo, pp. 391, 3 plates, 54 text-figures: 1907	12	0
Descriptive Catalogue of the Osteological Series. By Professor Owen. 2 vols. 4to, pp. 914: 1853	12	0
Catalogue of the Specimens illustrating the Osteology and Dentition of Vertebrated Animals, Recent and Extinct.		
Part I. Man. 2nd edit. 8vo, pp. 433: 1907	10	0
Part II. Mammalia. 8vo, pp. 779: 1884	10	0
Part III. Aves. By R. Bowdler Sharpe, LL.D. 8vo, pp. 469, 49 illustrations: 1891	12	0
Descriptive and Illustrated Catalogue of the Histological Series. By Professor Quekett. Vol. i. Elementary Tissues of Vegetables and Animals. 4to, pp. 305, 18 plates: 1850	10	0
Descriptive Catalogue of the Fossil Organic Remains of Reptilia and Pisces. By Professor Owen. 4to, pp. 184: 1854	5	0
Descriptive Catalogue of the Fossil Organic Remains of Invertebrata. By Professor Morris and Professor Owen. 4to, pp. 260: 1856	5	0
Descriptive Catalogue of the Fossil Organic Remains of Plants. By Professor Quekett and Professor Morris. 4to, pp. 94: 1859	5	0
Catalogue of Plants and Invertebrate Animals in a Dried State. Edited by Professor Quekett. 4to, pp. 514: 1860	10	0
Catalogue of the Specimens of Entozoa. By Dr. Cobbold. 8vo, pp. 24: 1866	1	0
Observations and Reflections on Geology. By John Hunter. 4to, pp. 58: 1859	2	6
Memoranda on Vegetation. By John Hunter. 4to, pp. 34: 1860	2	6
Memoir on the Pearly Nautilus (*Nautilus pompilius*, Linn.), with illustrations of its external form and internal structure. By Professor Owen. 4to, pp 63, 8 plates: 1832	3	0
Description of the Skeleton of an Extinct Gigantic Sloth (*Mylodon robustus*). By Professor Owen. 4to, pp. 176, 24 plates: 1842	10	0
List of Dissections and Models illustrating Normal Human Anatomy. Pp. 18 1896	1	0

B.—PATHOLOGY.

GUIDES.

THE LIBRARY.

The Library of the College dates from the year 1800, in July of which year the first grant of a sum not exceeding £50 was made for Library purposes. It had been the intention of the old Corporation of Surgeons to form a Library, but they failed to carry their intention into effect. In its early years the Library was considerably increased by presentations and bequests of books—the principal donors being Dr. Baillie, Sir Everard Home, Sir Charles Blicke, the widow of Mr. Sharpe, Sir Ludford Harvey, Dr. Fleming, Mr. Cotton, and Mr. Long. The Court of Assistants also directed from time to time the expenditure of small sums of money for the purchase of books. Sir Charles Blicke, in the year 1816, invested the sum of £300, the proceeds of which were to be devoted to the same object. By these means extensive purchases were from time to time made from the libraries of Mr. Pitt, Mr. St. André, Sir Anthony Carlisle, and others. The progress of the Library, however, for the first twenty-six years of its existence was very slow, but in 1827 great efforts were made to put it in a thoroughly good condition; in that and the two subsequent years the sum of £5269 was spent in the purchase of books, and in 1829 the first Librarian was appointed. The College was practically rebuilt by Sir Charles Barry in 1835–36, and during that period the Library was closed, the books being packed in cases and stored in the Museum Gallery. On the 15th of February, 1837, the Library was re-opened, the rooms in the new building allotted to this department being the Reading-Room and the Librarian's Room. From this date until 1888 very little extra accommodation had been provided for the Library, a small Committee-Room had been fitted up with shelves and room made for a few books under the Theatre.

The munificent gift of Sir Erasmus Wilson enabled the Council in 1888 very materially to increase the Library accommodation, and at the same time to improve and re-decorate the existing building. The residence of the Conservator of the Museum at the east end of the College was pulled down, and the building erected on its site was devoted to Library purposes. On a level with the old Reading-Room an extension was built, the two rooms being connected by four archways, two on the ground and two in the Gallery. Beneath this a handsome Book-Room was provided, and below that a spacious Store-Room. The new building, as at present shelved, gives accommodation for 26,000 volumes. The Librarian's Room was considerably improved by throwing into it a loft above the old ceiling and a passage which led into the Reading-Room.

The whole of the Library premises were re-decorated, and the Electric Light was installed throughout. The heating apparatus, which was under the floor at the south side of the Library, was all removed, and in its place a coil of hot-water pipes was placed in each window. The gallery railing, being in an unsafe condition, was replaced by one of a stronger pattern.

This extension of the Library made it possible to re-arrange the books in such a way as to render them more accessible to readers. In the Gallery of the Extension stand the books on Anatomy, Physiology, Pathology, Medicine and Surgery; round the Reading-Room are ranged sets of the Periodicals and Transactions in greatest demand. There is also a good collection of dictionaries, encyclopædias, systems and general books of reference, conveniently arranged for the use of readers. •

The lower room contains books on Chemistry and Physics, Materia Medica and Therapeutics, Forensic Medicine, Diseases of Women and Children, History of Medicine and Surgery, Biography and Bibliography. The basement is devoted to old sets of Journals and Transactions, a collection of Theses, and to miscellaneous books.

The Librarian's Room contains the books on Biology, and certain valuable works, including many Early Printed Books, which are kept in glass cases.

The current numbers of the Journals are displayed on tables down the middle of the Reading-Room : four of these are fitted with sliding trays, in which books too large for the wall-cases, and illustrated works still in progress, are kept. The new books are placed on a stand in the centre of the Room ; these are catalogued directly they are received, and are not at once available for readers. A list of the additions is posted in the Library.

The first Catalogue of the Library was issued in 1831. A classed Catalogue was prepared by Dr. Willis, and was in use in MS. for some years ; in 1838 a synopsis of it was printed, and the work itself was published in 1843. In 1853 an index of subjects was issued, and four supplements to the Author Catalogue were published between the years 1840 and 1860. In 1890 a List of Transactions, Periodicals, and Memoirs in the Library was published. A new Catalogue of Authors and Subjects on cards has been completed ; these are kept in cabinets at the west end of the Reading-Room, and are available for use by the readers. The cards can now be used as copy for the printers.

The Library is particularly rich in the Transactions of Societies, and in Periodicals relating not only to Medicine and Surgery, but also to the accessory sciences. The large illustrated works on Zoology, Anatomy, &c., are also well represented. There is a good and very large collection of Portraits of Members of the Medical Profession.

In December 1892 a Common Room for the use of Fellows and Members was opened in the Reading-Room adjoining the Entrance Hall.

A new Store-Room for books was fitted up in the basement in 1901, and in 1907 a new room with an annexe was added in proximity to the gallery of the large Library.

During the past year the supply of books and periodicals has been well kept up.

In the order of their arrival the important donations were as follows :— "Ophthalmology of General Practice," from the author, Dr. Malcolm Hepburn ; "Collected Papers of the Mayo Clinic," Vol. 13 ; "Cancer : its Causes, Treatment, and Prevention," from the author, Dr. A. T. Brand ; "American Journal of Diseases of Children," Vols. 16–17, from Dr. J. D. Rolleston ; Publications of the Ceylon Marine Biological Laboratory, from Mr. James Hornell, Madras ; "Le Petit Parisien," June-August, 1922, from the Editor ; Colorado State Medical Society Jubilee Volume, from the Secretary of the Society ; "On the Physiology of the Semi-circular Canals and their Relation to Sea-sickness," from the author, Dr. Joseph Byrne ; the "Festskrift" of the Medical School of Copenhagen, 1772–1922, from the Editor ; "Some Medical Aspects of Old Age" (Linacre Lecture.

1922), from Sir Humphry Rolleston; "Collected Papers of the Gynæcological Department of the Johns Hopkins Hospital and University," 1916–22, from the Secretary of the Johns Hopkins Hospital; "Bradykinetic Analysis of Somatic Motor Disturbances in Nervous Diseases," from the authors, Drs. Goodhart and Tilney; "Arboreal Life and the Evolution of the Human Eye" (Bowman Lecture, 1921), from Mr. Treacher Collins; "Harveian Oration on Medicine in the Century before Harvey," 1922, from Dr. Arnold Chaplin; "Royal Charities. Part IV. Touchpieces for the King's Evil," from the author, Miss Helen Farquhar; Italian medical works, from Dr. Da Fano; a work on Cancer Research in Sweden, 1922, from Prof. Nyström; reprints of papers on Primitive Trephining, from the author, Dr. Wilson Parry; the Linné Letters, Vol. 8, from the University of Uppsala; three Spanish works dealing with the history of Medicine in Spain, from Dr. Fernandez de Alcalde; six Reprints, from the author of the originals, Dr. Sepp Mittersteller, of Innsbruck; "Des Todes Bild," from the author of the English original, Dr. Parkes Weber, together with reprints of papers; "Cambridge University Medical Society Magazine," Easter Term, 1923, containing an account of the Society's visit to this College, from the Editor; "Recueil d'Ophthalmologie," 1873–82, containing Cuignet and Parents' original papers on Retinoscopy; "Notes on the Early Editions of Sir Thomas Browne," from the author, Prof. T. K. Monro; "Index-Catalogue of the Library of the Surgeon-Generals' Office, United States Army," Series 3, Volume III., 1922, from the Librarian, Brigadier General Noble; "Osteitis Fibrosa" (Hunterian Lecture), 1923, from Mr. Lawford Knaggs; "Liber Memorialis" of the Premier Congrès de l'Histoire de l'Art de Guérir, Antwerp, 1920, from the President of the Congress, Dr. Tricot-Royer; "Pasteur as Artist," from the author, Dr. Gustave Monod, M.R.C.S.; Viner Ellis's "Illustrations of Dissections," fol., 1867, from Mr. Herbert Friend; "Artificial Limbs and Amputation Stumps," from the author, Mr. Muirhead Little; "Duff House Papers," Vol. I., from the Managers of the Oxford Medical Publications; "Les Cercles Vicieux en Pathologie," translation from the author's English work, from Dr. Jamieson B. Hurry.

The following donations deserve special mention, and are noted in the order of their arrival :—

From the Wellcome Historical Medical Museum :—"Research Studies in Medical History, No. 1. De Arte Phisicali et de Cirurgia of Master John Arderne, Surgeon of Newark, dated 1412." Translated by Sir D'Arcy Power, K.B.E., F.R.C.S., from a Transcript by Eric Miller, M.A. Oxon. Coloured plates. 4to. London, 1922.

From Dr. S. D. Clippingdale :—"Medical Court Roll [of] Physicians and Surgeons and Some of the Apothecaries, who have attended the Sovereigns of England, from William I to George V, with a Medical Note on Harold." Original MS. in two volumes, folio.

From the President, Sir John Bland-Sutton :—Hoffmann's "Mortality of Cancer throughout the World," 1915.

From Sir Berkeley Moynihan, G.C.M.G., Vice-President :—his "Essays on Surgical Subjects" and Bradshaw Lecture, 1920.

From Sir Frank Swettenham, G.C.M.G., through Dr. Laing :—Sir Everard Home's "Comparative Anatomy," 6 volumes, 1814–28.

From Sir Rickman Godlee :—portrait of Lord Lister.

From Mr. MacLeod Yearsley, F.R.C.S. :—Volumes (40) of Congresses, Transactions, etc., to complete our sets.

: From Sir John Bland-Sutton as Hunterian Orator:—Léandre Le Gallen's "Belle-Isle," 1906.

From Mr. Alban Doran:—Bucknill's "Medical Knowledge of Shakespeare," 1860.

From Sir Squire Sprigge:—Adami's "Charles White of Manchester," 1922.

From Sir D'Arcy Power, Vice-President:—his "Dr. William Harvey as a Man and an Art Connoisseur."

From Mr. W. W. Keen, Hon. F.R.C.S.:—his "Papers and Addresses," 1923.

From Miss A. A. Leith:—water-colour drawings of Indian Cannibalistic Mendicants from the "Tyrrel Leith Papers."

From Sir Arthur Keith, Conservator:—the "Quekett Diaries" and "Catalogues," MSS., 8 volumes, as also Quekett's "Histological Lectures," 1852-53, MS., with the original drawings.

From the Librarian of the University College Hospital Medical School:— Volumes (13) of Old Medicine and Surgery.

From Lord Stanmore, Treasurer of Saint Bartholomew's Hospital:—"A Short History of St. Bartholomew's Hospital, 1123-1923" ("Past and Present," by Sir D'Arcy Power, K.B.E.; "The Future," by Mr. H. J. Waring).

From Dr. Janet Lane-Claypon:—"Transactions of the Fifteenth International Congress of Hygiene and Demography," 1913, Volumes I.-VI., and "Public Health Reports of the United States Public Health Service," 1920-23.

From Mr. D. Denham Pinnock, F.R.C.S.:—Volumes (24) from the Library of his late father, Dr. R. D. Pinnock.

From Mr. Jonathan Hutchinson:—his "Hernia and its Radical Cure."

From Professor Johan Nicolaysen:—Portrait medallion of his late father, Professor Dr. Julius Nicolaysen, of the University of Christiania.

The "Lives of the Fellows" have now been carefully indexed, and the process has brought to light a considerable number of references of interest to medical historians at large, but especially to those in search of information as to the history of operative methods, views on disease, and hygiene.

The valuable Collection of Letters relating to College affairs and medical politics during the last 80 years has now been catalogued and put in order.

During the past year the Library has been open 275 days, and the number of Readers has been 6169.

VICTOR G. PLARR,
Librarian.

1st August, 1923.

REGULATIONS RELATING TO THE LIBRARY.

The LIBRARY is open on each week-day, except Saturday, from 11 A.M. to 6 P.M. It is closed in September, on Bank Holidays, and on the Saturday before each Monday Bank Holiday. On Saturday the Library closes at 1 P.M.

The removal of any book from the Reading-Room by Readers is strictly forbidden.

Readers are permitted to take books from the shelves for use in the Reading-Room; but they are requested not to return the books to their places, but to leave them on the Table.

Members of the College have the privilege of personally introducing a Visitor.

Persons, not Members, desirous of admission, must make application in writing to the Librarian, specifying their Christian name and Surname, Rank or Profession, and Residence. The application must be accompanied by a letter from a Fellow or Member, recommending that a Ticket be granted to the applicant. Tickets of admission, which are not transferable, are granted for six months ; at the expiration of this time application must be made for their renewal.

In the case of Students the application must be made on a form, which may be obtained from the Librarian. Students' Tickets are granted for three months, and at the expiration of this time application must be made for their renewal.

The Catalogue is in Cabinets at the west end of the Room. Readers are requested to make personal application to the Librarian for any book they do not find in the Catalogue.

Readers, taking extracts from any book, may not lay the paper on which they write on any part of such book ; nor may tracings be taken from any plate without the permission of the Librarian.

No note or comment shall be written in or upon any book belonging to the College. Any one observing a defect in a book is requested to report the same to the Librarian.

Readers desirous of consulting works not in the Library are requested to enter their wants in a Book provided for that purpose, in order that the same may be reported to the Committee.

Every person before admission to the Library is required to write his name and address in a Book kept for that purpose in the Entrance Hall.

COMMON ROOM FOR FELLOWS AND MEMBERS.

(Closed until further notice.)

REGULATIONS.

1. The Common Room is open to Fellows and Members of the College only.

2. The Common Room is open on each week-day from 11 A.M. to 5 P.M., except Saturday, when it is open from 11 A.M. to 1 P.M. It is closed during September, and at such other times as the Council may direct.

3. No formal Meeting of any description may be held in the Common Room.

4. Fellows and Members writing letters at the College may not use the College as their Address.

Note.—Fellows and Members are reminded that Smoking is not permitted in any part of the College Premises.

REGULATIONS FOR ACADEMICAL COSTUME.

F.R.C.S.—A black stuff gown with a looped sleeve and crimson satin facings extending to the back of the gown. The facings shall not exceed six inches in the widest part.

M.R.C.S.—A black stuff gown similar in shape to the Fellows' gown but with a plain unlooped sleeve. The facings shall be of crimson satin of the same colour as on the Fellows' gown, but shall not extend to the back of the gown nor exceed two inches in the widest part.

CAPS :—Mortar-board with black tassel.

Robe-makers to the College :

Messrs. EDE, SON and RAVENSCROFT, 93 & 94 Chancery Lane, London, W.C. 2.

FORM OF BEQUEST.

I bequeath to the Royal College of Surgeons of England the sum of £   (free of legacy duty) ; and I direct the same to be paid out of such part of my personal estate as is by law applicable to that purpose.

I. WORKING RECEIPTS.   £ s. d. £ s. d. £ s. d. £ s. d.

A. Conjoint Examining Board. one half of Receipts :—
  1. Membership.
    a. Examination and Diploma Fees:

	£ s. d.	£ s. d.	£ s. d.	£ s. d.
First Examination	1,829 11 6			
Second Examination	3,241 11 6			
Third Examination	7,657 3 6			
Diploma Fees paid by University Candidates	6,444 7 6			
		19,171 14 0		
b. Incidental Receipts:				
Sale of Questions, Visitation Fees, &c.	47 7 5			
Hire of Rooms	932 16 10			
		980 4 3		
			20,151 18 3	
2. Diploma in Public Health:				
Part I. of Examination	417 18 0			
Part II. of Examination	450 9 0			
		868 7 0		
3. Diploma in Tropical Medicine and Hygiene :				
Fees		401 12 6		
4. Diploma in Ophthalmic Medicine and Surgery :				
Part I. of Examination	126 0 0			
Part II. of Examination	110 5 0			
		236 5 0		
5. Diploma in Psychological Medicine :				
Part I. of Examination	110 5 0			
Part II. of Examination	85 1 0			
		195 6 0		
			21,853 8 9	
B. Fellowship:				
Primary Examination Fees		2,000 5 0		
Final Examination Fees		2,318 8 0		
Completion Fees		294 0 0		
Election Fees		31 10 0		
			4,644 3 0	
C. Licence in Dental Surgery :				
Preliminary Science Examination Fees		1,590 15 0		
First Professional Examination Fees		3,479 14 0		
Second Professional Examination Fees		2,421 6 0		
Completion Fees		437 17 0		
			7,929 12 0	
D College Incidental Receipts :				
Sale of College Calendars, Museum Catalogues and Guides		54 11 5		
Sundry Receipts		12 12 0		
			67 3 5	
				34,194 7 2
II. RECEIPTS FROM HOUSE PROPERTY.				
Rent of House, No. 37 Lincoln's-Inn-Fields			450 0 0	
Rent of House, No. 38 Lincoln's-Inn-Fields			350 0 0	
Rent of House, No. 44 Lincoln's-Inn-Fields			430 0 0	
				1,230 0 0
III. RECEIPTS FROM INVESTMENTS.				
1. General Funds:				
Conversion 3¼ per cent. Stock (£1,000)		26 5 0		
5 per cent War Stock (£4,241 11s 5d.)		462 1 6		
Local Loans 3 per cent Stock (£30,000)		675 0 0		
Metropolitan Consolidated 3¼ per cent Stock (£12,600)		330 15 0		
London County 3 per cent. Stock (£14,000)		317 12 6		
Manchester Corporation 3 per cent. Stock (£4,000)		88 19 0		
Nottingham " " " (£8,000)		141 15 0		
Metropolitan Water " B " Stock (£10,000)		223 10 8		
Canada 3½ per cent. Registered Stock (£1,500)		39 7 6		
Ceylon 4 per cent. Inscribed Stock (£5,000)		150 0 0		
South Australia 4 per cent. Inscribed Stock (£5,000)		150 0 0		
Union of South Africa 4 per cent Inscribed Stock (£2,500)		75 0 0		
106 East India Railway B Annuities		79 3 6		
			2,759 9 8	
2. Erasmus Wilson Bequest :				
Guaranteed 2¾ per cent. Stock (£2,000)		41 5 0		
" 3 " " (£10,440 16s. 9d.)		234 18 6		
Bank of England Stock (£4,050 16s. 0d.)		349 7 8		
India 3 per cent. Stock (£40,000 0s. 0d.)		900 0 0		
Metropolitan Consolidated 3¼ per cent. Stock (£1,000)		26 5 0		
Manchester Corporation 3 per cent. Stock (£2,000)		44 9 6		
Birmingham Corporation 3 per cent Stock (£10,000)		225 0 0		
Edinburgh Corporation 3 per cent. Stock (£10,000)		228 15 0		
Canada 3½ per cent Registered Stock (£3,500)		91 17 6		
New Zealand 4½ per cent. Stock (£5,000)		131 5 0		
Straits Settlements 3½ per cent. Stock (£5,000)		137 16 3		
Midland Railway 2½ per cent. Debenture Stock (£16,000)		295 0 0		
Great Western Railway 4 per cent. Debenture Stock (£10,000)		245 0 0		
London & South Western Railway 3 p c Deb. Stock (£13,333)		288 0 1		
North Eastern Railway 3 per cent. Debenture Stock (£10,000)		221 5 0		
London and North Western Railway 3 p c Deb. Stock (£20,000)		442 19 0		
Great Northern Railway 3 per cent Debenture Stock (£10,000)		221 5 0		
Great Eastern Railway 4 per cent Preference Stock (£10,500)		309 15 0		
			4,483 14 6	
				7,243 4 2

TOTAL RECEIPTS IN RESPECT OF REVENUE...£42,967 11 4

EXPENDITURE.

WORKING EXPENSES

	£ s. d.	£ s. d.	£ s. d.	£ s. d.
A. Conjoint Examining Board.—One half of Expenses :—				
1. Membership				
a. Examiners' Fees :				
First Examination	276 12 0			
Second Examination	938 17 0			
Third Examination	5,468 2 0	6,683 11 0		
b. Examination Hall :				
Fees, Committee of Management	89 5 0			
Salaries, Wages, and Pensions	1,746 5 11			
Patients, Materials, &c. for Examinations	761 6 3			
General Expenses	1,387 3 3			
Rates and Taxes, and Insurance	598 1 9	4,582 2 2	11,265 13 2	
2. Diploma in Public Health				
Part I, Examiners' Fees		150 0 0		
Part II, Examiners' Fees		160 10 0		
General Expenses		86 16 3	397 6 3	
3. Diploma in Tropical Medicine and Hygiene :				
Examiners' Fees		215 0 0		
General Expenses		24 3 0	239 3 0	
4. Diploma in Ophthalmic Medicine and Surgery :				
Part I., Examiners' Fees		60 0 0		
Part II., Examiners' Fees		55 10 0		
General Expenses		11 0 0	126 10 0	
5. Diploma in Psychological Medicine :				
Part I., Examiners' Fees		48 0 0		
Part II., Examiners' Fees		39 0 0		
General Expenses		7 7 3	94 7 3	12,122 19 8
B. Fellowship :				
Primary Examination : Examiners' Fees	1,136 0 0			
" " Subjects, Patients, Instruments, etc.	70 16 11	1,206 16 11		
Final Examination : Examiners' Fees	1,756 13 0			
" " Subjects, Patients, Instruments, etc.	250 11 8	2,007 4 8	3,214 1 7	
C. Licence in Dental Surgery :				
Preliminary Science Examination Examiners' Fees		334 0 0		
First Professional Examination : Examiners' Fees		997 6 0		
Second Professional Examination : Examiners' Fees		1,134 8 0		
Patients, Materials, etc.		674 8 10	3,140 2 10	
D. House and Establishment Charges,				
1. General Working Expenses :				
Fees to Council	234 3 0			
Fees to Court of Examiners for special meetings	34 13 0			
Salaries and Wages	2,136 15 0			
Pensions	175 0 0			
Stationery, Printing, Advertisements, and Postage-stamps	965 0 5			
Law Expenses	34 17 8			
Fuel and Light	471 5 9			
Repairs, Painting, and Cleaning	608 9 3			
Rates, Taxes, and Insurance	2,842 10 9			
Furniture and Fittings	49 15 7			
Household Expenses and Miscellaneous Items	285 16 11	7,838 7 4		
2. Special Expenses of Museum :				
Salaries and Wages. (See also Trust Funds : Erasmus Wilson)	4,151 15 0			
Pensions	230 12 0			
Lectures	136 10 0			
Catalogues and Reports	303 12 1			
Specimens, Spirit, Glass, etc.	368 3 3			
Furniture and Fittings	304 16 10			
Household Expenses and Miscellaneous Items	142 14 2	5,638 3 4		
3. Special Expenses of Library :				
Salaries and Wages	1,109 2 0			
Purchases and Binding of Books, etc.	1,054 4 10			
Furniture and Fittings	24 4 8	2,187 11 6	15,464 2 2	34,141 6 3
. **EXTRAORDINARY EXPENDITURE :**				
New Heating Installation		3,044 9 0		
Basement Alterations		680 10 0		
Illuminated Address		52 10 0		
Hunterian Festival—balance of expenses		171 10 0	3,948 19 0	
TAL EXPENDITURE IN RESPECT OF REVENUE				38,090 5 3
LANCE CARRIED FORWARD TO GENERAL ACCOUNT				4,877 6 1
				£42,967 11 4

RECEIPTS AND EXPENDITURE

RECEIPTS AND EXPENDITURE ACCOUNT, TRUST FUNDS,

RECEIPTS.

UNEXPENDED INCOME BALANCES AT 24TH JUNE 1922.	£ s. d.	£ s. d.
Hunterian Fund	38 17 0	
Jacksonian Fund	1 3 8	
John Tomes Fund	10 2 4	
Blane Naval Medals	20 16 0	
Bradshaw Bequest	6 15 0	
Gale's Annuity	13 1 5	
Cartwright Medal	20 11 0	
Walker Fund	8 11 8	
Cline Trust	6 4 5	
Lister Memorial Fund	318 7 3	
Army Medical War Collection Fund	8 5 7	
		452 15 4

INTEREST ON INVESTMENTS (including Income Tax refunded):

	£ s. d.	£ s. d.
Hunterian Fund. £1,850 India 3 per cents. (Tax partially refunded)	44 2 6	
Jacksonian Fund. £616 13s. 4d. India 3 per cents	18 10 0	
Blicke Bequest. £300 India 3 per cents.	9 0 0	
John Tomes Fund. £337 6s. 7d India 3 per cents.	10 2 4	
Blane Naval Medals. £400 Metrop Consol. 3½ per cents.	10 10 0	
Bradshaw Bequest. £900 Metrop. Consol. 3 per cents.	27 0 0	
Erasmus Wilson Fund. £5,250 Metrop Consol. 3 per cents.	157 10 0	
Arris Bequest. £433 6s. 8d. Metrop. Consol. 3 per cents.	13 0 0	
Gale's Annuity. £703 0s. 1d. 2½ per cent. Consols	17 11 4	
Cartwright Fund. £822 8s. 7d. 2½ per cent. Consols	20 11 0	
Begley Bequest. £800 2½ per cent. Consols	20 0 0	
Arnott Bequest. £1,081 0s. 6d Transvaal 3 per cents.	32 8 6	
Walker Fund. Victoria Inscribed 3½ per cents. (£850 at this date)	29 11 2	
Cline Trust. 14,465 Francs French Rentes	230 12 8	
Lister Memorial Fund. £5,000 4 per cent. Stock	201 0 0	
Army Medical War Collection Fund. £10,000 2½ per cent. Consols	250 0 0	
„ „ „ Deposit Account	16 17 0	
		1,108 6 6
		£1,561 1 10

GENERAL ACCOUNT *from Midsummer-day* 1922

RECEIPTS.

	£ s. d.
Balance brought forward from Revenue Account.............	4,877 6 1
„ „ „ „ Receipts and Expenditure Account, Trust Funds	672 15 9
Sale of £9,241 11s. 5d. 5 per cent. War Stock.............	9,356 11 10
Payment of fraction of Stock on conversion	12 4
Deferred Income Tax on dividends not taxed by deduction charged to Revenue Account	98 3 7
Income Tax payable July 1, 1923, on Freehold House Property charged to Revenue Account	93 15 0
Balance as at Midsummer-day, 1922	3,116 5 7
	£18,215 10 2

We have examined the above account of Receipts and Expenditure with the books and vouchers of the College 4th June, 1923, and we certify that it is in accordance therewith. We further certify that we have satisfied ourselves Midsummer-day, 1923.

London, 12th July, 1923.

HE COLLEGE (*continued*).

Midsummer-day 1922 to *Midsummer-day* 1923.

EXPENDITURE.

EMENT OF FUNDS:

	£ s. d.	£ s. d.
Hunterian Fund—part expenses of Festival	82 19 6	
Jacksonian Prize	18 10 0	
Blicke Bequest—purchase of books	9 0 0	
Bradshaw Lecture	27 0 0	
Erasmus Wilson Lectures and part Salary of Curator	157 10 0	
Arris and Gale Lectures	20 0 0	
Begley Studentship	20 0 0	
Arnott Demonstrations	32 8 6	
Cline Trust—preparation of War Collection specimens	200 0 0	
Design and dies for Lister Medal	63 0 0	
Army Medical War Collection Fund—purchase of furniture	247 7 0	
ASE OF STOCK:		877 15 0
Walker Fund. £10 18s. 9d. Victoria Insc. 3½ per cents.	....	10 11 1

CE CARRIED DOWN TO GENERAL ACCOUNT:

expended Income at 24th June, 1923:

Jacksonian Fund	1 3 8	
John Tomes Fund	20 4 8	
Blane Naval Medals	31 6 0	
Bradshaw Bequest	6 15 0	
Gale's Annuity	23 12 9	
Cartwright Medal	41 2 0	
Walker Fund	27 11 9	
Cline Trust	36 17 1	
Lister Memorial Fund	456 7 3	
Army Medical War Collection Fund	27 15 7	672 15 9

£1,561 1 10

Midsummer-day 1923.

EXPENDITURE.

	£ s. d.
t due to Trust Funds Account at Midsummer-day, 1922	452 15 4
se of £15,000 3½ per cent. Conversion Stock	12,097 13 6
Medical War Collection—payment of balance of building costs	2,877 16 9
nt of Deferred Income Tax	455 0 0
e as at Midsummer-day, 1923	2,332 4 7

£18,215 10 2

ng thereto, and with the audited joint accounts of the Royal Colleges of Physicians and Surgeons dated correctness of the Cash Balance, and have verified the Investments in Government and other Stocks as at

COOPER BROTHERS & Co. }
Chartered Accountants. } *Auditors,*

1923.

2 R

BALANCE SH

Dr.   £   *s.*   *d.*   £   *s.*   *d.*   **£**   *s.*   *s*

	£ s. d.	£ s. d.	£ s. d.
To Income Tax payable on Dividends not taxed by deduction	....	....	155 18
To Income Tax payable on Freehold House Property	....	....	93 15
To Sundry Trusts. *See contra*	....	....	32,822 3
To Unexpended Income of Investments under Trusts:—			
Jacksonian Fund	....	1 3 8	
John Tomes Fund	....	20 4 8	
Blane Naval Medals	....	31 6 0	
Bradshaw Bequest	....	6 15 0	
Gale's Annuity...........	....	23 12 9	
Cartwright Fund	....	41 2 0	
Walker Fund	....	27 11 9	
Cline Trust	....	36 17 1	
Lister Memorial Fund	....	456 7 3	
Army Medical War Collection Fund	....	27 15 7	
		—— ——	672 15

To Principal or Capital, being the surplus Assets of the College at 24th June,
1923, exclusive of the contents of the Museum, Library, and General
Offices :—

As per last Account, 24th June, 1922 ....   368,353 10 1

     Add :—
Difference on Revenue Account:—

Receipts 42,967 11 4
Less Expenditure 38,090 5 3
                     4,877 6 1
rofit on sale of £9,241 11s. 5d. 5 per cent War Stock 648 0 10
                           —— —— 373,878 17

                                   £407,623 10

We have examined the foregoing Balance Sheet with the books of the College relating thereto, and with tl
  it is in accordance therewith. We further certify that we have satisfied ourselves of the correctness of tl

London, 12*th July.* 1923.

419

4TH JUNE, 1923.

Cr.

	£ s. d.	£ s. d.
ϝ CASH	....	2,332 4 7
ϝ ARMY MEDICAL WAR COLLECTION FUND:—		
Amount repayable from Fund	....	2,233 10 9

Y SUNDRY INVESTMENTS, at Cost or Market Value on date acquired :—

£ s. d.			
15,000 0 0	3½ per cent. Conversion Stock, after 1961	12,097 13 6	
2,000 0 0	Guaranteed 2¾ per cent. Stock, after 1933	1,180 3 0	
10,440 16 9	Guaranteed 3 per cent. Stock, after 1939	6,682 10 9	
30,000 0 0	Local Loans 3 per cent. Stock after 1912	19,343 3 6	
40,000 0 0	India 3 per cent. Stock after 1948	38,880 15 1	
4,050 16 0	Bank of England Stock	13,330 1 5	
13,600 0 0	Metropolitan Consolidated 3½ per cent. Stock 1929	13,549 9 8	
14,000 0 0	London County 3 per cent. Stock, after 1920	10,036 9 0	
10,000 0 0	Birmingham Corporation 3 per cent. Stock after 1947	10,775 2 0	
10,000 0 0	Edinburgh Corporation 3 per cent. Stock 1924	10,375 2 0	
6,000 0 0	Manchester Corporation 3 per cent. Stock after 1941	6,115 15 6	
6,000 0 0	Nottingham Corporation 3 per cent. Irredeemable Stock	4,386 13 0	
10,000 0 0	Metropolitan Water B Stock 1934-2003	8,448 19 0	
5,000 0 0	Canada 3½ per cent. Registered Stock 1930-1950	5,106 6 0	
5,000 0 0	Ceylon Government 4 per cent. Inscribed Stock 1934	5,518 16 6	
5,000 0 0	New Zealand 3½ per cent Stock 1940	4,912 11 0	
5,000 0 0	South Australian Government 4 per cent. Inscribed Stock 1940-1960	4,965 10 0	
5,000 0 0	Straits Settlements Government 4½ per cent. Inscribed Stock 1937-1967	4,925 1 0	
2,500 0 0	Union of South Africa Consolidated 4 per cent. Stock 1943-1963	2,024 0 0	
10,500 0 0	London and North-Eastern Railway 4 per cent. First Preference Stock	11,865 0 0	
20,000 0 0	London and North-Eastern Railway 3 per cent. Debenture Stock	21,332 13 3	
25,000 0 0	London, Midland and Scottish Railway 4 per cent. Debenture Stock	34,760 15 2	
10,000 0 0	Great Western Railway 4 per cent. Debenture Stock	12,400 0 0	
9,999 0 0	Southern Railway 4 per cent. Debenture Stock	13,007 18 0	
	106 East India Railway B Annuities of £1 each	3,595 11 6	

The market value of the above investments at the 22nd June, 1923, was £216,975 16s. 10d. — 279,615 19 4

IY INVESTMENTS UNDER TRUSTS, at Cost or Market Value on date acquired :—

£ s. d.			
1,850 0 0	India 3 per cent. Stock. (Hunterian Fund.)	1,809 15 8	
615 13 4	„ „ (Jacksonian Fund.)	571 10 8	
300 0 0	„ „ (Blicke Bequest)	304 4 7	
337 6 7	„ „ (John Tomes Fund)	335 0 0	
300 0 0	Metropolitan Consolidated 3½ p.c. Stock. (Blane Naval Medals)	289 18 1	
900 0 0	„ „ 3 „ (Bradshaw Bequest)	916 15 8	
5,250 0 0	„ „ 3 „ (Erasmus Wilson Fund.)	5,372 8 5	
433 6 8	„ „ 3 „ (Arris Bequest)	514 10 8	
703 0 1	2½ per cent. Consols. (Gale's Annuity.)	432 0 0	
822 8 7	„ „ (Cartwright Fund)	742 19 3	
800 0 0	„ „ (Begley Bequest)	713 10 0	
10,000 0 0	„ „ (Army Medical War Collection Fund)	5,269 3 0	
1,081 0 6	Transvaal Government 3 per cent Guaranteed Stock 1923-1953 (Arnott Bequest)	1,000 0 0	
850 0 0	Victoria 3½ per cent Inscribed Stock 1921-6 (Walker Fund)	808 16 3	
1,000 0 0	Canada 4 per cent. Registered Stock 1940-1960 (Lister Memorial Fund)	710 0 0	
1,000 0 0	Ceylon Government 4 per cent Inscribed Stock 1939 1959 (Lister Memorial Fund)	725 0 0	
1,000 0 0	New South Wales 4 per cent. Stock 1942-1962 (Lister Memorial Fund)	670 0 0	
1,000 0 0	Victorian Govt. 4 p.c. Consol Inscribed Stock 1940-1960 (Lister Memorial Fund)	670 0 0	
1,000 0 0	South Indian Railway 4 per cent Reg Deb Stock 1945 (Lister Memorial Fund)	595 0 0	
	14,465 Francs French 3 per cent. Rentes (Cline Trust)	10,566 11 6	

The market value of the above investments at the 22nd June, 1923, was £24,446 6s. 5d. — 32,822 3 9

ϝ FREEHOLD HOUSE PROPERTY IN LINCOLN'S-INN-FIELDS, at original cost	....	63,070 17 6
ϝ FREEHOLD HOUSE PROPERTY IN QUEEN SQUARE at original cost. one-half	....	27,548 14 4
		£407,623 10 3

audited joint accounts of the Royal Colleges of Physicians and Surgeons dated 4th June, 1923. and we certify that Cash Balance, and have verified the Investments in Government and other Stocks as at Midsummer-day, 1923.

COOPER BROTHERS & Co. } Auditors.
Chartered Accountants.

ANTHONY A BOWLBY, *President.*

REGULATIONS RELATING TO PRIZES.

Jacksonian Prize.

The Amount of the Dividend, £18 10s., received from the Trust.

THE SUBJECT FOR THE PRIZE FOR THE PRESENT YEAR, 1923, *IS—*

"THE PATHOLOGY AND TREATMENT OF MALIGNANT DISEASES OF THE TESTICLE."

THE SUBJECT FOR THE PRIZE FOR THE ENSUING YEAR, 1924, *IS—*

"THE PATHOLOGY, DIAGNOSIS AND TREATMENT OF ŒSOPHAGEAL OBSTRUCTION."

The Prize is to be written for under the following conditions:—

Candidates to be Fellows or Members of the College, not on the Council.

The Dissertations to be *typewritten* in English, and the number and importance of original facts will be considered principal points of excellence:—*cited cases to be placed in an appendix.*

Each Dissertation to be distinguished by a motto or device, and accompanied by a sealed envelope containing the name and residence of the Author, and having on the outside a motto or device corresponding with that on the Dissertation.

The Dissertations to be addressed to the Secretary at the College.

The Prize Dissertations and every accompanying drawing and preparation will become the property of the College.

Those Dissertations which shall not be approved, with their accompanying drawings and preparations, will, upon authenticated application within the period of three years, be returned, together with the papers, unopened, containing the names and residences of the respective Authors.

The unapproved Dissertations which shall remain three years unclaimed, with their accompanying drawings and preparations, will become the property of the College; at which period the papers containing the names of the Authors will be burnt, unopened, in the presence of the Committee.

The Dissertations for the Prize for the present year, 1923, must be delivered at the College not later than 4 o'clock P.M. on Monday the 31st of December, 1923.

The Dissertations for the Prize for the ensuing year, 1924, must be delivered at the College not later than 4 o'clock P.M. on Wednesday the 31st of December, 1924.

John Hunter Medal and Triennial Prize.

1. The John Hunter Medal executed in bronze shall be awarded with the Triennial Prize of Fifty Pounds.

2. The recommendation for the award shall be entrusted to a Committee, which shall consist of three Members of the Council, in addition to the President and Vice-Presidents, to be elected triennially at the Quarterly Meeting of the Council in the July preceding the year of award.

3. The award may be made triennially by the Council to a Fellow or Member of the College, not on the Council, who has, during the preceding ten years, done such work in Anatomy, Physiology, Histology, Embryology, or Pathological Anatomy as, in the opinion of the Committee, deserves special recognition.

4. The Committee shall report its recommendation to the Council not later than the Quarterly Council in April subsequent to the expiration of the Triennial period.

5. Should no work by a Fellow or Member of the College in the subjects selected be held by the Committee to be deserving of special recognition, the Committee shall report to the Council accordingly.

Walker Prize.

1. The Walker Prize shall be awarded for the best work in advancing the knowledge of the Pathology and Therapeutics of Cancer done, either partially or wholly, within the five years preceding the year in which the Prize shall be awarded.

2. The next award of the Prize shall be for the five years ending the 31st December, 1925.

3. The Prize shall consist of a gift of £100. A document declaratory of the award, sealed with the College Seal and signed by the President, shall be presented with the Prize.

4. The Prize shall be awarded by the Council on the recommendation of a Committee at the Quarterly Meeting of the Council in the April following the expiration of the quinquennial period. The Council shall not, however, award the Prize should they not consider any work deserving of it.

5. The Committee shall consist of five Members and shall be appointed by the Council not less than one year prior to the date of the award of the Prize. The Committee shall not of necessity be confined to Members of the Council.

6. The grounds upon which the Prize is awarded shall be made public at the time of the award.

7. The Prize shall be open to foreigners as well as to British subjects, and the Committee shall not be restricted in any way as to the selection of persons qualified to receive the Prize, with the exception that Members of the Council shall not be eligible.

NOTE.—It is not intended that Essays should be submitted in competition for this Prize, or that those who are anxious to obtain it should be called upon to submit their names as Candidates. It is hoped, however, that the knowledge of the reward which may be obtained, and the distinction which it will confer on its recipient, will prove an incentive to those who are occupied in the study of this disease.

John Tomes Prize.

1. The John Tomes Prize shall be awarded triennially.

2. The Prize shall consist of the amount of the interest accruing from the John Tomes Fund during the triennial period (about £30). A document, declaratory of the award, sealed with the College Seal, and signed by the President, shall be presented with the Prize.

3. The Prize shall be open to any person registered under the Dentists' Act of 1878, who shall hold a Diploma in Dental Surgery of one of the Licensing Bodies in Great Britain or Ireland included in the Schedule of the said Act.

4. The Prize shall be awarded for original or other scientific work, done either partially or wholly within the triennial period, on the subjects of Dental Surgery and Pathology, Dental Anatomy and Physiology (including Histology), or Dental Mechanics.

5. The Prize shall be awarded by the Council on the recommendation of a Committee at the Quarterly Meeting of the Council in the April following the expiration of the triennial period. The Council shall, however, withhold the Prize if, in the opinion of the Committee, no work within the prescribed time be of sufficient merit to justify its award, and in such case shall either invest the dividends to augment the capital of the Fund, or adjudge the Prize to the author of some original research, deserving recognition, in other than dental subjects, which may have been carried out by any person eligible for the Prize.

6. The Committee shall consist of five members, and shall be appointed by the Council not less than one year prior to the date of the award of the Prize. The Committee shall not of necessity be confined to Members of the Council.

7. No essays shall be submitted in competition for the Prize in the case of the next award, which shall be for the period ending the 31st December, 1923: but it shall be open to the Committee to recommend to the Council that essays should be called for before any subsequent award.

Cartwright Prize.

1. The Cartwright Prize will be awarded quinquennially, and the next award will be for the five years ending 31st December, 1925.

2. The Prize consists of a Medal executed in bronze and an honorarium of £85.

3. The subject for the essays to be submitted in competition for the Prize is "Variations in the form of the Jaws, with special reference to their Etiology and their relation to the Occlusion of the Dental Arches."

4. Candidates for the Prize must be persons engaged in the study or practice of Dental Surgery and possessing qualifications capable of registration under the Medical Acts of the United Kingdom. (*A Diploma or Licence in Dental Surgery without a Medical or Surgical Diploma or Degree will not be a sufficient qualification.*)

5. The Prize will be awarded to the author of the best essay written in English upon the proposed subject, if such essay is considered of sufficient merit.

6. Every essay must have a motto or device and must be accompanied by a sealed paper containing the name and address of the author, and having on the outside a motto or device corresponding with the motto or device on the essay.

7. Each essay must be addressed to the Secretary of the Royal College of Surgeons of England, and delivered at the College not later than 4 o'clock P.M. on the 31st December, 1925.

8. The manuscript Prize essay and every accompanying drawing and preparation will become the property of the Royal College of Surgeons of England.

9. Every unapproved essay which is unclaimed at the expiration of twelve months from the date of its receipt will be returned, with any accompanying drawing and preparation, to the author thereof at the address given in the sealed envelope.

Begley Studentship.

1. The Begley Studentship shall consist of the dividends derived from the Begley Bequest, viz.: £20 per annum, and shall be tenable for three years, subject to the conditions hereinafter mentioned.

2. The Studentship shall be awarded in April 1924, and thereafter triennially, or at such time as any Studentship may become vacant.

3. The Studentship shall be open, on the occasion of the sixth award, to any Candidate admitted to the Second Examination of the Conjoint Examining Board in England held in March or April 1924.

4. The Studentship shall be awarded to the Candidate, if any, obtaining the highest number of marks in the Anatomical part of the Examination.

5. If two or more Candidates in the Anatomical part of the Examination shall obtain an equal number of marks, being with respect to the other Candidates the highest number of marks obtained by any Candidate, reference shall be made to the marks obtained by them respectively in the Physiological part of the Examination, and on the combined result the adjudication shall be made ; and, if their marks shall still be equal, it shall be open to the two senior Examiners in Anatomy appointed by the Royal College of Surgeons to call upon such Candidates to present themselves for further examination, or to take such other steps as may enable them to adjudicate in the matter.

6. The examiners shall report their adjudication of the Studentship to the Council at the Meeting of the Council next succeeding the Examination.

7. The Stipend shall be paid yearly, and the Student shall receive the first instalment within three months after the award of the Studentship.

8. The Student shall be required, before payment of the second and third instalments respectively, to send to the Secretary of the Royal College of Surgeons of England a Certificate from the Dean of his Medical School to the effect that his conduct has been satisfactory and that he has been applying himself diligently to his studies, and should any Student fail to comply with this requirement he shall forfeit his Studentship and all future payments in respect thereof.

9. Words in these Regulations which import the masculine gender shall also import the feminine gender.

REGULATIONS OF THE COUNCIL RELATING TO MEETINGS OF FELLOWS AND MEMBERS.

1. A Meeting of Fellows and Members shall be summoned annually for the Thursday following the Ordinary Meeting of the Council in November, or for such other time as the Council may determine.

2. Other Meetings may be summoned, either with or without a requisition, at such times and for such objects as may by the Council be thought desirable.

3. Such requisition shall be signed by not less than 30 Fellows and Members, or Fellows or Members, and shall contain a statement of the object or objects for which the Meeting is requested.

4. At the Annual Meeting the Report of the Council shall be presented.

5. Motions introduced by Fellows or Members

    (*a*) shall have direct reference to the object or objects for which the Meeting has been summoned ;

    (*b*) shall be signed by the Mover, or the Mover and other Fellows or Members ;

    (*c*) shall be received by the Secretary not less than 10 days before the Meeting.

6. The President shall determine what Motions are in order and direct the arrangement of the Agenda.

7. The Quorum of each Meeting shall be 30, exclusive of Members of the Council, and if, at the expiration of 15 minutes from the hour for which the Meeting has been summoned, a Quorum be not present, the Meeting shall not take place. If, after the commencement of the Meeting, it shall be found upon a count that a Quorum be not present, the Meeting shall be dissolved.

8. The President or one of the Vice-Presidents, or in their absence the Senior Member of the Council present, shall be Chairman of the Meeting, and the Chairman's decision shall be final upon all points of order which may arise.

9. Not less than three weeks' notice of each Meeting shall be given by advertisement.

10. The Agenda paper shall be prepared 3 days before the Meeting, and shall be issued to any Fellow or Member who shall have applied for it.

11. A record of the proceedings shall be kept by the Secretary.

(See also Bye-Laws, Sect. XVII. p. lxxxix.)

INDEX

PRINTED BY TAYLOR AND FRANCIS, RED LION COURT, FLEET STREET.